Post-Keynesian Economics

Post-Keynesian Economics

New Foundations

SECOND EDITION

Marc Lavoie

Professor Emeritus, University of Ottawa, Canada
Professor Emeritus, University of Sorbonne Paris Nord (CEPN), France
FMM Fellow, Institut für Makroöconomie, Düsseldorf, Germany

Cheltenham, UK • Northampton, MA, USA

© Marc Lavoie 2022

All rights reserved. No part of this publication may be reproduced, stored in a retrieval system or transmitted in any form or by any means, electronic, mechanical or photocopying, recording, or otherwise without the prior permission of the publisher.

Published by
Edward Elgar Publishing Limited
The Lypiatts
15 Lansdown Road
Cheltenham
Glos GL50 2JA
UK

Edward Elgar Publishing, Inc.
William Pratt House
9 Dewey Court
Northampton
Massachusetts 01060
USA

A catalogue record for this book
is available from the British Library

Library of Congress Control Number: 2022932701

This book is available electronically in the Elgaronline
Economics subject collection
http://dx.doi.org/10.4337/9781839109621

ISBN 978 1 83910 961 4 (cased)
ISBN 978 1 83910 963 8 (paperback)
ISBN 978 1 83910 962 1 (eBook)

Typeset by Cheshire Typesetting Ltd, Cuddington, Cheshire
Printed and bound by CPI Group (UK) Ltd, Croydon, CR0 4YY

Contents

Notation used in the book	vii
Preface to the second edition	xv
1 Essentials of heterodox and post-Keynesian economics	1
2 Theory of choice	75
3 Theory of the firm	128
4 Credit, money and central banks	193
5 Effective demand and employment	296
6 Accumulation and capacity	370
7 Open-economy macroeconomics	497
8 Inflation theory	592
9 Concluding remarks	630
References	646
Name index	708
Subject index	718

Notation used in the book

		Chapter
a	real autonomous expenditures	5
A	nominal autonomous expenditures	5
A_{LT}	number of long-term securities	4
A_{ST}	short-term assets	4
ABP	accounting balance of payments	7
$AFAB$	accounting financial account balance (net foreign lending to the domestic economy)	7
B	debt of firms (or of households, Chapter 6)	3, 4, 6
B	bank loans	4, 6
BP	balance of payments	7
c_v	propensity to consume out of wealth	5, 6
C	consumption	4, 7
CAB	current account balance	4, 7
d	income share of direct (variable) labour	5
D	deposits	4, 6
DC	direct costs	3
e	estimate of a parameter	1
e	price elasticity of demand (its absolute value)	3
e	nominal exchange rate	7, 8
$\bar{e}$	fundamental exchange rate assessed by fundamentalists	7
e_R	real exchange rate	7, 8
$\bar{e}_R$	real exchange rate target	8
e^e_c	exchange rate expected by chartists	7
e^e_f	exchange rate expected by fundamentalists	7
e_w	Webb effect elasticity (efficiency wage effect elasticity)	5
E	rate of employment	6
f	ratio of overhead workers to variable workers at full capacity	5, 6, 8
f	forward exchange rate (in logs)	7
f_Ω	reaction parameter related to indexation of wages	8
f_ψ	reaction parameter of prices to changes in wages	8
F	financial assets	3
f_f	financial to tangible asset ratio	3
F	forward exchange rate (in level)	7
FC	full capacity of the firm	3
FC_{th}	theoretical full capacity	3
FY	net foreign income accruing to domestic residents	4, 7
FYI	foreign income accruing to domestic residents	7

FYO	income paid to non-residents	7
FAB	financial account balance in its economic sense	7
g	rate of capital accumulation (growth rate)	3, 6–8
g_B	balance-of-payments constrained growth rate	7
g_q	actual rate of growth of output	6
g_n	natural rate of growth	5–8
g_y	growth rates of sales	6
g_z	growth rate of autonomous consumption expenditures	6
g^i	investment function (in growth terms)	6–8
g^s	saving function (in growth terms)	6–8
g^s_w	saving function of workers	6
g^s_r	saving function of rentiers	6
G	government expenditure	4, 5, 7
h	annual number of hours worked per worker	5
h	number of houses	4
h	marginal propensity to invest of firms	5, 6
h_g	marginal propensity to spend of government	5
H	high-powered money (banknotes, reserves)	4
i	interest rate	3–6
i_B	interest rate on borrowed capital or loans	3, 4, 6
i_D	interest rate on bank deposits	4, 6
i_d	domestic interbank interest rate	7
i_F	interest rate on financial assets	3
i_f	foreign interbank interest rate	7
i_{fair}	fair rate of interest	4
i_R	real rate of interest	7
i_S	dividend rate on stock-market shares	3
i_{TSR}	rate of return on stock-market shares	4
i_{CB}	target interest rate of the central bank	4
i_{LT}	yield on long-term securities	4
i_{ST}	yields on short-term securities	4
I	investment expenditure	3–7
I_h	residential investment	4
I_f	investment by firms	4
IN	inventory stocks of firms	4
j	ratio of material costs to direct labour costs	3, 7, 8
J	$= (1 + j)$	8
k	number of machines per worker	1
K	capital stock	4, 6
K_B	capital borrowed through loans or bond issues	3
K_c	capital (or wealth) held by capitalists	6
KIF	gross financial inflows (net incurrence of liabilities)	7
KOF	gross financial outflows (net acquisition of financial assets)	7
K_S	capital owned by the shareholders (equity)	3
l	debt to capital ratio	3, 6

L	labour employment	1, 4, 5, 6
L_f	indirect labour, overhead labour	5
L_v	direct labour, variable labour	5
L_{fe}	full employment	5
L_v^{fc}	direct labour at full capacity	5
m	share of gross profits	3, 5
m_{va}	share of gross profits in value added	3
M	number of machines	1, 3
M_d	deflated capital	1
M	imports	4, 7, 8
MR	marginal revenue	3
MC	marginal cost	3
n	labour per unit of output $(= 1/y)$	3
N	active population	1, 6
NDC	normal direct costs	3
$NUDC$	normal unit direct cost	3
NUC	normal unit cost	3, 5
OF	own funds of banks	4
OR	official international reserves	7
p	price level	1, 5, 8
p_d	price of domestic goods	7, 8
p_f	price of foreign goods	7, 8
p_i	price of machines	3
p_h	price of housing	4
p_m	price of imports	7
p_x	price of exports	7
p_s	price of stock-market shares	4, 6
p_{LT}	price of long-term securities	4
P	profits	3, 5–7
P_c	profits of capitalists	6
P_w	profits of workers	6
P_D	dividends	4
P_{ND}	non-distributed profits (retained earnings)	4
q	output level	1, 3, 5, 7
q_d	deflated output	1
q^d	real aggregate demand	5
q^s	real aggregate supply	5
q_n	normal or standard level of output	3, 5
q_{fc}	full-capacity level of output	5
r	rate of profit	1, 6, 8
r^e	expected rate of profit	6
r_n	normal rate of profit, target rate of return on capital	3, 5, 6, 8
r_{ROE}	return on equity (ROE)	3
r_{ROA}	return on assets	3
r_{TSR}	total shareholder return (TSR)	3
s	spot exchange rate (in logs)	7

s	number of stock market shares	3, 4, 6
s_c	propensity to save of capitalists	6
S_c	saving of capitalists	6
s_f	retained earnings ratio	3, 6
s_h	propensity to save of households	6
s_p	(marginal) propensity to save out of profits	5–8
s_r	propensity to save of rentiers	5
S_w	saving of workers	6
s_w	propensity to save out of wages (or of workers)	5, 6
s_y	propensity to save out of income	5, 7
s_{yd}	propensity to save out of disposable income	5
S	spot exchange rate (in level)	7
S	saving of the private sector	4, 7
S_f	retained earnings of firms	3, 4
S_h	saving of the household sector	4, 7
SE	standard error of estimate	1
tb	trade balance ratio	7
T	taxes	4, 7
TB	trade balance	7
u	rate of capacity utilization	5–8
u^e	expected rate of capacity utilization	6
u^k	short-period Keynesian or Kaleckian equilibrium rate of capacity utilization	6
u_f	foreign rate of capacity utilization	7, 8
u_n	normal or standard rate of capacity utilization	3, 5–8
U	rate of unemployment	1
UC	unit cost	3
UDC	unit direct cost (or average variable cost)	3, 5
$UDLC$	unit direct labour cost	3, 7
UMC	unit material cost	3, 7
v	capital to full-capacity output ratio	3, 5–8
v_o	capital to output ratio	1, 7
v_m	material inputs to output ratio	7
v_r	valuation ratio (price-to-book ratio)	3, 6
V	wealth	4, 6
w	nominal wage rate	1, 3–6, 8
w_f	nominal wage of overhead labour	5, 6
w_M	mean nominal wage rate	5
w_v	nominal wage rate of variable labour	5, 6
x	units of consumer goods	2
x	proportion of investment financed by new share issues	3
X	exports	4, 7
y	output per worker (labour productivity)	1, 5, 6
y_f	labour productivity of overhead labour	5
y_h	hourly labour productivity	5
y_v	labour productivity of variable labour	5, 8

Y	individual income	2
Y	income (gross domestic product)	5, 7
Y_c	income of capitalists	6
Y_d	disposable income of the private sector	5
Y_{fe}	full-employment GDP	5
z	units of characteristics	2
z	ratio of autonomous expenditures to capital stock	6
Z	autonomous consumption expenditures of capitalists	6
Z	world income	7

Greek letters   Chapter

α (alpha)	output elasticity of labour	1
α	proportion of the feasible range of extra necessaries goods	2
α_1	parameter designed to calculate the natural rate of growth	6
α_i	parameters of a modified Phillips curve	8
β (beta)	output elasticity of capital	1
β_e	impact of an increase in the real exchange rate on the domestic rate of capacity utilization	7, 8
β_u	income elasticity of import demand in the domestic economy	7, 8
β_{uf}	income elasticity of import demand in the foreign economy	7, 8
γ (gamma)	parameter reflecting the animal spirits of firms or the trend growth rate of sales	6–8
γ_i	effect of the interest rate on the rate of accumulation	6
γ_r	effect of the profit rate or of the normal profit rate on the rate of accumulation	6
γ_u	effect of the rate of capacity utilization on the rate of accumulation	6–8
γ_v	effect of the valuation ratio on the rate of accumulation	6
γ_π	effect of the profit share on the rate of accumulation	6–8
Γ	adjustment coefficient related to the real exchange rate	7
ε (epsilon)	error term	1, 6
ε	price elasticity of demand (in absolute terms)	3
ε	Webb effect of the real wage on labour productivity	5
ε	world income elasticity of the demand for exports coming from the domestic economy	7
ε	admissible distance between the target and the actual real wage	8
ζ (zeta)	consumption emulation coefficient of workers	6
η (eta)	price elasticity of the demand for exports	7
η_1	effect of a change in the wage share on the growth rate of output	6
η_2	effect of technical progress on the growth rate of output	6
θ (theta)	percentage mark-up on direct costs (percentage gross costing margin)	1, 3, 5, 8

Θ	percentage net costing margin	3, 5
ι (iota)	reaction parameter tied to changes in expected spot rate	7
ι^T	target inventories to sales ratio	3
κ (kappa)	average markup of prices over unit labour costs	8
κ_c	proportion of capital (or wealth) held by capitalists	6
κ_d	proportion of bank deposits in household wealth	6
κ_s	proportion of stock-market shares in household wealth	6
λ (lambda)	growth rate of labour productivity	6
λ_g	Kaldor–Verdoorn effect of output growth on labour productivity growth	6
λ_k	effect of the growth rate of capital per head on labour productivity growth	6
λ_π	effect of the profit share on labour productivity growth	6
λ_ω	effect of real wage growth on labour productivity growth (dynamic Webb effect)	6
λ_{ij}	indicators of liquidity preference for various assets	4
μ (mu)	Hicksian measure of technical progress	1
μ	reaction of the rate of capacity utilization to excess demand	6
μ	propensity to import goods from abroad	7
μ_1	adjustment parameter tied to the expected rate of utilization	6
μ_2	adjustment parameter tied to the normal rate of utilization	6
ξ (xi)	implicit function indicating how the debt ratio changes as a function of itself and the growth rate of output	6
π (pi)	net share of profits in national income (or in value added)	5–8
π^d	net share of profits, from the demand side	5, 6
π^s	net share of profits, from the supply side	5, 6
Π	income elasticity of the demand for imports	7
ρ (rho)	ratio of the funds that can be borrowed to the retained earnings	3
σ (sigma)	risk and illiquidity premium or discount	4
σ	ratio of the wage of overhead labour relative to that of direct labour	5, 6
σ	reaction parameter tied to the retained earnings ratio	6
σ_B	illiquidity and risk premium on bank loans	4
σ_i	risk and illiquidity discounts associated with different assets	4
τ (tau)	weighted sum of the growth rates of the real wage and the profit rate	1
τ	tax rate	5
τ	tariff rate	7
υ_m (upsilon)	pass-through coefficient of export prices in domestic currency	7
υ_x	pass-through coefficient of import prices	7

ϕ (phi)	reaction of the profit share to excess demand	6
ϕ₁	adjustment parameter tied to the expected profit rate	6
ϕ₂	normal profit rate adjusts to the values taken by the realized profit rate	6, 8
ϕ_c	reaction parameter related to expectations of chartists	7
ϕ_f	reaction parameter related to expectations of fundamentalists	7
χ₁ (chi)	impact of the rate of capacity utilization on price inflation	6
χ₂	impact of the rate of inflation on the interest rate	6
χ₃	negative effect of the rate of capacity utilization on the trend rate of growth	6
χ₄	negative effect of an increase in the rate of employment on the trend rate of growth	6
χ₅	negative effect of an increase in the rate of unemployment on price inflation	6
χ₆	positive effect of the rate of unemployment on the profit share	6
χ₇	positive effect of an increase in the rate of employment on the rate of technical progress	6
χ₈	negative effect of an increase in the rate of unemployment on the rate of technical progress	7
ψ (psi)	implicit function indicating how the growth rate of output changes as a function of itself and the debt ratio	6
ψ	price elasticity of the demand for imports	7
ψ_i	(i = 1, 2, 3, 4) Harrodian destabilizing mechanisms	6
Ψ	parameters pertaining to price inflation	8
ω (omega)	real-wage rate (= w/p)	1, 8
ω	wage share	8
ω_f	real-wage rate targeted by firms	8
ω_h	hourly real wage	5
ω_M	mean real-wage rate	5
ω_w	real wage targeted by workers	8
Ω	parameters pertaining to wage inflation	8

Preface to the second edition

In the Fall of 2018, Alan Sturmer, on behalf of Edward Elgar, asked me whether I would consider writing a new edition. I thought this would be a nice project to get involved in, once I had retired from official teaching and administrative duties in May 2019. Also, it was likely to be worthwhile, since the book had attracted several citations, had received a prize from the *European Association for Evolutionary Economics*, and despite its size, has even generated a Chinese translation that came out in 2021. I had some hesitations in pursuing the project when I saw the book by Robert Blecker and Mark Setterfield, *Heterodox Macroeconomics: Models of Demand, Distribution and Growth* (2019), as I felt that their remarkable work already provided extensions and updates of my own book on several issues, but in the end I judged that there was nothing wrong in having another textbook dealing extensively with post-Keynesian themes. After all, at the time of the first edition, another substantial book devoted to post-Keynesian economics had been published nearly simultaneously, the book by Eckhard Hein, *Distribution and Growth After Keynes: A Post-Keynesian Guide* (2014).

The first edition of my book was published in 2014. At the time, we were still concerned with the Global Financial Crisis that had reached its apex in the Fall of 2008. Today, the main preoccupation is with the COVID-19 pandemic and its economic consequences, while climate change concerns are ever more present. As a consequence, Chapter 9 of the second edition contains an extended discussion of the relationship between post-Keynesian economics and ecological economics, more specifically ecological macroeconomics. Between 2014 and 2021, there has been an explosion of publications in post-Keynesian economics and related schools of thought, and so I have tried to take many of these new works into consideration. All chapters have been amended and extended, but those who know me will not be surprised to learn that the two chapters that contain the greatest modifications are the chapters on monetary economics (Chapter 4) and on growth and distribution theory (Chapter 6), which are my main fields of research. Nonetheless, there are also substantial additions to the chapters devoted to questions of methodology (Chapter 1) and to open-economy issues (Chapter 7).

Whatever the changes, however, the purpose of the book remains the same. Its objective is to provide a comprehensive access to post-Keynesian economics, a guide through the maze of publications, showing that it does have some coherence and provides a more realistic description of the world. The book is not an introduction to post-Keynesian economics; rather, I think it is fair to say that it assumes that students have some knowledge of alternative theories in economics, which many now acquire thanks to various resources on the internet. The book is mainly targeted at masters students, but I am sure that both honours students and PhD students can also benefit from reading it. It may as well be useful to scholars from other fields and to young colleagues in economics who, despite being trained in mainstream economics, are looking for an alternative view of the world.

It is traditional to thank colleagues who have read the manuscript, provided comments on it or spotted mistakes in the published version. I fear that I have not made a note of the names of all those who helped me in this regard for the first or the second edition, so I ask for forgiveness from whoever I might have forgotten in the following list: Olivier Allain, Robert Blecker, André Luis Cabral de Lourenço, Louison Cahen-Fourot, Brett Fiebiger, Eckhard Hein, Simon Julita, Antonio Carlos Macedo e Silva, John McCombie, Fabio Petri, Fabricio Pitombe Leite, Gilberto Tadeu Lima, Won Jun Nah, Mario Seccareccia, Mark Setterfield, Brenda Spotton Visano, Tom Stanley and Renaud du Tertre.

I also need to thank Louis-Philippe Rochon who helped me put together the two books which, in a sense, constitute an annex to the present book. These are *Post-Keynesian Monetary Theory: Selected Essays* (2020) and *Post-Keynesian Growth Theory: Selected Essays* (2022), which contain 20 and 18 of my essays respectively, sometimes with co-authors in the case of the collection on growth theory. These two books each contain a foreword, one by Louis-Philippe and the other by Eckhard Hein, and each book contains an introduction which provides a more personal note, as I explain how I got interested in these topics and how and why these papers came about. And while I am at it, I should also thank Louis-Philippe and his colleague Hassan Bougrine for having put together two books of contributions in my honour and that of my long-time colleague Mario Seccareccia, *Credit, Money and Crisis in Post-Keynesian Economics* (2020) and *Economic Growth and Macroeconomic Stabilization Policies in Post-Keynesian Economics* (2020). I am grateful to the authors of these contributions, whose contents might be considered as another annex to the present book.

1. Essentials of heterodox and post-Keynesian economics*

1.1 THE NEED FOR AN ALTERNATIVE

1.1.1 Winds of Change

Slightly more than a dozen years ago, the Western world was hit by the Global Financial Crisis. Since then, there has been a multiplicity of student-led initiatives devoted to enlarge the range of economic theories and approaches which students in economics could access. French students, who had already instigated a protest movement in 2000, got in action again with *Peps-économie* (2013). They helped launch an international call for more pluralism in the teaching of economics, the ISIPE call, *the International Student Initiative for Pluralism in Economics*. This was followed by other student movements, in particular *Rethinking Economics* and *Exploring Economics*, who provide information and documents on various theories alternative to mainstream economics. There are also the activities and conferences sponsored by the *Institute for New Economic Thinking* (INET) and organized through the *Young Scholar Initiatives* (YSI), as well as previously existing student organizations, such as *OIKOS International*, devoted to sustainability, which have also endorsed the call for more pluralism in economics. All this has been accompanied by an explosion of various highly-attended summer schools, which for a few days or even a full week, provide graduate students with instruction in alternative schools of thought.

The existence of these movements is proof that many students in economics wish to go beyond what they are usually being taught in most economics departments and are becoming aware that there exist alternatives; but it also demonstrates that not much has changed in academia, besides marginal additions to the curriculum.

Things have sometimes been more encouraging outside of academia, with developments within central banks or international organizations. The crisis has led to the reconsideration of many dogmas in macroeconomic and monetary theory. Perhaps, more importantly, it has led some researchers at large international organizations to question their entire philosophical stance. The Organization for Economic Cooperation and Development (OECD) has set up the New Approaches to Economic Challenges (NAEC) initiative, which gives more space to alternative views. The International Monetary Fund (IMF) has been criticized by its Independent Assessment Bureau for its tunnel vision, and as a consequence has attempted also to provide more space to internal critiques. As an example, Ostry et al. (2016) in an IMF journal devoted to a large readership, wonder whether neoliberal policies have been oversold. They examine two standard neoliberal policies geared to promote long-term growth: first, fiscal austerity, that is, the attempt to reduce fiscal deficits and public debt, notably by reducing the size of government expenditures (the so-called 'expansionary' fiscal consolidation); and second, the removal of restrictions on the mobility of capital across countries. Their argument is that these two policies did not increase economic growth, and that furthermore it did lead to more income and wealth inequality. Ostry et al. (2016, p. 38) conclude that 'instead of delivering growth, some neoliberal policies have increased inequality, in turn jeopardizing durable expansion'. This is a substantial turnabout.

Central bankers have also amended their views, now recognizing that inflation targeting is not a panacea, and that they may have claimed too much influence on the economy. Some central banks, such as the Reserve Bank of New Zealand who was first in adopting inflation targeting, have now moved to a dual mandate or toward a more flexible inflation targeting. In addition, many central banks, in particular the Bank of England, have been keen to criticize standard monetary theory as found in textbooks, such as the money multiplier story and the quantity theory of money, thus explaining the money supply process as post-Keynesians had done so for the last 50 years.

Under the pressure of some central bankers, many former compulsory components of macroeconomic theory are being questioned: the rational expectation hypothesis, the strong or semi-strong version of the efficient market hypothesis, the unbiased efficiency hypothesis in international finance, the assumption of perfect asset substitutability, Barro's Ricardian equivalence theorem, the idea of expansionary fiscal contractions based on the confidence fairy, the natural rate of unemployment and its NAIRU version as a unique (or even time-varying) attractor of the actual rate of unemployment – the vertical long-term Phillips curve and even the short-term downward-sloping Phillips curve (Lavoie, 2018). The Global Financial Crisis has completely undermined those hypotheses or assumptions, because, as reported for a while on a sidebar of the website of the *Financial Times*, 'the credit crunch has destroyed faith in the free-market ideology that has dominated Western economic thinking for a generation'.

Furthermore, the advent of the COVID-19 crisis, with governments daring to go into huge deficits to sustain economic activity or the purchasing power of households, has completely modified attitudes regarding public deficits and public debts, at least for a while. Economists and the public have taken notice that rising debt-to-GDP ratios and huge fiscal deficits did not generate rising interest rates. Whereas before the consensus was that monetary policy was all powerful while fiscal policy ought only attempt to balance the budget, there is now a recognition that fiscal policy is a powerful tool, in particular when provided support by the monetary authorities. In this regard, the unrelenting efforts of the advocates of Modern Monetary Theory (MMT) to convince their peers and the general public that federal governments have a large financial leeway to pursue expansionary policies did certainly help to discard deficit phobia.

1.1.2 Recantation

Critics of conventional economics have long argued that the regulations and economic policies put in place with the increased liberalization of the economy have been based on erroneous economic theories, and that these need to be scratched out. But with the advent of the Global Financial Crisis and the events associated with the COVID-19 crisis, a number of former partisans of mainstream economics have changed their mind and have been quite critical of standard theory.

Perhaps the most immediate and surprising such recantation was that of Richard Posner, a judge and a senior lecturer at the University of Chicago School of Law. Posner was a stern defender of free markets and of Milton Friedman's ideology. In his book titled *The Failure of Capitalism*, Posner (2009a) argues that deregulation went too far and that financial markets need to be heavily regulated, because banking has a systemic significance that other industries do not have. In a follow-up article, provocatively titled 'How I became a Keynesian', Posner (2009b) went further, arguing that 'we have learned since September [2008] that the present generation of economists has not figured out how the economy works'. Posner argued that Keynes's *General Theory*, despite its apparent antiquity, is the best guide to the crisis. Robert Skidelsky (2009, p. x), the historian biographer of Keynes, claimed that to understand economics it was better not to be a professional economist, the advantage being 'of not having been brainwashed to see the world as most economists view it'!

The strongest indictment of mainstream macroeconomic theory from the orthodox side was perhaps made by Willem Buiter, a former member of the Monetary Policy Committee of the Bank of England, and admittedly an early critic of the hypothesis of rational expectations. In a now famous blog, Buiter (2009) wrote that 'the typical graduate macroeconomics and monetary economics training received at Anglo-American universities during the past 30 years or so may have set back by decades serious investigations of aggregate economic behaviour and economic policy-relevant understanding'. Buiter (2009) referred to models based on New Classical and New Keynesian economics, as the kind of modelling that offers no clues as to 'how the economy works – let alone how the economy works during times of stress and financial instability'.

Besides heterodox economists such as Servaas Storm (2021a) who believe that it belongs to the *Museum of Improbable Economic Models*, several Nobel-prize recipients have been quite critical of the workhorse of mainstream macroeconomics – the Dynamic Stochastic General Equilibrium (DSGE) model. Robert Solow, who is sometimes considered as the father of DSGE models because of his famous 1956 neoclassical growth model, has also repudiated DSGE models, saying that its foundations were 'dumb and dumber macroeconomics' (Solow, 2003), and that adding realistic frictions did not make these models any more plausible (Solow, 2008, p. 244). Solow thus does not believe that recent efforts by DSGE advocates to add complex refinements to their models will make them any better or more realistic. Not unexpectedly, Joseph Stiglitz (2015, p. 43) has also argued that macroeconomics has done poorly over the years, as 'the models/theories that guided policy were not just innocent bystanders in the crisis that unfolded beginning in 2008. They were critical in the creation of the crisis and in the inadequate responses to it'. As to Paul Romer (2016, p. 1), the former chief economist at the World Bank, he provoked quite a stir when he wrote that he had 'observed more than three decades of intellectual regress' in macroeconomics, adding that it had turned into 'pseudoscience', targeting explicitly the work of Robert Lucas and that of the New Classical economists.

1.1.3 The Necessity of a Post-Keynesian Alternative

The argument put forward here is that the danger for policy makers of following bad advice has been greatly increased by the hegemony of mainstream economics. Dissent is also what is needed for a vibrant academic environment. It is our social duty as economists to develop an alternative outlook of the economic system. It is our duty to sustain and develop the heterodox traditions that question the efficiency and stability of unfettered markets, as we shall see in the following sections. Dissent, however, must go beyond criticism: a positive alternative must also be put forward. This is the main purpose of the book: to provide an alternative view and alternative models.

> Tearing down the monopoly of DSGE orthodoxy will be possible only if macroeconomists continue to build and maintain alternative models to inform and encourage policy discussions outside the path beaten by the macro-mainstream. In all this, there is a silver lining, however. The DSGE modeling project is programmed to continue going down the path toward irrelevance and, being unable of self-correction, it must at some point crash into this wall called 'economic reality'. This could take decades, but once the crash will have happened, there will be a demand for alternative, sensible, and more humane modeling approaches. It is vital, therefore, to maintain these initiatives in the meantime. (Storm, 2021b, p. 114)

Some eclectic mainstream economists, besides Stiglitz, have also recognized the necessity for alternative viewpoints. In an interview in the *IMF Survey Magazine*, Blanchard opened the door to alternative views, in particular those endorsed by long-time advocates of post-Keynesian economics:

> As a result of the crisis, a hundred intellectual flowers are blooming. Some are very old flowers: Hyman Minsky's financial instability hypothesis. Kaldorian models of growth and inequality. Some propositions that would have been considered anathema in the past are being proposed by 'serious' economists: For example, monetary financing of the fiscal deficit. Some fundamental assumptions are being challenged, for example the clean separation between cycles and trends: Hysteresis is making a comeback. This is all for the best. (Blanchard, 2015)

In this book, I wish to highlight the *post-Keynesian* tradition in economics. We shall see later that this school of thought can be subdivided into several strands. But for now, we can say as a first approximation that this tradition extends and generalizes the seminal ideas that were developed by the radical followers of John Maynard Keynes (thus the name *post-Keynesian*). These developments initially occurred mainly at the University of Cambridge, where Keynes was located. The originality of these ideas became pretty obvious in the 1950s, as researchers such as Nicholas Kaldor and Joan Robinson came to prominence. Of course, there were also other famous heterodox economists in Cambridge, most notably, Richard Kahn and Piero Sraffa. This generation was then followed by another one, that of Luigi Pasinetti, Geoffrey Harcourt, Wynne Godley, Robert Rowthorn and Ajit Singh, who came with ideas of their own, albeit compatible with this radical Cambridge tradition. Outsiders also made contributions to this tradition, the most notable one certainly being Michał Kalecki, the Polish economist, to whom we can add others such as Joseph Steindl, Augusto Graziani, Pierangelo Garegnani, Amit Bhaduri and Philip Arestis. Starting with the early 1970s, several American economists – such as Victoria Chick, Paul Davidson, Alfred Eichner, Jan Kregel, Hyman Minsky, Edward Nell and Sidney Weintraub – contributed in their own way to this tradition and helped to institutionalize post-Keynesian economics. Today, while not much remains of this tradition in the Faculty of Economics in Cambridge (Saith, 2022), the contributors to post-Keynesian economics can now be found in large numbers throughout the globe and in certain cases can be associated to other schools of thought, as was the case for John Kenneth Galbraith.

1.2 HETERODOX ECONOMICS

1.2.1 Heterodox versus Orthodox Economics

At this stage some definitions are required. Table 1.1 shows the alternative names that have been given to the two wide traditions that exist in economics. I chose to call these heterodox economics and orthodox economics; an economist who is not part of the heterodox group then by definition must belong to the orthodoxy. We shall see in the next section that these two traditions can be defined by key methodological characteristics and beliefs. Orthodox economics is often referred to as neoclassical economics, marginalism, the dominant paradigm or mainstream economics. Over the last two decades, various authors such as David Colander (2000) and John Davis (2006) have contended that all these terms are not synonyms. In particular, these authors have been arguing that important works in the orthodox tradition do not use some of the key assumptions that define neoclassical economics and the use of marginalist methods, making references to game theory, experimental economics, behavioural economics, neuroeconomics and non-linear complexity economics. While this may be true, particularly in the field of microeconomics, despite obvious elements of continuity with the neoclassical framework, it is clear that macroeconomics, with its current use of the representative agent with rational expectations (RARE, as John King (2012a) calls it), is still fully within the neoclassical berth. Hence, until contrary evidence is truly convincing, I see nothing wrong in assimilating orthodox economics to the neoclassical paradigm.

I have occasionally used the term 'unorthodox' or 'non-orthodox' economics in opposition to orthodox economics, but in the 1992 version of the book, I made references to the 'post-classical' paradigm, in opposition to the neoclassical paradigm, and also because some of the concerns of the post-classical economists reflected the concerns of classical economists such as Ricardo and Marx. The term *political economy* is often suggested, in an effort to encompass not only alternatives to mainstream economics but also the contributions that could arise from other fields in social sciences (Stilwell, 2019). There is a danger however in choosing such a term, because it has also been used by right-wing authors who are concerned with public choice, voting behaviour and the growth of the public sector. As a result, to avoid confusion, various authors have added qualifiers to the term. Heinrich Bortis (1997) has suggested the name *classical-Keynesian political economy* to represent what I called the post-classical paradigm. Malcolm Sawyer (1989) proposed the term *radical political economy* to identify a small subset of dissident schools. *Institutional political economy* and *heterodox political economy* have also been put forth

Table 1.1 Heterodox versus orthodox economics: alternative names

Heterodox economics	Orthodox economics
Post-classical paradigm	Neoclassical economics
Political economy	The dominant paradigm
Non-orthodox economics or unorthodox economics	Mainstream economics
Real-world economics	Marginalism
New paradigm economics	Old paradigm economics

by Nicolas Postel and Richard Sobel (in Labrousse and Lamarche, 2009) to describe a wide range of alternative schools of thought. These, in my view, are all acceptable denominations, but it may be better to avoid altogether the expression *political economy*, since terms such as *critical political economy* or *post-critical political economy* have also been utilized by some Marxists. To emulate the popular success of Modern Monetary Theory, one would be tempted to endorse the name *modern political economy*, but the term has already been taken by policists who wish to appropriate neoclassical theory!

Edward Fullbrook (2013) has suggested the use of two expressions, 'new paradigm economics' and 'old paradigm economics', proposing ten distinguishing characteristics. In his efforts to regroup all those frustrated with orthodox economy, and as a follow-up to the post-autistic economics movement, Fullbrook has created the *Real-World Economics Review*, the main publication of the World Economics Association. The converse of orthodox economics could thus also be called real-world economics.

I decided to adopt the denomination 'heterodox economics'. Over the years, in particular since the late 1990s, but even more so since the mid-2000s, the term 'heterodox economics' has become increasingly popular to designate the set of economists who view themselves as belonging to a community of economists distinct from the dominant paradigm (this can be seen by checking the Google Books Ngram Viewer). Indeed, there is now a huge *Heterodox Economics Directory* (Kapeller and Springholz, 2016), which provides useful information to all those young scholars looking for an alternative economics. As a result, I shall speak of 'heterodox economists', as has been suggested in particular by Frederic Lee (2009). While a number of heterodox economists dislike the name or find it awkward, as shown in interviews, I believe, as do many others, that it is still the best possible identifier (Mearman et al., 2019; Armstrong 2020).

Is it possible to summarize in a nutshell the difference between orthodox economics and heterodox economics? While much more will be said in the next section, at this stage we can focus on the definition of economics as an exemplar. The most accepted definition, which can be found in all orthodox textbooks, is that of Lionel Robbins (1932, p. 16), who defined economics as 'a science which studies human behaviour as a relationship between ends and scarce means which have alternative uses', summing this up by saying that economics is the study of 'behaviour conditioned by scarcity' (p. xxxi). When asked, some of my students defined neoclassical economics as the study of an upward-sloping supply curve with a downward-sloping demand curve! Lee (2013a, p. 108) by contrast defines heterodox economics as 'a historical science of the social provisioning process'. I find this rather ambiguous, and personally I prefer the definition offered by John Weeks (2012), who objects to the standard definition of economics based on scarcity, proposing instead that 'economics is the study of the process by which society brings its available resources into production, and the distribution of that production among its members'.

1.2.2 Heterodox Schools of Thought

Who are these heterodox economists? Frederic Lee (2009, p. 7), in his *History of Heterodox Economics*, lists the following: 'Post Keynesian-Sraffian, Marxian-radical, institutionalist-evolutionary, social, feminist, Austrian and ecological economics'. Table 1.2 gives a similar list of the various schools of thought that I have associated with

Table 1.2 Heterodox schools of thought in economics

School of thought	Associations
Post-Keynesians	Post-Keynesian Economics Society (PKES)
	Association des Études Keynésiennes (ADEK)
	Associação Keynesiana Brasileiro (AKB)
Radicals, Marxists, Marxians	Union for Radical Political Economy (URPE)
	Association for Heterodox Economics (AHE)
	International Initiative for Promoting Political Economy (IIPPE)
Institutionalists (old)	Association for Evolutionary Economics (AFEE)
	Association for Institutional Thought (AFIT)
Evolutionary political economy	European Association for Evolutionary Political Economy (EAEPE)
Feminist economics	International Association for Feminist Economics (IAFFE)
Social and humanistic economics	Association for Social Economics (ASE)
	Political and Ethical Knowledge on Economic Activities (PEKEA)
(Social) Ecological economics (green economics)	International Society for Ecological Economics (ISEE)
Development Structuralists	International Celso Furtado Center for Development Policies
Schumpeterian economics, innovation economics, evolutionary economics	International Joseph A. Schumpeter Society
French Regulation School	Association Recherche et Régulation
Social structure of accumulation school	
The economics of conventions	
Monetary circuit school	
Behavioural economics (old)	Society for the Advancement of Behavioral Economics (SABE)
Polanyi economics	Karl Polanyi Institute of Political Economy
Gesellian economics	
Ghandian economics	Ghandi Foundation
Georgian economics	Henry George Institute
Neo-Austrian economics (?)	Society for the Development of Austrian Economics (SDAE), Ludwig von Mises Institute
Agent-based modelling	
System dynamics	System Dynamics Society

heterodox economics in the past. Post-Keynesians are listed first, not because of their numerical importance, but rather because they are the subject of this book, although it should be pointed out that Radicals/Marxians are probably most numerous among heterodox economists, with the Institutionalists next. As we shall see later, these various schools of thought have methodological features in common, although this may not always be obvious because the members of each school usually specialize in different fields or because they provide different sorts of critiques against orthodox economics, so that the contacts between the various schools can be rather sparse.

As pointed out earlier, the financial crisis has given a boost to all alternative schools of thought, in particular heterodox Keynesian economics. In particular, it has brought to the fore the views of a well-known post-Keynesian economist – Hyman P. Minsky – to such an extent that journalists at the *Wall Street Journal* and other newspapers were making references to a 'Minsky moment'. Minsky conferences, organized by the Levy Economics Institute, now attract the presidents of some of the Federal Reserve banks in the USA. All this action around Minsky has led to new editions of three of his books, which for a while could be found even in airport bookstores.

But the revival of alternative economic thinking does not stop there. It extends to all brands of heterodox economics (see Table 1.2), in particular Marxism and the French Regulation School, whose credibility has also been given a boost. Indeed, in their explanations of the crisis, there are substantial similarities between the writings of several post-Keynesians, notably those concerned with the study of a monetary production economy, and those of members of the French Regulation School (for instance Robert Boyer, Jacques Mazier, Dominique Plihon, Frédéric Lordon), the French Convention School (notably André Orléan and his remarkably prescient 1999 book), and some Keynesian Marxians who share close ties with the post-Keynesian school (such as James Crotty and Gerald Epstein in the USA or Gérard Duménil and Dominique Lévy in France). A major reason why these authors of various backgrounds and traditions have a common understanding of the events of the last 15 years is that they hold a common view of what economics is all about.

Readers may have noted that Institutionalists and behavioural economists are listed in Table 1.2 with the additional 'old' qualifier. This is because, as we shall see, some of behavioural economics remains within the neoclassical tradition, while new Institutionalism is a variant of neoclassical economics. As a result, old Institutionalism and old behavioural economics could equally be called original Institutionalism and original behavioural economics. The labour economists of the old Institutionalist tradition helped to create a new field – industrial relations – which is still impervious to neoclassical influence (Kaufman, 2010a). Neo-Austrians carry a question mark, because, as we shall see in the next section, although they consider themselves as heterodox economists, they do not endorse the key features common to the other heterodox schools. The appearance of agent-based modelling, of which there are several brands, in this list may surprise some readers. But after discussion with some of these practitioners, I have come to the conclusion that several agent-based modellers share many of the criticisms that post-Keynesians would address to neoclassical economists, and that the key features of their models are genuinely of a heterodox nature. Indeed Corrado Di Guilmi (2017) shows that there can be a lot of cross-fertilization between agent-based modelling and post-Keynesian economics. As to system dynamics, Michael Radzicki (2008, p. 157) has persuasively argued that system dynamicists 'view the world through the same lens' as Institutionalists and post-Keynesian economists, and there are certainly tight links between the feedback loops and the stock–flow analysis promoted by system dynamicists and the stock–flow coherent analysis advocated by some post-Keynesians, as can be guessed by perusing the book edited by Cavana et al. (2021). Ecological macroeconomics, in contrast to environmental economics, has also adopted the stock-flow consistent approach.

1.2.3 Dissenters and Heterodox Economists

One problem in distinguishing heterodox and orthodox economics is that some orthodox economists, in particular New Keynesian economists such as Krugman and Stiglitz, are very critical of their orthodox colleagues. Some of their critiques are not dissimilar to those put forward by heterodox authors. Furthermore, sometimes the economic policies that they recommend are very similar to those that post-Keynesian economists advocate, albeit with less visibility. Thus one needs to make a further distinction, inspired by the proposals of Roger Backhouse (2004), whose article is devoted to understanding the nuances between disagreement, controversies and dissent in economics.

Besides heterodoxy and orthodoxy, economists can be divided into two broad groups: the mainstream and the dissenters. The mainstream essentially corresponds to the textbook view. 'Its existence as a coherent intellectual whole is generally most strongly expressed in textbooks at the upper undergraduate and at the graduate levels' (Colander et al., 2007–08, p. 306). The dissenters, as argued by Backhouse (2004), are themselves subdivided into two additional groups: the orthodox dissenters and the heterodox dissenters. Those three groups are represented in Figure 1.1, with the heterodox dissenters on the left, the mainstream on the right, and the orthodox dissenters in between the other two groups. Schools of thought such as the post-Keynesians, the Marxians, the Radicals and the old Institutionalists are clearly heterodox dissenters. Orthodox dissenters include authors such as the Institutionalist Oliver Williamson.

In his paper on the nature of heterodox economics and neoclassical economics, Davis (2006, p. 27) does not use the terminology proposed by Backhouse, but I think that this is what he has in mind when he says that 'heterodox economics post-1980 is a complex structure, being composed of two broadly different kinds of heterodox work . . . : the traditional left heterodoxy and the "new heterodoxy" resulting from other science imports'. His 'traditional heterodoxy' is Backhouse's heterodox dissent, while his 'new heterodoxy' (later called 'mainstream heterodoxy' in Davis (2008, p. 359)) is orthodox dissent. Similarly, those that Colander et al. (2007–08, p. 309) call 'outside the mainstream heterodox economists'

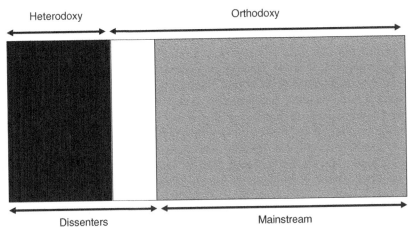

Figure 1.1   Orthodoxy, dissent and heterodoxy

are Backhouse's heterodox dissenters, while their 'inside the mainstream heterodox economists' are Backhouse's orthodox dissenters. Lawson (2009b, pp. 93–114), without, however, using the terms orthodox dissent and heterodox dissent, but obviously being in agreement with such a nomenclature, explains at length why Davis's new heterodoxy is not part of the heterodox programme, and why orthodox dissenters are instead committed to the methodological project pursued by mainstream economists.

Frederic Lee (2009, p. 4) also utilizes a slightly different nomenclature, a more provocative one as it is akin to religion, an analogy that, nevertheless, may be quite adequate for economics, calling 'heretics' those that Backhouse would name orthodox dissenters, while the heterodox dissenters are named 'blasphemers'. Here Lee uses the term heretics in a sense different from that of Keynes in the *General Theory*. In the context of economics, heretics believe in the mainstream and its methodology, but they advocate modifications to the doctrine. Thus they are not really a threat and are tolerated, the more so if they come from the upper ranks of the hierarchy. By contrast, the blasphemers are non-believers. They reject the core of the mainstream, deny its relevance and truth, and do not really wish to improve its doctrine. They have their own agenda, unrelated to that of the mainstream. They are apostates, who have apostatized from the mainstream, giving it up entirely. They are the heterodox dissenters.

Thus heterodox economists are dissenters in economics. But the concept of dissent is much broader than that of heterodoxy. Heterodox dissenters are unlikely to become part of the mainstream, and their position in the pecking order is likely to remain precarious. By contrast, orthodox dissenters may turn into heterodox dissenters or may become part of the mainstream, either from their own volition or because the bulk of the profession moved towards their propositions. Backhouse offers some examples of orthodox dissenters, such as the French Disequilibrium School in the late 1970s, with Malinvaud and Bénassy. Milton Friedman was certainly a dissenter in the 1950s, but then his views became mainstream in the late 1960s. Similarly, the New Consensus model, now best known as the dynamic stochastic general equilibrium model (the DSGE model), based as it was on a central bank reaction function involving the rate of interest rather than the money supply stock, was certainly considered as orthodox dissent at its beginning, but it is now the bread and butter of central bank researchers. Keynes himself, with the publication of the *General Theory* in 1936, was most probably perceived as an orthodox dissenter. As Herbert Simon (1997, p. 14) says, 'without the acceptance of the marginalist methods of thought, *The General Theory* would not have had the enormous and relative quick impact that it had on the thinking of mainstream economists'. This, by the way, raises a problem mentioned by Wladimir Andreff (1996) and by Earl and Peng (2012, p. 466): what if some heterodox dissenting stances were to become the most accepted paradigm? Could we still call them heterodox views? This is a somewhat rhetorical question, because, as pointed out earlier, it is a rather unlikely possibility now.

Other examples of orthodox dissent may include the work of authors as diverse as Colin Camerer, Harvey Leibenstein, Dan Rodrick, Herbert Simon, Ronald Coase, Wassily Leontief, Amartya Sen, George Akerlof, Paul Krugman, Joseph Stiglitz, Robert Shiller, Richard Thaler, Oliver Williamson or William Vickrey, most of them having won the Nobel Prize in economics. Some have explicitly stated that they certainly did not want to rock the mainstream boat. For instance Thaler, the behavioural economist, is cited as saying that he did not want 'to lay waste to the entire mathematical, hard science apparatus that economists had built after World War II' (Fox, 2009, p. 187). Others, like Simon and Vickrey, have turned towards heterodox economics.

1.3 PRESUPPOSITIONS OF THE HETERODOX AND ORTHODOX PARADIGMS

So far I have claimed that there exist two communities of economists, heterodox and orthodox. The philosophers of science would call these research programmes (Imre Lakatos) 'research traditions' (Laudan) or 'paradigms' (Kuhn). Both research programmes extend through all fields and domains of economics; within each field, each encompasses several theories or schools of thought; each theory entertains several models. Our task in this section is to identify the essentials of each of the two broad research programmes, what Leijonhufvud has called the presuppositions of a research tradition, that is, the set of commonly held metaphysical beliefs, which cannot be put in a formal form, and which are anterior to the constitution of the assumptions that rule specific models. These are the essentials of the research programme or their 'meta-axioms'. They are 'grand generalities somewhat in the nature of cosmological beliefs' (Leijonhufvud, 1976, p. 72). Tony Lawson (2006) expresses this by saying that orthodox and heterodox economists do not share the same 'ontology': they disagree on their preconceptions of the nature and structure of reality.

Although Marxians, Institutionalists, Structuralists, Evolutionarists, Socio-economists, the French Circuit and Regulation schools, Sraffians and post-Keynesians may have substantially different opinions on various topics, such as the theory of value or the relevance of long-period analysis, I believe they hold the same metaphysical beliefs, prior to the elements constituting the hard core of their respective theories. Similarly, Lawson (2009b, p. 123) argues that these various heterodox schools of thought hold a common implicit conception of social phenomena, and that to a large extent they can be mostly identified through the kind of questions that they ask, so that 'we can view the separate traditions as divisions of labour'. These heterodox economists are thus linked by something more than their dislike of neoclassical economics. If they dislike orthodox economic theory it is precisely because orthodox economics exudes presuppositions that are contrary to the metaphysical beliefs held by these economists. This is why they have become heterodox economists.

Showing that heterodox economists hold presuppositions that are different from those entertained in the mainstream will help to answer the main objection to the conception of an alternative to neoclassical economics. Mainstream economists rarely understand why any economist would want to work outside the framework of neoclassical economics. It is often believed that neoclassical theory offers the only viable approach to economic problems. Those who are not within the orthodoxy are said to be on the fringes of science. What is argued here is that there are two research traditions in economics, each with its own presuppositions, and that one cannot be called more scientific than the other, even though the orthodox research programme is much more in awe of formalization.

Several economists have attempted to identify what makes heterodox economics distinct from orthodox or neoclassical economics. This is not an easy task, as Andrew Mearman (2012a) reminds us. Over the last 30 years or so, I have argued that heterodoxy

Table 1.3 Presuppositions of the heterodox and orthodox research programmes

Presupposition	Heterodox schools	Orthodox schools
Epistemology/Ontology	Realism	Instrumentalism
Rationality	Environment-consistent rationality, satisficing agent	Hyper model-consistent rationality, optimizing agent
Method	Holism, organicism	Individualism, atomicism
Economic core	Production, growth, abundance	Exchange, allocation, scarcity
Political core	Regulated markets	Unfettered markets

and orthodoxy can be distinguished through four pairs of presuppositions, to which I have recently added a fifth one; all these can be found in Table 1.3. These five pairs result from my understanding of the two research programmes as well as from my reading of fellow economists interested in methodology, some of which, like Malcolm Sawyer (1989, pp. 18–21) and Mauro Baranzini and Roberto Scazzieri (1986, pp. 30–47), have suggested the same essentials. More recently, Mark Setterfield (2003) has endorsed these same presuppositions. I am not claiming that Table 1.3 represents the absolute truth, or that the pairs could not be rearranged, or new pairs put forward. I am only alleging that it is a convenient way to describe two broad visions of economics. Indeed, in trying, *a posteriori*, to verify if these presuppositions also applied to feminist and ecological economics, two fields about which I knew little, I discovered that these five presuppositions did a good job of describing these two traditions (Lavoie, 2003a; 2009a).

1.3.1 Instrumentalism versus Realism

Most outsiders would agree that 'economics should be about economic reality and should be demonstrably relevant to it' (Werner, 2005, p. 17). Some economic methodologists, most notably Lawson (1994), argue that the only crucial presupposition is that of realism. He argues that all the other presuppositions follow from it. This may be so, although Lawson himself seems to pay quite a bit of attention to another presupposition, atomicism, but I think it is worth spelling out all the others.

Realism and realisticness
Lawson, notably through his Cambridge Realist Workshop, has had a remarkable impact on economic methodologists in promoting the discussion of ontology, that is, the examination of the nature and existence of the phenomena under consideration, and some post-Keynesian economists have given explicit support to his philosophical views of transcendental realism and critical realism (e.g. Arestis, 1996; Dunn, 2008; Fontana, 2009). As Patrick Baert (1996, p. 513) has ironically written, 'a spectre is haunting the philosophy of the social sciences. It is called "critical realism", and, needless to say, it is spreading steadily throughout the academic community.' Indeed, several books in economics have been devoted to studies in critical realism and a full book has been devoted to a debate between Lawson and his critics on the topic of ontology and economics. In this book, Fullbrook (2009, p. 1) claims that Lawson's major point is 'that success in science depends on finding and using methods, including modes of reasoning, appropriate to the nature

of the phenomena'. Lawson believes that, although some stylized facts can be identified, a constant conjunction of events rarely occurs when analysing economic and social phenomena. As a result, the researcher must go beyond surface phenomena and find the true structures and causal mechanisms that explain the observed phenomena, by going to the essential rather than the most general. This, according to Lawson, is not what orthodox economists do.

If this sounds overly philosophical and vague – after all, it seems to me that everyone tries to go beneath surface phenomena – one may prefer instead to refer to the more down-to-earth concept of realisticness, with which I am more at ease. According to Muskali Mäki (1989, p. 179), when talking about the assumptions of a theory, 'we should not talk about "realism" of assumptions and theories, but rather about their realisticness ... "unrealisticness" means being not about reality or observables, being about inessentials, being false, disconfirmed in tests, idealizing, exaggerating, oversimplified, implausible, practically irrelevant. Both realisticness and unrealisticness are properties of representations'. Lawson (2009c, p. 171) himself agrees with this distinction, saying that 'realisticness' applies to the properties of actual theories, and suggesting that one should not say that mainstream theories lack realism, but rather that they lack realisticness.

There are certainly strong indications that heterodox authors attach great importance to discussing and modelling the economy on the basis of realistic assumptions. Caldwell (1989, p. 55) assesses that the most damning criticism of post-Keynesians against neoclassical economics is that it lacks realism, or rather that it lacks 'realisticness', arguing further that post-Keynesians value explanation rather than prediction, a characterization that can certainly also be applied to Institutionalists, who emphasize the storytelling method. Similarly, Morris Altman (2006, p. xvi), an author closer to the radical branch of behavioural economics, claims that 'what is critical to behavioral economics is the appreciation of the significance for economic analysis of the realism of one's modelling assumptions in terms of their behavioral and institutional dimensions'. Thus, as Lee (1994) says, theories should be 'empirically grounded'. And indeed, as Smithin (2009, p. 56) concurs, the 'emphasis on the realism of assumptions in macroeconomic models seems to be analogous to Lee's ... concept of grounded theory'.

Instrumentalism at work
By contrast, take the neoclassical presupposition of instrumentalism, defended by Milton Friedman (1953) in his famous essay on methodology. Instrumentalism is the belief that the truth of a theoretical statement is irrelevant. An assumption is sound when it allows precise predictions, in particular when it can help to find and calculate the value of an equilibrium position. Whether the assumption is realistic or not is irrelevant, and Friedman (1953, p. 14) even went so far as to argue that assumptions based on 'wildly inaccurate descriptive representations of reality' were more useful; ultimately, whether the prediction is accurate or not is also irrelevant (cf. Taleb, 2007, p. 280). The stance taken by Friedman, which Nathan Berg and Gerd Gigerenzer (2010) call 'Friedman's as if doctrine', gave neoclassical economists the freedom to start from wildly unrealistic foundations. Robert Lucas (1981, p. 270), the founder of New Classical economics, continued this tradition, claiming that 'insistence on the "realism" of an economic model subverts its potential usefulness in thinking about reality', adding that good models had to 'necessarily be artificial, abstract, patently unreal'.

By contrast, for (most) heterodox economists, a theory cannot be correct unless it starts from realist or realistic hypotheses, although it is recognized that assumptions are always abstractions and simplifications, and hence means to avoid cluttering a model with insignificant details. However, one should not start from assumptions that are descriptively false. The structure of a model cannot be built on foundations describing an imaginary or idealized economy. What is needed is an abstraction, not a fiction. Many heterodox economists would agree with Nicholas Georgescu-Roegen's (1971, p. 319) statement that 'when abstraction loses touch with reality, science becomes dogmatism'. The heterodox desire for realistic assumptions can be related to the fact that heterodox economists attach great importance to the storytelling method. An explanation has to be provided, usually associated with some causal mechanism, that goes beyond such simple claims as that supply or demand has shifted; therefore this or that has happened. Thus one has to go beyond surface phenomena, and examine the mechanisms or the structures that cause what is happening. What is required is an explanation of the causal processes at work. Obviously, if a story has to be told and explanations provided, one needs to pay more attention and scrutinize the starting assumptions, which need to be appropriately descriptive.

Heterodox economists are not interested in the counterfactual economies that have been the playground of researchers in general equilibrium theory such as Arrow, Debreu or Frank Hahn, and that are now the subject of state-of-the-art orthodox models. For instance, when Bliss (1975, p. 301) presents the intertemporal general equilibrium model, which is the twin of the now popular DSGE model, he claims that 'of course, that model does not serve to represent reality and that is not its purpose'. Hahn has made many similar claims regarding the irrelevance of his work for public policy. Unfortunately current neoclassical researchers do not appear to get this, as they maintain that variations on the Ramsey model, first designed to describe a planned economy, ought to be good enough to study capitalism.

Take as another example of neoclassical instrumentalism the so-called 'Gaussian copula function' that was used by financial engineers to model default correlation in the transformation of asset-backed securities (ABS) and the pricing of collaterized debt obligations (CDO), which were made up of tranches of ABS, and in the pricing of CDO-squared, which were made up of tranches of CDO (Salmon, 2009). As we know, these financial derivatives arising from securitized loans were at the core of the financial crisis. Instead of relying on the records of borrowers to assemble historical data about actual defaults to assess correlation and risk, finance economists looked instead at the evolution of the prices of credit default swaps (CDS) – the asset-backed securities index (ABX) – assuming that CDS markets can price default risk correctly. Another instance is the value-at-risk models that were based on high-frequency and very precise calibrated estimates; but they relied on samples that did not include catastrophic events and that were based on a particularly low volatility of the stock market, as pointed out by Boyer et al. (2005, p. 145). In those two instances we have instrumentalism in action. What counts most is to get a number. Whether that number is reliable is not so important. The fact that previous financial crises in the past, such as the Tequila crisis, have shown that markets do not necessarily correctly price risk is put aside; the fact that CDS markets had only been in existence for a short time, that is, only since housing prices had been on the rise, did not seem to matter either; the fact that the convenient normal distribution has long been shown by physicist Benoît Mandelbrot not to describe financial data, by under-representing extreme events, also seemed of little importance; and finally, the fact that the (recent) past is no guarantee of an uncertain future was also ignored.

Instrumentalism, in contradistinction to realism, implies, as sarcastically told by Anwar Shaikh (2016, p. 583), that 'one should not let realilty get in the way of rigor', or as Paul Davidson (1984, p. 572) would put it, that it is better 'to be precisely wrong rather than roughly right'. By contrast, post-Keynesians 'believe it is better to develop a model which emphasizes the special characteristics of the economic world in which we live than to continually refine and polish a beautifully precise, but irrelevant model' (ibid., p. 574). Nassim Taleb (2007, pp. 284–5) says nearly the same thing, arguing that heterodox economists 'want to be broadly right rather than precisely wrong', seeking 'to be approximately right across a broad set of eventualities' instead of being 'perfectly right in a narrow model, under precise assumptions'. Storytelling puts less emphasis on formalistic methods. For instance, Lawson (2009a) has argued, rightfully so it seems, that one could certainly put forward an adequate explanation of the Global Financial Crisis while omitting formal economics altogether.

Some may object that there is a good deal of realisticness in many mainstream models, in particular in the models put forth by New Keynesian authors. This can certainly be granted. Realisticness is integrated into the auxiliary hypotheses – asymmetric information, credit rationing, liquidity-constrained households, sticky prices. Some realism is also now being added to the state-of-the-art DSGE models, by introducing frictions in the financial system and by assuming the existence of banks (!). The main assumptions, however, defy common sense, based as they are on an all-knowing agent attempting to maximize some utility function by increasing work when she expects future taxes to rise and by increasing leisure time and reducing working hours when her real wage decreases. Orthodox economists, even many dissident orthodox authors, dress up their unrealistic foundations with realistic auxiliary hypotheses, such as the assumption that not all households can borrow funds at will. As Sebastian Dullien (2017, p. 243) puts it, adding heterodox assumptions to DSGE models based on highly implausible economic mechanisms are unlikely to make these models more plausible, except to students who have already been brainwashed by years of training in these models. The question, then, is whether it is possible to arrive at a model that describes the real world adequately by adding auxiliary realistic characteristics.

Nicholas Kaldor (1966, p. 310), for one, thought it was not possible: in an attempt to relieve the programme of its unrealistic foundations, the whole edifice would crumble. As he put it, removing the scaffolding 'is sufficient to cause the whole structure to collapse like a pack of cards'. Indeed, Kaldor thought that this defect of neoclassical theory was so important that he repeated the same argument six years later.

> The process of removing the 'scaffolding', as the saying goes – in other words of *relaxing* the unreal basic assumptions – has not yet started. Indeed the scaffolding gets thicker and more impenetrable with every successive reformulation of the theory, with a growing uncertainty as to whether there is a solid building underneath. (Kaldor, 1972, p. 1239)

This can certainly be observed of neoclassical macroeconomics, which strives on ever more extraordinary and unrealistic foundations. The same can also be said about new behavioural economists: while they intend to relax the most unrealistic features of the neoclassical model of the rational man, such as the belief that agents have access to all information at no cost, they are being forced to superpose other, even more unrealistic assumptions, as their utility-maximizing agents now need extraordinary computational abilities to handle their new information-costly environment.

1.3.2 Model-consistent Rationality versus Environment-consistent Rationality

Closely related to realism and instrumentalism is the kind of rationality that is assumed in our economic models. According to Hodgson (2019, p. 78), the crucial difference between orthodox and heterodox economics is the adoption or rejection of 'the assumption of utility-maximizing agents with preference functions', otherwise known as Max U. Following the rational expectations revolution, the only type of rationality admissible to mainstream macroeconomists is model-consistent rationality, which we can also call unbounded rationality or hyper-rationality (Shaikh, 2016, p. 78). Not only are economic agents assumed to know all contingencies, from now to eternity; since the rational expectations revolution they are further assumed to know how the world operates. Despite the fact that economists have been arguing with each other for centuries about the proper representation of the economy, modellers must assume that there is a single accepted model of the economy out there and that everyone agrees about how it functions. This is the RARE assumption of new consensus macroeconomics, as noted earlier. As Philip Mirowski (2011, p. 503) puts it, 'orthodox macroeconomists came to conflate "being rational" with thinking like an orthodox economist. What this implied was that agents knew the one and only "true model" of the economy (which conveniently was stipulated as identical with neoclassical microeconomics)'.

It is true that behavioural economists have tried to modify this by introducing heterogeneous agents into the realm of expectations, traders and chartists who rely on trends, alongside presumed truly rational investors who still look at the fundamentals, but they have made little headway in the more reputable journals. Most of the behavioural economists who have published in reputable journals agree with the as-if Friedmanian doctrine and argue 'that the goal of their models is not to provide a veridical description of the actual decision processes being used by economic agents, but to predict the outcome' (Berg and Gigerenzer, 2010, p. 159). Still, in my view, the more radical segment of behavioural economics – the group still devoted to a description of actual decision-making rather than to the study of biases relative to neoclassical rationality – must be classified under the umbrella of heterodox economics. This other group deals with what I call 'environment-consistent rationality'.

Economic agents, on this view, live in an environment either devoid of relevant information or characterized by an overload of unreliable information, and hence must follow some simple rules to make decisions without wasting too much time and resources. Agents attempt to achieve norms and will modify their short-run behaviour when these norms are not satisfied, thus reacting to what they perceive as disequilibria. In the long run, norms will be modified if they are continuously under- or over-achieved, or if changes in society at large have an impact on what is considered normal in the economic field. A good example of this is the gradual acceptance of the claim that a 'normal' return on equity, the famous ROE norm imposed by financial investors to managers, ought to be no less than 15 per cent, although this norm is incompatible with average macroeconomic conditions in Western economies, as has been demonstrated by Plihon (2002). More about reasonable rationality will be said in Chapter 2.

1.3.3 Atomicism versus Holism

The third pair of presuppositions concerns methodology: methodological individualism or atomicism versus holism or organicism. For Lawson, the conception of an economy based on isolated atoms is an essential feature of the lack of realism of orthodox theories. Atomicism, as practised by neoclassical economists, has a long history. Voltaire, in his famous novel, *Candide*, was already making fun through his Pangloss character of those who, like Leibniz, thought that non-interacting 'monads' ensure that we live in the best of all possible worlds. There is certainly a great deal of similarity with the neoclassical claim that all analysis must start at the level of the isolated optimizing individual and that competition between free atomistic firms will generate a Pareto optimum. Similarly, uncertainty in neoclassical analysis is often represented in terms of subatomic particles being subjected to a random Brownian motion. Within the framework of the subprime crisis, atomism is exemplified by the long-held belief that risk analysis could focus exclusively on individual firms and banks, without taking into account the macroeconomic conditions and implications, that is, by ignoring systemic risk. Another example would involve consumer behaviour: neoclassical authors assume that consumption expenditures are hardly influenced by marketing and publicity, and that consumers are not interdependent.

By contrast, heterodox authors have taken a more holistic approach. In relation to consumers, they have emphasized the predisposition to replicate the behaviour of others or to catch up with others, the search for status and positional goods, and the role of innovations in consumer credit. Many post-Keynesian authors see this interdependence as a driving force in the Global Financial Crisis, as low-income and median-income households, whose purchasing power has remained flat over the years, have attempted to keep up with the consumer and real-estate behaviour of upper classes, whose real incomes have quickly risen during the same time period (Brown, 2008; Barba and Pivetti, 2009; Zezza, 2008). Even more relevant to the crisis, perhaps, is the observation that herd or 'group behavior is the essence of financial markets' (Wojnilower, 1983, p. 179). This is related to what André Orléan (2014) has called *collective beliefs* or *conventions*, which are tied to the phenomena of mimetism and reflexivity, an example of which is the famous beauty contest story told by Keynes.

In (nearly) all heterodox models there are social classes, workers, capitalists, entrepreneurs, bankers and rentiers. The consideration of these classes, for income distribution purposes or for the theory of effective demand, arises from the presupposition that the definition of individual preferences is not sufficient to allow us to understand society. The consideration of individuals as social beings rather than atomistic ones allows not only for the explicit introduction of dominant and powerful institutions. But whereas mainstream economists view institutions as imperfections that prevent perfect competition, heterodox authors see them as providing some stability (Hodgson, 1989, p. 116). Stability, in a world of uncertainty, develops along the lines of organic interdependence, thanks to social conventions.

One may wonder how agent-based modelling fits within this atomistic/holistic dichotomy. On the one hand, agent-based modelling obviously starts with a multitude of atomistic agents, households or firms. On the other hand, modellers must design rules that their agents have to follow as they interact with each other. These rules constitute a social structure that is way more complex than the standard excess demand rules that are associated with orthodox economics, not to speak of the inanity of the single representative agent that populates DSGE models. In addition, a key characteristic of agent-based modelling is the 'emergence' of macroeconomic properties, which cannot be derived from the individual behaviour. From that perspective, it seems clear that agent-based modelling, or at least some versions of it, belongs to the heterodox tradition.

Emerging properties can be considered as macroeconomic paradoxes, or fallacies of composition, that contradict the pure aggregation of a representative agent. Heterodox authors pay considerable attention to these, and they are reminiscent of Marx's contradictions of capitalism. What seems reasonable for a single individual or nation leads to unintended consequences or even to irrational collective behaviour when all individuals act in a similar way. By way of example, Table 1.4 provides a list of general macroeconomic paradoxes that have been noted by post-Keynesian authors, such as Keynes's paradox of thrift. Table 1.5 will list paradoxes that can be associated more specifically with the financial system.

Some general macroeconomic paradoxes
Keynes's paradox of thrift says that an increase in the propensity to save will lead to reduced output. In its growth version, it says that it will lead to a decrease in the actual growth rate of output. With households being over-indebted, the paradox of thrift acts against the recovery, as households desperately try to restore their past levels of wealth by saving a larger proportion of their revenues. A quick check confirms that the notion of the paradox of thrift has now disappeared from most principles of economics textbooks.

Table 1.4 Holism: some general post-Keynesian macro-paradoxes

Paradox of thrift (Keynes, 1936; Robinson, 1956)	Higher saving rates lead to reduced output or reduced growth
Paradox of public deficits (Kalecki, 1971)	Government deficits raise private profits
Paradox of costs (Kalecki, 1969; Rowthorn, 1981)	Higher real wages lead to higher profit rates (wage-led growth regime)
The open-economy paradox (Blecker, 1989)	Higher real wages may lead to faster growth despite all countries being in a profit-led regime
The flexibility paradox I (Tobin, 1980; Caskey and Fazzari, 1987; Krugman, 2012)	The more flexible nominal wages and prices are, the more dramatic the perverse debt effects will be
The flexibility paradox II (Seppecher, 2012; Dosi et al., 2017)	The more easily employers can hire and fire employees, the less employment there is
The flexibility paradox III (Carnevali et al., 2020)	Sticky prices of exports stabilize the trade balance whereas exchange rate-sensitive export prices are destabilizing
The forecasting paradox (Dosi et al., 2020)	Better forecasting by individual firms may not lead to improved macroeconomic performance of the economy

The Global Financial Crisis illustrated the lack of awareness of this paradox, as several New Classical economists seemed to endorse Hayek's view that purchasing additional consumption goods would increase unemployment (Robinson, 1973, p. 94). Luckily, some decision-makers understood the paradox of thrift: Mark Carney (2008, p. 2), former Governor of the Bank of Canada and of the Bank of England, referred to it in a speech made during the financial crisis, when he pointed out that it would be 'individually rational for people to want to save more' in uncertain times, although if all individuals do so, then 'it becomes collectively irrational'.

The paradox of public deficits can be directly attributed to Kalecki (1971). He showed that higher government deficits play a role similar to that of higher net exports on corporate profits. Higher public deficits lead to higher corporate profits, just like higher public deficits lead to higher GDP and employment following the teaching of Keynes. While mainstream authors used to argue about the crowding-out effects of government activity, based on Ricardo-equivalence effects or rising real interest rates, several governments have engaged in expansionary fiscal policies in 2009 so as to sustain aggregate demand and corporate profits despite the financial crisis. When things go really wrong, as they did also during the COVID-19 crisis, neoclassical theories are thrown out of the window, being replaced by more pragmatic and realistic theories. It must be admitted, however, that pragmatism did not occur for long, as governments quickly called for fiscal consolidation programmes, especially in Europe.

The paradox of costs, in its static version, says that a decrease in real wages will not raise the profits of firms and will instead lead to a fall in the rate of employment. This was explained by Kalecki (1969, p. 26) in a Polish paper first written in 1939, where he concluded that 'one of the main features of the capitalist system is the fact that what is to the advantage of a single entrepreneur does not necessarily benefit all entrepreneurs as a class'. Its dynamic version has been proposed by Robert Rowthorn (1981). It says that rising real wages (relative to productivity) can generate higher profit rates. This flies in the face of a microeconomic analysis that would demonstrate that lower profit margins generate lower profit rates. But if higher real wages generate higher aggregate consumption, higher sales, higher rates of capacity utilization and hence higher investment expenditures, profit rates will be driven up. This of course is nothing else than a variant of Marx's problem of the realization of profit, underlined for instance by Amit Bhaduri (1986). In the midst of a crisis, it is important to resist calls to reduce labour costs in an effort to improve the profitability of individual firms. While this will be profitable to the firms that achieve the greatest real wage reductions, the overall effect will be detrimental to the overall economy, and most certainly to the overall world economy, as we shall discuss further in later chapters.

Related to the paradox of costs is the paradox of profit-led demand in an open economy. While a country taken in isolation may succeed in raising its net exports and its economic activity by imposing reductions in nominal and real wages, thus gaining a competitive advantage, this scheme will be unsuccessful if all other countries do the same. As will be discussed in Chapters 6 and 7, when only domestic demand is taken into consideration, thus omitting demand arising from abroad, all countries benefit from an increase in real wages (or in the wage share), mainly because of their positive impact on consumption expenditures. Because Planet Earth is a closed economy, the exports of one country are necessarily the imports of another country, and hence globally net exports are nil. Even though all countries may individually benefit from a change in income distribution towards profits, if other countries do not follow suit, such a change will have detrimental effects on the economic activity of the world economy if all countries pursue wage restrictions.

Three further paradoxes may be associated with the flexibility of nominal wages and prices or to the flexibility of the labour market. The first flexibility paradox claims that if a recession induces falling wages and prices, the recession will become even worse because households or firms which are indebted will become unable to pay back their debts, which is a fixed nominal amount, because of their falling nominal revenues. The more flexible prices and nominal wages are, the worse the recession will become. This is related to the objection that Kalecki made to the Pigou effect – the claim by Pigou that unemployment could not last because lower prices would raise real money balances and hence would eventually raise consumption. Kalecki argued that debts in real terms would also rise and hence would generate defaults and bankruptcies. Central bankers today seem to take this paradox very seriously, as they do all they can to avoid price deflation despite their liking for low inflation targets. The second flexibility paradox claims that if employers can hire and fire employees, the less employment there will be. Economies are more likely to go into a recession when workers are faster to adjust downward their reservation wage. By contrast more rigid labour markets and labour relations generate coordination successes leading to higher economic growth. This is an emerging property that has arisen in some agent-based models. This result goes against conventional beliefs, long held for instance at the OECD, which pretends that high unemployment in Europe is the consequence of excessive rigidity in the labour markets.

The third flexibility paradox concerns the behaviour of export and import prices. When a currency is devalued by a certain percentage, it is usually assumed by mainstream economists that exporting firms will lower the price charged in the currency of their foreign customers by the same percentage. In a two-country model where both real and financial effects are taken into account, Carnevali et al. (2020) show by contrast that the more exporters keep unchanged their foreign currency-denominated prices, the more likely it is that the deficits of the trade and current account balances will be erased, and the faster this will be achieved. Price stickiness generates stability. The final paradox, the paradox of forecasting, will be discussed in the next chapter.

Table 1.5   Holism: some macro-paradoxes related to financial crises

Paradox of debt (I. Fisher, 1933; Steindl, 1952)	Efforts to de-leverage might lead to higher leverage ratios
Paradox of tranquillity (Minsky, 1975)	Stability is destabilizing
Paradox of liquidity I (Dow, 1987; Orléan, 1999)	Efforts to become more liquid transform liquid assets into illiquid ones – the Minsky moment
Paradox of liquidity II (Minsky, 1986a; Nesvetailova, 2007)	Financial innovations seem to increase liquidity when in fact they end up reducing it
Paradox of risk (Wojnilower, 1980)	The possibility of individual risk cover leads to more risk overall
Paradox of degrading standards (McCulley, 2009)	Default rates are low because of the degradation of underwriting standards

Six paradoxes tied to the financial system

We now move on to macroeconomic paradoxes tied to the financial system, as shown in Table 1.5, and start with the paradox of debt. This paradox is also based on the concept of effective demand, and it was put forward by Joseph Steindl (1952, ch. 9), who was a follower of Kalecki. From a strictly microeconomic point of view, one would be led to believe that it is always possible for economic agents to reduce their debt or leverage ratios by simply deciding to do so. While this may be true for households, it may be quite difficult for firms and financial institutions taken as a group. To reduce the weight of indebtedness, firms may decide to cut their investment expenditures and hence the amounts they borrow. However, if all companies are pursuing this scheme, cutting back on borrowing and investment may not put matters right, for the slowdown in capital accumulation reduces the overall profitability of businesses and hence the accumulation of retained earnings. In the end, the actual leverage ratio may rise, moving in a direction that is the opposite of what is intended by the entrepreneurs. This is what Steindl (1952, p. 119) and Jan Toporowski (2005, p. 126) call 'enforced indebtedness'. The paradox of debt may also apply to governments: as they reduce government expenditures and pursue other austerity measures to reduce public debt, the government debt to GDP ratio may rise instead.

Something quite similar may happen to banks and other financial institutions as they try to reduce their leverage ratios. This is linked to Irving Fisher's debt-deflation effect. As banks sell some of their assets, in an effort to reduce leverage or recover liquidity, such forced sales bring down the price of these assets, which are now sold at a loss, thus reducing the banks' own funds, so that the leverage ratio is rising instead of falling. Other efforts to reduce the amount of loans may put borrowers in financial distress, as is observed in times of credit crunch, so that again individual attempts to reduce the leverage ratio (or to increase the capital to asset ratio) may indeed lead to the opposite macroeconomic effect. This can be associated with what we could call the paradox of banking refusal. When the economy is slowing down or is entering a recession, it may be rational for each individual bank to take protection measures against loan losses by rationing credit and refusing to grant new loans. But, as was recognized by central bankers, if all banks do the same, 'their actions will exacerbate the downturn and increase their eventual losses' (Carney, 2008, p. 2).

Also closely tied to the financial system is the paradox of tranquillity. This is an expression that I coined nearly more than three decades ago (Lavoie, 1986a, p. 7), when studying the works of Minsky. According to Minsky, a stable growing economy is a contradiction in terms. A fast-growing free-market economy will necessarily transform itself into a speculative booming economy. In a world of uncertainty, without full information about the fundamentals, a string of successful years diminishes perceived risk and uncertainty. People tend to forget the difficulties encountered in the past: turning points, falling asset prices, credit crunches and recessions. As time goes on, memories fade and economic agents dare to take on higher levels of risk. Or else, as time goes on, the risk level as computed by engineering models of finance, such as the very popular value at risk model, appears to get smaller because the last recession is just one remote observation among a series of more recent successful years. The longer an economy is in a tranquil state of growth, the less likely it is to remain in such a state. As Minsky himself says, 'each state nurtures forces that lead to its own destruction' (Minsky, 1975, p. 128). In three words, the paradox of tranquillity says that 'stability is destabilizing' (Minsky, 1982b, p. 26). Applied to a monetary economy, this implies that a string of successful financial operations will induce banks to indulge in ever riskier financial structures.

What Minsky was claiming 40 years ago seems quite prescient today: 'Over a period in which the economy does well, views about acceptable debt structure change. In the deal-making that goes on between banks, investment bankers, and businessmen, the acceptable amount of debt to use in financing various types of activity and positions increases' (Minsky, 1977, p. 24). The cushion for safety – the difference between the additional revenues expected from some new activity and the financial commitments required by this activity – gets reduced through time. For Minsky, instability and the rising fragility of the financial system are inherent features of an unregulated capitalist economy. Part of this destabilizing stability is tied to financial innovations, which will be introduced or expanded when things go well (ibid.). This view of the financial system is reminiscent of that of John Kenneth Galbraith, who, in his various books, most notably *A Short History of Financial Euphoria* (1990), has argued that speculative euphoria in market capitalism was an inevitable outcome, as speculators and bankers ride the wave by using leverage, and believe they become rich because they are smart.

The paradox of tranquillity is certainly at the heart of the Global Financial Crisis. But no less important for the subprime crisis is the paradox of liquidity. In modern finance theories of the neoclassical type, most assuredly the efficient-market hypothesis, liquidity is of little concern. It is assumed that well-informed market participants always manage to arrive at a transaction price reflecting the correct fundamental value of an asset. What is at issue is only the expected return and the estimated risk of the asset. By contrast, liquidity is a crucial element of post-Keynesian economics (Davidson, 2009). Investors should always be concerned about the impossibility of cashing in their assets. There must be some market-maker who guarantees to purchase assets if the market suddenly goes one way. These market-makers are dealers, with access to lines of credit issued by banks, or the banks themselves, with access to central bank liquidity.

The paradox of liquidity can be seen from two angles. First there is the obvious fact, also linked to Fisher's debt-deflation proposition, that the attempt of economic agents to become more liquid transforms previously liquid assets into not-so-liquid assets. The frenzy to get rid of assets drives down the price of these assets and may transform the markets for these assets into one-way markets, with no purchaser, leading to a total freeze, as occurred in some markets during the Global Financial Crisis. As Sheila Dow (1987, p. 85) says, 'attempts to increase the stock of liquid assets only succeed in reducing it; this is a paradox of liquidity on a par with Keynes' paradox of saving'. But there is a second paradox of liquidity, tied to innovations in the financial system that we just mentioned. Financial innovations seem to increase liquidity when they are really diminishing it. This second paradox was already pointed out by Minsky, but it has recently been underlined in a book. Anastasia Nesvetailova (2007, p. 78) claims that 'to Minsky and his followers, therefore, every institutional innovation that leads to both new ways to finance business and new substitutes for cash assets, *decreases* the volume of liquidity available to redeem the debts incurred'. Thus, she continues, 'in the process of financial expansion the financial system, contrary to appearances, becomes *progressively illiquid*'. The financial system gets ever more layered, with everybody thinking that they can easily access means of payment, but with virtually nobody holding safe assets without capital-loss risk.

The paradox of liquidity can be extended to a paradox of risk. Financial innovations designed to reduce risk at the microeconomic level, by spreading it over a larger number of financial institutions – as is the case with securitization, collaterized debt obligations, credit default swaps, equity default swaps, interest rate swaps, repo-based collaterized loans and the whole gamut of financial futures and financial derivatives – end up creating a larger amount of macroeconomic or systemic risk. For instance, it is now widely believed that the extensive use of mathematical models to quantify risk, yielding the illusion of precise and objective assessments, encouraged banks and other financial institutions to pursue more risky strategies and to use more leverage. Famous US regulators such as Alan Greenspan – the former Federal Reserve Chairman – and Tim Geithner – the former President of the New York Fed and former US Secretary of Treasury – both claimed as late as 2006 that credit derivatives were a stabilizing factor in the financial system, as they reduced the concentration of individual exposure to risk, spreading credit risk to those best able to handle it. Even left-wing economists such as Michel Aglietta (1996) argued that securitization would have beneficial effects on the economy. Each microeconomic agent believes that he or she is now covered against risk; but the risk is still there, in the form of counterparty risk. Indeed, even if the counterparty seems to be safe, the counterparty's counterparty may not be, and its failure may well spill over. The illusion of liquidity induces agents to take even more risky decisions. Thus risk-reducing microeconomic financial innovations end up producing a more risky macroeconomic environment. Derivatives were likened to the contingent markets of the general equilibrium model *à la* Arrow–Debreu. But we do not live in such a world. It is completely imaginary. We live in a world of fundamental uncertainty *à la* Keynes and Knight.

Derivative financial products do not stabilize the economy. While they are a tool of risk management, 'derivative markets actually increase the credit risks', since 'at the first whiff of crisis or instability, the first thing to evaporate is the liquidity' that these tools are supposed to provide (McKenzie, 2011, p. 212). Thus, ultimately, as summed up long ago by another Minsky follower, Albert M. Wojnilower (1980, p. 309), the 'supposed immunity to financial risk always turns out to be illusory, and the risks and costs of shattering the illusion may be considerable'. Wojnilower was particularly perceptive about this, since, as far back as 1984, he predicted the bailout of AIG from its CDS sales:

> The recent entry of major insurance companies into the business of insuring banks and bond investors against loan defaults represents another effort to stretch the safety net. Now, it can be presumed, the authorities will have to intervene to interdict a cascading of defaults only if to save the insurance industry. (Wojnilower, 1985, p. 356)

Finally, let us deal with the paradox of degrading standards, which can be attributed to Paul McCulley, himself a Minskyan and a former chief economist at PIMCO (one of the largest investment funds in the world), and the person who coined the *shadow banking* term. The paradox is there to explain how it is possible for banks and other financial institutions to keep providing loans to ever less qualified borrowers while everything seems to run smoothly. In the case of mortgages, as long as real estate prices keep growing, borrowers can easily refinance their loans or otherwise sell their residence with a capital gain, so that there are no defaults. The validation of previous lending decisions encourages the issuance of ever-riskier loans, but these loans in turn contribute to rising housing prices, until the market runs out of qualified buyers. Thus, as McCulley (2009, p. 268) puts it, 'Rating agencies thought the default rates would be low because they had been low. But they had been low because the degradation of underwriting standards was driving up asset prices'. In a sense, the paradox of degrading standards is a variant of the paradox of tranquillity.

1.3.4 Scarcity versus Abundance

I have already alerted the reader to the fact that the orthodox definition of economics focuses on the notion of scarcity, a definition that heterodox authors reject. Scarcity is the fulcrum of neoclassical economics. As Parguez (2012–13, p. 55) points out, scarcity in neoclassical economics plays a role akin to that of austerity in religion, where austerity is 'the supreme virtue of renouncing pleasures of worldly life to attain the joy of the afterlife'. Hayek (1941, pp. 373–7), when rejecting Keynes's economics, is precisely invoking the crucial importance of scarcity. To proclaim the existence of an economy of plenty or an economics of abundance, as did Keynes, was to negate the foundations of orthodoxy. A similar point is made by Galbraith (1958) in his book *The Affluent Society*. In the neoclassical model, the main feature of a capitalist market economy is the proper allocation of resources, real and financial. Prices, as emphasized by Hayek, are supposed to provide all the information required to make the market system function efficiently, because prices are the measure of scarcity, so that the knowledge of prices allows agents to respond to changes in scarce resources.

But is this really the case? Certainly, with respect to recent events, we can assume that prices did misallocate financial resources, as securitization provided misleading prices and too many financial resources were put into real estate. This had just been preceded by the stock-market crash of 2001, when stock markets worldwide took a beating, while the NASDAQ in particular plunged and never fully recovered. And then the real-estate bubble was immediately followed by the super-high prices in commodities, food products and oil, with these prices falling sharply just a few months later, thus giving a strong indication that these prices had risen only as a result of unwarranted speculative activity rather than as a consequence of changes in fundamentals. Indeed, it has been argued that high commodities prices have arisen from the efforts of financial managers to find new conduits that would be uncorrelated with the returns on bonds and equities. Thus high oil, commodities and food prices result from inflows of funds in the futures markets of these products, as fund managers follow a strategy of portfolio diversification that leads them to speculate on futures indices (Wray, 2008; Davidson, 2008). Again, one may think that these markets for derivatives have no influence on the real world; but they do, because, being more liquid, they induce economic agents to base their decisions on these futures markets, with the result that spot prices depend on futures prices, instead of futures prices being (only) dependent on expected spot prices.

Various conditions will be set in orthodox models to preserve scarcity outside the standard conditions of exchange economies where endowments are fixed: the stock of money will be assumed to be exogenous; full employment and full capacity utilization will be assumed at all times. The crucial assumption in most of modern orthodox macroeconomics, an assumption that drives all the standard results and policies, is the existence of a unique natural rate of unemployment (or of a single non-accelerating inflation rate of unemployment, the NAIRU). Whatever realistic feature is introduced in the model, the assumed uniqueness of the natural rate of unemployment will remove any room for alternative policies. The same can be said about the natural rate of interest: it forbids any imagination in central bank policy.

Scarcity justifies supply and demand analysis. It governs the behaviour of the economy. It explains why neoclassical economists attach such importance to the allocation of resources or why so many of them define the techniques of constrained optimization as the epitome of orthodox economics and a condition for scientific endeavour. When all resources are scarce, they are fully employed, and therefore all questions revolve around the proper use of existing resources, rather than around the creation of new commodities. Scarcity is particularly obvious in pure exchange models. The supplementary hypotheses that can be found in the various sophisticated neoclassical production models are, however, being introduced precisely to safeguard all the main conditions and results of the pure exchange model (Rogers, 1983; Pasinetti, 2007, p. 20). Production in neoclassical economics is a form of indirect exchange, between individual consumer agents who own resources that transit to the same individual agents, then christened producers. These producers are nothing but arbitragistes attempting to benefit from existing scarcities.

In the heterodox research programme, in particular in the post-Keynesian tradition, the notion of scarcity is put aside, while that of reproducibility is put to the forefront (Roncaglia, 1978, p. 5; Pasinetti, 1981, p. 24). With their emphasis on production, heterodox economists embark on the tradition of the classical economists, with their concern for the causes of progress and accumulation. In his review of the Cambridge critique, Rymes (1971, p. 2) makes clear that the Sraffian concern for reproducibility is in the lineage of the economic thought of Robinson, Kaldor and even Harrod. As pointed out by Pasinetti (1981, p. 7), classical authors, in particular Ricardo, focused on the permanent feature of reproducibility, considering that produced goods could be multiplied without limits, and thus judging that, besides land, scarcity conditions could only be of a temporary nature. Thus, for post-Keynesians, prices are not an index of scarcity in general; rather, prices reflect the unit costs of producing these reproducible goods or services.

In post-Keynesian models where output is not disaggregated, the emphasis on production appears through the assumption that in general neither capital goods nor labour is fully employed. In this sense, resources are not scarce. The major problem is not how to allocate them, but how to increase production or the rate of growth. It is generally possible to increase the rate of utilization of capacity and there are reserves of labour. The principle of scarcity is replaced by the principle of effective demand. The true constraint is not supply, but effective demand. Shiozawa et al. (2019, p. 140) insist that 'capitalism can be characterized as a *demand-constrained economy*', because sellers compete with each other to capture demand, whereas in a socialist economy buyers compete with each other for a restricted supply. As Kaldor (1983b, p. 6) says, 'for production to be demand-determined, excess capacity must exist as well as unemployed labour'. Arestis (1996, p. 112) concurs: 'Effective demand in post-Keynesian analysis implies that it is scarcity of demand rather than scarcity of resources that is to be confronted in modern economics, so that output is ordinarily limited by effective demand, although it is recognised that supply constraints are present in modern capitalist economies.' Today, one thinks mostly of ecological constraints.

I would be prepared to argue that, if orthodox economics is the research programme of a world of scarcity, heterodox economics is the research programme of a world of abundance (sometimes in the midst of poverty). John Weeks (2012) has put things in a more striking fashion: 'The economics of scarcity is pernicious foolishness. By contrast the economics of idle resources addresses reality. It is the same as the difference between alchemy and chemistry, astrology and astronomy, evolution and creationism.'

1.3.5 Unfettered Markets versus Regulated Markets

This leads us to the fifth and last of our key presuppositions, that of the role of markets relative to the role of the state. Mainstream economists exhibit great confidence in the ability of uninhibited markets to deliver stability and full employment, and to deliver solutions to any economic or social problem. The most extreme versions of neoclassical theory claim that instability and unemployment can prevail only when government interferes in the operation of markets, thus hampering the price mechanism from achieving equilibrium. In this version of orthodox economics, the market knows all and is the only provider of truth. All this is well expressed in the following quote:

> [The key beliefs of neoclassical economics] are that the pursuit of individual self-interest will lead to a better society, that government intervention beyond the narrow maintenance of law and order should be minimized if not eliminated and that the powers of unfettered markets should be unleashed in virtually every part of society, at home and abroad. For this purpose, structural reforms are recommended to deregulate, liberalize, privatize and open up as many industries and aspects of the economy as possible, as the beneficial forces of the invisible hand, if only allowed to operate freely, would improve people's lives, create wealth, produce prosperity and lead to maximum happiness. (Werner, 2005, p. 3)

By contrast, heterodox economists are very distrustful of unfettered markets. While post-Keynesian economists and their heterodox colleagues will recognize the creativity and dynamism imparted by entrepreneurship in a capitalist system, which along with Joseph Schumpeter they believe to be its main quality in opposition to static allocation efficiency, they question the wisdom of blindly relying on markets. They suspect their unfairness, their inability to self-regulate, their tendency for destabilizing paths and their squandering of resources. Capitalist economies cannot be left on their own devices. Indeed, some heterodox economists – Marxians and even more likely Marxists – would prefer to eliminate capitalism altogether.

Furthermore, heterodox economists believe that unbridled prices – highly flexible prices – generate instability rather than stability. By contrast, sticky prices with some inertia are more likely to generate stability. Thus they believe that state regulation is needed, both at the micro and macro levels, as the costs of such government intervention become dwarfed compared to the costs of unregulated capitalism. In the eyes of heterodox economists and some orthodox dissenters, it is no coincidence that the number of financial crises throughout the world in general and the USA in particular has occurred at such a rising rate ever since deregulation has spread over all economies in the early 1980s. Financial engineers – quants – made a mess of the financial system, as became obvious in 2007. Financial deregulation was based on the claim by orthodox economists that the regulators ought to leave finance to regulate itself because markets know the price of risk and allocate it efficiently, and that market discipline, along with the surveillance of shareholders, would keep a lid on excessive risk-taking. This intellectual edifice has collapsed, just as the intellectual edifice based on a self-adjusting system had collapsed in the 1930s, but the majority of economists still hold on to these ideas.

The fifth presupposition had been identified very clearly by Keynes himself 75 years earlier. Here is what he was saying then:

> I have said that we fall into two main groups. What is it that makes the cleavage which thus divides us? On the one side are those who believe that the existing economic system is, in the long run, a self-adjusting system, though with creaks and groans and jerks, and interrupted by time lags, outside interference and mistakes . . . On the other side of the gulf are those who reject that idea that the existing economic system is, in any significant sense, self-adjusting. (Keynes, 1973, xiii, pp. 486–7)

The post-Keynesian author Minsky has also been pretty clear about this divide between economists, focusing on the financial side:

> In a world with capitalist finance it is simply not true that the pursuit by each unit of its own self-interest will lead an economy to equilibrium. The self-interest of bankers, levered investors, and investment producers can lead the economy to inflationary expansions and unemployment-creating contractions. Supply and demand analysis – in which market processes lead to an equilibrium – does not explain the behavior of a capitalist economy, for capitalist economic processes mean that the economy has endogenous destabilizing forces. Financial fragility, which is a prerequisite for financial instability, is, fundamentally, a result of internal market processes. (Minsky, 1986a, p. 280)

Some readers may wonder whether it is really important to know whether the economy is stable or not. But think of it this way: how useful can be a theory that assumes from the start that financial markets can never be wrong, that they stabilize the economy, and that there can never be any defaults? Will such a theory be useful in designing rules to regulate the banking or the financial system? Another example could be the transition of Eastern European countries towards capitalism, as advisers and politicians did not seem to understand that capitalism has to be tamed and necessitates strong institutions (Marangos, 2004).

The divide here evoked by Keynes and Minsky is much more important now than it was 35 or 85 years ago. And the forces present are the same as those described by Keynes then, when he said that the 'self-adjusted school depends on its having behind it almost the whole body of organised economic thinking and doctrine' (1973, xiii, p. 488). This organized body today is made up of all the major US universities, along with foreign economics departments that attempt to imitate those renowned US economics departments, plus the myriad of well-endowed think-tanks devoted to market fundamentalism. On the side of the self-adjusted school we find the orthodox economists, who are a vast majority, controlling nearly all economics departments; on the side of the sceptics are the heterodox economists, who are a majority in only a handful of departments, and who are otherwise spread out in various economics departments, social sciences faculties and business schools.

1.3.6 Ideology

Another way to express the fifth set of presuppositions is to talk of ideology. Bernard Guerrien (2009), a French mathematical economist, agrees with Lawson and other methodologists that orthodox theories lack realisticness. In fact, he goes somewhat further than Lawson, claiming that the mainstream benchmark model, the neo-Walrasian perfect competition model, is not only unrealistic; it is completely irrelevant because, as pointed out earlier, it relies on mechanisms akin to a planned centralized economy and not on the adjustment mechanisms of a market economy. Guerrien wonders how such unwarranted conflations can be made. His answer is that orthodox economists are driven by ideology. Because they have conservative leanings, they wish to show that market economies, devoid of frictions and imperfections, yield efficient outcomes, even if this requires absurd assumptions. This thesis is also espoused by Marglin (1984a, p. 481), and no doubt by a large number of Marxian economists, who believe that ideology is the crucial element separating most orthodox economists from most heterodox economists.

Neoclassical theory is flexible enough, through the introduction of auxiliary hypotheses (externalities, imperfections, increasing returns, asymmetric information), to generate a large range of results so as to arrive at just about any sort of economic policy recommendation. New Keynesian economics is a good illustration of this phenomenon, and some orthodox dissenters, like Stiglitz, have clearly expressed that this was their academic strategy. This perhaps explains why many graduate students with left-wing inclinations do not object to being drilled through neoclassical economics. Thus the relationship between one's ideology and one's economic tradition may not be overly tight.

From a historical perspective, there is no doubt that neoclassical theory and hence today's orthodox theories have a link with ideology. In the midst of the various revolutionary waves that were hitting Europe in the second half of the nineteenth century, the simultaneous appearance of marginalist works, breaking away from several of the classical concerns and concepts, provided a breath of fresh air for the threatened political and economic establishment. Furthermore, marginalism, as it was then called, offered an alternative to Marx's extension of the classical school (De Vroey, 1975; Pasinetti, 1981, pp. 11–14). Because Marx's premises were similar to those of the classicals on so many points, it was difficult to reject his analysis and his conclusions altogether. Getting rid of the classical theory of value and of the classical explanation of the origin of profit by embarking on the path of marginalism was the answer of the European bourgeoisie. With the advent of Marx it became imperative for the establishment, long annoyed with some of the conclusions drawn from classical economics, to find a less class-conscious and more apologetic alternative.

The economists also embarked on the bandwagon, so that by the 1900s marginalism had swept over economics. There was a convergence in those days, perhaps still now, between the presuppositions and agenda of neoclassical economics and the interests of the political and industrial establishment, just as today there is an obvious convergence between economists and the financial establishment. As George Soros (2010, p. 86), the former speculator, says, 'by far the most powerful force working in favor of market fundamentalism is that it serves the self-interests of owners and managers of capital'. Indeed, the debates around the economic policies that should be or should have been pursued during and before the Global Financial Crisis, especially the debates that have raged around the consequences of budget deficits, the composition of tax cuts or tax increases, and the need for financial regulation, have clearly shown that ideology is a key determinant of the theoretical positions being advanced. 'Economists produce the sorts of knowledge that [their] patrons desire' (Mirowski, 2011, p. 508).

Perhaps there is an even simpler explanation. As the movie *Inside Job* highlighted, economists, or at least some of them, are driven by money. The popularity and the adoption of economic theories may depend more on their potential monetary rewards than on the search for truth. No less an author than Paul Samuelson (2007, pp. ix–x) has suggested that some theories take over others on the basis of the strength of political winds and monetary rewards, writing that 'what establishment economists brew up is as often what the Prince and the Public are already wanting to imbibe'. Samuelson thus reversed the causality invoked by Keynes (1936, p. 383), when, in an oft-rehearsed quote, he argued that: 'Practical men, who believe themselves to be quite exempt from any intellectual influences, are usually the slaves of some defunct economist. Madmen in authority, who hear voices in the air, are distilling their frenzy from some academic scribbler of a few years back.' Samuelson believes instead that 'madmen in authority can *self-generate* their own frenzies without needing help from either defunct or *avant-garde* economists'. This is confirmed by Paul Krugman (2013), who asserts that 'the austerity agenda looks a lot like a simple expression of upper-class preferences, wrapped in a facade of academic rigor. What the top 1 percent wants becomes what economic science says we must do.' Or perhaps this is an instance of two-way causality.

One would have thought that the development of statistical tools would have helped to limit the impact of ideology. But as Moosa (2017a, p. 242), himself an econometrician, says in a commentary, 'the contribution of econometricians is that they have provided the tools that allow anyone to prove anything, which can be rather "handy", particularly for those motivated by ideology'! Coming back to the statement of Samuelson, Fabo et al. (2020) show that empirical studies done by central bank researchers show a much greater positive effect of quantitative easing than studies done by other scholars, and that the greater the effect found the greater the probability of a promotion for its author within the central bank.

1.3.7 A Sixth Presupposition?

Could there be a sixth presupposition? Lawson, based on his view of critical realism, believes that orthodox economics is bankrupt precisely because it is using methods of formalism that are not adequate to study economic and social phenomena. For Lawson (2009d, p. 340), 'the reliance on formalistic models forces the mainstream on the path of irrelevance'. Earlier, he says that 'the insistence that mathematical methods should be everywhere used is not only mainstream doctrine; it is the cause of the discipline's continuing ills' (2009b, p. 109). Lawson claims that the unity and the stability of the orthodox school is based on this single edict – the requirement to put arguments in a mathematical–deductivist form. Thus, if we were to follow Lawson on this, we could argue that the requirement for formalism constitutes a sixth presupposition of orthodox economics, while 'the feature that characterises heterodoxy *qua* heterodoxy is opposition to the mainstream insistence that only formalism be used' (ibid., p. 106).

According to Lawson, heterodox schools of thought, in opposition to orthodox dissidents, would have arisen as a response to the failure of the formalistic methods in orthodox economics.

It is certainly tempting to follow Lawson on this formalization track. Indeed, it could be argued that neoclassical economics has gradually evinced non-neoclassical schools of thought from economics departments because most heterodox economists paid little attention to formalization. We know that the profession has become ever more technical and mathematized, preoccupied with ever more abstract and unrealistic assumptions, often devised to keep the mathematics tractable rather than be pertinent to the subject at hand. Skidelsky (2009, p.x) concurs, saying that he has 'come to see economics as a fundamentally regressive discipline, its regressive nature disguised by increasingly sophisticated mathematics and statistics'. Excessive formalization, as recognized in the speeches of many former recipients of the Nobel Prize in economics, is a scourge in the field of economics. As Leijonhufvud (1973, p. 329) recalled long ago, the priestly caste of mathematical economists occupies the highest caste-ranking. Their skills are looked at in awe by their colleagues. Indeed, as recalled by Beed and Beed (1996), 20 per cent of surveyed economists claimed to be familiar with a fictitious *Journal of Economic and Statistical Theory*, and placed it nearly in the top quarter of all listed journals, no doubt because of its mathematical-sounding name. Mathematics used to add some rigour to verbal arguments; now it plays a paradigm-preserving role. Formalization forces the focus of attention away from the larger issues and towards minute details. Such is their importance that the graduate students of the departments run by the invisible college now consider that being good at problem-solving and excellence in mathematics are more important for a successful academic career than a knowledge of the economy and of the overall economics literature (Klamer and Colander, 1990, p. 18). No doubt the situation has not improved since this survey was done more than 30 years ago.

How far do heterodox authors go, or how far should they go, in their distrust of mathematical methods? Sheila Dow (2000, p. 164) writes that 'the guiding principle of orthodox economics is mathematical formalism'. She seems to go too far when she adds that 'heterodox paradigms share a rejection of mathematical formalism'. And so does Lawson nowadays. While he used to deny that he is 'opposed to mathematical formalism per se' (Lawson, 2009e, p. 190), suggesting that what he is opposed to is 'the abuse of mathematical formalism', nowadays Lawson (in Mearman et al., 2019, p. 142) is complaining that some economists are 'claiming the heterodox label for themselves whilst allocating much of their time to mathematical modelling …. So heterodox contributions have become increasingly weak and of little relevance to the real world', adding that their models are 'worthless all the same because the methods are just irrelevant' since 'modelling necessitates false assumptions' (ibid., p. 144). These heterodox authors would be wasting their time and failing to see the true light. This has led one of his followers to make a distinction between *consistent* heterodox economists, who do not formalize, while those who do are said to be 'confused, inconsistent, heterodox economists' (Slade-Caffarel, 2019, p. 534).

As argued by Hodgson (2019, p.70), 'Lawson's argument concerning mathematics is not widely accepted, even in the heterodox community'. Harcourt (in Fullbrook, 2003, p. 70) considers that the issue of formalization in heterodox economics is a 'red herring', summing it up by saying that mathematics is 'a good servant but a bad master'.

All the heterodox schools of economics carry mathematically trained economists. Some heterodox economists have led the way in some research areas, such as non-linear and complexity dynamics. Several heterodox authors enjoy formalization, and some of them have regrouped under the informal term of 'analytical political economy' (Setterfield, 2003). The big difference, as Amitava Dutt (2003, p. 58) points out, is that the only mathematical modelling that is acceptable to both the mainstream and the orthodox dissenters ultimately relies on 'the use of the optimizing agent' instead of 'empirically-based behavioral relations'. It is the insistence on modelling and on this straitjacket of individual atomistic optimization that heterodox authors reject. Formalism should not be an end in itself. Formal models may illuminate comprehension. They provide some discipline. Thus several post-Keynesians endorse 'the cautious use of formal methods in economics' (Fontana, 2009, p. 39) or argue that 'formalism is fine, but it must know its place' (Chick, 1998, p. 1868). Indeed, Keynes (1973, xiv, p. 296) himself thought that 'economics is a science of thinking in terms of models joined to the art of choosing models that are relevant to the contemporary world'.

Another defining dichotomy between orthodox and heterodox economics, a candidate for a seventh presupposition, has been put forth by Lawson (1997) and Dow (2000). Heterodoxy would entail a belief in open systems, while orthodox economics would deal with closed systems. I have never been able to convince myself of the usefulness of such a dichotomy, even though some famous writers seem to approve of it. The distinction has been used by Stephen Pratten (1996) to argue that Sraffian economics was based on a law-like closed system, and therefore out of heterodoxy, despite the well-known fact that the profit rate in the Sraffian system is left up in the air, with no definite determinant. Indeed, Mearman (2006, p. 69) argues that there is a considerable amount of realism in Sraffian economics. The closed/open system dichotomy has also been used by Downward (2000) to argue that target-return pricing is not a truly heterodox theory, because it yields a determinate pricing formula, despite its kinship with Kalecki's or Gardiner Means's 'open' pricing proposals. Such pronouncements seem so obviously misleading that their open/closed basis cannot provide much useful information, a point also made earlier by John Smithin (2004, pp. 67–70) and by Mearman (2006).

1.3.8 Some Additional Reflections on Presuppositions

In the previous section, I asked whether neo-Austrian economists ought to be counted as orthodox or heterodox economists. On the matter of formalization just discussed, neo-Austrian economists clearly side with heterodox schools of thought, since neo-Austrians are rather sceptical about formalization in economics. Undoubtedly a large number of neo-Austrian economists consider themselves as heterodox economists, as they feel ostracized by their mainstream colleagues because of their lack of access to top academic journals. Various neo-Austrian economists have underlined the similarities between Keynesian uncertainty and Knightian uncertainty, Frank Knight being associated with the neo-Austrian tradition. Lawson (1994, pp. 533–4) and many others put the neo-Austrians in the heterodox camp.

Notwithstanding all of this, it remains that if the listed five presuppositions allow us to distinguish orthodox from heterodox economics, neo-Austrians do not fare well on at least three of these suppositions, being much closer to the atomistic, scarcity and self-adjusting presuppositions. Furthermore, a famous originator of neo-Austrian economics, Ludwig von Mises (1976, p. 228) has been very clear about this:

> we usually speak of the Austrian, the Anglo-American Schools and the School of Lausanne [the Walrasians] . . . These three schools of thought differ only in their mode of expressing the same fundamental idea and . . . they are divided more by their terminology and by peculiarities of presentation than by substance in their teaching.

This is also Davidson's (1989, p. 469) assessment; he says that 'the Austrians have neither logically differentiated themselves from the neoclassical approach, nor raised major problems in it'. Thus, all in all, I would say that it is best to consider neo-Austrian economists as orthodox dissenters. The same could be said about analytical Marxism (Wrenn, 2007, p. 102). Indeed, long ago, Hunt (1992, p. 105) considered analytical Marxism to be based on methodological individualism and 'to be a part of the long tradition of anti-Marxism', while more recently Shaikh (2016, p. 82) concurred, by calling it 'the most striking application of hyper-rationality'.

The situation is quite different for most of the other schools of thought mentioned in Table 1.2. This can be ascertained by looking at the descriptions provided by some journals or some of the associations. *The Review of Political Economy*, which used to include Austrian economics, now states that it welcomes 'contributions in all areas of political economy, including Behavioural economics, Ecological economics, Feminist economics, Institutional economics, Kaleckian economics, Marxian economics, Polanyian economics, Post-Keynesian economics, Schumpeterian economics, Sraffian economics, as well as in the tradition of the theory of the Monetary Circuit'. How about the *Cambridge Journal of Economics*? Its cover says that 'The *Cambridge Journal of Economics*, founded in the traditions of Marx, Keynes, Kalecki, Joan Robinson and Kaldor, welcomes contributions from heterodox economics as well as other social sciences disciplines.' As for the *Review of Radical Political Economics*, its short announcement says that 'the *Review* presents articles on radical political economy and applied economy from a wide variety of theoretical traditions – including Marxian, institutionalist, post-Keynesian and feminist'. Turning now to academic associations, perhaps the best example of an encompassing heterodox tradition is that of the European Association for Evolutionary Political Economy. On its website, when presenting its theoretical perspectives, the Association says: 'The Association accepts the relevance of writers as diverse as John Commons, Nicholas Kaldor, Michal Kalecki, William Kapp, John Maynard Keynes, Alfred Marshall, Karl Marx, Gunnar Myrdal, Edith Penrose, François Perroux, Karl Polanyi, Joseph Schumpeter, Herbert Simon, Adam Smith, Thorstein Veblen and Max Weber to institutionalist and evolutionary thought.'

All of this goes to show that there are tight links between the first three heterodox schools of thought identified in Table 1.2: the Marxians, post-Keynesians and Institutionalists. Indeed, it is sometimes said that Institutionalism provides the microeconomics of post-Keynesian economics while post-Keynesianism provides the macroeconomics of the Institutionalist School. From now on, we focus on the post-Keynesian School.

1.4 ESSENTIAL CHARACTERISTICS OF POST-KEYNESIAN ECONOMICS

1.4.1 A Very Short History of Post-Keynesian Economics

Before we move on examining what are the essential characteristics of post-Keynesian economics, that is, their own specific presuppositions relative to other heterodox traditions, we provide a very short history of post-Keynesian economics so as to give some background information to readers; afterwards, because post-Keynesians are not a homogeneous group, we present the various strands of post-Keynesian economics, hoping that this will help readers to find their way in the literature.

In his book on the *History of Post Keynesian Economics*, King (2002) believes that post-Keynesian economics started in the 1930s, when Keynes was testing his new ideas about depression economics with members of the Cambridge Circus, notably Joan Robinson and Richard Kahn. At the same time, Kalecki was creating his own version of effective demand, Kaldor (1934a) was already discussing multiple equilibria and path-dependence, two crucial heterodox concepts, and Robinson (1937) had written a toned-down version of Keynes's *General Theory*. It could also be tempting to say that post-Keynesianism started in 1956, when Kaldor and Robinson put forth what was then called the Cambridge, Anglo-Italian or neo-Keynesian theory of income distribution as an alternative to the neoclassical theory based on marginal productivity. For several years, this income distribution theory, based on effective demand, was the best-known contribution of these earlier post-Keynesians. Or it could be said that post-Keynesianism started in the 1960s, during the controversies on capital theory between the two Cambridges (in the UK and in Massachusetts), when Cambridge authors truly started to realize that they were putting forth a view of economic theory distinct from that of their neoclassical colleagues, even hoping that their critiques would destroy neoclassical theory (Mata, 2004). These key moments in the history of post-Keynesian economics are presented in Table 1.6, along with the main themes that were studied by post-Keynesians thereafter.

Table 1.6 The evolution of the main themes of post-Keynesian economics

Timeline	Main theme
1930s	Unemployment
1950s	Neo-Keynesian (Cambridge) models of growth and distribution
1960s	Capital controversies
1970s	Theory of the firm, pricing, employment theory, definition of a paradigm
1980s	Kaleckian models of growth, endogenous money, the financial fragility hypothesis
Late 1980s, early 1990s	Attempts at (a grand) synthesis and textbooks
1990s	Methodology, critical realism, history of economic thought
2000s	Economic policy, globalization, financialization, empirical and econometric work, the links between monetary and fiscal policies
2010s	Stock–flow real-financial coherence, agent-based models, path-dependence, financial instability, ecological economics, new attempts at synthesis

A somewhat different point of view is offered by Lee in his *History of Heterodox Economics*. Lee (2009, p. 11) argues that 'the history of Post Keynesian economics does not begin in 1936 with Keynes and the publication of the *General Theory*, but in the 1970s with the formation of a community of self-identified Post Keynesian economists in the United States who in part drew upon his ideas'. Lee shows that there were substantial and successful efforts at creating a community of post-Keynesian economists throughout the 1970s, notably by the Americans Alfred Eichner, Edward Nell and Paul Davidson. Social networking occurred in particular when American scholars visited Cambridge and when Joan Robinson visited the USA in the early 1970s. Institutionalization of post-Keynesian economics thus started in the 1970s, in particular with the creation of their two main journals, the *Cambridge Journal of Economics* and the *Journal of Post Keynesian Economics*, in 1977 and 1978.

Another major event at the time – one that had a profound influence on my own thinking – was the publication of the paper by Eichner and Kregel in the *Journal of Economic Literature*. There, they argued (perhaps with too much enthusiasm) that a new paradigm, that of post-Keynesian theory, was in the making, pointing out that post-Keynesian economics was much more than a negative critique of the neoclassical theory of capital, and that it was providing a strong positive and original contribution to the study of economics. They contended, in reference to our first heterodox presupposition, that the purpose of post-Keynesian theory 'is to explain the real world as observed empirically' and not 'to demonstrate the social optimality if the real world were to resemble the model' (Eichner and Kregel, 1975, p. 1309). This paper came out just as I was discovering, as an undergraduate, the existence of this alternative theory, and it had a strong impact on my views as I moved on with graduate studies and my early academic career. An interesting feature of the Eichner and Kregel article is that they provided alternatives on methodology and macroeconomics, but also in the field of microeconomics. Studies of the firm and of pricing procedures, as well as models of employment, were a key feature of the 1970s.

The 1980s saw the appearance of the stalwart of post-Keynesian modelling, the Kaleckian model of growth and distribution, which replaced the neo-Keynesian model of growth and distribution, as we shall see in Chapter 6. Monetary economics, with the hypothesis of endogenous money, as well as financial economics, with the development of the financial fragility hypothesis, were also in the forefront in the 1980s. Starting at the end of the 1980s, for about a decade several authors attempted to provide a textbook view of post-Keynesian economics (Reynolds, 1987; Eichner, 1987; Arestis, 1992; Carvalho, 1992; Lavoie, 1992b; Palley, 1996a; Nell, 1998). These efforts at creating a grand theoretical synthesis led Giuseppe Fontana and Bill Gerrard (2006) to refer to this period as the 'Romantic Age' of post-Keynesian economics in their short history of post-Keynesian economics.

This then gave rise, again according to Fontana and Gerrard, to the Age of Uncertainty, as the attention of post-Keynesians turned toward methodological issues, spearheaded by Lawson's fray into ontology and critical realism, as already discussed, as well as a re-examination of Keynes's writings and an analysis of his methodological views. This was accompanied by a renewed interest in the history of economic thought, as if several post-Keynesians and other heterodox economics feared to engage in policy debates and sought refuge from the attacks of their mainstream colleagues. Indeed, this led Fontana and Gerrard (2006, p. 69) to comment that 'Post Keynesian economists are seen to be more concerned with critique, methodology and the history of economic thought rather than the development of economic theory per se'. Indeed, an even harsher external appraisal was mentioned disapprovingly by Stephen Dunn (2000, p. 343): 'Post Keynesianism is commonly referred to as a disintegrating research program, more obsessed with the exegesis of the ideas of long dead economists than it is concerned with explaining new, novel empirical facts or contributing to the development of new policy.'

But, as can be clearly ascertained when participating to various post-Keynesian conferences throughout the world over the last 25 years or so, this has given way in the 2000s to a concern for policy relevance, at both the domestic and global level, accompanied by a revived interest in empirical studies and in applied econometrics, no doubt helped by the appearance of novel agnostic time-series methods, despite the methodological concerns of post-Keynesians about econometrics. Much has been written on monetary and fiscal policies, the links between monetary and fiscal operations through what has been called Modern Monetary Theory on the Web, and on globalization and financialization. There has been a clear shift from abstract methodological concerns towards more concrete ones. In other words, post-Keynesian economics today is not the same as it was 25 years ago, and it is not always clear that some of its critics are fully aware of this evolution.

Over recent years, tied in particular to the Global Financial Crisis, there has been renewed interest in the financial fragility hypothesis, in an attempt to integrate in a meaningful manner the analysis of the real and the financial sectors, particularly through what has been called the stock–flow consistent method, which will be discussed in Chapter 4. Post-Keynesians have also started to address the crucial environmental issue, linking up timidly with ecological concerns. This, in a reduced form compared to the story told in Lavoie (2011a), is my take on the themes that have marked the evolution of post-Keynesian theory, fully recognizing that this is a bird's-eye-view nomenclature, one based on readings, recollection and participation at conferences. A rather similar picture is offered by Fontana (2009, ch. 2) and Hein (2017).

1.4.2 The Presuppositions of Post-Keynesian Economics

A difficult question, which keeps haunting post-Keynesian economists, is: what are the contours of post-Keynesianism? A recurrent question is whether the Sraffian School should or should not be included within post-Keynesianism. We will come back to this question in the next subsection. But there are other contour questions, which are just as mesmerizing. Should we say that the French Regulation School is part of the post-Keynesian School, since Regulation authors use so many behavioural equations taken from Cambridge Keynesians, or should we say instead that post-Keynesianism is part of the Regulation School, since the latter takes a wider historical and institutional approach to analysing economic systems? Furthermore, what are the links between Radical Marxians and post-Keynesians? Lee (2009) shows indeed that there were warm working relationships between the two schools from the very beginning. Is it that the Radicals focus on cycles while post-Keynesians of the Cambridge variety have focused on trend growth? There are no easy answers.

There have been many proposals identifying the key characteristics of post-Keynesian economics since the first attempt by Eichner and Kregel (1975). A survey of these attempts yields Table 1.7.

Table 1.7 Presuppositions and key characteristics of post-Keynesian economics

Concept	Authors endorsing the concept
Heterodox presuppositions	
Realism	Arestis (1990, 1992, 1996), Arestis & Sawyer (1993), Chick (1995), Dostaler (1988), Dow (1991), Eichner & Kregel (1975), Fontana (2009), Holt (2007), Jespersen (2009), Norman (2008), Pasinetti (2007), Setterfield (2003)
Organicism	Arestis (1992), Arestis & Sawyer (1993), Chick (1995), Dow (1991), Jespersen (2009), Pasinetti (2007), Setterfield (2003)
Reasonable rationality	Arestis (1992, 1996), Brown (1981)
Production	Arestis & Sawyer (1993), Dow (1991), Henry & Seccareccia (1982), Setterfield (2003)
Disequilibria, instability	Arestis & Sawyer (1993), Brown (1981), Fontana & Gerrard (2006), Galbraith (1978), Lavoie (2006b), Norman (2008), Palley (1996a)
Post-Keynesian key characteristics	
Principle of effective demand	Arestis & Sawyer (1993), Arestis, Dunn & Sawyer (1999), Dunn (2008), Fontana & Gerrard (2006), Galbraith (1978), Jespersen (2009), Lavoie (2006b), Norman (2008), Palley (1996a), Sawyer (2010)
Monetized economy (monetary theory of production)	Arestis, Dunn & Sawyer (1999), Carvalho (1992), Davidson (1992), Dostaler (1988), Dow (1991), Eichner & Kregel (1975), Fontana (2009), Jespersen (2009), King (2015), Lavoie (2006b), Sawyer (2010)
Fundamental uncertainty	Arestis (1990, 1992, 1996), Arestis & Sawyer (1993), Danby (2009), Davidson (1992), Dunn (2008), Fontana (2009), Holt (2007), Jespersen (2009), Lavoie (2006b), Norman (2008), Pasinetti (2007)
Historical and irreversible time	Arestis (1990, 1992), Arestis & Sawyer (1993), Chick (1995), Danby (2009), Davidson (1992), Fontana (2009), Henry (1993), Henry & Seccareccia (1982), Holt (2007), Lavoie (2006b), Norman (2008), Robinson (1978), Pasinetti (2007)
Income distribution	Eichner & Kregel (1975), Norman (2008), Sawyer (2011), Hein (2017)

The presuppositions of post-Keynesian analysis can be divided into two groupings. The first five characteristics of Table 1.7 (realism, organicism, reasonable rationality, production, disequilibria and instability) correspond to what I have called the presuppositions of the heterodox research programme. This is not surprising since post-Keynesian economics is part of heterodox economics, and hence, as such, should share its presuppositions. For instance, dealing with realism, in a statement that applies just as well, and most likely much more, today as it did 47 years ago, Minsky (1975, p. 4) complained that 'academic economics has recaptured much of the sterility and irrelevance with respect to the operation of the real-world economy which characterized the discipline before the appearance of *The General Theory*'. The only characteristic in need of some explanation is the fifth one, which in Table 1.3 was described as 'regulated markets' and which here is presented as 'disequilibria and instability'. Post-Keynesian authors often consider that there are endogenous destabilizing forces at work and that price mechanisms cannot in general counteract these. As a result, multiple equilibria may arise, including of course financial crises and situations of unemployment, so that government intervention and the regulation of market forces are required.

About government intervention, a few more words may be required. I have already pointed out that post-Keynesians in general do not wish to eliminate capitalism; they wish to tame it, recognizing that it has important dynamic properties. While no doubt post-Keynesians do not hold homogeneous political views, my assessment is that the range of these views has tightened over the last two decades. Most post-Keynesians see some sort of alienation in both liberalism and socialism, and thus look forward to a 'humanistic' political system, which would constitute some 'middle way between liberalism and socialism' (Bortis, 1997, p. 33), as used to be found in Scandinavian countries, which, ironically, carry extremely few post-Keynesians in their ranks.

The second set of presuppositions is more specific to post-Keynesian economics. While different authors have identified different characteristics, Hein (2017, p. 135) defines five characteristics that help distinguish post-Keynesian economics from other heterodox schools, and 'which might apply to the different strands to different degrees, but on which all five strands might agree'. The first characteristic is the principle of aggregate demand which says that aggregate demand is the main force that determines output and employment. While most economists would agree or concede that the economy is demand-led in the short run, few would agree with the claim that the economy is demand-led even in the long run, and thus the assertion that the economy is demand-led both in the short and the long run is most likely a specific feature of post-Keynesianism. More concretely, this means that post-Keynesians believe that the actual path taken by the economy has an impact on the supply-side determinants of long-run growth.

The often-heard statement that investment determines saving is intimately linked to the principle of effective demand, and thus it is no surprise to see some authors (namely, Henry and Seccareccia (1982), Dostaler (1988), Henry (1993), Palley (1996a), Pasinetti (2007) and Sawyer (2010)) underlining this causality as a key feature of post-Keynesianism. Indeed, as pointed out early on by Nina Shapiro (1977), the autonomy of investment from the intertemporal decisions of households is most likely the revolutionary feature of post-Keynesian economics. This is even clearer now than it was then, with the focus of state-of-the-art orthodox macroeconomics on the representative agent and her maximization of intertemporal utility.

The next three characteristics – a monetized economy, fundamental uncertainty, historical and irreversible time – can be tricky to disentangle. The idea of a monetized economy could also be associated with the principle of effective demand since it is difficult to imagine an independent investment function without a monetized economy. In orthodox state-of-the-art macro models, such as the DSGE approach, there is no need for nominal magnitudes, nor for money. Some commodity acts as a numéraire or unit of account. As in neo-Walrasian models, everything is known until the end of time, with some probabilistic degree; in other words there is risk and no fundamental uncertainty. Time in such models is an artificial construct, since all decisions are taken on day zero. The introduction of nominal magnitudes and money adds friction and reduces welfare – a result that contradicts intuition and shows how counterfactual these models really are (Rogers, 1989; 2018).

In post-Keynesian models fundamental uncertainty is assumed from the start by considering that contracts, debts and assets are denominated in money terms, and by rejecting the possibility of proceeding to the maximization of intertemporal utility. Indeed, any model that rejects these state-of-the-art constructs integrates in some manner the concept of fundamental uncertainty, where, as Eichner and Kregel (1975, p. 1309) say, 'only the past is known, the future is uncertain'. More will be said about fundamental uncertainty in Chapter 2.

Post-Keynesians take the notion of time very seriously, making the distinction between historical time and logical time (Robinson, 1980). Historical time, or chronological time, is irreversible, in contrast to logical time. Post-Keynesians are very much influenced by Kalecki's (1971, p. 165) statement to the effect that 'the long-run trend is but a slowly changing component of a chain of short-period situations; it has no independent entity'. For Robinson, everything occurs in the short period. In their debates with their critics, post-Keynesians have underlined the need to consider and describe the transition from one position to another, recognizing that the conditions under which this transition occurs may affect the final position of equilibrium. As Halevi and Kriesler (1991, p. 86) claim, long-period analysis in logical time is relevant only when 'some coherent dynamic adjustment process is specified which can describe the *traverse* from one equilibrium position to another, without the traverse itself influencing the final equilibrium position, that is, without the equilibrium being path determined'. Thus post-Keynesians consider path-dependence and hysteresis phenomena as typical of their vision of economic phenomena set in historical time. As Robinson (1956, p. 58) put it, 'in most economic reactions the path the market follows, while it is adapting itself to a change, has a long-persisting effect upon the position that it reaches'. It may be that not all history matters, but certainly some does.

The importance of time is also related to the notion of non-ergodicity put forth by Davidson (1982–83), meaning that the time and space averages may not coincide, implying that we cannot rely on current or past averages to discover what ought to happen in the future. This concept has certainly attracted some attention with the subprime financial crisis, as it is associated with black swans and fat tails, as well as large switches in expectations and confidence, leaving little room for the empirical worthiness of rational expectations and the efficient-market hypothesis.

A third reason for which time needs to be taken seriously is that production takes time. As Kregel (2017, p. 884) puts it, 'this means that production requires financial commitments undertaken today to acquire the means of production that can only be verified by sales of produced output at some future date, contingent on the realization of the expectations that motivated the decision to initiate the production'. This implies that one should not dichotomize the real and the financial sides of the economy, as the two sides are necessarily intertwined.

The fifth specific feature of post-Keynesian economics according to Hein (2017) is the importance of distributional issues and distributional conflict, although one can say that it also figures prominently in both Institutional economics and Marxian economics. Still, functional income distribution was at the heart of post-Keynesian economics from the very beginning in the 1950s, and post-Keynesians very early on attributed the advent of the Global Financial Crisis to changes in income distribution – the increase in the profit share and the unequal distribution of the wage share. Post-Keynesians have indeed formalized previous concerns of under-consumptionists regarding the effect of unequal income distribution on aggregate demand. Early on, post-Keynesians have also expressed concerns regarding the role that monetary policy plays in potentially raising income inequality by favouring the rentiers – those who benefit from high interest rates or capital gains on financial assets. Income distribution conflicts can perform an important role for the determination of economic activity, employment and inflation.

Eichner and Kregel (1975), along with Lavoie (2006b), Norman (2008) and Sawyer (2011), have argued that post-Keynesian economics has its own specific microeconomic theory, and thus could constitute a sixth key characteristic. We shall say more about microeconomics in the next two chapters, when discussing the theory of choice and that of the consumer, and when dealing with the theory of the firm and pricing. Indeed, post-Keynesians have their own microeconomic theory.

Finally, some authors have claimed that post-Keynesian economics is associated with pluralism, as Dow (1991, 2005) and myself (Lavoie, 2006b) have argued in the past, as well as being associated with open systems, as claimed by Dow (2000, 2005) again and others (Brown, 1981; Dunn, 2008; Jespersen, 2009). I have already expressed my uneasiness regarding the relevance of the open system modelling condition. As Hodgson (2019, p. 58) says, this requirement seems 'more ceremonial than operational'. As to preoccupation for pluralism, whatever its merit, it does not appear as highly specific to post-Keynesian economics. It may have been the case in the past that pluralism – the Babylonian approach, as Dow (2005) calls it – could be specifically associated to the post-Keynesian school because it was one of the few schools of thought that was offering a 'broad tent' approach, accepting a variety of methods and theories as being scientific, but this certainly is no longer the case, as the idea of pluralism has been picked up by methodologists of all horizons.

To summarize so far, post-Keynesians embrace all five presuppositions associated with heterodox economics. In addition, post-Keynesianism can be distinguished from other heterodox schools by its focus on the principle of effective demand, in both the short and the long run, the study of a monetized production economy, an environment of fundamental uncertainty, the insistence that time is historical and irreversible, and the importance of income distribution issues.

The place of econometrics
One issue has been left aside, that of the place of econometrics in post-Keynesian economics. We discussed modelling when dealing with the issue of mathematical formalism and the presuppositions of heterodox economics, but what about econometrics? Here again it is convenient to refer to Lawson's position. Lawson argues that the nature of the phenomena to be studied in economics is rarely appropriate for the use of standard econometric methods. There are not enough event regularities in the real world for these techniques to be useful. The use of econometrics is not justified except in very specific conditions. One branch of post-Keynesian economists tends to agree with this assessment – the Fundamentalist strand, as we call it in the next subsection – and Keynes (1973, xiv, p. 320) himself was rather pessimistic about the use of econometrics in macroeconomics, going so far as to talk of 'statistical alchemy'. However, I think it is fair to say that, in general, post-Keynesians have embraced econometric methods, especially since 2000, although, from the very beginning, there have always been post-Keynesians who

'defend the use of econometrics vigorously' (Norman, 2008, p. 2), the best and earliest example, perhaps, being Kalecki.

As heterodox economists, and hence as naturally doubtful of the veracity of any statement, post-Keynesians are keenly aware that only a limited number of econometric results are robust and can be replicated, either because the stability of the calculated parameters is in question or because of excessive data-mining. They are cognizant that econometrics 'is very useful for those wantinig to prove a pre-conceived belief or find results that support an ideologically driven hypothesis (Moosa, 2017a, p. 18) They are also fully aware of the difficulties involved in using past econometric results to provide good predictions. 'While Post Keynesians should be skeptical about prediction, this does not mean that they should abandon all empirical work' (Holt, 2007, p. 101). As recalled by Bill Mitchell (2007), policy-makers require hard numbers for policy-making, and these can be provided either by back-of-the-envelope calculations or by econometrics. In addition, econometric results can offer a focus for thinking about a problem and for discussion. Econometric analysis, as a subset of empirical analysis, gives further ammunition in the heterodox quest for explanation and causal mechanisms – the two are certainly not incompatible. Another important and pragmatic argument is that econometrics is a powerful weapon in the battle of ideas. Economics is all about rhetoric, as Deirdre McCloskey (1983) has long argued, and econometrics is a potent rhetorical tool. Heterodox economists have to play this game, show their technical dexterity, even if empirical evidence rarely leads to changes in the dominant view (Mearman, 2012b).

The use of econometrics also provides a possible entry door in engaging with the mainstream. As Dullien (2017, p. 248) suggests, 'one form of engagement could be to focus on empirics and econometrics', more so than trying to emulate post-Keynesian versions of DSGE models.

It may thus be said that post-Keynesians (in contrast to most other heterodox schools of thought) have taken a middle of the road stance, believing that econometrics can be useful while recognizing that it has huge limitations, beyond those associated with forecasting or ideological bias. My own experience has shown that in some circumstances – for instance when assessing discrimination in professional ice hockey – results can be quite robust, whatever the specification, the estimation method and even the time period. Things are however quite different with respect to time-series macroeconomics, where a small change in either specification, estimation method, lag length, data set or time period, can lead to huge changes in the statistical results. More on this will be said later in the chapter, but in practice I think it is fair to say that contemporary post-Keynesians have endorsed the use of econometrics and other empirical and statistical tools, despite all of their shortcomings.

1.4.3 Strands of Post-Keynesian Economics

All post-Keynesians were not created alike. As of now, it is convenient to identify five strands within post-Keynesian economics: the Fundamentalists, the Sraffians, the Kaleckians, the Institutionalists and the Kaldorians, as described in the penultimate column of Table 1.8.

However, the best-known description of post-Keynesian economists is that of Hamouda and Harcourt (1988), also found in Table 1.8, who identify only three strands: the American post-Keynesians and the Sraffians at the two extremes, and the

Table 1.8 The various strands of post-Keynesianism

Hamouda and Harcourt (1988)	Arestis and Sawyer (1993)	Arestis (1996)	Lavoie (2011a)	King (2015)
American PK Kaleckians Sraffians	Marshallians Kaleckians Sraffians Institutionalists	Marshallians Robinsonians (Sraffians) Institutionalists	Fundamentalists Kaleckians Sraffians Institutionalists Kaldorians	Fundamentalists Kaleckians Minskyans

Kaleckians somewhere in the middle. The American post-Keynesians have elsewhere been called the Marshallian post-Keynesians (Arestis and Sawyer, 1993; Arestis, 1996), the Fundamentalist post-Keynesians (Lavoie, 2006b) or Keynes's School (Davidson, 1972). The main concerns of these authors are the descriptions of a monetized production economy, the fragility and instability of the financial system, questions tied to liquidity preference and fundamental uncertainty. As a result, they have also been referred to as Financial Keynesians or Monetary Keynesians (Fontana, 2009), which is probably a kinder denomination. The Fundamentalist post-Keynesians are those that are most likely to object to formalization or to the use of econometrics. An important concern of several of these authors is to amplify the true and fundamental meaning of Keynes's writings, and as a result their microeconomics (with the assumption of decreasing returns and pure (but not perfect) competition) is often tied to that of Alfred Marshall, of whom Keynes was a student, which explains why they are also called Marshallian post-Keynesians.

This branch is also named 'American' because its initial proponents – Sydney Weintraub, Paul Davidson, Hyman Minsky, Victoria Chick, Basil Moore – all came from the USA, although many supporters of this branch can now be found all over the world. Most work on post-Keynesian methodology is also associated with this branch, since a substantial amount of this work has been devoted to Keynes's writings on methodology and probability theory. The Italo-French monetary circuit theory, associated with authors such as Augusto Graziani and Alain Parguez, is closest to this strand, although it also has some strong Kaleckian components, so much so that Arestis (1996) includes the monetary circuit school in the Kaleckian strand, which we now discuss.

The Kaleckians are made up of authors such as Michał Kalecki, Joan Robinson, Joseph Steindl and Tom Asimakopulos, along with modern authors such as Amit Bhaduri and Malcolm Sawyer, to whom we could add younger authors such as Amitava Dutt, Eckhard Hein, Engelbert Stockhammer, Robert Blecker and Steve Fazzari, the latter two having been students of Donald Harris. All these authors have been mainly concerned with output and employment, like the American post-Keynesians, but also business cycles, growth theory and pricing issues, in particular the link between mark-ups and growth, and hence income distribution. The potential conflicts regarding income distribution are an important object of analysis. Another major concern is that of the realization of profit, using here Marxian terms. Arestis (1996) calls this group the Robinsonians, adding to them the monetary circuit school, as pointed out earlier, thus supplementing the Kaleckian strand with a more obvious monetary element, which can also be found in the work of Jan Toporowski (2000). I have also added Lance Taylor to the Kaleckians, although he is closely associated with the Development Structuralists of Table 1.2, because many of his models are indeed Kaleckian.

The place of Sraffians
The third strand described by Hamouda and Harcourt (1988) is that of the Sraffians – the followers of Piero Sraffa. They used to be called neo-Ricardians, somewhat ironically, because of Sraffa's resolve to solve the puzzles left by Ricardo (and indirectly by Marx), such as an invariable anchor of value, so that Dutt and Amadeo (1990) name them neo-Ricardian Keynesians. Many of the better-known Sraffians are Italians – Pierangelo Garegnani, Luigi Pasinetti, Alessandro Roncaglia, Neri Salvadori, Antonella Stirati, Sergio Cesaratto – but others are not, such as Ian Steedman, John Eatwell, Bertram Schefold and Heinz Kurz. Sraffians were very much concerned with the determination of relative prices, the choices of techniques, joint production and the interdependence inherent to the existence of a multisectoral production system, as in input–output analysis. These issues, according to Garegnani (1990b, p. 123), constituted the core of Sraffian theory, because he thought that definite answers could be offered. Questions related to output and employment, capacity and capacity utilization, or to money and interest rates were out of the core, although this did not mean that they were unimportant or not worthy of study. Indeed, modern Sraffians are now mostly dealing with these out-of-core issues.

Several post-Keynesian methodologists, for instance Stephen Dunn (2000, p. 350; 2008, p. 45), argue that Sraffians ought to be dropped from the post-Keynesian school, on the grounds that Sraffian economics does not fit the strictures of critical realism, and thus the inclusion of this strand into post-Keynesianism creates methodological confusion. Sending off the Sraffians, in their view, would help to bring more coherence to post-Keynesian economics. Even John King (2012b, p. 314) believes that 'almost no one today regards "Post Keynesian–Sraffian" economics as a single coherent school of thought'. I am among the few who still see some coherence, as do a number of researchers such as Harcourt (2001a, p. 275), Andrew Trigg (2008) and Gary Mongiovi (2012), and as I have tried to explain in detail (Lavoie, 1992a; 2011b; 2013b). On this, I have been given some mild support from Arena and Blankenburg (2013) and virtually no support from Hart and Kriesler (2016). So, what are the arguments in considering Sraffians as being part of post-Keynesian economics seen as a broad church?

First, as we saw in the previous subsection, Sraffians are intimately linked with post-Keynesian analysis by tradition and by history. Second, Sraffians are in close agreement with other post-Keynesians on crucial issues such as the causality between investment and saving, the role of effective demand in both the short and the long run, the endogeneity of the money supply and the possibility for the central bank to set short-run interest rates at levels of their choice (Dutt and Amadeo, 1990). Third, Sraffian views are not homogeneous and have evolved through time, so that the distinctions between the Sraffians and the other strands may no longer be so obvious. Modern Sraffians do not assume that the economy is always running at normal or full capacity. Many of them do not even assume that the economy is running at normal capacity in the long run. Fourth, the Sraffians provide equations that explain production and distribution in an interdependent setting, within a multisectoral framework, something that is generally lacking in the other strands. Sraffian price theory can be seen as an idealized administered pricing theory, a specific kind of benchmark pricing (Nell, 1998), which abstracts from imperfect information, past disequilibria, non-uniform profit rates or target rates of return, debt structures and so on. Those who are interested in the study of relative prices can add these complications at will. Fifth, Sraffians have made contributions to monetary analysis. The Sraffians were the first to claim that relative prices and real wages are affected by the trend level of the rate of interest, through its proportional impact on the normal profit rate, that is, the target rate of return embedded in the pricing mark-up.

There is also some wide agreement about policy issues and the need for government intervention. Fontana and Gerrard (2006, p. 51) present what they call the 'three interconnected characteristic Keynesian propositions': there can be involuntary unemployment; output and employment variations play the key role in macro adjustments; economic policy is effective and will stabilize the economy. Certainly, Sraffians agree with all three of these key Keynesian propositions, in part because, like other post-Keynesians, they see the problem of output determination as being separate from price determination (Bhaduri, 2011a, p. 95). Sraffians would also feel at ease with the three components of Keynesianism as defined by Palley et al. (2012, p. 3): '(1) holding that output and employment are normally constrained by aggregate demand; (2) holding that the problematic of aggregate demand shortage exists independently of price, nominal wage, and nominal interest rate rigidities; and (3) rejecting the claim that the real wage is equal to the marginal disutility of labor'.

For all these reasons the Sraffians are still present in my taxonomy and in that of Arestis and Sawyer (1993). They seem to be absent from the three-way taxonomy presented by Arestis (1996), but when he comes to the discussion of pricing, Arestis reintroduces Leontief, Sraffa and Pasinetti, that is, the Sraffians.

Two additional strands

As can be seen from Table 1.8, other taxonomies add a fourth strand, that of the Institutionalists. Arestis (1996) and Arestis and Sawyer (1993) give few examples of what authors they have in mind when they identify the Institutionalist post-Keynesians. They mention only Thorstein Veblen, and cite Hodgson's (1988) book, thus probably believing at the time that the Institutionalist tradition could reinforce the microeconomic analysis of post-Keynesians. Since John Kenneth Galbraith was the patron of the *Journal of Post Keynesian Economics*, I believe that it would be fair to present him as a main representative of the Institutionalist strand of post-Keynesianism, along with his son James Galbraith (2008). Within this strand one could include some works of the French Convention School, which deals with habits and routines. Some authors associate Minsky with an Institutionalist post-Keynesian school (O'Hara, 2007a; 2007b; Whalen, 2013; 2020). Some observers, such as King (2015), as shown in Table 1.8, believe that Minskyans constitute a strand of their own. Nikolaidi and Stockhammer (2017) show that indeed there exists a whole set of diverse Minskyan models.

Within the Institutionalist post-Keynesian branch, one could also include some of the more heterodox work in behavioural economics or psychological economics, some of which has been pursued or endorsed by post-Keynesians (Earl, 1986; Harvey, 1998; Fontana and Gerrard, 2004). There is also a substantial amount of work, linked to industrial organization, which examines the evolution of corporations in light of the financialization process and the development of new information and communication technologies. This work is at the juncture of the Marxian, Institutionalist and Regulation school traditions, and post-Keynesians certainly belong to this appraisal. Furthermore, the whole administered pricing literature – associated with Means, Andrews and Brunner, Kaplan and Lanzillotti – has been adopted by post-Keynesian authors such as Eichner (1976) and Lee (1998). Finally, the whole movement of the neo-chartalist school – nowadays better known as Modern Monetary Theory (MMT), as described in Wray (1998, 2012) and in the textbook of Mitchell, Watts and Wray (2019) – can be considered as part of the Institutionalist post-Keynesians, since the neo-chartalists base their policy recommendations on a detailed analysis of monetary institutions and implementation procedures. Some observers believe MMT has earned a branch of its own within post-Keynesian economics (LK, 2014), while some MMT authors give the impression that they are unrelated to any previous school of thought, as noted by Lavoie (2019a), despite Wray being a co-editor of the *Journal of Post Keynesian Economics*.

Hamouda and Harcourt (1988) wonder where, within their three-way classification, they should put authors such as Kaldor, Godley and Goodwin. One way out, suggested in Table 1.8, is to add a fifth strand, that of the Kaldorian post-Keynesians. This strand is mostly concerned with the constraints arising from open economy considerations, such as the balance of payments constraints or the fundamental identity that links private financial saving, public deficit and the current account balance. In the 1970s, this strand became known as the New Cambridge School. In addition, one can certainly draw a filiation from Kaldor, Harrod and Godley towards the work pursued by John McCombie and Anthony Thirlwall (1994) on these open economy issues, and their empirical work in return has inspired quite a large following. Furthermore, Kaldor's technical progress function and his empirical work on manufacturing growth and endogenous growth has generated a stream of research devoted to productivity regimes, which involved again McCombie and Thirlwall, authors such as Ro Naastepad and Servaas Storm, and also the French regulationists Robert Boyer and Pascal Petit. Indeed, as shown by Boyer (2011), the French regulationists cover both the Kaldorian and the Institutionalist strands of post-Keynesianism. One can also claim that the work being pursued on multiple equilibria, instability, path-dependence and hysteresis, initiated by Kaldor in the 1930s and 1940s and continued in the 1970s by John Cornwall (1972) and then in the 1990s by his student Mark Setterfield, is in this Kaldorian tradition, as is work on cumulative causation. I would also include Richard Goodwin within this broad Kaldorian strand, along with his student Vela Velupillai. Both Kaldor and Goodwin constructed growth models where the rate of capacity utilization is assumed to be equal to its normal rate, a tradition pursued by modern post-Keynesians such as Peter Skott and Tom Palley. Indeed, there is a truly huge literature on variations around the Kaldorian growth model (Baranzini and Mirante, 2013).

It should be made clear that the identification of these various strands is only indicative. Many eclectic and productive economists go across all or at least two of the categories discussed above, and so could not fit neatly into one of the strands. This is the case of key senior authors such as Philip Arestis, Geoff Harcourt, John King, Barkley Rosser Jr and Edward Nell, or somewhat younger ones like Steve Keen, Mathew Forstater, Matías Vernengo, Esteban Pérez Caldentey, Steve Pressman, Dany Lang, Ilene Grabel, Daniela Prates, Gennaro Zezza and Louis-Philippe Rochon. Several upcoming post-Keynesians feel at ease within all strands, taking the best elements from each. Some also look for cross-fertilization with other heterodox traditions. However, Table 1.9 attempts to recapitulate the major themes tackled by each strand, as well as the

Table 1.9 Post-Keynesian strands with main themes and authors

Strand	Major themes	Inspiration	Current authors
Fundamentalist Keynesians	Fundamental uncertainty Monetized production economy Financial instability Methodology	Fernando Carvalho Victoria Chick Paul Davidson Mark Hayes J.M. Keynes Hyman Minsky Basil Moore older Joan Robinson G.L.S. Shackle Sidney Weintraub	Jörg Bibow Victoria Chick David Dequech Sheila Dow Giuseppe Fontana Jan Kregel Edwin Le Héron André Orléan
Kaleckians	Income and distribution models The traverse Effective demand Class conflict Pricing	Amit Bhaduri Tom Asimakopulos Donald Harris Michał Kalecki younger Joan Robinson Joseph Steindl Lance Taylor	Robert Blecker Amitava Dutt Eckhard Hein Steve Fazzari Peter Kriesler Özlem Onaran Malcolm Sawyer Stephanie Seguino Engelbert Stockhammer Jan Toporowski
Sraffians	Relative prices Technical choice Multisectoral production systems Capital theory Joint production Long-run positions	Krishna Bharadwaj Pierangelo Garegnani Luigi Pasinetti Piero Sraffa Paolo Sylos Labini	Heinz Kurz Gary Mongiovi Carlo Panico Fabio Petri Massimo Pivetti Alessandro Roncaglia Neri Salvadori Bertram Schefold Franklin Serrano Ian Steedman Antonella Stirati
Institutionalists	Pricing Theory of the firm Monetary institutions Behavioural economics Labour economics	Philip Andrews Dudley Dillard Alfred Eichner John Kenneth Galbraith Frederic Lee N. Georgescu-Roegen Abba Lerner Gardiner Means Thorstein Veblen	Stephen Dunn Peter Earl Scott Fullwiler James Galbraith John Harvey Stephanie Kelton Mariana Mazzucato Pavlina Tcherneva Irene van Staveren Charles Whalen Randall Wray
Kaldorians	Economic growth Productivity regimes Open economy constraints Real–financial nexus	John Cornwall Wynne Godley Richard Goodwin Roy Harrod Nicholas Kaldor Anthony Thirlwall	Robert Boyer John McCombie Ken Coutts Ro Naastepad Neville Norman Tom Palley Pascal Petit Mark Setterfield Peter Skott Servaas Storm

authors who have inspired the current authors working within the strand, establishing a kind of who's who of post-Keynesian economics, although inevitably omitting some important contributors.

1.4.4 Controversies over the Definition of Post-Keynesian Economics

Narrow-tent versus broad-tent approach

One topic that has not yet been discussed is what spelling should be adopted, with or without the hyphen: 'post-Keynesian' or 'Post Keynesian', as in the *Journal of Post Keynesian Economics*. As recalled by King (2002, p. 9), the spelling advocated here, with a hyphen, was used by Kaldor and Robinson as early as 1956 and 1959. As mentioned earlier, the term 'post-Keynesian' to designate Cambridge Keynesians was then in competition with the term 'neo-Keynesian', which was used by Davidson (1972) among many others. Robinson, however, thought that the latter expression best applied to neoclassical Keynesians (Samuelson, Solow, Hicks, Tobin), so that by the late 1960s and early 1970s, as noted by Lee (2009, pp. 81–2), both Robinson and Eichner were promoting the use of 'post-Keynesian' to define Cambridge Keynesianism, an expression that was picked up by Kregel (1973) and Eichner and Kregel (1975), as well as most UK writers. 'Post Keynesian' without the hyphen was proposed by Davidson and Weintraub (1978) when founding their journal. Their motive was to come up with something that would be broader and more consensual than Cambridge Keynesianism, which at the time was associated with a left-wing view of the world, closest to the Sraffian and Kaleckian strands of the research programme, which, rightly or wrongly, were also accused of not paying enough attention to monetary economics. As a result the spelling without the hyphen was adopted by a large number of economists.

Strangely enough, the tables have recently been turned. The long-time editor of the *Journal of Post Keynesian Economics*, Paul Davidson (2003–04) has on occasion expressed some frustration over his unsuccessful efforts to convince his mainstream colleagues of the worth of what he calls Post Keynesian economics, blaming this failure on the fact that Post Keynesian economics is perceived as being incoherent because it incorporates too many different views. Davidson now wishes to redefine Post Keynesian economics, in the hope of stopping the marginalization of his ideas, by restricting its meaning to Fundamentalist Keynesianism (only the first strand of Tables 1.8 and 1.9), eliminating authors such as Eichner, Minsky, the Sraffians and all Kaleckians in the process (Lavoie, 2020). By doing so, Davidson (2003–4, p. 262) wishes to avoid what he calls a 'Babylonian incoherent babble', or a Tower of Babel. The '*true* Post Keynesian school' that Davidson (ibid., p. 258) refers to is what he used to call Keynes's school: 'Fundamental Keynesianism – what I would call Post Keynesianism – is based on throwing over the same classical axioms that Keynes discarded in the general theory' (ibid., p. 263). Ironically, Dutt and Amadeo (1990) had perceived this change of mind more than 30 years ago, since they assimilated Fundamentalist Keynesianism to the 'Post Keynesian' spelling. Thus we have gone full circle. The relevant taxonomy today seems to be that 'Post Keynesian' is a narrow-tent designation, while 'post-Keynesian' covers a broader tent. And this explains the use of the 'post-Keynesian' spelling in this book, a spelling also adopted by Harcourt (2006, 2012).

Personally, when analysing the contours of the post-Keynesian school, I tend to favour a 'broad-tent' approach. I am a 'lumper' more than a 'splitter', to use the expressions proposed by Mearman (2009), or, in the words of King (2002, p. 214), a 'synthesizer'. To some extent, it is in the nature of heterodox economists to be critical rather than constructive; this is why they have decided to reject mainstream economics. This may explain why a number of heterodox authors are busily criticizing each other or the mainstream, or even dead authors. Pasinetti (2007, pp. 38–9) believes that the failure of post-Keynesian economics to have had a large impact on economics can be explained in part by this personal feature of the founding members of Cambridge Keynesianism. King (2017) concurs with Pasinetti about this and notes its negative consequences. Pasinetti observes that too many post-Keynesians have been arguing with each other, 'disputing over who had which particular idea first'. Cambridge economists in particular did not spend much time trying to build bridges between themselves. Each one of them was too jealous of his or her intellectual independence. He also notes that too many of them showed a doctrinaire attitude, declining to enter into fruitful discussions with those holding slightly different views. 'What is not at all helpful is that economists following these different strands or approaches have so often attacked one another, stressing many times, even to the extreme, their differences and overlooking or rather refusing to investigate what they have in common' (Pasinetti, 2007, p. 46).

This, however, should not deter us from trying to link together contributions that differ but which were made in the same spirit. It is our task to generalize them and find extensions. One of the objectives of this book is to show that a synthesis of the various streams of post-Keynesian economics is possible. It is acknowledged that some of the contributions cannot be easily integrated, or that some of the authors may make strange bedfellows, although my position differs from that of Hamouda and Harcourt (1988), who believe that a search for a coherent vision is a futile endeavour, thus adopting a 'horses for courses' attitude. Rather than following the idiosyncrasies of one or the other, this book presents the views of a sort of representative post-Keynesian, taking what I believe to be the strongest contributions of each strand.

My position is closer to that of Eichner and Kregel (1975), who called for the adoption of a new paradigm unifying the main Sraffian and post-Keynesian concepts. Robinson, even after she had denied the importance of the capital controversies, also argued that the task of post-Keynesians was to reconcile Keynes and Sraffa, claiming that post-Keynesian theory had 'a general framework of long- and short-period analysis' that enabled it 'to bring the insights of Marx, Keynes, and Kalecki into coherent form' (Robinson, 1978, pp. 14, 18). My views are aligned with those of Arestis (1996, pp. 129–30), who concluded his survey on post-Keynesian economics by arguing that it 'draws on a body of method and theory which represents a consistent way of analysing economic phenomena', adding that post-Keynesian economics 'has now reached the stage of constituting a positive approach characterised by internal coherence'. Such a claim may, however, require relinquishing the most extreme views that cannot be entertained within the synthesis, however fundamental these views seem to be from the point of view of their proponents.

Let me illustrate all this. In his article on the definition of post-Keynesian economics, Davidson (2003–04, pp. 254–5) does not understand why colleagues like Minsky decline to make use of the aggregate demand–aggregate supply apparatus found in Keynes's *General Theory*, developed by Weintraub and later retrieved by Davidson himself. The reason, I submit, is that most post-Keynesians felt uncomfortable with this apparatus.

Keynes's treatment of price theory is deemed by many to be too closely associated with neoclassical views to be kept within a synthesis. Indeed, the endless debates about the appropriate representation of Keynes's aggregate supply function, or what has become the Z function, as well as the recursive and inconclusive debates about Keynes's classical postulates regarding the determination of employment, demonstrate that the adoption of neoclassical core assumptions within post-Keynesian economics leads only to sterile controversies, even if these assumptions are turned on their head. Indeed, the confusion about Keynes's aggregate supply function has been so great over the years that the editors of the *Cambridge Journal of Economics* have felt it necessary to issue a statement to the effect that they wished 'to discourage further submissions of comments on the Z function' (Editors, 2011, p. 635).

Keynes versus Kalecki

A number of observers have complained that heterodox economists, including post-Keynesians, tend to avoid questioning founding contributors, acting as self-appointed Guardians of the Temple, who are defending the true faith and the holy scriptures of their favourite authors. If Keynes did not abandon, but only modified, the quantity theory in his *General Theory*, thus being overly monetarist for contemporary post-Keynesians, as noted both by Kaldor (1982, p. 21) and the recanted Hicks (1982, p. 264), this does not mean that we must try to rescue him by making fancy distinctions between a 'constant' and a 'given' supply of money. If Keynes gave his seal of approval to the reserve position doctrine and to the money multiplier concept in the *Treatise on Money*, as recalled by Ulrich Bindseil (2004b), this does not mean that we must follow him blindly and ignore all the evidence provided by the new operating procedures that demonstrate that the purpose of compulsory reserves is not to restrain money creation.

If Keynes assumed decreasing returns when discussing employment in the *General Theory*, this does not mean that we have to follow him despite all empirical evidence to the contrary. As recalled by Simon (1997, p. 14), 'a large part of the book is an exercise in neoclassical analysis'. Keynes may have had good strategic reasons for presenting his analysis the way he did. These reasons are no longer valid. 'Keynes's choices probably were adequate to carry out a more convincing criticism of the neoclassical dominant paradigm. However, in my opinion, they cannot be regarded as acceptable when the emphasis of the analysis is shifted toward the explanation of how actual economies work' (Sardoni, 2002, pp. 10–11). In any case, this strategy turned out to be a failure because, as pointed out by the French translator of Keynes, the adornment of Marshallian microfoundations with diminishing returns in the *General Theory* 'made it possible to invoke the authority of the latter in favor of opinions directly contrary to its essential teachings' (de Largentaye, 1979, p. 9).

The purpose of post-Keynesian economics is 'to understand reality as a central point of its research and theory development' (Jespersen, 2009, p. 15). We must thus start the analysis with assumptions that are grounded in empirically observed facts, that is, use assumptions that are realistic. This is not the case of the neoclassical production function and the assumption of decreasing returns, which Keynes accepted (certainly until 1939, when Dunlop and Kalecki presented their objections to Keynes). As pointed out by Johann Deprez (1996, p. 141),

> [The] Davidsonian approach to the labour market is one true to Keynes's method of building with Marshallian tools and of giving the classicals as much as possible and still end up with unemployment conclusions. As such, it is not – nor is meant to be – a fully positive, descriptive approach to what actually happens in the labour market.

To understand the working of actual economies, these mainstream assumptions about the firm and production must be given up, as we shall discuss in Chapter 3. Kaldor (1983a, p. 10) issued a harsh warning when he wrote that 'so long as one sticks to neoclassical micro-economics, Keynesian macro-economics amounts to very little'.

It is for these reasons that a large number of post-Keynesians believe that the economics of Kalecki provide a preferable foundation for an alternative to orthodox theory, at least when dealing with problems tied to the concept of effective demand. It is clearly the opinion of Harcourt (1987, pp. xi–xii), who believes that 'Kalecki's analysis of the political economy of capitalism is the most profound of the twentieth century, as relevant today as when he originally developed it'. It is also the view of Bhaduri (1986, p. ix), according to whom the radical content of Keynesianism must be learned from Kalecki. Similarly, the historian of economic thought, Gilles Dostaler (1988, p. 134), maintains that 'Kalecki can be considered to be the real founder of post-Keynesian theory'. Even those who contributed to the development of the Keynesian revolution have passed similar judgements. Kaldor (1983a, p. 15) has noted that 'Kalecki's original model of unemployment equilibrium which takes monopolistic competition as its starting point, is clearly superior to Keynes's'. It can be said that, over time, both Kaldor and Robinson turned away from Keynes and tended towards Kalecki. Robinson (1977, pp. 14–15) has argued that, because 'Kalecki was free from the remnants of old-fashioned theory which Keynes had failed to throw off', he was better able 'to weave the analysis of imperfect competition and of effective demand together and it was this that opened up the way for what goes under the name of post-Keynesian theory'. Robinson (1973, p. 97) further argued that Kalecki's version of the *General Theory* was more coherent and 'was in some ways more truly a *general* theory', because it incorporated the influence of investment on profits. The economics of Kalecki are not, as Keynes (1973, xii, p. 831) once thought, 'esoteric abracadabra'.

The point I am trying to make here is that post-Keynesian economics is much more than a modernized version of the economics of a single contributor – Keynes. In some sense, post-Keynesian economics is a misnomer, because it encompasses several founding contributors besides Keynes. Indeed, this is why post-Keynesian economics can be said to be made up of five distinct strands. All strands have something important to contribute to the development of post-Keynesian economics. Some strands turn out to provide a stronger background for the study of some fields. For instance, although Sawyer (2001a) has shown that quite a lot could be said about the monetary theories of Kalecki, the Global Financial Crisis has demonstrated the particular relevance of Fundamentalist Keynesianism, notably with its emphasis on the fragility and instability of financial markets *à la* Minsky, as well as the need for liquid assets and the crucial role played by liquidity preference, a theme developed by Keynes, Davidson and several other authors in this tradition. Various historical events highlight the strength of different strands.

1.5 SOME LIMITS OF ORTHODOX ECONOMICS

Over the past 40 years, orthodox economic theories have faced three major setbacks. We have already discussed the first of these in Section 1.1 – the incapacity of state-of-the-art neoclassical models to make sense of the Global Financial Crisis and the incapacity of their authors to provide useful advice to policy-makers during the crisis. In addition, the crisis has demonstrated that markets do not behave in the way described by the fanciest orthodox theories. Enough has already been said about this. The other two setbacks have occurred at the theory level. The first of these two theoretical setbacks has to do with the stability of general equilibrium theory and is known as the Sonnenschein–Mantel–Debreu theorem. We shall also call it the impossibility theorem. The second theoretical setback involved Sraffian economists: it has mainly to do with production theory in aggregate models and is known under the name of the Cambridge controversies in the theory of capital. The denouement of the Cambridge capital controversies has involved empirical work, and so in this section we will also discuss some issues about econometrics, notably the following question: if orthodox theories rely so much on unrealistic assumptions, why is it that so many empirical studies seem to provide supportive evidence for these theories? We shall see that students of heterodox economics have no reason to be intimidated by those. We start with the Cambridge capital controversies.

1.5.1 The Cambridge Capital Controversies

The Cambridge capital controversies pitted a group of Cambridge Keynesians (Robinson, Sraffa and the Sraffians), in England, against a group of economists from the Massachusetts Institute of Technology (MIT), in Cambridge, near Boston, in the USA. Whereas the mainstream usually views the capital controversies as some aggregation problem, this is not the point of view of the Cambridge Keynesian economists, who see them as a more fundamental problem. Joan Robinson (1975a, p. vi), for instance, has clearly indicated that 'the real dispute is not about the *measurement* of capital but about the *meaning* of capital'. Nicholas Kaldor (1957, p. 595), who only briefly engaged in the controversies, nevertheless had a similar view when arguing that the distinction between the movement along a production function and the shift in the production function is entirely arbitrary.

The controversies arose as a combination of circumstances. The *coup d'envoi*, from the neoclassical side, was provided by Paul Samuelson's (1962) attempt to demonstrate that Robert Solow's growth model and empirical manipulations of the neoclassical production function were perfectly legitimate. Samuelson was also trying to respond to Joan Robinson, following her 1961 visit to MIT. One can suspect that this rare opportunity of exchange between rival research programmes was provided by the fact that both Robinson and Samuelson were dealing with linear production models, so that mainstream economists could grasp to some extent what the heterodox economists were up to (Backhouse, 2014). Robinson had in mind the Sraffian model that was then in the making (Sraffa, 1960), while MIT economists were working on linear programming and activity analysis (Dorfman et al., 1958). Samuelson (1962, pp. 201–2) claimed that the macroeconomics of aggregate production functions was 'the stylized version of a certain quasi-realistic MIT model of diverse heterogeneous capital goods' processes'. Through the construction of new tools which he called a surrogate production function and surrogate capital, he intended to show that complicated heterogeneous capital models behave as if they came from an aggregate neoclassical production function.

The controversies made use of static models based on profit maximization (which led the older Robinson (1975b) to argue that in the end the controversies were irrelevant), with fixed technical coefficients, but with several techniques, or even an infinity of techniques. It was finally resolved, among other things, that the main properties of aggregate production functions could not be derived from a multisector model with heterogeneous capital, nor for that matter even from a two-sector model with one machine, but several available techniques. This put in jeopardy the neoclassical concepts of relative prices as a measure of scarcity, substitution effects, marginalism, the notion of the natural rate of interest, and capital as a primary factor of production.

The controversies provided examples where standard results of neoclassical theory, as presented in undergraduate textbooks or when giving policy advice, were no longer true (Cohen and Harcourt, 2003). For instance, with aggregate production functions, it is usually argued that, economy-wide, the rate of profit is equal to the marginal productivity of capital, and that there exists an inverse relationship between the capital/labour ratio and the ratio of the profit rate to the real wage rate. Counter-examples were shown to exist and are well illustrated in Moss (1980), and more recently in Lazzarini (2011), Harcourt (2012, ch. 4) and Petri (2021, ch. 7). Here we mention three of them:

Reswitching: a technique which was optimal at high profit rates (or low real wages), and then abandoned, becomes optimal again at low profit rates (or high real wages); there seems to be a consensus now that reswitching is unlikely in practice;

Capital reversal, also called reversed capital deepening or negative real Wicksell effects: a lower profit rate is associated with a technique that is less mechanized (a lower capital/labour ratio), even without reswitching; this has been shown to be quite likely, first through simulations (Zambelli, 2004), and then in practice with the help of a new algorithm (Zambelli, 2018a);

Discontinuity or rejection of the discrete postulate: an infinitely small change in the profit rate can generate a large change in the capital/labour ratio, a phenomenon also observed in practice (Zambelli, 2018a).

Figure 1.2 illustrates the implications of these results for the theory of labour demand. Neoclassical authors thought that an infinite number of fixed-coefficient techniques would yield a labour demand curve that has the standard downward-sloping shape shown in Figure 1.2(a). However, Pierangelo Garegnani, who was a student of Sraffa, has shown that it is quite possible to build examples of a continuum of techniques that do not generate the downward-sloping curves that are needed by neoclassical theorists to assert their faith in the stability of the market mechanisms. Garegnani (1970) provides a numerical example that gives rise to the labour demand curve shown in Figure 1.2(b), and Garegnani (1990a) suggests the possible existence of a labour demand curve that would have the shape shown in Figure 1.2(c). Because the neoclassical theories of value and output are, nearly by definition, one and the same thing, it should be clear that these results have destructive consequences not only for neoclassical price theory but also

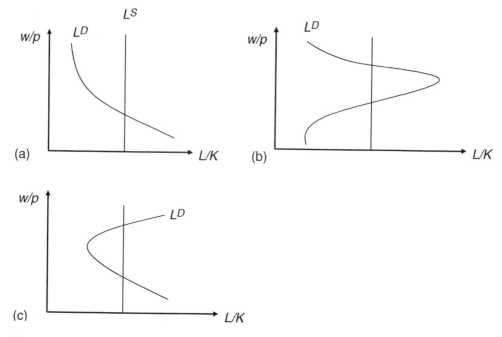

Figure 1.2 Labour demand curve: (a) assumed neoclassical relation; (b) simulated relation, Garegnani (1970); (c) simulated relation, Garegnani (1990a)

for neoclassical macroeconomic theory, which relies on substitution and relative price effects.

What has been the response of neoclassical authors to the Cambridge–Sraffian arguments? This response can be summarized under six headings:

1. neoclassical authors minimize the capital paradoxes, making an analogy with Giffen goods in microeconomics, which do not question the entire neoclassical edifice;
2. they look for the mathematical conditions that would be required to keep production functions 'well behaved', or they claim that this is a simple aggregation problem that can be resolved;
3. they claim that they have the 'faith';
4. they ignore these possible capital paradoxes altogether;
5. they claim that Walrasian general equilibrium theory is impervious to the critique;
6. they rely on empiricism (it works, therefore it exists).

Today, the last three responses are the most common ones; it is no longer fashionable to say that 'placing reliance upon neoclassical economic theory is a matter of faith' (Ferguson, 1969, p. xvii). Ignorance is the fad: aggregate production models with the standard neoclassical properties still abound, despite the results of the Cambridge capital controversies, with no apology. We discuss the last two responses in the next two subsections.

1.5.2 The Stability Nightmare of Neoclassical Theory

The consequences of the Cambridge controversies described above have also sometimes been perceived as a stability problem that would mar the results of an aggregate production economy. The Sraffians themselves volunteered this interpretation with some of their statements. For instance, Garegnani (1983, p. 73) argues that the Cambridge controversies 'deny plausibility to the traditional argument about a *long period* tendency towards the full employment of labour'. Colin Rogers (1989, p. 33) speaks of the 'problematic stability' of the long-period equilibrium solution. Nevertheless, the Sraffians have generally preferred to emphasize the fact that if the overall employment curve for labour looks the way it does in Figure 1.2(b) or 1.2(c), then one cannot really talk of a demand for labour as such. A claim is then made that demand and supply conditions, based on the flexibility of prices, can explain neither the prevailing wage rate nor the level of employment (Mongiovi, 1991, p. 28). Some other explanation, not based on these price functions, must then be the pertinent one, based on norms, conventions or notions of fairness. Another way to present this is to say that, since the Sraffians have shown that there can be unstable equilibria, looking at it from the point of view of standard supply and demand analysis, and since we observe no such blatant instability in the real world, the mechanisms at work must be something else than the standard supply and demand price theory.

A further debate has erupted concerning whether or not the Cambridge capital critique applies not only to the aggregate version but also to the intertemporal version of the neoclassical version, that is, the Walrasian general equilibrium model, which is still considered as the *nec plus ultra* of neoclassical theory. As we saw above, a major defence against the Cambridge critique was to suggest that the general equilibrium model was impervious to it. Sraffians have brought two sets of arguments to counter this claim, with Fratini (2019) providing a survey of this complicated topic.

But whatever is the case, results most damaging to the neo-Walrasian general equilibrium model, derived within the model, have been arrived at independently by three researchers, putting in jeopardy the stability of the model. The damaging result proven by Sonnenschein and others is the following (cf. Kirman, 1989; Guerrien, 1989; Rizvi, 2006). Starting from the usual maximizing behaviour of individuals, resulting from the assumptions required for the demonstration of the existence of a general equilibrium of the Arrow–Debreu type, it is shown that the excess demand functions satisfying Walras's law in an exchange economy can take almost any form. This is damaging to neoclassical theory because one would have hoped that the excess demand functions would always be downward-sloping. This would ensure that, when the price of a good is too low, and consequently the excess demand positive, the *tâtonnement* process leads to a decrease in the excess demand as a result of the *commissaire-priseur* calling higher prices. This is illustrated by Figure 1.3(a). What the so-called Sonnenschein–Mantel–Debreu theorem, or impossibility theorem, demonstrates is that nothing in the standard hypotheses of individual choice behaviour precludes the excess demand functions from looking like Figure 1.3(b). As can be seen, there are several equilibria, and increasing the price when at point A would initially increase excess demand to point B. Small changes in the value of the data may lead to large changes in prices, precisely what the Cambridge controversies had underscored in the context of long-period positions of aggregate production

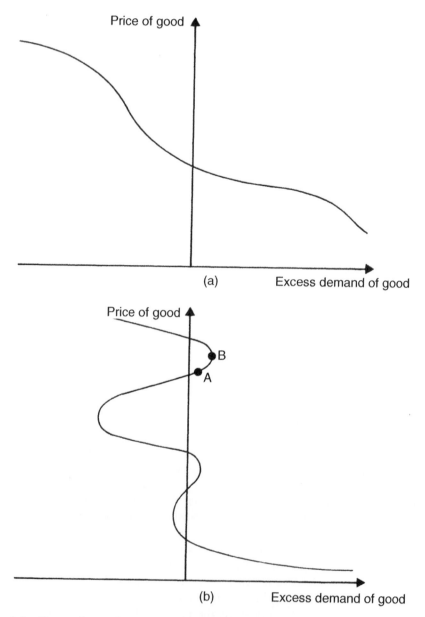

Figure 1.3   Excess demand curves in general equilibrium theory: (a) desired neoclassical relation; (b) possible relation arising from the impossibility theorem

economies. The only constraints on the shape of the function are that for some high price excess demand should be negative, and as price approaches zero the curve should tend towards infinity.

Neo-Walrasians may thus be able to prove the existence of an equilibrium, but they are unable to prove its uniqueness and its stability even in the simple case of an exchange economy without production. The same problem plagues the intertemporal model *à la* Arrow–Debreu and the temporary equilibrium models, where expectations of future prices add a further arbitrary dimension. Thus all comparative results become useless. This also implies that the invisible hand, even if prices are perfectly flexible, may be of no help in attaining an equilibrium, not to speak of the optimum one. This may explain, as pointed out by Abu Rizvi (2006, p. 230), that orthodox economists have virtually abandoned all research in general equilibrium theory, moving towards game theory and experimental economics, since the Arrow–Debreu research programme has reached a dead end. As Walsh (2011, p. 463) puts it, 'the canonical Arrow–Debreu model is a mansion deserted by its owners, the party is over, and the rigour has become rigor mortis'. Neo-Walrasian economics is no longer even taught in graduate programmes. Furthermore, and perhaps more damaging, the only way out of these negative results on stability seems to be to relinquish at least one of the four presuppositions on which the whole research programme is built, that of methodological individualism.

It has been noted that one way to get out of this impasse is to assume that all agents have identical preferences and equal income. One is back to the single representative agent, so much in vogue in DSGE modelling. This implies, furthermore, that the realms of microeconomics be left alone and that the methodology of building the foundations of economics from independent individuals be abandoned. The consequences have been well summarized by a participant to these negative theorems:

> The independence of individuals' behaviour plays an essential role in the construction of economies generating arbitrary excess demand functions. As soon as it is removed the class of functions that can be generated is limited . . . If we are to progress further we may well be forced to theorise in terms of groups who have collectively coherent behaviour. The idea that we should start at the level of the isolated individual is one which we may well have to abandon. (Kirman, 1989, p. 138)

The consequences of the Cambridge controversies were a setback for the neoclassical research programme, but it was said that they applied only to the aggregate versions of neoclassical theory. They dealt with production economies in steady states. The impossibility theorems demonstrated by Sonnenschein and others turned out to be a major setback for the neoclassical programme. The stability of the neoclassical model, whatever its degree of sophistication, the highbrow version or the vulgar one, thus cannot be demonstrated. This implies that comparative analysis cannot be performed within the standard neoclassical framework of supply and demand responding to market forces, at whatever level of aggregation. Furthermore, the standard assumptions made in macroeconomics or in partial equilibrium microeconomics have no justification whatsoever. Barring imperfections of all sorts, the flexibility of prices will not guarantee the attainment of the optimal Walrasian equilibrium. The problem is not one of imperfections; it is one of structure.

To get around the impossibility theorem, and avoid the near emptiness of general equilibrium theory, orthodox economists have adopted the unique representative agent. What have they done to get around the Cambridge critique affecting neoclassical aggregate models? They have adopted a pragmatic approach, claiming that the use of the neoclassical production model is justified because it 'works'.

1.5.3 Neoclassical Production Laws as Artefacts

Empiricism is the last line of defence of neoclassical economics, but we will show that it is a very weak one. As soon as MIT recognized its defeat over the Cambridge capital controversies in the 1966 symposium of the *Quarterly Journal of Economics*, neoclassical authors quickly moved on to the empirical front. Several orthodox economists have taken the view that the validity of neoclassical theory is an empirical question, not a logical one. One presumes that the stance implicitly taken is that neo-Walrasian theory does not have much to offer when it comes to more practical issues and that one then has to rely on the more pedestrian versions of neoclassical theory to be able to make any practical recommendations. What these authors then argue is that the Cambridge critique is right in a formal sense, but they deny that it has any real-world consequence. The empirical proof usually advanced to support this position is given by the numerous successful regressions that have been performed with various neoclassical production functions, with the regressions yielding the expected coefficients. Some orthodox economists were initially rather critical. Frank Hahn (1972, p. 8), a neoclassical economist from Cambridge, UK, claimed that the simplicity of the aggregate neoclassical theory 'is obtained at the cost of logical coherence' and that 'the view that nonetheless it "may work in practice" sounds a little bogus and in any case the onus of proof is on those who maintain this'. Nonetheless, in the end, the empiricist view has prevailed.

Modern orthodox authors justify their use of aggregate production functions on the basis of past successful regressions of neoclassical production functions. As Nobel Prize recipient Prescott (1998, p. 532) points out, 'the neoclassical production function is the cornerstone of the [neoclassical] theory and is used in virtually all applied aggregate analyses'. Without it, very little or no applied aggregate economic analysis can be pursued by orthodox economists. And very little policy advice could be offered, because, for instance, as again pointed out by Prescott (ibid.), 'the aggregate production function is used in public finance exercises to evaluate the consequence of alternative tax policies'. This is why it is so important for mainstream economists, even well-known ones such as Hamermesh (1986, pp. 454, 467), to claim that 'the estimated elasticities that seem to confirm the central prediction of the theory of labor demand are not entirely an artefact produced by aggregating data . . . The Cobb–Douglas function is not a very severe departure from reality in describing production relations.'

But is this the case because the world behaves as if it were a neoclassical Cobb–Douglas function, or is it for some other, more credible, reason?

One can draw up a long list of authors who have argued, in one way or another, and with more or less clarity, that neoclassical production functions (such as the Cobb–Douglas function, the constant elasticity of substitution (CES) function, or the translog production function) often provide good empirical results because they simply reproduce the underlying identities of the national accounts. The argument applies both to cross-industry estimates and to time series. The list goes back to Phelps-Brown (1957). It incorporates previous winners of Nobel Prizes in economics, Paul Samuelson (1979) and Herbert Simon (1979a), with the latter thinking that the issue was important enough to be mentioned in his Nobel Prize lecture. As one would suspect, some heterodox economists have driven the point on numerous occasions: Anwar Shaikh (1974; 1980a; 2005), John McCombie (1987; 1998; 2000–2001; 2001), McCombie and Dixon (1991).

Felipe and McCombie (2001; 2005; 2006; 2009; 2011–12) have written together numerous papers on this topic, which are recapitulated in their book (2013). I have myself dealt briefly with the subject in two of my books (Lavoie, 1987; 1992b) and more extensively in two articles (Lavoie, 2000a; 2008).

Orthodox authors often marvel at the apparent key result that their estimates of the output elasticities of capital and labour turn out to be nearly equal to the shares of profit and wages in national income. Since neoclassical theory predicts that this will be so in a competitive economy with diminishing returns and constant returns to scale, where firms are pursuing profit maximization and thus pay their production factors at the value of their marginal product, neoclassical economists usually conclude that, even though they know that the real world is made up of oligopolies and labour unions, as well as many other imperfections, in the end it behaves as if it were subjected to competitive forces. This assertion is rather hard to swallow, but all kinds of reasons will be advanced to justify such a result, such as the theory of contestable markets, whereby the threat of entry by newcomers will be sufficient to ensure that incumbent members of an industry behave in a competitive way. The (apparent) amazingly successful estimates of neoclassical production functions thus reinforce the belief of many neoclassical economists that the idealized supply and demand analysis is good enough to describe the real world, since economic agents ultimately behave as if pure competition prevailed. Similarly, in the realm of labour economics, when the profit-maximizing first-order conditions of a well-behaved neoclassical production function (with diminishing marginal product of labour, perfect competition, factor pricing at the value of the marginal product etc.) are fulfilled, the labour demand equation of Layard et al. (1991), which they call the price-setting equation, yields parameter values that are exactly reproduced in empirical studies. Researchers then marvel at how well neoclassical theory describes empirical reality.

The reality, however, is that the very same labour parameters can be obtained through the identity of the national accounts (Lavoie, 2000a). Similarly, Shaikh (1974) has shown that estimates of the production function based on deflated values simply reproduce the identities of the national accounts and that the pseudo estimates of the output elasticity of capital (labour) are really approximations of the profit (wage) share. The latter claim can be seen in the following way, by rewriting the Cobb–Douglas production function and the national accounts in logs or in growth terms. Start with the Cobb–Douglas function with technical progress, where q is real output, L the number of workers and M the stock of machines:

$$q_t = A_0 e^{\mu t} L_t^\alpha M_t^\beta \tag{1.1}$$

As is standard, α and β are presumed to be the output elasticities of labour and of capital respectively. Assume constant returns to scale, so that: $\alpha + \beta = 1$. Now consider output per head and capital per head, $y = q/L$ and $k = M/L$. Taking logs, the Cobb–Douglas function yields

$$\log y = \mu t + \beta \log k \tag{1.2}$$

Or, in growth terms, taking the log difference, $\Delta \log$, we have

$$\hat{y} = \mu + \beta \hat{k} \tag{1.3}$$

where the caret mark over a variable signals the growth rate of the variable.

We may now compare the two equations (1.2) and (1.3) with those obtained from the national accounts. Start with the national account identity, given by equation (1.4):

$$pq = wL + rpM \qquad (1.4)$$

where q, L and M are defined as before, and where p and w stand for prices and the nominal wage rate, while r is the profit rate. Thus pq is nominal GDP, wL is the wage bill and rpM are nominal profits. Now divide equation (1.4) through by the prices and the number of workers. One gets output per worker:

$$q/L = w/p + r(M/L) \qquad (1.5)$$

or

$$y = \omega + rk \qquad (1.6)$$

where y represents output per head, or labour productivity, ω is the real wage rate w/p, and k is the number of machines per worker. Taking the derivative of equation (1.6) with respect to time yields

$$dy/dt = d\omega/dt + k.dr/dt + r.dk/dt$$

This can be rewritten as

$$dy/dt = \omega(d\omega/dt)/\omega + kr(dr/dt)/r + rk(dk/dt)/k$$

We now divide this whole expression by y. Recalling that $(dy/dt)/y$ is the rate of growth of output per head, we get

$$\hat{y} = \left(\frac{\omega}{y}\right)\hat{\omega} + \left(\frac{rk}{y}\right)\hat{r} + \left(\frac{rk}{y}\right)\hat{k}$$

Denoting the profit share in national income by the Greek letter $\pi = rk/y$, the logarithmic derivative of equation (1.6) turns out to be

$$\hat{y} = \tau + \pi\hat{k} \qquad (1.7)$$

where

$$\tau = (1 - \pi)\hat{\omega} + \pi\hat{r} \qquad (1.7A)$$

Or else, by integrating, we have in logs

$$\log y = \tau t + \pi \log k \qquad (1.8)$$

Equations (1.7) and (1.8), derived from the national identities, are highly similar to equations (1.3) and (1.2), which came from the Cobb–Douglas production function. Thus it is not surprising that these equations will perform well, as long as technical progress μ in equations (1.2) or (1.3) is adequately represented. Indeed, Anwar Shaikh (1974; 1980a) has shown that even a production relation that would trace the word HUMBUG, with capital per head on the horizontal axis and output per head on the vertical axis, can be successfully represented by a Cobb–Douglas production function, using the method advocated by Solow (1957). Thus, as should now be clear following the exercises of Fisher (1971), any technological relation will yield the appearance of a Cobb–Douglas production function as long as its income shares are relatively constant.

Still, there are cases where Cobb–Douglas functions will yield nonsense, and hence are not 'verified', as pointed out by various authors such as Lucas, Romer and Solow, who try to justify such empirical tests. Such a situation does not normally occur when there is no technical progress. The problem is that technical progress is sometimes represented by a linear trend, whereas in reality the growth rate of labour productivity is highly variable, as shown by Shaikh (2005). Technical progress cannot be represented by some linear function; one must introduce a non-linear trend, given by a Fournier series or some trigonometric function, because the rate of technical progress is fluctuating in a wild way.

In the article that started the growth-accounting craze, Solow (1957) managed to overcome this problem by constructing a variable measuring technical progress. Solow's favourite equation is the log version of the Cobb–Douglas production function, given by equation (1.2) above, which we repeat here for convenience: $\log y = \mu t + \beta \log k$. Then, for each period, he introduces a value for the technical progress growth rate, μ, which he defines in a way that is analogous to equation (1.7A), thus deriving the measure of his μ parameter straight from the national accounts (more precisely, he derived it from the quantity dual of equation (1.7A)). In other words, Solow tested the national accounts identity, while claiming to have corroborated the neoclassical theory of income distribution and neoclassical production functions, as well as claiming to have found a simple way to distinguish between shifts of aggregate production functions and movements along the production function. No wonder he got a good fit!

Indeed, nowadays, neoclassical economists who still 'test' the Cobb–Douglas production function adjust the data by making corrections to the capital stock, deflating the capital index by taking into account the rate of capacity utilization, which is tightly correlated to the rate of technical progress, thus obtaining a good 'fit' with their regressions. Otherwise regression results of the Cobb–Douglas production function with technical progress would be catastrophic. If technical progress is misrepresented (for instance through a linear function in time, rather than by a non-linear one), the output elasticity estimates will not equal the profit and wage shares, and the elasticities may even turn out to be negative. This explains why Cobb–Douglas functions sometimes seem to misrepresent production relations, giving the illusion that neoclassical production functions can be falsified by empirical research.

All in all, the Shaikh and Solow episode has demonstrated that Kaldor's assessment of the neoclassical empirical work, as found below, was quite on the mark. Orthodox authors often 'decorate' their theories by calibrating them; they do not actually attempt to verify, let alone falsify, them.

In economics, observations which contradict the basis hypotheses of prevailing theory are generally ignored ... And where empirical material is brought into conjunction with a theoretical model, as in econometrics, the role of empirical estimation is to 'illustrate', or to 'decorate' the theory, not to provide support to the basic hypothesis (as for example, in the case of numerous studies purporting to estimate the coefficients of production functions). (Kaldor, 1972, p. 1239)

1.5.4 *'Reductio ad Absurdum'* Proofs against Neoclassical Empiricism

Students are rarely convinced by the demonstration found in the previous subsection. They need a proof that is more stunning. Here we present three successive *reductio ad absurdum* proofs, all related to the use of neoclassical production relations.

Shaikh's proof

We start with a proof offered by Shaikh (2005). He constructs a fictitious economy, where the value taken by variables through time is generated by data obtained from a Goodwin-cycle model, with Leontief input–output technology (fixed technical coefficients), Harrod-neutral technical progress and mark-up pricing. Hence none of the usual neoclassical constructs exists (diminishing returns, marginal productivity, marginal cost pricing). Still, once technical progress is introduced in an adequate way, any data can appear to be fittingly represented by a Cobb–Douglas function. This is the case of the US data also compiled by Shaikh, which yield a nearly perfect adjusted R^2 and an estimated output elasticity of capital that nearly perfectly equates the actual profit share, as neoclassical theory would have it; but more surprisingly, it is also the case of the Goodwin data, which, *by construction*, violate all the standard neoclassical assumptions.

One way to understand what is going on is to look at Figure 1.4, which represents a Leontief production function with fixed coefficients, with a dominant technology at each point of time. With technical progress arising at a constant capital to output ratio (given by v_o), that is, technical progress is of the Harrod-neutral sort, the real wage–profit frontier (here assumed to be linear for simplicity) rotates to the north-east, as shown on the left-hand side of the figure. On the right-hand side of the figure, one can observe the true relationship between output per head and capital per head: it is a simple straight line, $y = (1/v_o)k$. Neoclassical analysis, however, will assume that there exists a standard production function, with diminishing returns and the standard curvature, so that it needs to distinguish between a shift of the production function and a move along the production function, from k_0 to k_2. Even when technology is of the Leontief type, as depicted in Figure 1.4, neoclassical economists running standard regressions on deflated variables will manage to 'prove' the existence of a well-behaved pseudo-neoclassical production function.

McCombie's proof

We now move to the second *reductio ad absurdum* proof, this one offered by McCombie, who has devoted quite a bit of attention to these issues. McCombie (2001) takes two firms i each producing in line with a Cobb–Douglas function:

$$q_{it} = A_0 L_{it}^\alpha M_{it}^\beta \tag{1.9}$$

with $\alpha = 0.25$.

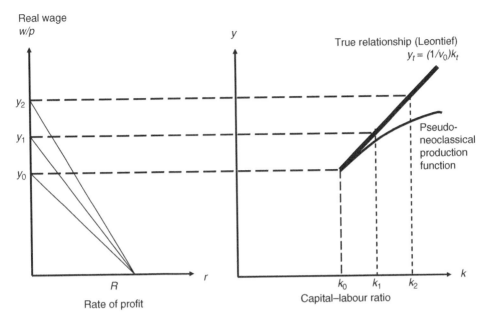

Source: Shaikh (1990, p. 193).

Figure 1.4 True Leontief technology and fitted neoclassical production functions

The other variables are defined as in previous equations. Thus α is still the output elasticity of labour and is equal to 0.25 for both firms. Similarly, for both firms, the output elasticity of capital, β, is equal to 0.75 since the sum of the two elasticities is assumed to be unity (there are constant returns to scale). Inputs and outputs of the two firms are perfectly identical. Hence there is no aggregation problem of the sort noted by Franklin Fisher (1971), which led him to conclude that if the Cobb–Douglas production produces good fits, it is because the share of wages is roughly constant, and not the other way around.

McCombie (2001) constructs a hypothetical economy, where L and M grow through time, with no technical progress, but with some random fluctuations. Running an econometric regression directly on this constructed physical data set (the q, L and M variables) yields an α coefficient close to 0.25, as expected. Running a regression over the equation in log values, McCombie obtains the following relationship (with the absolute *t*-statistics in parentheses):

$$\log q = -0.02 + 0.277 \log L + 0.722 \log M$$
$$(22.5) (55.5)$$

In this case, the estimate is based on physical data, and there is no problem: the regression estimates of the output elasticities correspond nearly exactly to those that exist by construction. With such a result, a neoclassical economist would conclude that neoclassical theory has been vindicated. Things turn out to be entirely different, however, when monetary values are used.

McCombie (2001) reconstructs the same hypothetical economy, with the same two firms, each again with identical output elasticities, but this time he tries to estimate an aggregate production function using deflated monetary values (also called constant-price values), as must always be done in macroeconomics and most often in applied microeconomics at the industry level. To do so, he assumes that firms set prices on the basis of the simplest of the cost-plus pricing procedures – a mark-up equation. Prices then depend on a percentage costing margin θ applied to unit labour costs (wL/q), about which we will say more in Chapter 3:

$$p = (1 + \theta)w(L/q) \tag{1.10}$$

McCombie assumes that firms impose a mark-up equal to 1.33 (the percentage costing margin $\theta = 0.33$). This implies that the wage share is 75 per cent and that the profit share is 25 per cent of national income. With this new regression, based on deflated monetary values, which we denote with the subscript d to make this clear, the regression yields an estimate of the α coefficient – the apparent output elasticity of labour – that turns out to be 0.75, as shown in the regression equation that follows:

$$\log q_d = +1.8 + 0.752 \log L + 0.248 \log M_d$$
$$(1198) \qquad (403)$$

Thus we started with production functions and physical data according to which we know that, by construction, the labour output elasticity α is 0.25. Yet the estimated aggregate production function (in deflated monetary terms) tells us that this elasticity is 0.75 – which is the wage share in income. In other words, estimates of aggregate production functions – at both the industry and macro levels, since they are necessarily based on deflated values and not on direct physical data – measure factor shares. They do not measure the output elasticities of factors of production, in contrast to what neoclassical authors would like us to believe. Disaggregation will not solve the problem in the least as long as deflated variables are used.

These empirical estimates of aggregate production functions are completely useless to provide any information about the kind of technology in use, or about the values of output elasticities and elasticities of substitution. McCombie (2001) provides additional proof of this. He starts with the base year data of the two firms mentioned above, but assuming now, by construction, that the inputs and outputs of these firms grow in a completely random way. Not surprisingly, when a regression is run on the physical variables of each firm, correlation coefficients are near zero and estimates of output elasticities are statistically insignificant, as they should be, since there is no relationship between inputs and output, by construction.

By contrast, when the same physical data set is combined with monetary value data obtained by assuming the same mark-up in each firm, with again a 75 per cent labour share and assuming a constant profit rate, the regression on the aggregated deflated values yields very promising results. The correlation coefficient is nearly unity, and the regression coefficients yield statistically significant values that reflect once more the labour and profit shares:

$$\log q_d = constant + 0.751 \log L + 0.248 \log M_d$$
$$(514) \qquad (354)$$

Thus, as McCombie (2001, p. 598) concludes,

> no matter what form the underlying micro or engineering production functions take, so long as the average mark-up is roughly constant over time (so that factor shares are constant), a reasonable fit to the Cobb–Douglas relationship will always be found. However, this says nothing about the underlying technology of the economy.

So even if technology is from Mars, and Martians manage to produce output independently of inputs, provided Martian firms follow some form of cost-plus pricing, the regressions over deflated data will tell us that Martians use Cobb–Douglas production technology, with diminishing returns, constant returns to scale, and factor pricing following principles of marginalism.

Why is this so? It turns out, as we saw in the previous subsection, that regressions over the deflated variables of production functions, when they are correctly estimated, reproduce only the relationships of the national accounts. If the wage share is approximately constant, and if there is no technical progress or, if technical progress is adequately estimated, one will always discover that a Cobb–Douglas production function provides a good fit. If the wage share is not constant, for instance when the wage share trends upwards along with the capital to labour ratio, the CES function will yield better fits. But the CES production function, along with the translog production function, are subject to the very same criticisms that apply to the Cobb–Douglas function (McCombie and Dixon, 1991; Felipe and McCombie, 2001).

Anyadike-Danes and Godley's proof
We now turn to a third and final *reductio ad absurdum* proof, provided by Michael Anyadike-Danes and Wynne Godley (1989). These post-Keynesian economists question the relevance of the kind of regression analysis that has been pursued by the economists who are convinced that overly high real wages are the main cause of the high European unemployment rates (Layard, Nickell and Jackman in particular, referred to as LNJ from now on). Godley and his associate intend to demonstrate that even when, by construction, there is no relationship whatsoever in a hypothetical economy between employment and real wages, standard econometric analysis (based on OLS (ordinary least squares) estimates) will give the impression that it verifies a negative relationship between employment and real wages.

Before we move on to their econometric results, we start by showing how easy it is to retrieve the labour-demand price-setting (PS) equation of the LNJ model. The PS equation of LNJ, obtained through an appropriate profit-maximizing behaviour of firms and other standard neoclassical conditions, is

$$(\log w - \log p) = U + (\log q - \log N) \qquad (1.11)$$

where U is the rate of unemployment and N is active population (in contrast to L, which is employed labour), while the other variables are defined as they were before. Equation (1.11) is usually interpreted, in particular in OECD offices, as saying that a higher rate of unemployment is being caused by higher real wages.

We simply wish to show that, by starting from the same mark-up pricing equation that McCombie used in his own proof, we will be able to arrive at LNJ's PS equation. Taking the log of the mark-up equation given by equation (1.10), we obtain

$$\log p = \log \theta + \log w - \log q + \log L \qquad (1.12)$$

or, rearranging in terms of labour employment, and dropping the constant, we get

$$\log L = -(\log w - \log p) + \log q \qquad (1.13)$$

Equation (1.13) reminds us that, for a given output level, we automatically get a negative relationship between employment and real wages when prices are set through a cost-plus procedure. But this negative relationship only reflects the fact, that, with a given costing margin, the real wage will be lower if labour productivity (measured by $\log q - \log L$) is lowered. It has nothing to do with a demand for labour function. It is simply an arithmetic relation that arises from the cost-plus pricing formula. Rewriting equation (1.12) yet once more, and dropping the constant, we see that

$$(\log w - \log p) = \log q - \log L \qquad (1.14)$$

LNJ arrive at their own PS equation by drawing on an approximation of the definition of the rate of unemployment U. They use equation (1.15):

$$U = \log N - \log L \qquad (1.15)$$

Combining equations (1.14) and (1.15), thus by combining two quasi-identities, we obtain LNJ's PS equation – equation (1.11). Thus, having started from the simple mark-up pricing equation, with no marginalism content whatever, we can recover the PS equation that attributes high unemployment to excessive real wages – a result that neoclassical economists attribute to the profit-maximizing behaviour of firms making hiring decisions. Felipe and McCombie (2009, p. 165) confirm that, in general, estimates of labour demand functions based on value data reproduce the identities of the national accounts and hence 'will always yield a negative relationship between the level of employment and the real wage'.

Anyadike-Danes and Godley (1989) go one step further. Here is their *reductio ad absurdum* proof. They start by assuming, by construction, that nominal wages, output and employment all grow independently of each other, with prices set on the basis of a mark-up on current and lagged labour unit costs (75 per cent of sales are assumed to be based on current output and 25 per cent of sales arise from held inventories, produced in the previous period, and hence, in the pricing equation below, $\varphi = 0.75$). Wage rates, output and employment are each assumed to grow at some specific trend rate (7 per cent, 5 per cent and 1 per cent respectively), with random fluctuations around it. We have:

$\log w = (1.07 + \text{random}) + \log w_{-1}$
$\log q = (1.05 + \text{random}) + \log q_{-1}$
$\log L = (1.01 + \text{random}) + \log L_{-1}$
$\log p = \log \theta + \varphi(\log w - \log q + \log L) + (1 - \varphi)(\log w_{-1} - \log q_{-1} + \log L_{-1})$

Anyadike-Danes and Godley then run a regression on the data generated by this hypothetical economy. They get the following result:

$$\log L = 1.3 - 0.94 (\log w - \log p) - 0.12 \log L_{-1} + 0.73 \log q + 0.01t$$
$$\quad\quad\quad\quad (7.4) \quad\quad\quad\quad\quad\quad (1.0) \quad\quad\quad\quad (1.0) \quad\quad (4.2)$$

According to the regression equation, employment seems to entertain a statistically significant negative relationship with real wages (nearly equal to unity, as expected from equation 1.14), as well as a positive time trend, as LNJ and their orthodox colleagues would like it to be. In addition, note that employment does not seem to depend on actual output q, in contrast to what post-Keynesians would argue, and that it does not depend on past employment L_{-1}, since these two variables do not have statistically significant coefficients in the regression.

But we know that, by construction, employment L is completely independent of real wages, and that the current level of employment depends only on past employment. This is what the regression should reflect. As Anyadike-Danes and Godley (1989, p. 178) put it, 'real wage terms turn out to be large, negative and strongly significant although we know, as Creator, that real wages have no direct causal role whatever in the determination of employment'. Thus empirical studies can manage to give support to the neoclassical theory of labour demand even in those cases where we know that, by construction, neoclassical theory is completely irrelevant (that is, when real wages and employment are independent of each other, while prices are set on a cost-plus basis and not on marginal-pricing principles).

Mainstream instrumentalism: not even wrong

Spurious correlation, as illustrated here, is an important problem in economics. It has been shown repeatedly that series of random walks that are absolutely independent of each other may exhibit high correlation coefficients. Granger and Newbold (1974), for instance, have shown that, on average, an R^2 of 0.59 could be obtained when regressing such a random walk over five variables also exhibiting a random walk. Variables that have nothing to do with each other may appear to have some economic relationship. Indeed, Hendry (1980) humorously showed that he could provide empirical support for a new theory of inflation by relating the price index P in the UK to an exogenous variable C – cumulative rainfall in the UK! For a while, one thought that cointegration analysis provided the means to identify genuine (long-run) relationships between two non-stationary variables. Unfortunately, a number of economists now question this claim, arguing that cointegration tests may fail to identify causal relations that we know are true while accepting as causal relations that we know cannot be true (Moosa, 2017a, p. 155).

This being said, the studies of Shaikh, McCombie, Felipe and others show that the econometric estimates of neoclassical production functions based on deflated monetary values, or constant-price value terms, as is the case at the macro and industry levels when direct physical data are not used, yield pure artefacts, that is, purely imaginary results. This affects all neoclassical applied aggregate work that relies in some way on well-behaved production functions and profit-maximizing conditions: NAIRU measures, labour demand functions and wage elasticities; investment theory; measures of multifactor productivity or total factor productivity growth; estimates of endogenous growth; theories of economic development; theories of income distribution; measures of output elasticities with respect to labour and capital; estimates of cost functions; measures of potential output; theories of real business cycles; estimates of the impact of changes in the minimum wage, social programmes, or tax rates. Even when setting aside problems of aggregation, these estimates are either completely off target (if the world is made up of neoclassical production functions) or imaginary (if economies are run on fixed technical coefficients, as most post-Keynesians believe). As Felipe and McCombie's (2013) book title says, neoclassical production theory is 'not even wrong': it is so useless that you cannot even prove it wrong!

As pointed out earlier, orthodox economics relies on instrumentalism, which claims that assumptions need not be realistic, as long as they help in making predictions. It combines the ability to start from idealized imaginary models and the need to resort to empiricism. In the case of well-behaved production functions and their implied labour demand functions, orthodox economists are pushing instrumentalism to the hilt. What counts is their ability to make predictions, based on estimates of elasticities, even if these predictions are meaningless because the estimates do not measure output elasticities, measuring instead factor shares! Neoclassical economists are claiming to measure something, but are really measuring something entirely different. Their theories, such as the necessary negative relationship between real wages and employment, seem to be supported by the data, whereas the negative relationship arises straight from the identities of the national accounts, with no behavioural implication for the effect of higher real wages on employment.

I have discussed these issues with a few of my neoclassical colleagues. The most genuine answers have been that without these elasticity estimates they could no longer say anything. But they would rather continue making policy proposals based on false information than make no propositions at all. In other words, they would rather be precisely wrong than approximately right. As Felipe and McCombie (2011–12, p. 290), conclude,

> given the importance of this critique, it is surprising that it has been almost totally ignored, misinterpreted, or even greeted with outright hostility within the mainstream profession. But perhaps on reflection it is not all that surprising. Few people are willing to concede that much of their academic work may be literally meaningless.

More than 60 years after the publication of Sraffa's (1960) book, it seems that this empirical critique of neoclassical production functions, based on *reductio ad absurdum* proofs, might be the most damaging one. In a string of papers, Schefold contends that the theoretical critique, based on Sraffian theory, has been blunted by the empirical discovery, through the manipulation of actual input–output tables, that wage–profit curves are nearly linear, that few of them appear on the envelope of efficient techniques, and that both capital-reversing and especially reswitching are unlikely phenomena (Schefold, 2013). It could be argued, however, that this critique is itself blunted by the fact that input–output technical coefficients are not obtained from direct observation of engineering physical data. They are derived instead from the computation of deflated values, and are thus potentially subjected to the same measurement problems associated with aggregate production functions (Felipe and McCombie, 2013, p. 42). Furthermore, as mentioned earlier, Zambelli (2018a) has shown, making use of actual input-output data, that the computation of the surrogate production function and surrogate capital, as suggested by Samuelson (1962), did not yield the well-behaved neoclassical properties – capital reversal was often present both at the macroeconomic and industry levels.

1.5.5 Further Limits of Orthodox Economics

Suspicion of publication bias
The multitude of research studies that supposedly demonstrate the validity of neoclassical theory in various fields of economics is one of the most puzzling features encountered by students dissatisfied with the mainstream approach. Whereas they confusedly perceive that several of the hypotheses that underlie the tested neoclassical models lack substance or realism, students are being swamped with successful tests of these models. It seems that the real world behaves according to these absurd hypotheses.

The preceding subsection has clearly shown that heterodox economists and their students need not fear the mountains of empirical evidence that seems to give support to neoclassical theory. Most, perhaps all, of this evidence is an artefact. The tons of regressions conducted on just-identified neoclassical production functions can provide estimates only of the model's parameters, but they can in no way provide support for the theory. Neoclassical production theory, and its offshoots, cannot be falsified by econometric research, and hence, if we are to believe the philosopher of science, Karl Popper, they are not truly scientific. Even worse than that, the experiments recalled here have shown that estimates based on constant-price values do not measure what neoclassical economists claim to be measuring. Policy advice based on these estimates is bogus.

A second cause of this proliferation of fortunate empirical studies is the manner in which empirical research is being conducted. This applies to orthodox researchers as well as to researchers of other persuasions. The typical economist draws up a theory, outlines a simplified functional form that could be empirically tested, and adds a few secondary variables that could be of significance. With the help of the computer and some arbitrary algorithms, the analyst then searches for the best equation. Several rounds might be needed to find regressions that offer any fit, and on the way several variables and several specifications will have been tested and discarded, bringing as well a revision of the theory. Furthermore, the data might be divided into subperiods, part of the data might be discarded, the data might be weighted in a useful manner, dummy variables might be introduced, and so on. In the end the theory claimed to be tested may have only a remote relationship with the one originally posited. This is the so-called interaction between data and theory. Some prefer to speak of 'data mining', 'data fishing' or 'data massaging'.

The famous study of Reinhart and Rogoff (2010) provides a striking example of data massaging. These two neoclassical economists have famously calculated that countries that run public debt to GDP ratios over 90 per cent grow much more slowly than countries with lower ratios. This study thus provided a convenient legitimacy to the calls for fiscal austerity and consolidation in the aftermath of the Global Financial Crisis. Notwithstanding the issue of reversed causality – slow or negative growth may generate high debt ratios rather than the converse – Herndon et al. (2014) show that if coding mistakes, omitted entries and a more conventional weighting method are taken into account, the growth rates of countries with high public debt to GDP ratios rise from −0.1 per cent to +2.2 per cent.

Here I wish to show that this is a generalized problem in economics, which questions several empirical results that seem to provide support for orthodox theory. In the 1992 version of this book, I asked: why do neoclassical theories always seem to be supported by some empirical evidence? Why do empirical facts in orthodox economic journals often appear to verify orthodox theory? Here is the answer that I then provided:

> The first thing to notice is that journals usually do not publish inconclusive results, except when they provide a scapegoat which can then be used to highlight the rival pet theory of their editors. As a consequence, authors do not bother submitting results which are inconclusive. Only a biased sample of the empirical work that is going on is thus published. Most of the unsuccessful attempts at verification go unnoticed, and a lot of the unsuccessful attempts at replicating published empirical models do not end up in the learned journals. (Lavoie, 1992b, p. 21)

Since this was written, a considerable amount of work has been devoted to this issue, that is, the problem of publication bias, sometimes called reporting bias, ideological bias or the file-drawer problem. In psychology, this is called confirmation bias. This is a well-known problem in medicine, where the results of studies of the effectiveness of medical drugs may mean substantial additional profits for the pharmaceutical companies. A further, but related, problem is that different investigators come up with quite different findings when trying to assess the same phenomenon. A standard remedy to this multiplicity of results is to do a literature review of these empirical studies, possibly by eliminating studies that are perceived to be badly done or by taking a count, of say the number of studies that find that the demand for water has a high price elasticity (in absolute terms) compared to those that find that its price elasticity is low. But these methods are rather rudimentary because, if economic theory says that the price elasticity ought to be high, then it is likely that many investigators will find just that. The problem also arises in the natural sciences: in their experiments researchers tend to find the same values for some scientific constant, until a breakthrough in technology allows someone to decisively affirm that a new value has been found, at which point other researchers also tend to find the same new value, as was the case with the speed of light.

Meta-regression analysis to the rescue
For a number of years now, Tom Stanley has been arguing that economists should proceed to meta-regression analysis, as has been extensively developed in psychology, educational research and medicine. Meta-regression analysis (MRA) is simply a regression on regression results and their characteristics. It has been largely developed by economists. 'Empirical models reported in economic journals are selected from a large set of estimated models. Journals, through their editorial policies, engage in some selection, which in turn stimulates extensive model searching and prescreening' (Stanley and Jarrell, 1989, p. 161).

There are two problems with the reporting of empirical results. The first problem is that 'researchers, reviewers, and editors are predisposed to treat "statistically significant" results more favorably; hence they are more likely to be published. Studies that find relatively small and "insignificant" effects tend to remain in the "file drawer". Such publication or selection biases make empirical effects seem larger than they are' (Stanley, 2005a, p. 310). There is a second problem, however, which is of particular concern for heterodox economists: 'reviewers and editors may be predisposed to accept papers consistent with the conventional view. Researchers may use the presence of a conventionally expected result as a model selection test' (ibid.). In other words, investigators will massage the data and search for new specifications until they get statistically significant results that fit conventional wisdom or their own views.

What can be done to gauge the true value of the parameter being investigated and to assess whether or not there is selection bias? At the heart of the identification of publication bias is the notion that investigators relying on smaller samples, with fewer degrees of freedom, will usually face larger standard errors. Hence the estimates of the parameter are likely to be less precise, and hence to be all over the map. Furthermore, to obtain statistically significant effects (say t ratios above 1.6), they will need to find large effects (recall that the t-statistic is the size of the coefficient divided by the standard error) and this may require quite a lot of tries with different specifications. By contrast, with large samples, the estimates are likely to be more precise. Also the standard errors will be smaller, and hence a statistically significant result can be achieved despite smaller values of the estimated parameter.

All this can be illustrated with the help of a graph, called a funnel plot. Figure 1.5 illustrates two such funnel plots, with the size of the estimated parameter on the horizontal

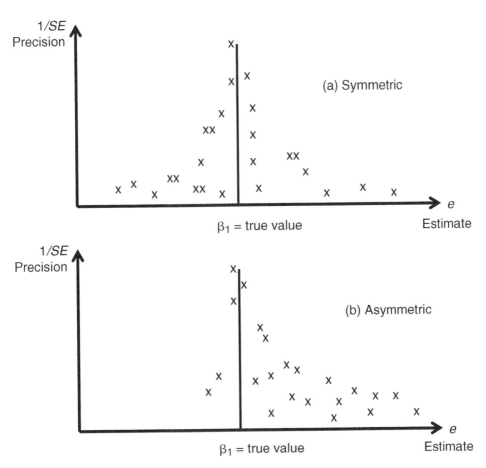

Figure 1.5 Funnel graphs: (a) symmetric, with no selectivity bias; (b) asymmetric, with selectivity bias

axis, and with a measure of the precision of the estimate e, measured by the inverse of the standard error SE. The doublets (e, SE) form a pyramid-looking set, with estimates being more spread out when the degree of precision is weak (when the standard error is high). Figure 1.5(a) shows the case devoid of publication bias: the various estimates (shown on the horizontal axis) are distributed symmetrically on both sides of the presumed true value of the parameter. By contrast, Figure 1.5(b) shows publication bias: the estimates are distributed in an asymmetric way; here most studies provide estimates that are much larger than the presumed true value (of course, we could also have asymmetry, with a large number of studies finding overly large negative values). An example of such asymmetry is research on the effect of an increase in the minimum wage rate on employment. If we express these variables in logs, then the parameter that we are looking for is the percentage increase in employment following a 1 per cent increase in the minimum wage rate. David Card and Alan Krueger (1995), two (until then) respected economists, provoked an economic earthquake when they contended that raising the minimum wage has almost no negative effect on employment, and that previous research was exhibiting publication bias.

While funnel graphs are highly useful, they are only a visual aid. Furthermore, it could be that different estimates are being found because the investigators have included different variables, have used different techniques or have worked on different countries or time periods. These meta-explanatory variables could thus be included in the meta-regression analysis and help explain the variations in parameter estimates. Here, however, we wish to focus only on the relationship between standard error SE and the parameter estimate e. If we invert the funnel graph, now putting the parameter estimate on the horizontal axis and the standard error on the vertical axis, we obtain Figure 1.6, which is the counterpart of Figure 1.5(b).

Figure 1.6 is the exact illustration of the simple meta-regression analysis, which is given by equation (1.16), with ε_i a random term:

$$e_i = \beta_1 + \beta_0 SE_i + \varepsilon_{1i} \tag{1.16}$$

What do the two coefficients β_1 and β_0 of this meta-regression represent? If the standard error SE is zero, then the estimate e will be equal to β_1. Thus β_1 represents the estimated true value of the parameter. We can then proceed to standard tests and check whether the null hypothesis H_0: $\beta_1 = 0$ can be rejected or not. If it cannot be rejected, then it means that there is no effect. In the case of research on the effect of the minimum wage, this is indeed what Doucouliagos and Stanley (2009) find: using both Card and Krueger's data and a much larger number of previous empirical studies, meta-regression analysis shows that increases in the minimum wage have no effect on employment. Thus, 'in spite of 678 reported statistically significant estimates of minimum wage's adverse employment effect' (Stanley et al., 2010, p. 75), no such effect exists. Ioannidis et al. (2017), in a meta-analysis that takes into account the concept of statistical power, assess that the true elasticity is 16 times smaller than the average value computed over all these studies. Furthermore, in a meta-regression analysis only dealing with studies from 2010 to 2014, Giotis and Chletsos (2015) also find no evidence of a negative relation between minimum wages and employment.

This in itself is interesting. But now we can focus on the meaning of the β_0 parameter. This parameter measures the extent of publication bias. If there is no publication

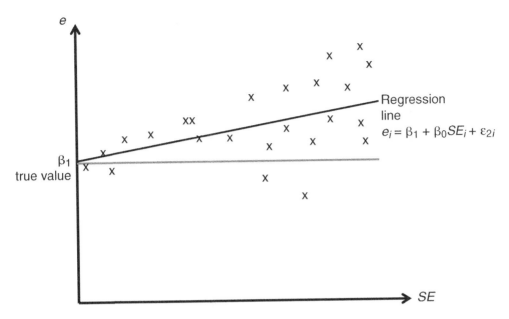

Figure 1.6   Illustration of the simple meta-regression analysis, in the case of selectivity bias

selection, the effects measured in the various empirical studies should vary randomly around the true value β_1, whatever the size of the sample and the standard error of the estimated parameter. Thus we can once more proceed to a standard test and check whether the null hypothesis H_0: $\beta_0 = 0$ can be rejected. If it can, then there is no publication bias in this field of research, or, possibly, the various forces which could lead to publication bias cancel each other out. If $\beta_0 \neq 0$, it means that the less precise studies tend to be more skewed, and hence there is evidence of publication bias. Again, Doucouliagos and Stanley (2009) show that this is the case with research on the effect of the minimum wage on employment.

In reality, because the regression equation given by (1.16) suffers from heteroscedasticity (there is more dispersion from the regression line for some of the observations), as is obvious from Figure 1.6, meta-regression analysis is usually conducted by using equation (1.17) below, which is obtained by dividing equation (1.16) by the individual standard errors SE_i, where t_i is the conventional t-value of the effect e_i. This provides a proper correction to heteroscedasticity, with the intercept and the slope now being reversed, but with the parameters β_1 and β_0 keeping their previous meaning.

$$(e_i/SE_i) = t_i = \beta_1(1/SE_i) + \beta_0 + \varepsilon_{2i} \tag{1.17}$$

Evidence of publication bias

The higher the absolute value of β_0 in equation (1.17), the greater the publication bias. Doucouliagos and Stanley (2013) look at 87 areas of economic research. They conclude that approximately 60 per cent of these suffer from severe or substantial publication bias. In microeconomics, the price elasticities of demand for residential water, tobacco, beer, spirits and alcohol all suffer from substantial or severe selectivity problems. They also show that these elasticities are very much overestimated, all of them being much below unity, so that the strength of substitution effects, which is at the heart of orthodox economics, is much weaker than usually described. Ioannidis et al. (2017) further find that in half of the areas of research, estimates of elasticities are exaggerated by a factor of 2 or more.

In macroeconomics, besides the issue of the minimum wage, the following fields suffer from severe publication bias: the inflation and the output coefficients in the Taylor rule equation of monetary policy; the wage curve (the (negative) relationship between unemployment rates and wages); business cycle correlations; and the (negative) relationship between unionization and productivity growth. The studies of the effect of central bank independence and inflation, as well as the field of the link between economic reform and economic growth, suffer from substantial publication bias, as does the assessment of the theory of efficiency wages. Krassoi-Peach and Stanley (2009) find that the estimated effect, the wage elasticity of production, corrected by the meta-regression analysis, turns out to be half the literature average measure (0.30 instead of 0.61), which now makes these estimates incompatible with the assumption of profit maximization, which requires that this elasticity be equal to the labour share (in analogy with what we have already discussed regarding neoclassical production functions).

Meta-regression analysis may also be useful even if there is no apparent publication bias. For instance, in the research field of the Ricardian equivalence theorem, that is, the claim that larger deficits will generate lower household consumption expenditures, publication bias is modest. Still, meta-regression analysis permits to falsify this mainstream belief (Stanley, 1998), which played an important role in the debate over the effectiveness of stimulus expenditure programmes during the Global Financial Crisis.

Similarly, with regard to the rate of unemployment, meta-regression analysis shows conclusively that the best studies (those that have the lowest standard errors) find coefficients of persistence closest to unity. This means that, in a simple autoregressive equation, as illustrated by equation (1.18), where U is the rate of unemployment, the coefficient β_1 is unity or nearly so:

$$U_t = \beta_0 + \beta_1 U_{t-1} + \varepsilon_3 \qquad (1.18)$$

This implies that there is unemployment hysteresis and thus that there is no natural rate of unemployment towards which the actual rate would be converging. This, plus another meta-regression analysis (Stanley, 2005b), which rejects the main assumption of the NAIRU hypothesis (that expected inflation leads to a one-on-one increase in the rate of inflation), leads Stanley (2004, p. 605) to conclude that the hypothesis of a natural rate of unemployment has been empirically and definitely refuted.

Doucouliagos and Stanley (2013, p. 318) observe that investigators often follow a 'stopping rule'. Just like other individuals, they 'satisfice': they cease to go through various specifications when they reach 'what they believe to be the "truth", or a sufficiently close approximation to it'. The truth, or admissible results, however, will depend on what economic theory claims. In the fields where theory is contested or where there are pluralistic views, the range of admissible results will be much larger, and there will be less selectivity bias. And indeed, this is what Doucouliagos and Stanley (2013) discover. This further justifies the importance and usefulness of pluralism in economic theory. Pluralism generates better economics. They further find that studies involving macroeconomics and calculations of demand elasticities are particularly subject to publication bias. Since various surveys show that there is less consensus in macroeconomics (Fuller and Geide-Stevenson, 2003), this result must be attributed to the greater role played by ideology in macroeconomics, again as was demonstrated during the Global Financial Crisis.

Another intriguing result is that the best-ranked journals are the worst offenders when it comes to publication bias. Costa-Font et al. (2013) find through a meta-regression that journals with the highest impact factors (the journals whose articles are most often cited) publish the studies that most overestimate the elasticities of health care and the use of prescription drugs. While such a result would need to be confirmed with other meta-analyses of the sort, there is logic to it. The top academic journals attract more submissions, and thus refuse a greater proportion of them. Thus editors and their reviewers can demand more spectacular empirical estimates. Those who submit to these journals also know it, and they will act accordingly. Thus the problems of data-mining, specification search and reporting bias are likely to be more severe for high-impact journals. The most highly regarded journals may turn out to be the worst ones!

1.5.6 Summing Up

Most post-Keynesians demonstrate scepticism when it comes to empirical and econometric research. Still, one cannot but be impressed by the huge quantity of empirical work that seems to provide support for orthodox theory. This section has shown that this cynicism with regard to orthodox econometric research is largely justified, as many of the studies that appear to verify or confirm orthodox theory are just artefacts. What is an 'artefact'? The most common definition, relevant to science, says that an 'artefact', or 'artifact', is a spurious finding caused by faulty procedures. Meta-regression analysis has certainly demonstrated that many of the empirical proofs of orthodox theory were phoney and arising from defective procedures. The word 'artefact' is also used in the fantasy and sorcery literature. There, an 'artefact' is a magical tool with great power, like a magic wand. This definition seems to be particularly relevant to neoclassical production functions since all the predictions that can be drawn from a model of perfect competition cannot be refuted, even when we know that the required conditions do not hold.

Heterodox and post-Keynesian economists can thus develop their own research programme and their theories without mental reservations. Their theories are just as scientific as those of the orthodoxy. Indeed, heterodox theories could even be said to be more scientific since they are founded on realistic hypotheses.

1.6   AN ANTIDOTE TO TINA

The Global Financial Crisis and the COVID-19 crisis have put in the limelight the huge debate that goes on in economics over whether austerity policies and low-wage policies are needed to achieve sustainable prosperity. On the one hand are those who claim that there is no alternative (TINA); this is the dominant view, which loses ground for a few months when a catastrophe seems imminent in the midst of the crisis. On the other hand are those who say that there is an alternative; these dissenters are a mixed bag of orthodox and heterodox dissenters.

Orthodox dissenters, such as Joseph Stiglitz, reject many of the free-market policies that were adopted in the 1980s and 1990s or the austerity policies that were advocated during or after the Global Financial Crisis, readily admitting that such policies rest on an oversimplified neoclassical theory. 'Stiglitz has admitted that his mission all along was to undermine free market fundamentalism from within' (Mirowski, 2011, p. 497). Orthodox dissenters argue that neoclassical models with more reliable and fancy assumptions convincingly demonstrate the limitations and errors of such policies. These critics start from the mainstream model and its tenuous theoretical foundations, on which they superimpose more realistic secondary assumptions. Yet this approach only yields models that are increasingly difficult to grasp. Although such an approach gets the hearing of economists heading large institutions, I do not think that offering a tortuous critique of the dominant view is the best strategy over time. While running with the (mainstream) pack, as Dullien (2017) calls it, by introducing some realistic or heterodox features within an otherwise doubtful model, may bring about some individual benefits, from a collective angle it is likely to be a guide towards paradigmatic incoherence and self-marginalization (Dobusch and Kapeller 2012).

The purpose of the book is to offer a clear-cut alternative. Post-Keynesian economics is an antidote to TINA – a clear example of this having been the specific proposals made by MMT advocates which have had quite a hearing in policy circles. Post-Keynesian economics is much more than a critique of mainstream economics. It provides realistic foundations for proposals of feasible alternative policies. The antidote, distilled in post-Keynesian articles, can now be found in a large range of journals. In alphabetical order, these are in particular: *Brazilian Keynesian Review, Bulletin of Political Economy, Cambridge Journal of Economics, Employment and Labour Relations Review, European Journal of Economics and Economic Policies: Intervention, International Review of Applied Economics, International Journal of Political Economy, International Papers in Political Economy, Journal of Economic Issues, Journal of Post Keynesian Economics, Metroeconomica, Paolo Sylos Labini Quarterly Review, Review of Evolutionary Political Economy, Review of Keynesian Economics, Review of Keynesian Studies, Review of Political Economy, Revue de la régulation, Structural Change and Economic Dynamics.*

NOTE

* Besides relying on and extending the 1992 *Foundations*, full sentences have been taken from the following publications: 'History and methods of post-Keynesian economics', in E. Hein and E. Stockhammer (eds), *A Modern Guide to Keynesian Macroeconomics and Economic Policies*, Cheltenham, UK and Northampton, MA, USA: Edward Elgar Publishing, 2011, pp. 1–33; 'Neoclassical empirical evidence on employment and production laws as artefact', *Economia Informa*, **351**, March–April 2008, pp. 9–36; 'The Global Financial Crisis: methodological reflections from a heterodox perspective', *Studies in Political Economy*, **88**, Fall 2011, pp. 35–57; 'Rethinking macroeconomic theory before the next crisis', *Review of Keynesian Economics*, 6(1), Spring 2018, pp. 1–21.

2. Theory of choice*

The objective of this chapter is to present how economic agents take their decisions in a post-Keynesian world. Since most of these decisions are set within a world of uncertainty, a concept that post-Keynesians have been keen to underline, the notion of uncertainty will be defined with care. Furthermore, although post-Keynesians have an organic view of the world, we shall pay a great deal of attention to the rationality underlying the actions of economic agents. Finally we shall deal with the much-neglected issue of consumer choice, about which we shall discover that, somewhat surprisingly, post-Keynesians hold a common view.

2.1 FUNDAMENTAL UNCERTAINTY

Before embarking on the study of how agents take decisions, it is necessary, as a preliminary step, to describe the environment in which these decisions are usually taken. In a sense, what we are doing is ontology, as defined in Chapter 1. We will discover that what can be called rational behaviour can be assessed only as a function of the environment in which the decision is being taken.

As pointed out in Chapter 1, many authors consider fundamental uncertainty – also called true uncertainty, radical uncertainty or irreducible uncertainty – to be a key characteristic of post-Keynesian economics. It is one of the few characteristics that draws a near-consensus among post-Keynesian authors. The notion of fundamental uncertainty is particularly associated with the Fundamentalist branch of post-Keynesian economics, notably Minsky (1975, chs 3 and 6) and Davidson (1972, ch. 2), who have stressed the role played by fundamental uncertainty, especially in conjunction with money and monetary economies. There is a debate within post-Keynesian economics about whether uncertainty is the result of the use of money or whether the use of money arises as a consequence of uncertainty, but this will not be discussed here. Rather, the aim of this section is to distinguish clearly between situations of risk, which are those usually described by mainstream authors, and situations of uncertainty, which are those faced by agents in a post-Keynesian world. My intention is to clear the confusion that the term uncertainty has generated.

2.1.1 Uncertainty versus Risk

The relevance of fundamental uncertainty, despite the post-Keynesian exhortations to include it in economic analysis, has not been taken very seriously by most mainstream economists. In fact, mainstream economists are often annoyed at being told that they do not deal with uncertainty. They point to the mainstream journals, the pages of which are filled with papers titled 'The economics of uncertainty of this or of that', which deal with asymmetric or incomplete information, stochastic elements of some sort, probability densities and so on. For mainstream economists, what is not certain is uncertain. There is thus a semantic confusion arising from the fact that the word uncertainty is being used both by post-Keynesian economists and mainstream economists, but with different meanings. What should really be said is that these mainstream papers are set in an environment of risk, or one of certainty equivalence. Annoyed mainstream economists thus do not recognize the distinction between risk and uncertainty.

Besides the neo-Austrians (Lachmann, 1977), or economists who have close links with them (Shackle, 1971; 1972; Loasby, 1976), there are also some orthodox economists who have acknowledged the importance of the distinction between risk and fundamental uncertainty. For instance, Roy Weintraub (1975, p. 530), perhaps influenced on that matter by his father Sidney Weintraub, while taking note that general equilibrium theory had not dealt with fundamental uncertainty, has written that Keynes's treatment of uncertainty is 'an innovation of sublime importance ignored for almost thirty years by most economists and still ignored by many'. He adds that 'there is no way uncertainty problems can be reduced to problems involving risk' (ibid., p. 532). Thus even those who make little use of the distinction recognize its significance and its importance. We shall deal later with the question of why enlightened neoclassical writers still leave aside situations of fundamental uncertainty.

Let us now see how uncertainty should be defined within a three-way taxonomy (Lavoie, 1985a).

1. There is *certainty* when each choice invariably leads to a specific outcome, the value of which is known.
2. There is *risk*, or certainty equivalence, when each choice leads to a set of possible specific outcomes, the value of which is known, each outcome being associated with a specific probability.
3. There is *uncertainty* when the value of an outcome is unknown, when the probability of an outcome is unknown, when the outcomes that can possibly result from a choice are unknown, or when the spectrum of possible choices is unknown.

There are thus three types of uncertainty. The first, uncertainty of value, when one ignores the values (presumably the monetary ones) attached to the different outcomes, can be easily brought back to a situation of risk by making use of sensitivity analysis. The second type of uncertainty, uncertainty of probability, is most often discussed in the economic literature. The question revolves around how one can get proper estimates of these probabilities. This is not considered to be a true problem by the mainstream. Estimates of probabilities can always be made, from a logical or subjective point of view. Alternatively, probabilities can be assigned to possible probability density functions. Dequech (1999) refers to this uncertainty of probability as 'ambiguity', making use of the term suggested by behavioural economists. However, as pointed out by Dequech (ibid., p. 415), 'a very important characteristic of ambiguity problems is that, even though the decision maker does not know with full reliability the probability that each state of the world will obtain, he or she knows *all the possible states of the world*'. The typical example of such an ambiguity problem is when an individual is told that there are red and black balls in an urn, five altogether, without being told how many of each. Obviously, possible events are predetermined, but the probability of drawing a red ball is unknown, although it would be simple to compute probabilities if the information were provided.

There is finally what one could call fundamental uncertainty, where the individual is ignorant of the available courses of action or of the extent of future states of the world. This form of uncertainty leads to unknown probabilities, or to what Keynes and others call non-measurable probabilities. This is the type of uncertainty that is the least likely to be subjected to standard analysis. This is what post-Keynesians mean when they speak of fundamental or true uncertainty, or of Knightian or Keynesian uncertainty.

It is not difficult to think of situations where the essence of the problem is to find the options that are available, and where all future prospects cannot be listed. Technological advancement is a good example of fundamental uncertainty, as emphasized by Schumpeterians, involving as it does the impossibility of knowing what the novelty will be, when it will appear, and how large its impact on society will be. Keynes and Knight underline fundamental uncertainty because they believe that it is a crucial element of our economic environment. When agents take decisions, they act according to this uncertain knowledge, rather than *as if* risky situations prevailed. Thus both Keynes and Knight were convinced that a radical distinction between situations of risk and situations of uncertainty had to be made, and that economic analysis had to take this distinction into consideration. Minsky (1995, p. 203) also believed so, arguing that 'units live in a world of intractable uncertainty: not only is their foresight imperfect, but sensate agents know that their foresight is imperfect'.

The various notions of uncertainty are well represented in the following quote from Donald Rumsfeld (2003), the former US defence secretary:

> Reports that say that something hasn't happened are always interesting to me, because as we know, there are known knowns; there are things we know we know. We also know that there are known unknowns; that is to say we know there are some things that we do not know. But there are also unknown unknowns – the ones we don't know we don't know.

The known unknowns could be unknown values of an action or their unknown probabilities. This is closest to the concept of ambiguity. The unknown unknowns would correspond to the unknown outcomes of a given action, or the possible states of the world about which we have no knowledge. We do not even know that they are possible or that they exist. Clearly, then, with unknown unknowns, we are within the realm of fundamental uncertainty. Why is this so?

2.1.2 The Realm of Fundamental Uncertainty

Ontological versus epistemic uncertainty
Broadly speaking, we can say that there are two kinds of fundamental uncertainty: there is 'ontological' uncertainty and 'epistemic' or 'epistemological' uncertainty. This corresponds roughly to what Rod O'Donnell (2013) calls the ergodic/non-ergodic approach and the human abilities and characteristics approach. Fundamentalist post-Keynesians emphasize ontological uncertainty. This is the case notably of Davidson (1996), Dunn (2001), and Fontana and Gerrard (2004). For these authors, true fundamental uncertainty is linked to the fact that the future cannot be known and that reality is transmutable,

because of the creativity of agents, because of the innovations of entrepreneurs, or because any decision taken by an agent is likely to transform the future. Since the future remains to be created, one cannot know what it will look like when a decision is being taken; indeed the chosen action may lead to changes that were not foreseen by those creating the change. This view of ontological uncertainty is closely related to the views of Shackle (1972), who emphasized the existence of *crucial* decisions, that is, decisions that destroy the present and modify the future. Davidson (1996, p. 485) speaks of a 'transmutable or creative reality' such that 'some aspects of the economic future will be created by human action today and/or in the future'. This view is also associated with the importance of providing the possibility of human agency and with the 'open systems' that were mentioned in Chapter 1. The future can be modified by human decisions. 'Individual freedom of choice is only compatible with a non-ergodic, path-dependent world subject to the continuous possibility of unpredictable structural change' (Fontana and Gerrard, 2004, p. 623).

The above quote brings us to the concept of non-ergodicity. We have already encountered this concept when discussing the key characteristics of post-Keynesian economics. The ontological view of fundamental uncertainty was further developed in Davidson's writings under the concept of non-ergodicity. According to Davidson (1982–83; 1996), the world is essentially non-ergodic, a term borrowed from statistics and physics, thus making an analogy that Carrión Álvarez and Ehnts (2016) question. A non-ergodic environment would be an environment of fundamental uncertainty. Roughly speaking, ergodicity implies that the time-series and cross-section (space) averages of a variable converge to each other, whatever sample is being assessed. 'If a stochastic process is ergodic, then, for an infinite realization, the space and time averages will coincide' (Davidson, 1993a, p. 310). The researcher can then confidently apply the empirical laws discovered from the past to the future, and 'the future is merely the statistical shadow of the past' (Davidson, 2009, p. 38). Or, as Basil Moore (2006, p. 114) puts it, 'past data can be treated as a sample drawn from the future'. Another way to put this is to say that 'even if a fully determined model's structure adequately represents outcomes in terms of a set of causal variables during a particular period of time, it will be inadequate during other periods' (Frydman and Goldberg, 2014, p. 13). This helps to explain the reluctance of Fundamentalist post-Keynesians to use econometrics. Davidson (1982–83, p. 189) believes that Keynes's analysis of an uncertain future is best understood as being based on non-ergodic stochastic processes.

There is, however, another view of fundamental uncertainty, based on epistemic considerations. This epistemic interpretation can itself be divided into two distinct sorts of fundamental uncertainty, which have been called substantive and procedural uncertainty, in an analogy with the terms proposed by Herbert Simon (1976) when discussing rationality. Substantive uncertainty is caused by a lack of information; procedural uncertainty is caused by an overload of information. This distinction was first proposed by Dosi and Egidi (1991, p. 149), who say that substantive uncertainty arises from 'the lack of all the information which would be necessary to make decisions with certain outcomes', while defining procedural rationality as being the consequence of the 'inability of the agents to recognise and interpret the relevant information, even when available'. With substantive uncertainty there is an information gap; with procedural uncertainty there is a competence gap, using the expression coined by Ronald Heiner (1983, p. 562), that is, a 'gap between an agent's competence and the difficulty of the decision problem to be solved'.

It is sometimes argued that epistemic uncertainty does not go far enough if it is not accompanied by ontological uncertainty with a transmutable future. Indeed, this is the argument that Davidson (1989; 1993b) tells against the neo-Austrian economists who see similarities between their views on uncertainty and those of post-Keynesians (Wynarczyk, 1999). Davidson's claim is that, eventually, in the long run, with an immutable reality, economic actors will either obtain enough information or will acquire the capability to process the existing information, and will thus remove epistemic uncertainty. But this is a strange argument. As argued in Chapter 1, the long run is just a succession of short runs. In every period, new crucial decisions need to be made, with the data and the circumstances having changed. In the real world, many important decisions are singular events that cannot be repeated. In addition, for epistemic uncertainty to disappear, one would need to assume that agents possess fantastic capacities, precisely those capacities that are usually assumed in mainstream economics, but denied by heterodox economists. The persistence of epistemic uncertainty, compatible with fundamental uncertainty, thus only requires that 'humans be credited with less than omnipotent powers of judgment' (O'Donnell, 1991, p. 85).

Given this understanding of the human mind and of the complexity of the world, my view is that epistemic uncertainty is just as conducive to fundamental uncertainty as is ontological uncertainty. Indeed, some authors go so far as to argue that ontological uncertainty cannot exist; there is only epistemic uncertainty. The argument is that 'if an event really is impossible, then it cannot become possible under any conditions' (Wilson, 2010, p. 52). If we do not know about some possible event, then it must be due to some lack of knowledge. O'Donnell (2013, p. 134) puts it somewhat differently, arguing that we do not have the capability of knowing if the world is ergodic or not. Those who rely only on ontological uncertainty declare 'that we know that we cannot know the future, because we know the nonergodic nature of reality makes such knowledge impossible'. By contrast, those who favour epistemic uncertainty declare 'that we know that we do not know the future, and we know that we have no means of acquiring such knowledge'. They would argue that we do not have the capability to assess whether the world is ergodic or not.

Chaos dynamics and black swans
Another subject of controversy is whether models of chaotic dynamics, arising from non-linearities, also called complex systems theory, can be included within the realm of fundamental uncertainty. Moore (2006, p. xxv) surely believes that it can, because he contends that arguing that 'economies are "complex systems" (rather than "based on non-ergodic distributions") will provide a more persuasive foundation for the necessary paradigm shift, and will finally enable Post Keynesians to mount a more convincing case to the profession'. By contrast, Davidson (1996, p. 492) objects to the association of chaos theory with fundamental uncertainty. He points out, rightly, that models of chaotic dynamics are deterministic. Once you know the equations and the initial conditions, you can find precisely the path that will be taken. So, in this sense, there is no ontological uncertainty, and the only problem is one of epistemic uncertainty, tied to the difficulty of assessing the equations and the starting point of a complex world.

Barkley Rosser Jr (1999), however, disagrees. The main feature of chaotic systems is their sensitive dependence on initial conditions. As is well known, a small change in the initial conditions, or in the conditions prevailing during a transitional phase, is likely to take two nearly identical systems far apart. Despite being deterministic, chaotic systems exhibit unpredictability, which can easily be confused with randomness, first through their own motion through time, with bifurcations, discontinuities, dissipative structures and fractals, and second through external shocks that can completely modify their trajectory. Rosser Jr (ibid., p. 299) thus concludes that 'one may have fundamental uncertainty *without* non-ergodicity' since some classes of models of chaotic dynamics generate ergodic chaotic outcomes. The fact that small changes to initial or existing conditions may provoke large changes, unrelated to the original trajectories, shows that chaotic dynamics 'may even be "effectively ontological" rather than merely epistemological'. From our perspective, the debate is rather moot, since we have already accepted that fundamental uncertainty can be associated with ontological or epistemic uncertainty. In addition, chaotic systems are usually non-ergodic, so they would seem to fulfil Davidson's main criterion!

A similar debate has erupted concerning the black swans made so popular by the book by Taleb (2007). Taleb argues that the mainstream in economics and finance assumes normal (Gaussian) probability distributions, whereas the world is characterized by power distributions, where the tails of the distributions are much fatter. Thus extraordinary events – black swans – that will have a permanent structural impact on our economies and our lives, are much more likely to happen than what is predicted by Gaussian distributions. Taleb relies on the work of Benoît Mandelbrot, already mentioned in Chapter 1, who has claimed that prices in competitive markets move in a discontinuous way, and who has introduced the notion of fractal geometry, and thus ultimately relies on chaos dynamics. Not surprisingly, Andrea Terzi (2010) and Davidson (2010) again claim that Taleb's black swans are a new variant of epistemic uncertainty, being already programmed from probability distributions. They are not compatible with ontological uncertainty, and hence do not belong to true fundamental uncertainty. My sentiment about black swans is the same as that about chaotic dynamics: epistemic uncertainty can also be fundamental uncertainty. Indeed Taleb (2007, p. 272) insists that extreme events cannot all be foreseen: 'a gray swan concerns modelable extreme events, a black swan is about unknown unknowns', just as Rumfeld would put it! In any case, when discussing economic variables and their relations, Taleb (ibid., pp. 239–40) describes a non-ergodic world without using the term when he says that 'the correlation measure will be likely to exhibit severe instability; it will depend on the period for which it was computed', adding that 'every sample will yield a different standard deviation'.

To conclude on this, Table 2.1 attempts to summarize the discussion so far by outlining the different degrees of uncertainty. As a conclusion, we may also refer to Robert Skidelsky (2009, p. 88): 'Is Keynes talking about epistemological uncertainty or ontological uncertainty? It is not clear.' So, if even the main biographer of Keynes is uncertain about his views on uncertainty, we are entitled to recognize that fundamental uncertainty can be of both an epistemological and ontological nature, and accept both approaches as representative of post-Keynesian theory.

Table 2.1   Different degrees of certainty

Certainty			
Risk			
Ambiguity			Uncertainty of probability
Fundamental	Epistemic	Procedural	Too much information
uncertainty			Competence gap
		Substantive	Lack of information
			Information gap
	Ontological	Complexity	Chaotic dynamics
		Unknown unknowns	Mutable and creative reality

2.1.3   The Weight of an Argument or the Credibility of Information

Over the years, several authors have attempted to underline the differences between Keynes's and Knight's accounts of uncertainty. Here I shall concentrate instead on the commonalities in the analyses of these two authors. My view is that fundamentally Keynes and Knight are in agreement. Both recognize that, for some experiences or decisions, the orthodox calculus of risk is the appropriate one, in particular in situations of scientific experimentations. O'Donnell (1991) calls this the determinate domain. Standard deviations can be computed and for point estimates we can even obtain a confidence interval, based upon the set probability of error. This can be linked to what Knight (1940, p. 226) calls the 'probability of error', and which Keynes (1973, viii, p. 82) names the 'probable error'. Both agree that in repetitive situations these probable errors are useful.

On the other hand, both Keynes and Knight would argue that, generally, decisions have to be taken under conditions where standard errors and probabilities are meaningless, even though they might be estimated and computed. This is O'Donnell's indeterminate domain. This is certainly the case of most long-term business decisions. To clarify this matter, in his 1921 *Treatise on Probability* Keynes defines a new concept, which he calls the 'weight of an argument'. As shown by Runde (1990), Keynes seems to oscillate between two definitions of the weight of an argument. In agreement with Runde, we adopt the one that says that the weight represents the relative amount of information available when a decision must be taken. It represents our relevant knowledge relative to our relevant ignorance (Keynes, 1973, viii, p. 77), or the degree of completeness of our knowledge (ibid., p. 345). A number of authors have endorsed a concept equivalent to the weight of an argument. Georgescu-Roegen (1966, p. 266) calls it the 'credibility' attached to a set of probabilistic expectations. Others have made reference to a measure of 'qualitat', 'acceptability' or 'epistemic reliability' (Anand, 1991, p. 200), or to 'credence' (Gerrard, 1995). One could define weight as the faith that an agent has in his or her own argument.

In some cases, the standard error of statisticians and the weight of an argument may be closely related. Where the law of large numbers applies, an increase in relative knowledge tends to reduce the standard error, without modifying the probabilities of the various outcomes. This is why in these cases one can associate the inverse of the standard error with the weight of an argument, as we assumed when discussing meta-regression analysis in Chapter 1. The credibility of the probability statement increases with the size of the sample. There is a practical connection between the two. It may be, however, that additional evidence leads to an increase in standard deviation, as Keynes (1973, viii, p. 82) shows. In general, the evolution of the weight and that of the standard deviation or standard error might thus diverge. Keynes believes that the former rather than the latter is then of significance. When probabilities are purely subjective, the standard deviation is without meaning, since it reflects only whether or not the agent has given high probabilities to the outcomes whose values are around the most likely value. An argument of high weight is not one in which the standard deviation is small.

The more relevant factor is the quality of information or the relative quantity of information that has led to the estimates of outcomes and probabilities. In truly uncertain situations, further information might reduce the degree of confidence without necessarily changing the assessed probabilities, in the case of political crises, for instance (Minsky, 1975, p. 65). There is new information, but this information has destroyed part of the past accumulated knowledge, or it has uncovered new aspects of unsuspected ignorance. The stock of relevant information relative to ignorance has then decreased. Evidential weight may decrease with the acquisition of new evidence and can thus be defined as 'the balance of the absolute amounts of relevant knowledge and relevant ignorance, on which a probability is based' (Runde, 1990, p. 290). Evidential weight would be a ratio, with relevant information in the numerator, and relevant ignorance in the denominator.

How can we relate the definition of evidential weight to our previous discussion of epistemic uncertainty? Recall that we defined substantive uncertainty by the lack of information and procedural uncertainty by the inability to handle the information, making reference to an information gap and a competence gap. The definition offered above by Runde seems to better characterize the information gap, the gap being a measure of relevant ignorance. It is possible, however, to combine the two gaps within a single definition of the concept of weight. We thus propose the following definition:

Weight of evidence = (Quantity of available relevant information that can be handled)/(Quantity of information that one would like to have and be able to process)

This definition incorporates both the information gap and the competence gap. In the numerator, we have the size of the relevant information that can be accessed and actually processed; this is the amount of knowledge that can be acquired by the economic actor. In the denominator, we have the amount of information that the agent would like to access and be able to process. The difference between the two is a measure of ignorance, due both to a lack of information and to the complexity of the problem to be solved. How much faith we have in our argument thus depends on how much relevant information we have and can handle relative to how much information we would ideally like to have and be able to process. But of course this measure of the weight of evidence is subjective; it is in the mind of the economic agent. Unless we are in situations of ambiguity, as defined earlier, we can never be sure how complete our information is.

Keynes thought that 'in deciding on a course of action, it seems plausible to suppose that we ought to take account of the weight as well as the probability of different expectations' (Keynes, 1973, viii, p. 83). The upshot of the matter is that situations of uncertainty cannot be reduced to situations of risk. When taking a decision in an uncertain world, a rational agent cannot rely only on the probability distribution that arises from past similar events or from subjective introspection. The credibility or the reliability of the acquired information, the degree of confidence in the assessed probabilities, must also be considered. Georgescu-Roegen (1966, p. 267) contends further that the lack of weight of an argument cannot be compensated by the high probability attached to the main outcome. Otherwise probabilities and weight could be summarized under one index, and we would be back to a revised form of expected utility theory. In the case of fundamental uncertainty, probabilities and the weight of the argument are independent properties. Knight comes to the same conclusion in his 1921 book. He also emphasizes the independent character of the weight of an argument and the probability distribution in situations of uncertainty. He is simply using words that will be later adopted by Keynes in the *General Theory* and after.

> The business man himself not merely forms the best estimate he can of the outcome of his actions, but he is likely also to estimate the probability that his estimate is correct. The 'degree' of certainty or of confidence felt in the conclusion after it is reached cannot be ignored, for it is of the greatest practical significance. The action which follows upon an opinion depends as much upon the amount of confidence in that opinion as it does upon the favorableness of the opinion itself ... Fidelity to the actual psychology of the situation requires, we must insist, recognition of these two separate exercises of judgment, the formation of an estimate and the estimation of its value. (Knight, 1940, p. 227)

We thus see that Knight calls the weight of an argument the degree of certainty or the degree of confidence, or the worthiness of a probability estimate. As is well known, when in *The General Theory* Keynes refers to uncertain factors, or to uncertainty, he quotes the chapter dealing with weights of arguments in his previous *Treatise on Probability*. The weight of an argument is then translated by the 'confidence' that economic actors attach to their assessment of the situation. The following quote shows clearly that Knight and Keynes are making the same distinction.

> The state of long-term expectations, upon which our decisions are based, does not solely depend, therefore, on the most probable forecast we can make. It also depends on the *confidence* with which we make this forecast – on how highly we rate the likelihood of our best forecast turning out quite wrong. If we expect large changes but are uncertain as to what precise form these changes will take, then our confidence will be weak. (Keynes, 1936, p. 148)

Dequech (1999) points out that we must be careful with the term 'confidence'. It can have two meanings. On the one hand, we can interpret the degree of confidence in estimates as the weight of evidence, as defined above; on the other hand, especially when Keynes talks about the 'state of confidence', what is at stake is rather business psychology, that is, the optimistic or pessimistic dispositions of economic agents (entrepreneurs, bankers, speculators), their spontaneous urge for action, their 'animal spirits'. Entrepreneurs may be highly optimistic, with high expectations, although these may be based on arguments of low weight, with little relevant information, and hence based on conventions that are not strongly anchored, and liable to violent changes.

2.1.4 Objections to Fundamental Uncertainty

It would seem that fundamental uncertainty is a pervasive phenomenon in real life. Why do mainstream authors mostly deny its existence? One argument they make is that probabilities constitute a code of coherence to apprehend a world without certainty. All situations can be described with the help of subjective probability distributions. If future outcomes or possible choices are unknown, as they would be in the case of fundamental uncertainty, risk analysis or expected utility theory can still be safeguarded by relying on the principle of insufficient reason, which imputes an equal probability to all uncertain states. By this principle, a given probability distribution corresponds to every situation. When further pressed, neoclassical authors observe that, if compelled to, a person will quote a betting quotient on any outcome.

We now understand why Knight and Keynes insist so strongly on the distinction between risk and uncertainty: they both reject the principle of insufficient reason on the grounds that it will not lead to rational decisions in an uncertain world (Knight, 1940, p. 222). As Blatt (1982, p. 267) says, 'This is a possible rule. But it is a fool's rule.' Keynes is pretty clear about this, both in the *Treatise on Probability* and in *The General Theory*. When future outcomes or choices are unknown, that is, when the set of known alternatives is not exhaustive, the principle of insufficient reason cannot be applied and therefore situations of uncertainty cannot be reduced to ones of risk.

> The recognition of the fact, that not all probabilities are numerical, limits the scope of the principle of indifference [insufficient reason]. It has always been agreed that a numerical measure can actually be obtained in those cases only in which a reduction to a set of exclusive and exhaustive *equiprobable* alternatives is practicable ... A rule can be given for numerical measurement when the conclusion is one of a number of equiprobable, exclusive and exhaustive alternatives, but not otherwise. (Keynes, 1973, viii, pp. 70, 122)

> Nor can we rationalise our behaviour by arguing that to a man in a state of ignorance errors in either direction are equally probable ... For it can easily be shown that the assumption of arithmetically equal probabilities based on a state of ignorance leads to absurdities. (Keynes, 1936, p. 152)

Keynes goes so far as to say that in such circumstances decisions 'cannot depend on strict mathematical expectations, since the basis for making such calculations does not exist' (ibid., p. 163). Mainstream analyses do exactly the opposite: they assume that decisions are taken on the basis of mathematical expectations and they do so as if the credibility of information were not an issue. Their reasons for doing so, assuming that they accept Keynes's critique of the principle of insufficient reason, must be linked to the last line of defence of the orthodox refusal to consider fundamental uncertainty. Mainstream authors argue that, if one were to discuss situations of fundamental uncertainty, rather than ones of risk, economics would be engaged on a nihilistic path. Robert Lucas (1981, p. 224) is famous for claiming so, alleging that, 'in cases of uncertainty, economic reasoning would be of no value'. Lucas further declares that business cycles must be seen as recurrent and essentially similar events, so that changes can be considered as risk events.

Orthodox authors thus continue to assume that knowledge of the future is perfect, or that all uncertain situations can be reduced to ones of risk. They do so as if agents could conceive of every possible event and assign probabilities to each of them, providing agents with the ability and competence to act upon these. They prefer to follow 'a passage more fertile in analytical results – rather than to face the delicate complexity of expectations and be content with making smaller, yet more relevant, strides' (Georgescu-Roegen, 1966,

p. 242). Readers will have recognized the instrumentalist posture of the orthodox research programme described in Chapter 1.

In the case of uncertainty, the justification for such an instrumentalist position is that the adoption of a realistic concept of uncertainty leads nowhere. Hodgson (2011) notes the virtual disappearance of fundamental uncertainty in top-tier mainstream journals and attributes this absence to the orthodox obsession with prediction rather than explanation. One must admit that some defenders of the notion of fundamental uncertainty, most notably Shackle (1984, p. 391), have left their readers with the impression that true uncertainty allows only nihilistic conclusions. But this is not the position of the majority of post-Keynesians, and certainly not the position taken in this book. The impact of uncertainty on economic analysis and on economic results depends on 'how individuals are supposed to respond to the fact of uncertainty' (Coddington, 1982, p. 482). Orthodox economics relies on a very specific sort of rationality – hyper-rationality, based on optimization under constraint. This is why it cannot make sense of situations of fundamental uncertainty. The argument of the following section will be that, once a different kind of rationality is introduced into the behaviour of agents, the presence of fundamental uncertainty does not prevent economic modelling and does not lead to nihilistic conclusions.

2.2 RATIONALITY

Now that we have defined the various environments in which economic agents operate, emphasizing that most of the time economic actors operate in a world of uncertainty, defined by either ambiguity or fundamental uncertainty, it is time to discuss how individuals, households, entrepreneurs, bankers or investors will take decisions within this environment. We need to discuss rationality. In Chapter 1, we devoted a few paragraphs to the concept of rationality, arguing that the way rationality is conceived is one of the five presuppositions that allows us to make a distinction between orthodox and heterodox economics. In Table 1.3 we opposed reasonable rationality on the heterodox side to hyper-model-consistent rationality on the orthodox side. We now need to make this distinction more precise.

2.2.1 Definitions of Rationality

In Chapter 1 we pointed out that 'old' behavioural economics was part of heterodox economics, while 'new' behavioural economics was not. My own view is that new behavioural economics is part of orthodox dissent, which explains why it has been so successful in attracting the attention of economists as well as that of politicians and policy makers, in particular through nudge-based policies. As Esther-Miriam Sent (2004, p. 753) puts it in a nutshell, 'behavioral economics has arrived'. Our discussion about definitions of rationality will help make this more obvious. Still, few post-Keynesian economists seem to have paid much attention to the work of behavioural economists. There are exceptions, most particularly the two books that Peter Earl (1983; 1986) devoted to the creation of a synthesis of behavioural economics and post-Keynesian economics, most particularly around consumer theory. More recently Harvey (1998), Fung (2006), Baddeley (2017) and Fontana and Gerrard (2004) have written articles to encourage post-Keynesian economists to take advantage of the works of new behavioural economics. There have also been two excellent surveys by Sent (2004) and Tomer (2007) on the various strands of behavioural economics and their links with heterodox economics. More recently still, King has written a short survey of the engagement between post-Keynesian economics and behavioural economics (Jefferson and King, 2010–11; King, 2013). As we do here, he argues that there is much to be gained from studying old behavioural economics, while the rewards from an association with new behavioural economics are more dubious. As for Davidson (2010–11), he argues that Keynes was the first (old) behaviourist economist, a claim also made earlier by Herbert Simon (1997, p. 16), who cautiously proposed that Keynes 'was the true originator of the economics of bounded rationality'!

We shall now define four views of rationality. The taxonomy adopted here, which is reflected in Table 2.2, takes its cue from the work of Gerd Gigerenzer, a German psychologist, who in my opinion has the best comprehension of the issue. Gigerenzer (2008, pp. 3–4) makes the case that economists and psychologists have proceeded in four ways: 'by (a) constructing *as-if theories of unbounded rationality*, by (b) constructing *as-if theories of optimization under constraints*, by (c) demonstrating irrational *cognitive illusions*, or by (d) studying *ecological rationality*'.

Unbounded rationality
The use of 'unbounded rationality' is now frequent in macroeconomics, and has been generalized when business cycle theories and the rational expectations revolution took over. Agents have a hyper-model-consistent rationality. General equilibrium theory is also the playground of unbounded rationality, as are DSGE models. As recalled in Chapter 1, in all these models, everything is known until the end of times, with some probabilistic degree. In all these models, the individual must gather information on all possible actions, all possible states of nature and therefore on all possible outcomes induced by the previous two sets. Probabilities, often complex conditional probabilities, must be ascertained for each outcome, and each outcome must be assigned numerical (monetary) values. On top of that, through a system of preferences, with or without utility measures, preferably with desired features such as transitivity, the agent must choose the most preferred action, the one that will optimize the situation. The agent must

Table 2.2 Four kinds of human rationality

Kind of rationality	Schools, individuals
(a) Unbounded rationality	Rational expectations, general equilibrium theory, efficient-market hypothesis, DSGE models, Lucas, Arrow, Woodford
(b) Bounded optimization	Pseudo-behaviourists, search theory, Stigler, Sargent
(c) Cognitive illusions	Heuristics and bias, Kahneman, Camerer, Thaler, Smith, Akerlof, Shiller
(d) Environment-consistent rationality	Keynes, Gigerenzer, Earl, Simon and the Carnegie School, Katona and the Michigan School, Nelson and Winter and evolutionary economics, Lutz and humanistic economics, Oxford price studies

thus consider all the various final outcomes, with their numerical counterparts, proceed to find out what possible results each initial action generates, and then compare these to find the action generating the optimal set of possible outcomes. Optimality necessitates recourse to a backward induction reasoning requiring a substantial amount of computations (Hey, 1982). The same huge computational capabilities are required in situations of certainty, when consumers make choices with respect to different goods, for instance. The stress put on human capabilities is not limited to probabilistic or uncertain situations. It affects most situations of certainty as well. In a way, this is a more destructive critique than the notion of uncertainty since it does not rely on the scarcity of information but rather on its over-abundance (Hodgson, 1988, p. 83).

As pointed out by Gigerenzer (2008, pp. 4–5), economic agents with unbounded rationality are endowed with three characteristics: they are omniscient (they have perfect knowledge, that is, they have access to all information at no cost); they are omnipotent (they have unlimited computational power to assess the most complex information); and they optimize (they maximize some function, for instance monetary gains or a utility function). Unbounded rationality, or hyper-model-consistent rationality, is obviously not realistic. It fully corresponds to the instrumentalist philosophy advocated by Milton Friedman, which is why it is identified as an 'as-if' theory. The purpose here is not to describe the process of actual decisions; rather, it is to answer the following question: if people were omniscient, omnipotent and were optimizing some function, what decision would they take? For several mainstream economists, this is the only possible definition of rationality: non-optimizing agents are classified as irrational beings.

Bounded optimization

The second kind of rationality, 'bounded optimization', or 'optimization under constraints', is also an 'as-if' theory, which falls into the same instrumentalist trap. The term 'bounded optimization' is a legacy of work started by Herbert Simon in the mid-1950s. As briefly mentioned earlier, Simon popularized the idea that economists ought to abandon 'substantive' or 'global' rationality, which corresponds to the description of unbounded rationality just given above, and adopt instead 'procedural' or 'bounded' rationality, 'a rationality that is consistent with our knowledge of actual human choice behavior, assumes that the decision maker must search for alternatives, has egregiously incomplete and inaccurate knowledge about the consequences of actions, and chooses actions that are expected to be satisfactory' (Simon, 1997, p. 17). Simon's bounded rationality has been understood in three different ways, which correspond to our other three definitions of rationality.

Bounded optimization rationality may thus be interpreted as an attempt by orthodox theory to introduce some realistic component into its theoretical edifice. The typical example of such an attempt is search theory, which its proponents consider to be a response to the criticisms of Simon. Bounded rationality is taken to mean optimization under the costly constraint of information-gathering. But the computations and the information required for the optimal resolution of this search are even more intricate. Ironically, the economic agent has to become smarter (Sargent, 1993, p. 2). 'Each new realistic constraint makes optimization calculations more difficult, and eventually impossible' (Gigerenzer, 2008, p. 6). It may have taken months for the theorist to find the optimal solution of the model, without even having had to gather concrete data. Whereas the proponents of models of bounded optimization claim that their new models allow them to get away from the assumptions of perfect knowledge, they are in fact taking the neoclassical programme further away from realism. 'The reason is that in order to apply the traditional optimizing concepts, the competence of the agent has been implicitly upgraded to handle the extra complexity resulting from an unpredictable future' (Heiner, 1983, p. 571). What these theorists basically do when they construct models is to match the computational capabilities and information-gathering abilities of the agents to the requirements of finding an equilibrium, preferably a unique one. Rationality is thus defined in accordance with the goals pursued by the modeller.

Furthermore, the optimizing approach leads to a problem of infinite regress (Gigerenzer and Selten, 2001, p. 5). To know whether or not the information search has been optimized, agents need to know beforehand the value of the information to be gathered. To argue that agents have a probabilistic view of the information to be gathered makes even more unlikely the practical possibility of such optimizing computations. There is thus the need for 'new kinds of omniscience, being able to foresee what additional information further search would bring, what it would cost, and what opportunities one would forgo during that search' (Todd and Gigerenzer, 2003, p. 146). Indeed, bounded optimization rationality can be seen as unbounded rationality in disguise. This is certainly not what Simon had in mind, and it is not what post-Keynesians are looking for. Indeed, bounded optimization rationality is a good example of Kaldor's description of the scaffolding surrounding mainstream theory.

Cognitive illusions or new behavioural economics

The third kind of rationality is associated with the highly active 'cognitive illusions' research programme, which is closest to what we can call new behavioural economics. This is the heuristics and biases programme, inspired from cognitive psychology, and pursued by Tversky and Kahneman, and many well-known researchers such as Colin Camerer, Richard Thaler, Matthew Rabin, Hersh Shefrin and Vernon Smith. It is this version of bounded rationality that most post-Keynesians have in mind when they envy the ability of behavioural economics to influence orthodox economics and finance. The claim of the cognitive illusions programme is that it provides an improved empirical realism, with more realistic assumptions. The main goal of the heuristics and biases school is 'to understand the cognitive processes that produce both valid and invalid judgments. Its second goal (or method to achieve the first one) is to demonstrate errors of judgment, that is, systematic deviations from rationality' (Gigerenzer, 2008, p. 6).

Various laboratory experiments conclude that individuals do not take decisions in the way described by standard neoclassical theory, in particular expected utility theory. The presence of various phenomena considered akin to cognitive illusions has been demonstrated, such as preference reversals, overconfidence, framing effects, anchoring, representativeness and availability. 'Legions of empirical psychologists and economists of the heuristics and biases school have shown that the model of rational behavior under uncertainty is not just grossly inaccurate but plain wrong as a description of reality' (Taleb, 2007, p. 185). Thus the main conclusion is that agents are not basically rational but are essentially irrational. Bounded rationality is here interpreted as the fact that 'humans have internal cognitive limitations, which express themselves in errors of judgment and decision making' (Todd and Gigerenzer, 2003, p. 146). For new behavioural economics, economic agents have inadequate foresight, they lack computational abilities and they let themselves be run by their emotions. However interesting the work of Akerlof and Shiller (2009) in macroeconomics, with their emphasis on Keynesian animal spirits, confidence, fairness and fraud, it falls into the same trap. For them, improving macroeconomics means taking into account irrational responses, and dealing with agents who have non-economic motives and are not fully rational.

The problem with this approach, from the post-Keynesian perspective, is that 'a systematic deviation from an "insane" standard should not automatically be called a judgmental error' (Gigerenzer, 2008, p. 86). The demonstrations of so-called irrationality, or cognitive illusions, derive from a comparison with a norm, founded on standard neoclassical optimization, and based on 'a process of weighting and averaging (i.e., integration) of all relevant pieces of information' (Berg and Gigerenzer, 2010, p. 136). In other words, the standard neoclassical model of decision is the benchmark of this literature. This problem has been well identified by Sent (2004, p. 743), who points out that new behavioural economics 'started from the rationality assumption that has characterized mainstream economics and next analyzed departures from this yardstick, as opposed to developing an alternative one'. New behavioural economists have not questioned the mainstream norms of rational behaviour.

This, despite the harsh conclusions that Taleb drew from the heuristics and biases studies, as recalled above, explains the ability of the cognitive illusions approach to get endorsed by orthodox economics. Indeed, those who did question the orthodox description of rationality and looked for alternatives – the old behavioural economists – failed to attract much attention from the mainstream. By contrast, orthodox economists are happy to embrace the psychological insights of new behavioural economists, because these insights do not threaten the orthodoxy. In other words, coming back to our taxonomy of Chapter 1, the heuristics and biases dissent is part of orthodox dissent. As pointed out by Berg and Gigerenzer (2010, p. 153), new behavioural economists quickly discovered 'that the easiest path toward broader acceptance into the mainstream was to put forward slightly modified neoclassical models based on constrained optimization . . . adopting Friedman's as-if doctrine'. This is demonstrated by several quotations taken from Sent (2004). For instance, Sent (ibid., p. 749) cites Camerer, Loewenstein and Rabin as claiming that the core of new behavioural economics 'is the conviction that increasing the realism of the psychological underpinnings of economic analysis will improve economics on its own terms . . . This conviction does not imply a wholesale rejection of the neoclassical approach to economics . . . The neoclassical approach is useful.' Sent (ibid., p. 743) also cites Camerer, according to whom the new psychology endorsed in the heuristics and biases approach 'provided a way to model bounded rationality which is more like standard economics than the more radical departure that Simon had in mind'. The heuristics and biases approach is no longer considered radical.

Sent (2004, p. 750) agrees that Simon's views were rapidly dismissed from the developments of new behavioural economics. How Simon reacted to the development of the heuristics and biases literature is interesting in its own right. Simon initially 'applauded the demonstrations of systematic deviations from expected utility' (Gigerenzer, 2008, p. 86), getting the impression that new behavioural economists had disproved the standard rationality model. Only later did he realize that the heuristics and biases programme had misappropriated his notion of bounded rationality, because although new behavioural economists dismissed optimization theory as a description of rational behaviour, they still hold it as the norm.

Some post-Keynesians may have had a reaction similar to Simon's initial reaction; they need to move on to his latter reaction and recognize that one must go beyond the cognitive illusions view, which Earl (1988) associated with a pseudo-behavioural approach. As Baddeley (2017, pp. 181–2) rightly points out, 'this connection between heuristics and bias does pre-suppose, however, that there is a stable point associated with the "correct" answer.... But in situations of fundamental uncertainty and complexity, there will be no anchor defining a correct answer'. Thus we must introduce the idea of environment-consistent rationality.

2.2.2 Environment-consistent Rationality

The three previous definitions of rationality all relied on model-consistent rationality as a description of actual behaviour or as-if behaviour, or as a prescription for behaviour. O'Donnell (1991, p. 81) refers to this orthodox view of rationality as hyper-rationality, ultra-rationality or pseudo-rationality. To this he opposes 'reasonable' or 'sensible' rationality, which he defines as the view of rationality that Keynes advocated when agents were facing ambiguity or fundamental uncertainty, that is, what O'Donnell calls the indeterminate domain. But we must go further. Reasonable rationality should characterize nearly all situations, that is, all the situations that are not overly simple and where the solution to the problem is not overly obvious, including situations of uncertainty. As already pointed out, Simon referred to the orthodox view as global or substantive rationality, while he called the alternative view bounded or procedural rationality.

Old behavioural economics

For Simon, a strategy is rational or irrational depending on the environment facing the economic agent. Using a Marshallian analogy proposed by Simon, there are two blades to the decision-making process: the internal limitations of the human mind; and the complexity of the tasks and of the setting in which the decision has to be made. A rational decision-making process will take both of these into consideration. Good decision mechanisms will be adapted to the informational environment. Thus a realistic concept of rationality is an environment-consistent rationality, which Gigerenzer calls an 'ecological' rationality. This kind of rationality is deemed to be ecological for two reasons: first, because it takes the informational environment into account; and second, because the decision rules followed will allow the decision-maker to save time and to access a limited amount of information. Indeed, Gigerenzer (2008, pp. 14–15) provides a table where he lists 12 examples of presumed cognitive illusions, identified by the heuristics and biases school, that can be revalued as reasonable decisions once the informational environment is taken into account.

Gigerenzer argues that decision-makers make use of an adaptive toolbox that relies on 'fast' and 'frugal' heuristics. Heuristics are short-cut decision processes. 'A heuristic is fast if it can solve a problem in little time and frugal if it can solve it with little information... Heuristics work in a real-world environment of natural complexity, where an optimal strategy is often unknown or *computationally intractable*' (Gigerenzer, 2008, pp. 7–8).

Homo heuristicus is the subject of ecological rationality. All that is needed are searching, stopping and deciding rules. *Homo heuristicus* has recourse to reasonable rationality in view of the complexity of the problem and the load of information. There is neither use nor time for optimization, which is considered a 'straitjacket' and 'a case of sterile modeling' (Taleb, 2007, p. 184). Optimization is intractable in most situations, in particular when there are multiple goals and when the problem to be solved is unfamiliar. By contrast, procedural rationality requires only appropriate reasoning. James March (1978, p. 590) says that agents develop procedures that are 'sensible' given the decisional constraints. In a similar spirit, Richard Cyert and Simon have offered the following extensive definition of procedural rationality in the case of businesses.

> The rationality of the business firm is a rationality that takes account of the limits on its knowledge, on its information, on its capacity for computation, and on its understanding of theory. It is a rationality that makes extensive use of rules of thumb where a more exact application of theory is impossible whether because the theory is not understood, because the data needed for estimating its parameters is not available, or because the decision must be made under conditions of uncertainty. (Cyert and Simon, 1983, p. 104)

The research programme that Gigerenzer advocates is no different from the one that post-Keynesians would put forward when discussing rationality. He wants to propose a realistic theory of the behaviour of economics actors, one based on their actual behaviour and on their actual informational environment, without the assumption of optimization.

> This program develops Herbert Simon's idea of studying the rational principles that underlie the behavior of real people, who do not optimize and, for the most part, do not calculate utilities and probabilities. Recall that this program differs from the optimizing program in that it analyzes the actual process – the heuristics – rather than constructing as-if models based on a convenient mathematical structure. Unlike the cognitive illusions program, it directly analyzes the decision process rather than trying to demonstrate violations of the assumptions underlying as-if models. (Gigerenzer, 2008, pp. 89–90)

Who, besides post-Keynesians, most notably Peter Earl, would endorse such a programme? As shown in Table 2.2, a number of strands in behavioural economics endorse environment-consistent rationality. These are mostly associated with what would be called old behavioural economics. This includes, of course, those associated with Simon at Carnegie, such as Cyert and March. But it also includes other strands of behavioural economics as defined by Tomer (2007), notably George Katona and the Michigan School, that emphasized the importance of consumer and business confidence in expenditure decisions, as well as the evolutionary theory of Richard Nelson and Sidney Winter, who made use of biological analogies to explain the evolution of businesses. Some authors, like Morris Altman, and Tomer himself, who drew inspiration from Harvey Leibenstein's X-inefficiency thesis, ought also to be added to this group. It is also clear that Institutionalists (as reflected, for instance, in the work of Hodgson), who are closely related to the work of evolutionary economics, as well as humanistic economics and socio-economics, have obvious ties with the research programme put forward by Gigerenzer. It could also be said that the proponents of multi-agent modelling, which make use of non-optimizing behavioural rules, would also endorse ecological rationality.

Finally, as we shall see when we discuss the theory of pricing, and as shown by Lee (1998), there are at least two traditions that endorsed non-optimizing pricing rules and hence were also clearly related to environment-consistent rationality, namely the Oxford Price Study Group in the UK and the researchers linked to administrative pricing in the USA.

Fast and frugal is better than sophisticated optimizing procedures

The fast and frugal heuristics put forward by Gigerenzer contain several surprising features, when compared to the heuristics and biases school. First, it is claimed that people rely on heuristics for both routine and important decisions. Second, behavioural rules are used because they allow economic actors to reach a decision even though the problem appears intractable and complex, while simultaneously saving time. Third, following simple rules often allows one to arrive at better results than making use of sophisticated optimizing rules that are subject to large estimation errors. Finally, it turns out that it may be more prudent to ignore part of the relevant information: less may be better than more. An obvious example of the latter feature relates to what we saw at the end of Chapter 1, when discussing meta-regression analysis. Stanley et al. (2010) have shown that, when there is a genuine empirical effect, accompanied by publication bias, it is best to discard 90 per cent of the studies and compute the average of the effect of the 10 per cent most precise studies. This will yield the most precise estimate of the true effect.

How can heuristic rules, processing less information, deliver better results than some optimizing procedures that process all information? Gigerenzer (2008, pp. 40–41) provides an example. The task was to predict the dropout rate in high schools. There were many explanatory variables, and rules of heuristics or optimization were derived from one half of the high schools, while prediction was assessed from the other half. The optimization rule was obtained by a multiple regression equation over all variables: one heuristic rule was a 'take-the-best' rule, based on a unique best predictor; a second heuristic rule was to take each variable and give each the same weight. Figure 2.1 shows the result of this exercise. The optimizing procedure yielded the best fit and had the highest percentage of predictive accuracy when testing on the first half. By contrast, when the three procedures were tested to predict the dropout rate in the remaining high schools, the accuracy of the optimizing procedure fell miserably, and its predictive accuracy fell below that of the two heuristic rules. This experiment was repeated for several other similar problems, with similar results.

The lesson to be drawn from this is that complex strategies, like multiple regressions, work well in predicting the past; they are no good at predicting the future. This resembles the critique that Keynes made about the use of time-series econometrics. It also resembles the problem observed with the use of DSGE models by central banks when the Global Financial Crisis hit in 2008. Because DSGE models are calibrated over several free parameters, they seem to perform well in fitting past data or in predicting the very near future. However, with the advent of the financial crisis, these optimizing models turned out to be completely useless. A very similar critique can be addressed to the numerous models proposed to replace expected utility theory. Besides regret theory, the best known of these models is prospect theory, promoted by Kahneman and Tversky (1979), which belongs as much to the as-if category as the model that it purports to replace, since it

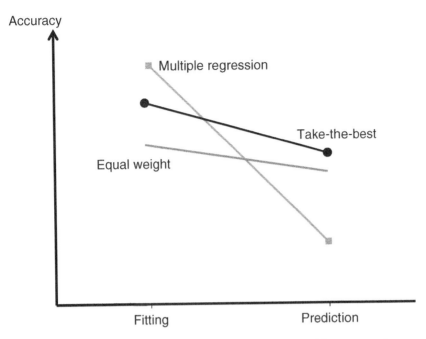

Figure 2.1 Fitting and predicting for optimizing procedures and heuristic rules

assumes that risky choices are the result of weighting and integrating all the available information. Models of new behavioural economics contain more free parameters than expected utility theory, and hence it is not surprising that they manage to explain a greater variety of choices. But once these free parameters are fixed (say through earlier experimenting), prospect theory predicts a smaller percentage of majority choices than simple heuristic rules, such as a rule of a lexicographic nature with no adjustable parameter (Berg and Gigerenzer, 2010, p. 143). Achieving a good statistical fit to past data is not the same thing as being able to predict behaviour.

Rather than trying to assess what agents should do, one should assess what they actually do to take decisions. Humans do not try to optimize; rather they make informed guesses, in line with ecological rationality. Todd and Gigerenzer (2003, pp. 148–9) argue that humans rely on four main heuristics to make appropriate decisions. First, they make choices based on recognition (of brand names, company names etc.). Second, they may take decisions based on a single cue, such as in the take-the-best heuristic. Third, they may proceed by elimination, such as suggested by Tversky's (1972) elimination by aspect model. Fourth, individuals set aspiration levels, so that the search for alternatives is brought to an end when the aspiration level is achieved. This is Simon's (1955) well-known concept of 'satisficing' (a neologism combining the words satisfy and suffice), the anti-thesis of optimizing. 'Experimenting evidence is growing that humans do indeed use simple heuristics to make decisions in an ecologically rational manner, using as little information as possible and tailoring their information and options search to the structure available in the environment' (Todd and Gigerenzer, 2003, p. 154).

Fast and frugal versus optimization procedures in macroeconomics

There is further evidence, at the macroeconomic level, that to follow simple rules in a world of complex structures – the indeterminate domain – might generate better results. Two examples can be provided. Andrew Haldane, a chief economist at the Bank of England, has been arguing that the experience with the exponentially rising complexity of the various versions of the capital adequacy rules imposed or suggested by the Bank for International Settlements (BIS) – the Basel I, II, III rules – has demonstrated that 'the more complex the environment, the greater the perils of complex control. The optimal response to a complex environment is often not a fully state-contingent rule. Rather, it is to simplify and streamline' (Haldane and Madouros, 2012, p. 115). Haldane further argued that 'complex environments often instead call for simple decision rules. That is because these rules are more robust to ignorance' (ibid., p. 112). It is said that Canadian banks avoided problems related to the Global Financial Crisis because, beyond the complicated risk weights defined by the BIS rules, they were submitted to a simple, unweighted, 20 to 1 asset to equity ratio.

To follow heuristics, or simple rules of thumb, is not suboptimal, in contrast to the message carried by the new behavioural research programme based on cognitive illusions. Dosi et al. (2020) show this by providing an interesting experience based on simulations done with their agent-based model, their so-called K+S model. This model is 'a bridge between Keynesian theories of effective demand generation and Schumpeterian theories of innovation and growth, with Minskyan financial dynamics' (ibid., p. 1489). Endogenous innovations create business cycles, with non-linearities, positive feedbacks, as in system dynamics, and structural breaks. Dosi et al. run their model with seven different rules regarding how firms forecast their own sales, namely naïve expectations, based on sales of the previous period; adaptative expectations (most often used in agent-based and stock-flow consistent models); weak and strong trend expectations, anchoring expectations where firms also take into account past macroeconomic data; and learning expectations where firms switch from one rule to another depending on their past success. Somewhat surprisingly, naïve and adaptative expectations clearly provide the best individual forecasts, and adaptative expectations are best to avoid GDP volatility and crises. Dosi et al. (2020) encounter a new macroeconomic paradox: expectation rules that provide the worse forecasts for individual firms do not necessarily generate the worse macroeconomic results in terms of unemployment rates, GDP volatility or the likelihood of crises. We called this the forecasting paradox in Table 1.4 of Chapter 1.

Perhaps even more interesting are the results obtained with the seventh process of expectations. Dosi et al. (2020, p. 1504) 'make agents learn *as if* they were econometricians', by using recursive least squares to assess the weighting parameter that splits expected demand in the current period between expected and realized demand of the previous period. In this case, the optimizing econometric rule generates both worse individual forecasts and worse macroeconomic functioning. Dosi et al. (ibid., p. 1507) argue that this poor performance 'boils down to the fact that it is not possible to bend complex, nonlinear worlds into a linear framework'. They conclude that in a world dominated by fundamental uncertainty where agents interact, the best response is likely to be the adoption of heuristics – rules of thumb – a kind of rationality which is consistent with the environment faced by financial and non-financial firms, central banks and other economic agents.

2.2.3 Rules of Procedural Rationality

Ecological rationality, in cases of uncertainty or of insufficient capability to process existing information, thus consists of means to avoid complex calculations and considerations, and of procedures enabling decisions to be taken despite incomplete information. Some of these procedures are conscious: we may then speak of rules; while others are unconscious: we may refer to them as habits (Hodgson, 2004). For instance, a large part of our spending as consumers is based on habits. Furthermore, short-cuts are used to arrive at quick decisions. Because these procedures do not rely on optimizing behaviour, they are usually considered as instances of market failure and are called, sometimes disdainfully, rules of thumb. However, in a world of ignorance and of complexity, these rules of thumb are rational, because 'they are modes of behavior that the firm (or individual) develops as guides for making decisions in a complex environment with uncertainty and incomplete information' (Cyert and Simon, 1983, p. 105). There are many examples of rules of thumb in the real world: pay-back periods for investment decisions; mark-up pricing or full-cost pricing for firms or retailers; the normal rate of capacity utilization; financial ratios of all sorts: the target rate of return, leverage ratios, cash ratios, liquidity ratios for firms; ratios of interest payments to gross income for households wanting to take a mortgage; all bureaucratic rules. The examples are endless. Rules allow individuals or institutions to take decisions without having to consider or reconsider all the available information.

On a more general plane, various procedures have been suggested by Keynes and Simon to handle the complexities of decision-making, especially in situations of fundamental uncertainty. These are:

1. When a satisfactory solution has been reached, stop searching.
2. Take the present and the recent past as guides for the future.
3. Assume that the present evaluation of the future is correct.
4. Follow the opinion of the majority.
5. Look for alternative actions when existing ones are too uncertain.
6. Take actions that reduce the amount of uncertainty.
7. When uncertainty is too large, postpone the decision.
8. Proceed to a partial adjustment.

The first rule, mentioned in the previous subsection, is in fact the core of ecological rationality. It presumes that the decision-maker sets aspiration levels that allow him to distinguish between what is acceptable and what is not. However, the problem of ranking all the possibilities is avoided since the agent is looking for one solution within the acceptable range, rather than the best among all solutions. All alternatives do not have to be considered in detail. This is the great advantage of satisficing.

The next three rules to deal with fundamental uncertainty were proposed by Keynes (1973, xiv, p. 114) in his famous 1937 *Quarterly Journal of Economics* article, where he insists that descriptions of economic behaviour must incorporate the concept of fundamental uncertainty. Rules 2 and 3 are somewhat reminiscent of an economic forecast with adaptive expectations, on to which the latest news would have been grafted. This is precisely what forecasting agencies generally have to offer and what firms are looking for. Keynes (1936, p. 152) makes clear that this is a 'convention', but one that can be precarious.

The fourth rule, relying on the opinion of the majority, is perhaps the rule whose implications are the most important. When the available information is not very reliable or too complex to be processed, it seems that a rational reaction is to rely on the opinion of others, whom we think are either better informed or representative of the majority view, that is the view that should prevail in the markets. As Keynes (1973, xiv, p. 114) said in the same 1937 article, 'knowing that our own individual judgment is worthless, we endeavour to fall back on the judgment of the rest of the world which is perhaps better informed'. The illusion of strong rationality in very uncertain situations will thus be safeguarded by mimicking others (Orléan, 1999). As Keynes says, as individuals copy others, society develops a conventional judgement. What we have here is a kind of super-convention, a societal convention that depends on the conventional view of others.

The rationale here is that there are fewer chances of getting burned when one is following the crowd. For instance, unless one is a speculator with a better-informed opinion, it is rational to launch a new product when others are optimistic, that is when one can expect effective demand to be strong. The less confident we are of our own views, the more we should rely on the judgement of others. Furthermore, as Keynes said (1973, ix, p. 156), a banker who has been ruined is a sound banker provided he has followed all the rules and traditions of the profession and has gone under with a few of his colleagues. This saying was certainly verified during the Global Financial Crisis. 'Worldly wisdom teaches that it is better for reputation to fail conventionally than to succeed unconventionally' (Keynes, 1936, p. 158). As Baddeley (2017, p. 188) puts it, Keynes 'focused on three main reasons why people herd with the crowd in a world of uncertainty: social learning, beauty contests and reputation'.

This type of imitative behaviour has strong consequences. The rules that we have mentioned, financial ratios and the like, will be normalized through imitation. Not only do they constitute helpful guidance for decisions, but they also become norms and conventions that must be respected. These norms are not necessarily the average of the aggregated opinion of all individuals, since the opinions of some are judged to be of more weight than those of others. As a consequence, these norms represent focal points, determined in great part by the opinions of some powerful and respected group. We have already associated ecological rationality with the presupposition of realism. Now we see that ecological or procedural rationality is consistent with the presupposition of organicism (Lawson, 1985; Winslow, 1989). When they take decisions, or even when they set their preferences, entrepreneurs and households rely on habits, customs, conventions, norms. This means that, to a large extent, when proceeding to analyse the overall economy we can dispense with going into the intricate details of individual behaviour and content ourselves with the study of the interaction between the various groups and classes of society based on received conventions. There is thus consistency between the presupposition of methodological organicism and that of ecological rationality. When the limitations of information processing are taken into consideration, the limits of methodological individualism are even more striking.

But imitation brings about a second important consequence. The conventional view transforms society; it transforms the economy. This was especially emphasized by Soros (2010), through his concept of 'reflexivity', formalized by Shaikh (2010). This can be associated to the 'beauty contests' that Keynes (1936, p. 156) was talking about, where investors try to anticipate 'what average opinion expects the average opinion to be'. In a world of fundamental uncertainty, where it is not clear what reality is and what the future states of nature will be, the existence of reflexivity – the imitation and the mimicking of the views and actions of others – will transform an already uncertain world into an even more uncertain one. Shackle's crucial decisions become all the more crucial and their proportion becomes ever larger.

Having established that conventions are the main response to uncertainty and excess information, it remains to discover when these conventions change. Rule 5 implies that, when the old routines cannot provide a satisfactory answer, they must be replaced. In particular, when the old routines imply too high a level of uncertainty, then some new information must be gathered and some new channels of thought must be found. Outlets for action that generate more confidence must be devised. For instance, when there are political or economic crises, uncertainty often rises, with the result that what earlier appeared as reasonable routines must now be discarded. This, of course, is the difficulty of post-Keynesian analysis: having established the importance of rules and conventions, when are these rules changed; when are the customs replaced? There must be some mechanism explaining the evolution of the customs, but besides external shock factors and some reference to endogenous innovation, post-Keynesians still have little to offer by way of an explanation (Bianchi, 1990). This, of course, should be the contribution of the Schumpeterians as well as that of the Institutionalists and their Veblenian evolutionary economics: explain why and how the convention gets modified – that is, provide a theory of creative rationality (Fernández-Huerga, 2008, p. 721).

Rules 6 and 7 provide the ultimate responses to uncertainty and insufficient capability. In general, agents try to avoid having to take decisions involving a substantial amount of uncertainty. As in the case of stuntmen, who do their best to eliminate imponderables (uncertainty) while knowing that they cannot eradicate all risks, firms attempt to reduce the extent of uncertainty by signing contracts and extending their domain of control. It could be said that the power of a firm is a measure of its command over uncertainty. In the end, when doubts are too large, it is always possible to delay a decision (Pasinetti, 1981, p. 234). This is rule 7. It explains to some extent the fluctuations of the economy. Investment requires a conscious decision to increase or replace the existing stock of capital. Furthermore, when consumers are in doubt as to the products upon which they should spend their newly increased income, they can always postpone their decisions by saving their incomes. This is consistent with theories of aggregate consumption based on habits (Marglin, 1984a, chs 17–18). If a decision must be taken in any case, the strategy of decision-making may change if the level of uncertainty increases. For instance, in classical decision theory, it is often assumed that risk-averse agents follow a maximin strategy; that is, they choose the action that minimizes the possible maximum losses, rather than pursuing a strategy that maximizes the minimum gains. I would argue that the choice of these strategies has nothing to do with the psychological character of the individual, but rather that the more risky strategy appears more appealing when the relative level of available pertinent information is sufficiently high. When uncertainty is greater, the more prudent strategy will usually be followed.

Finally, rule 8, the partial adjustment rule, says that agents will not fully respond to a change in conditions, either because they know that the change may be only a temporary one or because they are unsure of the quality of the information, so that their reaction will bring about only a partial recovery towards some norm. This rule is advocated in particular by Duménil and Lévy (1993, p. 184), who argue that 'adjustment is the crucial approach to . . . the behavior of economic agents confronting disequilibrium'. Although agents may also incorporate some forward-looking elements, they must rely essentially on objective backward-looking variables. This is questioned by New Keynesians who claim in their empirical studies of the new Phillips curve that expected inflation is a significant determinant of actual inflation. But when adjustment terms (error correction terms) are taken into consideration, the significance of the forward-looking term disappears, and only past inflation determines present inflation (Bjørnstad and Nymoen, 2008).

2.2.4 Implications for Theoretical Analysis

It is now time to evaluate the theoretical implications for economic modelling of accepting, on the one hand, the Keynesian/Knightian view of uncertainty, and on the other hand the concept of procedural rationality *à la* Simon. We have seen in the previous section that mainstream economists ultimately reject the adoption of fundamental uncertainty because they dread the nihilistic consequences for economic theorizing. Not only are they afraid that the standard optimizing tools cannot be utilized (they certainly cannot), but they are also fearful that introducing uncertainty will destroy any pretence at establishing laws and regularities. Furthermore, for neoclassical economists, models not based on microeconomic foundations of the constrained optimization sort are not scientific, for they do not rely on individual rationality. The rest of this section demonstrates that these fears are not substantiated.

Let us first tackle the question of the nihilistic component of fundamental uncertainty. As already pointed out, it must be admitted that those authors who have emphasized the importance of uncertainty have generally overestimated its destructive consequences for economic analysis. Two destructive paths have been pursued: one underlying the presumed irrationality of the agents; and the other the instability of the economic capitalist system. The reader should be convinced by now that ontological and epistemic uncertainty does not of necessity breed irrational behaviour. In fact, it can be argued on the contrary that, in both the *Treatise on Probability* and *The General Theory*, Keynes is striving to define a realistic and practical theory of procedural rationality based on the limitations of human knowledge and capabilities. When deprived of knowledge, reason cannot be based on simple probabilities and must turn to alternative strategies based on conventions and other procedures. In this context, 'Keynes may be viewed as basing the whole of economic theory on a single, broad, non-Neoclassical conception of agent rationality' (O'Donnell, 1989, p. 272).

The second path towards nihilistic conclusions follows some of Keynes's arguments. It has been assumed that uncertainty leads to instability since long-term decisions depend on flimsy foundations, subject to sudden changes (1973, xiv, p. 114). This has meant to some that a proper theory set in historical time, where these violent changes in opinions would have to be recorded, is beyond the reach of economics. Sticking to Keynes for the moment, it is well known that he also considered uncertainty to be a stabilizing influence on the economy, since a variety of opinions and the confidence with which they are held ensures mitigated aggregate reactions to news (Keynes, 1936, p. 172). The position taken here is that the presence of fundamental uncertainty, combined with a rationality based on procedures, generates regular patterns, except in exceptional crises (bifurcations and the like).

The basic argument is that the rules and conventions of procedural rationality spare the economic agents from reacting to every perturbation in the economic environment. Since agents are not assumed to be maximizing some objective function, they do not have to react to every little change in the parameters of the function, whether these changes can be ascertained objectively or be assessed from a hysterical subjective perspective. Provided that the new information leaves the agents in the satisfactory range, the existing procedures continue to be followed. As was said earlier, what counts with regard to the stable or unstable influence of uncertainty is how agents react to it. Uncertainty *per se* is no more a destabilizing force than a possibly stabilizing one. Only in situations of crisis, when all rules or conventions seem to go by the wayside, can uncertainty be a destabilizing force. In normal circumstances, uncertainty is a source of regularities, as shown by Heiner. He concludes that 'greater uncertainty will cause rule-governed behavior to exhibit increasingly predictable regularities, so that uncertainty becomes the basic source of predictable behavior' (1983, p. 570). This is a conclusion reached independently by other post-Keynesians: 'In the real world economic systems function coherently, insofar as they do, *because* of the bounds produced by imperfections of knowledge rather than, as in conventional theory, *despite* them' (Earl, 1983, p. 7).

Heiner's conclusions rest on the proposition that the greater the amount of uncertainty, the greater is the risk of taking the wrong decision; that is, deciding to change the procedures when this leads to losses or deciding not to change procedures when a move would have produced a gain. If the world was known with certainty, one would always recognize the proper time to make a move. However, when there is uncertainty and incomplete knowledge, many false signals are received and, as a consequence, changes to existing behaviour seem worthwhile only when there are substantial expected gains; that is when the gains (or the net gains compared to the no-change situation) and their probability are high. The argument of Heiner is thus based on some sort of compensatory calculus between the probability of an event and the weight of an argument, in the spirit of what Keynes seemed to have suggested in his *Treatise on Probability* when he said that, to make decisions, 'we ought to take account of the weight as well as the probability of different expectations' (1973, viii, p. 83).

The implications of all this are that models based on rules of thumb, such as mark-ups, target-return pricing, normal financial ratios, standard rates of utilization, propensities to consume, lexicographic rules and so on are perfectly legitimate since they rely on a type of rationality that is appropriate to the usual economic environment. In a world of uncertainty and of limited computational abilities, the economic agent cannot but adopt, except in the simplest of problems, a rationality that is of the procedural type. The models built on rules of thumb are not *ad hoc* constructions as the mainstream would like them to be because they are not derived from some axiomatic optimizing formalization. Rather, they reflect the rationality of reasonable agents. As such, they have microeconomic foundations that are more solid, from a realist point of view, than those of the standard mainstream models. Indeed, when one thinks about it, what is more *ad hoc*: to assume that economic agents follow some rules of thumb and are satisfied once they reach some threshold; or to assume that agents are omniscient, omnipotent and maximize some utility function that contains no conflicting goals, while at the macro level the representative agent acts as both a consumer and a producer? Heterodox economists must feel at ease in dismissing such accusations; it is orthodox theory that makes use of *ad hoc* methods (Amable et al., 1997). Making use of ecological rationality is perfectly legitimate because this is how people truly behave.

Post-Keynesians are sometimes asked about their response to the Lucas critique, presumed to damn all Keynesian analyses. Once more, what is more *ad hoc*? Is it to assume that all economic agents base their forecasts on the macroeconomic theory and causal structures advocated by the modeller, assumed to be *the* true model of the economy, with agents being able to take optimal decisions incorporating the rational expectations hypothesis? Or is it more reasonable to believe that agents base their expectations on the recent past or trends, using different strategies and sometimes making bold choices, disregarding conventional wisdom? There are many macroeconomic theories out there and even Lucasian advocates disagree on what are the essential frictions and imperfections. The Lucasian prescription cannot be right when applied to a real world where there is a divergence of opinions, views, forecasts and economic theories (Storm, 2021a).

2.3 A THEORY OF HOUSEHOLD CHOICE

While post-Keynesians have spent a great deal of effort on macroeconomics and monetary issues as well as methodological issues, they have devoted less attention to microeconomics, seemingly avoiding in particular the subject of consumer choice. For instance, in the two guides on post-Keynesian economics, published at a 20-year interval, there is no chapter devoted to consumer theory (Eichner, 1979; Holt and Pressman, 2001). However, despite its apparent neglect, there exists a post-Keynesian theory of consumer choice, based on the indications left by the best-known and most productive post-Keynesian authors, such as Joan Robinson, Luigi Pasinetti, Edward Nell, Philip Arestis and Alfred Eichner. These indications on consumer choice show a great degree of coherence, and in my opinion they fit tightly with the rest of post-Keynesian theory. Indeed, Drakopoulos (1992b) goes so far as to argue that Keynes himself had in mind such a heterodox consumer choice theory.

The purpose of the present section is to show what a research agenda on post-Keynesian consumer theory could look like, and to show that such an agenda offers plenty of synergies with research programmes by Institutionalists, social or humanistic economists, ecological economists, marketing specialists, the literature in economic psychology, and the work of some dissident mainstream economists.

2.3.1 The Coherence of Views on Post-Keynesian Consumer Choice Theory

As a general statement, one could claim that post-Keynesian economists, in contrast to their neoclassical colleagues, are very distrustful of the ability of the market price mechanism to solve most contemporary economic problems. This suspicion is based on a rejection, or at least a questioning, of the allocation role attributed to prices by mainstream authors. Post-Keynesian economists doubt the general validity of the principle of substitution. These doubts arise from the observation that factors of production are generally complementary, rather than substitutable, and also from the observation that most successful activities are pursued on the basis of cooperation and trust. Applied to the field of consumer theory, this lack of confidence in the principle of substitution implies that post-Keynesian authors doubt that price is often a key determinant of purchasing decisions, and hence they question whether consumers or individuals take decisions based on compensatory rules. As claimed by Arestis (1992, p. 124), 'The post-Keynesian theory of household demand begins with the fundamental assumption that in an economic system it is the income effects rather than the substitution effects which are most important'. This is true because of the lack of substitution but also because choices expand with rising incomes (Rassuli and Rassuli, 1988, p. 461).

The most detailed examination of a possible post-Keynesian consumer theory can be found in two books by Earl (1983; 1986), and the motivations supplied above are quite apparent there. Other specific contributions to post-Keynesian consumer choice theory can be found in the works of Arrous (1978), Eichner (1987, ch. 9), Drakopoulos (1990; 1992a; 1994; 1999), Lah and Sušjan (1999), Gualerzi (2001) and Fernández-Huerga (2008). A substantial amount of overlap with Earl's initial attempt at defining a specific post-Keynesian consumer choice vision is obvious. However, I consider that the first article that ought to be read to get a sense of what a post-Keynesian consumer theory implies is the one written by René Roy (1943; 2005) – an author unrelated to heterodox economics.

In his little-known article, Roy (2005) puts forward several propositions that would seem to constitute the core of a post-Keynesian theory of consumer choice and that are quite compatible with the rest of post-Keynesian theory. For instance, Roy denies that the preferences of consumers (demand) explain the prices of consumer goods, thus rejecting the neoclassical view of value based on scarcity. He rejects the generalized use of indifference curves, for he believes that such a representation is not a realistic representation of human needs. He argues that goods can be, to some extent, separated into groups of goods with common features, substitution effects playing an important role within a group, but not in-between groups. In addition, he believes that these groups can be ordered in a hierarchy, with consumers moving from one group of goods to another, as their most urgent needs are progressively satiated and as their incomes rise. Variations in the prices of goods located in core groups (the basic needs) will have an impact on the demand for the goods of peripheral or discretionary groups ('luxury goods'), but by contrast variations in the prices of goods located in discretionary groups will have no impact on the demand for the goods of core groups.

As will become obvious, there is a tight link between Roy's views and the common ground of post-Keynesian consumer theory, as represented below under the form of seven principles (Lavoie, 1994; Drakopoulos, 1999):

1. The principle of procedural rationality.
2. The principle of satiable needs.
3. The principle of separability of needs.
4. The principle of subordination of needs.
5. The principle of the growth of needs.
6. The principle of non-independence.
7. The principle of heredity.

These seven principles will be briefly explained in the next section, although their names are by themselves evocative. In the meantime, here are a few quotes from past and present leaders in the post-Keynesian field, which clearly illustrate the convergence of views mentioned in the introduction. The numbers in square brackets inserted within the quotes refer to the above list.

[6] There is a kind of competition in consumption, induced by the desire to impress the Joneses, which makes each family strive to keep up at least an appearance of being as well off as those that they mix with, so that outlay by one induces outlay by others ... [4] Generally speaking, wants stand in a hierarchy (though with considerable overlaps at each level) and [5] an increment in a family's real income is not devoted to buying a little more of everything at the same level but to stepping down the hierarchy. (Robinson, 1956, pp. 251, 354)

[4] Although possibilities of substitution among commodities are of course relevant at any given level of real income, there exists a hierarchy of needs. [5] More precisely, there exists a very definite *order of priority* in consumers' wants, and therefore among groups of goods and services, which manifests itself as real incomes increase. (Pasinetti, 1981, p. 73)

[3] Purchases of various consumption goods are thought to serve different physical needs so that substitution can only take place within extremely narrow subcategories. [6] Secondly, substitution possibilities are very much limited by social conventions and acquired tastes ... [4] Household expenditures are assumed to follow a lexicographic ordering. (Arestis, 1992, p. 124)

[3] As far as I can see, all theories of wants and their satisfaction (except the neoclassical) negate the generality of substitution and postulate hierarchies of needs and their satisfaction ... [4] To the extent that there is a hierarchy of wants, a system of preferences allowing the construction of a utility function with the appropriate properties of substitutability does not exist ... First elementary needs have to be fulfilled before there comes the turn of higher needs; in the extreme, there is no substitutability whatever between them (though there may be a substitutability between goods fulfilling the same need). (Schefold, 1997, p. 327)

[2] The moral is that price changes may have little or no effect over a substantial range, and then suddenly have large effects, sometimes in unexpected directions ... [6] Of course, even within a given lifestyle a social function can normally be filled in a number of alternative ways, substitutes for one another, so that price changes will lead to changes in consumption. [3] But these substitutes are all goods or services of the same *category* ... Within categories, substitution holds, but between categories complementarity tends to be the rule ... The more specific the good, the greater will be the possibilities of substitution, the more general the category, the more fixed the complementarity. (Nell, 1992, pp. 396–7)

[5] Post-Keynesians generally assume that, in an economy that is expanding over time, it is the income effect that will predominate over the relative price, or substitution, effects ... [3] Substitution can take place only within fairly narrow subcategories. [4] Consumer preferences are, in this sense, lexicographically ordered ... [6] A household's consumption pattern, at any given point in time, thus reflects the lifestyle of the households that constitute its social reference group. (Eichner, 1986a, pp. 159–60)

All these quotes help to show that post-Keynesians have a common vision of a heterodox consumer theory, and that this vision can be embedded within the seven principles listed above, which now need to be discussed. This is what we do, in general terms, in the next section. Examples will be provided in another section. As a warning, I should point out that in what follows I shall use the terms 'individual consumer' and 'household' interchangeably, which, given the concerns of feminist economists, is probably not appropriate (Danby, 2004, p. 62; Hanmer and Akram-Lodhi, 1998).

2.3.2 The Principles of Post-Keynesian Consumer Choice

Procedural rationality

We have already devoted a whole section to procedural or ecological rationality, so we shall say no more here. All we can add at this stage is that a large number of the fast-and-frugal rules used by consumers are based on non-compensatory procedures, where only some elements, or possibly a single one, are taken into consideration provided they reach a certain threshold, so that they 'satisfice' a given target. Rules are often based on a hierarchical design. The main advantage of non-compensatory rules is that, as recalled by Dhar (1999), they lead to more decisions than compensatory ones: when there is no decisive advantage, there is no choosing at all and the purchase decision is postponed.

Satiable needs

The second principle, that of satiable needs, can be likened to the neoclassical principle of diminishing marginal utility (or its non-satiable principle), but it takes a particular meaning in the post-Keynesian theory of the consumer. Here satiation arises with positive prices and finite income. There are threshold levels of consumption – satiation levels – beyond which a good, or its characteristics, may bring no satisfaction to its consumer. Beyond the threshold, no more of the good will be purchased, regardless of its price.

One has to carefully distinguish wants from needs, as do Lutz and Lux (1979). Following the psychologist Abraham Maslow (1954), and in line with the groups' classification proposed by Roy (1943), they argue that there is a hierarchy of needs, where some are more basic than others, which implies that they must be fulfilled in priority. In that sense all needs are not equal. Some needs are bound to be satiated much earlier than others. Needs are subjected to a hierarchical classification and are the motor of consumer behaviour. By contrast, wants evolve from needs. They can be substituted for each other and constitute 'the various preferences within a common category or level of need' (Lutz and Lux, 1979, p. 21). This distinction will be useful in defining the next two principles of a post-Keynesian consumer theory.

In standard economics, everything can usually be brought back under the label of utility. Every want can be compared to all the others, and in that sense all wants are equal. It is possible to rank the various wants, but this ranking depends solely on the ability of each want to create utility. This, however, was not the view of classical economists, nor initially that of the marginalist economists (Drakopoulos and Karayiannis, 2004). Both Karl Menger and Alfred Marshall considered a hierarchy of needs, that is, groups of wants that could be distinguished from each other. Menger proposed a list of needs of differential importance: water, food, clothing, lodging, transportation and tobacco (!), from the essential to the less essential (Lutz and Lux, 1979, p. 18). Marshall also recognized that there existed a variety of needs, some being more basic than others. From his discussion, we can identify the following hierarchy of needs: biological needs (food, clothing, shelter, variety); health, education and security; friendship, affection, belonging, conformity with social customs; distinction; excellence; morality (Haines, 1982, p. 111).

The above list looks strikingly like the pyramid of needs suggested by Maslow and his humanistic school of psychology. This pyramid is said to be constituted by five sets of needs, from the more basic to the highest: physiological needs (air, water, food, sex, sleep); safety needs (health, education, shelter, stability, protection); social needs, subdivided in two sets: belongingness and love needs on the one hand, and self-respect and the esteem of others on the other hand; finally the moral needs, which Maslow called self-actualization – that is, the search for truth, justice, aesthetics, the meaning of life, achievement (Lutz and Lux, 1979, p. 11; Lea et al., 1987, p. 499). Although there is little doubt that the two lists were constituted independently, the identified needs appear in the same order. We may thus suspect that the proposed order is of significance. This does not mean that all individuals have the same ranking, or that there is no interpenetration of the needs. But we can certainly presume that every individual entertains a ranking of the above sort. In fact, later research seems to demonstrate that needs are clustered around two or three levels: the lower level, which is represented by Maslow's first two layers of needs; and the higher level dealing with love, esteem and self-actualization (Lea et al., 1987, pp. 146, 501). These two layers broadly correspond to what we want to have and what we would like to be.

Separability of needs
The principle of the separability of needs asserts that categories of needs or of expenditures can be distinguished from each other. In the case discussed by Kelvin Lancaster (1971), with goods described by a matrix of consumption technology with various characteristics, a separate need will be associated with a submatrix of goods and characteristics arising out of a decomposable matrix. The principle of the separability of needs is illustrated by the widely used econometric models of consumer demand, which assume that broad categories of expenditures enter separately into the overall utility function. In the utility-tree approach of Strotz (1957), the principle of separability is pushed one step further, since these broad categories of expenditures are further subdivided into several branches.

The separability of needs allows the consumer to divide the decision-making process into a series of smaller multi-stage decisions, and is consistent with the 'hierarchic principle' designed by Simon (1962) to deal with complex systems or complex issues. The consumer first makes an allocation of his budget among needs, and then spends that allocation among the various wants or subgroups of each need, independently of what happens to the other needs. Changes in the relative prices of goods within a given category of wants will have no effect on the budget allocation between various needs, while a fall in the overall price of a group of goods corresponding to a given need will have repercussions on the budget allocation of all needs. The principle of the separability of needs imposes substantial restrictions on the neoclassical principle of price substitution (without dismissing it), since separability limits severely the degree of substitutability between goods in different groups.

Indeed, a substantial amount of empirical evidence shows that general categories of consumption expenditures have low own-price elasticities and cross-elasticities. Eichner (1987, p. 656) points out that most of these elasticities are not significantly different from zero, and he argues on technical grounds that all coefficients (their absolute values) are probably an overestimate of the actual values. This is consistent with results obtained through meta-regression analyses, as discussed in Chapter 1.

The subordination of needs

Further restraints may be added if one goes beyond the principle of separability of needs by introducing a fourth principle, the principle of the subordination of needs. With this principle, utility cannot be represented by a unique catch-all utility measure; it can be represented only by a vector, and there is no longer any continuity. The principle of the subordination of needs is often associated with the notion of a pyramid of needs – or a hierarchy of needs – as described by the humanistic school of psychology (Lutz and Lux, 1979). The integration of the principles of separability and subordination leads to Nicholas Georgescu-Roegen's (1954) principle of 'irreducibility'. Needs are irreducible. They are incongruous or incommensurable; that is, one metric (price or utility) is unable to capture their characteristics.

In the case of utility-tree analysis, the first-stage budgeting problem is now resolved by assuming that money is allocated first to necessities and then to discretionary needs. There is no substitution between the budget categories apportioned to necessary needs and to discretionary ones. All the principles previously invoked culminate in this hierarchy: needs are separable and the most basic needs are first taken care of in their order of priority until they are satiated at some threshold level. Several studies seem to offer some support to this principle of irreducibility, even when only material goods are concerned. For instance Johnson (1988) has shown that goods with a small number of common attributes are more likely to be ranked lexicographically when purchasing decisions are taken, regardless of price changes; consumers eliminate products depending on basic expenditure categories. Similarly, Sippel (1997, p. 1439) has found that 'every subject showed a marked preference for some of the goods, while other goods were not chosen at all, even at low prices'. Frequent substitution occurred, as one would expect, mainly in the case of goods fulfilling similar wants, such as Coke and orange juice. In general, subjects 'violated the axioms of revealed preference', those based on the neoclassical theory of the utility-maximizing consumer subject to a budget constraint. Besides arguing that these consumers are error-prone or irrational, a way out of these results is to suppose that many of these consumers acted on the basis of the principles of the separability and the subordination of needs.

While strict lexicographic ordering is unlikely, more sophisticated lexicographic approaches have been suggested, with consumers setting targets and threshold, that is, with the addition of the second principle of post-Keynesian consumer theory, that of satiation (Earl, 1986). These non-compensatory ordering schemes are not only reasonable but also compatible with procedural rationality, since a complete utility map is not required. Decisions about the most basic needs can be taken quite independently of the informational requirements of the higher needs. Consumers need know nothing whatsoever about the prices of the goods that are part of the higher needs, and they need not rank alternatives that they cannot attain or that are beyond their satiation levels (Drakopoulos, 1994).

Neoclassical authors deny that needs are subject to the principle of subordination. This, it must be presumed, is mainly due to the devastating consequences of the irreducibility of needs for neoclassical theory and its substitution principle. Irreducible needs imply that they are incommensurable and therefore that 'everything does not have a price'. A trade-off is not always possible. The axiom of Archimedes, so popular with choice theorists, no longer holds (Earl, 1986, p. 249), and nor does the axiom of gross substitution (Eichner, 1987, p. 632), so often invoked among general equilibrium theorists.

A large number of economists have been tempted to associate Georgescu-Roegen's combined principle of the irreducibility of needs with Lancaster's approach to characteristics. Lancaster (1991) himself has suggested such a move, which he calls 'dominance'. Such a combination had already been provided by Ironmonger (1972). Among post-Keynesians, Arrous (1978, p. 277) and Lavoie (1992b, pp. 78–85) have offered an analysis of irreducible needs tied to groups of characteristics. Other post-Keynesians have proposed adopting the radical form of Lancaster's analysis of characteristics, such as Pasinetti (1981, p. 75) and Nell (1992, p. 392).

A key consequence of the principle of subordination is that the utility index can no longer be represented by a scalar, but requires instead a vector, as can be expressed formally (Encarnación, 1964; Fishburn, 1974). The notions of gross substitution and trade-offs, which are so important for neoclassical economics, are reduced to a minor phenomenon, which operates only within narrow boundaries. In particular, it is presumed that the principle of subordination, or hierarchy, is especially relevant when dealing with moral issues, for instance questions of integrity, religion, or ecology. Past work in ecological economics has shown indeed that a substantial proportion of individuals refuse to make trade-offs with material goods when biodiversity, wildlife or forests are concerned. This has implications for cost–benefit analyses, based on willingness to pay or willingness to accept compensation, that attempt to take into account the non-market value of ecology or forestry preservation, as we shall see.

The growth of needs

Having assumed that there is a hierarchy of needs, how do consumers move up the steps of the pyramid, from the core basic needs to the higher but more peripheral ones? The basic answer is that individuals move upwards in the hierarchy due to income effects. (Joan Robinson says that consumers 'step down the hierarchy', meaning that basic or subsistence needs have top priority, while discretionary needs have lower priority!) Beyond the principle of satiation lies the principle of the growth of needs – the fifth principle of post-Keynesian consumer choice.

When a need has been fulfilled, or more precisely when a threshold level for that need has been attained, individuals start attending to the needs situated on a higher plane. There are always new needs to be fulfilled. If they do not yet exist, consumers will create them through innovation, but this may take time (Gualerzi, 2001). Needs, however, often require income to be satisfied. To go from one level of need to another demands an increase in the real income level of the individual. The fulfilment of new needs, and therefore the purchase of new goods or new services, is thus related to income effects. Goods offering specific characteristics will be purchased only when consumer income is greater than some threshold (Chattopadhyay et al., 2009). This is the microeconomic counterpart of the post-Keynesian focus on effective demand, that is, on macroeconomic income effects. What is being asserted is that income effects are much more important in explaining the evolution of expenditure on goods than are substitution effects. The latter play only a minor role in a static analysis of consumer behaviour, when similar goods or goods fulfilling the same wants are considered. Indeed, changes in relative prices have an impact on budget allocation between needs only in so far as they have an impact on real income. As argued by Pasinetti (1981) and Eichner (1987), the Engel curve – the relationship between the quantities demanded and real income – may provide the best explanation for the evolution of demand for various goods.

Many sociological or psychological explanations can be advanced to explain why consumers want to go beyond their physiological and most basic material needs. These are usually based on some comparison with the situation of other consumers. In the semiological view of consumption, consumer goods are a sign that tells the outside world which rank of the consumers' hierarchy the agent occupies (Baudrillard, 1972). This leads to a desire for belongingness, or for normality. The consumer wants to demonstrate that he or she belongs to a certain class of society, to a certain group within the hierarchy of consumers. This brings comfort to the consumer.

The emphasis of traditional theory on substitution effects has led to the neglect of the study of the hierarchy of consumption and of income effects. Beyond physiological needs, convention is the main reason for which it is believed that a hierarchy of needs will be more or less identical for all individuals of a similar culture. A household's pattern of consumption 'reflects the lifestyle of other households that constitute its social reference group' (Eichner, 1986a, p. 160); that is, 'the consumption of each class will be guided by a conception of its appropriate lifestyle, given its place in the social pyramid' (Nell, 1992, p. 393). The consumption pattern of individual households is thus influenced by the demand structure of households with similar incomes or similar types of jobs, as has been empirically shown (Alessie and Kapteyn, 1991).

Another issue related to the growth of needs principle is that of material versus moral needs. This is emphasized by Lux and Lutz (1999) in their entry on the dual self, and in the work of Etzioni (1988). While many would still doubt the possibility of a lexicographic ordering in the realm of material goods, a large number of authors seem to agree that, unless one is a rational fool, as Sen (1977) puts it, people will entertain lexicographic ordering when moral issues are at stake, and hence when moral issues are incommensurable with material goods. The use of lexicographic preferences now dominates the critiques of standard neoclassical measurements of contingency values in environmental studies (Gowdy and Mayumi, 2001; Spash and Hanley, 1995). A post-Keynesian consumer theory could become a strong (academic) argument for those favouring green choices.

Non-independence

Next is the principle of non-independence. The emphasis of traditional theory on substitution effects has also led to the neglect of the learning process in consumption theory. How do consumers rank their new spending opportunities? How do they learn to spend their additional buying power? The conventional view is that consumers obtain useful information that help them make enlightened decisions through the publicity provided by firms. The opposite view, that of John Kenneth Galbraith (1958, 1972), is that the purpose of publicity and marketing of large corporations is to manipulate and manage consumer demand for their products (Anderson and Dunn, 2006). As Robinson (1956, p. 251) puts it, 'good resolutions to behave in a thrifty manner are hard to keep when they are constantly assaulted by advertising and the temptation of new commodities'.

Beyond the obvious effects of advertising in inducing households to spend more and to purchase specific kinds of goods, consumers learn by watching and copying other consumers. Preferences are not innate; they are acquired by experience and by imitation of the consumption pattern of friends, social media influencers or of people of higher ranks in the consumers' hierarchy. Fads leading to large sales of specific products are thus explained by the informational content of consumption by neighbours, relatives, friends or acquaintances. The impact of socio-economic contact on purchases reinforces the belief that the composition of demand depends on socio-economic classes, as the philosopher Pierre Bourdieu would argue (Trigg, 2004). Decisions and preferences are not made independently of those of other agents. A household's pattern of consumption will reflect the lifestyle of the other households that constitute its social reference group. Marketing officers, through publicity, will attempt to induce households to follow the 'appropriate' lifestyle (Hanson and Kysar, 1999a; 1999b). Firms will make sure that households consume the goods that they produce. Firms do not ascertain wants; they create needs.

The term 'principle of non-independence' must be attributed to Galbraith (1958), who called it the dependence effect in his *Affluent Society*. But of course, as pointed out by Mason (1998), it must be related to the large amount of socio-economic studies on conspicuous consumption and lifestyles inspired by Thorstein Veblen (1899), Duesenberry (1949) and Harvey Leibenstein (1950), and their 'snob' and 'bandwagon' effects. Choices are dependent on the choices of others, and wealth and consumption relative to that of others is a key component of the degree of our satisfaction or happiness.

Members of the higher ranks of the consumer hierarchy attempt to distinguish themselves by their ostentatious consumption, while the consumers of the middle ranks try to transgress temporarily the limits of their rank. The norms set by the upper classes will in this case define the composition of this temporary consumption. In this spirit, Leibenstein (1950) has devised the 'snob' effect, where individual demands for a product are an inverse function of the overall aggregate demand for that product, and the 'Veblen' effect, where individual demand is an inverse function of the perceived price of the product. By contrast, other households will attempt to imitate what seems to be the consumption norm, to show that they belong to the appropriate rank of the hierarchy. This is what Leibenstein has called the 'bandwagon' effect or what Duesenberry referred to as the 'demonstration' effect, or still what modern authors denote by 'expenditure cascades'. All this has been summarized by marketing specialists under three headings. All consumers belong to a membership group (families, friends); all consumers have a reference group, a group to which they compare themselves; and all consumers have an aspirational group, a group to which they would like to belong (Goodwin et al., 2009, p. 255).

René Girard's 'envy' is the other sociological explanation of customized consumer behaviour. Girard's 'envy' is very similar to Runciman's concept of relative deprivation. Individuals feel relatively deprived when they want a certain good that a reference group possesses, and when they believe that it is feasible to obtain the good. Envy is defined as a desire to get what others have. It is thus distinct from jealousy, which is a desire to keep what you already have. The goal of publicity, besides the creation of purchasing habits, is to provoke envious feelings. Publicity makes one realize what the Joneses are up to, and indicates how to suppress the unhappy feeling of envy: the consumer need only buy the good that the Joneses have already incorporated into their structure of consumption (Dumouchel and Dupuy, 1979, p. 47). The norms of consumption are thus set either by imitation or by envy. Whatever the spring of action, the result is the same: the hierarchy of needs becomes the same for all, since all consumers try to emulate those who belong to the upper echelons of society's hierarchy. These consumer elites set the trends. 'Emulation effects normally follow the social hierarchy; the consumption styles of the rich and famous set standards to which the rest aspire (or, sometimes, against which they react)' (Nell, 1992, p. 396).

The non-independence effect, through marketing, emulation and envy, has generated an enormous literature over the last few years. Recent economic booms and their financial crisis consequences are explained by the attempt of households to keep up with the Joneses, especially in the real-estate market, something made temporarily possible by easy access to credit (Brown, 2008; Cynamon and Fazzari, 2008; Kapeller and Schütz, 2015; Setterfield and Kim, 2017). Furthermore, the economics of happiness has attempted to explain some paradoxes, for example the paradox that large increases in real income do not necessarily lead to higher happiness once a certain standard of living has been achieved. Drakopoulos (2008) explains this by arguing that while the fulfilment of basic needs (those that are at the bottom of the pyramid) brings about more happiness thanks to higher real incomes, this is not the case when one goes beyond those basic needs, since various elements of life, other than income, become more important. Another consequence of this analysis based on envy or on relative income positions is that happiness is a function of the rank occupied in the consumers' hierarchy. Individuals belonging to the upper income echelons generally consider themselves happier than those with low incomes (Scitovsky, 1976, p. 136).

Heredity or the endowment effect
The seventh and last principle is what Georgescu-Roegen (1950, p. 130) has called the 'heredity' postulate. One of the better-established facts in modern behavioural economics is that choices are not independent of the order in which they are made (or the method by which they are made), in contrast to the standard neoclassical assumption. Indeed, behavioural economists have rediscovered the heredity principle, making it known as the endowment effect (Kahneman, 2011, p. 292), and linking it to other behavioural theories, namely prospect theory and loss aversion. Tastes are not given. Preferences are endogenous and context-specific. Decisions depend on a reference point. In the case of loss aversion, the argument is that people dislike losing what they already have, even if they are being offered something of a higher value in exchange. The heredity principle incorporates historical time into choice theory. This implies that there is a kind of path-dependence. There is hysteresis in choice, perhaps the first kind of hysteresis discussed in economics, as pointed out by Crivelli (1993, p. 119).

Georgescu-Roegen was keen to point out that the non-independence principle had to be distinguished from the heredity principle, for the latter played a crucial role in a theory of choice that takes time into serious consideration: history matters.

> It should (however) be stressed that the hereditary mechanism just described must not be confused with the influence upon individual tastes due to exogenous (from the point of view of the individual) economic actions taken by others, such as advertising, conspiracy for creating false social distinctions, etc. The proper hereditary influences are an inborn feature of the individual. They are present irrespective of whether exogenous forces are at work or not. (Georgescu-Roegen, 1950, p. 128)

The hereditary effect can also be associated with learning. Consumers learn how to use certain goods. Their knowledge, or rather their lack of knowledge, limits the kinds of goods that they can use and purchase. Munier and Wang (2005) argue that this limits the strength of the non-independence effect in a knowledge economy.

The heredity principle, just like the non-independence principle, applies as well at the macroeconomic level. Duesenberry (1949, p. 1) argued that 'consumption relations are not reversible in time' and hence that consumers faced with a fall in their disposable income would attempt to maintain the consumption levels that they had achieved in the recent past. Trezzini (2011a, p. 539) thus contends that the irreversibility of consumption provides a source of demand-driven GDP growth, because 'during booms, consumers tend to acquire new and higher standards of consumption that are not readily reversed'.

2.3.3 Choices of a Lexicographic Nature

Let us assume that there exists a pyramid of needs. Within each need, say furniture, there is a wide variety of possibilities. How will rational households decide between these possibilities? We previously argued that economic agents follow rules of thumb to avoid time-consuming decisions. In the case of consumer behaviour, where a substantial amount of consumer expenditure is of the repetitive type, it can be presumed that a large portion of these expenditures is done through routines. There are also some expenditures, often the semi-durable or the durable goods, that are not the result of routine decisions and that require a conscious choice. Post-Keynesians would argue that in general the main rule of thumb is some sort of non-compensatory choice. These rules of a lexicographic nature actually apply at three levels. First, we have already seen that needs can be ordered, some having priority over others. Second, within a given category of need, there may be several types of sub-needs, for instance furniture within the need for lodging. One has to decide what kind of furniture has priority: beds, bedroom set, tables, dining set, kitchenware, bookshelves, sofas, paintings, various household appliances and gadgets. We may then speak of wants within sub-needs. At this level, it has been demonstrated that households establish a pattern of consumption (Paroush, 1965; Clarke and Soutar, 1981–82). Some types of goods are acquired before others in a consistent manner. Finally, lexicographic ordering also plays a role in the actual choice of the good, as already discussed in detail. This is what Earl (1986, p. 183) calls non-compensatory filtering procedures.

Orderings of a lexicographic nature may take several forms. The most extreme form is the naïve lexicographic rule, whereas choice is based on a single characteristic (Earl, 1986, p. 233). The product that scores best with respect to this characteristic is the one chosen regardless of the other characteristics, unless there is a tie, in which case the next characteristic in the priority list becomes the crucial one. This is illustrated in Figure 2.2, where point B is preferred to point A, since characteristic (or need) z_1 has absolute priority over characteristic (or need) z_2, but where C is preferred to B since there is a tie with respect to z_1.

Many more non-compensatory filtering rules that appear more reasonable are nevertheless possible. They may be called behavioural lexicographic procedures. Figure 2.3 illustrates such a possibility, which relies on a saturation or satiation level z_1^*. It is assumed that satisfaction S depends on characteristic z_1 only, up to the level z_1^*. Any higher level of z_1 is preferred over any level of z_2. On the graph, point B is preferred to

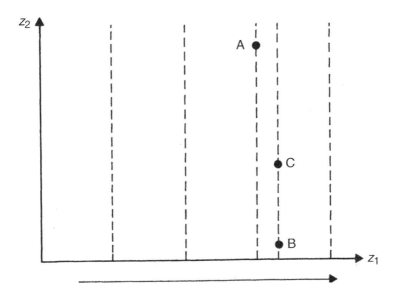

Figure 2.2   Naïve lexicographic ordering

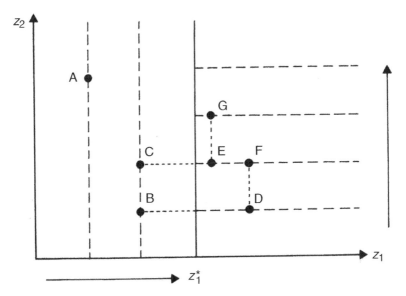

Figure 2.3   Ordering of a lexicographic nature, with saturation point

point A on the grounds of that priority, but points B and C would be indifferent. We may thus write

$$\text{If } z_1 < z_1^*, \quad S = S(z_1) \tag{2.1}$$

Turning now to the right-hand side of Figure 2.3, we suppose that the saturation level z_1^* has been exceeded and that in this case satisfaction depends on the saturation level z_1^* and on the second characteristic z_2. The order of preference between the various combinations indicated is given by the following inequalities: $G > F = E > D > C$. Note that the consumer would be indifferent between combinations F and E, since it is assumed that the characteristic z_1 does not matter once the saturation level z_1^* has been overcome. The level of satisfaction is

$$\text{if } z_1 \geq z_1^*, \quad S = S(z_1^*, z_2) \qquad (2.2)$$

In Figure 2.4, we suppose that z_1^* is not exactly a saturation level, but rather a threshold. This means that, although the consumer exceeds this threshold, resulting in characteristic z_2 becoming relevant, increases in z_1 provide supplementary satisfaction. Standard analysis could then apply beyond z_1^*, with the usual compensatory indifference curves. The following equalities or inequalities would hold: $F > D = E > C = B > A$. The level of satisfaction could be written as

$$\text{if } z_1 < z_1^*, \quad S = S(z_1)$$
$$\text{and if } z_1 \geq z_1^*, \quad S = S(z_1, z_2) \qquad (2.3)$$

Finally, we can present another kind of lexicographic ordering, suggested by Georgescu-Roegen (1954) and formalized by Encarnación (1964), and associated with Roy's (1943) description of consumer choice. It is illustrated by Figure 2.5, and it again corresponds to a threshold level rather than to a level of satiation. Below the threshold point of z_1^* corresponding to the first priority, preferences are ordered according to the highest level

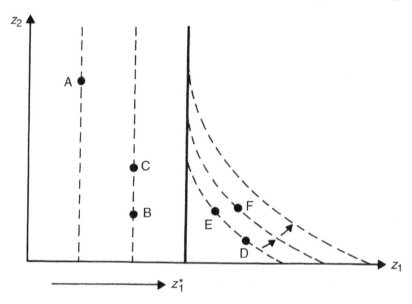

Figure 2.4 Ordering of a lexicographic nature, with indifference curves beyond the threshold

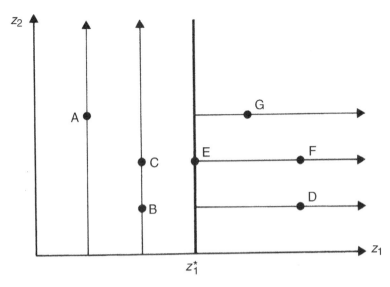

Figure 2.5 Ordering of a lexicographic nature, with Georgescu-Roegen's quasi-indifference curves

of characteristic z_1. However, for a given z_1, the agent prefers to have more of characteristic z_2 than to have less of it. Beyond the threshold point z_1^*, the reverse occurs: preferences are ordered according to characteristic z_2, but for a given z_2 the agent prefers to have more of z_1 than less of it. The lines so constructed represent 'quasi-indifference' curves, sometimes called 'behavioural' curves. All points on each of these curves are now unambiguously ordered. This is what the arrows are meant to represent, and this is how these quasi-indifference curves are differentiated from the standard flat or vertical indifference curves that would represent addictive behaviour. Suppose there are two goods, A and B, offering the characteristics z_1 and z_2. We can then write

$$\text{When } z_1 < z_1^*, S(z_1^B, z_2^B) > S(z_1^A, z_2^A) \text{ if } z_1^B > z_1^A \qquad (2.4)$$

$$\text{When } z_1 \geq z_1^*, S(z_1^B, z_2^B) > S(z_1^A, z_2^A) \text{ if } z_2^B > z_2^A$$

In the case of Figure 2.5, the following preferences hold: $G > F > E > D > C > B > A$. The standard utility analysis is now insufficient to represent this ordering. Satisfaction must be represented by a vector. From a mathematical point of view, this type of vectorial representation of preferences may appear more complex than the standard utility analysis where all characteristics or goods may be substituted for each other. From a decisional point of view, however, things are much simpler. The individual does not have to assess a myriad of possibilities to take a decision, trying to compute whether or not the loss of a characteristic can be compensated by the gain of another. No compensation must be performed. The individual simply has to assess whether the threshold has been attained or not. Furthermore, when individuals are regrouped within one household, lexicographic choice may be the main rule that solves inner conflicts and allows decisions to be taken (Earl, 1986, ch. 6).

While choices of a lexicographic nature have been emphasized here, it should also be recognized that some consumers may wish to consider all dimensions of a good (say cars of similar price) all at once. Kapeller et al. (2013) provide an interesting example of consumers having to choose between cars offering different levels of three characteristics – speed, safety and design. Assuming away compensatory choices, consumers will need to rely on aspiration levels – thresholds for a given characteristic that need to be attained for a car to remain as a contender. If more than one car fulfils all thresholds, the consumer will then need to raise at least one of these thresholds or else base the decision on some additional criterion.

2.3.4 Lexicographic Ordering and Ecological Economics

Ecological choices can provide good examples of lexicographic orderings of the kind illustrated in Figure 2.5. Post-Keynesian choice theory and ecological economics have much in common, both emphasizing the multidimensional feature of most choices. In what is probably the first post-Keynesian paper on environmental economics, Peter Bird (1982, p. 592) argued that, in contrast to neoclassical economics, 'the choice between alternative environmental policies must necessarily therefore be made in more than one dimension'. This theme is a recurrent one among the proponents of sustainable development and forest management. David Bengston (1994, pp. 523–5) for one claims that 'the multidimensional or pluralist perspective maintains that held values cannot be reduced to a single dimension and that all objects cannot be assigned value on a single scale – values are inherently multidimensional'. This is certainly an important feature of socio-economics (Etzioni, 1988), and has been endorsed by several ecological economists.

Lexicographic choices in the field of environment have been explicitly put forward by Edwards (1986), Stevens et al. (1991), Lockwood (1996), Spash and Hanley (1995), Spash (1998), van den Bergh et al. (2000), Gowdy and Mayumi (2001), and Kant (2003). The first five of these authors present a graphical representation of lexicographic choice, pointing out that it dismisses the neoclassical axiom of indifference (to which we referred as the Archimedes axiom or the axiom of gross substitution). These authors do not claim that all agents exhibit behaviour based on choices of a lexicographic nature. Rather they argue that a substantial proportion of the population – sometimes called ethicists or altruists – exhibit such a behaviour on matters tied to environment, and that neoclassical representations of these consumers are misleading, and lead to inadequate interpretation of surveys on the opinions of people about their environment. This applies in particular to the contingent valuation surveys.

As is well known, within the standard neoclassical choice theory framework, the willingness to pay (WTP) and the willingness to accept (WTA) (or willingness to sell, WTS) are well-defined measures of the Hicksian consumer surplus, which should be equal to each other (small income effects aside). Still, numerous studies have shown that WTA assessments largely exceed those of WTP. The discrepancy is easily a factor of three to ten (Knetsch, 1990, p. 228), and even a factor of 3 to 50 when environmental issues are considered (Gowdy, 1993, p. 236). Lockwood (1996, p. 91) points out that these discrepancies are particularly large when there are few substitutes for the good being valued, which is in line with the distinction we made about the separability of needs.

Various explanations have been offered for this phenomenon. The first obvious one is the heredity principle, according to which we hold on more dearly to something that we already have than to something we never acquired (Knetsch, 1990; Gowdy, 1993). The heredity principle can be easily illustrated with the help of Figure 2.6. Suppose, as proposed by Kahneman (2011, p. 290), that salaried workers are given the opportunity to get either a raise in their salary or an increase in the number of vacation days, or some acceptable combination of the two. These acceptable combinations will be represented by the standard indifference curve BB' shown in Figure 2.6, with the initial situation at A. Suppose two representative workers have chosen the extreme points B' and B respectively. The heredity principle says that, once the worker has experienced either B' or B, neither of them is likely to move towards any other point on the indifference curve BB', or even towards a point such as C, which in theory should lie on some higher indifference curve. The reason is that the worker at B' is unwilling to take a drop in salary, even though this would be accompanied by more vacation days, while the worker at B is unwilling to give up vacation days, even though her pay would be higher.

The second explanation has to do with lexicographic ordering. Consumers might be willing to give up a limited amount of money to improve their environment; but they would demand an unlimited amount of compensation to accept a reduction in the quality of the same environment. In fact, they might be unwilling to trade for any reduction in the quality of their environment.

This brings to the fore the large number of zero or infinite bids, as well as refusals to bid, that are encountered in contingency valuation studies. Zero bids or refusals to bid are often interpreted as signalling no interest in improving or preserving the quality of the environment. On the other hand, bids that appear absurdly high are waved off, on the basis that they cannot fit the neoclassical theory of consumer surplus. These anomalous

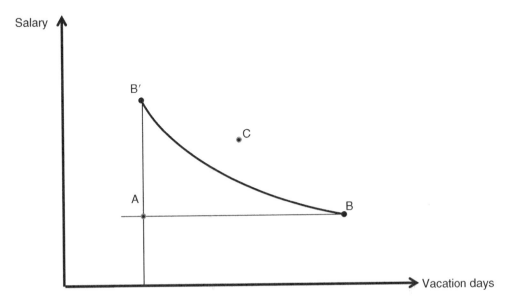

Figure 2.6   An illustration of the heredity principle or of the endowment effect

responses, however, are anomalous only within the strict neoclassical framework. As was first pointed out by Edwards (1986, p. 149), the willingness to sell will be undefined for agents who hold preferences of a lexicographic nature whenever their income exceeds their minimum standard of living. In that case, 'an altruist committed to the welfare of wildlife and future generations is expected to protest against contingent markets when asked for minimum WTS by either refusing to bid, bidding zero dollars, or bidding an extremely high amount'.

Some researchers have investigated these possibilities. Lockwood (1996, p. 99) concludes that his pilot study shows 'that some individuals do have complex preference maps which include regions of lexicographic preference for the protection of native forests from logging'. Stevens et al. (1991, p. 398) claim that most respondents gave answers that were inconsistent with both the neoclassical trade-off approach and the lexicographic theory. 'However, 80 percent of the remainder gave responses that were consistent with lexicographic preference orderings.' Spash and Hanley (1995) have investigated the motives behind zero bids. They found that almost none of the zero bids were given for reasons of zero value. Rather, some participants to the study said that they could not afford to pay anything, while most zero-bidders claimed that ecosystem rights ought to be protected at all costs, and hence should be protected by law. This is consistent with Kahneman and Knetsch (1992, p. 69), who claim that participants to contingency evaluation studies are bound to respond with indignation to questions about accepting more pollution over existing pristine landscapes, this indignation being expressed by 'the rejection of the transaction as illegitimate, or by absurdly high bids'.

Illustrations of the importance of lexicographic choice in ecological economics

As a comparative basis for these choices of a lexicographic nature, let us start with the illustration of the standard neoclassical case, with indifference curves. Let us assume that consumers are concerned with the income level that they can devote to private consumption as well as the quality of their environment, for instance the size of a neighbouring old-growth forest. Figure 2.7 is inspired by the graph provided by Edwards's (1986) pioneering article. Assume the existence of two well-behaved indifference curves, with the consumer being initially located at combination A on the U_0 utility indifference curve. Suppose the size of the environmental good is projected to be reduced from E_0 to E_d. As is well known, willingness to accept (WTA) is measured by the distance $(Y_d - Y_0)$. The consumer will be indifferent to combinations A and D. As a trade-off for the reduction $(E_0 - E_d)$ in the size of the environmental good, the consumer is willing to accept a monetary compensation of $(Y_d - Y_0)$. Alternatively, if consumers need to pay to preserve the quality of their environment, the consumer may either forsake environmental goods, in which case the person moves horizontally from combination A to combination B (on to the lower indifference curve $U-$); or the consumer may be willing to pay (WTP) an amount $(Y_0 - Y_c)$ to retain the quality of environment at E_0, in which case consumers move vertically from point A to point C (on the same lower indifference curve $U-$). With well-behaved indifference curves, WTP and WTA would be approximately equal, save for the decreasing marginal rate of substitution, as shown in Figure 2.7.

Let us now examine the case of choices of a lexicographic nature. Let us take the simplest case, beyond pure lexicographic choice. Assume that the primary element of choice, until income level Y^* is achieved, is the level of income. This means that, for any income

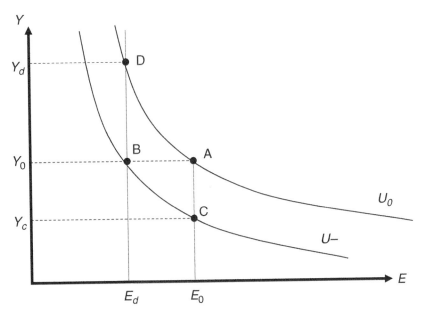

Figure 2.7 Neoclassical contingency value assessment, with indifference curves

level below Y^*, the combination with the highest level of income will be preferred, regardless of the size of the environmental good. The secondary element of choice, the size or quality of the environmental good E, plays a role only with combinations that feature equal levels of income. By contrast, once the threshold level of income Y^* is achieved (cf. Stevens et al., 1991, p. 398), the primary element of choice becomes the size of the environmental good, while private income reverts to a secondary element of choice, which plays a role only when combinations that feature equal environmental quality are compared. This algebraic example was proposed by Lockwood (1996, p. 89), and it corresponds to the graphical example provided by Edwards (1986, p. 148). Figure 2.8 illustrates this case. It is identical to the case illustrated by Figure 2.5 and equation (2.4), except that the axes are inverted, on the assumption that the z_2 characteristic, here income, is the primary element of choice until a threshold has been reached.

Below the threshold level of income Y^*, the quasi-indifference lines are horizontal, implying that the consumer prefers higher private consumption to lower private consumption, regardless of how much of the environmental good is being provided (D is preferred to F). The higher the horizontal quasi-indifference curve, the happier the consumer. However, for a given level of income, say Y_f, the person prefers more to fewer environmental goods (F is preferred to G). When the threshold level of income Y^* has been attained, the size of the environmental goods becomes the primary ordering criterion. The quasi-indifference curves become vertical. The further to the right the quasi-indifference curve, the better off the consumer is (bundle C is preferred to B). But for a given amount of environmental goods, say E_0, the higher the income level, the higher the satisfaction of the consumer (bundle A is preferred to C), which is what the arrows on each vertical quasi-indifference curve once again indicate.

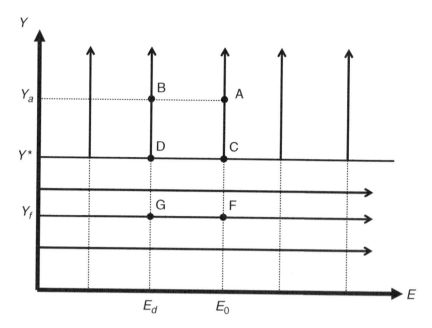

Figure 2.8 Contingency value assessment with choices of a lexicographic nature and quasi-indifference curves

What are the implications of such a preference set for contingency evaluation studies? Assume the consumer starts with combination A, with an income exceeding the threshold. Suppose this consumer is asked about a possible reduction in the size of the environmental good from E_0 to E_d. The likely willingness to pay (WTP) of this person will be $(Y_a - Y^*)$, that is, the entire discretionary income of the consumer, beyond the threshold income level. The consumer will drop down to combination C. Note, however, that the consumer is not indifferent between combination C and combination B, as was presumed in the neoclassical analysis of Figure 2.7. In Figure 2.8, the consumer still prefers combination C to combination B. The measured WTP thus underestimates the true value of environmental goods in the consumer mind. Note in addition that whatever the proposed reduction in the size of the environmental good, the income that can be given up remains the same, unless the reduction is so small that it does not trigger any negative feeling on the part of the consumer. On the other hand, if the consumer were to start with combination F, below the threshold level of income, WTP would be zero, or near zero, since more income is always preferred to less in this region.

What about the willingness to accept (WTA) compensation? Starting from the above-threshold combination A, the WTA is undefined, or it is infinite, since no amount of money will compensate for any loss in the quality of environment (Edwards, 1986, p. 148; Spash and Hanley, 1995, p. 193). Even an infinite amount of additional income will not procure enough compensation for the loss in the size of the environmental good to keep constant the consumer's level of satisfaction. Any reduction in the environmental good causes a reduction in the satisfaction of the consumer, since the environment is the primary criterion of choice above the income threshold.

Choices of a lexicographic nature thus explain why contingency valuation studies that solicit WTP and WTA estimates can arrive at widely different results. The use of one method, when the other is more appropriate, is not a matter of indifference. In addition, the WTP estimate does not correctly reflect the willingness to trade of the consumer. As Lockwood (1996, p. 92) points out, 'this sacrifice may not be regarded by the respondent as a transaction based on a free exchange, but as the payment of a ransom for recovery of a valued item'. Given all this, it is not surprising that several people surveyed in contingency valuation studies 'either refuse to participate in the survey, offer a protest response, try to play the game by inflating their response in an attempt to introduce their non-compensatory value into the process, or offer a WTP which is not a Hicksian measure of welfare change' (ibid., p. 91).

We thus have shown that there is a tight relationship between ecological and post-Keynesian economics, at least when it comes to methodology and choice theory, as recognized in particular by Mearman (2005) and Vatn (2009). Other works also underline the possible links between the two traditions (Kronenberg, 2010; Kesting, 2011).

2.3.5 Characteristics and Hierarchy

Consumption technology
The question now is: how do we formalize, to some extent, the principles developed in the previous subsections? Various formulations have been explicitly or implicitly suggested by various authors working outside the mainstream. In their presentation of humanistic economics, Lutz and Lux (1979) put together the Maslowian pyramid of needs with Georgescu-Roegen's plea to use lexicographic ordering or some form of it. In his search for more adequate foundations of consumer behaviour, Arrous (1978) proposes to put together Georgescu-Roegen's lexicographic ordering with Lancaster's analysis of the characteristics of goods. This approach is also the one that dominates Earl's latest essay on consumer behaviour (1986, p. 234), while Pasinetti (1981, p. 75) recommends making use of Lancaster's definition of a group of goods to identify a need. We will thus attempt to put together an analysis of needs that relies on an ordering of a lexicographic nature, where decisions are made on the basis of non-compensating priorities. The characteristics of the goods rather than the goods themselves will be the crucial distinctive elements, assuming, however, that goods can be joined together into groups.

It must be recognized that such a view is not totally novel, nor uniquely post-Keynesian. In their textbook on psychological economics, Lea et al. (1987, pp. 496–501) associate Lancaster's economics with Maslow's needs. In his own presentation, Lancaster (1971, pp. 146–56) recalls the importance of the hierarchy of needs (or of wants, as he calls them) as presented by certain earlier marginalists, relating these needs to sets of characteristics. Lancaster explains hierarchies by the possibility of satiation effects, when prices are positive and incomes finite. He establishes a link between the satiated needs of an individual and the income class to which that individual belongs, with the assumption that needs are partially ordered in a lexicographic way (Lancaster's 'dominance', as pointed out earlier). Similarly, Ironmonger (1972) proceeds to an analysis based on Georgescu-Roegen's distinction between utility and needs, using a technique reminiscent of Lancaster's. In Ironmonger's book, goods fulfil wants (Lancaster's characteristics), the latter being lexicographically ordered, with various satiation levels and income levels.

These non-orthodox views, however, have not been much disseminated among the mainstream, and as a result they can be considered as typically post-Keynesian.

Let us start by considering a consumption technology – that is, the relationship between goods and the characteristics that these goods provide. As a first approximation, one can think of these characteristics as being various wants. Let us suppose that there is a very simple consumption technology, with three characteristics, which we shall call z_1, z_2 and z_3, and four goods which we shall call x_1, x_2, x_3 and x_4. The technology matrix is given by $\mathbf{T}$ and the t_{ij}s indicate how many units of each characteristic are provided by one unit of each good. Prices are not considered at this stage. We thus have in matrix form

$$\mathbf{z} = \mathbf{T}.\mathbf{x} \qquad (2.5)$$

More explicitly, this equation looks like the following:

$$\begin{bmatrix} z_1 \\ z_2 \\ z_3 \end{bmatrix} = \begin{bmatrix} t_{11} & t_{12} & t_{13} & t_{14} \\ t_{21} & t_{22} & t_{23} & t_{24} \\ t_{31} & t_{32} & t_{33} & t_{34} \end{bmatrix} \begin{bmatrix} x_1 \\ x_2 \\ x_3 \\ x_4 \end{bmatrix}$$

If all t_{ij}s are positive, this means that each of the four goods contains all three characteristics. The four goods thus provide the same characteristics, but unless the t_{ij}s are proportional, the proportions in which these characteristics are provided by each good are different. Note that here it has been assumed that the consumption technology is linear; that is, doubling the quantity of a good doubles the amount of characteristics provided. This assumption is a simplifying one and is not very important, unless one attempts to derive from it conclusions about the shapes of demand curves, based on the optimality and uniqueness of the chosen bundles of goods (Watts and Gaston, 1982–83).

Let us now suppose that each good cannot fulfil all characteristics. Let us suppose further that we can separate goods according to the set of characteristics they fulfil – that is, goods that fulfil a given set of characteristics cannot fulfil other characteristics. These goods thus constitute an intrinsic group; that is, they respond to very precise and limited wants. The matrix of consumption technology is then said to be decomposable into submatrices. An example of such a decomposable matrix, with the previous notation, would be the following:

$$\begin{bmatrix} t_{11} & t_{12} & 0 & 0 \\ t_{21} & t_{22} & 0 & 0 \\ 0 & 0 & t_{33} & t_{34} \end{bmatrix}$$

Expanding the matrix, the relationship between the goods and the characteristics would then be the following:

$$z_1 = t_{11}.x_1 + t_{12}.x_2$$
$$z_2 = t_{21}.x_1 + t_{22}.x_2$$
$$z_3 = t_{33}.x_3 + t_{34}.x_4$$

In this example there are two distinct intrinsic groups. The first group is constituted by the goods x_1 and x_2, since they only cater to characteristics z_1 and z_2, while there are no other goods that can fulfil these two characteristics. We can also see that only goods x_3 and x_4 can provide characteristic z_3, and that these two goods provide no other characteristic. Therefore goods x_3 and x_4 also form a group, distinct from the first one. Lancaster's argument is then that one must distinguish between two types of substitution effects. Within a group, the increase in the price of a good might lead to its abandonment by all consumers since the other goods might eventually offer the same characteristics more efficiently, that is for a lower price. Lancaster calls this efficiency substitution. All consumers should act in a similar way within a group of goods. In the example above, in the second group, suppose that t_{33} is larger than t_{34}. This means that the price of good x_4 must be proportionally smaller than that of x_3 if both goods are to be part of the consumption basket. Otherwise, characteristic z_3 can be obtained from good x_3 at a lower cost than from good x_4, and the latter will not be bought at all. Efficiency substitution effects are based purely on technological parameters. They are not related to the preferences of individuals. Personal preferences play a role when it comes to comparing characteristics within a group or sets of characteristics between groups. For instance, if the agent has a strong preference for characteristic z_1, while good x_1 provides that characteristic at a low price, good x_1 may be preferred to good x_2, although the latter good provides characteristic z_2 very efficiently. Earl (1995, pp. 52–80) provides several visual examples of the use of an analysis based on characteristics, with or without preferences of a lexicographic nature.

We thus see that the combination of personal and efficiency substitution effects may provide the usual price substitution effects on which mainstream theory relies. Notwithstanding the fact that substitution within a group can be questioned when the technology of consumption is not linear, as was pointed out above, the notion of groups can be expanded in a direction that severely limits the extent of price substitution effects. Lancaster's analysis may be generalized to include the notion of needs and their irreducibility. Submatrices themselves can in fact be decomposed to form subgroups (Arrous, 1978, p. 259). We might thus suggest that efficiency substitution occurs only within subgroups. Each of these subgroups contains goods that are essentially identical, that is, the same goods under various brands (manufactured by different producers). Personal preference substitution occurs only between subgroups of the same group, while neither type of substitution can arise between goods of different groups. Irreducible needs are thus formally represented as sets of group characteristics, these sets showing no commensurability. Such a vision of consumer theory drastically reduces the extent and the power of price substitution.

Illustration of the irreducibility and overlap of needs
Figure 2.9 illustrates the decomposition of a matrix of consumption technology along the proposed lines. Within the technological matrix, the submatrices **A₁**, **A₂** and **A₃** of matrix **A** represent three subgroups. Within each of these submatrices, there can be efficiency and personal substitution. However, between the set of characteristics of **A₁** and that of **A₂** there can be only personal substitution. On the other hand, the matrices **A, B, C, D** and **E** are in order of dominance as they would be in Maslow's hierarchy of needs; that is, the characteristics of matrix **A** fulfil more basic needs than those of matrix **B**, while those of **B** fulfil more basic needs than do the characteristics of matrix **C**, and so on. The needs

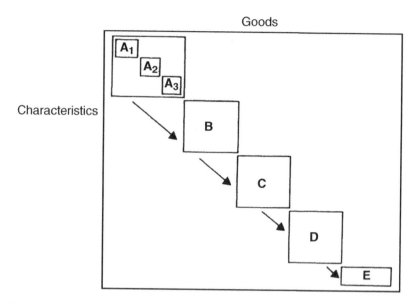

Figure 2.9 Subordination and irreducibility of needs: groups and subgroups of goods

corresponding to matrix **A** must be fulfilled; that is, the various thresholds and satiation levels must be attained before the consumer can start to consider the goods belonging to the groups of matrix **B**. To each of the five matrices within the matrix of consumption technology, one could attribute one of the five levels of needs ascribed to Maslow. We could thus say, following our earlier distinction in terminology, that the matrices **A**, **B** and so on represent needs for which there exists a hierarchy, while the submatrices A_1, A_2 and so on represent the various wants that can to a large extent be compensated.

We know that in reality things are not so simple. We have already seen that Maslow's hierarchy of needs has not been well demonstrated, and that it seems that only two or possibly three levels of needs can really be distinguished: one corresponds to the material needs and their social spin-offs, from which we can perhaps isolate the most necessary commodities; while the other coincides with the higher moral needs, the two levels being truly irreducible and independent of each other. Forgetting for now about the moral needs, one can also think of consumers as setting threshold levels for various types of expenditures, such as transport, lodging, vacations, entertainment and so on, and then deciding on a lexicographic order within each of these categories, as does Eichner (1987, p. 648) in his presentation of a decision tree. Let us call 'sub-needs' these various types of consumption expenditures that are ordered in a hierarchy. Consumers rank their possible expenditures over these sub-needs in a lexicographic pattern, each sub-need corresponding to a set of characteristics. While it is understood that the order is not irreversible, only the closest sub-needs may be substituted for each other. Each increase in income brings a revision of the thresholds, and therefore each consumer revises the same need on numerous occasions as income rises.

This type of behaviour is illustrated in Figure 2.10. Each of the three main matrices represents a category of expenditures, say food, lodging and entertainment. Each category of

Theory of choice 123

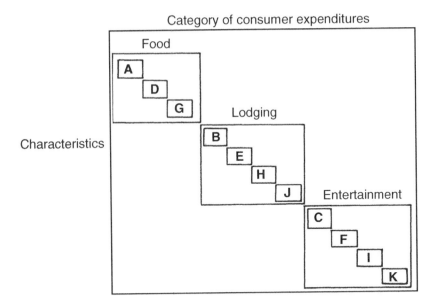

Figure 2.10 Subordination and overlap in needs: decision tree and sub-needs

expenditures presents characteristics that are linked to each other. The various submatrices **A, B, C** and so on represent the various sub-needs, each letter representing the rank of the sub-need. Consumers thus fulfil first their physiological needs, here food, then the other necessary ones, such as lodging. Entertainment is considered last, but then when some low thresholds have been reached, the consumer revises the criteria serving to appraise whether or not the need is being fulfilled, and new characteristics are then considered. The consumer may start looking for more sophisticated characteristics of food (submatrix **D**), instead of checking only the caloric intake. As income continues to rise, the criteria of acceptable housing, for instance, may be revised upwards and the consumer may start to look for some completely different type of housing, trying to fulfil the sub-need corresponding to submatrix **E**. All sub-needs are thus ordered in a lexicographic manner, but because of a considerable overlap between needs, as suggested by Joan Robinson in the passage quoted at the beginning of the section, consumers may visit each major need a considerable number of times. If the order is not perfectly lexicographic, as one would reasonably expect, one can imagine situations where sub-need **H** could be fulfilled before sub-need **G** but never before sub-need **F**. There would thus be some limited possibility of personal preference substitution between submatrices of adjoining rank, while efficiency substitution would be possible only within each submatrix.

2.3.6 Consequences for Price Theory

The subsidiary role of price substitution
The emphasis of orthodox theory on static behaviour has led to an excessive amount of research on substitution effects. On the other hand, income effects have been either neglected or assumed away. Whereas income effects used to be seriously considered, the

Engel curves being a well-known example of these dynamic effects, their importance in the eyes of most researchers has vanished. Those who have attempted to estimate the importance of pure substitution effects on the general categories of consumption expenditures, after having taken into consideration the income effects through time, have discovered that these substitution effects, own-price elasticities and cross-elasticities are quite negligible (Deaton and Muellbauer, 1980, p. 71). While the own-price elasticities of food, fuel, drinks, travel, entertainment and other services turned out to be negative, as expected, the absolute value of these elasticities was found to be no greater than 0.05. The price elasticity of clothing and housing was not statistically different from zero. These findings seem to correspond to the picture of consumer behaviour drawn in the preceding subsection. The cause of these small substitution effects, within the post-Keynesian framework, is that the large categories of consumer expenditures fulfil important needs that cannot be compensated one for another. Variations in their relative prices induce no change in consumption behaviour, or very small ones. Only within each one of these large spending categories could one possibly observe more substantial substitution effects. One can thus presume that the more disaggregated the analysis, the more likely we are to find high absolute values of price elasticities. However, the findings of Houthakker and Taylor (1970) show that even at a much more disaggregated level, that is with over 80 categories of consumer goods, consumption expenditures are mainly determined by habits and income effects, while price substitution effects play a fairly modest role.

The crucial issue here is that the fluctuations in the price of a good, unless they are really substantial, will not have much impact on the quantities sold. The major exception to this prediction is new goods being introduced to consumers. Innovations on the consumer market either create new needs or fulfil existing needs that were previously poorly met. Besides these innovative commodities, the reason that fluctuations of relative prices will have little impact on demand is that all goods respond to a need (or to a set of needs). Provided that these needs, or sub-needs, are arranged in a preset order, the decrease in the price of a good will only make it more attractive to consumers who have already attained that part of the pyramid. All those still trying to attain their threshold levels with respect to their basic needs will not be concerned by this price decrease. Furthermore, since a substantial amount of expenditure is made on the basis of habits and customs, the decrease in prices may go unnoticed unless it is heavily publicized. The decrease in the price of a good will have an impact only to the extent that it can replace other goods fulfilling the same needs, or more precisely what we have called the same wants. This is the traditional substitution effect, limited however to the goods that have similar characteristics. In classical theory, these goods were for practical purposes treated as identical (Schefold, 1985a, p. 112).

The symmetric consequences of the above is that changes in the prices of goods fulfilling needs at the higher levels of the hierarchy will have no impact whatsoever on the consumption of the goods at the lower levels of the hierarchy (Roy, 1943). The reason is that these goods are not part of the basket or of the hypothetical basket of consumption of all consumers who have not yet fulfilled the required thresholds of their lower needs. These poorer consumers just do not care about the prices of the goods that help to fulfil their higher needs since these goods cannot be acquired due to their budget constraint. On the other hand, if there is an increase (or a decrease) in the relative price of the goods that help to fulfil the more basic needs, this will have repercussions on the quantities sold of all goods belonging to the higher part of the hierarchy. A lower relative price will increase the real income of all households, leading to an increase in the consumption of all goods fulfilling the higher needs of the hierarchy.

Shaikh (2016, pp. 90–1) provides an interesting example of such a hierarchy. He assumes there are two groups of goods, necessaries and luxuries, which are consumed in quantities x_1 and x_2, with prices p_1 and p_2, under a budget constraint given by income Y. The maximum amount of necessaries that can be purchased is thus $x_{1max} = Y/p_1$. Shaikh then assumes that a minimum amount of necessaries, x_{1min}, will be consumed whatever the price. But how many more necessaries will be purchased if the consumer has an income greater than $p_1 x_{1min}$? Shaikh assumes that the consumer will add a proportion α of the feasible range of extra necessaries, $(x_{1max} - x_{1min})$, to her basket of necessaries. The consumption demand for necessary goods is thus

$$x_1 = x_{1min} + \alpha\left(\frac{Y}{p_1} - x_{1min}\right) \tag{2.6}$$

As to the consumption of luxuries, it can easily be computed from the budget constraint, $p_2 x_2 = Y - p_1 x_1$ and equation (2.6), so that we obtain

$$x_2 = -\left(\frac{p_1}{p_2}\right)(1-\alpha)x_{1min} + (1-\alpha)\left(\frac{Y}{p_2}\right) \tag{2.7}$$

Figure 2.11 illustrates the possible choices for such a consumer. It is obvious from equations (2.6) and (2.7) that the quantity x_1 of necessaries depends on p_1 but not on p_2, whereas the quantity of luxuries depends on both prices. From these equations, Shaikh (2016, pp. 92–93) computes the various elasticities of the two groups of goods – price

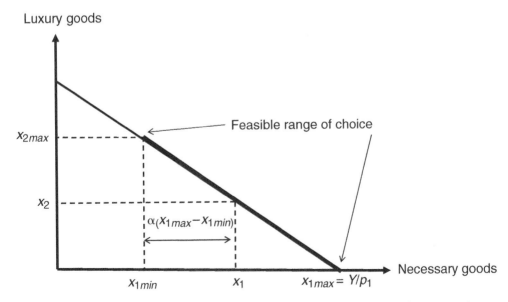

Figure 2.11 Asymmetric behaviour in the choice between necessary and luxury goods

elasticity, cross-elasticity, income elasticity – and finds established empirical results, for instance that the price and income elasticities of necessaries are smaller than unity, whereas the income elasticity of luxuries is greater than unity.

Ties with the classical and Sraffian analyses
What we have here is an asymmetric relation similar to the one established by the classical authors when they were discussing necessary goods and luxury ones (Roncaglia, 1978, p. 52). According to the classical classification, luxury goods were non-necessary goods that were not consumed by the workers. Only the rentiers and the capitalists could spend their income on luxury goods. Necessary goods, on the other hand, were consumed by both the workers and the upper classes. The consequence of this, according to Ricardo, was that changes in the production conditions of luxury goods or in their prices did not have repercussions on the overall rate of profit nor on the cost of producing necessary goods. On the other hand, changes in the prices or the production conditions of necessary goods had repercussions on the overall rate of profit and on the cost of production of luxury goods. The Sraffians have drawn similar conclusions from Sraffa's analysis of basic and non-basic commodities, the former playing the role of the necessary goods, so to speak, while the latter replaced the role played by luxury goods. Steedman (1980) has integrated the classical theory with the Sraffian approach by showing that in a world of heterogeneous labour, the rate of profit does not depend on the overall average real wage rate. Rather, only the real wage rate of workers producing goods consumed by workers is a determinant of the rate of profit.

There is thus a strong relationship between the classical and Sraffian asymmetric conception of the economy and the post-Keynesian theory of consumer behaviour, based on a hierarchy of needs and hence presumably on a hierarchy of goods, from the more basic necessaries to the products of high luxury. Whereas the Sraffian focus is on the consequences of this asymmetric relation for the determinants of relative prices, the impact of the asymmetry for the post-Keynesian theory is on the quantities consumed. Using the same conceptual framework that distinguishes between goods fulfilling lower needs and those responding to higher needs, the Sraffians tell us how a change in the conditions of production or in the composition of demand by the workers could affect relative prices or the purchasing power of consumers through the cost side. On the other hand, post-Keynesian theory shows how these changes in purchasing power are translated into increases in the quantities consumed of the various products, and how little substitution effects are induced by changes in relative prices, owing to the existence of hierarchical needs and sub-needs.

One may thus conclude that, when changes in relative prices are small, the substitution effects that they induce can be ignored, either because they are negligible, as in the case of goods fulfilling different needs, or because they concern goods that may be considered identical for all practical purposes. On the other hand, substantial changes in the relative price of a good are usually associated with novel products, which create new needs. Pure substitution effects in this case do not arise, since this consumption innovation needs to be incorporated within the hierarchy of needs and wants. This picture of the lack of importance of the substitution effect in consumer behaviour is certainly compatible with the views of Sraffian authors:

If the effect of the price on the quantity bought is not appreciable, then the effect can be ignored without great error. Alternatively, when the effect is important enough to need general consideration, it seems it will often be the case that the effect constitutes an *irreversible* change, which is incompatible with its treatment in terms of a demand function. That is, the effect will entail a permanent change in the habits of consumers, which even marginalist authors would have to treat as a change in 'tastes'. (Garegnani, 1990b, p. 131)

If one accepts the principles that are the building blocks of the post-Keynesian theory of consumer theory, macroeconomic constructions that focus on classes and groups of agents appear more reliable. We have seen that the stability of the neoclassical theory of the exchange economy depended in the end on assuming the existence of a representative agent, that is, on the assumption that all agents had identical preferences and identical incomes. Post-Keynesian analysis leads to the conviction that agents or households belonging to the same income class have a similar structure of consumption. We know, however, that agents do not have identical incomes. There is thus ample justification for utilizing income classes rather than the representative agent or a large number of differentiated individuals in macroeconomic studies. Furthermore, since income changes rather than price changes appear to be the main influence on modifications in the structure of consumption expenditures, the importance of the study of income effects in macroeconomics is reasserted.

Ironically, Eric Kemp-Benedict (2013) argues that post-Keynesian consumer theory as presented here provides an answer to the Sonnenschein–Mantel–Debreu impossibility theorem discussed in Chapter 1. Kemp-Benedict claims that interdependence in consumption and the presence of basic needs common to all consumers and representing a substantial portion of household expenditures even in industrialized countries provides a solution to the aggregation problem.

NOTE

* Besides relying on and extending the 1992 *Foundations*, full sentences have been taken from the following publications: 'Post-Keynesian consumer theory: potential synergies with consumer research and economic psychology', *Journal of Economic Psychology*, **25** (5), 2004, pp. 639–49; 'Post Keynesian consumer choice theory and ecological economics', in R.P.F. Holt, S. Pressman and C.L. Spash (eds), *Post Keynesian and Ecological Economics: Confronting Environmental Issues*, Cheltenham, UK and Northampton, MA, USA: Edward Elgar Publishing, 2010, pp. 141–57.

3. Theory of the firm*

3.1 A SHARED VISION

First-year students of economics are usually impressed by the symmetry of mainstream microeconomics. Firms maximize profits, just as households are assumed to maximize utility. After having mastered the shapes of the total utility curve and that of the indifference curves in the chapters covering consumer theory, students simply have to reproduce these curves to obtain the total product curve and the isoquants of production theory. The U-shaped cost functions are then derived. It is at this stage that the instructor has to be most vigilant, for students who have had working experience will object to the implication that average total costs eventually rise with sales. The law of decreasing returns has to be hammered in for order to be preserved. Nevertheless, when students enter intermediate microeconomics, these doubts about the coherence between reality and theory will be eliminated by the necessity of handling the required mathematics and Lagrangeans.

The objective of this chapter is to present a more realistic view of the typical firm and to show that this view is shared by all post-Keynesians. Four main themes will be tackled: the objectives of the firm; the shapes of cost curves and why there is excess capacity; the pricing procedures followed by firms and the possible determinants of the margins on costs when pricing decisions are made; and the links with the Sraffian prices of production.

To answer these questions, the contributions of authors from various heterodox schools will be considered. Although there is no necessary agreement on the details of the theory of the firm, these various authors share a vision. Post-Keynesian authors, at least since the late 1960s, conceived of the firm on similar grounds. The picture occasionally drawn by Kaldor and Robinson is consistent with that presented by Kalecki and the Kaleckians, such as Steindl. There is also much consistency with the then contemporary views of Oxford specialists of the firm, members of the Oxford Economists' Research Group such as Hall and Hitch, Harrod, Andrews and Brunner, as well as with the views that were associated a bit later with the Department of Applied Economics at Cambridge – Godley, Coutts and Norman. Indeed, Eichner (1978, p. 1436) writes that 'when the history of the post-Keynesian alternative to the orthodox theory comes to be written, it should be noted that the English roots of its microeconomics are to be found at Oxford, even more so than at Cambridge'.

There is also much consistency with the views of American Institutionalists, the specialists of administered prices, such as Means, Lanzillotti and Galbraith, and even those of Marxians Baran and Sweezy. More recently, the works of post-Keynesians, mainly Eichner and Lee, have highlighted the importance of non-neoclassical foundations of the theory of the firm, following in the footsteps of Sylos Labini. We shall also see that the framework developed by all these economists is quite coherent with the notions of uncertainty and bounded rationality presented in Chapter 2, and developed in the case of the firm in the so-called behavioural theories of Cyert and March or in the evolutionary theories of the firm associated with Nelson and Winter. It is of course possible to find other, perhaps lesser-known, authors who have developed various aspects of the post-Keynesian theory of the firm. We do not wish to deal strictly with economic history, however, and shall stick to the authors identified above.

Before we move to the crux of the matter, it may be worthwhile to consider a possible controversy tied to the history of economic thought. Both Lee and Irving-Lessmann (1992) and Marcuzzo and Sanfilippo (2009) have pointed out that there is some irony in noting that those usually considered to be the originators of the post-Keynesian school – Kahn, Robinson, Kalecki – were rather critical of the non-marginalist approach proposed by the members of the Oxford pricing study group in the 1930s and 1940s, namely Andrews as well as Hall and Hitch, adding that Kalecki himself, for a while, relied on marginalism. What is perhaps even more ironic is that just as the pricing views of the Oxford economists were gradually being rejected and marginalized by the economics profession in the 1950s, Kalecki repudiated marginalism and the hypothesis of profit maximization, while Robinson was slowly moving towards an Andrewsian view of pricing, which she fully endorsed in her *Accumulation of Capital* (1956), with her concept of the 'subjective normal price' (Lavoie, 1996a). Indeed, Lee (2011, p. 5) grants that 'Andrews's degree of competition and Kalecki's degree of monopoly are, once the ideology is ignored, more or less the same thing', and hence concurs with Eichner (1978, p. 1437), who wrote that 'if Kalecki had labeled the same set of factors "the degree of competition", it is doubtful that Andrews would have objected'. Today, as Eichner adds, 'anyone reading through all of Andrews's work and then comparing it with the post-Keynesian literature would be hard pressed to find any differences – except in terminology, emphasis, and the relative importance of various ideas'.

3.2 COMPETITION AND THE POST-KEYNESIAN FIRM

3.2.1 The Range of the Post-Keynesian Firm

To clarify matters, it might be appropriate at this stage to use Alfred Eichner's description of the four important characteristics of the relevant firm in the modern world, a firm that Eichner (1976) calls the megacorp. As its name indicates, this is a large firm: management is separated from proprietorship; marginal costs are approximately constant; and the firm operates in at least one industry of the oligopolistic type. Our discussion of the characteristics of the post-Keynesian firm will thus evolve around these four characteristics.

The main point of contention, related to the non-clearing aspect of prices, is whether or not the typical firm that post-Keynesians describe is necessarily set within an oligopolistic industry. It needs to be recognized that studying the behaviour of the price leader in an oligopolistic industry may lead to more satisfactory and more determinate results than if one studies the behaviour of a small firm operating in an industry where there is no dominant actor. Besides Eichner, several other post-Keynesians have noted that oligopolies constitute their representative post-Keynesian industry. Kaldor, for instance, has indicated on a number of occasions that the industrial model he is implicitly working with is 'a kind of oligopoly-cum-price-leadership theory' (1970a, p. 3), that is a theory where one assumes 'the prevalence of imperfect markets and oligopolistic competition, where prices are set by the leading firms, based on costs' (1978a, p. 21).

To argue that the post-Keynesian firm operates mainly in oligopolistic industries unnecessarily restricts the range of post-Keynesian theory. Means has denied that cost-plus pricing, or administered pricing, as he called it, applies only to monopoly: 'Administered prices should not be confused with monopoly ... In general monopolised industries have administered prices, but so also do a great many vigorously competitive industries in which the number of competitors is small' (quoted in Clifton, 1983, p. 24). Similarly, we can deny that cost-plus pricing applies only to monopolies and oligopolies. It has been recognized by several economists that the phenomenon of mark-up pricing, one of the important features of post-Keynesian firms, is 'simply too pervasive across the United States economy to be attributable to oligopoly' (Okun, 1981, pp. 175–6). Rigid cost-plus pricing is observed not only in the car or the computer industries but also in retail trades in which large firms do not dominate. This was one of the remarkable results of the survey by Hall and Hitch.

> The answers also suggest that the distinction between monopoly and monopolistic competition on the one hand and monopolistic competition with an admixture of oligopoly elements on the other is not of very great importance ... It proved to be extremely difficult in practice to distinguish between oligopolistic firms and others. The distinction seems to be almost entirely one of degree, for all firms were conscious to some extent of the presence of competitors and the possibility of reactions to changes in their price and output policy ... Where this element of oligopoly is present, and in many cases where it is absent, there is a strong tendency among businessmen to fix prices directly at a level which they regard as their 'full cost'. (Hall and Hitch, 1939, pp. 30–31)

The view taken here is thus the converse of that advanced by the advocates of contestable markets (Baumol, 1982; see Davies and Lee, 1988 for a critique). All markets, with the exceptions soon to be elaborated upon, can be brought back under the umbrella of imperfect markets, where prices in the short run basically depend upon costs, according to some principle of mark-up or full-cost pricing.

3.2.2 Alternative Ways to Differentiate Markets

The better-known distinction in analysing markets is probably that made by Hicks (1974), with his dichotomy of flexprice and fixprice markets. The latter are associated with normal costs, to be found mainly in manufacturing. Sylos Labini (1971, p. 245) adds the tertiary sector to fixprice markets. All this is consistent with Kalecki's opinion, according to which the prices of agricultural products and raw materials are determined by the interaction of supply and demand, mainly because any increase in production requires long delays, but also because, mining products being homogeneous, they are subject to speculation on futures markets. On the other hand, finished goods and industrial products are cost determined because there are reserves of capacity that allow flexibility in responding to demand changes. Kalecki (1971, pp. 43–5) adds that in these markets there must be some form of imperfect competition for excess capacities to prevail in the long run. While there is clearly an agreement as to whether the secondary and even the tertiary sectors fall under the domain of the imperfect market and therefore of the post-Keynesian firm, the case of the primary sector is less clear. In the case of mining products and even some agricultural goods (through marketing boards), competition does not always prevail and we should therefore expect prices to be fixed independently of demand. We could thus say that the representative post-Keynesian firm prevails everywhere, except in those industries where output is produced in batches, as in some areas of agriculture, or where output is not easily reproducible, as in the art market or for some commodities, or where prices are set in auction markets.

One could also link this post-Keynesian firm to the notion of reproducible goods: where products are reproducible, we should expect marginal costs to be linear up to capacity; that is, we should observe inverted L-shaped average variable cost curves. Commodities that are not reproducible, as is the case of natural resources, or that require long delays to increase their production – the case of agricultural goods – correspond to the U-shaped marginal cost curves of the standard neoclassical firm. The ability to fix prices, what Means has called administered prices, relies on something more than monopolistic power. It relies on the shape of the costs inherent to the type of technology in use. This is a point made by Means (1936, p. 35) himself, when he links the presence of administered prices, in opposition to flexible prices, to the existence of modern technology. We can relate this to Kalecki's distinction between cost-determined and demand-determined sectors, where 'it is clear that these two types of price formation arise out of different conditions of supply' (Kalecki, 1971, p. 43). According to Kalecki, there is a link between cost-determined prices or fixed prices, excess capacities, constant marginal costs and imperfect competition. On the other hand, prices that are sensitive to variations in demand are associated with rising marginal costs and homogeneous products, the latter being an element of traditional competition. The same link between administered pricing and the modern conditions of production of reproducible goods has been proposed by Kahn (1977).

As can be seen from Table 3.1, there are many ways in which markets and their products can be assessed, in addition to the first four already discussed. Coutts and Norman (2007) acknowledge that post-Keynesian pricing theory is more likely to apply when goods are heterogeneous and with product differentiation, a feature empirically verified by Henk-Jan Brinkman (1999). The additional four authors mentioned – Sawyer, Okun, Chandler and Melmiès – all relate their distinction to the kind of market involved. Thus one would presume that, in centralized markets, auction-market prices would be possible, and hence that we would observe market-determined prices, with firms being price-takers, so that one would have the impression that prices are determined by the invisible hand of markets. By contrast, decentralized markets would be associated with price-tag markets, with firm-determined prices, and hence with the visible hand of management. Sawyer (1995, p. 310) makes the further point that administered pricing is the result of a long-term strategy, a point endorsed by Gu and Lee (2012, p. 463) and by Shapiro and Sawyer (2003). We shall return to this issue when we discuss the determinants of costing margins.

We may thus sum up the issue of the domain of validity of the post-Keynesian firm by saying that post-Keynesians assert that there are hardly any markets, besides financial markets, where prices are not administered by firms. Administered pricing is a generalized phenomenon that goes beyond oligopolistic structures.

Table 3.1 Different approaches to markets

Author	Post-Keynesian theory	Orthodox theory
Kalecki (1971)	Cost-determined prices	Demand-determined prices
Means (1936)	Inflexible prices	Flexible prices
	Administered prices	Market-clearing prices
Hicks (1974)	Fixprice markets	Flexprice markets
Sraffians	Reproducible commodities	Non-reproducible goods
Sawyer (1995)	Firm-determined prices	Market-determined prices
	Long-term strategic prices	Short-term prices
Okun (1981)	Price-maker	Price-taker
	Price-tag markets	Auction-market prices
Chandler (1977)	Visible hand of management	Invisible hand of markets
Melmiès (2010)	Decentralized markets	Centralized markets
Coutts and Norman (2007)	Heterogeneous goods with product differentiation	Homogeneous goods

3.2.3 Non-price Competition

For post-Keynesians, competition does not occur so much through pricing. Rather, one could argue that it occurs through costs, by attempts to reduce unit costs and achieve greater profit margins than those of competitors. Competitive activities 'can create profound cost differences between enterprises so that many are driven from the market', and they 'center on investment decisions, on advertising decisions, on decisions regarding research and development, and on production decisions and controlling the production process' (Lee, 2013b, p. 169). Tuna Baskoy (2011; 2012) also argues that competition occurs through the access to financial resources and the use of discretionary expenditures such as advertising, marketing, research and development, and the investment in larger and more productive capacities. Firms improve their competitive position and their market shares through product differentiation, product improvements, and the creation of new and innovative products. A good example of this is the market for phone handsets, where the appearance of innovative products completely modifies market shares of cell phones.

Thus what we have here is a sort of neo-Schumpeterian view of competition, where firms rise or fall according to three main characteristics. As Metcalfe (2013, p. 119) puts it these characteristics are: 'differences in the quality and thus value of the goods being produced and in their methods of production; differences in the desire and capacity of the firms to expand; and differences in the desire and capacity to innovate in order to improve products and methods'.

Competition is a dynamic process, not an end-state or a static situation. Thus competition occurs mainly through non-pricing means, because price competition – price war – is likely to squeeze business profits, become ruinous, and lead to bankruptcies. In addition, price competition is likely to bring about behaviour that is overly risky. Too much competition may induce lower product quality, as the consequence of desperate attempts to cut into unit costs. In other words, too much competition, meaning too much competition through prices, is not optimal. Thus the post-Keynesian position on the value of competition is rather ambiguous. Post-Keynesians have an evolutionary view of competition, which resembles that of Schumpeter (1943, p. 639), according to whom 'perfect competition is not only impossible but inferior, and has no title to being set up as a model of ideal efficiency' – an argument that has recently been taken up by Lazonick (2022) under the name of the 'neoclassical fallacy'.

3.3 THE OBJECTIVES OF THE FIRM

3.3.1 Power

If one attempted to characterize briefly the received view of the objectives of the firm, one would draw the following picture: small firms operate in competitive markets and attempt to maximize profits, more specifically short-run profits; larger firms, because they operate in imperfect markets and because their management is divorced from ownership, generally pursue goals other than profit maximization, and hence pay incentives must be put in place to realign the interests of managers with those of owners. Here I argue that the objectives of firms are the same, irrespective of their size and of their type of control, and that this objective is not profit maximization. To the extent that profit motives have a substantial role to play, it will be argued that profits are means rather than ends.

The question of the objectives of the firm or those of their managers has generated a substantial amount of attention from economists. Various maximands such as sales, managers' utility and valuation ratios have been proposed, not to speak of goals of the satisficing type, such as normal rates of return or market shares. In front of this array of objectives, the only rational response is to assume that firms have multi-purpose objectives. This is the view that many empirical researchers take after having admitted that the empirical evidence is unclear (Koutsoyiannis, 1975, p. 258). Indeed, in surveys of their objectives, entrepreneurs often indicate several of them rather than the standard profit maximization hypothesis (Shipley, 1981, p. 442). Among post-Keynesians, while John Kenneth Galbraith (1975, p. 124) has claimed that it would be a serious error 'to seek a single explanation of how firms behave', Joan Robinson (1977, p. 11) has argued that firms have motivations that are multidimensional and that as a consequence 'it will never be possible to get a knock-down answer'. Besides the obvious fact that there is no reason to presume that different firms will behave identically, or that the various constituents of the modern firm pursue identical goals, the main cause of these distressing results is that the ultimate objective of the firm can be defined in only very general terms. The consequence of this is that various intermediate goals that serve to fulfil that ultimate objective will be proposed, by either the theoreticians or the business world itself.

My view is that power is the ultimate objective of the firm: power over its environment, whether it be economic, social or political. 'Power is the ability of an individual or a group to impose its purpose on others' (Galbraith, 1975, p. 108). The firm wants power over its suppliers of materials, over its customers, over the government, over legislation, and over the kind of technology to be put in use. Business firms 'make strategic decisions under uncertainty to pursue power over pricing, investment and financing' (Baskoy, 2011,

p. 124). The firm, whether it is a megacorp or a small family firm, would like to have control over future events, its financial requirements, the quality of its labour force, the prices of the industry, the possibility of takeovers. 'The firm is viewed as being able to exercise a degree of control over its environment through R&D, market development, interfirm cooperation, entry deterrence' (Davies and Lee, 1988, p. 21). Several authors have affirmed that 'power is the central concern of the Post-Keynesian theory' of the firm, because 'survival in the market requires market power; the enterprises that survive in the market are the ones that can affect its outcome' (Shapiro and Mott, 1995, p. 38).

Power and fundamental uncertainty
In his book on the economics of Galbraith, Dunn (2011) points to the importance of fundamental uncertainty in explaining megacorps and the role of power. 'The Galbraithian view of the firm is that it emerges in response to the uncertainties that surround major and complex, long-term investments', so that the firm is 'an institution for coping with, or getting rid of, market uncertainties' (ibid., p. 183). The corporation 'represents an enduring institutional response to an uncertain future specifically designed to mitigate its impact' (p. 203). 'To thrive, firms seek to control the market, growing through acquisitions and dominating the supply chain. The large firm thus emerges as a planning response to the uncertain nature of markets' (p. 333). Indeed, Dunn (ibid., p. 217) goes so far as to argue that the rise of large multinational firms is a response to the 'peculiar uncertainties and needs of international trade'. In a world without uncertainty, the notion of power dissolves and loses much of its importance. In such a world, for instance, firms always know if their investment projects will be successful and they have access to all the financial capital they require provided their investment project is expected to be profitable. The source of financing is indifferent and the Miller–Modigliani theorem would apply.

However, in a world where fundamental uncertainty prevails, firms must find means to guarantee access to financial capital, all their material inputs, or critical information. Powerful relations allow corporations to have access to scarce information without which firms would be immobilized. Furthermore, the control over events constitutes the means by which firms can evade the inaction that pervades uncertain situations. Power allows firms to 'control the consequences of their own decisions in order to prevent their desires being thwarted by others' (Dixon, 1986, p. 588). All firms thus look for more power over their environment. At a more fundamental level, perhaps, the search for power procures security to the individual owner or to the organization. Firms would like to ensure their long-run survival, the permanence of their own institution. 'For any organization, as for any organism, the goal or the objective that has a natural assumption of preeminence is the organization's survival. This, plausibly, is true of the technostructure' (Galbraith, 1972, p. 170). A powerful control over events and human actors provides the conditions for such long-run existential goals.

The notion of power, except when related to the case of the pure monopoly, has been systematically ignored in economics, with the exception of Institutionalists and Marxians. Among the former, Galbraith is probably the best-known exponent of the importance of power in the economic sphere. As argued above, the power that firms attempt to obtain is not limited to the market sphere: it extends to the political and the social spheres. Besides the implementation of new processes, the differentiation of old commodities, the marketing of new products, firms try to escape the established market structures and to act on them through the lobbying of public authorities and the formation of social norms. It is amusing to note that these strategies were outlined by French economist Jean Marchal, in an article published in the *American Economic Review*, to which the referee objected that power struggles pertained to Europe but not to the USA, where 'we have the purest of pure competition' (Marchal, 1951, p. 565). It is then easy to comprehend why Galbraith's vision of the American industrial state generated so much negative response from his fellow economists, as recalled by Dunn (2011, pp. 3, 54 and 174). Galbraith has emphasized the role of power for the megacorp along the lines suggested by Marchal. One should not forget, however, that this search for power is just as important for the small entrepreneurial firm that is trying to take off as it can be for the technostructure.

> The need to control environment – to exclude untoward events – encourages much greater size. The larger the firm, the larger it will be in its industry. The greater, accordingly, will be its influence in setting prices and costs. And the greater, in general, will be its influence on consumers, the community and the state – the greater, in short, will be its ability to influence, i.e., plan, its environment. More important, as organization develops and becomes more elaborate, the greater will be its freedom from external interference. (Galbraith, 1975, p. 56)

The quest for power and growth is as valid at the level of the organization as it can be at the level of the individual working within the corporation. Whereas a successful quest for power will endow the firm with stability and permanence, it will simultaneously endow the individual with a successful career, the opportunity of promotion, the availability of higher social status, respect of peers – all the items that comprise the upper echelons of Maslow's pyramid of needs. Thus we can understand the numerous studies that have underlined the maximization of managers' satisfaction, the so-called managerial theories of the firm. The gains from a more powerful corporation are not limited to the managers, however; they apply to the whole technostructure. Galbraith continues:

> As organization acquires power, it uses that power, not surprisingly, to serve the ends of those involved. These ends – job security, pay, promotion, prestige, company plane and private washroom, the charm of collectively exercised power – are all strongly served by the growth of the enterprise. So growth both enhances power over prices, costs, consumers, suppliers, the community and the state and also rewards in a very personal way those who bring it about. (Ibid.)

Management, ownership and financialization

This brings to the forefront the question of the separation between management and ownership, famous since the publication of the classic study of Berle and Means (1933), and known to Institutionalists as Veblenian 'absentee ownership'. Would the managers of a company still controlled by its owners behave any differently from those of a management-controlled one? Both Eichner and Galbraith imply that they would, insisting as they do on the consequences of the divorce between proprietorship and management. My opinion is that there is no need to emphasize that divorce. There is no or little evidence of performance differentials between owner-controlled and management-controlled corporations. Most studies seem to show that there is no discrepancy with respect to growth of sales and assets, advertising, salaries, the variability of investment and dividends. Most importantly, there is no differential with respect to profitability variables, such as earnings per share, return on equity and dividend per share. An argument could then be made, similar to that supporting the contestable-market hypothesis, that the forces of competition constrain management-controlled companies to behave as efficiently as firms controlled by their owners. It appears, however, that firms operating in concentrated industries and firms that are dominant in their markets do not exhibit any larger differentials than those operating under more competitive conditions, so that it must be concluded that '*competitive forces* are unlikely to be the *root* cause of similarity in owner-manager performance' (Kania and McKean, 1976, p. 288).

The Galbraithian view of the firm has been questioned by theoretical and actual developments in the governance of the firm. On the theoretical front, financial economists proposed agency theories, with a principal and an agent, the principal being the shareholder and the agent being the managers of firms. This led to the multiplication of stock-options pay schemes, in the hope of aligning the interests of the managers with those of the shareholders, giving rise to a principle of corporate governance according to which managers ought to maximize shareholder value, a principle that was even endorsed by the OECD. A series of changes and innovations in corporate governance and strategies took place, running from hostile takeovers (initially with the help of junk bonds), the creation of private equity funds, and the rising importance and influence of large financial institutions – banks, pension funds and mutual funds.

This was accompanied by a change in the mood of corporations, with a change in the regime of accumulation from 'retain and reinvest' towards a 'downsize and distribute' strategy, whereby American firms attempted to reduce costs by laying off a large number of workers, trying to achieve more with less, in an attempt to achieve high rates of return on equity (Lazonick and O'Sullivan, 2000; Dore, 2000). All this has been associated with the phenomenon of 'financialization', also referred to as 'marketization' or 'equitization' (Dore, 2002, pp. 116–17), or with the term 'money-manager capitalism' (Wray, 2008; 2009). This should be contrasted with managerial capitalism, in which 'the primary objective of top management is the *long-term reproduction, growth and safety of the firm itself*, and where 'stockholder interests are not an objective pursued by management but rather a constraint upon it' (Crotty, 1990, p. 533).

In the meantime, it can be pointed out that Galbraith himself did not seem much impressed by these theoretical and practical developments. In 2004, when the regime of money-manager capitalism seemed to be in full force, Galbraith (2004) was still arguing that the control of firms by shareholders was a myth – an innocent fraud. For Galbraith, meetings of the boards of directors or the general annual meetings are a sideshow. Despite the strength of the finance sector and the pressures exerted by institutional investors, the power still resides with the managers of firms (financial and non-financial ones). The proof, according to Galbraith, is that top managers still determine their own remuneration and now extract ever higher salaries and bonuses, and that this upward spiral in remuneration seems unrelated to the profits achieved by the firm.

Making the same point, Pascal Petit (2005) adds that 'the financialization of company governance is largely triggered by the managers of the financial sector who derive an advantage from that situation, in particular through restructuring operations'. Galbraith's technostructure may have lost some of its influence, but core or top management has not. As Boyer (2005, p. 8) puts it, 'managers have used the pressures of institutional investors and diverted them to their own benefit', adding that even takeover operations were mostly beneficial to top managers, and not to the shareholders. Dunn, providing support to the Galbraithian view, also expresses doubts as to whether the new age of financialization and money-manager capitalism has truly modified the relationship between owners and managers. Dunn (2011, p. 9) thinks 'it is far from clear that the modern firm is now effectively policed by investors and stockholders alike'. All these sceptics about the rise of a new capitalism point to the numerous inside frauds committed by management that were uncovered in the early 2000s, with Enron, Worldcom, Tyco, Palmalat, Nortel, and their accounting firms. Perhaps more than anything, what has changed and gone downwards is the regulation of economic activity and the ethics of those running businesses, who are now more concerned with their own wealth than that of their firms or that of other stakeholders, in particular the workers of the firm.

Studies on pay compensation of executives also provide some support to the Galbraithian firm. It is a well-known fact that 'compensation rises, on average, proportionately with the logarithm of company size, for chief executives' (Simon, 1997, p. 67). Studies still show that for both non-financial and financial firms, 'the primary factor related to executive pay appears to be firm size' (Gregg et al., 2012, p. 117). While it is often argued that the executive pay packages are overly aligned towards short-run goals and the stock market performance of the firm, it turns out that the most important incentive, as reflected in Gregg et al.'s regressions, remains that the assets of the firm should be as large as possible. Furthermore, surprisingly, these authors find little evidence of an upward trend in pay-performance elasticities over time. Sonenshine et al. (2016) find however that the compensation of chief executives after the 2008 financial crisis became more strongly linked to firm performance, such as stock returns and earnings per share.

That managers are paid more as a function of the size of their firm than as a function of their financial results may not be such a bad thing. Experiments have shown that large financial stakes lead to big mistakes. Excessive monetary rewards lead to a decline in performance that draws on motor skills, memory and creativity (rather than pure physical strength). It may thus be that pay schemes based on performance bonuses and stock options have perverse effects, so that, in the language of agency theory, as Ariely et al. (2009, p. 467) put it, over-motivated principals (the investors in stock market shares) have to be aware of 'the performance-debilitating effects of high incentives' for their agents (the managers).

3.3.2 Growth

Assuming that power is indeed the ultimate objective of almost all types of firms (perhaps with the exception of small family-run firms, which just strive to survive and of private equity firms, whose purpose is to dismantle acquired firms (Reardon, 2009)), how can this objective be met? The answer is simple: to become powerful, firms must be big; to become big, firms must grow. As a first approximation, it may then be said that if firms attempt to maximize anything, they will try to maximize their rate of growth. The compelling need to survive, says Galbraith (1972, p. 174), requires 'to achieve the greatest possible rate of corporate growth as measured in sales'. Thus he concludes, 'the primary affirmative purpose of the technostructure is the growth of the firm' (1975, p. 116). This is not surprising: the larger the firm, the easier it is to overturn market forces, and 'the greater the scope for conscious planning of economic activity' (Penrose, 1959, p. 15). Besides Galbraith, and also historian Alfred Chandler (1977, pp. 8–10), several economists of the managerial school have emphasized the importance of growth as the major measurable objective of the firm, Marris (1964a) being the prime example. The short-run equivalent of the targeted growth of sales is Baumol's (1959) sales maximization – with Chirat (2022) showing that Baumol and Galbraith corresponded and influenced each other.

Growth is also a recurrent theme of post-Keynesian economics. Post-Keynesians have consistently asserted that firms maximize the rate of growth, subject to various constraints, or that the main analytical objective of the firm is to grow. Survival and growth are often associated, in opposition to the neoclassical viewpoint. This is asserted at both the microeconomic and macroeconomic levels. For the latter, for instance, Robinson (1962, p. 38) indicates that 'the central mechanism of accumulation is the urge of firms to survive and to grow'. A similar view can be found in Kaldor (1978a, p. 16), for whom 'the individual enterprise – for reasons first perceived by Marx – must go on expanding so as to keep its share in the market'. The reasons attributed to Marx, but also to Allyn Young, are the existence of increasing returns to scale, which give a cost advantage to firms holding large shares of the market. Increasing returns to scale preclude the neoclassical concept of the optimal firm size. It may be that the managerial coordination of activities becomes increasingly difficult as the firm gets bigger, but this is largely compensated by the increasing returns experienced on other inputs and through power. Growth, then, ensures economic power for those who already have it, no less than for those who strive for it. Indeed, growth simultaneously provides for the survival of the firm, the satisfaction of the managers and the hopes of the employees within the technostructure.

> For the executives who exercise effective control of the megacorp, the growth of the firm over time, because of the increase in power, prestige and remuneration which it brings in its wake, is the most important desideratum . . . It turns out that those megacorps which are most likely to survive in the long run are the megacorps which have attempted to grow at the highest possible rate by continuously diversifying and expanding into newer, more rapidly growing industries. Thus it is the need to ensure survival that dictates maximum growth as the goal of the firm. Those firms which fail to expand apace with the economy are likely to find themselves at an increasing disadvantage on a number of fronts. (Eichner, 1987, pp. 360–61)

I earlier asserted that the structure of control of the corporation would not have any noticeable impact on the behaviour or the goals of the firm. To acquire power, the ultimate objective, the decision-makers of the modern megacorp try to expand as quickly as is reasonably possible. The objective of growth, rather than the consumption of profit, is predominant, irrespective of the size of the firm. Adrian Wood, a post-Keynesian economist, has also emphasized the universality of the motive of growth, valid for the small as well as for the large firm, for the owner-controlled as well as for the management-controlled corporation.

> The basic goal of those in charge of the firm is to cause sales revenue to grow as rapidly as possible . . . But I do not agree with Marris that this pattern of behaviour is caused by the separation of ownership from control. Instead, I believe it to reflect the fact that (in so far as the two conflict) the urge for power is stronger than the urge for money. As a result, growth maximisation is a phenomenon which is to be observed in (all except the smallest) unincorporated firms and in closely owned companies as well as in large quoted companies with widely dispersed ownership. (Wood, 1975, p. 8)

This type of behaviour is not something entirely new, however. 'At all stages of capitalism development the growth of the firm has been the requisite for survival among competing firms' (Clifton, 1977, pp. 147–8). The old tycoons, so well described by Veblen, also strove for power and growth; and we may even presume that growth was the main objective of the small family firm of yesterday, despite being the neoclassical ideal of competition and the free market. Joan Robinson has admirably summed up this point of view in a long paragraph, which is worth reproducing in full here.

> Why do firms grow? Some contemporary writers are inclined to treat growth as a specially modern phenomenon arising from the divorce between control and property in the modern corporation, legally owned by a floating population of shareholders and operated by a cadre of salaried managers; they seem to suggest that there was a past period to which the textbook scheme applied. Yet obviously the successful family businesses of the early nineteenth century must have been just as keen on growth as any modern corporation. Anyone who is in business naturally wants to survive (particularly if his own heirs and successors are involved) and to survive it is necessary to grow. When a business is prosperous it is making profits; for that very reason it is threatened with competition; it would be feckless to distribute the whole net profit to the family for consumption; part must be ploughed back in increasing capacity so as to supply a growing market, to prevent others coming in, or to diversify production if the original market is not expanding. Any one, by growing, is threatening the position of others, who retaliate by expanding their own capacity, reducing production costs, changing the design of commodities, or introducing new devices of salesmanship. Thus each has to run to keep up with the rest. (Robinson, 1971, p. 101)

3.4 THE CONSTRAINTS ON GROWTH

Now that the primary objectives of the post-Keynesian firm have been established, these objectives being the acquisition of power and the expansion of the firm, what of the neoclassical concern with profit maximization? What is the role of profits in the post-Keynesian theory of the firm? What is the role, if any, of the shareholders?

3.4.1 The Importance of Retained Earnings

Satisficing and procedural rationality
The standard critique of the neoclassical theory of the firm is that profit maximization is not possible because of the lack of pertinent knowledge due to an uncertain environment. The claim is that both family businesses and corporate managers do not try to maximize anything, attempting instead to achieve various aspiration levels. This is the so-called behavioural model of the firm associated with Simon (1979b) and Cyert and March (1963). As summarized by Anna Koutsoyiannis (1975, p. 389), 'the firm in the behavioural theories seeks to *satisfice*, that is, to attain a "satisfactory" overall performance, as defined by the set of aspiration goals, rather than maximize profits, sales or other magnitudes'. This may include a satisfactory level of production, a satisfactory level of share of the market, a satisfactory level of profit, a satisfactory amount devoted to research and development, a satisfactory public image, a satisfactory amount of perks and other 'slack' payments. Satisficing occurs, first because firms are a coalition of groups with conflicting interests, and second because managers must take decisions that reconcile these interests based on information that is hard to get and can be hard to process. Managers are 'people

with limited time at their disposal, have limited and imperfect information and limited computational ability. Hence it is impossible for them to examine all possible alternatives open to them . . . Instead they . . . choose the "best" given their limited time, information and computational abilities' (Koutsoyiannis, 1975, p. 390). The problem is not so much that of a scarcity of information; rather the problem is an overload of complex information within an uncertain environment, and the difficulty in assessing which information is truly relevant. We discussed these issues in Chapter 2.

This view of the firm is certainly valid. In particular, it reflects the need for managers to achieve a high enough rate of return to satisfy the pressures of investors and to provide a constant stream of dividends to shareholders in order to keep them quiet. This satisficing view of profits must, however, be reassessed in a context of growth. The consensus opinion among post-Keynesians is that profits are the means that allow firms to grow. Of financial necessity, profits cannot be disconnected from investment and growth. The growth objectives set by decision-makers are constrained by the financial requirements of profitability, past and expected. There is thus strong opposition to the neoclassical view of perfect capital markets, according to which all that needs to be demonstrated is the seriousness and the future expected profitability of the projected investment. This sounds very much like the 'new economy' craze, with its free-wheeling financing of Internet and software start-ups, which lasted until the NASDAQ crash of 2000, and which resurfaces on occasion.

Post-Keynesians believe that bankers lend money only to those who already have it. Outside the neoclassical world of certainty or certainty equivalence, the biblical principle 'unto every one that hath shall be given' generally applies, as pointed out by Kaldor (1978a, p. 16): 'Finance raised externally – whether in the form of loans or of equity capital – is complementary to, not a substitute for, retained earnings.' To be financed externally, firms must prove their capacity to generate profits. Banks and financial institutions are much more reluctant to finance upcoming firms than they are to finance well-established firms because the latter have already demonstrated their ability to run successful projects and to make profits. This is a typical example of procedural rationality. Bankers make use of one of the rules of thumb identified in Chapter 2. Uncertainty about the future, as well as lack of relevant knowledge about the competence of the managerial team and about the profitability of the project, forces bankers to rely on the performance record of the past – that is, the profits generated in the past by the firm. As will be argued in Chapter 4, this does not mean that investment is objectively constrained in the aggregate by a fund of savings that the firms would acquire through their retained earnings. Rather, it means that corporations can safeguard their financial independence by either generating themselves the funds necessary for their expansion projects, or by staying within the borrowing norms set by the financial system. Put briefly, growth is the objective, and profits are the means to realize this objective.

> The key strategic variable becomes the level of capital expenditures derived from the investment plans of firms, with competitive rivalry focused on relative growth rates and relative market shares. Rather than making short-run profit maximization an end in itself, firms see profits as a means to an end, that of enabling them to expand over time, preferably by increasing their market share. Post-Keynesian writers argue that the behavioral goal of the firms is to maximize the growth in sales revenue over time, subject to a minimum constraint. (Kenyon, 1979, pp. 37–8)

Growth maximization versus profit maximization

One may wonder whether there is any practical difference between the post-Keynesian hypothesis of maximizing growth and the neoclassical hypothesis of profit maximization. The truth of the matter is that, in the long run, in part because imperfections and uncertainty will transform any maximizing behaviour into an *ex post* satisficing one, there will not be much practical difference between the consequences of maximizing profits and those of maximizing growth, nor will it be possible to empirically distinguish between the two kinds of maximand. This has been readily admitted by several post-Keynesian and Institutionalist writers (Eichner, 1976, p. 24; Sylos Labini, 1971, p. 251; Harcourt and Kenyon, 1976, p. 451; Galbraith, 1975, p. 132). According to Kenyon (1979, p. 38), 'industrial economists have found, of course, that it is hard to distinguish empirically between growth measured in terms of sales revenue and growth measured in some other manner – for example, in terms of profits over time'.

What do the managers themselves say? A most interesting, though somewhat dated, study is that of Arthur Francis (1980), who first asked what objectives were most important in the long run. The top two objectives were clearly maximizing growth in total profits and maximizing the rate of return on capital. As a distant third, with nearly equal importance, came a variety of goals: maximizing the rewards for employees; maximizing growth in sales and in assets; maximizing growth in dividends and the price of company shares. Surprisingly, however, when managers were asked to choose between competing objectives, a majority of them responded that they would maximize the growth of the business instead of maximizing the rate of return on capital. Francis pursued this further by asking why companies were interested in pursuing a high level of profitability (high rates of profit). Strikingly, the main reason, by far, was to provide finance for expansion. Thus there is a circular relationship between sales growth and profitability, because when managers were asked why their companies were interested in pursuing a high rate of growth in sales, the top reasons offered were that it helped secure or increase future profits and that no growth meant an eventual decline. Profitability and expansion are thus tightly related. Firms can grow because they make profits that allow them to finance their expansion. But, reciprocally, the growth of firms allows them to be profitable. Clearly it may be difficult in reality to disentangle long-run maximization of profit and growth maximization.

It may be preferable at this stage to present a simple model illustrating the theses put forth in this section. To be able to do so, we must deal, as a preliminary issue, with the question of the shareholders' dividends. In the Galbraithian firm, shareholders play a purely passive role. There are two major causes for this compliance, each more pertinent depending on the size of the firm. With respect to the megacorp, the lack of information is certainly the most crucial element. Decision-making in huge corporations relies on various committees, which spend days gathering the necessary knowledge. Shareholders or their elected directors just do not have the time to be overloaded with the necessary information that full-time staff take months or years to absorb. In the case of smaller firms, shareholders quickly come to understand that, without retained earnings, the expansion possibilities of the firm are severely limited, and that as a consequence the dividend payout must be an indicator of the wealth of the corporation rather than a truly significant revenue to the owner. The result of mingling these two causes is that dividend payments become not very different from interest payments on borrowed funds

(Robinson, 1956, pp. 247–8). 'On this view, dividends would be looked on as a cost to be kept at a level no higher than necessary to keep investors happy' (Penrose, 1959, p. 28). The rate of dividends is a convention (Robinson, 1962, p. 38), but one that may have changed upwards since the 1980s.

As already pointed out, the relevance of the Galbraithian firm for modern-day capitalism has been questioned by a number of post-Keynesian authors. The issue here is that financial investors are looking beyond dividends, hoping for capital gains on the stock market. The new convention is not so much the dividend rate but rather that firms should make a sufficiently high return on equity (ROE), the famous 15 per cent ROE norm. It is in this sense that shareholders are not passive, in contrast to what was earlier the case.

3.4.2 The Finance Frontier

We are now in a position to analyse the relationship between profit goals and growth objectives in the post-Keynesian firm. This relationship, as previously outlined, is based on the hypothesis that firms will dare to borrow only to the extent that they have been accumulating their own means to finance investment, and, similarly, that banks and other financial institutions will grant loans or finance share and bond issues only to the extent that their corporate customers have been profitable in the past. The fact that a firm can or is willing to borrow only limited amounts, related to its previously accumulated internal funds, is known in post-Keynesian circles as Kalecki's 'principle of increasing risk'. Several interpretations of this principle abound in the literature, and we shall employ Kalecki's later version of it.

The principle of increasing risk is based on the intuitive notion that the higher the gearing or leverage ratio – that is, the higher the proportion of outside funds financing investment – the larger the potential fluctuations of earnings net of interest payments. In general, at least as long as it is still concerned with the continued existence of the firm, the management of the firm will self-impose stricter limits, being more cautious in its borrowing than lenders about lending (Wood, 1975, p. 31). This means that firms will be free to borrow as much as they desire within the limits that they themselves have set, based presumably on some multiple of their retained earnings.

In periods of crises, the reverse may occur. In such cases, it might be impossible for firms to borrow as much as they would like to, constrained as they are by the leverage ratio judged acceptable by the banks, with firms thus facing credit rationing. Corporate borrowers will be unsatisfied, whatever the expected profitability of their planned investments and whatever rate of interest companies are willing to pay for borrowed funds. In the orthodox literature, the problem facing the bank and its customer, or the capital markets at large, is called moral hazard. In standard terms, the supply of finance is infinitely elastic up to some multiple of the retained earnings of the firm, at which point it becomes infinitely inelastic. More will be said on that topic when we discuss money and credit in Chapter 4. For the moment, note that, as early as 1937, Kalecki (1937) had made clear the presence of moral hazard, while he later insisted on the necessity of retained earnings and the innocuousness of the interest rate as a market mechanism.

> It would be impossible for a firm to borrow capital above a certain level determined by the amount of its entrepreneurial capital. If, for instance, a firm should attempt to float a bond issue

Theory of the firm 143

which was too large in terms of its entrepreneurial capital, the issue would not be subscribed in full. Even if the firm should undertake to issue the bonds at a higher rate of interest than that prevailing, the sale of bonds might not be improved since the higher rate in itself might raise misgivings with regard to the future solvency of the firm ... It follows from the above that the expansion of the firm depends on its accumulation of capital out of current profits. This will enable the firm to undertake new investments without encountering the obstacles of the limited capital markets or 'increasing risk'. Not only can savings out of current profits be directly invested in the business, but this increase in the firm's capital will make it possible to contract new loans. (Kalecki, 1971, pp. 105–6)

A very similar prescription is offered by Davidson:

In an uncertain world, firms must guard against illiquidity while creditors fear the inability of firms to meet long-term obligations. Thus both entrepreneurs and lenders are anxious to see that some portion of investment is funded internally. In an uncertain world, therefore, internal and external finance are complements rather than substitutes and a firm's access to the new issue market will normally be limited by institutional rules about gearing ratios ... (Davidson, 1972, p. 348)

We can now formalize the relationship between the total funds available to finance expansion and the realized profits of the firm, along the lines suggested by Sylos Labini (1971). Let P be the gross profits of the firm, before dividends and interests are paid out. Let us call K_S the capital owned by the shareholders (the own funds or equity of the firm) and K_B the capital borrowed through loans or bond issues – that is, its debt – while i_S and i_B are the dividend rates on shares and the rate of interest on borrowed capital. The retained earnings of the firm, which are in fact additions to the capital owned by the shareholders, are then equal to

$$\Delta K_S = P - i_S K_S - i_B K_B \qquad (3.1)$$

As a simplification, let us assume that the dividend rate and the interest rate are equal to each other. This is not an overly unrealistic simplification, as we have argued that the dividend payout is a quasi-contractual obligation of the firm. It is safe for firms to adhere to the conventions, one of which must surely be the rate of interest on bonds. Under this assumption, equation (3.1) becomes

$$\Delta K_S = P - iK \qquad (3.2)$$

Kalecki's principle of increasing risk then tells us that the maximum amount of capital that can be newly borrowed is a multiple of the current level of retained earnings:

$$\Delta K_B = \rho(P - iK) \qquad (3.3)$$

The multiple ρ is an example of a conventional rule of thumb, as outlined in Chapter 2, the convention being determined by the interaction of the lender's risk as perceived by the banks and other financial actors and of the borrower's risk as perceived by the managers of the non-financial firms. Let us assume that the firm borrows up to its maximum and that all financial resources are used to purchase fixed capital goods (and no financial assets). In that case, from the previous two equations, we get the relationship between investment (I) and profits, that is, equation (3.4) below. Dividing this equation by K, we get its dynamic equivalent, that is, the relationship between the rate of growth ($g = I/K$) of the company and its rate of profit ($r = P/K$).

$$\Delta K = I = (P - iK) + \rho(P - iK) \tag{3.4}$$

$$I/K = g = (1 + \rho)[(P/K) - i]$$

$$r = i + \frac{g}{(1+\rho)} \tag{3.5}$$

Equation (3.5) is known as the finance constraint of the firm; a similar constraint may be found in Marris (1964a, p. 9). It tells us that if the firm desires to grow at a faster rate, it must collect a higher rate of profit, given the average rate of interest payable on its capital and given the proxy ρ of the leverage ratio that is admissible. Incidentally, one can note that a higher rate of interest will require a higher rate of profit for growth to keep up at the same rate, while a higher permissible leverage ratio (measured here by its proxy ρ, representing the ratio of the funds that can be borrowed to the retained earnings) will naturally allow for a lower required profit rate.

Figure 3.1 on page 147 illustrates the meaning of this finance constraint. The hatched area under the financial constraint curve (here a straight line) is not accessible to firms. Companies that happened to be in this zone for some time could not sustain their rate of growth since external financing would no longer be forthcoming. Firms that stretch their financial capabilities to the limit would lie on the financial constraint curve. In the long run, firms must therefore lie either on the financial constraint curve or above it, where there is some financial room (meaning that either firms borrow less than the maximum that they or their lenders feel is reasonable, or they store the excess financial resources into financial assets, for instance bank deposits or treasury bills).

The financial constraint is, however, better known as a slightly revised version, that presented by Wood (1975). In his formulation, the crucial parameter is the retention ratio s_f of firms. The retention ratio is the ratio of retained earnings to gross profits, that is

$$s_f = \frac{P - iK}{P} \tag{3.6}$$

In that formulation, retained earnings are thus equal to

$$\Delta K_S = s_f P = P - iK \tag{3.7}$$

Assuming still that borrowed funds are a multiple of retained earnings, that is, by combining equations (3.3) and (3.7), we get another form of the financial constraint:

$$I = (1+\rho)s_f P$$

$$r = \frac{g}{s_f(1+\rho)} \tag{3.8}$$

Equation (3.8) closely resembles Wood's formulation of the finance frontier, one that can also be found in the macroeconomic models of Kaldor (1966) and Moss (1978). In these models it is assumed that firms decide or are allowed to finance a percentage x of their investment from external sources, more precisely share issues in the Kaldor case. Investment expenditures are thus partly financed by retained earnings ($s_f P$) and partly by borrowing (xI), such that

$$I = xI + s_f P \tag{3.9}$$

Dividing through by K and rearranging yields the expression of Kaldor's famous neo-Pasinetti theorem, but here limited to the microeconomics of the firm:

$$r = \frac{g(1-x)}{s_f} \tag{3.9A}$$

If we wish to assume in addition – a highly realistic assumption – that firms wish to invest in new financial assets, say as a proportion f_f of their investment in physical assets, then we must write

$$I + f_f I = xI + s_f P \tag{3.10}$$

so that the finance frontier becomes

$$r = \frac{g(1-x+f_f)}{s_f} \tag{3.10A}$$

This is the exact form of the finance frontier found in Wood (1975, p. 81), with the caveat that he presents it with respect to a profit margin rather than a profit rate. Comparing equations (3.8) and (3.9A), we see that the share of investment that is financed by inside sources, $(1-x)$, is equivalent to the ratio $1/(1+\rho)$, expressed in terms of the proportion of outside funds that can be matched to net retained earnings. Since equation (3.9A) is strongly reminiscent of the standard Cambridge equation relating the macroeconomic rate of profit to the overall rate of growth, as we shall see in Chapter 6, it has usually been the preferred version of the finance frontier among post-Keynesian authors. An advantage of equation (3.5) is that the rate of interest appears explicitly as a determinant of the finance frontier, thus showing the possible impact of monetary policy. Equation (3.10A) is also interesting because it highlights the role of financialization, here taken as meaning that firms acquire large amounts of financial assets through the f_f parameter. A more complex financial frontier can be found in Dallery (2009).

We can combine all the previous forms of the finance frontier in the following way. There is a rate of interest i_B on the debt of firms, which we call B, and which is made up of bank loans and of bonds. Firms retain a proportion s_f of their profits, but the proportion is out of profits net of interest payments on debt and net of interest payments received on their financial assets F, this rate of interest being i_F. Note that P stands for the profits on tangible capital only. We further assume, as in equation (3.9A), that firms issue new shares as a proportion x of tangible investment, and that they acquire financial assets as a proportion f_f of tangible investment. What the firms cannot finance through retained earnings and new share issues is financed by borrowing from banks or the bond market. The finance constraint of the firm then becomes

$$I + f_f I = xI + s_f(P - i_B B + i_F F) + \hat{B}B \tag{3.11}$$

where $\hat{B}$ is the growth rate of the debt of firms, and hence where $\hat{B}B$ is the increase in debt. This equation will also be used in Chapter 6, in a macroeconomic framework.

Assume now that the firm is on a long-run equilibrium growth path, with a constant debt to capital ratio equal to $l = B/K$, and with a constant financial assets to tangible capital ratio equal to $f_f = F/K$. The constancy of the former ratio implies that debt B grows at the same rate as capital, at the rate g, so that $\hat{B} = g$. Dividing through by K, we obtain the long-run finance frontier:

$$r = \left(i_B l - i_F f_f\right) + \frac{g\left(1 - x - l + f_f\right)}{s_f} \tag{3.11A}$$

The finance constraint is not a far-fetched notion. Fazzari and Mott have shown in a cross-section study that firms with high internal finance (net of dividend payments) have high investment. They note that 'internal finance is quite important for explaining why different firms invest different amounts at any point in time' (1986–87, p. 184). They also show the importance of interest payments and capacity utilization for investment decisions. Similar results are also achieved in many other empirical studies, in particular by Ndikumana (1999). More recently, Brown et al. (2009) show that empirical evidence providing support to the view that cash flows matter for investment and access to external finance is quite compelling.

3.4.3 The Expansion Frontier

We now turn to the other major constraint facing the firm. Looking at Figure 3.1, it would seem that there is no difference between the goal of maximizing the rate of profit and that of maximizing the rate of growth. The finance constraint is not, however, the only constraint facing the firm. Companies are further constrained by what Wood (1975, p. 63) calls the opportunity frontier, also named the efficient demand-growth curve by Marris (1964a, p. 250). We shall call it the 'expansion frontier'. Whereas the finance frontier indicated the various profit rates required to sustain growth strategies, the expansion frontier associates to each growth strategy the profit rate that can optimally be realized. The shape of a typical expansion frontier is represented in Figure 3.2.

In a certain sense, the expansion frontier of the firm is a denial of the orthodox view of the firm. The latter considers that firms reach finite optimal sizes, as in the case of standard U-shaped long-run total average cost curves. The grounds for this shape are the limitations in the ability of the managerial factor of production to coordinate activities within large organizations. The proposition was denied very early on by various post-Keynesians: both Kaldor (1934b) and Kalecki (1971, p. 105) argued that managerial coordination could be achieved by proper delegation of decision-making and decentralization. To this we can add hierarchal structures and routines. Thus, although each plant may have a technologically defined optimal size, the optimum size of a multi-plant firm is

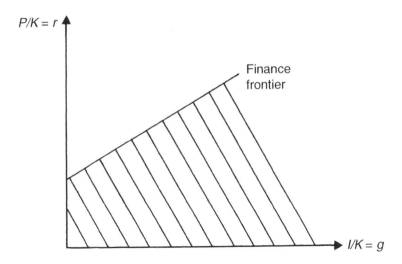

Figure 3.1   The finance frontier of the firm

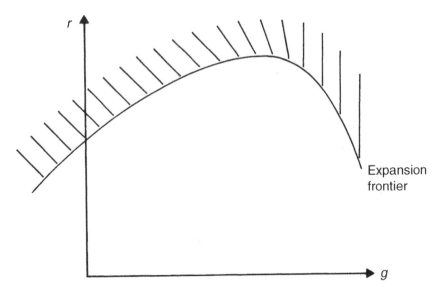

Figure 3.2   The expansion frontier of the firm

either indeterminate or infinite. Empirical evidence seems to show that there are no diseconomies of scale. In his summary of the evidence, Johnston (1960, p. 168) noted that the most obvious element was 'the preponderance of the L-shaped pattern of long-run average cost that emerges so frequently from the various long-run analyses'. The limits of managerial coordination are therefore not to be found in the absolute size of the firm, but rather in its rate of expansion. There are no managerial diseconomies of scale, but there are increasing costs to growth. The descending segment of the expansion frontier as drawn in Figure 3.2 is thus due in part to the inherent difficulties of management to cope efficiently with change and expansion.

The negative relationship between the growth rate and the rate of profit is known as the Penrose effect, since Edith Penrose (1959) was the first to clearly illustrate the limitations of management in handling the speed of expansion, in contrast to the absolute size of an organization. Growing firms must integrate new managers within the organization and train them to handle the complexities of the business. This settling-in is time consuming, in particular for existing management, and consequently it is costly to the firm. There are also further reasons, partially related to these managerial limits. When firms expand, they may do so either internally or externally. In the latter case, the diversification into foreign markets and the diversification into other products are confined by the management's lack of knowledge about these new markets or products. Indeed, many self-made millionaires have lost their shirts by venturing into markets about which they had little knowledge. When firms expand internally, attempting to increase the share of their main market, profit margins and hence profit rates may have to be cut back. More likely, non-pricing forms of competition will be used, with firms engaging in costly advertising, promotion, product innovation, and research and development (Wood, 1975, p. 66). These expenditures are then likely to increase unit costs compared to rivals, and lead to lower profits per unit.

The reader may wonder what accounts for the ascending portion of the expansion frontier. Three reasons may be advanced, all mainly related to internal growth. First, investment allows for the introduction of new and more efficient means of production. Growing firms will find it easier to incorporate technological advancements as they replace their old plants or as they build new ones. This will permit lower unit costs compared to those of slower-growing rivals and will lead to higher profit rates. Second, in the oligopolistic environment with uncertainty, which characterizes the real world, the profitability and survival of the firm and its control over events depend on sheer size. The control of the firm over events therefore depends on its share of the market. To grow slowly implies reducing market shares, such that 'an individual firm's profit rate may also be negatively related to the rate of growth of its competitors' (Moore, 1973, p. 539). Third, when firms expand through diversification, they may encounter novel products where temporary monopoly profits can be earned (Marris, 1964a, p. 251). These positive influences of the rate of growth on the rate of profit are exactly balanced by the Penrose effects at the top of the expansion frontier.

As before, the hatched area in Figure 3.2 represents the combinations of profit and growth rates that are not accessible to the individual firm. Those firms that are efficient, from the point of view of both selling and producing, will lie on the expansion frontier. Those that suffer from X-inefficiency, *à la* Leibenstein (1978), or that attempt simply to satisfice, *à la* Simon, will lie below the expansion frontier.

Assuming for now that firms attempt to maximize their rate of accumulation, we can see, by combining the two frontiers, that the hypothesis of growth maximization is not the same as that of profit maximization, even in the medium run. Figure 3.3 combines the finance constraint with the expansion frontier. Profit maximization would lead to point R on the expansion curve, where the rate of profit is maximized at its rate r_r. At that point, the rate of growth, g_r, would be smaller than the possible maximum rate of growth, g_g, given by the intersection of the two finance and expansion frontiers at point G. We can see that the difference between the two types of firms, the one maximizing

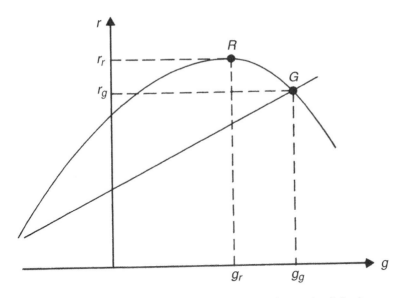

Figure 3.3   Maximum rate of profit and maximum rate of growth of the firm

profit and the other maximizing the rate of growth, is that the former does not attempt to take advantage of all the borrowing leverage that is available to it, since it lies above its finance frontier. This means that profit-maximizing firms avoid becoming involved in investment or advertising expenditures that have low rates of return, although they could obtain the borrowed funds necessary to finance these expenditures. On the other hand, growth-maximizing firms engage in all expansion projects, provided these projects generate a rate of profit that is sufficient to provide the necessary internal and external finance.

Furthermore, the notion of a growth-maximizing firm provides us with some elements of a pricing theory. Although Figures 3.1, 3.2 and 3.3 have been expressed in terms of profit rates, one could also label the vertical axis by using the profit margin. It then becomes clear that the margin of profit set by the firm is the result of two conflicting pressures, both associated with growth maximization. On the one hand, businesses would like to reduce their profit margin in order to steal customers from their competitors, mainly through advertising and the conception of new products. On the other hand, profit margins must be sufficiently high to generate enough retained earnings and sustain the ability of the firm to borrow from outside sources. The profit margin finally chosen must strike a balance between those two considerations (Wood, 1975, p. 86; Shapiro, 1981, p. 88). In a world of uncertainty and of bargaining, the behaviour described above can, of course, be only approximated. To achieve their goals, firms will set targets, knowing that these targets will often not be reached and will sometimes be largely surpassed.

To conclude this section, we may return to the notion of non-price competition. As argued earlier, while all firms in a sector may set the same price, the one with lower unit costs benefits from an outward shift of its expansion frontier. Making use of Figure 3.4 as an illustration, this firm will be at G″ while its competitors will stand at G′. It will be able to earn a higher profit rate, and 'will have a natural tendency to expand relatively to other firms' (Steindl, 1952, p. 41). The higher profit rate will allow this firm to engage into

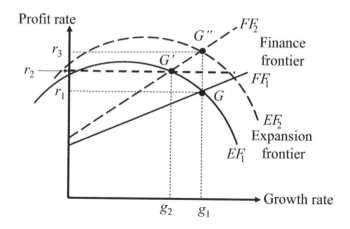

Figure 3.4 Two possible effects of financialization

larger sales efforts or in developing new products, thus progressively achieving a larger share of the market.

3.4.4 Alternatives to the Galbraithian Firm

As pointed out earlier, a number of authors have questioned whether the Galbraithian firm described above is still relevant in the current world of financialization, where financial investors put pressure on corporate managers to achieve high enough rates of return on equity and refuse to remain passive. These authors argue that managerial capitalism is a history-specific construct, so that the theory of firms under managerial capitalism either does not apply or needs to be modified to take into account the modern developments towards a new form of finance capitalism. As Engelbert Stockhammer (2004, p. 133) puts it, 'we would expect that managers and consequently non-financial businesses identify increasingly as rentiers and consequently will also behave as such. We would expect higher dividend payout, lower growth and more financial investment of non-financial businesses.'

There are several ways in which the move towards financialization or money-manager capitalism can be interpreted. For instance, Stockhammer (2005–06) relies on a utility function of managers, the arguments for which are the growth and profit rates, with the weight of each component depending on shareholder power. Another possibility is that financialized firms give themselves a hurdle rate. A new investment will only get the go-ahead from managers if its prospective rate of profit is higher than a certain threshold in the rate of return – the hurdle rate. For instance, if the finance and expansion frontiers are given by FF_1 and EF_1 in Figure 3.4, a growth-maximizing firm will nonetheless constrain itself to operate at point G' if the hurdle rate is given by r_2. The move towards financialization, as illustrated by this minimum hurdle rate, will thus induce a slowdown in accumulation, from g_1 to g_2. Studies by J.P. Morgan (2016) indeed show that the hurdle rate relative to the cost of funds is much higher now than it was 20 years ago.

Here we focus on two proposals made by Dallery (2009). First, we can assume once again that the move towards financialization does not change the essential feature of the

Galbraithian growth-maximizing firm, and that it changes only the value of the parameters of the finance frontier, described by equation (3.11A). As recalled by Rabinovich (2021), there are two broad channels. The first channel is the drain side of financialization (Fiebiger, 2016b). It involves two parameters: an increase in the dividend payout ratio (that is, a fall in its complement, the retention ratio s_f), and a fall in the x ratio, the proportion of investment which is financed by the issue of new shares. Indeed, as managers decide to buy back shares in an attempt to crank up the stock market value of the firm, the short-term value of the x ratio may become negative. Both of these actions drain financial resources away from the firm. The second channel is the pull side of financialization (Fiebiger, 2016b), also called the financial turn of accumulation (Rabinovich, 2019), which involves an increase in the f_f ratio, that is, an increase in the proportion of investments going to financial assets. The impact of all these presumed effects of financialization is illustrated by the upward rotation of the finance frontier, shown by the dashed FF_2 line in Figure 3.4. As long as the firm is operating on the downward-sloping portion of the expansion frontier, financialization will raise the profit rate of a firm (from r_1 to r_2) and will lead to a slowdown in growth (from g_1 to g_2). The firm will be moving from point G to point G'. Furthermore, an increase in interest rates, as occurred in the 1980s, is likely to shift upward the finance frontier.

This, however, is not the only possible effect of financialization. As Stockhammer (2004, p. 132) points out, the move towards money-manager capitalism and the achievement of shareholder value will induce managers to reduce slack or X-inefficiency, and to proceed to a more rigorous exploitation of the resources of the firm, namely to an increased exploitation of ordinary workers. We have already evoked the move towards a regime of 'downsize and distribute', meaning that managers attempt to reach their profit objectives by reducing their workforce and reducing the relative wages of their workers. In other words, managers will attempt to raise the profit margins of their firms, for a given rate of growth, by transferring the pressures exercised by institutional investors on to workers. This will be done by circumventing the bargaining power of unions by lobbying for changes in labour law, thus achieving a reduction in labour costs. As an example, suggested by Dallery (2009, p. 504), it may be that managers still want to achieve the same growth rate g_1 as before, but with the new parameters of the finance constraint they will need to shift up the expansion frontier from EF_1 to EF_2 so as to attain the higher rate of profit r_3 now necessary to achieve the original growth rate g_1. The firm will thus move from point G' to point G''.

Finally, let us consider a possible third effect of financialization. Whereas in the two preceding instances financialization was associated with a change in the constraints facing the growth-maximizing firm, let us now consider the case where financialization leads to a change in objectives, that is, the abandonment of the main objective of the Galbraithian firm – growth – with the main objective of the firm now being the profit rate. What the shareholders are really interested in is the rate of return on equity, but let us assume that corporate managers take the profit rate as a proxy for it, and hence operate the firm in such a way that the realized growth rate and profit rate of the firm are g_r and r_r – the maximum profit rate that can be found on the expansion frontier. What can we say? This new situation is shown in Figure 3.5. The achieved profit rate is r_r but the minimum profit rate required to finance the growth rate g_r is only r_f, as can be read from the finance frontier.

Profit rate r_f suffices to make interest payments on debt, pay fair dividends, and retain a sufficient amount of earnings to obtain the residual amount of loans or other liabilities

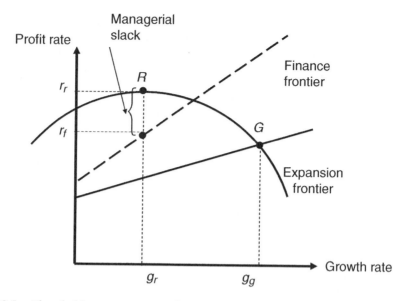

Figure 3.5 Shareholder governance with managerial slack appropriation

necessary to finance tangible investment and obtain the targeted amount of new financial assets. The firm is thus left with a surplus amount ($r_r - r_f$) which can be used to engage in stock market share buy-backs, or which is appropriated by upper-rank managers in the form of stock options, bonuses and outrageous salaries. This is called the managerial slack in Figure 3.5. The figure thus helps to explain the paradox of the governance scheme based on shareholder value. On the one hand it is said that finance and shareholders now have much better control of the corporate firm and its managers, so that managerial capitalism is a thing of the past. On the other hand, corporate executives have defrauded owners for amounts that are larger than they ever were (Black, 2005). Upper management has collected payrolls that are way beyond anything that could have been imagined before the new governance schemes were put in place (Stockhammer, 2005–06, p. 199).

The huge managerial emoluments can even be increased if the firm pursues a downsizing strategy, thus pushing its expansion frontier upwards, as in Figure 3.4, and raising both the maximum profit rate and the differential between the maximum profit rate and the profit rate minimally required to finance growth. However, another, opposite, effect may also occur. As noted earlier, Ariely et al. (2009) have shown that large financial rewards to enhance effort may lead to a decline in performance, meaning that bad decisions by managers under finance capitalism may ultimately lead to a downward shift of the expansion frontier of a firm, for instance because managers take overly risky decisions.

3.4.5 Shareholder Value

There is an additional possible feature of financialization that we have not yet considered and this is the possibility that firms may wish to raise their ratio of external borrowing, the *l* ratio in equation (3.11A), so as to pump up the rate of return on equity – the famous *ROE* – and achieve the well-known 15% benchmark associated with this *ROE*. In this case, an increase in the debt to capital ratio will lead to a downward rotation of the finance frontier, but because interest payments will have to be made on this debt, it will also shift the finance frontier upwards. As explained by Dallery (2009), the 15% *ROE* is a financial convention – a norm – that signals that the managers of the firm are concerned about the financial wealth of the shareholders.

Renaud du Tertre and Yann Guy (2019) have devoted a considered amount of attention to the relationships between the profit rate and various accounting or financial rates of return. To ascertain them, we can start from a highly simplified balance sheet of the firm. On the asset side, the firm has tangible capital K and financial assets F. As to the liability side, as we did when first discussing the finance frontier, it can be split into two components: the own funds of the firm, K_S, and borrowed capital, $K_B = B$. We may thus say that the equity of the firm is equal to:

$$K_S = K + F - B \qquad (3.12)$$

In the case of a firm producing goods or services, the rate of return on equity, r_{ROE}, is the net operating income of the firm (its earnings rK), to which we add the interest payments received and to which we subtract the interest payments made, divided by the equity of the firm. We thus have:

$$r_{ROE} = \frac{rK + i_F F - i_B B}{K + F - B} = \frac{r + i_F f_f - i_B l}{1 + f_f - l} \qquad (3.13)$$

Taking the partial derivatives, it can easily be seen that for a given profit rate on tangible capital r, the rate of return on equity can be increased by raising the debt to capital ratio l or by decreasing the financial asset to tangible capital ratio f_f.

Another accounting measure of profitability is the return on assets, the *ROA*. The denominator of this rate of return is instead all the capital resources mobilized by the firm. This is the measure of the overall profitability of the firm as an institution. We get:

$$r_{ROA} = \frac{rK + i_F F - i_B B}{K + F} = \frac{r + i_F f_f - i_B l}{1 + f_f} \qquad (3.14)$$

The rate of return on equity is obviously higher than the rate of return on assets, thanks to the leverage effect, provided the rate of profit on tangible capital is large enough to keep the numerator positive, hence large enough to offset the high net interest payments that could arise when the interest rate i_B on borrowed funds encounters a sudden rise.

Finally, we may consider the total shareholder return, the *TSR*. Shareholders are mostly concerned with this financial rate, but its evolution greatly depends on what happens on the stock market, and hence firms have much less control on this rate of return. They can only hope that achieving a high rate of return on equity will help them achieve a good rate of return for their shareholders. Following du Tertre and Guy (2019), the total shareholder return is made up of two components, with the second component consisting as we shall see of two sub-components. The first component is the dividend per share, the number of shares being denoted by s, while the second component is the capital gain per share, in other words the growth rate in the price p_s of shares. Recalling that a proportion $(1-s_f)$ of overall profit goes into dividends, the dividend component of the total shareholder return is thus equal to:

$$dividend\ rate = \frac{(1-s_f)(rK + i_F F - i_B B)}{p_s s} = \frac{(1-s_f)(rK + i_F F - i_B B)}{(v_r)(K + F - B)} \quad (3.15)$$

where v_r is the price-to-book (PTB) ratio, which we will again encounter in a slightly different form in Chapter 6. The price-to-book ratio is a variant of what Kaldor (1966) called the valuation ratio and of Tobin's (1969) q ratio. The price-to-book ratio compares the stock market value of the firm to the book value of its own funds (its equity), so that:

$$v_r = p_s s / (K + F - B) = p_s s / K_S \quad (3.16)$$

The dividend rate can thus be written as a function of the ROE, making use of equations (3.13) and (3.16), thus underlining the importance of the rate of return on equity for the determination of returns to shareholders:

$$dividend\ rate = \frac{(1-s_f) r_{ROE}}{v_r} \quad (3.17)$$

We now focus on the second component, the capital gain per share. This is the growth rate of the price of shares. We can again make use of equation (3.16), which can be rewritten as:

$$p_s s = v_r K_S \quad (3.16A)$$

Taking growth rates and rearranging, we get:

$$\hat{p}_s = \hat{v}_r + (\hat{K}_S - \hat{s}) \quad (3.18)$$

Thus, the capital gain per share is equal to the growth rate of the price-to-book ratio plus the growth rate of the own funds per share, in other words, the growth rate of own funds minus the growth rate of the number of shares in circulation. All in all, the total shareholder return, which we denote by r_{TSR}, is thus equal to:

$$r_{TSR} = \frac{(1-s_f) r_{ROE}}{v_r} + \hat{v}_r + s_f r_{ROE} - \hat{s} \quad (3.19)$$

We thus see that the return on equity r_{ROE} plays an important role in determining the total shareholder return r_{TSR}, or what Lavoie and Godley (2001–2) simply called the rate of return on the equities of shareholders. This underlines the relevance of the 15% ROE benchmark. Equation (3.19) also shows that both dividends and retained earnings play a role in determining the total shareholder return, although a slightly different one. Looking at its last term, equation (3.19) also shows why firms would buy back shares ($\hat{s} < 0$) in an effort to raise the total shareholder return. Most importantly perhaps, this total shareholder return also depends on the evolution of the price-to-book ratio, and this evolution, as pointed out by du Tertre and Guy (2019), is contingent on macroeconomic considerations, such as overall credit conditions and the perceptions and state of confidence of financial operators. Those factors are beyond the power of the individual firm.

3.5 COST CURVES AND EXCESS CAPACITY

3.5.1 Some Required Definitions

As mentioned in the introduction to this chapter, one feature at odds with business intuition and experience is the neoclassical presumption, based on the standard U-shaped cost curves, that profitable firms face increasing average costs as they augment sales. In this section, I wish to point to three stylized facts about the post-Keynesian firm that will be of fundamental importance when we discuss macroeconomics. These three facts, naturally restricted to the domain of validity of the post-Keynesian firm identified previously, are the following: first, short-run average costs are generally decreasing; second, marginal costs, and hence average variable costs, are roughly constant up to full capacity; third, firms generally produce at levels where there are reserves of capacity. Although these three stylized facts have been repeatedly observed – leading eclectic authors such as Koutsoyiannis (1975, p. 114) to refer to them as the modern theory of costs or modern microeconomics – they have not been incorporated in traditional economics.

At this stage it may be a good idea to establish a few definitions, taken from Andrews (1949). British authors often refer to 'direct costs' or 'prime costs', and hence to 'unit direct costs', which we can write as 'UDCs'. These include wages, the cost of raw materials and intermediate goods directly linked to the making of the product. As long as they are constant, UDCs and marginal costs are equal. In fact, we can claim that UDCs are nearly identical to the average variable costs found in traditional microeconomics.

To get the 'unit cost', denoted 'UC', we need to take into account general shop and enterprise expenditures. These are often called the 'overhead costs' or 'indirect costs'. They include costs linked to supervision of the production process, as well as administrative and other possible costs related to the manufacturing of the product, such as the costs incurred to bring the product to its purchasers. The 'unit cost' is thus the sum of the 'unit direct cost' and the 'unit overhead cost'. It decreases up to full capacity. The unit cost is similar (but not identical) to the average total cost found in traditional microeconomics (which is the sum of the average variable cost and the average fixed cost). Yet, contrary to average total cost, the unit cost does not include normal profits per unit produced, which are supposed to cover at the very least the amortization of fixed capital.

As in orthodox theory, the shape of the cost curves essentially depends on the technology in use. In the traditional view, substitution between the various inputs is always possible, both in the short run and in the long run. In the short run, for instance, mainstream textbooks claim that it is always possible to increase production by having more labour working on the same machine, thus reducing the capital/labour ratio and therefore the marginal physical product of labour. This was denied early on by post-Keynesian authors. Kaldor (1938), for instance, argued that factors of production showed specificity and complementarity, and hence that if more labour were to be employed, more raw materials and more machines would be required.

In post-Keynesian theory, although some form of substitution can be contemplated in the long haul, through innovation and technical progress, no substitution is possible in the short run. Whether variable factors or fixed factors are considered, fixed technical coefficients prevail. As argued by Eichner (1976, pp. 28–30), plants, or, more precisely, segments of plants, are designed to operate with a given crew, using the most efficient quantity of raw materials. Even where machinery is so designed by engineers that variations in the number of operators may be considered, bureaucratic rules imposed by management will generally lead to a standard ratio of combined inputs. Once these standards are known and win the tacit approval of the workers involved, they become work rules, enforced by collective bargaining. Of course the enterprise may wish to experiment with new combinations, trying to find more efficient ones. However, this may have nothing to do with substitution effects as such, and does not address the short run.

Emerging from those fixed technical coefficients of production is thus a set of plant segments, each designed to operate at the most efficient level of output per unit of time. This level of output, which takes into consideration the necessary breaks in production to execute repairs and regular maintenance, is called the 'engineer-rated capacity' (Eichner, 1976, p. 62) or the level of 'practical capacity'. Steindl (1952, p. 7) defines practical capacity as 'the output achieved with normal length of working time, with sufficient shut-downs to allow for repairs and maintenance, and without disturbance in the smooth running of the production process'.

This practical capacity must be distinguished from 'theoretical capacity', which is the highest degree of production that could be attained if regular maintenance and its accompanying shut-downs did not hinder production and if no breakdown occurred while the plant or its segment was operated at a rate higher than that designed for. While any level of output below practical capacity corresponds to marginal costs that are relatively easy to ascertain and that are constant as a result of the fixed coefficients, levels of output in between practical and theoretical capacities are associated with the traditional increasing marginal costs. These rising costs are due to overtime payments, the damage to machines arising from the speed-up of operations, and the disproportionate reduction in the useful life of equipment as a consequence of its lack of repairs (Steindl, 1952, p. 7). The exact rise in marginal cost is fairly difficult to estimate, because entrepreneurs have generally no experience of production at those high rates of production, and they cannot measure in advance the costs induced by the intensified use of machinery and the supplementary faulty work, breakdowns or accidents that will occur as a result of this overworking (Harrod, 1952, p. 154).

A firm, unless it is of the small entrepreneurial family type, will thus be composed of several plants, each having a number of segments with their own practical capacity. The practical capacity of a plant will thus be the sum of the practical capacities of its segments; and the 'full capacity' of a firm will be the sum of the practical capacities of its plants. Whereas there is no flexibility in the use of plant segments, unless one is prepared to go beyond practical capacity or unless one closes the segment on some days of the week or some weeks of the month, there is a substantial amount of flexibility at the level of the plant and at that of the firm. The reason is that management can increase or reduce production by reopening or closing plant segments or entire plants.

3.5.2 The Shape of Short-run Cost Curves

Figure 3.6 illustrates the relationship between marginal costs (or, for that matter, average variable costs or unit direct costs) and the level of output of the firm, given the levels of practical capacity of its various plants or plant segments, and given the fixed technological conditions prevailing at each plant. The full capacity of the firm, noted *FC*, is the sum of the engineer-rated capacities of each segment, denoted PC_i. The marginal cost curve here is represented as a step function, under the assumption that various plants will not necessarily be of the same vintage, having been built at different points in time (Eichner, 1987, p. 292). Unless there is no technological progress, or unless technical improvements can be simultaneously embodied within the older plants, such a step function will necessarily prevail (Eichner, 1976, p. 34; Rowthorn, 1981, p. 37). However, the differentials in efficiency from one plant to another might not be important, since parts of the technical improvements are diffused to older plants. For this reason, and for simplification purposes, we shall assume away the upward drift of the marginal cost function and set the marginal cost, and hence unit direct costs, as a constant in the rest of the book. The relevance of this simplification will be further discussed at the end of the section.

We are now in a position to represent the shape of the cost curves of the typical post-Keynesian firm. Assuming that unit direct costs are constant up to full capacity, it follows that unit costs (the average total costs) in the short run are necessarily decreasing up to full capacity. Only beyond that point may marginal costs and unit costs increase in the traditional manner. Figure 3.7 illustrates the cost curves of the typical post-Keynesian firm. Beyond full capacity, noted *FC* on the graph, more output can be forthcoming only by over-utilizing the machinery of the various plants above practical capacity. This can be done until theoretical full capacity, noted FC_{th} in Figure 3.7, is reached. There

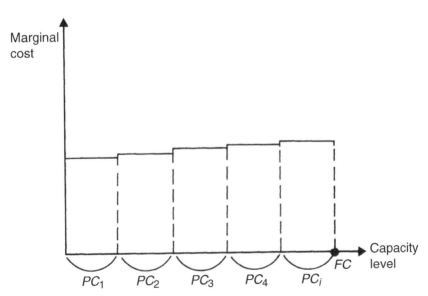

Figure 3.6 Upward drift of the constant marginal cost segments of the firm

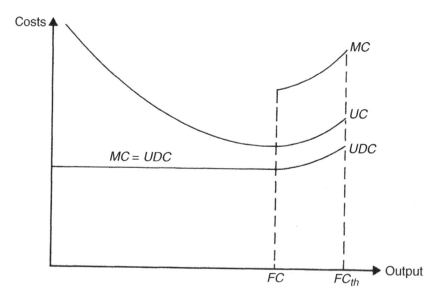

Figure 3.7 Marginal costs (MC), unit direct costs (UDC) and unit costs (UC) of the post-Keynesian firm

is a discontinuity in the marginal cost curve because, as noted above, it is assumed that the over-extensive use of machines will drastically swell replacement costs and because workers will most likely have to be paid overtime. Whether there is a discontinuity or not is not, of course, fundamental.

What is more important is that firms will generally not be producing at levels of output where the marginal cost – and therefore also the unit cost – is increasing. The rising portions of the marginal cost curve, so fundamental to orthodox microeconomics, are for all practical purposes irrelevant to the analysis of the post-Keynesian firm, since the enterprise will absolutely avoid producing in this area. In general, the firm will be operating at output levels where unit direct costs are constant and where unit costs are decreasing, that is, below full capacity as we have defined it. This means that the firm generally operates with reserves of capacity. Large companies plan the presence of excess capacity, operating at rates of utilization of practical capacity that oscillate between 65 and 95 per cent, and aiming for normal rates of utilization in the 80 to 90 per cent range (Eichner, 1976, p. 37; Koutsoyiannis, 1975, p. 273). The normal rate of utilization of capacity is also called the 'load factor on the capacity' or the 'standard operating ratio'. It is defined as the percentage of total practical capacity at which the firm can expect to operate on average over the business cycle (Eichner, 1976, p. 62). The rate of utilization at which the firm is planning to function in the coming period is the expected rate.

As mentioned above, there has long been a vast empirical literature, both in the UK and in the USA, covering statistical and econometric studies as well as case studies and studies based on questionnaires, which demonstrates the irrelevance of the neoclassical U-shaped assumption of cost curves while supporting the L-shaped long-run total average cost curve and the constant average variable cost curve (see, among many others, the surveys of Johnston, 1960 and Lee, 1986). Typical conclusions of these surveys or of original studies are that 'an absolute majority of the answers supported the view that the variable costs are proportional to output [while] quite a number held the belief that variable costs were moderately regressive, at least until close to capacity' (Fog, 1956, p. 46). Johnston (1960, p. 168) resolves firmly that 'the various studies more often than not indicate constant marginal costs and declining average costs as the pattern that best seems to describe the data'.

These results have been confirmed by the interview study conducted by Alan Blinder et al. (1999), who contacted 200 executives of companies with sales of more than $10 million in a Federal Reserve sponsored study devoted to an understanding of price stickiness. Since one of the hypotheses being tested was whether price stickiness could be attributed to constant marginal costs, Blinder et al. endeavoured to find the shape of the marginal cost curve, asking respondents about the behaviour of their 'variable costs of producing additional units as production rises' (ibid., p. 216). This question turned out to be much more difficult to answer than Blinder et al. expected, as several executives declined to send back an answer or had to be poked to provide one. In the end, only 11 per cent answered that marginal costs were rising; 40 per cent said they were declining, and 49 per cent said they were constant. It is somewhat surprising that so many replied that marginal costs were declining, but in view of the difficulty of many executives to understand the question, it is likely that several respondents confused marginal costs or average variable costs with average total costs, that is, the unit cost curve UC in Figure 3.7. Blinder et al. (1999, p. 105) conclude that the managers' answers 'paint an image of the cost structure of the typical firm that is very different from the one immortalized in textbooks'. Ironically, despite all this, when Baumol and Blinder (2006, p. 126), present U-shaped cost curves based on the law of diminishing returns in their first-year textbook, they assert that 'this so-called law rests simply on observed facts; economists did not deduce the relationships analytically'!

By contrast, post-Keynesian authors have been quite keen to accept and disseminate the empirical findings on the shape of cost curves. Graphical representations of the 'modern' theory of costs can thus be found in the works of Davidson (1972, p. 37), Kregel (1973, p. 139), Robinson and Eatwell (1973, p. 168), Harris (1974) and Eichner (1976). The most famous proponent of the cost curves presented in Figure 3.7 is, however, Kalecki (1969, p. 51), who as early as the 1930s proposed a macroeconomic theory built upon the microeconomic foundations of a constant marginal cost with excess capacity. There was also such a tradition at Oxford University, where researchers also came to adopt the hypothesis of constant unit direct costs, as can be seen in the work of Harrod (1952, p. 154) and in that of Andrews (1949, p. 102) and his associate Brunner (1975). With Kalecki, Kaldor is the other post-Keynesian who, from very early on, has attempted to rebuild macroeconomics on the basis of modern microeconomic foundations. Drawing a graph similar to Figure 3.7, Kaldor (1961, p. 197) assumes that 'average and marginal prime costs are constant up to the point where the optimum utilization of capacity is reached'.

3.5.3 Causes of Planned Excess Capacity

While Kaldor has long been explicit in his recognition of constant direct costs below full-capacity output, he has also been quite explicit about the need for firms to keep reserves of capacity under all circumstances. It is not enough to show that marginal costs can be constant for some scale of production: one must show that firms stay below the point of full capacity, in the region where marginal costs are constant.

> The motives which cause firms, in a world of imperfect competition, to maintain capacity ahead of output – the motive of being in a position to exploit any chance increase in selling power – operate just as powerfully in times of full employment as at other times . . . It is perfectly consistent to assume that, in long-term equilibrium, both output and output capacity should grow at the same rate, without implying that the one is equal to the other. (Kaldor, 1970a, p. 4)

> The manufacturing sector is the archetypal case of fix-price market . . . In markets of this type uncertainties concerning the future growth of demand mainly affect the degree of utilization of capacity; it pays the manufacturers to maintain capacity in excess of demand and keep the growth of capacity in line with the growth of demand. (Kaldor, 1986, p. 193)

Besides the chance to exploit increases in selling power, due to random variations or seasonal fluctuations, various reasons have been advanced to justify the continuous existence of reserves of capacity. For Sylos Labini (1971, p. 247), excess capacity is a deterrent to entry by new or outside firms. It is part of the defensive strategy to limit entry into the industry, since any potential producer knows that existing firms have the ability to increase output and cut prices without necessarily incurring losses. Thus Joan Robinson (1969, p. 261) connects the presence of imperfect competition to the existence of excess capacity, and the latter to a market that 'is not exactly foreseeable for the individual seller'.

Steindl (1952, p. 2) has linked the presence of reserves of capacity to the presence of fundamental uncertainty, and this may be the best explanation of excess capacity. Whereas households have cash holdings to satisfy their liquidity preference, firms hold excess capacities to face an uncertain future. The presence of excess capacities evidently allows firms to respond quickly to a boom in the demand for their product. It is true that this flexibility is also acquired through the existence of inventories. The problem, however, is that inventories can be used only once, as a temporary response. Furthermore, when the evolution of consumer demand requires minor alterations to the style of the product being sold, reserves of capacity allow firms to continue the production of the standard good while modifying the design of idle plants. Reserves of capacity thus provide flexibility in the face of uncertainty about the exact composition of forthcoming demand. 'Demand is distributed between diverse types and qualities of output which require separate facilities, and this distribution of demand between types cannot be correctly foreseen. Therefore a reserve of capacity is necessary to take care of possible shifts in the pattern of demand' (Steindl, 1952, p. 8). As pointed out by Pasinetti (1981, p. 233), the future composition of demand is uncertain, not only because it may be difficult for managers to foresee the preferences of consumers, but also because the consumers themselves, when their incomes are increasing, may be uncertain about what they want to purchase next. In this sense, excess capacity is truly analogous to precautionary demand for liquidity.

There are further reasons explaining the prevalence of excess capacity. They have to do with technological aspects. There is some indivisibility of plants and equipment. The most efficient plant or plant segment may require a minimum level of practical capacity, because of economies of scale up to this minimum level. The installation of a new plant may thus temporarily bring an excess of capacity over demand, which should then be eliminated through the secular increase in demand; but for the reasons outlined above, the temporary reserve will in effect be a permanent one, the firm consistently making sure that its capacity is ahead of demand in order to avoid the risk of losing its customers to more provident producers. The fact that producers carry excess capacity is also related to the technological fact that production takes time: plants cannot be built instantaneously; machinery cannot be stacked in inventories, since machines are often specific to the task at hand, and are therefore made to order. As a consequence, capacity cannot be increased overnight. The irreversibility of time lies in production, not in demand. A desired volume of unused capacity quiets managers' concern about the possibility of losing the goodwill of customers as a consequence of the over-delayed delivery of promised goods. Firms know that their customers have no patience for delivery lags and delays.

One could argue that firms could always take advantage of the excess of the theoretical capacities over the practical capacities, and aim at operating at the least costly level of production, that is at point *FC* in Figure 3.7. Forbidding excesses in capacity due to indivisibilities, firms would thus generally attempt to operate at full capacity, where they would minimize unit costs. If demand randomly increases beyond full capacity, this increase in demand could usually be taken care of by the excess of theoretical capacity over practical capacity, along the rising portion of the marginal cost curve. Besides Sylos Labini's objections to such a short-run strategy, there are practical technical reasons that explain why such a strategy will not be pursued.

First, collective bargaining may have prohibited the extensive use of overtime work, or the possibility of night shifts. As Marris (1964b, p. 22) notes, 'in practice, most societies do collectively decide . . . to live with a fairly low rate of capital utilisation, and thus ensure that shift-work is a minority experience'. Second, when capacity is overworked, machines are more likely to break down for lack of regular maintenance, and accidents are more likely. There is thus a danger for the firm, because of disruptions in the production process, of being incapable of responding to demand, and thus, once more, of losing its share of the market and the goodwill of its customers. As Downward and Lee (2001, p. 469) point out, in the Blinder et al. (1999) survey, '85 percent of sales represented repeat business', so that most of the activity occurs between businesses. It is thus particularly important not to antagonize customers and preserve goodwill by being always able to respond to orders.

Furthermore, even if such production disruptions were not feared, increased production could only be achieved at higher unit costs and, unless prices were increased, with generally diminishing profits. The financial capacity of the firm to expand its output potential would thus be curtailed precisely when funds were most required for expansion. A firm without reserves of capacity would thus be at a cost disadvantage *vis-à-vis* its competitors, and the alternative solution of raising prices would again run the risk of losing the goodwill of customers, who could find elsewhere the same product at a non-increasing price. All this has led various authors to associate rational behaviour, including long-term profit maximization, with excess capacity (Skott, 1989a, p. 53). Even Kaldor (1961, p. 207), in contrast to the quotation above, has at one point argued that 'under conditions of imperfect competition it is perfectly compatible with "profit-maximizing behaviour" to suppose that the representative firm will maintain a considerable amount of spare capacity'.

To conclude on the issue of excess capacity, we may say that there are good theoretical and practical reasons, as well as good strategic and technical ones, to explain why corporations generally aim at operating much below their full capacity, in the range of constant unit direct costs. Whatever one may think of the rationality of such behaviour, one must recognize, as post-Keynesians do, that firms consistently function with large reserves of capacity, and that any analysis of the firm must take that fact into account.

3.5.4 Constant Marginal Costs: Myth or Stylized Fact?

Before closing this section on the costs of firms, we should clear up an issue that, in previous discussion, has been neglected. More specifically, we need to come back to the issue of the step function representing the marginal cost curve of the firm, as illustrated in Figure 3.4. As argued then, the rising steps from one segment of the curve to the other are due to the differentials in efficiency of the various plants owned by the firm, these differentials being caused by the various vintages of the plants. Furthermore, as mentioned earlier, the Blinder et al. (1999) survey found that a fairly large proportion of firms claimed that marginal costs were decreasing. It has been frequently argued by Lee (1986; 1988; 1994) that it is an error to assume constant unit direct costs, since several case studies have shown that unit direct costs or marginal costs could be either decreasing or increasing at the level of the individual plant. As a consequence, to describe the overall marginal cost of the firm as a constant up to full capacity would be as misleading as using the traditional U-shaped curve.

What are we to make of this criticism of a core assumption in post-Keynesian economics? With respect to the individual plant, it has been answered by Yordon (1987) that the evidence in favour of increasing marginal costs was rather tenuous. As to the case of decreasing marginal costs, a pre-eminent case if judged by the results obtained by Fog (1956) and Blinder et al. (1999), Yordon explains how they can in fact be reconciled with constant marginal costs. When post-Keynesians claim that marginal costs, unit prime costs, unit direct costs or average variable costs are constant up to full capacity, they exclude from these costs the overhead labour costs. These include the managerial staff but also the supervisors and foremen assigned to the various segments of the plant. There is a certain ambiguity with respect to overhead labour costs. These salaries are not exactly fixed costs, since they could be cut substantially if the firm were to close, but neither are they variable costs, since, once the plant has been started up, they 'remain roughly stable as output varies' (Kalecki, 1971, p. 44). As shown by Steindl (1952, p. 8) and confirmed by Elizabeth Brunner (1975, p. 32), the salaries of overhead labour represent a substantial portion of labour-earned income, and as such they should not be ignored.

We shall see later that the distinction between direct and indirect labour, an underrated distinction according to Brunner (1975, p. 32), can play a key role in the macroeconomics of income distribution. In empirical work, however, as well as for accountants, it is often very difficult to disentangle the salaries paid to overhead staff from the wages paid to labour directly involved with production. Since overhead staff does not increase with production, but rather with capacity, the practical impossibility of differentiating between direct labour and some of overhead labour will lead to apparently slightly diminishing average variable costs, although pure direct costs are indeed constant. Some authors speak of 'paying-out', or 'cash', costs (ibid.). Other authors speak of start-up costs, saying that prime costs consist of both marginal costs and overhead start-up costs. As Robinson (1969, p. 261) says, 'There is always an element of quasi-fixed cost which must be incurred when a plant is kept in running order. Thus average prime cost falls with output up to full capacity' (cf. Asimakopulos, 1970, p. 172; Kaldor, 1964b, p. xvi). On the basis of this proper distinction between true variable costs and start-up costs, we may thus conclude that, at the level of the plant, there is strong evidence to believe that marginal or pure direct costs are constant.

Now what about the differentials in productivity between plants? Kaldor (1961, p. 198) argued a long time ago that the increased productivity of labour, due to the existence of overhead labour, precisely compensates for the diminishing productivity of equipment brought about by various vintages. Such an answer to Lee's objections to a constant marginal cost is not acceptable, however, if we want to continue to differentiate between direct and indirect labour, as we shall. Eichner's reply (1986b) to Lee's critique was to argue that without technical progress the overall marginal cost curve would be horizontal up to capacity, and that it is useful to assume it so. Lee's anticipated answer (1986, p. 409) to that reply was that instrumentalism could not be part of a post-Keynesian theory of the firm.

There is, however, a much more valid reply to Lee's criticism. Yordon (1987, p. 596) notes that, when they reduce production, firms do not necessarily close down the least efficient plants. Mainly because of transportation costs, a general reduction in the demand for the products of a firm will be met by closing down segments of all plants, rather than closing down all segments of the least efficient plant. The step-wise representation of marginal costs given by Figure 3.6 is thus an abstract one. The more concrete representation of marginal costs, its depiction in historical time, is the one offered by Figure 3.7, since it corresponds to the actual sequential behaviour of marginal and unit costs when firms increase or reduce their level of output.

A similar objection, and also a similar answer, can be made at the industry level. As Davidson (1960, p. 53) recalls, even if all firms do have constant marginal costs, this does not imply that the industry supply curve is horizontal, as post-Keynesians in the Kaleckian tradition would have it, since there may be low-cost as well as high-cost firms. This point has recently been reasserted by Allain (2021a). In the following chapters, we shall assume nonetheless that the industry supply curve is a horizontal cost curve, because we shall presume that firms operate in parallel fashion, sharing in the variations of total output. For instance, when demand falls, the reduction in output is spread more or less proportionately over all firms. The least efficient firms do not bear the brunt of the reduction in activity unless they are forced to go under. Inefficiency is reflected in profits per unit, rather than in prices. Symmetrically, when demand expands, unit costs for each firm go down, and hence 'productivity rises because the rise in output following the rise in demand is shared among *all* firms, not concentrated among the marginal firms' (Kaldor, 1985, p. 47). It is the existence of excess capacity that allows such behaviour, as well as the irrelevance of the marginal pricing rule.

This brings to the forefront the question of pricing, which we must now tackle.

3.6 PRICING THEORY

3.6.1 Some Preliminary Statements

Following a distinction made by Eichner (1987, p. 338), post-Keynesian authors like to distinguish 'pricing' theories from 'price' theories. A theory of prices is a theory that ascertains the price of a product relative to other prices. It is an economy-wide theory of relative prices. It yields an equilibrium configuration of prices, which would occur if all adjustments and various time lags could be dispensed with. More recent work in price theory has dealt with the issue of dynamic stability: are there mechanisms, everything else being constant, that would drive actual prices towards the equilibrium configuration? On the other hand, a pricing theory is a statement about the behaviour of price-making agents. It discusses how price decisions are actually taken; it deals with the process of price-setting; it might also make explicit the information basis on which the pricing decisions are taken. There may be several post-Keynesian theories of prices, but all these theories are based on the same pricing theory – the cost-plus pricing approach. What are the ultimate determinants of pricing is another issue, about which there is less agreement.

Firms have two kinds of decisions to make: costing and pricing. Agreement or disagreement between various authors may thus arise from both the costing and the pricing sides:

> Costing refers to the procedures that a business enterprise employs to determine the costs that will be used in setting the selling price of a good before actual production takes place and hence the actual costs of production are known ... Pricing refers to the procedures the business enterprise uses to set the price of a good before it is produced and placed on the market. That is, starting with the costs determined by its costing procedures, the business then adds a costing margin to costs or marks up the costs to set the price. (Lee, 1998, p. 10)

Whereas neoclassical pricing theory relies on the equality of marginal cost and marginal revenue, post-Keynesians rely on the generic principle of 'cost-plus pricing'. There are several variants of cost-plus pricing, but all share a few salient characteristics (Shapiro and Sawyer, 2003; Gu and Lee, 2012).

First, prices are set by firms; they are not determined by invisible market forces or by a fictitious and omniscient auctioneer. Prices are cost-coverers and not resource-allocators; they are not indices of scarcity. Second, managers fix prices based on some measure of what they consider to be normal costs, to which they then add a markup or a costing margin; prices do not depend on actual costs. Third, prices are reproductive prices. Their purpose is to recoup the expenditures of the firm (Shapiro and Mott, 1995, p. 36). Firms must secure enough revenues to be viable financially and to grow. Fourth, prices are stable. They are not set as a one-shot profit-maximizing affair; rather, they are often set within a framework of repetitive transactions with purchasers, where firms must avoid giving the impression that they are overcharging. To help preserve goodwill, prices are usually maintained for some period of time. Furthermore, the stability of prices reduces the probability of price wars, which are always destructive. Indeed, following the Blinder et al. (1999) study, several central banks have conducted enquiries into price stickiness; these studies have confirmed that 'prices are rarely reviewed, and even more rarely changed' (Melmiès, 2010, p. 450).

Fifth, not unrelated to the previous feature, firms seem to set prices independently of a presumed inverse price–sales relationship, seemingly implying that price elasticity is very low. Sixth, prices are not market-clearing prices. The 'costing margins', which yield the *ex post* 'profit margins' (the realized margins), are added *ex ante*, before the firm can find out what the actual costs or demand conditions are. Prices are administered to the market and are set before transactions take place. As a large share of costs comes from intermediate inputs, the prices of which may not be known with certainty when firms set their own prices, costing margins are likely to diverge from actual profit margins. The importance of intermediate goods in the costs of firms underlines the interdependence of prices – the seventh attribute of post-Keynesian pricing. This is reflected in input–output models of the Sraffian sort, for instance, or in other multisector pricing models. Finally, we may say that post-Keynesian prices are strategic prices, which are set by firms to fulfil some purpose, which may differ in time and space. This also applies to costing, in particular overhead expenditures, which may be allocated to the different products produced by the firm in a strategic fashion, a feature that Andrews called the 'plasticity' of overhead costs.

We can mention two additional features of cost-plus pricing as underlined by Coutts and Norman (2013). Indirect taxes will be fully shifted into prices, since they appear as a cost to the firm; the same will happen with tariffs on imported materials that are a cost to the firm. By contrast, at least in advanced industrialized nations, domestic prices will be impervious to changes in the exchange rate or in the tariff on rival imported goods.

3.6.2 Variants of Pricing Procedures

Cost-plus pricing, or what Okun (1981, p. 153) calls cost-oriented pricing, includes five variants: mark-up pricing, full-cost pricing, normal-cost pricing, historic normal-cost pricing, and target-return pricing. I shall argue that there is no fundamental difference between these five variants, which have a substantial amount of overlap. Extended presentations of these variants can be found in Lee et al. (1986), Reynolds (1987), Downward (1999) and especially Lee (1998). Lavoie (2016a) provides an analysis of Lee's legacy on the subject of pricing theory.

Mark-up pricing
The simplest cost-plus pricing procedure is the Kaleckian mark-up approach, or direct cost pricing. It assumes that a gross costing margin is added to unit direct costs or average variable costs. The pricing equation is then

$$p = (1 + \theta)UDC = (1 + \theta)DC/q \qquad (3.20)$$

The price variable is p; UDC stands, as before, for unit direct costs (or average variable costs); the percentage mark-up on direct costs is θ; and the gross costing margin is $\theta(UDC)$. DC and q stand for direct costs and the output level. Figure 3.8(a) illustrates the mark-up procedure of equation (3.20).

While simple mark-up pricing – also called direct-cost pricing – is quite popular among post-Keynesian macroeconomists, some authors, notably Lee (1985; 1994) have argued that mark-up procedures are much less prevalent today than in the past, as a result of

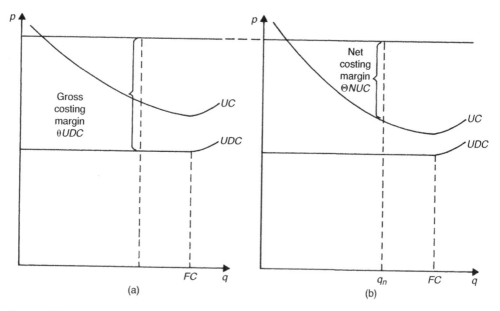

Figure 3.8 (a) Mark-up pricing and gross costing margin; (b) normal-cost pricing and net costing margin

the increased sophistication of accounting techniques within firms. Whereas, earlier, accountants had only very rough estimates of unit overhead costs, including depreciation costs, this has not been the case for quite a long time. Most firms, large ones in particular, have accurate estimates of unit overhead costs, having found means to attribute to each branch or product the overhead shop and factory costs incurred. Lee (1998, p. 206) points out that only 20 per cent of firms surveyed utilized direct-cost pricing, most of them being small enterprises.

Since many authors assume that unit prime costs are constant up to or near full capacity, and since most firms try to avoid operating beyond full capacity, the level of capacity utilization at which these unit prime costs are computed is of little importance. Still, mark-up pricing assumes that a certain gross costing margin is added to unit prime costs, thus yielding the price of the concerned good, but that gross costing margin must be related in some way to a specific output level if the margin is to cover both overhead costs and some profit target (Brunner, 1975, p. 29). Thus, as argued earlier, even in the case of direct-cost pricing firms need to set prices on the basis of some normal or standard level of output. As Andrews (1949, p. 110) pointed out, for pricing, 'it is the normal level of average direct costs that will be the important thing'. Then, whether the unit direct cost curve is flat or not becomes a secondary issue, at least at the microeconomic level. As Lee (1994, p. 314) points out, 'since the costs used for pricing are based on estimated production or normal capacity, the question of the shape of the average direct cost curve is immaterial for pricing purposes'. If the unit direct cost curve is not flat on the relevant segment, DC and UDC will be replaced by NDC and $NUDC$ in equation (3.20), where NDC and $NUDC$ stand for normal direct costs and normal unit direct cost, and where

q_n is normal or standard output (Gu and Lee, 2012, p. 456). So interpreted, the mark-up pricing equation becomes

$$p = (1 + \theta)NUDC = (1 + \theta)NDC/q_n \qquad (3.21)$$

Lee (1994, p. 305) has also noted that, in most aggregate models, like those in the spirit of Sidney Weintraub (1978), the mark-up is imposed upon unit labour costs, thus ignoring material costs. This may be a misleading simplification, at least within a multisectoral framework, since the costs of intermediate inputs often constitute a much larger proportion of direct costs than do labour costs. We can ascertain this by computing first the share of gross profits in sales, and then the share of gross profits in value added.

The share of gross profits in sales, also equivalent to the degree of monopoly in Kalecki's terminology, is equal to

$$m = \theta/(1 + \theta) \qquad (3.22)$$

The percentage mark-up θ can be considered as a proxy for the share of gross profits in sales, since the former can be written as a function of the latter:

$$\theta = m/(1 - m) \qquad (3.23)$$

However, things are slightly different if we look at the share of gross profits in value added (Hein, 2012, pp. 22–3). We must now distinguish between unit direct labour costs (*UDLC*) and unit material costs (*UMC*), with the mark-up price equation becoming

$$p = (1 + \theta)(UDLC + UMC) \qquad (3.24)$$

Then the share of gross profits in value added, m_{va}, is the ratio of gross profits to the sum of gross profits and direct labour costs, so that

$$m_{va} = \frac{\theta(UDLC + UMC)}{\theta(UDLC + UMC) + UDLC} \qquad (3.25)$$

Dividing throughout this equation by *UDLC*, and denoting the ratio of material costs to direct labour costs by $j = UMC/UDLC$, one obtains

$$m_{va} = \frac{\theta(1+j)}{1+\theta(1+j)} \qquad (3.26)$$

The derivative of equation (3.26) with respect to j turns out to be always positive

$$\frac{dm_{va}}{dj} = \frac{\theta}{\{1+\theta(1+j)\}^2} > 0$$

Thus, with a constant mark-up θ on unit direct costs, an increase in the ratio of material to direct labour costs will raise the share of gross profits in value added m_{va}. Thus, again under the assumption of a constant percentage mark-up θ, workers can reduce the share of profits in value added by negotiating higher nominal wage rates. This will reduce the j ratio in equation (3.26) and lead to a lower m_{va} value. *A fortiori*, if firms pass on the cost increase without applying the mark-up on it, aggressive nominal wage bargaining can succeed in increasing the wage share in value added, even if material unit costs rise, as perhaps happened in the 1970s (McCombie, 1987, p. 1132).

Full-cost pricing

A second approach to cost-plus pricing, *full-cost pricing*, was first presented by Hall and Hitch (1939). Using this approach, firms fix prices by taking into account all their costs, and not just direct costs. In the full-cost approach, as initially defined, prices were said to depend on actual unit costs. Indeed, Hall and Hitch (1939, p. 20) indicated that about half the firms surveyed were using either actual or expected output. Indeed, Brierley et al. (2006) report that a number of UK firms still compute unit overhead costs on the basis of budgeted output, finding it convenient to use the annual forecast of activity made as part of the planning exercise. This is thus a form of full-cost pricing. But since unit costs are falling, up to full capacity, the idea has fallen into disrepute among scholars, because it meant that prices had to fall with rising production or higher expected sales – a case of perverse pricing, as Gardiner Means (1992, p. 326) called it. As Robinson (1977, p. 11) recalls, 'the old full cost doctrine . . . appeared to hold that prices of manufactures . . . fall when demand increases because overheads are spread over a larger output'.

Looking at it the other way, with falling production or lower expected sales, perverse pricing may imply the *death spiral*, as the calculated higher unit cost implies higher prices and hence potentially a further fall in sales, which would induce another rise in the estimated unit overhead cost, and so on (Brierley et al., 2006, p. 60). In addition, full-cost pricing *stricto sensu* meant that actual unit costs (prime costs plus overhead costs) had to be known in advance: this was deemed to be impossible. Whereas the expression full-cost pricing is still used occasionally by various authors, it may be best to leave it aside, and move to the next variant.

Normal-cost pricing

The predominant pricing procedure is now a close alternative to the full-cost approach and to mark-up pricing – the normal-cost pricing procedure described by Andrews (1949), Brunner (1952) and Andrews and Brunner (1975). Normal-cost pricing emphasizes the fact that firms fix prices by adding a costing margin to unit costs that have been computed at some normal level of output (Lee et al., 1986, p. 24). Hence prices are not set according to realized costs; rather they depend on some conventional measure of costs – the normal or standard cost. In the work of Andrews himself, a gross costing margin was presumed to be added to unit direct costs, assessed at some normal output. Andrews and Brunner recognized, however, that many larger firms set prices by adding a net costing margin to normal unit costs, that is, a cost measure that includes both direct and overhead unit costs, estimated at normal output. More recently, normal-cost pricing tends to be associated with the latter rather than with the former view (Rowthorn, 1981, fn 4; Bhaduri, 1986, p. 76; Lee, 1994).

Normal-cost pricing in its modern incarnation is thus similar to the full-cost approach, but unit costs are computed at some conventional level of output. This conventional level can be either full-capacity output or a standard level of output, based on a standard rate of utilization of capacity. Managers need not know the value of unit costs for all levels of output; they need this value only for the conventional level of output.

Costing procedures are facilitated when some trade association sets the convention, for instance by providing a value for the normal degree of utilization of current capacity that might be used to compute unit overhead costs.

It turns out that most authors who gave their support to normal-cost pricing have based the unit cost on a normal level of output (q_n), consistent with what we have called above the standard operating ratio or the normal degree of utilization of capacity (Brunner, 1975, p. 27; Sylos Labini, 1971, p. 247; Harrod, 1972a, p. 398; Wood, 1975, p. 61; Lee, 1985, p. 206). As Harrod (1952, p. 165) remarks, this is a 'modification of the full cost principle *stricto sensu*'. Normal-cost pricing with its net costing margin is illustrated with the help of Figure 3.8(b). Normal-cost pricing must thus be understood as a percentage net costing margin Θ imposed on normal unit costs NUC, as shown in equation (3.27)

$$p = (1 + \Theta)NUC \qquad (3.27)$$

As Lee (1998, p. 205) points out, in reality, firms may impose two mark-ups, one to cover overhead costs (denoted by θ' in equation 3.28), and then another one to cover profits (denoted by Θ, as it was in equation 3.27), so that normal-cost pricing may be instead represented by

$$p = (1 + \theta')(1 + \Theta)NUDC \qquad (3.28)$$

Historic normal-cost pricing

This is a complexified variant of full-cost pricing or of normal-cost pricing. This variant was put forward by Nordhaus and Godley (1972) and Coutts et al. (1978), and much later by Godley and Lavoie (2007a, ch. 8). Coutts et al. (1978, p. 1) rely on what they call a 'normal price hypothesis'. For them, this means that 'the normal value of a variable is defined as the value that variable would take, other things equal, if output were on its trend path' (Nordhaus and Godley, 1972, p. 854). This thus corresponds to computing a normal cost, that is, a unit cost at a normal level of output. The historic component arises from the fact that they consider that the 'output price is set by taking a constant percentage over average normal historical current cost', the historical cost being 'the sum of costs of different inputs, the cost of each category being calculated at the time of purchase' (ibid.).

Because firms hold inventories of produced goods, the sales in any period may reflect goods that have been produced in the previous or in the current period. The cost of production of a particular unit depends on when the good was produced. For instance, with wage and commodity inflation, and without technical progress, a good produced in the previous quarter will have a lower cost than the same good produced in the current quarter. Goods sold this quarter will be made up of goods produced at two different periods of time, and the single price at which all these goods are sold currently should reflect this composition.

What will be the normal proportion of the goods produced last quarter among all the goods sold this quarter? The answer is fairly simple: it will correspond to a target ratio, given by the stock of end-of-period inventories relative to the flow of expected quarterly sales, say ι^T. Therefore, if prices are reviewed and possibly changed every quarter, prices based on the normal historic unit cost will depend on the weighted average of the normal unit cost of the previous period and that of the current period, as shown in the equation below:

$$p = (1 + \Theta)[(\iota^T NUC_{-1} + (1 - \iota^T)NUC] \qquad (3.29)$$

An interesting consequence of historic normal-cost pricing is that changes in costs are not fully transferred to prices, because of the lag imposed by the existence of stocks of goods that have been previously produced.

Target-return pricing

The fifth and last variant of cost-plus pricing is target-return pricing. This again is a variant of normal-cost pricing. This procedure was identified by Kaplan et al. (1958) in their study of large firms, but was also found to be used by many small firms (Haynes, 1964; Shipley, 1981, p. 430). This pricing method seems the most prevalent. In the target-return procedure, given unit direct and indirect costs, prices are set to yield a target rate of profit on the capital assets of the company whenever sales correspond to the output produced at the standard rate of capacity utilization. As Lanzillotti (1958, p. 923) puts it, 'margins added to standard costs are designed to produce the target profit rate on investment, assuming standard volume to be the long run average rate of plant utilization'. Bhaduri and Robinson (1980, p. 107) propose an identical pricing procedure: 'gross margins in each line are fixed up in such a way as to cover costs and yield a "subjective-normal" rate of net profit at a standard level of utilisation of capacity'. This also corresponds closely to what Robinson (1956, pp. 185–6) had defined earlier as a *'subjective-normal price*, which is such that gross profit margin entering into it is calculated as to yield a profit that the entrepreneurs concerned have come to regard as attainable ... calculated upon the bases of an average or standard rate of output'.

The advantage of target-return pricing is that it provides an explanation of what the percentage net costing margin ought to be. Target-return pricing is thus the most sophisticated approach, for accountants must have a precise idea of the worth of capital or of the value of the newly built plant. A well-known example of target-return pricing, if a somewhat outdated one, is that of General Motors, where a unit cost, including a prorated overhead, was calculated based on the assumption of a standard volume, which was assumed to be 80 per cent of output capacity; a costing margin was then added to this normal unit cost so as to achieve a 15 per cent target rate of return after taxes on invested capital (Scherer, 1970, p. 174). This seems to be roughly equivalent to what we earlier called the return on assets – the *ROA*.

One can show that target-return pricing is a specification of normal-cost pricing. Suppose that the target rate of return or the normal rate of profit is r_n and the value of the stock of capital is $p_i M$, where M is the number of machines and p_i the price of machines. Required profits for the period are then $r_n p_i M$. Let us assume a capital to full-capacity output ratio (M/q_{fc}) of v. If the standard or normal rate of utilization of capacity is u_n, corresponding in the period to a level of output of q_n, the required profits for the period must be equal to $r_n v p_t q_n/u_n$. This must be equated to the profits obtained by the product of the net costing margin and sales at the standard level of output q_n, the net costing margin being itself the product of the percentage net costing margin and normal unit costs, that is, unit costs at the standard rate of utilization of capacity: $\Theta(NUC)(q_n)$. Thus we need to have

$$r_n v p_t q_n/u_n = \Theta(NUC)(q_n)$$

This done, we find that the previously identified mark-up Θ of equation (3.27) must be equal to

$$\Theta = (r_n v/u_n)(p_t/NUC) \qquad (3.30)$$

The larger the target rate of return and the larger the capital to capacity ratio, the higher the required percentage net costing margin Θ.

3.6.3 Which Pricing Variant is Best?

Accounting
Cost-plus pricing is prevalent among firms because it constitutes a convenient rule of thumb in making what would otherwise be complex and difficult decisions in a world of uncertainty. This is particularly clear in the case of retailers who, without their customary margins, would be forced to take thousands of decisions. Cyert and March (1963) have shown that, knowing the unit cost of various products, they could predict quite precisely almost all prices set by a large retail store with the help of a few simple rules, including a fixed percentage cost margin. The neoclassical theory of the firm assumes that entrepreneurs have knowledge of things of which the entrepreneurs themselves claim to be ignorant (marginal revenue, rising marginal cost schedules, the exact shape of the demand curve that they face). Post-Keynesians, instead, base their theory of pricing on the knowledge that managers of firms are likely to be able to rally in an uncertain and complex environment. As is the case for consumers when they make their choices, there is a strong element of convention in the price decisions of firms. Pricing by custom is 'an indispensable simplification of what otherwise would be an inordinately complex task' (Galbraith, 1952, p. 18).

This being said, which pricing variant is best? The exact pricing variant chosen by a firm depends on the accounting procedures and cost information available to decision-makers. The fact that various cost-plus pricing rules, such as mark-up, full-cost, normal-cost and target-return pricing, have been used through time or are still being used is related to the availability of data on cost and to the proper accounting conventions to distribute overhead costs to the appropriate lines of product. When seen in this light, it is even more obvious that these pricing formulae are variants of the same general procedure, and that 'the differences between them is explainable entirely in terms of the cost accounting procedures used in their formulation' (Lee, 1985, p. 206). Where, for instance, data only on direct costs are accessible or reliable – the less advanced accounting situation – one would expect mark-up pricing rather than full-cost pricing to be prevalent.

Various post-Keynesians or other eclectic authors have used one or the other formulation of cost-plus pricing. Lee (1998, ch. 12) constructs a multisector model, which he calls the empirical pricing model, with a mix of pricing procedures: some industries relying on a mark-up approach, others on various specifications of the normal-cost approach and so on. Mark-up pricing today is mainly associated with the names of Kalecki (1954), Weintraub (1958) and Okun (1981). In addition, as shown by Lee (1994), most post-Keynesian macroeconomic models are built around the notion of a fixed mark-up over unit direct labour costs. New Keynesians also rely on the same approach, a mark-up over constant marginal costs, when they formalize their macroeconomic models of imperfect competition. This is because most macroeconomists prefer the simplicity of the mark-up approach, since it allows them to tackle complex macro questions without being impeded by a more complicated pricing procedure. Lee has argued repeatedly that those who are using only mark-up pricing are showing a lack of understanding of actual pricing practices, since firms now make use of more sophisticated accounting procedures incorporating unit material costs and unit overhead costs, and also because there has been undeniable evidence that firms mostly rely on normal-cost pricing or target-return pricing. In addition, large firms, which are most likely to operate in oligopolistic industries, are also most likely to use normal-cost pricing. There is thus a contradiction in using mark-up pricing to depict imperfect competition. Should all simple mark-up models be forsaken?

The difference between mark-up and other cost-plus models should not be exaggerated. For instance, when Kalecki himself (1971, p. 51) attempts to differentiate his mark-up model from the full-cost one, he indicates that in his model the price of a firm is influenced by the prices of other firms and that it may (not that it must) be influenced by a change in its overhead costs. To that effect, he even mentions that there is a tendency for the mark-up to rise during the slump. But once the influence of overhead costs is accepted, very little difference remains between the mark-up procedure and other cost-plus rules, in particular all the variants of normal-cost pricing. A typical example is when Asimakopulos (1975, p. 319) sets up what he calls a Kaleckian mark-up on unit direct costs. His explanation of the value taken by the mark-up resembles a target-return pricing procedure: 'These mark-ups are designed to cover, over time, both overhead costs and profits. Their values would thus be dependent on the standard rates of utilization of productive capacity used to calculate standard costs as well as on some expected rate of return.'

Still, as we shall see in later chapters in the case of one-sector models and as was shown by Lavoie and Ramírez-Gastón (1997), Kim and Lavoie (2016; 2017) and Fanti and Zamparelli (2021) in the case of two-sector models, it is possible to construct and run macroeconomic models using fancy target-return pricing procedures. Their models also show, on some issues, that using normal-cost pricing can yield results that are distinct or that contradict models based on simple mark-ups. An example of target-return pricing in a two-sector model is presented in a later section of this chapter.

Complications

Some economists have questioned the validity of cost-plus pricing, perhaps because it seems to undermine the virtues of capitalism and its underlying faith in competition between firms. After all, it seems difficult to believe that all firms can always simply decide to change their prices whenever their unit costs change. Indeed, Shapiro and Sawyer (2003, p. 356) insist that 'prices are not decided by costs alone' and that 'there is no automatic transmission of costs into prices'. The mark-up may instead be adjusted, because, as we pointed out earlier, prices are also the result of strategic choices. Still, Coutts and Norman (2013, p. 446) insist that 'cost movements, meaning *shifts* in NUC, *always* lead to price adjustments in the same direction'.

At this stage of the discussion, we need to distinguish between the price-leader, who sets prices, and the price-taker, who follows the lead of the price-leader. The price-leader may be the biggest firm of the industry (the dominant firm), the most innovative one, or firms may take turns. The price-leader may also be a 'barometric' firm, that is, a firm that is representative of the costs of the industry and is convenient for others to follow. Cost-plus pricing procedures explain how price-leaders – those firms that either dominate the market or serve as leaders – set their own prices. Smaller firms, or those considered to be price-takers, may well adopt the same procedures, but they also have to consider the prices set by their price-leaders.

This helps to explain why foreign firms may or may not pass on higher costs, depending on whether they are price-leaders or price-takers on foreign markets. In industries where products are homogeneous and traded at international prices and where foreign firms dominate, the latter tend to pass on to foreign customers their domestic cost increases as well as the effects of changes in exchange rates – the so-called pass-through effects. Domestic firms then need to adjust their prices to those of foreign competitors, in which case mark-ups are flexible. On the other hand, in industries where domestic firms dominate, the mark-ups of domestic firms are constant, and foreign firms fix their prices on the basis of domestic prices. These foreign companies either absorb losses or post windfall profits when exchange rates fluctuate (Bloch and Olive, 1996). In a major econometric study of domestic and foreign firms operating in the UK manufacturing market, Coutts and Norman (2007) show that most domestic firms hardly respond to changes in exchange rates, even when foreign firms change their prices. Thus they conclude that cost-plus pricing with fairly stable mark-ups still holds despite the globalized economy. In other words, the law of one price, so dear to mainstream economists in international trade, does not hold.

How about less efficient firms that face higher unit costs? As such, they will be unable to set costing margins in ways that will generate a normal target rate of return. They will have to put forth competitive prices, similar to those of their rivals. In the short run, they will thus be able to maintain their market share and respond to any sudden increase in demand. But in the medium and long run, market forces will take their toll, unless the high-cost firm is somehow able to redesign its product and reduce its unit costs. Only then will the less efficient price-taker be able to impose normal costing margins. Otherwise, competition will impose financial constraints on inefficient firms by limiting their ability to pursue investments in their productive capacity or in research and development (Steindl, 1952; Kaldor, 1985, p. 47). Because of the financial constraint, high-cost firms will be forced to reduce their growth rate, thus diminishing their market share and, ultimately, leading to their disappearance.

In his review of the studies on pricing conducted by 12 central banks, Melmiès (2010, p. 455) finds that the most frequent reason for price increases is changes in material costs, followed by changes in labour costs. This is because 'the implicit understanding among rivals is that all have similar cost conditions and little risk is attached to moving prices when costs move' (Coutts and Norman, 2013, p. 446). The most important factor for price decreases is competitor pressures, followed by changes in material costs. This gives some credence to Kalecki's (1971) views; he argued that prices essentially depend on unit direct costs and the prices set by rival firms. In fact, in both competitive and oligopolistic surroundings, all firms will tend to set a similar price for a given product.

In his review of central bank studies on price stickiness, Melmiès (2010) also shows that two explanations of price stickiness predominate: cost-based pricing and implicit contract theory. Thus firms, of their own account, explain that they do not change prices when demand increases because pricing is based on unit costs, which do not necessarily change when demand changes, as we shall discuss in the next subsection. Furthermore, firms decline to increase prices when demand increases because they have an implicit contract with their customers, meaning that 'producers seek to build a long-term relationship with customers' (Melmiès, 2010, p. 448). By keeping prices stable, they minimize the risk that their customers will look for other providers. Thus an important facet of the pricing behaviour of firms is that they do not want to antagonize their customers, a feature emphasized by Blinder et al., (1999, p. 308) and which, as pointed out by Downward and Lee (2001), had long been underlined by Hall and Hitch (1939) when they referred to 'goodwill'.

Goodwill, or brand loyalty, is the rule of thumb that says there is no need to try other suppliers as long as the current price appears to be fair and the product satisfying. This applies to both consumers and industrial purchasers. Firms must avoid giving the impression that they are overcharging (Okun, 1981, p. 178; Kaldor, 1985, p. 48). To retain fair prices, firms seek price similarity with their rivals or try to stabilize prices with respect to unit costs, thus keeping constant the percentage costing margin. To set fair prices, firms rely on fair or reasonable target rates of return on investment (Lanzillotti, 1958, p. 931; Shipley, 1981, p. 432). Sticky prices thus play two roles: they help to retain goodwill; and they help to avoid price wars, which observers usually refer to as cut-throat competition or destructive competition, thus highlighting its undesirable characteristics. This is particularly the case during recessions.

3.6.4 Prices and Variations of Demand

We have seen how prices are normally set. What happens when economic conditions are such that firms consistently produce below either the expected rate of utilization of capacity or the standard rate? What if the actual rate of utilization of capacity is above the standard rate? In other words, what happens to prices and the margins of profit during the business cycle? What would the post-Keynesian model of pricing predict? It all depends on the variant used. The answer may also change depending on whether the variables looked at are prices or mark-ups.

Let us first assume that variations in the sales of firms of an industry have no impact on its direct unit costs; that is, the price of raw materials and the nominal wage rate are not influenced by these variations in output. Any change in the industry price would thus be a consequence of a change in the mark-up or in average indirect cost. Let us consider the case of a downturn. Four models of pricing may be considered. In the mark-up model, since the gross margin of profit is over prime costs only, variations of output should have no impact on prices unless the mark-up is changed. In the full-cost model *stricto sensu*, that is, in its old version, since overhead costs are spread over a smaller level of output, unit costs increase in the downturn. With a given net costing margin, we should thus expect prices to go up in a recession. In the normal-cost model, with the net costing margin calculated over normal or standard unit costs, a downturn accompanied by a constant mark-up should lead to constant prices. This is because standard unit costs are independent of variations of output by definition. The same can be said of target-return pricing if the downturn has no impact on the conventional rate of return and the conventional rate of utilization that determine the mark-up. The net costing margin may change if the downturn is perceived as a secular downfall in the rate of growth of the economy or of the industry. This is the effect emphasized by Eichner in particular, who conjectures that a fall in the perceived secular rate of growth of sales leads to a lower mark-up, presumably through the downward adjustment of the target rate of return. This effect on the pricing formula may nevertheless be compensated by a simultaneous fall in what is considered to be the normal rate of utilization of capacity.

All three possible effects of output variations on prices can thus be entertained within the various post-Keynesian variants of pricing. The main view that emerges from this quick assessment is that cost-plus pricing generally leads to the belief that output fluctuations have no effect on costing margins. If prices fall in a recession, this may be due only to a fall in direct costs, that is, wages and raw materials, the latter fact having been noted by Kalecki (1969, p. 53). Various empirical studies seem to demonstrate that all three possible effects of output variations on margins of profit are observed. The empirical studies performed by Coutts et al. (1978), by Sawyer et al. (1982) and by Domowitz et al. (1986) all highlight the fact that margins of profit can stay constant, increase or decrease in recessions. The same diversity of behaviour occurs during expansions. These studies conclude, nonetheless, that the impact of demand on prices or margins is small and that, overall, the number of cases where prices decrease in a recession compensates for the number of cases where prices increase. The response to changes in demand is predominantly a quantity response, not a price one. The conclusions reached by Coutts et al. are in clear support of normal-cost pricing or of any other similar procedure based on standard costs.

> The central tendency of these estimates, as well as the absolute size of even the most extreme estimates, indicate that there is no general or economically significant tendency for prices to change relative to normal costs over the course of the business cycle ... The evidence did not support the view that demand affects prices relative to normal unit costs: the effect of demand on the mark up was both statistically and economically insignificant. (Coutts et al., 1978, pp. 72, 139)

The lesson to be drawn from all this is that it is a good approximation to assume that firms fix prices by adding a constant percentage mark-up to their normal unit costs, calculated at a conventional rate of utilization of capacity and with a target rate of return in mind. The cause of this is that prices are not designed to be market-clearing prices; rather they are reproductive prices. The purpose of prices is to ensure that efficient or average firms generate enough profits through the cycle to finance or obtain finance for the required investments. When firms keep their margins of profit constant through the business cycle, their flow of profit varies in proportion to their immediate needs. When capacity is strained to the limit, total profits and the share of profits are high; when production is below standard capacity, total profits and the share of profits are low. Total profits and retained earnings thus move procyclically although prices and margins of profit may stay constant as demand varies. This is due to the constant or slightly decreasing direct unit costs and to the spread of fixed costs over a larger output.

Figure 3.9 illustrates this direct relationship between output and profits or the share of profits in the value of sales when the mark-up is constant. At the normal level of output q_n, normal unit direct costs are equal to OD, overhead unit costs are DF, and normal unit costs are OF. The net costing margin is set at Fp and thus the price is set at p. If sales turn out to be equal to standard output, the realized net profit per unit will turn out to be equal to the net costing margin. The share of profits in sales is precisely equal to the share of the net costing, Fp/Op. The value of profits is then equal to the large hatched rectangle area. However, when actual sales do not correspond to standard output, the net profit per unit and the costing margin do not correspond to each other. Figure 3.9 illustrates the case of a recession, when the output level of the firm falls to q_r. Unit direct costs stay the same, but unit fixed costs increase to DR and the share of indirect costs in the value of output increases to DR/Op. As a consequence, net profits per unit of output fall to Rp. The realized share of profits out of sales decreases to Rp/Op, and total profits shrink to the area covered by the smaller doubled-hatched rectangle. The converse happens when output increases. In contrast to orthodox theory, profits necessarily increase when the output of the firm increases, provided the firm stays beneath full capacity.

These effects of variations in the rate of utilization of capacity will be further analysed in Chapter 5, with the help of a simple algebraic form. Meanwhile, we can make use

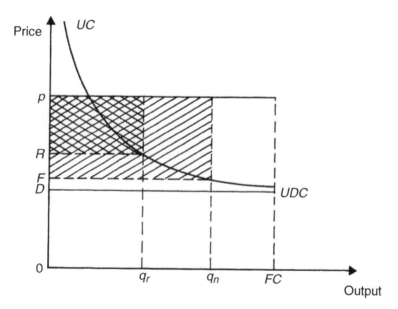

Notes: OD = normal direct unit costs ($NUDC$); DF = normal overhead unit costs; OF = normal unit costs (NUC); Fp = net costing margin ($\Theta.NUC$); Fp/OF = percentage net costing margin (Θ); Dp = gross costing margin ($\theta.NUDC$); Dp/OD = percentage gross costing margin (θ); Rp = realized net profit margin; Rp/OR = realized percentage net profit margin; Rp/Op = realized net profit share in sales.

Figure 3.9 Procyclical variations in profits with cost-plus pricing

of an illustration provided by Coutts and Norman (2013). In Figure 3.9, we assumed away shifts in labour costs or raw materials. Here, with Figure 3.10, we consider the case where cyclical fluctuations in the economy cause changes in labour and material costs. As Coutts and Norman (2013, pp. 447–8) note, 'wage rates may increase as the labour market tightens at a higher level of economic activity. Also, the general increase in demand across the economy may put upward pressure on material prices that are traded on markets where prices move significantly with demand.' This will be particularly so if the increase occurs worldwide, so that the prices of raw materials, which are determined in world markets, are likely to rise.

This wage inflation and raw material price inflation will lead to an increase in actual unit costs and in unit costs calculated at normal output. With a fixed costing margin or a fixed percentage mark-up, as it should be with normal-cost pricing, this will be reflected in higher prices for the goods manufactured, which will thus be mildly procyclical, as shown in Figure 3.10. By contrast, actual unit costs are shown to be countercyclical, as actual costs mostly reflect the variations in rates of capacity utilization and hence the countercyclical changes in overhead unit costs. As a consequence, as was the case with Figure 3.9, the actual profit margin will move in a procyclical fashion despite the fixed mark-up over normal unit costs. This is completely at odds with the New Consensus claim that costing margins or profit margins decline during an expansion.

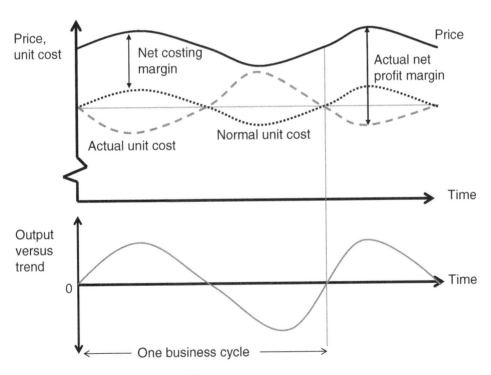

Source: Coutts and Norman (2013, p. 448).

Figure 3.10   Prices, normal unit costs and actual unit costs through the business cycle

3.6.5 Determinants of the Costing Margin

Rejecting an implicit form of profit maximization
We have not yet discussed the determinants of the costing margins, except to say that they should depend on the target rate of return. The major criticism of cost-plus pricing, seen from the neoclassical side, is that it really is nothing else than profit maximization in disguise. The claim was made from very early on, in the 1940s, when the so-called marginalist controversies were raging (Lee, 1984). The claim has been resuscitated with the New Keynesian use of mark-up pricing in its macro models. As explained by Kriesler (1987), Kalecki himself, at some point, adopted the method of profit maximization, although he quickly dismissed it explicitly. Even today, some post-Keynesians (Cowling, 1982; Moore 1988, p. 213), as well as eclectic economists who show some sympathy for cost-plus pricing (Koutsoyiannis, 1975, p. 281; Tarshis, 1980, p. 11), conclude that it is a trial-and-error or routine version of profit maximization. Others argue that, since Kalecki has always denied the importance of overhead costs for pricing, he must have assumed at all times short-run profit maximization (Carson, 1990). One of the drawbacks of cost-plus pricing is that its earlier proponents have generally been silent about the determinants of the mark-up. This silence led Kaldor (1956, pp. 92–3) to reject initially cost-plus pricing as some kind of tautology, and it has helped neoclassical critics to reduce cost-plus pricing to marginalism. We first show how this can be so, and then we discuss alternative determinants of the mark-up.

The proof of the equivalence of marginalist pricing and mark-up pricing is very simple. Profit maximization requires the equality of marginal revenue with marginal cost.

$$MR = MC$$

As is well known, marginal revenue can also be expressed as a function of the price charged and of the (absolute value of the) price elasticity of demand e.

$$MR = p(e-1)/e$$

Since cost-plus proponents usually assume constant marginal costs, direct unit costs and marginal costs are equal, so that the profit-maximizing condition may be rewritten as

$$p(e-1)/e = UDC$$

The profit-maximizing price can thus be rewritten as

$$p = [e/(e-1)]UDC = (1 + \theta)UDC$$

We are back to the mark-up variant of cost-plus pricing, given by equation (3.20). Solving for θ, we have $\theta = 1/(e-1)$, or, solving for e, we get $e = (1 + \theta)/\theta$. Marginalists argue that the lower the price elasticity of demand, that is, the less sensitive is demand to price variations, the higher is the profit-maximizing mark-up that firms will eventually adopt through trial and error. Neoclassical authors thus claim that, while managers report that they are using cost-plus procedures, they are in fact maximizing profits in the orthodox marginalist manner without knowing it. Marginal cost and marginal revenue are equated at the appropriate gross profit margin.

The equivalence of mark-up and marginalist pricing requires, however, that the (absolute value of the) price elasticity of demand be above unity. Otherwise, marginal revenue is negative and thus cannot be equated with marginal cost, which is necessarily positive. It turns out that in many oligopolistic industries the empirical estimate of the price elasticity of demand e is below unity (Koutsoyiannis, 1984). If we assume that there is a price-leader in these industries, and that other firms follow the leader, thus keeping market shares constant, the price elasticity measured for these industries is exactly equal to the price elasticity of demand faced by the individual price-leader, which is thus also much below unity. Neoclassical authors respond to this by saying that, if oligopolies behave as competitors, with N firms, the price elasticity of demand faced by each firm will then be eN, so that below-unity industry elasticities need not imply incompatibility with profit maximization. This response is highly dubious, however, because the Blinder et al. (1999) survey showed that over 80 per cent of respondents implied that their price elasticity of demand was below unity. We may thus conclude that the marginal revenue at current prices of the price-leader is negative, and that as a consequence price maximization as a hypothesis cannot be entertained (Steindl, 1952, pp. 15–17; Eichner, 1976, p. 48). The mark-up equation cannot be interpreted as trial-and-error profit maximization.

We have not yet spoken of normal-cost pricing. Can it also be subsumed to implicit profit maximization? The answer is an obvious no. Marginalism implies that changes in fixed costs have no impact on the pricing decision. With full-cost pricing, normal-cost pricing or target-return pricing, an increase in overhead costs implies an increase in prices. Normal-cost pricing is thus totally incompatible with marginalism and profit maximization. Since most large companies practise normal-cost pricing, the hypotheses of profit maximization and of marginal pricing in disguise cannot be sustained.

The expansion and finance frontiers again

If the mark-up does not depend on profit-maximization considerations, what determines it? The target-return pricing approach offers the beginning of an answer. Equation (3.30) shows that the percentage net costing margin Θ depends in particular on the target rate of return and the capital to capacity ratio, or more precisely the capital to normal output ratio (v/u_n). The higher the capital to capacity ratio, the higher the mark-up over unit costs. Or, as Eichner (1986a, p. 49) would put it, the higher the incremental capital to capacity ratio, when new additions to capacity only are taken into consideration to cover fixed capital costs, the higher the mark-up over unit costs. In Marxian terms, the mark-up depends on the organic composition of capital.

While there can be little disagreement about the relevance of the capital to capacity ratio or of the capital to normal output ratio, the determinants of the major component of the target-return approach – the target rate of return itself – are more controversial. In the very abstract, the answer lies at the intersection of the finance and expansion frontiers, as described earlier with the help of Figure 3.3. As long as firms try to grow as fast as they can, their managers perceive that with the existing constraints (finance, but also competition, technology, knowledge, labour unions), there is a certain rate of profit that can and must be realized for all the constraints to be met. This corresponds to the rate of profit r_g in Figure 3.3. This constrained rate of profit is the standard rate of return of the pricing formula.

What determines the target rate of return? Post-Keynesians have offered four answers, as shown in Table 3.2, which can be associated with four traditions. These four answers can be related to our little model of the expansion and finance frontiers, the answer of each tradition being associated with a particular component of the two frontiers. Thus, at the microeconomic level, the profit rate that a firm can achieve is tied to the shape of its expansion frontier, determined by its market power and its ability to control its costs. This is thus related to the Kaleckian and the Marxian determinants of the target rate of return, that is, the degree of monopoly in the former case, and class struggle in the latter case.

The next two explanations are better linked to the finance frontier, which we repeat below for convenience. The Cambridge explanation says that the growth rate of the firm determines its target rate of return, while Sraffians argue that the trend long-term interest rate is the main determinant of the target rate of return. If we are to believe in the finance frontier, we could say that both the growth rate g and the interest rate i are determinants of the profit rate required to fulfil the finance frontier and hence are determinants of the rate of return that ought to be targeted by the firm. But similarly, as equation (3.11A) shows, reproduced here, other elements, such as the trend debt ratio l that is permissible or considered safe, along with other variables such as the retained earnings ratio s_f as well as the propensities to issue new shares or to purchase new financial assets, x and f_f, will have an impact on the required profit rate.

$$r = \left(i_B l - i_F f_f\right) + \frac{g\left(1 - x - l + f_f\right)}{s_f} \qquad (3.11A)$$

The dominant explanation of the target rate of return

The dominant view within post-Keynesian economics remains the one that sees a cost-plus price as a 'reproductive price and a growth price' (Lee, 1985, p. 209; cf. Lee, 2013b). Pricing is linked with investment decision. When Lanzillotti (1958, pp. 938–40) presented the results of his survey on the price behaviour of firms, he concluded by linking pricing to the planned profits required for investment and growth. This view has been developed in the models of Wood (1975), Eichner (1976), Harcourt and Kenyon (1976), Shapiro (1981) and Capoglu (1991). All these authors present a variant of the model of the firm that has been suggested earlier, where the growth of the firm is restricted by the intersection of the finance frontier with the expansion frontier. This line of thought is consistent with the old Cambridge growth models of the mid-1950s, *à la* Robinson and Kaldor. In these models, higher growth rates were presumed to be accompanied by higher realized

Table 3.2   The various determinants of the target rate of return

Tradition	Determinants
Marxian	Class struggle
Kaleckian	The degree of monopoly and the ability to prevent the entry of potential rivals
Cambridge	The growth rate of capital
Sraffian	The rate of interest set by the central bank

profit rates – a result of the higher costing margins generated by the improved demand conditions. Within the framework presented here, the higher profit margins are not the result of demand and supply forces in the goods market; rather they arise as a result of the discretionary decisions of the price-leaders over costing margins, on the basis of the improved prospects with regard to the secular growth rate. This link between profit and growth is also consistent with the 'natural system' developed by Pasinetti (1981; 1993), where the profit rate and the growth rate are assumed to be equal within each of his hyper-vertically integrated sectors.

All this did not impress upon Robinson (1977, p. 11), who argued that 'such theories can never be quite convincing, for motivation in business is multi-dimensional and cannot be squeezed into a simple formula', thus being consistent with her previous claim that the profit margin 'depends very much upon historical accident or upon conventional views among business men as to what is reasonable' (1966, p. 78). Kaldor, however, endorsed an account of the mark-up based on the finance and the expansion frontiers.

> This objective – maximizing the attainable rate of growth – can mean several things. First, it means aiming at a price that will maintain, and, if possible, improve on their *share* of the market. This consideration would suggest that they should choose a price and hence a markup that is as *low* as they can make it.
>
> Second, they must choose a markup that allows them to increase their *own* capital, by means of ploughed-back profits as much as possible ... Their main motive in all this is to prevent a situation where they become restricted in their expansion by a financial constraint ... This second consideration taken by itself suggests making the markup as high as possible, since the higher the markup, the higher the rate at which their own capital accumulates at any given plough-back ratio ... So these opposing considerations should determine the firm's judgment as to what the optimum markup should be. (Kaldor, 1985, pp. 50–52)

Of course firms never know exactly the shape of their finance and expansion frontiers, and hence the exact value of their constrained optimal rate of profit r_g. Furthermore, it can be presumed that the strength of the constraints frequently changes, thus modifying in Figure 3.3 the shape and the slope of the frontiers. The target rate of return that results from these considerations is thus a conventional rate of profit, the equality of which with the realized rate of profit cannot be presumed, neither in the short run nor in the long run. This is why, in the words of Joan Robinson (1971, p. 94), the profit margins of full-cost pricing procedures 'are set at a level calculated to yield a satisfactory return on some normal or standard average level of utilization of capacity'. The firm can know only what the past rates of return have been; it can know neither what the present nor the future rates of profit will be. It must thus rely on some conventional measure of the rate of return that will fully recover part of both past and future expansion costs.

Ironically, it should be mentioned that, while several present post-Keynesian authors believe that target-return pricing as here redefined through the finance frontier applies mostly to oligopolistic industries and their price-leaders, earlier exponents of target-return pricing thought that it applied with more force to competitive manufacturing industries. When discussing an industry with plenty of small producers, Steindl (1952, p. 51) resolves that competitive pressures are such that the margin of profit is just sufficient to cover the financial costs of expansion, given the acceptable gearing ratio. In the case of oligopolies, Steindl believes that since firms possess some monopoly power, they are able to remain beyond their finance frontier, maximizing neither profits nor growth.

Alternative explanations of the target rate of return

This brings us to the other post-Keynesian views about the determination of the mark-up on direct or unit costs. Steindl's theory of pricing, which he tried to substantiate in his book, was basically that higher margins of profit could be associated with higher industrial concentration ratios (1952, pp. 70–71). This, of course, is a development of Kalecki's degree of monopoly, that is 'the semi-monopolistic influences ... resulting from imperfect competition or oligopoly' (1971, p. 160). The height of the mark-up in each industry depends on the monopoly power of its firms, measured by the industrial concentration ratio or a proxy thereof. This view, now known as the monopoly power model (Dutt, 1987b, p. 65), or the monopoly capital model (Baran and Sweezy, 1968), relies in its microeconomic incarnation on some empirical evidence showing a positive relation between mark-ups and concentration ratios (Weiss, 1980).

A variant of the monopoly power view of the determination of mark-ups, also derived from Kalecki (1971, pp. 51, 156–64) and the work of neo-radical authors, can be similarly integrated. In this variant, monopoly power is not associated with concentration ratios, but with the corporate power of the firm over the whole economy (Dutt, 1987b, p. 71). As noted by a number of commentators, in his later writings Kalecki has associated the degree of monopoly power not only with the struggle between competing firms, but also with the intensity of the struggle between social classes (Jossa, 1989). The size of the mark-up on direct costs is in inverse relation with the bargaining power of the trade unions. Reciprocally, the more successful the class struggle from the point of view of the workers, the higher the real wage rate and the lower the mark-up (Dutt, 1987a). This can easily be seen from the mark-up version of cost-plus pricing as shown in equation (3.11A). If average variable costs there are assumed to consist only of wages (the wage rate multiplied by the number of workers), a higher wage rate at fixed prices necessarily entails a lower mark-up and higher real wages. Again, from the point of view of the individual firm, this class-bargaining variant of the monopoly power view can be interpreted as shifts of the expansion frontier in Figure 3.3. In its modern incarnation, class bargaining extends to overhead costs, as increases of manager emoluments occur through an increase in overhead costs and hence an increase in the gross costing margin.

A final explanation for the value taken by the target rate of return has been provided recently. This explanation was mainly endorsed by a group of Sraffian authors, in particular Garegnani (1979, p. 81) and Pivetti (1985), following a suggestion made by Sraffa (1960, p. 33), according to whom the rate of profit is 'susceptible of being determined from outside the system of production, in particular by the level of the money rates of interest'. They argue that the target rate of return, or what they usually call the normal rate of profit, is determined to a large extent by the real rate of interest that arises from the monetary regime put in place by the central bank. All else equal, when interest rates rise, prices rise. Sraffian authors argue that the normal rate of profit is made up of two components: the rate of interest that needs to be paid to lenders and that constitutes an opportunity cost; and the net entrepreneurial premium, which is a kind of liquidity premium, designed to compensate for the trouble and risk of engaging in entrepreneurial activity. While the premium would vary from industry to industry, depending on the variability of its returns or the height of its barriers to entry, the rate of interest would affect all industries. A monetary regime with very high real rates of interest, as the one we have known during most of the 1980s and 1990s, would thus be conducive to higher target rates of return. Simply put, interest payments are seen as a cost to the firm, a cost incorporated into the target rate of return.

This view has a long history among heterodox economists: Thomas Tooke and the Banking School in the nineteenth century; Harrod, Kaldor, Sylos Labini, Graziani and even for a time Robinson have taken this view. The impact of interest rates on target rates and prices has also been noted by Smithin (1997), Taylor (2004, pp. 88–90) and Hein (2008). Kaldor (1982, p. 63) argued that 'interest costs are passed on in higher prices in much the same way as wage costs', while Harrod (1973, p. 111), through his work with the Oxford Economists' Research Group, acquired the conviction that 'sustained low rates of interest will presumably in the long run reduce the normal rate of profit'.

The upshot of all this is that the four explanations of the target rate of return are not incompatible. All four explanations may affect simultaneously the actual value of the target rate of return. More importantly, all these explanations are unrelated to marginalism.

3.7 COST-PLUS PRICES AND PRICES OF PRODUCTION

3.7.1 Similarities

In Chapter 1 we noted that Sraffian economists were concerned with relative prices and multisectoral models. But we also noted that some methodologists are reluctant to include Sraffian economics within post-Keynesian economics. What is the relationship between cost-plus prices and the prices of production of Sraffian economists?

There are basically four points of contact between cost-plus prices and prices of production: (1) both visions of prices are cost oriented; (2) they are reproductive prices; (3) market clearance is not an issue; (4) prices are based on normal conditions.

First, and very obviously, neither of these types of prices equates marginal costs to marginal revenues. In cost-plus prices as well as prices of production, the centre of attention is the cost of production. As Wiles (1973, p. 386) says, 'the main function of prices is not to be resource-allocators but cost-coverers'. Cost-plus prices and prices of production are not indices of temporary scarcity, in opposition to neoclassical prices. As is clear in the model of Pasinetti (1981; 1993), prices of production are correctly weighted indices of labour costs. Demand plays no role, except in peculiar circumstances such as joint production, or the role of demand is an indirect one. For instance, the rate of growth of demand may have an impact on the target rate of return or the uniform rate of profit, something that can be interpreted as the need for more hyper-indirect labour.

Second, there is the reproductive quality of cost-of-production prices and cost-plus prices. We have already seen that cost-plus prices could not be associated with short-run profit maximization. We have underlined in particular the importance of the expansion and the financial constraints on the mark-up decision of the firm. Prices must allow growth. In Sraffian models, reproduction is also *the* crucial element. Reproducibility enters through the explicit interdependent connections between the various products: the reproduction of commodities by means of commodities so central to Sraffian analysis. The technological matrix – the input–output matrix – takes care of this interdependence. Some outputs are the inputs of other products, and therefore the variations in prices of these commodities have feedback effects. In cost-plus pricing, the interdependence is made implicit only: each firm is assumed to fix its prices according to its costs, that is, according to the prices of its inputs; but the prices of these inputs are themselves the result of a mark-up procedure.

Third, we know that cost-plus prices are non-clearing prices. As such, they are not market prices, but administered ones. Cost-plus prices are not influenced by short-run variations in demand. Furthermore, they certainly do not ensure that in the short run demand will equate the standard rate of utilization of capacity; but as the case of General Motors illustrated, the same can be said even in the long run: the average actual rate of utilization of capacity is not necessarily the standard rate. A similar claim has been made for Sraffian prices. When they are interpreted as a photograph at a given moment of time, with given levels of output, 'there is no reason to suppose that prices of production should equate the quantity demanded with the quantity supplied for any commodity in the long period' (Roncaglia, 1978, p. 16).

The similarities between cost-plus prices and prices of production are most obvious in the target-return pricing approach (Reynolds, 1987, p. 179). In the canonical version of Sraffian prices of production, it is assumed that best-practice technological coefficients are calculated at standard levels of capacity utilization, and the rates of profit imposed upon fixed capital (or variable capital) are assumed to be uniform across industries. This rate of profit is thus the normal rate of profit, and output corresponds to the normal rate of utilization of capacity, each plant or segment of plant being operated at its optimal engineer-rated capacity. This is quite similar to the target-return view: standard or normal output, that is the normal rate of utilization, helps to determine unit costs and the mark-up; the latter also depends on the normal rate of profit that corporations wish to obtain in the long run on their investments and capital. The target rate of return thus plays a similar role to that of the uniform rate of profit in prices of production.

Still, there is no obligation to impose a uniform rate of profit. Several authors deal with prices of production models that assume neither the uniformity of the rate of profit nor the uniformity of the industry rates of growth. This is the case, among others, of Pasinetti (1981) and Eichner (1987, ch. 6). Indeed, from the very beginning, various authors have asserted that the uniformity of the rate of profit is only a convenient hypothesis to make, and that differentiated rates of profit due to oligopolistic conditions and barriers to entry are perfectly compatible with the Sraffian model (Sylos Labini, 1971, p. 270; Roncaglia, 1978, p. 29). More recently, Zambelli (2018b) has reasserted that Sraffa himself assumed a uniform rate of profit and did not say that it had to be so to explain self-reproducing prices, while Ricardo recognized that the classical natural prices entertained differentiated profit rates. To those that believe that the explicit introduction of financial markets would generate profit rate equalization, Dutt (1990a, p. 131) has replied that 'this is by no means obvious: the incorporation of financial capital in the model can result in the equalization of financial rates of return without equalizing rates of profit'. In terms of what we discussed earlier in section 3.5.4, financial considerations may generate the equalization of the total shareholder return r_{TSR}, but of neither the profit rate of firms r nor the return on total assets r_{ROA}.

Prices based on target rates of return are the behavioural counterpart to Sraffian prices; they are what Nell (1988, p. 195; 1998, p. 394) calls 'benchmark prices'. With non-uniform rates of profit, which correspond to the differentiated target rates of return of each firm or industry, and assuming that the technological coefficients are those of the firms that act as price-leaders, the Sraffian multisector price model becomes the relative price version of the target-return pricing approach. The study of the properties of target-return pricing models, within a system-wide model, has been analysed in particular by Boggio (1992). His conclusion is that, in these target-return pricing models, the convergence of relative prices towards constant values requires very few assumptions, in contrast to the conditions required to obtain convergence in standard Sraffian models. Some post-Keynesians, however, dispute the relevance of such studies, since convergence requires a large number of periods, during which time the assumed constant data set – production conditions and target rates of return – is most likely to change continuously (Lee, 1994).

3.7.2 Target-return Pricing and Prices of Production

The purpose of this subsection is to show the algebraic similarities between Sraffian prices of production and target-return pricing, a resemblance noted by a number of authors (Earl, 1983, ch. 2; Semmler, 1984; Eichner, 1987; Levine, 1988). To illustrate this similarity we will construct a two-sector model based on target-return pricing. We start with a simple description of Sraffian prices of production, which excludes intermediate goods, but with fixed capital (see Pasinetti, 1977). These Sraffian prices are given by the following equation. It says that the value of a product is equal to the sum of the costs in terms of wages for labour and profits on capital:

$$\boldsymbol{p} = w\boldsymbol{n} + r\boldsymbol{M}\boldsymbol{p} \tag{3.31}$$

Letters in bold indicate a vector or a matrix: $\boldsymbol{p}$ is a column-vector of prices, w is the wage rate, $\boldsymbol{n}$ and $\boldsymbol{M}$ are a vector and a matrix of technical coefficients representing respectively labour per unit of output and the amounts of each kind of machines per unit of output. Finally, r is the uniform profit rate. We can rewrite the above equation as

$$\boldsymbol{p} = w\boldsymbol{n}\,[\boldsymbol{I} - r\boldsymbol{M}]^{-1} \tag{3.32}$$

We can recover a very similar one-sector equation from our target-return pricing procedure by combining equations (3.27) and (3.30), assuming that all goods have a unique price, $p = p_i$, and that normal unit costs come down to direct unit wage costs, so that $NUC = wL/q = wn$, where n is labour per unit of output, that is, $n = 1/y$, where y was defined as output per worker, as per equation (1.6). This being the case, we get

$$p = u_n wn (u_n - r_n v)^{-1} \tag{3.33}$$

The last two equations are essentially identical, once we note that in these kinds of equations Sraffians assume that the normal rate of capacity utilization u_n is unity. In addition, the Sraffian uniform rate of profit is what Sraffians also call the normal profit rate, which is no different from the target rate of return r_n of the normal-cost pricing procedure. The similarity between target-return pricing can be further shown by constructing a two-sector target-return pricing model, with a consumption sector and an investment sector (Lavoie and Ramírez-Gastón, 1997; Fanti and Zamparelli, 2021). The latter provides the machines required to produce goods in both sectors, so that the investment good is a basic good, as the Sraffians call it. Making the same assumptions that we made to obtain equation (3.33), and using nearly the same notations (n for a normal value is now a superscript instead of a subscript), we can write the pricing equation of both j sectors, with subscripts i for investment goods and c for consumption goods, and with unit labour costs wn_j, each sector having its own percentage costing margin θ_j, in analogy with equation (1.10) of Chapter 1:

$$p_j = (1 + \theta_j)wn_j \qquad (3.34)$$

As pointed out earlier, the mark-up in each sector must be such that sales corresponding to the normal degree of capacity (q_j^n) must provide enough profits to fulfil the target rate of return (r_j^n). As Bhaduri and Robinson (1980, p. 107) put it, 'gross margins in each line are fixed up in such a way to cover costs and yield a "subjective-normal" rate of net profit at a standard level of utilization of capacity'. In a given period, it follows that the standard flow of profits for the j sector may be written, from equation (3.34), either as

$$P_j^n = \theta_j w n_j q_j^n \qquad (3.35)$$

or as

$$P_j^n = r_j^n p_i M_j \qquad (3.36)$$

Here the notation is still similar to what has been used previously. Defining for each j sector, the capital to full-capacity output ratio $v_j = M_j/q_j^{fc}$, and the standard rate of capacity utilization $u_j^n = q_j^n/q_j^{fc}$, equation (3.36) can be rewritten as

$$P_j^n = \frac{r_j^n p_i v_j q_j^n}{u_j^n} \qquad (3.37)$$

Combining equations (3.35) and (3.37), we find:

$$\theta_j = \frac{r_j^n p_i v_j}{u_j^n n_j w_j} \qquad (3.38)$$

Inserting equation (3.38) into equation (3.34) when they apply to the investment sector, we get the percentage costing margin in the investment sector:

$$\theta_i = \frac{r_i^n v_i}{u_i^n - r_i^n v_i} \qquad (3.39)$$

Under the assumptions of the model, the percentage costing margin θ_i of the investment sector depends solely on its own standard rate of capacity utilization and target rate of return, as well as on its own capital to full-capacity ratio. To find the percentage costing margin θ_c of the consumption sector, we must first know the price p_i of investment goods, as is obvious from equation (3.38). Knowing θ_i and hence p_i, the price of the machines, we can now compute the percentage costing margin of the consumption sector required for firms of that sector to achieve the profits necessary to attain their target rate of return when sales correspond to the standard rate of utilization of capacity.

The mark-up is obtained by applying equations (3.34) and (3.38) to the consumption sector, making use of equation (3.39) and of the fact that $p_i = (1 + \theta_i)w_i n_i$. The percentage costing margin in the consumption sector is thus

$$\theta_c = \left(\frac{r_c^n v_c}{u_i^n - r_i^n v_i}\right)\left(\frac{u_i^n}{u_c^n}\right)\left(\frac{n_i}{n_c}\right)\left(\frac{w_i}{w_c}\right) \tag{3.40}$$

Equation (3.40) provides an answer to the critique of Kaleckian models by Ian Steedman (1992), who argued that mark-ups in the various sectors could not be independent of each other. Here, equation (3.40) reflects the interdependence between sectors. The costing margin in the consumption sector also depends on what occurs in the investment sector. Any change in the determinants of the costing margin of the basic good, or even in its wage costs, will have an impact on all costing margins and hence on all prices. Obviously, there is no reason for the two mark-ups to be equal, even if the two target rates of return are equal to each other and if the same wage rate is being paid in both sectors.

What the above shows is that it is perfectly possible to construct an interdependent multi-sectoral model of relative prices based on target-return pricing. In the canonical Sraffian model, the target rates of return embedded in prices are assumed to be uniform. But this does not need to be the case, especially if different sectors or industries are growing at different rates. The other issue is whether realized rates of profit will correspond to the target rates. For this to be so, there must be some mechanism that will drive the actual and the normal rates of capacity utilization towards each other.

There are other ways to incorporate sectoral interdependence in Kaleckian models of pricing and thus to counter Steedman's critique. Fujita (2019) presents a two-sector model that shows some similarities with equation (3.32), with firms setting prices as a markup on unit direct costs that incorporate labour costs and the costs of intermediate inputs. The latter are assumed to be produced by the other sector, so that both goods are basic goods.

3.7.3 Gravitation or Not?

The remaining question is whether prices of production, or their target-return version, ever come about. This is the issue of the gravitation around prices of production or that of the convergence towards prices of production. A number of Sraffian and Marxian authors believe that competitive forces bring about a tendency towards an equality of normal profit rates throughout industries, and that such a tendency operates through a reaction of produced quantities to discrepancies between the actual profit rate and the normal profit rate. Now, as summed up by King (1995, p. 246), there is 'little enthusiasm for any notion of long-period "prices of production" as centres of gravitation towards which short-period or market prices are supposed to tend. The unreconstructed "neo-Ricardians", of whom Pierangelo Garegnani is the most resolute example, are increasingly isolated on this question.'

Classical economists believed that market prices converge towards prices of production, and so did the Sraffians such as Garegnani. It took some time for conditional proofs of such a process to be put forward. Duménil and Lévy (1990) have presented a neat summary of the various kinds of convergence processes that have been proposed. The first convergence models, proposed mainly by French authors, assumed that market prices in a given period were clearing prices, prices that equated demand to the given supply of the period. The discrepancy between the market price and the natural price, or rather between the actual profit rate and the uniform normal profit rate, then generated capital mobility and hence quantity adjustments. As these modern 'classical' models of convergence sounded rather Walrasian, they were progressively replaced by cross-dual models, with clearing prices being replaced by prices based on their value in the previous period and on the observed disequilibria in quantities (excess demand). These cross-dual models were then supplemented with various mechanisms, including a Keynesian increase in output in the case of excess demand.

The problem with these convergence models is that they undermine their own foundations. This is pointed out by Bertram Schefold (1984, p. 1), a Sraffian economist himself, who argues that

> classical economists sometimes adopt neoclassical conceptual tools for the analysis of supply and demand in individual markets (e.g. in the analysis of the gravitation of market prices towards prices of production) and are then led towards models of at least superficial similarity with neo-classical general equilibrium in consequence of the attempt to analyse the interdependence of the various markets.

It follows that 'some of the work by modern classical economists on the convergence of market prices towards prices of production tends to undermine its own foundations by generating systems in which supply and demand are dominating forces' (ibid., p. 2). This is quite obvious with convergence models based on clearing market prices, while non-supplemented cross-dual models must rely on substitution effects in demand to achieve convergence – a rather ironic feature. These criticisms are also made by Adriano Boggio (1986, p. 84), when he mentions that 'the whole disequilibrium process' of classical convergence models is 'dominated by price reactions to excess demand and by consumption reactions to price changes', as it would in mainstream models. In addition, Boggio (1990, p. 56) says, several of the models assume that economic agents know the long-run or equilibrium values of prices and quantities, a rather unKeynesian assumption since this implies that the long-run position is known before actual short-period values occur. These formalized models also imply that quantities are brought back to their 'normal' levels or to their normal rate of capacity utilization. Finally, convergence is always conditional.

Thus, if one wishes to connect Sraffian economics with the other strands of post-Keynesian economics, one needs to examine prices of production in a different light, not as long-run or long-period centres of gravitation to which market prices tend. This alternative view is tied to the contributions of Boggio (1980, 1986, 1990). His relative price models are full-cost models. He assumes, as does Nisticò (2002), that firms set output prices on the basis of wage costs and the commodity prices of the previous period, with a mark-up designed to achieve an exogenously given target rate of return (the normal profit rate). These models are very robust, in the sense that they converge to a steady set of relative prices without the need to impose almost any restriction. One can assume from the start that the target rate of return is the same in each sector; or we can assume differential target rates of return, in which case one might wish to add a slow reaction process, perhaps akin to the excess demand mechanism described by the Sraffian dominant strand, that would explain the evolution of these target rates (Boggio, 1986).

Boggio's full-cost prices are cousins of Roncaglia's interpretation of Sraffa's prices. For Roncaglia (1995, p. 114), 'Sraffa's "outputs" should not be identified with those actually observed at any point in the historical development of the economy'. Instead, costs ought to be computed, 'not for current output levels, but for a "normal" degree of capacity utilisation' (ibid., p. 115). This is consistent with a statement of Joan Robinson (1978, p. 16) that 'each firm is assumed to reckon its costs on the basis of a standard ratio of utilization of its plant'. And of course it is also consistent with target-return pricing, as described by Lanzillotti (1958), according to whom unit costs are assessed on the basis of a standard rate of capacity utilization that is only roughly related to actual rates of capacity utilization.

There is thus a need to reconsider what prices of production are, adopting a point of view closer to that of the dissident Sraffian strands. For authors such as Pasinetti, Roncaglia or Schefold, in a sense prices of production arise both in the short and in the long period; they do not entail a uniform profit rate. Prices set on markets of reproducible goods and services are *quasi* prices of production. Leading firms administer prices, taking into account costs assessed at the normal rate of capacity utilization, with some target rate of return. Sraffian prices should be reinterpreted as normal-cost prices, where 'the price of each commodity is simply determined by its production cost – measured at the normal level of utilization of capacity – plus a target rate of return' (Boggio, 1990, p. 47). Inequalities between supply and demand are resolved mainly through changes in stocks of inventories or in the rate of utilization, not by changes in market prices. Actual prices are not market prices that would clear excess demand at each period (Arena, 1987, p. 205). As pointed out by Shiozawa (2016), the reason for which Ricardo mentioned market prices is because in his day the most important industrial product and input ingredient was cotton textile, an agricultural product subjected to the law of supply and demand. This is not the case anymore, so that there is no need for the study of the long-run convergence of market prices towards production prices. Normal prices based on standard unit costs *are* actual prices. If one avoids the so-called process of gravitation, it then becomes clear that prices of production and cost-plus prices are compatible with each other and part of the same conceptual framework. The following quote by a well-known Sraffian tries to make the point:

> The mark-up on unit costs will have to be such that normal profits corresponding to the prevailing rate of profit are obtained at the normal level of capacity utilisation. This approach allows to give a rationale for the rule of full cost pricing, but only in a very simple case. The merit of this application is to clarify the conditions under which full cost pricing is consistent with a given rate of profit in a classical long period position (Or, in an obvious extension, there may be a hierarchy of such rates of profit . . .). One may say that normal prices are here calculated on the basis of a given normal utilization of capacity, and that changes of capacity are used to adapt supply to demand at unchanged prices . . . Actual prices are therefore equal to prices of production but utilization fluctuates around a normal level. (Schefold, 1984, p. 4)

A similar interpretation was offered by John Hicks (1990, p. 102) when he argued that Sraffa's prices were 'based on costs, not of actual outputs but of "normal" outputs'. This, according to Hicks, helped to explain the mystery of the '(apparently uniform) rate of profit in Sraffa's system', which had to be considered 'as a mark-up, established by convention' (Hicks, 1990, p. 100). Hicks (1985, p. 306) made an earlier similar statement as shown below:

> [Sraffa's prices] seem to be prices which are set upon products, by their producers, according to some rule. Now it is perfectly true that we are nowadays familiar with that method of price-fixing, by 'mark-up'; but when that method is used, the rate of profit that is used to establish the mark-up is conventional. Now it may be that Sraffa wants us to think of his rate of profit as being conventional; and that the uniformity of the rate of profit throughout his system, of which he makes so much, is just a uniformity of conventions.

Thus here Hicks interprets Sraffian prices as cost-plus prices, where adjustments occur through over-utilization or under-utilization of capacity, and this in my view is the correct interpretation of what prices of production ought to be. As long as one avoids the so-called process of gravitation, it becomes clear that prices of production and cost-plus prices are identical concepts, set at different levels of abstraction.

3.7.4 Quantity Adjustments versus Price Adjustments

Neoclassical economics assumes that price flexibility is at the core of a market economy and that, without it, adjustments to demand changes would be next to impossible. It is often argued that a complex market economy only avoids chaos thanks to these flexible price adjustments, and this would justify the use of the neo-Walrasian model as a rigorous benchmark model. By contrast, the whole chapter has suggested that firms generally wish to avoid price competition, so as to avoid destructive price wars. Leading firms try to stick to their costing margins while peripheral firms match the prices of the price leader, so that competition occurs through lower unit costs, investment and innovation. With the exception of raw materials, prices hardly react to demand changes and only react to changes in their unit costs. One may thus wonder whether a world which consists of such firms relying on cost-plus pricing, and with limited information as argued in Chapter 2, can truly constitute an adequate representation of a reality made of a highly complex and diversified set of interdependent firms and sectors where chaos is avoided. Herbert Simon certainly thought so.

> Price provides only one of the mechanisms for coordination of behavior, either between organizations and within them. Coordination by adjustment of quantities is probably a far more important mechanism from a day-to-day standpoint, and in many circumstances will do a better job of allocation than coordination by prices.... Quantities of goods sold and inventories, not prices, provide the information for coordinating these systems... Many observers of business scheduling and pricing practices have claimed that (with the possible exception of agricultural and mining sectors) models that use quantities as signals approximate first-world national economies more closely than do models in which prices are the principal mechanisms of coordination. (Simon, 1991, p. 40)

The question has recently been tackled in a book by Shiozawa, Morioka and Taniguchi (2019). They contend that capitalism is by nature a 'sellers' market' – a demand-constrained economy – as opposed to the supply-constrained socialist economy described by Janos Kornai (1980). They link this claim to Sraffa's 1926 statement that the expansion of firms is not limited by rising unit costs but rather by the difficulty of attracting more customers. The separation of price and quantity adjustments is a fundamental principle. Quantities reflect changes in demand. Prices provide the criterion to judge if a new production technique is better than previously existing ones. Prices are regulated by production costs, that is, the minimum cost for a given markup structure. What we have here is a Sraffian theory of prices, slightly reinterpreted. The reinterpretation is based on three features: there is no uniform profit rate; the normal price, based on the normal unit cost, *is* the actual price, that is, cost-of-production prices are not prices achieved only in the long run; fixed capital is not associated with joint production, on the grounds that such joint production accounting is not practised in actual accounting, thus setting the unit depreciation cost on the basis of the normal volume.

Shiozawa et al. (2019) construct multi-sectoral models, each sector with several different firms, each firm of a sector disposing of a finite set of fixed-coefficient production techniques. Prices are set by firms on the basis of normal-cost pricing, where prices only change when unit costs change and not when demand or the proportion of demand attributed to each product changes. Production takes time – there is a time sequence, forecast and orders, then production, and finally delivery and sales – so production cannot immediately respond to changes in demand, and hence there must be a buffer, which are the stocks of inventories, for both intermediate inputs and produced outputs. Finally, as argued in section 3.5.3, firms have excess capacity.

Shiozawa et al. (2019) show that supply adjusts to demand in a converging process, despite the complete lack of reaction of prices to the evolution of sales and inventories, under minimal conditions: production must be equal or higher than the break-even point given by the markup, so that firms do not go bankrupt; banks provide credit on demand; inventory buffers must be large enough, and there must be sufficient smoothing in forecasting demand. These forecasts are based on data that are easily obtainable, and the computations that are assumed to be made by firms require little capability.

The message being conveyed by their book should by now be clear: the results achieved by Shiozawa et al. (2019) constitute a great breakthrough – an achievement of paramount importance as the authors say – for the analysis of the modern industrial economy (the financial sector requires a completely different story). The authors claim that their results are comparable to those of Arrow–Debreu, but obtained within the completely realistic framework of a production economy where agents dispose only of local information and frugal capabilities. Prices are not scarcity indices: changes in prices are not signalling changes in demand relative to supply. They are a tool to assess the best production method, as improvements or new combinations will be reflected by a decrease in unit costs. The information conveying changes in demand is transmitted and assessed through quantity signals – sales and changes in inventories – but not through prices. A key achievement of the authors is the demonstration that a multi-sectoral economy, where production takes time and with produced inputs, can adjust to changes in demand through the realistic decisions of managers to change quantities without any change in prices – something that previously was not thought to be possible. The only drawback of Shiozawa et al.'s book is the lack of aggregate demand feedback, which will be the main subject of the remaining chapters.

NOTE

* Besides relying on and extending the 1992 *Foundations*, full sentences have been taken from the following publications: 'Pricing', in Ric Holt and Steve Pressman (eds), *A New Guide to Post Keynesian Economics*, London: Routledge, 2001, pp. 21–31; 'Should Sraffians be dropped out of the post-Keynesian school?', *Économies et Sociétés*, série *Histoire de la pensée économique*, **45** (7), June–July 2011, pp. 1027–59.

4. Credit, money and central banks*

We now enter macroeconomics. It may seem bizarre to start off by dealing with the topic of credit and money. Students who receive instruction in orthodox economics are used to tackling money as an afterthought, once all the real phenomena have been taken care of. The ordering of topics proposed here is nonetheless perfectly legitimate. The principle of effective demand, which is an essential feature of post-Keynesian economics, with causality running from investment to saving, is best understood within the context of a macroeconomic explanation of a monetary production economy. Although investment is not constrained by saving, production needs to be financed, and this is why it is preferable to start with the monetary dimension of macroeconomics before proceeding to an explanation of employment and growth. Indeed, in Chapter 3, we already had to touch upon the borrowing possibilities of the firm in its attempt to expand production. Although one firm may conceivably be able to avoid borrowing, we shall see that, from a macroeconomic point of view, firms overall must get into debt for expansion to proceed. This chapter is concerned with domestic matters; money in an international context will be dealt with in Chapter 7.

4.1 BACKGROUND INFORMATION

4.1.1 Endogenous Money to the Forefront

Going over the post-Keynesian view of money and credit will give us, once more, the opportunity to take note of the internal coherence of post-Keynesian economics. Post-Keynesians of various strands hold views on monetary matters that have a common core, whether they are Sraffians, French and Italian circuitists, Kaleckians, Fundamentalist Keynesians or neo-chartalists – the branch of post-Keynesian monetary economics that has attracted considerable attention on the worldwide web by putting forth specific theoretical and policy proposals known as Modern Monetary Theory (MMT). All these economists agree that the supply of money is endogenous and demand-led. Indeed, an Italian post-Keynesian, Paolo Sylos Labini (1949, p. 240), argued, more than 60 years ago, that money has been endogenous for over 200 years. Wynne Godley (2012, p. 91) has illustrated the thesis of endogenous money supply with a rather ironic statement: 'Governments can no more "control" stocks of either bank money or cash than a gardener can control the direction of a hosepipe by grabbing at the water jet.' This is in clear contrast and opposition to the quantity theory of money, monetarism, and what can be found in nearly all contemporary mainstream textbooks, where the supply of money is exogenous and depicted as a vertical line in money and interest rate diagrams.

The endogeneity of the supply of money, and hence the reversed causation between money and income, has been most clearly presented in an article by Kaldor (1970b), who was responding to the claims of Milton Friedman. The endogenous money thesis was further developed in books by Kaldor (1982) and Moore (1988), where the latter opposed Horizontalists and Verticalists – those who think that the money supply is endogenous and those who believe that it is exogenous. Other important post-Keynesian contributions to the theory of endogenous money at the time included those of the French economist Jacques Le Bourva (1992), as early as 1959 and 1962, Weintraub and Davidson (1973), Eichner (1986a) and Wray (1990). Indeed, Cambridge post-Keynesians all expressed clearly their rejection of the quantity theory of money and their adhesion to the endogenous money hypothesis, as can be ascertained by the contributions of Robinson (1956, chs 22–3; 1970), Kahn (1972, chs 4 and 7), Tony Cramp (1971), Godley and Cripps (1983), and Kaldor and Trevithick (1981). John Hicks (1982) can also be put in that camp. I myself engaged with this literature when I wrote two surveys on the post-Keynesian views of money and credit (Lavoie, 1984; 1985b), spurred in part by the critiques of traditional theory by the French circuitists.

While a considerable amount of space was devoted in the past to arguments and statements supporting the claims of money supply endogeneity, this is no longer required. There are essentially two reasons for this. First, many central banks have changed the way they implement monetary policy. Their behaviour is now much more transparent, and no veil is hiding the way they are conducting monetary operations. In particular, the interest-rate targeting procedures of central banks are now explicit, corresponding to what several post-Keynesians had been claiming all along. It has thus become much more difficult to argue against the view that the money supply is endogenous and demand-led. Indeed, even researchers at well-known financial institutions are now giving their full support to post-Keynesian monetary theory (Sheard, 2013). These changes in operating procedures have been followed by changes in monetary theory within orthodox economics. While these changes are only entering a limited number of mainstream textbooks, the more advanced macroeconomic models do make room for endogenous money.

This is the case of the so-called New Consensus model, also called the New Neoclassical Synthesis, which arose in the late 1990s and early 2000s, and which combines the hyper-rational behaviour of real business cycle theory with the rigidities of New Keynesian theory (as in the DSGE models). In these models, actual interest rates are determined by a central bank reaction function, and the supply of money is assumed to adjust to the demand for money at the set interest rate. From the standpoint of endogenous money theory, as argued in the book edited by Fontana and Setterfield (2009a), there is a great deal of similarity with the monetary views that post-Keynesians have been advocating for more than 40 years, although the mechanisms underlying the rest of the New Consensus models are entirely different from those that post-Keynesians have in mind, as explained by Sebastian Dullien (2010; 2011; 2017). For instance, both post-Keynesians and New Consensus authors believe that higher real interest rates will slow down the economy. But while post-Keynesians argue that this is because high interest rates are likely to discourage investment or to have a detrimental impact on income distribution, New Consensus authors think that high interest rates ensure higher future income out of present savings, thus diminishing the need to work now to acquire assets, so that the reduction in the supply of labour leads to a reduction in current output.

In addition, while money is endogenous in New Consensus models, it plays no role, being only a money of account.

4.1.2 Historical Background

New Consensus authors usually do not attribute the rediscovery of endogenous money theory to the works of post-Keynesians, paying reverence instead to Fisher Black (1970), the co-author of the Black–Scholes formula now so much used in finance for the calculation of the prices of derivatives. Black described a world without central bank money. More knowledgeable New Consensus authors also sometimes link their monetary views to the endogenous view of money that was pursued in the early twentieth century by authors from the Austrian tradition, namely Ludwig von Mises, Friedrich Hayek and Joseph Schumpeter (Lakomski-Laguerre, 2016), as well as their Swedish predecessor, Knut Wicksell (Seccareccia, 1994; Bellofiore, 2013). Indeed, Cambridge authors were also exposed to these views, since Hayek taught Kaldor when they were at the London School of Economics in the early 1930s, while Kahn translated Wicksell from German into English. But this Austrian view of endogenous money also nearly disappeared, with the advent of the exogenous money supply found in Keynes's *General Theory*, the rise of Friedman's monetarism and his advocacy of money supply growth targets, and the full acceptance of the money-multiplier story where bank reserves, controlled by the central bank, are said to allow the creation of credit and money by banks.

The vagaries of the thesis of endogenous money should not entirely surprise students of the history of economic thought, as they know that economic theory is infected by fashions and fads. Ideas that have long been abandoned suddenly reappear. As was pointed out by Cramp (1971, p. 62), 'Economic ideas, the Cambridge economist D.H. Henderson once remarked, move in circles: stand in one place long enough, and you will see discarded ideas come round again . . . And nowhere is this more true than in respect to monetary theory and the associated theory of monetary policy.'

Most of the modern monetary controversies between mainstream economics (monetarism in particular) and post-Keynesian economics can be brought back to the Currency and Banking schools' debates of the early nineteenth century (Arnon, 2011). Ricardo and the Currency School argued that only coins and Bank of England notes could be considered as money, that this stock of money determined aggregate demand, and that aggregate demand determined the price level, thus giving support to the quantity theory of money. The Banking School, with John Fullarton, Thomas Tooke and John Stuart Mill, argued instead that the definition of money was much more complicated, that aggregate demand determined the stock of money, and that if controls were needed to influence prices, these controls should be imposed on credit aggregates. The Banking School also put forth the 'reflux principle', arguing that if too many banknotes were created, its holders would bring them back to the issuer, and hence the excess would disappear. The Banking School thus supported endogenous money, reversed causality and the need to focus attention on credit instead of money aggregates, just as modern post-Keynesians do (Panico, 1988; Wray, 1990).

Another well-publicized debate occurred in the late 1950s, during the hearings of the Radcliffe Commission in England. Two opposite views were then expressed, that of academics and that of central bankers. Academics defended the mainstream view, advocating money supply control through the provision of reserves by the monetary authorities, claiming that the velocity of money and the money multiplier were constant or predictable variables, and arguing that causality ran from money to prices. Central bankers, on the other hand, supported by post-Keynesians Kaldor and Kahn, argued instead that the operating tool of central banks was interest rates, having only an indirect effect on monetary aggregates. They further claimed that the velocity of money was unstable, appealing instead to the importance of 'general liquidity'. They added that monetary policy had only a moderate effect on inflation, because it depended on many other factors, and evoked the possible necessity of credit controls. The Radcliffe Commission dismissed the mainstream view and endorsed those of central bankers and of post-Keynesians. This choice certainly looks like the right one now, as argued by central banker Bindseil (2004b), but at the time the Commission was lambasted by mainstream Keynesians such as Samuelson (1969b, p. 7), who called it 'one of the most sterile operations of all time', opening the gates for the revival of the quantity theory of money and the advent of Friedman's monetarism in the 1970s. Thereafter, as recalled by a high official at the Bank of England, 'in separate acts of folly a quarter of a century or so ago, the monetary authorities sought to hide the fact that they were setting rates' (Tucker, 2004, p. 369). This was the case not only in the UK, but all over the world.

Until 1970, it was not perfectly clear that post-Keynesians held a theory of money that was much different from that of the mainstream. Until then the main criticisms against the quantity theory of money were based on the instability of the velocity of money or that of the money multiplier (Minsky, 1957; Kaldor, 1964a). Only Kahn (1972, ch. 7), in his 1958 submission to the Radcliffe Commission, and Robinson (1956), in her book *Accumulation of Capital*, had a clear understanding of what was at stake. Unfortunately, Robinson's exposition of modern post-Keynesian monetary theory is contained in chapters at the end of her book, after a complex description of growth theory, value theory and technical change, so that readers were too exhausted by then to pay any attention to her monetary theory. But as a direct response to the rise of monetarism and its widespread acceptance by central bankers and academia, the more important issue of reversed causality was simultaneously brought to the forefront by post-Keynesian authors, as already mentioned, and by a few central bankers (Holmes, 1969; Lombra and Torto, 1973; Goodhart, 1984; and now McLeay et al., 2014; Ábel et al., 2016; Bundesbank, 2017).

Over the last 30 years, there have been in my view three major contributions to our understanding of monetary economics. First, Rochon (1999) has provided an extended survey of post-Keynesian monetary economics, showing in particular the similarities and differences with the works of some New Keynesian authors, in particular the New Paradigm Keynesians (Stiglitz and Greenwald, 2003) – a comparison which is still valid today. Second, while circuitist authors emphasized the links between producers and commercial banks, and post-Keynesians underlined the links between commercial banks and the central bank, Wray (1998; 2012) has focused attention on the links between the government, the central bank and the clearing and settlement system, thus giving rise to what is now called Modern Monetary Theory (MMT). Third, Godley (1996; 1999a) has provided a framework that allows us to study together the real and the financial sides of the economy, thus greatly enhancing the comprehensiveness of post-Keynesian theory, and providing a true study of monetary production economies, giving rise to what is now called the post-Keynesian stock–flow consistent approach – the SFC approach. Besides these post-Keynesian contributions, I should also mention the works of Bindseil (2004a; 2004b; 2014), who has produced an enlightening revision of our understanding of monetary policy implementation by central banks over the last 100 years.

4.2 THE MAIN CLAIMS

I have argued that post-Keynesian monetary economics has a common core. But of course, as is the case in mainstream economics, there is a degree of heterogeneity among the views held. In particular, for many years a debate occurred between 'horizontalist' and 'structuralist' post-Keynesians, as they were called. I think it is fair to say that most of the first exponents of money endogeneity were 'horizontalists': Robinson, Kahn, Le Bourva, Kaldor, Weintraub, Moore, Godley, as well as the French circuitists (Parguez and Seccareccia, 2000). However, as various authors examined in more detail the alternative monetary theory put forward by these post-Keynesian authors, some of their claims and simplifications were questioned. This internal critique came to be known, following Robert Pollin (1991), as the 'structuralist' view, because it was claimed by the critics that money endogeneity arose mainly from structural changes in financial conditions, and only meagrely from the accommodative behaviour of central banks (hence the name 'accommodationists' sometimes attributed to 'horizontalists'). Critics included authors as diverse as Chick, Dow, Peter Howells, Le Héron, Palley and Wray, many of whom got their inspiration from the previous works of Minsky (1957) and Stephen Rousseas (1986). The disputes between the structuralists and the horizontalists generated an enormous amount of literature, followed by many attempts to produce syntheses of the two views (Rochon and Rossi, 2017).

Moore has called the controversy 'a tempest in a teapot' (1991, p. 405) or 'a quintessential storm in a teacup' (2001, p. 13). I prefer to be more positive and accept Fontana's (2003, p. 309) assessment of it, and say instead that 'structuralists took over where the accommodationists had stopped'. The structuralists brought some clarifications and provided new details to the basic horizontalist story. For instance, they insisted that spreads between interest rates could quickly vary, in particular due to sudden changes in default assessments, the degree of uncertainty, confidence and liquidity preference. Wray (2006a, p. 271) now believes that 'for the most part . . . this particular debate was at best a result of misunderstanding', wishing that 'it had died a more timely death'. To a large extent, the debate has petered out, because many of the structuralist arguments regarding central bank behaviour simply cannot hold up in light of the recent developments in monetary policy implementation, notably the changes that have transformed murky central bank procedures into more transparent ones. I have given my own views on this in previous works (Lavoie, 1996d; 2006d), so those looking for further details are referred to these works and those of Rochon (1999; 2001) and Wray (2006a), although some of the debates will be evoked later in the chapter.

4.2.1 Credit and Money

Despite all this, I take the risk of devising three tables that attempt to summarize the main differences in monetary theory between the post-Keynesian school on the one hand and mainstream economics on the other hand. As already pointed out, the concept of a demand-led endogenous supply of money is dear to post-Keynesians and makes their views distinct from the mainstream ones. However, since neo-Austrians and New Consensus economists now also recognize that money is endogenous, this cannot be the only distinctive feature of post-Keynesian monetary economics. Table 4.1 provides some additional general distinctions. Post-Keynesians, especially since the advent of the SFC approach, pay particular attention to the counterparties of the stock of money, especially the loans or credits granted by the banking system. By contrast, mainstream authors often just throw a stock of money into their models, as if it were dropped from a helicopter, as Friedman once famously said, or like manna from heaven. This explains in part why the main concern of post-Keynesians about the financial system resides in the availability of credit for productive activities and in the stock of debts held by the various agents, as debt can generate financial instability, whereas mainstream authors focus on the real balance effects of wealth or of money balances, thinking that they will stabilize the economic system.

Another key difference between post-Keynesians and mainstream authors is related to one of the presuppositions discussed in Chapter 1. The focus on production rather than exchange is a fundamental feature of heterodox economics relative to orthodox economics. This is reflected in explanations of why money is needed. In the mainstream tale, money arose as a facilitator of exchange relations, as an improvement over barter invented by economizing individuals. From this view follows the mainstream story, whereby commodity money and coins emerged spontaneously, with goldsmiths eventually realizing that they could issue promissory notes in excess of the gold entrusted to them, thus leading to fractional reserve banking. In the mainstream story, commodity money, based on silver or gold, emerged first, followed later by coins and tokens, with the final appearance of scriptural money such as bank deposits, which became accepted as a convention. Many mainstream economists wish for the return to a system where scriptural money would behave as if it were scarce commodity money. Because of the disastrous consequences of the Global Financial Crisis, some heterodox economists also seem to favour this approach, in an attempt to restrict the credit-creating ability of banks, advocating schemes similar to full-reserve banking (Laina, 2019), sometimes under the name of 'sovereign money' (Dyson et al., 2016), but these proposals have generated

Table 4.1 Main features, money and credit

Features	PK School	Mainstream
The supply of money is . . .	endogenous and demand-led	exogenous
Money . . .	has counterpart entries	falls from a helicopter
The main concern is with . . .	debts, credits	assets, money
Money is tied to . . .	production and social relations	private exchange
Monetary causality	Credits make deposits	Deposits allow credits
Banks are . . .	creators of credit flows	merely financial intermediaries
Reserve mechanism at work, if any	Divisor	Multiplier
Credit rationing is due to . . .	lack of confidence	asymmetric information

heated responses from post-Keynesians who emphasize the necessary elasticity of credit (Fontana and Sawyer, 2017; Nersisyan and Wray, 2017).

Post-Keynesians theorize a monetary system that has been developed by bankers for centuries, based on scriptural means of payment. Indeed, economic historians argue that scriptural credit money, providing a general unit of account and tracking credits and debts, preceded fiat money and coins (Innes, 1913; Copeland, 1974; Courbis et al., 1991). Money originated as a vehicle to settle debts. A proof of the above is that most of the so-called modern financial innovations, based on scriptural manipulations, were known since antiquity and were in practice just before and during the Renaissance. In the post-Keynesian approach, money is a social relation, with two somewhat different justifications. The first one says that credit money requires a property-based society, where pledges based on legal property – collateral – permit the expansion of loan contracts (Heinsohn and Steiger, 1983; de Soto, 2000). The second justification is based on the tax-driven approach, also called the chartalist view following Knapp (1924), which is at the heart of the MMT reconstruction of monetary theory. It says that the general acceptance of a non-metallic form of money is due to the fact that the state requires taxes to be paid in this medium (Wray, 2000). The usefulness of chartal money is derived from the state's authority to impose and collect taxes.

Keynes (1930a, pp. 4–5) himself takes the middle ground, claiming that modern money is 'a creation of the State', and 'beyond the possibility of dispute, chartalist', meaning that the state not only enforces the delivery of money contracts but also decides 'what it is that must be delivered as a lawful or customary discharge of a contract which has been concluded in terms of the money-of-account', making only a brief footnote reference to tax liabilities. Davidson (1994, p. 223) concurs, pointing out that 'the internal medium of contractual settlement is not only whatever is declared to be legal tender by the State, but also anything the State or the Central Bank undertakes to accept from the public in payment of obligations'. As to Kregel (2019), he seems to give major importance to confidence in bank money and the essential nature of the clearing house, while downplaying the role of tax liabilities. His views look similar to those of the French Institutionalist theories of money, which rely on trust, based on ethical confidence, convertibility and the security of payments (Alary et al., 2020).

Also from Table 4.1 we can see that, for post-Keynesians, the main causality runs from credits to deposits, meaning that bank deposits are created the moment a new bank credit is granted. There is reversed causation. This also ties in with the statement that banks are not merely financial intermediaries that would arbitrage between short-term and long-term assets, as many mainstream economists still believe. Banks, in the post-Keynesian view, are creators of credit and of purchasing power – a vision also found in Schumpeter (1934). When banks increase their assets and liabilities by granting a loan, they create new means of payment. These can be used to increase aggregate demand. This goes beyond the mainstream belief that banks merely transfer funds from patient individuals, who decide to save more and accumulate deposits, towards impatient individuals, who wish to spend more than their income and take loans to do so.

The peculiar credit-creating role of banks has been reaffirmed recently by several post-Keynesian authors (Bertocco, 2011; Bianco and Sardoni, 2018; Bouguelli, 2018; 2020; Lavoie, 2019b), thus rejecting Tobin's (1963) so-called new view, which became highly influential among orthodox authors and which claimed that banks were subjected to the same constraints as other financial institutions, and hence had to be considered as just another financial intermediary. The post-Keynesian view of banks as credit-creating institutions that are to be clearly distinguished from other financial institutions has recently been given full support by some lawyers (Rahmatian, 2020, pp. 73–4) and a number of central bankers (McLeay et al., 2014; Jakab and Kumhoff, 2015; 2019; Ábel et al., 2016; Borio, 2019).

Furthermore, the causality associated with bank reserves is also reversed, with reserves being endogenous and demand-led, thus being a fraction (the divisor) of deposits, instead of deposits being a multiple of bank reserves (when these exist, which is no longer the case in several countries). Post-Keynesians thus reject the standard money-multiplier story, also known as the fractional-reserve banking theory of credit creation. This will be discussed in more detail in the next section. Finally, for post-Keynesians, if credit rationing occurs, it is mainly because of a lack of confidence on the part of the banking or financial system, and not so much because of asymmetric information. Indeed, in a world where so much information is now at the disposal of anybody with access to the Internet, it would be surprising to have asymmetric information as the main cause of such a recurrent phenomenon. Credit rationing, that is, credit restraints, will also be discussed later.

4.2.2 Interest Rates

Table 4.2 focuses on the characteristics of interest rates. Post-Keynesians view interest rates as a distribution variable that, to some extent, can be controlled by the monetary authorities. Thus the overall level of interest rates is not exclusively the result of market forces. The overall level of the rate of interest depends partly on policy choices about the way income will be distributed between borrowers and lenders. It is clear that there is a base rate of interest that is exogenous, in the sense that the central bank is able to set the base rate at the level of its choice. The central bank is a price-maker and a quantity-taker, at least under normal circumstances, as will be shown later. The base rate is the target interest rate of the central bank. This base interest rate is usually a short-term interest rate. Thus what can be considered to be an exogenous rate is this short-term rate. In the past it used to be the one-month or three-month yield on Treasury bills. Nowadays the target interest rate is the overnight rate – the federal funds rate in the USA, ESTER (Euro short-term rate) in Europe. In normal times, all short-term interest rates follow very closely the evolution of the overnight rate, and the latter is very close to the target rate set by the central bank. In unusual times, the evolution of short-term interest rates

Table 4.2   Main features, interest rates

Features	Post-Keynesian School	Mainstream
Interest rates . . .	are distribution variables	arise from market laws
Base rates . . .	are set by the central bank	are influenced by market forces
Liquidity preference . . .	determines the differentials relative to the base rate	determines the interest rate
The natural rate . . .	takes multiple values or does not exist	is unique, based on thrift and productivity

on private assets may diverge from that of the overnight rate and from the interest rates on government assets. Mainstream authors believe that market forces, as measured by longer-term interest rates, are the determinant of the base rate, while some structuralist post-Keynesians argue that these market forces constrain the ability of central banks to set their target of choice.

The relationship between the short-term target interest rate and long-term interest rates, especially rates on securities issued by the private sector, is much looser. Thus, while the short-term interest rate can be considered for all practical matters as being determined exogenously, this is far from the case for other rates, including bank lending rates and in particular long-term rates. Liquidity preference is reflected in the differentials between all these other interest rates, including bank lending rates, and the target interest rate set by the central bank. Liquidity preference, in contrast to the textbook model of interest rate determination, does not affect the base rate, unless we extend the concept of liquidity preference to the interest-setting behaviour of the central bank.

The last row of Table 4.2 deals with the notion of the natural rate of interest. This is the rate of interest that would exist if there were no money. It is determined by the confrontation of the productivity of capital and the time preference of economic agents. As Hubert Henderson, a friend of Keynes, put it: 'The rate of interest (like a price) is determined at the point of intersection of a demand curve and a supply curve ... Behind the demand curve is the productivity of capital for investment; behind the supply curve is the disposition and ability to save' (Keynes, 1973, xxix, p. 226). The natural rate is the key element of the New Consensus model. For orthodox authors, the long-term interest rate, deflated by expected price inflation, is the closest measure of this natural rate of interest. Thus short-term interest rates cannot deviate too much from the long-term rate, as otherwise the actual real rate of interest will diverge excessively from the natural rate of interest, thus creating disequilibria in the economy, in particular changes in inflation rates, as Wicksell would argue. Wicksellians thus contend that central banks are heavily constrained in their choice of the base rate of interest, and that the natural rate of interest, through the long-term interest rate and other market-determined interest rates, causes the base rate – an argument that is similar to the critique that Pollin (1991) was addressing to horizontalist post-Keynesians. Indeed, as Smithin (1994, p. 112) crucially points out, 'the usual argument that central banks *cannot* affect the real rate is based on the assumption that there *is* a natural rate from which the financial real rate must not deviate'.

Thus, as Mario Seccareccia (1994, p. 70) points out, we cannot just assert that 'it is money-supply endogeneity which fundamentally distinguishes the neoclassical from the post-Keynesian conception of money, one would like to think that there is substantially more than the endogeneity/exogeneity issue that separates them'. What truly distinguishes (horizontalist) post-Keynesians from orthodox dissenters (for instance New Consensus authors), who also recognize the endogeneity of the money supply, is the post-Keynesian rejection of the concept of the natural rate of interest (Rogers, 1989). This is a point that I first made fleetingly (Lavoie, 1985b), and then in more detail (Lavoie, 1997). Keynes (1936, p. 243) himself pointed out that he was 'no longer of the opinion that the concept of a "natural rate of interest" ... has anything very useful or significant to contribute'. Post-Keynesians either completely reject the validity of the natural rate of interest, or consider that there exists a multiplicity of such natural rates of interest (Lavoie and

Seccareccia, 2019; Levrero, 2021). The belief or disbelief in the validity of the concept of the natural rate of interest is what allows or disallows the central bank to set the standard for all interest rates and pursue full-employment policies instead of focusing exclusively on inflation targeting. As Smithin (1996, p. 93) again puts it,

> in the absence of a natural rate of interest, it can be argued that central bank control over short real rates will ultimately influence the entire structure of interest rates in the economy, including long rates ... Eventually, the real economy must adjust to the policy-determined interest rate, rather than vice-versa. This is therefore the precise opposite to the natural rate doctrine.

4.2.3 Macroeconomic Implications

Table 4.3 summarizes the main macroeconomic implications of the two approaches to monetary theory. Post-Keynesians truly adopt the monetary analysis advocated by Schumpeter (1954, p. 277) and his student Minsky, by contrast with the real analysis that dominates orthodox theory. As already pointed out, post-Keynesians are concerned with a monetized production economy, where money is neither neutral nor an inessential veil. As a result, post-Keynesians believe that a restrictive monetary policy will have negative consequences on an economy, both in the short run and in the long run, meaning that it is likely to raise unemployment rates and possibly reduce real growth rates. Similarly, financial disturbances are likely to have both short- and long-run effects. Ironically, central bankers, imbued with the assumption of money neutrality and New Consensus dogma, used to swear that anti-inflation austerity policies could not have any negative long-term effects on the economy and that the best that central bankers could do to help the economy achieve its full potential was to make sure that inflation rates remained low and stable. Their tune changed after the 2008 financial crisis, as central bankers started arguing that the crisis had reduced the growth rate of potential output, something that was deemed impossible before the crisis. Anti-inflation policies, when real growth rates are still low and when unemployment rates are still high, are thus justified by orthodox authors on the grounds that the natural rate of unemployment is now higher than it was before the crisis.

Post-Keynesians hold two further claims of reversed causality, as shown in Table 4.3. Observing the statistical relationship between money aggregates and price inflation, post-Keynesians attribute the growth in money aggregates to the growth in output and

Table 4.3   Main features, macro implications

Features	Post-Keynesian School	Mainstream
Schumpeter's distinction	Monetary analysis	Real analysis
Financial disturbances ...	have effects both in short and long run	have effects only in the short run
Inflation causality	The growth in money aggregates is mainly caused by the growth in output and prices	Price inflation is caused by an excess supply of money
Macro causality	Investment determines saving	Saving (loanable funds) determines investment

prices, thus objecting to the mainstream assertion that price inflation is a monetary phenomenon. This will be discussed in more detail in Chapter 8. Finally, as said at the beginning of the chapter, post-Keynesians argue that investment is not constrained by previous saving, but that instead investment determines saving – a claim that many regard as the key presupposition of post-Keynesianism. This reversed macroeconomic causality is evidently closely related to the monetized production economy, where banks can grant loans without disposing of previously acquired deposits. As Kregel (1973, pp. 159–60) put it, 'the availability of finance in excess of earnings (and without reference to savings) allows investment to be a truly independent and autonomous variable in the system'.

It is perhaps worth dwelling on this last point. In Chapter 3, when dealing with the firm at the microeconomic level, we argued that individual firms faced financial constraints. Here, at the macroeconomic level, we argue that investment drives saving. At first sight, it would seem that a contradiction arises from these two statements. But this is not the case. Finance is not saving. The fact that households are saving or that firms are accumulating retained earnings does not mean that there will be more investment. This is a point that Keynes tried very hard to get across. We have already mentioned the paradox of thrift, which will be developed further in Chapter 5. An increase in the propensity to save will lead only to larger stocks of unsold goods in the very short run, and it will lead to a reduced level of output, with no increase in saving in the short run, when production is readjusted to aggregate demand. The fact that various individuals wish to save more does not mean in any way that firms will wish or will be able to invest more. As Keynes (1973, xiv, p. 222) put it in response to his critics and introducing his finance motive,

> the public can save *ex ante* and *ex post* and *ex* anything else until they are blue in the face, without alleviating the problem in the least . . . The investment market can become congested through shortage of cash. It can never become congested through shortage of saving. This is the most fundamental of my conclusions in the field.

What 'cash' means here is that firms are able to invest if they hold money balances or if banks are ready to grant advances. More saving by the public will not help at all. In fact it will make matters worse.

What if prices were flexible? Would this make any difference to the paradox of thrift? Keynes (1930a, pp. 176–7) dealt with this when providing his 'banana parable'. Keynes's answer was essentially that if a thrift campaign got going, the reduced demand for bananas would lead to a fall in the price of bananas and to monetary losses for banana producers. Virtue would seem to be rewarded: households would accumulate their saving as deposits in bank accounts. But these deposits would then be the counterpart of the loans that banks would have to make to the banana producers so that they could cover their losses. The increased saving by banana consumers would be compensated by the financial loss of banana producers, and there would be no increase in the net wealth of the community. The saving, once again, would not help investment in the least. It is rather unlikely that loss-making producers would believe that current household saving would give rise to future consumption and invest in new facilities (Skidelsky, 1986, pp. 323–5).

4.3 UNDERSTANDING ENDOGENOUS MONEY

When students enter a post-Keynesian class in monetary economics, their minds have been so much distorted by the neoclassical fallacy of an exogenous supplied stock of money that they find it difficult to understand even the simplest story about demand-led endogenous money. The purpose of this long section is to present elementary features of a modern financial system that will help to explain the meaning of an endogenous money supply. To do so, the T-accounts of banks and central banks, where assets must by necessity balance with liabilities, will be presented in a systematic way, starting from the simplest pure credit economy, with a single bank and without central banks and outside currency. Complications will be gradually introduced, such as competing private banks, a central bank and its reserve requirements, and then, at a later stage, the state with its financial requirements and its issues of government bonds. Recent developments in banking, such as capital adequacy ratios, zero-reserve requirements and electronic money, will also be discussed within the framework of the T-accounts.

4.3.1 A Pure Credit Economy, with a Single Bank

We start with a pure credit economy, in which there is a single bank engaged in credit and debit operations, and where the unit of account has already been determined by the state. There is no other financial institution, and producing firms are forbidden to issue shares, bonds or commercial paper. This single bank may be a private bank, set up by some private entrepreneurs, with the imprimatur of the state that grants it a charter, or it may be an institution set up by the state itself. Whatever the case may be, we assume that the state has no budget, and hence that it spends nothing and taxes nothing. There is no currency money issued by the state, no reserve requirements, no financial markets and no central bank. The economy is also a closed one: there are no foreign transactions, no foreign reserves and no exchange rates. Neither gold nor silver is considered as reserve assets. Finally, in this 'perfect' world, selected borrowers never default, as in all DSGE models before the 2008 debacle.

Within such a financial system, all financial transactions would have to transit through this single bank. There could be no leaks, and no inflows, apart from the new credits granted by the bank. Everyone would have an account at the single bank. That account could be either a debit, in which case the bank would make a loan B to the individual household or firm, or it could be a credit, in which case the individual household or firm would be holding a bank deposit, D, that is, money. Because there are no leaks, whatever amount of credit exists must be equal to the amount of debit; that is, $B = D$.

In a sense, today we are nearly in the situation described above. Many countries have no compulsory bank reserves, for instance there are no reserve requirements in Canada since 1994 and the US Federal Reserve has entirely removed its reserve requirements in March 2020 (Ihrig and Wolla, 2020, p. 25); few transactions are made with cash, most of them being done through electronic transfers, credit cards and debit cards. There are several banks, but all transactions are eventually netted in a single institution – the clearing house. Furthermore, in some countries, all banks 'move forward in step' as Keynes (1930a, p. 26) put it, so that 'there is no limit to the amount of bank-money which the banks can safely create'.

Let us now assume that some agents, most likely firms, but perhaps also household consumers, wish to increase the amounts they borrow. Where are these loans going to come from? In the mainstream story, starting from fully loaned banks, new credits can be granted only when banks are the recipients of new deposits, a situation that occurs when the central bank purchases government bonds (from banks or from the general public) on the open market, thus giving rise to the creation of excess reserves. But in this pure credit economy there are neither government bonds nor a central bank. How can the banks create new loans?

The post-Keynesian answer to this query is rather simple. Loans are created *ex nihilo*, at the stroke of a pen, or by punching a key on the computer, as long as the borrower is creditworthy, that is, as long as the borrower can show some collateral. The main limit to this process is given by the amounts of loans that can be granted to creditworthy borrowers. This depends on the willingness of borrowers to borrow, on the amount of collateral they can show, and on the willingness of banks to grant creditworthy status to their customers. The last factor may be influenced by the liquidity preference of the bank, to be defined in a later section. In a sense, loans are not truly created *ex nihilo*, since they generally require collateral.

The simplest arrangement for banks and their customers is to set up credit lines, or overdrafts, which Keynes (1930a, p. 41) defined as 'an arrangement with the bank that an account may be in debit at any time up to an amount not exceeding an agreed figure, interest being paid not on the agreed maximum debit, but on the actual average debit'. When the credit line is pulled on, the additional loan awarded to the borrower has an immediate counterpart in the liabilities of the bank, by the creation of an equivalent additional deposit. Thus, in Table 4.4, both loans and deposits would simultaneously increase by the same amount. The additional deposits would then change hands, as the borrower would presumably use the newly created deposit to pay for some goods or services.

In our modern world, just as in Keynes's time, it is not necessary to have money deposits to be able to spend. 'A customer of a bank may draw a cheque against his deposits, thus diminishing his *credit* with the bank; but he may, equally well, draw a cheque against his overdraft, thus increasing his *debit* with the bank' (Keynes, 1930a, p. 41). The same point was made by Robinson (1956, p. 19) when she said that 'overdraft facilities are just as good a source of purchasing power as a bank balance'. Similarly, recipients of cheques may use the funds to increase their credit balances at the bank, that is, their deposits; or they may use the funds to reduce their debit balances, that is, the used portion of their credit line.

This is what currently occurs with the use of debit cards. For instance, when customers use their debit cards to purchase goods, they may hold no bank deposits (no money), and hence the used portion of their credit line will be increased as the transaction occurs. Similarly, some sellers may also be in a debit position *vis-à-vis* the bank, and hence the payments received will be automatically applied to reduce the amounts due, as shown in Table 4.5. In these circumstances, no change whatsoever will occur in the amount of

Table 4.4   Simple balance sheet of the unique bank

Assets	Liabilities
Loans B	Deposits D

Table 4.5   Payments through debit balances

Bank assets	Bank liabilities
Debit position of purchaser +100	
Debit position of seller −100	

Table 4.6   Taking explicit account of credit lines

Bank assets	Bank liabilities
Loans (used overdraft facilities)	Deposits
Unused overdraft facilities (potential loans)	Unused overdraft facilities (potential deposits)

deposits held by each transactor. This is a clear example of the reflux principle emphasized by the Banking School and Kaldor (Kaldor and Trevithick, 1981).

Agents who desire to spend can thus do so in two ways. Either they spend by depleting their money balances (the bank deposits), or they maintain their money balances while increasing their debit at the bank. As Keynes pointed out, the potential for purchasing goods and services, or what he calls the cash facilities, is made up of two components, the money deposits held and the unused overdraft, that is, the portion of the credit line that has not yet been drawn on. 'Properly speaking, unused overdraft facilities – since they represent a liability of the bank – ought . . . to appear on both sides of the account' (Keynes, 1930a, p. 42). If we were to keep track of these unused overdraft facilities, as some regulators suggest, then bank accounting would look as shown in Table 4.6.

Although unused overdraft facilities are still considered as off-balance-sheet loan commitments, some countries, namely the USA, have some statistical data on these (Moore, 1988, p. 25). Unused credit lines at the time represented approximately half of the narrowly defined money stock, and twice the amount of used overdraft facilities. In the UK, 'about 60 per cent of overdraft facilities are in use at any one time' (Howells, 2010, p. 171). It is thus clear that those who have credit-line arrangements have access to an endogenous source of credit-money. Indeed, the Bank for International Settlements (BIS) considers that formal standby facilities and credit lines of banks must be taken into consideration when assessing minimum liquidity requirements (BIS, 2013a, p. 32).

4.3.2   A Pure Credit Economy, with Privately Issued Banknotes

Let us now assume that the customers of the unique bank would like to benefit from the convenience offered by banknotes when making their transactions. In other words, rather than having all transactions going through a scriptural system of accounts, some transactions, presumably the smaller ones, could be made without the bank being an intermediate. In our modern financial systems, we are accustomed to banknotes being backed by the central bank or by the Treasury of the central government. Here, neither of these institutions exists. Where will the banknotes come from? They will be issued by the private bank.

Table 4.7 Balance sheet of the unique bank, with banknotes

Assets	Liabilities
Loans B	Deposits $D' = D - H$
	Banknotes H

In the past, privately issued banknotes were quite common. The state would grant some banks the right to issue them. Indeed, some economists believe that banks, and not the government, ought to issue banknotes, a position known as free banking. In our pure credit economy, banknotes would be issued by our unique bank, on demand. In other words, whenever a customer desires to have a deposit transformed into banknotes, these would be created by the bank. Banknotes are purely endogenous. Their supply is demand-led. The new T-account of the bank would look as in Table 4.7.

Banknotes issued by the unique bank are a liability of the bank. The bank transforms one kind of liability, the deposits, into another kind of liability, the banknotes. There is no limit to the amount of banknotes that can so be created. If customers of the bank were to bring back the banknotes, they could be exchanged only for deposits at the very same bank. There cannot be an excessive creation of banknotes, in line with the reflux principle underlined by Kaldor, Robinson (1956, p. 227) and Le Bourva (1992). It could happen, however, that credit is granted to finance inflationary expenditures or wage increases. This explains why the best-known exponent of the reflux principle – Thomas Tooke, who was in favour of free enterprise in all aspects of economic life – argued in his later work that while banknotes need not be regulated, credit and loans ought to be (Arnon, 1993).

It should be noted that banks should be highly favourable to the issue of private banknotes. Whereas banknotes carry no interest rates, bank deposits do or can easily do so. As a consequence, for a given mark-up between the loan and the deposit interest rates, the higher the proportion of money in the form of banknotes, the larger the profits of banks. As a result, one should expect banks to favour any technological change that would transform bank deposits into privately issued banknotes. This is the case of smart cards, electronic wallets or electronic purses.

4.3.3 The Profits and Bad Loans of Banks

One issue that has been ignored up to now is that of bank profits. Obviously, in a perfect world where financial transactions could be conducted at no cost, and where there would be no default risk on the part of borrowers, the condition of zero profit for the bank would be equivalent to a situation where the interest rate charged is equal to the rate of interest paid on deposits. In the real world, borrowers are sometimes unable to face their debt commitments and must default on their loans. Banks must thus set a spread between the lending and the deposit rates, to compensate for this risk. In addition, banks, like all firms, must pay salaries to their employees, they must service the cost of their fixed equipment, and they must turn a profit for their owners. Indeed, banks, like all firms, have a certain target rate of return, and the differential between the lending and the deposit rate (on top of service charges, now a key component of bank profits) will be such that banks achieve this target rate of return on the capital of their owners in normal times, net of the losses due to loan defaults.

If all the profits are redistributed to the households who own the banks, then the simple equality of Table 4.4 will still be relevant. This can be seen with the help of Table 4.8. Assume that the rate of interest on loans is i_B, while the rate on interest on deposits, which is lower, is i_D. By the end of a year, unless interest payments have been made by the borrowers or loans have been reimbursed, outstanding loans will now amount to $B(1 + i_B)$. On the liability side, outstanding deposits will have increased to the amount $D(1 + i_D)$. This implies, assuming that in the initial state deposits and loans were of equal amounts, that the profits of the banks are now of an amount $D(i_B - i_D)$. These profits, as shown in the first line of Table 4.8, will now be added to the bank's own funds – to their equity capital. If all the profits are redistributed as dividends, which are now held by the bank owners as bank deposits, then we are back to the second line of Table 4.8, where deposits and loans are once more equal, as they were in Table 4.4.

It should also be clear, even though loans and deposits appear to grow at a rate equal to the rate of interest on loans, i_B, that there is no need for loans and money deposits to grow at that rate. For instance, if the households who are the owners of the banks decide not to save their dividends in the form of deposits, but rather decide to spend them all on consumption goods, the loans due by the non-financial firms will be reduced by an equivalent amount, and hence there will be no growth whatsoever in the amount of outstanding loans. Thus, although post-Keynesians keep saying that 'loans make deposits', implying that granting a new loan will lead to the creation of new money deposits, readers need also be aware that if households decide to increase their spending, the money balances of the purchasers will flow into the money balances of the sellers. This will allow the producers selling their wares to use their newly acquired bank deposits to reduce the size of their debt *vis-à-vis* the bank, and thus reduce the amount of outstanding loans, if the producers prefer to reduce their money balances. Thus there is a possible two-way link between bank loans and bank deposits. To sum up, the operating profits of the bank are added to the own funds of the bank, while the reimbursement of a bank loan is accompanied by a reduction in bank deposits.

In general one would expect the administrators of the bank to retain part of the profits, so as to increase their own funds and constitute a buffer against expected losses. Retained profits are added to the funds initially put up by the owners of the bank when starting business. Broadly speaking, it is the bank's net worth, although things in real life are a bit more complicated (see Fullwiler, 2013, p. 174). The own capital of the bank constitutes a liability to itself. It represents the funds that the firm owes to its owners. In general, the bank's own funds play a role similar to deposits in the hands of the owners. The own funds, just like the deposits or the credits, are an accounting entry, but in contrast

Table 4.8 Banks with own funds distributed as dividends

Assets	Liabilities
Loans $B(1 + i_B)$	Deposits $D(1+ i_D)$
	Own Funds (equity capital) $OF = D(i_B - i_D)$
Loans $B(1 + i_B)$	Deposits $D(1+ i_B)$

Table 4.9 Banks with own funds and loan defaults

Assets	Liabilities
Loans B	Deposits D Own funds OF
Loans $B' = B - BLWO$	Deposits D Own funds $OF' = OF - BLWO$

to deposits, they cannot be drawn down by the owners. They are reduced whenever the bank pays out dividends or whenever a borrower defaults on a loan. In the latter case, an identical amount is deducted from the loan assets and from the own funds liabilities when the bad loans need to be written off (that is, when the accountants of the bank consider that the borrowers are unable to service the interest payments on their loan and will never be able to pay back the loan).

This is shown in Table 4.9, under the assumption that an amount $BLWO$ of bad loans is being written off. When there are too many bad loans, the amount of own funds, that is, the net worth of the bank, can become negative. This occurs when the amount of defaulting loans exceeds the amount of own funds of the bank, thus reducing the value of assets below that of liabilities, in which case the bank becomes insolvent. This, however, has no impact on the day-to-day operations of the bank, unless someone takes notice of the insolvency. As Neilson (2019, p. 73) puts it, 'one can quite easily be liquid but not solvent.... As long as lenders are willing to put up cash, [borrowers] are able to make their payments'. In other words, while insolvent banks should legally go bankrupt, they are forced to do so only if the insolvency or the danger of insolvency makes the bank illiquid, that is, unable to cover deposit withdrawals and unable to settle in the payment system. During the Great Depression of the 1930s, concerns about US banks being insolvent generated hundreds of bank runs (where clients withdraw their deposits and where lenders recall their loans and refuse to do business). In Europe and in Canada many banks were no doubt insolvent, but no one cried 'fire' and so there was no stampede to the exit – no bank run – and banks eventually recovered when the economic situation improved.

In the case of a unique bank, with a total monopoly on financial assets and liabilities, it is difficult to conceive why insolvency should create an illiquidity problem. The unique bank *is* the payment system, and clients can withdraw only those banknotes issued by the bank itself. Agents have nowhere else to put their savings. The situation of central banks is quite analogous to that of our unique bank, and hence fears of possible default by an insolvent central bank seem unwarranted in general. There are exceptions to this claim, however, for instance if a central bank has borrowed funds in a foreign currency, or if a country were to leave the eurozone while its central bank held a large debit position in the TARGET2 system.

4.3.4 Bank Liquidity, Bank Solvency and the Capital Adequacy Ratio

Another interesting feature of the pure credit economy, with no government bonds on the books of commercial banks, which is indeed representative of several financial systems in the world, is that the liquidity of a bank is rather difficult to assess from the standard point of view. In the standard view, the liquidity of a bank is measured by the ratio of its safe to total assets, or else by the ratio of its liquid to illiquid assets. This standard view of liquidity has already been criticized by those who point out that, through liability management, it is (nearly) always possible for large banks to obtain the funds that they need to settle their accounts (Moore, 1988, p. 33).

In the pure credit economy, there are no safe assets since banks hold no government bonds and since there are neither reserves nor central bank cash. The lending behaviour or the liquidity of a bank thus cannot be based in general on the proportion of cash or government bonds that the bank holds in its asset portfolio. Such a ratio would always be equal to zero. The only option left, then, is to measure the liquidity of a bank by the proportion of its own funds. It is the own funds of a bank, rather than its reserves or safe assets, that may play a key role in a theory of endogenous money (de Boyer, 1998). The relevant ratio to measure risk would be the *B/OF* ratio, that is, the ratio of loans to own funds. Alternatively, if the real assets of the banks are taken into account, it would be the asset to own funds ratio.

Lately, this ratio, or rather its inverse, the own funds to assets ratio, has become the subject of intensive scrutiny, under the guidance of the BIS. The BIS has designed a 'capital adequacy ratio' that private banks ought to respect, under the guidance of central banks or their supervising agencies. The minimum ratio suggested by the BIS used to be 8 per cent, but it is now quite complex. Roughly speaking, it is the ratio of the own funds of the banks (their capital) to a weighted measure of their assets, the weights being based on a conventional assessment of the risks associated with each kind of assets, and even off-balance items (BIS, 2013b).

Some economists have argued that the maximum asset to own funds ratios that arise from the imposition of minimal capital adequacy ratios may replace the role of reserve multipliers in a world without reserve requirements (Dow, 1996, p. 499; Nell, 2003, p. 196; Descamps and Soichot, 2003). For Borio and Disyatat (2010, p. 77), 'the main exogenous constraint on the expansion of credit is minimum capital requirements'. This new multiplier would be equal to the allowed assets to own funds ratio. For instance, it has been argued that the incapacity of the Japanese economy to move out of economic stagnation since the 1990s has been due to the low net worth of the Japanese banks, following the huge losses that these banks had to absorb as a consequence of substantial defaults on loans (mainly related to land and construction speculation). Because of their low net worth, it was said that Japanese banks were prevented from granting new loans because of binding capital adequacy ratios. A similar argument has been made with regard to European and American banks since the 2008 financial crisis.

A few objections can be made in this respect. It should be noted first that the capital adequacy ratios have been set in such a manner that they would only be binding for the most risky banks. Second, solvent and profitable banks accumulate retained earnings that are added to their net worth, and they should have no trouble in inducing economic agents to either forego deposits or take loans to purchase newly issued bank shares, thus allowing these banks to improve their own funds to assets ratio. Third, as I was told by a central banker, the BIS rules gave flexibility in how to evaluate the riskiness of assets, making it possible for accountants to devise means to transform the capital adequacy ratios of banks into good-looking ratios. Fourth, a bank can grant loans to investors for the purpose of purchasing newly-issued shares of the bank (Werner, 2016;

Rahmatian, 2020, p. 80). The reluctance of banks to accept strict capital adequacy ratios may have more to do with their desire to achieve high rates of return on equity than with their fear of being unable to grant new loans. Indeed, Panagopoulos and Spiliotis (2017, p. 139) conclude from their empirical analysis, that 'the equity multiplier is operational and reversed (loans cause equity)'.

What happens, however, if all banks incur large losses, pushing the asset to own funds ratio beyond its maximum value, but without being insolvent, so that no private agent would be willing to buy bank equity? In such a situation, there is only one way out. The government or the central bank has the responsibility to purchase new equities issued by banks, thus proceeding to partial or full nationalization. If such action were taken by the central bank, the banks would increase both their own funds and their reserves at the central bank. This would allow them, as we shall see in later sections, either to reduce their borrowing from the central bank or to acquire safe assets such as government securities. They could then resume their business of granting loans to all creditworthy customers.

Some post-Keynesian authors argue that when banks grant new loans they are automatically reducing their liquidity and hence their liquidity preference, since the ratio of loans to own funds is immediately rising (Wray, 1995; Fontana, 2009, p. 103). This would be one possible cause of an upward-sloping supply curve of credit. That it is true, in some sense, can be seen immediately from the first line of Table 4.9. At the very moment that a new loan is granted, the bank commits itself to a more illiquid position. The amount of loans rises while that of own funds remains the same. Thus, at the very moment when a new loan has been granted, the bank is in a more risky position.

This situation is, however, only a temporary one, for the larger stock of loans and deposits will allow the bank to rake up additional net interest revenues (unless the new loans are being defaulted on in unusual proportions), as shown in Table 4.8. These additional revenues, when they are due and integrated with the retained earnings, will thus bring the *B/OF* ratio back to its initial level. At the end of the year, the balance sheet of the bank has increased in size, but the liquidity of the bank may remain the same. In other words, at the macroeconomic level, there is no upward pressure on interest rates charged on loans when additional loans are granted.

4.3.5 A Pure Credit Economy, with Two Sets of Banks

What happens when there are two banks or more? New institutions will need to be created: a clearing house and an interbank market. Let us still assume that there is no central bank and no government expenditures. Let us further assume that there are two banks, one specialized in making loans to corporations, and the other specialized in collecting deposits from households. In a sense, this corresponds to the institutional framework of many financial systems. In the USA, for instance, banks located in New York have specialized in making large loans to big business, while the so-called country banks specialize in collecting deposits. Similarly in France, for a long time specialization was institutionalized, with business banks (*banques d'affaires*) and deposit banks (*banques de dépôt*) (Marchal and Poulon, 1987). Godley and Cripps (1983, p. 77) call them loan banks and deposit banks.

With this division of the banking business, it is impossible for each bank to reach an approximate equality between loans and deposits. The deposit bank (Bank D)

Table 4.10 Two banks in a pure credit economy

Bank B		Bank D	
Assets	Liabilities	Assets	Liabilities
Loans to non-financial agents	Deposits	Loans to non-financial agents	Deposits
	Funds owed to Bank D	Advances made to Bank B	
	Own funds		Own funds

consistently has excess deposits, while the business bank (Bank B) continuously has an excess of loans over deposits. In other words, at the end of each day, Bank B realizes that the payments made by its customers in favour of the customers of Bank D are of an amount that exceeds the cheques drawn the other way. The positive balances of Bank D at the clearing house are exactly matched by the negative balances experienced by Bank B. At the end of the day, to settle the payments that have cleared, Bank B must obtain a loan from Bank D. Thus, over time, Bank B is indebted *vis-à-vis* Bank D, and Bank D holds an asset against Bank B, as shown in Table 4.10. In a system with only two banks, it cannot be otherwise. Still, if Bank D consents to grant loans to Bank B, the accounts at the clearing house will balance at the end of each day, and such a situation can perpetuate itself. As Godley and Cripps (1983, p. 77) say, 'once a system of inter-bank credits is in existence, there is no logical or institutional constraint on the extent to which the whole banking system can supply additional loans, thereby simultaneously expanding the stock of money held by the public'.

The two banks B and D, or the two sets of banks, need only make sure that they agree on a rate of interest that will be profitable to both of them. In other words, the interbank interest rate, that is, the rate of interest charged by Bank D to Bank B on the amounts due, must be somewhere in between the (low) rate of interest on deposits that Bank D is paying to its depositors, and the (high) rate of interest on loans that Bank B is charging to its borrowers. If the interbank rate is set in an appropriate fashion, the rate of return of both banks will be the same, and hence the ratio of own funds to assets of both banks will be the same. Similarly, the loans to own funds ratio will also be the same in both banks, where loans now include the loans made to other banks. Both banks will also engage in longer-term arrangements, discussed next.

4.3.6 Certificates of Deposits and Securitization

Although the above direct lending arrangements between banks are perfectly legitimate, some observers of the banking scene may find it rather worrying that some banks are heavily in debt in respect of other banks or other financial institutions. Overnight lending is only for a day, and needs to be renewed daily. It is thus safer to look for longer-term arrangements. Besides the obvious solution of attracting more deposits, and especially more time deposits, a series of arrangements has been designed, two of which we shall briefly outline.

An option for business banks, that is, the banks that specialize in lending to firms, is to issue certificates of deposit (CDs). Bank B, the business bank, is attracting an insufficient

Table 4.11 Two banks, certificates of deposit

Bank B		Bank D	
Assets	Liabilities	Assets	Liabilities
Loans to non-financial agents	Deposits	Loans to non-financial agents	Deposits
	Sold CDs	Purchased CDs	
	Own funds		Own funds

amount of deposits. Bank B may thus issue certificates of deposit, which will be purchased by Bank D, which has positive balances. The issued certificates of deposit would thus appear on the liabilities side of the balance sheet of Bank B, replacing the amounts due to Bank D, while the purchased certificates of deposit would appear on the assets side of the balance sheet of Bank D, taking the place of the loans made to Bank B. This is shown in Table 4.11, which is barely different from Table 4.10. But now Bank B no longer 'borrows' from Bank D, or so it appears from a legal point of view, and in any case the CD secures funds for more than one night.

The above presentation makes clear that credit relations are based on creditworthiness. As long as Bank D believes that Bank B is able to provide interest payments on its commitments, there is no reason for Bank D to refuse extending loans to Bank B, or purchasing certificates of deposit from Bank B. The same occurs at the level of the customers of a bank. Banks grant loans and renew lines of credit as long as they have faith in the ability of the borrower to make interest payments. Similarly, depositors have no hesitation to leave their deposits at a bank as long as they believe that their orders to transfer these deposits will be honoured. The creditworthiness of a bank thus ultimately depends on the creditworthiness of its borrowers and the confidence of its depositors. Creditworthiness and trust are the key elements of the financial system.

It should be emphasized that there are no safe assets in this pure credit economy. When deposit banks lend to business banks, collateral in the form of risk-free government assets cannot be provided since they do not exist by definition. The creditworthiness of the loans granted by the banks is the only collateral available. Conventions based on trust and confidence rule the banking system.

The sale of certificates of deposit used to be the main tool of liability management by banks. Broadly speaking, liability management refers to the ability of banks to increase their lending activity by borrowing funds that appear on the liability side of their balance sheet, without being forced to sell some of their marketable assets – mainly Treasury bills. This gives rise to another fashionable arrangement, 'securitization'. It should be made clear that securitization has two different meanings. In the case of mortgages, securitization in its old meaning implied that banks would keep the mortgage on its books on the asset side, but that the bank, instead of looking for deposits, would issue securities based on these loans, with the mortgage-based securities now appearing on its liability side. Securitization in this first sense is thus part of liability management. To finance their loans, instead of looking for new deposits or issuing certificates of deposit (CDs) that are of a relatively short duration, banks issue long-term bonds that have the additional advantage that they help them cover term risk. This kind of arrangement was first put in place in nineteenth-century Germany, where the securities are known as *Pfandbrief* bonds, and it was used in the USA as a means to help mortgage issuers, the thrift industry and home owners, in the hope of lowering mortgage interest rates. Only mortgage loans conforming to strict norms and insured by some government agency were eligible for such conversions, so there was very little risk for the investors. In and of itself, this first kind of securitization is of little consequence and has been practised successfully for decades – and still is.

Securitization is now mainly understood in its second meaning, which is related to asset management. Securitization may be defined as the transformation of an asset that was not previously marketable into a marketable one. In other words, the securitization of an asset implies that this asset can now be sold on some market. Securitized assets go beyond mortgages and include student loans, car loans and even credit card balances. A typical example of securitization is the sale of a set of loans, previously granted by a commercial bank or a mortgage bank, to a special purpose entity, or special investment vehicle. The loans are then transformed into securities (the asset-based securities (ABS) and the collaterized debt obligations (CDO)) with the help of investment banks – in the case of the USA these were the Wall Street banks (Morgan Stanley, Bear Stearns, Lehman Brothers and Goldman Sachs) – which also act as the underwriter. Part of these long-term assets are ultimately financed by short-term assets – asset-based commercial paper (ABCP). The buyers are other financial institutions, non-bank financial intermediaries such as money market funds, mutual funds, pension funds, trust companies and insurance companies, which collect vast amounts of savings from households and from non-financial firms with large money balances. This process, 'originate and distribute', as is well known now, contributed to the 2006 housing crash in the USA and to the 2008 debacle of the Wall Street banks. Minsky (1991) considered securitization as another example of endogenous money, whereby financial innovation helps to create portfolio assets that appear to take the characteristics of money as a safe and liquid store of wealth.

Once again, this kind of arrangement arises as a result of specialization. Other bank or non-bank financial intermediaries specialize in collecting long-term savings from households and corporations. The lender banks specialize in finding borrowers that seem to be creditworthy. This specialization creates an imbalance in the balance sheets of banks and financial intermediaries, similar to the one shown in the top part of Table 4.12. This imbalance could be solved by banks issuing certificates of deposit, which would be bought by financial intermediaries, but securitization quickly became the new fad in finance, allowing financial wizards to show their skills.

In the case of securitization, banks typically sell a portion of their loans to a financial intermediary that has collected a large amount of time deposits or other liabilities of a similar nature. The loans thus disappear from the balance sheet of the bank, and appear on that of the financial intermediary. In the example in Table 4.12, 70 per cent of the loans end up being securitized. The net result for the bank is a reduction in the size of its balance sheet: the loan made to a non-financial institution is gone, but so is its liability to financial intermediaries. The bank is forgoing the future interest revenues to be obtained from the borrower, but it has collected up-front fees when initially granting the loan and selling it. In addition, the bank is now in a better position with regard to its capital adequacy ratios, as previously discussed. It has collected fees when making the loan,

Table 4.12 Securitization

Bank B		Financial intermediary FI	
Assets	Liabilities	Assets	Liabilities
Loans to non-financial agents +100	Deposits +30		Deposits +70
	Funds owed to FI +70	Advances made to Bank B +70	
Loans to non-financial agents +30	Deposits +30	Securitized loans (basic paper) +70	Asset-based commercial paper (derivative paper) +70

and it can repeat the operation without having to worry about the BIS-imposed capital adequacy ratios, thus circumventing them.

Securitization, just like lending between banks, requires confidence. Bunches of loans can be repackaged and sold only as long as the purchasers of these loans are confident that the loans will be repaid and the interest payments will be made.

4.3.7 Multiple Banks, the Clearing House, the Central Bank and Repos

Things are just slightly more complicated in a multi-bank system. Payment orders will clear at a clearing house, usually run by the association of domestic bankers, or else the central bank will act as the clearing house. In the first case, the clearing system is likely to be a deferred net settlement (DNS) system, where payments are cleared on a net multilateral basis, but where final settlement occurs only at the very end of the day; in the second case, it is likely to be a system based on real-time gross settlement (RTGS), where participants need to hold sufficient balances at the central bank for each payment, with settlement occurring at the same time as the payment is made, and with clearing balances being moved from one bank account to another at the central bank. Obviously, the DNS system requires no or few reserves at the central bank, while the RTGS system necessitates much larger reserves (or else large daytime overdrafts from the central bank, as in the US system). There are also hybrid systems, as in Canada's large-value transfer system (LVTS), where payment is final the moment it clears while netting occurs on a multilateral basis. It is this system that we describe below, run with a private clearing house, and with the central bank playing a role only at the very end of the day.

A single bank may at the same time owe funds to a bank and be owed funds by another bank. The clearing house is designed to net out these balances, and bring together all the main participants to the clearing system. By the end of the trading day, each participant bank knows its clearing-house balance, that is, the amounts that it can lend to those in deficit or the amounts that it must borrow from those in surplus. The clearing house may then act as a broker between the deficit and the surplus banks. An example with four banks and their gross flows of payment is provided in Table 4.13. What should be noted is that, as long as commercial banks issue their own banknotes and as long as the transactions involve only commercial banks, and not the central bank, whenever a bank

Table 4.13 The clearing house in a multi-bank system

Owed to → Owed by ↓	Bank A	Bank B	Bank C	Bank D	Σ amounts owed by (debits)	Σ amounts owed to (credits)	Clearing balances
Bank A		15	20	20	55	60	+5
Bank B	30		40	35	105	90	−15
Bank C	20	50		10	80	85	+5
Bank D	10	25	25		60	65	+5
Σ amounts owed to	60	90	85	65	300	300	0

has a clearing-house deficit balance, there is another bank, or a group of banks, that has an identical surplus balance. In other words, the net overall balance of all banks taken together under these conditions is zero at all times. In the case illustrated by Table 4.13, Bank B (the business bank) would need to borrow 15 monetary units from the other three banks on the interbank market by the end of the day, in order to be able to settle its payments.

If one of the other three banks (say Bank A) declines to lend its surplus funds, then for final settlement to occur, Bank B will need to borrow funds from the central bank, while Bank A will have no choice but to deposit its surplus funds at the central bank. These are the so-called liquidity facilities of the central bank: the borrowing and the deposit facilities. The central bank acts as the lender of last resort, making a loan to ensure that payments are indeed settled.

In reality, during the course of the day, banks will estimate their position at the clearing house, and, instead of borrowing on the overnight market (for one night), may decide to engage in repurchase agreements, also called repos or RPs. For instance, when Bank B sees that it will end in a negative position at the clearing house, it will offer to sell some of the securities that it has on its balance sheet, but promise to buy them back – say the next day, in a week or in two weeks – at a pre-agreed price. From the point of view of the organization granting the liquidity – the party that buys the security and promises to sell it back – this agreement is called a reverse repo. This is tantamount to a loan, secured on collateral. Indeed, this is how the BIS (2013a, p. 41) views repos. A one-week repurchase agreement is equivalent to a one-week collaterized loan. But with a repo, the security is held and owned for the duration of the repo by the lender, not by the borrower. Since capital adequacy ratios attach no risk to this kind of asset, loans based on repos can totally circumvent the capital adequacy requirements and have thus become highly popular. In the example of Table 4.13, if Bank B manages to sell 15 units worth of securities to the other banks, it will manage to bring its clearing-house balance back to zero (Rochon and Rossi, 2004).

In reality, repos are often based on government securities, mostly Treasury bills, but we have not yet introduced the government and the central bank, so here we assume that they are based on securities issued by private agents! While the system of repos seems to be highly useful, we shall deal later in this chapter with its possible drawbacks.

4.3.8 The Central Bank in an Overdraft Economy

An interesting classification, underlined by several post-Keynesian authors, is the distinction between 'overdraft economies' and 'auto-economies', a distinction first made by John Hicks (1974, p. 51). In the auto-economy, agents sell their liquid assets to finance new ventures, or they issue new bonds or shares. For this reason, these economies are often called 'financial-markets economies', but we shall call them 'asset-based economies' to underline the fact that firms in such economies are said to own the financial resources required to make their investment expenditures, while banks are said to sell their liquid assets (mainly Treasury bills) to obtain central bank money.

In the overdraft economy, by contrast, firms or households pull on their lines of credit with commercial banks when they require new financing means. The same distinction applies to the financial sector. In an overdraft economy, commercial banks need to take advances from the central bank. As a result, when the focus of the analysis is on the balance sheet of the central bank, the distinction between an overdraft economy and an asset-based economy depends on whether the central bank has claims over the domestic financial sector. 'The overdraft economy is thus defined by a double level of indebtedness: that of the firms to the banks and that of the banks to the central bank' (Renversez, 1996, p. 475). This distinction will be quite useful in the discussions that follow.

Let us start, then, with the simpler of the two systems, the overdraft system. The overdraft system is an extension of the pure credit economy, to which a central bank is added. In the overdraft system, the operations of central government, beyond those of the central bank, may still be assumed away, and this is mainly why the overdraft system is easier to describe than the asset-based system.

Let us then assume the existence of a central bank, and that of a network of commercial banks, consolidated into a single conglomerate for simplification. In this more realistic financial system, we assume that private banks can no longer issue banknotes. Only the central bank can issue banknotes. Suppose that we start from the situation described by Table 4.4. The private bank conglomerate has loans on the asset side, and deposits on the liability side (own funds are set aside for simplification). Its depositors now wish to split their money holdings into bank deposits and banknotes. How will the banks provide their customers with the banknotes issued by the central bank?

The mainstream answer, provided within the framework of an asset-based financial system, is that the banks must sell to the central bank some of the government securities they hold, thus obtaining the central bank banknotes they need. These banknotes, which are said to be part of the money supply, are also part of what is called high-powered money, that is, money issued by the central bank, or central bank money. But here, in this pure overdraft economy, there is no government sector (beyond the central bank) and there are no government securities lying around. And we assume, in line with present institutions (in normal times), that central banks just will not buy any privately issued asset. Still, banks are required to obtain the banknotes, for their customers will lose all faith in the banking system if it cannot provide the banknotes they want. How can the banks obtain the banknotes?

If banks cannot sell any asset to the central bank, the only way they can obtain the banknotes is by borrowing them from the central bank. This is what used to be known

Table 4.14 Overdraft economy, with banknotes

Commercial banks		Central bank	
Assets	Liabilities	Assets	Liabilities
Loans B	Deposits $D' = D - H$ Funds H borrowed from central bank	Advances H made to commercial banks	Banknotes H

as a 'discount window operation', whereby banks borrow from the central bank, now known as a 'borrowing standing facility'. This is shown in Table 4.14. The amount borrowed is exactly equal to the required amount of banknotes, that is, the amount of central bank money. The central bank has a monopoly over the provision of banknotes. As long as there is a demand for central bank banknotes by their customers, commercial banks are forced to go into debt *vis-à-vis* the central bank. Commercial banks cannot but be indebted *vis-à-vis* the central bank.

4.3.9 Liability Management and the Overdraft Economy

The overdraft economy is the ultimate example of liability management. Several authors have argued that liability management is the latest stage in the historical development of banking systems, where money is seen as an evolutionary process (Chick, 1986). Before the advent of liability management, banks would passively wait for deposits, and only expand their lending activity if new depositors emerged. The attracted deposits were taken as a pool of funds, available for lending.

There is, however, another view of liability management – the radical view, akin to what Rochon and Rossi (2013) call the revolutionary view of endogenous money. According to this new view, liability management is not an innovation that would have transformed the process of banking intermediation. Rather, liability management is a permanent feature. Banks are perpetually engaged in passive liability management, as they must first consent to loans, and later search for funds to finance the currency drain (deposits that become banknotes). All overdraft systems are compelled to practise liability management as a logical necessity. Any adjustment is made on the liability side, simply because no adjustment from the asset side is possible. Banks as a whole, when they are in need of banknotes for their customers, or in need of compulsory reserves, as we shall soon see, cannot get them by selling liquid assets to the central bank, either because banks just do not hold Treasury bills or because the central bank declines to purchase government securities, as was the case in many emerging countries and with the European Central Bank until May 2010. Banks must obtain all their high-powered money by borrowing it from the central bank. The argument, to be found in the traditional view, that liability management would be a new phase in the development of financial systems thus does not seem to be a correct assessment of the actual evolution of financial systems throughout the world.

An interesting feature of the overdraft economy is that it shows clearly that money and high-powered money are endogenous variables that cannot be under the control of the

Table 4.15 Overdraft economy, with compulsory reserves

| Commercial banks || Central bank ||
Assets	Liabilities	Assets	Liabilities
Loans B Reserves H	Deposits D Funds H borrowed from central bank	Advances H made to commercial banks	Deposits of banks (reserves) H

central bank. In the present overdraft economy, with a demand for central bank banknotes, the banknotes must be provided and the central bank has no choice but to provide the commercial banks with the loans they ask for (unless it wishes to create chaos in the economy, as ATMs get empty). The central bank is left, however, with a powerful tool: setting the rate of interest at which the commercial banks will be forced to borrow the required amounts of banknotes.

The situation is identical when compulsory reserves are taken into consideration. Suppose that we are in an economy where customers wish to use only scriptural money and no banknotes. Is it still possible for the central bank to force indebtedness on the part of private banks? The obvious solution is for the central bank to impose compulsory reserve requirements. It does not matter whether the reserves are imposed on deposits, as they are in most countries, or on loans or other assets, as they used to be in France and in other European countries and as is now suggested by Palley (2006). Reserve requirements have consequences similar to those of central bank banknotes on the accounting structure of banks. Again, because banks in an overdraft system have no assets to sell to the central bank, banks have no choice but to borrow the required reserves, at the rate of interest charged by the central bank. As shown in Table 4.15, the adjustment to the compulsory reserve requirements is made through the liability side.

4.3.10 The Overdraft Economy, with Two Banks or Sets of Banks

Finally, let us consider the case of two banks, or two sets of banks, within an overdraft economy. Let us sweep away, again for simplification, all the complications associated with compulsory reserves and banknotes issued by the central bank, as well as the own funds of banks. In a previous section, we also considered the case of two sets of banks, but in the absence of a central bank. All discrepancies in the net claims of each bank had to be made good by banks borrowing or lending funds to each other, usually with the help of some clearing agent, the clearing house. Let us now consider the case where the clearing house is the central bank, with no interbank market.

The advantage of such a system is that the commercial banks need not enter into contracts with each other. In other words, the risk of lending to another bank is now taken over by a public institution, the central bank. Suppose again that there are two kinds of bank, the business bank and the deposit bank. The business bank will consistently run negative balances at the clearing house, while the deposit bank will consistently accumulate surpluses. The clearing house is now the central bank, and what the central bank can do, in contrast to the private clearing house, is itself be the counterpart to the required lending and borrowing operations of the banks when accounts have to be settled at the end of the day.

This is shown in Table 4.16. The discrepancy, for Bank B, between loans and deposits is exactly equal to the discrepancy, for Bank D, between deposits and loans. And this discrepancy is exactly balanced on the books of the central bank. Provided there is only a small difference between the penalty rate charged on negative settlement balances (the advances provided by the central bank to banks showing a deficiency of funds) and the rate of interest offered by the central bank on the positive settlement balances (the rate of interest on the surplus funds that banks with excess funds deposit at the central bank), there is no incentive for banks to look for the private arrangements described in Table 4.10, such as overnight lending. In other words, provided the central bank is content with making a small profit when running the clearing house, there is no need for commercial banks to settle their accounts between themselves before relying on the facilities of the central bank for final settlement.

An interesting feature of this overdraft system without an overnight market and with a central bank is that it clearly shows that the amount of high-powered money (here excluding banknotes and including only the amount of deposits held at the central bank – the reserves) has no relationship whatsoever with the total amount of money, or money deposits, in the system. This amount of high-powered money depends mainly on how extensive are the specializations of the private banks into loan-making and deposit-attracting activities. When all banks move together in step in their lending and deposit businesses, the required amount of high-powered money is quite low, and may even approach zero. When banks specialize heavily, the amount of high-powered money will be large relative to economic activity.

The amount of outstanding reserves, relative to economic activity, will also rise when the overnight market breaks down, because participants lose confidence in each other. This was precisely the case of the eurozone from 2010 to 2012. Investors moved their deposits from banks situated in the south towards banks situated in the north of the eurozone. Because of the lack of confidence in the solvency of banks situated in the south (Greece, Spain, Portugal, Italy), the overnight market was not functioning properly, so that banks in the north (mainly Germany) preferred to hold their positive settlement

Table 4.16 Overdraft system, with two banks and no overnight market

Bank B		Bank D		Central bank	
Assets	Liabilities	Assets	Liabilities	Assets	Liabilities
Loans to non-financial agents +100	Deposits of non-financial agents +80	Loans to non-financial agents +70	Deposits of non-financial agents +90		
	Advances from the central bank (negative settlement balance) +20	Deposits at central bank (positive settlement balance) +20		Advances to Bank B +20	Deposits of Bank D +20

balances as deposits at the European Central Bank (ECB) rather than lending them on the overnight market. Something similar happened in the USA in September 2008, as banks became reluctant to lend overnight on the uncollaterized fed funds market, leading to an increase in deposits at the Fed (by banks with positive settlement balances) and in advances made by the Fed (to banks with negative settlement balances).

4.3.11 The Central Bank in an Asset-based Economy: The Neo-chartalist View

Let us now abandon the overdraft economy for a while and deal with the asset-based financial system. In an asset-based economy, there are large stocks of accumulated public debt. In the past, central governments have run public deficits, and as a result there is an outstanding stock of government securities, which is held by the central bank and by private agents, non-financial and financial ones, banks in particular.

New debt is issued when past issues have come to maturity and the central government is unable to reimburse the debt-holders: this is the case of the rollover. New debt is also issued when the government runs a deficit. There are two views with regard to the financing of government deficits. According to the first view, the Treasury, the fiscal arm of government, is best seen as drawing cheques from its account at the central bank, and selling securities to the central bank in order to replenish its bank account at the central bank. This view is endorsed in particular by the post-Keynesian advocates of Modern Monetary Theory – also known as the neo-chartalists (Wray, 1998; 2012; Mosler and Forstater, 1999; Bell, 2000). According to the second view, it is best to imagine that the Treasury sells securities to commercial banks (or more precisely to primary dealers). This second view – let us call it the post-chartalist view for taxonomic purposes – sees government expenditures in a light akin to that of expenditures by private firms: firms need to borrow from banks to make their expenditures. The bonds issued by government and purchased by banks play a role similar to that of the advances made by banks to firms (Lavoie, 2003d).

Let us start with the web-popular neo-chartalist view. Let us suppose that the government is running a deficit, say equal to 100 units, and hence issues Treasury bills (short-run government securities) to that amount, the bills being bought by the central bank, in line with the neo-chartalist view. Table 4.17 illustrates the neo-chartalist story. The first row of Table 4.17 shows the impact of the initial sale of Treasury bills on the accounts of the central bank. This sale has no impact whatsoever on the money supply and the private economy as long as the newly acquired government deposits are not spent in the

Table 4.17   *The neo-chartalist story: Treasury bills are first sold to the central bank*

Central bank		Commercial banks	
Assets	Liabilities	Assets	Liabilities
Treasury bills +100	Government deposits +100		
Treasury bills +100	Deposits of banks +100	Reserves +100	Household deposits +100
Treasury bills +19	Banknotes +10	Treasury bills +81	Household deposits +90
	Deposits of banks +9	Reserves + 9	

economy. Once the expenditures of government have actually occurred, the deposits of government at the central bank are now held by households or firms as deposits at private banks. But since the cheques were drawn on the central bank, the banks, the customers of which received the cheques, see their clearing balances at the clearing house increase by 100 units. If nothing else happens, by the end of the day, these balances will be deposited at the central bank, where they will enlarge bank reserves at the central bank by 100 units, as shown in the second row of Table 4.17.

Banks now dispose of excess reserves of 100 units. In the mainstream story, these 100 units of excess reserves would allow the commercial banks to provide new loans and start the money-multiplier process. The post-Keynesian story at this stage is entirely different, however. In the post-Keynesian view, banks provide loans first, and search for reserves later. Banks do not wait for excess reserves to be provided like manna from heaven. They grant loans whenever a creditworthy customer shows up or if they find one. It follows that, when banks wind up with excess reserves, they have already granted all the loans they could have made. The fact that they now have excess reserves, or positive settlement balances, does not make their potential customers more creditworthy.

What, then, will banks do with their excess reserves – their extra deposits at the central bank? Banks that hold these additional deposits will try to lend them to banks that have an insufficient amount of reserves or that are in a deficit position within the clearing house: they will try to lend them on the overnight market. But, as we have seen in a previous subsection, the overall net position of banks in the clearing house cannot but be zero as long as there is no transaction involving the government or the central bank. This means that, when the government spends through its account at the central bank, the overall net position of banks in the clearing house is necessarily positive. Taken as a whole, banks have no reason to borrow reserves. As a consequence, the overnight rate (the federal funds rate in the USA) must fall (Mosler, 1995). To stop it from falling, and to keep the overnight rate at its target level, the central bank must engage in a countervailing action. There are several possibilities, including the textbook one, which is to pursue open-market operations, with the central bank selling government securities. Open-market operations occur on secondary markets; that is, they deal with second-hand securities, which have already been issued and sold.

If there are no reserve requirements and if there is no demand for additional central bank banknotes by the bank customers, banks will use the entire reserve amount of 100 units to purchase Treasury bills. In the present case, let us assume that households now wish to hold 10 extra units of banknotes, and keep only 90 units in the form of bank deposits. Let us also assume that there is compulsory reserve ratio of 10 per cent on deposits. Banks will thus need to use 10 units of their reserves to acquire the banknotes and will need to keep nine units to fulfil their reserve requirements. The bank can thus trade the remaining 81 units of reserves by purchasing 81 units of Treasury bills from the central bank, as shown in the last row of Table 4.17.

4.3.12 The Central Bank in an Asset-based Economy: The Post-chartalist View

Let us suppose again that the government is running a deficit, say equal to 100 units, and hence issues Treasury bills to that amount, the bills being bought by a commercial bank, in line with what we called the post-chartalist view (we omit the complication brought

Table 4.18 The post-chartalist story: Treasury bills are first sold to the commercial banks

Central bank		Commercial banks	
Assets	Liabilities	Assets	Liabilities
		Treasury bills +100	Government deposits +100
		Treasury bills +100	Household deposits +100
Treasury bills +19	Banknotes +10	Treasury bills +81	Household deposits +90
	Deposits of banks +9	Reserves +9	

about by the fact that the bills are more realistically purchased by dealers, who are often affiliated with a bank, and who require bank advances). The counterpart to this purchase is the deposits that are now credited to government. This is shown in the first row of Table 4.18. In the second stage, however, the deposits will revert to households as soon as the planned government expenditures are made good, as shown in the second row. We can assume again that that households wish to keep 90 per cent of their additional money holdings in the form of bank deposits, and 10 per cent in the form of banknotes issued by the central bank.

The question arises again as to how the commercial bank will be able to obtain their required reserves and the banknotes demanded by its customers. In this asset-based financial system, banks need simply to sell to the central bank some of the Treasury bills that are part of their assets. In the present case, since households desire 10 units of additional banknotes and with banks being submitted to a 10 per cent reserve ratio on the remaining 90 units of deposits, banks will be selling 19 units worth of Treasury bills to the central bank on secondary markets, as shown in the third row of Table 4.18. Is the final situation any different from the one described by the neo-chartalists? The answer is no; ultimately it is not. The last row of Table 4.18 is identical to the last row of Table 4.17. Whether the Treasury bills used to finance government expenditures are initially sold to the central bank or to commercial banks makes no difference whatsoever to the final requirements of the banking system. Thus, the fact that most central banks cannot purchase government securities on the primary market, only being allowed to do so on secondary markets, seems to be a useless institutional constraint, as MMT advocates would claim.

Which view best describes the financial relationship between government and the banking system: the neo-chartalist view of Table 4.17 or the post-chartalist view of Table 4.18? It really does not matter. Each view may best correspond to the existing institutional arrangements. In Canada, the central bank makes direct purchases of up to 20 per cent of the securities newly issued by the federal government. The neo-chartalist view would thus seem to apply to that country. By contrast, the post-chartalist view seems more appropriate for the eurozone and the USA. In the eurozone, until the sovereign debt crisis that started in 2010, the European Central Bank declined to purchase any government security, either directly from governments (it is prohibited from doing so) or indirectly from financial institutions. Eurozone governments must sell their securities to commercial banks, and these banks must then take advances from the European Central Bank to acquire reserves or banknotes, as described in Tables 4.14 and 4.15. In the USA, there are also restrictions on direct purchases of government securities by the Federal Reserve – the central bank in the USA (Akhtar, 1997, p. 37).

In reality, things are even more complicated, and correspond neither to what we called the neo-chartalist story nor to the post-chartalist story. First, the newly issued securities are purchased by dealers, which are not necessarily banks. Second, most of the funds so acquired by the government are normally repatriated on the books of the central bank, so that the financial sector must borrow funds from the central bank to settle its position at the clearing house. The resulting balance sheet is thus some intermediate step between the neo-chartalist and the post-chartalist stories (Lavoie, 2013a, p. 15).

MMT authors have attracted a considerable amount of attention, but also of puzzlement, by making statements such as 'the Treasury does not "need" to borrow in order to deficit-spend' (Wray, 1998, p. 117), 'taxes do not finance spending' (Forstater and Mosler, 2005, p. 538) or 'the federal government is not dependent on revenue from taxes or borrowing to finance its spending' (Kelton, 2020, p. 9). These statements rely on the neo-chartalist description of Table 4.17. But they implicitly omit the first transaction of this table, which is that the Treasury must first borrow funds, or rather sell bonds or bills to the central bank. Neo-chartalists rationalize this omission and their surprising statements by resorting to the consolidation of the government's financial activities with the central bank's operations. By doing so, the activities of the central bank are turned over to the Treasury. It is said that the sale of government securities to the central bank has no impact on the economy as long as the government does not spend the proceeds of this sale – certainly a correct claim – so that consolidation is justified. A number of post-Keynesian economists counter this by arguing that consolidation and its associated description of how governments finance their expenditures are counterfactual and likely to create confusion (Armstrong, 2020; Fiebiger, 2016a; Lavoie, 2013a).

4.3.13 The Government in an Overdraft Economy

MMT authors argue that consolidating the government and the central bank and making use of the neo-chartalist process shown in Table 4.17 is justified by the fact that 'even after adding the self-imposed constraints and going through the minute details of Fed-Treasury operations, we find that the basic claims made in the much simplified model hold' (Wray, 2012, p. 108). The case of overdraft economies, where central banks are prohibited by law or by convention to make any purchases of government securities on both the primary and secondary markets, illustrates the importance of taking into account operational and institutional reality. In overdraft economies, an institutional configuration encouraged by the IMF, the central bank acts as a lender of last resort to the banks, but not as a purchaser of last resort for the government securities. For instance, the constitutional act of the central bank of Chile says that 'no public expenditure or credit of whatsoever nature may be financed with loans granted, directly or indirectly, by the Bank' (Banco Central de Chile, 2016, p. 17). Several central banks from emerging economies face legal constraints or even bans on bond purchases. If MMT is truly 'a *description* of how a modern fiat currency works' (Kelton, 2020, p. 233), then it must also consider this third configuration.

The self-imposed constraints of such an overdraft economy will have repercussions on the ability of the government to pursue expansionary policies and handling its debt, despite the fact that such a framework seems to fit the requirements of what Wray and Nersisyan (2020, p. 262) define as a *sovereign currency*, where the country, as is Chile, is a *currency issuer* rather than a *currency user*: the State chooses the money of account; the State imposes taxes that must be paid in the money of account; the State issues bonds in its own currency; the central bank issues the currency that must be accepted for payment; the country is on a flexible exchange rate. MMT authors argue that such a sovereign state 'can always meet its obligations denominated in its own currency' and 'can set the price/interest rate on any obligation it issues' (ibid., p. 263). But we can see, with the help of Table 4.19, that this will not necessarily be the case.

Again, we assume that the government is running a deficit of 100 units, financing it through the issue of securities, which in this overdraft economy can only be bought by the commercial banking sector. We retain the assumption that the central bank is the bank of the government, so that the proceeds of the bond sale are repatriated at the central bank. This puts the banks in a negative position at the clearing house, forcing them to take advances from the central bank, or else to enter into a repo agreement with the central bank, using the Treasury bills as collateral for the repos. This corresponds to the second row of Table 4.19. Thus, in contrast to the neo-chartalist and post-chartalist stories, government deficit-spending will tend to raise overnight interest rates, unless the central bank proceeds to liquidity-providing operations. The government then uses its deposits at the central bank to pay households, who get bank deposits, transforming 10 per cent of their new balances into banknotes, while the banks must keep a 10 per cent reserve to deposit ratio, as we assumed in the previous two tables. This leaves us with the third row of Table 4.19, where in contrast to the last row of Tables 4.17 and 4.18, the central bank holds no government securities.

Within this configuration, as exemplified by Chile, there is no workaround the self-imposed constraint. While it is true that the central bank keeps some control over short-term rates of interest, through the rate that it sets on its loans to the banks, within this configuration the central has little or no control over long-term rates if financial markets are determined to speculate against the sovereign bonds. Providing advances or repos – of short or long duration – to the financial markets is not the same thing as purchasing bills and bonds outright on the secondary markets. Interest rates will rise if banks or bond dealers are reluctant to purchase the securities when they are newly issued and when investors refuse to rollover the securities that come to maturity. Within this overdraft configuration, the central bank can only *encourage* financial markets to keep

Table 4.19 *An anti-chartalist story: Treasury bills are never sold to the central bank*

Central bank		Commercial banks	
Assets	Liabilities	Assets	Liabilities
		Treasury bills +100	Government deposits +100
Advance (repos) +100	Government deposits +100	Treasury bills +100	Advance (repos) +100
Advances (repos) +19	Banknotes +10 Deposits of banks +9	Treasury bills +100 Reserves +9	Household deposits +90 Advances (repos) +19

or purchase the securities since it does not act as a purchaser of last resort (Oreiro and Costa Santos, 2020).

The arch-typical example was the eurozone crisis, between 2010 and 2012. Financial markets took into consideration the fact that, *by convention*, the European Central Bank (ECB) only provided repos based on rated collateral and did not make outright purchases of sovereign debt on secondary markets. When it became clear with the Greek case that the ECB was willing to abandon the convention and use its constitutional right to engage in outright open-market operations, the financial markets then realized that the ECB was itself reluctant to do so in full force, in part because Bundesbank officials still insisted that the convention ought to be upheld, and so the crisis extended to other countries and kept dragging on. The financial crisis only came to a halt when the new President of the ECB, Mario Draghi, insisted that the central bank from then on would purchase a 'whatever it takes' amount of sovereign bonds. MMT advocates argue that the crisis occurred because financial markets took note that countries within the eurozone did not have their own currency and were *currency users*. I would argue instead that the crisis occurred because financial investors took note of the constraints imposed by the conventions tied to the overdraft configuration of the eurozone system.

4.3.14 Reverse Operations and Transfers of Government Deposits

In previous sections we saw that commercial banks as a whole have a net zero position at the clearing house as long as there are no transactions involving the central bank. Such transactions will occur if commercial banks need to acquire reserves or banknotes issued by the central bank. They will also occur whenever payments are moving in and out of the government account at the central bank; that is, whenever the government is paying for its expenditures by drawing on its deposits at the central bank or when tax payments are made by the private sector and the payment is deposited at the government's account at the central bank. In a fixed exchange rate regime, as will be discussed in Chapter 7, the interventions of the central bank on foreign exchange markets also generate transactions between the central bank and the commercial banks. A payment involving the central bank and a commercial bank will also occur when a government security matures and the security has to be redeemed. Whenever such transactions occur, they affect the overall net clearing position of banks at the clearing house, and hence the amount of bank reserves at the disposal of the banking system. These various transactions and their effects on reserves and on the overnight interest rate are shown in Table 4.20.

As Peter Howells (2010, p. 169) says, 'in the course of a normal working day, there will be large spontaneous flows between the public and the private sectors'. These payments can involve large sums of money and thus can have a sizeable impact on the amount of outstanding reserves. If the central bank did not intervene, these payments would generate huge daily fluctuations in the overnight rate of interest. As Bindseil (2004a, p. 17), an ECB and formerly Bundesbank central banker, puts it, 'if the central bank does not systematically neutralize exogenous money market shocks, short-term rates would regularly be either zero or be extremely high'. Thus, in contrast to what is believed by mainstream authors, the main role of central banks is essentially a defensive one, as we shall see in more detail in the next subsection. The central bank must assess the size and the

Table 4.20 Impact of various transactions on reserves and overnight interest rates, with possible compensatory measures

Action	Reserves (settlement balances)	Overnight interest rates	Possible compensating measures
Citizens and corporations pay their taxes, which are deposited at the account of the government at the central bank Central bank sells banknotes to banks Government sells securities to the private sector and deposits the proceeds in its account at the central bank Central bank sells foreign currency on foreign exchange markets Banks wish to acquire more reserves	Fall (banks make a payment outflow involving the central bank)	Tend to rise	Central bank buys government securities or other financial assets Central bank provides advances to banks Central bank provides repos to banks or dealers (liquidity-creating reverse operations) Central bank moves government deposits at the central bank towards government accounts at banks
Government purchases goods and services out of its account at the central bank Government securities mature and central bank redeems them out of government account at the central bank Central bank buys foreign currency on foreign exchange markets	Rise (banks receive a payment inflow involving the central bank)	Tend to fall	Central bank sells government or central bank securities Central bank provides reverse repos to banks or dealers (liquidity-absorbing reverse operations) Central bank moves government deposits at banks towards government account at central bank

amplitude of the payments that are likely to go through its accounts during each day, and be ready to take compensating measures.

In some countries, such as Canada, the central bank is in a position to know with perfect certainty the size of the net payments that go through its accounts. As a result, and because there are no reserve requirements in Canada, in normal circumstances the central bank is able to bring back to zero its position at the clearing house, so that the net position of the private banking system is also brought back to zero at the end of each day. In that case, the central bank can achieve nearly perfectly its target overnight rate. In other countries, such as the USA or the UK, things are more complicated, as the central banks do not have perfect information about the drains on reserves that must be compensated for. They also lack information about the demand for free reserves and the extent of discount window borrowing. As a consequence, these central banks cannot perfectly equate the supply of and the demand for reserves at the target interest rate, so that the actual overnight rate can wander away from its target.

As indicated in the last column of Table 4.20, central banks can take various compensatory measures to absorb fluctuations in reserves caused by daily transactions between the central bank and the banking system. Mainstream textbooks emphasize the open-market operations mentioned in the previous sections. Open-market operations are usually understood as outright purchases or sales of government securities by the central bank. As we saw earlier, however, a large proportion of open-market operations are conducted on different terms, on the basis of reverse operations. Repurchase agreements add flexibility and security to the conduct of monetary policy. With repurchase agreements, central banks can add to or subtract liquidities from the financial system, but on a temporary basis, say for one week. So, if at the end of the week central bankers desire to call back the previously injected liquidities, they need do nothing; the adjustment will be automatic. 'Under the RP agreement, the Desk buys securities from dealers who agree to repurchase them at a specified price on a specified date. The added reserves are extinguished automatically when the RPs mature' (Akhtar, 1997, p. 37). Liquidity-absorbing repos do the opposite: they allow the central bank to reduce the liquidities that would be temporarily in excess amount, and to reverse this operation automatically at the end of the purchase and resale agreement.

Repos operations should be understood for what they are: both the central bank and the banks are perfectly willing to engage in these special kinds of open-market operations. In the case of liquidity-absorbing repos, for instance, the central bank wants to drain excess reserves in order to maintain the overnight rate at the level of its choice. The banks, on the other hand, want to get rid of excess funds that would draw either no interest rate (as was the case in the USA until 2008) or a rate of interest below market rates (as in Canada) if it were to be deposited at the central bank. Repos operations have replaced outright open-market operations. We shall discuss repos further when tackling the shadow banking system.

There are, however, other means, besides open-market operations, repos or direct advances, at the disposal of the central bank to add liquidities to or subtract them from financial markets. Some central banks, such as the Bank of England, have issued their own bills, which they sell to banks or dealers. Several central banks – in particular the Bank of Canada – now use transfers of government deposits between the books of the central bank and those of commercial banks as the main tool to control the amount of settlement balances in the system. To increase liquidities in the banking system, government deposits are transferred from the central bank to private banks; to subtract liquidities, government deposits are transferred the other way. These government deposit transfers are often used to compensate the flows originating from government expenditures and collected taxes. We have already seen, with the help of Table 4.17, that government expenditures financed by cheques drawn on the central bank automatically lead to the creation of reserves. Reciprocally, taxes collected from private agents and deposited as government deposits in the accounts of the central bank withdraw reserves from the banking system. An obvious way to neutralize these effects is to transfer government deposits the other way. For instance, if, near the deadline for income tax collection, payments made by households to the order of the tax-collecting government agency have been settled at the clearing house, the liquidities of the banks may be replenished by the central bank, simply by moving government deposits back to the accounts at the commercial banks.

Table 4.21   Transfers of government deposits

Central bank		Commercial banks	
Assets	Liabilities	Assets	Liabilities
	Government deposits +100 Deposits of banks −100	Reserves −100	Household deposits −100
	Government deposits 0 Deposits of banks 0	Reserves 0	Household deposits −100 Government deposits +100

This is shown with the help of Table 4.21. Suppose households have paid their taxes with cheques worth 100 units. Commercial banks then lose the equivalent of 100 units of reserves or clearing balances, as shown in the first row of Table 4.21. But the loss can be made good by the autonomous transfer of government deposits from the books of the central bank to those of the private banks, as shown in the second row of Table 4.21. Reserves will then come back to their zero level.

4.3.15   The Defensive Role of Central Banks

It is now time to summarize what we have learned so far. Causality is probably the most crucial aspect of economics: this is how, in many instances, theories can be distinguished from one another. The T-accounts that have been presented must be comprehended with the causal story appended. This causal story underlines the importance of the autonomy of credit creation from the previous existence of bank deposits. The coherence of the described financial system also relies on the law of reflux, the existence of credit lines and the acquisition of own funds.

Our study of the banking system has shown that lending and borrowing between banks is an inevitable feature of financial systems. The banking system is a system that relies entirely on trust. Banks must make loans and purchase financial assets to make profits. Nothing limits the creation of credit and money other than the prudence of the bankers and the self-restraint of borrowers. When confidence falters, financial institutions will decline to lend to each other, and financial markets, notably the interbank market, will freeze. In times of crisis, there is thus a need for a special operator that can intervene as a lender of last resort – the central bank.

In normal times, the role of central banks in their day-to-day operations is also a defensive one. The central bank must neutralize, or sterilize, the net inflows or outflows of the clearing and settlement system. Otherwise there would be wild gyrations in the amount of outstanding reserves and in the overnight interest rate, as was pointed out more than 100 years ago by Walter Bagehot (1873).

> Day-to-day monetary policy implementation *means maintaining some level of short term interest rates by permanently adjusting quantities with regard to high frequency, partially transitory shocks, which are not or only marginally related to macroeconomic developments* . . . Any attempt to control in the short run the monetary base leads to extreme volatility of interest rates since the market will, due to stochastic and seasonal fluctuations in the demand for base money, permanently be short or long of reserves, as already observed by Bagehot (1873). (Bindseil, 2004b, p. 18)

Why have central bankers focused on interest-rate targeting instead of money targeting throughout history, except for the brief stint with monetarism? Two justifications have been proposed. The most famous one is that of Poole (1970). It is a macroeconomic justification. It says that if the LM curve is more unstable than the IS curve, meaning that the demand for money is volatile, interest-rate targeting will produce less output variability than monetary targeting. The other explanation is the microeconomic one proposed in the quotation above; it is associated with the post-Keynesian view. It is tied to the inner functioning of the clearing and settlement system, and linked to the day-to-day operations of the central bank, as explained in the previous section, and as accounted for by central bank economists (Bindseil, 2004a at the ECB; Clinton, 1991 at the Bank of Canada; Holmes, 1969 at the Fed). It is this microeconomic explanation that is the relevant one. As Fullwiler (2013, p. 178) puts it, 'when analysing monetary policy, the better starting place is the modern central bank's role in the national payment system'.

Thanks to the works of MMT scholars – Mosler (1997–98), Wray (1998) and Fullwiler (2003; 2006) – post-Keynesians now have a much better understanding of the defensive operations conducted by central banks and the technicalities involved in the interaction between the Treasury and the central bank when taxes are collected and when public expenditures arise. It needs to be said, however, that the first post-Keynesian to provide an in-depth understanding of the defensive role of central banks was Alfred Eichner.

Through his empirical work, Eichner discovered that there was no correlation whatsoever between changes in the holdings of government securities by the Federal Reserve and the reserves of the commercial banks.

> No matter what additional variables were included in the estimated equation, or how the equation was specified (e.g., first differences, growth rates, etc.), it proved impossible to obtain an R^2 greater than zero when regressing the change in the commercial banking system's nonborrowed reserves against the change in the Federal Reserve System's holdings of government securities. (Eichner, 1986a, p. 111)

This lack of correlation led Eichner to look for an alternative explanation for the changes in the balance sheets of central banks – an explanation that he found in the work of Lombra and Torto (1973), whose article covered the defensive operations of the Fed, in addition to the endogenous money and reverse causation arguments put forward by post-Keynesian authors. Their explanation was fully endorsed by Eichner (1987, p. 849), who later claimed that 'the Fed purchases and sales of government securities are intended primarily to offset the flows in and out of the domestic monetary–financial system and thereby hold bank reserves constant', just as we have argued in this section.

As pointed out earlier, the implementation procedures of central banks have changed and are now much more transparent, reflecting the actual behaviour of central bankers. Those who have tracked these changes are fully aware that central banks do not attempt to exert quantity constraints on bank reserves, as is still claimed by some post-Keynesian structuralists. Still, this does not mean that central banks fully accommodate the private sector. Accommodation, as already explained by Eichner (1987, p. 847) and Rochon (1999, p. 164), should take on a meaning unrelated to quantitative adjustments. It should refer to whether or not the central bank is pegging the target interest rate, whatever the economic conditions. When central banks are not accommodating, they are pursuing what Chick (1977, p. 89) calls 'dynamic' operations, increasing or reducing the target interest rate. This is a topic for the next section.

4.4 NEW DEVELOPMENTS IN MONETARY POLICY IMPLEMENTATION

4.4.1 Interest-rate Targeting

As a consequence of recognizing the total failure of monetarism from the mid-1970s to the early 1980s, central bankers have thought hard about how monetary policy strategy and monetary policy implementation ought to be changed. Perhaps the best-known change is the explicit or implicit adoption of inflation targeting as a new monetary policy strategy by a number of central banks. Just as important, however, have been the changes in monetary policy implementation, in particular the explicit recognition of interest-rate targeting. Although the new procedures are not that much different from previous ones, it is easier to pierce through their veil. In the case of the USA, for instance, as demonstrated by the description of the central bank reaction function by J.B. Taylor (1993), which became known as the Taylor rule, the behaviour of the Federal Reserve can be interpreted as one of interest-rate setting, long before it announced official targets. As Mosler (2002, p. 419) puts it, 'the federal Open Market Committee's target rate has been the focus of activity under previous Fed policies as well, and the difference is that prior to 1994 the target rate was known only to the Fed, whereas currently it is disclosed to the general public'. The procedures of some central banks are more transparent than those of others, making the horizontalist story more obvious, as is the case of Canada, New Zealand or Sweden. In other cases, such as the American system before 2008, some further investigation is required, but it can soon be demonstrated that the operational logic is identical to that of the more transparent central banks.

The Cambridge hare that was evoked by Robertson is very much present: today's principles of central banking are no different from what they were before the advent of monetarism. 'Today's views and practice on monetary policy implementation and in particular on the choice of the operational target have returned to what economists considered adequate 100 years ago, namely to target short-term interest rates' (Bindseil, 2004a, p. 10). These principles, following Fullwiler (2017), can be summarized in the following five statements:

1. The operating target is necessarily an interest-rate target.
2. Daily operations of central banks are about the payment system, not reserve requirements.
3. The operations of central banks accommodate the banks' demand for reserves by offsetting changes to its balance sheet that are inconsistent with such accommodation.
4. Compulsory reserves are means to smooth the demand for reserves; they have nothing to do with controlling monetary aggregates.
5. The implementation of a new overnight rate target does not require any change in the supply of reserves.

The fifth principle will be explained next. We can add a sixth principle: the ability of the central bank to fix interest rates is not so much related to its monopoly over the issue of high-powered money; rather, it has to do with the fact that the central bank is part of the clearing-house arrangement, and that ultimately banks and other direct clearers are required by law to settle their clearing accounts on the books of the central bank (Lavoie, 2003d, p. 538; Rochon and Rossi, 2011, p. 111). The central bank has the power to corner the market, forcing all banks to borrow from the central bank at the interest rate of its choice. Thus, in contrast to what was claimed by a number of economists, even heterodox ones, the advent of electronic money, the abandonment of compulsory reserve requirements and the reintroduction of private currency cannot undermine the power of central banks to control the overnight rate.

Four different kinds of operating system can be designed to steer interest rates with interest-rate targeting: a symmetric corridor system, a no-interest-on-reserves system, a floor system and a ceiling system. Before the advent of the Global Financial Crisis, the symmetric corridor system appeared to become the standard for monetary policy implementation. But with the 2008 financial crisis, several central banks have moved towards a floor system, and many more made the move towards this system when central banks responded to the financial and economic consequences of the COVID-19 crisis.

4.4.2 The Symmetric Corridor System

In the symmetric corridor system, the central bank announces a target overnight rate, with a symmetric corridor around it. The corridor system is also called the channel or the tunnel system. The top of the band is the lending facility rate – the old discount rate – at which commercial banks are free to borrow overnight as much as they wish, provided they have adequate collateral. Banks are also free to take daylight advances when payments go through the clearing house. The bottom of the band is the interest rate paid on the positive clearing balances (reserves) that commercial banks keep overnight at the central bank; this is the deposit facility rate, which Americans call interest on reserves (IOR). The symmetric corridor system is illustrated in Figure 4.1. Here it is assumed that there is no reserve averaging. The curve in bold illustrates what happens to the overnight rate as a function of the discrepancy between the amount of non-borrowed reserves supplied and the demand for reserves (these are called settlement balances in Canada and clearing balances in many other countries). In the particular case of Canada, where there are no reserve requirements since 1994 and where a corridor system has been in place, except for one year, between 1999 and 2020 when the COVID-19 crisis started, banks do not wish to hold any reserves under normal circumstances, so that the daily demand for reserves is zero. As a consequence, the supply of reserves is normally set at zero as well.

But what if it turns out that at the end of the day the Bank of Canada has not completely neutralized the effect of its transactions with the private sector and the commercial banks as a whole are left in a negative position at the clearing house, lacking enough clearing balances to settle payments, so that we are on the left of the zero point on the horizontal axis? In this case, some banks will be forced to borrow funds from the Bank of Canada. The banks that are in a negative position in the clearing house, as illustrated for instance in Table 4.11, will compete with each other to borrow clearing balances from the

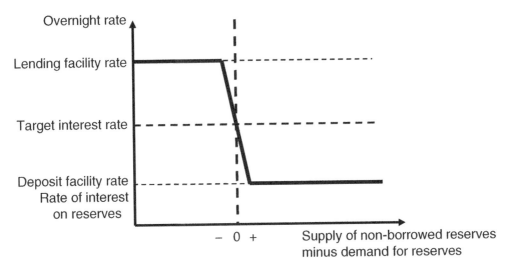

Figure 4.1 The symmetric corridor system

banks that have excess clearing balances. Not all such banks will be successful, however, and some will end up being forced to borrow from the central bank at the lending facility rate. The successful banks will manage to borrow funds on the overnight market, but at an interest rate that is likely to be somewhere between the target interest rate and the lending facility rate. If the deficiency in reserves is large, the overnight rate will reach the lending facility rate, illustrated in Figure 4.1.

Symmetrical effects will occur if the private banking system has been left with a positive amount of clearing balances at the end of the day, so that the banking system lies to the right of the zero point. The greater this excess amount, the more likely it is that the overnight interest rate will fall towards the deposit facility rate, as more of the excess clearing balances will find no borrower and will be deposited at the central bank for the night. Note the causality involved here. It is not that higher overnight rates relative to the lending facility rate induce banks to make more use of the borrowing facility or the discount window at the central bank, which is the usual interpretation of American scholars, an interpretation that Bindseil (2004a, p. 138) calls the reverse causation fallacy; rather, it is the lack of available clearing balances that forces banks to borrow funds from the central bank, thus pushing up the overnight rate in the process, as banks compete to obtain clearing balances.

The slope of the curve shown in Figure 4.1 depends on technical features, such as whether a bank has some market power – for instance if a single bank holds excess reserves while a large number of banks are in a deficit position in the clearing house. It will also depend on the strength with which clearing participants hold the convention regarding the target interest rate. For instance, if banks believe that the central bank has the ability and the information required to keep the overnight rate on target, the slope is likely to be flatter: the discrepancy between the supply of (non-borrowed) reserves and the demand for them will have to be large to raise or bring down the actual overnight rate towards the ceiling or the floor of the corridor.

Under normal circumstances, the overnight rate will be positioned in the middle of the corridor, a few basis points or less away from the target overnight rate. This is because overnight market participants know that they can rely on the deposit rate of the standing facilities at the bottom of the corridor if they have positive clearing balances and that, conversely, they can rely on the lending rate of the standing facilities at the top of the corridor if they have negative clearing balances. With enough competition and confidence in the participants to the clearing house, the overnight market rate ought to gravitate around the middle of the band, that is, around the target set by the central bank, as it does in Canada, within a couple of basis points. The standard differential between the top and the bottom of the corridor is 50 basis points.

As noted by Fullwiler (2013, p. 182), even with an inadequate knowledge of money-market conditions, a 'central bank could very precisely achieve its target rate simply by narrowing the corridor system between its lending rate and the remuneration rate', reducing the differential to ten basis points, for instance. Central bankers are, however, reluctant to do so, because they fear that banks might stay away from the money markets, using instead the standing facilities of the central bank, as they believe that money markets provide information about the health of their participants. Mosler (2010, p. 103), by contrast, argues that 'the interbank market serves no purpose', so that we might as well have banks depositing all their surplus clearing balances at the central bank and borrowing all their missing funds from the central bank, at a single target rate – a kind of degenerated corridor system.

Bindseil (2004a, p. 252) claims that 'the simplest system for controlling short-term interest rates is that with a symmetric standing facilities corridor around the target rate'. The reason for this assessment is that within a symmetric corridor system 'changes to the monetary policy stance, that is, of the target short-term interest rate, may be made without any change in reserve market conditions by simply moving the standing facilities corridor in parallel with the target rate' (ibid.). In other words, as confirmed by Borio and Disyatat (2010, p. 56), 'Crucially, the interest rate can be set quite *independently* of the amount of bank reserves in the system. *The same amount of bank reserves can coexist with very different levels of interest rates; conversely, the same interest rate can coexist with different amounts of reserves.*' This is what they call the 'decoupling principle'. We shall come back to this principle when we discuss the extraordinary measures that have been taken by a number of central banks since the beginning of the Global Financial Crisis and because of the COVID-19 crisis. In the meantime we can note that, with the symmetric corridor system, to change short-term interest rates, the central bank needs only to announce a new target overnight rate. The actual overnight rate will immediately adjust to the new target.

4.4.3 The US System until 2008

Things are not so simple in systems where reserves are not remunerated. The American procedures followed before 2008 are the typical example of such an asymmetric setup, as illustrated in Figure 4.2. This system is characterized by the availability of a discount window, where banks can borrow at the lending facility rate, and by the feature that bank reserves or bank deposits at the central bank get no remuneration. If banks are truly free to borrow from the central bank when the overnight rate reaches the lending facility rate,

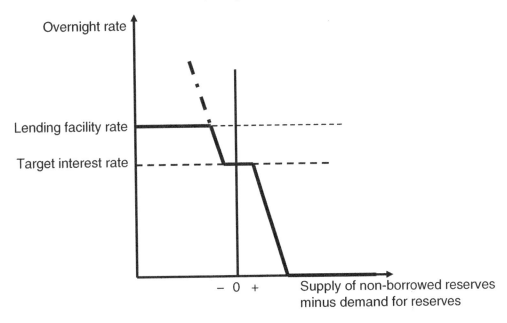

Figure 4.2   The no-interest-on-reserves system

then the overnight market interest rate cannot exceed the discount rate. This became (nearly) the case in the USA starting in 2002, when the discount rate was relabelled the 'primary credit rate'. Before that, because borrowing at the discount window was frowned upon, the actual overnight rate could exceed the discount rate, as shown by the dotted line, the spread between the two rates being assessed as the value of 'frown costs'. This also reflected in part the fact that the Federal funds rate is a rate without collateral (in contrast to the repo rate), whereas banks borrowing at the discount window have to show proper collateral.

The curve shown in Figure 4.2 reflects again the impact of the differential between the supply of non-borrowed reserves and the demand for reserves on the overnight rate. The curve has three flat segments. Besides the flat portions at the zero rate and at the lending facility rate, with averaged reserve requirements the curve should exhibit a flat portion around the target overnight rate, or rather at the expected overnight rate. On the last day of the averaging period, however, the demand for reserves should become inelastic and this flat portion should disappear (Whitesell, 2006; Ennis and Keister, 2008; Fullwiler, 2013). In any case, what Figure 4.2 aims to show is that interest-rate targeting is not an easy task with such a system because, unless the flat middle portion is sufficiently large, the central bank needs to supply an adequate amount of reserves to the system for the target interest rate to be achieved.

The range of possible overnight rates is wide, the more so if there are frown costs attached to the discount window. An additional difficulty is that the target overnight rate is usually set near the interest rate on lending facilities, so that there is asymmetry, as the target is not half-way between the two extreme possible values that can be taken by the actual overnight rate. This approach 'is much more challenging for the central bank and less transparent, especially if the central bank's target rate is not published' (Bindseil, 2004a, p. 87), which was the case in the USA before 1994. It should also be noted that, for changes in the target interest rate to be achieved, the central bank needs to modify the supply of reserves. It is this absence of the decoupling principle in the US monetary system, plus the lasting influence of the reserve-position doctrine – advocated by Keynes, American scholars and even American central bankers, as reflected in procedures such as 'borrowed reserve targeting' in place in the USA between 1979 and 1982 – that may have led some structuralist post-Keynesians to claim that central banks could exert quantity constraints on bank reserves.

4.4.4 The Floor and the Ceiling Systems

The subprime financial crisis and the delirium caused by the failure of the Lehman Brothers investment bank forced the Fed to modify its implementation procedures. The crisis provoked large fluctuations in the fed funds rate. In an effort to regain proper control over short-term interest rates, the Fed adopted the corridor system in October 2008. But just a month later, it moved to a new system, the 'floor system', which is still in force at the time of writing (2022). This eventually became the zero-interest policy (ZIRP), as the floor was set at zero (within a range of 0 to 0.25 per cent!).

With the floor system, the central bank sets the target overnight rate of interest at the level of the rate of interest on deposits at the central bank. In fact, the floor system is nothing new: it was in place in the USA between 1933 and 1951, when short-term interest rates were driven down to zero. Japan, attempting to come out of its balance-sheet recession (Koo, 2009), has long been on a floor system. Moreover, the floor system was adopted by New Zealand and Norway before the financial crisis. Six major central banks, including the ECB and the Bank of England, were on the floor system in 2016; due to the COVID-19 crisis, more central banks, including the Bank of Canada, have recently joined that group.

In Figure 4.3, the supply of clearing balances is set so that it largely exceeds the demand for reserves (to the right of the zero vertical line in the figure). Thus the actual overnight rate is always equal, or nearly so, to the interest rate on deposit facilities at the central bank, now also the target interest rate. There are two advantages to this procedure. First, central banks do not need to worry about being precise in their actions to neutralize autonomous flows of payments, in contrast to what is needed within the corridor system. Provided it is large enough, the supply of reserves can be of any amount. Second, central banks can let their balance sheet balloon and force banks into using their deposit facilities without worrying about the impact on overnight interest rates. This is particularly useful during a financial crisis when central banks wish to use all possible tools.

Otherwise, the floor system retains some of the advantages of the symmetric corridor system. It retains the decoupling principle. The target interest rate can be raised or lowered, with actual overnight rates responding fully to this change without having to tamper with the supply of reserves. It should be noted that the floor system was advocated before it was implemented in the USA, both by post-Keynesian authors (Fullwiler, 2005) and by central bankers (Keister et al., 2008). The only drawback of the floor system is that it creates worries among ignorant investors and mainstream economists, who believe that large amounts of excess reserves will generate price inflation.

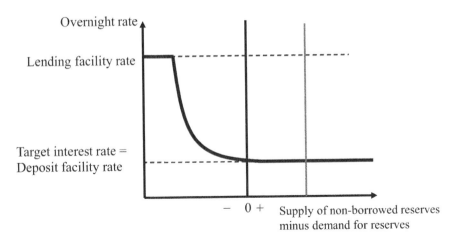

Figure 4.3 The floor system

A symmetric alternative to the floor system is the 'ceiling system'. In this interest-setting system, the central bank compels commercial banks in the aggregate to use the lending facilities. This is done by supplying at all times an insufficient amount of clearing balances, forcing the commercial banks to borrow them from the central bank (the system is always on the left of the zero vertical line in Figure 4.4). This was indeed a typical feature of overdraft economies, within which as we saw when discussing the anti-chartalist story, central banks do not acquire any government securities, forcing banks to take advances from the central bank, and hence, as was said, 'to be in the Bank'. Most continental European countries were in this situation until asset-based systems became the fashion because overdraft economies were perceived to be more inflation-prone. Different rates could be charged to the borrowing banks, depending on how much they had already borrowed.

Figure 4.4 illustrates the ceiling system, with the supply of reserves set at such a low level that banks taken overall are forced to come to the central bank. With the target interest rate equal to the lending facility rate, this ensures that the actual overnight rate approximates the ceiling rate. Although the ECB is usually depicted as operating within a corridor system, I would argue instead that the ECB was operating under a modified ceiling system until its sovereign debt crisis. This is because the target interest rate of the ECB was the minimum bid rate, which is the rate at which banks could engage in repo operations with the ECB, under the main refinancing operations. As was pointed out earlier, repurchase agreements are equivalent to loans. Thus, overall, eurozone banks were structurally indebted to the ECB, with the actual supply of reserves, not counting the borrowed ones, equivalent to the supply of reserves shown in Figure 4.4. With the eurozone crisis, the monetary market became fragmented, with Southern eurozone banks still borrowing from the central bank, while Northern eurozone banks were flooded with reserves (Febrero et al., 2018).

The ceiling system, just like the floor system or the symmetric corridor system, displays the decoupling principle. The target interest rate can be modified without any change in the outstanding amount of reserves. While Minsky (1986a, pp. 282, 361) advocated a return to the ceiling system, most observers today believe that a floor system is preferable

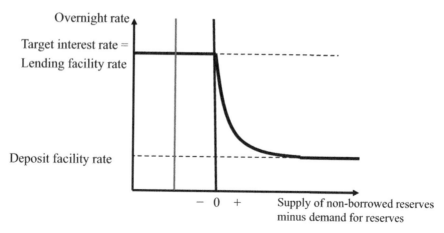

Figure 4.4 *The ceiling system*

to a ceiling system because in the former case commercial banks carry central bank assets rather than central bank liabilities.

The new developments in monetary policy implementation over the last 25 years and as a consequence of the financial crisis have certainly vindicated the post-Keynesian theory of endogenous money. The simplest representation of this theory is to draw a horizontal supply of high-powered money, set at the target overnight rate. This representation can also be found in a few orthodox textbooks (Cecchetti, 2006, p. 463). This is meant to represent the claim that, between meetings of the interest-setting committee of the central bank (the FOMC in the USA, for instance), the monetary authorities will supply any amount of reserves corresponding to the target overnight interest rate that they wish to achieve. The shape of this supply curve was the subject of an intense debate among post-Keynesian economists, as many argued that the central bank reaction function ought to make it upward-sloping when several periods came to be considered (Fontana, 2009, p. 115). By contrast, one could take the view here that, from a daily perspective, the supply of clearing balances is a vertical line, as the central bank has substantial control (as in the USA or Europe) or perfect control (as in Canada) over the supply of non-borrowed reserves.

In past writings of post-Keynesians, mine included, this distinction was not always made clear. Along with others, I used to argue that central banks have little control over the overall supply of reserves (the sum of borrowed and non-borrowed reserves). For instance, when sitting on the left of the zero line in Figure 4.2, banks access the discount window and get the reserves they need. This has been verified time and time again, in particular when the Fed attempted to reduce the overall amount of reserves by cutting into the amount of non-borrowed reserves, only to find no change in the overall amount as banks made use of the lending facilities. If too many (non-borrowed) reserves were provided, banks that had previously taken advances at the central bank would use these extra reserves to reduce their indebtedness *vis-à-vis* the central bank – the case of overdraft economies with a ceiling system – thus getting the supply of reserves equal to the demand for reserves through a kind of Kaldorian reflux mechanism. But with the floor system, the central bank is able to achieve its target interest rate while simultaneously setting an amount of excess reserves of its choosing.

4.4.5 Credit Easing and Quantitative Easing

A look at the strategies pursued by the Fed

What remains intriguing is the case of the floor system when the central bank is flooding the banking system with excess reserves in an asset-based economy. In this case, one cannot say that the supply of reserves is demand-led. Banks do not necessarily wish to hold these huge amounts of reserves. In that sense, the supply of reserves is not necessarily equal to the demand for reserves. There is nothing that banks can do in the aggregate to remove excess reserves as long as they are not indebted to the central bank or as long as there are no compulsory reserves. Thus our monetary principles need to be slightly modified: the supply of reserves can be said to be demand-led, but only in so far as the target interest rate is not set at the bottom of the corridor.

The floor system has been accompanied by quantitative easing policies, which have generated many questions among economists and the general public. What can post-Keynesian theory say about these? The first obvious question relates to the purpose and efficiency of quantitative easing policies. Ironically, these policies, based on monetary aggregates, as were monetarist policies, are now called non-conventional policies, because they do not rely on interest-rate targeting. To some extent, they seem to be a remnant of the academic belief in the quantity theory of money.

Some authors distinguish between credit easing and quantitative easing. In the case of credit easing, the central bank proceeds to a swap, borrowing or purchasing illiquid private assets or long-term government securities that are less liquid in exchange for highly liquid Treasury bills. This helps those banks and other financial institutions that lack liquidity, as they can now use the liquid Treasury bills to borrow funds from more liquid banks through repurchase operations. The swap corresponds to situation A in Table 4.22: Treasury bills and private assets are exchanged between the central bank and the commercial banks. This is what the Federal Reserve did for about a year, between August 2007 and September 2008. The swaps have no repercussions on reserves, because the purchases of private assets by the central bank are 'sterilized' by the sale of Treasury bills to the commercial banks. This, however, cannot go on for ever, because at some point the central bank will run out of Treasury bills.

Table 4.22 Accounting for balance-sheet changes during the Global Financial Crisis

Central bank (the Fed)		Commercial banks	
Assets	Liabilities	Assets	Liabilities
(A) T-bills: −100	(B) Govt deposits: +100	(A, B) T-bills: +100	Deposits Own funds
(A, B, D) Private assets or long-term securities: +100	(C, D) Reserves: +100	(C, D) Reserves: +100	(C) Fed credit: +100
(C) Advances: +100		(A, B, D) Private assets or long-term securities: −100	

This is why the Fed adopted a new credit-easing scheme. While it continued to purchase (or borrow) private assets from financial markets, it asked for the collaboration of the US Treasury, requesting it to auction equivalent sums of Treasury bills that were sold to financial institutions. This was the so-called Treasury Supplementary Financing Program (SFP). The proceeds of these Treasury-bill sales were then repatriated in the form of government deposits at the Fed, thus draining the reserves created by the use of the various credit facilities of the central bank. Other central banks, such as the Bank of Canada, organized identical transactions. This scheme, which was also pursued in the Spring of 2020, at the beginning of the COVID-19 pandemic in North America, produces a swap that is no different from the previous one: the central bank takes in illiquid private financial assets while the private sector acquires liquid short-term government securities. But this time, in contrast to what had occurred previously, the size of the Fed's balance sheet rose precipitously: the rise in its holdings of private assets was not compensated by a decline in its holdings of government securities; instead it was accompanied by a rise in its liabilities – the increased deposits of the federal government at the central bank. This corresponds to situation B in Table 4.22.

This new scheme lasted only a few weeks, however, as American authorities started to worry about the approaching US government debt ceiling. Just before adopting the floor system, the Fed gave up on sterilization, as banks and other financial institutions started to borrow huge amounts from the Fed, thus creating reserves and boosting the size of its balance sheet. This is shown by case C in Table 4.22. As the use of credit programmes declined, the Fed switched to quantitative easing in 2009, by purchasing large amounts of private assets, thus creating reserves, still without attempting to sterilize them. This is case D in Table 4.22. Further episodes of quantitative easing then followed whenever the Fed felt that the US economy was moving away from recovery.

The new normal: a floor and a sub-floor at the Fed

Fed officials had some trouble in explaining the new monetary policy operational framework and its consequences to people trained in mainstream economics. Fed officials now distinguish between *limited-reserves* regimes and *ample-reserves* regimes, with the former corresponding to Figure 4.2 while the latter corresponds to Figure 4.3 and what we called the floor system. Indeed, the Fed has now decided that despite planning to gradually diminish the size of its balance sheet after the COVID-19 shock, 'the level of reserves will be such that the Fed continues to implement policy with an ample level of reserves' (Ihrig and Wolla, 2020, p. 22). The new normal at the Fed is thus a floor system.

In fact, this floor system had to be slightly modified, as Fed operators kept facing a puzzle. While theory would tell us that the federal funds rate cannot fall any lower than the interest rate on reserves (the IOR), the reality was that with the IOR at 0.25 per cent the federal funds rate oscillated between 0.05 and 0.20 per cent. The reason, it was found, is that government-sponsored enterprises (such as Fanny Mae or Freddy Mac) could not receive interest payments on their reserve balances at the Fed, so that, lacking bargaining power, they were offering them to other financial institutions at a rate between zero and the IOR rate.

When, in 2014, the Fed started considering raising the target interest rate, which happened in 2016, it became concerned with this slack control over the fed funds rate as it feared that raising the floor rate might not succeed in achieving its new targets. The Fed thus set up a sub-floor, by providing reverse repos to financial institutions who were denied, by law, access to interest-paying reserve accounts at the Fed, such as the said government-sponsored enterprises and money market funds. These reverse repos were called overnight reverse purchase agreements (ON RRP). The rate paid on ON RRP transactions is set at 25 basis points below the interest rate on reserves. In terms of Figure 4.3, the target federal funds rate would be in between two horizontal lines at the low end of the graph. The ON RRP thus acts as a supplementary tool for the successful operation of the US floor system, as the effective federal funds rate gravitates in between the floor and the sub-floor (Ihrig and Wolla, 2020; Grossman-Wirth, 2019). Another puzzle occurred in 2019 and 2020 when both the federal funds rate and one-day repo rates went above the top of this floor corridor, thus inducing the Fed in 2021 to institute a standing repo facility, which allows banks to convert government bonds to reserves on demand at an administered rate.

Purpose and puzzles of quantitative easing
While credit-easing operations had the obvious goal of supporting the prices of faltering private assets and providing liquidity to the financial sector, thus avoiding a complete meltdown, the justification for quantitative-easing policies when conditions have stabilized is not so clear. Once there is a large amount of reserves in the private banking system, ensuring that the overnight rate stays at the floor of the corridor, there is no obvious justification for handing out reserves exceeding the required amount by a factor of 20 or 30.

Once the financial crisis has been contained, there are three broad transmission mechanisms that might justify quantitative easing operations (Fiebiger and Lavoie, 2020; 2021). The first set of mechanisms can be associated with post-Keynesian theory. The second mechanism relies on some sort of signalling. As to the third mechanism, it relies on Friedman's monetarism.

We start with the first transmission mechanism. The purchases of government bonds or of private financial assets support the prices of these assets, thus reducing long-term yields and allowing companies to issue bonds and shares at a lower cost to finance their investments. The purchases may also generate capital gains for rentiers, or help them avoid capital losses, thus inducing them to increase their consumption. Keynes (1930b, pp. 370–1) himself mentions these two effects when he argued that in conditions of acute slump central banks could conduct open-market operations *à outrance*. This in addition would bring short-term rates to zero. From a post-Keynesian perspective, there is nothing wrong with these two claims, which are similar to those of credit easing, although the ultimate effects on aggregate demand are likely to be modest. In an open economy, the low interest yields may also generate a depreciation of the currency, as domestic agents may use their newly-acquired money balances to rebalance their portfolio by purchasing foreign financial assets.

The second transmission mechanism is based on various signalling effects. It is said that quantitative easing will engender a rise in expected present or future inflation, and thus an increase in actual inflation and a decrease in expected real interest rates. It is also thought that by boosting asset prices, it will increase the collateral values of borrowers and the equity of lenders. These latter effects are associated with the bank lending channel of New Keynesians. Post-Keynesians have little confidence in these. As to the third transmission mechanism, it relies on the standard monetarist story and the intellectual influence of Milton Friedman. It is said that the sellers of the private assets will deposit the proceeds in banks, which will now have more funds and more reserves at the central bank to make loans. Such proponents of quantitative easing then rely on the standard money multiplier story, itself based on the myth of the fractional reserve system, claiming that the new deposits will permit a multiple expansion of credit and money aggregates, and hence increases in nominal GDP, in total contradiction to post-Keynesian theory.

Two phenomena associated with quantitative easing have been puzzling for mainstream observers of monetary aggregates. First, as bank reserves of ever greater size accumulate at the central bank, observers complain that commercial banks are refusing to collaborate or are somehow constrained and unable to use them to provide new loans. This was notably the case in the USA. By contrast, within the eurozone, which was an overdraft system, quantitative easing was not necessarily associated with rising reserves, as several European banks used instead their newly acquired clearing balances to reduce their debt *vis-à-vis* other banks, thus allowing the latter to reduce their overdrafts at the ECB. There is no puzzle from the post-Keynesian point of view: holding extra reserves at the central bank will not induce banks to find more creditworthy borrowers.

A second puzzling feature, noted particularly in the UK, is that increases in the official definitions of the money supply, however measured, seem to be much smaller than increases in bank reserves. This is puzzling to most observers, because they would argue that 'surely the central bank remains able to *increase* the supply of money and credit to the economy, for instance by autonomously deciding to step up its purchases of private sector assets (such as bills, commercial paper, bonds, equity, real estate, and so on)' (Werner, 2005, p. 59). But this second puzzle is easy to resolve if one is aware of the reflux principle put forth by the Banking School and Kaldor. This is shown in Table 4.23, where it is assumed that non-bank agents are the sellers of the financial assets purchased by the central bank, here assumed to be gilts (government long-term securities) or asset-based securities (ABS). Indeed, in reality, non-bank agents rather than banks often were the main counterparty to the quantitative-easing operations of central banks. This was a conscious decision of central bankers, as they thought that in previous quantitative easing operations the banks had declined to grant more loans despite the presence of excess reserves. The idea was thus to directly provide firms and households with additional money balances.

Table 4.23 *Balance sheet of commercial banks and sellers of illiquid assets following a quantitative-easing operation*

Commercial banks		Sellers of financial assets	
Assets	Liabilities	Assets	Liabilities
Reserves +100	Deposits +100	Gilts and ABS −100 Deposits +100	
Reserves +100 Loans −90	Deposits +10	Gilts and ABS −100 Deposits +10	Loans −90

When the central bank purchases financial assets, the sellers deposit the proceeds of the sales at their commercial bank, and banks acquire reserves through the clearing house. This is non-controversial and shown in the first row of Table 4.23. But why do private agents accept to sell their financial assets? It may be because they are only too happy to get rid of illiquid assets at what they think is a good price. It may also be because they wish to deleverage and reduce their debt. The effect of such a decision is shown in the second row of Table 4.23. While banks are still holding 100 units in reserves, it may be that 90 per cent of their clients have decided to use their newly acquired deposits to reduce the amount of bank loans that they had previously taken. In this case, a quantitative-easing operation of £100 billion sterling will only lead to an increase of £10 billion sterling in the money supply. Richard Koo (2009), an iconoclast economist working for a financial firm, explains that this is likely to happen in a balance-sheet recession during which agents do their best to pay down their debt, as is the case in Japan, the USA and the UK. Thus there is no mystery here.

Quantitative easing appears as a desperate attempt by monetary authorities and some economists still adhering to monetarism to demonstrate that monetary policy is always effective. Quantitative easing is often justified by the belief that loan officers check the reserves position of their bank before making new loans. Until 2001, Japanese central bankers were reluctant, and rightly so, to pursue quantitative-easing operations, because the 'Bank of Japan argued vigorously that such measures would be meaningless' (Koo, 2009, p. 73). The reason, as Koo (ibid., p. 75) explained, is that 'borrowers – not lenders, as argued by academic economists – were the primary bottleneck in Japan's Great Recession'. This is tied to the sayings that 'you can't push on a string' or that 'you can bring a horse to water, but you can't force it to drink'. This explains the first puzzle noted above. Now, as Fullwiler (2013, p. 184) remarks, 'whereas this might have been a time for economists to consider that perhaps the money multiplier model and the Quantity Theory of Money have causation wrong, instead the lack of impact from increased quantities of excess reserves is often blamed on IOR [interest on reserves]'.

Alternative versions of quantitative easing
While quantitative easing, as presented here, has been applied in several countries, a number of economists and activists have been advocating variants of quantitative easing. Table 4.24 sketches some of these alternatives (Fiebiger, 2016a; Lavoie and Fiebiger, 2018). In all cases it is assumed that households wind up with the proceeds of the fiscal or monetary intervention, and hence improve their net worth position. Case 1 corresponds to a standard fiscal operation, where the government spends by issuing bonds, here held by banks. Case 2 corresponds to the standard case of quantitative easing, where the issued bonds are purchased back by the central bank. Case 3 describes a proposal made by a number of European economists (Couppey-Soubeyran, 2020), in an attempt to circumvent Maastricht rules and provide more fiscal space to eurozone countries: the central bank cancels the government debt that it holds on its balance sheet. As shown, this leads to a drop in its net worth, while the debt of the government disappears. Case 4, which in an accounting sense, is identical to case 3, corresponds to what has been called quantitative easing for the people or also helicopter money. Here, the central bank – instead of the government – sends funds to households, thus creating again a hole in its net worth.

Table 4.24 Fiscal operation, quantitative easing and alternatives

Case	Government Assets	Government Liabilities	Central bank Assets	Central bank Liabilities	Commercial banks Assets	Commercial banks Liabilities
1		Bonds B +10 Net worth −10			Bonds B +10	Household deposits +10
2		Bonds B +10 Net worth −10	Bonds B +10	Reserves H +10	Reserves H +10	Household deposits +10
3, 4				Reserves H +10 Net worth −10	Reserves H +10	Household deposits +10

What are the flow consequences of these various actions? In case 1, the government has to make interest payments equal to $i_{LT}B$, where B is the amount of the debt and i_{LT} is the long-term rate of interest on bonds. In case 2, the government needs to make the same interest payment as in case 1. The central bank receives a flow of $i_{LT}B$, but it has an interest outflow equal to $i_{TR}H$, where H is the amount of bank reserves (with $H = B$) and i_{TR} is the target rate of interest, that is, the rate of interest on reserves. The central bank thus makes a profit of $(i_{LT} - i_{TR})B$, which can be transferred to the account of the government. The net cost of case 2 for the government is thus $i_{TR}B$. As to cases 3 and 4, the government makes no interest payment, but the central bank needs to make interest payments equal to $i_{TR}H$. These payments will diminish the profits of the central bank by the same amount, thus reducing the dividends that it can send back to the government. The net cost of cases 3 and 4 for the government is thus $i_{TR}B$ – the same cost as in case 2. In a world where central banks pay interest on reserves, cancelling the government debt held by the central bank or going for helicopter money thus makes no difference whatsoever in terms of flow payments compared to a standard quantitative easing operation. And it makes very little difference compared to a standard fiscal operation. What really counts for flow payments is the actual level of the interest rate. Somehow, the debt is always there and cannot go away.

4.5 LIQUIDITY PREFERENCE

The efficient-market hypothesis sees agents in financial markets acting essentially as arbitragists who intervene when they see small deviations in the prices of financial assets. They are actors who make sure that financial resources are *allocated* efficiently – note that nothing is created here. The arbitragists ensure that prices move smoothly, in a continuous way. In his excellent critique of rational financial markets, Justin Fox (2009) recalls how Lawrence Summers (1985, p. 634) depicts the rational-market hypothesis. Its adherents 'have shown that two quart bottles of ketchup invariably sell for twice as much as one quart bottles of ketchup except for deviations traceable to transaction costs . . . They ignore what seems to many to be the more important question of what determines the overall level of asset prices.'

There is another element that seems to be entirely absent from the efficient-market hypothesis: liquidity. It is all very well, as mainstream authors do, to claim that markets find the correct price at all times. Let the prices fall and someone will be willing to buy, they say. But this occurs only if there is enough liquidity (Davidson, 2009). If all orders go one way, as everyone wants to sell assets, the market will freeze unless there is a market-maker out there who is willing to swim against the tide. The importance of liquidity can be recalled through the following story, told by Paul Jorion (2008). Take a bull livestock breeder. Suppose he owes $10 000 to his banker. Now comes the time to pay. He doesn't have the cash to pay back the loan so he proposes to his banker that he will raise the money by auctioning off one of his bulls. The auction market is full of livestock breeders. Nobody, however, is willing to buy at $10 000, nor at $9000, and nor at $8000. The banker tells the breeder to forget it, and to leave the auction. The livestock breeder insists that pretty soon someone will buy his bull at a fair price. Then the banker says. 'Don't you understand? All the livestock breeders here owe me money!' As Keynes (1936, p. 155) says, the objective of most participants in financial markets is 'to pass the bad, or depreciating, half-crown to the other fellow', as was pretty obvious during the subprime financial crisis.

So far most of our attention has been devoted to the links between the banking system and the central bank. Not much has been said about the behaviour of commercial banks or about the determination of interest rates – the target rate of the central bank and other interest rates. And hardly any space has been devoted to the concept of liquidity preference. We remedy to this in the present section.

4.5.1 Some Controversies over Liquidity Preference

The rate of interest, but which one?
Many of the controversies between structuralist and horizontalist post-Keynesians arose, in my view, from two related misunderstandings. There has been confusion about the meaning of 'the' rate of interest; and there has been confusion about the meaning of 'liquidity preference'. Broadly speaking, I think it is fair to say that horizontalist post-Keynesians have the target rate of interest of the central bank in mind when they talk of 'the' rate of interest. This for them is the base rate – the benchmark rate. On the other hand, structuralist post-Keynesians view the long-term rate of interest as 'the' rate of interest. Obviously, to talk of 'the' rate of interest is a simplification, and this possible confusion illustrates only too well that economists should be more careful and differentiate clearly between the two rates, and possibly even more rates, as emphasized by James Tobin (1982).

The confusion over 'the' rate of interest may perhaps be attributed to Keynes (1936, p. 167), who found it convenient 'to mean by the rate of interest the complex of the various rates of interest'. Thus, when Keynes himself says that liquidity preference determines 'the' rate of interest, it is not quite clear whether he means the short-term rate, the long-term rate, or the spread between the short- and the long-term rates. I tend to favour the last of these three possibilities, since although Keynes (ibid.) says that he will assume that 'money is co-extensive with bank deposits', he also recognizes that he could just as well include instruments such as Treasury bills in the definition of money.

For instance, Keynes's concept of the liquidity trap cannot apply to the short-term rate, which we know can be brought down to zero; rather it must apply to the long-term rate or to the spread between the short- and the long-term rates. The proper view of the liquidity trap is thus a situation where the central bank gets the base rate down, but without much impact on other interest rates. The cause of the liquidity trap, as explained by Keynes, is twofold: when interest rates are low, even a small change in the yield on bonds will produce a large capital loss (Godley and Lavoie, 2007a, pp. 167–8); furthermore, even if the central bank provides advances at zero per cent while deposits at banks are remunerated at zero per cent, banks still face fixed costs that need to be covered through interest rates on loans or other charges. Still, amazingly, many eurozone governments had negative interest rates on their 10-year bonds, and in 2021 only German bonds of a 30-year duration carried a positive interest rate, thus questioning Keynes's liquidity trap!

Keynes's view of the liquidity trap is thus different from its orthodox interpretation, according to which the liquidity trap is associated with the 'zero lower bound' – the fact that short-term nominal interest rates cannot fall below zero (Krugman, 1998). Post-Keynesians like Moore (1988, p. 264) had long recognized that, because the 'zero nominal floor on deposits imposes a positive nominal floor on bank lending rates', expansionary monetary policy was rendered ineffective 'during periods when prices are falling'.

When horizontalist post-Keynesians claim that 'the' interest rate is exogenous, they refer to the target interest rate set by the central bank, as well as the short-term interest rates that should gravitate around it. This makes structuralist post-Keynesians uneasy because for them the key rate of interest is the long-term rate, and that rate is obviously neither exogenous nor under the direct control of the central bank. Similarly, when horizontalist post-Keynesians like Kaldor (1982, p. 26) affirm that 'liquidity preference turns out to have been a bit of a red herring', leading some post-Keynesians to complain that horizontalists leave 'no room for liquidity preference in the determination of interest rates' (Wray, 1989, p. 1187), what the horizontalists have in mind is the target interest rate set by the central bank. This rate is not determined by the liquidity preference of the public. Dow and Dow (1989, p. 148) understood this well when they wrote that, if liquidity preference is understood in a narrow way, as the determinant of the rate of interest on short-term assets, then it is 'not of much interest' and 'the liquidity preference theory of interest becomes irrelevant' since 'the monetary authorities can, and normally do, set short-term rates in any case'.

To understand the role of liquidity preference, its meaning has to be enlarged to all agents of the economy and to all financial instruments, as Keynes had it in his *Treatise on Money*, rather than being limited to households and money, as in the *General Theory* or the standard IS/LM model. Such a generalization was proposed early on under various guises by several post-Keynesian authors (Kregel, 1984–85; Mott, 1985–86; Le Héron, 1986; Wray, 1992a; Brown, 2003–04). Besides the impact on the lending activity of banks and their lending rates, which will be discussed in a later section, several authors have suggested, following Hicks (1974, p. 45), that, broadly speaking, liquidity preference is measured by the differential between short and long interest rates: 'liquidity preference determines not the long rate of interest but the spread between the short and the long rates' (Wells, 1983, p. 533). As Dow and Dow (1989, p. 148) again rightly put it, 'liquidity preference, then, in practice determines the difference between the interest rate on liquid deposits and on less liquid substitutes. The monetary authorities set the rate at the short-term end of the spectrum; liquidity preference (along with other considerations) determines the mark-up to long-term rates.'

Thus it would seem that there was not much to quarrel about on this front. Still, a controversy erupted about the determination of the base rate itself. Whereas it could be recognized that the monetary authorities set a target rate of interest, it could also be contended that 'market opinion', or the financial lobby, determines the conventional rate that the central bank wishes to establish. Indeed, for a number of years, especially in the 1980s, when they imposed high nominal and real interest rates, central bankers in many countries were setting the discount rate equal to the Treasury-bill rate plus a certain number of basis points, pretending then that they were in no way responsible for the high Treasury-bill rates. Indeed, Paul Tucker (2004, p. 359), from the Bank of England, recognized that the monetarist episode 'had the unfortunate effect ... of clouding the Bank's thinking about the feasible role of open market operations in the framework for setting interest rates'. This led Moore (1991, p. 412) to retort that 'central banks must be held accountable for the ruling level of short-term interest rates, no matter how much they disavow'.

What rate of interest causes the others?
This lack of transparency, plus the misunderstandings just evoked, led to a controversy over causality. Both Moore (1988) and Pollin (1991; 1996; 2008) ran Granger–Sims causality tests that showed bidirectional causality between long-term market rates and the discount rate or the federal funds rate. Pollin (1991) also ran Granger–Sims causality tests between the federal funds rate and the discount rate, which at the time could be said to play the role of the target rate. Pollin (ibid., p. 390) then argued that 'the predominant causality runs from the federal funds rate to the discount rate', and from his further tests he concluded that there was support for interactive causality, 'with primary influence running from the market to the Fed' (Pollin, 1996, p. 510). Pollin's (2008) newer tests again showed two-way causality between long-term interest rates and the federal funds rate, with the stronger effect often going from the former to the latter.

Using a different method, Atesoglu (2005) concludes instead that there is unidirectional causality from the federal funds rate to the AAA bond yield and the 30-year Treasury-bond yield, a result similar to the unidirectional causality going from fed fund rates to mortgage rates found by James Payne (2006–07), with a complete pass-through (Cook, 2008). Finally, both Pollin (2008) and Atesoglu (2003–04) agree that the prime rate (the rate at which banks lend funds to good customers) has been clearly determined by the federal funds rate since the mid-1990s and during the 2000s. This is not surprising because, since the early 1990s, banks in the USA set the prime rate simply by adding 300 basis points to the target federal funds rate.

There has been a revival of interest for this causality issue. As one would expect from these delicate time-series tests, results have been disparate despite involving only US data. Rahimi et al. (2016), by combining linear and non-linear Granger causality tests, conclude the federal funds rate causes the 10-year Treasury-bond rate, the more so during recent business cycles. Rahimi et al. (2017), with another econometric strategy, find instead more evidence of bi-directional causality. Levrero and Deleidi (2021), using yet another method, find bi-directional causality when the long-term interest rate is the 10-year sovereign bond, but find instead unidirectional causality going from the federal funds rate to the 10-year AAA corporate bond. As to Kim (2019), looking at the 2004–2008 period only but using several different long-term rates, he finds a long-run bi-directional causality between the federal funds rate and long-term rates, while in the short run there would be a unidirectional causality going from the federal funds rate to long-term rates.

Moore's (1991) and Palley's (1991) interpretation of Pollin's (1991) results was that long-term rates partly reflect future expected short rates, as in the Hicksian expectations theory of long-term interest rates, and this is why they carry information about future federal funds rates. This, as pointed out by Pollin (2008) and Kim (2019), seems a rather weak explanation for the two-way causality linking short and long rates. Anyway, recent evidence shows that investors are totally unable to correctly anticipate future long-term interest rates just one semester or one year ahead (J.P. Morgan, 2016). If we accept that this two-way causality exists, a possible alternative explanation is that both rates respond to a third variable, for instance inflation. An even better explanation, as was clear during the subprime financial crisis and also in March 2020 at the beginning of the COVID-19 crisis, is that, when the economy is faltering, long-term interest rates and yields on private assets tend to increase, due to rising uncertainty and rising default risks. This induces the central bank to reduce the target federal funds rate in an attempt to bring down long-term rates and yields on private assets. The fact that long rates 'cause' short rates does not necessarily mean that rising long-term rates induce the central bank to raise targets on short-term rates; it may mean instead that rising long-term rates trigger a reaction from the central bank, which attempts to stop the increase in most of the spectrum of interest rates by lowering short-term rates.

The argument built around expectations makes more sense when we try to understand why, sometime in the past, federal funds rates appeared to 'cause' the discount rate. As Mosler (2002, p.420) points out, 'markets anticipate Fed action'. This, however, as he continues, 'is in sharp contrast to the notion often supported by the media that market rates, rather than anticipating Fed action, contain information as to where the Fed should target the federal funds rate', the target being roughly the discount rate at the time that Pollin (1991) was writing. Pollin (ibid., p.389) seemed somehow to accept the media view – that is, the view that market opinion pushes the central bank around, when he made the surprising claim that 'although the Fed autonomously sets the discount rate, it does so not simply to influence the market but to keep apace with it'.

In his latest review of the topic, Pollin (2008) seems to acknowledge that, despite his evidence of two-way causality, the federal funds rate can be considered as an exogenous variable, under the control of the Fed. But he adds that this rate has little influence on long-term rates, especially those on private assets, which are essentially determined by liquidity preference features, such as risk of default assessment. Thus, once again, when all is said and done, there seems to be little to disagree about. Horizontalists are likely to claim that, if monetary authorities are sufficiently insistent and consistent, a shift in interest-rate differentials can only be temporary. Summoning Keynes's authority, it could be said that the convention established in the prevailing spread 'will not be always unduly resistant to a modest measure of persistence and consistency of purpose by the monetary authority' (1936, p.204). In the case where long-term rates were high relative to short rates, financial operators would come to realize that substantial profits could be made by borrowing short and lending long. Eventually, unless 'the authorities' nerves are shaken by the ferocious growls with which the bears have been deafening them all this time', the convention enshrined in the base rate should prevail, and the liquidity premium should be back to its normal level (Robinson, 1952, p.30).

Fullwiler (2013, p.192) suggests that the monetary transmission towards long rates would be improved if central banks were to announce long-term interest-rate targets.

Indeed, Keynes (1936, p. 206) made the same suggestion when he wrote that 'perhaps a complex offer by the central bank to buy and sell at stated prices gilt-edged bonds of all maturities, in place of the single bank rate for short-term bills, is the most practical improvement which can be made in the technique of monetary management'. At this stage, Pollin's (2008) and Cömert's (2013) argument is that deregulation and financialization have weakened the ability of the monetary authorities to influence long-term rates as described above by Keynes and Robinson, and hence that rules and regulations should be introduced to help the central bank steer long-term rates towards values that are compatible with the targeted short-term rates. Indeed, extraordinary measures have been taken by central banks, and this may explain why, contrary to predictions, they have retained influence over long-term rates.

4.5.2 The Reaction Function of the Central Bank

Let us now assume that indeed the central bank has the power to set the target overnight interest rate at the level of its choice. In the previous section we examined the implementation procedures that the central bank can put in place to ensure that the actual overnight interest rate is equal to the target interest rate set by the central bank. But we have not discussed what this target rate of interest ought to be. The fact that the base rate of interest is considered to be exogenous in post-Keynesian theory does not mean that it should remain forever pegged at a constant level. Ever since the appearance of J.B. Taylor's (1993) paper on the Fed's reaction function, much attention has been devoted to how central banks set their target rate of interest. In post-Keynesian terms, within the generalized liquidity preference approach suggested by the post-Keynesian structuralists, the central bank reaction function can be interpreted as a formalization of the shape taken by the liquidity preference of the central bank. Rochon and Setterfield (2008) have proposed an excellent survey of the various ways in which the target interest rate could be set by the central bank. The present subsection is very much inspired by their paper.

The countercyclical approach
At the most global level, central banks can follow either a countercyclical policy or an income-distribution approach, which Rochon and Setterfield, not quite appropriately, call the 'activist' and the 'parking-it' approaches. A countercyclical policy means that the central bank attempts to fine-tune some economic aggregate by changing the target nominal interest rate, possibly changing the real interest rate as well. In the case of the parking-it approach, the central bank sets the nominal or the real rate of interest without attempting to fine-tune macroeconomic conditions. The countercyclical policy corresponds to the current behaviour of central banks. The income-distribution approach is more akin to a post-Keynesian view that sees fiscal policy, instead of monetary policy or interest-rate policy, as the main tool for fine-tuning the economy.

Currently, most central banks seem to pursue an activist policy based on inflation targeting. This is so, even though, as is the case of the ECB and the Bank of Canada, the statutes of these central banks do not specify a single mandate. On the other hand, the Federal Reserve in the USA has had an explicit dual mandate since 1977, based on price stability and maximum employment, and it can be argued that this is reflected in Taylor's (1993) assessment of the Federal Reserve reaction function. Giovannoni (2008) even shows empirically that output forecasts, rather than inflation forecasts, have driven changes in federal funds rates. As readers should expect by now, a number of post-Keynesians have argued that central banks should be concerned with unemployment rates and rates of capacity utilization, rather than with inflation. It has also been suggested that target interest rates take into account, or should take into account, the evolution of exchange rates and the rate of asset inflation, in particular on the stock market. The Global Financial Crisis has also underlined the weaknesses of a monetary-policy regime unconcerned with financial stability. In any event, there is little evidence that inflation targeting per se has really been responsible for contemporary low inflation rates (Tatliyer, 2017), while it may have slowed down GDP growth in emerging economies (Khan, 2022).

Rochon and Setterfield point out that Basil Moore, who is often depicted as assuming a constant target interest rate, can be seen as being part of the activist policy camp. They claim that Moore (1989, p. 487) argued in favour of 'a central bank reaction with short-term interest rates as the dependent variable', which would depend on 'the future state of the domestic economy (demand factors)', as well as on the goals of the monetary authorities including 'full employment, price stability, growth, balance of payments, terms of trade, exchange rates, the distribution of income'. Moore (1988, p. 264) mentions in addition foreign exchange reserves and foreign exchange rates as determinants of a central bank reaction function. Indeed, Moore (1988) was quite confident that the central bank could achieve fine-tuning, although he was somewhat less confident 20 years later (Moore, 2006).

If a central bank pursues countercyclical policies, should it target a real interest rate or a nominal rate? In the New Consensus analysis of the central bank reaction function, the target is a real interest rate set around the natural rate of interest, with the target set above or below the natural rate depending on whether the central bank wishes to diminish or increase the rate of price inflation. Alan Haight (2007–08) argues instead that the fight against overly high inflation rates does not require increases in real interest rates; it is enough to raise nominal interest rates by less than the rise in inflation. The rise in nominal interest rates will be enough to slow down the economy.

Why is this so? As we will note in Chapter 6, in North America the cyclical behaviour of the economy is driven to a large extent by the housing market. In that market, prudent borrowers rely on monthly payment to monthly income ratios, which depend on nominal interest rates and not on real rates. In addition, at least until the advent of subprime mortgages and NINJA loans (no income, no job and assets), it is standard practice in the industry to determine the maximum possible mortgage on the basis of this monthly payment to monthly income ratio. As a consequence, 'higher nominal rates lead (as any realtor knows) to smaller mortgages and smaller new homes' (Haight, 2007–08, p. 262). Because individual nominal incomes normally rise through time, most of the risk of default occurs during the early years of the mortgage, so that taking into account the nominal rate, rather than the real rate, is rational, as debt burdens will be front-loaded. The housing market is thus driven by these mortgage payments to income norms and by nominal interest rates. Indeed, in an empirical analysis of the euro area, Deleidi (2018) shows that higher interest rates do slow down loans provided to the housing market while there is no significant effect on loans granted to firms. Still, Fazzari et al. (2008, p. 560) argue that nominal interest rates, at constant real rates, also slow down business investment because firms rely on internal cash flows to finance their investments, and higher nominal interest rates on debt do reduce cash flows.

Two points can thus be made. First, the central bank reaction function does not have to be as steep as portrayed by the New Consensus. Second, low inflation targets with equivalently low interest rates generate conditions conducive to predatory lending, since they are likely to lead to overly large mortgages.

The income-distribution approach
The current view of post-Keynesians seems to trend towards the income-distribution approach. There are three reasons for this. The first reason, which has been developed by Arestis and Sawyer (2006) in several papers, is that monetary policy has only an indirect effect on inflation rates, so that inflation control can be achieved only at the cost of large losses in economic activity. The second reason is that the countercyclical approach has some ties with the natural rate of interest, a concept that the post-Keynesians reject, and that in any case has been proven to be impossible to measure with sufficient precision for actual use in central bank decisions. The third reason is that the interest rate is viewed by post-Keynesians as a distribution variable, as pointed out at the beginning of the chapter. Eichner (1987, p. 860) is quite clear about this when he says that the base rate of interest 'is a politically determined distributional variable rather than a market determined price'. Changes in real interest rates caused by inflation targeting produce changes in income distribution, affecting in particular the share of income going to rentiers. Monetary policy should thus focus on achieving rates of interest that are consistent with an appropriate income distribution. 'Monetary policy should not be designed so much to control the level of activity, but rather to find the level of interest rates that will be proper for the economy from a distribution point of view' (Lavoie, 1996e, p. 537). As Rochon and Setterfield (2008) indicate, at least three rules have been suggested in the past.

The first rule, which they call the Kansas City rule, since its proponents came from the University of Missouri in Kansas City (UMKC), simply says that the overnight interest rate ought to be zero. In its original version, the rule was to target 'a low and stable base rate' (Wray, 1997, p. 569). Forstater and Mosler (2005), supported by other neo-chartalists such as Éric Tymoigne (2009, p. 114), argue, making use of the neo-chartalist story developed with the help of Table 4.17, that if the government runs a deficit financed by the central bank, overnight interest rates will tend towards zero, and hence that this ought to be the normal case. Other rates of interest would adjust to this zero base rate. There are three problems with this proposal. First, as follows from our discussion of the previous section, it is not clear that the normal overnight rate is zero, even if the government is running a deficit. Second, the proposal, in a world where inflation is not nil, is likely to bring the euthanasia of the rentier. While Keynes (1936, p. 376) thought that this was likely to happen, for other reasons, however, the low interest rates that a number of economies have been experiencing since the Global Financial Crisis have clearly created sustainability problems for workers' pension funds. Third, in normal times, with some price inflation, near-zero interest rates will induce agents to purchase and hold real physical durable goods (real estate, precious metals), instead of holding financial assets as hedges against inflation, which is likely to lead to real asset inflation and possibly to financial instability (Epstein, 2019, ch. 6).

The next two rules ensure that real interest rates remain positive. Rochon and Setterfield (2008) call the first of these two rules the 'Smithin rule'. This is because John Smithin (1994, p. 199) has been arguing for more than 25 years that 'the most sensible advice for central banks to follow would be to stabilize real interest rates at low but still positive levels'. This advice has been reasserted by Smithin (2020) more recently. He argues that when monetary authorities act on countercyclical lines they tend to produce excessive fluctuations in real interest rates, moving from overly low real rates, as was the case in the 1970s, to overly high real rates, as was the case in the 1980s and 1990s (the break occurring around 1979–80). We may add that the Global Financial Crisis has led many central banks to adopt zero-interest-rate policies or quasi zero-interest-rate policies, with negative real interest rates. Smithin believes that these regime switches harm the economy, in particular when a regime of high real rates of interest is imposed on society. This, he says, is the result of years of zero or negative real rates of return on bonds, which correspond to the euthanasia of the rentiers. This, however, cannot but be followed by years of 'revenge of the rentiers', when the regime of high real interest rates prevails.

The solution for Smithin (1996, p. 86) is thus for the central bank to abandon inflation targets and instead

> to stabilize after-tax real interest rates at low but still positive levels (say no more than 1 per cent or 2 per cent) . . . Under such a regime, the already-rich may not become very much richer, but, as long as real returns remain positive, at least they would not suffer the erosion of capital which was the original source of the anti-inflationary agitation.

Sawyer (2011, p. 286) has proposed an alternative, with the real interest rate set equal to or just below the trend growth rate of real output, so as to provide some room for fiscal policy without fearing explosive debt ratios. Hein (2012, p. 138) has made a proposal that sits somewhere between the second and third rule, by advocating 'a slightly positive real rate of interest, below the long-run rate of productivity growth'.

The last of three distributional rules is the rule based on a *fair* interest rate. This rule was proposed by Lavoie and Seccareccia (1999; 2019). The concept of a fair rate of interest has resurfaced under the (unfortunate) appellation of the 'natural' rate of interest in the works of Luigi Pasinetti (1981, ch. 8; 1993, ch. 6), who has given it a very precise meaning. According to Pasinetti (1981, p. 174), the fair rate of interest 'stems from the principle that all individuals, when they engage in debt/credit relations, should obtain, at any time, an amount of purchasing power that is constant in terms of labour (a labour theory of income distribution)'. The fair rate of interest, or what Pasinetti (2002) himself later called the *just* rate of interest, thus maintains the purchasing power, in terms of command over labour hours, of funds that are borrowed or lent, and preserves the intertemporal distribution of income between borrowers and lenders. Thus the fair rate of interest 'means a zero rate of interest in terms of labour' (Pasinetti, 1993, p. 92). The fair rate of interest, in real terms, should be equal to the rate of increase in real wages. In an economy where the share of profit remains roughly constant, this growth rate would simply equal the growth rate of labour productivity. With price inflation, the fair rate of interest, in nominal terms, would be equal to the average rate of wage inflation, that is, the growth rate of labour productivity plus the rate of price inflation. Formally, we have

$$i_{fair} = \hat{y} + \hat{p} \tag{4.1}$$

where, as in Chapter 1, $\hat{y}$ is the growth rate of labour productivity, and $\hat{p}$ is the rate of price inflation. Thus, in a world with no technical progress and no inflation, the nominal interest rate ought to be zero, as was argued by the Church at the time when these conditions were roughly fulfilled.

The constancy of the profit share is not a stylized fact anymore. Several OECD countries since the late 1980s have seen a slow secular rise in the profit share. Under these circumstances, nominal wages will grow at a rate which is smaller than that determined by equation (4.1). Lavoie and Seccareccia (2019) show that the fair nominal rate of interest then ought to be:

$$i_{fair} = \hat{w} = \hat{y} + \hat{p} - \hat{\pi}\pi / (1 - \pi) \tag{4.1A}$$

where $\hat{w}$ is nominal wage inflation and where π is the profit share, with $\hat{\pi}$ the growth rate of the profit share.

A numerical example may help to clarify the notion of the fair rate of interest. Take an economy with a 5 per cent rate of price inflation. Suppose that the average wage is initially $10 per hour. Suppose furthermore that a borrower contracts a $10000 loan. This person has thus borrowed the equivalent of 1000 hours of labour time. Suppose now that labour productivity has risen by 2 per cent during the year, and that the average real purchasing power of wages has also risen by 2 per cent. Nominal wages have thus risen by 7 per cent, reaching $10.70 per hour a year later. If the rate of interest charged to the borrower is also 7 per cent, that is, if it is equal to the growth rate in nominal wages, the borrower will have to reimburse an amount of $10700 at the end of the year. However, since the average nominal wage rate has now risen to $10.70 per hour, the amount given back by the borrower is still equivalent to 1000 hours of labour time. As long as the actual rate of interest is equal to the fair rate of interest, as defined above, the purchasing power temporarily exchanged between the borrower and the lender remains constant in labour time.

In practical terms, the Smithin rule and the fair-rate rule may not be very different. Labour productivity has been growing at around 1 or 2 per cent per year in most industrialized countries, which is the premium suggested by Smithin. It seems that Keynes (1936, p. 221) had an even simpler rule, with a real interest rate equal to zero, when he says that 'a man would still be free to accumulate his earned income with a view to spending it at a later date. But his accumulation would not grow.' The other practical difficulty is to identify the interest rate that we are talking about. Both Keynes and Pasinetti seem to refer to the 'pure' interest rate, one devoid of default risk. This would imply the interest rate on government securities, either short-term or long-term ones. One could also argue that the most relevant variable is the mortgage rate, since mortgages are generally the most important personal liability.

4.5.3 The Liquidity Preference of the Public

While risk assessment, or rather underestimated risk, has been in the news during the Global Financial Crisis, post-Keynesians have associated the concept of liquidity preference with an environment of fundamental uncertainty. Within that environment, economic agents do not know probability distributions, they are aware that past sequences of events may not reoccur, they hope to learn more in the near future, and they may therefore delay decisions. This sort of liquidity preference is inversely related to the degree of confidence, to the reliability of beliefs, to Keynes's weight of an argument and animal spirits, as we explained in Chapter 2, and as it has been pointed out in particular by Jochen Runde (1994). A generalized theory of liquidity preference is thus intertwined with a generalized theory of rational behaviour in an environment dominated by uncertainty. But how do we express this concretely and in a simple manner? How will an increase in liquidity preference express itself? How will the rush towards liquid assets be absorbed? Here we consider the case of the liquidity preference of the public, looking at the management of households' (or their representatives') portfolio of assets.

A pricing adjustment mechanism of portfolio choices

Broadly speaking, we can say that there are two possible answers to these questions. An increase in the liquidity preference of the public, that is, an increase in the demand for safe and liquid assets, can be handled either through a change in the prices of the assets, and thus in the yields of these assets; or it can be handled through a change in the supply of these assets. Household portfolios will contain real assets, equities, bonds, Treasury bills, money-market instruments, bank deposits and cash. The case of cash, meaning here banknotes issued by the central bank, is peculiar. We know that cash is provided on demand by banks, in exchange for bank deposits. We know further that banks can procure cash to their clients either by getting advances from the central bank or by selling Treasury bills to the central bank (or through the repo market), which will necessarily be done unless the central bank wishes to create chaos in the economy. Thus an increase in the demand for cash will be absorbed by an increase in the supply of cash.

How about the other elements of the public's portfolio? There are two ways to see the necessary portfolio adjustments required by a change in liquidity preference. The first framework, the simplest one, is provided by Carlo Panico (1985). It is inspired by Keynes's chapter 17 of the *General Theory*. The idea is that the rates of return of all assets, modulated to take into account both their risk and their illiquidity (including the risk of a capital loss), need to be equalized. Each asset thus carries a risk and illiquidity discount, which we will call σ. In the case of money deposits, the risk and illiquidity discount may in fact be a positive liquidity premium. Once the portfolio has been modified to reflect the risk and illiquidity discounts, from the point of view of individual investors, the following equality should thus be realized:

$$i_{CB} = i_D - \sigma_D = i_{ST} - \sigma_{ST} = i_{LT} - \sigma_{LT} = i_{TSR} - \sigma_{TSR} \qquad (4.2)$$

where i_{CB} is the target overnight rate of the central bank, i_D and σ_D are the interest rate and illiquidity discount on bank deposits, i_{ST} and i_{LT} are the yields on short-term and long-term securities and i_{TSR} is the rate of return on stock market shares, while σ_{ST}, σ_{LT} and σ_{TSR} are their respective illiquidity discounts.

Equation (4.2) can be interpreted as follows. The central bank sets i_{CB}, which is the base rate of the system. The other rates adjust to it, the independent variables being the risk and illiquidity discounts σ_i associated with each kind of asset. An increase in the illiquidity discount associated with long-term assets will lead to an increase in i_{LT} – the yield required to hold on to long-term assets. Thus a reduction in the base rate of the system, i_{CB}, will succeed in reducing long-term rates if the illiquidity discount does not change; but it could also lead to an increase in long-term rates if the decrease in the base rate induces an even bigger increase in the illiquidity discount on long-term assets (for instance because of fears of inflation). The low long-term rates that were observed in the US in the 2000s, before the financial crisis, can be explained by this phenomenon: low and reduced illiquidity discounts on long-term bonds.

We may thus concur with Amstad and Martin (2011, p. 2) when they say that if 'credit-risk premia ... and the term structure of interest rates are sufficiently stable, intervention in the overnight market ... will allow the central bank to steer longer-term rates'. By contrast, 'in times of market stress ... stabilizing the overnight rate will not prevent longer and more economically relevant interest rates from fluctuating with credit-risk or liquidity premia'.

An alternative adjustment mechanism of portfolio choices
There is a second way in which the portfolio choice and portfolio adjustment can be conceived. This second framework was first proposed by Tobin (1969) and slightly modified by Godley (1996). It also bears some resemblance to the asset price model proposed by Wray (1992a). The implicit assumption of their models is that assets are imperfect substitutes, and that people will not put all their eggs in the same basket, even when there are still differentials in rates of return net of the illiquidity discounts. Here, for simplicity, we provide an example with only three assets: bank deposits, short-term assets, D and A_{ST}, as well as a number of long-term securities, A_{LT}, the price of which is p_{LT}, which is inversely related to its yield. In matrix form, we have the following representation of the demand for assets:

$$\begin{bmatrix} D \\ A_{ST} \\ p_{LT} A_{LT} \end{bmatrix} = \begin{bmatrix} \lambda_{10} \\ \lambda_{20} \\ \lambda_{30} \end{bmatrix} V + \begin{bmatrix} \lambda_{11} & \lambda_{12} & \lambda_{13} \\ \lambda_{21} & \lambda_{22} & \lambda_{23} \\ \lambda_{31} & \lambda_{32} & \lambda_{33} \end{bmatrix} \begin{bmatrix} i_D \\ i_{ST} \\ i_{LT} \end{bmatrix} V + \begin{bmatrix} \lambda_{14} \\ \lambda_{24} \\ \lambda_{34} \end{bmatrix} Y \qquad (4.3)$$

The various λ_{ij} parameters act as indicators of liquidity preference for the various assets. For those not at ease with matrices, the first row simply says that the demand for bank deposits D is such that

$$D = (\lambda_{10} + \lambda_{11} i_D + \lambda_{12} i_{ST} + \lambda_{13} i_{LT}) V + \lambda_{14} Y \qquad (4.4)$$

This means that the demand for deposits is a proportion of wealth V and of income Y (the transaction demand for money), and that the proportion of wealth is given by the parameter λ_{10}, but that this proportion is modulated by the rates of interest on deposits, short-term assets and long-term assets. The λ_{11} parameter is positive, as a higher rate of interest on deposits should induce portfolio-holders to hold more deposits, while the λ_{12} and λ_{13} parameters are negative since higher interest rates on other assets should induce investors to keep less of their wealth in the form of deposits. The λ_{14} parameter is also positive, as a higher income is likely to require transactions of a higher value and hence larger balances in bank accounts. The other two rows can be interpreted in a similar way.

There are compulsory restrictions on the various λ_{ij} parameters – the so-called adding-up conditions. These can be split into vertical conditions, as described by Tobin:

$$\lambda_{10} + \lambda_{20} + \lambda_{30} = 1$$
$$\lambda_{11} + \lambda_{21} + \lambda_{31} = 0$$
$$\lambda_{12} + \lambda_{22} + \lambda_{32} = 0$$
$$\lambda_{13} + \lambda_{23} + \lambda_{33} = 0$$
$$\lambda_{14} + \lambda_{24} + \lambda_{34} = 0$$

and into horizontal conditions, as described by Godley (1996, p. 18):

$$\lambda_{11} = -(\lambda_{12} + \lambda_{13})$$
$$\lambda_{22} = -(\lambda_{21} + \lambda_{23})$$
$$\lambda_{33} = -(\lambda_{31} + \lambda_{32})$$

The first vertical adding-up condition simply says that the total of the desired proportions of each asset must sum to unity. In other words, the sum of the demands must be equal to wealth V, so that $D + A_{ST} + p_{LT}A_{LT} = V$. You can have more of one thing by having less of another. The other vertical conditions arise from the same constraint. The horizontal adding-up conditions mean that the effect on an asset of an increase in its own rate of interest, with all other rates remaining constant, should not be any different from that of a fall, of the same size, in all the other rates, with the own rate staying the same. The horizontal constraints can be replaced by symmetry constraints, in which case the horizontal conditions will hold. Symmetry means that, in the main matrix, we have $\lambda_{ij} = \lambda_{ji}$ for all $i \neq j$, as proposed by Karacaoglu (1984). For instance, the equality $\lambda_{12} = \lambda_{21}$ implies that an increase in the interest rate on short-term assets will generate a drop in the demand for deposits of the same amplitude as the drop in the demand for short-term assets generated by an identical increase in the rate of interest on deposits. All these adding-up conditions ensure coherence of the analysis.

In the Godley and Lavoie (2007a) models, the demand for assets, given by equation (4.3), is confronted with the supply of assets. In contrast to equation (4.2), where the adjustment is presumed to occur only through prices, that is, through the values taken by the interest rates, here adjustments to portfolio preferences can occur either through the supply of the assets or through prices. In the case of equation (4.3), this implies changes in interest rates, but also changes in the price of long-term assets. For instance, looking at equation (4.4), if there is a rise in liquidity preference that compels households to wish to hold more bank deposits at the current rates of interest i_D, i_{ST} and i_{LT}, while the other agents in the economy do not accommodate by modifying the net supply of these corresponding assets, then the demand for bank deposits will have to adjust itself to the existing stock of bank deposits, through a decrease in the interest rate on deposits and an increase in the interest rate of the other two assets. Wray (1992a, p. 79) believes that this is the most likely effect of an increase in liquidity preference 'because private institutions are not likely to issue more money in response to rising liquidity preference'.

Naturally, it should be emphasized that here we are looking at instantaneous changes in portfolio considerations. We are not concerned with the case where households acquire bank deposits through their pay cheques and their saving over the period, or where households reduce their money balances by purchasing goods, while firms reduce their money balances by paying down their outstanding debt with the proceeds of these sales – a case associated with the Kaldorian reflux mechanism.

In Godley and Lavoie (2007a), it is assumed, except in the case of the market for stock market shares, that the adjustment to changes in liquidity preference occurs mainly through changes in asset supplies. Besides the case of stock market prices, adjustments through prices can also occur, but only in a subsidiary manner. There are two reasons for this. First, their models assumed that banks administer the rate of interest on deposits and on loans, while the central bank targets the interest rate on (short-term) Treasury bills. Second, the models purported to show that the monetary authorities, with the collaboration of the government, were able to set both the short-term and the long-term interest rates. Thus banks and the monetary authorities will modify interest rates only in so far as the actual values of the target ratios that they have assigned to themselves depart from an acceptable range. This can happen because of changes in liquidity preference (the λ_{ij} parameters of equation (4.3), in particular the λ_{i0} parameters) but also because of changes in the real economy.

Examples of changes in the liquidity preference of the public
Let us examine what can happen within such a framework if households modify their liquidity preference parameters. Let us assume that households wish to move the contents of their portfolio towards money (cash and bank deposits) and away from short-term and long-term assets, which we shall call here bills and bonds. Let us further assume, for good measure, that there is a 10 per cent compulsory reserve ratio on bank deposits, calling HPM (high-powered money) the sum of cash and reserves. Thus, let us assume that, at the current yields on assets, households as a whole wish to acquire 10 additional units of cash and 90 units of bank deposits, while getting rid of 20 units of bills and 80 units of bonds. This is shown in the first column of Table 4.25 (items [1] to [4]). Note that an increase in the holdings of an asset is represented by a plus sign, while the decrease of an asset is represented by a minus sign. It should further be noted that the increase in a liability is represented by a minus sign, while the decrease in a liability carries a positive sign. To help readers, liabilities are shown in parentheses.

The matrix accounts for changes in the stocks of assets that are made through actual transactions outside each sector. It does not include capital gains, so that both the columns and the rows of the matrix must sum to zero. In other words, if only other households purchase the bonds that households wish to discard, households as a whole will manage to reduce the proportion of bonds in their portfolio, but only through a capital loss on bonds, the prices of which will fall. In other words, the reduction in the value of bonds will imply a reduction in the wealth of households, and will not allow households to hold more of the other assets. How important this restriction is will become obvious as we go through the examples.

Here in Table 4.25, we assume that the central bank takes the necessary measures to absorb whatever change in the demand for bonds [5] and bills, at the current rates of interest, by being the counterparty to the sales, which allows the households to acquire the cash and the deposits they long for. The banks thus wind up with 90 units of extra deposit liabilities [6], forcing them to acquire an extra 9 units in reserves [7]. Banks will also purchase 81 units of bills [8]. How is that? This can be understood from the

Table 4.25   An accommodated increase in the liquidity preference of households

Assets	Households	Government	Central bank	Banks	Σ
HPM	+10 [1]		(−19) [9]	+9 [7]	0
Deposits	+90 [2]			(−90) [6]	0
Bills	−20 [3]		−61 [10]	+81 [8]	0
Bonds	−80 [4]		+80 [5]		0
Σ	0	0	0	0	0

clearing-house equations. As households initially sell 100 units of bonds and bills that are purchased by the central bank, banks acquire 100 units of clearing balances at the clearing house, as was shown earlier. However, banks must deposit 9 units at the central bank, as reserves, and they must acquire 10 units of cash to give to their depositors, so they are left with 81 units of clearing balances, which they use to purchase the bills. As to the central bank, it must increase its reserves and banknote liabilities by 19 units [9]. Having bought 80 units of bonds, its balance-sheet adding-up conditions thus imply that it must have net sales of 61 units of bills [10]. These correspond to the 20 units they bought from households and the 81 units they sold to the banks. Thus, as Bibow (2009, p. 122) puts it, the bearishness of the investors and the increased liquidity preference will 'impact on the rate of interest only to the extent that the banks', and here the monetary authorities, 'do *not* offset such a move by enlarging the pool of liquidity'.

Table 4.25 could be taken as a sketchy description of the activities of the Federal Reserve following the 9/11 terrorist attack on New York City, which have demonstrated that a central bank can avoid large price adjustments 'by reducing the outstanding supply of securities available for sale to the general public. The public can then satisfy its increased bearish tendencies by increasing its money holdings without depressing the market price for financial assets in a disorderly manner' (Davidson, 2009, p. 91).

The construction of Table 4.25 raises several questions. What if banks decline to buy the Treasury bills, keeping their 81 units of clearing balances as excess reserves? Then the overnight rate would quickly drop down, making this a poor decision. What if the central bank starts to run out of Treasury bills, having sold all its stock? Then we need the collaboration of the government. The government needs to restructure its portfolio of liabilities by buying back the bonds that households wish to sell and by issuing the equivalent value of bills (which are bought by the banks or their dealers). This corresponds to the description given by Robinson (1952, p. 29): in attempting to keep long rates down, the authorities 'issue bills in order to buy bonds, the quantity of money being adjusted to whatever level is required to keep the bill rate at its bottom stop'. All this is shown in Table 4.26. In this case, the central bank acquires 19 units of bills [11], instead of being constrained to sell them, as in the previous case.

What if banks consider that they are acquiring an overly large amount of safe assets (Treasury bills) relative to bank loans, a possibility examined by Godley (1999a)? Then they might decide to lower the interest rate on deposits so as to encourage households to hold on to their bills, thus making an adjustment through an indirect price mechanism. Similarly, the government in Table 4.26 may feel that its bills-to-bonds liability ratio

Table 4.26 *An accommodated increase in the liquidity preference of households, but with the central bank running out of Treasury bills*

Assets	Households	Government	Central bank	Banks	Σ
HPM	+10 [1]		(−19) [10]	+9 [8]	0
Deposits	+90 [2]			(−90) [7]	0
Bills	−20 [3]	(−80) [6]	+19 [11]	+81 [9]	0
Bonds	−80 [4]	(+80) [5]			0
Σ	0	0	0	0	0

becomes overly tilted towards short-term liabilities. It may then decide to stop supporting the price of long-term bonds, letting long interest rates rise. The changes in interest rates, through equation (4.3), will thus induce households to weaken their desire to move towards the most liquid assets.

Another situation of this sort can be envisaged. What if the economy is of the overdraft type, with the central bank not holding any government securities? Then the banks would have to buy the securities, and get advances from the central bank. From this we can see once more why a sovereign debt problem can arise within the eurozone, where the ECB and its national central banks by convention did not purchase any government securities. In normal times, banks purchase the bills and bonds that investors no longer want to hold, getting the advances that they need from the central bank, as shown in Table 4.27. But if banks refuse to purchase the securities, for instance because they fear a sovereign default, then all the adjustment to changes in liquidity preference will fall on asset prices and interest rates. The adjustments in prices and yields will be such that households will be induced to hold their assets in the same proportions as before their change of preferences.

There is a final case worth considering, that of a diversity of opinion within the same sector. Let us split households into bears and bulls, the bears being willing to divest themselves of bonds, and the bulls being keen to purchase them. This situation corresponds to the case discussed by Bibow (2009, pp. 103–4), based on Keynes's *Treatise on Money*, when Bibow says that 'the banking system . . . may facilitate a changing degree of diversity of opinion within the general public . . . by providing advances ("financial loans") to the "bulls" who therewith buy out the "bears", the latter being content, for the time being, with holding more saving deposits at rising security prices'. The situation is described with the help of Table 4.28. Banks agree to make advances to the bulls, who will now have the funds necessary to purchase bonds. Thus, relying again on Bibow (2009, p. 122), we can say that 'the banking system plays a key part in determining financial conditions'.

Indeed, one could argue that Table 4.28 describes the standard case, if we reinterpret the bulls as the specialist traders, because, as argued by Christopher Brown (2003–04, p. 334),

> a sell-off of any significant magnitude . . . will force specialist traders to access 'contingent capital', which most often takes the form of pre-negotiated lines of credit with commercial banks. Thus the money supply is likely to expand endogenously in consequence of the intense selling pressures as specialists draw on overdraft privileges to make the market.

Table 4.27 *An accommodated increase in the liquidity preference of households within an overdraft system*

Assets	Households	Government	Central bank	Banks	Σ
HPM	+10 [1]		(−19) [9]	+9 [8]	0
Deposits	+90 [2]			(−90) [5]	0
Bills	−20 [3]			+20 [6]	0
Bonds	−80 [4]			+80 [7]	0
Advances			+19 [10]	(−19) [11]	0
Σ	0	0	0	0	0

Table 4.28 *Bulls get bank advances to purchase the bonds that bears no longer wish to hold*

Assets	Bears	Bulls	Central bank	Banks	Σ
HPM			(−10) [9]	+10 [7]	0
Deposits	+100 [5]			(−100) [6]	0
Bills			+10 [10]	−10 [8]	0
Bonds	−100 [4]	+100 [3]			0
Loans		(−100) [2]		+100 [1]	0
Σ	0	0	0	0	0

Davidson (2009, ch. 6) makes the point that it is precisely the breakdown of these liquidity arrangements that led to chaotic financial markets during the Global Financial Crisis, as market makers were either unable or unwilling to absorb sales. Daniel Neilson (2019, p. 89), an advocate of Perry Mehrling's (2017) *Money View* makes the same point: market liquidity – the relationship between dealers and their customers – requires funding liquidity, that is, the willingness of banks always to abide by their line-of-credit agreements with dealers.

We can also interpret Table 4.28 in the opposite way. It could be that bulls are now wishing to purchase bonds, getting the funds to do so through bank loans. In that case, the transactions described by Table 4.28 will occur only if the prices of bonds rise, as the bears will agree to divest themselves of their bonds only if they make a capital gain, since their portfolio coefficients have not changed. In that situation, the value of bonds and the amount of money in the economy will both rise. This case illustrates clearly how asset price inflation can occur when financial investors have easy access to bank credit (Toporowski, 2000).

4.5.4 The Liquidity Preference of Banks

During our discussion of the public's liquidity preference, we referred to the behaviour of banks. The liquidity preference of banks can be and has been understood in two ways. The first way is analogous to the liquidity preference of households. Le Héron and Mouakil (2008) thus put forward a set of equations similar to those of equation

(4.3), where banks choose between making loans and purchasing corporate paper, bills or bonds. Liquidity preference may also be assessed by some ratios. This was mentioned when pointing out that banks might wish to achieve a range of safe assets to deposits ratio. When discussing Table 4.26, we pointed out that banks may wish to achieve or raise this ratio by raising the interest rate on deposits, thus purchasing bills from investors lulled into bank deposits by their higher yields. The size of the banks' balance sheets would thus rise in this case. An alternative would be for banks to securitize their loans, to get them off their balance sheet, in which case the size of their balance sheet would be reduced.

The liquidity preference of banks can also be interpreted in a second sense, defined by the state of banking entrepreneurs' animal spirits. This is tied to the issue of credit rationing, which Keynes (1930b, p. 364) described by saying that 'there is normally a fringe of unsatisfied borrowers' who believe that they should be able to get more loans from banks. Banks with high liquidity preference are reluctant to increase loans or to take on new customers. Hence we can use the concept of liquidity preference in the banking industry to measure the willingness of banks to extend credit to potential borrowers. It represents the confidence banks have about an uncertain future. By this definition, a fall in banks' liquidity preference implies that banks are more willing to grant loans, or are willing to grant them on easier conditions. This second meaning is the focus of the current subsection.

Horizontalism was always associated with creditworthiness and credit restraints

The consideration of banks' liquidity preference and of credit restraints has given rise to another controversy between horizontalist and structuralist post-Keynesian economists, but in my view an unnecessary one. Some post-Keynesian authors have depicted horizontalist banks as 'passive' (Dow, 1996, p. 497), or 'mere ciphers' (Cottrell, 1994, p. 599). There is now a large body of evidence to show that this never was the case (Rochon, 1999, pp. 169–73 and ch. 8). Horizontalists such as Moore and Kaldor have emphasized the elasticity of the supply of credit by banks and their accommodating behaviour ('non-discretionary'), through overdraft arrangements, for instance, rather than the credit-rationing aspects. But this is to be expected since these authors were initially trying to convince their readers that money was endogenous. However, both Kaldor and Moore underlined the possibility of credit restraints and the importance of finding creditworthy borrowers. Indeed, creditworthiness is a crucial feature of money endogeneity, and it ties in with the property and collateral requirements of bank lending as emphasized by Heinsohn and Steiger (2000). Indeed, as Minsky (1986a, p. 256) explains, 'the fundamental banking activity is accepting, that is, guaranteeing that some party is creditworthy'. The following quotes demonstrate quite clearly that earlier horizontalist authors paid attention to the issue of credit restraints and creditworthiness:

> The banking system fixes a rate (or a set of rates) for the money market and then lends however much borrowers ask for, provided that they can offer satisfactory collaterals. (Le Bourva, 1992, p. 449)

> Changes in the stock of loans and money will be governed solely by the demand for loans and the *credit-worthiness* of would-be borrowers. (Godley and Cripps, 1983, p. 77)

At any one time the volume of bank lending or its rate of expansion is limited only by the availability of credit-worthy borrowers. When trade prospects are good or when the money value of borrowers' assets (collateral) rises as a result of a rise of prices, the demand for bank credit rises but by the same token the credit-worthiness of potential borrowers also improves, so that the demand for and the supply of credit move simultaneously in the same direction. (Kaldor, 1981, p. 15)

Banks are not inclined to approve bank loan applications just because they have excess reserves. They will, in fact, be willing to grant loans only to those who can demonstrate that they are 'credit-worthy', and once this demand for loans has been satisfied, no additional credit is likely to be extended. (Eichner, 1987, p. 854)

Commercial bank loan officers must ensure that loan requests meet the bank's income and asset collateral requirements. They must in general satisfy themselves as to the credit-worthiness of the project and the character of the borrower. It is precisely for these reasons that banks develop client relationships with their borrowers. (Moore, 1988, p. 24)

Banks ... attempt to meet all customer loan requests up to some prearranged credit ceiling, provided that the latter meet the bank's minimum collateral and risk requirements. (Ibid., p. 57)

Banks establish individual borrowers' credit limits according to their estimates of borrowers' credit worthiness, and then are price setters and quantity takers in their retail loan and deposit markets. Bank borrowers ordinarily do not fully exhaust their credit commitments ... This is not to deny that many small borrowers are effectively credit-constrained. New businesses and poor households in particular do not possess the income, assets, and credit records criteria that banks require in order to make profitable and financially sound loans (the banks' three C's: credit, collateral and character). (Moore, 1994, p. 123)

How best can we represent the concept of credit rationing? Before we propose what I think is the most enlightening representation, a few preliminary remarks are in order. Nowadays, most businesses hold a credit line with a bank, and financial institutions have credit lines with each other. Many individuals also have automatic access to advances, through their credit cards, their bank account, or with their house as collateral. Lines of credit, which are a contract between a bank and a borrower, play an important role in the initial financing of production, since they provide flexible access to finance. By agreeing to a credit line, firms enter into a contractual agreement with the bank that specifies the maximum amount that can be borrowed when needed, the conditions under which access to the line is given, as well as the rate of interest on the amount being drawn down (Wolfson, 1996).

The rate may be fixed, in which case the borrower pays some fee to guarantee the fixed rate; or the rate may vary, in which case its level will be set as a mark-up over some market rate, say the Treasury-bill rate, or even the target rate of the central bank. This mark-up is a risk premium imposed by banks to cover default risks as well as administrative costs. As a result, the interest rate on credit lines tends to follow the general evolution of market rates, as formalized by Lavoie and Reissl (2019), but of course, each category of borrowers will be facing a different interest rate. Thus a small firm with a low debt to equity ratio is likely to face higher interest rates than a large corporation with a high debt to equity ratio. With otherwise identical firms, banks will necessarily impose a higher interest rate on those firms burdened by a heavier debt load, due to the perceived higher risk. The same kind of rating will occur when firms issue commercial paper or corporate bonds on

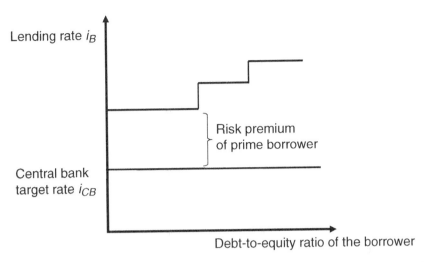

Figure 4.5   Kalecki's principle of increasing risk, understood at the microeconomic level

the financial markets. This instance of Kalecki's principle of increasing risk is illustrated in Figure 4.5. This must be understood as a cross-section of firms, not as an evolution through time.

Credit rationing with notional and effective demand for credit

The main characteristics of credit-line contracts are that they specify the interest rate charged and the maximum amount that can be borrowed, as was argued in a different format with equation (3.3) when discussing the finance frontier of firms. At some point, the banks or the markets will simply refuse to lend any longer. How can this be represented graphically? Some authors suggest drawing an upward-sloping supply curve of credit; others propose a truncated supply curve, or one that suddenly becomes vertical.

I have argued in the past that credit constraints have nothing to do with the slope of the credit supply curve. This was pointed out in Lavoie (1985c, p. 845), where the conditions imposed on borrowers ('profitability, collateral and the like') were considered as 'shift parameters'. Arestis and Eichner (1988, p. 1010) also consider that credit rationing acts as a shift variable in regression analysis. But the appraisal of what a good borrower is must be partly subjective. Borrowers and lenders may have a quite different opinion about this and about how much can be lent to a good borrower. In Lavoie (1992b, pp. 177–8), I refer to the 'effective' demand for credit curve, based on the 'existing collateral and risk requirements for borrowing. When these requirements are modified, say relaxed, they shift upwards the effective demand curve for credit.' In another article, I refer to 'solvent' demand, claiming that 'more exacting norms will shift the solvent demand for credit curve to the left' (Lavoie, 1996d, p. 287). Wolfson (2012) refers to '*creditworthy* demand' within the same context. One thus needs to make a distinction between the demand curve for loans, as perceived by the borrowers, and the demand curve for loans that is judged to be effective, solvent or creditworthy in the eyes of the lenders.

Borrowers who do not meet the banks' criteria simply do not receive credit. As long as borrowers are credible – that is, perceived as being able to reimburse their debt – banks will agree to lend to them. Hence, as Robinson (1952, p. 29) puts it, 'the amount of advances that banks can make is limited by the demand from good borrowers'. The obvious question then is whether banks can tell who is creditworthy. Banks have developed a number of sophisticated ways to do this. For instance, they will rate borrowers into various risk categories, based on the borrowers' history, their past relationship with the bank, the value of their collateral, the kind of project to be financed, a number of debt and liquidity ratios, including the borrowers' cash flow relative to the estimated interest burden. Those borrowers who do not meet the criteria or who decline to fulfil the collateral requirements will be turned down (or rather should be turned down, which was not the case during the years leading to the subprime financial crisis!). Individuals or firms meeting all conditions will be given access to a line of credit that will cover their normal financial needs.

A good example of all this occurred right after the default of the investment bank Lehman Brothers. Firms were suddenly unable to access some of their funds deposited in the shadow banking system and could not finance their expenditures by selling corporate paper, as nobody dared to purchase what was suddenly considered unsafe assets. For a few weeks, several firms suffered from a credit crunch, as banks were reluctant to lend to new customers or to increase lending to customers who had not made adequate credit-line arrangements.

Martin Wolfson (1996), who once worked for the Federal Reserve, has written what I consider to be the best post-Keynesian article on the issue of credit rationing. As pointed out in Wolfson (2012, p. 117), his purpose was 'to develop a framework to analyse credit rationing that incorporates a horizontal endogenous money supply curve'. For a borrower of a given risk class, Wolfson (1996) draws a horizontal credit-supply curve, at the rate of interest relevant to this risk class. There are then two credit-demand curves, in analogy with the notional and effective labour-demand curves that will be described in Chapter 5. There is a 'notional' demand curve, which corresponds to the demand for loans by entrepreneurs, according to their own expectations. There is then another demand curve, the 'effective' demand curve, which takes into account only the demand that responds to the conditions and expectations of the bankers. The terms 'notional' and 'effective' are also endorsed by Gillian Hewitson (1997, p. 132). The horizontal distance, at the existing lending rate, between the notional and the effective demand curves is a measure of the extent of credit rationing. In other words, from the perspective of the bankers, the effective demand curve for credit is the demand curve arising from creditworthy borrowers. Credit supply is demand-led, but subject to the assessment of creditworthiness, which depends on both objective and subjective criteria. We may say that it depends on the liquidity preference of bankers or their animal spirits.

Figure 4.6 illustrates the two types of demand for credit. The total demand for credit, which includes the demand from those who are creditworthy and those who are not, can be called the 'notional demand' for credit. Yet, since banks consider only those who meet their creditworthiness criteria, and since they impose limits on the amounts that can be borrowed even by creditworthy borrowers, for all practical purposes the only relevant demand is the 'effective demand' for credit. It should be noted that, as the interest rate on loans increases, a widening gap arises between the notional and the effective demand curve. This may happen because of an adverse selection problem – only those who have no intention of reimbursing the loan will agree to pay high interest rates – as New

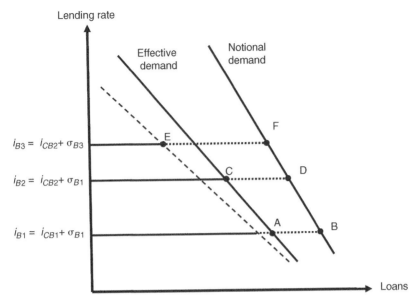

Figure 4.6 Credit rationing with notional and effective demand curves for credit

Keynesians have pointed out; or it may happen simply because the higher interest rate makes it more difficult for the borrower to fulfil his or her debt obligations, a point made earlier by Kalecki (1971, p. 105) when he noted that 'the higher rate in itself might raise misgivings with regard to the future solvency of the firm'.

As to the rate of interest on loans, we can divide it into two components. As was the case with equation (4.2), there is a component i_{CB} reflecting the benchmark rate of the central bank and hence the prevailing money-market rates (such as the Treasury-bill rate or the overnight rate, or the rate at which banks can borrow on wholesale markets), while the second component reflects the illiquidity and risk premium, σ_B. Hence we can write the following:

$$i_B = i_{CB} + \sigma_B \tag{4.5}$$

We thus see that interest rates on loans can increase from two sources. First, since lending rates are essentially based on the benchmark interest rate set by the central bank, any increase in the benchmark will lead to an increase in lending rates. This is illustrated in Figure 4.6, with the move of the lending rate from i_{B1} to i_{B2}. In this case, fewer firms and fewer households will want to borrow, given the higher costs of borrowing. This is reflected by the negatively sloped notional demand curve. Yet, at the same time, a greater number of borrowers will not meet the banks' criteria. In other words, fewer borrowers will be creditworthy, and, as a result, a greater number of borrowers will be turned down. Thus credit rationing, measured by the horizontal distance between the two demand curves, will increase from AB to CD.

A different case arises when banks see their confidence falter, as they decide to increase the average spread between the lending and the benchmark rates, thus raising the risk and illiquidity premium σ_B. This is illustrated in Figure 4.6 by the increase in the lending rates from i_{B2} to i_{B3}. The increase in the risk premium and in the lending rate is then accompanied by a leftward shift of the effective demand curve, which is now the dotted line, as banks are in effect strengthening the criteria needed to get a loan. Credit rationing is now measured by the distance EF. As Wolfson (1996, p. 461) puts it, 'interest-rate spreads, nonprice standards, and credit rationing increase together'. Hence, for every different level of the illiquidity and risk premium, there exists a specific effective demand curve for credit.

In mainstream economics, credit rationing occurs because of asymmetric information. While this may indeed play a role, particularly in interbank lending, post-Keynesians focus instead on the role played by divergent expectations between banks and the consumers or entrepreneurs who wish to obtain loans to finance their activities. When credit markets freeze, it is not because there is a sudden rise in asymmetric information; rather it is because the degree of uncertainty has been rising, generating a loss of confidence and an increase in the liquidity preference of bankers, whose expectations regarding the future are not as rosy as they were. Banks and financial markets will enforce existing criteria or will impose more stringent criteria for lending. As a consequence, a number of borrowers will now be denied a loan: they simply are no longer considered creditworthy. Also, since banks are less confident about the future and expect more defaults on loans, they will want to protect their own rate of return by increasing the illiquidity and risk premium to compensate for the perceived increased risk, which is consistent with Wray's (1992b, p. 1161) claim that the interest spread depends on the perception of lender's risk. Indeed, risk premia are lower, not higher, during expansions (Robinson, 1956, p. 230).

Of course, we can also look at the other side of the credit market, when risk and liquidity premia decrease and when nearly all the notional demand for credit is fulfilled and is judged to be creditworthy. This corresponds to the case where liquidity seems abundant, meaning that banks and other financial institutions are quite willing to provide credit, at low spreads, and may even encourage households and firms to borrow funds. Still, no one is forced to borrow, but marketing and bank offers may change the preferences of agents, as was argued in Chapter 2. This situation has been well described by Minsky, as will be discussed in the next subsection.

The complete model

How are we to summarize graphically all that we have said so far about interest rates, reserves, bank deposits and bank loans? Structuralists used to favour a continuous upward-sloping supply curve in the reserves and interest plane (Palley, 1994; Pollin, 1996, p. 505), as well as a rising credit supply curve. Horizontalists, as their name indicates, have instead supported a horizontal supply curve of reserves, at the target rate of interest, or, as Kaldor (1983a, p. 22) has put it, as a 'set of horizontal lines, representing different stances of monetary policy'. Fontana (2003; 2009, p. 108), as a compromise, proposes a step function that rises with an increasing amount of reserves, meaning that, as more reserves need to be provided, the target interest rate set by the central bank rises in a discontinuous way. This aims to represent the countercyclical behaviour of the central bank and its reaction function. But then it should be clear that this can be the result only of a particular kind of feedback rule. Furthermore, how does that make any sense in countries where banks do not hold reserves and where banknotes are supplied on demand? It is a bit disconcerting to see that a number of orthodox authors have adopted the horizontal supply of reserves at the target rate of interest as a pedagogical tool while some post-Keynesians are still hesitant to embrace it.

If there now exists a consensus among post-Keynesians, the apparatus shown in Figure 4.7 provides it. This is a four-quadrant figure initially developed by Palley (1996b, p. 588). Nearly the same figure can be found in more recent post-Keynesian works, for example those of Hein (2008, p. 45), Fontana (2009, p. 114), Fontana and Setterfield (2009b, p. 134), Howells (2009, p. 178) and Deleidi (2020, p. 158). To read the graph, start from the target interest rate set by the central bank, i_{CB}. Through equation (4.5), this determines the interest rate that banks charge on their loans, i_B, once we know what the illiquidity and risk premium σ_B is equal to. Given the effective demand curve for loans, we then know the actual amount of loans in the economy. This amount then helps to determine the stock of bank deposits, depending, however, on the liquidity preference of the public as measured by the slope of the BD line. This slope may also be influenced by a variety of interest rates, but what is at issue is the spread between deposit rates and market rates. Assuming that banks hold reserves, either because they are compulsory or for prudential reasons, we can then derive the amount of reserves in the system.

Howells (2009, p. 183) adds an additional quarter in the north-east corner that depicts the relationship between the lending rate and economic activity. One would think, however, that it is the amount of loans, or rather the amount of new loans, that would best predict the level of economic activity or its change. Indeed, forecasting models that

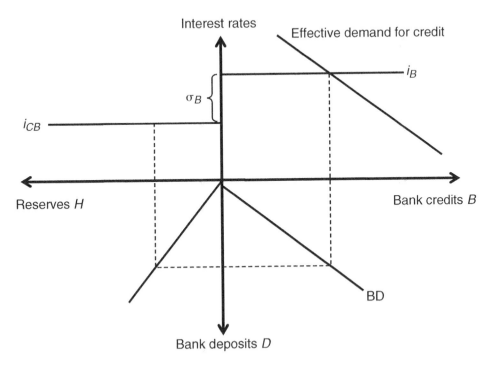

Figure 4.7   The complete model, with loans, deposits and reserves

incorporate the change in household debt and in business debt do well in foretelling economic activity (Godley et al., 2008; Werner, 2012). It should be kept in mind that the effective demand for credit may shift inward not only because banks are less confident, but also because non-financial firms have lost their own animal spirits or have become reluctant to borrow and engage in new projects.

4.5.5 Financial Instability

The introduction of the liquidity preference of banks thus enriches considerably the theory of endogenous money. First, it shows that the focus of our attention should be on the credit market, rather than on the money market. This important point has been made by a number of post-Keynesians, notably Wojnilower (1980) and more recently Peter Howells (2009; 2010) and Steve Keen (2017), because, except when the central bank intervenes when the liquidity preference of the public increases, it is the expansion of bank loans that generates increases in the supply of money. As Eichner (1987, p.158) puts it, 'it is the demand for credit rather than the demand for money that is the necessary starting point for analyzing the role played by monetary factors in determining the level of real economic activity'. Second, as pointed out by Dow and Dow (1989, p.158), 'an interest rate set by the monetary authorities is consistent with varying rates on bank loans, depending on the state of liquidity preference'. Finally, it is clear that, for a given stance from the central bank and a given interest rate on loans, several levels of loans and credit aggregates are possible, depending on the liquidity preference of banks broadly defined.

Minsky's thesis
Indeed, financial instability may be attributed to the large shifts in the liquidity preference of banks (and those of other economic agents). We discussed this in some detail in Chapter 1, when introducing the paradoxes of tranquillity and liquidity. These paradoxes and the concept of the liquidity preference of banks are closely related to Minsky's financial instability hypothesis, also sometimes referred to as the financial fragility hypothesis. Minsky had clearly established the main points of his thesis in the 1960s, before the post-Keynesian resurgence:

> The broadest hypothesis is that the behaviour of an economic system with respect to the real variables is not independent of the financial structure of the economy . . . [The second hypothesis] is that the likelihood of a financial crisis occurring is not independent of the financial structure of the economy and the financial structure reflects the 'past' of the economy. The third hypothesis . . . is that the financial changes that take place during a sustained boom . . . are such that the domain within which the financial structure is stable is decreased as the boom lengthens . . . If in addition it is assumed that a sustained boom will not be broken by . . . any deficiency in demand, then it follows [the fourth hypothesis] that if a sustained boom is to be broken it must be broken by a financial crisis. (Minsky, 1964, p.175)

The first hypothesis, that real and financial variables are interdependent, will be taken up in the last section of this chapter. The second hypothesis exemplifies the importance of time in post-Keynesian economics. The third hypothesis is split into two elements. The first element – in my view the crucial contribution of Minsky – restates the paradox of tranquillity, and says that any economy is likely to experience structural changes in its financial ratios and its balance sheets as time goes by, as a result of financial innovations and changes in the behaviour and standards of agents when faced with a string of good years. This is the essence of the financial fragility hypothesis, and it is the common feature leading to all financial crises.

As the expansion proceeds, a series of successful experiences validates the expectations of the most optimistic actors. 'Success breeds a disregard of the possibilities of failure' (Minsky, 1986a, p. 237). Disbelief is suspended as those who warn about impending disasters and plead for more caution are proved wrong time and time again. 'Stability – even in an expansion – is destabilizing in that more adventuresome financing of investment pays off to the leaders, and others follow' (Minsky, 1975, p. 127). This is particularly the case within financial institutions where 'lenders/money managers are "rewarded" for riding speculative waves and indeed are compelled to engage in these activities in order to cement their institutional position' (Grabel, 1996, p. 22). In an environment of fundamental uncertainty, validation of optimistic expectations leads to a disregard of contrary opinion, as many market participants believe that a new era has arrived and that the old rules no longer apply. This is facilitated by the fact that people, and bankers in particular, tend to forget events long past – a key feature of Minsky's fragility hypothesis. Financial agents suffer from myopic hindsight.

The second element of the third hypothesis is the financial instability hypothesis as such: it says that balance sheets and financial ratios will deteriorate. This will be modelled in Chapter 6, where it will be seen that the debt ratios of overconfident households are more likely to deteriorate in a boom, whereas the aggregate financial ratios of firms may or may not deteriorate with faster growth, a feature that Minsky (1986a, p. 237) anticipated when he conceded that, at least for a time, 'internal financing through retained earnings is greater than anticipated, and the push towards a greater use of short-term debt in liability structures is frustrated'.

As to the fourth hypothesis – the advent of a financial crisis – Minsky (1982a, pp. 7, 83, 107) seems to blame the upper turning point on the inevitable tendency of interest rates to rise towards the end of the boom, either as a consequence of the rise in debt ratios (which may or may not happen) or because of the monetary restrictions imposed by the central bank, either as a preventive strike against inflation or as a consequence of actual demand inflation. But then, as pointed out by Toporowski (2005, p. 146), 'it requires an explicit *policy* decision to raise interest rates', and we can no longer say that the financial crisis is self-generating or that the turning point is fully endogenous. In any case, once the crisis is there, we may have what the financial press has called 'a Minsky moment'. The financial crisis becomes a debt-deflation vicious circle of falling asset prices and forced sales, caused by margin calls resulting from the falling value of collateral, unless the government acts with determination.

There are some complications that cannot be easily handled in a simple macroeconomic model. In the real world, financial fragility is associated with shorter-duration finance, relaxed banking standards, less intense credit evaluations, more reliance on collateral than on cash flows, the creation of financial innovations to avoid regulation, and a decrease in perceived risk. Aggregates usually deal with net ratios. It should be clear, however, that the robustness and resilience of a financial system are not independent of the gross liabilities or savings of each agent or each sector of the economy. Through leveraged buyouts, firms may accumulate debt in an effort to buy each other, with no increase in output and profits. As another example, it is quite possible for the net flow of new consumer credit to double or triple, although net household saving and national income stay constant. For instance, it may be that rich households are saving more, while poor ones are getting more into debt. This can be seen by making use of the following two identities:

Consumption + Gross saving = Household income + Net additions to consumer's debt

Net saving = Gross saving − Net additions to consumer's debt

The fragility of the financial system with high consumer credit is much higher than one with low consumer credit. In a period of tranquillity followed by a period of financial euphoria, it is quite possible for gross liability and gross saving to outrun the growth of income and profits, thus leading to a multi-level financial structure – a financial bubble – with a large number of intertwined cash-flow requirements. Minsky has identified the fragile consequences of such layering, in particular the domino effect that it may lead to, as counterparties are unable to deliver funds when they are asked to do so. 'Liabilities (debts) are issued to finance – or pay for – positions in owned assets . . . In a layered financial structure, the unit acquiring liabilities may have liabilities of its own, and its ability to fulfil its obligations depends upon the cash flow it receives from its assets, i.e., other units' liabilities' (Minsky, 1975, p. 87).

Another simple example of the fallacy of net measures is the case of credit default swaps (CDS) – a derivative that emerged in the mid-1990s. CDS were originally designed to hedge against risk: for a small premium, the CDS buyer was purchasing protection against possible losses due to a particular bond default. But in the 2000s, 'naked' CDS became fashionable, meaning that investors who did not hold bonds would purchase CDS, gambling that they would default, while CDS sellers – the insurers – were betting that there would be no bond default. Since this is a zero-sum game, it could be said that net risk is zero. But obviously it is not: if there are multiple defaults and the insurer goes bankrupt, the CDS buyer will not get compensation and its problems may spread to other counterparties. Thus, as pointed out in Chapter 1, the existence of protection may actually increase risk rather than diminish it.

The third hypothesis relies crucially on an understanding of financial agents. There are no limits to the amount of credit that can be granted by the banking system. Credit creation depends on the liquidity preference of banks and the confidence of borrowers. Banking is based on trust and confidence, so that if a bank believes that it can be profitable to lend more, it can always do so, as long as it maintains the trust of other banks. The business of banking is essentially a trade-off between the appeal of profits and the fear of losses. Profits are made by lending more, and by innovating in providing new financial products. The fear of losses will gradually vanish in good times, so that banks will encourage potential borrowers to take on loans by offering low interest rates based on low spreads because they assess low default risks. As the boom proceeds, banks will dare to target higher leverage ratios on their equity, and in addition their equity will be growing quickly thanks to the rising profits that are retained.

Hersh Shefrin (2016, p. 133) argues that 'the global financial crisis provided a dramatic out-of-sample test of Hyman Minsky's ideas, which he developed based on events he observed between 1960 and 1990'. Shefrin shows that there are many similitudes between

Minsky's insights and the explanations that have been provided by the 2011 report of the Financial Crisis Inquiry Commission which investigated the American 2008 financial crisis.

Alternatives and implications

It should be said, however, that there are alternative post-Keynesian views about the financial behaviour of (non-financial) entrepreneurs. Myron Gordon (1987) argues instead that when entrepreneurs have gone through a series of successful years, they tend to become more prudent, saving more and borrowing less, in order to protect the wealth that they have accumulated during these good years. It is the switch towards this more prudent behaviour, rather than continuing reckless behaviour, that will be at the origin of the downturn. Similarly, Toporowski (2005, p.146) believes that the boom ends as firms become more prudent and start hoarding financial assets, using them as a buffer against a possible future inability to service their debt, and thus diminishing their tangible investments in the process. This kind of behaviour is supported by the prospect theory of new behavioural economics, which presumes that 'an individual's degree of loss aversion increases as her forecast of the size of the potential loss increases' (Frydman and Goldberg, 2014, p.16).

In the case of the subprime financial crisis, Minsky was certainly right with regard to financial institutions and households, although he himself tended to emphasize the indebtedness of firms, which was not really at stake during that crisis, since much of the borrowing in the private sector was done by households, who ended up as the Ponzi sector that could not service its debt (Brown, 2007; McCulley, 2009). We can also say that the fourth hypothesis came true – interest rates set by the Federal Reserve did rise in the mid-2000s, helping to cause the fall in real-estate prices that precipitated the subprime financial crisis and then the Global Financial Crisis.

Minsky's thesis regarding the transformation of financial structures is very close to that of Keynes. Both described a Wall Street or City view of financial markets, peopled by speculators. Keynes compared the financial markets, and especially the stock market, to a giant casino, where all agents try to outguess each other, and where market evaluations depend on the state of confidence, waves of pessimism and optimism, fads and conventions. Keynes provides the analogy of the beauty contest to show that financial markets are reflexive and prone to mimetism, as participants try to guess the average opinion to assess the overall level of asset prices, since the so-called fundamental determinants are themselves only partly objective (Fung, 2006). Orthodox dissidents also recognize that financial markets exhibit bubbles, fads, overshooting and possibly financial crises when corrections occur, but they blame these on information asymmetry whereas post-Keynesians attribute them to the normal behaviour of financial actors and financial markets.

An obvious conclusion from this is that banks and financial markets need to be closely regulated, as was argued by Minsky (1986a), even though the imposed rules and regulations may not succeed in avoiding bubbles and even crises. While this may restrain the entrepreneurial spirit of bankers, it may slow down the creation of innovations of 'massive destruction', as they have been called. Another reflection is that if lenders are so hard to restrain, then the restrictions ought to be imposed on the borrowers (Minsky, 1975, p.168; Pollin, 1996, p.503; Toporowski, 2000, p.123). This would weaken the ability and the desire of financial institutions to modify their own liquidity preference.

For instance, strict regulations on downpayments required to purchase residential units and be eligible for mortgages have proven to be quite effective in slowing down housing speculation and construction. With respect to financial speculation, tight regulations on margin requirements should also help in avoiding instability.

A further proposal in this direction is that monetary authorities ought to bring back credit controls, which have been known in the past under various names, such as credit ceilings, lending ceilings, the corset or window guidance (Werner, 2005, p. 269). There is a long tradition in post-Keynesian writings in favour of credit controls (Lavoie, 1996e, pp. 540–41). Credit controls have been advocated by Kahn, Le Bourva, Kaldor, Rousseas and Minsky. As argued by Wojnilower (1980, p. 307), credit controls can have 'startling potency'. Werner (2005, p. 280) also believes that credit controls are 'the most effective and also the most important tool of monetary policy'. There is a danger, however, that of evasion through disintermediation, moving financial activity from the regulated banking system towards the deregulated financial sector. We discuss this in the next subsection, in the context of the rise of credit aggregates.

4.5.6 The Shadow Banking System

Minsky and shadow banking

Before the advent of the subprime financial crisis, it seemed that financial institutions, particularly in the USA, were 'awash with liquidity'. This led to what we called the paradox of liquidity in Chapter 1, with liquidity quickly evaporating just when it is most needed, when confidence collapses. This is tightly linked to the views of Minsky, who emphasized the development of near monies in his explanation of the endogeneity of the money supply and of the increase in the fragility of the financial system. These near monies are liabilities issued by what has come to be known as the shadow banking system. Minsky (1975, ch. 4) associates the rise in financial asset prices with the rise in money aggregates and in credit instruments. When banks and the shadow banking system become more optimistic and less wary of possible losses, there is an increased layering of the financial system, more liquidity is created, more loans are granted, and financial asset prices rise. This gives rise to a virtuous circle. The purpose of this short subsection is to explain how this virtuous circle can arise in the modern financial world.

Minsky (1975, p. 90) explains that an increase in the price of the stock market shares of a firm 'decreases the ratio of cash-payment commitments . . . to the market valuation of the firm. To bankers and other financers, such increased market valuation implies that the firm can issue more debt – undertake additional commitments.' The virtuous circle is also helped by the fact that the financial assets, the prices of which have risen, will also generate more collateral, thus helping to purchase further assets and push prices even higher.

This phenomenon also applies to financial institutions, in particular non-bank financial institutions that hold a large fraction of their assets in the form of shares or securities that can be traded on exchanges. When the value of the assets that they hold goes up, the net value of these institutions goes up as well, and they are encouraged to expand their balance sheets. Defining the leverage ratio as the ratio of the value of assets to the difference between assets and debts (excluding equity), as shown for instance in Table 4.8), we can say that, *ceteris paribus*, when financial asset prices rise, the leverage ratio of these financial firms diminishes. Thus, under circumstances of rising financial asset prices, financial institutions will attempt to increase the size of their balance sheet by looking for new borrowers, and in the case of non-banks, by searching for more funds to finance the acquisition of new liabilities, so as to bring leverage ratios to their previous historical values.

Adrian and Shin (2010) show, however, that financial institutions, and in particular investment banks, go beyond that. They show that leverage ratios tend to rise when their balance sheet expands, and that leverage ratios diminish when balance sheets contract. This means that financial institutions and investment banks in particular take discretionary decisions in an attempt to increase their leverage ratio when the prices of financial assets are booming. The targeted leverage ratios of these financial institutions are thus procyclical, a feature also noted by the BIS for its new Basel III regulations. Minsky (1986a, p.117) had made exactly this point when, just like Adrian and Shin, he tied the instability of the financial sector to the possibility of upward-sloping demand curves, writing that 'a rise in the relative prices of some set of financial instruments or capital assets may very well increase the quantity demanded of such financial or capital assets'. Adrian and Shin (2010, p.428) also point out that the 'adjustment in the fluctuations of balance sheets is through repos' – the very short-term collaterized loans that we discussed earlier. But how can the shadow banking system end up creating more liquidity, when we have asserted earlier that it is only official banks that have been granted the power to create money deposits?

Banks versus non-bank financial institutions

Before we can answer this question, let us look in more detail at the distinction between banks and non-bank financial institutions. Bouguelli (2020) points out that the mainstream literature on the shadow banking system identifies three distinctive attributes relative to banks: shadow banks are not regulated, they do not have access to the lending facilities of the central bank, and their liabilities are not insured by the government. Bouguelli contends that these are non-essential distinctions, based on the assumption that banks, like shadow banks, are only financial intermediaries, and that the shadow banking system – now often called the market-based credit system – has supplanted the bank-based credit system, an assumption which can also be found in the *Money View* advocated by Perry Mehrling (2017, p.4), according to whom 'today the quintessential form of banking is so-called "shadow banking" – a money market funding of capital market lending'. In what follows, by contrast, I wish to identify the essential distinctive traits of banks.

First, in contrast to other financial institutions, banks can provide new credit without having earlier collected funds or without having to borrow from some other agent. As central bankers McLeay et al. (2014, p.15) point out, 'rather than banks receiving deposits when households save and then lending them out, bank lending creates deposits.... Indeed, viewing banks simply as intermediaries ignores the fact that, in reality in the modern economy, commercial banks are the creators of deposit money'. Similarly, Jakab and Kumhoff (2015, p.3) note that 'in the real world, the key function of banks is the provision of financing, or the creation of new monetary purchasing power through loans.... The bank therefore creates its own funding, deposits, in the act of lending'.

The second specific feature of banks is that their deposits are part of the payment system. They are the means through which debts are irrevocably discharged. Non-banks ultimately have to transfer funds to some bank account for the final payment to go through. Payment is final, or settlement occurs, once the bank payment goes through the books of the central bank, or in some countries through the clearing house run by a bankers' association, as in Canada. As Michell (2017, p. 363) states, this is not the case for non-banks, as they 'fund themselves by issuing liabilities which cannot be used for settlement purposes'. This second feature was underlined by Davidson (1972, p. 157), when he wrote that 'the difference between the liabilities of non-bank financial intermediaries and commercial bank liabilities is that clearing institutions exist for the latter which permit them to be a perfect substitute for legal money'. By contrast, the liabilities of non-banks 'cannot be used in settlement of an obligation' and cannot 'be generally used to discharge a contract'.

It follows that 'as long as banks create credit at the same rate as other banks, and as long as customers are similarly distributed, the mutual claims of banks on each other will be netted out and may well, on balance, cancel each other out. Then, banks can increase credit creation without limit and without "losing any money"' (Werner, 2016, p. 373). This was recognized long ago by Keynes (1930a, p. 26), and then Le Bourva (1992, p. 461), who argued that with the compensation occurring at the clearing house, there would be no limit to the amount of loans that banks could create, provided that these banks 'are all moving in step, with no one bank getting ahead or lagging behind'. For Unger (2016, p. 5), from the Bundesbank, this implies that 'credit expansion in the traditional banking system is not subject to the laws of supply and demand to the same extent as it is for other parts of the financial system'.

This is not the case for non-banks, since, as we shall see, if they wish to create more credit, they must first get either more deposits from the public or new loans from banks. Tobin (1963), when claiming that banks were no different from other financial institutions, argued that banks face the same constraints as other financial institutions, because bank deposits are also subjected to the portfolio decisions of households. In particular, when depositors decide to transfer their bank deposits at accounts in other banks or in non-banks, then the originating bank in its turn will need to borrow funds. The difference, however, is that non-banks need *financing* to start with; when banks grant loans, they create their own finance; if the created deposits leak out, then financing will be needed, but this will occur *afterwards*. This is the distinction made by post-Keynesian circuitists (Botta et al., 2015), inspired in particular by Graziani (2003). Credit creation by banks is associated with *initial finance*; the funds that might be needed to be recovered afterwards are *final finance* or *funding*.

Because of their emphasis on the special role of banks, post-Keynesians are sometimes accused of not realizing that non-banks can also provide credit, so that in a modern monetary economy, bank credit is in competition with other sources of financing. Some past authors have been quite clear about the limitations of non-bank financial institutions. Eichner (1987, p. 825), for instance, has written that: 'It is only through a bank loan that the amount of funds circulating as checkable deposits can increase. If, instead, funds are borrowed from a nonbank financial intermediary, the latter will need to draw down its cash balance at some bank.... This is why the existence of nonbank financial intermediaries can usually be ignored and the flow of funds model simplified by eliminating the nonbank financial sector'.

In view of the rise of the shadow banking system, this quote might be perceived as an overly extreme statement of the post-Keynesian view on this topic. There have always been post-Keynesian authors taking a more balanced position. Edwin Le Héron (1986), has noted that non-banks could create credit. Palley (1996a, p. 128) made a similar critique, under the guise of the *endogenous theory of finance*, when he contended that both versions of endogenous theory, the horizontalist and the structuralist ones, 'are flawed because of their exclusive attention to the banking system'. Palley (1996a, p. 133) argued that insofar as 'the activity of direct capital markets are pro-cyclical', non-bank financial institutions will also influence economic activity.

These critiques have recently been resurrected by Nersisyan and Dantas (2017, p. 281), who argue that non-banks, just like banks, have the power to change the level of economic activity. Their view is based on an extension of the idea of a hierarchy of money, which can be attributed to Minsky. They claim that banks and non-banks provide liquidity transformation, accepting to convert into liquid debts the less liquid debts of those institutions sitting at the bottom of the monetary hierarchy. They contend that non-bank financial institutions are 'liquidity creators', the activities of which 'affect the real economy', and thus 'they can be a source of instability'. Thus, for these two authors, the claimed specificity of banks relative to non-bank financial institutions 'does not capture the elasticity of finance, or the financial fragility that may arise due to the activities of these institutions.... The ability of the financial sector to create liquidity is much more elastic than the endogenous money theory allows for' (Nersysian and Dantas, 2017, pp. 297–8). Similar arguments are made by advocates of *critical macro-finance*, who argue that the definition of money must be extended to include repos, and possibly the shares of money market funds and asset-backed commercial paper (Gabor, 2020; Murau and Pforr, 2020).

While one can readily admit that non-bank financial institutions have the power to affect the stability of the economy, it still seems appropriate to consider banks as very special institutions, different from other financial institutions. Bouguelli (2018, p. 653), in a comment on Nersisyan and Dantas (2017), argues that 'making a sharp distinction between commercial banks and other financial institutions' provides a 'framework that has the advantage of clarity'. Bouguelli (2020) also provides a table where he identifies how mainstream and critical macro-finance advocates on one hand, and post-Keynesian authors on the other hand, differ in their understanding of shadow banking. Bonizzi and Kaltenbrunner (2020) concur with Bouguelli, arguing that the special role of banks in determining credit conditions is being underplayed by advocates of critical macro-finance and of Mehrling's *Money View*, who believe that shadow banking is now the centrally important channel of credit. In the next subsection, I try to illustrate the usefulness of this distinction with the use of several examples, once more with the help of T-accounts. The main objective is to understand how non-bank financial institutions can originate credit of their own accord, while still being dependent on the traditional banking system.

Examples of credit creation and securitization
In the first example, a non-bank financial institution (NBFI), in this case an investment bank, desires to lengthen its balance sheet. How can it do it? The simplest solution is to draw on its credit line with a commercial bank, as shown on line 1 of Table 4.29. This then allows the investment bank to provide credit to a non-financial agent, as shown on line 2, by purchasing newly-issued securities. There have been two sources of credit, one from the bank loans and the other because of the bonds acquired by the investment

bank. Note that the commercial bank could have just as well purchased the security, avoiding an additional layer of debt. Note also the investment bank needed first to obtain a loan from the commercial bank.

In the second case, we assume that a non-bank issues money-market funds (MMF) deposits that are desired by some wealth holders. Start with a bank that makes a loan to a non-financial agent who desires to acquire some liquid assets (bank deposits) for future use. This is the first line of Table 4.30. Assume now that the depositor transfers 20 units to a non-bank financial intermediary by purchasing shares in a MMF (we could have assumed just as well that the non-bank is a finance company that issues commercial paper bought by the non-financial agent). This implies that the non-bank now has 20 units of deposits at the commercial bank, which it may decide to transform into a certificate of deposit (CD). This occurs in line 2 of the table. The non-bank is now in a position to provide credit to some other non-financial agent, for instance by purchasing securities worth 15 units, thus reducing its certificate of deposit at the bank by 15. Line 3 shows the consequences of such a move. Whereas we started with bank loans of 100 units, we now have 115 units of credit: 100 units of bank loans and 15 units of sold securities. As to the non-financial sector, it now holds 95 units in bank deposits and 20 units as money-market shares for a total of 115 units of liquid assets, while the non-bank financial sector is left with 5 units of CDs.

To sum up: the overall amount of credit in the economy has risen; the amount of bank deposits has not; and the amount of liquid assets held by the non-financial sector has also risen. Thus, the non-bank financial system has contributed to the creation of liquidity, and has provided new credit, just as Le Héron, Palley or Nersysian and Dantas would have it. Note that, once more, the additional credit could have been provided just as well

Table 4.29   Credit creation by an investment bank

Case	Banks		NBFI (Investment bank)		Non-financial agents (NFA)	
	Assets	Liabilities	Assets	Liabilities	Assets	Liabilities
1	Loan +100	Deposit of NBFI +100	Deposits +100	Loan +100		
2	Loan +100	Deposit of NFA +100	Securities +100	Loan +100	Deposit +100	Securities +100

Table 4.30   Credit creation by a money-market fund

	Banks		NBFI (money market fund)		Non-financial agents	
	Assets	Liabilities	Assets	Liabilities	Assets	Liabilities
1	Loan +100	Deposit +100			Deposit +100	Loan +100
2	Loan +100	Deposit +80 CD +20	CD +20	MMF share +20	Deposit +80 MMF +20	Loan +100
3	Loan +100	Deposit +95 CD +5	CD +5 Security +15	MMF share +20	Deposit +95 MMF +20	Loan +100 Security +15

by the banking sector. Note further that the non-bank financial institutions would have been unable to provide any credit unless non-financial agents had previously transferred some of their bank deposits to the non-banks. Still, it is clear that in this second case the additional credit has originated from the non-bank financial institution, and not from a bank. A counterpoint, however, is that the funds acquired by the non-banks have arisen initially from some previous loan granted by a bank.

We move on to a third case, tied to securitization, as described by Unger (2016). Here, start with a bank that grants a mortgage to some household; this is the first row of Table 4.31. In row 2, it is assumed that the real-estate builder is paid and acquires the deposits that were initially in the hands of the purchaser of the residence. A public institution or semi-public institution, such as a government-sponsored enterprise (GSE) in the United States or the Canadian Mortgage and Housing Corporation, issues commercial paper (CP) which is bought by real estate builders who swap part (say 70 per cent) of their bank deposits for commercial paper. In row 3, with the proceeds, the GSE is now in a position to purchase the mortgage loans and ease the maturity position of the commercial banks. Finally, 'the loans are bundled together to form an asset-based security (ABS) which are then retained on the GSE's balance sheet' (Unger, 2016, p. 7). In Table 4.31, these are described as mortgage-based securities (MBS).

In the case described by Table 4.31, loan origination (initial finance) is performed by banks, not by non-banks. However, funding (final finance), as it will appear at the end of the process, is now partly in the realm of the *market financial system*. It seems that banks are losing out to non-banks: this is true from the standpoint of *stocks*, but it is not when considering *flows*: the flow of credit does indeed originate from banks.

We can look at another case of securitization, as described by Table 4.32. Start again with mortgage loans being granted by a bank to some households. The deposits so created end up in the bank account of the real-estate constructor. In the second step, shown in row 2, 70 per cent of the mortgages are securitized and sold to a non-bank financial institution, this time a bank-sponsored conduit – a Structured Investment Vehicle (SIV). The SIV purchases the mortgage-based securities (MBS) by getting a temporary loan from its sponsoring bank. In addition, in the last step, shown in row 3, the conduit manages to sell 60 units of asset-backed commercial paper (ABCP) to real-estate builders, whose bank deposits then fall down to 40 units.

In this case of securitization, it is clear once again that the loan originates from the banks; furthermore, the conduit needs to have access to bank loans to handle

Table 4.31 Securitization with government-sponsored enterprises (GSE)

	Banks		NBFI (GSE)		Non-financial agents (NFA)	
	Assets	Liabilities	Assets	Liabilities	Assets	Liabilities
1	Mortgage +100	Deposit +100			Deposit +100	Mortgage +100
2	Mortgage +100	NFA Deposit +30 GSE Deposit +70	Deposit +70	CP +70	Deposit +30 CP +70	Mortgage +100
3	Mortgage +30	NFA Deposit +30	MBS +70	CP +70	Deposit +30 CP +70	Mortgage +100

Table 4.32 Securitization with a conduit

	Banks		NBFI (SIV)		Non-financial agents (NFA)	
	Assets	Liabilities	Assets	Liabilities	Assets	Liabilities
1	Mortgage +100	Deposit +100			Deposit +100	Mortgage +100
2	Mortgage +30 Loan to SIV +70	NFA Deposit +100	MBS +70	Loan +70	Deposit +100	Mortgage +100
3	Mortgage +30 Loan to SIV +10	NFA Deposit +40	MBS +70	ABCP +60 Loan +10	Deposit +40 ABCP +60	Mortgage +100

discrepancies between its purchases of mortgage-based securities and its sales of asset-backed commercial paper. For Unger (2016, p. 14), in agreement with what seems to be the consensus post-Keynesian position on this issue, 'the largest part of the shadow banking system enters the credit intermediation process only after the loans to the ultimate borrowers and the means of payment to finance them have already been created'. Thus, for Sissoko (2017), the expansion of securitization and the quasi-monetary liquidity of repos and corporate paper is only made possible through the credit enhancement and guarantees provided by commercial banks.

This is the *originate-and-distribute* model of banking, which makes the chain from the initial borrower to the ultimate fund holder longer, more complex and more opaque. It is also likely to make the system more fragile. While even some heterodox authors thought that securitization would diminish the overall risk of credit (Aglietta, 1996, p. 572), Minsky (1986b, p. 14) by contrast feared that 'fraud and incompetence will intrude in the long chain of securitization', as risk is being passed along by the originator to agents who may lack a proper understanding of the characteristics of the financial asset, with all the risks of contagion that this entailed. Securitization enhanced the globalization of financial markets and thus contributed to the lack of appreciation of the risks involved. The new originate and distribute banking model allowed lenders to avoid, at least in the short run or even medium run, the destructive consequences of the decline in underwriting standards.

We conclude this subsection by coming back to the question that motivated its existence: is the shadow banking system conducive to more credit? When Palley (1996a, p. 133) highlighted endogenous finance and securitization, he argued that 'raising finance in capital markets ... is more expansionary [than bank loans] because it by-passes the monetary constraint imposed by reserve requirements .... By taking transactions out of the banking system, this reduces the need for bank services and helps circumvent emerging liquidity shortage within the banking system'. Today, this regulatory arbitrage argument is based on capital adequacy requirements. When discussing the BIS rules earlier in the chapter, we already contended that the main purpose of securitization was instead to raise returns on bank equity, and not necessarily to provide more credit. Nonetheless, it can be conceded that insofar as 'non-bank financial intermediaries are able to obtain additional bank credit which could not be made directly available to entrepreneurs' through bank loans (Davidson, 1972, p. 183), the presence of securitization and of the shadow banking system may indeed lead to increased credit. But this may be due to degrading lending standards more than anything else.

Repos and the shadow banking system

We discussed earlier, with the help of Table 4.29, how an investment bank could decide to lengthen its balance sheet. Besides obtaining a loan from a commercial bank, the investment bank could also engage itself in a repo operation. Suppose the investment bank feels that its leverage ratio is too low, either because the prices of its assets have gone up or because it is willing to take more risk. It will be on the lookout for both investors and borrowers. One way to attract funds is to offer reverse repos, collaterized by its holdings of government bonds, to a non-financial firm that holds deposits at a bank, perhaps by offering a higher rate of return than that on deposits. This is shown in the first line of Table 4.33. The non-financial agent, say General Motors (GM), now has less bank deposits but more of a highly liquid asset, the repo. It feels as liquid as before, while the investment bank now has cash – deposits held at the commercial bank. Additional liquidity has thus been created, without the involvement of commercial banks.

The next step is for the investment bank to decide what it will do with its new money balances. Row 2a shows one possibility. The investment bank could purchase a security that was issued by another non-financial agent, say IBM. Credit aggregates have thus risen, again without the apparent involvement of the banking sector. Row 2b shows another possibility: the investment bank could instead acquire mortgages initially granted by banks. In this case, there is no net credit creation: what has been gained by the investment bank has been lost by the commercial bank.

One is tempted to deduce from the above table that these repo operations make murkier the distinction between *bona fide* banks and non-bank financial intermediaries. We are left with two alternative views of the shadow banking system. The first view, which is the mainstream view, is that financial markets and economic growth would collapse without the presence of market-based lending based on repos, securitization and the originate and distribute model. The second view is that market-based lending is more dangerous than bank-based lending and depends on the latter, and hence that monetary authorities should promote a return to bank-based lending. We already outlined the fact that securitization tends to induce lenders to be less rigorous in their

Table 4.33 Extending credit through repos

	Banks Assets	Banks Liabilities	NBFI (Investment bank) Assets	NBFI (Investment bank) Liabilities	Non-financial agents (NFA) Assets	Non-financial agents (NFA) Liabilities
1		NFA Deposit −100 NBFI Deposit +100	Deposit +100	Repo +100	Deposit −100 Repo +100	
2a		GM Deposit −100 IBM Deposit +100	Security +100	Repo +100	GM Repo +100	IBM Security +100
2b	Mortgage −100	NFA Deposit −100	MBS +100	Repo +100	Deposit −100 Repo +100	

analysis of creditworthiness. The use of repos has also several drawbacks. While repos offer safety to the repo lenders, as we pointed out earlier since the lender holds and owns the collateral for the duration of the repo, borrowers bear an enormous risk (Gabor, 2016; Sissoko, 2019).

The repo, as explained earlier, is like a time-limited loan, based on the value of a collateral, usually a security. Before the 2008 financial crisis, these securities could be private asset-based securities, thus creating a linkage between securitization and repos, but now they are mostly safe government-issued securities, often long-term ones. What we have not yet pointed out is that the loan is provided with a haircut, meaning for instance that, notwithstanding the interest rate charged, the borrower will only obtain a loan of 95 units in exchange for a security worth 100. Because the collateral is based on daily mark-to-market values, this means that if the value of the security falls below 100, the borrower will be subjected to a collateral call and being asked to provide additional collateral. If the call is not met, the lender sells the security, settles the loan, and sends the remaining proceeds to the borrower. In this sense, a properly arranged repo contract is safer for the lender than an uninsured bank deposit.

The risk of changing circumstances, however, is entirely born by the borrowers, who are always subjected to the possibility of forced selling. In addition, the repo may not be rolled over, or it may be offered to be rolled over based on considerably larger haircuts. Such events lead to collapsing financial markets, as financial institutions, one after the other, are unable to face their settlement constraints. The collateral then needs to be sold, its price declines, leading to further increases in haircuts, with the repo market whirling into a death spiral. Sissoko (2017; 2019) argues that contemporary repos are similar to the margin-call bank loans that were popular in the 1920s and which precipitated the Great Depression crisis of the 1930s. Market-based lending based on repos is thus pro-cyclical. When trust and confidence vanish, holders of large financial assets move away from the shadow financial system. Just as easily as liquidity was created, liquidity vanishes, thus creating problems for the shadow banks as well as those institutions that relied on the shadow banking system to obtain funding, forcing them back into the fold of commercial banking or requiring the intervention of the central bank. Repo funding looks good from a microeconomic point of view, but it ends up being dangerous at the macroeconomic level.

4.6 A SYSTEMIC VIEW OF THE MONETARY ECONOMY

We pointed out towards the end of the previous section that Minsky emphasized that the real and the financial sides of the economy could not be treated separately if one wanted to have a full picture of how modern economies function. Besides Minsky, Davidson and Eichner are two other post-Keynesian economists who contributed to the development of an integration of the monetary and real sides of the economy. But Godley is probably the one who worked hardest at providing a formalized version of this integration of the real and financial sides. We already had a glimpse of this work when we examined the liquidity preference of the public. Here we look at the overall picture, in what we shall call the stock–flow consistent approach. But before we do so, we examine the aggregate financial balances that have been proposed by Godley and that have illuminated his forecasting work, in particular for the Levy Economics Institute.

4.6.1 Financial Balances: The Fundamental Identity

Around 1974, in his efforts to make better conditional forecasts in the context of what became known as the New Cambridge model, Godley put forward what he called a three-sector financial balances model, which is now known by many as the 'fundamental identity'. These financial balances, although they are simply a flow-of-funds accounting identity, help to provide some rigour in what can and cannot be said. Once we know the financial position of the private sector, there is a constraint on what the external and government deficits can be. The framework, used extensively by Godley in his conditional forecasts of the US economy, has been adopted by several researchers in universities and in financial institutions, notably by Jan Hatzius at Goldman Sachs, since the late 1990s. The three sectoral balances, or the fundamental identity, are usually written as

$$(S - I) = (G - T) + CAB \tag{4.6}$$

where S stands for the saving of the private sector, I is the non-financial investment of the private sector into tangible fixed capital goods (including dwellings) and inventories, G is government expenditure, T are taxes, and CAB stands for the current account balance. All these variables are understood to be expressed in nominal terms (e.g. in dollars).

In the terminology used by Godley, $(S - I)$ is the net accumulation of financial assets of the domestic private sector ($NAFA$), $(G - T)$ is the government deficit or what used to be called the public sector borrowing requirement ($PSBR$), while CAB is often referred to as the external balance. Godley (1999c, p. 8) interprets equation (4.6) as saying that public deficits and current account surpluses create income and financial assets for the private sector, whereas budget surpluses and current account deficits do the opposite. Of course, we could also rewrite equation (4.6) in a more neutral, standard national accounting, form:

$$(S - I) + (T - G) - CAB = 0 \tag{4.7}$$

In words, using national accounting expressions, equation (4.7) says:

Domestic private net lending + Domestic public net lending + Foreign net lending = 0

What is saved but not used to purchase new tangible investment goods must have been saved in the form of financial assets. Thus $(S - I)$ can also be interpreted as the 'net financial saving' or 'net financial investment' of the domestic private sector. This is the amount that is lent to the other two sectors. When the amount is negative, it is the 'net borrowing' of the domestic private sector. The domestic private net lending is in fact made up of two components: the additions to financial assets, from which are subtracted the additions to financial liabilities. Thus, if an individual purchases $100 worth of bonds by borrowing $100 from the bank, the addition to financial assets is $100, the addition to financial liabilities is $100, while net lending and net financial investment ($NAFA$ in Godley's terms) are zero.

In a similar way, the government surplus $(T - G)$ is the domestic public net lending. Finally, the negative of the current account balance CAB is the current account deficit.

This means that the country has an equivalent financial account surplus (which used to be called a capital account surplus), which is net foreign lending, that is, the net amount that the domestic economy has to borrow from abroad. In other words, if the private and the public domestic sectors cannot fund their own expenditures (both running a deficit), they must borrow funds from the foreign sector. Thus the expression 'foreign net lending' means net lending to the domestic economy by non-residents.

Equation (4.6) (or 4.7) is highly useful because it shows clearly the constraints that any economy faces. This is not a matter of opinion. The equation, or rather the fundamental identity, is derived from the national accounts identity. It is a matter of accounting, not economics. Using standard notations, and noting that M now stands for imports, and not machines as it did in earlier chapters, gross domestic product, GDP, is defined as

$$GDP = C + I + G + X - M$$

We move from the gross domestic product to gross national income, GNP, by taking into consideration net foreign income accruing to nationals, FY, so that GNP equals

$$GNP = C + I + G + X - M + FY$$

We subtract taxes T from both sides, and move private expenditures:

$$(GNP - C - T) - I = (G - T) + (X - M + FY)$$

$(GNP - C - T)$, income less consumption and taxes, is simply private domestic saving. The term $(X - M)$ is net exports, or the commercial balance, while $(X - M + FY)$ represents the current account balance. We have thus recovered equation (4.6).

We can further split the private sector into two components, the business sector and the household sector. Doing this from equation (4.7), we obtain a four-sector fundamental identity instead of a three-sector fundamental identity:

$$(S_f - I_f) + (S_h - I_h) + (T - G) - CAB = 0 \qquad (4.8)$$

The f and h subscripts refer to firms and households, S_f thus being the gross retained earnings of the firms, while I_h is gross residential investment.

The fundamental identity in the form of equation (4.8) was proposed by Steindl (1982) when he tried to assess the impact of household financial saving. Parguez (1980) used an equation such as (4.8) to find the determinants of the retained earnings of firms. We shall also see in Chapter 5 how Kalecki started from the national accounts to identify the determinants of business profits.

One could also have a five-sector fundamental identity by distinguishing between the financial business sector and the non-financial business sector. This would be important when attempting to distinguish between the accumulation of retained earnings by production firms and banks, as we know that with financialization a large proportion of business profits have ended up in the coffers of financial institutions (Fiebiger, 2016b). We may thus insert S_b as the gross retained earnings of banks (more precisely, the overall financial sector), while I_b stands for fixed capital investment of the banking sector. Assuming $(T - G) = CAB = 0$, in order to get to the heart of the matter, we have

$$(S_f - I_f) + (S_h - I_h) + (S_b - I_b) = 0 \quad (4.9)$$

It is then clear that if the private non-financial sector invests more than it saves, thus spending more than its income of the current period, it must be a net borrower; and net lending here can come only from the banking sector. The $(S_b - I_b)$ amount tells us whether the retained earnings of the financial sector exceed their expenditures in tangible capital. The financial saving of the financial sector could go into direct loans or into the purchase of financial assets issued by the non-financial business sector. This amount is only indirectly related to the new creation of credit and deposits. For instance, households could decide to put all their current financial saving into bank deposits, so that bank credit to the non-financial business sector would have to be much larger than $(S_b - I_b)$.

Two special cases can be drawn from equation (4.6). The first case is known as the 'twin deficit', and is at the heart of the so-called consolidation programmes of the International Monetary Fund (IMF) and at the heart of the old Washington Consensus. If net lending by the private sector is assumed to be nil, then equation (4.6) becomes

$$(G - T) = - CAB \quad (4.10)$$

The IMF asserts that, by restraining government expenditures and imposing austerity programmes, both the government deficit and the external deficit will be solved at once, thus killing two birds with one stone (and the economy as well, post-Keynesians would say!).

The second special case assumes away the external sector, and allows us to focus on the domestic economy. With $CAB = 0$, equation (4.6) can be reduced to

$$(S - I) = (G - T) \quad (4.11)$$

In this case, the government deficit is the mirror image of the private domestic surplus. When considering these balances as a percentage of GDP, if the current account balance is fairly stable, these two balances will move together, without being equal to each other, as happens in several countries, Canada in particular.

At the world level, where by definition the current account balance overall must be nil, this implies that any private financial surplus must be accompanied by a government deficit. MMT post-Keynesians take this as meaning that, if the private sector wishes to accumulate additional safe government assets, as should be the case in a growing economy, the government cannot but run a deficit. Arguing for balanced budgets over the business cycle thus makes no sense in a growing economy, since it means a diminishing proportion of safe assets in the portfolios of the private sector. It is important to understand, however, that households can accumulate new financial assets even if the government is not running a deficit. This can be seen by relying on the fundamental identity given by equation (4.8). Assuming that $(G - T) = CAB = 0$, and assuming in addition that

$I_h = 0$, so that S_h represents both the saving and the net lending of the household sector, we get another special case:

$$S_h = I_f - S_f \tag{4.12}$$

As one would expect, households can have a positive financial balance and accumulate new financial assets even though the government is running a balanced budget, provided business firms have investment expenditures. It should thus be clear that the household sector can accumulate financial assets without the government sector running a deficit. Equation (4.12) can also be read in reverse. It is then clear that, for a given amount of investment, an increase in the saving of the household sector will lead to a decrease in the saving of the business sector (their retained earnings). Thus, as Eichner (1987, p. 831) puts it, 'should a nonfinancial sector reduce its current outlays as the means it has chosen to increase its net savings, the gross income of some other non-financial sector will necessarily fall by the same amount'. This will be noted again in Chapter 5.

These important clarifications being made, the implication of equation (4.11) in light of the subprime financial crisis is shown in Figure 4.8, inspired from Krugman (2009). Assume that private saving and taxes are positively linked to GDP, while investment and government expenditures are exogenous variables. The private financial balance is thus shown as the upward-sloping line, while the public deficit is represented by its mirror image, the downward-sloping curve. Figure 4.8 assumes that the world economy was at point E before the crisis, at the intersection of the two continuous lines, with a balanced government budget. As a consequence of the financial crisis, the private sector invests less and there is a sudden shift in thriftiness, so that the line representing the private financial

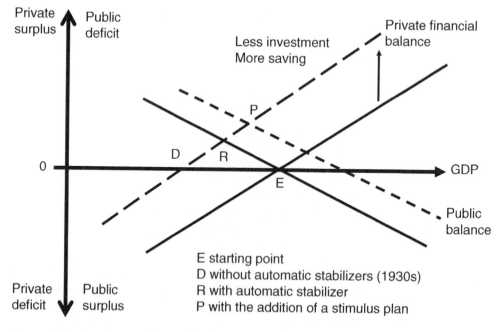

Figure 4.8 A two-sector financial balance model, when the crisis hits

balance shifts up to the dotted upward-sloping line. Letting the automatic stabilizers do their work leads the economy to point R. If deficit hawks had had their way, forbidding any public deficit, the economy would have been propelled to point D, in a state of deep depression, where the public budget is balanced, but with an economy so depressed that financial saving would have been brought back to zero, despite the greater degree of thriftiness – the famous Keynesian paradox of thrift. Finally, with a stimulus plan, that is, a discretionary increase in the government deficit, the economy ends up at point P, at the intersection of the two dotted lines, and in a mild recession. We could also draw a graph representing the fundamental identity in its three-dimensional case, but we shall wait until Chapter 7 to do so.

4.6.2 The Principles of a Systemic Monetary Analysis

While the financial balances presented above have proven to be useful, it is time to discuss monetary transactions from a less aggregated point of view. The French circuit writers have always advocated a mesoeconomic approach, that is, the study of structural – or macroeconomic – laws, independent of the behaviour of agents. Mesoeconomics is found halfway between the macroeconomic emphasis on effective demand and the microeconomic analysis of agents. With respect to technical conditions and relative prices, Leontief's and Sraffa's input–output models can be considered as examples of mesoeconomic analysis. Here we wish to study the interactions of sector-based balance sheets and financial flows.

Over the last 15 years, a number of post-Keynesians have adopted the use of matrices to better explore mesoeconomic relations. Inspired largely by the work of Wynne Godley (1999a) and Lance Taylor (2004), but also by that of Eichner (1987), I believe that such an approach constitutes an important new way of unifying all heterodox macroeconomists, helping to replace and dismiss the neoclassical concept of constrained maximization. This new approach, developed in Godley and Lavoie (2007a), also shares many points of interest with the macroeconomic work of James Tobin (1982), himself a neoclassical synthesis Keynesian. In fact, in his Nobel Prize acceptance speech, Tobin explained why his approach is different from that of the standard neoclassical model. According to Tobin, a proper macroeconomics must entertain four important characteristics, which can be summarized as follows:

1. Stocks and flows must be fully integrated into the analysis, and their accounting must be done in a fully coherent manner.
2. All models should include a multitude of sectors and of assets, each with its own rate of return.
3. It is important to incorporate all monetary and financial operations, and thus integrate the central bank and commercial banks.
4. There cannot be any 'black holes': all flows must inevitably have an origin and a destination; and all budget and portfolio adding-up constraints must be respected, both for behavioural relations and for the actual values of the variables.

Because Tobin was at Yale University, in New Haven, Connecticut, this approach is often referred to as the New Haven School. At the very same time, in the 1970s, a closely related methodology and approach were independently developed and advocated by Godley and his colleagues in the Department of Applied Economics at the University of Cambridge, leading to the creation of the so-called New Cambridge approach (Godley and Cripps, 1983). What Godley's and Tobin's analyses emphasize is the need for a coherent macroeconomic framework that links together the flow dimension of macroeconomics with the stock dimension of real capital, financial assets and debts, with their corresponding rates of return, while also taking into account the interrelationships and correspondence between the various sectors of the economy. While neoclassical economists have rejected Tobin's approach and have fallen back on the unrealistic 'representative agent', where consumers and producers are one and the same, some post-Keynesians have embraced Tobin's approach, incorporating it, however, into a monetary production economy where the supply of money is endogenous and where behavioural equations respond to Kaleckian or Keynesian precepts rather than neoclassical ones.

This approach has become known as the stock–flow consistent approach, or the SFC approach. 'SFC models are necessarily based on social accounting frameworks that consistently "integrate" conventional product and income accounts with "flows of funds" accounts and a full set of balance sheets' (Dos Santos, 2006, p. 543). Thus, as Taylor (2004) shows, SFC models make use of the social accounting matrices (SAM) of national accounting, which also arose from the work being conducted at the Department of Applied Economics at Cambridge, under the initial leadership of Richard Stone. Indeed, the accounting of the SFC models is inspired by the System of National Accounts of the United Nations, as described in its 1968, 1993 and 2008 versions, whereas orthodox macroeconomics is still based on the outdated 1953 version. Some of the users of the SFC approach hope that SFC models will become the locus of some form of post-Keynesian consensus in macroeconomics, as it allows us to entertain both monetary and real issues within a single model. Nikiforos and Zezza (2017) provide a survey of this rapidly expanding field of research.

In fact, the SFC approach is perhaps a misnomer, as several other theories relate stocks and flows in a consistent way. The peculiarity of the post-Keynesian SFC approach is that its models truly integrate the real and the monetary sides. To get a gist of what this SFC approach truly implied for Godley and his collaborators, we should recall some of the other names that were initially suggested, such as the 'real stock flow monetary model' (Godley, 1993, p. 63), or names that Godley and I juggled with during the 2000s, such as the 'financial stock–flow coherent' approach or the 'sectoral stock–flow coherent' approach, to emphasize that stock–flow consistency is not limited to the trivial link between real investment and tangible capital, but involves most importantly the interrelated financial flows and stocks of assets and liabilities of the main economic sectors of the economy, including those of the all-important banking sector (Dos Santos, 2006, p. 543). These models also attempt to integrate both short-run and long-run dynamics (Macedo e Silva and Dos Santos, 2011).

In attempting to provide a useful model of the economy that deals with both the real and the monetary factors, economists face various difficulties. They have to identify the structural framework that they believe is relevant to the problem at hand. This means that they have to choose the number of sectors that they wish to consider: firms, banks with or without non-bank financial institutions, the government, a central bank, the external sector, households, split or not into two categories, say workers and capitalists. From there, the modeller must choose what assets and liabilities ought to be included in the model, and whether an asset or a liability can be omitted without much damage from a particular sector. For instance, should banks be assumed to hold long-term bonds or be assumed to issue equities, and should firms be assumed to issue corporate paper or be assumed to hold financial assets such as Treasury bills? These choices lead to the construction of a balance-sheet matrix, which ensures that the model starts out in a coherent way. A proper balance-sheet matrix also helps in designing a proper transactions–flow matrix, which will take into consideration all the financial flows associated with the assumed stocks. The same transaction–flow matrix also ensures that each sector fulfils its budget constraint. To take into account capital gains, a third matrix, a re-evaluation matrix, is also needed.

Finally, appropriate behavioural equations must be inserted within the framework so defined. Different closures of the model will bring about a different choice of endogenous and exogenous variables. For instance, we are likely to suppose that the government deficit is an endogenous variable. But we could also suppose that the government wishes to achieve a given deficit and will do everything to achieve this target, in which case the deficit variable is an exogenous variable, implying that some other exogenous variable will need to become endogenous. This gives rise to two different scenarios in forecasting exercises.

4.6.3 Examples of Balance-sheet and Transactions–Flow Matrices

Besides the revaluation matrix, Godley's systemic approach rests on two matrices: a balance-sheet matrix and a transactions–flow matrix. Balance sheets deal with stocks, both tangible and financial. Tangible stocks include machines and buildings (the fixed capital of firms), as well as the value of real estate held by households. Tangible stocks also include durable goods such as cars still in circulation. We may also wish to include the inventory stocks of firms (IN) – goods that are produced but have yet to be sold. These tangible stocks have no counterpart in the balance sheet.

Financial assets, on the other hand, do have a counterpart, which is debt, and which appears on the liability side of another agent's or sector's balance sheet (household, producing firms, banks, the government or the central bank). For instance, loans made by banks are an asset for the bank, but a liability for the borrower. Where do these stocks come from? The answer is that they are either the result of flows, which are added to the existing stocks; or they result from the re-evaluation of certain assets, an exercise that is excluded from the transactions–flow matrix. Each stock is then associated with a given flow through a dynamic equation, which links the past and the present. For instance, the value of all shares held by households at the end of a given year is equal by definition to the stock of shares held at a given time, s, and the price of the shares, p_s, as shown in Table 4.34. This value can be said to arise from three distinct sources: the value of the shares held at the end of the previous year (that is, at the beginning of the year at stake); the value of the new shares issued by firms and purchased by households at market prices during the current year; and the capital gain resulting from the increase in the price of the shares that were held at the beginning of the year during the course of that same year. Long-term bonds are also subject to capital gains.

Table 4.34 shows a simple balance sheet, where inventories have been added to the balance sheet used in the Lavoie and Godley (2001–02) growth model. Obviously, the

Table 4.34 Modified balance-sheet matrix of the Lavoie and Godley (2001–02) model

	Households	Firms	Banks	Σ
Fixed capital		$+K$		$+K$
Inventories		$+IN$		$+IN$
Deposits	$+D_h$		$-D$	0
Loans		$-B_f$	$+B$	0
Shares	$+s \cdot p_s$	$-s \cdot p_s$		0
Balance	$-V_h$	$-V_f$	0	$-(K+IN)$
Σ	0	0	0	0

matrix omits important features of present-day capitalism. As pointed out earlier, all assets appear with a positive sign in the matrix, while liabilities carry a negative sign. The horizontal sum of all assets and liabilities must be zero, except for tangible assets, as explained earlier. The vertical sum for each sector yields the net worth V of the individual sector, which, as was also explained earlier, carries a negative sign as it is part of the liabilities and net worth of the balance sheet. Note that the net worth of firms seen from the perspective of the national accounts is different from net worth seen from the business perspective, as the latter would not consider the value of shares as a liability.

We shall start from the balance sheet of Table 4.34 to show the transactions-flow matrix that corresponds to it. The transactions-flow matrix, here given by Table 4.35, is an interesting tool because it can link all the important aggregates of the National Income and Product Accounts (NIPA) to the financial flows that affect balance sheets. The matrix describes a vertically integrated production economy, dealing with value-added only, as in NIPA, abstracting from the maze of interdependencies associated with intermediate production. To simplify further, we also assume that banks do not make profits (we set the rate of interest on loans, i_B, equal to the rate of interest on bank deposits, i_D).

One of the advantages of using accounting matrices is that they guarantee that nothing gets lost in the discussion: as stated above, all flows must come from somewhere and must end up somewhere. This explains why each line and column adds to zero: the matrix is perfectly balanced. Horizontally, each flow has an equivalent counterpart. Overall, the rows describe the nominal amounts that are exchanged from one sector to another. The equality between the inflow and the outflow arises for one of the following three reasons. First, supply may always adjust itself to demand, either because production adjusts or through changes in inventory stocks; second, demand may be rationed (as in the case of credit rationing); third, market prices may provide for an instantaneous adjustment between supply and demand (as in financial markets). Vertically, each transaction must be financed. The columns sum to zero and represent the budget constraints that each of the sectors must respect.

Let us begin the examination of the transactions–flow matrix given by Table 4.35 by considering households, which face an obvious budget constraint: they receive interest payments ($i_D \cdot D_{(-1)}$), dividends (P_D) and wages (wL), with which they can consume (C), increase their bank deposits (ΔD), or purchase newly issued shares on the financial market ($p_s \Delta s$). In the flow matrix, all components with a negative sign represent a use of

Credit, money and central banks 289

Table 4.35 The transactions–flow matrix in a closed economy without government

Account	Households	Firms		Banks		Σ
		Current	Capital	Current	Capital	
Consumption	$-C$	$+C$				0
Investment		$+I$	$-I$			0
Δ inventory stocks		$+\Delta IN$	$-\Delta IN$			0
Wages	$+wL$	$-wL$				0
Net profits	$+P_D$	$-(P_{ND}+P_D)$	$+P_{ND}$			0
Interest on loans		$-i_B \cdot B_{(-1)}$		$+i_B \cdot B_{(-1)}$		0
Interest on deposits	$+i_D \cdot D_{(-1)}$			$i_D \cdot D_{(-1)}$		0
Δ in loans			$+\Delta B$		$-\Delta B$	0
Δ in deposits	$-\Delta D$				$+\Delta D$	0
Shares	$-p_s \Delta s$		$+p_s \Delta s$			0
Σ	0	0	0	0	0	0

funds, while a positive sign represents a source of funds. For instance, wages, given by wL, which is the product of nominal wages, w, and employment, L, is a source of funds for households. Yet they also represent a use of funds from the point of view of the production sector, and so carry a negative sign when entered in the column of the firms.

The situation of firms is slightly more complicated. While they sell consumption goods (C) to households, they also sell investment goods (I) to each other, as well as finished goods not yet sold to customers, ΔIN. The income generated from these sales, either realized or based on an accounting entry, must always equal the wage and interest payments, plus the net profits from the private sector. These profits can be further divided into two components: dividends P_D to households, and retained earnings, P_{ND}, which is a component of the final financing of fixed capital and inventory stocks, all of these three elements appearing in the capital account of firms.

The middle of the matrix shows the interest payments that need to be paid at the beginning of the period, based on the stocks outstanding at the end of the previous period. The bottom of the matrix represents changes in claims and liabilities. Inasmuch as households increase either their holdings of stock market shares or of bank deposits, this implies a use of funds and therefore a negative sign. But when a firm gets a new bank loan, ΔB, which increases its stock of debt, it becomes a source of funds for the production sector, meaning that it should carry a positive sign. This is usually somewhat confusing to students since the bank deposits of households carry a positive sign in the stock matrix while the stock of loans taken by firms carries a negative sign. Similarly, when firms issue new shares, the proceeds $p_s \Delta s$ appear with a positive sign in the transactions–flow matrix. When firms buy back shares, as many of them do to sustain share prices, a negative number appears in the capital account of firms.

Readers should note that the terminology 'source and use of funds' may lead to an additional confusion when discussing the role of banks. When a bank lends and, in doing so, increases the stock of outstanding loans, the additional loans are assigned a negative sign in the transactions–flow matrix. The corresponding deposits that are created as a result carry a positive sign. In this sense, we can claim that from the point of view of the banking sector, deposits are a 'source' of funds whereas loans are the 'use' of funds. A note of caution is required here: this may give the impression that deposits are therefore required to make a loan, but this would be a misleading inference. Rather, as we argued earlier in this chapter, loans make deposits. In other words, while the increase in deposits may be seen as a source of funds from a financial perspective, the causal element remains nevertheless the loans initially granted by banks. These loans are created *ex nihilo* at the request of firms considered creditworthy by banks.

The SFC approach presented here is certainly consistent with the integration of the real and financial analysis advocated by some of the key Fundamentalist post-Keynesians. For Minsky (1975, p. 118), for instance, 'an ultimate reality in a capitalist economy is the set of interrelated balance sheets among the various units. Items in the balance sheet set up cash flows.' The quote below describes well what an SFC model could or should look like.

> It will be the objective of the historical model developed below to provide a simple analysis of capital accumulation by blending the stock and flow elements in the demand and supply of (i) real capital, (ii) money, and (iii) securities . . . with the more familiar concepts . . . of effective demand developed in the *General Theory*. Within such a framework it is possible to provide more perspective on the interplay among organized security exchanges, corporate financing policy, investment underwriters and the banking system in channeling the financial funds necessary for capital accumulation. Regrettably this is an analysis which is virtually ignored in most 'analytical' post-keynesian models. (Davidson, 1972, p. 31)

4.6.4 Monetary Creation in a Monetized Production Economy

The monetary circuit and the finance motive

Table 4.1 claimed that a distinct feature of post-Keynesian monetary theory is that it sees money as arising from the production process, since post-Keynesians, as discussed in Chapter 1, are concerned with a monetized production economy. Still, so far, while we have emphasized the role of banks in creating credit and in responding to the liquidity desires of the public, we have not paid a great deal of attention to the relationship between production firms and the banking sector. Yet there is a key relationship between firms and banks, which fund the production activities of non-financial firms. The essential consideration here is time. The production of goods and services takes time, and firms must be in some way able to remunerate their employees and pay their suppliers in advance of sales receipt. While firms generally hold financial assets that allow them to meet their regular monetary obligations, several firms rely on bank loans to start production. This is called 'initial' finance. Firms, whether they produce consumption goods in advance of demand or whether they produce investment goods to order, must be able to rely on bank credit. This logic applies equally well to growing or stationary economies, since in the latter case the banks must also agree to roll over debt. The logic of the monetary circuit has been well explained by Godley himself, in his tribute to Augusto Graziani.

> In order to finance production, the entrepreneur must obtain the funds necessary to pay his workforce in advance of the sales taking place. Starting from scratch, he must borrow from banks, at the beginning of each production cycle, the sum which is needed in order to pay wages, creating a debt for the entrepreneur and, thereby, an equivalent amount of credit money, which sits initially in the hands of the labour force. Production now takes place and the produced

good is sold at a price which enables the debt to be repaid inclusive of interest, while hopefully generating a surplus – that is, a profit – for the entrepreneur. When the debt is repaid, the money originally created is extinguished. An entire monetary circuit is complete. (Godley, 2004, p. 127)

Post-Keynesians, and in particular circuit theorists, as alluded to earlier, thus make a distinction between 'initial' and 'final' finance (Graziani, 1984; 2003). This distinction has recently been reasserted by Cesaratto and Di Bucchianico (2020). Initial finance is usually short-term finance, through bank loans and corporate paper. Final finance refers to more long-term market instruments. Davidson (1992) refers to 'construction finance' and 'investment funding' to distinguish the two steps of the financing process. Firms that purchase capital goods must be able to finance them. Besides their retained earnings, firms must capture the savings of households, either directly or indirectly, through the banking system or other financial institutions such as mutual funds and insurance companies. This final finance phase of the production process closes the monetary circuit of production.

Table 4.35 helps us to make the distinction. The production sector of the transactions-flow matrix is subdivided into a capital account and a current account. Both accounts must sum to zero. The capital account column describes the components of final finance. In this simple model, the accumulation of fixed capital or the increase in inventories of firms at the end of the period, say a quarter or even a year, is financed by only three possible sources: new share issues, new borrowing from banks, or undistributed profits (retained earnings).

By contrast, the grey cells in the matrix represent initial finance. At the beginning of the production process, as the monetary circuit begins, firms must borrow the funds needed to pay wages to employees, and begin the production of new goods, ΔIN (recall that we assume a closed vertically integrated production economy, where the only costs are wage costs). The amount borrowed is exactly equal to total wages in the current period. It is the first stage of the monetary circuit of production. It does not matter whether loans are taken for the production of consumption or investment goods: both in fact require initial finance, as explained by Keynes (1973, xiv, p. 220) when in 1937 he added the 'finance motive' to his scheme.

At the very beginning of the circuit, therefore, firms have a debt towards banks but also a claim in the form of a bank deposit. This first stage is in fact very short: firms will draw on their line of credit only when they need to pay wages and begin production. This is done either through cheques or through electronic transfers, as is usually the case nowadays. But as soon as wages are paid, they become an income for households and workers. At the very moment they are paid, and hence before households begin consuming the newly received income, these funds simultaneously become household saving, kept in the form of bank deposits, ΔD. The grey cells depict this second stage. The third stage – final finance – as already pointed out, is represented by the capital account of the production sector, when firms collect back funds from households.

Making use of the grey cells of matrix 4.31 allows us to fall back on some useful accounting principles, especially when considering the operations of firms. As goods are produced but remain unsold, they become an additional component of inventory stocks, ΔIN. Consistent with the best accounting practices, it is important that inventory goods be valued at their current production costs (at their replacement cost, and not at their expected sale price). In our vertically integrated economy, the cost of production of these stocks is exactly equal to the wages paid to households within this period. In this sense, the value of the increase in inventories, ΔIN, is exactly equal to wL, which is what emerges from the grey cells in the current account column of the firms.

This illustrates the 'quadruple accounting' principle that was put forward by Morris Copeland (1949) and is highlighted in the System of National Accounts (SNA) of the United Nations (2009). This principle is also mentioned by Minsky (1996, p. 77). Since each column and each row must sum to zero at all times, any transaction requires at least four recorded changes for the matrix to balance out. For instance, if a bank decides to grant a loan ΔB to the production sector, it must also create, as a counterpart, deposits ΔD of an equal amount. The capital account column of the banking sector then sums to zero. Moreover, the new loan must also be recorded as an additional liability in the capital account of the producing sector. This ensures that the row of loans sums to zero. But a fourth entry must be changed to take into account the fact that the producing sector now holds an additional amount of bank deposits, which allows the row of deposits to sum to zero as well. As a result, we have a minimum of four accounting records for each transaction. In Table 4.35, the operation requires even more entries, because the firms immediately dispose of their deposits by paying wages to their employees, who then deposit the funds in their own bank accounts.

A balance-sheet matrix with shadow banking

The role of the shadow banking sector relative to *bona fide* banks was assessed in the previous section. Quite a bit of effort has been devoted over the last few years to incorporate the shadow banking sector and its various components to stock-flow consistent models. Indeed, initially, Taylor (2008) complained that even the more complex models in the book of Godley and Lavoie (2007a) only handled a plain banking sector. Lavoie (2009d) provided an initial answer, showing how aspects of shadow banking could be introduced within a balance-sheet matrix. Since then, several such balance-sheet matrices have been proposed, and in some cases modelled, such as those found in Nikolaidi (2015), Botta et al. (2015), Sawyer and Passarella (2017), Caverzasi et al. (2019) and Botta et al. (2020).

Table 4.36, taken from Lavoie (2022), presents such an institutionally-rich balance sheet. While there are three tangible assets – inventories, fixed capital and houses h priced at p_h, there is a multitude of financial assets to which households, firms and also financial institutions have access. A key feature is the way in which securitization has been handled, taken from Botta et al. (2015). It is assumed that a proportion z of the mortgages and of other loans granted by banks is being passed on to special purpose vehicles (SPV), who then transform them into asset-based securities (ABS), while the amount of mortgages and loans left on the balance sheets of commercial banks is reduced by the percentage $1-z$. Structured investment vehicles (SIV), who are pure intermediaries, purchase part of these long-term asset-based securities and finance their acquisition by issuing short-term asset-based commercial paper (ABCP), which are themselves purchased by firms and money market funds in search of yields comparable to those of treasury bills.

As discussed earlier, investment banks purchase treasury bills and the securitized assets, essentially through their own funds and repos. These repos are mostly issued by money market funds, who get their funds from households and firms that have large cash

Table 4.36 A balance-sheet matrix incorporating the shadow banking system

	Households	Firms	Commercial banks	Investment banks	SPV	SIV conduits	Money market funds	Central bank	Govt	Σ
Tangible Capital		$+K$								$+K$
Inventories		$+IN$								$+IN$
Homes	$+p_{lr}h_h$									$+p_{lr}h_h$
Cash	$+HPM_h$		$+HPM_b$					$-HPM_{cb}$	$+HPM_g$	0
Deposits	$+D_h$		$-D$	$+D_{ib}$						0
MM funds	$+MMF_h$	$+MMF_f$					$+D_{mmf}$			0
Mortgages	$-MO$		$+(1-z_1)MO$		$+z_1MO$		$-MMF$			0
Loans	$-B_h$	$-B_f$	$+(1-z_2)B$		$+z_2B$					0
ABS/CDO				$+ABS_{ib}$	$-ABS$	$+ABS_{siv}$				0
ABCP		$+ABCP_f$				$-ABCP$	$+ABCP_{mmf}$			0
Repos			$+R_b$	$-R_{ib}$			$+R_{mmf}$			0
Corporate paper		$-CP$	$+CP_b$				$+CP_{mmf}$			0
Shares	$+p_s s_h$	$-p_s s_f$	$-p_s s_b$	$-p_s s_{ib}$						0
T-bills		$+TB_f$	$+TB_b$	$+TB_{ib}$			$+TB_{mmf}$	$+TB_{cb}$	$-TB$	0
Advances			$-A$					$+A$		0
Net worth	$-NW_h$	$-NW_f$	$-NW_b$	$-NW_{ib}$	$-NW_{cpv}$	$-NW_{siv}$	$-NW_{mmf}$	$-NW_{cb}$	$-NW_g$	$-(K+IN+p_{lr}h_h)$
Σ	0	0	0	0	0	0	0	0	0	0

balances and wish to obtain better rates of return on them. As one can see by looking at their column, money market funds in counterpart hold several different liquid financial assets, such as bank deposits, treasury bills, asset-backed corporate paper, corporate paper, and repos. Finally, there is a central bank, that provides cash to households, reserves and advances to banks, and deposit facilities to the government. Despite the complexity of the matrix relative to that of Table 4.34, there are still components missing, such as hedge funds and long pools of cash such as mutual funds. Still, Table 4.36 helps to see how interconnected are the balance sheets of the various financial institutions.

4.6.5 The Limits of SFC Accounting

Alongside sector-based balance-sheet matrices, sectoral transactions–flow matrices provide the core relationships of monetary production economies. To these, along with the dynamic equations that link stocks and flows, we need to add behavioural equations pertaining to each sector of the economy. Any model offers specific behavioural equations that provide the closure of the model and account for its particular results and derived conclusions. Nevertheless, post-Keynesians like Godley believe that the core accounting equations and the dynamic stock–flow equations actually constitute a framework that constrains the range of possible results. In other words, certain configurations or dynamics are just plain impossible, because they contradict the accounting core. As pointed out by Taylor (2004, p. 2), stock–flow consistent macro modelling and the core accounting equations 'remove many degrees of freedom from possible configurations of patterns of payments at the macro level'.

According to Godley and Cripps (1983), any fully coherent model that adequately represents a monetary economy of production will necessarily give some medium- and long-term results that are essentially identical, irrespective of the values given to the various parameters. Such a model must be able to provide a linkage between all stocks and flows, while taking all transaction flows into account, including the budget constraints. In addition, stock constraints must be accounted for, such as the portfolio constraints and asset adding-up constraints that we have already discussed. Economic agents target certain ratios that will guarantee the confluence of both stocks and flows, for instance desired sales to inventory stocks ratio in the case of firms. In fact, this may arise without the expressed knowledge of agents. For example, when households consume each year a given ratio of their income and of their wealth, they implicitly define a long-term steady relationship between wealth (a stock) and disposable income (a flow).

Unfortunately, things are not so simple. While it may be relatively easy to agree on the main structural features of a simplified economy, different economists see the behaviour of firms or banks or even households in many different ways. Despite a possible common structural framework that should constrain the range of possible results, as Godley and Cripps (1983) initially hoped when they proposed a first version of the stock–flow consistent approach, it turns out that different economists will still disagree on behavioural equations and the appropriate closure of the model. Thus the results obtained with these different models will differ, as has been confirmed when new SFC models, with assumptions slightly different from those of the earlier ones, produced different trajectories. Moreover, Kappes and Milan (2020) show that, even within the same model, in this case the GROWTH model of Godley and Lavoie (2007a), different weights used in the adaptative expectations of a single equation generate different transitional paths as well as different steady-state ratios of household wealth to corporate capital stock. This shows that the tested SFC model is subjected to path-dependency, thus underlying once more that time is important in post-Keynesian models.

Notwithstanding the above, models or analyses based on proper accounting and flow-of-funds are more likely to provide useful information than models that ignore the interdependence of the real and the financial sides of the economy. Indeed, Bezemer (2010) argues that those making use of such tools hold a much better record in predicting financial crises and their possible causes and consequences.

NOTE

* Besides relying on and extending the 1992 *Foundations*, full sentences have been taken from the following publications: 'Money, credit and central banks in post-Keynesian economics', in Eckhard Hein and Engelbert Stockhammer (eds), *A Modern Guide to Keynesian Macroeconomics and Economic Policies*, Cheltenham, UK and Northampton, MA, USA: Edward Elgar Publishing, 2011, pp. 34–60; 'A primer on endogenous credit-money', in L.P. Rochon and S. Rossi (eds), *Modern Theories of Money: The Nature and Role of Money in Capitalist Economies*, Cheltenham, UK and Northampton, MA, USA: Edward Elgar Publishing, 2003, pp. 506–43.

5. Effective demand and employment*

The focus of this chapter is the labour market and the employment of labour. The analysis will be pursued within the short-run framework, assuming given monetary conditions and a fixed level of investment. Long-run conditions will be studied in Chapter 6. Here we start by discussing the main characteristics of the so-called labour market. We then present two simplified versions of the post-Keynesian labour market model – the Marshallian and the Kaleckian versions. This Kaleckian version will then be subjected to a deeper analysis.

5.1 CHARACTERISTICS OF THE LABOUR MARKET

5.1.1 General Characteristics

For mainstream economics, labour is a commodity no different from any other, and hence labour markets should be explained through the usual laws of supply and demand. This is certainly not the view of post-Keynesian and Insitutionalist economists. The major characteristics of the post-Keynesian labour market are the following: the labour market does not truly exist; the wage rate is not just another ordinary price: it has much influence on the overall economy; workers are not commodities: norms rule over forces of supply and demand; the demand for and the supply of labour are not well behaved (Appelbaum, 1979; Seccareccia, 1991a; Prasch, 2004).

Ironically, the major aspect of the post-Keynesian view of labour markets is that such markets do not really exist. Whereas one may admit that there is a market for peanuts or for bananas, with possibly well-behaved supply and demand curves, the same hypothesis cannot be made in the case of labour. On the demand side, we have already seen in Chapter 3 that machines and labour are in fixed proportion in the short run. One cannot increase production by putting more workers on the same machine. No such substitution is possible. As to the longer run, we saw in Chapter 1 that the Cambridge controversies on capital have ramifications for all standard scarcity relationships, even at the industry level. *A fortiori*, at the aggregate level, one should not expect to find a continuous negative relationship between the demand for labour and the aggregate real wage, as was illustrated in Figure 1.2 of Chapter 1.

A further difference between the market for peanuts or broccoli and the market for labour is that the former deals with things whereas the latter deals with human beings. This is why Eichner (1986a, ch. 4) calls the post-Keynesian approach an anthropogenic approach to labour. Two essential distinctions between labour and commodities, also emphasized by Robert Prasch (2004), are that labour cannot be separated from its provider and labour cannot be stored. The productivity of labour depends on how healthy and motivated the labour force is. Also, if labour is not used in one period because of cyclical unemployment, it is lost forever. Even worse, the skills and the productivity of the unemployed labour force depreciate through lack of use, whereas they generally appreciate when they are being utilized, in obvious contrast to physical capital. Furthermore, in contrast to mainstream economics, work does not necessarily carry disutility; it also brings satisfactions. Work in itself can be rewarding.

The market for labour has to deal with labourers, which 'bring with them not only their labour-power but also their past history and norms of justice in the workplace' (Seccareccia, 1991a, p. 45). We mentioned in Chapter 3 that the notions of fairness and justice often permeate the determination of the prices of things, in particular the prices of manufactured goods. The question of justice and of norms is even more fundamental in the so-called market for labour. These norms enter into all dimensions of labour: the real wage and also the relative wages to be paid, as was emphasized by Keynes (1936, p. 14); the duration of the contract; the level of work effort or of productivity; the range of activities that can be assigned to the worker; the duration of the working week; the safety of the job, its security in the face of cyclical fluctuations, and so on. Using the terms proposed by Wood (1978), one could argue that in most markets anomic pressures overshadow normative ones, whereas in labour markets it is the reverse. In the market for labour, normative pressures, that is, pressures linked to customs and equity, have much more importance than anomic pressures, that is, pressures that lack organizational content such as market forces and conjectural forces. In this chapter, we shall deal with one aspect of these normative pressures – the impact of higher wages on the work effort of the workers, or what is known in the neoclassical literature as the efficiency wage hypothesis, but which we can also relate to X-efficiency (Altman, 1998). The consequences of normative pressures for the determination of money wage rates, and hence the importance of relative wages, will be discussed in Chapter 8, when the topic of inflation will be pursued.

5.1.2 A Segmented Market

A particular striking example of normative forces is those forces at work within the core economy of the now widely accepted dual labour market hypothesis. The labour market is assumed to be segmented in two submarkets, as has long been argued by Institutional labour economists and also by neo-radical ones (Gray and Chapman, 2004). One of the submarkets corresponds to the core economy, where wages and productivity are relatively high, as are the requirements and the costs of labour training, as well as the costs of monitoring work. Within this economy, there is a well-structured wage or salary scale, where experience and seniority are given prominence, and there can be a high degree of unionization. Also, each organization within the core economy tries to develop a sense of affiliation among its staff and workers. The other labour market is the peripheral one, where little training is required, where the monitoring of work is inexpensive, and where wages are systematically low. In the organizations of the peripheral economy, the turnover of employees is often encouraged.

To some extent, the core economy corresponds to the sectors where prices are administered and under oligopolistic control, and hence where sufficient profits can be generated to introduce more productive machinery, while the peripheral economy corresponds to products sold in more competitive markets with few possibilities to introduce up-to-date technology, but this correspondence is imperfect (Reich, 1984). In particular, within the same industry, some jobs may be within the core economy while others are at the periphery. Large firms of the core economy may contract out work to non-unionized peripheral firms. Even within the same firm, some jobs may belong to the core and others to the periphery. In universities, for instance, professors who have tenure or who have a tenure-track position are part of the core economy. By contrast, many university teachers move from one temporary position to another, or, worse, barely survive as part-time lecturers, taking on a full teaching load, sometimes in different universities, at salaries two or three times lower than their more lucky young colleagues, despite having similar qualifications. Similar situations arise in all sectors, even in government services. It is of no use for those without a permanent job in the core sector to propose their services at a salary lower than the ruling one: they will not be offered the job.

The present chapter will focus on the macroeconomics of employment. There is no specific post-Keynesian view of the microeconomics of labour markets. However, I think it is fair to say that post-Keynesians essentially endorse the views put forward by Institutionalist labour economists or industrial relations labour economists of the 1950s, such as John Dunlop, Clark Kerr, Lloyd Reynolds or Richard Lester, or by more recent ones, such as Lester Thurow, Michael Piore, Peter Doeringer, Barry Bluestone, David Howell and Frank Wilkinson. Bruce Kaufman (2004) identifies seven principles that define the contribution of Institutionalist economists, many of which are related to what we discussed in Chapter 2. The first principle is tied to humanistic economics, and says that the goals of economic activity must go beyond efficiency and include equity and self-realization. The second principle is that satisfaction goes beyond the consumption of goods and must include conditions and experience of work. The third principle is that behaviour is interdependent and that decision-making or satisfaction depends on relative comparisons. The fourth principle is that the labour market is the antithesis of a perfect market, being plagued by asymmetric information, significant costs of mobility and large externalities. All these 'imperfections' create an inequality of bargaining power – an asymetric relationship between the employer and the worker – and that is the fifth principle. The sixth principle is that the marginal productivity theory does not hold, workers being usually underpaid. The seventh principle is that labour markets are unlikely to clear, because lower wages are unable to reduce unemployment; they will lead to a reduction in aggregate demand and hence a decrease in employment.

5.1.3 The Role of Effective Demand

Kaufman (2004, p. 22) contends that 'the early institutionalists were "proto-Keynesians" in that they believed the level of output and labour demand were primarily a function of the level of purchasing power, so they concluded that wage cuts often exacerbate the level of employment'. Institutionalists thus rejected and still reject the standard demand and supply analysis with well-behaved curves. The relationship with modern post-Keynesians is thus quite evident. For post-Keynesians, employment in the labour market is essentially determined by effective demand in the goods market. The lack of employment has nothing to do with excessive real wages or with a lack of wage flexibility. It is instead, in general, a demand-led phenomenon. Indeed, in several versions of the post-Keynesian short-run model of employment, higher real wages are conducive to higher levels of employment.

This is not to say that there never arise supply-side constraints to employment, such as a lack of productive capacity for a given labour force, which is associated with Marxian unemployment. This was pointed out by two famous post-Keynesians. Joan Robinson in a 1977 interview said that 'unemployment in most developing countries is not due to a deficiency of effective demand, but rather to a deficiency of equipment. Keynesian remedies can be effective as a solution to a problem of under-utilization of capacity, but it is evident that they cannot create a capacity that doesn't already exist' (Pizano, 2009, p. 96). Kalecki, in 1966, as reported by Feiwel (1972, p. 19), made the exact same claim: 'The cardinal problem of the underdeveloped (or less developed) economies is the deficiency of productive capacity rather than the question of its variable utilization (underutilization).... This is not to deny that an underdeveloped country may suffer from a deficiency of effective demand and underutilization of even its meager capacities'. However, it should be pointed out that, by contrast, Taylor (1983, pp. 13–14) asserted that 'countries at middle or low levels of gross domestic product per head operate in a state of excess or spare capacity'.

Thus the problem of a lack of aggregate demand may plague countries at all levels of development. Post-Keynesians in general argue that, in most circumstances, the problem will be one of unutilized labour resources accompanied by under-utilized production capacities, due to a lack of effective demand. As an illustration, scholars pondered for many years why the unemployment rate in the USA was systematically lower than in Canada, using sophisticated econometric analysis to identify causes such as the percentage of the population being incarcerated, unemployment benefits, taxation rates, and other kinds of supply-side phenomena. When the subprime financial crisis hit the American economy, the unemployment rate in the USA jumped way ahead of that in Canada, thus showing that a lack of aggregate demand may be the simplest and best explanation of the discrepancy between the rates of unemployment in the two countries. A similar explanation is likely to apply to the high rates of unemployment in Europe.

Just as neoclassical macroeconomics can be split into at least two branches – the New Classical and the New Keynesian schools, or the clearwater and the saltwater versions of neoclassical macroeconomics – the post-Keynesian theory of employment can also be subdivided into two branches, the Marshallian and the Kaleckian, corresponding to the Marshallian and Kaleckian strands identified in Chapter 1. And just as the New Classical and the New Keynesian schools share some tools, the Marshallian and Kaleckian branches also share some features. Thus although, like Stockhammer (2011), we will be presenting two different models of the labour market, each associated with one branch of post-Keynesianism, those two models will be sharing their depiction of aggregate demand.

A key feature of post-Keynesian economics is its rejection of Say's law. There is no insurance that all the goods produced will be sold. This is akin to the Marxist problem of profit realization, as clearly explained by Bhaduri (1986). Whatever is produced will not necessarily be sold. One has to take into account the effective demand constraint – the constraint that aggregate supply needs to equal aggregate demand. The effective demand constraint will impinge upon the level of employment. The shape of the aggregate supply curve will distinguish the Marshallian and the Kaleckian models. But aggregate demand is perceived by Keynes and Kalecki in the same terms.

As often claimed by Davidson (2000, pp. 11–13), Keynes (1936, ch. 3) distinguishes between autonomous and induced components of effective demand, which allows him to reject Say's law. By induced expenditures, we mean the components of current aggregate demand that are dependent upon current economic activity. In contrast, autonomous expenditures are independent of current output. Autonomous variables may themselves be endogenous, as long as they don't depend on the level of current output (Allain, 2021b). In a closed economy with no government, which we will initially assume, the only remaining components of aggregate demand – GDP seen from the expenditure side – are consumption and investment. Note that, in such an economy, GDP seen from the income side must be equal to wages plus profits:

$$Y = \text{Consumption} + \text{Investment} = \text{Wages} + \text{Profits} \tag{5.1}$$

For Keynes, investment is basically an autonomous variable, which depends on the long-run expectations of entrepreneurs and on interest rates. Consumption, however, is partially induced. In fact, this approach is largely consistent with that of Kalecki (1971, ch. 8), who considers investment to be independent of current output, and who divides consumption into two components: consumption out of wages (workers) and consumption out of profits (capitalists). Whereas the former component of consumption is induced, the latter is an autonomous variable according to Kalecki since it is presumed to depend on lagged realized profits and influenced by expectations. A similar view is endorsed by Robinson (1956, p. 284) when she argues that rentiers' consumption is not closely tied to their receipts for the period.

To make our forthcoming basic models as simple as possible, let us assume that aggregate demand is made up of only two components: wages, which are entirely consumed (the propensity to consume out of wages is unity), and some autonomous expenditures, which can be said to cover investment expenditures and consumption out of profits. We are thus left with aggregate demand AD being equal to

$$AD = wL + A = wL + ap \tag{5.2}$$

where w is the nominal wage rate and L is the amount of employment while a represents the given amount of real autonomous expenditures, and hence $A = ap$ is nominal autonomous expenditures (Lavoie, 1986b; Dutt, 1987c).

The position taken at this stage is that investment in the short run is based on past historical considerations as well as on animal spirits, both of which cannot easily be modelled in a simple short-period model of effective demand (see Dutt (1991–92), Setterfield (1999) and Lainé (2017) however). Knowing in addition that the determinants of investment are a highly contentious subject, we shall take investment expenditure as an exogenous variable. It is also assumed that consumption out of profits depends on profits collected in a previous period and not on current profits. Thus we assume implicitly that the propensity to save out of wages s_w is zero, while the propensity to save out of current profits s_p is unity. This, as we shall see later, can be easily modified to include more realistic values of these propensities to save. But most of the results obtained here will hold as long as the propensity to save out of profits is larger than the propensity to save out of wages. We can be quite confident about this assumption because the discrepancy $(s_p - s_w)$ on average seems to be around 0.41 for OECD countries (Storm and Naastepad, 2012, p. 130); it is 0.43 for the eurozone, and in that range for all other countries of the G-20, except South Africa and Argentina where the difference is around 0.15 (Onaran and Galanis, 2012, p. 12).

When considering investment expenditures as autonomous, two possibilities may prevail. One is to suppose that investment expenditures are fixed in nominal terms. The other is to consider that investment expenditures are given in terms of increases in capacity, and hence that they are given in real terms. This is what Kalecki (1971) and Robinson (1962, p. 46) do, as well as several post-Keynesian authors of models of the type presented here (Harcourt, 1972, p. 211; Harris, 1974). Consequently, autonomous expenditures will be assumed to be given in real terms.

Equation (5.2) will be the driver of many important results of our post-Keynesian short-run models of employment, because aggregate demand will depend on income distribution variables; that is, it will depend on the distribution between wages and profits and hence on the value taken by the real wage. This is obviously true of the Kaleckian and Kaldorian strands, but even fundamentalist post-Keynesians can rely on statements from Keynes, according to whom the distribution of income has an impact on the average propensity to consume and effective demand (Keynes, 1973, xiv, p. 271). Post-Keynesian models of employment are thus a formalized version of underconsumptionist ideas that were familiar to several Institutionalists and to early socialist economists (see Bleaney, 1976). As pointed out in Chapter 1, a number of post-Keynesians believe that a key feature of post-Keynesian economics is the importance given to the role of income distribution, in particular when discussing issues tied to aggregate demand, and even more so when discussing the determinants of employment. We shall now see what mechanisms are at play, as examined recently by Fernández-Huerga (2019).

5.2 THE MARSHALLIAN POST-KEYNESIAN MODEL

I define as the Marshallian version of the post-Keynesian model a model that retains the properties of the standard production function of neoclassical analysis, most notably the assumption of diminishing returns. We shall consider two variants of this model: a flexible-price variant, which can be attributed to Keynes himself and to some of his most faithful followers, such as Paul Davidson (1998; 1999) or Victoria Chick (1983); and a fixed-price variant, which can be associated with the work of the so-called French disequilibrium school. In both variants, we will have to distinguish between the 'notional' demand for labour and the 'effective' demand for labour, along the lines first developed by Patinkin (1965, ch. 13) and then by Barro and Grossman (1971). The model presented here owes a great deal to Schefold (1983) and Fujimoto and Leslie (1983), and it relies on the formulation of Nell (1978), Lavoie (1986b; 2003b) and Dutt (1987c).

Since this Marshallian version incorporates diminishing returns, which we dismissed under normal circumstances in Chapter 3, this version can be valid only when modern firms operate beyond full capacity or as a model of things past. So why do we discuss it? The Marshallian model is presented here for three reasons: it illustrates what Keynes could have had in mind; it represents what a number of Fundamentalists have in mind; and it will help us understand in what ways the post-Keynesian model of employment, in both its variants, differs from the mainstream model.

5.2.1 The Notional and the Effective Labour Demand Curves

The production side of the model assumes a standard aggregate neoclassical production function, with a decreasing marginal product of labour and decreasing returns. Aggregate supply, in nominal terms, is thus simply given by

$$AS = pq^s = pq(L) \qquad (5.3)$$

where p is the price level, q^s is the real output being supplied, and L is labour. As usual, we suppose that the first derivative of this production function is positive, $q'(L) > 0$, and the second derivative negative, $q''(L) < 0$, which implies that the marginal product of labour is decreasing with respect to labour. It must be pointed out that for Keynes (1936, p. 42) decreasing returns arose for Ricardian reasons rather than for neoclassical ones: as employment increased, firms would be forced to hire second-rate, less trained and less productive workers, just as farmers would be forced to use less productive land as the market expanded. This being said, as is standard in neoclassical economics, let us assume that firms are attempting to maximize profits. Their constrained optimization problem, when faced with a nominal wage w, which is the cost of labour, is thus to choose the level of employment L that maximizes real profits P, such that

$$P = q(L) - (w/p)L \qquad (5.4)$$

Differentiating the above equation with respect to L and setting the result equal to zero yields the standard condition that says that the profit-maximizing employment level needs to be such that the marginal product of labour is equal to the real wage rate:

$$q'(L) = w/p \qquad (5.5)$$

from which follows the standard downward-sloping demand for labour curve. This, however, should be considered only as the 'notional' demand for labour, in the terminology of Barro and Grossman (1971), because this labour demand curve takes no account of effective demand. For a given real wage, the chosen level of employment maximizes only potential profits, that is, the profits that would be realized if everything produced were actually sold. To underline the notional aspect of this demand for labour, we may thus rewrite the previous condition as

$$(w/p)_{not} = q'(L) \qquad (5.6)$$

There is, however, another demand for labour, which will be called the 'effective' demand, which takes into account the fact that what is produced must be sold. This effective demand constraint is the equilibrium locus on the goods market, and is obtained by equating aggregate demand with aggregate supply, that is, equations (5.2) and (5.3):

$$wL + ap = pq(L) \tag{5.7}$$

Equation (5.7) highlights an interesting feature of the specification of aggregate demand that we have adopted in equation (5.2). In this vertically integrated economy, where the value of output can be reduced to wages and profits, realized profits, when the effective demand constraint is being fulfilled, can be quickly computed. Profits are the difference between the value of sales ($wL + ap$) and the wage costs (wL), that is ap, so that realized real profits are simply equal to real autonomous expenditures, a macroeconomic feature pointed out by Kalecki (1971, ch. 7) in 1942 and later reasserted by Kaldor (1956):

$$P = a \tag{5.8}$$

We will make further use of this relationship later. In the meantime, note that this equation provides some justification for assuming that investment is purely autonomous, as changes in the real wage will not modify real profits of firms as long as firms do not modify their real investment expenditures. Solving equation (5.7) for the real wage, we obtain the effective demand constraint, or the effective labour demand curve, that is, the locus of combinations between the real wage and the level of employment that ensure that whatever is being produced is sold (a sort of IS curve, since on this curve investment will equal saving):

$$(w/p)_{eff} = \frac{q(L)-a}{L} \tag{5.9}$$

The real wage rate that allows the goods market to be in equilibrium, for a given level of real autonomous expenditures and a given technology, is thus a function of the level of employment. Now, as shown by Schefold (1983) and Fujimoto and Leslie (1983), this non-linear function reaches its maximum when it equals the notional demand for labour function. In other words, the effective labour demand curve reaches its highest point when it is intersected by the notional labour demand curve. This can be seen by taking the first derivative of the effective demand for labour:

$$\frac{d\left(\frac{w}{p}\right)_{eff}}{dL} = \frac{q'(L)L - [q(L)-a]}{L^2} \tag{5.10}$$

and setting it to zero, which happens when

$$q'(L) = \frac{q(L)-a}{L} \tag{5.11}$$

The term on the left of the above equation is the notional labour demand; the term on the right is the effective labour demand – equation (5.9). It can be shown that the second derivative of the effective labour demand equation is negative when evaluated at its extremum, thus indicating that the extremum is a maximum. What this all means is that the effective demand curve reaches its maximum when it crosses the notional demand curve. Thus, at low levels of employment, an increase in employment and hence in output requires an increase in real wages for the additional supply of goods to be absorbed by aggregate demand. After a while, however, the impact of decreasing returns is such that the additional output is too small relative to the associated additional employment and wage payments, and as a consequence real wages must fall for aggregate supply and demand to equate each other on the goods market.

We are then able to draw the two labour demand curves, shown with thick lines in Figure 5.1. The plane can further be divided into three areas. Along the $L^D_{effective}$ curve, $AD = AS$; above the curve, there is excess demand on the goods market, $AD > AS$; and below the curve, there is excess supply, $AD < AS$. These inequalities are obvious. For instance, if, at the current level of employment L, the real wage on the effective demand constraint is just sufficient to equate demand to supply, an increase in the nominal wage w (an increase in the real wage) will increase aggregate demand without modifying aggregate supply. Thus, above the effective demand constraint there is excess demand on the goods market.

Looking at equation (5.9), we can also see that higher autonomous expenditures, for a given level of employment, imply a lower real wage if the effective demand constraint is to be fulfilled. This means that when there are higher autonomous expenditures, the effective labour demand curve shifts down. But we also know, from equation (5.8), that the concave effective labour demand curve describes an iso-profit curve, as pointed out by Dalziel and Lavoie (2003). On all points of the $L^D_{effective}$ curve, real profit is constant and equal to a. Thus, as the effective labour demand curve shifts down with larger expenditures, we also know that the new, lower, curve represents a higher level of real profits. But we already know this from the notional demand curve for labour that maximizes potential

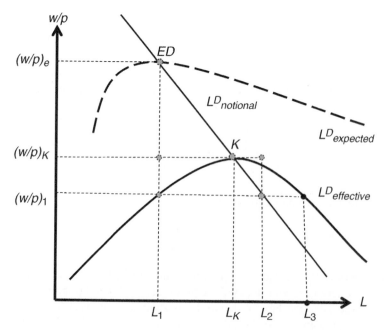

Figure 5.1 The notional and the effective labour demand curves, and the point of effective demand in the Marshallian post-Keynesian model of employment

profits. For a given real wage rate, say $(w/p)_K$, profit would be maximized at employment level L_K. Any other level of employment, at that real wage rate, say L_1 or L_2, would generate a lower profit level. And this is why the effective labour demand curve, which is also the iso-profit curve, reaches its maximum when it crosses the notional labour demand curve (Chick, 1983, p. 166). By contrast, to keep realized profits at a, while not producing at the profit-maximizing output, would require firms to lower real wages, say at $(w/p)_1$ with employment at L_1 or L_3.

The model, as constructed here, with its two distinct labour demand curves, is common to both variants of the Marshallian labour market model that we will now examine.

5.2.2 Keynes's Flexible Price Model

Keynes's flexible price model in a competitive goods market has been put forth by post-Keynesian authors such as Deprez (1996), Dutt (1987c) and Palley (1996a), and is in line with the interpretation of Allain et al. (2013). In these models of Keynes's effective demand model of *The General Theory*, firms are assumed to be atomistic: there is pure rather than perfect competition, in the sense that firms do not know the market price; they can have only expectations about it. These market prices are not known to entrepreneurs until the end of the market period, in contrast to what is assumed in the New Classical model, where only households ignore what realized prices will be. To make their employment decisions, firms must have expectations about the price level. It is assumed that nominal wages are set at the beginning of the market period, before entrepreneurs know the realized price level. We will see later why assuming a fixed wage has no detrimental effect on the generality of the model. In the meantime we can say that, on the basis of the expected real wage, firms make their employment decisions, in accordance with the notional demand curve (Dutt, 1987c, p. 276; Deprez, 1996, pp. 129–30).

The expected price and the chosen level of employment, given the wage level, embody all the information that corresponds to what Keynes (1936, p. 25) called 'the point of effective demand'. It is to be found at the intersection of the aggregate supply function and what Keynes called the aggregate demand function, which deals with the proceeds that the entrepreneurs expect to receive from the employment of L workers. This intersection, says Keynes, is where expectations of profits will be maximized. In Figure 5.1, the point of effective demand, in Keynes's initial terminology, is given by the point ED, at the intersection of the notional demand curve for labour and the expected effective demand constraint, here called $L^D_{expected}$ and shown as a dotted line. At a low expected price level, the expected real wage corresponding to these expectations about proceeds is high and equal to $(w/p)_e$, and hence aggregate employment is L_1, as given by the profit-maximizing decisions of firms.

With this combination, however, since the economy is above the effective demand constraint given by $L^D_{effective}$, there will be an excess demand for goods. Prices will rise until aggregate demand and supply are equated, that is, until the economy is back on the effective demand curve for labour. Market prices will thus be such that the realized real wage rate, compared with the expected real wage, has fallen to $(w/p)_1$ in Figure 5.1. Thus, as Davidson (1999, p. 584) and others have emphasized, in Keynes's model, Marshall's adjustment mechanisms have not been reversed. Prices react first, within the market period, and quantities will react later, in the next period (cf. Harcourt, 2001b, p. 118). In

Marshall's market period, which some authors call the ultra-short period (Skott, 1989a, p. 63), output and employment are fixed by definition, and the adjustment is made through prices, demand adjusting to the supply of goods.

Although the goods market clears, the situation as illustrated is inconsistent with short-period equilibrium, since price expectations are not fulfilled. Firms will thus revise their expectations. If, as Keynes (1936, p. 51) says, 'it is sensible for producers to base their expectations on the assumption that the most recently realised results will continue', expectations are adaptative, and the expected price will be the price realized in the previous period. Hence the newly expected real wage will be $(w/p)_1$, and reading off the notional labour demand curve, the new level of employment by firms will be L_2. At that combination, there is an excess supply of goods, and prices will fall somewhat, with the realized real wage rate standing somewhere between $(w/p)_1$ and $(w/p)_K$. There will thus be a succession of oscillations in employment, as mentioned by Keynes (1936, p. 49). Intuitively, we can see that point K will eventually be reached, where price expectations are achieved.

The short-period equilibrium is thus given by point K, where the notional and the effective labour demand curves intersect. Point K is what Davidson (1998, p. 822) calls the 'point of effective demand', which 'represents equilibrium in the product market where the expectations of sales by profit maximizing entrepreneurs are just being met by the spending decisions of buyers'. At point K, as Davidson says, there are no endogenous forces that would lead the entrepreneurs to alter their 'production, pricing and hiring decision', as long as the determinants of the notional and effective labour demand curves remain unchanged. If firms know how a demand-constrained economy works out, and if they have perfect knowledge of both the notional and effective labour demand curves, anticipations based on rational expectations should lead them right through point K.

Now, as is well known, Keynes felt that his presentation of *The General Theory* could have been much improved. On the matter of effective demand, Keynes (1973, xiv, p. 181) wrote:

> I now feel that if I were writing the book again I should begin by setting forth my theory on the assumption that short-period expectations were always fulfilled; and then have a subsequent chapter showing what differences it makes when short-period expectations are disappointed... For the theory of effective demand is substantially the same if we assume that short-period expectations are always fulfilled.

Thus Keynes was essentially saying that his theory would be much clearer if he were to cut through the ultra-short-period haggling, and assume right away that the economy is at point K, where the expected proceeds are the realized ones. In other words, the exposition of the principle of effective demand would be much simpler if point K were defined as the point of effective demand, as Davidson does, and if all disequilibrium ultra-short-period states were left aside, allowing us to concentrate on the changes of the short-period equilibrium induced by modifications in the determinants of the notional and effective demand for labour. This is what we shall do from now on.

It also appears that Keynes and Davidson are mainly right when they claim that the (realized) real wage does not determine the level of employment, but rather that the level of effective demand determines the real wage. Out of equilibrium, the expected real wage, via the expected price level, which is a function of the level of the expected aggregate demand, determines the level of employment, read off the notional demand curve for labour. This chosen level of employment then determines the realized real wage, given the realized aggregate demand. The realized real wage is thus endogenous. Similarly, in the equilibrium state, at the K equilibrium, the real wage rate is also endogenous and dependent on the effective demand constraint. The model is also consistent with Keynes's claim (1936, ch. 2) that firms are on their labour demand curve (the notional demand curve), thus fulfilling what he called the first postulate of (neo)classical economics.

In this model, the oft-made claim that there is unemployment because real wages are too high is thus erroneous. Entrepreneurs have no incentives and no means to lower real wages, given the existing effective demand conditions, since real wages are determined by the (newly defined) point of effective demand. It follows that real wages can fall and full employment L_{fe} can be restored only if effective demand increases; that is, if the effective labour demand curve shifts down, intersecting the notional demand curve at point W. This is shown in Figure 5.2, under the simplifying assumption of a vertical labour supply curve L^S. Point W is the Walrasian equilibrium, with both the goods and the labour markets clearing. In the present simplified model, the downward shift of the effective demand curve can occur only if real autonomous expenditures a increase, as is obvious when taking the derivative of equation (5.9) with respect to a.

Two well-known automatic mechanisms have been contemplated in the mainstream literature to restore full employment, both related to falling nominal wages, accompanied by falling prices, and which are at the heart of the assumed downward-sloping aggregate demand curve in the AD/AS model in the price and output space. The first mechanism is

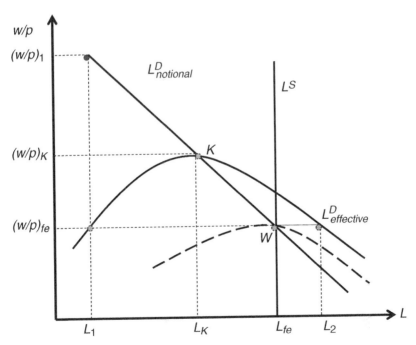

Figure 5.2 *Achieving full employment in the Marshallian post-Keynesian model, in its fixed-price and flexible-price variants*

the Keynes effect, whereby the fall in prices will diminish the demand for money needed for transaction purposes, leading to a fall in interest rates and hence an increase in the investment part of our parameter a. The second mechanism is the Pigou effect, whereby the fall in prices will lead to an increase in real money balances and hence to an increase in the autonomous consumption part of parameter a. Post-Keynesians believe that neither automatic mechanism is credible, first, because money and credit are endogenous variables, so that there is no exogenous stock of money out there, and second, because falling prices generate debt deflation, bankruptcies and adverse expectations – as argued in great detail by Keynes (1936, ch. 19) and Kalecki (1944), and later by Minsky (1975) and Tobin (1980), and as recollected in Lavoie (2010a) – so that lower prices will not increase real autonomous demand. Indeed, Fazzari et al. (1998, p. 551) 'find no empirical basis for the nearly universal assumption that lower prices stimulate spending'. Furthermore, the experience of the Japanese economy since the early 1990s has reasserted the dangers of debt deflation, often associated with balance-sheet depression (Koo, 2009), and it was clear during the subprime financial crisis that central bankers were quite fearful of price deflation, doing all they could to avoid its appearance.

In fact, if any mechanism exists, it is a conscious one, based on the reaction function of the central bank, which reduces interest rates when economic activity and inflation or prices are falling, in the hope of boosting aggregate demand. But this mechanism is also dubious. We are back to Keynes's position: the a parameter can be increased, and full employment can be restored, only by government taking the discretionary decision to increase its autonomous expenditures and create a fiscal deficit.

Still, due to the standard assumption of diminishing returns made about the production function, full employment must be accompanied by a lower real wage – here in Figure 5.2, at the level $(w/p)_{fe}$. In this model, there is a negative correlation between real wages and the level of employment, when considering the various K equilibria corresponding to different determinants of aggregate demand, although one cannot say that high real wages have caused low levels of employment.

5.2.3 The Marshallian Model with Fixed Prices

In our description of Keynes's model, it was assumed that any discrepancy between aggregate demand and aggregate supply would be quickly made good by a variation in prices. In a world of imperfect competition, and also in most markets of today, prices are set in advance, and hence they do not adjust immediately to possible discrepancies between supply and demand. Most of the adjustment is then accomplished by changes in inventories and in flow production. This is precisely what is being assumed in the next variant of the Marshallian model, where it is supposed that wages and prices are fixed, at least in the short period. The model is based on the equations presented above, and on the arguments offered by the economists of the so-called French disequilibrium approach, as can be found in the writings of Bénassy (1975) and Malinvaud (1977). In their models, adjustments are made through quantities, rather than prices. And as long as firms are able to sell whatever they produce, firms are on their notional labour demand curve.

These economists consider that there are two kinds of unemployment: classical unemployment and Keynesian unemployment. Classical unemployment occurs when real wages are too high. This would be the case in Figure 5.2, if the real wage set by the decisions of firms were anywhere above $(w/p)_K$. Being above the effective demand constraint, there is excess demand on the goods market, and since prices are not flexible, inventories get depleted: this is the case of so-called repressed inflation. There is classical unemployment because a fall in real wages, say from $(w/p)_1$ to $(w/p)_K$, would allow employment to increase from L_1 to L_K as firms move down their notional labour demand curve.

Note that, as Kahn (1977) was quick to point out, the relevance of this sort of classical unemployment appears unlikely. If there is excess demand on the goods market and excess supply in the labour market, one would think that, eventually, prices would rise while nominal wages would drop (or rise more slowly than prices), thus gradually leading the economy to point K. In other words, classical unemployment here is an unstable situation, although one could also argue that it may take a long time to move back to the effective labour demand curve if there is real wage resistance.

Increases in real wages in this model may also allow for increases in employment, however. This is the so-called case of Keynesian unemployment. Suppose that real wages are set below $(w/p)_K$, say at level $(w/p)_{fe}$ in Figure 5.2. Following profit-maximizing behaviour, firms would initially choose the level of employment L_{fe}. At this combination of real wages and employment, the goods market is not in equilibrium, since the economy is not on the $L^D_{effective}$ curve. Two different levels of employment, at the real wage $(w/p)_{fe}$, could clear the goods markets: these are L_1 and L_2. But below the effective labour demand curve, goods are in excess supply. Oligopolistic firms in a fixed-price world will thus reduce production, at a constant real wage, until aggregate demand and supply are equated, that is, until the economy moves back horizontally to the effective labour demand curve, and hence until employment is down to L_1. In this case, because of fixed prices, firms cannot be on their profit-maximizing notional labour demand curve. For any real wage below $(w/p)_K$, the effective labour demand curve is the relevant constraint, and any increase in real wages will generate an increase in employment, as firms respond to the new aggregate demand conditions by moving up, along their effective labour demand curve.

Still, ultimately, to wipe out all unemployment, real wages have to decrease (unless it is assumed that the labour supply curve cuts the effective labour demand curve to the left of the K equilibrium point). As in the previous model, an increase in autonomous demand a, such as an increase in government expenditures, will be required, and this will have to be accompanied by a fall in real wages, from $(w/p)_K$ to $(w/p)_{fe}$. Thus, in this model, as in Keynes's model, getting rid of all unemployment requires lower real wages.

5.2.4 Alternative Means to Present the Principle of Effective Demand

The non-linear shape of the effective labour demand curve is surprising at first sight, and not very intuitive. One purpose of the present section is to consider alternative presentations of the principle of effective demand that may be either more intuitive or more familiar to students of economics.

Let us first consider the graphs proposed by Nell (1978; 1988) over the last 40 years. Nell's intention is mainly to present what he considers to be the model relevant to contemporary economies, one devoid of decreasing returns, but he also considers the case of the so-called 'craft' economies, where diminishing returns are still present. Nell's graphs can easily be linked to Figures 5.1 and 5.2, and they will provide an intuitive understanding of the bell-shaped curve of the effective labour demand curve. Nell's graphs are normally in the employment/proceeds space, but things can be even clearer if proceeds and wage payments are deflated by the price level, thus considering real output and real wages.

Nell's presentation, as related to the notional and effective labour demand curves suggested in the preceding sections, can be found in Figure 5.3. The bottom part of the graph represents a standard neoclassical production function, with output q being a function of employment L, under the assumption of decreasing returns. Wage costs $(w/p)L$, in real terms, are shown by a straight line arising from the origin, assuming away overhead labour and under the assumption that all workers are paid the same real wage, whatever the production level. These real labour costs also represent the first component of aggregate demand, since, in line with our initial aggregate demand formulation, it is assumed that all wages are consumed. Total aggregate demand in real terms is thus given by an RAD curve, which includes both real consumption out of wages and real autonomous expenditures:

$$q^d = (w/p)L + a \qquad (5.12)$$

It is clear from the top part of Figure 5.3 that, when the real wage is $(w/p)_0$, firms would like to hire the amount L_3 of workers, because this is where they could maximize their potential profits (in real terms). This is where the distance between real output and real

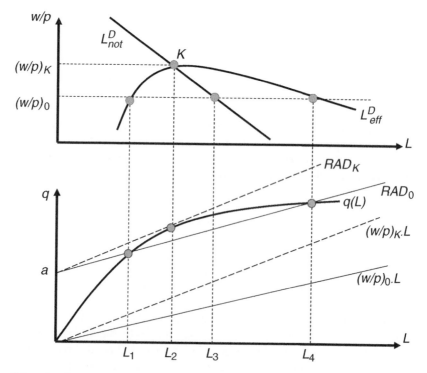

Figure 5.3 Combining the Marshallian model with Nell's alternative presentation of the relationship between real wages and employment

wage costs is the greatest, as illustrated in the bottom part of Figure 5.3. However, at that real wage rate, the potential profits at an employment level L_3 would not be realized, given the existing autonomous component of aggregate demand. It is clear that, at the going wage $(w/p)_0$, there are two short-period-equilibrium levels of employment at which real aggregate demand RAD_0 equals real aggregate supply: L_1 and L_4. These equilibria correspond to the fixed-price model described in the previous section. Only the L_1 employment level, however, would be stable, since at L_3, as is obvious from the bottom part of the graph, supply exceeds demand, so that firms would tend to reduce output and employment until L_1 is reached (Nell, 1978, p. 23).

On the other hand, the Keynes equilibrium, given by point K in the top part of the graph, would correspond to a real wage equal to $(w/p)_K$. At that real wage, real aggregate demand RAD_K in the bottom part of the graph would be tangent to the production function, and hence there would be just one equilibrium level of employment, where aggregate supply is equal to aggregate demand. At that level of employment L_2, potential profits are maximized and they are also realized, as Keynes would have them.

I would also like to consider the case where the value of real wages has no impact on the level of effective demand. This is implicitly the stance taken by Davidson (1998; 1999) in his graphs of effective demand: the employment level, constrained by the effective demand for labour, is a vertical line and hence is impervious to the realized real wage rate. It is also the implicit assumption of those post-Keynesians who claim that the aggregate demand curve 'should be considered vertical in the price-output space' (Moore, 1988, p. 384; cf. King, 2001, p. 70). In several Keynesian or post-Keynesian models, we thus have an aggregate demand function that does not depend on the level of the real wage. For instance, we could have

$$AD = (1 - s_y)Y + ap \qquad (5.13)$$

Here aggregate demand depends on real autonomous expenditures and on the propensity to consume out of aggregate income. There is no distinction between wage and profit income: it is assumed that the propensity to save s_y out of both sorts of income is identical. In this case, the equilibrium level of output, which equates the aggregate supply and demand on the goods market, is $q_{eff} = a/s_y$, and hence there is a unique level of employment corresponding to the effective labour demand curve, given by $L^D_{effective} = q^{-1}(a/s_y)$. Under these conditions, it is possible to represent the effective demand for labour as a vertical line in the employment and real wage space, as shown in Figure 5.4. I would argue that this is not an adequate representation of Keynes's view since Keynes (1936, pp. 91, 373) contended that income distribution is an important determinant of the average propensity to consume.

In the case of Figure 5.4 it is easier to make the claim that real wages do not determine the level of employment, since the latter is determined independently of the level of real wages. The actual real wage is clearly endogenous, resulting from the application, at the level of employment determined by the effective demand for labour, of the profit-maximizing constraint given by the notional demand curve for labour. One can also see why some heterodox economists are determined to forego terms such as 'demand for labour'. Davidson (1983) has an article whose title is precisely 'The marginal product curve is not the demand curve for labor'. He further insists that 'neither a marginal

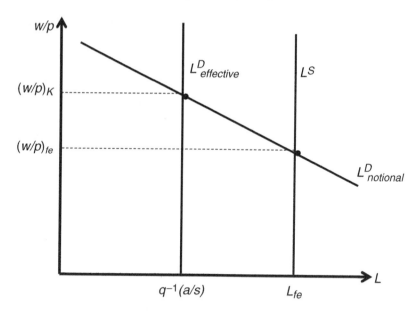

Figure 5.4   Davidson's oversimplified case: the effective demand for labour is impervious to changes in income distribution

productivity for labor function ... nor any other productivity based labor-demand analysis can provide an *aggregate demand for labor*' (Davidson, 1999, p. 581). These strong statements are based on the simplified characterization of Figure 5.4, where the notional demand for labour plays no role whatsoever in the determination of the level of employment. But, as we have seen in the previous sections, this recursivity is only a special case. In general, at least in Keynes's model with flexible prices, the notional and the effective demand curves for labour determine simultaneously the level of employment and the real wage rate. However, with a vertical effective labour demand curve, and assuming that firms are always at the point of effective demand (the K point), it is easier to understand Davidson's claim (1972, p. 124) that in Keynes's model 'short-run adjustments to disequilibrium occur primarily via changes in output and employment'. As we shall see, in the Kaleckian model, adjustments also occur through quantities.

5.3   THE KALECKIAN VERSION OF THE POST-KEYNESIAN MODEL

The hybrid model described in the previous sections, with an effective demand constraint associated with a neoclassical production function and market-clearing through changes in prices, is not necessarily a realistic one. Thus, for Nell (1998), this hybrid model applies only to a world of 'craft' technologies, which operated in the past and which might be said still to operate in a small subset of industries. 'Transformational growth' has led modern economies on the path to 'mass production' technology – manufacturing, the service sector and the so-called new economy of the Internet – based on constant or increasing returns, where prices are not market-clearing, and which has given rise to the Kaleckian branch of post-Keynesian economics. It is this Kaleckian version of the labour market that we now investigate.

5.3.1 Simple Analytics of the Kaleckian Model

The utilization function

As pointed out earlier, the structures of the Marshallian and Kaleckian versions of the post-Keynesian labour model are identical. The only difference is their production function. Kaleckians reject the assumption of diminishing returns and assume constant marginal costs (up to full capacity), as discussed in Chapter 3. Technical conditions, job definitions and management constraints are such that technical coefficients of production can be assumed to be fixed. Labour cannot be substituted for capital and vice versa. Still, it is possible to modify the rate of employment in the short run, despite no possibilities of substitution because various segments of plants can be closed down or opened up. With a given stock of capital, more labour can be employed because a larger portion of the machinery is utilized. While there is no production function in the neoclassical sense, there is in post-Keynesian theory a 'utilization function' relating output to employment, as suggested by Robinson (1964, p. 25), whereby a higher rate of utilization of capacity is associated with higher employment (Nell, 1978, p. 7).

Following Kalecki (1971, p. 44), Kaleckians divide labour into direct and indirect labour. Direct labour is proportional to production whereas indirect labour is proportional to productive capacity. One advantage of making this distinction is that Okun's law arises as a natural outcome. Another advantage is that the macroeconomic consequences of the currently observed shift in wage distribution between non-supervisory and managerial labour can be analysed under different pricing procedures. We shall make use of these distinctions later in the chapter and in Chapter 6. In the present section, however, we shall omit the distinction and assume only the presence of direct labour, as this will simplify the analysis without losing the main message of the Kaleckian model of employment. This simplified Kaleckian aggregate supply function can thus be written in line with our new utilization function, thus having

$$AS = pq^s = pLy \qquad (5.14)$$

where y is output per worker or labour productivity (as defined in Chapter 1), which is assumed constant (also $y = 1/n$, where n was defined in Chapter 3).

Once again, we assess the effective demand constraint, that is, the equilibrium locus on the goods market, by equating aggregate supply (equation 5.14) with aggregate demand (equation 5.2):

$$wL + ap = pLy$$

and thus, solving for the real wage rate, we obtain

$$(w/p)_{eff} = y - \frac{a}{L} \qquad (5.15)$$

This equation is the effective labour demand curve. It represents all the combinations of employment levels and real wage rates such that the goods market is in equilibrium. This equation is illustrated by Figure 5.5. Note, in contrast to what occurred in the case of the Marshallian variant, that the Kaleckian labour demand curve is always upward-sloping, up to its asymptote given by y. So, as long as firms operate below full capacity, the effective labour demand curve does not have a downward segment; it is only upward-sloping.

Now what about the notional labour demand curve, dear to neoclassical economists? The notional demand for labour vanishes. Provided we accept the empirical evidence about constant or decreasing direct costs, with falling unit costs if overhead costs are taken into consideration, at any given price firms will not self-impose restrictions on the amounts that they produce. As more is produced and sold, the realized profit per unit does not fall, and overall profits made by the firm will rise. There is no longer any profit-maximizing constraint that limits production and employment. The crucial constraint is given by sales: it is an effective demand constraint. Thus, even if unit costs are rising, say because the labour wage rate has risen, the firm is still compelled to produce as much as it can sell at a given price. The crucial constraint is demand, or the lack thereof. In general, higher real wages will not necessarily entail a reduction in production and employment, unless the real wage is so high that it is no longer profitable to produce; that is, unless the real wage is higher than labour productivity.

In other words, for every real wage–employment combination on this effective labour demand curve, all produced goods are sold at the price set by firms, as shown in Figure 5.5. The area below the curve represents a situation of aggregate excess supply in the goods market, while the area above the curve depicts a situation where aggregate demand is greater than aggregate supply (investment exceeds saving). As long as firms react to a

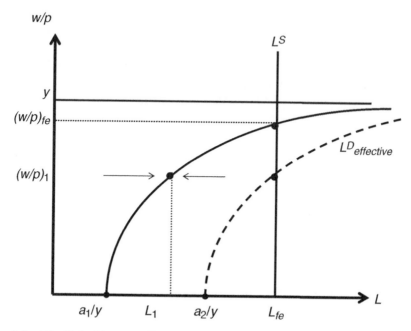

Figure 5.5 The Kaleckian post-Keynesian model of employment

situation of excess supply (demand) on the goods market by reducing (increasing) production, rather than changing the mark-up and hence prices, the economy will move horizontally towards the locus of equilibria, that is, towards the effective labour demand curve. In other words, the model exhibits stability under these conditions. Henceforth we will presume, when doing comparative analysis, that the period under consideration is long enough for firms to adjust their production to actual demand, and hence that the economy always operates on the effective labour demand curve. Note that Figure 5.5 is the inversed graphical representation of the Kaleckian model that Robinson and Harcourt showed to generations of students at Cambridge, who saw instead the price to wage ratio (rather than the wage to price ratio) on the vertical axis (Harcourt, 2006, pp. 11–12).

The model in the ultra-short period

More formally, the move towards equality between production and sales can be seen in the following way. Assume some lag between the production decisions of firms and the corresponding sales. In a given period, output supply is given at $\bar{q}^s$ with a level of employment equal to $\bar{L} = \bar{q}^s/y$. Real aggregate demand, arising from equation (5.12), can thus be written in this particular case as

$$q^d = \left(\frac{w}{p}\right)\bar{L} + a = \left(\frac{w/p}{y}\right)\bar{q}^s + a \qquad (5.16)$$

Real aggregate demand is a positive function of real wages and of the given level of output supply. This is illustrated by the q^d line in Figure 5.6. With a higher real wage rate relative to labour productivity, the q^d line would be steeper; and with higher real autonomous expenditures, the intercept with the vertical axis would be higher. Here, the fixed level of output (in the ultra-short period) is q_0. At the current real wage relative to productivity, realized aggregate demand within this ultra-short period is q_0^d, so that the economy is in a situation of excess supply on the goods market: sales are inferior to production, and firms in the aggregate are accumulating unsold goods. For given values of the real wage, productivity and real autonomous expenditures, the short-run equilibrium level of output is q^* in Figure 5.6, which will eventually be attained if firms reduce their output and employment. If they do so, aggregate demand and aggregate supply will equate each other, equation (5.15) will be fulfilled, and the economy will end up on its effective labour demand curve in Figure 5.5. Ideally, a formal model would take into account changes in inventories, in which case the level of output would depend on expected sales plus the desired change in the stock of inventories, but we will avoid this complication although a small number of authors deal with inventories (Duménil and Lévy, 1993; Godley and Lavoie, 2007a).

It should be noted that not all post-Keynesians have adopted this view. Just as we had a fixed-price and a flexible-price version of the Marshallian model, we could have a Kaleckian model with flexible prices, where output and employment are assumed to be given, and where prices adjust to equate demand to the fixed supply. As Narciso Tuñez-Area (2006) points out, this is precisely what Minsky (1986a) does when he defines consumer prices, and it is also a possibility suggested by Seccareccia (1984) and Graziani (2003). In this case, the economy will move vertically towards the locus of equilibria in Figure 5.5. But we shall not discuss this case any further.

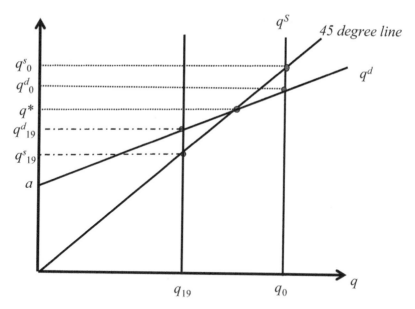

Figure 5.6 Effective demand in a Kaleckian model where output is given in the short period

Figure 5.6 can also illustrate what happened during the first few months of the COVID-19 pandemic. Assuming that just before the outbreak the economy was at its equilibrium output q^*, the lockdown of the economy brought production down to q_{19}^s. Normally, the level of demand should have been q_{19}^d, but because most stores were closed, there was forced saving, roughly equivalent to the difference $q_{19}^d - q_{19}^s$. Mehlum and Torvik (2021) provide an even better illustration of the consequences on aggregate demand of this supply shock, based on a simple two-sector Keynesian model. The unavailability of goods or services in the first sector, due to the lockdown, generates forced saving à la Kornai and a reduction in the income of agents of this sector. This induces a reduction in the demand for the goods of the other sector, which itself induces in turn a negative feedback effect on the demand for firms that still operate in the first sector. Charles et al. (2021) also provide a graphic illustration of the impact of the COVID-19 lockdown.

Employment as a positive function of the real wage
Assuming an adjustment through quantities, the consequences of this Kaleckian model of employment are pretty straightforward. For a given real autonomous component of aggregate demand, and for a given labour productivity, higher real wages will generate more employment. Higher real wages translate into an upward movement along the effective labour demand curve. For instance, if in Figure 5.5 real wages move from $(w/p)_1$ up to $(w/p)_{fe}$, employment will rise from L_1 to L_{fe}. This is true as long as firms operate below full capacity and as long as real wages do not exceed labour productivity. The Kaleckian model thus offers a complete reversal of the neoclassical theory of employment and of some of the claims made by advocates of TINA (There Is No Alternative). An objection to the positive relationship between real wages and employment could be that firms may

decide to restrain their investment expenditures if their profit margins are reduced by the higher real wages, thus leading to a reduction of the assumed autonomous term *a* defining aggregate demand. This is certainly a possibility and it will be discussed in detail in Chapter 6.

Otherwise, the effective labour demand curve reproduces standard Keynesian results. As one would expect, any increase in real autonomous expenditures will have a positive impact on employment, as can be asserted by inverting equation (5.15) and writing it as an employment function:

$$L^D_{eff} = \frac{a}{y - \left(\frac{w}{p}\right)} \qquad (5.17)$$

Indeed, the value of the employment multiplier depends inversely on the difference between labour productivity and the real wage rate; that is, it depends on income distribution between wages and profits. The impact of increasing autonomous expenditures is shown in Figure 5.5: when these are increased from a_1 to a_2, the effective labour demand curve shifts towards the right, and at a given real wage $(w/p)_1$, employment rises from L_1 to L_{fe}. But, as pointed out by Nell (1978), whereas the value of the multiplier depends on some psychological propensity to save, here the multiplier depends only on income distribution.

The employment equation (5.17) can be rewritten in a form that is closer to the standard Cambridge equation endorsed by post-Keynesian authors such as Kaldor and Robinson in the mid-1950s. Assume for simplification a closed economy without government. Assume further that real investment, noted *I*, is the only autonomous expenditure, and that wage-earners consume all their income while profit-earners save a proportion s_p of their income, given by $pq - wL$. The aggregate demand curve now takes the form

$$AD = wL + (1 - s_p)(pq - wL) + pI \qquad (5.18)$$

Things could be made slightly more complicated by introducing saving out of wages, as does Andini (2009), but we will stick to equation (5.18). Combining this equation with the Kaleckian utilization function (equation 5.14), and setting $AS = AD$, the equilibrium level of output is

$$q = \frac{Iy}{s_p\left(y - \frac{w}{p}\right)} \qquad (5.19)$$

from which we can derive the effective demand for labour:

$$L^D_{eff} = \frac{I}{s_p\left(y - \frac{w}{p}\right)} \qquad (5.20)$$

The output multiplier can be easily derived from equation (5.19). The employment multiplier is now slightly more complex, as it depends on income distribution, proxied by the difference between the productivity of workers and their real wage rate, as well as on the propensity to save out of profits. An increase in this propensity to save will lead to a reduction in output and employment – a variant of Keynes's paradox of thrift mentioned in Chapter 1.

Minimum wage and heterogeneity of unit costs
The Kaleckian model shown here provides a possible explanation of why increases in the minimum wage show no negative effect on employment according to meta-regression studies, as we saw in Chapter 1. Schütz (2021) provides a variety of explanations, based on different schools of thought, using for each a diagram with causal mapping. Kaufman (2020) recalls that scholars in industrial relations, such as Richard Lester, already took a position similar to that of post-Keynesians, arguing in the 1940s about the positive effects of higher wages on aggregate demand that would compensate for the possible negative effects of higher unit costs. Kaufman (2020, p. 1020) mentions however that the 'largest source of negative minimum wage employment effect, is in the bottom-end competitive fringe of firms/facilities – nearest the short run shut-down point.... Some of these employers are forced out of business by the minimum wage increase and their employment drops to zero'. There is thus an additional issue when there is heterogeneity in the unit costs of firms. Steindl (1952, pp. 40–45) refers to the same phenomenon, but looking at it from the opposite angle. He mentions that progressive firms will manage to decrease their unit costs by implementing the use of a more efficient technology, and will thus impose lower prices to the industry, forcing out of business the highest-cost producers.

On account of this effect, within our Kaleckian model of the labour market, could it be that an increase in real wages would not lead to an increase in employment? Allain (2021a) has recently tackled this question. We mentioned earlier that the model was valid as long as firms operate below full capacity and provided the real wage remains below labour productivity. With heterogeneous firms, an increase in nominal wages may bring the real wage to a level which is higher than the labour productivity of the least efficient firms. These firms will then have to close down. As long as their market share is taken over by the more progressive firms, the positive effect of higher real wages will be sustained. Allain (2021a, p. 561) notes however that there is a limit to this, when the number of high-cost firms going under is so large that the progressive firms taking their place reach full capacity and can't replace exiting firms: 'the whole economy faces a supply constraint: profitable firms are at full capacity while there is an excess in aggregate demand'. One is tempted to ascertain that while such a situation could occur in a single industry, it is unlikely to happen for the whole economy.

5.3.2 Technological Unemployment

In this section we show that resolving the problem of technological unemployment may not be as easy as it seems. We start again from the effective labour demand curve, as represented by equation (5.17). As illustrated with the help of Figure 5.7, an increase in labour productivity from y_1 to y_2, accompanied by an unchanged real wage set at $(w/p)_{fe}$, will lead to a reduction in output and employment, here from L_{fe} to L_2, as the effective labour demand curve is shifted up by the increase in productivity. It is intuitive that, with improved labour productivity, the same amount of goods can be produced with a smaller

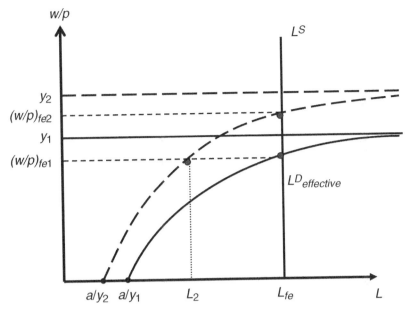

Figure 5.7 Effect of an improvement in labour productivity on employment in the Kaleckian model

labour force. But the ensuing decrease in aggregate demand becomes an additional source for the reduced demand for labour. The fall in aggregate demand arises from the change in income distribution that makes workers relatively worse off; since their propensity to consume is higher than that of profit recipients, aggregate demand falls. The negative effect on employment is compounded because, as a consequence of technical progress, a given amount of output can now be produced with fewer workers. Technological unemployment is thus a possibility that cannot be denied in a post-Keynesian model.

Thus, all else constant, whenever there is an increase in productivity, there must be some increase in real wages to keep employment from falling. Looking at the employment equations (5.17) and (5.20), it is obvious that, to maintain current employment levels, the difference between productivity per worker and real wages must be kept constant. Indeed, even when the real wage to productivity ratio remains constant, meaning that real wages and productivity per worker increase at the same rate and hence that costing margins and the profit share remain constant, which we can consider the most likely scenario, we will still need an increase in real autonomous expenditures to keep employment at a constant level and avoid technological unemployment in a stationary economy. As pointed out by Nell (1988, p. 124), 'in the short run increasing real wages in step with productivity will reduce employment'.

This can be confirmed by assuming that prices are set on the basis of a simple mark-up θ on unit labour costs, given by w/y, as we assumed in equation (3.26). In this case, prices are equal to

$$p = (1 + \theta) w/y \qquad (5.21)$$

Hence real wages depend on this mark-up, and are set as

$$w/p = y/(1 + \theta) \qquad (5.22)$$

Combining equations (5.20) and (5.22) to obtain equation (5.23) below, we get an alternative specification of the effective labour demand function, where it is clear that higher labour productivity will have a detrimental effect on employment, even if real wages increase in step with productivity as firms keep the percentage costing margins constant. There is thus some similarity with Ricardo's revision of his views 'on machinery' and the impact of technical progress in the third edition of his 1817 book: Ricardo (1951) thought that, despite the rise in their real wages, the working class as a whole would be worse off because of a fall in the demand for labour.

$$L_{\mathit{eff}}^{D} = \frac{I(1+\theta)}{s_p y \theta} \qquad (5.23)$$

In the build-up to the subprime financial crisis, it is a well-investigated fact that the share of profits in national income (here $\pi = \theta/(1 + \theta)$) kept rising, thus requiring compensating changes in other components of aggregate demand to keep employment up. As is well known, compensating changes were observed in the propensities to save (here s_p), thanks in part to the growing indebtedness of households made possible by easier access to bank credit.

5.3.3 Work-sharing

The high levels of unemployment, especially in Europe, have induced many left-of-centre and social economists to propose some innovative policies aimed at reducing unemployment. One such policy is work-sharing, whereby workers reduce their hours of work with the objective of increasing overall employment – a policy incidentally considered by Keynes (1936, p. 326) with little enthusiasm. Ecological economists who wish to see reduced growth rates of economic activity, zero-growth policies or even de-growth have also proposed work-sharing as a way to contain the likely increases in rates of unemployment that would arise as a result of the economic slowdown.

Work-sharing rests on the hypothesis that firms require a certain number of work-hours in order to meet their production goals. It presumes that if workers reduce the length of their work-day or work-week, firms will have no choice but to hire additional workers. Yet work-sharing has important consequences for the hourly productivity of workers, besides its impact on employment and on weekly or monthly wage income. Many firms claim that the adoption of a four-day work-week, as an alternative to a five-day week, has led to an increase in hourly productivity. In the best of circumstances, workers are able to achieve in four days what they would otherwise do in five days.

If this is indeed so, and assuming further that workers have accepted a 20 per cent reduction in their weekly or monthly pay, since they have reduced their work-week by one day, it implies that unit labour costs are being reduced by 20 per cent while hourly productivity is rising by a similar percentage. A work-sharing programme is also likely to lead to similar effects: the reduction in the number of working hours per week may also lead to increases in productivity rates. But, as we have seen in the previous subsection,

Effective demand and employment

any increase in productivity is bound to have negative effects on employment unless it is compensated by an increase in real wages. In the extreme case of the four-day week considered above, where workers do in four days what they used to do in five, there would be no effect whatsoever on the number of employed workers, if effective demand remained the same. But effective demand will fall, since hourly productivity rises while the hourly real wage does not.

Work-sharing, or the four-day work-week, can have favourable effects on employment only if hourly wages w/p are increased, at least in proportion with productivity gains. Otherwise, if such policies are accompanied by a reduction in weekly or monthly wages, because workers are working fewer hours at the same pay rate, then they will have no beneficial effect on the demand for labour.

To be successful, a work-sharing policy must therefore be accompanied by an increase in hourly real wages, so that the annual purchasing power of each worker is maintained, thus also sustaining aggregate demand. Otherwise, the increase in hourly productivity likely to arise from such programmes will lead to a decrease in effective labour demand. The best way to achieve this increase in the hourly wage is to preserve the existing weekly (or monthly) wage, despite the reduction in the official number of hours on the job. Post-Keynesians endorse work-sharing programmes and their reduced work-week only when they are accompanied by an increase in the hourly real wage; that is, when the weekly wage is kept constant despite the reduction in the work-week.

In our previous equations, since all variables were implicity expressed as flows per year (e.g. output per year), y stood for the output per worker per year, that is annual labour productivity, while w/p stood for the annual real wage income of a worker. Since we now consider changes in the number of hours of work per week or per year, we must redefine these two variables to take into account changes in the length of the work-week. Let us then define: $y = y_h h$ and $\omega_h = (w/p)/h$, where h is the average annual number of hours worked per worker, y_h is hourly labour productivity and ω_h is the hourly real wage. The effective labour demand equation, given by equation (5.17), can now be written as

$$L^D_{eff} = \frac{a}{(y_h - \omega_h)h} \tag{5.24}$$

Let us consider two extreme cases. If there is a reduction in the work-week, that is a reduction in the annual number of hours worked per worker, h, with no change in both hourly productivity y_h and the hourly real wage ω_h, this will obviously lead to an increase in the overall level of employment L, and such a work-sharing programme will succeed in achieving its intended results.

Suppose, however, as another extreme case, as was our four-day-week example, that the reduction in the length of the working week is entirely compensated by an increase in hourly productivity, so that there is no change in annual productivity y. Also, suppose, as we did with that example, that the hourly real wage ω_h is kept constant. This implies that the annual wage income of each worker, $(w/p) = \omega_h h$, is now lower than before (h, the average number of annual hours of work, used to be, say, 2000 hours, at 40 hours per week for 50 weeks, whereas with the new four-day week it is 1600 hours, at 32 hours per week for 50 weeks). If the annual wage income of each worker had been kept at its initial level, employment would have neither increased nor decreased.

Let us now consider what could be the general case. When entrepreneurs keep their costing margins θ constant despite productivity increases; that is, when hourly real wages increase in proportion to the hourly productivity gains, the effective labour demand equation (5.23) becomes

$$L_{eff}^{D} = \frac{I(1+\theta)}{s_p h y_h \theta} \tag{5.25}$$

What equation (5.25) shows is that employment increases whenever annual productivity (hy_h) decreases, that is, whenever workers cannot accomplish in the shortened work-week all the work they used to do with longer hours. The positive effects of work-sharing thus require that firms do not use it as a pretext to increase their costing margins. Firms need to adjust hourly real wages in line with the gains in hourly productivity. From the standpoint of environmentalists, this is an interesting solution, since output will remain constant despite the increases in productivity and employment. Under the conditions that led to equation (5.25), the rate of output fulfilling the effective demand constraint will simply be

$$q = I(1+\theta)/s_p\theta \tag{5.26}$$

5.3.4 Aggregate Demand and Aggregate Supply

One may wonder how different the short-run macroeconomic Kaleckian model is from the standard aggregate demand and supply framework, which is usually set in the price and output space. This can be assessed by rewriting the effective demand constraint as assessed by equation (5.17) and making use of the definition of labour productivity, $y = q/L$, and now solving in terms of the price variable. We obtain

$$p = \frac{wq}{y(q-a)} \tag{5.27}$$

This equation represents what is usually called the aggregate demand curve, with the price variable on the vertical axis, and the quantity variable on the horizontal axis. As one could have guessed from the previous analysis, this curve is downward-sloping, because a decrease in prices, *ceteris paribus*, is associated with a higher real wage rate, and hence with higher output and employment levels. Taking the derivative of equation (5.27), this is indeed what we get:

$$\frac{dp}{dq} = \frac{-wa}{(q-a)^2} \tag{5.28}$$

The aggregate demand curve in a Kaleckian model thus has the same downward slope as the mainstream aggregate demand curve. The mechanism explaining this negative slope is, however, quite different. Here it is due to the increased consumption demand generated by increases in real wages. In the mainstream model, these income distribution effects are not taken into consideration. As mentioned earlier, the mainstream downward slope is attributed to the Keynes effect or the Pigou effect; that is, it is due to the presumed exogeneity of some money or wealth aggregate. In models related to the New Consensus, it is attributed to the reaction function of the central bank, which raises interest rates when prices are higher. More specifically, in the inflation and output space privileged by some New Keynesian authors, the downward slope of the aggregate demand curve is caused by the actions of the central bank, which raises real interest rates when inflation rates are higher, thus reducing output.

The Kaleckian aggregate demand and supply model differs in another respect. In the Kaleckian model, the aggregate supply curve is flat for all levels of output beneath full capacity as a result of the hypothesis of constant returns. An increase in demand will not lead to an increase in prices (unless this leads to an increase in the prices of raw materials). As is obvious from equation (5.27), an increase in the nominal wage rate w, at a given price level, leads to an outward shift of the aggregate demand curve, in the manner shown in Figure 5.8(a). This will lead to an equivalent increase in output and employment. Similarly, the same increase in output could be achieved with an increase in the real wage generated by a fall in the mark-up and hence in the price level, at a constant nominal wage rate, leading to a downward shift of the aggregate supply function, as shown in Figure 5.8(b). By contrast, in the mainstream model, an increase in the wage rate would generate an upward shift of the aggregate supply curve, and a reduction in output.

Finally, we may wish to consider the case where, as mentioned earlier in the chapter, any possible Pigou effect or real wealth effect would be thwarted by debt effects. In his critique of the Pigou effect, Kalecki argued that the bigger part of the money stock was made up of bank deposit money, and that bank loans were the counterpart of these bank deposits. Kalecki (1944, p. 132) thus concluded that 'to the gain of money holders there corresponds an equal loss to the bank debtors'. As a consequence, the lower prices that were called for to restore full employment 'would increase catastrophically the real value of debts, and would consequently lead to wholesale bankruptcy and a "confidence crisis"'.

Ironically, Keynes (1936, p. 264) had himself put forth a similar argument in *The General Theory*, arguing that 'the depressing influence on entrepreneurs of their greater burden of debt may partly offset any cheerful reactions from the reduction of wages', so much so that entrepreneurs 'may soon reach the point of insolvency – with severely adverse effects on investment'. Keynes also pointed out that the lower prices would increase 'the real burden of the national debt', thus proving 'very adverse to business confidence'. Thus, even before Pigou and Patinkin put forth their arguments in favour of the positive real wealth effects on consumption, Keynes had already focused on the other side of the balance sheet – the liability side – underlining the dangerous and detrimental effects of falling prices for those holding debt. Indeed, other famous authors at the time had also underlined the increased debt burden arising from price deflation, most notably Irving Fisher (1933). For this reason, the negative effects of lower prices on aggregate demand are often referred to as the Fisher (debt-deflation) effect. It has also been called the reverse Pigou effect, or we might prefer to call it the real debt effect. Few authors have underlined these negative effects, among whom we can mention Minsky (1975), Tobin (1980), Dutt (1986–87), Smithin (1988), Palley (1996a, ch. 4) and Fazzari et al. (1998).

A further point that needs to be made is that, while nominal debt is unlikely to decrease when output prices are falling, the same cannot be said of nominal wealth. The debt of households and firms is usually fixed in nominal terms, set by contract. Firms still need to

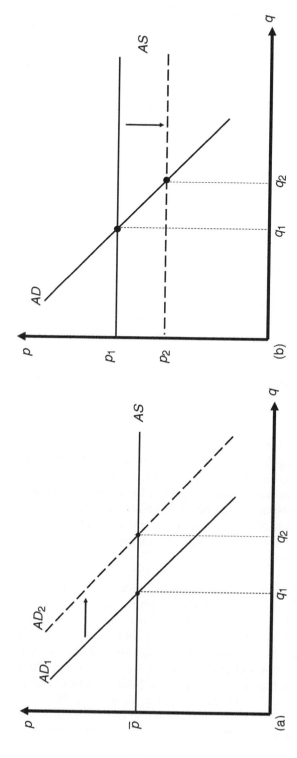

Figure 5.8 (a) The impact of an increase in the nominal wage in the Kaleckian AS/AD model; (b) the impact of a decrease in the price level in the Kaleckian AS/AD model

make interest payments on the bank loans that they have contracted in the past or on the bonds that they have issued. Similarly, households have contracted mortgage loans, car loans or credit-card loans in nominal terms. All these debts remain unchanged in nominal terms but they rise in real terms when prices fall. In addition, unless interest rates change quickly, the real burden of these debts is likely to rise. As prices fall it becomes harder to service corporate debt, and if wages fall along with prices, it will also become harder to service household debt.

Notwithstanding the above, the real wealth effect is likely to be further neutralized by the fact that nominal wealth often falls when output prices fall. With unemployment and reduced economic activity, real-estate prices and stock market prices are bound to drop, and hence real-estate wealth and stock market wealth, in nominal terms, will also fall, leaving no or little room for a positive real wealth effect (Davidson, 1985, p. 382). Thus the real wealth effect can be supported only by that small part of household wealth that corresponds to currency backed by the central bank. Furthermore, even if one believes that falling prices simply lead to a redistribution from debt-holders to wealth-owners, it is quite likely that the propensity to consume of debt-holders is higher than that of wealth-owners (Tobin, 1980, p. 10). As a consequence, even if the increase in real debt is entirely compensated by an increase in real wealth, the Pigou effect would be overwhelmed by the Fisher effect, a feature that even New Keynesians have found relevant enough to be modelled (Eggertsson and Krugman, 2012).

It is thus quite possible that the Fisher effect overtakes both the real wealth effect and the distribution effect. In this case, the aggregate demand curve will have a positive slope. An increase in nominal wages at constant prices will still lead to an increase in output, as shown in Figure 5.8(c). But an increase in real wages due to lower prices will now induce a fall in output as a consequence of the strong real debt effects, as shown in Figure 5.8(d), as the aggregate supply curve shifts from AS_1 to AS_2. *A fortiori*, as shown in Lavoie (2010a), with an upward-sloping aggregate demand curve, falling wages and prices, at constant real wages, will have a perverse effect on output and employment. The perverse effects will be even greater if lower or falling prices induce less investment, as investment is likely to be postponed (Keynes, 1936, p. 263). The more flexible wages and prices are, the more dramatic the perverse Fisher debt effect will be. Krugman (2012, p. 46) calls this the 'flexibility paradox'.

In the story now told by New Consensus authors, a positive aggregate demand curve can appear only when the negative shock on the economy is so large that real interest rates are still too high even when the central bank pushes the nominal interest rate all the way to its zero lower bound (Buttet and Roy, 2014; 2015). In this case, which the New Keynesians call a liquidity trap, any reduction in the rate of inflation (deflation) increases the real interest rate, thus reducing output further. By contrast, the post-Keynesian story based on the perverse Fisher debt effect does not rely on the strong interest elasticity of private expenditures.

5.3.5 Efficiency Effects and Labour Demand

Alternative explanations of efficiency effects
We now deal with what some nineteenth-century American economists used to call the economy-of-high-wages (Hudson, 2010). This doctrine establishes a link that goes from

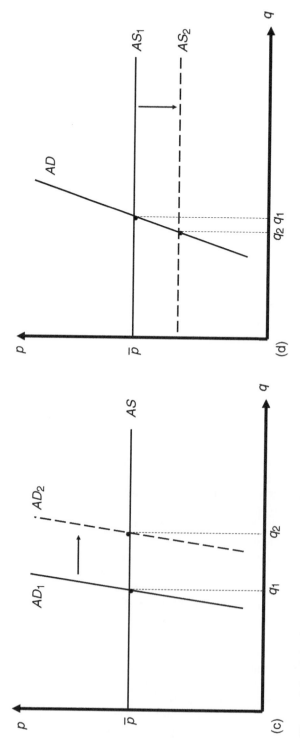

Figure 5.8 (c) The effect of an increase in the nominal wage rate in the Kaleckian model with an upward-sloping AD curve; (d) the effect of a decrease in the price level in the Kaleckian model with an upward-sloping AD curve

higher real wages to faster productivity. These effects are now known in mainstream theory as wage efficiency effects, but we shall refer to them as the Webb effect (see below).

In their search for a neoclassical theory of involuntary unemployment, New Keynesian authors such as Shapiro and Stiglitz (1984) have assumed the existence of a positive relationship between the productivity of workers and their real wage rate, with changes to the latter variable causing changes in the former. This relationship goes beyond the standard relation that says that more productive economies allow for higher real wages. Krassoi-Peach and Stanley (2009) find that the Webb effect still exists when reverse causality is taken into account and Marquetti (2004) even finds unidirectional causality going from real wages to labour productivity.

Neoclassical authors have thus adopted the Marxian distinction between labour power and labour, the former corresponding to the potential number of hours of work, the potential work effort and the quality of work included in the explicit or implicit labour contract, while the latter is the actual number of hours on the job and the actual work effort of the employee (Hodgson, 1982, p. 219). In the Marxist view, labour productivity is not given by the existing technology. The actual technical coefficients depend on various socio-economic determinants, in particular the real wage rate. The difference between labour and labour power may also be explained by an inappropriate social organization of production (e.g. a hierarchal organization that leads to a lack of motivation among workers, because of a lack of labour participation in the decision-making process).

In both the neoclassical and the radical approaches, the crucial element explaining efficient labour units is the expected cost of job loss. This cost depends on the probability of being caught loafing and losing one's job. It also depends on the differential between income earned on the job, on the one hand, and income earned on another job or while unemployed, on the other hand. The rate of unemployment or the average duration of unemployment, or sometimes the rate of increase of these two variables, the availability of social security benefits and the level of wage rates are thus important determinants of work effort (Schor, 1987). In the neoclassical version, utility functions are usually invoked to justify the shirking behaviour of workers and explain the absolute level of productivity per worker. The excessively high wage rate paid in the core economy induces workers to stop shirking, but simultaneously creates unemployment, which increases the expected cost of shirking. In the radical version, class struggle and class conflict explain the resistance to innovations designed to enhance efficiency or work intensity, and hence the rate of growth of labour productivity. Strikes, slowdowns, sabotage and absenteeism are all reduced when there is a large reserve army of unemployed workers (Naples, 1987). Discipline is upheld by high unemployment rates and high wages, or, in a dynamic world, by high increases in unemployment and in the cost of job losses.

On the whole, the reasons presented above to justify the positive relationship between real wages and productivity seem to overemphasize the disutility of work. The positive impact of increased real wage rates on labour productivity may also be given other interpretations. Some authors, such as Akerlof (1982), have suggested social underpinnings that are more in line with heterodox theory or old behavioural theory, pointing out that work can bring satisfaction. This satisfaction is to a large extent a function of the interpersonal relations among fellow employees, but also a function of the status of the job. Increased earnings, or increases in earnings relative to other groups of workers, boost the morale of employees. They reinforce the feeling of affiliation of the employee for the firm and enhance the satisfaction for a job well done.

Similarly, improved working conditions, which are part of the implicit wage rate, create a working environment that is more conducive to high productivity and satisfaction since workers will not dread coming to work. Employees with better morale are more likely to set themselves higher work norms, and they require less monitoring. In a dynamic framework, it is the rate of growth of real wages that leads to increases in the rate of change of productivity. Storm and Naastepad (2012, p. 57) call this the degree of wage-led technological progress. Within the statics of the short period, a higher real wage rate, compared to the previous one, would boost the morale of employees. Higher real wages are thus associated with higher effort intensity and a higher level of worker productivity. The static framework based on workers' morale is, however, harder to justify: if the wage increase occurs for all workers, no relative increase occurs; also, after a while, the spirit-boosting effect of the new salary should vanish.

It may thus be preferable to rely on a third group of reasons for labour productivity to be positively related to the level of real wages. These reasons were underlined a long time ago by Sidney Webb (1912, p. 984), in discussions in favour of higher minimum wages. In a more technical sense, higher real wages may lead to the elimination of firms or of plants that have low productivity. Firms for which average costs rise above the price set by the price-leader, because of general higher real wage rates, must close down, as we discussed earlier. On average, the disappearance of firms whose productivity is low would lead to higher output to labour ratios, since demand would be redistributed towards more efficient firms. The technical coefficients of our utilization function would change. The positive relationship between higher real wages and labour productivity can thus be explained by low-productivity firms being weeded out of the market (Nell, 1988, p. 236). In the longer run, higher real wages also induce management to search for more efficient methods of production and to cut down on wasteful processes, in particular X-inefficiency (Leibenstein, 1978; Altman, 1998). As a result, overall productivity rises. Because of his earlier appreciation of the positive impact of higher real wages on labour productivity, we denote this relationship the Webb effect.

The Webb effect in the Kaleckian model

Whatever cause of variable productivity one prefers to adopt, we may easily graft its effects on to our simple Kaleckian model. Let us thus assume that there is a positive feedback between the real wage rate and the productivity of workers. Making use of a linear formulation, labour productivity, which we previously assumed to be a constant, may now be written as

$$y = y_0 + \varepsilon(w/p) \tag{5.29}$$

Replacing y by its new definition in equation (5.17) yields a new employment function that incorporates the positive impact of higher wages on productivity. The new effective labour demand relation becomes

$$L_{eff}^D = \frac{a}{y_0 - \left(\dfrac{w}{p}\right)(1-\varepsilon)} \tag{5.30}$$

Taking the derivative of this equation with respect to the real wage, we get

$$\frac{dL^D_{eff}}{d\left(\frac{w}{p}\right)} = \frac{a(1-\varepsilon)}{\left\{y_0 - \left(\frac{w}{p}\right)(1-\varepsilon)\right\}^2} \qquad (5.31)$$

It is clear from equation (5.31) that the positive relationship between real wages and the level of employment will persist as long as the reaction parameter ε is smaller than unity. If this is the case, the employment function may still be described by a curve that is similar to the one previously drawn in Figures 5.5 and 5.7. Figure 5.9 illustrates the impact of the Webb effect when the reaction parameter is smaller than one. The employment function, which incorporates the impact of higher real wages on labour productivity, is denoted by WE, for Webb effect (or for wage efficiency effect). The curve is asymptotic to the straight line, noted y, which represents what is now an endogenous labour productivity variable, resulting from changes in the real wage rate. Two partial equilibrium employment curves are also drawn. One assumes that the productivity of workers stays at the level determined by a wage rate of $(w/p)_1$, whatever the actual real wage rate; similarly, the other partial equilibrium employment curve is based on the productivity set by a real wage of $(w/p)_2$. At the initial wage rate $(w/p)_1$, the level of employment is L_1. An increase to $(w/p)_2$ would drive the employment level to L'_2 if there were no efficiency effects. The increase in the wage rate, however, drives up the productivity of labour, and consequently the partial equilibrium employment function shifts up, as we saw in Figure 5.7. The global impact of the rise in the real wage rate is thus finally a smaller increase in the level of employment from L_1 to L_2. This is what the WE curve incorporates.

Although the situation described by Figure 5.9 is the more likely case, it is not the only possible one. If increased wages induce a strong positive productivity effect; that is, if the reaction parameter ε is so large that equation (5.31) has a negative sign, then the Kaleckian employment curve takes on a negative slope. The description of Figure 5.10 is similar to that of Figure 5.9. This time, however, the negative impact on employment of the induced increase in labour productivity, $L'_2 - L_2$, overtakes the positive effect on employment of the raised real wage, $L'_2 - L_1$. The resulting change in the level of employment is then negative. As a result, the employment curve that incorporates efficiency effects, the WE curve, has a downward slope. In such an economy, the demand for labour curve would have all the orthodox characteristics since a decrease in the wage rate would help return towards full employment. Obviously if $\varepsilon = 1$, then the effective demand curve for labour will be vertical, and real wages will have no impact on employment.

Note that the introduction into our post-Keynesian model of the efficiency wage hypothesis in its strongest version has turned the neoclassical theory of involuntary unemployment upside down. The hypothesis was introduced in neoclassical models to allow for involuntary unemployment. With large real-wage-induced productivity effects, the hypothesis destroys the possibility of involuntary unemployment in post-Keynesian models! The question that thus arises is whether the ε parameter can take large values, greater than unity, or not.

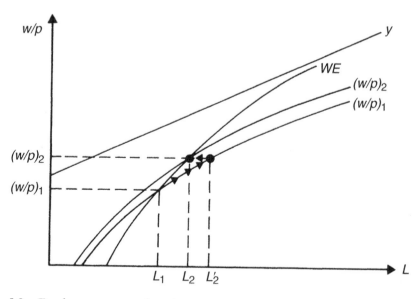

Figure 5.9 Employment curve when the parameter of the Webb effect is below unity

Seccareccia (1991b) has empirically tested a model for Canada that is very similar to the one presented here. He finds a Webb effect, the elasticity of which is 0.34. He further finds that the real wage rate has a positive and statistically significant impact on labour employment in the overall industrial sector. An increase of 10 per cent in the level of real wages leads to an increase of 1.3 per cent in the level of employment or the number of

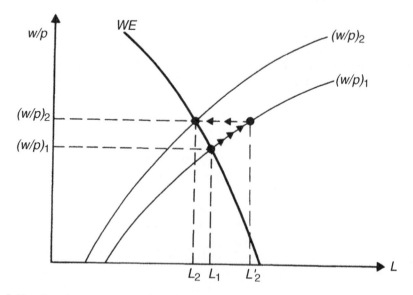

Figure 5.10 Employment curve when the parameter of the Webb effect is above unity

hours worked. These results provide empirical support for the existence of an upward-sloping employment curve WE, as described in Figure 5.9, despite an important Webb effect. Incidentally, in their meta-regression analysis, Krassoi-Peach and Stanley (2009) find that the best estimate of the Webb effect elasticity (the efficiency wage effect elasticity) is around 0.31, as already pointed out in Chapter 1. Writing the real wage as $\omega = w/p$, we know that the Webb effect elasticity is $e_w = (dy/y)/(d\omega/\omega)$. From equation (5.29), we also know that $\varepsilon = dy/d\omega$, so that $\varepsilon = e_w y/\omega$. Thus, since the share of labour in national income is roughly 60 per cent at worst, this implies that ω should be no larger than 0.50, and hence smaller than unity. We can thus accept Figure 5.9, rather than Figure 5.10, as the general depiction of the employment curve.

Whereas this on its own seems reasonable, a negative relationship between real wages and employment is not impossible when additional factors are taken into account. Naastepad and Storm (2010) show that, while high real wages can have favourable effects on aggregate demand, faster growth and higher real wages together combine to generate large increases in productivity that might reduce employment growth despite the increase in aggregate demand. Thus, things may not be as simple as we would wish.

5.3.6 Profits and Profit Shares

Profit identities
An essential feature of the Kaleckian approach is that it provides a macroeconomic explanation of profits in national income, an explanation based on the national accounts with the addition of a few assumptions. We start with the simple case of a closed economy without government, and will then move on to a more realistic world. We shall also discuss the relationship between profits and profit shares.

First, recall equation (5.1), which splits the national product from an incomes approach and an expenditure approach:

$$Y = \text{Consumption} + \text{Investment} = \text{Wages} + \text{Profits} \qquad (5.1)$$

Given the subdivision of consumption between profit recipients and wage recipients that we have introduced, we may write the following:

$$\text{Wages} + \text{Profits} = \text{Consumption out of wages} + \text{Consumption out of profits} + \text{Investment}$$

Assuming, as we did, that workers spend all their income, that is, they have no savings, we can write

$$\text{Consumption out of wages} = \text{Wages}$$

Plugging this into the previous equation yields Kalecki's famous profit equation, which he first outlined in Polish in 1939:

$$\text{Profits} = \text{Consumption out of profits} + \text{Investment}$$

This is exactly what we obtained when we assumed in equation (5.2) that autonomous expenditures were made up of investment expenditures and of consumption out of previously acquired profits, thus obtaining equation (5.8), such that, in real terms, $P = a$. But what is the exact meaning of this equation, and what can we say about the causality it implies? How can we interpret its conclusions? This is a question that Kalecki asked, and to which he provided the following answer:

> What is the significance of this equation? Does it mean that profits in a given period determine capitalists' consumption and investment, or the reverse of this? The answer to this question depends on which of these items is directly subject to the decisions of capitalists. Now it is clear that capitalists can decide to consume and to invest more in a given period than in the preceding one, but they cannot decide to earn more. It is, therefore, their investment and consumption decisions which determine profits, and not vice versa. (Kalecki, 1971, pp. 78–9)

We can summarize this macroeconomic theory by referring to an aphorism made famous by Kaldor (1956, p. 96), although often wrongly attributed to Kalecki: 'Capitalists earn what they spend, and workers spend what they earn.' This statement highlights an important asymmetry: capitalists and entrepreneurs can always decide to spend more (provided banks accept to finance them), whereas workers cannot easily decide to earn more, since this depends essentially on the employment they are being offered by entrepreneurs.

Manipulating the definitions of the national accounts, Kalecki (1971, p. 82) further shows that the profit equation in the general case comes down to

Profits net of taxes = Consumption out of profits + Investment + Budget deficit + Net exports − Saving out of wages

This equation is an antidote to the crowding-out effect, so popular in mainstream textbooks, according to which expansionary fiscal policies designed to support aggregate demand are doomed to fail. The crowding-out effect is the modern version of the 'Treasury View', against which Keynes was arguing in the 1930s. By contrast, the above equation says that, all else equal, the profits of the private sector rise when the government runs larger deficits. Both Kalecki and Keynes were, however, aware that the use of expansionary fiscal policy to combat unemployment and falling profits could generate disapproval from the business community. Keynes (1936, p. 120) issued the following warning: 'With the confused psychology which often prevails, the government programme may, through its effect on "confidence", increase liquidity-preference or diminish the marginal efficiency of capital, which again, may retard other investment unless measures are taken to offset it.' Indeed, mainstream economists have taken up this idea, arguing that restrictive fiscal policy could be expansionary, as the reduction in deficit would raise business confidence, triggering what Krugman has called the 'confidence fairy', recently criticized in a model by Botta (2020).

Profits in the simple model
Let us come back for a while to the closed economy without government. We already know that in such an economy firms cannot increase their profits unless they spend more. As long as autonomous expenditures are given, if firms manage to raise their share

of profits, by increasing their mark-ups θ, in the hope of making more profits, this will lead only to a reduction in the quantities sold, without any increase in the real amount of profits. We already know this from equation (5.8). We can obtain the same result by starting from equation (5.18), which represents the standard Cambridge expression of aggregate demand, where profit recipients save a proportion s_p of their current profit. We repeat it here for convenience, denoting again real profits by P:

$$AD = wL + (1 - s_p)pP + pI \qquad (5.18A)$$

The equality between aggregate demand and aggregate supply can be expressed as an equality between investment and saving, made up of saving out of profits. In real terms, we have

$$I = s_p P \qquad (5.32)$$

from which we immediately see that the amount of profits in real terms is determined by the level of real investment and the propensity to save out of profits:

$$P = I/s_p \qquad (5.33)$$

This is the so-called Cambridge short-period profit equation found in Kaldor (1956, p. 96), who ties this equation to Kalecki's profit equations and to Keynes's (1930a) 'widow's cruse' analogy. Keynes was then making a reference to the Old Testament story found in the First Book of the Kings, whereby a widow was assured that her barrel of meat and jar of oil would never get depleted. Keynes (ibid., p. 139) argued that, 'however much of their profits entrepreneurs spend on consumption, the increment of wealth belonging to entrepreneurs remains the same as before. Thus profits, as a source of capital increment for entrepreneurs, are a widow's cruse which remains undepleted however much of them may be devoted to riotous living.' As Kaldor points out, the same can be said about the investment of entrepreneurs.

Equation (5.33), however simple it is, helps to explain a puzzle that arose with the advent of financialization: why did firms make large profits despite the fact that they did not seem to engage in large investment expenditures? One answer is to be found in the denominator of equation (5.33). We are not in a pure capitalist economy where workers spend all their wages and where capitalists save and reinvest all their profits. If firms distribute more dividends and retain fewer profits, then the s_p parameter will be smaller and profits will be larger for a given level of investment. The same effect will occur if households spend a larger proportion of the dividends and interest payments that they receive. Cordonnier and Van de Velde (2015) argue that this is exactly what happened during decades, thus solving the puzzle. An alternative answer is that the puzzle arises from a statistical illusion: firms do invest, but they do so abroad (Fiebiger, 2016b; Rabinovich, 2019).

Still assuming that there is only direct labour and that prices are set as in equation (5.21), with a mark-up θ and hence a profit share $\pi = \theta/(1 + \theta)$, it follows that real profits are a proportion π of output q, so that real output is

$$q = I/s_p\pi \qquad (5.34)$$

The higher the profit share π, the lower the level of output (and hence of employment), for a given amount of real investment (Lavoie, 1998). This, according to Andrew Trigg (1994, p. 97), represents the true picture of Kalecki's economics. As he says, 'The relative share of profits in income must increase in response to the higher degree of monopoly. Since profits are determined by investment ... the level of profits does not change.' Changes in the profit share (or in the costing margin or in the so-called degree of monopoly) have no effect whatsoever on the level of profits.

On the other hand, an increase in the costing margin or in the profit share, for a given level of investment, leads to a reduction in the level of output. Trigg (1994, p. 98) made it quite clear: 'An increase in monopoly power generates a reduction in output that increases the profit share without changing the absolute volume of profits.' Higher costing margins thus induce lower rates of capacity utilization, for the same level of profits. This result can be directly attributed to Kalecki (1954, p. 71): 'The level of income or product will decline to the point at which the higher relative share of profits yields the same absolute level of profits.' The decreased output and employment that are assumed to accompany a redistribution of income towards profit-earners (or an increase in the bargaining power of firms) is illustrated in Figure 5.11. The effective demand condition, given by the last equation above, is represented by a rectangular hyperbola to the horizontal axis.

Profits in a model with government and saving out of wages

Let us now see whether these simple results (with a given investment level) still hold when the public sector (or the foreign sector, for that matter) is introduced. Let us assume that the government spends G in real terms and that there is a tax rate τ that applies on all income. The equality between investment and saving, still in real terms, now involves private saving by profit recipients out of their disposable income and public saving when the government is running a surplus:

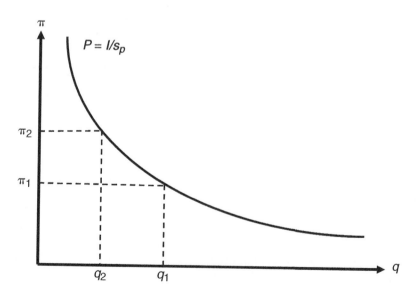

Figure 5.11 The profit share in a simple Kaleckian closed economy without a public sector

Effective demand and employment

$$I = s_p(1 - \tau)P + (\tau q - G) \quad (5.35)$$

Solving for q, the equilibrium level of output is still an inverse function of the costing margin (here the profit share π), as it was in the closed economy. As one would expect from a standard Kaleckian or Keynesian model, output (or employment) depends positively on government expenditures and negatively on the tax rate. We have

$$q = \frac{I+G}{s_p(1-\tau)\pi+\tau} \quad (5.36)$$

Looking now at profits, it is clear that, as Kalecki (1971, p. 85) would put it, a budget deficit 'permits profits to increase above the level determined by private investment and capitalists' consumption'. On the other hand, when taking changes in costing margins into consideration, profits do not behave in the manner that most Kaleckians would expect. The level of profits is now given by the equation:

$$P = \frac{I+G}{s_p(1-\tau)+\tau/\pi} \quad (5.37)$$

The above equation shows that, in contrast to what occurred in the closed economy without government, any increase in the mark-up θ and hence in the profit share π leads to an increase in the level of profits P, as illustrated in Figure 5.12.

The economic logic of the above result is simple. When firms decide or manage to increase their costing margins, effective demand is reduced and this leads to a decrease in income and output. The fall in income induces a fall in the yield of taxation, thus leading to an increase in the public deficit, assuming there is no change in government expenditures. The increase in government deficit, for a given level of private investment, thus generates in the end an increase in corporate profits. The redistribution of income

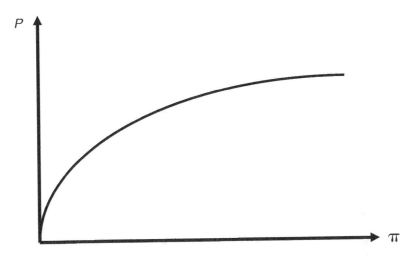

Figure 5.12   Profits and profit share in a model with an endogenous budget deficit

towards profit-earners is thus achieved through the accumulation of debt by the public sector. Profit-earners are targeting higher profits, and are achieving them. The situation was different in a closed economy without government. There, capitalists could realize these higher profits only by increasing investment and private debt. With the existence of the public sector, the higher profits can be achieved instead by an endogenous increase in the debt of the public sector. A very similar result would be achieved in an open economy, if net exports were a function of income.

It is clear that introducing a public sector, with an endogenous budget deficit, does change some of the fundamental results of the Kaleckian model. The profitability constraint, also called the reproducibility condition by Bowles and Boyer (1990), plays no role in the simple Kaleckian model of employment (Mason, 1993). The profitability constraint is that firms should achieve a minimum amount of profits, or rate of profit, for them to keep producing or to invest. Profitability becomes a concern in a model that includes a foreign sector or a government sector. In the simple model, higher real wages that are lower than labour productivity, through higher effective demand, can always improve employment because realized profits remain the same whatever the costing margin. However, once the budget deficit is made endogenous to economic activity, or once saving out of wages is introduced, the profitability constraint may become binding. This much can be ascertained by looking at Figure 5.13: high real wages (low profit shares) generate high economic activity and budget surpluses, which diminish business profits.

At some point, increases in real wages, even if they remain below labour productivity, become impossible because they would induce overly low corporate profits. This much can be surmised from Kalecki's general profit equation, where profits also depend negatively on the government budget surplus and saving out of wages. This can be assessed in our little model by adding saving out of wages. With the propensity to save out of wages, $s_w < s_p$, equation (5.35), which yields the investment and saving equality, becomes

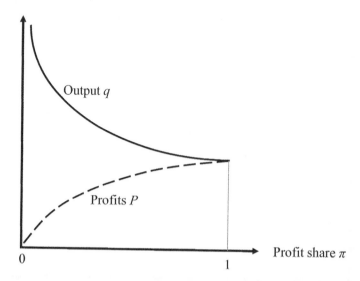

Figure 5.13   *The levels of output and of profits for different profit shares in a Kaleckian model with an endogenous budget deficit*

Effective demand and employment

$$I = s_p(1-\tau)\pi q + s_w(1-\tau)(1-\pi)q + (\tau q - G) \tag{5.38}$$

And the real output and profits equations become

$$q = \frac{I+G}{(s_p - s_w)(1-\tau)\pi + s_w(1-\tau) + \tau} \tag{5.39}$$

$$P = \frac{I+G}{(s_p - s_w)(1-\tau) + [s_w(1-\tau) + \tau]/\pi} \tag{5.40}$$

Thus a reduction in the share of profit π leads to an increase in aggregate demand, real output and demand-determined employment; however, with given amounts of autonomous expenditures, the decrease in the costing margins also leads to a reduction in overall profits as long as income is taxed or wage-earners save part of their income. This can help to explain why business would be opposed to a high-wage macroeconomic strategy: unless there are induced effects on investment, a reduction in the costing margins will indeed lead to a reduction in the overall profits of business, in contrast to what happens in the simple Kaleckian model. This point, which is sometimes missed, had been clearly outlined by a Kaleckian author:

> Kalecki's proposition that the degree of monopoly can affect the profit share but not the level of profits, is not valid in his more general model of an open economy with government taxation and expenditure and workers' saving ... The 'class struggle' could affect not only income shares by altering markups in manufacturing industries but also the level of profits because of their effect on the trade balance, the government deficit, and workers' saving. (Asimakopulos, 1988, pp. 140, 152)

Gilberto Tadeu Lima has brought to my attention a 1946 article by Thomas Schelling – the Nobel Prize winner – who tackled precisely this issue with what we could call a Kaleckian model, asking himself whether the claim that profits can be raised through higher wages could hold true. As we just did, he found that 'so long as government expenditure and investment are constant a rise in wage rates at the expense of profits will increase aggregate income but decrease profits' (Schelling, 1946, p. 227). What, however if investment and government expenditure respond to the GDP level? In other words what happens if firms have a marginal propensity to invest h and the government has a marginal propensity to spend h_g? If these new parameters are large enough, the term between squared brackets can become negative, as can be checked from equation (5.40A). Then, higher real wages will lead to higher profits. Schelling believed however that this was unlikely.

$$P = \frac{I_0 + G_0}{(s_p - s_w)(1-\tau) + [s_w(1-\tau) + \tau - h - h_g]/\pi} \tag{5.40A}$$

5.4 THE SUPPLY OF LABOUR

Nothing has been said so far about the supply of labour. As noted by Janet Yellen (1980, p. 18), a former chair of the Federal Reserve, 'one thing notably absent from the

Post-Keynesian model is a labor supply function'. Without necessarily providing one, we shall nevertheless discuss this labour supply function. Mainstream macroeconomists generally assume that the supply of labour is well behaved; that is, they assume that the supply of labour has a positive slope, the substitution effect overcoming the income effect. Leisure is assumed not to be too strongly an inferior good. As recalled by David Spencer (2006, p. 462), unemployment in neoclassical economics looks like a desirable state of affairs. This, combined with the standard assumptions ruling the demand for labour, produces the orthodox labour market, where the forces of supply and demand necessarily lead to an equilibrium wage rate. In the long run, if not in the short run, the labour market clears.

Neoclassical labour economists take a more prudent view about the shape of the supply of labour. Many empirical studies have shown that the income effect of a change in the real wage rate is more significant than the substitution effect. In particular, in the case of men, it is often found that when the real wage rate is decreased, hours worked increase (Pencavel, 1986). Although the lower price of leisure should induce people to work less or to stop working, they end up working more hours to compensate for the loss of income due to the lower hourly wage rate. Still, for a neoclassical economist, the presence of a backward-bending supply curve of labour is not detrimental to the standard demand and supply analysis, even though the demand and supply curves may intersect twice. While there may be two equilibria, the labour supply curve will have its standard upward slope in the vicinity of the stable equilibrium and that equilibrium will provide the higher of the two full-employment equilibrium levels.

5.4.1 Supply of Labour and Consumers' Hierarchy

The outline of a post-Keynesian theory of the supply of labour could be presented along the following lines. Decisions to work and decisions to consume are not unrelated. The crucial objective of most individuals or of most households is to keep their position within the consumers' hierarchy, as explained in Chapter 2. As a consequence, households feel an obligation to retain the levels of income to which they have been accustomed. Furthermore, households, like firms, have contractual obligations (Rima, 1984a, p. 68; Appelbaum, 1979, p. 112). They have borrowed in the past to acquire housing, cars, electric appliances, furniture and other semi-durable consumption goods, as well as to pay for their holidays and the education of their children. Households are thus compelled for normative and cash-flow reasons to maintain customary income levels. The level of non-wage income being given, and the level of income of other households being given, the standard of living of an individual or of the household can be represented by a rectangular hyperbola in the plane described by the real wage rate and the number of hours worked, as shown in Figure 5.14 (Nell, 1988, p. 123; Mongiovi, 1991, p. 39; Sharif, 2003, p. 202). A more formal version of this approach can be found in Schoder (2017, pp. 178–9), while Fernández-Huerga et al. (2017) provide a general survey.

Any increase in the standard of living will be associated with another rectangular hyperbola, denoted SL', above the previous one, called SL. An increase in the real wage rate that is considered temporary, that is, which does not change the customary standard of living, may then induce a worker to reduce the number of hours offered from h_0 to h_1, moving along the hyperbola. Only if the change in the real wage rate is considered to be

Effective demand and employment 339

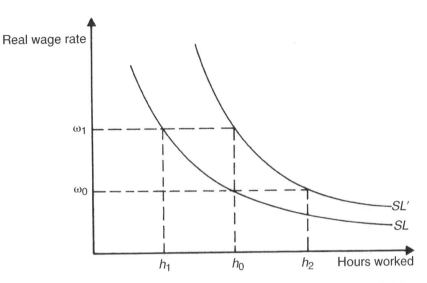

Figure 5.14 Downward-sloping labour supply curve at two different norms of living standards

a permanent one – the worker feels that a higher rank of the consumers' hierarchy can be attained – will the desired number of hours of work stay the same, the individual shifting up to the *SL'* curve. The main cause of this is that when the household feels that a permanently higher level of income can be maintained, it will modify its borrowing behaviour accordingly, by increasing its liabilities and its cash-flow requirements. A higher real wage rate associated with a higher standard of living and consumption norm will not modify the number of hours worked as the worker will conform to the existing social norm.

The supply of labour thus depends in large measure on the normal standard of living of a household relative to that of other households. The supply of labour depends on the perceived mean income of the reference group against which a particular household is comparing itself, that is, on the perceived mean wage rate and the perceived social norm regarding the number of hours worked per week (or per year). For instance, in Figure 5.14, if an individual believes that the mean income of the reference group has increased from *SL* to *SL'*, while this individual feels that he should still belong to that reference group, he will attempt to increase the number of hours worked from h_0 to h_2 in order to remain at the same rank in the hierarchy of consumers. The supply of labour thus depends, both at the individual level and in the aggregate, on the perceived wage rate of the reference group and on the past standard of living. One would expect the amount of labour supplied to increase when a household is subjected to a drop in the real wage rate and when a drop in standards of living relative to the reference group is perceived. These two assumptions are the mainspring of the inflation theory to be developed in Chapter 8.

In brief, then, the supply of labour of an individual depends on her customary consumption level, as well as on her wage rate relative to that of other workers (Rima, 1984b, p. 541). The post-Keynesian view of the supply of labour is closely related to the post-Keynesian approach to consumption developed in Chapter 2: both underline the importance of peer groups and that of past income levels (Baxter, 1988). What explains the social norm regarding the average number of weekly working hours may be harder to identify. One must certainly fall back on cultural explanations, which have little to do with constrained individual behaviour. For instance, why is it that professors or business leaders now work more hours than they used to half a century ago (Schor, 2008)? This may have to do with the downfall of the leisure class and the reinforcement of the work ethic: all have to work, even those who do not need labour income.

5.4.2 Alternative Heterodox Views on the Supply of Labour

The previous analysis of the labour supply is still quite idealistic. It assumes that individuals have a choice regarding the number of hours they can work. This may be true for independent professionals, those in business, self-employed people or university professors, and also for those who work part-time. In general, however, employers offer full-time jobs with a fixed number of hours of work per week, and a fixed number of weeks of work per year (Eichner, 1987, p. 883). The choice is simply between working the number of hours imposed by the institutional norm and turning down the employment. As a result, any change in the real wage rate is unlikely to lead to a different decision. Some flexibility may be added by searching for different employers, offering the optimal combination of wages and hours of work, although most companies of the core economy will tend to gravitate around the socially accepted norm. Flexibility in the number of hours worked may also be obtained by taking up part-time jobs with other employers, but the additional income, once additional income taxes and lost marginal benefits are taken into account, is usually much reduced compared to the real wage rate of a full-time job.

Part-time jobs are seldom offered in the core economy, which explains why so many women, who are constrained to search for part-time jobs when they rear young children, are found working in the peripheral economy. This last point highlights a last possibility of flexible hours: within the household, one of the two main members of the household may choose to work part-time rather than full-time, or may choose not to work at all. Indeed, it is well known that the supply of labour of married women increases in recession times, in an attempt to sustain the monetary standard of living of the household. On the other hand, the costs to enter the labour market are often significant for the second main member of the household, generally women. A high wage rate is more conducive to induce participation. As a consequence, researchers have often found a positive relationship between wages and the supply of labour in the case of women.

A short survey of the heterodox literature on the shape of the supply curve of labour is not fully conclusive. Besides the view illustrated with the help of Figure 5.14, three opinions can be found, all based on non-linear representations. Prasch (2000, p. 686) draws a labour supply curve that is relatively vertical, but that swirls with successive upward- and downward-sloping segments. Mohammed Sharif (2003, p. 202) and Roger Johnson (2010, p. 248) both draw labour supply curves with a forward-falling segment, as shown in Figure 5.15. At low real wage rates, so their arguments go, workers are faced with subsistence needs or with financial obligations that force them to target a level of earnings and thus work more hours if real wages are lower, as was assumed in Figure 5.14. However, at higher real wages, these constraints slacken off, as workers can afford to work less if they find that their real wage diminishes. The substitution effect takes over and the

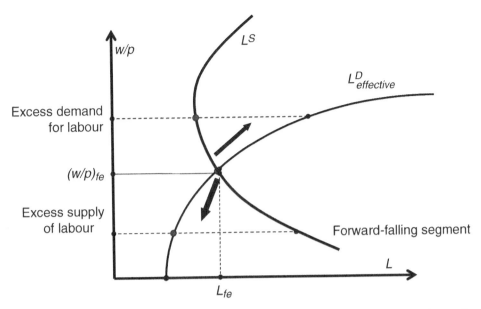

Figure 5.15 Instability in the labour market with a Kaleckian effective labour demand curve and a forward-falling segment of the labour supply curve

supply curve takes its standard upward-sloping shape. What Figure 5.15 shows, when the Kaleckian labour demand curve is integrated into the figure, is that there is instability in the labour market. And this instability would also arise with a vertical labour supply curve, or an upward-sloping one.

If the real wage is below its full-equilibrium level, market forces will tend to push the economy away from full equilibrium, because too low a wage rate will be associated with an excess supply of labour, so that a labour market with no impediments would drive down real wages and move the economy away from full employment. Market mechanisms are helpless in the case of Keynesian unemployment, as is the case here in Figure 5.15. Letting real wage rates fall in line with the hypothetical market forces would lead to perverse results, as the rate of unemployment would increase with falling wages. This theory of labour demand thus reinforces Keynes's contention (1936, ch. 19) that a flexible wage rate would be detrimental to employment, and cannot help to restore full employment. Similarly, if the real wage is higher than its full-employment level $(w/p)_{fe}$, market forces left on their own will tend to push the real wage even higher, and thus are likely to induce cost-push inflation.

There is a third view, however, according to which the labour supply curve is backward-bending, with the bottom part of the curve having a traditional upward slope, while it takes a negative slope at high real wages, as argued by Altman (2001, p. 208). He posits that, as wages rise, workers are induced to work more as they attempt to reach an ever-rising income target; then when this target is achieved, workers will work less if real wages keep rising, which drives the backward-bending part of the curve. The argument then is that, with high real wages, having attained a decent living standard, households prefer to enjoy more leisure rather than pile up more income. The backward-bending curve, already drawn by Joan Robinson (1947, p. 122), is still quite popular, and indeed, at some

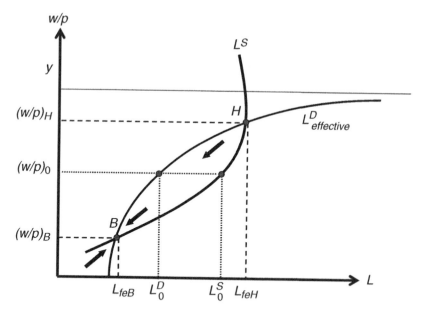

Figure 5.16 Multiple equilibria with the Kaleckian effective labour demand curve and a backward-bending labour supply curve

point it was claimed that 'the "backward-bending" supply curve of labor is now accepted as a matter of course by most economists' (Barzel and McDonald, 1973, p. 621).

If we now combine this backward-bending supply curve of labour with the Kaleckian effective demand curve for labour, we obtain multiple equilibria, that is, two real wages for which the demand for and the supply of labour are equated, as first suggested by Seccareccia (1991b). This is illustrated with the help of Figure 5.16. There is a bad equilibrium, given by point B, at which real wages and (market) employment are low; and there is a high equilibrium, given by point H, where real wages and employment are high. In both instances we can say that the economy operates at full employment, since the labour demanded at the given real wage is equal to labour supplied at that wage rate. However, the high equilibrium clearly dominates the bad equilibrium.

Given these two possibilities, which of the two equilibrium positions, B or H, has the highest probability of being realized? To answer this, let us consider an initial arbitrary real wage, $(w/p)_0$, which is half-way between the two full-employment real wage rates. At this initial real wage, the amount of labour supplied is L_0^S, whereas the amount of labour demanded is L_0^D, if we still assume that within the short period the economy is always on the locus of points where the goods market is in equilibrium (on the effective labour demand curve).

At $(w/p)_0$, the goods market is thus in equilibrium, but there is unemployment, since the labour supplied is greater than the labour demanded. For post-Keynesians, this situation could very well persist, because entrepreneurs' expectations about sales are realized and they have therefore no incentives to modify their labour-hiring decisions. As for the real wage, provided there are sufficient institutional rigidities, it has no tendency to change as long as unemployment remains relatively stable. This said, if labour markets were deprived of conventions, rules, regulations or institutional anchors, market forces would push down the nominal wage, w. By contrast, the prices of goods would tend to remain stable since aggregate demand and supply are equalized, provided of course that the economy is still on its effective labour demand curve. Hence, in such a flex-price economy, with falling nominal wages and stable prices, the real wage would tend to fall until it reaches $(w/p)_B$, which corresponds to the low full-employment equilibrium.

Given the analysis presented above, we can conclude that, if left to themselves, market forces will have a tendency to generate a full-employment equilibrium with low levels of real wages, output and employment – point B in Figure 5.16. For a given population level, this suggests therefore that living standards would be much lower than would otherwise be the case if the economy were at point H, where high levels of real wages $(w/p)_H$, and high levels of output and employment N_{feH} can be enjoyed by all.

Our analysis shows that the 'high' equilibrium is unstable, whereas the 'low' equilibrium is stable. In a world devoid of rigidities, market forces will push the economy away from the high equilibrium towards the low equilibrium, as indicated by the arrows in Figure 5.16. In other words, market forces will push the economy towards the suboptimal equilibrium. So, in contrast to what TINA advocates claim, market forces and price flexibility need not generate the best of possible solutions. In this context, in times of unemployment, by preventing real wages from falling, powerful unions have beneficial effects on overall employment, production and living standards.

Since the high full-employment equilibrium is unstable, only sustained state intervention can succeed in maintaining the economy near that level of employment. In fact, the state must intervene in order to keep real wages high, even in times of rising unemployment. This could be done through minimum wage laws or living-wage ordinances (Pollin, 2005; Kaufman, 2010b), with higher minimum wages pushing upwards the entire wage structure. The state can also increase wages in the public service, and pass laws that encourage stronger unions, which provide a countervailing force to the power of large corporations. While the Kaleckian multiple-equilibrium model shows that market forces can push the economy towards a low equilibrium with low levels of wages, output and employment, it also shows that adequate legislation and institutions can pull the economy towards higher levels of employment, higher real wages and higher living standards.

5.4.3 The No-shirking Constraint

One can describe another instance of multiple equilibria in the labour market. We have already discussed the efficiency wage hypothesis, when arguing that higher real wages could lead to higher labour productivity, thus affecting the shape and position of the effective labour demand curve. Still, we assumed that the actual real wage was given by historical or institutional factors, and was thus considered exogenous. An alternative to this is to consider the case of an all-or-nothing effort function, where workers provide or not the required normal effort, as in Shapiro and Stiglitz (1984). In this case, firms face a no-shirking constraint (*NSC*). This constraint is such that, for each level of expected aggregate employment, firms find the minimum real wage that will induce workers to provide the normal level of effort, without any shirking. The higher the level of expected aggregate employment, the lower the expected rate of unemployment, and

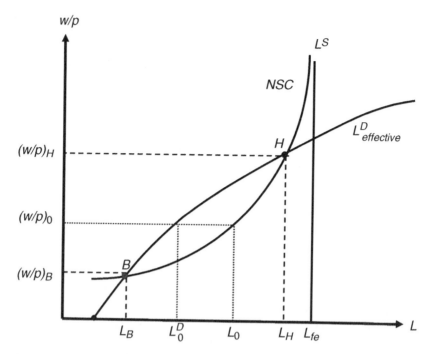

Figure 5.17 Multiple equilibria with the Kaleckian effective labour demand curve and a no-shirking constraint arising from the efficiency wage hypothesis

hence the higher the required real wage, the idea being that if the unemployment rate is low, workers are unlikely to be as disciplined, because they will not fear being let go. It is usually assumed that low rates of unemployment require especially large increases in real wages, thus generating the upward-rising no-shirking constraint (*NSC*) curve shown in Figure 5.17. This no-shirking curve is asymptotic to the labour supply curve, here assumed to be vertical.

With the curvature of the no-shirking constraint curve, and the curvature of the Kaleckian effective labour demand curve, as also shown in Figure 5.17, the two curves will generally intersect twice (Bowles and Boyer, 1990, p. 205). There are thus two points of equilibrium, a good one and a bad one, given by points *B* and *H*. This is where the expectations of workers and entrepreneurs, regarding the expected level of aggregate employment, are fully realized. In Figure 5.17, these employment expectations are fulfilled for two real wage levels, a high one $(w/p)_H$, and a low one $(w/p)_B$. For any other real wage, the expectations about the aggregate level of employment would not be fulfilled. Suppose, as is the case in Figure 5.17, that workers and firms expect the level L_0 of employment. At this level, the *NSC* curve is telling us that cost-minimizing firms would set the real wage at the level $(w/p)_0$. But at that real wage rate, only L^D_0 workers would eventually end up in employment, as a result of the effective demand constraint. Now realizing that employment is much lower than previously expected, firms and workers would revise their expectations about aggregate employment and the rate of unemployment, and as a result firms would now set an even lower real wage. This would lead to still lower realized employment. In other words, the high employment and high real wage equilibrium, given by L_H and $(w/p)_H$ in Figure 5.17, is not stable. In contrast, the low employment and low real wage equilibrium, given by L_B and $(w/p)_B$, is stable.

We thus have a situation similar to the one that occurred with the backward-bending labour supply curve. Once again, government intervention is required to ensure that social conventions are such that the high real wage and low unemployment equilibrium is enforced. Otherwise, if market forces are left to themselves, they will drive the economy towards a low level of employment and low standards of living (low real wages). Market forces thus lead the economy towards a sub-optimal equilibrium.

One way to avoid shirking, and thus extracting acceptable levels of work effort from employees is to have piece-based compensation, where the remuneration of workers is directly tied to what they contribute. Today, this is associated with new technologies and to platform-based businesses like Uber, sometimes called the sharing economy, where workers provide their own tools (such as a car or a bike), with on-call contingent labour. Some observers believe that this evolution is inevitable, because it would be associated with the spread of digital technology, and that the change is welcomed, because workers become independent and free to move from one job to another. Jim Stanford (2017), by contrast, argues that such *gig work* existed in the early stages of capitalism, that for good reasons it was replaced by standard employment contracts, and that gig work is not the inevitable consequence of digital technology. He contends that the rise of platform-based work is just another ploy to manage labour effort extraction, and that from the standpoint of workers taken as a class, the negative consequences of such precarious work far exceeds any advantage that could be associated with the presumed freedom associated with gig work.

5.5 THE KALECKIAN MODEL WITH OVERHEAD COSTS

We noted earlier that Kalecki and Kaleckians consider that labour ought to be divided into direct and indirect labour. So far, however, we have considered only direct labour because the points we wished to make could be made more simply without having recourse to this distinction. It is now time to consider the additional insights provided by the addition of indirect labour. Another way to put this distinction is to talk of variable and fixed labour, also referred to as blue-collar and white-collar workers or else as non-supervisory and supervisory positions. Oxford economists, like Kaleckians, also paid much attention to indirect labour. Brunner (1975, p. 32) talked of overhead labour and overhead costs, pointing out that because of staff salaries, 'a high proportion of labour is in fact overhead, and especially in modern industry'. Among Kaleckians, Steindl (1952, p. 46; 1979, p. 3), Asimakopulos (1970; 1975), Harris (1974) and Rowthorn (1981) have popularized the relevance of indirect labour in economic analysis. It must be recognized, however, that few have walked in their footsteps when formalizing the economy: the list probably stops with the following authors: Myatt (1986), Kurz (1990), Nichols and Norton (1991), Dutt (1992a; 2012), Lavoie (1995a; 1996b; 1996–97; 2009b; 2017a), Sasaki et al. (2013), Nikiforos (2017) and Lavoie and Nah (2020). In all these works, overhead labour is indeed a fixed cost and 'assumed to move in proportion to productive capacity' (Steindl, 1979, p. 3). A few other authors, such as Palley (2005; 2017), also consider two sets of workers, but they assume that employment in both sets moves in proportion to output, so that the second set cannot really be considered as being overhead labour.

The distinction between direct labour and overhead labour is all the more relevant given the recent evolution of macroeconomic income distribution. The last three decades, especially in the USA, have witnessed an unprecedented change in income distribution, with a large redistribution towards the upper ranks of the managerial bureaucracy, as already discussed in Chapter 3. This managerial-friendly regime based on large pay packages for upper-level managers and the overall managerial class has been studied and called *cadrisme* by Duménil and Lévy (2004, ch. 7), from the French *cadre*, which means managerial staff. Ordinary employees and workers, as a counterpart, have seen their real purchasing power stagnate. Indeed, based on the data gathered by Simon Mohun (2014), who has long studied the evolution of non-supervisory and supervisory workers, in 2010 the average annual wage income of a supervisory worker was four times that of a non-supervisory worker, whereas that ratio was only 2.3 to 1 in the mid-1960s. Thus, because overhead labour is a substantial part of labour cost, nearly half of it now, and because its share of income has risen over time, it is certainly important to look at its impact on various variables of the economy.

5.5.1 The Supply Side and Labour Productivity

The utilization function
We first look at the supply side, examining the production relationships that can be observed with overhead labour. We have already pointed out that post-Keynesians object to the standard neoclassical production function, and represent short-run production relationships through a utilization function, which relates employment to the level of output or to the level of capacity utilization. To obtain this utilization function we need to make three definitions. The firm thus hires two kinds of labour. On the one hand, we have direct labour, which is the variable factor of production, and which is directly linked to production. We shall denote it by L_v. On the other hand, there are managerial positions that are part of the overhead costs. Indirect labour depends on the level of full capacity, rather than on the level of production. Indirect labour includes permanent staff: administrative officers, accountants, the firms' lawyers and so on. In the short run, since the level of capacity is fixed, the salaries of white-collar workers are a fixed component of costs. We shall thus denote them by L_f. With q the level of output and q_{fc} the full-capacity level of output, as was the case in Chapter 3, and L the overall level of employment of this firm, and with y_v and y_f the respective constant indices of labour productivity, we have the following three equations:

$$L = L_v + L_f \qquad (5.41)$$
$$L_v = q/y_v \qquad (5.42)$$
$$L_f = q_{fc}/y_f \qquad (5.43)$$

From the above equations, the utilization function may thus be written as

$$q = \{L - (q_{fc}/y_f)\}y_v \qquad (5.44)$$

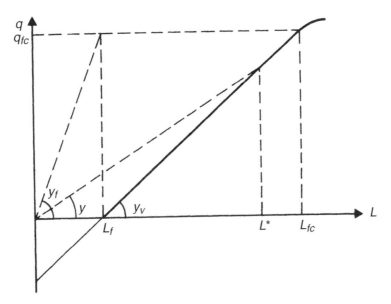

Figure 5.18 Short-run post-Keynesian utilization function

This peculiar production function is illustrated graphically in Figure 5.18. As long as the level of employment is below L_f, no output can be forthcoming. The relationship between output and employment is linear up to the level of full capacity q_{fc}, after which one may presume, as we did in Chapter 3, that the laws of diminishing returns take over. However, as long as aggregate demand is such that production never exceeds what we have defined to be full capacity, the above equations fully apply.

The marginal physical product of labour is represented in Figure 5.18 by the slope of the utilization function, as shown by the tangent of angle y_v. The tangent of angle y_f represents the productivity of overhead labour. If the angle were to increase, the amount of fixed labour required for a given level of capacity would decrease, and hence the productivity of overhead labour would rise. As a consequence, when the productivity of overhead labour changes, the whole utilization function shifts; whereas when it is the productivity of direct labour that changes, the slope of the utilization function changes.

Okun's law

A peculiar characteristic of the above production function is the evolution of the overall productivity per worker as the rate of utilization of capacity increases, shown by the tangent of angle y in Figure 5.18 for a given level of employment L^*. Let us make use of the following two definitions. The overall productivity per worker is now

$$y = q/L \tag{5.45}$$

And the rate of utilization of capacity is simply

$$u = q/q_{fc} \tag{5.46}$$

Making use of these definitions and of equations (5.41) to (5.43), the employment of overhead labour may be written as $L_f = q/(uy_f)$, and the overall productivity per worker y may be written as a function of the rate of utilization of capacity.

$$y = \frac{L_v y_v}{L_v + L_v y_v / uy_f}$$

$$y = \frac{q}{L} = \frac{y_v}{1 + (y_v / y_f)/u} \qquad (5.47)$$

The overall productivity per worker is an increasing function of the rate of utilization of capacity, as can be seen by taking the first derivative of equation (5.47):

$$dy/du = (y_f y_v^2)/(y_f u + y_v)^2 > 0 \qquad (5.48)$$

Taking the second derivative by using the chain rule shows that the productivity per worker is rising at a decreasing rate as the rate of utilization of capacity increases up to unity.

$$d^2y/du^2 = -2y_v^2 y_f^2/(y_f u + y_v)^3 < 0 \qquad (5.49)$$

Output and productivity are thus positively related in the short run. Figure 5.19 illustrates the labour productivity curve as a function of the rate of utilization of capacity. This productivity curve looks much like the standard production function of comparative statics. It has the same look of diminishing returns. The variable on the vertical axis, the level of output per unit of labour, is also identical to the one that can be found in

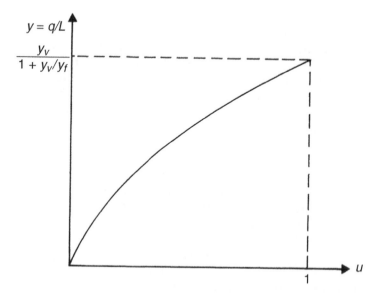

Figure 5.19 Average productivity of labour as a function of the rate of utilization of capacity

production functions. The variable on the horizontal axis, however, is different from the one to be found in production functions. In the traditional analysis, the capital/labour ratio would be the variable of the horizontal axis. Here, we have the opposite: it is the level of employment, for a given stock of machinery, that is on the horizontal axis. Although the productivity curve may look like a neoclassical production function, the relationship underlying the former curve is completely different from the one underlying traditional analysis. Whereas production functions usually rely on decreasing returns, we have here a type of short-run increasing returns to the use of labour. All these remarks could apply equally to the microeconomics of the firm as to the macroeconomics of the economy. We now turn more specifically to the latter.

Taken together, equation (5.47) and Figures 5.18 and 5.19 also illustrate Okun's law, which asserts that a fall in the unemployment rate of 1 per cent is accompanied by a much greater percentage increase in output, in the range of 2 per cent depending on the estimates. This means that, in the short run, an increase in employment is accompanied by a much faster increase in output; that is, the output to labour ratio increases, as it does in equation (5.47) and in Figure 5.19 when the rate of utilization of capacity rises. In post-Keynesian theory, Okun's law is a natural outcome of the theory, whereas in neoclassical economics, *ad hoc* assumptions, severe restrictions, lags and extremely complex stories are necessary to integrate the well-verified empirical results of Okun to the standard decreasing returns. With the post-Keynesian utilization function, the presence of overhead labour, emphasized by Okun himself, combined with a constant marginal physical product of variable labour, yields Okun's law without any additional assumption. 'Demand expansion . . . has a positive cyclical effect on productivity' (Jean and Vernengo, 2008, p. 240), as also verified empirically by Cauvel (2019).

Indeed, Okun's law reinforces the constructions proposed in Chapter 3, in particular the hypothesis that the marginal cost of multi-plant firms may be considered constant despite plants or segments of plants of different vintage and productivity. The presumption made in Chapter 3 was that firms, at the microeconomic level, do not necessarily close down their less efficient plants when the rate of utilization of capacity decreases. Similarly, at the macroeconomic level, firms of different efficiency share all increases in total output, as underlined by Asimakopulos (1975, p. 322) and also by Kaldor (1985, p. 47) when he discusses the theoretical underpinnings of Okun's law. The cause of this sharing, except when prices fall so low relative to costs that the least efficient firms have to go under, is that in imperfect competition all firms adjust their prices to those set by the price-leaders of the industry, with all firms operating with some excess capacity. This post-Keynesian view can be contrasted with the standard view, according to which reduced aggregate demand implies the disappearance of the least efficient firms or the unemployment of the least efficient workers, a view that Keynes (1936, pp. 397ff.) accepted until he was confronted with contrary evidence. In actual economies, the most efficient firms are not operating at full capacity; and the least efficient firms do not operate only when the more efficient ones cannot respond to increased demand.

We should close this section by noting that any increase in the y_v coefficient of direct labour has automatic repercussions on the y_f coefficient of overhead labour. If an identical number of variable workers, with the same equipment or even with new machines, can now produce a larger output, this implies that full-capacity output is now larger. If the same number of overhead workers is required to supervise an equal number of direct labour workers when the machinery is functioning at full capacity, this means that the ratio of full-capacity output to overhead labour has increased. The productivity of fixed labour has grown in the same proportion as the productivity of variable labour. This can be seen in Figure 5.20. The increase in the productivity of variable workers shifts the utilization function counterclockwise. With the same number of operatives as before, if the plants were functioning at full capacity, the full-capacity level of output would jump from q_{fc1} to q_{fc2}. Assuming no change in the number of required overhead workers L_f, the productivity of this fixed labour necessarily rises, as shown by the increase in the angle y_f. Algebraically, recalling the definitions of y_v and y_f, we may take note of the following relations:

$$ f = \frac{y_v}{y_f} = \frac{q/L_v}{q_{fc}/L_f} = \frac{q_{fc}/L_v^{fc}}{q_{fc}/L_f} = \frac{L_f}{L_v^{fc}} \qquad (5.50) $$

The f variable represents the ratio of the productivity of variable labour to the productivity of fixed labour at full capacity. This ratio is also equal to the ratio of the number of overhead workers to the number of direct-labour workers when the firm or the economy is functioning at full capacity (Rowthorn, 1981, p. 4). As we can see in Figure 5.20, when this is the case, the number of workers L_f and L_v^{fc} does not change regardless of the induced change in the marginal product of variable workers. We must thus conclude that any change originating from the productivity of variable labour induces a proportional change in the productivity of fixed labour. The ratio f is a constant, regardless of the changes in the productivity of variable labour, unless there are other independent modifications in the number of overhead staff required to manage the existing capital stock. Looking again at equation (5.47), which defines the overall labour productivity ratio,

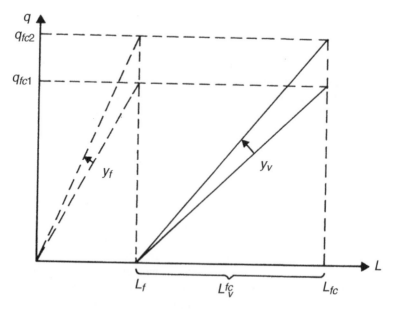

Figure 5.20 Impact of a change in the productivity of the blue-collar workers on the productivity of the white-collar workers

we see that it can be further simplified by making use of the relationship noted above in (5.50).

$$y = \frac{q}{L} = \frac{y_v}{1+f/u} \qquad (5.51)$$

Although we may look at y_v as a variable that may vary because of the Webb effect, we may still regard the ratio $f = y_v/y_f$ as a constant that is independent of the variations of y_v induced by the Webb effect or any other cause. We shall make use of this relationship in the next subsection and in Chapter 6. We omit a complication, that is, a possible relationship between the productivity of variable workers and the proportion of managers in the workforce, as suggested by Tavani and Vasudevan (2014).

5.5.2 The Mean Real Wage

We have seen in Chapter 1 that it is relatively easy for neoclassical economists to find an inverse relationship between real wages and employment. As explained there and in Felipe and McCombie (2009), this is because many estimates of labour demand functions are mere statistical artefacts. There are also many studies that find no relationship between real wages and employment, to such an extent that Peter Riach (1995, p. 173) concludes that 'in post-Keynesian analysis ... there is no dogmatic position on the consequences for employment of higher real wages'. The intention of this subsection is to show that the Kaleckian model can explain the apparent approximate independence between the real wage rate and the level of employment. This is done by distinguishing between the base real wage and the mean real wage. While the former sets the whole structure of wages, the latter depends on the composition of the labour force. This composition changes as output increases, or as the economy goes through the business cycle. Thus, while employment and the base real wage rate are positively correlated, as shown in previous sections, it is simultaneously possible for the mean real wage rate and the level of employment to be negatively correlated, as argued by Lars Osberg (1995, appendix 2).

What we need to do is distinguish between the nominal wage rate of variable labour, which is w_v, and the nominal wage of fixed workers, w_f. It is further assumed, as shown in equation (5.52), that the latter is σ times the level of the former; in other words, the wage of overhead labour is higher than that of direct labour. Since the mean wage is a weighted average of w_v and w_f, the mean wage will thus change with the composition of overhead and variable labour, as the level of output changes. Calling w_M the mean nominal wage rate and ω_M the mean real wage rate, we have

$$w_f = \sigma w_v \qquad \sigma > 1 \qquad (5.52)$$

$$w_v = w \qquad (5.53)$$

$$\omega_M = \frac{w_M}{p} = \frac{wL_v + \sigma w L_f}{pL} \qquad (5.54)$$

Let us still assume that all wages, even those of indirect labour, are spent on consumer goods. Aggregate demand in nominal terms, the equivalent of equation (5.2), is now given by

$$AD = w_M L + A = wL_v + \sigma w L_f + ap \qquad (5.55)$$

while aggregate supply, as a small variant of equation (5.14), is given by

$$AS = pq^s = pL_v y_v \qquad (5.56)$$

Equating these two equations, we get the effective demand constraint, that is, the new employment curve, for direct labour:

$$L_v = \frac{a + \sigma \omega L_f}{y_v - \omega} \qquad (5.57)$$

where $\omega = w/p$ is the base real wage rate, that is, the real wage rate of direct labour. Making use of equation (5.41), we get the employment curve for total labour:

$$L = \frac{a + L_f \{y_v + \omega(\sigma - 1)\}}{y_v - \omega} \qquad (5.58)$$

This equation has the same properties as our previous Kaleckian effective labour demand curves. It is upward-sloping and asymptotic to the productivity of variable demand. Thus there exists a positive relationship between the base real wage and employment. But what about the relationship between the mean real wage and employment? Combining equations (5.57) and (5.54), we find an implicit relationship between the mean real wage and total employment:

$$\omega_M = \omega + \frac{\omega(\sigma - 1) L_f}{L} \qquad (5.59)$$

This negative relationship is depicted in Figure 5.21, by the *MRW* (mean real wage) curve. It is this relationship that gets picked up in a number of empirical studies supporting conventional policy analyses recommending a decrease in real wages in order to improve employment. If the Kaleckian model shown here adequately describes stylized facts, one must conclude from it that lower real wages do not cause higher employment; rather lower mean real wages arise from changes in the composition of the labour force consequent to increases in the level of output and employment.

The determinants of the mean real wage rate can be given in explicit form, by combining equations (5.58) and (5.59). One finds:

$$\omega_M = \omega + \frac{\omega(\sigma - 1)(y_v - \omega) L_f}{a + \{y_v + \omega(\sigma - 1)\} L_f} \qquad (5.60)$$

Obviously, any increase in autonomous expenditures will reduce the mean wage rate by increasing employment and the proportion of low-paid variable or temporary workers in the active labour force. This, in Figure 5.21, is represented by a downward move along the *MRW* curve. A further look at the above equation also shows that an

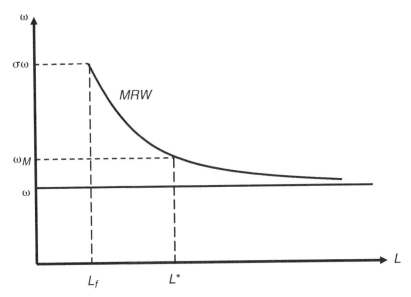

Figure 5.21   The mean wage rate as a function of employment, for a given base real wage rate

increase in the base real wage rate may or may not give rise to an increase in the mean real wage. The impact of an increase in the base real wage would be represented in Figure 5.22 by an outward shift of the *MRW* curve, with the mean real wage rate varying as indicated.

Any of the three outlined possibilities could occur, depending on the exact values of the parameters. The increase in the base real wage leads to an increase in the mean real wage, at a given level of employment. But the increased base real wage induces an increase in the level of employment, thus producing a change in the composition of labour towards a greater proportion of low-paid variable or temporary workers. At the new higher level of employment L^{**}, the mean real wage rate may thus rise (point A in Figure 5.22), stay constant (point B), or fall (point C). This explains why it may be difficult empirically to find a positive relationship between real wages and employment. Variables reflecting aggregate demand, for instance rates of capacity utilization, have to be taken into account when assessing the impact of real wages on employment.

5.5.3   Cost-plus Pricing Revisited

We start by showing how the cost curves and the price behaviour of firms, informally discussed in Chapter 3, are related to the Kaleckian utilization function. We identified three main variants of cost-plus pricing procedures. These were mark-up pricing, normal-cost pricing, and target-return pricing. All these procedures are variations on the same theme, and we show here that they are amenable to a similar algebraic core. The simplest of these variants is mark-up pricing, based on unit direct costs, which we can write now as

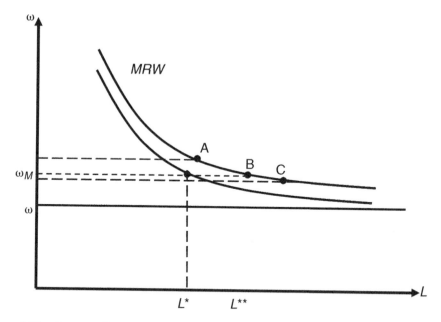

Figure 5.22 Impact of an increase in the base real wage on the mean real wage

$$p = (1 + \theta)UDC = (1 + \theta)w/y_v \qquad (5.61)$$

Normal-cost pricing is based on normal unit costs, that is, unit costs computed at the standard rate of capacity utilization. The normal unit cost in this vertically integrated economy is equal to the sum of unit direct labour cost and unit overhead labour cost, computed at standard output. Making use of equations (5.42), (5.43) and (5.50), we find that unit costs are

$$UC = (wL_v + \sigma wL_f)/q = w(1 + \sigma f/u)/y_v \qquad (5.62)$$

Remembering that u_n is the normal rate of utilization of capacity, we can write the normal-cost pricing relationship as

$$p = (1 + \Theta)NUC = (1 + \Theta)(1 + \sigma f/u_n)(w/y_v) \qquad (5.63)$$

We now have expressed unit costs as a function of the rate of utilization of capacity. Naturally, as can be seen from equation (5.62), the higher the rate of utilization, the lower are unit costs. These unit costs fall until the rate of utilization reaches 100 per cent, at which point they become equal to $w(1 + \sigma f)/y_v$. For a firm to make net profits, net profits being defined as the excess of the value of sales over total labour costs, the price must exceed the unit cost. In the present instance, the rate of utilization must be above $\sigma f/\theta$. All these relations are shown in Figure 5.23, which replicates Figure 3.9, but this time with the appropriate algebraic figures. The graph also shows that the share of direct labour in the value of output is equal to $1 - m$, while the share of the sum of overhead

Effective demand and employment

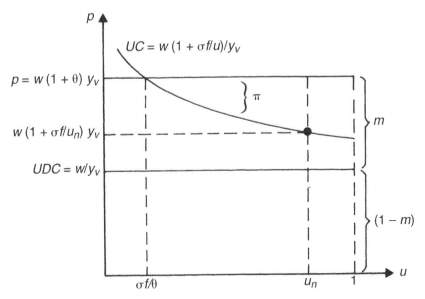

Figure 5.23 Share of gross profits, unit cost and share of net profits according to the rate of utilization of capacity

costs and profits is equal to m. This m is the share of gross profits. The share of net profits is also indicated in Figure 5.23. It is represented by the letter π, and it obviously changes, in contrast to the share of gross profits, with the rate of utilization of capacity. If capacity were to fall to $\sigma f/\theta$, net profits would drop to zero. We shall later see how that can occur. As to the share of managerial labour, it corresponds, by residual, to the difference $m - \pi$.

It is easy to find the mark-up on average variable costs that will yield the same price as the full-cost principle (Rowthorn, 1981, p. 36). By equating the prices of equations (5.61) and (5.63), we see that, given a percentage markup of Θ on normal unit costs, the same price would be obtained from a percentage mark-up on direct costs only if the mark-up were equal to

$$\theta = (1 + \Theta)(1 + \sigma f/u_n) - 1 \tag{5.64}$$

It is also possible to derive the same equivalence in the case of target-return pricing. We looked at this in Chapter 3, and considered the case where the price of capital goods and of output are the same, as in equation (3.31), which described the investment sector. When this is the case, to obtain a target rate of return r_n on investment, v being the capital/capacity ratio, the value of the markup Θ on normal unit costs must be equal to

$$\Theta = \frac{r_n v}{u_n - r_n v} \tag{5.65}$$

Naturally, for this to make sense the denominator must be positive, $u_n - r_n v > 0$, which simply means that profits ought not be larger than value added. As Asimakopulos (1975, p. 319) points out, 'these mark-ups are designed to cover, over time, both overhead costs and profits'. By combining equations (5.64) and (5.65), we see that, to arrive at an identical price, given the value of the markup Θ on normal unit labour costs arising from the target-return pricing decision, the mark-up θ on unit direct costs would have to be equal to

$$\theta = \frac{r_n v + \sigma f}{u_n - r_n v} \tag{5.66}$$

Combining equations (5.66) and (5.61), we find the explicit pricing equation based on target-return pricing procedures:

$$p = \left[1 + \frac{r_n v}{u_n - r_n v}\right]\left[\left(1 + \frac{\sigma f}{u_n}\right)\left(\frac{w}{y_v}\right)\right] = \left[1 + \frac{r_n v + \sigma f}{u_n - r_n v}\right]\frac{w}{y_v} = \left[\frac{u_n + \sigma f}{u_n - r_n v}\right]\frac{w}{y_v} \tag{5.67}$$

And hence the share going to variable labour is:

$$d = \frac{(w/p)L_v}{q} = \frac{(w/p)}{y_v} = \frac{u_n - r_n v}{u_n + \sigma f} \tag{5.67A}$$

We have thus obtained a very simple expression relating prices to unit direct costs w/y_v, although the assumed pricing behaviour of firms is of the sophisticated target-return pricing type. The advantage of equation (5.67) is that it shows that target-return pricing can be rewritten as a function of unit direct costs. This proves that using the simpler mark-up model is appropriate, even if firms make use of more complex accounting and pricing procedures, as long as there is no change in the normal ratio of overhead to variable labour, the relative wage rate between overhead and direct labour, the capital to capacity ratio, the standard rate of utilization of capacity and the target rate of return.

5.5.4 Mark-up Pricing and Net Profit Shares

In the previous sections of this chapter, the principle of effective demand was seen through the employment function. Changing the real wage rate, or other parameters, we examined the consequences for the level of employment. Here, we explore the principle of effective demand through its impact on the rate of utilization of capacity and the net profit share.

We can see the profit share from two angles. From the demand side, we already know that the total amount of real profits is a given, set by the amount of real autonomous expenditures a. From equation (5.8) we already know that

$$P = a \tag{5.8}$$

The share of profits in national income, seen from the demand side, is thus

$$\pi^d = a/q = a/uq_{fc} \tag{5.68}$$

Effective demand and employment 357

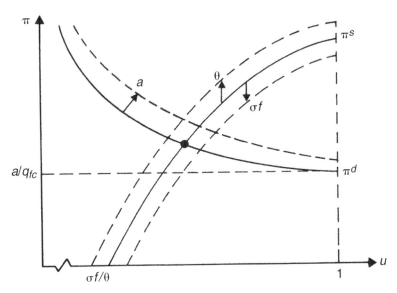

Figure 5.24 Impact of increases in various parameters on the rate of utilization of capacity and the net share of profits in national income

The above equation shows that, when the rate of utilization of capacity u is higher, the given amount of real profits is spread over a larger output, and as a consequence the net share of profits seen from the demand side diminishes with rising rates of utilization. This is only one part of the story, however. This share of profits must be equal to the share of profits determined from supply-side considerations. This share of profits results from the difference between the value of output and the total cost of producing that output, in other words the difference between the price and the realized unit cost. We have

$$\pi^s = (p - UC)/p \qquad (5.69)$$

Making use of mark-up equation (5.61) and the definition of unit cost, equation (5.62), we find that the net share of profits seen from the supply side is

$$\pi^s = \frac{\theta - \sigma f/u}{1+\theta} \qquad (5.70)$$

This equation tells us that, looking at it from the supply side, the share of profits increases as the rate of utilization rises. This is of course consistent with the cost curves drawn in Figure 5.23, and the remarks made there. Equations (5.70) and (5.68) are illustrated in Figure 5.24 with the curves π^s and π^d respectively. The intersection of the two curves yields the equilibrium rate of utilization of capacity. The same intersection yields the actual share of profits in national income, as well as the share of net profits in the value of output at the level of the representative firm when the aggregate level of sales is equated to the aggregate value of output. The advantage of such a presentation in the present context is that each relevant parameter is to be found in only one of the two curves, so that only one curve shifts as one of the parameters changes.

It is obvious from equation (5.68) that, if the level of autonomous expenditures rises, for a given level of utilization of capacity, the share of profits from the demand point of view must rise. The curve π^d would then shift up, as shown by the dotted π^d curve in Figure 5.24. At equilibrium, the rate of utilization and the share of profits would be higher, as shown by the new intersection of the two curves. We may now look at the factors affecting the π^s curve, as shown by equation (5.70). A rise in the f ratio, that is, the ratio of overhead workers to the number of variable workers that would operate at full-capacity output, leads to a downward shift of the π^s curve, as shown by one of the dotted π^s curves in Figure 5.24. The hiring of more overhead labour would thus induce a rise in the degree of utilization, but it would also cause a fall in the share of net profits. Exactly the same occurs with an increase in the σ parameter, that is, if the relative wage of overhead labour increases relative to that of direct labour (for a given base real wage).

Finally, an increase in the mark-up θ, that is, a decrease in the base wage rate relative to productivity, would provoke an upward shift of the π^s curve. At the new equilibrium, the rate of utilization would be lower, but the share of profits in aggregate income, as well as the share of net profits in the sales value of firms, would be higher. As we saw earlier, capitalists are able in the short run to increase their share of profits by increasing the mark-up on costs, but they do so at the expense of the rate of utilization of capacity. Symmetrically, increased real wages relative to productivity lead to a higher degree of utilization of capacity and allow more workers to be employed, as we have seen in previous sections. These higher wages, however, force down the share of profits. This inverse relationship is extensively used by authors close to the Marxian tradition, as we shall see in Chapter 6.

The lesson to be drawn from the above exercise is that the share of profits varies according to various parameters, including the mark-up on direct unit costs and the level of autonomous expenditures. In particular, the model determines simultaneously the share of profits and the level of output, which contradicts Kaldor's earlier presumption that the theory of effective demand could not simultaneously determine employment and distribution (Kaldor, 1956, p. 94). Indeed, it is this presumption that led Kaldor to assume full employment in his earlier models of growth and distribution. In his and other earlier post-Keynesian models, such as those of Robinson (1956), variations in the distribution of income following changes in the rate of investment were obtained by changing the mark-up, that is, the costing margin. The idea was that a higher level of activity would bring about higher prices relative to wage rates. The model with overhead labour costs also provides a response to the critique of overdetermination evoked by Janet Yellen (1980, p. 17).

It should now be clear that Kaldor's and Robinson's earlier beliefs are incorrect when one takes overhead labour costs into account. This was recognized by Asimakopulos (1970) when he formalized remarks made by Joan Robinson. Her remarks were to the effect that, with target-return pricing, super-normal profits are made in a seller's market, 'through changes in output at constant prices, instead of through changes in prices, as must be supposed to occur under perfect competition' (Robinson, 1969, p. 260). This is due, she said, to an element of quasi-fixed cost which is such that the 'average prime cost falls with output up to full capacity' (p. 261). Recalling that both Robinson (1956, p. 183) and Kaldor label as prime costs all the costs related to running a plant, rather than resting it, it is obvious that the average prime cost that Robinson is talking about is the unit labour cost of the vertically integrated firm of our model. The presence of overhead labour costs allows for variations in the shares of wages and profits, although the investment to output ratio, unit direct costs and the mark-up on unit direct costs are all constant. Similarly, an increase in the share of investment in output leads to an increase in the share of profits, although the mark-up is constant. Overhead labour costs thus play a major role, as emphasized in the present section.

Not surprisingly, as early as 1964, Kaldor recognized that he had been mistaken in assuming that the mechanism of effective demand could not simultaneously deal with the determination of the output level and that of the distribution of income. He attributed this earlier erroneous conception to the oversight of overhead labour costs. Without these, the share of profits could not go up when investment went up, unless the mark-up changed, and the mark-up could change automatically only in situations of full utilization of capacity.

> The one important respect in which I would now amend the exposition of the [previous theory] ... relates to the assumption of constant (short-period) prime costs. I did not realise then that this assumption – which makes a constant 'markup' equivalent to a constant *share* of profit in income – was not just a simplification, but was definitely misleading. In industry, short period labour costs per unit of output are not constant, but falling (mainly on account of the influence of 'overhead labour'); as a result of this, changes in the ratio of investment to output can elicit corresponding changes in the *share* of profits (and hence in the savings ratio) even if the 'markup' is constant; it follows from this that it is not *necessary* to assume full employment in order that the 'Keynesian' mechanism of adjusting the savings ratio to the investment coefficient should operate. (Kaldor, 1964b, pp. xvi–xvii)

It is clear from this quote that Kaldor had in mind all the ingredients that led to the construction of the present model of effective demand. Steindl was also fully aware of the role played by overhead costs.

> The net profit margin can, in fact, change for two quite different reasons: either because of a change in utilisation of capacity, with an otherwise unchanged structure of costs and prices; or the net profit margin can change at a given level of utilisation of capacity. The latter change will take place, for example, if gross profit margins change, while overhead costs at any given level of utilisation remain constant. (Steindl, 1952, p. 46)

The first case arises with a change in aggregate demand, and hence a shift of the π^d curve in Figure 5.24, so that the economy moves along the π^s curve, with an unchanged mark-up. The second case is represented by an increase in θ and hence a shift of the π^s curve.

5.5.5 Target-return Pricing and Net Profit Shares

One may wonder whether the results obtained so far depend on the assumed pricing procedure. Until now, our attention has been devoted to the simpler mark-up pricing procedure. What if corporations use target-return pricing? It should be obvious that the pricing procedure has no impact on the effects of an increase in autonomous demand in this short-period model. One may doubt, however, that an increase in overhead labour

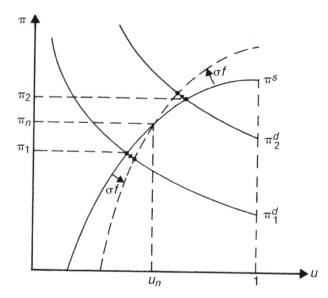

Figure 5.25 Impact of an increase in overhead costs on the rate of utilization of capacity and the net share of profits in national income when target-return pricing procedures are in use

costs still leads to an increase in the rate of utilization of capacity when pricing is done on the basis of unit costs rather than on the basis of direct costs. One may also wonder about the effect of larger overhead costs on the realized net profit margin when firms set prices on the basis of target-return pricing: do such increases in overhead costs still necessarily lead to a fall in the net share of profit?

This can be accounted for by integrating the target-return pricing procedure, given by equation (5.67), with the definition of the net profit share seen from the supply side, given by equation (5.69). Doing so, we obtain

$$\pi^s = \frac{(\sigma f + r_n v)u - (u_n - r_n v)\sigma f}{u(u_n + \sigma f)} \tag{5.71}$$

To find out about the impact of overhead costs on the net profit share, we take the derivative of equation (5.71) with respect to $f\sigma$, and get a surprisingly simple expression:

$$d\pi^s/d(\sigma f) = \frac{(u - u_n)(u_n - r_n v)}{u(u_n + \sigma f)^2}. \tag{5.72}$$

We can observe in Figure 5.25 the consequences of increasing overhead unit costs. As before, the π^s curve is upward-sloping while the π^d curve is downward-sloping. When overhead costs are increased; that is, when f or σ is higher, the π^s curve is displaced, but whether it is displaced up or down depends on whether the economy operates above or below the normal rate of capacity utilization. When the actual rate of utilization of capacity u is smaller than the normal rate of utilization u_n, the π^s curve shifts down, as can be read from equation (5.72). The consequence of larger overhead unit costs is that the net profit share is smaller and the rate of utilization of capacity is larger than in the initial position, as can be seen in Figure 5.25, when autonomous expenditures are such that the π_1^d curve is the relevant one. Reciprocally, if the actual rate of utilization of capacity u is larger than the normal rate of utilization u_n, then higher overhead unit costs lead to an upward shift of the π^s curve. This happens when, as can be seen from Figure 5.25, autonomous expenditures are such that the relevant curve is the π_2^d curve, and when the actual share of profit π_2 is larger than the target share of profit π_n. As a consequence of this shift, when overhead unit costs increase, the share of net profits increases while the rate of utilization of capacity decreases. Indeed, it cannot be otherwise since the total amount of profits is given by the amount of autonomous expenditures in this simple model, so that the rate of profit is constant for a given stock of capital. Thus, if the share of profits rises, the rate of utilization must fall.

The introduction of target-return pricing thus gives rise to interesting comparative statics, as its introduction may lead to the disruption of previous results and to conditional results. In particular, the increase in overhead costs does not necessarily lead to increased economic activity. This occurs even if we omit the possibility of saving out of overhead salaries, which would otherwise reduce aggregate demand, and which we did not consider here.

One may be puzzled as to why higher unit overhead costs would have a positive effect on the cost-side profitability of firms when the actual rate of capacity utilization exceeds its standard rate, whereas it would have a negative effect on cost-side profitability when the actual rate of capacity utilization is below the standard rate. The cause of this is that overhead labour costs are spread over different levels of output. Following an increase in managerial labour costs, prices are raised just enough to maintain the customary rate of return when the firm is operating at the standard rate of utilization of capacity. When the firm is operating beyond the standard rate of utilization, the hike in prices more than compensates for the increase in unit costs. Reciprocally, when the firm is operating below the standard rate of utilization, the hike in prices does not fully compensate for the increase in unit costs.

This can be seen in Figure 5.26, where the cost curves of the representative Kaleckian firm have been drawn with direct labour costs shown as constant per unit of output, while total unit costs incorporating the fixed managerial overhead labour costs are represented by a rectangular hyperbola. Sticking to a partial equilibrium analysis, the increase in the overhead labour costs is shown here by the upward shift of the unit cost curve. At the standard rate of capacity utilization u_n, the vertical distance between unit costs and the price level remains the same, before and after the change, indicating that the rate of profit on capital remains at r_n. By contrast, at $u_B > u_n$, this vertical distance increases, showing that profitability is now higher than when overhead labour costs were lower. At $u_A < u_n$, the vertical distance diminishes, indicating that profitability is dropping at that rate of utilization. An extreme instance of this case is given at rate u_C, where profitability was zero and now becomes negative because of the increase in overhead costs.

As a final remark, it should be said that the model is only one among several possible formalizations. In the present model, the real wage of managers was a multiple σ of the real wage of workers. As a consequence, an increase in the target rate of return of corporations would have led to an increase in the mark-up and hence to a reduction in the real wage of both the workers and the managerial staff. In a *cadrisme* regime of accumulation,

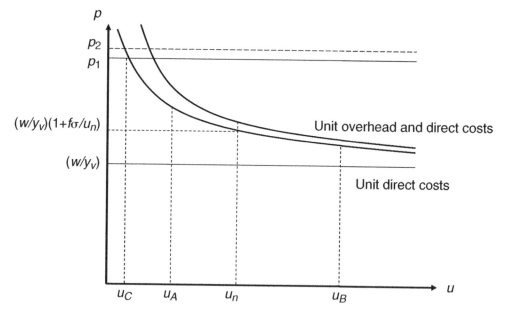

Figure 5.26 Microeconomic impact of an increase in managerial costs, with target-return pricing

where finance and managers join forces to appropriate potential income shares, it might be more relevant to assume instead that the real wage of managers is a given, for instance a multiple of labour productivity. With this alternative closure, the wage multiple σ becomes an endogenous variable, which depends on the target rate of return set by managers and on the real salaries that they assign to themselves through control of the corporate board of directors. This alternative closure, however, generates results that are similar to those shown here, as demonstrated in Lavoie (2009b, pp. 390–91).

5.6 FISCAL POLICY AND FULL EMPLOYMENT

5.6.1 Sound Finance and the New Fiscalism

We have so far argued that we could not rely on market forces to bring the economy back to a position of high aggregate demand and full employment. It was further argued that increases in employment could be generated by increases in autonomous expenditures and real wages. Introducing the possibility of endogenous government budget balances and endogenous trade balances did, however, weaken the strength of the argument in favour of real wages, since with constant autonomous expenditures, an increase in real wages (or a fall in the profit margins) led to a fall in overall profits, as shown in equations (5.37) and (5.40), despite the favourable impact of higher real wages on real output and employment. Lower profits could thus induce a negative reaction on the part of business firms, which could decide to reduce their autonomous investment expenditures, which would then further hurt profits and possibly reduce output despite the higher real wages. Higher real wages thus cannot be used as a panacea against unemployment. Higher real wages must be accompanied by higher autonomous expenditures, arising from either the consumption or the government sectors. The Global Financial Crisis has certainly made us aware of the dangers of autonomous consumption expenditures financed by consumer debt, so the alternative is expansionary fiscal policy, conducted along Keynesian lines.

Within the mainstream New Consensus, the responsibility for achieving the appropriate amount of employment, compatible with the natural rate of unemployment and stable inflation, is attributed to monetary policy. While the major instrument for macroeconomic management is monetary policy, fiscal policy has been relegated to a very secondary role. Mainstream economists have been arguing that fiscal policy should broadly aim at balanced budgets, it being understood that endogenous fluctuations in the budget balance were permissible, and that budget deficits generated by the automatic fiscal stabilizers could occur when the economy was hit by a negative shock. Roughly speaking, this meant that public budgets had to be balanced over the business cycle. Some politicians have gone one step further, putting forth rules that force governments to avoid budget deficits altogether in any given year, thus pursuing procyclical budget policies by reducing government expenditures when the economy is doing poorly, and pursuing relentlessly what could be called 'sound finance'. All this seemed to fit well with the fear that a Keynesian approach to fiscal policy would encourage profligacy by irresponsible politicians.

Larger government deficits, all else equal, help sustain aggregate profits. But, as we have seen earlier in the chapter and as noted by Keynes, the business community may misunderstand how aggregate profits are generated. Kalecki (1971, p. 139) went one step further. As did Keynes, he argued that, with capitalism, 'the level of employment depends on the so-called state of confidence', but he further contended that this gives 'to the capitalists a powerful indirect control over Government policy: everything which may shake the state of confidence must be carefully avoided because it would cause an economic crisis. The social function of the doctrine of "sound finance" is to make the level of employment dependent on the "state of confidence".' Thus Kalecki claims that governments know how to achieve full employment, but that they may decide not to use this knowledge, fearing the reaction of the business community, thus reverting to 'sound finance' policies.

The Global Financial Crisis (and later, the recession induced by the COVID-19 pandemic) has put a momentary halt to the calls for sound finance. For a year or so, starting around November 2008, the consensus at the IMF, among central bankers and among G-20 leaders evolved towards a new story line, which was dubbed 'new fiscalism' by my colleague Mario Seccareccia (2012). Advocates of the new fiscalism argued that government deficits arising from the automatic stabilizers could be enlarged by discretionary expansionary fiscal measures when a large recession was caused by a financial crisis, something we could also call contingent Keynesianism. The economic rationale for such a change of mind was that monetary policy having reached its zero lower bound, fiscal policy could be efficient in recovering economic activity, since rising inflation and interest rate hikes were unlikely. Still, despite the low interest rates, it was believed that they would end up rising in the medium run, and hence advocates of the new fiscalism were quick to call for responsible fiscal policies, with measures of fiscal consolidation – a disguise for fiscal austerity – thus ensuring fiscal sustainability and a return to balanced budgets (Fiebiger and Lavoie, 2017). By June 2009 expansionary fiscal policies were all but forgotten by the very important people. The problems encountered by eurozone countries, starting with Greece in December 2009, seemed to validate their concerns and those of the new fiscalists. What then has been the position of post-Keynesians on fiscal policy?

5.6.2 Functional Finance

Although post-Keynesians have been influenced by the focus on monetary policy of the mainstream New Consensus, they have always remained faithful to the importance of discretionary fiscal policy. For instance, Nell (1988) wrote a whole book on the importance of the government sector and the necessity of government deficits, and several edited books have been produced around these topics. William Vickrey (1997), the Nobel Prize recipient who turned towards post-Keynesian economics in his older years, also gave his support to functional finance. Other post-Keynesians, such as Arestis and Sawyer (2003; 2004; 2010) have been quite clear about the relevance of countercyclical fiscal policy, at a time when mainstream economists claimed that Keynesian expansionary policies were rendered ineffective by equivalent reductions in private aggregate demand. These were said to be caused by crowding-out effects, which would raise interest rates and reduce loanable funds available for investment by the private sector, and by the Barro–Ricardo equivalence effects, which were said to reduce consumption, as consumers would save more now in order to pay the higher taxes that would later be generated by the higher budget deficits. Despite the fact that 'it is the anti-Keynesian economists, the high priests of rational expectations, Ricardian equivalence, and other mumbo-jumbo who have failed to connect with the common sense of ordinary people' (Galbraith, 1994–95, p. 257), mainstream economists and think tanks have had great success in convincing the general public about the virtues of sound finance by using slogans such as 'it is high time to put the government house in order' or 'the government ought to do like any household does: it should balance its budget'. Post-Keynesians did not buy these arguments, and have continued to argue instead that government expenditures could raise actual and potential output.

> Conventional claims about the impotence of Keynesian fiscal policy are largely unfounded ... Our current state of knowledge provides no reason to reject Keynesian demand management principles as the appropriate response to an economy operating with substantial idle resources. Furthermore ... effective Keynesian fiscal policy may raise potential output, as well as addressing problems of underutilized resources. (Fazzari, 1994–95, p. 233)

As Arestis and Sawyer (2004, p. 63) say, post-Keynesian fiscal policy is based on one form or another of 'functional finance', advocated by Abba Lerner (1943). Post-Keynesians still agree with Keynes (1936, p. 129) that it is absurd to waste labour resources because public expenditures are presumably unprofitable and inefficient: one might as well have the government put cash in bottles, bury them in the ground, and have the private sector dig to uncover the cash, thus providing employment and profits to the private sector. But we can do much better by claiming unutilized labour and capital capacity to build or repair houses, buildings, bridges, roads, sewers, or by hiring less skilled labour to clean up the environment or provide other community services or improvements. MMT authors have been highly vocal about the latter, arguing that the government should act as an employer of last resort (ELR); that is, it should provide employment to anyone willing but unable to find work in the private sector (Forstater, 1998; Wray, 1998; Kelton, 2020; Tcherneva, 2020). This policy stance, which relies on direct employment policies, is also known as a job-guarantee programme or a buffer-stock employment programme. Its main advantage, relative to standard expansionary fiscal policies, is that it would be geographically concentrated in the areas with low economic activity, rather than being spread out all over the country, including in regions where resources are nearly fully employed (Mitchell and Muysken, 2008). As a consequence, this is sometimes referred to as spatial Keynesianism. Whatever the choice made, direct employment policies or infrastructure expenditures, the key common-sense argument is that labour is a flow and not a stock: 'If resources are left idle, output is lost forever. It is not stored up for later use' (Littleboy, 2013, p. 126).

While functional finance, as opposed to sound finance, has won the approval in one way or another of all post-Keynesians, functional finance as strictly described by Lerner (1943) himself has been particularly endorsed by the neo-chartalist branch of post-Keynesianism – the MMT school (Nell and Forstater, 2003). Lerner is essentially making three claims. His first claim is that a government budget surplus or deficit, in and of itself, is neither good nor bad. The purpose of fiscal policy should not be the attainment of a particular budget position, such as a balanced budget, over a year or over a business cycle. Rather, the goal of fiscal policy ought to be the achievement of the proper level of employment, one that can provide for full employment, without inflation. As Lerner (1943, p. 39) puts it,

> the central idea is that government fiscal policy, its spending and taxing, its borrowing and repayment of loans, its issue of new money and its withdrawal of money, shall all be undertaken with an eye only to the *results* of these actions on the economy and not to any established traditional doctrine about what is sound or unsound.

The second essential claim of Lerner (1943) is that the government is not helpless and unable to raise funds. There is no financial constraint on a government backed by a central bank. This is, or should be, the case of central governments, such as the federal governments in the USA or in Canada. This second claim means that such central governments can always get the financial resources they need from their central banks. This is compatible with the story told by Table 4.17, which we have called the neo-chartalist view. As confirmed by Lerner (1947, pp. 313–14), the view here is that 'money is a creature of the State', which has the 'power to create or destroy money'. As long as there exists collaboration between the central bank and the government, and as long as the government does not borrow funds in a foreign currency and is not forced to support the value of its currency on foreign exchange markets, the government cannot 'run out of money'. This point has been made again and again by the neo-chartalists, and it now seems to be accepted once again by a large number of post-Keynesian and Keynesian economists: it is said that in such a case the government benefits from a 'sovereign currency' (Wray, 1998; 2012; Tcherneva, 2006; Kelton, 2020). If there is a constraint, it is a real resources constraint (capital and/or labour), but in this case this constraint is also faced by the private sector, and then by definition we must be at full employment of resources.

The third essential claim of Lerner (1943) is that, even if the government engages in functional finance and deficit-spends in the attempt to achieve full employment, the public debt will not rise forever. In modern terms, we would say that the public debt to GDP ratio will converge to a finite value. There are two main reasons for this. Assuming a closed economy, as the public debt rises, the wealth of the private sector rises, as we showed in equation (4.11). Thus, first, as wealth and interest payments out of the public debt increase, households will spend a greater proportion of their private income; second, as interest payments rise, so will tax payments out of these interest payments, thus reducing the public deficit relative to GDP. The claim here is that government deficits, at least in a closed economy, can be sustainable. As Lerner (1943, p. 49) puts it, 'as the national debt increases it acts as a self-equilibrating force, gradually diminishing the further need for its growth and finally reaching an equilibrium level where its tendency to grow comes completely to an end'.

While the first and the second essential claims of Lerner, as I see them, are relatively uncontroversial, the third claim, about the unconditional sustainability of the debt ratio, is more dubious. We thus examine it in the next subsection.

5.6.3 The Sustainability of Functional Finance

Sustainability can be defined in several different ways. Here we define the sustainability of public debt as whether the debt to GDP ratio converges either towards zero or towards a constant value. The standard argument regarding the sustainability of public debt is that the real rate of growth of output ought to be larger than the real rate of interest on debt (Domar, 1944). More precisely, what is at stake is the real rate of interest net of taxes. If this stringent condition is not realized, meaning that the growth rate of output is smaller than the rate of interest net of taxes, then the government ought to pursue austerity policies and achieve a large enough primary budget surplus, that is, a large enough difference between tax revenues and government expenditures from which interest payments are omitted. While there is some sense in these rules, it can be shown that a government that pursues a full-employment policy, increasing or reducing its expenditures so as to achieve an output and a growth rate of output compatible with full employment of a growing labour force, will see its debt to GDP ratio converge to a constant value under fairly weak conditions.

Recent papers based on the stock–flow-consistent approach that was developed in Chapter 4 have provided an algebraic proof of the above under more general conditions (Cassetti, 2020; Ryoo and Skott, 2013). Here we offer a highly simplified version, based on Godley and Lavoie (2007b) and on Martin (2008). We assume away inflation, and we assume further that government debt is the only available asset, so that household wealth V is exactly equal to government debt. Suppose that the government is successfully pursuing functional finance, so that government expenditures take up any slack between private expenditures and full-employment output, so that full employment is achieved in each period. Actual output then grows at the rate g_n that ensures full employment of the labour force. This means that actual output is independent of private expenditures and is such that GDP is equal to full-employment GDP, so that $Y = Y_{fe} = (1 + g_n)Y_{fe-1}$. The disposable income of the private sector, which we call Y_d, is thus equal to full-employment GDP net of taxes plus the interest payments net of taxes that the private sector is getting

Effective demand and employment 367

out of the government debt. Defining i as the interest rate, these interest payments are thus iV_{-1} before tax, and $(1 - \tau)iV_{-1}$ after tax, so that disposable income in any one period, for a given income tax rate τ, can be written as

$$Y_d = (1 - \tau)Y_{fe} + (1 - \tau)iV_{-1} \tag{5.73}$$

Let us now assume that the private sector saves a proportion s_{yd} of its disposable income, and that it dissaves a proportion c_v of its past accumulated wealth. Empirically, c_v has been estimated to be around or less than 5 per cent. The saving of the private sector during this period, or the increase in its wealth for the period (omitting capital gains), is thus equal to

$$V - V_{-1} = s_{yd}Y_d - c_vV_{-1} = s_{yd}[(1 - \tau)Y_{fe} + (1 - \tau)iV_{-1}] - c_vV_{-1} \tag{5.74}$$

The above equation can also be rewritten as

$$V - V_{-1} = c_v\left(\frac{s_{yd}}{c_v}Y_d - V_{-1}\right) \tag{5.74A}$$

This implies that the private sector has an implicit target level of wealth, which is given by $(s_{yd}/c_v)Y_d$. It means that the private sector is saving so as to gradually achieve this target stock of wealth, which is thus a function of disposable income (which is itself growing). The wealth accumulation towards the target proceeds at a certain rate, determined by a partial adjustment parameter, which is given by c_v.

Since the liability of the government – its public debt – is equal to the assets held by the private sector – its wealth V – the increase in government debt in a given period is equal to the saving of the private sector during that same period, as given by equation (5.74). We can rewrite this equation by regrouping all the V_{-1} terms together, so as to obtain a difference equation of the form $V = A + BV_{-1}$:

$$V = s_{yd}(1 - \tau)(1+g_n)Y_{fe-1} + [1 - c_v + s_{yd}(1 - \tau)i]V_{-1} \tag{5.75}$$

What is of concern however is whether the public debt to GDP ratio converges. Thus, we ought to divide the previous equation by Y, and check instead:

$$\frac{V}{Y} = s_{yd}(1-\tau)(1+g_n)\left(\frac{Y_{fe-1}}{Y}\right) + \left[1 - c_v + s_{yd}(1-\tau)i\right]\left(\frac{V_{-1}}{Y}\right) \tag{5.76}$$

Since we assume that $Y = Y_{fe} = (1 + g_n)Y_{fe-1}$, the above equation can be rewritten as:

$$\frac{V}{Y} = s_{yd}(1-\tau) + \left[\frac{1-c_v + s_{yd}(1-\tau)i}{1+g_n}\right]\left(\frac{V_{-1}}{Y_{-1}}\right) \tag{5.76A}$$

This difference equation would lead to an explosive path when B is greater than one; it yields a non-oscillatory convergent path whenever B takes a positive value less than one. This means that the public debt is converging to a constant value whenever $0 < B < 1$. Convergence of the public debt to GDP ratio requires that the term within the squared brackets be smaller than one. The public debt to GDP ratio will thus converge to a constant number if the following inequality is realized:

$$(1-\tau)i < \frac{c_v + g_n}{s_{yd}} \tag{5.77}$$

Condition (5.77) is thus much weaker than that considered to be Domar's standard condition on the sustainability of public debt. Furthermore, the steady-state public debt to GDP ratio can be calculated from equation (5.76A). One obtains:

$$\left(\frac{V}{Y}\right)^* = \frac{s_{yd}(1-\tau)(1+g_n)}{g_n + c_v - s_{yd}(1-\tau)i} \tag{5.78}$$

It can readily be seen that an increase in the interest rate or in the propensity to save out of disposable income leads to a higher steady-state public debt ratio, while an increase in the tax rate or in the propensity to consume out of wealth will induce a lower steady-state public debt ratio. More computations show that a faster growth rate g_n will be associated with a lower steady-state public debt ratio.

What the above shows is that Lerner's third essential claim seems to be validated. Even if the rate of interest net of taxes reaches a level as high as 10 per cent, condition (5.77) is very likely to be realized. As we said earlier, the propensity to consume out of wealth c_v is often estimated at around 5 per cent. The propensity to save out of current income, taking into account saving out of retained profits, is unlikely to be any higher than 25 per cent. Thus, even if the sum of the growth rate of the economy and of the propensity to save out of wealth were only 3 per cent, the term on the right-hand side of equation (5.77) would still be above the rate of interest net of taxes. Unless the central bank is determined to have interest rates skyrocketing so as to scare the government and force it to adopt austerity policies, functional finance is a viable strategy.

5.6.4 Fiscal Policy versus Monetary Policy and Final Warnings

Readers may wonder how such a surprising result has been achieved. The reasoning that arrives at condition (5.77) is built upon a stock–flow-consistent approach that takes into account the dynamic evolution of public debt and the generation of interest payments. As Bill Martin (2008, p. 653) points out, 'in stock–flow models, it is well-known that the rate of interest has an apparently perverse effect on the level of aggregate demand', so that 'in stock–flow consistent equilibrium, the debt interest rate effect will always be dominant'. This has long been recognized, for instance by Blinder and Solow (1973), but seems to have been omitted from many practical discussions. Even though higher interest rates will have a short-run and medium-run negative effect on aggregate demand, by curbing consumption and investment expenditures and by inducing capital losses on the value of bonds and other such financial assets, the additional government debt interest payments end up raising the flow of disposable income (Godley and Lavoie, 2007a).

The result achieved through condition (5.77) provides strong support to the pursuit of full employment through a functional finance approach. It also provides an additional insight regarding the debate between advocates of fiscal policy versus those favouring monetary policy for stabilization purposes. When the public debt to GDP ratio is low, the positive effects of interest payments on aggregate demand are likely to be wiped out by the negative effects of high interest rates on investment in fixed capital and housing. However, by contrast, when the public debt to GDP ratio is high, as has been the case of Italy for a long time, the positive effects of higher interest payments on debt are likely to kick in much earlier, as pointed out by Bell-Kelton and Ballinger (2006).

Monetary policy is thus likely to be relatively ineffective under circumstances of high public debt ratios. When this is the case, zero-interest-rate policies, ZIRP, are unlikely to be effective because over time they greatly reduce the amount of public interest payments that are added to private income and thus constitute the base for disposable income and consumption. This helps to explain further why post-Keynesians do not have much faith in the ability of monetary policy to control economic activity and thus, indirectly, the level of inflation. Post-Keynesians prefer to support an active fiscal policy. Indeed, in his various writings, Godley has emphasized the significance of what he has called the fiscal stance, which is the ratio of pure government expenditures to the average tax rate. The trend value of GDP is always some function of this ratio, G/τ (Godley and Lavoie, 2007a, p. 116). This provides a long-run view of the importance of fiscal policy, by contrast with the standard countercyclical view.

To conclude, two warnings regarding all this must be issued. The equations that led to condition (5.77) were based on a closed-economy model. In an open economy, or more specifically one where some of the public debt is held by foreigners, part of the interest payments on public debt will flow abroad and will not be part of domestic aggregate demand, as alluded to by Lerner (1943, p. 43). Furthermore, a full-employment policy may lead to current account deficits, especially if other countries are instead pursuing austerity policies, and these may raise additional concerns from financial observers. The decisions of policy-makers will not be as simple as depicted here.

The final warning is related to income distribution matters. The higher the debt to GDP ratio, the higher the interest payments, relative to GDP, received by households that save – the rentiers in short. The higher the debt to GDP ratio, the higher will be the share of disposable income going to rentiers and hence the lower will be the share of disposable income going to other households. Thus, although it is very likely that the debt to GDP ratio will be stabilized when the government runs public deficits in its efforts to sustain full employment, even if interest rates are high, one cannot remain indifferent to the levels that interest rates can reach since they play an important role with regard to income distribution and since they may push up the costing margins of firms. The same reasoning applies to tax rates, since lower tax rates drive up the steady-state debt to GDP ratio when a pure functional finance policy is being pursued, thus also raising the share of full-employment output that will be consumed by rentiers. If one is concerned by these long-run consequences on income distribution, one should not advocate tax cuts to fight unemployment.

NOTE

* Besides relying on and extending the 1992 *Foundations*, full sentences have been taken from the following publications: 'Real wages and unemployment with effective and notional demand for labor', *Review of Radical Political Economics*, **35** (2), Spring 2003, pp. 166–82; 'Real wages, employment structure and the aggregate demand curve in a Kaleckian short-run model', *Journal of Post Keynesian Economics*, **19** (2), Winter 1996–97, pp. 275–88.

6. Accumulation and capacity*

As was briefly mentioned in Chapter 1, one of the objectives of post-Keynesian theory is to combine the classical concerns for growth and distribution with the Keynesian principle of effective demand. Indeed, this was Joan Robinson's explicit objective in her famous *Accumulation of Capital*, where she pointed out that her intention was to develop 'a generalisation of the *General Theory*, that is, an extension of Keynes's short-period analysis to long-run development' (1956, p. vi). Similarly, the aim of the present chapter is to extend to the long period the results of Chapter 5, which were obtained within the framework of the short period, with a focus on the level of employment and the level of output. Here the focus will move towards rates of growth of output, rates of profit and rates of utilization of capacity, as is done in Hein (2014).

The method of analysis to be employed is that of comparative dynamics. A number of post-Keynesian and heterodox economists (Peter Flaschel, Steve Keen, Peter Skott, Barkley Rosser, Lance Taylor) have for some time insisted that dynamic analysis ought to be conducted with the tools of differential equations and non-linear dynamics, on the grounds that these tools better reflect the world as we know it. Still, except for a few sections, most of what follows will rely on comparative dynamics based on linear relations. The main justification for doing so is pedagogical. The use of differential equations confers an extra degree of difficulty, which is ill suited to the readership targeted in this book. A second justification is that a fair amount can be said with the simple use of comparative dynamics, as we shall see.

The focus of our long-run analysis will be once more the Kaleckian model. Thus our analysis of accumulation will be based almost exclusively on extensions of the Kaleckian model developed in Chapter 5 for the short run. We will pursue the same strategy as the one we used in that chapter; that is, we will start with a simple model, which we will call the canonical model, to which we will gradually add complications as the need arises, either as a way of taking into account additional factors or as a way to introduce and deal with criticisms of the model. A study of other post-Keynesian or heterodox growth models, such as neo-Goodwinian or neo-Harrodian models, can be found in the recent book of Blecker and Setterfield (2019).

6.1 THE NEO-KEYNESIAN MODEL: THE INFLATIONIST VERSION

For a long time post-Keynesian economics was mostly known for the models of growth and distribution that were developed at the University of Cambridge by Robinson, Kaldor and Pasinetti in the late 1950s and in the early 1960s. Furthermore, as pointed out by Baranzini and Mirante (2013) in their survey of the various lines of research that these growth models gave rise to, more than 200 scholars have made contributions to these Robinson–Kaldor–Pasinetti growth models. For these reasons, it is important to distinguish between these Cambridge models of growth and the models of growth associated with the Kaleckian foundations emphasized in Chapter 5. We shall call the former 'neo-Keynesian', and the latter 'Kaleckian' models. There are two major related differences between the two groups of models to note. First, the neo-Keynesian models, because they are inspired by the framework developed by Keynes, are basically set in a world of competition, whereas the post-Keynesian models of Kaleckian inspiration are part of an oligopolistic framework. The second difference between the two models is that the older neo-Keynesian model implicitly assumes that in the long period the rate of utilization of capacity is fixed at its normal level, whereas in the newer post-Keynesian model the rate of utilization of capacity is presumed to be endogenous, even in the long period. There are important consequences to the adoption of these differing assumptions, despite the other similarities of the two models.

6.1.1 The Stability of the Model

The most famous feature of the neo-Keynesian model of growth and distribution is that the rate of profit does not depend on microeconomic technical conditions or on relative physical endowments, but solely on macroeconomic variables, namely the rate of growth of the economy and some variable related to the propensity to save out of profits. This is true either under the classical saving assumption that is, when assuming that all wages are consumed, or under the Pasinetti assumption, that is, assuming that wages can be saved while adding conditions regarding the rate of return on savings of different social classes, in which case it is the propensity to save on profits by the capitalist class that determines the rate of profit (Pasinetti, 1974, ch. 5). We shall examine this second case later. Turning to the classical saving assumption, the principle of effective demand requires that investment and saving be equal, the latter being equal only to saving on profits. This condition has already been encountered in Chapter 5 under equation (5.32), which can now be rewritten as:

$$I = s_p P \tag{6.1}$$

The Cambridge equation is simply the dynamic version of this simple expression of the principle of effective demand. Dividing both sides of equation (6.1) by K, the stock of capital, and rearranging, one gets the overall rate of profit r as a function of the overall rate of accumulation g and of the propensity to save on profits:

$$r = g/s_p \tag{6.2}$$

Although simple, the Cambridge equation raises several controversial issues. In its standard interpretation by Kaldor, Pasinetti and Robinson, it is the rate of growth that determines the rate of profit. This interpretation arises from the short-run Keynesian causal scheme, where investment is given and hence considered the exogenous variable. A natural development of this short-run causality is thus to suppose that the rate of growth of investment is the exogenous factor, while the rate of profit is the endogenous one. 'Thus, given conditions to save from each type of income (the thriftiness conditions) the rate of profit is determined by the rate of accumulation of capital' (Robinson, 1962, p. 12). Conversely, a number of heterodox economists, mainly Marxians, believe that an exogenous rate of profit determines the rate of growth. We shall see later that both variables may be seen as being endogenously determined. We could then just as well rewrite equation (6.2), denoting it as g^s to indicate that it describes the rate of growth of the supply of savings.

$$g^s = s_p r \tag{6.3}$$

One simple way to have both variables endogenous, while preserving the one-way causality from output variables (the rate of investment) to price variables (the rate of profit), is to keep equation (6.2) while making the rate of growth decided by entrepreneurs a function of the expected rate of profit on future investment. This is precisely what Robinson (1962, pp. 47–8) proposes. She has a 'double-sided relationship between the rate of profit and the rate of accumulation', which gives rise to her famous banana-shaped diagram. On the one hand, the actual rate of profit is determined by the rate of accumulation decided by entrepreneurs and their firms. On the other hand, the rate of accumulation depends on the expected rate of profit, at a decreasing rate, generating the banana-shaped diagram. Here we shall present only a linear version of this latter relationship, as does Amadeo (1986, p. 86), for instance. Calling r^e the expected rate of profit, and γ the rate of growth if no profit were expected, we have the investment function in a dynamic mode, which we denote g^i:

$$g^i = \gamma + \gamma_r r^e \tag{6.4}$$

Both coefficients γ and γ_r may be said to reflect the intensity of the animal spirits of the entrepreneurs. In particular, the γ_r parameter reflects the sensitivity of the rate of growth decided by entrepreneurs to changes in the expected rate of profit. The double-sided relationship between the rate of profit and the rate of accumulation is illustrated in Figure 6.1. It has been supposed that the slope of equation (6.3) – the saving function – is steeper than that of equation (6.4), which represents the investment function. This means that the sensitivity of investment decisions to changes in the expected rate of profit is less than the sensitivity of saving to changes in the actual rate of profit. We shall soon see the importance of this assumption.

To comprehend how the model functions, start with an arbitrary expected rate of profit, say r_0^e as in Figure 6.1. At that expected rate of profit, investment decided by entrepreneurs will be such that the rate of accumulation will be g_0, as shown in the figure. Assume now that investment turns out to equal saving. This means that the economy will be at point A on the saving curve, that is, on the line given by equation (6.3). As we know from equation (5.16) and Figure 5.6, this is not an obvious assumption to make, because in the ultra-short period, firms may be in a situation of excess supply or excess demand. Thus we need to assume the existence of a price or quantity mechanism that will bring about the equality between investment and saving, pulling the economy on to the saving curve g^s. This is an assumption often made by post-Keynesians, who ignore the ultra-short-period haggling that could occur, setting aside the questions that were posed

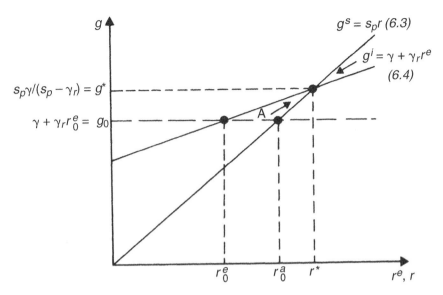

Figure 6.1 Determination of the desired rate of accumulation when the neo-Keynesian model is stable

by Harrod (1973). Assuming that the economy has indeed reached the point where investment equals saving, the economy thus being on its effective demand curve, the actual rate of profit is given by the g^s curve. Robinson (1962, p. 48) makes this assumption in her original analysis, and this is why the g^s curve of Figure 6.1 is often called the profit realization curve (Harris, 1978, p. 189). With the rate of accumulation at g_0, the actual profit rate is r_0^a. The realized profit rate is thus larger than the expected profit rate r_0^e. Provided the new expected rate of profit responds positively to the actual rate of profit, the expected rate of profit will rise, eventually reaching the value r^*, at which point the expected rate of profit will turn out to be equal to the actual rate. For the model to be complete, we thus need one more equation that relates the expected rate of profit at time t to the actual rate of profit at time t_{-1}. Several formulations are possible. We may write this as some adaptive process compatible with reasonable rationality:

$$r_t^e = (1 - \phi_1)r_{t-1}^e + \phi_1 r_{t-1}, \text{ with } 0 < \phi_1 < 1 \qquad (6.5)$$

When the actual rate of profit at period t_{-1} is equal to the expected rate of profit of the same period, there is no change in the expected rate. We may then speak of an equilibrium rate of profit. The rate of growth g^* that corresponds to this value of the rate of profit in Figure 6.1 is called by Robinson the desired rate of growth. This rate of growth is such that the expectations of the entrepreneurs are fulfilled. Equations (6.3) and (6.4) thus jointly determine an endogenous rate of accumulation and an endogenous rate of profit, assuming that in long-run equilibrium the expected and the realized rates of profit are identical. The desired rate of growth is thus equal to

$$g^* = s_p\gamma/(s_p - \gamma_r) \tag{6.6}$$

while the equilibrium rate of profit, such that $r = r^e$, is given by

$$r^* = \gamma/(s_p - \gamma_r) \tag{6.7}$$

It can be seen from equation (6.6) that for the desired rate of accumulation to be positive, both the denominator and the numerator must be positive or both must be negative. Figure 6.1 corresponds to the case where both are positive. Let us now consider the case where $\gamma_r > s_p$; that is, investment decisions are more sensitive than saving to changes in the rate of profit. This case is illustrated in Figure 6.2, with a value of γ that is negative. There the slope of equation (6.3), the saving function given by g^s, is less steep than that of equation (6.4), the investment function given by g^i. Let us suppose, as we did in Figure 6.1, that the expected rate of profit r_0^e is initially inferior to the equilibrium rate of profit r^*. Since firms expect a rate of profit of r_0^e they set a rate of growth of g_0, which causes a realized rate of profit of r_0^a. As can be seen in the graph, the realized rate of profit is in this case smaller than the expected rate of profit. According to the adaptative process of equation (6.5), this should induce entrepreneurs to expect a smaller rate of profit in the next production period. The new growth rate decided by the entrepreneurs will be even further away from the equilibrium desired rate of growth. The model pictured by Figure 6.2 is unstable: once we are out of equilibrium, we are getting away from it, rather than converging to it. If the initial expected rate of profit had been higher than the equilibrium rate of profit, the realized rate of profit would have been higher than the expected one, thus again leading the economy away from equilibrium. By contrast, when

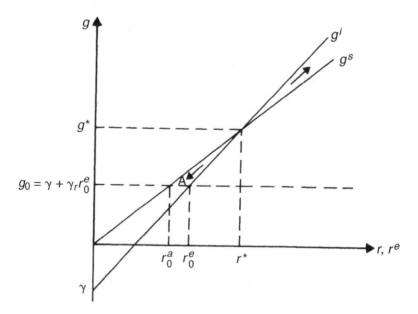

Figure 6.2 Instability of the growth model when investment is more responsive than saving to changes in the profit rate

the rate of investment is less sensitive than saving to changes in the rate of profit, as can be seen in Figure 6.1, the model is stable. Expectations of rates of return that would be too optimistic, compared to the equilibrium rate of profit, would eventually lead firms to adopt the desired rate of growth. For the Robinsonian model of growth to be stable, we thus need the following inequality, which can be found in various forms in several post-Keynesian models, for instance Pasinetti (1974, p. 114):

$$\gamma_r < s_p \tag{6.8}$$

The stability of the model requires the slope of the investment function, with respect to the rate of profit, to be smaller than the slope of the saving function. This does not necessarily mean that the above inequality is verified under all circumstances. It may be that structural crises, such as that of the 1929 crash, correspond to unstable systems. There could be accumulation regimes that are structurally unstable, and that precipitate the economic system into big depressions (Boyer, 1988). In the latter case the unstable model would correspond to a temporary situation. For our present purposes, we shall, however, suppose that the economy, and hence its model, is structurally stable, and shall assume the realization of the inequality given by (6.8) or of other similar stability conditions. Let us then study some more implications of the model illustrated by Figure 6.1, taking into account the desired rate of accumulation and its corresponding equilibrium rate of profit.

6.1.2 The Paradox of Thrift and Constant Normal Rates of Utilization

One of the major features of the neo-Keynesian model is that it transposes Keynes's paradox of thrift to the long period. As we saw in Chapter 5, any increase in the propensity to save leads to a reduction in the level of output or of employment. In the simple neo-Keynesian model of growth and distribution presented here, an increase in the propensity to save on profits leads to a reduction in the desired rate of growth and in the equilibrium rate of profit. This can be easily checked by inspection of equation (6.7) in the case of the profit rate. As to the growth rate, taking the derivative of equation (6.6) with respect to s_p, we get

$$dg^*/ds_p = -\gamma_r/(s_p - \gamma_r)^2 < 0 \tag{6.9}$$

But how does this adjustment proceed? It was mentioned at the beginning of this section that one ought to distinguish between the old neo-Keynesian models of growth and distribution, where the rate of utilization of capacity was assumed to be fixed in the long run, and the newer models of Kaleckian inspiration, where rates of utilization are endogenous. As pointed out in Chapter 5, it seems that earlier post-Keynesians were initially convinced that there are two uses to the principle of effective demand. It could be put to work in the short period, to determine real income by 'varying the level of utilization of given capital equipment' (Robinson, 1962, p. 11); or it could be put to work in the long period, by modifying the level of prices relative to wages and hence changing the distribution of income and the share of saving relative to income (ibid., p. 12). These two uses of the multiplier and of the principle of effective demand were not seen as incompatible as long as 'one is conceived as a short-run theory and the other as a long-run theory' (Kaldor, 1956, p. 94). The cause of this dichotomy, as argued earlier, is that earlier post-Keynesians considered the share of profits to be the main regulator of the economy. They associated a higher share of profits with a higher share of investment.

Both the earlier Kaldor and Robinson go to great lengths to ensure that in the long period firms have no undesired excess capacity. Indeed, both authors suppose that in the long period firms operate at full capacity (where the rate of utilization is equal to 100 per cent), something that Kaldor (1961, p. 199) calls full employment, and Robinson calls normal capacity. In the case of the former author, a tentative proof, based on the instability of excess capacity situations when output is growing, is offered to sustain the belief that in the long run firms are necessarily operating at full capacity, and that, consequently, changes in prices are the means by which saving is adjusted to investment decisions. Skott (1989b, p. 79) is not convinced, however, saying that 'Kaldor's theoretical explanation of full employment suffers from several shortcomings'. In contrast, Robinson offers no proof. She relies upon the forces of competition to arrive at the same result, supposing that 'competition (in the short-period sense) is sufficiently keen to keep prices at the level at which normal capacity output can be sold' (Robinson, 1962, p. 46). The issue then is to find out what Robinson means by normal capacity. She says that the limit of the normal capacity of a plant is reached when 'any increase in the weekly rate of output would involve a rise in prime cost per unit of product' (Robinson, 1956, p. 184). This corresponds to what we have called, in Chapter 3, the practical capacity of a plant. Since Robinson generalizes this concept to the firm as a whole, normal capacity must be understood as the sum of all the practical capacities, that is, the full capacity of a firm. It is the point at which there is a discontinuity in marginal costs and where they start rising, as shown in Figure 3.7.

Now there is something bizarre in this neo-Keynesian model. Post-Keynesians usually emphasize the predominance of quantity changes when adjustments to demand are required. As first pointed out by a puzzled Davidson (1972, pp. 124–5), the neo-Keynesian view seems to be instead that 'adjustments are made via demand prices, profit margins and income distribution'. Thus, as Roberto Ciccone (1986, p. 22) concludes, 'although variations in the degree of utilization of capacity are admitted in the short period, Robinson excludes them as far as the long period is concerned'. Marglin (1984b, p. 125) also wonders about the Keynesian pedigree of the neo-Keynesian model, noting that 'the key assumption is that the rate of capacity utilisation varies on the transition path between steady-growth configurations, but not across steady-growth states'. In another publication, he puts it even more clearly: 'In the short run ... the rate of capacity utilisation changes in accordance with aggregate demand ... But in the long run ... there is no excess capacity to accommodate demand. Distribution must bear the brunt of adjusting aggregate demand to aggregate supply' (Marglin, 1984a, pp. 474–5).

There are substantial consequences to the assumption that the rate of utilization of capacity across long-run positions is a constant (here equal to unity). We shall underline two of them. The first one is that changes in the distribution of income can occur only through changes in the price level relative to wages, that is, in the mark-up on unit costs. A higher level of demand, that is, a higher rate of growth, is absorbed by higher prices. This is why the neo-Keynesian model is called an 'inflationist' theory of growth (Rowthorn, 1981, p. 31). Note that the neo-Keynesian model is consistent with Eichner's view of the firm, according to which prices are set in response to investment financial needs. In the Eichnerian firm, a higher rate of investment requires higher profits and induces a higher mark-up, and hence higher prices relative to wage costs. This is a profit inflation theory of growth, which can be found in various guises among several other post-Keynesian authors (Seccareccia, 1984; Minsky, 1986a), briefly alluded to in Chapter 5. The only difference between the Eichnerian model and the neo-Keynesian one is that in the latter, competition prevails, changes in prices being induced by demand and the forces of competition, while in the former, megacorps dominate oligopolistic markets, taking discretionary decisions when they change prices and income distribution to sustain their financial needs ensuing from accumulation.

The tricky aspect of the neo-Keynesian model can also be illustrated with the help of Figure 6.3. The top part of the graph reproduces Figure 6.1. The bottom part shows the relationship between the profit rate r and the rate of capacity utilization u. This relationship is given by equation (6.10), which will prove highly useful. The profit rate can be expressed as the product of three ratios: the profit to output ratio, which is the share of

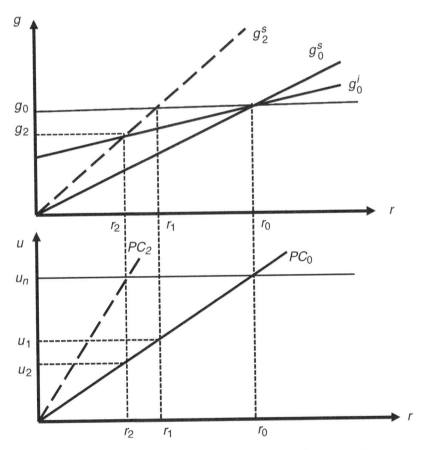

Figure 6.3 Short-run and long-run impact of an increase in the propensity to save on utilization rates and profit shares

profit π; the output to full-capacity output ratio, which is the rate of utilization u; and the inverse of the capital to full-capacity output ratio, which we called v in Chapters 3 and 5. This is often referred to as Weisskopf's (1979) decomposition of the profit rate:

$$r = \left(\frac{P}{q}\right)\left(\frac{q}{q_{fc}}\right)\left(\frac{q_{fc}}{M}\right) = \frac{\pi u}{v} \quad (6.10)$$

In the bottom part of the figure, the relationship is reversed, written as: $u = rv/\pi$, and represented by the PC curve, the profit curve seen from the cost side. Now start from the g_0, r_o and u_n position, where profit expectations are realized and where firms are at their desired rate of accumulation. Suppose there is an increase in the propensity to save s_p, so that the saving curve rotates upwards, as shown at the top of the graph. In the short run, firms will not yet modify their rate of accumulation, so that the rate of accumulation will remain at g_0. With the reduction in consumption due to the higher propensity to save, the top part of the figure shows that the realized profit rate will fall to r_1. In a Keynesian or Kaleckian world, as described in Chapter 5, this will occur through a reduction in output and employment, and hence through a reduction in the rate of utilization, which will fall from u_n to u_1, as shown in the bottom part of the graph. This is the paradox of thrift revisited. Indeed, this is what Robinson (1962, p. 46) admits, saying that 'firms may be working plants below designed capacity and still charging the "full cost" prices at which they were earlier able to sell their normal capacity output'.

In a longer run, investment will adjust to the new realized profit rate, entrepreneurs will modify their expected rate of profit as prescribed in equation (6.5) and in Figure 6.1, and hence the economy will end up in a new equilibrium with a lower growth rate g_2 and a lower profit rate r_2. This is the long-run version of the paradox of thrift. One would expect the rate of utilization to fall all the way to u_2, but this is not what Robinson (1962, p. 46) puts forward, arguing instead that competition 'is sufficiently keen to keep prices at the level at which normal capacity output can be sold'. Thus, what is assumed instead in the neo-Keynesian model is that the rate of utilization is brought back to its normal level u_n, through a fall in the mark-up, which reduces the share of profits π, thus leading to a counterclockwise rotation of the PC curve, as shown in Figure 6.3. For a given technique, the lower rate of accumulation is necessarily associated with a higher real wage; and reciprocally, 'a higher rate of accumulation means a lower real-wage rate' (Robinson, 1962, p. 58). Thus, within this framework, it is not the abstinence of the capitalists that allows for faster growth; rather it is the sacrifices of the workers, through their lower real income. Later in the chapter we will refer to such a negative relationship between growth and real wages as a profit-led growth regime.

The dichotomous adjustment mechanism, through quantities in the short run, and through prices in the long run, is rather surprising, the more so because Robinson (1962, p. 65) herself recognizes that price competition does not hold, arguing that, 'in reality, of course, markets for manufacturers are highly imperfect, prices are fairly sticky and changes in investment are generally accompanied by changes in output and employment'. Things get even more awkward when the adjustment mechanisms have to be assessed within a two-sector model, where the sizes of the consumption and investment sectors, their labour and their machines, have to be reproportioned in such a way that full-capacity output is recovered in both sectors. When he attempts to describe along

Robinsonian lines the return to full utilization of capacity when growth rates change, Fernando Vianello (1985, p. 82) is forced to describe the traverse as a path 'along a more or less tortuous route'.

6.1.3 The Inflation Barrier

The second consequence of assuming full-output capacity or a continuous normal rate of utilization is that the paradox of thrift may not hold after all. There exists a post-Keynesian tradition according to which more thriftiness leads to faster accumulation (Asimakopulos, 1986, pp. 87–9). This tradition is associated with Joan Robinson's 'inflation barrier', which turns upside down the causality associated with the Cambridge equation, bringing forth a closely resembling Marxian view of accumulation and income distribution. As pointed out above, a higher rate of accumulation is associated with a lower real wage because, for a given propensity to save, the higher rate of growth is tied to a higher profit rate and profit share. With a single rate of utilization, there is a unique inverse relationship between the real wage rate and the rate of profit, as illustrated at the bottom of Figure 6.4. This is the wage/profit frontier, a well-known relation among

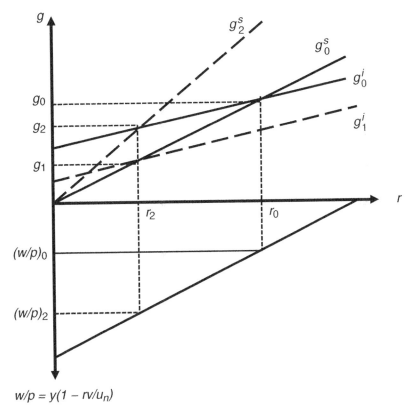

Figure 6.4 The inflation barrier, or the demise of the paradox of thrift in neo-Keynesian models

neoclassical, Marxian and Sraffian authors. The wage/profit frontier is usually shown using prices of production in two-sector or more complex models; it may, however, also be shown from the national accounts within the context of a one-sector model (Amadeo, 1986). As we saw in Chapter 1, the national revenue can be written as the sum of wages and profits on capital:

$$pq = wL + rpM \qquad (1.4)$$

This can be rewritten as

$$p = w(L/q) + rp(M/q)$$

Within the framework imposed by Kaldor and Robinson on long-period analysis, there is no overhead labour, so that output per unit of labour q/L is a constant equal to y. Furthermore, for the earlier Kaldor and Robinson, the rate of utilization of capacity is assumed to be equal to its normal or standard rate (or unity), so that the capital output ratio M/q is another constant, equal to v/u_n. In the context of the neo-Keynesian model, equation (1.4) may thus be rewritten as

$$p = (w/y)/(1 - rv/u_n)$$

Rearranging the above equation, one gets the inverse relationship between the real wage rate and the rate of profit, the wage–profit frontier:

$$w/p = y(1 - rv/u_n) \qquad (6.11)$$

We are now ready to explain Robinson's inflation barrier. We know that a higher rate of growth causes a higher rate of profit, which itself induces a lower real wage rate because of equation (6.11), given the conditions imposed by the earlier post-Keynesians, that is, a fixed rate of utilization. The inflation barrier also requires the reasonable hypothesis that workers refuse to have their real wages squeezed out by a higher rate of profit, induced by a faster rate of growth. There is then a minimum acceptable real wage rate (Kaldor, 1956, p. 98). If this minimum wage rate is reached, the neo-Keynesian model turns into a Marxian model, where the real wage rate is given and determines the other variables of the system (Marglin, 1984b). The conflict between the growth objectives of the firms and the minimum standards of living of the workers cannot be resolved, and inflation sets in. When this happens, says Robinson (1956, p. 238; 1962, p. 60), monetary authorities raise interest rates until the animal spirits of the entrepreneurs are dampened and investment is curtailed. At that point, inflation pressures are eliminated. The inflation barrier and its detrimental consequences on accumulation could have been avoided, however, if the propensity to save had been higher.

> In any given situation, the lower the level of expenditure on consumption by rentiers the further out the inflation barrier lies, and the higher the rate of accumulation that is possible. When entrepreneurs, taken as a whole, are aiming at a high rate of accumulation, and are held in check only by the inflation barrier, the more thrifty everyone is the better it suits them. (Robinson, 1956, pp. 53–4)

The standard Keynesian causal sequence is thus reversed. The rate of investment depends on the height of the acceptable real wage rate and on the degree of thriftiness. The higher the propensity to save, the higher the rate of accumulation. Indeed, in a later work, Robinson (1962, p. 63) neatly summarizes her views of the inflation barrier: 'When it is the real wage which limits the rate of growth, greater thriftiness makes more investment possible in a perfectly straightforward and unambiguous sense.' This is consistent with Richard Kahn's (1972, p. 202) claim that, in this situation, 'thrift can now be regarded as an influence on the rate of growth . . . greater thriftiness means a higher rate of growth'.

The mechanism at work in the case of the inflation barrier may be interpreted graphically in Figure 6.4. Suppose that initially the saving function is given by g_0^s while the investment function is given by g_0^i. The equilibrium position, if there were no inflation barrier, would be given by the desired rate of growth g_0. This rate of growth would, however, require a profit rate equal to r_0 and a real wage rate equal to $(w/p)_0$. Suppose, however, that there is a minimum acceptable real wage rate, say $(w/p)_2$, which is greater than $(w/p)_0$. To the minimum real wage rate $(w/p)_2$ corresponds a maximum attainable profit rate r_2. At this maximum rate of profit r_2, firms would be willing to accumulate at rate g_2, but only the growth rate g_1 is achievable under current circumstances. Any attempt to grow at a rate above g_1 creates a conflict over the distribution of the surplus and generates inflation, since investment is greater than saving. Assuming that inflation brings about monetary austerity policies, the effect of these policies is to dampen animal spirits and to shift the investment curve from g_0^i to g_1^i. The consequence of the inflation barrier is to bring down the desired rate of growth to g_1 and the actual rate of profit to r_2 by shifting the investment function and making investment compatible with the saving rate and the given real wage rate.

What Kahn, Robinson and then Asimakopulos (1986) have been telling us is that if instead the degree of thriftiness s_p had been sufficiently high, no such restraint would have been necessary. The saving equation would have shifted up from g_0^s to g_2^s and with the initial animal spirits, embodied in the investment function g_0^i, the equilibrium desired rate of growth would have been higher, at g_2. When there is real wage resistance on the part of the workers, a higher propensity to save on profits is favourable to the economy since it allows a higher rate of growth at a given rate of profit, that is, at a given real wage rate. When the inflation barrier has been reached, higher thriftiness generates a higher rate of accumulation by avoiding monetary restraints.

The case of the inflation barrier rests on the negative relationship between the real wage and the rate of growth. This is evidently true if one assumes that the economy always lies on the wage/profit frontier; that is, if one assumes that in long-run analysis the rate of utilization of capacity is fixed at its normal or full-capacity level. In answer to Marglin (1984b), who was comparing the neoclassical, Marxian and neo-Keynesian models, all based on the hypothesis of a fixed degree of utilization of capacity, and thus reasserting the importance of the negative relationship between real wages and growth implicit in such a hypothesis, post-Keynesian authors have questioned the validity of this assumption (Nell, 1985; Dutt, 1987a). Once the variations in the rate of utilization of capacity are taken into account, in the long run and not only in the short run, the inverse relationship between the real wage rate and the rate of growth may not hold. There may then be no inflation barrier, and Keynes's paradox of thrift may then prevail in all circumstances, even in the long run. This is what we shall now see by studying the models of growth and distribution in the Kaleckian tradition. By contrast with the earlier neo-Keynesian models, the newer post-Keynesian models show no discrepancy between the behaviour of the economy in the short run and in the long run. They generally leave no room for thriftiness and austerity policies.

As was argued in Chapter 5, there is evidence that both Kaldor and Robinson abandoned their neo-Keynesian models at the end of their career, advocating instead a more Kaleckian approach. The newer post-Keynesian models in the Kaleckian tradition, rather than the neo-Keynesian ones, should therefore be viewed as the best representation, within one-sector models of growth, of the matured Kaldorian and Robinsonian heritage.

Somewhat surprisingly, in view of our discussion of the various strands of post-Keynesianism, a large number of Sraffians agree with Kaleckians over the rejection of an analysis conducted under the assumption of a normal or full degree of capacity. Following Garegnani (1992), Palumbo and Trezzini (2003) and Serrano and Freitas (2017) argue forcefully against the Cambridge theory of income distribution, meaning the neo-Keynesian growth model presented here, with its constant normal rate of capacity utilization. They reject the notion that higher rates of accumulation require lower real wages. They also question the idea that the rate of accumulation could determine the normal rate of profit associated with the normal rate of capacity utilization.

These Sraffians argue that what they call the Keynesian Hypothesis, that is, the premise that it is saving that adjusts to investment, applies both in the short and in the long period, and that this Keynesian Hypothesis is unlikely to be compatible with the 'normal utilization hypothesis'. In the following quote, Garegnani, the Sraffian economist, objects to the pricing mechanism of the neo-Keynesian model, and finds that those using the neo-Keynesian model are not Keynesian enough!

> It seems that once the Keynesian Hypothesis is accepted, the margins of unutilized capacity which are normal in a capitalist system make it plausible to think that, in the long period, even more so than in the Keynesian short period, autonomous changes in the incentive to invest will usually generate the corresponding amount of savings through changes in output rather than through changes in the real wage and normal rate of profits. (Garegnani, 1992, pp. 62–3)

6.2 THE KALECKIAN GROWTH MODEL

The newer post-Keynesian model of growth and distribution is an extension of the short-run Kaleckian model developed in the preceding chapter. According to Edward Amadeo (1987, p. 75), it seems that the Kaleckian model of growth and distribution was originally developed independently by Bob Rowthorn (1981) and Amitava Dutt (1984). Early formulations of the model were also provided by Lance Taylor (1983; 1985), Amadeo (1986) and Marco Committeri (1986). The most intriguing result of all these Kaleckian models is that higher costing margins, that is, lower real wages, lead to lower rates of utilization, lower growth rates and lower realized profit rates. These results, however, were also arrived at by Alfredo Del Monte (1975), in an earlier paper published in Italian and designed to explain industrial organization in an oligopolistic world, as was pointed out by Joseph Halevi (1985, p. 122), according to whom these results are 'the most important implication of the Kalecki–Steindl–Baran–Sweezy interpretation of contemporary capitalism'.

The Kaleckian model of growth and distribution has progressively become quite popular among heterodox economists concerned with macroeconomics and effective demand issues. As argued in Lavoie (2006a), the model has provided common ground and has proven to be highly flexible. For instance, Hein (2020) has shown how issues and consequences related to a gender wage gap could be introduced into a Kaleckian model of growth and distribution, while Codrina Rada (2017) did the same in the case of pension funding. This neo-Kaleckian model has also been used to assess the macroeconomic impact of organized crime (Astarita et al., 2018). The Kaleckian model has generated substantive interaction between economists of different economic traditions, with various versions having been developed by post-Keynesian, Structuralist, Sraffian and Marxian economists alike. In addition, it has been shown how post-Keynesian economics and its Kaleckian model of growth and distribution, could contribute to the literature on comparative political economy and more specifically to the studies devoted to varieties of capitalism (Behringer and van Treeck, 2019; Hein et al., 2021; Hein and Martschin, 2021; Stockhammer, 2022; Stockhammer and Kohler, 2022). As a consequence of this popularity, the Kaleckian model has been subjected to criticisms, and one of the objectives of the chapter will be to go over these.

There are four crucial aspects according to which the forthcoming model may be unambiguously called a Kaleckian model of growth and distribution. First, there is the investment function, which may depend on several variables, one of which must be the rate of capacity utilization. Second, prices relative to direct costs are assumed to be given, dependent on conventional forces instead of market forces. Prices are of the cost-plus type. Third, saving out of wages is often assumed to be nil, although it is sufficient to assume that the propensity to save out of wages is smaller than that out of profits, as in the neo-Keynesian growth model. Fourth, in contrast to the early Kaldorian hypotheses, the rate of utilization of capacity is assumed to be generally below unity, and labour is assumed not to be a constraint. This is an obvious Kaleckian feature, as the following quote demonstrates.

> A considerable proportion of capital equipment lies idle in the slump. Even on average the degree of utilization throughout the business cycle will be substantially below the maximum reached during the boom. Fluctuations in the utilization of labour parallel those in the utilization of equipment... The reserve of capital equipment and the reserve army of the unemployed are typical features of capitalist economy at least throughout a considerable part of the cycle. (Kalecki, 1971, p. 137)

The Kaleckian assumption that the rate of capacity utilization may diverge from its normal or full-capacity rate even in the long run is questioned by a number of heterodox authors, as will be seen later in the chapter. This is an old controversy, however. Keynes (1973, xii, p. 829) himself objected to Kalecki precisely on those grounds: 'Is it not rather odd when dealing with "long-run problems" to start with the assumption that all firms are always working below capacity?'

6.2.1 The Canonical Kaleckian Growth Model

In this subsection, we present what we may call the canonical Kaleckian model of growth and distribution. There are several variants of the Kaleckian model. Here we choose as the canonical model the variant suggested by Amadeo (1986; 1987), and picked up by Dutt (2011) and Hein et al. (2011). The model, in nearly all its variants, is made up of three equations that involve income distribution, saving and investment. We have already encountered the first two equations, which we repeat here for convenience. As we did with the neo-Keynesian model, we will assume away overhead labour costs for now, and hence the share of profits is a constant such that $\pi = \theta/(1 + \theta)$, where θ is the percentage mark-up on unit direct costs. The third equation is the new investment equation, which substitutes the rate of utilization for the profit rate of the Robinsonian investment equation (6.4) that we had earlier:

$$r = \pi u/v \qquad (6.10)$$
$$g^s = s_p r \qquad (6.3)$$
$$g^i = \gamma + \gamma_u(u^e - u_n) \qquad (6.12)$$

As before, γ is a parameter reflecting the animal spirits of firms, for instance expectations about the future trend rate of sales growth. The parameter γ_u represents the sensitivity of the rate of accumulation to changes in the expected rate of utilization of capacity u^e, while u_n is the normal or standard rate of utilization of capacity. The idea is that, if the actual or expected rate of utilization is higher than the normal rate, firms will speed up accumulation in an effort to bring back the actual rate towards the normal rate. More will be said about the meaning of these parameters in the next section, when some of the questions and controversies surrounding the Kaleckian model will be discussed. It should be said that, although both Kalecki and Steindl doubted the ability of the economy to converge towards a given rate of utilization in the long run, they did not hesitate to refer to a normal rate. Steindl (1952, pp. xiv and 12) talks about a planned or intended level of capacity utilization, while Kalecki (1971, pp. 169, 171, 173, 175) mentions a standard rate of profit as well as a 'trend degree of utilisation of equipment' (ibid., p. 181).

As we pointed out in Chapter 5, one of the most contentious issues in economics is the way investment decisions are determined. The controversies arise at both the theoretical and empirical levels. The first Kaleckian models of growth and distribution incorporated a slightly different investment function, which included both the rate of capacity utilization and the rate of profit, as was informally proposed by Kaldor (1957, p. 601), and could thus be seen as some generalization of the Robinsonian investment function. As found in Rowthorn (1981), Taylor (1983), Dutt (1984), Agliardi (1988), Blecker (1989), Lavoie (1992b) and Allain (2009), this investment function was instead

$$g^i = \gamma + \gamma_u u + \gamma_r r \qquad (6.13)$$

The above equation is a simplification of the investment function advocated by Steindl (1952, pp. 127–9). For this reason in particular, Dutt (1990a) speaks of a Kalecki–Steindl closure. Steindl himself considers that a host of factors influence investment decisions, most of which are endogenous to the economic system. These factors are the retention ratio, the debt leverage ratio, the rate of profit and the rate of utilization of capacity. Steindl believes that none of these factors alone can explain investment by firms. Although they are interrelated, each factor plays an independent role. Still, here, since we intend to present the simplest Kaleckian model, introducing complications at a later stage, we rely on investment equation (6.12), which depends only on the rate of capacity utilization. It turns out that the crucial results of the Kaleckian model of growth are obtained indifferently with either investment equations, (6.12) or (6.13). These equations reflect empirical work that has consistently shown that the most important explanatory variable of investment is the rate of capacity utilization (or sales) and cash flow (or profits). Thus, whereas investment is driven by prices (the interest rate) in neoclassical economics, in post-Keynesian economics investment is essentially driven by quantities and finance.

How can this little three-equation model be solved? First note that, by incorporating equation (6.10) into the saving equation, it can be rewritten as a linear function of the rate of utilization, with the share of profits as one of the parameters:

$$g^s = s_p \pi u / v \qquad (6.14)$$

We thus have two growth equations as a function of the rate of utilization. These two equations are illustrated in Figure 6.5. They are drawn in such a way that the slope of the saving function is steeper than that of the investment function, as was the case in the neo-Keynesian model. This condition is what is called the Keynesian stability condition, which says that saving reacts more than investment to changes in the rate of utilization. With the specification of our two functions, this comes down to the inequality shown below, which is assumed for now:

$$s_p \pi > v \gamma_u \qquad (6.15)$$

The model reaches its long-run equilibrium when the two curves of Figure 6.5 cross each other. When this occurs, expectations regarding the rate of utilization are realized;

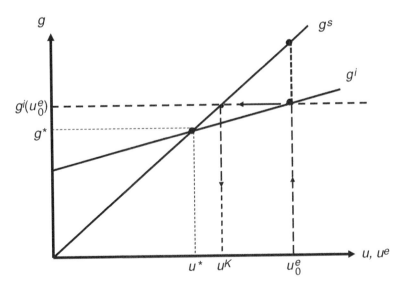

Figure 6.5 The canonical Kaleckian growth model with an expected rate of capacity utilization

that is, when $u = u^e$, we obtain the equilibrium rate of utilization, and investment equals saving. We thus also obtain the equilibrium rate of growth and rate of profit of our little model. The rate of utilization is obtained by combining the investment and saving equations (6.12) and (6.14):

$$u^* = \frac{(\gamma - \gamma_u u_n)v}{s_p \pi - v\gamma_u} \tag{6.16}$$

The denominator of this expression is the stability condition; for this solution to make sense, we need the rate of utilization to be positive, so that both the denominator and the numerator must be positive. The issue of short-run stability can be seen in two ways. One possibility is to assume a disequilibrium mechanism, whereby the level of output is given in the ultra-short period. This means that in the ultra-short period the actual level of utilization is also assumed to be a given, with $u = \bar{u}$. In general, there will be a discrepancy between desired investment and saving at this given level of output. Firms will then adjust the level of output to the disequilibrium observed in the goods market, and will thus increase output and hence the rate of capacity utilization whenever aggregate demand exceeds aggregate supply, in which case we have

$$\dot{u} = \mu(g^i - g^s), \mu > 0 \tag{6.17}$$

with the dot on the variable representing the change in that variable.

When the initial rate of utilization u_0 is too high relative to the equilibrium rate u^*, as shown in Figure 6.5, saving at that rate of output is higher than investment, and, as a consequence, firms will reduce their rate of utilization of capacity. This will bring the economy towards u^* provided the saving curve is steeper than the investment curve.

Another way to see Keynesian instability is to imagine a pure adjustment process, assuming that firms are always able to adjust production to sales within the period, thus assuming that the goods market is in equilibrium in each period. This is what Duménil and Lévy (1993) call equilibrium dynamics. Firms make their investment decisions on the basis of the expected rate of capacity utilization u^e, which is set at the beginning of the investment period (Amadeo, 1987), but they have enough time to adjust production to the actual sales that occur, thus ensuring within each short period that aggregate supply equals aggregate demand, and hence that saving equals the investment expenditures that were activated on the basis of the expected rate of utilization. In other words, making reference to Chapter 5, we assume that firms are on their effective demand curve. The rate of utilization u^k (k for Keynesian or Kaleckian equilibrium) that will be realized in each short period will thus be given by equating equations (6.12) and (6.14), but this time without assuming $u = u^e$, thus obtaining

$$u^k = \frac{\gamma + \gamma_u(u^e - u_n)}{s_p \pi/v} \tag{6.18}$$

We can envisage an adjusting mechanism, such that

$$\dot{u}^e = \mu_1(u^k - u^e), \mu_1 > 0 \tag{6.19}$$

With Keynesian stability, as illustrated with Figure 6.5, this adjustment mechanism will bring the expected rate of utilization closer to the realized rate of utilization in the short period, and bring the economy towards the equilibrium utilization rate given by equation (6.16). Note that this adjustment process is no different from the adaptive process that we had assumed for the expected profit rate in the neo-Keynesian model, because equation (6.19) can be rewritten as

$$u_t^e = (1 - \mu_1) u_{t-1}^e + \mu_1 u_{t-1}^k \tag{6.19A}$$

At this stage, we can make two remarks. First, from now on, except when we deal once more with the issue of stability, we shall assume that either the economy has reached the short-period equilibrium utilization rate u^k or that enough time has passed for the economy to reach the long-run equilibrium u^*. The second thing to notice is that all the adjustment is done through quantities, through the rate of utilization, as was the case in Chapter 5.

6.2.2 Comparative Dynamics in the Canonical Kaleckian Model

In this section, we consider two paradoxes, the paradox of thrift and the paradox of costs. Before we do so, we construct an additional relationship, the relation between the rate of profit and the rate of utilization when the expected and the realized rate of utilization of capacity are equal. Equating the saving equation (6.3) and the investment equation (6.12) under the assumption that $u = u^e$, we get what Rowthorn (1981, p. 12) calls (mistakenly, we think, as noted by Committeri, 1986) the realization curve, but which we will call the effective demand curve ED. This curve is found in the bottom part of Figure 6.6, and has to be contrasted with the profit cost curve PC, which also illustrates a relationship between the profit rate and the rate of utilization, but seen from the cost side and given by equation (6.10). In the case of Keynesian stability, because of the restrictions imposed by condition (6.15), the slope of the effective demand curve is necessarily less steep than that of the profit cost curve. In other words, looking at equation (6.20), we have $\gamma_u/s_p < \pi/v$ or $s_p\pi > \gamma_u v$ as in condition (6.15). The equation of the effective demand curve is

$$r = \frac{\gamma - \gamma_u u_n + \gamma_u u}{s_p} \tag{6.20}$$

Let us now examine what happens when there is an increase in the propensity to save out of profits. In the top part of Figure 6.6, assume that we start from the equilibrium position given by g_0^*, u_0^* and r_0^*. The higher propensity to save means that the saving curve rotates leftwards from g_0^s to g_1^s. Once again, we can assume that the rate of accumulation will not change in the short period, remaining at g_0^*. The short-period Kaleckian rate of utilization u_1^k will thus be found at the intersection of the saving curve and the horizontal line representing the given rate of accumulation. At this lower rate of utilization, the realized profit rate will also be lower, at r_1, and given by the profit cost curve PC, as can be read from the bottom of the figure. Over time, the lower realized rate of utilization and the lower realized rate of profit will induce entrepreneurs to slow down accumulation, and this will occur until the saving and investment functions intersect each other at the

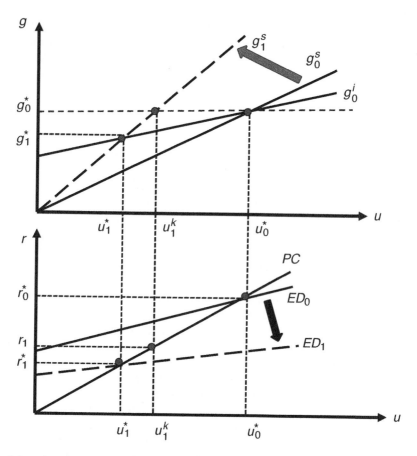

Figure 6.6 The paradox of thrift in the Kaleckian model

new long-run equilibrium growth rate g_1^* and the new rate of utilization u_1^*. The higher propensity to save also provokes a downward shift in the intercept and the slope of the effective demand curve in the bottom part of the graph, as can be assessed from equation (6.20). The new intersection of the PC and ED curves will yield the new equilibrium profit rate r_1^*.

Thus, in the Kaleckian model, the paradox of thrift holds, meaning that a higher propensity to save leads to a lower growth rate, and this will be accompanied by lower rates of profit and of capacity utilization. In contrast to the neo-Keynesian model, however, all of this happens without any change in the costing margins or in real wages.

Let us now deal with the paradox of costs, as first explicitly outlined by Rowthorn (1981, p. 18), according to whom, 'under the assumed conditions, higher costs lead to higher profits'. More precisely, within the framework of the model, what is meant here by the paradox of costs is that a lower costing margin, that is, higher real wages in given technical conditions, leads to a higher realized profit rate. Mathematically this can be shown by combining equation (6.16) and equation (6.10). We obtain

$$r^* = \frac{\gamma - \gamma_u u_n}{s_p - \gamma_u v/\pi} \qquad (6.21)$$

Obviously, when the mark-up is higher, that is, when the share of profits π is higher and real wages lower, the profit rate r^* is lower; and reciprocally, when the share of profits π is lower and real wages higher, the profit rate r^* is higher. The latter case is illustrated with the help of Figure 6.7, with the profit cost curve and the effective demand curve shown once more at the bottom of the graph. Both the saving curve and the profit cost curve rotate downwards, as a consequence of the reduction in the costing margin. Assuming once more that the rate of accumulation remains at its initial position g_0^* in the short period, as shown at the top of the graph, the short-period rate of utilization u_1^k is to be found at the intersection of this given rate of accumulation and of the new saving

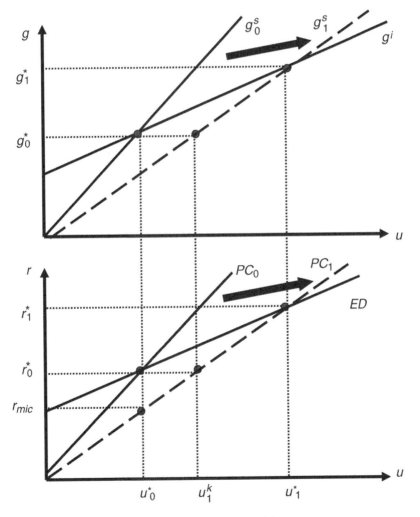

Figure 6.7 *The paradox of costs in the Kaleckian model*

function g_1^s. Thus the rate of profit also remains at its initial value r_0^* in the short period, as shown at the bottom of the graph. With the higher realized rate of capacity utilization, the expected rate of utilization will be larger, and firms will be induced to invest faster. This process will go on until finally all three endogenous rates move up to u_1^*, g_1^* and r_1^*, at which point the expected and realized rates of capacity utilization will be equal. This was all described by Del Monte, in the first formalization of the Kaleckian model of growth and distribution:

> Our model confirms what is usually observed in the real world, that is, an increase in the degree of monopoly diminishes the rate of utilization of plants and the rate of growth... When firms decide to reduce the real wages of workers, the result is not an increase in the rate of profit, but rather a decrease in the rate of profit, because the higher degree of monopoly has led to a fall in the rate of utilization of capacity. (Del Monte, 1975, p. 243, my translation)

We have achieved what we believe to be the most puzzling result of the Kaleckian model of growth and distribution, as announced at the beginning of this section. Higher labour costs, that is, higher real wages, are in the end conducive to higher profit rates. This is achieved because the higher real wages drive up consumption and hence rates of utilization, which induces faster rates of accumulation and thus higher profit rates. As discussed in Chapter 1, this is a typical example of a macroeconomic paradox, where what is true for one entrepreneur is false for all of them taken together. Going back to Figure 6.7, we see that if a single firm were to reduce its costing margins, the rate of utilization would remain at u_0^* and the realized profit rate would fall to r_{mic}, which is what a partial equilibrium microeconomic analysis would depict. But the actual degree of capacity utilization does not remain at its initial level when we accept the macroeconomic implications of the assumed general increase in real wages. If a single firm raises real wages and reduces its costing margins, everything else being equal, it will obviously make less profit and it will face a reduction in its profit rate (unless there are wage efficiency effects). But if all firms increase their real wages together, this will generate a higher rate of capacity utilization for the whole economy, and, through the induced effects, linked to a sort of accelerator effect, it will lead to a higher macroeconomic profit rate. Thus, while it may be beneficial to an individual firm acting alone to reduce its costs of production and to increase its profit margins by reducing real wages or shedding employment (as long as this does not affect negatively the productivity of the remaining workers), the profit rate at the aggregate level would be greater if all firms agreed to increase real wages and reduce their costing margins.

The paradox of costs and the paradox of thrift are both key features of the canonical Kaleckian model of growth. A reduction in the propensity to save leads to a higher rate of accumulation, while a rise in real wages gets translated into a higher profit rate at the macroeconomic level. Both results are in direct conflict with neoclassical theory and TINA (There Is No Alternative). In fact, these two paradoxes are very good examples of what happens when one does not assume full employment of labour and capacity as the starting point of economic analysis. They emphasize the importance of effective demand and that of real-world adjustments through quantities instead of prices. Most importantly, they underline the shortcomings of an analysis that would rely solely on individual behaviour within microeconomic markets, while ignoring their macroeconomic consequences. Fallacies of composition are always lurking when unintended consequences due to macroeconomic forces are not taken into account.

It should be pointed out that the paradox of cost is valid only as long as the rate of utilization of capacity stays below unity. The other parameters being given, it requires that the real wage rate does not exceed a certain critical value. The range of relevance of the model is thus limited. There is an upper bound to the values that the real wage rate can take, or in other words there is a lower bound to the values that the profit share can take, and, as in Robinson's inflation barrier, the constraints on the real wage are less stringent if the propensity to save out of profits is higher.

6.3 VARIANTS OF THE KALECKIAN MODEL

The canonical Kaleckian model of growth and distribution just described has been subjected to a number of critiques, from very early on. Some of these critiques can be viewed as proper extensions of the canonical model. In this section, we will deal with two of these critiques. First we will analyse what happens when saving out of wages is taken into consideration. Second, we will provide a more in-depth discussion of the investment function by entertaining an alternative suggested by Bhaduri and Marglin, which will be called the post-Kaleckian model.

6.3.1 Adding a Propensity to Save Out of Wages

We have so far assumed that there was no saving out of wages. While there is some truth in this simplifying assumption when one excludes compulsory contributions to private and public pension funds from saving out of wages, there are bound to be countries and time periods where such savings are positive and possibly substantive, even though the propensity to save out of wages s_w is significantly lower than that out of profits. Do the paradoxes of thrift and of costs still hold when the propensity to save out of wages is positive?

There are reasons why post-Keynesians have been somewhat reluctant to consider the case where $s_w > 0$. First, if workers save some of their wages, then they must also earn some capital income, and hence one may feel obliged to consider two classes of households, workers and capitalists, as does Pasinetti (1974). Second, there are complications brought about by aggregation problems, when one goes beyond an aggregated one-sector economy and moves to a two-sector model similar to the one described in Chapter 3. For instance, while the positive relationship between the rate of growth and the rate of profit holds under all circumstances when $s_w = 0$, this is not necessarily the case when $s_w > 0$. With positive saving out of wages, an increase in the propensity to save out of profits or out of wages, at a given rate of growth, may or may not generate a reduction in the profit rate, as Sraffians have shown, depending on whether one sector is more mechanized (with a higher machine to labour ratio) than the other (Spaventa, 1970; Hagemann, 1991). Things are somewhat different in a Kaleckian two-sector model, because adjustments are done through quantities rather than through prices, as is the case in the Sraffian two-sector model, but this is still worrying, as faster growth would necessarily entail a redistribution of activity from one sector to another.

Let us remain within the confines of a simple one-sector model and examine what happens when there is saving out of wages, assuming that all households earn wages or salaries, and are able to differentiate between their wage income and their profit income when they make their saving decisions. This has been examined by a number of authors, namely Amadeo (1987), Taylor (1990), Sarkar (1993), Mott and Slattery (1994) and Blecker (2002). The saving function is split between two components, the share of profits π and the share of wages $(1 - \pi)$, so that the saving function now becomes

$$g^s = s_p \pi u/v + s_w(1 - \pi)u/v = \{(s_p - s_w)\pi + s_w\}u/v \qquad (6.3A)$$

Note that this new saving equation still starts from the origin, since all terms depend on u. It is rather obvious that, within the confines of the canonical Kaleckian model, a decrease in the profit share π still leads to an increase in the long-run rate of growth and rate of utilization despite the presence of saving out of wages. This is because the saving function rotates downwards, while the investment stays put, as was the case in Figure 6.7. To get some ambiguous results, we thus need an investment function that includes the profit share, either directly, or indirectly, as is the case of the other typical Kaleckian investment function, given by equation (6.13), repeated here for convenience, but making the presence of the profit share variable explicit by writing it out as

$$g^i = \gamma + (\gamma_u + \gamma_r \pi/v)u \qquad (6.22)$$

Equating this revised investment function with the new saving equation (6.3A), we get the equilibrium rate of capacity utilization:

$$u^* = \frac{\gamma v}{\left(s_p - s_w - \gamma_r\right)\pi + s_w - v\gamma_u} \qquad (6.23)$$

The rate of utilization is positive provided both the numerator and the denominator are larger than zero, the later requirement constituting again the stability condition of the model. Can we still be sure that an increase in the profit share π will lead to a fall in the equilibrium rate of capacity utilization? The answer is that we are no longer sure. Taking the derivative of equation (6.23) with respect to the profit share, we find

$$du/d\pi = -\gamma v(s_p - s_w - \gamma_r)/D^2$$

where D is the denominator of equation (6.23).

Thus the result of the canonical Kaleckian model, that is, higher costing margins reduce the long-run rate of utilization, still holds provided $s_p - s_w > \gamma_r$. Indeed, Mott and Slattery (1994, p. 75) argue that since $s_p - s_w$ is roughly 0.5, this inequality is fairly likely to be realized. Note in addition that, if investment depends only on the rate of utilization, and not on the profit rate, which was the case in our canonical Kaleckian model, then $\gamma_r = 0$, and the above condition gets reduced to $s_p - s_w > 0$, which we know is empirically true. Hence this confirms what we affirmed earlier: in the canonical Kaleckian model (where $\gamma_r = 0$), higher real wages still generate higher rates of utilization, despite the presence of saving out of wages (Amadeo, 1986, p. 94).

What about the paradox of costs, that is, the inverse relationship between the share of profits and the rate of profit? Combining equations (6.10) and (6.23), we can easily compute the equilibrium profit rate:

$$r^* = \frac{\gamma \pi}{\left(s_p - s_w - \gamma_r\right)\pi + s_w - v\gamma_u} \quad (6.24)$$

Taking the derivative with respect to the profit share, we find

$$dr/d\pi = \gamma(s_w - v\gamma_u)/D^2$$

where D is the denominator of equation (6.24).

The paradox of costs still holds as long as the propensity to save out of wages is not too large, that is, as long as $s_w < v\gamma_u$. If the inequality is reversed, the paradox of costs does not hold. Looking at the condition, we see that the paradox of costs may not hold when there is saving out of wages even in the canonical Kaleckian model. Indeed, if raising the profit share leads to an increase in the rate of utilization, it will necessarily lead to an increase in the profit rate, because of the definition of the profit rate, and because of the requirements of the stability condition. This leads Sarkar (1993) to assert that the paradox of costs is more likely to hold in developing countries, because propensities to save out of wages ought to be low in these countries.

Thus, to conclude, all we can say is that the introduction of saving out of wages brings complexity to the Kaleckian model of growth and distribution. The paradox of thrift still holds – increasing either propensities to save will lead to a reduction in the rates of growth, profit and capacity utilization – but increasing the profit share may or may not have these negative effects. The final word may thus have to come from the empirical side.

6.3.2 The Post-Kaleckian Model

There is a critique of the standard or canonical Kaleckian model that has given rise to such a highly popular variant of the Kaleckian model that it is worth giving that variant a name: we will call it the post-Kaleckian model. That highly popular variant is the one provided by Bhaduri and Marglin (1990), which I first saw presented in a conference honouring Kaldor in New York in 1987. At the same conference, there was also a presentation of a highly similar variant, by Heinz Kurz (1990), which got less attention, probably because it involved a more fancy three-dimensional diagram. All this goes to show that the Kaleckian growth model has attracted the attention of heterodox economists of all strands, because while Bhaduri is considered to be a Kaleckian, Marglin belongs to the Marxian school and Kurz is a well-known Sraffian. One can also throw in Rowthorn (1981) for good measure, a Marxian who is one of the originators of the Kaleckian model of growth and distribution.

The Bhaduri and Marglin investment function
The point made by Kurz, as well as by Bhaduri and Marglin, and a number of other Sraffian authors such as Ciccone (1986) and Vianello (1989), is that investment depends

on expected profitability and that the usual investment functions of Kaleckian models, such as equations (6.12) and (6.13), fail to incorporate expected profitability in a proper way. This is obviously the case of equation (6.12), which excludes by definition the impact of the profit rate. But what about the other equations originally in Kaleckian models, equation (6.13) in particular, which we repeat here for convenience, combined with its extended version, equation (6.22):

$$g^i = \gamma + \gamma_u u + \gamma_r r = \gamma + (\gamma_u + \gamma_r \pi/v)u \qquad (6.13)$$

Bhaduri and Marglin (1990) argue that equation (6.13) imposes restrictions on the relative response of investment to the two main constituents of the profit rate: the profit share and the rate of capacity utilization. They question what is implicit in equation (6.13), that an increase in the rate of utilization will generate additional investment even if the profit rate remains constant. The reasoning of Bhaduri and Marglin (1990) is that if the rate of profit is constant, despite the rise in the rate of capacity utilization, this implies that the profit share must have fallen. But the fall in the profit share ought to have a negative impact on investment, and there is no *a priori* ground, they say, to suspect that the positive impact on investment of the higher rate of utilization will be any higher than the negative impact of the lower profit share. But this is precisely the sort of question that equation (6.13) denies, even though it incorporates the profit rate and indirectly the profit share, because of the restrictions it imposes. As a solution to this, Bhaduri and Marglin propose an alternative investment equation, where investment depends on two separate components, the rate of utilization and the share of profit, both carrying different parameters.

$$g^i = \gamma + \gamma_u u + \gamma_\pi \pi \qquad (6.25)$$

Bhaduri and Marglin's (1990) investment equation was quickly adopted by a number of heterodox economists (Taylor, 1991; Epstein, 1994; You, 1994). As mentioned before, Sraffians were arguing along similar lines at the time. Kurz (1990), for instance, introduces real wages as an argument of the investment function, in place of the profit share. Other Sraffians were also making similar arguments. Their main point was that investment depends on expected profitability, computed at normal prices based on the normal rate of utilization. This means that the investment function depends on the expected normal rate of profit rather than on the actual rate of profit. The justification for this is that entrepreneurs cannot make plans under the assumption that capacity will be perpetually over-utilized or under-utilized in the future. Plans must be made according to profitability assessed at the standard rate of capacity utilization. The rate of profit that represents 'the guiding light for investment and pricing decisions, cannot possibly be either an abnormally high or an abnormally low one' (Vianello, 1985, p. 84). Sraffians, Vianello (1989) in particular, thus argue that Kaleckians fail to understand that expected profitability is hindered by a rise in real wages, even if actual profitability stays constant in the short period. Thus their argument is no different from that of Bhaduri and Marglin (1990). Garegnani (1992, p. 62) puts it this way: 'the normal rate of profits will be that on which [the entrepreneurs] will base their decision to invest – a rate which . . . need bear no close relation to a ratio between aggregate actual net profits and aggregate existing capital'.

If we are to interpret the argument of Sraffian critics, what they are saying comes down to either of the following two investment functions:

$$g^i = \gamma + \gamma_r r_n \tag{6.26}$$
$$g^i = \gamma + \gamma_u u + \gamma_r r_n \tag{6.27}$$

where r_n is the normal rate of profit.

With the first of these two investment equations, equation (6.26), we get a hybrid form of the Keynesian and Marxian models. On the one hand, higher animal spirits, through the γ and γ_r parameters, lead to a higher rate of accumulation; on the other hand, higher real wages or a lower normal profit rate discourages entrepreneurship and leads to a lower rate of accumulation.

The second Sraffian investment equation, equation (6.27), is perhaps more interesting because it resembles the Bhaduri–Marglin equation so closely, and thus can be considered as a variant of the post-Kaleckian model. This can be seen by recalling what the normal rate of profit is. The normal rate of profit is the profit rate that will be achieved for a given mark-up (and thus for a given profit share in an economy without overhead labour costs) when the economy is running at its normal rate of capacity utilization. One has

$$r_n = \pi u_n / v \tag{6.28}$$

As long as normal capacity utilization u_n and the capital to capacity ratio v are constant, any change in the costing margins, that is, in the profit share π, implies a change in the normal rate of profit r_n. Clearly, then, the investment function proposed by Bhaduri and Marglin as a replacement for the Kaleckian investment function is a variant of the Sraffian case against the use of current profitability as an argument of the investment function. Bhaduri and Marglin (1990, p. 388), as well as Vianello (1989, p. 183), argue that Kaleckians have omitted the depressing cost effects of higher wages on economic activity. Equation (6.28) makes clear that the proponents of equation (6.25) suppose that, if the rate of profit is to be taken into consideration in addition to the rate of capacity utilization, it should be calculated at the normal rate of utilization. Those who say that the share of profit π, rather than the actual rate of profit r, should enter the investment function in addition to the rate of utilization of capacity are making an argument that is no different from the assertion that the normal rate of profit r_n, rather than the actual one, should be included in the investment function in addition to the rate of utilization of capacity. The Sraffian and the Marxian objections to the Kaleckian investment function are thus in the end identical. While the Sraffian equation (6.27) probably makes more sense from a theoretical point of view, the Bhaduri and Marglin investment equation (6.25) is more useful from a practical point of view. This is because in empirical work it is much easier to get measures of profit shares, whereas it is much more perilous to get estimates of the normal profit rate or of expected profitability.

Consequences of the Bhaduri and Marglin investment function

The consequences brought about by the post-Kaleckian investment function are quite dramatic, because the positive effects induced by higher real wages and lower costing margins on the rate of utilization, the growth rate and the profit rate that occurred in the canonical Kaleckian model then only become one case among many in the post-Kaleckian model arising from investment equation (6.25). In other words, the positive effects of higher real wages on consumption may be overtaken by the negative effects that higher real wages, and hence a lower profit share, may have on investment expenditures. This is well explained in the following:

> Any increase in real wage rate, depressing profit margin and profit share ... must decrease savings and increase consumption to validate the under-consumptionist thesis ... Nevertheless, aggregate demand (C + I) may still rise or fall depending on what impact that lower profit margin/share has on investment. Since it is plausible to argue that, other things being equal, a lower profit margin/share would weaken the incentive to invest, the contradictory effects of any exogenous variation in the real wage on the level of aggregate demand become apparent. A higher real wage increases consumption but reduces investment, in so far as investment depends on the profit margin. (Bhaduri and Marglin, 1990, p. 378)

We can formalize the impact of an increase in the profit share by examining the solution of the post-Kaleckian model. Making use of equations (6.25) and (6.14), we get the equilibrium rate of capacity utilization:

$$u^* = \frac{(\gamma + \gamma_\pi \pi) v}{s_p \pi - v \gamma_u} \quad (6.29)$$

Taking the derivative with respect to the profit share, we find

$$\frac{du}{d\pi} = \frac{-(\gamma_\pi \gamma_u v + \gamma s_p) v}{(s_p \pi - v \gamma_u)^2} \quad (6.29A)$$

At first sight it would seem that it is impossible for the profit share to have a positive effect on the rate of utilization (Blecker, 2002, p. 137; Dutt, 2011, p. 68). But with the post-Kaleckian investment equation, the parameter γ no longer needs to be positive for the model to make sense, because there is a second (positive) constant term in the numerator of the equilibrium value of the rate of utilization. Thus, with $\gamma < 0$, expression (6.29A) could be positive and an increase in the profit share could have a positive effect on the rate of utilization.

The conditions required for the profit share to have a positive effect on the profit rate (and hence on the growth rate, since $g = s_p r$), thus denying the paradox of costs, seem less stringent. From (6.29) and (6.10), we get

$$r^* = \frac{(\gamma + \gamma_\pi \pi) \pi}{s_p \pi - v \gamma_u} \quad (6.30)$$

and

$$\frac{dr}{d\pi} = \frac{-\gamma \gamma_u v + (s_p \pi - 2\gamma_u v) \pi \gamma_\pi}{(s_p \pi - v \gamma_u)^2} \quad (6.30A)$$

Figure 6.8 illustrates how the post-Kaleckian model works. Start from the initial position given by u_0^* and g_0^*. Assume now an increase in the costing margin and hence an

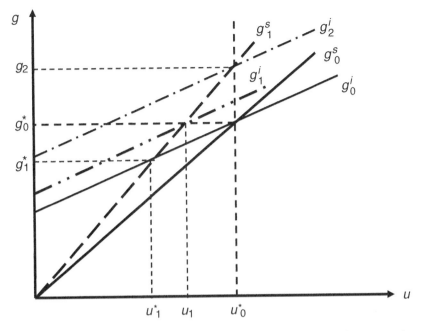

Figure 6.8 Impact of an increase in the profit share in the post-Kaleckian growth model

increase in the profit share. This provokes a counterclockwise rotation of the saving curve from g_0^s to g_1^s. In the canonical Kaleckian model, the rate of utilization and the growth rate would fall to u_1^* and g_1^*. In the post-Kaleckian model, however, this is not the end of the story. Here, the increase in the profit share creates an upward shift of the investment curve since investment is assumed to respond positively to increases in the profit share or in the normal profit rate. Depending on the size of the shift of the investment curve relative to the rotation of the saving curve, three configurations can occur. If the shift is less than that shown by g_1^i in Figure 6.8, the results of the canonical Kaleckian model are preserved and the paradox of costs still holds. If the shift occurs somewhere between the investment curves g_1^i and g_2^i, the rate of growth and the rate of profit rise as a consequence of the increase in the profit share, although the rate of utilization does not. Finally, if the shift brings the investment curve beyond g_2^i, then even the rate of utilization rises.

A confusing terminology followed by a debate

The three possible cases, and the names that they were originally given by the authors of the post-Kaleckian model, are shown in Table 6.1. It should be said, however, that the terminology has evolved over time, in part because it was a bit confusing, but also because of all the empirical work that has been performed to identify which case seems to be verified in a given country. As shown at the bottom of each of the three relevant cells, the most common terminology today is to speak of a wage-led regime when an increase in real wages or in the share of wages leads to a positive effect on the variable being considered; and reciprocally, when an increase in real wages or in the share of wages, that is, a decrease in the share of profits, leads to a negative effect on the variables under

Table 6.1 *Regimes tied to income distribution, with their different names*

		\+	−	
Effect of an increase in real wages on the rate of growth and the rate of profit	(+)	Cooperative stagnationism	Impossible	Bhaduri and Marglin (1990)
	(+)	Underconsumption		Kurz (1990)
	(+)	Wage-led demand with wage-led investment		Lavoie and Stockhammer (2013a)
	(−)	Conflicting stagnationism	Exhilarationism	Bhaduri and Marglin (1990)
	(−)	Overaccumulation	Keynesian neoclassical	Kurz (1990)
	(−)	Wage-led demand with profit-led investment	Profit-led demand with profit-led investment	Lavoie and Stockhammer (2013a)

(Column header spanning + and −: Effect of an increase in real wages on the rate of utilization)

consideration, then we have a profit-led regime. This is also the terminology adopted here. Thus, for instance, if an increase in real wages or the share of wages leads to an increase in the rate of capacity utilization, then we will say that this economy operates within a wage-led demand regime.

The advantage of the Bhaduri and Marglin investment function is that it enriches the post-Keynesian models of growth and distribution based on effective demand and endogenous rates of utilization of capacity. The canonical Kaleckian model then becomes one of three cases that arise from an investment function incorporating as an argument the normal rate of profit. The investment functions given by equations (6.25) or (6.27) may be considered as the answer of the Sraffians and Marxians to the post-Keynesian critique of their models, in particular the objection that, if the rate of utilization is considered to be endogenous in the long run, increasing real wages may induce a higher rate of profit and of accumulation (Nell, 1985; Amadeo, 1986; Dutt, 1987a). The investment function based on the normal rate of profit and on the rate of utilization introduces a variety of results, compatible with previous Marxian, post-Keynesian and even neoclassical models, although effective demand, rather than profit maximization or scarcity, is the major principle invoked.

> Particular *models* such as that of 'cooperative capitalism' enunciated by the left Keynesian social democrats, the Marxian model of 'profit squeeze' or even the conservative model relying on 'supply-side' stimulus through high profitability and a low real wage rate, fit into the more general Keynesian theoretical scheme. They become particular *variants* of the theoretical framework presented here. (Bhaduri and Marglin, 1990, p. 388)

A number of Kaleckians have been reluctant to accept the post-Kaleckian investment function. As Mott and Slattery (1994, p. 72) put it, 'it is not clear to us why the level of the profit share, or height of the mark-up, should influence investment by itself'. The main concern of Mott and Slattery (1994), which can also be found in Agliardi (1988), is that retained earnings depend on actual profits, not on normal profits, and it is these cash flows that will determine the capacity of firms to obtain advances and funds from banks and the financial markets. Actual retained earnings are thus an important element of the investment function, independently of any effect that a high rate of utilization may have on the desire to invest. Be that as it may, econometricians have taken such an interest in the post-Kaleckian investment function that it can be considered as nearly part of the canonical Kaleckian model.

6.3.3 Wage-led or Profit-led Demand?

So, are modern economies in a wage-led or profit-led regime? A fairly large number of empirical studies have been conducted since the mid-1990s to determine whether various countries are running under a wage-led or a profit-led demand regime. As one would expect, various studies use different econometric approaches and model specifications, so that they do not all reach the same results, even when studying the same country. Blecker and Setterfield (2019, pp. 235–251) present the main econometric methods that have been used, namely the structural and aggregative approaches, with their advantages and drawbacks, along with a summary of the results of the main studies. Also, more Marxian-oriented authors tend to conclude that economies are profit-led, as this sits well with their views about the contradictions of the capitalist economy and their explanation of business cycles based on profit squeeze (Lavoie, 2017a).

However, some broad lessons can be drawn from the empirical studies based on the structural approach, as summarized by Onaran and Galanis (2012, appendix D, pp. 58–9) in a study that was done for the International Labour Office. Nearly all studies conclude that every country studied has wage-led domestic demand. This means that the impact of higher real wages on the sum of consumption and investment demand is positive, as described in the canonical Kaleckian model. There is one factor, however, that we have not yet considered: the impact of higher real wages on the trade balance. When the impact of net exports on demand is also taken into account – the sum of the effect on domestic demand and on net exports is called total demand – then the results of empirical studies are much more mixed, depending of course on the country under consideration, but also within a given country, as is the case notably for the USA.

In any case, Onaran (2016) argues that while the world economy and large economic areas are wage-led, the income-distribution effects are of a modest size. Wage-led demand effects will be more substantial if they are accompanied by increases in public investment. In a recent empirical work, Oyvat et al. (2020) conclude that countries are more likely to be in a profit-led demand regime if their economy is more open to international trade. Profit-led demand is also more likely when there is more wage inequality, as we shall discuss later, and also when there is a high private debt to GDP ratio. The latter case can be explained by the fact that heavily-indebted households are prone to reduce their propensity to spend out of wages because of their high interest payments.

To their credit, it must be said that Bhaduri and Marglin (1990, p. 385) did not put much weight on their investment function to justify the possibility of a profit-led demand regime. Rather, they considered that their arguments would be more compelling when associated with an open economy. Their argument, and that of Blecker (1989), was that the income elasticity of imports could eventually lead to a deterioration of the trade balance, annihilating the expansionary effects of higher real wages on domestic demand. Also, higher wages, associated with somewhat higher prices, could lead to a deterioration of the competitive position of a country. The results mentioned here, and those of several other studies, support this interpretation, and we shall discuss it further in the chapter on the international economy. What we can say so far, although it is still a contentious statement among some heterodox economists, is that closed economies face a wage-led demand regime; the case of open economies is an open question! Whether the economy is wage-led or profit-led is evidently a crucial question, with important ramifications for economic policy.

Obviously, if a country is in a wage-led demand regime, it would be best to pursue distributional policies that are favourable to labour, for otherwise the economy might stagnate or spiral into instability. Table 6.2, inspired from Lavoie and Stockhammer (2013a, pp. 19–20) describes the likely relationships between distributional policies and demand regimes. It is important not to confuse these two concepts. While the government of a country may decide to pursue distributional pro-capital policies the objective of which is to increase the profit share, it may well be that such a country is in a wage-led demand regime, thus implying that these policies will have a detrimental effect on the economy. It should also be pointed out that the demand regime is to some extent endogenous. For instance, increases in the tax rate on profits and capital gains will increase the likelihood of a wage-led regime. Also, a distributional change favourable to the poor may reduce the propensity to import and may transform a profit-led regime into a wage-led one. On the policy front, an increase in the wage share or a reduction if the dispersion of wages would require the adoption of pro-labour distributional policies such as 'increasing or establishing minimum wages, strengthening social security systems, improving union legislation and increasing the reach of collective bargaining agreements' (Lavoie and Stockhammer, 2013a, p. 34). King (2019, p. 317) is rather pessimistic about the possibility of reversing past neoliberal policies, arguing that 'there is no single dramatic event to focus public attention on the need for reform'. But such an event, the COVID-19 crisis, has now occurred.

6.4 THE ISSUE OF STABILITY

In this section, we return to a controversial issue, which was momentarily set aside – that of whether or not stability should be assumed. This, as we shall see, is tied to another

Table 6.2 Viability and actual growth regimes and strategies

		Distributional policies	
		Pro-capital	Pro-labour
Demand regime	Profit-led	Profit-led growth process *Trickle-down capitalism*	Stagnation or unstable growth *Doomed social reforms (TINA)*
	Wage-led	Stagnation or unstable growth *Debt-led growth, export-led growth*	Wage-led growth process *Post-war Golden Age*

Source: Adapted from Lavoie and Stockhammer (2013a, Table 1.4).

controversial issue – that of whether there ought to be adjustment mechanisms that bring the actual rate of utilization towards the normal or standard rate of capacity utilization, which will be dealt with in the following section.

6.4.1 Keynesian versus Harrodian Instability

We have so far assumed that the economy described by the Kaleckian growth model exhibited Keynesian stability; that is, we assumed that the saving function would react more strongly than the investment function to changes in sales or in the rate of utilization of capacity. However, a number of critics of Kaleckian models doubt that this stability condition holds. Or they will say that, even if Keynesian stability holds in the short run, the Kaleckian model is likely to succumb to the problem of 'Harrodian' instability, an issue underlined by Roy Harrod (1939).

Figure 6.9 illustrates Keynesian instability, where investment reacts more than saving to changes in the rate of utilization. Entrepreneurs overestimate the equilibrium rate of capacity utilization ($u^e > u^*$), but the realized short-run rate of utilization is even higher than the overestimated rate ($u^K > u^e$), so that entrepreneurs are induced to raise the expected rate of utilization even more, thus moving away from the long-run equilibrium u^*.

Whereas Keynesian instability arises when the investment function is steeper than the saving function, Harrodian instability arises because the γ parameter of the investment function is unstable and rises (decreases) whenever the rate of capacity utilization exceeds (lies below) its normal rate. Thus one may have simultaneously Keynesian stability and Harrodian instability. Formally, critics of the Kaleckian model represent Harrodian instability as a difference or a differential equation, where the change in the rate of

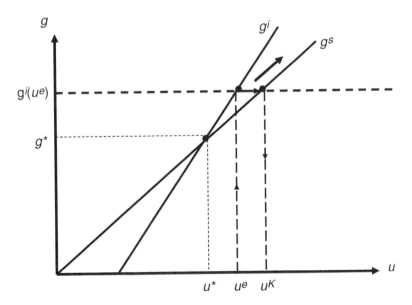

Figure 6.9   The case of Keynesian instability

accumulation is a function of the discrepancy between the actual and the normal rates of capacity utilization (Skott, 2012; Skott and Ryoo, 2008; Dutt, 2010).

$$\dot{g}^i = \psi_1(u^* - u_n), \psi_1 > 0 \tag{6.31}$$

But what this really means in terms of our little Kaleckian model is that the parameter γ gets shifted as long as the actual and normal rates of capacity utilization are unequal:

$$\dot{\gamma} = \psi_1(u^* - u_n), \psi_1 > 0 \tag{6.32}$$

The reason for this is that, in investment equation (6.12), the γ parameter can be interpreted as the assessed trend growth rate of sales, or as the expected secular rate of growth of the economy. When the actual rate of utilization is consistently higher than the normal rate ($u > u_n$), this implies that the growth rate of the economy is consistently above the assessed secular growth rate of sales ($g > \gamma$). Thus, as long as entrepreneurs react to this in an adaptive way, they should eventually make a new, higher, assessment of the trend growth rate of sales, thus making use of a larger γ parameter in the investment function.

This is similar to the original Harrodian knife-edge problem. Harrod (1939) starts from a full-equilibrium position, at the normal rate of utilization of capacity. If entrepreneurs expect a growth rate of sales that is higher than what Harrod called the warranted rate of growth, and thus set accordingly a high rate of capital accumulation, then the realized growth rate of sales will exceed the expected growth rate (Sen, 1970, pp. 11–12). In other words, the income-multiplier impact of investment will exceed the capacity-creating impact of investment so that the rate of utilization of capacity will rise beyond its normal level. This can be seen by recalling the definition of the rate of capacity utilization, $u = q/q_{fc}$, and looking at growth rates. As long as we exclude any change in the capital to capacity ratio, we have, as already pointed out in Lavoie (1995a, p. 799):

$$g_y = g + \hat{u} \tag{6.33}$$

where g is still the rate of accumulation of capital, while g_y is the rate of growth of sales and $\hat{u}$ is the growth rate of the rate of capacity utilization.

For Harrod, there is an inherent principle of dynamic instability, because the higher sales growth expectations will generate even higher realized growth rates of sales and higher rates of capacity utilization, thus leading entrepreneurs to speed up accumulation even more in the next period. This will be reflected in equation (6.32) as the upward shift in parameter γ, and this may be interpreted as a slow process. This is illustrated with the help of Figure 6.10. Once the economy achieves a long-run solution with a higher than normal rate of utilization, say at $u_1 > u_n$ (after a decrease in the propensity to save in Figure 6.10), the constant in the investment function moves up from γ_0 to γ_2 and γ_3, thus pushing further up the rate of capacity utilization to u_2 and u_3, with accumulation achieving the rates g_2 and g_3, and so on. In line with equation (6.33), as the rate of capacity utilization rises, the growth rate of sales in each period will exceed the growth rate of capital. Thus, according to some of its critics, the Kaleckian model gives a false idea of what is really going on in the economy, because the equilibrium described by the Kaleckian model (point B in Figure 6.10) will not be sustainable and will not last.

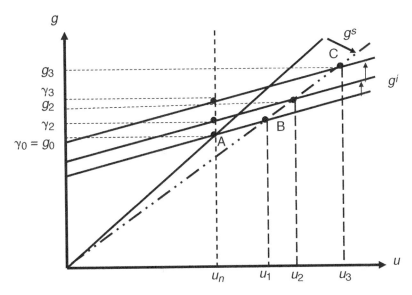

Figure 6.10 The Harrodian principle of dynamic instability in a Kaleckian model

Whether the simple Kaleckian model 'suffers' from Keynesian instability or Harrodian instability (with Keynesian stability), the consequences are nearly identical when the economy is subjected to a decrease in the propensity to save or a decrease in the profit margin. With Harrodian instability, there will be a succession of equilibria with ever-rising rates of accumulation and capacity utilization. With Keynesian instability, the new equilibrium is at a lower rate of utilization and a lower rate of accumulation; but since the economy is moving away from this equilibrium, the actual rates of utilization and accumulation are ever-rising (as indicated by the arrow in Figure 6.9), as in the case of Harrodian instability.

However, despite similar consequences, Keynesian and Harrodian instability give rise to different issues. In the rest of this section, we deal with the question of Keynesian stability. How Harrodian instability can be handled will be discussed in the next section, together with the question of whether a discrepancy between actual and normal rates of capacity utilization can be sustainable.

6.4.2 Expectations and Instability

The problem of Keynesian instability is driven by the fact that investment may respond strongly to changes in current values, more specifically those of the actual rate of capacity utilization. The Keynesian stability condition, given by equation (6.15), is such that: $s_p \pi > v \gamma_u$. With stylized facts such as $v = 3$, $\pi = 0.4$ and $s_p = 0.6$, there is not much room left for the γ_u parameter, which reflects the sensitivity of investment to changes in the rate of utilization. With the above numbers, one would need $\gamma_u < 0.08$, a number that seems rather low. The same point, with different parameter values, is made by Skott (2012), who also shows that the income multiplier is too large. Even if Keynesian stability is acquired, finding reasonable values for the rate of utilization, as given by equation (6.16) for the canonical model, isn't obvious.

This problem of stability and appropriate calibration is investigated in great detail by Botte and Dallery (2019) in the case of the post-Kaleckian model and equation (6.29), with quite pessimistic conclusions. One must not forget, however, that our little models are *prototypes* which abstract from several key determinants of the real world and thus are not designed to mimic actual data (Lavoie, 2017b, p. 195; Dutt, 2019, p. 298). Besides, Franke (2017a, p. 65) shows that a proper calibration and appropriate multipliers can be achieved by adding capital depreciation and especially taxes proportional to income, concluding that 'the introduction of the proportional taxes provides a simple and suitable way to overcome the problems that arise from the Keynesian stability condition'. In particular, Franke (2017b) affirms that empirical measures of the output to capital ratio of the non-financial corporate business sector is barely above 1, which implies that the capital to capacity ratio is likely to be around 0.8 and not 3 as is often assumed.

Another way out of this conundrum is to remember that our investment equations rely on the expected rate of utilization and not on the actual rate of utilization. Thus, when we write the stability condition as $s_p \pi > v \gamma_u$, we are in fact assuming that the investment equation (6.12) is written as

$$g^i = \gamma + \gamma_u (u - u_n) \tag{6.12A}$$

whereas the actual investment function was written as a function of the expected rate of utilization:

$$g^i = \gamma + \gamma_u (u^e - u_n) \tag{6.12}$$

with the expected rate of utilization assumed to be given by equation (6.19A), repeated here for convenience:

$$u^e_t = (1 - \mu_1) u^e_{t-1} + \mu_1 u^k \tag{6.19A}$$

Combining these two equations, the stability condition is weakened and now becomes

$$s_p \pi > \mu_1 v \gamma_u \tag{6.34}$$

When the actual rate of utilization is inserted in the investment function and the stability condition is described as equation (6.15), it is implicitly assumed that $\mu_1 = 1$. If μ_1 is reduced to one-half, then the γ_u parameter can become twice as big.

We may also follow the suggestion of Lima and Setterfield (2008, 2016). They argue that expectations about a variable depend on past realized values but also on some conventional anchor. For instance, this could be the rate of inflation targeted by the monetary authorities. In the present case, it could be either the normal rate of capacity utilization u_n that firms target, or it could be some rate of capacity utilization that the monetary authorities consider adequate for their purposes, with the firms being informed of this target level. This should further weaken the μ_1 parameter, and hence make the Keynesian stability condition less demanding.

6.4.3 A Dual Adjustment Process

Whether Keynesian stability is likely to hold or not, is there any way for Kaleckian models to retain stability, despite the failure of the Keynesian stability condition? One possibility has been explored by Bruno (1999) and Bhaduri (2008), and is the subject of this section. It requires slightly more involved algebra.

Both Bruno and Bhaduri study the post-Kaleckian model, where investment depends on the rate of utilization of capacity and the share of profits, as given in equation (6.25). This is also what we do here. They start away from the equilibrium dynamics model, assuming the absence of market-clearing in the short period. Thus, in the short (or ultra-short) period, (intended) investment and saving are not equal. Capacity utilization is fixed, as are profit margins. But let us assume that both quantities and prices react to disequilibria, so that two adjustment mechanisms get going simultaneously, one tied to quantities, which we have already defined as equation (6.17), and another linked to an adjustment in costing margins, as shown in equation (6.35):

$$\dot{u} = \mu(g^i - g^s), \quad \mu > 0 \tag{6.17}$$

$$\dot{\pi} = \phi(g^i - g^s), \quad \phi > 0 \tag{6.35}$$

One would presume that the ϕ parameter is necessarily positive. When output demand is above production ($g^i > g^s$), prices and profit margins rise, leading to a rise in the profit share π (or in the normal profit rate r_n). This case corresponds to the standard classical price adjustment mechanism, and it also corresponds to the Cambridge adjustment mechanism, found in the earlier neo-Keynesian growth models à la Kaldor and Robinson, and associated with forced saving. Bhaduri (2008), however, argues that the alternative, with $\phi < 0$, is not inconceivable. With excess demand, firms must raise rates of capacity utilization and hence employment rises faster than capacity, and this may generate a stronger bargaining position for workers. Thus, in some circumstances, when output demand is above production, it may be that real wages rise and hence that profit margins and the profit share fall. We shall call this the Radical case, since this kind of profit-squeeze behaviour has been underlined mostly by Radical economists (Bowles and Boyer, 1988; Gordon, 1994; Barbosa-Filho and Taylor, 2006), but also by Kalecki and Goodwin.

Because equations (6.17) and (6.35) turn out to be a non-linear system of differential equations in u and π, we examine the local stability of this system by linearizing it, making use of partial derivatives and computing its Jacobian matrix J at the equilibrium. Omitting the constant terms, the system can be written as

$$\begin{pmatrix} \dot{u} \\ \dot{\pi} \end{pmatrix} = \begin{pmatrix} \mu\left(\gamma_u - \frac{s_p \pi}{v}\right) & \mu\left(\gamma_\pi - \frac{s_p u}{v}\right) \\ \phi\left(\gamma_u - \frac{s_p \pi}{v}\right) & \phi\left(\gamma_\pi - \frac{s_p u}{v}\right) \end{pmatrix} \begin{pmatrix} u \\ \pi \end{pmatrix} \tag{6.36}$$

Because the change in the two relevant variables depends on the same functional form, the determinant of the matrix is zero, implying that this system has a zero root and hence there is a multiplicity of equilibria on a single demarcation line, with $\dot{\pi} = (\phi/\mu)\dot{u}$. Whether this locus of equilibria is stable or not depends on the sign of the trace of the matrix. The post-Kaleckian model as modified here is stable whenever the trace is negative, and unstable whenever the trace is positive. The trace of the matrix is equal to the sum of the two terms on the main diagonal:

$$Tr\ J = \mu(\gamma_u - s_p\pi/v) + \phi\ (\gamma_\pi - s_p u/v) \qquad (6.37)$$

Keynesian stability, or 'stability in dimension', requires that the first term of the trace be negative. Given that $\mu > 0$, it means that $\gamma_u - s_p\pi/v$ must be negative. This implies that inequality (6.15) must be verified, as we already know from our previous study of the Keynesian adjustment process.

Stability in proportion requires that the second term of the trace, associated with changes in costing margins, be negative. Two cases need to be considered. In the case of the classical or Cambridge adjustment process (with $\phi > 0$), this will occur whenever investment does not react too briskly to changes in costing margins, that is, when

$$\gamma_\pi - s_p u/v < 0 \qquad (6.38)$$

When equation (6.38) is verified, excess demand leads to an increase in profit margins and profit shares, with a moderately positive impact on investment, and a more important impact on saving, thus bringing together saving and investment, and bringing the economy towards equilibrium. With no quantity adjustment (with $\mu = 0$), this process through price adjustment guarantees the stability of the system.

By contrast, in the Radical case, with $\phi < 0$, excess demand leads to a fall in profit margins and profit shares. To reduce the discrepancy between investment and saving, investment must react strongly to the fall in the profit share, decreasing faster than saving does, and thus, in this alternative case, stability in proportion requires that equation (6.39) be fulfilled:

$$\gamma_\pi - s_p u/v > 0 \qquad (6.39)$$

With both the quantity and the price mechanisms in action, no fewer than eight cases, all shown in Table 6.3, become possible when dealing with the post-Kaleckian model. With stability in both dimension and proportion, the trace is necessarily negative, and stability is unconditional; there are two such cases. Symmetrically, with instability in both dimension and proportion, the trace is necessarily positive, and the model is unstable. In the other four cases, stability is conditional. Thus, in the absence of Keynesian stability, the post-Kaleckian growth model may still be stable. When we restrict the analysis to the canonical Kaleckian model, with the investment function not being dependent on the profit share ($\gamma_\pi = 0$), only four cases are possible, since we must have $\gamma_\pi - s_p u/v < 0$. With the Cambridge price adjustment, despite the lack of Keynesian stability (instability in dimension), the model may still exhibit stability. This point was made early on by Marglin and Bhaduri (1990, p. 165), who pointed out that 'the Keynesian Stability Condition, though standard in the texts, is necessary for stability only in a model which

Table 6.3 Stability in dimension and in proportion, Cambridge vs Radical price adjustment mechanisms, and wage-led vs profit-led regimes

Sign of $\gamma_u - s_p\pi/v$	Sign of $\gamma_\pi - s_p u/v$	Classical or Cambridge case: $\phi > 0$	Radical case: $\phi < 0$	$\dfrac{du^*}{d\pi^*} = -\dfrac{\gamma_\pi - s_p u/v}{\gamma_u - s_p \pi/v}$
(−) Stability in dimension	(−)	(A) $\phi(\gamma_\pi - s_p u/v) < 0$ Stability in proportion Tr $J < 0$ Unconditional stability	(B) $\phi(\gamma_\pi - s_p u/v) > 0$ Instability in proportion Tr $J = ?$ Conditional stability if μ is large	(−) Wage-led locus
	(+)	(C) $\phi(\gamma_\pi - s_p u/v) > 0$ Instability in proportion Tr $J = ?$ Conditional stability if μ is large	(D) $\phi(\gamma_\pi - s_p u/v) < 0$ Stability in proportion Tr $J < 0$ Unconditional stability	(+) Profit-led locus
(+) Instability in dimension	(−)	(E) $\phi(\gamma_\pi - s_p u/v) < 0$ Stability in proportion Tr $J = ?$ Conditional stability if ϕ is large	(F) $\phi(\gamma_\pi - s_p u/v) > 0$ Instability in proportion Tr $J > 0$ Unconditional instability	(+) Profit-led locus
	(+)	(G) $\phi(\gamma_\pi - s_p u/v) > 0$ Instability in proportion Tr $J > 0$ Unconditional instability	(H) $\phi(\gamma_\pi - s_p u/v) < 0$ Stability in proportion Tr $J = ?$ Conditional stability if ϕ is large	(−) Wage-led locus

abstracts from all determinants of equilibrium but the level of output, and in particular, one which abstracts from the impact of the distribution of income'.

6.4.4 Profit-led and Wage-led Regimes Revisited

Table 6.3 also highlights the fact that, whether the economy is wage-led or profit-led in terms of aggregate demand, that is, relative to the rate of utilization, depends on the signs of the first two columns. This can be seen by taking the total differentials of the saving and investment equations (6.14) and (6.25), each evaluated at a position of equilibrium ($g^i = g^s$), thus obtaining

$$dg^s = s_p(\pi/v)du^* + s_p(u/v)d\pi^*$$

$$dg^i = \gamma_u du^* + \gamma_\pi d\pi^*$$

Equating the above two equations, we obtain the equation in the last column of Table 6.3. Thus, unless we have *a priori* opinions about the values taken by the parameters in the investment and saving functions, for instance because of results arising from previous empirical work, a wage-led demand regime is as likely as a profit-led demand regime. It is interesting to note that some configurations are impossible. For instance, a stable wage-led economy with a classical or Cambridge price adjustment mechanism is compatible only with stability in dimension. Similarly, a stable profit-led economy with a Radical or profit-squeeze price adjustment mechanism requires stability in dimension.

Figures 6.11 to 6.14 illustrate the transition dynamics in the various cases. Figures 6.11 and 6.12 illustrate the Keynesian or dimension stability cases. When there is excess demand, the rate of utilization rises, and this will tend to bring the economy towards the equilibrium locus in the Keynesian stability case. When the economy is wage-led, the addition of the Cambridge price adjustment mechanism (rising profit margins with excess demand) will reinforce this tendency, as shown with the A arrow in Figure 6.11 (which corresponds to the (A) entry in Table 6.3). But with a Radical price adjustment mechanism (falling profit margins with excess demand), stability may either occur (arrow B_S) or not occur (arrow B_U). When the economy is profit-led, the reverse occurs, as shown in Figure 6.12. With the addition of the Cambridge price adjustment mechanism,

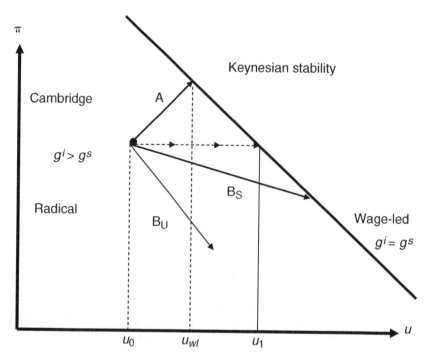

Figure 6.11 A wage-led regime with stability in dimension

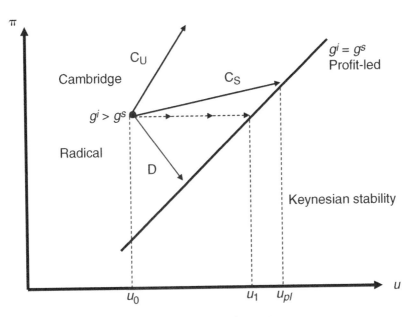

Figure 6.12   A profit-led regime with stability in dimension

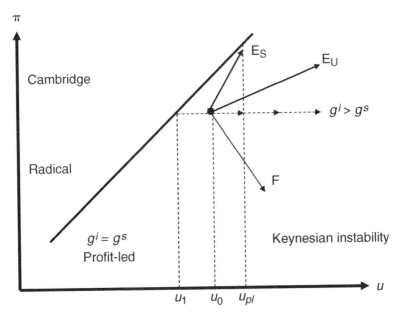

Figure 6.13   A profit-led regime with instability in dimension

convergence may either occur (arrow C_S) or not occur (arrow C_U), whereas it will always occur with the addition of a Radical price adjustment mechanism (arrow D).

Keynesian instability is illustrated in Figures 6.13 and 6.14. This time, when there is excess demand, increases in rates of utilization drive the economy away from the

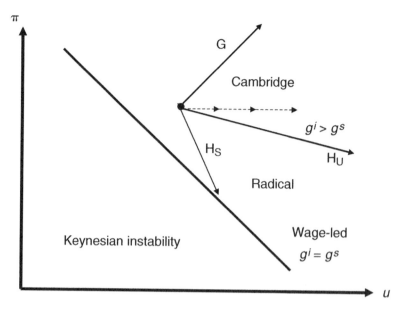

Figure 6.14 A wage-led regime with instability in dimension

equilibrium locus. When the economy is profit-led, as in Figure 6.13, the addition of a Cambridge price adjustment mechanism provides for conditional stability (arrow E_s), whereas the addition of a Radical mechanism makes the model completely unstable (arrow F). With a wage-led regime, as in Figure 6.14, it is the Cambridge price adjustment mechanism that will make the model unconditionally unstable (arrow G). With a Radical mechanism, convergence may either arise (arrow H_S) or not occur (arrow H_U).

6.5 CONVERGENCE TOWARDS THE NORMAL RATE OF CAPACITY UTILIZATION

As pointed out earlier, a key feature of the Kaleckian model is that the rate of capacity utilization is endogenous. In the canonical model, or even in the post-Kaleckian model, there is thus nothing that will bring back the actual rate of capacity utilization towards its normal value. This criticism of Kaleckian models was made early on by Auerbach and Skott (1988) and Committeri (1986; 1987). In their view, the normal rate of capacity is an optimal rate of utilization that firms try to achieve, at least over the long run. Therefore entrepreneurs will not be content unless the targeted rate of capacity utilization is realized: 'It is inconceivable that utilization rates should remain significantly below the desired level for any prolonged period' (Auerbach and Skott, 1988, p. 53). The only possible steady state is one in which the actual rate of utilization is equal to its normal or targeted level. This leads to the belief that the only consistent steady-state analysis is one where those two rates are equal. This is what Vianello (1985) calls 'fully adjusted positions'. In these positions, the actual rate of profit will also turn out to be equal to the normal rate of profit; otherwise it will not, as pointed out in the following quote:

The possibility of capacity utilization being different from its planned degree in the long run would have an important implication for theories of distribution and accumulation ... The *realized* rate of profit emerging from the interplay between distribution and effective demand may not be inversely related to the real wage, even in situations that the authors seem not to think limited to the short period; another way to say this is that the ... normal rate of profit r_n (i.e. the rate of profit technically obtainable at the normal utilization degree with [the real wage rate] taken at its current level) may diverge from its realized rate, even for long periods of time. Now, we do not wish to quarrel with this reasonable proposition: the *observed* rate of profit is very unlikely to coincide with r_n, even in terms of averages covering long periods of time, although we might suspect that after all, there must exist *some* connection between the two rates. The model, however, contains no element for the exploration of this connection, as it implies a persistent and systematic divergence between [the actual and the normal degree of capacity utilization]. (Committeri, 1986, pp. 170–71)

If the actual rate of capacity must eventually be equal to a given normal rate, then the rate of utilization is no longer an endogenous variable in the long period, which is likely to put in jeopardy many of the results achieved by the Kaleckian model. This objection to the Kaleckian model is highlighted by the use of investment equation (6.12) or (6.12A), which makes an explicit reference to a normal rate of utilization or to a 'planned' degree of utilization of capacity, as Steindl (1952, p. 129) calls it. This investment function, reproduced below, is based on the distinction between undesired and desired excess capacity, or between the actual rate and the normal rate of capacity utilization, respectively denoted by u and u_n:

$$g^i = \gamma + \gamma_u(u - u_n) \tag{6.12A}$$

It is obvious from the above equation that if the actual rate of utilization turned out to be equal to the normal or desired rate, the actual rate of growth would be equal to γ. As Committeri (1986, p. 173) and Caserta (1990, p. 152) point out, if firms are content about the degree of capacity utilization that is being achieved and do not desire to have it changed, one may conclude that the rate of accumulation desired by firms should be equal to the expected growth rate of sales. It is clear from equation (6.12A) that the exogenous parameter γ then represents this expected growth rate of sales. If it is assumed that the actual rate of capacity utilization u is larger than the planned rate u_n, the actual rate of growth g must be larger than the expected growth rate of sales γ. Committeri argues that this cannot be a consistent solution: in a proper steady-state model, expectations of sales growth and of spare capacity should be realized. When using investment equation (6.13), this objection seems much weaker, but there remains the issue of the normal rate of capacity utilization.

Several answers, consistent or inconsistent with Kaleckian analysis, have been provided to this conundrum, and in the rest of this section we outline some of them.

6.5.1 Provisional Equilibria in the Medium Run

The critique of the Kaleckian model assumes that there exists a given and unique normal rate of capacity utilization, or a given target rate of utilization perceived by firms when making investment decisions. However, not all post-Keynesians would agree that normal or target rates of utilization are unique. Neither would all post-Keynesians agree that economic analysis must be conducted under the restriction that some mechanism brings the economy back towards normal rates of utilization.

Chick and Caserta (1997), among others, have argued that expectations and behavioural parameters, as well as norms, change so frequently that long-run analysis, defined as fully adjusted positions at normal rates of capacity utilization, is not very relevant. Instead, they argue that economists should focus on short-run analysis and what they call medium-run or provisional equilibria. These are defined as arising from the equality between investment and saving, or between aggregate demand and aggregate supply. These short-run and medium-run equilibria are what we have previously defined as the u^K and u^* equilibrium values of the rate of utilization. In the view of those who support the analysis of provisional equilibria, these equilibria lend themselves more easily to the study of endemic conflicts and behavioural norms that characterize real historical episodes.

There is another post-Keynesian way out to avoid the need to examine mechanisms that would bring rates of utilization back to their normal value. As pointed out by Palumbo and Trezzini (2003, p. 128), Kaleckian authors tend to argue that 'the notion of "normal" or "desired" utilisation should be defined more flexibly as a range of degrees rather than as a single value'. Hence, according to Dutt (1990a, pp. 58–60), firms may be quite content to run their production capacity at rates of utilization that are within an acceptable range of the normal rate. On this interpretation, the normal rate of capacity utilization is more a conventional norm than a strict target. If this is correct, provisional equilibria could be considered as long-run fully adjusted positions, as long as the rate of capacity utilization remains within the acceptable range. Indeed, John Hicks (1974, p. 19) himself seems to have endorsed such a viewpoint. He points out that

> The stock adjustment principle, with its *particular* desired level of stocks, is itself a simplification. It would be more realistic to suppose that there is a range or interval, within which the level of stock is 'comfortable', so that no special measures seem called for to change it. Only if the actual level goes outside that range will there be a reaction.

Dutt (2010) has provided some justification for this type of behaviour. He appeals to economic agents with cognitive limitations and refers to Shackle's theory of potential surprise, so that decision-makers require drastic changes in their environment to modify their behaviour. As Dutt (ibid., pp. 242–3) puts it, 'to use Shackle's approach we could assume that firms have a band of values within which they expect capacity utilization to be, and if actual capacity utilization falls within that expected band they will not change their behaviour'. This thus produces a corridor of stability, a zone of inertia, from which Harrodian instability is excluded. Based on Simon's concept of satisficing, Setterfield (2019) also argues that there must exist a range of rates of capacity utilization around the normal rate such that investment behaviour is unlikely to change. Indeed, Setterfield (2019, p. 451) contends that 'one needs to look no further than Harrod himself' to respond to the critiques for Harrod (1972b, p. 129), in an essay in honour of Shackle, wrote that the knife-edge vision 'is really a caricature of my whole position', preferring an analogy with a 'fairly flat shallow dome', which he associated with the generic uncertainty faced by entrepreneurs.

Thus, as long as rates of utilization remain within the acceptable range, firms may consider discrepancies between the actual and the normal rates of utilization as a transitory rather than a permanent phenomenon. As a consequence, the Harrodian instability mechanism, which would induce firms to act along the lines of equation (6.32), accelerating accumulation whenever actual utilization rates surpass the normal rate, might be very slow, implemented only when entrepreneurs are persuaded that the discrepancy is persisting. Given real-world uncertainty and the fact that capital decisions are irreversible to a large extent, firms may be very prudent, so that the Harrodian instability may not be a true concern in actual economies, at least within a reasonable range of values taken by the rate of utilization.

A further point needs to be made. Some authors, such as Skott (1989a), have argued that if firms behave along profit-maximizing lines, there will be a unique profit-maximizing rate of capacity utilization (for a normal profit rate), corresponding to the optimal choice of technique. Kurz (1986), who is often cited as a reference for those insisting on normal capacity use, studies reserve capacity in a first sense, meaning the duration or the intensity of operation of a plant during a day. Franke (2020, p. 64), however, argues that even when holding this Sraffian understanding of reserve capacity, 'deviations of actual from desired utilization may appear rather inessential to the firms and, therefore, may well persist'. His arguments are somewhat related to the downward shape of the expansion frontier of the firm of Chapter 3. His idea is that the relation between the conjectured profit rate and utilization rate is likely to be non-linear, so that there may exist a corridor of utilization rates such that the conjectured profit rate is not much different from the optimal rate. Higher sales may require reduced markups and higher marketing efforts. Steindl (1952, pp. 41–2) makes the very same claim, contending that the capture of a larger market share will require 'a special sales effort', 'lower prices' or an engagement in 'quality competition'. Franke thus concludes, like Dutt and Setterfield, that Harrodian instability is unlikely to occur within a fairly large range of utilization rates.

In addition, as Caserta (1990, p. 151) points out, reserve capacity can be understood through a second meaning. What Kaleckians have in mind is instead idle capacity, as defined in statistical surveys of capacity use. They believe that each plant or segment of plant is usually operated at its most efficient level of output per unit of time. As Eichner (1976, p. 29) puts it, 'from basic engineering studies . . . it will be determined what is the most efficient size crew to operate the machinery, together with the most efficient quantity of raw materials to be fed into or through it'.

However, some plants or segments of plants are not operated at all. Firms are cost-minimizers, but they have little control over the rate of capacity utilization as defined by Kaleckians. It is telling to note that Kurz (1994, p. 408) is very clear about this when he studies reserve capacity in the second sense: 'There is no reason to presume that productive capacity will be exactly utilized at that level which, in conditions of free competition, cost-minimizing producers desire to realize and which will be called the "normal degree of utilization".' And later in the same paper he writes:

> It is virtually impossible for the investment-saving mechanism, as it is conceptualized in this section along non orthodox lines, to result in an optimal degree of capacity utilization. It is, rather to be expected, that the economy will generally exhibit smaller or larger margins of unutilized capacity over and above the difference between full and optimal capacity. (ibid., p. 414)

In other words, the actual degree of capacity utilization is likely to be different from its normal (optimal) level. Elsewhere, Kurz (1993, p. 102) insists that 'one must keep in mind that although each entrepreneur might know the optimal degree of capacity utilization, this is not enough to insure that each of them will be able to realize this optimal rate' (translated from French).

Joseph Steindl (1952, p. 12) concludes similarly when he says that 'the degree of utilisation actually obtaining in the long run, we must conclude, is no safe indication of the *planned* level of utilisation'. Thus what we have here is another example of macroeconomic paradox. As Caserta (2002, p. 177) puts it, ' firms are trying to create the appropriate amount of capacity, but by doing so they generate an outcome that in the aggregate reproduces exactly the same situation as before . . . The aggregate results of purposeful individual actions constantly frustrates the ultimate objective of those actions.' This is something that the critics of the Kaleckian model do not always seem to keep in mind.

Another line of response to the challenge that the normal rate of capacity utilization is a stock–flow norm and hence ought to be achieved in steady-state growth (Shaikh, 2009) is to argue that firms have several important objectives, and hence several targets or norms, as we saw in Chapter 3. As a consequence, it may not be possible for firms to achieve all of them simultaneously. This argument has been pursued in some detail by Dallery and van Treeck (2011). They argue that firms may need to trade off the utilization rate target against other targets, as was also argued in Lavoie (2003c). In particular, they discuss the frictions around the target rate of return, which is subject to a confrontation between workers and shareholders.

This being said, although all the above statements represent strong enough arguments to claim that steady growth may occur within a range of rates of capacity utilization that are different from a given normal rate, I do not wish to 'sweep the problem of the long run relevance of Kaleckian models under the carpet' (Commendatore, 2006, p. 289). I recognize the relevance of the concerns of those economists who object to provisional Kaleckian equilibria as the final word.

In the past, several heterodox economists, most of them Marxian and Sraffian, have argued that long-run analysis should be conducted on the basis of fully adjusted positions, that is, on the basis of an economy being run at its normal rate of capacity utilization. The problem, however, was that these economists did not explain how one could move from a world dominated by short-run Keynesian or Kaleckian demand-led mechanisms towards a world led by supply-side mechanisms. In other words, how can one move from a world where rates of utilization are endogenous towards a world where the rate of utilization is assumed to be equal to its normal value? In their critique of this dichotomy, Joseph Halevi and Peter Kriesler (1991, p. 86) wrote that the Sraffians argue that 'variations in the degree of capacity utilization are seen to occur only in the short run. However, to maintain this position, they must postulate a long-run adjustment of capacity to demand so that the actual rate of utilization tends towards the desired one.' This, they continue, is unacceptable 'until some coherent dynamic adjustment process is specified which can describe the "traverse" from one equilibrium position to another, without the traverse itself influencing the final equilibrium position, that is, without the equilibrium being path determined'. The task of the next subsections is thus to discuss mechanisms that have been offered as ways to achieve convergence towards a normal rate of utilization. In all that follows, we shall assume the existence of Keynesian stability.

6.5.2 The Cambridge Price Mechanism

The most obvious mechanism that can bring the economy back towards its normal rate of utilization is the Cambridge price mechanism. We have already discussed this mechanism in the first section of this chapter, when we presented the neo-Keynesian growth model of Robinson and Kaldor, and in particular when we looked at what we considered to be its main drawback, and also when we discussed the possibility of both prices and quantities adjusting together. Within the present context, the Cambridge price mechanism may be represented by either one of the following two differential equations:

$$\dot{r}_n = \phi_2(u^* - u_n), \phi_2 > 0 \tag{6.40}$$

$$\dot{r}_n = \phi_2 \frac{u_n}{r_n}(r^* - r_n), \phi_2 > 0 \tag{6.41}$$

Looking at equation (6.40), the Cambridge price adjustment mechanism implies that profit margins and hence prices relative to wages rise as long as the actual rate of utilization exceeds the normal rate of utilization, in an effort to bring the rate of capacity utilization to its normal value. Looking now at equation (6.41), the Cambridge price mechanism can be understood as an adaptive mechanism, whereby firms raise profit margins, and hence what they consider to be the normal profit rate, whenever the actual profit rate exceeds the previously assessed normal profit rate. This brings the rate of capacity utilization back towards its normal value as a side effect.

We already know the effects of such an adjustment mechanism in the case of the neo-Keynesian growth model, since we observed them in Figure 6.3. With an increase in the propensity to save, the rate of capacity utilization and the rate of profit are driven to below-normal values. As a result, the profit cost curve PC rotates up in the lower part of the figure, bringing the actual rate of utilization back towards u_n. But this change in the components of the profit rate has no impact on the Cambridge investment function (6.4), so that the growth rate and the profit rate remain at their lower values, g_2 and r_2. Despite the fully adjusted position, the paradox of thrift is sustained in the long run, but of course there can be no paradox of costs.

However, if we combine the Cambridge price adjustment with the Kaleckian canonical investment function, given by equation (6.12A), then the paradox of thrift also vanishes in the long run. This is obvious from the fact that if $u = u_n$ in investment equation (6.12A) where $g^i = \gamma + \gamma_u(u - u_n)$, then the equilibrium growth rate cannot but be equal to the assumed constant γ, whatever the propensity to save. This can be seen with the help of Figure 6.15. The increase in the propensity to save leads to an upward shift in the saving function in the top part of the figure (from g_0^s to g_1^s), and it leads to a downward shift in the effective demand curve in the bottom part of the figure (from ED_0 to ED_1), as shown by the dark arrows. The lower realized rates of profit and of capacity utilization then induce a reduction in costing margins and in the normal profit rate, thus leading to a countervailing rotation of the saving curve and to a downward shift of the profit cost curve (from PC_0 to PC_1), as shown by the light arrows. At the end of the process, the rate of utilization is back to its normal value u_n, while the normal profit rate is now lower than it was at the very start of the process (at r_{n2} instead of r_{n0}).

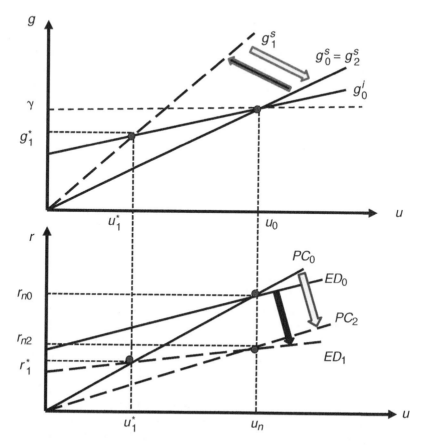

Figure 6.15 The Cambridge price mechanism within the canonical Kaleckian model

Several modern post-Keynesian authors have picked up some form or another of the Cambridge price mechanism: authors such as Harcourt (1972, p. 211), Wood (1975), Eichner (1976) and Kaldor (1985, p. 51) have argued that oligopolistic firms raise profit margins when faced with fast sales growth and high rates of capacity utilization. Indeed, this is why Wood (1975, p. 129), for instance, says that his model is a 'long run model of the determination of the share of profits at normal capacity use'. Other post-Keynesians have been critical of the mechanism however. Besides Davidson's (1972) irritation with the Cambridge price mechanism, Steindl (1979, p. 6), Garegnani (1992, p. 63) and Kurz (1994, p. 410) have all argued that rising costing margins were unlikely to be associated with high rates of capacity utilization, and hence with low unemployment and stronger labour bargaining power. A similar argument can be derived from Kalecki (1954, pp. 11–41; 1971, pp. 161–3), according to whom the bargaining power of labour unions should increase in an economic upswing with rising employment, thus implying instead a countercyclical movement of the mark-up. If this is so, the Cambridge price mechanism would have to be replaced by what we called the Radical price adjustment. Thus it is not clear that the Cambridge price adjustment can realistically provide the mechanism that would systematically bring the economy back towards a fully adjusted position. But more will be said about this mechanism at the very end of the chapter.

6.5.3 An Endogenous Retention Ratio

With the Cambridge adjustment mechanism, the saving curve rotates back to its original position, thus bringing the economy back to its normal rate of capacity utilization, thanks to a change in income distribution. An alternative to this is to assume that the saving curve rotates back to its initial position thanks to an endogenous change in the propensity to save. This is the solution adopted by Anwar Shaikh (2007a; 2009, pp. 477–82), a Marxian economist who has long defended the classical approach, or what he has also called a Harrodian approach. Shaikh's objective is to find a mechanism that will drive the economy back towards the normal rate of utilization in the long run, as desired by many Marxian and Sraffian critiques of the Kaleckian model, while safeguarding some Keynesian or Kaleckian features. Shaikh (2007a, p. 6) claims that 'this classical synthesis allows us to preserve central Keynesian arguments such as the dependence of savings on investment and the regulation of investment on expected profitability, without having to claim that actual capacity utilization will persistently differ from the rate desired by firms'. Shaikh's saving and investment equations are variants of those found in the canonical Kaleckian model:

$$g^s = s_f r + s_h \left(\frac{u}{v} - s_f r \right) \tag{6.42}$$

$$g^i = \gamma_r r_n + \gamma_u (u - u_n), \quad \gamma_r > 0, \gamma_u > 0 \tag{6.43}$$

The saving equation (6.42) is new. It reflects the fact that saving in modern economies is made up of two components. The first component corresponds to retained earnings, here represented in growth terms by $s_f r$, with s_f standing for the retention ratio of firms on profits, as was the case in Chapter 3. The second component assumes that households save a proportion s_h of their wage and dividend income. This is in line with Robinson's (1962, p. 38) claim that 'the most important distinction between types of income is that between firms and households'.

Investment equation (6.43) is a specific version of the canonical Kaleckian investment function (6.12A). As in the latter case, there is a catch-up term based on the discrepancy between actual and normal rates of utilization. But the equation also borrows from the post-Kaleckian model by making investment a function of profitability, as measured by the normal rate of profit, that is, the profit rate at the normal rate of capacity utilization. The introduction of normal profitability in the investment function is fully in line with arguments previously made by Sraffians and by Bhaduri and Marglin, their argument being that entrepreneurs do not base their investment decisions on the rate of profit realized on past investments but rather on the profit rate that they believe can be realized on newly created capital under normal conditions, as described with the help of investment equation (6.27). Thus, as was the case with the post-Kaleckian model, Shaikh's model can give rise to a wage-led or a profit-led regime in the medium run.

Shaikh's addition to all this is that the retention ratio of firms, s_f, is endogenous, as also can be found in the models of Sébastien Charles (2008) and Cédric Rogé (2020). Shaikh assumes that it reacts to a discrepancy between the current rate of capacity utilization and the normal rate of capacity utilization as conceived by the firm when making investment decisions, and, hence, between the actual rate of accumulation and the rate of accumulation induced by normal profitability at the normal or target rate of capacity utilization of firms. Shaikh suggests the following equation:

$$\dot{s}_f = \rho(u^* - u_n), \quad \rho > 0 \tag{6.44}$$

The consequences of such a differential equation are shown in Figure 6.16. The economy is initially at its normal rate of capacity utilization u_n and at the rate of growth g_0. Let us then imagine an increase in animal spirits, which in the present model can be proxied by an increase in the value of the γ_r parameter; for a given normal rate of profit, entrepreneurs decide to accumulate at a faster pace. As a result, on the basis of Keynesian dynamics, the economy moves up to a rate of utilization u_1 and a rate of accumulation g_1. As the slowly moving adjustment process suggested by Shaikh proceeds, the retention ratio of firms goes up, pushing the saving function upwards until finally the economy is back to the normal rate of capacity utilization u_n. Still, despite this, the economy in the new fully adjusted position has a rate of accumulation g_2, which is superior to the initial rate g_0.

We may thus conclude that, indeed, saving depends on investment in this model – a Keynesian feature – despite actual rates of capacity utilization being brought back to

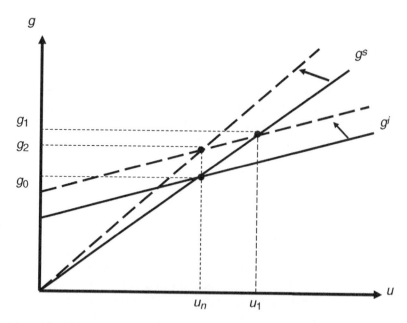

Figure 6.16   *Shaikh's adjustment mechanism through the endogeneity of the retention ratio of firms*

their normal values, and Keynesian animal spirits do play a positive role on economic activity. However, the paradox of thrift and the paradox of costs have disappeared in the fully adjusted positions. A decrease in the propensity to save of households will generate a compensating rise in the retention ratio of firms, with no change in the long-run rate of accumulation. As to the paradox of costs, an increase in the normal profit rate, and hence a fall in real wages, necessarily leads to a higher rate of accumulation in fully adjusted positions, at least in the case of Keynesian stability.

This can be readily seen by going back to equation (6.43) and assuming that the economy has reached its fully adjusted position, such that $u^* = u_n$. Because the saving function adjusts to the investment function, as shown in Figure 6.16, the long-run value of the rate of accumulation is entirely determined by the investment equation, so that the fully adjusted rate of growth depends positively on animal spirits, proxied by γ_r, and on the normal profit rate. In the long run, we have

$$g^{**} = \gamma_r r_n \qquad (6.45)$$

If Shaikh had adopted instead the canonical Kaleckian investment function (6.12A), the results would be nearly identical to those of the Cambridge price adjustment (we would have again $g^{**} = \gamma$). The only difference would be that the necessary long-run negative relationship between the rate of accumulation and real wages would disappear, since all the adjustments are done through the retention ratio and not through costing margins. Thus we can presume that this modified model would please modern Sraffians, who deny the existence of this negative relationship.

The only remaining issue is whether one can provide economic justifications for the adjustment mechanism given by equation (6.44). Shaikh (2009, p. 478) invokes various heterodox authors, arguing that retained earnings ought to respond to the financial needs of business investment. For instance, Robinson (1962, p. 61) argues that 'a high propensity to accumulate may have some effect in making thriftiness higher, in so far as it causes firms to distribute less to rentiers in order to finance investment from their own net profits'. But the point made by Kaleckian authors is precisely that, with higher rates of utilization, higher profits are forthcoming without a higher retention ratio or a higher mark-up! An alternative justification would be a ratchet effect, whereby firms set dividends on the basis of normal profits, retaining an ever-larger proportion of their profits when rates of capacity utilization exceed their normal rate. But this mechanism is far from obvious. It is easier to believe that firms have a *higher* retention ratio, instead of a *rising* retention ratio, when rates of utilization and hence accumulation rates are above normal. Finally, taking a more historical point of view, Dallery and van Treeck (2011) argue that, while the retention ratio may be endogenous, under the current paradigm of shareholder value orientation, managers may not be able to change the retention ratio on the basis of the discrepancy between the actual and the normal rates of capacity utilization because the decision to distribute profits is likely to be determined by the shareholders' claims on profitability.

All in all, we may prudently conclude that the adjustment mechanism based on an endogenous retention ratio may have some role to play in moderating the fluctuations of the rate of utilization away from its normal value, but it is unlikely to bring it back there.

6.5.4 Kaleckian in the Short Period, Classical in the Long Period

Duménil and Lévy's adjustment process

Another quite different dynamic adjustment path has been proposed by two French economists, Duménil and Lévy (1999). These two Marxians have long argued that Keynesian economists are mistaken in applying to the long run results arising from the short run. Their claim, in short, is that one can be Kaleckian or Keynesian when dealing with the short run, but that one ought to adopt a classical viewpoint when dealing with long-run issues. What they mean by this is that, in the long run, the economy will be brought back to normal rates of utilization – fully adjusted positions, as the Sraffians would say – and that, in the long run, classical economics is relevant again. Put briefly, this implies that, in the long run, a lower propensity to save will drive down the rate of growth of the economy, and that a lower normal profit rate (that is, higher real wages and a lower profit share, for a given technology) will also drive down the rate of accumulation. These authors thus reject both the paradox of thrift and the paradox of costs. Duménil and Lévy are more classical than Shaikh because for the latter a decrease in the propensity to save of households will have no long-run impact on the growth rate of the economy whereas for the former it will lead to a reduction in the fully adjusted growth rate.

Duménil and Lévy (1999) provide a simple mechanism that ought to bring the economy back to normal rates of capacity utilization. They consider that monetary policy is that mechanism. Their model, as shown by Lavoie (2003c) and Lavoie and Kriesler (2007), is strongly reminiscent of the mainstream New Consensus model, but there is also a great deal of resemblance with Joan Robinson's inflation barrier and the reaction of the monetary authorities which she describes (1956, p. 238; 1962, p. 60) and which we outlined at the beginning of this chapter. A simplified version of their model can be provided as follows. They start with the three main equations of the canonical Kaleckian model, to which they add two equations, given below. Equation (6.46) says that price inflation $\hat{p}$ is a function of the discrepancy between the actual and the normal rates of capacity utilization. This is simply a kind of Phillips curve, where the role of the rate of employment is replaced by the rate of utilization. The crucial addition is equation (6.47), which can be interpreted as saying that the monetary authorities will impose ever more restrictive monetary policies that will reduce the animal spirits of entrepreneurs as long as the rate of inflation is not brought back to zero.

$$\hat{p} = \chi_1 (u^* - u_n), \quad \chi_1 > 0 \qquad (6.46)$$

$$\dot{\gamma} = -\chi_2 \hat{p}, \quad \chi_2 > 0 \qquad (6.47)$$

Equation (6.47) can be understood as the reduced form of the impact of the reaction function of the monetary authorities. If we wish to make this more explicit, we could say, as do Duménil and Lévy in the working-paper version of their article, that parameter γ depends on the real rate of interest i_R and that the real rate of interest is raised by the central bank as long as the rate of inflation does not come back to zero. We then have

$$\gamma = \gamma_0 - \gamma_i i_R \qquad (6.47A)$$

$$\Delta i_R = +\chi_2 \hat{p} \qquad (6.47B)$$

Combining equations (6.46) and (6.47), we get equation (6.48), which says that a positive discrepancy between the actual and the normal rates of capacity utilization will lead to a reduction in the γ parameter:

$$\dot{\gamma} = -\chi_1 \chi_2 (u^* - u_n) \tag{6.48}$$

This equation looks very much like equation (6.32), which described Harrodian instability, except that here the sign of the equation is the opposite of the sign corresponding to Harrodian instability. The mechanism provided by Duménil and Lévy (1999) is thus a stabilizing mechanism, which brings the economy back towards its normal rate of utilization of capacity whenever the short-run rate of utilization ventures away from its normal value.

Figure 6.17 illustrates this adjustment mechanism. Suppose that this economy behaves along Keynesian or Kaleckian lines in the short run and exhibits Keynesian stability, while inflation only kicks off with a lag. A decrease in the propensity to save will rotate the saving function downwards, bringing the rate of capacity utilization from u_n to u_1. Through equation (6.46), this generates demand inflation, which induces the central bank to raise real interest rates, as shown by equation (6.47B). Interest rates will keep on rising as long as inflation is not brought back to zero. As a consequence, the investment function g^i shifts down gradually. It will stop shifting only when it returns to the normal rate of utilization u_n, because this is where inflation is brought back to zero. The end result, however, as can be read off Figure 6.17, is that the economy now grows at a slower rate, g_2 instead of g_0.

The lesson drawn from this graph is that the economy might be demand-led in the short run, but in the long run it is supply-led. In the long run, the growth rate is determined

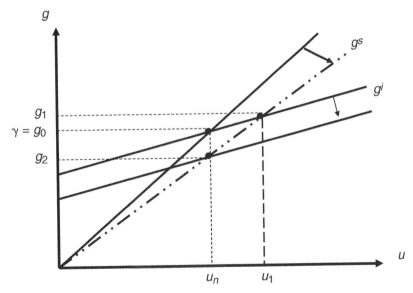

Figure 6.17 Duménil and Lévy's adjustment mechanism through a reaction function of the central bank

by the saving function, calculated at the normal rate of capacity utilization, and hence calculated at the normal profit rate. The long-run solution of the model is thus

$$g^{**} = s_p r_n \qquad (6.49)$$

Inspecting equation (6.49), it is then obvious that a reduction in s_p or r_n, that is, a decrease in the propensity to save or in the normal profit rate, induces a slowdown of the rate of accumulation in the long run. This is a standard result among Marxian (or classical) economists. We are back to the 'dismal' science. The paradoxes of thrift and of costs disappear in the long run. In addition, the model recovers the results of loanable funds theory: with a fall in the propensity to save, real interest rates need to be raised, thus recovering the scarcity interpretation of interest rates that is at the core of loanable funds theory. This can be seen by equating the long-run solution of the model with the extended investment function at its normal rate of utilization:

$$s_p r_n = \gamma_0 - \gamma_i i_R + \gamma_u (u_n - u_n)$$

so that the long-run equilibrium rate of interest is indeed a negative function of the propensity to save out of profits:

$$i_R^{**} = (\gamma_0 - s_p r_n)/\gamma_i \qquad (6.50)$$

Duménil and Lévy (1999) thus provide a simple and intuitive adjustment mechanism that can tame Harrodian instability, while simultaneously providing a traverse from a short-run Keynesian or Kaleckian equilibrium towards a classical long-run equilibrium. Two main critiques can be addressed to their proposed mechanism. The first one is that they assume away the presence of cost inflation, and assume a zero per cent target inflation rate, with actual inflation being at zero per cent when the actual rate of utilization equates the normal rate. Lavoie and Kriesler (2007, p. 591) show that when the target rate of inflation and the rate of cost inflation do not correspond to each other, the long-run rate of utilization will not be brought back to its normal level. This is indeed recognized by Duménil and Lévy (1999, p. 712) themselves when they say that 'economic policies may direct the system toward targets other than the stability of the general price level . . . It would be easy to show in the model that, if such targets are defined, long-term equilibrium will be shifted to another position deviating from the normal utilization of capacity.'

The second criticism is that a number of empirical studies have shown that the Phillips curve is non-linear and exhibits a horizontal segment, as first established by Eisner (1996), and found again by Filardo (1998), Barnes and Olivei (2003) and by Peach et al. (2011). If there is a horizontal segment in the Phillips curve, then it means that there is a range of rates of utilization where the inflation rate remains constant and hence where the monetary authorities will not feel the need to impose more restrictive policies, so that the usual Kaleckian results – the paradoxes of thrift and of costs – will hold within that range, despite the kind of mechanisms described by Duménil and Lévy. Moreover, and this is the third criticism, when interest payments to households are taken into consideration, and as already discussed in Chapter 5 when dealing only with interest payments from the government, it is not clear that higher interest rates will have the expected restrictive impact on the economy (Hein, 2008, chs 16 and 17; Franke, 2018).

Shaikh's second adjustment process
Before closing this subsection, we should mention another adjustment mechanism that arrives exactly at the results achieved by Duménil and Lévy (1999). This is the second mechanism proposed by Shaikh (2009). He claims that Harrodian instability is not a problem as long as a proper investment equation is being used. Shaikh proposes what he calls a Hicksian stock–flow adjustment equation, which he defines as

$$g^i = g_q + \gamma_u (u - u_n), \quad \gamma_u > 0 \quad (6.51)$$

where g_q is the rate of growth of output, by contrast with g^i, which is the rate of accumulation or the growth rate of capital (and also the growth rate of capacity, assuming away any change in the capital to capacity ratio).

Shaikh assumes the existence of a Kaleckian/Keynesian mechanism, whereby output adjusts to sales within the period (in the ultra-short run), so that the growth rate of sales and the growth rate of output are identical. But we already know that, by definition, as long as we exclude changes in the capital to capacity ratio, we have

$$g_q = g + \hat{u} \quad (6.33A)$$

Combining equations (6.51) and (6.33A) we get

$$\hat{u} = -\gamma_u (u - u_n) \quad (6.52)$$

Thus, with investment equation (6.51), the rate of utilization converges towards its normal value u_n, since the derivative of equation (6.52) with respect to u is negative. The Harrodian instability problem would thus be avoided through the use of investment equation (6.51). Dynamic stability prevails. Shaikh (2009, p. 464) claims that this adjustment mechanism renders the Harrodian 'warranted path perfectly stable'.

Whenever the rate of utilization wanders above its normal value as a consequence of an increase in real wages or a decrease in the propensity to save, the investment function shifts down, as it did in the Duménil and Lévy model. Despite the fact that the growth rate of sales during the transition that led to the higher rate of utilization (for instance at u_1 in Figure 6.17) has exceeded the initial growth rate of the economy (γ in Figure 6.17), the investment function is such that entrepreneurs must now expect a growth rate of sales and output that is lower than this initial growth rate, implying that the investment function in Figure 6.17 must now shift down. This process will continue until the rate of capacity utilization is brought back to its normal level, u_n, at which point all growth rates – of capacity, sales and output – will be brought down to g_2. Thus, once again, in the long run, at $u = u_n$, the rate of accumulation is simply determined by equation (6.49), and hence $g^{**} = s_p r_n$. There is no longer a paradox of thrift in the long run, and neither is there any paradox of costs. Thus Shaikh (2009) can conclude, as Duménil and Lévy (1999) did, that economists ought to be Keynesian for the short run but of classical obedience in the long run.

While the informational requirements in the Kaleckian model are very weak, things are completely different in the case of the Hicksian investment function proposed by Shaikh. Hein et al. (2011, p. 607) argue that firms must know the value of the current growth rate of output, and hence the current growth rate of sales, that is g_y, when they make their investment decisions and hence set g. They must also know the current rate of capacity utilization. They must make no mistakes. For if they do, say because they base their estimates of the current growth rate of sales on past growth rates, as they will if they behave in an adaptive manner, then the Hicksian stabilizing mechanism will not work and the model will become unstable. In other words, there is a kind of saddle-path equilibrium, as in the neoclassical models with rational expectations. In a sense, this is not surprising, since firms with investment equation (6.51) must be endowed with perfect foresight, being able to correctly assess future growth rates of sales while making them coherent with their investment decisions, something that is possible for firms only if they have a full understanding of the underlying structure of the economy. The informational requirements are thus huge, because the growth rate of sales depends on what all other firms are doing, as also pointed out by Palumbo and Trezzini (2003, p. 119) in their critique of Shaikh-like adjustments towards fully adjusted positions. Hence there is a coordination problem, which is swept away by Shaikh. Skott (2010, p. 129) gives the following critical assessment of Shaikh's adjustment mechanism:

> This argument is correct but is based on the assumption of fulfilled expectations at all times, and the Harrodian instability argument is precisely that when all firms reduce investment in order to raise their utilization rate, the outcome will be an unanticipated decline in aggregate demand and a fall in the utilization rate. Shaikh circumvents the instability by *assuming* that the economy is always on the warranted path . . .

Reiner Franke (2015) has constructed formalized discrete time versions of Shaikh's mechanism, with explicit time periods. He confirms that the mechanism is operative when rational expectations are assumed, that is, when firms know output and sales over the *next* period and thus the future growth rate of sales and the current rate of utilization. Surprisingly, the mechanism also holds in the case of myopic foresight, that is, when firms know output and sales of the *current* period, and hence the growth rate of sales of the current period, when they make their investment decisions at the *beginning* of the current period. Still, as contended by Franke (2015, p. 12) 'the myopic perfect foresight of sales requires capabilities of acquiring and processing information from the firms that cannot be too easily taken for granted' since firms must know what their sales will be before they have actually engaged in their investment decisions of the period. Finally, as argued by Hein et al. (2011), in the case of static or adaptive expectations, when firms only know the sales of the previous period and can make mistakes in assessing expected sales, Shaikh's mechanism cannot dodge Harrodian instability.

6.5.5 Entrepreneurs Fear High Rates of Utilization

Peter Skott has proposed some adjustment mechanisms of his own. Ever since Auerbach and Skott (1988), he has been a critic of the Kaleckian investment function and the idea that the rate of capacity utilization could be endogenous in the long run. In several papers he has argued that 'the current dominance of the Kaleckian model ... is unfortunate' (Skott, 2010, p. 127), claiming that models based on Harrodian instability provide a better fit with empirical evidence. According to Skott (2012), while the Keynesian/Kaleckian stability condition might hold in the short run, it will not do so in the long run. Thus, for him, both the simple Kaleckian model and the post-Kaleckian model suffer from Harrodian instability. However, Skott, like Fazzari et al. (2013), sees this as a real-world feature rather than as a drawback of the models. The main remaining task, according to Skott, is to develop models that may be locally Harrodian unstable but globally stable. Therefore one needs to find the mechanisms that might contain Harrodian instability.

Skott's main model has three different time periods, as can be understood from his previous work (Skott, 1989a). First, there is an ultra-short run in which the capital stock and output are given, while demand and supply in the goods market are adjusted by a fast price mechanism. This mechanism modifies income distribution in a Kaldorian way; that is, excess demand causes rising prices and a higher profit share. This corresponds to what we called Keynes's flexible price variant of the Marshallian post-Keynesian model of employment in Chapter 5. Second, there is a short run, where the growth rate of the capital stock is predetermined, and where output can be adjusted, under the assumption that the higher the profit share, the higher the growth rate of output. The rate of capacity utilization is thus an endogenous variable in this short run, but not as it would be defined in a Kaleckian model. Third, there is a long run, during which firms adjust the capital stock in order to achieve their desired rate of capacity utilization. It is this long-run adjustment process that may give rise to Harrodian instability and that needs to be tamed.

Skott (2010) discusses several variants of a Harrodian model: labour supply may or may not be perfectly elastic, thus giving rise to his 'dual' and 'mature' economies; and the adjustment speed of prices may be faster or slower than the adjustment speed of quantities, giving rise to what Skott calls the 'Kaldor/Marshall' analysis and to the 'Robinson/Steindl' approach, the latter being the closest to the Kaleckian model. By crossing over all these cases, one gets four variants. However, the underlying assumption, in particular regarding the three time periods mentioned above, are not always made transparent. In the 'Kaldor/Marshall analysis' with perfectly elastic labour supply, the relatively faster price adjustment mechanism seems to be valid for all three runs, thus preventing Harrodian instability and stabilizing the system through the Cambridge price mechanism previously described. Alternatively, with slow price adjustment (the 'Robinson/Steindl' approach), stability in the 'dual economy' requires a sluggish adjustment of the rate of capital accumulation to changes in the profit rate, which implies that the Robinsonian stability condition has to hold. Therefore this adds nothing new to our discussion of stability based on the dual adjustment process with both prices and quantities. It would seem that somehow Skott's 'Kaldor/Marshall' corresponds roughly to case (E) of Table 6.3, with instability in dimension and a strong stability in proportion.

In the 'mature', labour-constrained economy, as described by Skott, another mechanism containing Harrodian instability is supposed to be at work. This is indeed the mechanism already proposed in Skott (1989a). In the 'mature economy', the employment rate is entered as a negative determinant of the willingness of firms to expand their output. Skott's arguments are as follows. When the economy moves beyond u_n and growth exceeds the (exogenous) growth of labour supply, unemployment falls, firms have increasing problems in recruiting additional workers, labour unions are strengthened *vis-à-vis* management, workers' militancy increases, monitoring and surveillance costs rise, and hence the overall business climate deteriorates. This negative effect of increasing employment finally dominates the production decisions of firms, output growth declines, capacity utilization falls, investment falters, and finally profitability declines. Under certain parameter conditions this mechanism gives rise to a Goodwin-like limit cycle around the steady growth path given by labour supply growth, marrying Harrodian instability with a stabilizing Marxian labour market effect. The integration of a stabilizing Marxian labour market effect into a Kaleckian model suffering from short-run Harrodian instability thus again requires the addition of equation (6.48) to the model:

$$\dot{\gamma} = -\chi_3 (u^* - u_n), \quad \chi_3 > 0 \tag{6.48A}$$

Formally, this extension is exactly equivalent to the integration of the Duménil and Lévy (1999) policy rule introduced into the Kaleckian model in the previous subsection. The difference, however, is the interpretation of equation (6.48). Whereas the Duménil and Lévy model generates a downward shift in the investment function through the imposition of a restrictive monetary policy that purports to fight inflation, in the Skott model it is capitalists themselves who cause the downward shift in the investment function when $u^* > u_n$. If the unemployment rate falls below its steady-state value, capitalists reduce output growth, sales growth declines and the constant γ in the investment function starts to shrink, driving the economy towards u_n.

As detailed in Hein et al. (2011), Skott's approach also suffers from major problems. A most obvious problem is that the models lack clarity: they are rarely easy to understand, in contrast to the Kaleckian or post-Kaleckian models, which are much more pedagogical. Second, the 'Marshall/Kaldor' variant is hard to swallow: it is difficult to understand how an author who claims 'plausibility' and realisticness can assume that prices adjust instantaneously to equate aggregate demand with a fixed level of output. Such a price-clearing mechanism is certainly antagonistic to everything we learned in Chapter 3 on pricing. Third, the mechanisms described in the case associated with an inelastic supply of labour – the so-called case of a mature economy – are also unconvincing. It is not at all clear why falling unemployment rates, accompanied by more powerful workers and labour unions, should induce individual capitalists to reduce output growth, as assumed by Skott and as reflected by equation (6.48A). One would, rather, be tempted to assume that it would increase the bargaining power of labour, thus leading to rising nominal wage growth and possibly higher real wages, generating what we have called a Radical price adjustment mechanism. Output expansion as a positive function of the profit share and a negative function of employment seems to exclude Kaleckian results by assumption.

6.5.6 Endogenizing the Normal Rate of Capacity Utilization

So far we have considered mechanisms that drive the actual rate of capacity utilization towards the normal rate of utilization. But what if, instead, the causality of the adjustment mechanism were reversed, with the normal rate of capacity utilization tending towards the actual rate? As Park (1997, p. 96) puts it, 'the degree of utilisation that the entrepreneurs concerned conceive as "normal" is affected by the average degree of utilisation they experienced in the past'. Indeed, Joan Robinson herself has argued that normal rates of profit and of capacity utilization are subjected to adaptive adjustment processes, as the following quote shows:

> Where fluctuations in output are expected and regarded as normal, the subjective-normal price may be calculated upon the basis of an average or standard rate of output, rather than capacity... profits may exceed or fall short of the level on the basis of which the subjective-normal prices were conceived. Then experience gradually modifies the views of entrepreneurs about what level of profit is obtainable, or what the average utilisation of plant is likely to be over its lifetime, and so reacts upon subjective-normal prices for the future. (Robinson, 1956, pp. 186–90)

While this adaptive process seems hard to swallow for those who see economic agents as beings who follow constrained maximization, there is another tradition, related to the behavioural theories of the firm as developed by Herbert Simon and his followers, as we saw in Chapter 2. The behavioural theory of the firm sees the firm as an organization facing internal conflicts of interest and conflicting goals, as pointed out earlier in this section. Firms act within an environment of fundamental uncertainty and an overload of information. Firms or their managers are 'satisficers', rather than maximizers. They set themselves goals that take the form of aspiration levels defining a satisfactory overall performance. The crucial point made by behavioural economists in relation to Robinson's quote is that 'if goals are not met the firm readjusts downwards its aspiration levels' (Koutsoyiannis, 1975, p. 397). Because the arguments used to justify an endogenous normal rate of utilization are similar to those that we used previously to justify the lack of reaction when the actual rate diverges somewhat from the normal rate, it is not always easy to disentangle these two behaviours.

We can imagine various adaptive mechanisms that take into account both the flexibility of the normal degree of capacity utilization and the Harrodian instability principle. One possible mechanism, which we present here, deals only with the investment function (Lavoie, 1995a, pp. 807–8; 1996c; Hein et al., 2012). Sticking with saving equation (6.14) and with the canonical Kaleckian investment function given by equation (6.12A), the γ parameter in the investment function is interpreted as the secular growth rate of the economy, or the expected growth rate of sales. One would think that the expected trend growth rate is influenced by past values of the actual growth rate. Similarly, it may be that the normal rate of capacity utilization is also influenced by past actual rates. If this is so, we can write two dynamic equations such that

$$\dot{u}_n = \mu_2 (u^* - u_n), \quad \mu_2 > 0 \tag{6.53}$$

$$\dot{\gamma} = \psi_2 (g^* - \gamma), \quad \psi_2 > 0 \tag{6.54}$$

Formally, it would make more sense to use actual output growth, as defined by equation (6.33), instead of the rate of capital accumulation, but here and elsewhere we shall keep to this simplification. Making the proper substitutions, with the help of equation (6.16), these two equations get rewritten as

$$\dot{u}_n = \frac{\mu_2 (\gamma v - s_p \pi u_n)}{s_p \pi - v \gamma_u} \tag{6.53A}$$

$$\dot{\gamma} = \frac{\psi_2 \gamma_u (\gamma v - s_p \pi u_n)}{s_p \pi - v \gamma_u} \tag{6.54A}$$

and hence the differential function relevant to the perceived growth trend is

$$\dot{\gamma} = \frac{\psi_2 \gamma_u}{\mu_2} \dot{u}_n \tag{6.55}$$

We now have a continuum of equilibria, such that $\dot{u}_n = \dot{\gamma} = 0$, shown in Figure 6.18, and which corresponds to the long-run equilibrium:

$$g^{**} = \gamma^{**} = s_p \frac{\pi}{v} u_n^{**} \tag{6.56}$$

With a decrease in the propensity to save s_p, or with a decrease in the profit share π (or the normal profit rate r_n), the continuum of long-run equilibria rotates downward, and two cases arise. When dynamic equations (6.53) and (6.54) describe a stabilizing process, the normal rate of utilization and the perceived growth trend rise to a point such as A_S in Figure 6.18. The paradoxes of thrift and of costs thus still hold, even in the fully adjusted positions where $u = u_n$. The dynamic process, however, may be unstable, as shown by arrowhead A_U. The process will be stable provided the transitional path has a smaller slope than that of the new demarcation line; that is, provided we have $d\gamma/du_n = \psi_2 \gamma_u/\mu_2 < s_p \pi/v$, which means that $s_p \pi/v > (\psi_2/\mu_2)\gamma_u$. If the Keynesian stability condition given by equation (6.15) holds, then a sufficient condition for dynamic stability is simply $\mu_2 > \psi_2$. In other words, the Harrodian instability effect, represented by equation (6.54), which tells us that entrepreneurs will raise their expectations about future growth rates whenever current realized growth rates exceed the current trend estimate, must not be too large.

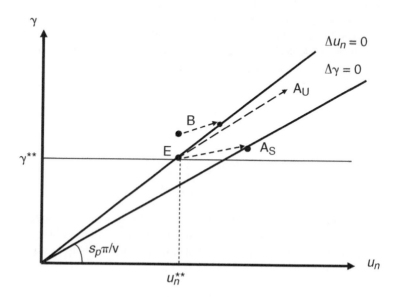

Figure 6.18   The normal rate of utilization adjusts to the actual rate

An interesting characteristic of the present model is that it features what Setterfield (1993) calls 'deep endogeneity'. The new fully adjusted position depends on the previous fully adjusted position. Very clearly, it also depends on the reaction parameters (the ψ_2 and μ_2 parameters) during the transition or traverse process, and hence we may also say that it is path-dependent. We may thus speak of a 'possibility devoid of definite solutions' (Lavoie, 1995a, p. 807), or what Kaldor (1934a, p. 125) characterized as 'indeterminate' equilibria. Commendatore (2006, p. 289) believes that 'the Keynesian nature of the analysis is severely reduced' with the adoption of these dynamic equations. This is not so. For instance, an increase in the animal spirits of the entrepreneurs or in their expectations with regard to the future growth of sales would be reflected in an independent upward shift of the γ parameter, which would drive the economy up, away from point E, and then along the B arrow in Figure 6.18.

A few other similar models, with an endogenous normal rate of capacity utilization, have been constructed, notably by Dutt (1997; 2010). One can also consider models where the endogenization of parameters can be extended to the pricing equation (Lavoie, 1996c; 2010b), a suggestion that seems to be approved by Park (1997). There is also the model of Dallery and van Treeck (2011), with firms facing multiple and competing targets, which was mentioned earlier. Perhaps the most complete model is that of Cassetti (2006), where the trend growth rate γ, the normal rate of capacity utilization u_n, and the normal profit rate r_n are all endogenized, reacting to their past values, while in addition the rate of capital scrapping gets speeded up as long as the actual rate of capacity utilization lies below its normal rate. Cassetti also finds path-dependence effects, with the saving paradox prevailing, while the paradox of costs may or may not occur in fully adjusted positions.

The topic of an endogenous normal rate of utilization, moving towards the actual rate of utilization or along with the growth rate of the economy, has generated quite a lot of attention lately. Needless to say, critics of the Kaleckian model such as Skott (2012) or Shaikh (2016, pp. 595–6) remain unconvinced. As a response to these doubts and believing that one should go beyond the idea that the normal rate is just a mere adaptative convention, Nikiforos (2013; 2016) has proposed a sophisticated microeconomic explanation and empirical evidence to justify the adjustment of the normal rate of utilization towards the actual rate. This proposal, however, has been strongly criticized both by Girardi and Pariboni (2019), and Fiebiger (2020). Since the arguments are rather involved, we will leave it at that, letting interested readers consult the papers, and move on to another new suggestion. Picking up on the idea briefly mentioned long ago by Ciccone (1986, pp. 26–7) and Amadeo (1987, p. 79), Setterfield and Avritzer (2020) argue that the level of the normal rate of capacity utilization depends on the volatility (the standard deviation) of the actual rate. They show empirically that periods of high volatility are associated with low rates of capacity utilization while periods of low volatility are connected to high rates of utilization. They then design a model where firms switch between two regimes, one with a low normal rate and the other with a high normal rate, when volatility moves out of given thresholds, thus creating a model of *strong* hysteresis where variations in the normal rate are slow, discrete and bounded. Whether their theoretical argument is convincing or not, notably because one may wonder whether filtered values of actual rates can be presumed to be proper estimates of the normal rate of utilization, one thing is certain: the trend rate of capacity utilization cannot be considered to be roughly constant anymore. Both Setterfield and Avritzer (2020) and Fiebiger (2020) provide definite empirical evidence that the secular average rate of utilization and the growth rate of aggregate demand move together and have trended downwards.

6.5.7 Heterogeneous Firms

So far, we have implicitly assumed that firms were homogeneous. Unless one brings in one of the taming mechanisms mentioned above, the addition of equation (6.32) or any variant of it will generate Harrodian instability within the canonical neo-Kaleckian model of growth and distribution. But what if firms are heterogeneous, either because actual rates of utilization are different for each firm or because their managers hold different views regarding future expected rates of growth of sales? This possible heterogeneity has recently attracted the attention of a few researchers. It turns out that such heterogeneity is another taming mechanism.

Setterfield (2019) has examined the case where there are several different industries, each with their own rates of capacity utilization. He assumes the existence of a range of rates of capacity utilization around the normal rate such that the Harrodian mechanism of equation (6.32) will not be triggered. Based on his statistical assessment of this range for each industry in the US economy, he shows that variations within 'the range of observed values of aggregate capacity utilization that might be regarded as normal', will 'not excite economy-wide changes in investment behaviour of the sort associated with the onset of Harrodian instability' (Setterfield, 2019, pp. 459–60).

Franke (2021) also built a canonical neo-Kaleckian model with an infinite number of firms. He assumes that all firms run at the same rate of capacity utilization, but with each firm holding a different view about the future growth rate of sales, as represented by the γ variable in the investment equation (6.12A). Individual firms switch randomly between an optimistic and a pessimistic view of the future growth rate, where the transition probabilities depend on the discrepancy between the actual and the normal rate of utilization. The model is calibrated as was Franke's (2017a) model, with taxes on income and production. Franke shows that the economy will reach a steady state if firms react relatively weakly to variations in the utilization gap; in this steady state, the actual utilization rate diverges from the normal rate; and the paradoxes of thrift and of costs still hold. Thus, once again, heterogeneity tames Harrodian instability.

Finally, we may consider the results of a full-blown agent-based model constructed by Emanuele Russo (2020), with a finite number of firms which receive a fraction of total demand according to their market share. Following an increase in real wages, if all firms are identical and do not modify their view of the future growth rate of sales, the average rate of utilization converges to a higher steady-state level. Russo then verifies that Harrodian instability occurs when these identical firms have adaptative expectations of future growth rates of sales (given by γ) and react along the lines of the Harrodian mechanism previously described by equations (6.32) and (6.54), now rewritten as:

$$\gamma_t = \gamma_{t-1} + \psi_3 (g_{y\,t-1} - \gamma_{t-1}) \tag{6.54B}$$

Russo (2020) thus can conclude that his agent-based model is indeed isomorphic to the standard aggregate model. He then examines what happens if heterogeneity is included, with firms having heterogeneous expectations, including a normally distributed idiosyncratic noise which may capture the firm-specific factors that could also affect sales expectations. We thus have:

$$\gamma_{i,t} = \gamma_{i,t-1} + \psi_3(g_{yi,t-1} - \gamma_{i,t-1}) + \varepsilon_i \qquad (6.54C)$$

Russo (2020) finds that for a significantly large set of values the model will not display instability. A non-trending process with endogenous oscillations emerges. Provided the random biases ε_i play a large enough role relative to the adaptative term in determining sales expectations, the model will avoid Harrodian instability and on average firms will not achieve the target rate of utilization. This result is consistent with the results obtained by Dosi et al. (2020), which we mentioned in Chapter 2: what seems like mistaken or naïve forecasts at the individual level tend to generate macroeconomic stability. Russo further finds that his agent-based model with heterogeneous expectations as designed by equation (6.54B) recovers the macroeconomic paradoxes of thrift and costs of the canonical neo-Kaleckian model.

6.5.8 An Exogenous Growth Component

The Sraffian supermultiplier approach
There remains a final adjustment mechanism to consider, a mechanism which Mongiovi (2012, pp. 503–4) deems to be a key component in reconciling and integrating Sraffian economics to the rest of post-Keynesian economics. This is the mechanism tied to an exogenous growth component. This mechanism was proposed by Franklin Serrano (1995a; 1995b) under the name of the Sraffian supermultiplier, in reference to Hicks's (1950) and Kaldor's (1970c) use of the term supermultiplier when describing an economy where the growth rates of induced expenditures become attuned to the growth rate of the autonomous components of demand. His intention is to show that some Keynesian results will still hold despite the actual rate of capacity utilization being brought back to its normal level in the long run. There are two Sraffian positions on this issue. There are those Sraffians who support the analysis of the supermultiplier with its normal rate of capacity utilization, such as Serrano, Bortis (1997), Sergio Cesaratto (2015a) and Oscar Dejuán (2005); and there are those, like Man-Seop Park, Antonella Palumbo and Attilio Trezzini, who, despite many similarities in their analyses, deny that rates of utilization are at their normal levels, either at all time or on average (Trezzini and Palumbo, 2016).

The crucial point made by Serrano is that the average propensity to save will move endogenously when there are autonomous consumption expenditures, even if the marginal propensity to save and the profit share are constant. This will be the case both in the short run, when autonomous consumption is a given, and in the medium run, when growth occurs, with autonomous consumption growing at some given rate different from the rate of accumulation. The simplest way to put this is to write a modified saving equation:

$$g^s = s_p \pi u / v - z \qquad (6.14A)$$

with $z = Z/K$, where Z are the autonomous consumption expenditures of the capitalists, and hence where z is the ratio of autonomous expenditures to the capital stock.

There is thus some similarity between this variable Z and the autonomous expenditures that we called A or a in equation (5.2) when dealing with our model of employment in Chapter 5. The main difference is that Z contains only autonomous expenditures that do not create productive capacity. It should further be noted that here the marginal propensity to save out of profits is s_p, the marginal propensity to save out of national income is $s_p\pi$, while the average propensity to save out of national income is $s_p\pi - zv/u$. Thus even if s_p and π, as well as the rate of utilization are constant, or even if there is a single marginal propensity to save on all components of income as assumed by Freitas and Serrano (2015), the average propensity to save will be endogenous as long as z is itself endogenous.

The main point that Serrano (1995b) wished to make is that saving can adjust to investment even when assuming that the marginal propensity to save, income distribution and the rate of utilization are all constant. The argument is thus that the 'Keynesian Hypothesis' (saving adjusts to investment) is more general than previously thought, since it does not need to rely on an endogenous rate of utilization in the long run (as in the Kaleckian approach); nor does it need an endogenous profit share (as in the neo-Keynesian approach).

Serrano (1995b) however made a second point. He argued that, as long as demand expectations by entrepreneurs are not systematically biased, the average rate of capacity utilization will tend towards the normal rate of utilization and hence that the economy will tend towards a fully adjusted position. While other Sraffians have been happy to endorse Serrano's first point, a number of them have questioned Serrano's second claim, arguing that it was at best dubious, due to unstable dynamics away from the fully adjusted position. Freitas and Serrano (2015) have however provided a conditional proof showing that over time an economy with autonomous consumption expenditures (and hence with saving equation (6.14A)) would converge towards the growth rate of these autonomous expenditures as well as converge towards the normal rate of capacity utilization. Their proof crucially relies on an investment function based on the assumption that investment is entirely induced, with a flexible propensity to invest h, given by the following equations in continuous time:

$$I = hq \qquad (6.57)$$

$$\hat{h} = \psi_4(u - u_n) \qquad (6.57A)$$

This says that firms will increase their investment to output ratio h whenever the actual rate of utilization exceeds the normal rate. Now one may wonder whether in discrete time the individual attempts to increase the share of investment in income would be successful in actually achieving this result in the aggregate since firms, when they make their investment decisions, do not actually know what sales there will be. In other words, does equation (6.57) succumb to a macroeconomic paradox? It turns out that the equations are verified in the aggregate. Freitas and Serrano (2015) further show that the mechanism will indeed bring the economy towards its fully adjusted position (at the normal rate of capacity utilization) provided the expanded propensity to spend (the sum of the marginal propensity to consume, the propensity to invest at normal utilization and the propensity to invest during the transition) is smaller than unity. Serrano et al. (2019, p. 276) later point out that their mechanism also requires that the growth rate of autonomous demand g_z not be excessive. Blecker and Setterfield (2019, pp. 351–362) place the Sraffian supermultiplier in a wider context.

As we shall see later, models based on autonomously growing expenditures that do not by themselves create production capacity have generated a lot of interest lately. Can all this be somewhat modelled within a neo-Kaleckian model of growth and distribution? Olivier Allain (2015) first put forward the formalization of a Kaleckian model based on autonomous government expenditure, showing that the addition of a slow Harrodian mechanism would bring the economy towards its normal rate of capacity utilization, thus providing another mechanism to tame Harrodian instability. Allain's formalization is thus distinct from what Serrano first proposed and different from what is proposed below based on Lavoie (2016b), but Allain's (2015) approach is the inspiration for all that follows in this subsection.

Modelling exogenous expenditures within the Kaleckian model
We thus start with the canonical Kaleckian investment function, given by equation (6.12A), $g^i = \gamma + \gamma_u(u - u_n)$, and the new saving equation, given by equation (6.14A). In the short run, nothing special happens and all the standard Kaleckian results, such as the paradoxes of thrift and of costs, hold. This is obvious from looking at the short-run solution for the rate of utilization, when the ratio z has not had time to change:

$$u^* = \frac{(\gamma - \gamma_u u_n + z)v}{s_p \pi - v\gamma_u} \tag{6.58}$$

Let us now consider what we shall call here a medium run. The key idea here is that autonomous consumption expenditures grow at a certain rate g_z, which we assume given by outside circumstances. As Serrano (1995a, p. 84), puts it, it is usually assumed that autonomous components of aggregate demand grow in line with the capital stock, but 'it seems that it is rather the size of the economy itself that depends partially on the magnitude (and rates of growth) of these autonomous components of final demand'. Serrano refers to Kaldor (1983a, p. 9) to provide support for this reversal of causality. Other post-Keynesians also assume that autonomous expenditures are the driving force: in Godley and Lavoie (2007a, ch. 11), it is autonomous government expenditures; in Trezzini (2011a), it is consumption expenditures. With consumer credit and lines of credit based on the value of real estate, it is clear that consumption expenditures can grow independently of income to a large extent, at least for some time (Barba and Pivetti, 2009). This increase in autonomous consumption can also be tied to the attempt to keep up with the Joneses and to 'invest' in an appropriate lifestyle, as discussed in Chapter 2 and to be discussed further in a forthcoming section on household debt.

Assuming that Z grows at the constant rate g_z means that the ratio $z = Z/K$ must be changing over time, through the following law of motion that defines the growth rate of z:

$$\hat{z} = \frac{\dot{z}}{z} = \hat{Z} - \hat{K} = \bar{g}_z - g = (\bar{g}_z - \gamma) - \gamma_u(u^* - u_n) \tag{6.59}$$

434   Post-Keynesian economics

The last equality is derived from the investment equation, $g^i = \gamma + \gamma_u(u - u_n)$. The bar over g_z is there to recall that the growth rate of autonomous expenditures is an unexplained constant. What we wish to know is whether the behaviour of z is dynamically stable or not; that is, whether it will converge to a stable value. This will happen if $d\hat{z}/dz$ is smaller than zero. From equation (6.58), we can compute what the term $(u^* - u_n)$ is equal to:

$$u^* - u_n = \frac{(\gamma + z)v - s_p \pi u_n}{s_p \pi - v \gamma_u} \tag{6.60}$$

Combining equations (6.60) and (6.59) we get

$$\hat{z} = \dot{z}/z = (\bar{g}_z - \gamma) - \gamma_u \left[\frac{(\gamma + z)v - s_p \pi u_n}{s_p \pi - v \gamma_u}\right] \tag{6.61}$$

Naturally, $\dot{z} = 0$ if $z = 0$. More interesting is the non-trivial solution, and taking the derivative of $\hat{z}$ with respect to itself, we find that

$$\frac{d\hat{z}}{dz} = \frac{-\gamma_u v}{s_p \pi - v \gamma_u} < 0 \tag{6.62}$$

The derivative is always negative, as long as the denominator is positive, that is, as long as there is Keynesian stability. This means that z will converge to an equilibrium value z^{**}, at which the growth rates of capital and aggregate demand will be the same as the given growth rate of autonomous consumption expenditures. This also means that the medium-run solutions that one could find, by assuming that at some point the growth rate of capital equates the growth rate of autonomous consumption, will indeed be realized if given enough time. In the long run, $g^{**} = \bar{g}_z$, and hence making use first of the investment equation, and then of the saving equation, we can derive the two equilibrium values:

$$u^{**} = u_n + \frac{\bar{g}_z - \gamma}{\gamma_u} \tag{6.63}$$

$$z^{**} = \frac{s_p \pi u^{**}}{v} - \bar{g}_z \tag{6.64}$$

Combining the above two equations, we get an explicit form for the share of autonomous consumption:

$$z^{**} = \frac{s_p \pi(\gamma_u u_n - \gamma) + (s_p \pi - v \gamma_u)\bar{g}_z}{v \gamma_u} \tag{6.65}$$

For this share to be strictly positive, note that the growth rate of the autonomous component must be high enough. We need:

$$\bar{g}_z > \frac{s_p \pi (\gamma - s_p \pi u_n)}{s_p - v \gamma_u} \tag{6.65A}$$

At this stage, three remarks can be made. First, the the introduction of an autonomous non-capacity expenditure does not on its own achieve a normal rate of capacity utilization, since $u^{**} \neq u_n$. For $u^{**} = u_n$ to be achieved, the γ parameter in the investment equation would need to equal g_z. In other words, entrepreneurs would need to assess the trend growth rate of sales as being equal to the growth rate of autonomous consumption expenditures. Dutt (2019, p. 291) believes that this apparent case of perfect foresight is not unreasonable, because entrepreneurs only need to know the growth rate of autonomous expenditures, and not the entire structure of the model. This case would be particularly plausible whenever the government announces the secular growth rate of its expenditures in its budgetary exposés. If not, then we need some additional adjusting mechanism to achieve the normal rate of utilization.

Second, almost by definition, with this mechanism we can have neither a wage-led nor a profit-led regime, as we defined them earlier, since the growth rate of capital and of output eventually adjusts to the given growth rate of autonomous consumption expenditures, and also because the long-run value of the rate of utilization depends neither on the profit share nor on the marginal propensity to save out of profits. As long as there is no change to any of the four parameters in equation (6.63), any change in the profit share or in the marginal propensity to save will have no effect on the long-run value of the rate of utilization.

This leads, however, to a third remark. While the paradoxes of thrift and of costs have disappeared in the long-run version of this model, reducing the profit share or reducing the marginal propensity to save out of profits will have a positive effect on the levels of capital, capacity and output. This is a point that Cesaratto (2015a) has emphasized recently, and it is precisely the point that was initially made by Serrano:

> That lower marginal propensity to save will increase the level of induced consumption and aggregate demand, and, consequently, also the long-period level of productive capacity. However, this will be a once-and-for-all effect. Once capacity has adjusted to the new (higher) level of effective demand implied by the higher (super) multiplier, the economy will settle back to steady growth at the unchanged rate given by the growth of autonomous expenditures. Therefore, on the demand side, a decrease in the marginal propensity to save brought about by the rise of the real wage will have a positive long-period level effect (on capacity output), but will have no effect on the sustainable secular rate of growth of capacity. (Serrano, 1995b, p. 138)

A fourth remark is now in order. By a strange turn of events, whereas Sraffians are usually accused by other post-Keynesians of focusing on fully adjusted positions, several Sraffian authors have criticized Kaleckians for focusing unduly on steady states, arguing that steady-state analysis ought to be jettisoned (Trezzini, 2011b, p. 143). In the example provided above by Serrano and in our little model, while the rate of capacity utilization will be the same at the beginning and at the end of the process, it will be higher during the transition process. Thus, on average, the rate of utilization and the growth rate of the economy are higher than at the starting and terminal points of the traverse. Thus, what these Sraffians are telling us is that more attention should be paid to the average values achieved during the traverse than to the terminal points. This is a recommendation with which all post-Keynesians could certainly agree (see for instance Henry, 1987), and it is one made quite explicitly by Park (1995, p. 307), who argues that the moving averages of key variables are quite distinct from their potential steady-state values.

The Serrano–Allain adjustment mechanism and the appeal to average values can be illustrated with the help of Figure 6.19. Let us assume that the economy starts from a steady state where the rate of accumulation is exactly equal to the growth rate of autonomous consumption expenditures, with a rate of utilization of u_0^{**}. Let us now suppose that there is a decrease in the marginal propensity to save out of profits or in the share of profits. This will be associated with a rotation of the saving curve, from g_0^s to g_1^s, as shown with the help of the dark arrow, since the slope of the curve will now be smaller. In the short run, as in all Kaleckian models, this will generate an increase in the growth rate of capital and in the rate of utilization, which move to g_1 and u_1 in the short run. But the new equilibrium is only a temporary one, as the new discrepancy between g_1 and g_z will generate a reduction in z through equation (6.59). The saving curve will thus gradually shift up through time, as shown in Figure 6.19 with the help of the light arrow, until the saving curve reaches g_2^s at which point the rate of accumulation equates the given growth rate of autonomous consumption. As to the rate of utilization, it will be back to its initial equilibrium position such that $u_2^{**} = u_0^{**}$. The change in income distribution or in the marginal propensity to save has had no impact on the equilibrium rate of utilization. However, the average rate of utilization and the average rate of growth achieved during this whole episode are higher, the economy having been run between u_0^{**} and u_1 and g_z and g_1 respectively during the whole transition. As a consequence, the level of output and of capacity will be higher than if there had been no increase in real wages or no decrease in the marginal propensity to save.

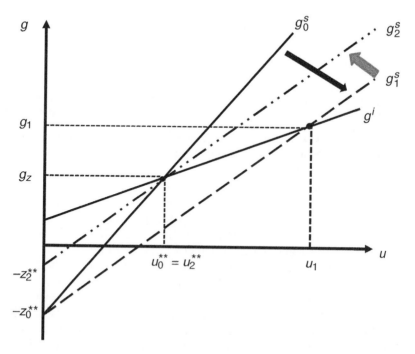

Figure 6.19   *The impact of autonomous non-capacity-creating expenditures in the Kaleckian model*

A Harrodian mechanism to achieve convergence towards normal utilization

The topic of this subsection is whether there is convergence towards the normal rate of capacity utilization. It is not yet the case. We need an additional mechanism. Allain (2015) proposes to add such a mechanism, which ironically consists of a Harrodian reaction function, similar to the one we have already encountered with equation (6.54), where the secular growth rate γ rises when the actual growth rate exceeds the secular growth rate previously considered. The complete model is then made up of two differential equations:

$$\dot{\gamma} = \psi_2(g^{**} - \gamma) = \psi_2 \gamma_u (u^{**} - u_n) \quad (6.54)$$

$$\dot{z} = z(\bar{g}_z - g^{**}) = z(\bar{g}_z - \gamma) - z\gamma_u(u^{**} - u_n) \quad (6.59A)$$

The second equation is non-linear since z also enters into u^{**}. We may now check local stability by computing the partial derivatives near the equilibrium given by u^{**} in equation (6.58). We obtain:

$$\frac{\partial \dot{\gamma}}{\partial \gamma} = \psi_2 \gamma_u \frac{\partial u^{**}}{\partial \gamma} = \frac{\psi_2 \gamma_u v}{s_p \pi - v \gamma_u}$$

$$\frac{\partial \dot{\gamma}}{\partial z} = \psi_2 \gamma_u \frac{\partial u^{**}}{\partial z} = \frac{\psi_2 \gamma_u v}{s_p \pi - v \gamma_u}$$

$$\frac{\partial \dot{z}}{\partial z} = -z^{**} \gamma_u \frac{\partial u^{**}}{\partial z} = \frac{-z^{**} \gamma_u v}{s_p \pi - v \gamma_u}$$

$$\frac{\partial \dot{z}}{\partial \gamma} = -z^{**}\left(1 + \gamma_u \frac{\partial u^{**}}{\partial \gamma}\right) = -z^{**}\left(1 + \frac{\gamma_u v}{s_p \pi - v\gamma - u}\right)$$

$$J(\gamma, z) = \begin{pmatrix} \dfrac{\psi_2 \gamma_u v}{s_p \pi - v \gamma_u} & \dfrac{\psi_2 \gamma_u v}{s_p \pi - v \gamma_u} \\ -z^{**}\left(1 + \dfrac{v\gamma_u}{s_p \pi - v\gamma_u}\right) & z^{**} \dfrac{-\gamma_u v}{s_p \pi - v \gamma_u} \end{pmatrix} \quad (6.66)$$

To find how the system described by (6.66) behaves, we need to look at the determinant of the 2×2 Jacobian matrix, called J, and at its trace. For the system to exhibit stability and converge to equilibrium, the determinant needs to be positive and the trace needs to be negative. We get:

$$\mathrm{Det}J = \frac{z^{**}\psi_2 \gamma_u v}{s_p \pi - v \gamma_u} > 0$$

$$\mathrm{Tr}J = \frac{\gamma_u v(\psi_2 - z^{**})}{s_p \pi - v\gamma_u}$$

The determinant is positive whenever the Keynesian stability condition is fulfilled. The trace is negative if $\psi_2 < z^{**}$. Thus, the system is stable as long as the effect of Harrodian instability is weak. If this is so, this system will go towards its fully adjusted position, where $u^{**} = u_n$ and where $g^{**} = \gamma^{**} = g_z$, and hence where $z^{**} = s_p \pi u_n - \bar{g}_z$. Obviously, for the share of autonomous expenditures to be positive, the growth rate of autonomous expenditures can neither be too small (because of condition (6.65A) nor too large. The following condition must also be fulfilled:

$$\bar{g}_z < s_p \pi u_n \tag{6.67}$$

This exact same condition is also required in the model of Freitas and Serrano (2015). More information, discussions and graphic representations about the above model can be found in Lavoie (2016b; 2017b) and Skott (2017).

More on autonomous expenditures and the supermultiplier
The recent rediscovery of the importance of autonomous non-capacity creating expenditures for the stability of demand-led models has generated a lot of interest among post-Keynesian authors. The first such model, that of Allain (2015), dealt with the consequences of autonomous government expenditure when the public budget is fully balanced. In that model, the share of government expenditure relative to capital plays the role of the z variable in the models of Freitas and Serrano (2015) and Lavoie (2016b). Because a higher government share requires a higher tax rate, the saving function takes a form similar to equation (6.14A) and plays a similar role. Allain (2015) showed that by combining these autonomous expenditures and the Harrodian reaction function, the economy could conditionally converge towards the normal rate of utilization. Since then, well-known authors such as Dutt (2019), Fazzari (in Fazzari et al., 2020), Hein (2018) and Palley (2019) have designed models with autonomous non-capacity creating expenditures growing at a constant rate. Fazzari et al. (2013), in models entertaining Harrodian instability, had already recognized the relevance of the growth in government expenditure to provide a floor to downward spirals. In their new model, Fazzari et al. (2020) provide their own complex formalization of an economy driven by Harrodian instability but tamed by the growth rate of some autonomous expenditure, and underline the similarities with the Sraffian multiplier and the neo-Kaleckian version of it, carefully taking into account what firms control and know relative to what they don't know and can only expect in a given time period.

Dutt (2019) recalls that the modified neo-Kaleckian model and the Sraffian supermultiplier model can be said to be isomorphic. Furthermore, he shows that 'wage-led growth occurs (in the sense that the *average* growth rate *along the adjustment path* increases after the increase in the wage share, though not in the sense of a change in the long-run *equilibrium* position) despite the imposition of the condition that growth occurs in the long run with normal capacity utilization (and that the long-run *equilibrium* growth is exogenously given), holds in a class of models' (Dutt, 2019, p. 293). I venture to claim that the main difference between the neo-Kaleckian model thus modified and the Sraffian supermultiplier approach lies in their investment function, where investment is entirely induced, with no autonomous term in the Sraffian model. In growth terms comparable to the canonical neo-Kaleckian investment function (6.12A), investment equation (6.57) of the Sraffian supermultiplier can indeed be rewritten as:

$$g^i = hu/v \qquad (6.57\text{B})$$

The consideration of growing autonomous non-capacity creating expenditures have given rise to a whole new spectrum of demand-led models within the post-Keynesian literature. For instance, Nah and Lavoie (2017; 2019a; 2019b) and Lavoie and Nah (2020) have written a series of models focusing on different issues and drivers, and so have Allain (2019; 2021b) and Hein (Hein, 2018; Hein and Woodgate, 2021). Some of their results will be dealt with in the sections of the chapter that consider these issues, for instance when discussing technical progress or Harrod's second problem, that of equating the growth rate of the economy with the growth rate of potential supply. A special mention at this stage goes to the model of Riccardo Pariboni (2016a), because it uncovers a paradoxical result. He applies the idea of a growing autonomous consumption to the post-Kaleckian model of Bhaduri and Marglin (1990), thus making use of investment equation (6.25). As is the case for other similar models, growth is neither wage nor profit led, since the growth rate of the economy comes back to the growth rate of the autonomous component. The paradox, however, is that Pariboni (2016a, p.426) finds that 'an increase in the profit share leads to a reduction in the equilibrium degree of capacity utilization, regardless of the relative magnitudes of the parameters involved'. Profit-led *demand* is impossible in this modified post-Kaleckian model.

Some authors have created full-scale stock-flow consistent versions of supermultiplier models that allow to tame Harrodian instability mechanisms, such as Mandarino et al. (2020), who study the evolution of the debt of workers. The first of these SFC models was the one by Lídia Brochier and Antonio Macedo e Silva (2019). The autonomous consumption component in their model is consumption out of wealth of the previous period, thus implicitly implying that households have a stock-flow norm – a target wealth to income ratio (Godley and Lavoie, 2007a, p.74). One can debate whether consumption out of wealth is truly an autonomous component since it is an endogenous variable, but if we stick to our definition of Chapter 5, we may say that it is since it does not depend on current income. The authors use investment equation (6.57), adding to it Setterfield's range of rates of capacity utilization around the normal rate where the mechanism of equation (6.57A) is not triggered. Despite a return to normal utilization, their simulations generate the paradox of thrift and wage-led growth in the new equilibrium, and not just as an average during the transition. There is no paradox of costs however, as the higher real wages are accompanied by lower profit rates.

In a model that entertains a Harrodian instability mechanism and fully induced investment, Thompson (2020) also combines constant growth in autonomous non-capacity creating components, which he calls Luxemburg's external demand, with consumption out of wealth. He demonstrates both local and global stability. Making external demand proportional to productive capacity instead of being autonomous, as do Brochier and Macedo e Silva (2019), does not alter convergence; the steady-state growth rate will be an increasing function of this (constant) proportion defining the desired wealth to income ratio, consumption out of wealth thus again playing an essential role as it allows the average saving rate to be endogenous. What seems to happen is that an increase in the rate of accumulation caused by the higher animal spirits of the entrepreneurs will generate a temporary fall in the wealth to income ratio. This will induce a rise in the average propensity to save, as households attempt to recover their targeted wealth to income ratio, thus neutralizing the assumed Harrodian instability.

Despite the rising popularity of these supermultiplier and modified neo-Kaleckian models, some objections have been raised. As with the standard neo-Kaleckian models, Skott (2019) has argued that it was difficult to find plausible numbers when doing calibration, but this critique has already been dealt with before. Another critique was that in the real world one could not expect any autonomous demand component to grow at a constant rate, or that all variables were endogenous (Nikiforos, 2018; Skott, 2019). Obviously, nobody believes that g_z (whether it is exports, government expenditure or consumption) will remain constant forever and will be entirely impervious to changes in the economic situation. Again, these models are prototypes. In any case, in the more sophisticated SFC models there seems to be no need for an autonomous expenditure growing at a constant rate. For these reasons, Fiebiger and Lavoie (2019) prefer to refer to 'semi-autonomous' expenditures, tied to the external markets of Rosa Luxemburg, as did Kalecki. Related to this, critics have asked whether there was any evidence of these semi-autonomous expenditures impacting the economy. Girardi and Pariboni (2020) provide such statistical evidence. The econometrician Edward Leamer (2015) has long argued that housing activity was the leading indicator of the business cycle in the USA, a claim upheld by Fiebiger (2018) who shows that business activity always lags consumer credit and expenditure on housing.

A final critique is that the supermultiplier and the modified neo-Kaleckian models would 'eliminate all role for uncertainty and animal spirits in long run growth', thus jeopardizing the Keynesian message (Oreiro et al., 2020, p. 521). This is a debatable point. A first counter-argument would be that an increase in the expected secular rate set by entrepreneurs will have a temporary positive effect on the economy and the average growth rate. Furthermore, several economic variables besides business investment may influence the 'semi-autonomous' growth rate and are subjected to fundamental uncertainty, notably mortgage credit and consumer credit as just pointed out, which are influenced by the liquidity preference of the banking sector and the animal spirits of households. It must be granted however that under the new approach, the focus is less on business investment and more on residential investment, consumer credit, government expenditure and exports as drivers of aggregate demand.

6.6 RECONCILING THE GROWTH OF AGGREGATE DEMAND AND AGGREGATE SUPPLY

6.6.1 Preliminaries

Having dealt at long last with the issue of the normal rate of capacity utilization, we can now tackle another objection to the Kaleckian growth model that also requires some kind of adjustment mechanism. Critics point out that, unless the growth rate of the economy happens by chance to equal the natural rate of growth, the rate of unemployment will keep increasing or decreasing, depending on whether this natural growth rate is above or below the growth rate of the economy. This is Harrod's second problem. As Dutt (2006a, p. 322) says, 'the model may be considered problematic, both because one does not observe indefinite increases or decreases in the unemployment rate in reality and also because it seems theoretically implausible to have a long-run equilibrium in which the rate of unemployment does not arrive at some equilibrium value'.

While the issue of reconciling aggregate demand and aggregate supply is certainly an important one, here we shall make only a few observations and sketch possible solutions. First, we should point out that there are basically two ways to ensure that the actual growth rate of the economy is roughly equal to the natural rate of growth, so that the rate of unemployment is approximately constant. The first one is to provide a mechanism that will drive the actual rate of growth towards the natural rate of growth; the second one is to design a mechanism that will pull the natural rate of growth towards the actual growth rate of the economy; and of course there could be a combination of the two mechanisms that would drive the two growth rates towards each other. Post-Keynesians, who argue that aggregate demand is the key variable both in the short and in the long run, would tend to favour the second mechanism, pointing out that there are forces that would tend to pull the natural growth rate towards actual growth rates. In this subsection, we will not provide formal proofs, relying instead on intuition.

Before we start, let us recall or make some definitions. Output per unit of labour, or labour productivity, was defined as $y = q/L$ in equation (5.45). Thus the growth rate of employment is defined by the growth rate of output q, which we called g_q in equation (6.51), minus the growth rate of labour productivity, which we designated $\hat{y}$ in Chapter 1, and which we define as λ from now on:

$$\hat{L} = \hat{q} - \hat{y} = g_q - \lambda \tag{6.68}$$

The natural rate of growth g_n is the sum of the growth rate of active population and the growth rate of labour productivity:

$$g_n = \hat{N} + \hat{y} = \hat{N} + \lambda \tag{6.69}$$

The rate of employment is defined as $E = L/N$. Putting together equations (6.68) and (6.69), we see that the discrepancy between the growth rate of employment ($\hat{L}$) and the growth rate of active population ($\hat{N}$) is the discrepancy between the growth rate of output and the natural rate of growth. In the steady state, with $\hat{u} = 0$, and assuming no change in the capital to capacity ratio, this discrepancy will also be equal to the difference between the rate of accumulation and the natural rate of growth. Using equation (6.33A):

$$\hat{E} = \hat{L} - \hat{N} = g_q - g_n = g + \hat{u} - g_n \tag{6.70}$$

Roughly defining the rate of unemployment by $U = (N - L)/L$, provided it is not too large, it can be shown that its change is approximately equal to

$$\dot{U} \cong \hat{N} - \hat{L} = g_n - g_q \tag{6.71}$$

6.6.2 A Reconciliation towards the Supply Side

Dutt (2006a) analyses several possible mechanisms that might do the trick of reconciling aggregate demand with aggregate supply. His first mechanism is of the first nature, and would bring the actual growth rate towards the natural rate of growth. Dutt assumes the following relationship between the growth rate of the γ parameter in the investment equation and the discrepancy between the growth rate of the employed labour $\hat{L}$ and the growth rate of active population $\hat{N}$, thus implying that the growth rate of the γ parameter depends negatively on the growth rate of the employment rate, from equation (6.70):

$$\hat{\gamma} = -\chi_4(\hat{L} - \hat{N}) = -\chi_4 \hat{E}, \chi_4 > 0 \tag{6.72}$$

How is this justified? Dutt (2006a, p. 323) provides an explanation that resembles somewhat that of Duménil and Lévy (1999). As the rate of employment E rises (and as the rate of unemployment falls), the monetary authorities are likely to impose restrictive policies and higher real interest rates, which will slow down capital accumulation and the economy. As shown in Lavoie (2009c, pp. 201–2), this could be based on the assumption that the change in the rate of inflation depends on the change in the rate of unemployment, instead of its level, as would be the case in the mainstream accelerationist hypothesis. This would mean that there is unemployment hysteresis, a hypothesis put forward by both New Keynesian and post-Keynesian economists, and for which there is considerable evidence (Cross, 1995; Stanley, 2004; Mitchell and Muysken, 2008; Lang, 2009). Monetary authorities will impose austerity as long as the rate of inflation is not stabilized. Formally, we have

$$\Delta \hat{p} = -\chi_5 \dot{U} = -\chi_5(\hat{N} - \hat{L}) = \chi_5(g_q - g_n) \tag{6.73}$$

Equation (6.72) also fits quite well the arguments provided by Skott, presented in a previous subsection, and that are based on the notion that entrepreneurs get discouraged by rising or high rates of employment. Indeed, in equation (6.72), one could assume that the level of the employment rate is the key variable, thus replacing $\hat{E}$ by $(E - E_n)$, where E_n would be a normal rate of employment corresponding to a rate of unemployment that would stop the central bank from taking further action or that would leave entrepreneurs indifferent. Whether the natural rate of growth or the normal rate of employment is the target, it will be achieved with this kind of mechanism as the fall in the rate of accumulation (through a lower γ) will generate a fall in the growth rate of output and hence a fall in the growth rate of employment. But with this mechanism, the supply side takes over in the long run, and effective demand loses its dominant role.

Another mechanism, also of the first nature, has been proposed by Stockhammer (2004, ch. 2). Stockhammer starts from the post-Kaleckian model, which can be either wage-led or profit-led. Stockhammer assumes the existence of some sort of Radical price mechanism or modified Goodwinian effect, where the share of profit is positively linked to the rate of unemployment U. We thus have

$$\pi = \pi_0 + \chi_6 U \qquad (6.74)$$

Thus it follows that, at least as an approximation:

$$\dot{\pi} = -\chi_6 \dot{U} = -\chi_6(\hat{N} - \hat{L}) = -\chi_6 \hat{E} \qquad (6.75)$$

As long as the growth rate of employment is decreasing because the growth rate of the economy is too low, costing margins rise and the profit share increases. Equation (6.75) is based on the intuitive notion that the bargaining power of labour unions and employees is weakened when unemployment is rising or when unemployment is high. The consequences of assuming the mechanism described by equation (6.75) are fairly obvious: with a profit-led growth regime, the rising costing margins will induce faster growth and hence a faster growth of employment, until the growth rate of employment attains the growth rate of active population, thus achieving a stable rate of unemployment. By contrast, in the wage-led growth regime, the converse will happen, and the rate of unemployment will not stabilize. Thus, as Stockhammer (2004, p. 53) concludes, 'in the profit-led regime, there is a stable equilibrium rate of unemployment . . . In the wage-led regime, the rules of the game change. The long-run rate of unemployment is not stable. The long run is thus but a succession of short-run equilibria.'

A simple solution to have the growth rate of the economy converge to its natural value in the case of no technical progress would be to 'assume that the government sets the rate of growth in public expenditures in accordance with the demographic rate of growth', as mentioned by Allain (2019, p. 88). He proposes instead an entirely different mechanism to bring the growth rate of the economy towards the natural growth rate. His model is however of a Keynesian nature since there is nothing in his model to achieve full employment. Allain (2019) assumes that society grants consumption of a minimum subsistence level to all members of the labour force, not unlike the necessary goods that we discussed in Chapter 2. Employed workers must thus transfer part of their wages to the unemployed in the form of unemployment benefits which are all consumed. Employed workers also consume these necessary goods and then have a marginal propensity to consume out of their leftover income, while profits are entirely saved. The result of all this is that the saving function takes a form similar to that of equation (6.14A), where the autonomous component z is proportional to population. The model thus has an autonomous non-capacity creating growth component – the growth rate of population – with an average saving rate which is endogenous, as discussed in section 6.5.8. As is usual with this kind of model, there is convergence towards the exogenous growth rate, provided the Keynesian stability condition holds, so that in this case there is convergence of the actual growth rate towards the natural rate of growth.

Allain (2021b) presents a similar model, with somewhat similar results, but this time with technical progress, so that the minimum subsistence level determined by society grows at the same pace as the real wage, itself determined by the rate of technical progress. The latter rate is itself influenced by the actual growth rate of the economy, so that one could say that there are reciprocal influences, but Allain (2021b, p. 625) insists that his model 'provides theoretical support for the growth rate of the autonomous component to be equal to the natural rate of growth. It is the (natural) growth rate of the autonomous component that exerts a force of attraction on the economic rate of growth'.

6.6.3 A Reconciliation towards the Demand Side

Finally, we may consider mechanisms of the second nature, those that bring the natural rate of growth towards the actual growth rate of the economy. Dutt (2006a) proposes the following relation:

$$\hat{\lambda} = \chi_7 (\hat{L} - \hat{N}) = \chi_7 \hat{E} = \chi_7 (g_q - g_n), \chi_7 > 0 \qquad (6.76)$$

This says that the change in the growth rate of labour productivity depends positively on the growth rate of output, or more precisely that it depends on the difference between the growth rate of output and the natural rate of growth. Because the growth rate of labour productivity λ is one of the two components of the natural rate of growth, as shown in equation (6.69), whenever the natural rate of growth is too low, the mechanism of equation (6.76) will drive up the natural rate of growth towards the actual growth rate of the economy. The same mechanism, sometimes formalized slightly differently or incorporating an effect on the growth rate of the workforce, has also been suggested and analysed by Lavoie (2006c), Bhaduri (2006), Sasaki (2011), Palley (2019), Nah and Lavoie (2019b) and Fazzari et al. (2020).

Here it is the supply side that adjusts to effective demand in the long run, so that the Kaleckian growth model is left untouched. This is consistent with the long-standing tradition in post-Keynesian growth theory described by Setterfield (2002, p. 5), who contends that the natural rate of growth is not a strong attractor in demand-led growth models: 'The natural rate of growth is ultimately endogenous to the demand-determined actual rate of growth.'

Several reasons could be offered for this phenomenon. Fast growth rates of demand imply fast growth rates of output; the latter encourage learning by doing but also a fast pace of capital accumulation, which on its own drives up the rate of technical progress. Kaldor (1957), with his technical progress function, very clearly established such a relationship at the theoretical level: he assumed that higher capital accumulation per head would generate a faster rate of growth of output per head, and hence a faster rate of technical progress. This is also tied to an empirical variant of Kaldor's technical progress function, Kaldor–Verdoorn's law, which has been verified in various incarnations, and which will be the focus of a forthcoming section.

Also, faster growth rates encourage potential workers to enter the workforce, and they encourage foreign workers to migrate to the area where growth proceeds at a faster pace, as evidenced by John Cornwall (1977). Indeed, the Great Recession has illustrated this phenomenon: the financial crisis has provoked large displacement movements in the workforce, and rates of participation of the active population have fallen dramatically. This mechanism is invoked by Nah and Lavoie (2019b) and Fazzari et al. (2020) in models led by non-capacity generating autonomous expenditures where the long-run solution implies a constant demand-determined rate of unemployment. The two main components of the natural rate of growth, the growth rate of the labour force and the rate of technical progress, are thus positively linked to the rate of growth of demand. The mechanism described by equation (6.76) or some similar mechanism truly can be said to lie at the heart of the debate between neoclassical growth economists on the one hand, who treat the rate of growth of the labour force and labour productivity as exogenous to the actual rate of growth, and economists in the Keynesian/post-Keynesian tradition, who maintain that growth is primarily demand driven because labour force and productivity growth respond to demand growth. (León-Ledesma and Thirlwall, 2002, pp. 441–2)

Historically, post-Keynesians have been keen to underline the possibility of endogenous changes in the natural rate of growth and in the rate of technical progress in particular, as shown by the statement of Robinson in her *magnum opus* and that of Kaldor in a 1954 lecture:

> But at the same time technical progress is being speeded up to keep up with accumulation. The rate of technical progress is not a natural phenomenon that falls like the gentle rain from heaven. When there is an economic motive for raising output per man the entrepreneurs seek out inventions and improvements. Even more important than speeding up discoveries is the speeding up of the rate at which innovations are diffused. When entrepreneurs find themselves in a situation where potential markets are expanding but labour hard to find, they have every motive to increase productivity. (Robinson, 1956, p. 96)

> The stronger the urge to expand ... the greater are the stresses and strains to which the economy becomes exposed; and the greater are the incentives to overcome physical limitations on production by the introduction of new techniques. Technical progress is therefore likely to be greatest in those societies where the desired rate of expansion of productive capacity ... tends to exceed most the expansion of the labour force (which, as we have seen, is itself stimulated, though only up to certain limits, by the growth in production). (Kaldor, 1960, p. 237)

An interesting empirical study that extends the above arguments has been made by León-Ledesma and Thirlwall (2002). They have shown that the natural rate of growth is endogenous to the rate of growth of output demand, demonstrating that the natural rate of growth rises in booms, and falls in recessions. As they say, 'growth creates its own resources in the form of increased labour force availability and higher productivity of the labour force' (2002, p. 452). Similar studies have yielded similar results for the three countries of North America (Perrotini and Tlatelpa, 2003), for Latin America (Libânio, 2009), and for Asia (Dray and Thirlwall, 2011). These studies are based on an empirical version of equation (6.71), $\dot{U} \cong g_n - g_q$. An intuitive understanding of the test is the following. First, omitting the random term, the following equation is estimated:

$$\dot{U}_t = \alpha_0 - \alpha_1 g_{qt}$$

When $\dot{U}_t = 0$ it can be ascertained that the actual rate of growth equates the natural rate of growth. This means that the natural rate of growth is such that $g_n = \alpha_0/\alpha_1$. The same regression can then be run by using a dummy variable to take care of time periods during which the actual growth rate exceeds the natural rate initially computed. The dummy is usually positive and significant, meaning that the newly computed natural rate of growth for these time periods is larger, showing that high growth rates pull up the natural rate of growth.

6.6.4 Reciprocal Influences

Naturally, as suggested by Dutt (2006a), we can combine his two mechanisms, given by equations (6.72) and (6.76). We then have a system of two differential equations. As we noted twice before, because the change in the two relevant variables depends on the same functional form, the determinant of the matrix of this system is zero. This implies that the system has a zero root and hence that there is a multiplicity of equilibria on a single demarcation line. We could also verify that the trace of the matrix of the system is negative, thus showing that this dynamic system is stable, but the stability is fairly obvious. Figure 6.20 illustrates the effect of combining the two mechanisms. Here, for simplicity, we examine the evolution of the actual growth rate g_q and that of the natural rate of growth g_n.

When the economy happens to be at point B, the actual rate of growth is lower than the natural rate. The first mechanism (equation 6.72) will push up the actual rate of growth along the horizontal arrow; the second mechanism (6.76) will pull down the natural rate of growth vertically. Thus the two rates will traverse towards each other, to a value determined by the strength of the parameters tied to each of the two mechanisms. Similarly, starting from point A, where the actual rate of growth is higher than the natural rate, the two rates will converge to some undetermined value such as A*, above A. Thus, as Dutt

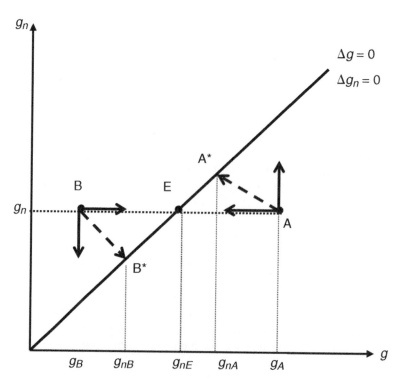

Figure 6.20   Combining supply-side and demand-side mechanisms to achieve an endogenous natural rate of growth

(2006a, p. 326) concludes, 'expansionary policies and other positive aggregate demand shocks have long-term expansionary effects, although not as strong as short-run expansionary effects'.

6.7 THE KALECKIAN MODEL WITH OVERHEAD COSTS

In Chapter 5, we extended the short-run Kaleckian model by adding overhead labour costs. This led to some interesting results with regard to the impact of changes in the base real wage on the average real wage. The addition of target-return pricing to overhead labour costs also led to some peculiar results when considering the impact of an increase in managerial costs on the share of profits, as we showed that this had a negative effect on the profit share when the actual rate of utilization was below its normal value, while it had a positive effect when the rate of utilization was above its normal value. Here we pursue this kind of analysis, but this time within the context of a growing economy.

Recall from Chapter 5 that the percentage mark-up over unit direct labour costs w/y_v, could be written as

$$\theta = \frac{r_n v + \sigma f}{u_n - r_n v} \quad (5.66)$$

The formula given by equation (5.66) clearly shows how additional costs associated with overhead labour will be passed on to consumers, in the form of higher prices. It does not matter whether managerial and supervisory staff are now paid higher wages relative to variable labour (a higher σ ratio), or whether more managerial staff have been hired relative to the number of blue-collar workers (a higher f ratio). The result is the same: mark-ups will be raised, and hence prices will increase, *ceteris paribus*, relative to the wage of direct labour. In a world dominated by megacorps that endorse pricing procedures based on target-return pricing, higher managerial staff costs are necessarily associated with higher prices, as well as higher gross costing margins at standard capacity utilization, unless firms simultaneously decide to reduce their target rates of return.

6.7.1 The Paradox of Costs Reconsidered in the Case of Overhead Costs

In the canonical Kaleckian model, any increase in unit costs will lead to an increase in economic activity and hence in profitability, as shown by Dutt (1992a) where this is applied to managerial costs. Without target-return pricing, higher unit overhead costs lead to a downward shift of the *PC* curve, with the old and new *PC* curves being parallel to each other. This is shown in Figure 6.21, where the *PC* curves start from below the origin, thus reflecting the presence of overhead costs. The rise in f or in σ means that the break-even rate of capacity utilization, for a given markup θ, is now higher than before, as shown on the horizontal axis of the figure. The redistribution of income away from profits generates higher rates of utilization and a higher profit rate, here shown as u_2 and r_2. In a comment on this claim, Paul Burkett (1994, p. 119) has wondered 'whether firms are able to pass on unproductive outlays as higher prices'; that is, whether firms are able to pass on to consumers additional managerial costs. If this is so, as would be

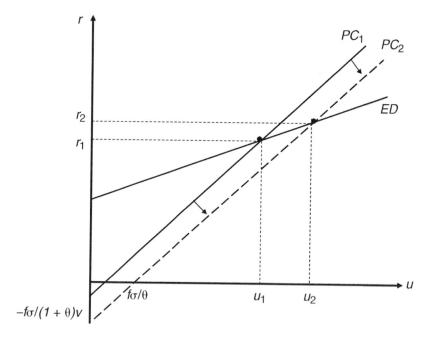

Figure 6.21 Macroeconomic impact of an increase in managerial overhead costs, without target-return pricing

the case with target-return pricing, the higher prices 'could limit the positive impact of such expenses on effective demand in the economy as a whole'. Higher managerial costs could thus be associated with lower realized profit rates and rates of accumulation. The paradox of costs, as applied to managerial costs, would vanish, even without saving out of labour income. This is what we now explore, in analysing instead what happens when firms follow target-return pricing procedures.

The question at stake is whether an increase in f or in σ, that is, in the relative importance of managerial labour or in its relative remuneration, still leads to an increase in effective demand, and hence to an increase in the rate of capacity utilization, the rate of profit (and the rate of capital accumulation). To find out, we must take the derivative of the profits cost function with respect to σ (or indifferently with respect to f, since the two parameters play a symmetric role). The profits cost function can be derived from the net profit share seen from the cost side, given by equation (5.71) of Chapter 5:

$$\pi^s = \frac{(\sigma f + r_n v)u - (u_n - r_n v)\sigma f}{u(u_n + \sigma f)} \tag{5.71}$$

Since we know that the profit rate is $r = \pi u/v$, it is simple to compute the profit rate of the economy, also seen from the cost side, as

$$r^{PC} = \frac{(\sigma f + r_n v)u - (u_n - r_n v)\sigma f}{v(u_n + \sigma f)} \tag{6.77}$$

Accumulation and capacity 449

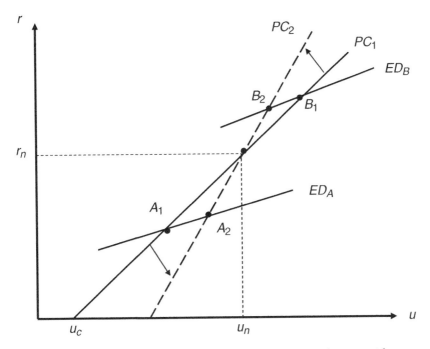

Figure 6.22 Macroeconomic impact of an increase in managerial costs, with target-return pricing

That equation is upward-sloping with respect to u. The derivative of the profits cost function is thus

$$dr^{PC}/d(\sigma f) = \frac{(u-u_n)(u_n - r_n v)}{v(u_n + \sigma f)^2} \tag{6.78}$$

The partial derivative is positive whenever the actual rate of capacity utilization is above the normal rate. Equation (6.78) shows that, when there is an increase in overhead costs in a model in which firms practise target-return pricing, the profits cost curve spins counter-clockwise around the fixed point determined by the target rate of return and the normal rate of capacity utilization. What happens to the rate of profit from the cost side is indeed identical to what happened to the share of profits from the cost side as described earlier with Figure 5.25. What is different is what happens on the demand side. With a given amount of autonomous expenditures, the π^d curve was necessarily downward-sloping, whereas here the effective demand curve, given by equation (6.20), is upward-sloping.

Two graphical solutions are offered in Figure 6.22: one where the economy stands beneath the average standard rate of capacity utilization (point A_1, given by the intersection of PC_1 and ED_A), and the other where the economy operates beyond the average standard rate of capacity utilization (point B_1, given by PC_1 and ED_B). With a higher unit overhead cost, the profits cost curve rotates towards the PC_2 curve. The impact of the rise in overhead costs on the rates of profit and of capacity utilization depends on the actual rate of capacity utilization compared to the standard one. Where this actual rate of utilization stands depends on the position of the effective demand curve, ED_A or ED_B. As can be seen, the equilibrium rate of utilization and rate of profit move together in the same direction.

6.7.2 The Impact of Higher Overhead Costs on the Net Profit Share

What about the net profit share? We already know the shape of the net profit share seen from the cost side, π^s, from equation (5.71) and Figure 5.25. We need only to find the shape of the net profit share seen from the demand side. We get it from the equation determining the effective demand curve of the canonical model, equation (6.20), remembering once more that $r = \pi u/v$:

$$\pi^d = \frac{(\gamma - \gamma_u u_n)v}{s_p u} + \frac{\gamma_u v}{s_p} \tag{6.79}$$

With a model without overhead labour costs, the first term of equation (6.79) has to be positive, because the saving curve necessarily arises from the origin, so that stability and a positive rate of utilization requires a positive intercept for the investment function. This means that the γ term has to be positive. Hence the profit share from the demand side necessarily has a downward slope, as it did in Chapter 5. The behaviour of the equilibrium net profit share is illustrated for the long run with the help of Figure 6.23.

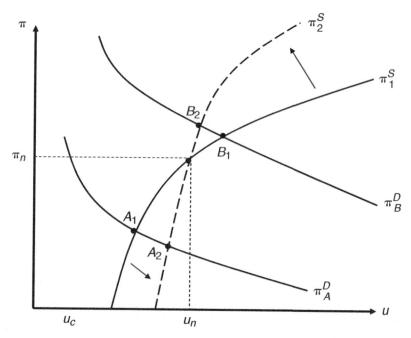

Figure 6.23 Impact of an increase in managerial costs on the net profit share, with target-return pricing, when the investment constant is positive

However, with overhead labour costs, this need not be the case, and the constant γ parameter can take a negative value for a range of different investment functions. This can occur with equation (6.13), given by $g^i = \gamma + \gamma_u u + \gamma_r r$. Similarly, if we adopt the investment function of the post-Kaleckian model, $g^i = \gamma + \gamma_u u + \gamma_\pi \pi$, the constant parameter γ could also be negative. When this is so, as can be asserted from equation (6.80) below in the case of equation (6.13), there is a positive relationship between the profit share seen from the demand side π^d and the rate of capacity utilization, as shown in Figure 6.24 (Rowthorn, 1981, p. 21; Lavoie, 2009b, p. 381). With a negative constant term, the effects of an increase in overhead costs on the equilibrium net profit share will be reversed, as shown in Figure 6.24.

$$\pi^d = \frac{\gamma v}{(s_p - \gamma_r)u} + \frac{\gamma_u v}{s_p - \gamma_r} \qquad (6.80)$$

The lesson to be drawn from all this is that the net profit share can go in any direction. By contrast, as pointed out earlier by checking equations (5.66) and (5.67A), an increase in managerial costs necessarily leads to a reduction in the income share of workers and to an increase in the gross profit share, as recalled in Table 6.4. This implies that an increase in managerial costs leads to an increase in the labour share of the managerial staff under all circumstances, whatever happens to the rate of utilization and the profit share.

In addition, the net profit share is a poor indicator of the potential profitability of firms. Take the case of an increase in the target rate of return r_n. A quick examination of

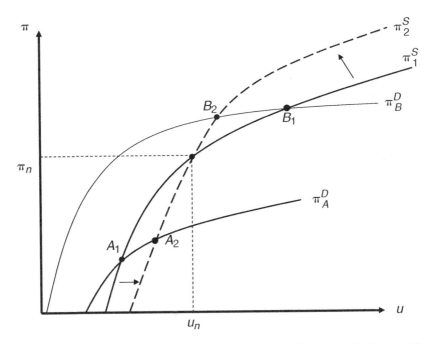

Figure 6.24 Impact of an increase in managerial costs on the net profit share, with target-return pricing, when the investment constant is negative

Table 6.4 *Effect on the various income shares of an increase in managerial costs*

Income share	Conditions		Effect of higher managerial costs
Workers share $1 - m$	$\forall u$		−
Share of managerial salaries $m - \pi$	$\forall u$		+
Gross profits share m	$\forall u$		+
Net profits share π	$u > u_n$	$\gamma > 0$ or no growth	+
		$\gamma < 0$	−
	$u < u_n$	$\gamma > 0$ or no growth	−
		$\gamma < 0$	+

equation (5.71) reveals that such an increase will induce an upward shift of the entire π^s curve. Figure 6.25 illustrates the fact that an increase in the target rate of return will lead to an increase in the share of profit when the constant term in the investment function is positive. However, when the constant term in the investment function is negative, as it can be in a more general investment function, the higher target rate of return induces lower net profit shares. This is shown in Figure 6.26. Thus net profit shares can either

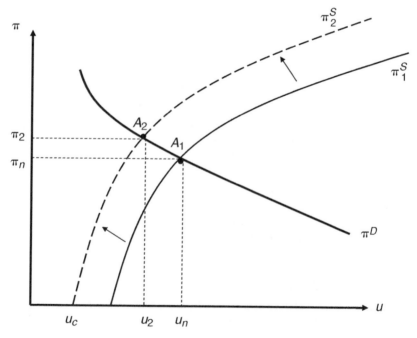

Figure 6.25 *Impact of an increase in the target rate of return on the net profit share when the investment constant is positive*

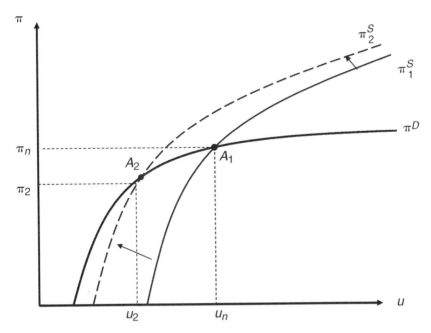

Figure 6.26 Impact of an increase in the target rate of return on the net profit share when the investment constant is negative

increase or decrease when firms manage to implement higher costing margins or higher target rates of return into their prices, and hence reduce real wages. As Rowthorn (1981, p. 21) puts it, 'this all goes to show how misleading it can be to argue in terms of the profit share, rather than the rate of profit, when the economy is operating below full capacity'.

6.7.3 Possible Implications for Empirical Studies

What this demonstrates is that the slope of the π^d curve is not a reliable indicator of whether the economy is profit-led or wage-led. It is usually asserted that a negative slope is indicative of a wage-led economy while a positive slope is indicative of a profit-led economy. The slope of the the π^d curve is positive in Figure 6.26, and hence the economy would be defined as a profit-led regime according to the usual standards. But this economy is instead wage-led: the reduction in real wages leads to a reduction in the rate of utilization and in the profit share. The real wage (with the productivity of direct labour remaining constant) and the wage share move in opposite directions. Nikiforos and Foley (2012) also show that the slope of the π^d curve can be a misleading indicator of the regime when the π^s curve is non-linear.

This demonstrates that the net profit share is not a reliable indicator of potential profitability when there are managerial costs, and hence there is no compelling reason to incorporate the profit share in an investment equation, as Bhaduri and Marglin (1990) do. Rather, if one is keen to eliminate the actual profit rate because it doubles with the effect of the rate of utilization, it is the target rate of return, or the rate of profit calculated at normal use of capacity, as suggested by Sraffians, that should be included in investment functions. Thus, in contrast to what seems to be the implicit assumption of a large number of empirical studies, the evolution of wage shares or profit shares is not necessarily an appropriate indicator of the bargaining power of labour or of capitalists, unless one succeeds in taking adequate care of cyclical effects by incorporating the evolution of overhead labour, which is indeed what Weisskopf (1979) did by measuring corrected profit rates and profit shares. Unfortunately, it seems that only the USA has adequate data on the labour share of supervisory workers, most likely a good enough proxy for overhead labour (Brennan, 2014).

It was argued by Nichols and Norton (1991, p. 53) that 'stagnationist models can be easily generalized to include a third class of overhead workers, a class important in modern capitalism'. This is what we have done in this section, taking up the challenge offered by Nichols and Norton (ibid.), who further claimed that 'a stagnationist model so generalized is capable of yielding a broader range of capitalist dynamics than the traditional stagnationist framework allowed'. Things can be made fancier by examining what happens when managers save part of their income, as do Lavoie and Nah (2020) by using a variant of the saving function suggested by Shaikh (2009), where saving is split between the retained earnings of firms and the amounts saved by managers on the sum of their labour and dividend income. The results of Table 6.4 are then complexified.

The addition of overhead labour costs brings about a further complication. Palley (2005, p. 216; 2017, p. 60) has proposed models where labour is split between workers and managers, but where the latter group is not treated as overhead labour. As long as the propensity to save of workers is weaker than that of the latter, Palley concludes that a reduction in wage inequality (a redistribution within the wage share, without reducing the profit share) will have a positive effect on aggregate demand through a reduction in the average propensity to save, even if the economy is profit led. While this seems intuitive, it is no longer necessarily true when managers are treated as overhead labour, as illustrated with Figures 6.23 and 6.24. However, when growing autonomous non-capacity creating expenditures are added to overhead labour, Lavoie and Nah (2020, pp. 527–8) show that a reduction in wage inequality will always increase the average rate of accumulation during the traverse, thus supporting the prospect for a 'wage equality-led growth'.

6.8 BUSINESS CYCLES

It was said at the beginning of the chapter that we would avoid using fancy mathematical tools; however, we made use of a few differential equations. But nothing has yet been said about business cycles, crises or cyclical behaviour. This can be explained by the fact that most of the earlier post-Keynesians focused their analysis on balanced growth, and the present chapter reflects this tendency to a large extent. As pointed out by Goldstein and Hillard (2009, p. 6), this tendency has 'generated a split in long period analysis between growth theorists and crisis theorists' and, given Marx's preoccupation with economic crises, this division between business cycles and balanced growth has 'tended to run along Marxian and post-Keynesian lines'. A number of Marxian authors have also studied the empirics of business cycles in great detail, generating their own controversies, in particular as to the cause or causes of downturns. There are of course exceptions to this division, as some post-Keynesians, usually of the Kaleckian branch, have endeavoured to produce business cycle models. And of course, out of Cambridge, there is the famous Goodwin (1967) model – the prey–predator model – which combines growth and cycles, based on the notion of the profit squeeze, that is, the claim that, eventually, further increases in economic activity reduce the profit share.

This has given rise to the idea that, even assuming constant labour productivity, real wages cannot be assumed to remain constant as the employment rate or the rate of capacity utilization changes, and hence that wage shares and profit shares in national income ought to be treated as endogenous variables. *A fortiori*, with increases in labour productivity, the share of profits may move one way or another, thus leading to the notion of what Taylor (2004, p. 236) calls a 'distributive' curve, similar to our π^s curve, with the rate of utilization on the horizontal axis. More recently, several heterodox or post-Keynesian economists, usually with some Marxian background, have developed what we can call cyclical growth models based on this idea (Skott, 1989a; Taylor, 2004, ch. 7; 2012; Flaschel, 2009; Nikiforos and Foley, 2012). Their goal is to provide a unified theory of growth and cycles.

The purpose of this section is to look at the stylized facts of business cycles, and to check whether they could be explained within the Kaleckian model with overhead labour costs that we developed in the previous section, with the addition of a few reasonable assumptions. Thus, although fully aware of the controversies that have arisen among business cycle observers (Goldstein, 1999), we start by relying on the stylized facts identified by Howard Sherman (2010), and then we look at how these could fit with a standard Kaleckian model of growth and distribution, accompanied by changes in some of its parameters.

Sherman (2010) studies the evolution of a number of variables through the various stages of a business cycle. As does the National Bureau of Economic Research (NBER), he defines peaks and troughs, and periods of expansion and of recession, which cover nine stages altogether. The trough occurs in the first and the ninth stage, while the peak is in the fifth stage. The middle of the expansion is stage three, while stage four can be characterized as the beginning of the slowdown, when the economy is still growing but more slowly, on its way to the peak of economic activity, when economic growth falls to zero. Figure 6.27 is a stylized representation of the nine stages of the business cycle, based on the study of five US business cycles since 1970 (Sherman, 2010, p. 33).

Sherman (2010) then examines the evolution of each important macroeconomic variable at each stage of the business cycle. The crucial variable for Marxian economists is the profit rate. Checking the profit share as a proxy for it, the profit share rises from the first to the third stage of the cycle, remains roughly constant between the third and the fourth stages, and decreases before the peak, after which it goes down sharply. In other words, the profit share increases during the early expansion, while it remains steady or decreases in the second half of the expansion. It keeps decreasing during most of the recession (Sherman, 2010, p. 51). Unfortunately, Sherman (2010) does not provide a series for rates of utilization, but once again let us use a proxy, which will be GDP as a relative percentage of cycle average. We thus obtain a graph that illustrates the co-variation between the profit share and the rate of utilization, shown in Figure 6.28. The numbers represent the stages of the business cycle identified in Figure 6.27.

Note the direction of the arrows. Here, with the rate of utilization and the profit share, the economy is running around the ellipse in a clockwise direction (taking the profit share

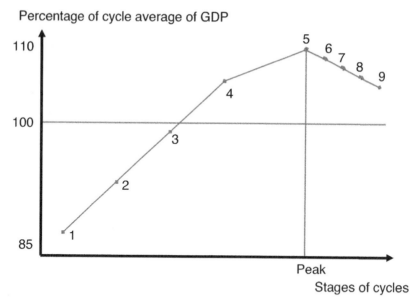

Source: Sherman (2010, p. 33).

Figure 6.27 GDP in the nine stages of the business cycle

as the key variable). This is consistent with what is asserted by students of the business cycle such as Skott (1989a, p. 101) and Taylor (2004, p. 286; 2012). Now what is the cause of this cyclical evolution? Sherman (2010, p. 88) argues that 'at the end of every expansion, profit is reduced both by stagnant demand for goods and services, and by rising costs of production. Profit is squeezed like a nut in a nutcracker at the end of expansion, causing a recession or a depression.' But why is this so? Looking at Sherman's graph, it is clear that an explanation of the business cycle must go much beyond the variables that we have dealt with in our simple Kaleckian growth model. Neither household consumption nor business investment can really be blamed for the slowdown and the recession, as they keep rising until the peak. As to the profit share, it falls after the slowdown has begun, so rising real wages may not be at fault. The culprits need to be found elsewhere. The evidence seems to point in three directions: first, interest rates rise briskly during the second half of the expansion; second, as a consequence, there is a downturn in housing construction, which is a relatively important industry in North America, starting with stage four; and third, tax revenue increases sharply throughout the first stages of the expansion, so that the government fiscal deficit decreases (or its surplus increases), thus withdrawing aggregate demand from the economy.

Is it possible to reproduce, at least roughly, the evolution described by Figure 6.28 with a Kaleckian growth model with overhead costs, without resorting to tricky dynamics and differential equations? There are two possibilities, since the curve representing the profit share seen from the demand side can be either upward-sloping or downward-sloping, depending on the value taken by the constant in the investment function. Figure 6.29 illustrates one possibility, assuming the π^d curve is downward-sloping. The Kaleckian

Accumulation and capacity 457

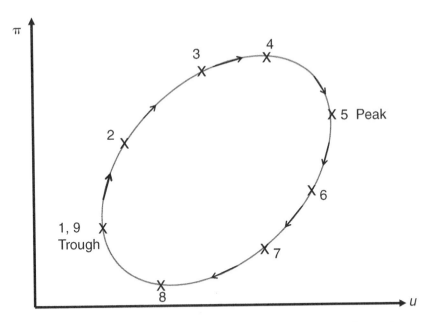

Figure 6.28 Schematic evolution of the profit share and of the ratio of capacity utilization during the stages of the business cycle

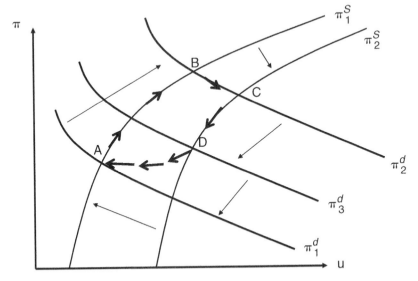

Figure 6.29 Clockwise evolution of the economy with a downward-sloping π^d curve

model with a wage-led economy can reproduce the clockwise evolution of the economy by assuming first that autonomous aggregate factors (which would be reflected in the constant of the investment equation, for instance) would push the π^d curve outwards, moving the economy from point A to point B. In a second step, higher economic activity, through a Radical distributive mechanism, would then push real wages up and profit shares down, moving the economy from B to C, point C being the peak. In the third step, fiscal and monetary policies slow down the economy, shifting the π^d curve inwards, provoking the recession. Then, in the fourth step, the combination of discouraged entrepreneurs and powerless workers drives both the π^d and π^s curves back to their original positions, at A.

A nearly similar story can be told with an upward-sloping π^d curve, as shown in Figure 6.30. The first and second steps are similar to those previously described, with the economy moving from A to B, then to C, the peak point of the cycle. In the third step, once again, the austerity policies pursued by the monetary authorities and the fiscal drag due to rising surpluses shift the π^d curve inwards, inducing the recession and forcing the economy to move to point D. In the fourth step, the bad economic conditions drive the π^s curve back to its original position.

6.8.1 Past and More Recent Evidence About the Clockwise Cycle

We saw earlier that there has been a great deal of controversy regarding whether economies are in profit-led or wage-led demand or employment regimes, ever since the mid-1990s with the advent of the first econometric studies on this topic. As reported by

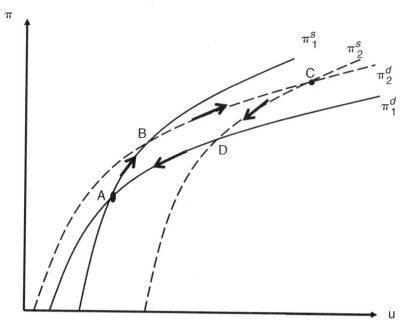

Figure 6.30 *Clockwise evolution of the economy with an upward-sloping π^d curve*

Lavoie (2017a), these controversies go back to the empirical controversy surrounding the Marxian profit-squeeze view advocated by Boddy and Crotty (1975). They found, as described by Figure 6.28, that the profit share rose during the first part of the upswing and fell in the latter part of the upswing. This was interpreted as meaning that higher economic activity caused a squeeze of profits as a consequence of a depleted Marxist reserve army of unemployed workers. The increase in the wage share, by disrupting the spirits of capitalists, would eventually induce a recession. These results were at the heart of the economic policies promoted by members of the Social structure of accumulation (SSA) school, who argued that besides getting rid of capitalism, 'the most obvious exit from the crisis is that pointed out by the right: strengthen the capitalist class, restore profits and rekindle the capitalist accumulation process' (Weisskopf et al., 1985, p. 261). These policies were also advocated by a number of other important Marxist-influenced authors, such as Marglin (1984b, p. 142), who argued that 'a Left program must therefore accept limitations on real wages' or Taylor (2004, p. 305) who warned that 'wage increases as advocated by people on the Left cannot restore aggregate demand if it is in fact profit-led'. These views today are enshrined in the neo-Goodwinian belief that the cyclical behaviour of the economy is the joint product of an aggregate demand which is profit led and of a distributive curve which is based on a profit squeeze mechanism, as reflected in the results of the aggregative econometric studies that make the rate of utilization a function of the profit share while the profit share is itself a function of the rate of utilization (Barbosa-Filho and Taylor, 2006; Kiefer and Rada, 2015).

Kaleckians as well as Keynesian-influenced Marxians have questioned this interpretation of the data that generates Figure 6.28 and its schematic evolution of the profit share and of capacity utilization during the business cycle. Stockhammer and Michell (2017) have constructed a model that generates what they call pseudo-Goodwin cycles generated by a Minskyan process, where high rates of utilization induce more debt and fragility in the economy, associated with a profit-squeeze mechanism attributed to a reserve army effect, even though income distribution has no impact on aggregate demand. Pseudo-Goodwin cycles can keep on being generated even when aggregate demand is wage led by construction. The authors conclude that the existence of a clockwise loop relating output and the profit share cannot be regarded as proof of the existence of a profit-led demand regime. Similarly, in a model with autonomous expenditures, overhead labour, target-return pricing and wage-led growth, Nah and Lavoie (2018) provide figures illustrating numerical simulations which show that changes in the target rate of return or in the wage premium of overhead labour can produce transitional dynamics that generate a clockwise loop in the (u, π) space, and thus loops similar to those defending the neo-Goodwinian profit-led/profit-squeeze story, thus generating a pseudo-Goodwin loop.

Fiebiger (2018) has also presented another explanation of these loops which is not associated with the standard Marxian interpretation. He shows that there exist systematic clockwise cycles between the corporate profit share and the output shares of household fixed investment and semi-autonomous expenditures with respect to the rate of employment and the rate of utilization, whereas the profit share does not closely follow the output share of corporate fixed investment, especially around troughs. Indeed, he shows that while the growth rates of corporate fixed investment are strongly correlated with past GDP and corporate profits, the growth rates of economic activity and corporate profits are themselves most strongly correlated with contemporaneous household

Table 6.5 *Average annual rates of growth of the three components of the profit rate through the three phases of the business cycle, unadjusted and corrected for overhead labour costs*

	Early expansion		Late expansion		Recession	
	U	C	U	C	U	C
Profit rate	+26.8		−10.1		−25.3	
Profit share	+17.0	+3.4	−8.8	−9.7	−15.6	+4.7
Utilization rate	+10.8	+27.4	+0.5	+1.4	−11.9	−32.1
Capacity/capital	−1.1	−1.1	−1.8	−1.8	+2.1	+2.1

C = corrected for overhead labour costs; U = unadjusted.

Source: Weisskopf (1979: Tables 4 and 7), adapted by Lavoie (2017a, p. 211).

fixed investment expenditures and household semi-autonomous expenditures. Thus, according to Fiebiger, the investment of the corporate sector is essentially reacting to the evolution of its sales. The business cycle is driven by the fluctuations in the fixed investment of households and their debt-financed consumption, with the cyclical evolution of the profit share being essentially explained by the existence of overhead labour costs.

The COVID-19 pandemic provides a clear example of the importance of overhead labour costs in the determination of the profit share. In the spring of 2020, at the height of the first wave, when output in Canada in the second quarter declined by 12 per cent, the wage share went up from 56 to 64 per cent, with similar changes in the USA. A naïve interpretation of this data, taking the change in distribution as an exogenous shock, would be that the economy is obviously in a profit-led demand regime. The more reasonable argument is to say that the fall in economic activity raised the share of overhead labour costs and as a consequence diminished the share of profits.

Strangely, while it seems to be ignored today, overhead labour was seriously taken into account in the earlier studies on the characteristics of business cycles. In his careful study of business cycles, Weisskopf (1979) proceeded to compute a 'true' wage share, corrected for the effect due to overhead labour. Table 6.5 shows the evolution of the various components of the profit rate, as estimated by Weisskopf (1979), uncorrected and corrected for the impact of overhead labour. With unadjusted data, it would seem indeed that the profit squeeze plays a substantial role. Once the correction is made, however, it appears that changes in the profit rate during the first phase of the upswing and during the downswing are nearly entirely due to changes in the rate of capacity utilization. Only in the second phase of the upswing do we see changes in the (falling) profit share playing a role in the determination of the profit rate.

Reading the row dealing with profit rates makes the neo-Goodwinian story told by authors such as Skott and Taylor difficult to swallow. First, why would firms expand productive capacity at troughs when they are bulging in idle capacity? Second, profitability is 35 per cent lower in the trough of the cycle than it was at the beginning of the second phase of the expansion, when presumably low profitability starts discouraging corporate investment. Why should low profitability encourage firms to speed up investment, as must be the case in the neo-Goodwinian story? The answer to this puzzle was provided above: there must exist external drivers – Fiebiger's (2018) semi-autonomous expenditures – that provide firms with rebounding sales.

Sherman (1979) immediately interpreted Weisskopf's findings as a dismissal of the Boddy and Crotty thesis, as well as a proof that a rise in aggregate demand and the rate of utilization produces an enormous rise in labour productivity, essentially due to the relative decline of overhead labour. As to the fall in the profit share near the peak, it was interpreted as being caused by the slowdown in productivity growth and the lagged catch-up in real wages. Cauvel (2019) has recently highlighted the importance of taking into account these endogenous changes in productivity when looking for demand regimes. He points out that aggregative studies use a restrictive specification, such that 'the utilization rate does not have a contemporaneous effect on the wage share'. Under this condition he finds the usual profit-led/profit-squeeze results. However, when that restriction is removed, he finds that 'an increase in the wage share is generally found to have a positive effect on the utilization rate.... The response of the wage rate to a utilization rate shock is generally small and insignificant' (Cauvel, 2019, p. 30). He gets similar results when dealing with an adjusted wage share and adding the cyclical component of labour productivity. Cauvel thus concludes that the Goodwin cycle story, based on profit-led demand and profit-squeeze distributive effects, is spurious. Figure 6.28 should be best characterized 'as a combination of wage-led demand and procyclical productivity effects' (ibid., p. 39).

That the Goodwinian cycle story is likely to be spurious also arises from the work of Lilian Rolim (2019). Using the standard aggregative approach, she gets the usual Goodwinian results – a profit-led/profit-squeeze regime. With the data on income shares provided by Mohun (2014), she is able to split the wage share into the income shares of non-supervisory and supervisory workers. She finds that a positive shock to the workers' share leads to an increase in capacity utilization, while the same shock to the supervisors' share leads to a decrease in capacity utilization. 'There is evidence that both the workers' and supervisors' shares Granger-cause capacity utilization and that capacity utilization Granger-causes the supervisors' share' (Rolim, 2019, pp. 765–6). Interestingly, there does exist a profit-squeeze mechanism, but the squeeze appears through the supervisors' salaries and not through the wages obtained by non-supervisory workers. It is the increase in the wage-income share of managers, presumably obtained through various bonuses and salary boosts when the economy is doing well, that leads to an eventual fall in the rate of capacity utilization.

6.9 TECHNICAL PROGRESS

We mentioned that real wages could not be assumed to remain constant for long. One reason is that technical progress occurs through time, thus changing unit costs, and possibly real wages or costing margins. The issue of technical progress is quite a complex one, with several ramifications. Indeed, there is a whole school of thought – Schumpeterian economics or evolutionary economics – devoted to the issue, and a whole book would not be sufficient to deal with the topic (Dosi et al., 1988). Thus what we propose is a preliminary look at the possible causes and consequences of technical progress, set at the macroeconomic level. We shall deal with only one kind of technical progress, the so-called labour-saving technical progress or Harrod-neutral technical progress, which will be reflected in a higher coefficient of labour productivity, assuming that the capital to capacity ratio remains the same, an assumption that is perhaps not as solid as Kaldor (1961, p. 178) thought when he identified it as one of his stylized facts.

We have already discussed the possibility of endogenous technical progress in the section devoted to ways to reconcile the growth rate of aggregate demand with the natural rate of growth, in particular when we presented some evidence that faster growth induces a faster rate of technical progress. In the present section, we look at the elements that could possibly affect the growth rate of labour productivity, notably what is called the Kaldor–Verdoorn law. This section will thus be particularly inspired by the Kaldorian branch of post-Keynesian economics. We shall then present a model, inspired by Naastepad and Storm (2010) and Storm and Naastepad (2012), which combines productivity and aggregate demand effects. Among other things, we shall see whether the consideration of productivity effects can modulate the results that we obtained in a world dealing only with effective demand effects. We shall leave aside one important question, that of the effect of technical progress on the rate of depreciation of capital, mainly because we have left this variable out of our model. We shall also skip a discussion of how technical progress has been introduced in the new models with autonomous non-capacity creating expenditures, as can be found in Nah and Lavoie (2019a), Caminati and Sordi (2019), Brochier (2020) and Allain (2021b).

6.9.1 Verdoorn's Law and the Technical Progress Function

Probably the most-researched empirical question in post-Keynesian economics is the Kaldor–Verdoorn law. There have been hundreds of studies validating this relationship (McCombie and Thirlwall, 1994; McCombie, 2002). The law, at first applying only to the manufacturing industry, as reinterpreted by Kaldor (1978b), can be written as follows:

$$\hat{y} = \lambda = \lambda_0 + \lambda_g g \tag{6.81}$$

This says that the growth rate of output per labour, that is, labour productivity or the rate of technical progress, which as before we represent by the Greek letter λ, is a positive function of the growth rate of the economy (which we assume to be the same as the growth rate of capital). This makes technical progress an endogenous variable. Although Kaldor himself nowhere links this version of Verdoorn's law to his own previous work, it is clear that the above equation is close to Kaldor's technical progress function. As McCombie (2002, p. 99) puts it, 'the basis of the Verdoorn Law would seem to be a linear Kaldorian technical progress function with an allowance for increasing returns'. Kaldor postulates a positive relation between the rate of technical progress and the rate of accumulation of capital per head, which we denoted by $\hat{k}$ in Chapter 1. The rationale for this relation is that innovations and improvements are more likely to be infused into the productive system when new investments are made and when entrepreneurs are more dynamic. Technical progress depends on the rate of progress of knowledge as well as on the speed with which innovations are introduced, that is, with the pace of investment (Kaldor, 1961, p. 207). In its linear form, the technical progress function is

$$\lambda = \lambda_0 + \lambda_k \hat{k} \qquad (6.82)$$

This relationship allowed Kaldor to avoid distinguishing between a move along a production function and a shift of the production function, a distinction that Kaldor (1957, p. 595) and all those within the Cambridge tradition reject (Rymes, 1971). Still, we see right away that there is no difference between: (i) Kaldor's linear technical progress function; (ii) the Cobb–Douglas production function in its dynamic version with appropriate restrictions; and (iii) the dynamic version of the national accounts. This can be seen by recalling from Chapter 1 that the dynamic expansion of the Cobb–Douglas function and of the national accounts identity yielded respectively:

$$\hat{y} = \mu + \beta \hat{k} \qquad (1.3)$$

$$\hat{y} = [(1 - \pi) \omega + \pi \hat{r}] + \pi \hat{k} \qquad (1.7)$$

where π still stands for the profit share while $\hat{\omega}$ and $\hat{r}$ still represent the growth rates of real wages and of the profit rate.

This shows again the weakness of instrumentalism. The same mathematical regressions may arise from different theories: prediction would be helpless in identifying the right one. The above also shows that one should beware of some of the successes of Kaldor–Verdoorn's law for precisely the same reason that led us to question the apparent successes of the neoclassical production function. It could also be an artefact.

We can combine the technical progress function with Verdoorn's law: one gets what Michl (1985) calls the augmented technical progress function, which he shows to be similar to the dynamic expansion of a Cobb–Douglas function with returns to scale. When the λ_g parameter is positive, there would be increasing returns to scale.

$$\hat{y} = \lambda = \lambda_0 + \lambda_g g + \lambda_k \hat{k} \qquad (6.83)$$

Michl shows that both the λ_g and the λ_k parameters are significant when regressions are run on this augmented technical progress function. It is a bit disconcerting to note that the value of the λ_k coefficient is very close to the share of profits in manufacturing national accounts, between 0.38 and 0.40, exactly what one would expect if the augmented technical progress function turned out to be an artefact. Furthermore, one would expect the rate of change of the rate of profit $\hat{r}$ to be close to zero, since there is usually no trend in the rate of profit. This is precisely what Michl gets: the λ_0 coefficient in his regressions is not significantly different from zero. The regression, however, even if Verdoorn's law depends on an algebraic fluke, would seem to add one piece of information. By comparing equations (6.83) and (1.7), we see that faster rates of growth of output g take the place of faster rates of growth of real wages ω. The national accounts predict that the growth rate of labour productivity is tied to the growth rate of real wages. Equation (6.83) says that the growth rate of economic activity increases the growth rate of labour productivity, and is thus a peculiarity of Verdoorn's law.

McCombie and Spreafico (2016) have recently tackled the possible relationship between the Kaldor-Verdoorn law and the identity of the national accounts, by providing a *reductio ad absurdum* proof, similar to those that we looked at in Chapter 1. To do so, they once more resort to the use of the constructed data of a hypothetical economy, thus knowing the true data that underlies the estimates that are being calculated. They test the Kaldor-Verdoorn relation given by equation (6.81) on 15 hypothetical regions, over ten years. In the first experiment, they assume by construction the existence of a Kaldor-Verdoorn effect, that is, they assume that there is a positive relationship between the growth rate of output and the growth rate of labour productivity. In the second experiment, McCombie and Spreafico (2016, p. 1130) construct the data in a similar manner, 'with the exception that for any given productivity growth rates of a particular region, the output growth rates were random', making the Kaldor-Verdoorn effect absent by construction. In both experiments, assuming that the constant λ_0 is allowed to vary for each region, the regression reflects the national accounting identity, as the estimate of the constant is captured by the growth rate of real wages, while the estimate of λ_g is statistically no different from zero.

However, when it is assumed that the exogenous constant of technical progress is the same for all regions, as is usually done in this kind of study, the Kaldor-Verdoorn effect is captured in the first experiment, and its value is nearly the value with which the data was generated by construction. By contrast, in the second experiment, the regression based on equation (6.81) has a very poor fit, with the R^2 being close to zero, and the estimate of λ_g is not statistically different from zero, as it should be since the Kaldor-Verdoorn effect had been excluded by construction. We can thus conclude that the Kaldor-Verdoorn relation is not an artefact, since the relationship between productivity growth and output growth is not verified when it is excluded by construction. We can thus agree with Kaldor in believing that Verdoorn's law is not just a measure of the economies of large-scale production. It is a dynamic relationship 'between the rates of change of productivity and of output, rather than between the *level* of productivity and the *scale* of output' (Kaldor, 1978b, p. 106). It reflects dynamic increasing returns.

The close relationship between the growth of output and the growth of labour productivity – the Kaldor–Verdoorn law – is a key relationship of post-Keynesian economics. There are three ways in which it can be incorporated into the rest of the post-Keynesian analysis. The first way, privileged by McCombie and Thirlwall (1994), is to link it to the balance-of-payments constraint approach, which is another major Kaldorian topic. We shall not do this here. The second way was adopted by Rowthorn (1981), Lavoie (1992b) and Cassetti (2003): it incorporates the addition of technical progress straight into a standard Kaleckian model of growth and distribution, or even incorporates it into a post-Kaleckian growth model, as done by Hein and Tarassow (2010). We shall not pursue this avenue here either. The third way is to construct a reduced-form model, as done by Storm and Naastepad (2012), and as was initially suggested by Boyer (1988) and Boyer and Petit (1988). That model will include the productivity effects of faster growth, but also the income distribution effects on both labour productivity and effective demand.

6.9.2 The Storm–Naastepad Growth Model

The Storm–Naastepad reduced-form model is made up of two equations. The first one determines the growth rate of labour productivity, while the second one determines the growth rate of output. We have

$$\hat{y} = \lambda = \lambda_0 + \lambda_g g + \lambda_\omega \hat{\omega}, \quad \lambda_g > 0, \quad \lambda_\omega > 0 \qquad (6.84)$$

$$g = \eta_0 + \eta_1(\hat{\omega} - \lambda), \quad \eta_1 \lessgtr 0 \qquad (6.85)$$

Equation (6.84) is an extension of the Kaldor–Verdoorn relationship. It says that the growth rate of labour productivity depends positively on the growth rate of output and on the growth rate of real wages. We have already encountered the second effect within the static framework of Chapter 5, when we assumed a positive relationship between labour productivity and real wages, due to what we called the Webb effect, also sometimes named the Marx effect. In theory, higher real wages could encourage or discourage firms to invest in labour-saving technologies, so that the λ_ω parameter could be positive or negative, but in practice we know that the direct effect of real wage growth on productivity growth is positive, so that we shall assume that the λ_ω parameter (the dynamic Webb effect) is indeed positive, as do Storm and Naastepad (2012) and Hein and Tarassow (2010). One may question the relevance of incorporating the $\hat{\omega}$ term in equation (6.84), since one could argue just as well that causality goes the other way and that rising real wages are a consequence rather than a cause of increases in labour productivity. Marquetti (2004), however, finds that, while real wages appear to Granger-cause productivity, the reverse is not true – there is unidirectional causality. This would thus justify the inclusion of the growth rate of real wages as a determinant of technical progress.

It should be mentioned that Cassetti (2003) and Hein and Tarassow (2010) write down a nearly identical extended Kaldor–Verdoorn relationship in their Kaleckian model with technical progress, where the growth rate of real wages is replaced by the level of the profit share. This is because they relate their technical progress equation to an explicit Kaleckian growth model, as does Hein (2012, ch. 4). They have

$$\hat{y} = \lambda = \lambda_0 + \lambda_g g - \lambda_\pi \pi, \quad \lambda_g > 0, \quad \lambda_\pi > 0 \qquad (6.84\text{A})$$

Coming back to the Storm–Naastepad model, as said before, equation (6.85) is a kind of reduced form of our post-Kaleckian growth model. It is not exactly so because in the post-Kaleckian model the equilibrium growth rate of the economy depends on the level of the profit share, or inversely on the labour share, whereas the term $(\hat{\omega} - \lambda)$ in equation (6.85) represents instead the growth rate in the labour share (this can be seen by noting that the labour share is $wL/pq = (w/p)/(q/L) = \omega/y$). When the economy is in a wage-led growth regime, the η_1 parameter is positive; when the economy is in a profit-led demand regime, the η_1 parameter is negative. Note that the Storm–Naastepad model is set in the medium term, since the profit share is not constant, but changes continuously.

The combined productivity and demand growth regimes
Each of the two equations (6.84) and (6.85) can be represented in a graph, with the growth rate of labour productivity on the horizontal axis and the growth rate of output on the vertical axis. Equation (6.84) will be called the productivity regime, and will be illustrated by the *PR* curve. Equation (6.85) represents the demand regime, and is illustrated by the *DR* curve. While the sign of the slope of the *PR* curve is always positive, the slope of the *DR* curve can be either positive or negative, depending on the sign of the η_1 parameter in equation (6.85). When $\eta_1 > 0$, the demand regime is wage-led and the slope of the *DR* curve is negative (because then output growth g is a

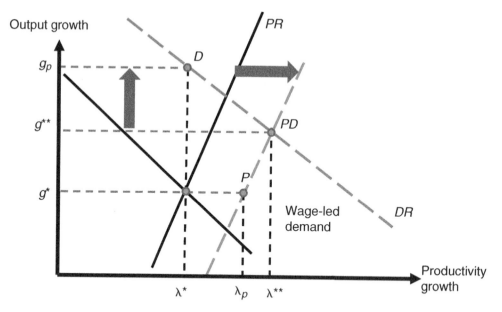

Figure 6.31 The impact of an increase in the growth rate of real wages in a wage-led demand regime

negative function of technical progress λ). This case is first illustrated with the help of Figure 6.31.

What happens if there is an exogenous rise in the growth rate of real wages and hence an increase in the share of wages? We can look at it from two angles. We start from the intersection of the two curves, at g^* and λ^*. First, looking at the effect on output growth, the demand regime curve DR will shift up. Keeping labour productivity constant for now, the economy moves to point D, with a much higher growth rate g_p, which reflects the partial effect induced by effective demand alone. However, faster growth will induce faster technical progress; this in turn will reduce the share of wages, and induce a downward move along the new demand regime curve. Once the direct and induced effects on effective demand are taken into account, the economy reaches point PD and the growth rate of output is brought back to g^{**}. The consideration of productivity effects thus reduces the amplitude of the positive impact on aggregate demand of an increase in real wages in a wage-led economy. Could this reduction be so big that the new growth rate of output would end up being lower than its initial value? In other words, could we have $g^{**} < g^*$? To find out, we need to solve the system of the two equations (6.84) and (6.85), the growth rate of real wages being considered as the exogenous variable. We get

$$\lambda^* = \frac{\lambda_0 + \lambda_g \eta_0 + (\lambda_g \eta_1 + \lambda_\omega)\hat{\omega}}{1 + \lambda_\omega + \lambda_g(\eta_1 - \eta_2)} \quad (6.86)$$

$$g^* = \frac{\eta_0(1+\lambda_\omega) + \lambda_0(\eta_1 - \eta_2) + (\eta_1 + \lambda_\omega \eta_2)\hat{\omega}}{1 + \lambda_\omega + \lambda_g(\eta_1 - \eta_2)} \quad (6.87)$$

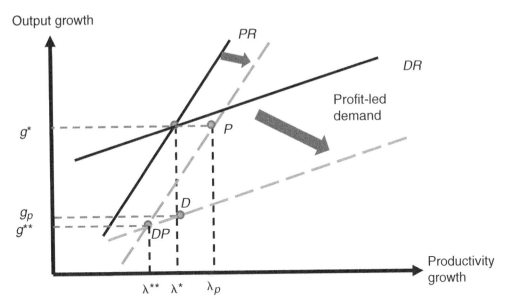

Figure 6.32 *The impact of an increase in the growth rate of real wages in a profit-led demand regime*

The denominator of these equations is necessarily positive, even if η_1 is negative, for all values within the range of empirical research. Inspecting equation (6.87), since $\eta_1 > 0$ in the case of the wage-led demand regime, the impact of an acceleration in the growth rate of real wages is positive as long as $\lambda_\omega < 1$. This means that the direct impact of the growth rate of real wages on the growth rate of labour productivity must be less than one for one, which sounds like a reasonable restriction, as already discussed in Chapter 5. Graphically, this means that the shift of the *PR* curve must be smaller than that of the *DR* curve.

We can also look at things the other way around. Start again from g^* and λ^*. Keeping aggregate demand constant, assume real wages rise faster. The *PR* curve shifts outwards. This generates a positive direct but partial effect on the growth rate of labour productivity, which moves from λ^* to λ_p at point P in Figure 6.31. However, faster-growing real wages induce a rise in aggregate demand, which feeds back into an even faster growth rate of labour productivity, through the Kaldor–Verdoorn effect. Once the direct and induced effects are taken into account, the growth rate of labour productivity moves up to λ^{**}. Thus, with wage-led growth, the consideration of effective demand effects increases the amplitude of the positive effects of real wage growth on labour productivity growth, as can be garnered from equation (6.86).

A similar exercise can be conducted in the case of a profit-led demand regime. It turns out, as already pointed out by Boyer (1988), that for the model to be stable the productivity regime curve must be steeper than the demand regime curve. With $\eta_1 < 0$, the demand regime is profit-led and the slope of the *DR* curve is positive (because then output growth g is a positive function of technical progress λ). This case is illustrated with the help of Figure 6.32. Start again from the intersection of the two curves, at g^* and λ^*. First, looking at the effect on output growth, the demand regime curve *DR* will shift down, as a higher growth rate of real wages will slow down aggregate demand. Keeping labour productivity constant for now, the economy moves to point *D*, with a lower growth rate g_p. Looking now at the direct effect on productivity growth, the higher real wages will spur more productivity-enhancing investment, so that the direct effect of faster growth in real wages will be to bring the productivity growth to λ_p at point *P*. The slower output growth, however, induces slower technical progress, through the Kaldor–Verdoorn effect, and this slowdown may be so large that the overall effect of the increase in the growth rate of real wages may be to reduce the growth rate of labour productivity from λ^* to λ^{**}. This case is illustrated in Figure 6.32. We can thus conclude that, in the case of the profit-led demand regime, an increase in the growth rate of real wages will always have a negative effect on the growth rate of output, while it may have a positive or a negative effect on the growth rate of labour productivity. Inspection of equation (6.86) reveals that the effect is negative if $|\lambda_g \eta_1| > \lambda_\omega$, that is, if a strong profit-led regime is accompanied by a strong Kaldor–Verdoorn effect, while the dynamic Webb effect is weak.

The combined productivity and demand impact on employment growth
We have not yet discussed what happens in the labour market. The impact of faster growth rates of real wages on the growth rate of employment can be assessed by making use of equation (6.68), $\hat{L} = \hat{q} - \hat{y} = g - \lambda$. Figure 6.33 clarifies the complexity of the combined demand and productivity effects of an increase in the growth rate of real wages on the growth rate of employment, when both the Kaldor-Verdoorn and Marx-Webb effects are taken into consideration. Making use of the equilibrium values of *g* and λ in equations (6.86) and (6.87), we find

$$\frac{d\hat{L}}{d\hat{\omega}} = \frac{\eta_1 \left(1 - \lambda_g - \lambda_\omega\right) - \lambda_\omega}{1 + \lambda_g \eta_1} \tag{6.88}$$

Once more, because the denominator is necessarily positive, we need only be concerned with the numerator of equation (6.88). Assume that the terms between parentheses in the numerator are positive. Obviously, in the case of a profit-led demand regime, with

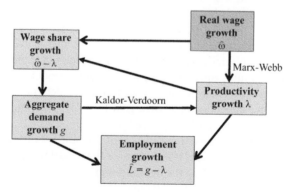

Figure 6.33 A diagram of the determination of employment growth in the Storm-Naastepad growth model

$\eta_1 < 0$, an increase in the growth rate of real wages has a negative impact on the growth rate of employment $\hat{L}$ (unless it turns out that $\lambda_p + \lambda_\omega > 1$). Things would appear to be more ambiguous in the case of the wage-led demand regime, which, as we saw earlier, is the more frequent case for G-20 countries. The overall effect of a higher growth rate of real wages on the growth rate of employment will be positive only if the numerator of equation (6.88) is positive, that is, if

$$\eta_1 > \frac{\lambda_\omega}{\left(1-\lambda_g-\lambda_\omega\right)} \qquad (6.89)$$

This will tend to be the case in a strong wage-led demand regime (with a large η_1 coefficient), accompanied by a dynamic Webb effect that is not too large (a low λ_ω coefficient) as well as a Kaldor–Verdoorn effect that is not overly large (a low λ_g coefficient) leading Bowles and Boyer (1995, p. 145) to state that 'if productivity growth is strongly wage-led, it is unlikely that employment will be wage-led. But how large is large?

Storm and Naastepad (2013) have made such calculations. From previous empirical research, they believe that it is reasonable to assume that, on average, in OECD countries, the Kaldor–Verdoorn coefficient and the dynamic Webb coeffiecient are respectively $\lambda_g = 0.46$ and $\lambda_\omega = 0.38$. If this is so, then the effect of faster growth rates on real wages will be positive if $\eta_1 > 2.37$. In other words, a one percentage point increase in real wage growth must lead to more than a 2 percentage point increase in output growth, which is totally unrealistic. Assigning a value of $\eta_1 = 0.30$, Storm and Naastepad (2013) estimate from equation (6.88) that a one percentage point increase in the growth of real wages leads to a fall of 0.29 percentage point in the growth of employment. They thus conclude that, even in countries that are in a wage-led demand regime, the effects of faster growth of real wages are very likely to be negative for the growth rate of employment. They give as an example of this dilemma the fact that their country – the Netherlands – has enjoyed a job recovery thanks to very slow growth in real wages, despite being in a wage-led demand regime. This has been achieved because the slow growth in real wages has induced very slow growth in labour productivity, and hence few job losses associated with technological progress. The Hartz reforms of the Schröder government in Germany are another example of wage restraints ending up with higher job growth (Storm and Naastepad, 2017). These results are confirmed by Vergeer and Kleinknecht (2010–11): they show that Anglo-Saxon countries appeared to have some success in job creation because their GDP per working hour grew at a slower rate, not because of high growth rates in real GDP.

Storm and Naastepad thus conclude that, while a wage-led strategy is good for productivity increases and possibly output growth, and thus for increases in living standards, the growth of employment requires additional policies. They thus insist that growth recovery necessitates something more than a reshuffling of primary income distribution towards wages. Supportive macroeconomic policies must also be put in place, such as expansionary fiscal policies and a more progressive taxation system, which will raise both the η_0 and η_1 parameters. 'A strategy of wage-led growth can only work in conjunction with a supportive macroeconomic policy geared towards full employment, for example, active demand management' (Storm and Naastepad, 2017, p. 18). Onaran (2016) has also underlined the the need for a wage-led recovery to be accompanied by an expansionary fiscal policy. In a way, these results are not surprising: we obtained very similar results in a static context in Chapter 5, where it was shown that higher labour productivity, even if accompanied by higher wages and constant mark-ups, would bring down the level of employment, unless there was a rise in autonomous expenditures.

6.9.3 The Productivity and Demand Regimes Revisited

The empirical results arrived at by Storm and Naastepad (2013; 2017) are rather disconcerting from a Kaleckian viewpoint: even economies in a wage-led demand regime are unlikely to be in a wage-led employment regime. This is the 'dismal science' all over again! Is there any way to weaken condition (6.89)? Is there any mechanism that could raise the probability that faster growth in real wages would improve the growth rate of employment?

Two such mechanisms have been proposed in the past by Kaleckian authors, and they are integrated in equations (6.84) and (6.85) as follows:

$$\hat{y} = \lambda = \lambda_0 + \lambda_g g + \lambda_\omega (\hat{\omega} - \lambda) \tag{6.84B}$$

$$g = \eta_0 + \eta_1 (\hat{\omega} - \lambda) + \eta_2 \lambda \tag{6.85A}$$

Let us start with equation (6.85A). A large number of authors, starting with Rowthorn (1981, p. 23), have argued that the rate of technical progress λ ought to be included in the investment function and hence in the equation determining output growth (Boyer and Petit, 1988; Lavoie, 1992b, p. 318; Cassetti, 2003; Rada and Taylor, 2006; Hein and Tarassow, 2010). This is a classical Schumpeterian proposition: the optimism of firms and that of their bankers rides on waves of innovation. One might add that it is also a Kaleckian proposition. Kalecki (1971, p. 151) endorses such a view, arguing that 'capitalists investing "today" think to have an advantage over those having invested "yesterday" because of technical novelties that have reached them'. Furthermore, Steindl (1979, p. 7) considers the pace of innovations to be a shift parameter of the Kaleckian investment function in his more recent work. There is an additional reason for which one would think, on logical grounds, that the rate of technical progress ought to be an argument of the function determining the rate of output. In a true long-period analysis, one would think that the share of wages ought to be constant, so that $\hat{\omega} = \lambda$. But this then implies that in the long run the rate of technical progress has no feedback effect whatsoever on the rate of investment and the rate of output growth in the original model, which seems a bit odd, as noted by Hein and Tarassow (2010, p. 729).

The second modification occurs in equation (6.84B). The term $(\hat{\omega} - \lambda)$ replaces the term $\hat{\omega}$. The justification for such a change is provided by Hein and Tarassow (2010, p. 735): 'We hold that real wage growth will only give an additional push to capitalists' efforts to implement technical progress if it exceeds productivity growth and downward pressure on the profit share or on unit profits is exerted.' Making these two changes makes the system of equations symmetric, but also makes the empirical estimation of the two equations more difficult since this creates a problem of identification. But here we are concerned with theory. Solving for the rate of technical progress and for the rate of accumulation, we get two expressions which are more complicated than the ones arrived at originally with equations (6.86) and (6.87):

$$\lambda^* = \frac{\lambda_0 + \lambda_g \eta_0 + (\lambda_g \eta_1 + \lambda_\omega)\hat{\omega}}{1 + \lambda_\omega + \lambda_g (\eta_1 - \eta_2)} \tag{6.86A}$$

$$g^* = \frac{\eta_0 (1 + \lambda_\omega) + \lambda_0 (\eta_1 - \eta_2) + (\eta_1 + \lambda_\omega \eta_2)\hat{\omega}}{1 + \lambda_\omega + \lambda_g (\eta_1 - \eta_2)} \tag{6.87A}$$

Relative to those of the original model, the solutions of the new model both have a slightly different denominator, which is still positive for observed parameter values. What is of interest, however, is the numerator of g^*. While the numerator of λ^* is not modified, the numerator of g^* has three new additional positive terms. We can thus already guess that, with such changes, the growth rate of employment is more likely to react positively to changes in the growth rate of real wages. Computing again this solution to the growth rate, and taking its derivative, we now get

$$\frac{d\hat{L}}{d\hat{\omega}} = \frac{\eta_1 (1 - \lambda_g) - \lambda_\omega (1 - \eta_2)}{1 + \lambda_\omega + \lambda_g (\eta_1 - \eta_2)} \tag{6.88A}$$

Relative to equation (6.88), in the numerator of equation (6.88A) there is now one less negative term while the remaining negative one is smaller. Thus, in a wage-led regime, the addition of our two mechanisms – to assume that the growth rate of labour productivity has a positive effect on output growth (through the new parameter η_2), and to assume that labour productivity growth reacts to the growth rate of the labour share (rather than to changes in growth rate of real wages) – increases the likelihood that faster growth in real wages will generate faster growth in employment. The new condition for equation (6.88A) to be positive in a wage-led regime is

$$\eta_1 > \frac{\lambda_\omega (1 - \eta_2)}{(1 - \lambda_g)} \tag{6.89A}$$

Presuming that the parameters computed for the old model are still valid for the new model, and assuming for demonstration purposes that the effect of the growth rate of labour productivity on output growth is $\eta_2 = 0.20$, we can compute that the condition for a wage-led employment regime gets reduced to $\eta_1 > 0.56$ whereas it was $\eta_1 > 2.37$ in the original model. If $\eta_1 = 0.30$, equation (6.88A) yields that a one percentage point increase in the growth rate of real wages will lead to a 0.10 percentage point fall in the growth rate of employment instead of a fall of 0.29 percentage point obtained earlier with equation (6.88). If the estimates of the Kaldor–Verdoorn and Webb effects turn out to be somewhat lower, and if it happens that $\lambda_g = \lambda_\omega = \eta_1 = \eta_2 = 0.30$, then the effect of an increase in the growth rate of real wages on the growth rate of employment will be perfectly neutral. Adopting the amended model of equations (6.84B) and (6.85A) thus weakens the dismal results obtained by Storm and Naastepad, and makes it more likely that a growth strategy based on policies favourable to labour will be successful.

We can conclude this section by noting that real wage growth has been particularly dismal in countries where labour markets are flexible, that is, in countries with weak labour unions, easy firing and modest social benefits (Vergeer and Kleinknecht, 2010–11). Indeed, Storm and Naastepad (2012, p. 103) show that 'higher employment protection and more extensive labor market regulation are associated with higher labor productivity growth'. It follows that 'rigid' labour markets are not the cause of slow growth, and that, contrary to the views championed by the OECD, 'unregulated labor markets, weak employment protection, low taxes, high earnings inequalities, and weak unions are not at all necessary to sustain high rates of labor productivity growth; in actual fact, they are detrimental to technological dynamism' (ibid., p. 108). This is confirmed by Kleinknecht (2020), who also finds that supply-side labour market reforms have detrimental effects on productivity growth in high-tech industries.

6.10 BUSINESS DEBT

6.10.1 Earlier Thoughts

Thus far nothing much has been said about a monetary growth model, except when discussing mechanisms that could bring the economy back towards normal rates of capacity utilization and when discussing the business cycle. Furthermore, nothing has been said about firms needing bank credit or about business debt, and nothing has been said about the liquidity preference of households. All this is rather odd within post-Keynesian theory since post-Keynesians attach so much importance to the monetary and financial aspects of the economy, but this, to some extent, is a symptom of the difficulties that post-Keynesians have had in the past in conflating the real and the financial sides of the economy. Indeed, some of the initial frictions between Fundamentalist post-Keynesians *à la* Davidson and Minsky and the Cambridge or Kaleckian strand of post-Keynesianism can be attributed to this absence of explicit monetary variables in growth models. This has led Jan Kregel (1986) to compare Cambridge growth models without money to *Hamlet* without the Prince, and to call for the introduction of Bulls and Bears into heterodox Keynesian analysis.

Still, there has always been some effort at least to discuss the implications of a monetary economy in growth models. Robinson (1956) devotes several chapters to financial issues, but at the very end of her book. Robinson (1956, p. 231) points out that the amounts lent to households and firms depend on the 'interest coverage ratio', that is, the ratio of (profit) income to due interest payments. She also points out that the borrowing power of entrepreneurs depends on 'the strictness of the banks' standards of creditworthiness' and the state of mind of individual investors, as well as 'the subjective attitude of potential lenders' (ibid., p. 244). All this is clearly reminiscent of Robinson's (1952, p. 81) discussion of finance as a possible bottleneck to expansion, where she claims that a shortage of finance may limit investment plans:

> It shows itself in a high risk premium on industrial securities and in difficulty in arranging new loans, and it may be caused by a general lack of confidence on the part of owners of wealth, or by the fact that too small a part of total wealth is owned by actual or potential entrepreneurs.

Such a statement could just as well have been written during the subprime financial crisis. It also reminiscences Kalecki's (1937) principle of increasing risk, which inspired Minsky (1975) in his analysis of financial instability.

Kalecki's follower, Steindl (1952, ch. 9), was also much concerned with financial issues. He devotes an entire chapter to what he calls the gearing ratio of firms, which is a variant of their debt ratio. In particular he emphasizes a problem left in the dark by Minsky: how can the decisions of entrepreneurs regarding the relative size of the debt that they are willing to take on be reconciled with the decisions of households regarding their desired wealth? For instance, when there is an economic slowdown and when profit rates decline, how do firms manage to reduce their gearing ratio? Steindl's answer is that this may not be so easy, especially if household saving is less responsive than investment to changes in profits. In this case, says Steindl (1952, p. 114), the realized gearing ratio is likely to rise, so that 'the entrepreneurs, even apart from their desire to reduce the initial gearing ratio, will soon be inclined to check this relative growth of their indebtedness, and their only possible reaction against it will be to reduce investment. This however will not put matters right.' This is the paradox of debt that was described in Chapter 1, and Steindl's arguments gave rise to an interesting attempt by Dutt (1995) to deal with financial and leverage issues within an otherwise Kaleckian model, mixing financial and real possible sources of instability.

For a long time, there were only two attempts to introduce financial factors into Cambridge growth models. Pasinetti (1974, ch. 6) distinguished the rate of return on the assets held by workers from that obtained by capitalists. He assumed that workers held only money deposits or bonds, while capitalists held stock market shares. This allowed him to differentiate the overall profit rate of the economy from the interest rate, and the rate of return of capitalists. The other Cambridge growth model with finance was Nicholas Kaldor's (1966) neo-Pasinetti model. Pasinetti (1974, ch. 5) had shown in 1962 that, with workers getting wages and profits while capitalists only got profits, the propensity to save of workers has no impact whatsoever on the overall rate of profit in the very long run under fairly simple conditions. A proof of this result will be offered in the last section of the current chapter. Kaldor's 1966 model drew its name from the fact that Kaldor showed similarly that in a world of corporations and households, where households spend a portion of their capital gains, the propensity to save of households has no impact on the rate of profit. The problem with Kaldor's neo-Pasinetti model, as was pointed out by Paul Davidson (1972), is that it assumes that all saving is done in the form of share purchases. There is no money in the model, and hence no portfolio choice on the part of investors.

This problem was remedied by Skott (1989a) in his synthesis extension of Kaldor's neo-Pasinetti model. Skott introduced a budget constraint on firms, investment being financed by retained earnings, stock issues or new loans. Households' consumption depends on their wealth, and they make a portfolio choice by deciding to hold fixed proportions of their wealth in equities and money. The money supply is endogenous and demand-led in the main variant of Skott's model. The price of equities depends on demand and supply, with the former itself depending on the level of net profits of firms. Despite its interesting features, in particular the fact that it is fully stock-flow-consistent, the model did not attract much attention, for the reasons outlined in a previous section. An updated version of the model has been constructed by Skott and Ryoo (2008).

Most influential, perhaps, in its attempt to tie together Cambridge or Kaleckian growth models and Minsky's concerns about finance was the paper by Taylor and O'Connell (1985). They had investment as a function of the discrepancy between the expected profit rate of firms and the interest rate, with this expected profit rate being the sum of the actual profit rate and some confidence indicator. While this in itself was innovative, the true innovation of the Taylor and O'Connell (1985) model is the introduction of portfolio choice. Households hold cash money, interest-paying bills and stock market equities, and their choice is influenced by the values taken by the interest rate and the expected profit rate of firms (the fundamentals, rather than the rate of return on equities!). A third innovation of the Taylor and O'Connell (1985) model is the introduction of cyclical dynamics by adding a differential equation, which says that the confidence indicator rises as long as the interest rate is below some normal interest rate. Franke and Semmler (1991) constructed a somewhat similar model, incorporating the three mentioned innovations, and adding an explicit account of the evolution of the leverage ratio of firms. One of the drawbacks of both models, however, was that the supply of money was not demand-led, in contrast to what was argued in Chapter 4.

Over the past few years there has been an explosion of different ways in which monetary and financial matters can be introduced into a growth model in general and into a Kaleckian growth model in particular. Obviously, we cannot deal with all of them here, and we shall focus on only one of them. There are many possible candidates, most of them having several points in common. The first one is a Kaleckian growth model that would incorporate some kind of central bank reaction function that determines the rate of interest, as first presented by Setterfield (2006) and for which there are now several variants, for instance Rochon and Setterfield (2012). These models are explicit or implicit answers to the New Consensus models developed by New Keynesian authors and are vaguely related to the stabilizing mechanisms described by Duménil and Lévy (1999).

A second candidate consists of the many Kaleckian models developed by Hein (2008; 2012; 2014, ch. 9–10), where profit recipients are split between firms and rentiers, as in Shaikh's (2009) model discussed earlier. Because firms retain a given proportion of their profits net of interest payments, an increase in the rate of interest may reduce overall saving since the propensity to save out of the retained earnings of firms is equal to one by definition, whereas that of rentiers is smaller than one. Hein's models also examine the possibility that higher interest rates could lead to higher costing margins – a sort of interest rate cost-push effect that we described in Chapter 3. Hein's models, initially inspired by those of Dutt (1992b) and Lavoie (1995b), take into account the leverage ratio of firms. Depending on the parameters of the investment and saving functions, an increase in the rate of interest may lead to a decrease in the rate of accumulation – the normal case; but it may also lead to an increase in the rate of accumulation – the puzzling case. These models thus show that the leverage ratio may or may not (as pointed out by Steindl) move procyclically with the growth rate of economic activity, thus questioning Minsky's financial fragility hypothesis, which is often interpreted as meaning that faster business investment leads to higher debt ratios.

Despite the high relevance of household debt models, at least since the Global Financial Crisis, I deal first with corporate debt. I have chosen to present a model inspired by the stock–flow-consistent growth model of Lavoie and Godley (2001–02), solved by numerical simulations. This model is inspired by Kaldor's (1966) neo-Pasinetti model, and thus is consistent with the finance frontier portrayed in Chapter 3. Bank deposits and Kaleckian behavioural equations have been added to Kaldor's model. Taylor (2004, pp. 272–8) has built a slightly modified analytical version of the Lavoie and Godley (2001–02) model, and it is this version that is shown here. Taylor's version contains the standard Kaleckian investment and saving functions; the portfolio choice and liquidity preference of households play a role; and the dynamics of the debt ratio of firms can be assessed under a number of different regimes, thus justifying its choice as a representative Kaleckian growth model with financial variables. Still, the presentation of the model is slightly more involved than that of models without explicit monetary variables. Another variant of the same model can be found in Taylor and Rada (2008).

6.10.2 Bears and Bulls

We thus present what Taylor (2004, p. 273) calls a 'parsimonious' post-Keynesian model of business borrowing. Because the model fully integrates the real and the monetary sectors, it is a stock–flow consistent model, as defined in Chapter 4. The stock and transactions matrices of the model are essentially those given as examples in Tables 4.34 and 4.35. There are thus three sectors in the model: households, firms and banks. There are four kinds of assets: tangible capital (machines), and three financial assets – equities, bank deposits and bank loans. Here, for simplicity, it is assumed that the rate of interest on deposits is equal to the rate of interest on loans, so that banks make no profits (and hold no capital of their own). There is only one class of households, thus omitting the distinction between rentiers and workers that can be found in van Treeck (2009) in a similar simulated model. We first deal with the portfolio choice of households. In the second stage, we shall deal with the saving and the investment functions, as well as the debt ratio of firms.

As we saw in our example of Chapter 4, it is assumed that households hold only two kinds of assets, bank deposits D and stock market shares. The value of the wealth that households hold in the form of equities is $p_s s$, where s is the number of shares out there and p_s is the price of each share. The wealth of households is thus $V = D + p_s s$. But this is also the market value of firms, because, from the identities of the balance-sheet matrix given in Table 4.34, bank deposits D of households cannot but be equal to the bank loans B made to firms, and hence $D = B$. We may now compute a useful ratio, which we have already encountered in Chapter 3. This is Kaldor's valuation ratio, named v_r, which we define here as the market value of firms divided by the replacement cost of their tangible capital. We have

$$v_r = \frac{V}{K} = \frac{D + p_s s}{K} \tag{6.90}$$

And thus the market value of firms and the wealth of households can be expressed as $v_r K$. Following Skott (1981, p. 571), Wray (1992a, p. 71) and Taylor (2004, p. 277), we can make use of highly simple portfolio equations, assuming that the demand for bank deposits and for shares is a proportion κ_d and κ_s respectively of household wealth V (with $\kappa_d + \kappa_s = 1$):

$$D = \kappa_d v_r K \qquad (6.91)$$

$$p_s s = \kappa_s v_r K = (1 - \kappa_d) v_r K \qquad (6.92)$$

At any moment of time, the number of shares outstanding and the amount of bank loans and hence of bank deposits are given. Any change in portfolio choice is thus accommodated through changes in share prices. We can solve for p_s and v_r, and, recalling that $D = B$, and hence that $D/K = B/K = l$, where l is the debt ratio of firms, we obtain

$$p_s = \left(\frac{1-\kappa_d}{\kappa_d}\right)\left(\frac{D}{s}\right) \qquad (6.93)$$

$$v_r = \frac{D}{\kappa_d K} = \frac{l}{\kappa_d} \qquad (6.94)$$

We have thus managed to introduce the bears and the bulls that Kregel (1986) was talking about. When economic agents are willing to hold a smaller proportion κ_d of their wealth in the form of bank deposits, the price p_s of shares rises and so does the valuation ratio v_r. Thus what we have here is a liquidity preference theory of asset prices, with the price of equities being determined by the willingness of households (or of the managers of their wealth) to hold equities and to forego the quietude of money (that is, bank deposits), thus acting as bulls instead of bears. But what is the effect of such changes in liquidity preference on the debt ratio of firms and on the real variables of the economy? To find out, we now turn to the saving and investment functions of the model.

6.10.3 Debt-led or Debt-burdened Regime?

The saving function of this model, given by equation (6.95) below, has some resemblance to equation (6.42) because, as was the case with Shaikh's model, we split saving into corporate and household saving. This time around, however, we take into account the interest payments that firms must make on their debt. We thus assume, as when we derived equation (3.11A) of the finance frontier in Chapter 3, that firms keep a proportion s_f of their profits net of interest payments as retained earnings. This is the first term of the saving equation (6.95). The second term consists of the saving out of the revenues of households. The propensity to save out of the income flows of households is assumed to be s_h, whatever the source of their income. The income of households is made up of three components: wages, which are the first term inside the squared brackets; dividends, which are the second term; and interest payments on their bank deposits – the third term. Because $D = B$, interest income on bank deposits can be represented by $il = i(B/K) = i(D/K)$. The saving function contains an additional term, already introduced at the end of Chapter 5. This term represents dissaving out of household wealth V, that is, $c_v v_r$, where c_v is the propensity to consume out of wealth, while v_r is Kaldor's valuation ratio. In absolute terms, in addition to their consumption out of their regular income flows, households consume $c_v V$.

$$g^s = s_f(r - il) + s_h[(u/v - r) + (1 - s_f)(r - il) + il] - c_v v_r \qquad (6.95)$$

Because the model will be solved in terms of the rate of utilization and the debt ratio, u and l, the terms of the saving equation can be reshuffled. Remembering that $r = \pi u/v$, we get

$$g^s = \left[s_f(1-s_h)\pi + s_h\right](u/v) - s_f(1-s_h)il - c_v v_r \qquad (6.95A)$$

We now move to the investment function. The investment function is constructed to show some symmetry with the saving function. It relies on empirical studies that show that interest payments and the rate of utilization are key determinants of investment decisions, although the influence of the valuation ratio is unclear (Ndikumana, 1999; Arestis et al., 2012). We thus write a Kaleckian investment function that, in addition to reacting to the rate of utilization, depends positively on the valuation ratio and negatively on interest payments. The investment function thus has some Minskyan content, as it depends on the sentiment of the financial markets, as reflected by the stock market value, and on the burden caused by the financial obligations associated with the existing debt:

$$g^i = \gamma_0 + \gamma_u u - \gamma_l il + \gamma_v v_r \qquad (6.96)$$

We first look at the short-run solution of this model, when $g^s = g^i$, assuming that the debt ratio is a constant in the short run. Solving for the rate of utilization, and remembering from equation (6.94) that $v_r = l/\kappa_d$, we find

$$u^* = \frac{\gamma_0 + \left[s_f(1-s_h) - \gamma_l\right]il + \left[(c_v + \gamma_v)/\kappa_d\right]l}{\left[s_f(1-s_h)\pi + s_h\right]/v - \gamma_u} \qquad (6.97)$$

As usual, Keynesian stability requires that the denominator be positive, and we assume that it is. Also, as usual in Kaleckian models, we can see that the equilibrium rate of utilization is inversely related to the profit share π. In addition, we can see immediately that an increase in the valuation ratio v_r (or a decrease in the desired proportion κ_d of bank deposits in household wealth) has a positive impact on the rate of utilization, since both consumption and investment should respond positively to the change. More surprisingly, perhaps, inspection of equation (6.97) reveals that an increase in interest rates may either reduce or increase the rate of utilization depending on the sign of the expression in square brackets in the numerator. This is because an increase in interest payments by firms, while it reduces their inducement to invest, also redistributes gross profits from firms towards households, with firms saving all their net revenue while households spend only part of their dividend and interest income. This is a feature common to all post-Keynesian models incorporating interest payments, and it can be found in the models of Skott (1989a), Lavoie (1995b) and Hein (2008; 2012). Focusing now on the role of the debt ratio l, we see that only one of the four terms involving it in the numerator has a negative impact on the rate of utilization. Right away, we can thus distinguish two cases, one where effective demand conditions yield a positive relationship between the rate of utilization and the debt ratio l, and another case where this relationship is negative, which will mainly happen when the γ_l parameter is large. Taylor (2004, p. 275), in analogy with wage-led and profit-led regimes, calls the positive case a 'debt-led' demand regime while the negative case corresponds to a 'debt-burdened' demand regime. We could also solve for g^*, and find two debt growth regimes, but obviously the solution would be complex.

6.10.4 Minsky or Steindl Debt Dynamics?

What will be the evolution of the debt ratio towards its long-run value, when both debt and capital grow at the same rate? To find out, we have to go back to the finance frontier of firms derived in Chapter 3, which can also be obtained from a flow-of-funds analysis. Starting from equation (3.11), but removing placements in financial assets, we obtain

$$I = xI + s_f(P - iB) + \hat{B}B \tag{6.98}$$

where $\hat{B}$ is the growth rate of the outstanding stock of bank loans taken by firms, and where keen readers may recall that x is the proportion of investment that is financed by new issues of equities. Investment in tangible capital is thus financed by new share issues, retained earnings and new bank loans. Dividing through by K, we get

$$g = xg + s_f(r - il) + \hat{B}l$$

Remembering that $\dot{l}/l = \hat{l} = \hat{B} - \hat{K} = \hat{B} - g$, after some manipulation we find the differential equation that describes the evolution of l through time:

$$\dot{l} = g(1-x) + (s_f i - g)l - s_f \pi u / v \tag{6.99}$$

Expanding the above equation by using investment equation (6.96), we get

$$\dot{l} = (\gamma_0 + \gamma_u u - \gamma_l il + \gamma_v l / \kappa_d)(1 - x - l) + s_f il - s_f \pi u / v \tag{6.99A}$$

For dynamic stability, we need $d\dot{l}/dl < 0$. However, since u itself depends on l and since expression (6.99) contains a multiplicative term in l, little simple can be said, and we shall do as Taylor (2004) and assume away the cases where there is dynamic instability. As to the slope of the demarcation line – the steady-state locus where $\dot{l} = 0$ – we can look at the partial derivative of $\dot{l}$ with respect to u. We have

$$\frac{d\dot{l}}{du} = \gamma_u(1 - x - l) - \frac{s_f \pi}{v} \tag{6.100}$$

Obviously, once more, there are two possible cases. The effect of higher economic activity will lead to rising debt ratios when the share of retained earnings in national income is low, when the proportion of investment financed by share issues is low, and when the current debt ratio is low. This is the case that corresponds to the main interpretation of Minsky's financial instability hypothesis. Faster growth and higher economic activity generate higher debt ratio. This will thus be called the Minsky regime. The demarcation line then has a positive slope. By contrast, when the derivative of equation (6.100) is negative, the slope of the demarcation line is negative: higher economic activity generates lower debt ratios, a possibility underlined by Steindl (1952), which we discussed in Chapter 1 under the topic of the paradox of debt. This will thus be called the Steindl regime.

Crossing over the Steindl and Minsky regimes with the debt-led and debt-burdened demand regimes, we thus have four possible cases (there could be more if we took into account dynamically unstable configurations). These four cases are illustrated with the help of Figure 6.34. In these figures we assume that the economy starts from a full-equilibrium position, given by point A, on the effective demand curve and with a constant debt ratio. We then suppose that there is either an increase in the animal spirits of entrepreneurs (the γ_0 constant in the investment function goes up) or a decrease in the liquidity preference of households (the κ_d proportion of equation (6.91) goes down), boosting the valuation ratio and hence the wealth of households. As a consequence, the effective demand curve shifts towards the right, and in all four cases the rate of utilization increases in the short run, at a constant debt ratio, reaching position B. In the two Minsky configurations, the debt ratio l rises as the economy reaches its new stationary state at point C. By contrast, in the two Steindl configurations, the debt ratio is lower in the new configuration, at point C, than in the initial one, at point A, despite the higher level of economic activity. This is the paradox of debt, evoked in Chapter 1.

These results provide some support for the critique of Lavoie and Seccareccia (2001) and that of Toporowski (2008), who argued that Minsky (1975) based part of his financial instability hypothesis on a microeconomic view of the firm, overlooking the macroeconomic consequences of larger investments on retained profits. With the Steindl configuration, firms may be willing to raise their debt ratios when economic activity grows and investment accelerates, but the macroeconomics will be such that the debt ratio will instead end in going down. Naturally, in what we have called the Minsky configuration, Minsky's hypothesis is vindicated. Pedrosa and Lang (2021), in an agent-based SFC model, show that individual firms may exhibit a Minskyan or a Steindlian behaviour, depending on the distribution of profits and hence on the cost competitiveness of each firm. They warn that the aggregate leverage ratio may be a poor indicator of actual financial fragility.

Another line of defence of the financial instability hypothesis has been that steady-state models cannot claim to be faithful to Minsky's views, since a crucial feature of these is that 'stability is destabilizing', as already pointed out in Chapter 1. We turn to a study of such a notion.

6.10.5 A Minsky Cycle Model

Taylor (2004, ch. 9) suggests an extension of the Lavoie–Godley model to formalize Minsky's views as a cycle model. What follows is inspired by this suggestion, although its graphical representation is different. The proposed model is a system of two differential equations, which involves the growth rate of the economy and the debt ratio. At the most abstract level, we can write two implicit functions such that

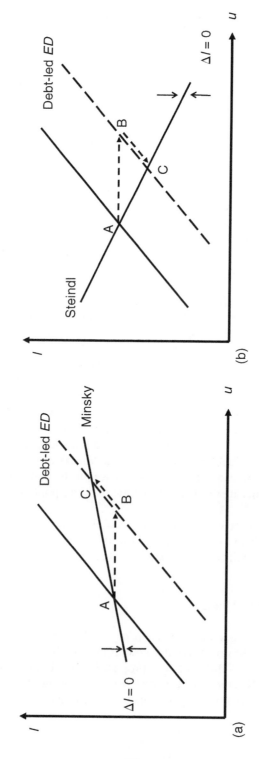

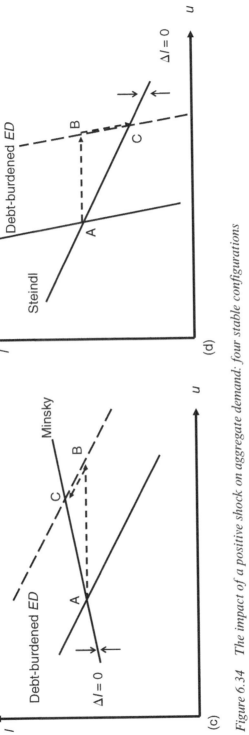

Figure 6.34 The impact of a positive shock on aggregate demand: four stable configurations

$$\dot{g} = \psi(g, l) \tag{6.101}$$
$$\dot{l} = \xi(g, l) \tag{6.102}$$

We can presume that the behaviour of equation (6.102) follows from our previous analysis. The novelty is equation (6.101). As in Taylor and O'Connell (1985), where it was based on a 'state of confidence' variable, Taylor (2004, p. 303) assumes that there exists a self-reinforcing mechanism that drives up the growth rate of the economy when this rate is already high. This is the 'stability is destabilizing' notion that Minsky emphasized so much. As the economy grows, financial norms change. Banks are likely to rely on stricter norms in bad times, and they tend to loosen their rules in good times, both lenders and borrowers believing that the economy is now in a new era, where the old rules no longer apply. It will thus become easier for firms to obtain credit and accelerate investment expenditures when the growth rate of the economy is high. There are thus cumulative processes at work, mainly driven by finance, that create virtuous or vicious circles. The higher state of confidence will be reflected in a higher parameter γ_0 in the investment equation and will thus raise the growth rate of the economy. In addition, the same positive feedback mechanism of high economic growth can also be presumed to affect households, which will take more risky positions, increasing the proportion of their assets held in the form of equities, thus raising the valuation ratio and hence output growth. This, I think, is compatible with what Palley (2011) calls the Minsky super-cycle.

We can examine the local stability of this system of differential equations by linearizing the system at the equilibrium (g^*, l^*), thus obtaining

$$\begin{bmatrix} \dot{g} \\ \dot{l} \end{bmatrix} = \begin{bmatrix} \dfrac{\partial \dot{g}}{\partial g} & \dfrac{\partial \dot{g}}{\partial l} \\ \dfrac{\partial \dot{l}}{\partial g} & \dfrac{\partial \dot{l}}{\partial l} \end{bmatrix} \begin{bmatrix} dg \\ dl \end{bmatrix}_{(g^*, l^*)}$$

The 2 × 2 matrix is the Jacobian J of the system, with elements j_{ij}. The two demarcation lines are thus such that

$$\dot{g} = j_{11} dg + j_{12} dl = 0$$
$$\dot{l} = j_{21} dg + j_{22} dl = 0$$

From the above, the slopes of these two demarcation lines can be computed as being equal to

$$\left. \frac{dl}{dg} \right|_{\dot{g}=0} = -\frac{\partial \dot{g} / \partial g}{\partial \dot{g} / \partial l} \tag{6.103}$$

$$\left. \frac{dl}{dg} \right|_{\dot{l}=0} = -\frac{\partial \dot{l} / \partial g}{\partial \dot{l} / \partial l} \tag{6.104}$$

Accumulation and capacity

What do we know so far? We know that there is a destabilizing Minskyan self-reinforcing effect on output growth, so that $\partial \dot{g}/\partial g > 0$. We also know that $\partial \dot{l}/\partial l < 0$ as was assumed in the previous subsection, for otherwise the trace of the Jacobian, tr $J = j_{11} + j_{22}$, could never be negative and the system could not be stable around its equilibrium. Finally, since we are trying to model Minsky insights, we also need to assume the presence of the Minsky regime, so that $\partial \dot{l}/\partial g > 0$. What can be said about $\partial \dot{g}/\partial l$? To avoid a saddle-point, the determinant must be positive, so that Det $J = j_{11} j_{22} - j_{12} j_{21} > 0$. Since j_{11} is positive while j_{22} is negative, this means that the product $j_{12} j_{21}$ must be negative, so that we need to have $\partial \dot{g}/\partial l < 0$. In other words, the economy must be in a debt-burdened demand regime, output growth being negatively influenced by debt. Furthermore, the absolute value $|j_{12} j_{21}|$ must be larger than the absolute value $|j_{11} j_{22}|$. This implies that the demarcation line given by $\dot{l} = 0$ must have a slope in absolute terms that is greater than that of the demarcation line given by $\dot{g} = 0$. Also, given all this, the slopes of the two demarcation lines must be positive.

Figure 6.35 illustrates the business cycle thus generated. As the economy starts growing from its lowest point (point A), the debt ratio falls, but then it rises during the rest of the growth expansion, and this is what eventually stops the acceleration of output growth and slows down the economy. As the economy starts slowing down, the debt ratio keeps rising, but eventually, with an even greater slowdown, the debt ratio falls, along with the falling growth rate of output. By increasing the strength of the self-reinforcing effect on output growth, the model can be made to explode. This toy model and Figure 6.35 are thus, I think, a fair formal representation of Minsky's views, although many others are possible and can be found in the literature recently surveyed by Nikolaidi and Stockhammer (2017). Still, it should be pointed out that a Steindl regime, with a debt-led demand regime, where we have instead $\partial \dot{l}/\partial g < 0$ and $\partial \dot{g}/\partial l > 0$, can also generate a stable cyclical behaviour, as shown in Figure 6.36. With these new conditions, and keeping as

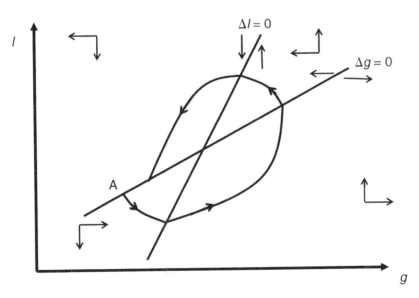

Figure 6.35   Cyclical behaviour in a debt-burdened Minsky regime

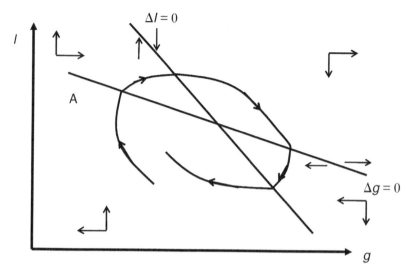

Figure 6.36 Cyclical behaviour in a debt-led Steindl regime

before $\partial \dot{g}/\partial l > 0$ as well as $\partial \dot{l}/\partial l < 0$ the negative slopes of the two demarcation lines can be derived from equations (6.103) and (6.104), while the relative size of the absolute values of the slopes is derived from the condition that the determinant of J be positive.

6.11 HOUSEHOLD DEBT

So far, no mention has been made of household debt, which has been at the core of the recent subprime financial crisis. It can also be argued that household debt, in particular consumer debt, was a crucial element of the causes of the Great Depression in the 1930s, as household debt in the USA rose roughly from 20 to 50 per cent of GDP between 1922 and 1929, while the debt ratio of non-financial firms was nearly constant. Indeed, it could be argued that Minsky's financial fragility hypothesis applies best to households and financial institutions, although as recalled by Lavoie (2020, pp. 90–91), Minsky (1982a, p. 30) himself wrote that 'the typical financing relation for consumer and housing debt can amplify but it cannot initiate a downturn in income and employment'. It was left to Palley (1996a, p. 202) to claim that 'the focus on household debt accumulation represents a theoretical innovation that contrasts with, and complements, existing Minskyan models which focus on the corporate debt–investment spending nexus'.

Palley (1996a) assumes that there are two classes of households. One class is made up of borrowers, who must make interest payments. Their consumption depends on their income net of interest payments, plus the new loans that they get. They have a given debt to gross income ratio that they achieve in each period. The other class is made up of lenders, who receive interest payments, and who make new loans. Their consumption is a function of their overall income, minus the loans that they allow to the borrowers. It is assumed that borrowers have a higher propensity to consume than lenders. Thus, initially, the higher debt taken on by borrowers leads to higher economic activity, because borrowed funds are all spent. But then, as more interest payments must be made, this slows down economic activity.

Various other models incorporating growth and household debt have been proposed by Bhaduri et al. (2006), Bhaduri (2011b), Dutt (2006b), Godley and Lavoie (2007a, ch. 11), Palley (2006; 2010), and van Treeck (2009). Isaac and Kim (2013) even produced a highly complex model that handles corporate debt and consumer debt simultaneously, while Zezza (2008) also deals with the real-estate market. Nikolaidi and Stockhammer (2017) show that this is a quickly expanding field of research. Here, however, we shall provide only the gist of the relationship between household debt for consumption purposes and effective demand in a Kaleckian model. To do so, we shall rely on a variant of the models proposed by Hein (2012, ch. 5) and by Kim (2012), the two models achieving similar results, despite the fact that Hein's model constrains the amount that workers can borrow to the savings that rentiers do not pass on to firms (Pariboni, 2016b, p. 217). We make several simplifying assumptions, with the objective of achieving some results quickly.

6.11.1 The Accounting Famework

As in the model describing the evolution of corporate debt, the economy is made up of three sectors: firms, banks and households. The household sector, however, is split into two groups: the workers and the rentiers. The stock–flow matrix of the present model, described by Table 6.6, shows some differences with that of Table 4.34, since it is assumed that firms run no debt. Only workers get into debt, and they hold no assets. By contrast, rentiers have financial assets: they hold equities and deposits. Banks take the deposits of rentiers and make loans to workers.

Next we examine the transactions–flow matrix of our model, given by Table 6.7. Firms distribute all their profits in the form of dividends, and they issue new shares, as required by their investment expenditures. Banks make no profits and hence the rates of interest on loans B and deposits D are identical. As already said, workers save nothing; they spend all they can. This means that they spend all their wages, net of the interest payments that they must make on their accumulated debt. However, in any given period, worker households can spend more than that by borrowing from the banks. Rentiers save a proportion s_r of their income. They purchase all the new shares issued by the firms and they put the rest of their saving into bank deposits.

Table 6.6 Balance-sheet matrix of the consumer debt model

	Households		Firms	Banks	Σ
	Workers	Rentiers			
Fixed capital			$+K$		$+K$
Deposits		$+D_r$		$-D$	0
Loans	$-B_w$			$+B$	0
Shares		$+s \cdot p_s$	$-s \cdot p_s$		0
Balance	$-V_w$	$-V_r$	$-V_h$	0	$-K$
Σ	0	0	0	0	0

Table 6.7 The transactions–flow matrix of the model with household debt

	Households Workers	Households Rentiers	Firms Current	Firms Capital	Banks Current	Banks Capital	Σ
Consumption	$-C_w$	$-C_r$	$+C$				0
Investment			$+I$	$-I$			0
Wages	$+wL$		$-wL$				0
Net profits		$+P$	$-P$				0
Interest on loans	$-i \cdot B_{(-1)}$				$+i \cdot B_{(-1)}$		0
Interest on deposits		$+i \cdot D_{(-1)}$			$-i \cdot D_{(-1)}$		0
Δ in loans	$+\Delta B$					$-\Delta B$	0
Δ in deposits		$-\Delta D$				$+\Delta D$	0
Shares		$-p_s \Delta s$		$+p_s \Delta s$			0
Σ	0	0	0	0	0	0	0

All this can be formalized in our standard notation. We assume an even simpler investment equation:

$$g^i = \gamma + \gamma_u u \qquad (6.105)$$

The saving function is made up of two components: the saving of the rentiers, g_r^s, and the saving of the workers, g_w^s, which is in fact their dissaving:

$$g^s = g_r^s + g_w^s \qquad (6.106)$$

The saving of the rentiers is a proportion s_r of their profit and interest income, where $l = B/K$, and hence where the debt of households (for reasons of convenience) is normalized by the value of the capital stock:

$$g_r^s = s_r \left(\frac{\pi u}{v} + il \right) \qquad (6.107)$$

We follow Kim (2012) in assuming that workers in each period borrow a flow of funds which is a proportion ζ of the consumption of the rentiers. This is the dissaving of workers. There is thus a flow–flow norm. It is assumed that workers attempt to emulate the consumption expenditures of the richer rentiers, along the lines set out long ago by Veblen (1899) and Duesenberry (1949), with workers imitating the conspicuous consumption of rentiers as explained in Chapter 2 at the individual level. The proportion ζ depends on social norms, but also on the willingness of banks to grant creditworthiness status to the borrowers. As Dutt (2006b, p. 347) says, the level of borrowing 'can be interpreted as being determined by lenders, by borrowers or by both'. As a simplification, we assume that the ζ parameter is exogenous, not influenced by other variables such as the debt ratio of worker households. The saving of workers is thus equal to:

$$g_w^s = -\zeta(1 - s_r)\left(\frac{\pi u}{v} + il \right) \qquad (6.108)$$

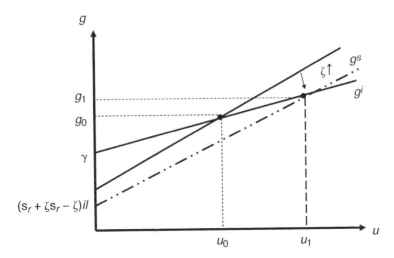

Figure 6.37 The short-run impact of an increase in the emulation parameter

Given equations (6.107) and (6.108), the saving equation (6.106) is:

$$g^s = (s_r + \zeta s_r - \zeta)(\pi u/v + il) \qquad (6.109)$$

6.11.2 The Short-run Solution

Looking for the equilibrium level of capacity utilization by equating the saving function (6.109) with the investment equation (6.105), we get:

$$u^* = \frac{\{\gamma - (s_r + \zeta s_r - \zeta)il\}v}{\pi(s_r + \zeta s_r - \zeta) - \gamma_u v} \qquad (6.110)$$

Making use of equation (6.105), we can also compute the equilibrium rate of growth:

$$g^* = \frac{(\gamma\pi - \gamma_u vil)(s_r + \zeta s_r - \zeta)}{\pi(s_r + \zeta s_r - \zeta) - \gamma_u v} \qquad (6.111)$$

As usual, the model is stable if the denominator is positive. This implies the following necessary but insufficient condition:

$$\zeta < s_r + \zeta s_r \qquad (6.112)$$

which we can also write as $\zeta(1 - s_r) < s_r$.

Looking back at the two saving equations (6.107) and (6.108), this means that an increase in the saving of rentiers, due to an increase in their income, must not be overtaken by an increase in the dissaving of workers induced by this increase in rentier income. For instance, for a given u, if there is an increase in the profit share π going to rentiers, thus generating more income and saving for them, the additional dissaving by workers must not generate a lower average propensity to save of the economy. In all likelihood, this condition was not fulfilled in the USA during the build-up towards the subprime financial crisis, since more inequality in income distribution was associated with lower overall saving rates (Brown, 2008, ch. 4; Cynamon and Fazzari, 2008; van Treeck and Sturn, 2012). We shall nonetheless stick to the stability case and assume that the denominator is positive. Then, for the rate of utilization to be positive (if $u > 0$, then $g > 0$), the numerator of equation (6.110) also needs to be positive, which means that

$$\gamma > (s_r + \zeta s_r - \zeta) il \tag{6.113}$$

Figure 6.37 illustrates the model in its short-run configuration. The standard results of the canonical Kaleckian model are recovered: an increase in animal spirits γ or a decrease in the profit share and in the propensity to save of rentiers have a positive effect on the rate of capacity utilization. An increase in the emulation parameter ζ, and thus in the potential dissaving of workers, leads to an increase in effective demand and in the rate of capacity utilization. This is what is shown with the dotted line representing the saving function. There is plenty of evidence to show that indeed the emulation parameter in the USA has risen over the years and is now much higher than it used to be. By contrast, a higher interest rate i or a higher debt ratio for workers, associated with higher debt payments, reduces effective demand and the short-run rate of capacity utilization. Thus, as in several other such models, the flow of borrowing increases economic activity, but the stock of debt reduces it.

6.11.3 Long-run Effects and Dynamic Stability

We now wish to know what happens in the long run, when the debt ratio of household, l, is no longer a given. In other words, we wish to find the long-run equilibrium value of l and to examine the dynamic stability of the model. We first need to recall once more that $\hat{l/l} = \hat{l} = \hat{B} - \hat{K} = \hat{B} - g$. Note also that the growth rate of household debt can be manipulated as follows:

$$\hat{B} = \frac{\Delta B}{B} = \frac{\Delta B}{K}\frac{K}{B} = -\frac{g_r^s}{l} \tag{6.114}$$

Plugging the value of u^*, given by equation (6.110), into equation (6.108), and making use of equation (6.114), we obtain the growth rate of household debt:

$$\hat{B} = \frac{\zeta(1-s_r)(\gamma\pi - \gamma_u vil)}{l\{\pi(s_r + \zeta s_r - \zeta) - \gamma_u v\}} \tag{6.115}$$

The debt ratio of worker households becomes a constant when $\hat{l} = \hat{B} - g = 0$. Making use of equations (6.115) and (6.110), this will happen when

$$\hat{l} = \hat{B} - g^* = \frac{\{\zeta(1-s_r) - l(s_r + \zeta s_r - \zeta)\}(\gamma\pi - \gamma_u vil)}{l\{\pi(s_r + \zeta s_r - \zeta) - \gamma_u v\}} = 0 \tag{6.116}$$

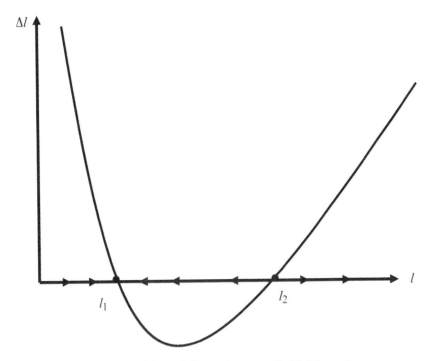

Figure 6.38 The dynamic stability of the worker household debt ratio

There are thus two solutions to this equation, since the numerator of the above equation can become zero for two different values of the household debt ratio:

$$l_1^{**} = \frac{\zeta(1-s_r)}{(s_r + \zeta s_r - \zeta)} \qquad (6.117)$$

$$l_2^{**} = \frac{\pi\gamma}{\gamma_u iv} \qquad (6.118)$$

The second solution corresponds to a rate of accumulation $g^{**} = 0$, and thus to a rate of capacity utilization that would be negative when short-run stability holds. As there are two possible solutions, one of them is dynamically stable and the other is not. Indeed, the first solution, given by l_1^{**} is the stable one. This can be ascertained by checking the equation of $\dot{l} = \hat{l}/l$ which is a polynomial of the second degree, with a positive l^2 term (assuming still short-run Keynesian stability), meaning that it has a U-shape, as shown in Figure 6.38. Somewhat surprisingly, the stable long-run equilibrium of the worker household debt ratio depends only on the propensity to save of the rentiers and on the emulation parameter. There is no paradox of debt here: if households wish to borrow more, as proxied by the ζ parameter, this will indeed drive up the long-run value of the worker household debt ratio. Taking the derivative of l_1^{**} with respect to s_r, it can also be shown that, if rentiers have a higher propensity to save, it will lead to a lower long-run value of the worker household debt ratio. The long-run value of the rate of capacity utilization, u^{**}, could be calculated by substituting l in equation (6.110) by its long-run value in (6.117).

The other parameters of the model have an impact only on l_2^{**}; that is, they have an influence on the range of stable debt ratios that are possible within the model. For instance, an increase in the rate of interest i will diminish l_2^{**} and will thus increase the likelihood of the model falling into dynamic instability. With his model, which is closely related to the one shown here, Hein (2012, ch. 5) describes, through graphs and algebra, the impact of various parameters on the shape of the dynamic stability curve of Figure 6.38. Naturally it should be understood that the present model is rudimentary, with a number of overly simplifying assumptions.

A number of post-Keynesian authors have pointed out that consumer credit has helped to offset the decrease in the share of wages and of direct labour in particular. Brown (1997) has argued, however, that consumer credit is liable to household-debt deflation when consumers lose confidence in a downturn, thus leading to a brisk fall in our ζ parameter. This effect could be further reinforced by changes in the creditworthiness standards set by banks and other financial institutions.

6.11.4 Some Additional Thoughts About Household Debt

Many studies have underlined how household debt and inequality in personal income distribution have become more obviously intertwined over the last decades, especially with the easier access to consumer and residential credit. This has also been related to the issue of whether economies are in a wage-led or a profit-led demand regime. The empirical work of Oyvat et al. (2020) show that higher household debt ratios raise the probability of being in a profit-led regime. It decreases the wage-led component of an economy, just as income inequality does.

Two models, by Kapeller and Schütz (2015) and Setterfield and Kim (2016), produce a consumption-driven profit-led growth regime which corresponds to these empirical findings. Both models split workers into production workers on one side and supervisor workers on the other side. When the profit share increases, it is entirely at the detriment of the production workers. This group of workers is then forced to borrow to upkeep their consumption norms or consumption target, which is said to depend on the consumption of the other group of workers. With high enough emulation effects, the increase in the profit share will generate an increase in economic activity and thus an apparent profit-led regime. This is so even if the economy, without consumer credit, had been assumed to be impervious to changes in income distribution or even wage-led, thus creating yet another paradoxical behaviour.

Consumer credit has also been introduced in Sraffian supermultiplier models with investment equation (6.57) and (6.57A). Pariboni (2016b) assumes the presence of an autonomous consumption component, arising from consumer credit obtained by workers, whose debt is thus growing at the constant rate g_z. As in other such models, he shows under similar conditions, that the growth rate of the economy tends towards g_z and that the debt ratio converges to a stable value. An increase in the profit share in his model leads to an increase in the steady-state debt ratio of workers. A similar supermultiplier model, within a more complete SFC setup, devised by Mandarino et al. (2020, p. 358), shows that, except at the moment of the shock, 'higher consumption financed out of credit never leads to higher indebtedness, provided consumption is the sole autonomous variable in the model'.

The importance of stock-flow consistency, where there are no black holes, must be reiterated, because the models of Pariboni (2016b) and Kapeller and Schütz (2015) assume that workers save part of their income but omit the fact that they ought to receive earnings on their savings; or else the authors implicitly assume that workers hold all of their wealth in the form of bank deposits that earn an interest rate of zero per cent. The importance of linking saving to accumulated wealth will be the topic of the next section.

Meanwhile, recall that nearly all previous models came to the conclusion that an increase in the debt ratio of households led to a reduction in economic activity since it meant an increase in the plight of debt servicing. Setterfield and Kim (2016) show, however, that this is not a foregone conclusion. Borrowers who do not save and who try to emulate the consumption norms of rich lenders *must* reduce their consumption flow when debt servicing costs rise. This was the standard assumption in earlier models. However, if workers borrow funds and at the same time save part of their income, they may decide instead to give priority to their consumption target and reduce their saving flow when faced with higher debt servicing obligations.

6.12 WEALTH DISTRIBUTION AND PERSONAL INCOME DISTRIBUTION

6.12.1 The Pasinetti Paradox

We mentioned that some authors seem to have forgotten that if workers save then they must receive some of the capital income distributed by firms. As Setterfield and Kim (2017, p. 48) recall, 'when workers save, they amass a stock of assets from which they subsequently derive income in proportion to what they own'. They must thus get a share of the profits. This was pointed out in 1962 by Pasinetti (1974, ch. 5) when he questioned Kaldor's (1956) model of growth and distribution. In section 6.3.1, we did examine the case of saving out of wages, assuming a one-class society, collecting both wages and profits. It was then presumed that the propensity to save out of profits was higher than that out of wages because firms retain part of their profits. This was the justification provided by Kaldor (1966) in response to Pasinetti, and this kind of saving equation was made explicit in equation (6.42).

The work of Thomas Piketty (2014) has however triggered a renewed interest for the study of personal income distribution and wealth distribution within social classes, going beyond functional income distribution which, except for overhead labour, has been our main focus so far. One of the reasons for which the work of Piketty has attracted the attention of post-Keynesians has been his claim that if the rate of profit is higher than the rate of GDP growth, $r > g$, which he called the fundamental inequality, 'then it logically follows that inherited wealth grows faster than output and income' (ibid., p. 26), implying 'that capitalism automatically generates arbitrary and unsustainable inequalities' (ibid., p. 1). Within post-Keynesian theory, however, this is a dubious assertion. The inequality need not generate rising inequalities with an ever-rising concentration of wealth in the hands of a few investors.

To show this, we start by showing how Pasinetti (1974, ch. 6) recovers the Cambridge equation when households are split into capitalists, who only receive profits, and workers, who receive wages but also profits from their accumulated savings. Omitting the presence of retained earnings, where the c and w subscripts refer to capitalists and workers, the saving function of the economy can thus be written as:

$$S = S_c + S_w = s_c P_c + s_w \left(wL + P_w\right) \tag{6.119}$$

Saving propensities are thus split according to the propensities to save of capitalists and of workers, instead of being split between the propensities to save out of profits and out of wages. Pasinetti assumes that workers manage to get the same rate of return as capitalists on their capital. Baranzini and Mirante (2013, p. 294) provide a long list of authors who have introduced differentiated rates of return, but we will stick with the uniform rate of return, equal to the rate of profit. This then implies that:

$$r = \frac{P}{K} = \frac{P_c}{K_c} = \frac{P_w}{K_w} \tag{6.120}$$

Pasinetti then assumes that the economy has reached a long-run equilibrium, where the wealth of each class grows at the same rate. We thus have:

$$g = \frac{I}{K} = \frac{S}{K} = \frac{S_c}{K_c} = \frac{S_w}{K_w} \tag{6.121}$$

Dividing through these two equations, we get:

$$\frac{P_c}{S_c} = \frac{P_w}{S_w} \tag{6.122}$$

Making use of equation (6.119), we can rewrite the above equation as:

$$\frac{P_c}{s_c P_c} = \frac{P_w}{s_w \left(wL + P_w\right)} \tag{6.122A}$$

This implies that:

$$s_c P_w = s_w \left(wL + P_w\right) \tag{6.122B}$$

And hence equation (6.119) now becomes:

$$S = S_c + S_w = s_c P_c + s_c P_w = s_c P \tag{6.119A}$$

Dividing through by K, we recover the Cambridge equation, but this time without having to assume that the propensity out of wages is nil. The profit rate in this long-run equilibrium only depends on the growth rate of the economy and the propensity to save of capitalists, regardless of the propensity to save of workers. We have:

$$r^{**} = g/s_c \tag{6.2A}$$

This result seemed paradoxical, since the decisions of workers appeared to have no impact on the macroeconomic rate of profit and thus was named the Pasinetti paradox.

Readers should be reminded however that this result holds only in the long-run steady state. In the short run, the propensity to save of workers is still relevant. Also, depending on how differentiated rates of return are introduced, the paradox may vanish. In any case, equation (6.2A) shows that even when the rate of profit is higher than the growth rate of the economy, wealth distribution will remain steady when the reinterpreted Cambridge equation is verified, in contrast to the claim of Piketty.

6.12.2 Pasinetti's Social Classes in a Neo-Kaleckian Model

As recalled earlier, there are many different ways in which households could be split. We will stick however to Pasinetti's distinction between capitalists, who only receive profits, and workers who receive wages and profits. A number of authors have combined this way of organizing social classes with the neo-Kaleckian model of growth and distribution. As was the case with many other topics, Dutt (1990b), more than 30 years ago, was the first author to conduct such an exercise, assuming in addition the presence of retained earnings. He has been followed recently by Palley (2012), Kumar et al. (2018) and Ederer and Rehm (2020). All these authors have shown how wealth distribution is endogenous and changes through the transition towards the long-run steady state.

The approach being taken by these authors is similar, but they use different investment functions. Ederer and Rehm (2020) adopt the post-Kaleckian investment equation (6.25), Kumar et al. (2018) use the Robinsonian investment function (6.4), while Dutt (2017) prefers the Steindl-Kalecki investment function (6.13). To avoid complications, we use a simplified version of the canonical Kaleckian investment function, also used by Dutt (1990b), so that:

$$g^i = \gamma + \gamma_u u \qquad (6.12B)$$

The saving function is derived from Pasinetti's equation (6.119) and its assumptions. Defining the share of capital (or of wealth) held by the capitalists as $\kappa_c = K_c/K$, the saving function is then a variant of equation (6.3A), found on page 392, which, with our usual notation, can then be written as:

$$g^s = \{s_c \kappa_c \pi u + s_w [(1-\pi)u + (1-\kappa_c)\pi u]\}/v \qquad (6.123)$$

Combining equations (6.12B) and (6.123), and taking the share κ_c as a constant for now, we can solve for the short-run rate of utilization, which is equal to:

$$u^* = \frac{\gamma v}{s_w + (s_c - s_w)\kappa_c \pi - v\gamma_u} \qquad (6.124)$$

As usual, the denominator must be positive for the rate of utilization to be positive and to achieve Keynesian stability. Nearly by definition, the model is wage-led, at least provided we assume as usual that $s_c > s_w$, since an increase in the profit share π would lead to a fall in u^*. Under the same condition, we can also see that if the capitalist class has a bigger share κ_c of total wealth, this will also imply a lower rate of utilization. Thus, wealth distribution matters for economic activity, at least in the short run.

But what about the long run? In the long run, the shares of wealth become endogenous variables, and we should recover Pasinetti's paradoxical equation. We start from the definition of the capitalist share of wealth, and from the definitions that we used to derive Pasinetti's result, we get:

$$\dot{\kappa}_c = \hat{K}_c - \hat{K} = s_c r - g = \frac{s_c \pi u}{v} - g \qquad (6.125)$$

Using equation (6.12B), we can also rewrite the above equation as:

$$\dot{\kappa}_c = \left(s_c \pi u / v - \gamma - \gamma_u u \right) \kappa_c \qquad (6.125A)$$

and the steady state is thus achieved either when $\kappa_c = 0$, or when the long-run value of the rate of utilization is given by:

$$u^{**} = \frac{\gamma v}{s_c \pi - v \gamma_u} \qquad (6.126)$$

We focus on this second possibility, which also requires that $s_c \pi > v \gamma_u$. Thus, in the long run, the rate of utilization does not depend on the share of capital held by the capitalists, and neither will the growth rate (because of equation 6.12B). In addition, as we already knew, the profit rate does not depend on the propensity to save of workers.

$$r^{**} = \frac{g}{s_c} = \frac{\pi \gamma}{s_c \pi - v \gamma_u}$$

This will be achieved when the stocks of wealth of both workers and capitalists grow at the same rate. Plugging the long-run value of the rate of utilization into its short-run value, by combining equations (6.124) and (6.126), we get the steady-state share of wealth in the hands of the capitalists:

$$\kappa_c^{**} = \frac{s_c \pi - s_w}{\left(s_c - s_w \right) \pi} \qquad (6.127)$$

For this share to be positive, the condition $s_c \pi > s_w$ needs to be fulfilled. Otherwise, the capitalists will eventually get wiped out by the savings of the workers. This is what Dutt (2017, p. 183) calls the 'asymptotic euthanasia of the capitalists'. By calculating the derivatives, we can grasp, as one would expect, that the share of wealth belonging to the capitalists will be higher when their propensity to save and the profit share are higher, although this will lower the rate of utilization, the profit rate and the growth rate.

These steady-state values and the transitional dynamics can be represented with the help of Figure 6.39. The downward-sloping curve shows the negative relationship between the capitalist share of the capital stock and the rate of capacity utilization whenever the economy is in a short-run equilibrium. It is thus the locus of all the possible short-run equilibria, and thus represents a sort of effective demand curve, which can call ED. There is a single rate of capacity utilization, u^{**}, given by equation (6.126), such that the shares of capital stay steady, given by the vertical line $\dot{\kappa}_c = 0$. The intersection of these two curves yields the long-run equilibrium share of capital held by capitalists, κ_c^{**}, towards which the economy will tend. It will do so because when the rate of utilization is higher than u^{**}, κ_c rises, and vice-versa. This can be verified by looking at equation (6.125A). At the long-run

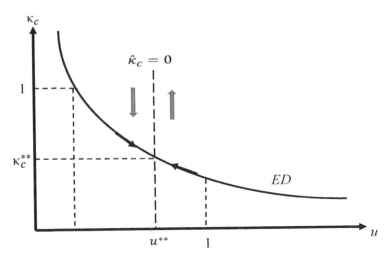

Figure 6.39 Long-run dynamics determining the rate of utilization and the share of wealth going to the capitalist in a neo-Kaleckian version of the Pasinetti theorem

equilibrium, $s_c \pi u^{**}/v = \gamma + \gamma_u u^{**}$. Hence, with a higher u, the term on the left-hand side is necessarily larger than the one on the right-hand side (since the denominator of equation (6.126) must be positive for the long-run rate of utilization to be positive).

It is also easy to compute the long-run share of total income acquired by the capitalists. They get κ_c^{**} per cent of all the profits. And since profits are π per cent of total income, using equation (6.127), the share of income going to capitalists in the steady state is equal to:

$$\frac{Y_c}{Y} = \kappa_c^{**} \pi = \frac{(s_c \pi - s_w)}{(s_c - s_w)} \qquad (6.128)$$

Thus, although the propensity to save of workers does not have an impact on the profit rate in the long-run equilibrium, it does play an important role with regards to the respective shares of wealth (the stocks) and shares of income (the flows) towards which the economy will converge over time. Through a higher propensity to save, workers can obtain a higher share of income and a higher share of wealth, as can be verified by computing the derivatives of equations (6.128) and (6.127) with respect to s_w.

Going back to our discussion in section 6.3.1 about the consequences of adding a propensity to save out of wages within a model containing the Steindl-Kalecki investment function (6.13), readers may recall that this addition could generate a profit-led demand regime (in the short run). However, as recalled by Dutt (2017, p. 184), when the dynamics of the shares of wealth are taken into account, utilization and growth in such a model become unambiguously wage-led in the long run an increase in the profit share π leads to a fall in the long-run value of the rate of utilization given by equation (6.126).

It cannot be overemphasized that all these results are highly abstract. As said earlier, we have not taken into account differentiated rates of return, due to the fact that workers are more likely to hold a large proportion of their wealth in the form of low-risk assets such as bank deposits, while capitalists are more likely to hold stock-market shares. As can be ascertained from section 3.4.5 of Chapter 3, the rates of return of capitalists are thus more likely to benefit from the optimism of the stock market and from the retained earnings accumulated by firms. Dutt (1990b) indeed shows that the long-run capitalist share of wealth is higher when the share of retained earnings that they get attributed is raised.

NOTE

* Besides relying on and extending the 1992 *Foundations*, full sentences have been taken from the following publications: 'The Kaleckian model of growth and distribution and its neo-Ricardian and neo-Marxian critiques', *Cambridge Journal of Economics*, **19** (6), December 1995, pp. 789–818; 'Surveying short-run and long-run stability issues with the Kaleckian model of growth', in M. Setterfield (ed.), *Handbook of Alternative Theories of Economic Growth*, Cheltenham, UK and Northampton, MA, USA: Edward Elgar Publishing, 2010, pp. 132–56; E. Hein, M. Lavoie and T. van Treeck, 'Some instability puzzles in Kaleckian models of growth and distribution: a critical survey', *Cambridge Journal of Economics*, **35** (3), May 2011, pp. 587–612; E. Hein, M. Lavoie and T. van Treeck, 'Harrodian instability and the normal rate of capacity utilization in Kaleckian models of distribution and growth – a survey', *Metroeconomica*, **63** (1), February 2012, pp. 39–69; M. Lavoie, 'The origins and evolution of the debate on wage-led and profit-led regimes', *European Journal of Economics and Economic Policies: Intervention*, **14** (2), 2017, pp. 200–221.

7. Open-economy macroeconomics*

Dealing with an open economy is not an easy task. First, there is a great deal of confusion regarding international monetary relations, as can be ascertained by readings and policy discussions on global imbalances, the possible destabilizing impact of incoming financial flows, the role of the US dollar, the impact of rising foreign exchange reserves, the causes of exchange rate changes, the effects of currency devaluation, the advantages of dollarization or of euroization, not to mention the impact of free trade, tariffs and many other subjects related to international trade. Second, there is no consensus post-Keynesian view on open-economy macroeconomics, so this makes it rather difficult to present what ought to be 'the' post-Keynesian foundations of open-economy theory within a single chapter. Bonizzi et al. (2021) also make note of this difficulty while attempting to identify the main elements of the post-Keynesian literature on foreign financial flows, exchange rates and emerging economies.

While wishing to avoid being unjust to anyone, I think it is fair to say that post-Keynesians have mostly written about two topics in the field of international macroeconomics: the reform of the international payment system, along the lines suggested by Keynes – the Keynes Plan; and the balance-of-payments constraint on growth, known as Thirlwall's law. In the 1970s, Sraffians applied the Cambridge capital critique to theories of international trade (Steedman, 1979a; 1979b; Evans, 1981; Henry, 1991); but these contributions will be left aside. More recently, the three-balance approach of Godley, which includes foreign lending or borrowing, has been in the limelight, as noted in Chapter 4. The Keynes Plan and Thirlwall's law will thus be presented here, but I shall also handle a few more topics, in a slightly iconoclastic form, such as the compensation thesis, the theory of forward exchange markets, and the Kaleckian growth model in an open economy. Similarly to the approach to macroeconomics in the closed economy, I start the discussion of open-economy macroeconomics with monetary matters and deal with the real economy in the second stage.

7.1 SOME INTERNATIONAL ECONOMY ACCOUNTING

As in Chapter 4, we first identify essential mechanics of international monetary relations. We start with the accounting of the balance of payments. We will then examine how international payments, involving or not involving currency exchange, are made between banks. We shall end with a graphical representation of Godley's three-balance approach that was introduced in Chapter 4, extending Figure 4.8 to include the international component.

7.1.1 The Balance of Payments

Here we recall the main components of the balance of payments. We begin with the three financial balances – the fundamental identity – that we used in Chapter 4, where once again the various variables of the equation are expressed in nominal terms:

$$(S - I) + (T - G) - CAB = 0 \qquad (4.7)$$

CAB stood for the current account balance, and we determined that $-CAB$ was net foreign lending, that is, lending to the domestic sector by non-residents. Omitting errors and omissions, we may thus define the following identity:

$$ABP = CAB + AFAB = 0 \qquad (7.1)$$

where ABP is the accounting balance of payments, which must necessarily sum to zero, and where I define $AFAB$ as the accounting financial account balance (using the terminology of the national accountants). This implies that $AFAB = -CAB$, and hence this accounting financial account balance is none other than net foreign lending to the domestic economy. It is the 'accounting' financial account balance in the sense that it includes the flow of increases in the official international reserves (ΔOR) of the central bank. Now an increase in official reserves means that the central bank is lending funds to other countries. So if we subtract the gain in official reserves from $AFAB$, we obtain the financial account balance in its economic sense (FAB), which used to be called the capital account, so that the balance of payments, again in its economic sense, is equal to

$$BP = CAB + FAB = \Delta OR \qquad (7.2)$$

In a fixed exchange rate regime, or in a managed float regime, both the current account and the financial account may turn out to be in a positive (negative) position, so that the central bank would be accumulating (losing) official exchange reserves. With a pure floating regime, the current account balance (CAB) has to be equal to the negative of the financial account balance ($-FAB$). Table 7.1 recalls the main components of the (accounting) financial account.

Over the last few years, a number of scholars have paid a great deal of attention to gross capital flows, instead of just looking at the net financial account balance (Kohler, 2020). We can expand equation (7.1) by splitting $AFAB$ into gross financial inflows (KIF) minus gross financial outflows (KOF), corresponding respectively to the right and left columns of Table 7.1. We can also recall from Chapter 4 that the current account balance CAB is net exports ($X - M$) plus net foreign income FY. The latter can be split into foreign income inflow (FYI) minus foreign income outflow (FYO), essentially interest payments and other capital income arising from foreign assets and received by domestic residents, minus payments made to non-residents arising from domestic liabilities. Combining all this, we get:

$$X + FYI + KIF = M + FYO + KOF \qquad (7.3)$$

Table 7.1 Components of the accounting financial account balance

Net acquisition of financial assets (monetary outflows)	Net incurrence of liabilities (monetary inflows)
Direct investment abroad	Direct investment in the domestic economy made by non-residents
Portfolio investment abroad	Portfolio investment in the domestic economy made by non-residents
Change in official international reserves	
Other investments (bank loans made to non-residents or increases in deposits held abroad)	Other investments in the domestic economy made by non-residents (loans from foreign banks or increases in deposits held by non-residents

Note: AFAB = Net incurrence of liabilities − Net acquisition of financial assets = Net foreign lending to the domestic economy.

The three components on the left-hand side of equation (7.3) will tend to lead to an appreciation of the domestic currency, while the three components on the right-hand side will tend to generate a depreciation of the domestic currency.

As we shall soon see, the last row of Table 7.1 comprises a component that accommodates changes in the components found above it, as well as the components of the current account balance. This explains why identity (7.1) is always verified, especially in a flexible exchange regime, without the intervention of the central bank and even possibly without any adjustment in the exchange rate. Indeed, Godley and Lavoie (2007a, p. 464) show within the confines of a stock–flow consistent two-country model that it is perfectly possible to have a fixed exchange rate regime without any change in central bank reserves by letting long-term interest rates absorb the necessary adjustment. This is the point made repeatedly by Taylor (2004, ch. 10): in a fully coherent model, there is no balance of payment *per se*. 'The widely used Mundell–Fleming IS/LM/BP model makes no sense because there is no independent equation for the home country's external balance or "BP"' (Taylor, 2008, p. 656).

7.1.2 The Fundamental Identity in a Three-dimensional Framework

We attempt to provide a graphical representation of the fundamental identity in a three-dimensional framework, drawing on the insightful analysis of Robert Parenteau (2010). We can rewrite what we have called the fundamental identity, given by equation (4.7), as equation (4.7A), which says that the private sector, taken as an aggregate, can accumulate net financial savings when the current account surplus is larger than the government surplus, or, put otherwise, when the government deficit is larger in absolute terms than the current account deficit:

$$(S - I) = CAB - (T - G) \tag{4.7A}$$

Figure 7.1 provides this three-dimensional representation of the fundamental identity. Each 45-degree line represents the combinations of current account and fiscal balances

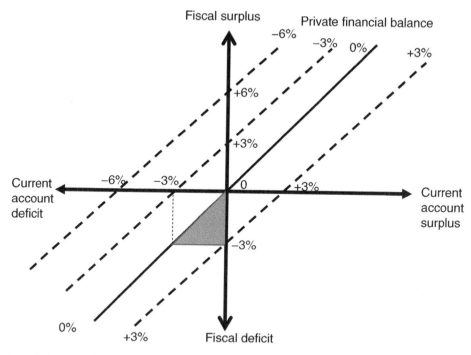

Figure 7.1   The three dimensions of the fundamental identity

that will yield a given private surplus in percentage points as a function of GDP. Thus, as we already know, when the twin deficit property is verified, the current account balance and the fiscal balance being equal to each other, net lending of the private sector is zero. As an example, a current account deficit of 3 per cent, accompanied by a balanced government budget, will yield a −3 per cent private financial balance. To achieve a given percentage of net lending in terms of GDP by the domestic private sector, any increase in the fiscal deficit must be compensated by a decrease in the current account surplus. Thus, as we move towards the right, the probability that the private sector will be accumulating net financial assets rises. What the figure clearly illustrates is that countries running a current account surplus have plenty of possibilities for the private sector to achieve a positive net lending position. This was the case of several Asian countries before the Global Financial Crisis. The room to do so is necessarily reduced if fiscal deficits cannot be any larger than 3 per cent, as was the case with the Maastricht Treaty. The figure also shows that this room becomes really small – it gets reduced to the triangle shown in the figure – for countries that happen to have current account deficits, while simultaneously being constrained to fit the 3 per cent Maastricht rule on fiscal deficits.

7.1.3   A Transaction Initiated by the Banking Sector

We first deal with a transaction initiated by the banking sector. The purpose of this example is to show that such transactions have no impact on the net financial account balance, as far as the transaction is concerned. Thus let us assume that some American bank, say CityBank, decides that it would be a good idea to lend American dollars to a Mexican bank, say Banamex. The account of Banamex at CityBank is called a nostro account for Banamex, while it is a loro-account for CityBank. The loro-account is thus part of CityBank's foreign liabilities, while the nostro account of Banamex is part of its foreign assets. The impact on balance sheets of this operation is shown in row 1 of Table 7.2. We may then presume that Banamex agrees to take in the loan because it knows that some Mexican residents would like to borrow US dollars. The newly created dollars are now held by the Mexican residents. This is shown in row 2.

So far, there has been no impact on the net financial account balance. There has been an increase in the 'other investment' component of the incurrence of liabilities (KIF), but this has been compensated by an increase in the 'other investment' component of the acquisition of financial assets (KOF). If the Mexican residents decide to buy shares on the US stock market, the financial account balance still remains at zero, as the increase in other investment liabilities of the Mexican bank will now be compensated by an increase in the 'portfolio investment' component of the acquisition of financial assets. The Mexican residents may also decide to import US goods with their US dollars, in which case the current account balance will be negative ($CAB < 0$) while the financial account balance will become positive ($FAB > 0$), the impact on balance sheets being shown in row 3 (assuming the exporter's bank is the correspondent bank of Banamex). Clearly, there is no downward pressure on the peso, since the increase in net liabilities of the Mexican economy has fully accommodated the increase in imports.

The above, and Table 7.2, may help to explain why it is difficult to find a link between the 'fundamentals', such as the current account balance, and the evolution of the exchange rate. Besides the role played by expectations, we see that current account deficits are not necessarily associated with downward pressures on the domestic currency, depending on how and in what currency it is financed.

A fair question to ask is whether the principle of endogenous money still holds. Some economists would say that it does not, in that it could be argued that the funds lent by CityBank to Banamex have allowed it to make a loan to its Mexican client. Another

Table 7.2 *US bank lends US dollars to Mexican bank, which lends it back to Mexican resident, who ends up importing US goods*

	CityBank		Banamex	
	Assets	Liabilities	Assets	Liabilities
1	Loan to Banamex +$100	Loro-deposit of Banamex +$100	Nostro-deposit at CityBank + $100	Funds borrowed from CityBank +$100
2	Loan to Banamex + $100	Deposit of Mexican resident +$100	Loan to Mexican resident +$100	Funds borrowed from CityBank +$100
3	Loan to Banamex +$100	Deposit of US exporter +$100	Loan to Mexican resident +$100	Funds borrowed from CityBank +$100
4		Loro deposit of Banamex −$100	Nostro deposit at CityBank −$100	
		Deposit of US exporter + $100	Loan to Mexican resident +$100	

perspective is to argue that Banamex could have made the loan to its client before, without having to borrow funds from CityBank. It could have made the loan in pesos, in which case the Mexican importing firm would have had to ask its bank to purchase US dollars, thus putting downward pressure on the peso, however. Thus the principle of endogenous money still holds. The only thing we can say is that the lending operation initiated by CityBank facilitates things for Banamex. But everything in the end (meaning row 3), would have been the same if the Mexican importers had come first to their bank, asking and getting a loan in US dollars, while Banamex would get the funds by borrowing them from CityBank. An alternative is also shown in row 4, which assumes that Banamex already had some deposits in US dollars at CityBank, drawing down these to provide the funds to the importer, who then pays the exporter. In this case, Mexico does not have an increase in its other investment liabilities, but it has a decrease in its other investment acquisition of assets. Some authors, such as Castillo-Palermo and Schmidt (2019), would then argue that the need for domestic banks of peripherical countries to acquire foreign currency puts pressure on the domestic interest rate.

7.1.4 A Foreign Exchange Transaction Initiated by a Client

What happens when the importer or some investor wishes to have foreign currency? Large transactions occur through bank accounts, possibly with the help of brokers. Figure 7.2 shows schematically what happens. Suppose Bank C, located in Canada, initiates a foreign exchange transaction and wishes to obtain yens for its clients, in exchange for Canadian dollars which are being purchased by Bank J, located in Japan. Bank C will transfer dollar funds to the correspondent bank of Bank J in Canada – J's nostro bank. This will

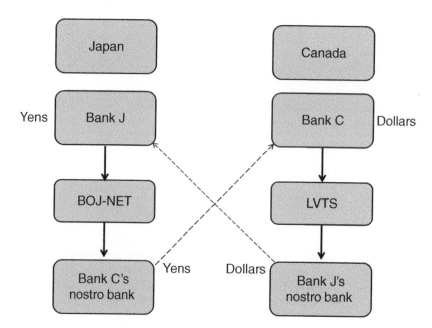

Figure 7.2   Bank C in Canada buys yens from and sells dollars to Bank J in Japan

Table 7.3 Bank C in Canada buys yens from and sells dollars to Bank J in Japan

	Bank C		Bank J's nostro bank	
	Assets	Liabilities	Assets	Liabilities
1	Nostro deposits in yens ≈ +$100 Settlement balances −$100		Settlement balances + $100	Loro deposits of Bank J +$100
2	Settlement balances −$100	Deposits of client −$100	Settlement balances + $100	Loro deposits of Bank J +$100

be done through the large-value transfer system in Canada, called the LVTS, which is the Canadian equivalent of the US Fedwire or CHIPS. Thus, Bank J will now be credited with the dollars on its nostro account at its correspondent bank. Simultaneously, Bank C will be credited with yens on its nostro account with its correspondent bank in Japan. Thus Bank C is credited with yens, but it is debited with dollars in the LVTS, as shown in row 1 of Table 7.3. Bank C is covered against exchange risk since its clients will now obtain the yens while they will see their dollar account being debited, as shown in row 2.

The situation of Bank J is more ambiguous. If Bank J does not have clients that wish to purchase dollars, it might decide to keep the dollars, in which case it has an open position since it owes more funds to the Japanese clearing house BOJ-NET, while it holds more assets denominated in Canadian dollars. Otherwise Bank J will try to get rid of its dollars, thus starting a cascade of foreign exchange transactions, pushing up the yen and pulling down the dollar. If the Bank of Japan does not like to see the yen going up, it will intervene, purchasing the dollars from Bank J or other banks, and thus crediting with yens the account of the Japanese bank or that of the correspondent bank of the foreign bank selling the Canadian dollars. The Japanese central bank thus acquires foreign currency while the settlement balances or reserves of the Japanese banking system rise. We shall see what happens under such a regime of managed float or of fixed exchange rate in the next section.

In the meantime, we can say that the intervention of commercial banks on the foreign exchange market does not lead as such to any change in the financial account balance of a country. Their liabilities and assets rise simultaneously. Only transactions initiated by non-financial agents will have an impact on the net foreign assets of banks. Thus it is the decisions of the non-financial agents to hold assets in the domestic or foreign currencies that generate changes in the net foreign assets of banks. This is the accommodating item in the balance of payments (Bakker, 1993; Chaundy, 1999).

7.2 THE COMPENSATION THESIS IN FIXED EXCHANGE RATE REGIMES

We start by considering how the concept of endogenous money – a demand-led supply of money – is being extended to the open economy. Historically, this extension is known as the 'compensation' thesis. The compensation approach is the open-economy version of the 'reflux' principle, put forth by Thomas Tooke and the Banking School, as it applies to the central bank. The compensation thesis states that fluctuations in the foreign reserves of a central bank will be compensated by opposite movements in other elements of its balance sheet. This is particularly important in the case of fixed exchange rate regimes or in the case of a managed float.

7.2.1 A Critique of the Mainstream View

Fiscal policy in a Mundell–Fleming model revisited by post-Keynesians
To help highlight the post-Keynesian view on monetary economics in an open economy, it is perhaps useful to briefly recall the textbook mainstream view. The workhorse of neoclassical economics when it comes to short-run open-economy macroeconomics, both in textbooks and in policy advice, is the Mundell–Fleming IS/LM/BP model. Modern reincarnations of this model yield similar results. Briefly, the model says that, in the case of flexible exchange rates, monetary policy is effective while fiscal policy is ineffective or weakly effective, because, for instance, an expansionary fiscal policy is likely to lead to higher interest rates, which will cause an appreciation of the domestic currency, thus reducing both investment and net exports and counteracting expansionary fiscal policy. We can quickly dismiss this claim. Within a post-Keynesian open-economy model, an expansionary fiscal policy does indeed stimulate economic activity. As Bougrine and Seccareccia (2004, p. 666) point out, this is because 'there is no reason why, in a Post Keynesian endogenous money world, there ought to be any accompanying upward pressure on interest rates that would supposedly "crowd out" other components of aggregate spending'. An expansionary fiscal policy thus does not lead to higher interest rates and an appreciation of the domestic currency. This is confirmed by the stock–flow consistent analysis of Godley and Lavoie (2005–06), who show instead that higher government expenditures lead to a depreciation of the domestic currency, because of the induced trade deficit caused by the higher level of economic activity, while the central bank can continue to peg interest rates at a constant level. Thus, from a post-Keynesian standpoint, the stimulating effects of an expansionary fiscal policy are reinforced by a floating exchange rate regime, since the consequent depreciation of the domestic currency ought to further stimulate exports and aggregate demand. Thus, in opposition to the standard Mundell–Fleming view, within a flexible exchange rate regime, 'fiscal policy would probably be an even more effective tool at the disposal of policy-makers' (Bougrine and Seccareccia, 2004, p. 666).

This claim is illustrated with the help of Figure 7.3, with the standard *IS*, *LM* and *BP* curves representing balance in the money market, internal balance for goods and the external balance. The *LM* curve is flat, since the central bank sets and pegs the interest rate. The expansionary fiscal policy is shown by a move from IS_0 to IS_1, with GDP moving from q_0 to q_1. At the constant rate of interest and with the level of output corresponding to the internal equilibrium, the economy is below the *BP* curve and hence the balance of payments will be in deficit (this can continue only so long as the central bank has enough foreign exchange reserves). The floating exchange rate regime makes the domestic currency depreciate, which leads to a downward shift of the *BP* curve towards BP_2 and a rightward shift of the *IS* curve towards IS_2 due to higher exports. In the end, the expansionary fiscal policy pushes GDP all the way to q_2. Had the country been in a fixed exchange rate regime, GDP would have remained at q_1 and the balance of payments would remain in a deficit position. This argument thus provides some further

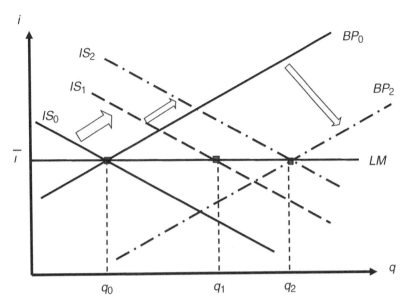

Figure 7.3 Expansionary fiscal policy with flexible exchange rates within a post-Keynesian interpretation of the Mundell–Fleming model

ammunition to MMT advocates who contend that functional finance should rely on floating exchange rates, as we shall note later.

Monetary policy in a Mundell–Fleming model revisited by post-Keynesians
Within the Mundell–Fleming model, with fixed exchange rates, monetary policy is said to be ineffective while fiscal policy is effective, meaning that only fiscal policy can achieve its goal of lower or higher output. In the case of monetary policy, it is said, for instance, that a deflationary monetary policy, with higher interest rates, will be counterproductive because the higher interest rates will lead to net financial inflows, which will increase the foreign reserves of the central bank, thus leading to an increase in high-powered money and in the money supply, bringing back interest rates to their starting level. From the mainstream point of view, the supply of money and of high-powered money is endogenous, being driven by the fluctuations in the foreign exchange reserves of the central bank. But this endogeneity is quite different from that underlined by post-Keynesians. In the Mundell–Fleming case, it is a supply-led endogeneity, whereas for post-Keynesians the endogenous supply of money is demand-led.

The mechanism described by Mundell and his followers in the case of the fixed exchange rate is an indirect version of the old 'price-specie flow' mechanism, associated with a gold standard. Indeed, this mechanism corresponds to the 'rules of the game'. As Ethier (1988, p. 341) describes them, 'a balance of payments deficit should be fully reflected in a reduction in the supply of money, and a surplus should be fully reflected in an increased money supply'. The purpose of the rules of the game is to mimic the effects of gold flows, eventually through an 'income–specie flow mechanism', as Mundell (1961a, p. 159) calls it. While more sophisticated open-economy models have since been discussed in the literature, such as the portfolio approach, the positive link between balance-of-payments surpluses and increases in the monetary base and the money supply is held by all to be an adequate representation of this portion of the story.

The standard view about fixed exchange rates has been put in a nutshell by Obstfeld and Rogoff (1995, p. 75): 'The key lesson is that a government that fixes its currency's exchange rate loses control of the domestic money supply.' This is the theory. In practice, Obstfeld and Rogoff continue, 'central banks often try to influence the exchange rate without fully committing monetary policy by using *sterilized* exchange market intervention'. Sterilization, as usually understood, means that the increase (decrease) in the stock of base money arising from a purchase (sale) of foreign currency could be undone by a sale (purchase) of government securities by the central bank. But Obstfeld and Rogoff (ibid., p. 76) conclude nevertheless that 'for all the fanfare and attention they sometimes receive, sterilized intervention operations are largely smoke and mirrors . . . Sterilized interventions can do little, if anything, to break the tight link between monetary policy and exchange rate.' This has led Obstfeld et al. (2005) to put forth the so-called trilemma or impossible trinity, according to which countries can have only two of the following three features: monetary independence, control over exchange rates and financial integration (free capital mobility).

Such statements confuse 'perfect capital mobility' with 'perfect asset substitutability'. Capital mobility refers to whether or not there are restrictions on capital flows. It may be that capital is perfectly mobile, while asset-holders do not consider assets to be perfectly substitutable. In this case, rates of return need not be equal, as we argued in Chapter 4, so that portfolio decisions correspond to an open-economy variant of equation (4.3) rather than to that of equation (4.2). This implies that domestic interest rates need not be equal to world rates, and that uncovered interest parity need not hold. This is why the *BP* curve in Figure 7.3 is not drawn as a flat curve, in contrast to what is often assumed in standard representations of the Mundell–Fleming model. Thus, in the case of perfect capital mobility accompanied by imperfect asset substitutability, sterilized interventions are possible and will have some effect. But the mainstream view remains that 'the effects on exchange rates of sterilized market interventions are both weak and short-lived' (McCallum, 1996, p. 138). Such statements sound strange in view of the evidence that has been accumulating in the 2000s regarding the ability of several countries to maintain managed exchange rates while sterilizing enormous amounts of newly acquired foreign exchange reserves (Aizenman and Glick, 2009).

The post-Keynesian view of the mechanics of an open economy is different from that of the Mundell–Fleming model for essentially two reasons. First, Mundell (1963) assumes perfect capital mobility and perfect asset substitutability, whereas post-Keynesians assume only the former, so that capital flows generated by differing rates of return cannot go on forever. Second, Mundell (1963) and Fleming (1962), along with their textbook representations, assume that monetary policy is best represented by purchases and sales of securities on the open market, whereas, as clarified in Chapter 4, post-Keynesians assume that interest rate targeting best represents monetary policy. It is interesting to note that this second distinction was recognized by earlier Keynesian authors, such as James Meade. As Allen and Kenen (1980, p. 8), point out, 'Meade instructs the central bank to maintain a constant interest rate; the bank's open market operations offset changes in the supply of money caused by movements of reserves and offset changes in the demand for money caused by the movements in domestic income.' As a matter of fact, Fleming

(1962, p. 370), who is associated with Mundell as the founder of the standard IS/LM/BP model, recognizes that 'the only clear-cut alternative would appear to be that of defining constancy of monetary policy as the maintenance of a constant rate of interest', giving Mundell (1961b) as an example of this choice. It must be pointed out that Mundell (1961a), whose other works are often invoked to justify the relevance of the 'rules of the game' in textbooks and the IS/LM/BP model, was himself aware that the automaticity of the rules of the game relied on a particular behaviour of the central bank. Indeed, he lamented the fact that modern central banks were following the 'banking principle' instead of the 'bullionist principle', and hence adjusting 'the domestic supply of notes to accord with the needs of trade' (1961a, p. 153), which is another way of saying that the money supply was endogenous to its demand and that central banks were concerned with maintaining the targeted interest rates. This was in 1961!

We may once more offer a post-Keynesian interpretation of the Mundell–Fleming model, dealing this time with an expansionary monetary policy, as illustrated in Figure 7.4. Such a monetary policy will be reflected by the central bank pegging a lower interest rate, and hence by a downward shift of the flat LM curve. GDP as a result will move from q_0 to q_1 and the economy will find itself at an internal equilibrium that is below the BP curve, thus inducing a deficit of the balance of payments and downward pressures on the domestic currency. By contrast with the standard story, the loss of reserves in a post-Keynesian fixed exchange rate model will not drive the LM curve back to its starting position and will not imply a return to the initial higher interest rate. This is because the change in foreign reserves will be either sterilized or automatically compensated, as we shall see. The economy will thus remain at q_1 when the economy is in a fixed exchange rate regime (as long as there are reserves left). In the case of the flexible exchange rate regime, the positive

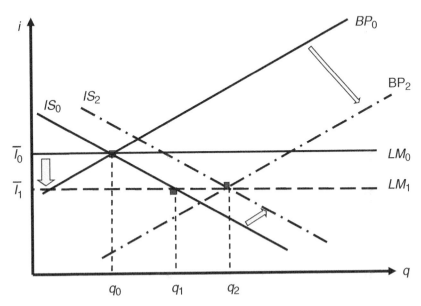

Figure 7.4 Expansionary monetary policy within a post-Keynesian interpretation of the Mundell–Fleming model

effects of the lower interest rates will be enhanced, as is usually pointed out by central banks when explaining their monetary transmission mechanism, and hence both the *IS* and *BP* curves will shift rightwards, eventually bringing GDP to q_2. Godley and Lavoie (2005–06), however, show that this additional impact is likely to be temporary.

7.2.2 The Balance Sheet of Central Banks

The Mundell–Fleming and the post-Keynesian stories can be more easily understood and distinguished if one examines the balance sheet of a central bank. Table 7.4 illustrates this balance sheet as usually found in textbooks, while Table 7.5 describes a more realistic balance sheet.

With the balance sheet of Table 7.4, since bank reserves plus currency in circulation equate the monetary base, there has to be a one-to-one relation between the size of the assets of the central bank and the monetary base (currency plus bank reserves), unless sterilization, initiated by open-market operations over domestic government securities, compensates for the movements in foreign reserves. Table 7.4 can be said to be the illustration of an 'asset-based' financial system, where banks can extend their activity and acquire reserves at the central bank by selling to it financial assets – government securities. While this may represent, to some extent, the characteristics of Anglo-Saxon monetary systems, it certainly oversimplifies the majority of monetary systems found in the world. It thus yields a misleading interpretation of the functioning of most monetary systems. The correct balance sheet of most central banks looks more like the one shown in Table 7.5.

On the asset side, claims on domestic private banks are the crucial addition. In most monetary systems, central banks provide advances to private banks. This was the case of nearly all European banking systems until the eurozone crisis, as well as those in Mexico, China and Korea (Lavoie, 2001). These commercial banks are structurally in debt *vis-à-vis* the central bank, and will thus attempt to reduce this debt whenever they can. These monetary systems are 'overdraft' systems, as explained in Chapter 4, because private banks can make use of a kind of overdraft by pulling on a line of credit at the central

Table 7.4 Textbook balance sheet of central banks

Assets	Liabilities
Foreign reserves	Currency in circulation
Domestic government securities	Bank reserves

Table 7.5 A more realistic balance sheet of the central bank

Assets	Liabilities
Foreign reserves (claims on non-residents)	Currency in circulation
Domestic government securities	Bank reserves
Claims on domestic banks	Government deposits
	Central bank bonds
	Equity capital (own funds)

bank, provided they show appropriate collateral. On the liability side of the central bank balance sheet, three additional items have been included. Besides the equity capital of the central bank, there are central bank bonds and government deposits. As also pointed out in Chapter 4, a central bank can move government deposits around, as it wishes, between its own central bank account and the accounts that government agencies hold at the various private banks. In addition, in several (developing) countries, central banks issue their own securities, called central bank bills or central bank bonds, since domestic financial markets often perceive these securities as carrying less risk than government securities.

An increase in foreign reserves can thus be sterilized – compensated – in at least three additional ways: there can be a reduction in advances to domestic banks or in claims on the central government; or there can be an increase in government deposits at the central bank and in the outstanding amount of securities issued by the central bank. The additional entries in the central bank balance sheet disrupt the straightforward relation between the size of the assets of the central bank and the monetary base. The main argument of the compensation approach is that, in the external surplus case, when commercial banks wind up with additional reserves, having sold their newly acquired stocks of foreign currency to their central bank, they will do their best to get rid of these additional reserves. Because banks do not wait for extra reserves to make new loans to creditworthy borrowers, they have already granted all the loans that they could make to creditworthy borrowers when foreign currency piles up in their accounts. Hence the banks will usually comply in getting rid of these excess reserves, either by reducing the advances that they have taken from the central bank or by purchasing risk-free assets, such as government securities or central bank bonds, since there will be an opportunity cost in holding reserves at zero or low interest rates.

In countries where the overnight rate is clearly under the control of the central bank, the central bank will initiate the sterilization process, for instance by transferring government deposits or through repo operations, removing the excess liquidity through the clearing and settlement system. In one of its background papers, the Bank of Canada (2004) explains that, when it conducts exchange rate operations to slow down the appreciation of the dollar, thus selling Canadian dollars on the exchange markets and acquiring foreign currency, 'to prevent downward pressure on Canadian interest rates . . . the same amount of Canadian-dollar balances are withdrawn from the financial system'. This is done by removing government deposits at commercial banks and re-depositing them on the books of the central bank. Thus sterilization is not a matter of choice; it is a necessity as long as the central bank wants to keep the interest rate at its target level. Indeed, as Craig and Humpage (2001, p. 1) point out, 'When a country's central bank maintains an unchanged interbank rate as the intermediate operating target for its monetary policy, it automatically offsets (or sterilizes) the impact of any exchange-market intervention on its monetary base.'

Extreme historical instances of compensation
Tables 7.6 and 7.7 present extreme instances of the compensation mechanism. The first example is that of the German Bundesbank, when the European Monetary System was under attack in September 1992 and August 1993. The financial markets and their speculators were expecting major realignments of the European currencies, and believed that

510   Post-Keynesian economics

Table 7.6 *The compensation effect at work at the Bundesbank, in billions of Deutschmarks*

	31 August 1992	30 September 1992	15 July 1993	7 August 1993
Foreign reserves	104	181	108	160
Domestic credit	237	144	236	174
Assets total	341	325	344	334

Source: Claassen (1996, p. 57).

Table 7.7 *Sterilization through government deposits by the Bank of Canada, in billions of Canadian dollars*

	1995	1996
Assets	50.9	59.2
Foreign assets	20.8	28.2
Claims on central government	30.1	31.0
Liabilities	50.9	59.2
Monetary base	32.1	33.4
Government deposits	17.8	25.0
Other items	1.0	0.8

Source: Lavoie (2001).

the Deutschmark would be revaluated upwards compared to the other main European currencies. Although there were substantial changes in the composition of the balance sheet of the Bundesbank before and after each of the two crises, its overall size hardly changed, as can be ascertained from Table 7.6. Since the German financial system is of the overdraft type, the change in domestic credit essentially reflects the change in advances to German banks. As a consequence of financial inflows, the commercial banks became loaded with excess reserves that they did not wish to hold, and as a result did not renew the loans that they had previously contracted to fulfil their compulsory reserve requirements and to acquire the banknotes (issued by the central bank) demanded by their customers.

The second example comes from an asset-based financial system and is provided by the Bank of Canada before it decided to have a pure floating exchange rate. Between 1995 and 1996, there was a large increase in the foreign reserves held by the Bank of Canada. In the mainstream story, this should have led to a large increase in the monetary base, unless the central bank pursued an active sterilization policy by selling government securities in the open market. The figures in Table 7.7 show, however, that there has not been any decrease in the claims on government. The Bank of Canada did not sell any of the government securities that it held. Instead, it moved a large amount of government deposits held at chartered banks, shifting them to its own account at the central bank, thus sterilizing the increase in foreign reserves. As a result, the amount of high-powered money (the monetary base) hardly increased (it did so by one billion dollars), despite the large change in official reserves and in the size of the central bank balance sheet (about eight billion dollars extra).

This is fully consistent with Tables 4.20 and 4.21, which underlined that the transfer of government deposits towards the central bank reduces the reserves available to the banking system, and that the central bank needs to neutralize the impact of autonomous flows on clearing balances if it wishes to achieve its target overnight rate in a corridor system.

Kaldor (1980, p. 309) and Marselli (1993) were the first authors to provide some econometric evidence in support of the principle of compensation. More recently, Stefan Angrick (2018) has provided concrete examples of the compensation thesis through an econometric analysis of five East Asian economies, finding that sterilization or compensation is the norm rather than the exception. Lavoie and Wang (2012) and Li et al. (2021) both found a tight relationship between Chinese foreign reserves and the amount of central bank securities, while there is no such relationship between foreign reserves and the monetary base.

7.2.3 The Compensation Thesis in Retrospect

The compensation thesis has a long tradition, despite being ignored in textbooks. It is valid in the current environment, where central banks target interest rates, as well as in the gold standard period. The compensation thesis is also sometimes called the 'Banque de France view' because in its modern incarnation it was endorsed by Pierre Berger, who was the general director of research at the Banque de France. Berger (1972a, p. 94; 1972b, p. 171) observed that peaks in the gold reserves of the Banque de France were accompanied by troughs in credits to the domestic economy, as was already the case in the nineteenth century. Despite the wide fluctuations in gold reserves, variations in the monetary base and the money supply were quite limited.

This analysis is confirmed by studies on the gold standard period, between 1880–1913 and 1922–38. Bloomfield (1959, p. 49) shows that, when looking at year-to-year changes in the period before the First World War – the heyday of the gold standard – the foreign assets and the domestic assets of central banks moved in opposite directions 60 per cent of the time. Foreign assets and domestic assets moved in the same direction only 34 per cent of the time for the 11 central banks under consideration. The prevalence of a negative correlation thus shows that the so-called rules of the game were violated more often than not, even during the heyday of the gold standard. Indeed, 'in the case of *every* central bank the year-to-year changes in international and domestic assets were more often in the *opposite* than in the same direction' (Bloomfield, 1959, pp. 49–50). Godley and Lavoie (2007a, ch. 6) provide a stock–flow consistent model of a fixed exchange rate regime, where foreign reserves are held in gold, and where indeed the central bank retains control of the interest rate, despite fluctuations in gold reserves at the central bank, through countervailing changes in its claims on the domestic economy.

Almost identical results were obtained in the case of the 1922–38 period. Ragnar Nurkse (1944, p. 69) shows that the foreign assets and the domestic assets of 26 central banks moved in opposite directions in 60 per cent of the years under consideration, and that they moved in the same direction only 32 per cent of the time. Studying the various episodes of inflows or outflows of gold and exchange reserves, Nurkse (ibid., p. 88) concludes that 'neutralization was the rule rather than the exception'. Without saying so, Nurkse adopts the compensation principle as the phenomenon ruling central banks in an open economy. The rules of the game as they were to be endorsed in the modern IS/LM/BP models of Mundell are an erroneous depiction of reality.

> There is nothing automatic about the mechanism envisaged in the 'rules of the game'. We have seen that automatic forces, on the contrary, may make for neutralization. Accordingly, if central banks were to intensify the effect of changes in their international assets instead of offsetting them or allowing them to be offset by inverse changes in their domestic assets, this would require not only deliberate management but possibly even management in opposition to automatic tendencies. (Ibid.)

Nurkse's account of the negative correlation between foreign and domestic assets of central banks in various dramatic instances is particularly interesting because he rejects the standard interpretation in terms of a 'sterilization' operation initiated by the central bank. Nurkse considers that it would be 'quite wrong to interpret [the inverse correlation] as a deliberate act of neutralization' on the part of the central bank. To the contrary, Nurkse considers that the neutralization of shifts in foreign reserves is caused by 'normal' or 'automatic' factors, and that the compensation principle operates both in the overdraft financial systems and in the asset-based ones. In the overdraft system, Nurkse (ibid., p. 70) notes that 'an inflow of gold, for instance, tends to result in increased liquidity on the domestic money market, which in turn may naturally lead the market to repay some of its indebtedness to the central bank', a fact also noted by Gyöngyössy (1984, p. 132).

But Nurkse also observed compensating phenomena that were consistent with the operation of an asset-based financial system. In the case of an inflow of gold and foreign exchange, foreign investors (or the banks where their deposits would be held) would purchase new government securities. This would allow government to reduce its debt to the central bank, as would be the case in an open-market operation. However, as Nurkse (1944, p. 77) points out, in contrast to the usual open-market operation, the manoeuvre 'did not come about at the Bank's initiative'. Alternatively, as Nurkse (ibid., p. 76) points out, gold inflows could also be neutralized by an increase in government deposits held at the central bank, as the Bank of Canada does nowadays.

Nurkse's analysis can easily be extended to the current context, with central banks setting high interest rates to attract foreign capital and achieve a balance-of-payments surplus. Suppose foreigners borrowed funds at home at low interest rates and sold their foreign currency to acquire Brazilian money deposits. They now need to purchase Brazilian Treasury bills to take advantage of the high interest rates (the 'carry trade', as it is known). If they acquire these bills directly from the Brazilian central bank, the increase in the foreign reserves of the central bank is fully compensated by the decline in the credits granted to government; that is, sterilization is automatic and at the initiative of the foreign investors. The Brazilian government may also decide to issue new securities and sell them directly to the foreign investors, in which case the money deposits of the latter would now be held by the government. Once again, compensation is complete provided the newly held bank deposits are shifted to the government's account at the Brazilian central bank. A third possibility is for the foreign investors to purchase the securities from the bank at which they have deposited the proceeds of their foreign exchange transactions, in which case the bank is left with excess reserves that it can remove by purchasing securities from the government or the central bank.

Finally, it should be mentioned that Keynes (1930b, p. 230) was also keenly aware of the compensation phenomenon. He points out that year after year the Bank of England would gain huge amounts of gold in the spring and lose a similar amount in the autumn. This should have caused concern to all, but it did not, because these inflows and outflows were compensated by corresponding seasonal outflows and inflows arising from the Treasury. In the spring, with the receipts of income tax, the Treasury would buy back its securities from the public and from the Bank of England, thus reducing the domestic credit entry in the balance sheet of the Bank of England.

7.2.4 Limitations to the Compensation Thesis

It is often argued that sterilization cannot occur on a long-term basis. In other words, there are limits to sterilization. This implies that there are limits to the compensation principle, or so it would seem. Most analysts make no distinction between a balance-of-payments surplus and a deficit position. It is understandable that an economy in an external deficit position and a fixed exchange regime will eventually run out of official reserves, or will need to borrow them. Clearly this process cannot go on forever. But as long as the central bank under attack has foreign reserves left, or the creditworthiness to borrow them, it can compensate for their loss. Although the external deficit position can last for a long time if foreign reserves are substantial and the deficit is meagre, it will not be sustainable forever, and hence, at some point, something will need to break: the currency will be devalued, interest rates will be pushed up, the government will have expenditure cut-backs, or quotas or financial controls will need to be imposed.

By contrast, it is hard to see what limits there are when an economy is in an external surplus position. Why should there be any limits to the amount of foreign reserves held by the central bank of an economy with a recurrent balance-of-payments surplus (Keynes, 1973, xxv, p. 29)? Is there any such limit in the case of the Chinese economy, which piled up huge surpluses for over a decade?

Some authors argue that sterilization in countries with external surpluses cannot go on forever because rates of interest on the liabilities of the central bank are bound to be higher than rates of interest on US Treasury bills; this, it is argued, would lead to operating losses (or opportunity costs) to the sterilizing central bank (Aizenman and Glick, 2009). For instance, in the context of Latin American countries, Frenkel (2006, p. 587) writes that sterilization operations 'consist in the selling of public-sector or central bank papers with the objective of money absorption. They imply a financial cost to the treasury or the central bank, proportional to the difference between the interest rate of those papers and the interest rate earned by the central bank's international reserves'. This argument certainly does not apply to countries such as China, where interest rates are administered, and can be set at levels lower than in the USA or Europe, notwithstanding the extraordinary low interest rates prevailing in the USA since 2008 and in the eurozone since 2014. In a later paper, Frenkel (2007) reconsiders this issue, and recognizes that sterilization of excess foreign currency can be sustainable under some conditions even if home interest rates are higher than the rate of return obtained on foreign reserves. He also rejects the impossible trinity when countries are running external surpluses. Indeed, there is now a realization among post-Keynesians that the concept of the trilemma needs to be rejected (Serrano and Summa, 2015; Angrick, 2018; Cömert, 2019).

What happens when there is a balance-of-payments surplus? This situation can arise for at least four reasons. There may be a financial crisis abroad, and the domestic currency is considered to be safe, thus inducing substantial capital inflows. Second, exports may be strong, and exporters receive large amounts of foreign currencies compared to the amounts required by importers. Third, foreign investors may find domestic interest rates high and attractive, as discussed in the previous subsection. Finally, it may be that domestic firms consider domestic interest rates to be too high, as would be the case when domestic monetary policy is highly restrictive; these domestic firms would then borrow funds from foreign markets, at lower interest rates, while accepting the risk that the domestic currency could depreciate in the future, before the debt can be reimbursed.

This fourth case is somewhat different from the first three, because the compensation principle does not play a role. The financial account surplus is induced by the attempt of the central bank to slow down the economy. What we have here is a typical instance of structural endogenous money. The central bank sets high interest rates in an attempt to slow down the growth rates of credit, money, output and prices. Banks try to evade the restrictions by inducing their customers to borrow abroad, from their correspondents, at the lower world rates, as happened for instance in the case of emerging European countries (Radonjić and Kokotović, 2014). Whether the exchange rate is fixed or not is irrelevant. The same would occur in a world of flexible exchange rates. Banks and their customers would still attempt to avoid the constraining monetary policy. In any case, even if there exists this endogenous inflow of foreign capital, it is not certain that it will lead to an increase in the monetary base and the money supply. Firms may prefer to borrow in other currencies on the euro-markets to take advantage of the low rates of interest. But they may use the proceeds to repay their indebtedness *vis-à-vis* domestic banks, 'so that neither money supply nor effective demand for goods and services increase' (Coulbois and Prissert, 1974, p. 303).

Reverting now to the case where a currency is under attack, the domestic central bank may in fact take measures that run counter to the endogenous compensation principle. The central bank may then pursue a deliberately restrictive monetary policy, pushing up overnight rates of interest, not so much to induce incoming capital flows as to increase the cost of outgoing capital transfers (Coulbois, 1982, p. 200). The increase in the rate of interest is not the endogenous result of the capital outflow. Rather, it is an economic and political decision of the central bankers. The central bank has a choice. By hiking up rates of interest, the central bank wishes to increase the opportunity cost of borrowing domestic funds to purchase foreign funds, thus increasing the cost of speculation against the domestic currency. Speculation may become unrewarding. It is clear, however, that such an interest rate policy needs to be drastic: a 1 per cent change in the exchange rate within a month will be sufficient to cover a 12 per cent interest rate differential. Clearly, capital controls or penal taxes on short-term capital flows are a better alternative.

It has been argued by some critics of the compensation approach that as soon as exporters receive their foreign currency, the money supply increases, even though banks wipe out their excess reserves, since the currency from abroad will be transformed immediately into deposits in local currency. But such a claim is misleading. The reflux principle applies equally well to foreign and to domestic receipts. Exporters, who now get paid for their exports, previously incurred expenditures when producing these export goods, and probably had to borrow to do so. As a result, when they transform their foreign receipts into domestic deposits, these deposits are utilized to pay back their debt *vis-à-vis* the banks. This was underlined by Le Bourva (1992, pp. 462–3):

> Moreover, notice that an initial compensation occurs in the accounts of productive businesses before doing so in those of financial establishments. If the businesses obtain the funds needed for the payments of their means of production by foreign and not domestic sales, they present foreign currencies instead of regular bills of exchange to their bankers.

As a result, one can say that the compensation principle occurs at two levels: at the junction between the public and the banks, and at the junction between the banks and the central bank. Thus, as rightly noted by Arestis and Eichner (1988, p. 1004), 'any money creation emanating from fiscal or debt management operations initiated by the authorities or from a favourable balance of payments, can be neutralized through an equivalent reduction in commercial bank credit brought about by the actions of private economic agents'.

In any case, most economies operate with growing figures. In general, a balance-of-payments surplus, through the compensation principle, will diminish the rate of growth of the debt owed by the banks to the central bank, or it will diminish the needs of banks to sell government securities to acquire their growing requirements in high-powered money. Thus, while a negative correlation between foreign and domestic assets of central banks disproves the operation of the rules of the game, a positive correlation does not disprove the operation of a compensation mechanism.

Finally, we should consider the remarks of Taylor (2008, p. 660) regarding full compensation as it arose in two-country stock-flow consistent models when he commented on the book of Godley and Lavoie (2007a). On the basis of his knowledge of emerging economies, Taylor doubted that financial inflows would have no or little effect on these economies. The discrepancy between actual experience and the results of the model can be explained in the following way. Most open-economy SFC models dealt with only one type of security per country. When there are two sorts of securities, it may well be that the central bank is able to control the short-term rate of interest through compensation or sterilization, but in all likelihood the long-term rate of interest will be left as an endogenous variable. This is indeed what happens in one of the two-country SFC models of Godley (1999b), where the long-term interest rate falls, as long as a country enjoys a balance-of-payment surplus, unless fiscal policy becomes more expansionary. The falling long-term rate of interest may generate greater economic activity, thus reconciling the model with actual experience, and hence underlining a limit to the compensation thesis.

7.2.5 A Special Fixed Exchange Rate Regime: The Currency Board

There is a special fixed exchange rate regime – the currency board regime – which is often said to behave according to the rules of the game. Is this really the case? The argument here is that the currency board also functions in line with the compensation thesis.

Currency boards were first set up in colonial times, in the first half of the nineteenth century, when Britain wished to reduce the costs and inconvenience generated by the use of its currency by the far-away colonies of its huge empire. Currency boards were highly popular until the end of the Second World War, at which stage they went out of fashion, being a symbol of outmoded colonialism, and were replaced by standard central banks. Except for Hong Kong and Singapore, currency boards virtually disappeared until 1991, when Argentina adopted a currency board monetary arrangement, which was then imitated by a few other countries, such as Bulgaria, North Macedonia and Lithuania. As we all know, the Argentine experiment, after a string of relatively successful years, came to a disastrous and chaotic end in 2002.

Currency boards have been proposed as a quick-fix solution to the recurrent problems of various countries to maintain price and exchange rate stability, in particular in South America and in Eastern Europe, especially in Russia. The currency board promises to supply or redeem bank reserves and domestic cash against a foreign currency without restrictions, at a fixed exchange rate. Currency boards are said to provide credibility to a currency, since, at least in theory, the issue of currency in a currency board regime is limited by the availability of foreign reserves, since sterilization is forbidden. In other words, domestic currency is entirely backed by foreign reserves. 'Pure' currency boards hold a single type of asset – foreign reserves, gold or foreign currencies such as the American dollar or the euro. They provide no domestic credit. Currency boards, in contrast to central banks, make no advances to the domestic private sector; nor do they hold domestic government assets. The asset side of the balance sheet of the currency board is strictly limited to official foreign reserves. Any increase in the stock of high-powered money must be accompanied by an influx of foreign reserves; that is, the country must run a favourable balance of payments ($BP > 0$).

Currency boards, according to its proponents, are thus the means to restore the automatic adjustment mechanisms that neoclassical economists have been longing for. The currency board is said to restore the rules of the game that ought to regulate any properly designed open financial system, notably one based on the gold exchange standard. Within such a system, any deficit in the balance of payments would generate gold losses, which are then said to induce reductions in the money supply and higher interest rates, and hence a slowdown in economic activity and in imports, and ultimately a newly equilibrated balance of payments. Clearly the rules of the game provide a mechanism that is little different from the one envisaged in the standard IS/LM/BP model, where balance-of-payments deficits generate reductions in the money supply and higher interest rates, and hence reductions in economic activity.

Pure currency boards do not exist, however. A real currency board does not quite behave in this simple way. Its functioning, contrary to appearances, is no different from that of an ordinary central bank. The currency board functions along the lines of an endogenous-money economy, responding to the compensation thesis, but it does so within a much narrower zone.

There are three possible elements of flexibility in the currency board system. First, when the needs for domestic currency are growing at a faster rate than that of foreign reserves, the currency board may acquire the needed foreign reserves by borrowing them from foreign commercial banks. Of course, when foreign reserves are growing too fast relative to the need for domestic cash, the process can be inverted and the central bank can reimburse the loans it took from foreign banks. Second, when foreign reserves are large, larger than the demand for compulsory reserves and cash, the government takes up the slack by accumulating deposits at the currency board. Indeed, this is precisely the arrangement adopted by some countries that have taken up the currency board arrangement, such as Bulgaria and Lithuania. In Bulgaria, for instance, government deposits represented about 40 per cent of the foreign exchange reserves found on the other side of the balance sheet of the currency board (Dobrev, 1999, p. 21). The government deposits play 'the role of a buffer between changes in the monetary base and foreign exchange reserve dynamics ... Essentially it performs sterilizing functions and injects or withdraws liquidity in and out of the economy' (Nenovsky and Hristov, 1998, p. 18). Finally, some currency boards, such as the one in Hong Kong, deal with excess foreign reserves by issuing currency board bills. Although the currency board may have a single kind of asset on its balance sheet, it could have as many as four different kinds of liabilities that break the one-to-one link between foreign reserves and base money. Besides base money, these are the funds borrowed from abroad, the government deposits and the currency board bills.

As shown in the stock–flow consistent model of Lavoie (2006e), the currency board can control interest rates despite defending a fixed exchange rate on the one hand, and refusing on the other hand to allow loans to its domestic economy. This is recognized by the officials of some currency boards. In the case of Bulgaria again, although there are no open-market operations, since these are prohibited by law, the currency board can set interest rates. The Bulgarian National Bank 'announces the base interest rate', whereas the standard belief is that, under a currency board or more generally a fixed exchange rate, 'the market alone should determine interest rates' (Dobrev, 1999, p. 14).

The currency board regime is little different from a strict fixed exchange rate regime. In the latter case, when the central bank is about to run out of foreign reserves, some large structural change must be imposed, such as import controls, capital controls, fiscal and monetary austerity policies, unless foreign reserves can be borrowed from abroad or from some international institution such as the IMF. With the currency board arrangement, a structural change may need to occur even though there are still plenty of foreign exchange reserves left, because the currency board is an institution that guarantees 100 per cent backing of its high-powered money by foreign reserves. The second difference is that the currency board is committed to a fixed exchange rate, whereas a central bank can decide either to devalue its domestic currency or to let it float. These options are not open to the currency board, since the inconveniences of a currency board are precisely there to persuade international speculators that these two options are not considered.

A structural change took place in the case of Argentina. For a while, despite a current account deficit, Argentina managed to keep a non-negative balance of payments by privatizing public companies and selling them off to foreign investors. The proceeds of these sales also gave the impression that the government was running a budget surplus. At a later stage, when Argentina started running a balance-of-payments deficit, the country was able to sustain its level of foreign reserves by having the currency board itself borrow foreign reserves from large foreign banks – a behaviour contrary to pure currency board rules. An alternative was for the Argentine government to issue securities denominated in a foreign currency (the dollar), these securities being purchased by foreign investors. The government would then deposit the proceeds at the central bank, raising foreign reserves in the process (De Lucchi, 2013). When the foreign debt of the government became too high, confidence waned, and these sources of funds started to run out. Argentina had to take extreme measures, which eventually led to the abandonment of the fixed exchange rate and its currency board regime.

7.2.6 Consequences for Theory

The essential features of the post-Keynesian horizontalist approach to monetary economics are that credit and money are demand-led endogenous variables, and that central banks have the ability to set interest rates (even real interest rates), at a level of their choice. This choice, of course, is constrained by the objectives pursued by the central bank and the economic conjuncture.

The same features still characterize an open economy operating in a world where capital is mobile (but where asset substitutability is imperfect). As Serrano and Summa (2015, p. 266) put it, 'even in an open economy with free short-run capital mobility, the short-term basic interest rate is exogenous, in the sense of being operationally an economic policy variable, directly controlled by the central bank'. Through the compensation principle, which is a variant of the reflux principle, balance-of-payments disequilibria have no effect on the overall monetary base or money supply, even with fixed exchange rates. Money aggregates are still determined by demand-led factors. The only difference is that these foreign-induced disequilibria will change the composition of the balance sheet of the central bank.

Balance-of-payments disequilibria have no endogenous effect on the level of short-term interest rates. For instance, external deficits do not lead to reduced internal liquidity and higher interest rates. This conclusion is confirmed by various stock-flow consistent models of a two-country economy with mobile capital where the compensation mechanism within the balance sheet of central banks is indeed observed (Godley and Lavoie, 2005–06; Godley and Lavoie, 2007a, ch. 12). The central bank, however, may decide to hike up interest rates when it feels uncomfortable with its falling foreign reserves. But there is nothing automatic about such a change in interest rates: it does not result from market supply and demand forces; it is a discretionary decision of the central bank. However, as was the case in a closed economy, long-term interest rates are more likely to move as a function of demand and supply, and are thus susceptible to change as a consequence of financial flows.

We conclude, as do Arestis and Eichner (1988, p. 1015), that, 'so long as it is recognized that money supply is credit-driven and demand-determined, the exchange rate regime is of absolutely no consequence in the determination of money and credit'. It also follows that countries running trade surpluses or benefiting from net capital inflows are not prone to inflationary forces since there is no supply-led endogenous creation of money. As Prissert (1972, p. 302) notes, there is no such thing as imported inflation in a fixed exchange regime. In a world where growth is demand-led, countries with external surpluses should have no hesitation in pursuing expansionary policies to help countries that experience slowdowns because their growth has been constrained by balance-of-payments difficulties. The compensation principle is thus fully consistent with Paul Davidson's (1994, p. 265) insistence, following Keynes, that the burden of adjustment to international disequilibria should fall on creditor countries rather than on debtor ones.

7.3 INTEREST PARITY

We argued in the previous section that central banks were at liberty, to some extent and within the limits associated with their exchange rate objectives, if any, to set interest rates of their choice, both within flexible exchange rate regimes and within fixed exchange rate regimes. Mainstream economists and a number of heterodox economists object to such a statement on account of interest parity relations. In the present section we analyse interest parity conditions, and we present an alternative interpretation of covered interest parity (CIP), which we call the 'cambist' view, and which fits pretty well with the rest of post-Keynesian monetary theory. This view is also sometimes called the bankers' view or the dealing-room view.

Because the forward exchange rate plays an important role in the story we wish to tell, it is probably a good idea to recall what the forward exchange rate is. Suppose that you are a European wholesaler, importing goods from abroad, which will have to be paid in US dollars in three months' time. You could borrow euros and purchase dollars, leaving them in some euro-dollar account until the bill is due, thus knowing exactly what the cost of your imports is in euros. But it would be much simpler to purchase dollars on the forward exchange market, through your bank, thus engaging in a contract whereby you promise to deliver a given amount of euros in three months, while the bank promises to deliver in exchange a given amount of dollars, also in three months. Similarly, if you are a European producer who exports goods abroad, to be paid in US dollars, you would like to be sure of the amount of euros that these sales will generate when the exports get paid for three months later. Again, all you need to do is purchase euros on the forward exchange market, promising to deliver dollars in three months' time (those dollars that you will obtain when you get paid by your client) while the bank promises to provide you with euros at an exchange rate which is decided now, thus eliminating your exchange rate risk.

Forward foreign exchange markets are over-the-counter trades. There are also foreign exchange futures, the purpose of which is similar, but with fixed trade units and where contracts are usually closed before physical delivery is required. The futures are mostly used for speculative purposes, in an attempt to profit from price changes. Here we focus on the forward exchange market.

7.3.1 Interest Parity Relations in a Nutshell

The crucial relation in mainstream open-economy macroeconomics is the real interest parity (RIP) condition, which says that (expected) real interest rates should be equalized across countries. This means that, within the context of an open economy, without capital controls, the central bank is not at liberty to set real interest rates as it wishes for domestic reasons, since such a central bank is constrained by the RIP condition, and is forced to set its real interest rate in line with the world real interest rate, that is, the real interest rates that prevail in the biggest economies. RIP is often invoked to argue that 'There Is No Alternative' (TINA) within a globalized economy. As Smithin (2002–03, p. 224) mentions, RIP 'in effect transfers the doctrine of the "natural rate of interest" to the international setting'. It is thus quite important to verify whether RIP relies or not on unsubstantiated hypotheses, since the belief in the existence of a natural rate of interest, as was pointed out at the beginning of Chapter 4, is the crucial point of differentiation between post-Keynesians and orthodox authors in monetary economics. As Smithin (2002–03) continues, 'if the RIP condition holds, then this will preclude the domestic central bank from having any influence over the real rate of interest in its own jurisdiction, and, hence, makes redundant any analysis of monetary policy worked out in the closed economy context'.

Four key relations for real interest rate parity

We now look at the implications of RIP, or, more precisely, the reasons why RIP may fail. The real rate of interest is usually written as the difference between the nominal interest rate and the expected rate of inflation (although this is an approximation; see Godley and Lavoie, 2007a, p. 274). In what follows, we assume realized values rather than expected values. If there is a discrepancy between the real rates of interest in the domestic economy and the real rate of interest in the rest of the world, in other words, if RIP does not hold, this differential, by definition, can be written as

$$i_{Rd} - i_{Rf} = (i_d - \hat{p}_d) - (i_f - \hat{p}_f) \tag{7.4}$$

As before, i and $\hat{p}$ stand for the nominal rate of interest and the rate of price inflation, while i_R is the real rate of interest. The subscripts d and f refer to the domestic and foreign values of these variables. RIP of course implies that $i_{Rd} = i_{Rf}$.

The differential in real interest rates can further be decomposed into two or three components. To see this, we make the following four definitions. Because we are running out of names, we will be forced to use some letters used in other chapters to define other variables. With s denoting the spot exchange rate in logarithmic terms, the purchasing power parity (PPP) in its relative version can be written as

$$s_{t+1} - s_t = \Delta s = \hat{p}_d - \hat{p}_f \tag{7.5}$$

Thus, if the rate of price inflation is higher at home than abroad, the exchange rate s goes up, meaning that the local currency is depreciating and that s stands for the value of the foreign currency expressed in units of the domestic currency. If the domestic currency is the dollar and the foreign currency is the euro, s tells us how much one euro is worth in dollars. If s goes up, the dollar is depreciating. Thus we adopt the non-intuitive way of defining the exchange rate that is standard among economists.

The second relation is that of uncovered interest parity (UIP); it requires that

$$i_d - i_f = s_{t+1} - s_t \tag{7.6}$$

UIP is generally understood as a relationship involving expectations, in particular the expected value of the spot exchange rate in the next period (s^e_{t+1}), since decisions to hold assets from one country or another have to be forward-looking. With this alternative understanding, UIP gets rewritten as

$$i_d - i_f = s^e_{t+1} - s_t \tag{7.6A}$$

The third relation is that of covered interest parity (CIP), with f standing for the logarithmic value of the forward exchange rate:

$$i_d - i_f = f_t - s_t \qquad (7.7)$$

The fourth relation is called the forward market unbiasedness hypothesis, or the unbiased efficiency hypothesis (UEH). It says that the forward premium ought to be equal to the change in the exchange rate, or, in other words, that the one-month forward exchange rate obtained today ought to equal the spot rate realized in one month. The forward rate is said to be 'an unbiased and efficient predictor of the spot rate prevailing in the future (on the maturity of the underlying forward contract)' (Moosa, 2004, p. 396). The forward exchange rate, on this interpretation, is the expected future spot rate ($f_t = s^e_{t+1}$), which will indeed be the realized future sport rate if expectations are unbiased. UEH thus implies

$$f_t = s_{t+1} \qquad (7.8)$$

The above equation will be verified, and hence UEH holds, if both UIP and CIP are verified together (if both equations 7.6 and 7.7 hold).

We are now in a position to assess why RIP could possibly not be verified. Equation (7.4), which defines the real interest rate differential, can be rewritten as

$$i_{Rd} - i_{Rf} = [(i_d - i_f) - (s_{t+1} - s_t)] + [(\hat{p}_f - \hat{p}_d) - (s_t - s_{t+1})] \qquad (7.9)$$

The first term between brackets measures the deviation from UIP, while the second term measures the deviation from relative PPP. Thus RIP will not be realized if either UIP or PPP does not hold, or if both conditions do not hold. We can modify equation (7.4) further by adding and subtracting the forward exchange rate f, thus getting three components of RIP on the right-hand side:

$$i_{Rd} - i_{Rf} = [(i_d - i_f) - (f_t - s_t)] + [f_t - s_{t+1}] + [(\hat{p}_f - \hat{p}_d) - (s_t - s_{t+1})] \qquad (7.10)$$

The third term between brackets is still the deviation from PPP. The first and second terms between brackets are now the deviation from CIP and the deviation from UEH. Thus another way to put things is to say that RIP will not be realized if PPP, CIP or UEH do not hold; we can also say that UIP does not hold if either CIP or UEH does not hold (or if neither holds!).

It is a well-known fact that absolute and relative purchasing parity relations do not hold; at best it is conceded that equation (7.5) roughly holds over the long run only. There is also the issue of causality: it may be that changes in exchange rates influence relative inflation rates, rather than relative inflation rates determining exchange rates. Whatever the case, PPP is not observed in the short and medium run, thus giving some room to central bankers.

Uncovered interest parity does not hold
Leaving aside real interest parity, orthodox models in open-economy macroeconomics all assume that uncovered interest parity holds. UIP is 'a constituent of virtually all

contemporary exchange rate models, from small-scale theoretical systems ... to large-scale econometric system constructed and tended by teams of researchers employed by organizations such as the IMF' (McCallum, 1996, p. 191). The inclusion of UIP in orthodox models is not based on empirical evidence; rather it is based on an instrumentalist philosophy, discussed in Chapter 1, according to which it is better to be precisely wrong than vaguely right. UIP is used as a means to close open-economy models. Even some heterodox authors do so. For instance, while Lance Taylor (2004, p. 315) acknowledges that UIP 'does not fit the data', he introduces UIP to close his model on the grounds that UIP relies on 'arbitrage arguments that should be true' (ibid., p. 333).

In any case, as soon as UIP does not hold, UEH cannot hold either, as can be ascertained by comparing equations (7.6) and (7.8) with equation (7.7), here rewritten as equation (7.7A).

$$f_t = s_t + (i_d - i_f) \qquad (7.7A)$$

As pointed out earlier, in the minds of neoclassical authors the forward exchange rate ought to be equal to the expected future spot rate. Neoclassical authors thus imagine two mechanisms through which the values of the forward exchange rate f found in equations (7.7A) and (7.8) will get equalized. This mechanism operates through arbitrageurs and speculators. In the neoclassical account of the forward exchange market, the expectations concerning the change in the future value of the spot rate, Δs^e, are said to determine the value of the forward exchange rate, f, relative to the current spot rate. Start from a situation where domestic and world interest rates are equal, and where the spot and the forward exchange rates are equal. Suppose now that the central bank, for some reason, decides to reduce the domestic rate of interest. For the neoclassical economist, the following sequence of events will occur. It now becomes profitable for arbitrageurs to enter into covered arbitrage (there is an intrinsic interest differential). In this case, arbitrageurs sell the domestic currency spot (buy foreign currencies spot), and buy back the domestic currency forward. For neoclassical economists, there is now a tendency for the domestic currency to depreciate on the spot market (s increases) and to appreciate in the forward market (f decreases). As pointed out by Coulbois and Prissert (1974, p. 300), this analysis resembles the one proposed by Keynes (1973, iv), but this does not make it right.

The process described above is said to go on until the negative spread ($f - s$) becomes equal to the differential ($i_d - i_f$). If the central bank intervenes and resists the depreciation of its domestic currency, it will be losing foreign reserves, and as a consequence the money supply will decrease and hence the spread between domestic and world interest rates will be reduced, along the lines of Mundell's story recalled in the previous section, until the two rates are back to equality. If the forward exchange rate is any different from the future spot rate expected by speculators, the latter will also intervene in the forward exchange market until the two rates are equal. Thus, to the neoclassical economist, the forward exchange rate and the expected future spot rate get equalized and, with proper expectations, equation (7.8) will be verified as well.

We know, however, that there is little empirical support for UIP, despite clear evidence that CIP holds. It would thus seem that the above story and UEH are not valid. As a consequence, as a last resort, *ad hoc* defence of UIP, neoclassical authors have added a twist to their story, modifying UEH and arguing that there exists a risk premium σ so that

$$s_{t+1} = f_t + \sigma \qquad (7.11)$$

thus deriving a modified UIP relationship:

$$i_d - i_f + \sigma = s_{t+1} - s_t \qquad (7.12)$$

We shall further discuss this modification later. An alternative point of view – the one defended in the next subsections – is that, while CIP is true, UEH is false. Leaving aside the risk premium story, and if we accept the post-Keynesian claim that nominal interest rates are essentially exogenous variables, it is clear that CIP and an unmodified UEH cannot be true simultaneously. In other words, equations (7.7) and (7.8) cannot both be true at the same time.

This is what we now develop, under the name of the 'cambist' view.

7.3.2 The Cambist View

The cambist view is based on an analysis of the forward exchange market proposed by Coulbois and Prissert (1974; 1976; see also Lavoie, 2000b; 2002–03; Smithin, 2002–03; Moosa, 2002; 2004; 2017b). This alternative view is reinforced by an interpretation of the large amount of empirical work regarding the determinants of exchange rates and the relevance of the covered and uncovered interest parity relations.

The post-Keynesian account of the forward exchange rate – based on the cambist view – is entirely different from the one described in the previous subsection. According to post-Keynesians, (short-term) interest rates are not endogenous but are the result of the decisions taken by the monetary authorities. Central banks are the ultimate providers of liquidity, and hence have the ability to set short-term interest rates. This view of the determination of interest rates extends to the forward exchange market. According to Prissert (1972) and Coulbois and Prissert (1974; 1976), the spread between forward rates and spot exchange rates is administratively set by foreign exchange dealers, on the straightforward basis of the interest rate differentials on the euro-currency markets that are accessible to the banks making the deal.

In other words, in the eyes of Coulbois and Prissert, covered interest parity always holds perfectly, by definition. The forward exchange rate is not an expectational variable; it is instead the result of a simple arithmetical operation. Except when they themselves speculate by carrying open-exchange positions, banks do not make money on any intrinsic interest differential; rather they make a profit by setting a small profit margin between the selling and the buying price, which they quote to their customers on the forward exchange market. 'Cambists' profits stem from the bid-ask spread' (Coulbois, 1982, p. 199). The forward exchange rate itself is endogenous, and is computed by the banks by simply reversing equation (7.7) and using equation (7.7A), or, to be more precise, by using equation (7.7B), where F and S are the actual values of the forward and spot exchange rates rather than their logarithmic values:

$$F_t = S_t \frac{(1+i_d)}{(1+i_f)} \qquad (7.7B)$$

The arguments of Coulbois and Prissert are summarized in the following quote:

> Equilibrium on the forward exchange market is not brought about by the intervention of arbitrageurs, but simply by that of banks, which cover on the spot market the excess forward orders, borrow the currency which is sold and lend the currency which is bought ... Banks charge to their customers forward rates which simply reflect the interest rate differential ... It follows from the cambist analysis that forward market equilibrium does not require the appearance of an intrinsic premium and that average forward rates are always at the level dictated by the interest rate differential which exists in the markets where banks are lenders or borrowers. (Coulbois and Prissert, 1974, p. 290)

The cambist interpretation of equation (7.7) explains why all studies of the covered interest parity relation have always shown that the relation holds very well – often perfectly well. The cambist view of the forward exchange market gives a much simpler explanation of these empirical results: the forward exchange rate is determined mechanically by equation (7.7B). The forward exchange rate, or rather its premium or discount relative to the spot rate, is not determined by demand and supply forces. It is set by bank dealers at a rate that will allow banks to cover their costs, and the mark-up is given by the interest cost differential. The forward exchange rate, relative to the spot exchange rate, is a straightforward example of a cost-determined price! The forward exchange rate results from a simple arithmetical operation based on euro-deposit rates and the spot exchange rate, an operation that does not involve expected future spot rates!

As pointed out by Moosa (2004, p. 402), the deterministic CIP equation is the result of a hedging operation by banks, rather than the consequence of an operation pursued by arbitrageurs. An obvious implication of the cambist view of forward exchange markets is that covered interest arbitrage has no impact whatsoever on flows of funds or on foreign reserves, even when exchange rates are fixed. When covered arbitrageurs decide to sell spot and buy forward (domestic currency), commercial banks take the 'buy forward' order of their customers and are the counterpart to it. To cover themselves, banks buy domestic currency on the spot market. The cover operation of the banks cancels the initial operation of the covered arbitrageur, so that 'the spot market remains unaffected, and hence official reserves as well as the domestic money supply ... There is no international net movement of capital' (Coulbois and Prissert, 1974, p. 296).

Another obvious consequence of the cambist view is that 'the spot–forward relationship is contemporaneous, not lagged, as the unbiased efficiency hypothesis suggests' (Moosa, 2004, p. 404). Moosa (2004) checks which relationship is best supported by statistical analysis. His results show that the link between the forward rate and the spot rate is best explained by a contemporaneous relationship, as in equation (7.7A) or (7.7B). Empirical analysis also fails to achieve a one-to-one relationship between the forward rate and the future spot rate, and the lagged relationship requires the addition of time-varying parameters that presumably reflect the risk premium introduced in equations (7.11) and (7.12). However, when the spot rate of the current period is explained by the spot rate of the previous period and the forward rate of the previous period, the latter being said to forecast the spot rate of the current period, the risk premium proxy loses its statistical significance. Moosa (ibid., p. 416) concludes the following:

> The finding that the spot rate is related to the contemporaneous rather than the lagged forward rate implies the failure of the unbiased efficiency hypothesis. Given that it is a necessary condition for RIP to hold, this finding implies the empirical failure of RIP, irrespective of the validity of PPP (which is another necessary condition). If this is the case, then the Post Keynesian view that the monetary authorities can control domestic interest rates is valid, or at least that the opposite mainstream view is invalid.

As pointed out by Smithin (2002–03, p. 232), it should be noted that within the cambist view, CIP holds at all times, regardless of the efficiency of capital markets, and whether or not there is perfect capital mobility, in contrast to the mainstream view on this. Coulbois and Prissert (1974, p. 291) explain that researchers who did not find a perfect fit did not use the interest rates that were relevant to banks operating on the forward exchange markets (at the time, many authors used the rates of return on Treasury bills, whereas euro rates were the relevant rates). The only restriction that could be made is that, with capital controls, the forward rate paid by a national resident might be different from that paid by a foreign customer, because foreign banks will have access only to euro-markets, which, because of capital controls, will be partly disconnected from the domestic money markets. As a result, in particular when a currency is under attack, money market rates on euro-markets might rise above those of the domestic money market, thus leading to two distinct forward rates. It is this feature of capital controls that may have led some authors to deny that covered interest parity holds at all times.

Despite the fact that the guides to practitioners adopt the cambist view of the determination of the forward exchange rate, tests of CIP continue unabated. The criticisms concerning the validity of the CIP relation have become more intense since the 2008 financial crisis, and even before in the case of Japan, several authors claiming that CIP has been repeatedly violated (Stenfors, 2019). Despite the fact that more fancy data is now collected, the explanation for these apparent deviations is based, as before, on the discrepancy between the rates effectively used by foreign exchange dealers in the monetary markets that they can access and the published data accessed by researchers. 'Deviations are bound to be found if the tests are based on published rather than transaction data' (Moosa, 2017b, p. 472). In particular, because of the newly-imposed regulatory costs, there can be a breakdown between onshore and offshore dollars, so that published information is unlikely to reflect the differentiated rates. In addition, in times of turbulences and one-way markets, bid/ask spreads are likely to be larger and asymmetric relative to the mid rate, and thus create apparent intrinsic premia. This was a point already made by Coulbois and Prissert (1974, p. 291) when they wrote that 'exchange and interest rates used in calculations are middle rates, whereas dealers take into account the rates that are effectively paid and received at one particular moment'. There is a bid/ask spread for both the forward rate and the spot rate, as well as for swap rates. The consequence of the existence of these bid/ask spreads is that when they are taken into account, there is no way that arbitrageurs can make a profit next to the covered interest parity condition, whereas hedging banks will (Moosa, 2017b). Thus, the achievement of the CIP condition arises from hedging, as the cambists say, and not from arbitrage. As Moosa (2017b, p. 474) puts it, fully endorsing the cambist view, 'commercial banks simply quote a forward rate on the basis of the known interest differentials and spot exchange rate to ensure that CIP holds. This means that CIP is an identity'.

7.3.3 The Cambist View in a Flexible Exchange Rate Regime

As suggested by equations (7.11) and (7.12), the failure of UIP may be attributed to the presence of risk premia. We have already discussed the fact that perfect capital mobility is not the same as perfect asset substitutability. In its open-economy variant, the Tobin–Godley approach to portfolio choice leads to rates-of-return differentials, even between no-risk Treasury bills of different countries, simply because asset-holders will not want to put all their eggs in the same basket. An interest differential will not induce infinite and never-ending capital flows. Portfolios will adjust, and then stay put, leaving interest differentials as they are. The difference with the closed economy is that there is an additional element influencing the expected rate of return on assets – expectations about future exchange rates. The proportions of each asset being held will be changed accordingly; but this can be done without any change in the rates of interest on the assets under the control of the respective monetary authorities, as long as the monetary authorities are determined to keep interest rates as they are. Thus, with imperfect asset substitutability, UIP does not prevail.

In other words, the uncovered interest parity theorem could hold (in general) only in a world of perfect asset substitutability, devoid in addition of any currency risk or credit risk, and devoid of any fundamental uncertainty. Uncovered interest parity does not hold because uncovered positions carry currency risk. Portfolio-holders who act as arbitrageurs that wish to take advantage of divergent expected rates of return on safe assets can do so only as far as they are willing to face exchange risks. This is an inescapable conclusion.

Still, what would happen in a world devoid of risk premia, where both the cambist theory of the forward exchange rate and the uncovered interest parity held? This is a question that justifiably bothers Smithin (2002–03, p. 226), for he writes that, in his view, 'it seems unlikely that there should be no relationship whatsoever between the forward rate and the expected future spot rate. If the expectations are firmly held and do differ from the quoted forward rate, there is nothing to prevent "speculators" from taking uncovered positions to take advantage of this.' This is certainly a valid point. In contrast to arbitrageurs, the pure speculator cares neither about the expected change in spot exchange rates nor about the yield of an asset. The pure speculator is solely concerned with the difference between the forward exchange rate and the future spot rate that is expected to occur when the forward contract comes due for delivery. In theory, speculators need no financial resources of their own, since this is just a forward contract. In practice, a deposit will have to be provided, representing 10 to 20 per cent of the value of the contract (Coulbois, 1979, p. 183), as it would be the case with foreign exchange futures, thus putting a limit on the possible leveraged position when rules are not circumvented. Nowadays, to provide the 10 per cent margin, speculators may simply lend to the banks the Treasury bills that they hold, thus using the repo market, and encountering hardly any opportunity cost.

For instance, if the consensus is that the American dollar ought to be 1.50 Canadian dollars in three months' time, while the forward exchange rate is at 1.48, there is an incentive to speculate against the Canadian dollar by selling Canadian dollars forward. At delivery time three months later, with 148 Canadian cents the speculator would get one American dollar, which he or she could immediately transform back to 150 Canadian cents on the spot exchange market. This would seem to imply that, as long as the forward rate of the Canadian dollar is below the expected future spot rate, there is an inducement to speculate against the Canadian dollar on the forward exchange markets. How is this compatible with the cambist view?

Figure 7.5 helps to explain what would occur in such a situation. Start from a situation where the interbank interest rates are equal, $i_{d0} = i_f$, the former rate being the Canadian rate while the latter is the rate in the USA – the world rate. In the initial situation, assuming away any risk premium, the forward exchange rate, the spot rate and the expected future spot rate are all equal, $f_0 = s_0 = s^e$. Suppose now that the governor of the Bank of Canada decides to lower the target overnight rate, which leads to a fall in all short-term Canadian rates, including the interbank rates. In this new situation, $i_{d1} < i_f$, as shown on the graph. Since cambists fix the forward rate simply by marking up the current spot rate on the basis of the interest cost differential, they use equation (7.7A), represented by the upward-sloping f curve in Figure 7.5, as a result of which the forward rate drops to f_1.

Now, as was pointed out by Smithin, this situation could not last forever. If the expectations about future spot rates (s^e) are held with sufficient conviction, speculators will take uncovered positions and will sell Canadian dollars forward, in the hope of making a quick profit. If these expectations reflect a consensus, the forward market will become a one-way market, banks will be unable to find clients willing to purchase Canadian dollars forward, and hence will be forced to find cover by selling Canadian dollars spot, acquiring immediately the American dollars that they will have to provide to the speculators within three months' time. Unless the central bank intervenes on exchange markets, the Canadian dollar will depreciate, meaning that its s value will rise. We have

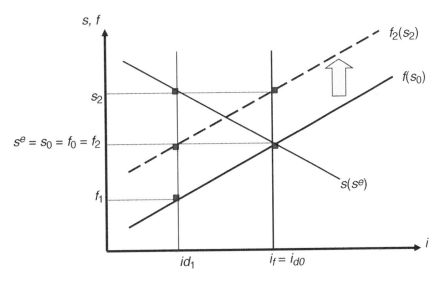

Figure 7.5 Impact of lower domestic interest rates on the forward and spot exchange rates with risk-neutral speculators in a world of perfect asset substitutability and perfect capital mobility

$$\Delta s = \mu\left(s^{e}_{t+1} - f_{t}\right) \tag{7.13}$$

This implies that the f curve will now be shifting upwards (check again equation 7.7A). Provided there is no change in the future expected spot rate, speculators will sell Canadian dollars forward and the spot rate will rise until the forward rate is equal to the expected rate; that is, until we have $f_2 = s^e$ with the notations of the graph. This implies that, at that point, both CIP and UIP, in its forward-looking version, are verified, meaning that both equation (7.7) and equation (7.6A) are verified. Still, at that point, UEH (equation 7.8) is not verified: the expected spot rate is not equal to the realized one, since the new spot rate will have risen to $s_2 = s^e - (i_{d1} - i_f)$, as shown on the downward-sloping s line. Thus, even in this case, there is room for domestic monetary autonomy.

The same mechanism could be described in a world where speculators are risk-averse. We could again imagine that speculators sell Canadian dollars forward as long as the expected future spot rate is higher than the forward rate. This would induce an upward move in the Canadian exchange rate (a depreciation of the Canadian dollar).

We could suppose, however, that speculation, with the consequences outlined by equation (7.13), is actually carried on only when the absolute value of the discrepancy between the expected future spot rate and the forward rate is large enough to compensate for a possible loss due to mistaken expectations (or possibly due to a transaction tax), that is, only if

$$\left|s^{e}_{t+1} - f_{t}\right| > \sigma \tag{7.14}$$

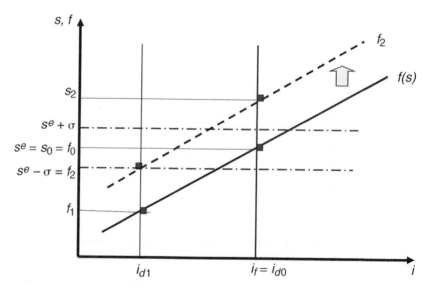

Figure 7.6 Impact of lower domestic interest rates on the forward and spot exchange rates with currency risk

The horizontal dotted lines below and above s^e, in Figure 7.6, would then represent the threshold points beyond which speculators would stay put. In this case, only the covered interest parity would hold, and the depreciation of the Canadian dollar would not be as large as in the perfect mobility case; pressures on the spot exchange rate would end as soon as the forward rate reached the threshold, $f_2 = s^e - \sigma$, as given by the f_2 upward-sloping line. The currency risk premium σ underlines the fears that speculators may have regarding mistaken exchange rate expectations. The greater the confidence with which the expectations are held (the weight of evidence, as we called it in Chapter 2), the smaller σ will be. The freedom of central banks to set interest rates of their choice is even more obvious in this case.

Uncovered interest parity was propelled to the forefront by economists propounding models with a single interest-earning asset (the so-called monetary approach to the balance of payments). But how is uncovered interest parity to be interpreted in a world with a multiplicity of income-earning assets, including equities? Low real interest rates may help to generate high growth rates, and hence high rates of return on equities. Bibow (2002) argues that the interest rate hikes of the European Central Bank (ECB) in 1999 and 2000, which were intended to stop the depreciation of the euro relative to the American dollar, had the exact opposite effects. The euro plunged with each euro interest rate hike because, Bibow says, the markets were more concerned with growth prospects than with inflation-netted money market rates. Presumably, international financial operators were mostly attracted by fast-growing economies that had the potential to deliver high rates of return on equity assets. Rising interest rates weakened growth prospects. In that time period at least, it would seem that if the uncovered interest parity had any validity, it was associated with equity returns, not with yields on short-term assets. This implies that the covered interest parity theorem and the uncovered interest parity theorem deal with different assets and different rates of return. They are not commensurate. A somewhat similar point was made by Coulbois (1972, p. 58). Translated, he says: 'One would need to construct as many graphs – and as many arguments – as there are possible financial investments, which would take away any significance to the theory.'

7.3.4 The Cambist View in a Fixed Exchange Rate Regime

One may wonder what is left of the cambist view and the forward exchange market when an economy is in a fixed exchange rate regime. Smithin (2002–03, p. 229) seems to believe that the central bank loses quite a bit of autonomy relative to world interest rates, as he argues that, 'in a "credible" fixed exchange rate regime with capital mobility . . . domestic authorities entirely lose control of the domestic rate of interest'. He is careful to point out that what he means by a credible fixed exchange rate in that context is 'a regime, which, without reservation, is confidently expected to hold' (ibid.). For domestic interest rates to diverge from world rates, Smithin (ibid., p. 233) argues that there have to be 'separate currencies, with either floating exchange rates, or a fixed rate regime in which some adjustments/revaluations are to be expected', concluding that 'in a common currency or similar environment . . . there would be no forward market'.

No one would wish to argue with the fact that within the common-currency eurozone there is no room for forward exchange rates, no more than there is between the various states in the USA. But what about standard fixed exchange rate regimes? According to

Isard (1995, p. 25), 'countries rarely seek to keep their exchange rates rigidly fixed. To do so would be almost an impossible task in a country where residents had the freedom to exchange currencies with each other.' Thus, if there is capital mobility, in practice the fixed exchange rate arrangements 'provide for a limited degree of flexibility by defining fluctuation ranges or bands around the central parities'. In the case of the Bretton Woods arrangements, as is well known, the currencies were pegged to the US dollar with fluctuation margins of 1 per cent on each side of the central parity, and hence fluctuation margins twice that size between currencies other than the US dollar (except for the period near the end of the system, when the margins were widened). Were there forward markets then?

We know that there were. In normal periods, these forward exchange markets played a stabilizing role. Why is this so? Suppose that stable views on fixed exchange rates prevail, and a one-to-one fixed parity, with 1 per cent fluctuation bands, has been established between the euro and the American dollar. When the forward exchange rate of the euro hits the bottom band, say 0.99 euro per dollar, domestic European exporters who expect to be paid in US dollars for their exports in one month's time will not take cover, for they know that they will not get any less than 0.99 euro on the spot market one month later. By contrast, European importers who must pay their goods in US dollars will all be purchasing US dollars forward, and hence will be selling the euro forward, for otherwise, if they pay for the goods using the spot market one month later, they will have to fetch at least the same 0.99 euro per dollar, and perhaps as much as 1.01 euro, so that the spot cost of imported goods could turn out to be more expensive. We thus have a one-way forward exchange market. As a result, all banks will sell the domestic currency spot to cover themselves, and hence both the spot and the forward euro exchange rates will depreciate towards the parity level. Leads and lags stabilize the currency back towards its parity rate. Symmetric effects will arise when the currency hits the top band. Thus, in theory, both the forward rate and the spot rate cannot move out of the fluctuating band. The forward exchange market, when parity is believed to be one of the 'fundamentals', in this case provides a stabilizing force.

However, what occurred in reality was very different. In the Bretton Woods era, currencies that nearly reached the bands for some time were usually subjected to intense speculation, as is well known from the British episode with speculator George Soros (who now objects to unfettered financial markets). Weak currencies were generally associated with high interest rates, while strong currencies had low rates. Figure 7.7 illustrates two examples. On the left-hand side of the figure, the spot value of the domestic currency is on its lower band, and it is about to appreciate (say the German mark). Its forward rate is below the spot rate, because German interest rates are much lower than US rates. On the right-hand side, the spot value of the currency is on its upper band, and it is about to be devalued (say the pound sterling). Its forward rate is above the spot rate, because British rates are much higher than those in the USA. The problem was that, for most operators, the expected future exchange rate of the German mark was even lower than the forward rate; similarly, the expected future exchange rate of the British pound was even higher than the forward rate, thus leading to the pressures described by equation (7.13). The presence of forward exchange markets exacerbated the problem. Leads and lags transactions operated in reverse gear, and pure speculators making outright transactions could use forward exchange markets to leverage their own bets.

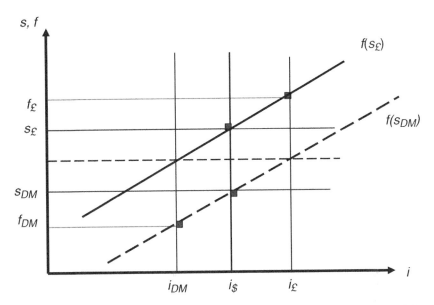

Figure 7.7 Forward exchange markets with large destabilizing expectations and fixed exchange rates

The point I wish to make, however, is that, even with fixed exchange rates, there were wide variations in interest rates across countries. The presence of forward exchange markets did not prevent these variations. These could be explained to some degree by variations in inflation rates, the perspective of future modifications to the parity rate, and the highly imperfect mobility of capital for several countries; but the interest differentials also depended on the monetary policy pursued by the monetary authorities. One could say, as Smithin (2002–03) did, that the scope for interest changes with fixed exchange rates depends on the fixity being imperfect in some sense, and of course that different currencies still exist. So there can be scope for policy under fixed rates; but the more rigid the fixed exchange rate, the less scope there is, unless this rigidity is compensated by imperfect portfolio substitutability.

Forward exchange markets are useful even when small variations in exchange rates are expected. Interest differentials of 12 per cent and 4 per cent generate one-month and three-month forward exchange rates that are different from spot rates by only 1 per cent – which is half the size of the exchange variations allowed by the Bretton Woods arrangements. If cover for longer time periods pushes the forward rate way out of its fluctuation bands, this particular forward market might simply vanish. But this is of little importance, since 'forward exchange markets do not exist as such'; in the words of a cambist, Pierre Prissert, 'a forward exchange order is really a spot exchange order where the customer, instead of arranging the funding of the operation, leaves it to the bank which got the order' (Coulbois, 1972, p. 114).

In this sense, there is wide scope for domestic monetary policy within a fixed exchange rate system, as long as there is imperfect asset substitutability; the more so when financial market operators are less concerned with short-term yields than with long-term growth prospects, as has apparently been the case since the end of the 1990s, in the belief that we have entered the age of a new economics, where production growth spurs productivity growth, quashing inflation forces, as suggested by the Kaldor–Verdoorn law.

7.3.5 Practical Consequences of the Cambist View

We have already underlined one practical consequence of the cambist view: covered interest arbitrage has no impact on either the spot or the forward exchange rate, since the spot and forward transactions compensate for each other. Since about half of the transactions on foreign exchange markets are covered, this means that about half of these transactions have no impact whatsoever on exchange rates. By contrast, if speculators decide to sell the domestic currency forward, banks will need to cover themselves by selling the domestic currency spot, and this will have an immediate impact on the spot rate or on foreign reserves. It is sometimes argued that 'central banks are able to manipulate the forward–spot differential by intervention in the foreign exchange market' (Moore, 1988, p. 273), but the real purpose of these forward exchange market interventions is to counter the sales of the domestic currency on the spot market without immediately losing foreign exchange reserves. These operations on the forward exchange market have no impact whatsoever on the forward–spot differential unless they are accompanied by discretionary changes in relative interest rates. Hence only uncovered forward operations induce inflows and outflows, and these can be countered by forward exchange market interventions by the central bank. Monetary authorities can renew these operations as long as they have the nerves to face the possibility of losing their foreign reserves in the future.

Since only uncovered forward operations have an impact on the spot exchange rate and hence on the amount of official reserves that a central bank would hold in a fixed exchange rate regime, a well-determined central bank, which does not face an exchange rate crisis in a world of turbulence, could thus impose low real rates of interest if it so desires. International turbulence, however, seems to be a systemic feature of modern economies, and in the case of exchange crises, capital controls are most probably required to retain control over domestic interest rates. But these financial storms may also blow over the central banks that obediently follow the market conventions.

The empirical failure of uncovered interest parity, combined to the cambist causal explanation of the covered interest parity relation and the post-Keynesian view of the foreign exchange market, sustains the notion that central banks can set real rates of interest that are lower (or higher) than those ruling on average in the rest of the world. This result does not necessarily rely on some risk premium or discount. Rather, the ability of central banks to set their own interest rates relies on the behaviour of the dealers and participants to the exchange markets, the nature of which is fundamentally uncertain.

Suppose a central bank were to impose systematically low real rates of interest. Short-term investors who agree to gamble on uncovered arbitrage, thus acting as speculators, would be tempted to invest abroad, where rates are higher. This would induce either a depreciation of the local currency, or a balance-of-payments deficit. If the local currency depreciates, there will be pressures on the inflation rate, and, as a consequence, for a given nominal interest rate, real rates will have a tendency to fall, not to rise.

In the fixed exchange regime, because of the operation of the reflux principle and the compensation thesis, a thesis to which Coulbois and Prissert (1974, p. 303) also adhered, there is no endogenous reduction in the monetary base or the money supply, as was argued extensively in the preceding section. As a consequence, even if low real interest rates induce short-term capital outflows, there is no endogenous inducement for the money supply to decrease or for interest rates to rise. There are no mechanisms that would automatically pull up the domestic real rate towards the levels reached in the rest of the world. Indeed, a fast-growing economy, so driven by low real interest rates, might entice long-term investors to invest in that economy, and these long-term capital movements could compensate for the outflows induced by the low short-term interest rates.

There is a problem with any story based on uncovered interest parity, the unbiased efficiency hypothesis and the purchasing power parity relation. The problem is that none of these relations holds in empirical work. It is highly dubious that any financial actor would wish to conduct his or her exchange operations on their basis. But these relations are the theoretical foundations upon which is built the mainstream assertion that central banks cannot set domestic real interest rates that are any different from world rates.

The essential features of the post-Keynesian approach to monetary economics are that credit and money are demand-led endogenous variables, and that central banks have the ability to set interest rates, and even real interest rates, at a level of their choice. This choice, of course, is constrained by the objectives pursued by the central bank and the economic conjuncture. In a modern monetary production economy, there is no such thing as a natural rate of interest, towards which the central bank must necessarily align its target rate. The same features still characterize an open economy operating in a world where capital is mobile. Through the reflux principle, balance-of-payments disequilibria have no effect on the overall monetary base or money supply, even with fixed exchange rates. Money aggregates are still determined by demand-led factors. The only difference is that these foreign-induced disequilibria will change the composition of the balance sheet of the central bank. Also, in an open economy, the central bank can set domestic interest rates of its choice, in line with its assigned economic objectives, one of which now includes the foreign exchange rate. Just as there was no necessity for the bank rate to equal the natural rate in a closed economy, there is no requirement for domestic interest rates to equal or to stay in line with the rates prevailing elsewhere in the world. This is because the uncovered interest parity theorem, in contrast to the covered interest parity relation, cannot hold, either in theory or in practice.

7.4 FOREIGN EXCHANGE RATES

7.4.1 Exchange Rate Determination

Is there a post-Keynesian theory of exchange rate determination? Post-Keynesians are just as puzzled as are orthodox economists about the fluctuations and volatility of foreign exchange rates. The mainstream view seems to be that variations in interest rates, and hence portfolio decisions, will be the major determinant of exchange rates in the short term, that trade balances and current account balances will determine exchange rates in the medium term, and that the relative purchasing power parity will be the main determinant in the (very) long term. There would thus be different 'fundamentals', depending on the time period considered.

Expectations and financial flows

John Harvey is the only author who has written consistently on this topic. Harvey (2012, pp. 186–7) says that 'Post Keynesians argue that currency prices are a function of international investors' portfolio decisions . . . In summary, the Post Keynesian view of exchange rates is based on the empirical fact that currency prices are driven by short-term capital flows. Those flows are in turn a function of agents' expectations'. With regard to very short-term movements, Harvey (1991; 1998–99) puts a substantial amount of weight on the decisions taken by foreign market dealers, whose expectations about future values of exchange rates are influenced by the news in the financial press. Thus a run of 'good' news is likely to drive up the value of a country's currency, and this might be reinforced by the technical analysis and the rules or algorithms pursued by several foreign exchange dealers. News is somewhat related to fundamentals: Harvey (1993) shows that news announcing higher current account balances, interest rates and growth rates leads to an appreciation of the currency. News about world politics also has some influence. The Global Financial Crisis has highlighted the importance of liquidity preference: currencies of peripheral countries faced depreciation, while the speculative capital of offshore hedge funds flew back to the USA and other advanced economies, in the belief that this was the thing to do and that others would do it.

In a world dominated by fundamental uncertainty, Harvey (1993, p. 517) shows that '*actual* changes in the exchange rate are a function of how dealers *expect* the rate to change over the short and medium term', a statement that seems fully consistent with Keynes's (1936, p. 156) contention that financial markets operate as a beauty contest, where participants try to find out 'what average opinion expects average opinion to be'. Traders look at the decisions and the positions taken by their colleagues, notably those of the large offshore traders.

Moosa (2002, p. 449), like Harvey, believes that one must distinguish between short-term and medium-term views. Moosa maintains that 'short-term expectations are based on technical factors, whereas medium-term expectations are based on signals arising from asset and goods markets'. He further points out that survey-based studies of exchange rate expectations show that 'expectations are extrapolative over short periods of time and regressive over longer periods of time. This means that if a currency is appreciating then it should continue to appreciate in the near future (in the short term) and to depreciate after that (in the medium term)'. This view corresponds to behavioural finance as applied by De Grauwe and Grimaldi (2006, ch. 2) to foreign exchange markets. Exchange rate movements are said to be driven by two types of economic agents, the 'chartists' and the 'fundamentalists'. The chartists expect the latest change in the exchange rate to be repeated in the next periods. The chartists, in this formalization, are trend-following speculators who push the price up after an initial price increase. The fundamentalists trade in a manner that puts pressure on the exchange rate to go back to some exogenously defined fundamental rate. The expectations about changes in exchange rates of the chartists and of the fundamentalists can each be described by the following two difference equations:

$$de^e_{c,t} = +\phi_c de_{t-1} \qquad (7.15)$$

$$de^e_{f,t} = -\phi_f \left(e_{t-1} - \bar{e}\right) \qquad (7.16)$$

where e_t is the exchange rate at time t, $e^e_{c,t}$ and $e^e_{f,t}$ are the exchange rates expected by chartists and fundamentalists, while $\bar{e}$ is the fundamental exchange rate assessed by fundamentalists. The change in the exchange rate expected by the market is thus a weighted average of these two difference equations, depending on the proportion of traders who act as chartists and fundamentalists, as well as the strength of their beliefs. The proportion may reverse itself, the reason being that when an economy benefits from financial inflows, the foreign debt of this country rises, so that, at some point, the decisions of some traders will be more driven by the dangers of this rising stock of debt than by the incoming financial flows.

It cannot be overemphasized that the use of the term *fundamentals* is likely to be misleading. First, 'many now believe that macroeconomic fundamentals do not play an important role in currency movements' (Frydman and Goldberg, 2014, p. 20). Second, while 'movements in macroeconomic fundamentals *do* influence exchange rates', they are likely to do so 'in different ways during different time periods' (ibid., p. 21). Many different fundamentals have been proposed in the past by various neoclassical authors, such as inflation rates, the growth rate of the money supply, real GDP growth rates, stock market prices or interest rates. Because post-Keynesians doubt that it is possible for traders to identify a *fundamental* value of the exchange rate even if there exists one when exchange rate expectations are neutralized, it may be best to replace the term *fundamentals* by the term *conventions*.

Current account flows
While expectations and portfolio decisions have no doubt a substantial impact on the spot exchange rate of a currency, there is another tradition in post-Keynesian economics that puts a substantial amount of weight on trade flows. This is the post-Keynesian tradition associated with Harrod's import multiplier, which, in its growth version, is known as Thirlwall's law. A whole section will be devoted to Thirlwall's law later in this chapter, so we shall say no more at this stage. However, we recall some of the results achieved within post-Keynesian stock-flow consistent two-country models, which also belong to this Harrodian open-economy tradition.

Godley (1999b) produced the first version of a post-Keynesian stock-flow consistent two-country model with flexible exchange rates, and a somewhat similar model with flexible exchange rates can be found in Godley and Lavoie (2007a, ch. 12) and in Carnevali (2021). These models, as discussed earlier, incorporate stocks and flows of both the real and the financial sides of the economy, but here within the framework of two countries having trade and financial relationships. The models thus incorporate trade relations that depend both on income and relative prices, as well as on portfolio decisions, which depend on income as well as expectations about asset returns at home and abroad. The striking lesson to be drawn from such models is that a permanent change in the parameters driving the trade equations will have a gradual but persistent impact on the exchange rate; on the other hand, a permanent change in the parameters associated with portfolio decisions will have an immediate and brisk impact on the exchange rate, but this impact will gradually vanish over time. Indeed, the reversal will be so complete that a short-term positive shock to the exchange rate caused by portfolio decisions will turn out to have a (small) negative long-term effect. This is because the temporary positive financial account balance creates additional debt-servicing costs, which require a depreciation of the exchange rate large enough to generate a trade account surplus that will compensate for the higher interest payments on external debt. This result seems to be consistent with what we said about exchange rate expectations being extrapolative in the short term but regressive over the medium or long term. Thus, in a flexible exchange rate regime, expectations and portfolio decisions have a substantial impact in the short term, but over the long haul the exchange rates will have to be such that the current account balance is back to equilibrium. This has been clearly expressed by Godley himself:

> Finally if we make the assumption that a change in expectations alters the relative demand for one country's assets ... the effect on the exchange rate, though it may be large and immediate, is essentially self-reversing because of the feedback from trade, though the re-achievement of 'equilibrium' may take a long time. Hence while hardly anything has been said about expectations in this paper, I incline to the view that their role (though very important) is somewhat exaggerated in much contemporary discussion of exchange theory. (Godley, 1999b, p. 23)

We could thus say that expectations, portfolio decisions and monetary policy changes move the exchange rate up and down, but that the overall trend of the exchange rate is given by what happens to the current account. This is essentially verified in the model of Lavoie and Daigle (2011), which is the Godley and Lavoie (2007a, ch. 12) model to which equations (7.15) and (7.16) have been added in an effort to assess the role of exchange rate expectations. As long as the proportion of chartists is low enough, the qualitative variations in the exchange rate are identical to those of a model without expectations. The fundamental exchange rate, as assessed by fundamentalists, which Lavoie and Daigle (2011) call the 'conventional' exchange rate, will have an impact, however, on the actual exchange rate towards which the economy will tend. Interestingly, when the long-run value of the exchange rate is underestimated, the economy tends towards a value that is above its trend value without expectations, and vice versa. In general, the presence of exchange rate expectations slows down the convergence process towards the long-run value of the exchange rate. In addition, when chartists are overly dominant, the cyclical behaviour of the exchange rate imparted by expectations leads to non-converging cycles, and the relationship between trade fundamentals and the exchange rate breaks down. If this SFC model has any validity, we can say that there is thus some legitimacy in claiming that capital account flows led by trend-following investors may destabilize exchange rates.

Summing up, we may thus say that flexible exchange rates over the long term are determined by the fundamentals associated with trade parameters and stocks of assets and debts previously accumulated – the current account balance. Expectations about future exchange rates, through their effects on stocks of foreign assets and liabilities, will also have an impact on the actual trend value of the exchange rate, although their effects in the long term are likely to be the opposite of their short-term effects. Finally, speculative behaviour, of the sort described by equation (7.15), when excessive, can destabilize flexible exchange rates. In any case, as pointed out by Jacques Mazier (2020, p. 82) and Emilio Carnevali (2021), in a pure floating regime, at each moment of time, the exchange rate will have to be such that equation (7.3) is realized, so that both trade flows and capital flows play a role, while recognizing that these variables are themselves endogenous.

7.4.2 Fixed or Flexible Exchange Rates?

The choice of the appropriate exchange rate regime is without a doubt an object of controversy among post-Keynesians, who clearly do not speak in a single voice on this issue. It can be noted that orthodox authors also disagree about what the most appropriate exchange rate regime ought to be, although a majority probably supports a flexible exchange rate regime on the grounds that markets always know best. As Smithin (2001, p. 118) says, the 'debate crosses over party lines'. Whether there is truly a better exchange rate system is doubtful. In the end, what may matter most is the overall exchange rate arrangement that generates the fastest growth in world effective demand. These doubts are best expressed by changes in the position taken by Kaldor with regard to exchange rate regimes. Before the end of the Bretton Woods system in 1973, with its exchange rates fixed to the US dollar within small bands, Kaldor was in favour of flexible exchange rates, believing that changes in relative prices brought about by changes in exchange rates would be enough to bring current account balances back towards equilibrium. Kaldor (1978c, p. xiii) changed his mind in the late 1970s, realizing that he had 'greatly overestimated the effectiveness of the price mechanism in changing the relationship of exports to imports at any given level of income'. Kaldor thus moved back towards a position that had been defended by Harrod in the 1930s, thus claiming 'that trade is kept in balance by variations of production and incomes rather than by price variations: a proposition which implies that the income elasticity of demand of a country's inhabitants for imports and those of foreigners for its exports are far more important explanatory variables than price elasticities' – a proposition that will be examined in detail in another section of this chapter and that is compatible with the post-Keynesian emphasis on income rather than price effects. Kaldor thus came to favour a fixed exchange rate regime, possibly accompanied by restrictions on imports, so as to control, if needed, this income elasticity of demand.

Tilting towards fixed exchange rates

The main post-Keynesian advocate of a regime of fixed exchange rates has always been Davidson (1992). The main argument in favour of fixed exchange rates is the reduction in uncertainty. Although the relative value of a currency may suddenly and drastically change at times, following a devaluation or revaluation, in general, uncertainty is greatly reduced in a fixed exchange rate regime compared to the case of a flexible exchange rate regime. With fixed exchange rates, producers in general and exporters in particular can more easily plan their sales or purchases, as well as their investment decisions, since they have a fairly good idea of the price and profit margins that their products will fetch. They can ascertain with much more confidence whether or not they will be able to compete and win contracts in foreign markets. As Dow (1999, p. 162) put it, 'where there is scope for variation in exchange rates between currencies, there is an additional layer of uncertainty to contend with'. The excessive and unpredictable currency movements involved with flexible exchange rates interfere with the planning decisions of firms. The kind of uncertainty generated by typical fluctuations in floating exchange rates seems much greater than any indecision brought about by changes in inflation rates. Still, orthodox economists claim that price inflation and changes in price inflation distort economic decisions because entrepreneurs become unable to discern the correct relative prices. But those who favour flexible exchange rates seem to be oblivious to the planning difficulties caused by fluctuating exchange rates. The point is made very neatly in the following quote from Wray (1999, p. 196):

> It is ironic that orthodox economists are so concerned with the uncertainty generated in the domestic economy by inflation but are so willing to sweep aside the uncertainty caused by fluctuations in exchange rates, even when theory and evidence suggest that the uncertainty caused by moderate inflation is minuscule when compared with that generated by wildly fluctuating exchange rates.

Davidson (1994, p. 232) provides a related argument in favour of fixed exchange rates, here meaning an exchange rate that moves around a targeted value, with a band of a few percentage points. Davidson argues that the target provides an anchor, a normal exchange rate, around which expectations of traders can concur. With a fixed exchange rate, expectations are likely to be inelastic; their elasticity may even approach zero, so that random changes in the exchange rate will not generate further changes in the same direction. Because of the existence of the anchor, 'portfolio transactions create forces that tend to move the price back towards the original fixed exchange rate after the temporary decline' (ibid.). By contrast, Davidson says, in a flexible exchange rate regime, elasticities of expectations are likely to be high and to generate instability: 'The more flexible the exchange rate is perceived to be, therefore, the more likely an apparent weakness in a currency will induce perceptions of greater uncertainty about the ability of that currency to maintain its value relative to other currencies' (ibid., p. 233). In such a case, just because of precautionary motives, asset-holders are likely to move their assets towards the appreciating currency, and through leads and lags, even assuming away speculation, cumulative causation movements in the exchange rate may ensue. Davidson (ibid., p. 237) further argues that, even if some participants to the foreign exchange market, such as large international banks, have a view of what is the true fundamental value of a currency, there are few incentives to act on the basis of this view, because uncertainty and discontinuities prevail in foreign exchange markets, while the threat of bankruptcies is always looming.

Both Davidson (1994) and Wray (1999) thus argue in favour of a fixed exchange rate regime, based on their belief that such a regime provides for more stability than floating rates, both because less speculative activity in currency markets will ensue and because it provides stability of the units of accounts in which contracts are written. A further argument against floating exchange rates is that, since the end of the Bretton Woods arrangements, there has been an unending series of financial crises throughout the world, although it is not clear whether these have been caused by the presence of flexible exchange rates or rather by the move towards free capital movements, financialization and financial deregulation. Finally, some authors, such as Moore (2004, p. 632), claim that flexible exchange rate regimes exacerbate the deflationary bias that global imbalances impart to the world economy because capital flight is more likely with floating exchange rates, since future values are more uncertain in such a regime.

Tilting towards flexible exchange rates
Some post-Keynesians hold exactly the opposite view, this alternative view having been held most consistently by Smithin (1994, ch. 7; 2001). It is argued instead that fixed

exchange rate regimes impose the largest deflationary biases. Negative external shocks are likely to exercise the largest reductions in effective demand when the domestic economy operates within a fixed exchange rate regime. With such a regime, the authorities become fixated on the evolution of the balance of payments, so as to avoid losing foreign exchange reserves. With a flexible exchange rate, the monetary and fiscal authorities benefit from an extra degree of freedom. Expansionary policies can be pursued in a single country, even if the rest of the world does not follow, as the only drawback will be a depreciation of the home currency. This does not ensure that Keynesian macroeconomic policies will be implemented within the framework of a flexible exchange rate regime, but at least the ability to do so will be increased. Indeed, as is well known, Keynes himself was opposed to the fixity of the exchange rate inherent in the gold standard, and in *The General Theory* he gave a short nod to fluctuating exchange rates (Keynes, 1936, p. 270).

New arguments in favour of flexible exchange rates have been recently proposed. Wray (2006b; 2012), just like Kaldor in the 1970s, has made a complete turnabout on exchange rate regimes, but in his case moving his support from fixed exchange rates to flexible exchange rates. As argued previously by Smithin, Wray (2012, pp. 151–2) now believes that 'a *floating* currency provides more *policy space* – the ability to use domestic fiscal and monetary policy to achieve policy goals'. The golden rule is that governments and the private sector should never borrow funds denominated in a foreign currency: 'it is critical that sovereign nations avoid the temptation to directly (or indirectly) take on foreign currency-denominated debt' (Wray, 2006b, p. 225). Countries must avoid what Eichengreen et al. (2002) have called 'the original sin'. If this is so, meaning that the domestic currency is truly 'sovereign', in the term used by MMT economists, any devaluation of the domestic currency due to expansionary fiscal or monetary policies can have only limited unfavourable effects on the economy and the current account balance, since the government and the domestic agents will not be hurt by an increased debt burden consequent to a currency devaluation. The authorities thus have more room to pursue Keynesian expansionary policies. With flexible exchange rates and no foreign debt in a foreign currency, the central bank is free to keep the target interest rate at the level of its choice since interest rates need not be used as an instrument to safeguard the level of its foreign exchange reserves. Indeed, Moore (1988, p. 274) has long argued that 'the true advantage of flexible exchange rates is that they permit national monetary authorities a greater range of discretion in setting nominal domestic interest rates, thus increasing the power and independence of domestic monetary policy'.

Furthermore, we saw in the previous section that within a post-Keynesian framework the favourable effects of a given expansionary fiscal policy on economic activity are likely to be stronger with flexible than with fixed exchange rates. The government can thus engage in expansionary fiscal policies, with whatever levels of fiscal deficits or public debt necessary to achieve full employment. In other words, macroeconomic policies based on the functional finance approach *à la* Lerner are much easier to achieve in a flexible exchange rate framework than in a fixed exchange rate system. The authorities cannot run out of money, so to speak, because, whatever level the deficit or the public debt achieves, the central bank can always intervene and keep interest rates at a stable level, and it cannot run out of foreign reserves since it does not attempt to peg the exchange rate. Thus the government with a sovereign currency and a flexible exchange rate cannot default on its debt. Provided speculators understand that the risk of default is practically nil, they should exercise no additional pressure on the exchange rate and on interest rates, so that long-term rates should remain within the realm of the short-term interest rate targeted by the central bank.

In the case of a fixed exchange rate regime, when the domestic currency is under attack or simply facing a negative external shock, the authorities have essentially three choices: they can watch their foreign exchange reserves become depleted; they can raise interest rates to generate capital inflows or a reduction in the current account deficit that will bring the balance of payments towards equilibrium; or they can pursue fiscal austerity, to slow down the economy and, it is hoped, reduce the current account deficit. It is as if the government faced a budget constraint forbidding it to spend as much as needed to eliminate unemployment, or as if the government was operating within the confines of the loanable funds model.

The situation is, however, quite different for a country that has set an undervalued currency and that benefits from a structural balance-of-payments surplus. In that case, the central bank intervenes to stop the domestic currency from appreciating: the central bank purchases foreign currency with its domestic currency. The ability to stop a currency from appreciating was demonstrated when in 2011 the central bank of Switzerland decided to stop the Swiss franc from rising relative to the euro. In that case, the central bank disposes of unlimited supplies of domestic currency to keep the peg at its target level. The Swiss National Bank could thus purchase unlimited quantities of foreign currencies since the central bank was itself issuing and selling the Swiss currency desired by foreigners.

The advantages and disadvantages of the exchange rate regime are thus heavily dependent on circumstances. Fixed exchange rates seem highly constraining, but countries on a fixed exchange rate that are piling up foreign exchange reserves are free to pursue monetary and fiscal policies of their choice. Flexible exchange rates seem least restraining, but countries that have taken loans in a foreign currency, as all countries with a few exceptions must do when they borrow on international financial markets, will face heavier debt burdens in addition to increased inflationary pressures if they pursue macroeconomic policies that induce a depreciation of their currency. There is possibly no best solution, only second-best ones.

MMT and the hierarchy of currencies
The question of whether the advantages of a flexible exchange rate regime also apply to developing or emerging economies has generated a lot of debates lately among heterodox economists. Wray (2012, p. 216) affirms that 'most of the developed nations have a sovereign currency'. Although they sometimes add nuances to their claims, MMT advocates contend that countries with a sovereign currency, as defined in section 4.3.13 of Chapter 4, face no or little financial constraints in trying to achieve growth and full employment provided they adopt flexible exchange rates. 'The two principles of functional finance apply most directly to a sovereign nation operating with a floating currency' (Wray, 2012, p. 211). This is because states with a sovereign currency cannot become insolvent and because 'a *floating* currency provides more *policy space* – the ability to use domestic fiscal and monetary policy to achieve policy goals' (ibid., pp. 151–2). However, as Kregel (2020, p. 287) notes, 'proponents of Modern Monetary Theory

frequently use the slogan that a nation State that issues its own currency possesses monetary sovereignty. The problem with this definition is that most countries issue their own currency.... However, the external constraint faced by most open economies does limit monetary sovereignty, irrespective of the exchange rate regime adopted'.

The crux of the matter, so it seems, is that the external constraints faced by developing economies are not the same as those of advanced economies, upon which are based most of the arguments put forth by MMT scholars. A number of post-Keynesian economists have developed the concept of a hierarchy of currencies, so much that one could speak of a currency hierarchy school (Fritz et al., 2018). How high the currency stands in the hierarchy depends on how much the currency is being demanded on international markets to fulfill the standard properties of money (means of payment, unit of account and store of value). This will be reflected, for instance, in the currency composition of trade invoicing, the composition of foreign exchange reserves, and the denomination of the cross-border claims of banks. The currencies at the top of the hierarchy benefit from a liquidity premium, as their position guarantees deep markets, so that the currency can be safely exchanged. There is thus a strong macroeconomic asymmetry on international markets.

The US dollar is obviously at the top of the hierarchy, followed by a handful of centre currencies, in particular the euro, and then the Swiss franc, the Japanese yen, the British pound, the Canadian dollar, the Australian dollar, as well as the Chinese renminbi. At the bottom of the hierarchy are the currencies of developing countries, with the currencies of emerging countries in between. While these latter countries may possess a sovereign currency as defined by MMT, they are subjected to substantial external constraints, including speculative attacks and unstable exchange rates, due to their place in the international monetary and financial system. In addition, as pointed out by Bonizzi et al. (2019), the lack of confidence in many peripherical currencies, caused by previous devaluations or depreciations, induces the residents of these countries to hold their wealth in a foreign currency, thus further jeopardizing the efforts of the monetary authorities to mitigate the effects of global liquidity cycles.

Those economists who support the concept of a hierarchy of currencies thus believe that in the case of peripherical economies, pure floating regimes are no better than managed floating regimes or fixed exchange rates, and do not provide more policy space. Indeed, there is even a fear of floating. The trilemma is gone. The refusal of peripherical countries to adopt floating rates does not arise from self-imposed constraints; rather, it is a consequence of the additional constraints arising from being at the bottom of the currency hierarchy (Vergnhanini and De Conti, 2018; Prates, 2020).

Vernengo and Pérez Caldentey (2020, p. 333) explain that the main financial problem of peripherical countries is to obtain the core foreign currencies that will allow them to pay for the imported intermediary and capital goods that they need to develop and transform their industrial structure; without these essential imported products, the country is at risk of paralysis. Since most developing countries are still unable to borrow funds in their own currency in international markets, as explained above, they must submit themselves to the *original sin* and borrow funds in foreign currencies, and will thus also require foreign currency to service their debt. These funds are not necessarily borrowed by the state; they may be borrowed by banks, non-financial firms or even households. Whatever is the case, if for whatever reason the domestic currency depreciates, there will be negative consequences as the burden of the debt valued in the local currency will rise: the government may have to default on its foreign debt; banks or firms may wind up in a dire situation, with their foreign debt being taken over by the state; households may have to make large cuts in their consumption expenditures to avoid being insolvent. Even if these peripherical countries and firms can borrow from abroad in their own currency, they are likely to do so at very high interest rates so as to cover the depreciation risk inherent to weak currencies as well as the liquidity risk inherent to small debt issuers, thus ultimately inducing them to borrow in a foreign currency.

Furthermore, Lerner (1943, p. 43) himself, when discussing his principles of functional finance, recognized that public debt issued in the domestic currency but held by foreigners could become problematic, while Wray and Nersisyan (2020, p. 278) affirm that whether the holder of the debt is a resident or a non-resident is irrelevant. But in the case of the non-resident, income taxes cannot be levied on the interest payments and a refusal to rollover the debt will tend to depreciate the domestic currency.

In contrast to what is asserted by Wray and Nersisyan (2020, p. 266) who only rely on evidence pertaining to advanced economies, peripherical countries, whose markets are dominated by foreign corporations and who must import intermediary goods, are subjected to significant pass-through effects as noted in Chapter 3, meaning that inflation responds strongly to depreciation. This may generate restrictive fiscal or monetary policies that would jeopardize any full-employment policy. In addition, as also pointed out by Serrano and Summa (2015, p. 263), in and by itself the depreciation of the domestic currency is likely to be contractionary, in particular because real wages will decrease, bringing down consumption and aggregate demand, notwithstanding the rising debt burden already alluded to. For all these reasons, letting the home currency depreciate without limits as suggested by MMT advocates is unlikely to be an appropriate strategy. It is preferable for peripherical countries to adopt a managed floating regime, possibly accompanied by capital controls.

7.4.3 The International Financial Architecture

While both flexible and fixed exchange rate regimes appear unsatisfactory, are there other alternatives? We have already discussed the currency board and its flaws, and hence no more will be said about them here. Three other possibilities have been under discussion by various post-Keynesians: dollarization, an international clearing house, and a common currency area. We discuss these in turn.

Moore (2004) has presented what most would consider a rather surprising position. In a nutshell, his argument is that a global economy ought to have a global currency. In the most extreme form of this argument, Moore recommends that all countries adopt what is already the *de facto* international currency, the US dollar. If they do this, exchange rates no longer exist, the uncertainty caused by unpredictable fluctuations in exchange rates disappears as well, as do the financial and real costs of converting currencies. Moore (2004, p. 638) also claims that, with global dollarization, 'the current account deficit or surplus becomes a matter of supreme indifference', as is already the case of provinces or states that form part of country sharing a currency. Moore recognizes that a country that accepts to dollarize its economy loses the possibility of having an independent monetary policy, or, in the words of Smithin (1994, p. 124), 'it effectively abandons control over its own economic destiny'. Moore believes, however, that less developed countries do not have such control anyway and might as well dollarize and enjoy the removal of the external balance constraint. As a compromise, Moore proposes to have two or three large currency areas, based on the dollar, the euro and either the yen or the renminbi.

A common currency area: the eurozone
The mention of the euro brings to mind the huge financial difficulties met by several members of the eurozone since 2010. While Moore may be right in claiming that intra-eurozone current account balances as such ought to be of no or little concern to financial analysts, dollarization or euroization, if it eliminates currency risk, does not eliminate country risk due to possible defaults on debt (Wray, 2006b, p. 225). In the case of a dollarized country, there is no purchaser of last resort for the securities issued by the government that took the decision to dollarize, and thus interest rates in such a country are entirely under the control of financial markets. Dollarized countries must pursue fiscal policies that satisfy the whims of financial actors, otherwise they will get punished, meaning that interest rates on domestic government securities will rise.

There was a belief, nourished by reliance on the efficient-market hypothesis and the assumption that markets are self-righting, that with the strictures and obligations of the Maastricht Treaty, eurozone countries would never run into any sort of financial trouble. As explained in section 4.3.13 of Chapter 4, by both design and convention, the ECB and its national central banks did not act as a purchaser of last resort for sovereign securities, or rather did not do so until it was too late and until interest rates of several eurozone countries escalated to unsustainable levels, driven up by the feverish sentiments of speculators and the fears caused by a sovereign debt no longer deemed default-free. The convention held by the creators of the eurozone, as Sawyer (2001b, p. 188) points out, was that interest rates are set by a 'loanable funds consideration', so that 'there must be limits on the borrowing of each government, as "excessive" borrowing by one government in euros would bid up the interest rate paid by other governments, also borrowing in euros'. To avoid distortions in the financial markets, it was thus decided that it was best for the ECB not to purchase any sovereign debt at all. All the predictions of this loanable funds approach turned out to be wrong, as we now know. There was financial trouble, the ECB launched itself into huge purchases of government and corporate bonds, and long-term interest rates of all eurozone countries eventually became either negative or not very far from zero, despite the public debt to GDP ratio of the whole euro area being much higher than that commanded by the Maastricht Treaty.

A number of post-Keynesian authors (Bell, Forstater, Kregel, Palley, Pivetti, Simonazzi and Vianello, Wray) were quite critical of the eurozone setup and how the ECB and national central banks were being constrained. The most explicit critics were perhaps Godley and Parguez, who were quite prescient about the flaws of the eurozone setup and their damning consequences, although it took nearly ten years for these flaws to become obvious. Their statements speak for themselves.

> It needs to be emphasized at the start that the establishment of a single currency in the EC would indeed bring to an end the sovereignty of its component nations and their power to take independent actions on major issues . . . The power to issue its own money, to make drafts on its own central bank, is the main thing that defines national independence. If a country gives up or loses this power, it acquires the status of a local authority or colony. Local authorities

and regions obviously cannot devalue. But they also lose the power to finance deficits through money creation while other methods of raising finance are subject to central regulation. Nor can they change interest rates. (Godley, 1992, p. 3)

Member states will have to be granted credit by private banks . . . Their ability to borrow will depend on the ability and willingness of private banks to finance government expenditures . . . A credit-worthy state should pledge to balance its budget, to get to a zero ex post deficit, so as to protect the banks against the risk of accumulating public debt. Government bonds will no longer be liquid assets . . . The fate of the euro will depend upon the fiscal austerity rules. States could not be granted credits by private banks if they do not meet the constraint of running a balanced budget or a fiscal surplus. To comply with this constraint, states will have to slash their social expenditures because they are the most adverse to the brutal instincts of financial investors . . . Contrary to the hopes of its architects, the Euro will increase financial instability in the world economy. By exporting its self-imposed deflation, Europe will, like in the early 1930s, accelerate the pace of the world crisis. (Parguez, 1999, pp. 73–4)

The eurozone setup should have incorporated a central government that can pursue expansionary fiscal policies, targeting in particular the countries that are most hurt by a recession. With the present setup, individual countries are prevented from doing so on their own, first because they might be punished by financial markets if the central bank stands still, and second because the various European treaties – starting with Maastricht in 1992, moving on to the Stability and Growth Pact, and culminating in the 2012 Fiscal Compact – forbid large fiscal deficits. The eurozone setup should also have incorporated a central bank that purchases large amounts of securities issued by the participating national governments, thus allowing the ECB to acquire the securities of the countries whose yields are rising and to sell its holdings of securities whose yields are decreasing (Godley and Lavoie, 2007c). The convention that the ECB should provide instead advances to commercial banks, acting for them as the lender of last resort, turned out to be insufficient and even totally inept in times of crisis, for, as noted by Sawyer (2001b, p. 188), 'bonds issued by different national governments, denominated in euros, may attract different credit ratings and hence different interest rates'. Deprived of their ability to devaluate, eurozone countries in crisis seem to be stuck in a 'low' equilibrium. They are in a much more difficult situation than countries in a standard fixed exchange rate regime that still have the possibility of recourse to a unilateral devaluation.

Keynes's Plan

The austerity policies proposed by mainstream economists as a solution to the eurozone crisis exemplify the main drawback of current fixed exchange rate regimes, be they of the standard sort or currency unions such as the eurozone: the burden of adjustment falls on the country that is running a current account deficit. The alternative to the Bretton Woods system that Keynes (1973, xxv) had put forward in 1941 was precisely based on the opposite principle: it is the country running the current account surplus that ought to defend the parity of the exchange rate. In other words, Keynes wanted the burden of adjustment to fall mostly, or at least equally, on the creditor, and not on the debtor. This became known as Keynes's Plan. Davidson (1992; 1994) has been a long-time advocate of such a plan, or more precisely of a modified version of it, and a somewhat similar plan has also been proposed by Jane D'Arista (2000; 2004). As was pointed out earlier, the reason for which the creditor – the country running a current account surplus – ought to provide support for exchange rate parity is that it is much easier to stop a currency from appreciating than it is to stop it from depreciating. In the former case, the central bank can buy foreign exchange without limit by issuing its own money. The country running a surplus can sell unlimited amounts of its own currency and thus preserve an exchange rate peg. By contrast, the debtor with a current account deficit, or more precisely with a balance-of-payments deficit, will eventually run out of foreign exchange reserves. Furthermore, as argued by Bagnai and Rieber (2019), restrictive fiscal policy by the weaker country to retrieve a balanced current account will generate a reduction in the growth rate of both countries; by contrast, an expansionary fiscal policy by the country enjoying a current account surplus will be benefical to both countries while also bringing both current account balances back to equilibrium.

The main feature of Davidson's (1994, p. 269) plan is to have 'a *closed*, double-entry bookkeeping clearing institution to keep the payments "score" among the various trading regions plus some mutually agreed rules to create and reflux liquidity'. The unit of account, which Davidson calls the International Money Clearing Unit (IMCU), and which Keynes called the bancor, would be held only by the central banks, and not by the public or private financial institutions. The parities would first be set in accordance with the existing exchange rates, exactly as when the conversion rates towards the euro were decided in January 1999, and would then be modified, according to circumstances, by following pre-established rules. Both Davidson (1994, p. 269) and D'Arista (2004, p. 570) indicate that major international payments would have to go first through the national central banks, which would then clear and settle on the books of what D'Arista calls the international clearing agency (ICA) and which Keynes called an international clearing bank. An English importer of Chilean wines would pay for the wine in pounds, from his or her account at a UK bank; the payment would go through the Bank of England, which would be debited at the ICA in units of the IMCU. The Chilean central bank would then be granted a credit at the ICA in the same unit, and would credit the account of the Chilean exporter in Chilean pesos. From Keynes's (1973, xxv, p. 212) standpoint, the advantage of such a procedure is that it facilitates the imposition of capital controls and increases the likelihood of getting rid of currency speculation.

In D'Arista's (2000) plan, all national central banks hold reserves at the ICA, which they acquired by selling securities issued by their respective governments to the ICA. If a country is running out of ICA reserves, because of a consistent deficit of its balance of payments, its reserves can be replenished by further sales of government securities to the ICA. If Chile kept selling wine to the UK, the ICA would purchase securities issued by the UK government to replenish the reserves of the UK at the ICA; symmetrically, the ICA would sell some of its holdings of Chilean securities so as to stop Chilean reserves at the ICA from accumulating. In Davidson's (1992) plan, the ICA would act as a true clearing house: countries with surpluses in their balance of payments would accumulate credits at the ICA, while countries with deficits in their balance of payments would accumulate overdrafts at the ICA. The latter would be the financial claim that countries with a current account deficit must relinquish in exchange for their net imports (Rossi, 2006, p. 196). What rate of interest would be paid on credits, if any, and what interest rate would be charged on advances in the IMCU, and how it would be determined, is not very clear, however. Both Keynes and Davidson proposed various rules to stop countries from piling up credits and overdrafts, including adjustments to exchange rates. To encourage surplus countries to pursue more expansionary macroeconomic policies, excessive credits could be confiscated and redistributed to debtors.

Davidson's plan offers resemblances to two existing institutions. Since 2002, there has been a special private international institution – the CLS Bank – which settles foreign exchange transactions occurring in nearly 20 major currencies. The main purpose of the CLS Bank is to eliminate the so-called 'principal Herstatt risk', which exists because national settlement systems have different operating times: it could happen that a counterparty provides the sold currency without receiving the bought currency. The risk is eliminated because the central banks involved with the major currencies have agreed to keep a continuously linked settlement service with the CLS Bank. Figure 7.8 illustrates a foreign exchange transaction when the CLS Bank is involved. Things are slightly more complicated than the case illustrated in Figure 7.2. Bank C, the Canadian commercial bank, wishes once more to buy yens and sell Canadian dollars. It will provide the dollars, the 'pay-ins', by making a payment through the clearing house, here the LVTS, to the Bank of Canada, which will deposit the dollars in the account of the CLS Bank at the Bank of Canada. Bank J, on the other hand, will make a pay-in in yens, through the Japanese clearing and settlement system, to the Bank of Japan, which will deposit the yens in the account of the CLS Bank at the Bank of Japan. Once both pay-ins are made, the CLS Bank can then proceed to the 'pay-outs'. The nostro bank of

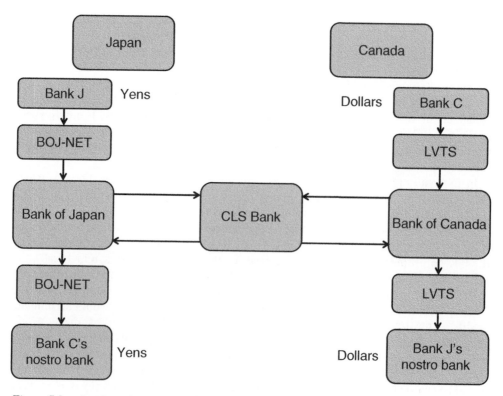

Figure 7.8 A private international clearing agency: the CLS Bank

the Japanese commercial bank, Bank J, will receive the dollars through the Canadian clearing and settlement system, while the nostro bank of the Canadian commercial bank will receive the yens through the Japanese clearing and settlement system. At the end of the day, nothing will be left on the books of the CLS Bank. To some extent, the CLS Bank plays the role of Davidson's international clearing agency: transactions have to go through the central banks, and the CLS acts as a clearing house. Here, however, the central banks are not a counterparty to any foreign exchange transaction; they act as a pure intermediary.

TARGET2 as a European version of Keynes's Plan
The second institution having some resemblance to Keynes's plan is the TARGET2 clearing and settlement system that has been put in place in the eurozone (Cesaratto, 2013; Lavoie, 2015a; 2015b). In a sense this is not surprising since the eurozone is a peculiar instance of a fixed exchange rate. Of course, things are simplified in the case of the eurozone since the IMCU is also the currency used for private transactions – the euro. While there is much talk about the ECB and its decisions to set the target interest rate and to provide various special lending facilities to the banks, most of the actual operations occur through the national central banks of the countries that are part of the eurozone. When it comes to monetary transactions involving banking systems located in different countries of the eurozone, the ECB operates in a way that is very similar to Davidson's version of the international clearing agency or bank: the ECB lets national central banks accumulate surpluses or overdrafts on their accounts at the ECB. This can be shown with the following example.

Suppose that some Italian company imports goods from Germany and makes its payment through its Italian bank, here the Banca Nazionale de Lavoro (BNL). The payment goes through TARGET2, and, ends up as a credit on the account of the German exporting firm, at its German bank, here the Deutsche Bank (DB). At this stage, the Italian bank has a debit position at the Bank of Italy, while the German bank has a credit position at the Bundesbank. Furthermore, the Bundesbank debits the account of the Bank of Italy. All this occurs smoothly as national central banks of the eurozone provide unlimited and uncollaterized lines of credit to each other. All these debit and credit accounts are recorded in the first row of Table 7.8. However, by the end of the day, national central banks must also settle with each other. All the debits and credits are netted on the books of the ECB, where each national central bank then acquires a net position *vis-à-vis* the rest of the European System of Central Banks (ESCB). This is shown in the second row of Table 7.8. Moreover, as one would expect within the confines of a theory of endogenous money and the reflux principle, the Deutsche Bank will most probably use its positive clearing balances (or reserves) to reduce its overdraft position *vis-à-vis* the Bundesbank. This is also shown in the second row of the table.

There is no limit to the debit position that a national central bank can incur on the books of the ECB; that is, its liabilities with respect to the rest of the eurosystem are not limited. 'These liabilities can be carried indefinitely as there is no time prescribed for the settlement of imbalances' (Garber, 2010, p. 2). Additionally, national central banks in debit are charged the main official rate, which is also the rate gained by those with claims on the eurosystem (Whelan, 2014, p. 88). Thus these imbalances could go on forever, as (coming back to the example) the BNL would be taking advances from the Bank of

Table 7.8 The eurozone clearing and settlement system when Italy imports goods from Germany

Banca Nazionale del Lavoro (BNL)		Bank of Italy (BI)		Deutsche Bank (DB)		Bundesbank (BB)		ECB	
Asset	Liability	Asset	Liability	Asset	Liability	Asset	Liability	Asset	Liability
	Deposit importer −10 Advance from BI +10	Advance to BNL +10	Advance from BB +10	Reserves at BB +10.	Deposit exporter +10	Advance to BI +10	Deposit of DB +10		
	Deposit importer −10 Advance from BI +10	Advance to BNL +10	Due to the eurosystem +10		Deposit exporter +10 Advance from BB −10	Claims on the eurosystem +10 Advance to DB −10		Debit position of BI +10	Credit position of BB +10

548

Italy at 1.5 per cent (if this is the main refinancing rate), while the Bank of Italy would be accumulating liabilities within the eurosystem at the same pace, also at a 1.5 per cent interest rate.

What has been shown above demonstrates that imbalances within the eurozone ought not to be a problem, besides the obvious fact that a trade deficit has a negative impact on economic activity. A current account deficit of Spain or Italy with respect to the rest of the eurozone is no more meaningful than the current account deficit of the Mezzogiorno relative to northern Italy. The problem is that there are no federal transfer payments from the surplus to the deficit countries to help compensate the negative impact of trade deficits on GDP and budget balances.

In the example of Table 7.8, we assumed that German banks would not provide overnight lending or longer-term lending to Italian banks. But if they were to do so, as they did before 2007, the current account deficit of Italy would be compensated by a financial account surplus, arising from the last row of Table 7.1. There would be no increase in the balance sheet of the ECB. But if the overnight market within the eurozone is partially frozen, as was the case starting in 2007, then the second row of Table 7.8 is indeed the most likely result of imbalances in current accounts. Similar changes to the balance sheet of the ECB will also occur if economic agents lose confidence in the Italian banking system and decide to move their funds to German banks. Again, balance sheets will get modified as shown in the second row of Table 7.8.

There are thus great similarities between Davidson's plan and the functioning of the payment system in the eurozone, since both setups envisage an international clearing bank that grants advances to deficit countries, with no timeline for reimbursement. Keynes's Plan and Davidson's plan are thus in the realm of the possible. Indeed, some heterodox economists argue that the structure of the eurozone could be modified so as to incorporate other features of Keynes's Plan, in particular the possibility, even the obligation, to revise the existing parities within the eurozone (to devalue or revalue all contracts and financial assets held in a given country of the eurozone). The ECB would still be handling the external value of the euro (Mazier, 2020, ch. 6).

Was the eurozone crisis a balance-of-payment crisis?
I have argued above that a eurozone country could suffer from balance-of-payment deficits without any financial consequences. Deficit countries can accommodate capital flight or current account deficits without incurring a financial crisis. The country will not be losing any foreign exchange reserves, or rather it is as if foreign reserves are constantly being replenished through the mechanism of the negative TARGET2 balances that the deficit country would accumulate within the eurosystem along with the refinancing operations of the ECB. Still, a number of economists, both mainstream and heterodox, have argued that the eurozone crisis was either a balance-of-payment crisis or something akin to a balance-of-payment crisis. How can this be, given the existence of the TARGET2 mechanism within the currency union?

The first argument is that, except for Ireland, all the countries found in the middle of the storm of the eurozone crisis between 2010 and 2012 were countries that had run current account deficits. The argument is thus that Greece, Portugal, Spain and Italy, just like emerging economies subjected to balance-of-payment crises, went through a sequence of financial liberalization, associated with the obvious fixed exchange rate of the eurozone, with financial flows going from the core of the eurozone towards these more peripherical countries, followed by rising wage and price inflation, current account deficits and rising indebtedness towards foreign institutions, culminating with fears of default on these debts and sudden stops or reversals of financial flows, accompanied by rising interest rates on sovereign bonds. In emerging economies, the IMF is called to the rescue, which imposes conditionality programs based on cuts in public expenditures and wage deflation. This is obviously what happened to Greece, and to a lesser extent to the other GIIPS countries, through the threats of the ECB to pull the plug on banks if their governments did not follow fiscal rules. Austerity policies are being imposed by surplus countries as a means to generate future current account surpluses so as to ensure that the external debt of GIIPS countries can be serviced and even reduced. Cesaratto (2013; 2015b; 2017) has been the main advocate of this view among heterodox economists.

The alternative view, found in various blogs of Randall Wray, and in Lavoie (2015a; 2015b) and Febrero et al. (2018), is that the eurozone financial crisis was essentially the consequence of flawed institutional arrangements, notably the lack of a proper federal government that could engage in stabilization policies, the absence of a banking union and the convention that the ECB would pursue monetary operations by the exclusive use of advances or repos, and not through outright bond purchases. There was some uncertainty even regarding the ECB as a lender of last resort to the banking system since the ECB refinancing operations through collaterized credit were subjected to minimum credit-rating requirements, in an effort to impose fiscal discipline on eurozone countries. Eventually, during the crisis, rating requirements were diminished and then even suspended, but as pointed out by Gabor and Ban (2016, p. 629), the ECB decided to impose higher haircuts on repos, including those based on sovereign bonds, thus dealing 'a heavy blow to low-rated governments, increasing the cost of using their government bonds as collateral'. Hedge funds and other financial institutions became fully aware of these flaws that made eurozone governments no longer default-risk free. Investor funds proceeded to speculative attacks, first against the countries whose bond markets lacked liquidity, then against those that were most susceptible to the doom loop of commercial-bank insolvency and sovereign-debt illiquidity. The ECB had already acted too little and too late in 2010, and had been under tremendous pressure from the German media and German institutions not to act as a purchaser of last resort of sovereign bonds. The attacks stopped in July 2012 with Draghi's famous 'whatever it takes' statement, which was understood as a significant turnaround in ECB policy, thus vowing to act as a purchaser of last resort. Speculators immediately relented, and yield spreads declined without the ECB actually buying any bond. In addition, the ECB later engaged in huge quantitative easing operations, which brought the bond yields of *all* eurozone countries below those of American bonds, showing that the eurozone crisis could have been averted by adequate actions.

Since these two views of the eurozone crisis are based on a similar understanding of their authors about endogenous money and the TARGET2 system, can they be reconciled? One could argue that denomination risk was the main reason for which yields on sovereign bonds of the eurozone south rose to unsustainable levels. For Cesaratto (2020, pp. 180–1), the main cause of spread increases was the investors' fear that the eurozone would implode and that countries would revert to their own currencies. What makes it a balance-of-payments crisis, from this perspective, is that the periphery high spreads were caused by the denomination risk generated by the belief that the GIIPS would decide or would be forced to leave the monetary union as a consequence of the fiscal straitjacket imposed by the various fiscal pacts. There was thus a convertibility risk, the risk that the sovereign debts would be converted from the euro to a domestic currency that would suffer depreciation relative to the euro. But there also could be a default risk, if the exiting countries became unable to modify the denomination of their debt and be forced to default on a currency that would become a foreign one. The higher interest rates were thus there to cover both risks. Kelton and Wray (2009, p. 13) in their *Can Euroland Survive* paper, said something very similar: rising austerity measures 'intensify frustration among member states and fuel speculation that some states may simply abandon the euro. Financial markets can hedge against the risk of default (as a consequence of leaving the euro) by purchasing CDSs'.

7.5 IMPEDIMENTS TO INTERNATIONAL TRANSACTIONS

Orthodox economists, save for some of their dissenters, would argue today that the best international architecture is a world of flexible exchange rate regimes, with unrestricted international capital flows and liberalized trade: in short, free trade and no capital control. This view of international transactions is based on the presupposition underlined in Chapter 1: the belief that markets, and financial markets in particular, are essentially stabilizing institutions that provide for optimal efficiency. The liberalization of international capital flows is justified on several grounds: it makes for a better allocation of savings; it allows capital to move towards the projects with the highest returns; it spreads risks; it sparks underdeveloped financial sectors; and it disciplines profligate governments. The liberalization of trade is said to provide similar advantages: through specialization and through higher competitive pressures, it makes economic activity more productive, and it is said to speed up growth by getting access to international markets.

7.5.1 Capital Controls

There is a long tradition of open opposition to fully liberalized trade and capital flows within post-Keynesian economics. This opposition goes all the way back to Keynes, although his objections to international capital mobility were much more systematic than his support for tariffs on imported goods, which evolved with time and circumstances (Eichengreen, 1984; Bibow, 2009, chs 7 and 8). In his proposal for an international clearing union, Keynes (1973, xxv, p. 185) quite clearly stated that 'control of capital movement, both inward and outward, should be a permanent feature', arguing that 'there is no country which can, in future, safely allow the flight of funds for political reasons or to evade domestic taxation'. Elsewhere, Keynes (ibid., p. 149) comments that 'freedom of capital movements is an essential part of the old *laissez-faire* system', but he obviously rejected that part of the neoliberal doctrine, on the grounds that capital controls allow central banks to set interest rates to achieve domestic objectives such as full employment, a task that he deems impossible with pegged exchange rates and no impediment to capital flows.

The essential post-Keynesian argument against unrestricted international capital flows and hence in favour of capital controls is that unfettered financial liberalization leads to financial crises – a kind of Minsky's financial fragility hypothesis applied at the international level (Bonizzi and Kaltenbrunner, 2021). Freely moving capital flows facilitate speculative activity and herd behaviour. International capital flows are procyclical. They provoke asset bubbles and make for worse downturns. According to Ilene Grabel (1996; 2006), financial liberalization makes countries more vulnerable to financial crises – associated with both banking crises and currency crises. This is particularly true for developing economies, but even fully industrialized countries have had to face devastating financial crises. These crises have involved large-scale depreciations of the domestic currency, maturity mismatches, currency mismatches between assets and debts, capital withdrawals by both foreigners and residents, contagion effects when neighbour countries started to run into difficulties, and extraordinary increases in interest rates. In most cases, financial liberalization and its subsequent crises have led to IMF intervention and the imposition of all the standard IMF austerity measures, with their now well-known disastrous consequences for economic activity and employment. The purpose of capital controls, what Grabel (2006) calls trip-wires and speed-bumps, is to reduce the frequency and depth of financial crises.

For post-Keynesians, financial efficiency as defined by neoclassical authors, with its highly liquid assets, is a recipe for disaster. The Global Financial Crisis has shown once more that the countries that were most open to outside financial flows are those that suffered the most from the world crisis. The destabilizing effects of unpredictable capital flows were all there to be seen in the cases of Mexico in 1994–95, East Asia in 1997–98 and Argentina in 2000–01. Taking a more structural long-term view, post-Keynesians interpret historical evidence as giving credence to the idea that successful nations, those that have managed to create an industrial base, had state-imposed constraints on finance and in particular international finance. The state had a strong influence on the domestic financial sector, which was essentially closed to the outside world. South Korea and Japan had stringent capital controls when their economies took off, and the same may still be said today about China. Capital controls have also been imposed quite successfully in recent years by countries such as Chile, Colombia, India, Malaysia, Singapore and Taiwan, and indeed, in light of all this historical experience, even the IMF had to recant its previous objections to capital controls (Grabel, 2015; Gallagher, 2015; Ostry et al., 2016).

Gerald Epstein (2010) provides a list of various capital management techniques that can be put in place to tame international flows. These capital controls can be price-based or quantity-based; they can affect inflows or outflows; they may even be related to prudential regulations of the domestic banking sector, such as limitations on the maturity structure of assets and liabilities. In the case of controls over outflows, the main aim is to stop the currency from devaluing and to create some room for expansionary policies by neutralizing the threat of capital flight. Capital controls over inflows can have several different objectives: they help manage the exchange rate in the hope of keeping a competitive rate; they promote desirable types of investments: those that create employment, and are long-term, stable and sustainable. Price-based controls on inflows may include taxes or unremunerated reserve requirements on capital inflows; quantity-based controls on inflows can include quantitative limits on funds borrowed from abroad or quantitative limits on foreign ownership of domestic companies, in all sectors or in specifically important sectors. The Tobin tax, applied on all foreign exchange transactions, would be a price-based control affecting both inflows and outflows.

As Epstein (2010, p. 303) concludes, 'capital management techniques are no panacea for economic problems ... For countries navigating the treacherous waters of international finance, however, they can be useful components of the macroeconomic toolkit.'

7.5.2 Absolute Advantage versus Comparative Advantage

Trade protection is certainly not part of conventional wisdom. Still, Ha-Joon Chang (2003; 2008) provides detailed historical evidence that the current big players of international trade did not industrialize by following the precepts of free trade. These countries have jockeyed for technological superiority by putting in place protectionist measures, thereby obtaining an absolute advantage at the expense of other nations during certain historical periods. Western European countries and the USA, along with Canada and the more recent Asian tigers, and now China, moved up the ladder by exporting more while providing trade protection and state support to industry. They did not play by the rules that are now advocated by the USA and international organizations such as the World Trade Organization (WTO), the International Monetary Fund (IMF) or the World Bank, and imposed on the developing countries that attempt to industrialize in their turn. As the title of one of Chang's (2003) books says, rich countries are 'kicking away the ladder' when they pressure developing countries to adopt free trade and the elimination of all trade impediments. Or, as Robinson (1973, p. 12) put it, 'it seems after all that the free-trade doctrine is just a more subtle form of mercantilism. It is believed only by those who will gain an advantage from it'. Bhaduri (1986, p. 147) agrees, writing that 'freer trade merely sets the rules for the economically stronger nations to capture a large share of the international market'.

Post-Keynesians have for a long time shown a degree of scepticism with regard to the claims of free traders (Rider, 1982). The free trade doctrine is based on the law of comparative advantage, the understanding of which used to be the litmus test to distinguish true economists from amateur ones. Most economists will thus assert that trade restrictions reduce global welfare, although this assertion will be qualified by recognizing that some groups may be losing out when trade is liberalized (Blecker, 2005, p. 334). While the theory of comparative advantage is unassailable on its own grounds, its critics question the assumptions that underlie the conclusions drawn from it (Prasch, 1996). The theory of comparative advantage relies on at least four assumptions, which are not always obvious to students: the theory assumes that trade occurs between nations; it assumes full employment and full capacity utilization; it assumes the existence of a mechanism that will bring the trade balance into equilibrium; and it assumes away increasing returns or increasing returns to scale.

The rejection of these four hypotheses has led post-Keynesian and other heterodox economists to adopt an alternative approach to trade theory – the principle of absolute advantage (Shaikh, 1980b, 2007b; Milberg, 1994; Cagatay, 1994; Onaran, 2011). The critics argue that international trade does not occur between nations but between firms. International trade is not some kind of barter between two nations. It involves firms that trade with each other but that also compete for shares on world markets, just as they compete for shares on domestic markets.

Firms do not take their purchasing decisions on the basis of comparative advantage; their decisions are based on absolute advantage. In a given country, as long as transport costs are not overly high, all else equal, firms will produce the products that have the lowest costs. Regions that have low unit costs, either because they have low wages or because their plants are more productive, will be able to export more. The same will occur with regions that are able to produce quality products not found elsewhere. Economic activity and employment will rise in this region. The fact that another region has some comparative advantage in the production of widgets will not help that other region one bit, as long as these widgets are produced at a higher unit cost. If interprovincial or interstate free trade is implemented, trade will go only one way, employment will rise in the low-cost region and it will decrease in the high-cost region. Thus, while employed workers in the high-cost region will indeed benefit from the lower prices of the imported goods, thus gaining higher real wages and higher living standards, the number of unemployed workers in the high-cost region will rise and their standard of living will plunge. In the low-cost region, more people will be able to find jobs and hence family incomes will rise.

The principle of comparative advantage assumes the existence of full employment and full capacity in the two regions or the two countries that are trading. It assumes that the low-cost region is unable to produce, simultaneously, more of everything. In the language of microeconomists, it assumes that economies are always on their production possibility frontiers, so that the only way to increase overall production and consumption is to abandon production in sectors where each region has a relative disadvantage, and to increase production in sectors where each region has a relative advantage. Full employment, however, is not the usual situation, neither in industrialized nations nor in less developed countries where there is a mass of unemployed or sub-employed workers and where there is a problem of insufficient aggregate demand. With labour unemployment and excess capacity, more of everything can be produced without the reallocation of production.

Is it appropriate to make an analogy between interregional provincial trade and international trade? Critics such as Shaikh (1980b; 2007b) believe that it is, because they contend that there are no automatic mechanisms, beyond changes in economic activity, that will bring the trade balance back to equilibrium. They argue, both on theoretical and historical grounds, that the automatic mechanisms that are meant to transform some of the absolute advantages into merely comparative ones do not exist, or else may take too much time to produce their effects. Countries that suffer from absolute disadvantages will thus face persistent trade and current account deficits.

Free trade advocates argue that trade deficits lead to falling exchange rates or to falling domestic prices that transform the weaker country into a competitive one by lowering its costs relative to those of their foreign competitors. Post-Keynesians question whether this is necessarily so. Take the case of a fixed exchange rate regime. According to the rules of the game that we discussed earlier, trade deficits ought to lead to a loss of gold or of foreign exchange reserves, thus generating a decrease in the supply of money and hence, in line with the quantity theory of money, a decline in prices and unit costs. The compensation thesis that we described in an earlier section of the chapter shows that the first stage of this automatic adjustment mechanism – the decrease in the money supply – does not arise in the post-Keynesian model with reflux. We also saw that the reflux mechanism, applied to international payments, already existed even at the time of the gold standard, and hence that a return to such an international monetary system would not help to enforce the so-called rules of the game. The compensation thesis, based on the reflux mechanism and on the other features of the post-Keynesian theory of endogenous money, thus puts in jeopardy both the theory of comparative advantage and the self-adjusting mechanisms that are taken for granted in mainstream theories of open economies in a fixed exchange rate regime. An example of this nowadays is the current account imbalances that existed before and during the Great Recession within the eurozone, which is a special case of a fixed exchange rate arrangement. Adjustments so far have occurred mainly on the quantity side, through reductions in economic activity.

7.5.3 Trade Protection

The New Cambridge support for tariffs and quotas
All this helps to explain why, despite the opprobrium associated with trade protection measures, a number of post-Keynesians, including Robinson and Kaldor, have expressed some sympathy for the use of tariffs and quotas. New Cambridge – the members of the Cambridge Economic Policy Group – became well known for its endorsement of tariffs and quotas on imports in the UK in the 1970s. Cripps and Godley (1978) argued that, once a country started running systematic trade deficits with high unemployment, being what they called a 'relatively unsuccessful country', few options were open to remedy this situation. At the time, after the fall of the Bretton Woods agreement, the UK pound sterling had joined the European 'serpent', along with the Deutschmark, the French franc and the Italian lira. With such pegged exchange rates, expansionary policies could not be pursued because they would worsen the external deficit. With import controls, domestic production, substituting for imports, would increase and expansionary fiscal and monetary policies would be made possible as the external constraint would be uplifted. The argument made by Cripps and Godley (1978, p. 327) was that 'the use of import controls with fiscal expansion to raise the level of activity need not be a "beggar-my-neighbour" policy', and that such a policy could achieve full employment in countries that happen to be relatively unsuccessful with regard to their trade performance.

But what about the other options – devaluation or else letting the domestic currency depreciate within a floating exchange regime? At the time, Cripps and Godley (1978, p. 329) argued that 'devaluation quickly raises export and import prices in sterling relative to home costs, but only slowly changes export market shares or import propensities'. Their argument relied on the belief that difficulties encountered with the trade balance had more to do with the quality and design of the products being exported than with their relative prices. Thus, from their standpoint, a devaluation would not bring the trade balance back to equilibrium in the short run, so that expansionary policies could not yet be conducted since a country on a pegged exchange rate would still be losing foreign exchange reserves. This behaviour of the trade balance came to be known as the J-curve effect. They further thought that devaluation would cause an increase in import prices, and hence trigger a wage–price inflationary spiral (McCombie and Thirlwall, 1994, p. 452), through the real-wage resistance argument that will be outlined in Chapter 8, so that even long-term effects on the trade balance were questionable. In the view of Cripps and Godley, wage resistance was more likely in the case of a devaluation than in the case of tariffs because in the former case exporters would be able to increase their export prices and thus make higher profits, which would induce unions to ask for higher wages in accordance with Kaldor's (1959) theory of wage inflation. Thus, once again, a policy of tariffs and quotas so as to reduce the propensity to import looked preferable.

Norman (1996) has proposed what he calls a post-Keynesian theory of protection. He makes the following two propositions, which are derived from the post-Keynesian theory of cost-plus pricing discussed in Chapter 3. First, let us examine what happens if a tariff is imposed on foreign finished products. Norman argues that domestic firms will not change their prices, since they are based on normal unit costs. He further argues that the tariff (or the quota) will give a boost to domestic production in accordance with the size of the tariff and of demand substitutability. Second, let us examine what occurs if a tariff is imposed on imported raw materials or intermediate products. From equations (3.16) and (3.18), remembering that the ratio of unit material costs to unit direct labour costs is $j = UMC/UDLC$, and calling the tariff rate τ, the prices of finished products produced domestically are given by

$$p = UDLC\{1 + \theta[1 + j(1+\tau)]\} \tag{7.17}$$

Because tariffs on imported intermediate products raise unit costs, they will lead to an increase in the prices of domestic finished products. However, the increase is likely to be relatively small, since its impact will depend on the size of the mark-up and on the relative importance of material costs. It is also possible that the exporters of the intermediate goods will take a cut in their profit margins, or that the importers will do so, 'pricing to market', so to speak, thus making the impact even smaller. Summing up all this, 'post-Keynesians contend that protection on final demand leads to higher output. Domestic firms will increase output when tariffs are raised on final demand imports because of shifting demand but will increase their prices if tariffs are leveled on intermediate imports because it is a cost increase' (Brinkman, 1999, p. 98). All this is consistent with the empirical evidence uncovered by Coutts and Norman (2007, p. 1221), who show that 'price effects of global competition on domestic markets are normally *not* dominant' and 'contrast to the core postulates of standard trade and tariff theory'. This may not be the case in semi-industrialized countries, however, where the price leaders are likely to be foreign firms, which explains why the depreciation of domestic currency in these countries is accompanied by a high pass-through rate and accelerated price inflation.

We still have to discuss the option of having a flexible exchange rate regime. Free trade advocates would argue that these trade deficits lead to falling exchange rates that transform the relatively unsuccessful countries into competitive ones, by lowering their costs relative to those of their foreign competitors. Shaikh (2007b) denies this and argues instead that the trade deficits will be compensated by capital inflows, with foreign companies purchasing the domestic assets of the relatively unsuccessful countries, thus hindering the exchange rate from adjusting to the trade deficit. As a result, rich industrialized countries or successful exporting nations reap most benefits of free trade: they improve the employment situation of their workers at home, and their capitalists make more profits and acquire foreign assets at bargain prices. To this we may also add the problems caused by the depreciation of the domestic currency that we have already mentioned, namely the acceleration of inflation and the additional debt burden associated with liabilities denominated in a foreign currency.

When discussing the impact of an expansionary fiscal policy within the Mundell–Fleming model, we saw that Godley ended up taking a more optimistic stand on the capacity of flexible exchange rates to bring the current account balance back to equilibrium. In Godley (1999b) and in Godley and Lavoie (2007a), flexible exchange rates are quite successful at absorbing negative shocks on trade performance. Why this may be so in the eyes of Godley will be discussed briefly in the next section.

Increasing returns and increasing returns to scale
Before closing this section, we must bring back the fourth important assumption that sustains the law of comparative advantage, the assumption of constant returns to scale. The rejection of this hypothesis is closely related to an old argument for trade protection – the 'infant-industry' argument, which was used both by the USA and Germany in the nineteenth century, and which was developed by Friedrich List and the American School of Political Economy (Hudson, 2010). As early as 1841 the German economist List was claiming that advanced economies were trying to 'kick away the ladder' by preaching in favour of free trade and against trade protection (Chang, 2003, p. 3). The argument has now become the infant-economy argument, based on the fact that firms face declining unit costs, both in the short run, as we saw in Chapter 3, but also in the long run.

For many products, comparative advantage is no longer given, in contrast to the case of agricultural products; rather, the comparative advantage is created, as is the case of many high-tech products. We already know from Chapter 3 that firms face declining unit costs in the short run. But it is also usually asserted that, whereas firms taken individually benefit from approximate constant returns to scale, the average costs of domestic industry could be decreasing. This happens as a result of external economies, whereby, for instance, the expansion of the industry generates better knowledge and improved technology for all the participants of the industry. This argument can also be extended to a dynamic framework, in which case it is related to the Kaldor–Verdoorn effect that we presented in Chapter 6: faster growth in manufacturing will generate faster technical progress overall. The existence of increasing returns to scale at the industry level has implications for the optimality of unrestricted free trade. It has led to the definition of the infant-economy argument, whereas all manufacturing industries of a developing nation ought to benefit from tariff or quota protection so as to reach the scale necessary to achieve lower unit costs. The COVID-19 pandemic has reasserted the relevance of this, for security reasons. Palley (2008) has recently dealt with the role of increasing returns to scale.

Figure 7.9 illustrates what can happen when industries benefit from increasing returns to scale. Take two countries, say countries D and U (the developed and underdeveloped countries). Suppose that the unit cost curve of producing some specific high-tech gadget in country D, given by UC_D in Figure 7.9, lies above the unit cost curve of the same gadget produced in an underdeveloped country U, given by UC_U. Suppose further that the companies from country D started to produce and market the gadget ahead of companies from country U, so that their industry output stands at q_D, having taken over the entire market. Companies from country U that try to enter the market will be unable to compete unless they produce more than q_C units, because at any lower sale level their unit cost will be higher than that of the industry in country D. As Robinson (1973, p. 24)

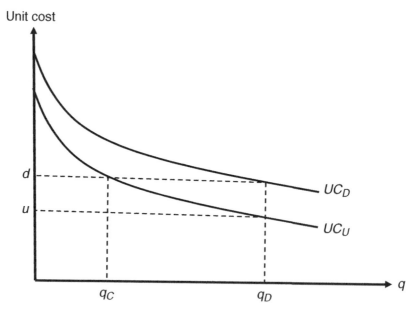

Figure 7.9 The infant-economy argument and increasing returns to scale

comments, 'the doctrine of the advantages of free trade favoured the country which was first in the field with manufacturing industry'. If the industry in country U benefited from some protection, it could reach this level of output by operating on its domestic market. Without protection, it will never achieve it, and the world market for this gadget will remain cornered by the companies of country D. Whereas it would be best for the global economy to have companies from country U produce this product at a cost of $$u$ per unit, companies from country D will retain the whole market, at $$d$ per unit.

The infant-economy argument will turn out to be especially relevant in view of what we discuss in the next section. If growth is limited by balance-of-payments constraints, it is important to export products whose demand is quickly rising. This is unlikely to be the case of agricultural products, in contrast to several kinds of manufactured goods. Trade protection is thus likely to be needed to develop manufacturing industries.

New developmentalism
New developmentalism, as presented mostly by Brazilian authors who inspire themselves from post-Keynesian economics and Latin American Structuralism, is an open-economy macroeconomic theory devoted to the problems specifically faced by middle-income economies (Bresser-Pereira, 2020a; 2020b). A major plank of this theory of development is that the exchange rate plays a critical role. A key argument is that Latin American countries are exporters of raw materials and agricultural products and consequently tend to suffer from the Dutch disease. Because natural resources take such a substantial share of exports, the exchange rate tends to be over-valued from the standpoint of the domestic manufacturing industry, even when the current account is in balance. This overvaluation gets larger when there is a rise in the price of raw materials, since it signifies a rise in the

demand for these commodities and thus an upward pressure on the current account. This over-appreciation of the domestic currency has a twin effect on the domestic manufacturing industry. First, it becomes less competitive relative to foreign firms, because of the exchange rate; second, it becomes less competitive relative to the domestic firms operating in the natural resources industry, as the latter are able to achieve much higher profit rates. This is bad news, presumably because, as claimed earlier, growth in manufacturing promotes innovation and growth in overall productivity.

There is also a relationship between New developmentalism and another theoretical contribution of Latin American economists to the field of open-economy macroeconomics – the theory of the hierarchy of currencies. Besides the real effects already identified, the rise in the world price of commodities also tends to attract financial flows to the countries endowed with these natural resources. This puts further pressure towards the over-appreciation of the exchange rate, and further exacerbates the Dutch disease. While the exchange rate of these countries tends to slowly appreciate through time during the upward phase of the business cycle, when the world economy enters into a recession the currencies which are low in the hierarchy will briskly depreciate, provoking acute problems and possibly generating a financial crisis, especially if firms and governments owe large foreign debts.

There are obvious similarities between List's infant industry argument and the Dutch disease. In both cases, the manufacturing industry of middle-income or under-developed economies suffers from a detrimental impact if market forces are left unfettered. As well, the remedies look somewhat similar. To neutralize the Dutch disease or to protect the infant manufacturing industry, one can impose tariffs on imports (and possibly subsidize manufacturing exports). To reduce the negative impact on manufacturing of the high profit rates in the primary sector, one can also impose export taxes on that sector, which will reduce its net profit rate. But the favourite recommendation of New developmentalism scholars is to maintain a competitive exchange rate by relying on a managed exchange rate regime and thus avoiding the gradual appreciation of the exchange rate during the booming phase of the business cycle (as well as accumulating foreign exchange reserves). In addition, to help the management of the exchange rate, it is suggested to impose capital controls on incoming financial flows, thus also avoiding an accumulation of foreign debt. Both of these policies also ought to minimize the impact of sudden stops in capital flows.

New developmentalism is only one of several varieties of developmentalism (Amado and Mollo, 2015; Palley, 2021). While all these approaches are based on the idea that market mechanisms are insufficient to achieve development and that the State should take an active role, they differ about the importance of State involvement and in their views about the key ingredient. New developmentalism relies on an under-valued exchange rate, favours fiscal austerity and private-sector led industrialization in order to minimize government debt, and seems to be based on the assumption of a profit-led demand regime due to external markets. By contrast, advocates of Social developmentalism argue that there can be state-led industrialization through the provision of infrastructures, and that development can or should be achieved by promoting growth in domestic mass consumption based on a more equitable income distribution. Whether an under-valued exchange rate will have the described favourable impact is also debatable. While Boggio and Barbieri (2017) find that it will be so, Ribeiro et al. (2020) uncover that real exchange rate undervaluation has a detrimental effect on the economy, essentially because of its negative impact on real wages.

7.6 HARRODIAN MODELS OF AN OPEN ECONOMY

We have been slowly drifting from international finance theory towards international trade theory. The last sections of the chapter are devoted to the real side of an open economy. This side of post-Keynesian theory has been explored mainly by the Kaldorian branch of post-Keynesianism, but we shall see in the next section that Kaleckians have also devoted some of their attention to the open economy. In the present section we discuss what I call Harrodian models of the open economy. All these models have a point in common: they are extensions of Harrod's foreign trade multiplier.

7.6.1 Harrod's Foreign Trade Multiplier and Kaldor's Supermultiplier

While the income multiplier is usually attributed to Keynes (1936), it is also known that Richard Kahn put forward the idea of an employment multiplier as early as 1931. What was less known is that Roy Harrod (1933) proposed the notion of a foreign trade multiplier in his book on *International Economics*. Harrod, who was a close friend of Keynes and his first biographer, intended to challenge the standard balance-of-payments mechanism based on price adjustments, the assumption of full employment and the rules of the game associated with the gold standard. He puts forward a simple model, with no investment or government expenditure, but assuming the existence of an import function similar to those shown in first-year courses, which here we write as

$$M = \mu Y \tag{7.18}$$

where M, as in Chapter 4, represents imports while Y and μ stand for GDP and the propensity to import goods from abroad.

Harrod assumes that economic agents spend all their income either on home consumption goods or on imports. Since there is no saving and no investment, and no government sector in this open economy, it must be the case that the current account balance and here the trade balance is always in equilibrium, so that exports and imports are equal to each other at all times, as we already know from the fundamental identity given by equation (7.3). Thus, with X standing for exports, Harrod has

$$X = M \tag{7.19}$$

Putting together equations (7.18) and (7.19), we get

$$Y = X/\mu \tag{7.20}$$

Harrod's foreign trade multiplier is thus $\Delta Y/\Delta X = 1/\mu$. As McCombie and Thirlwall (1994, p. 238) put it, the multiplier 'will always bring the balance of payments back into equilibrium through changes in income following a change in exports'.

This static foreign trade multiplier can be made dynamic by proceeding to the following transformation. Because of equation (7.19), we can write

$$\frac{\Delta Y}{\Delta X}\frac{X}{Y} = \frac{\Delta Y}{\Delta M}\frac{M}{Y} \qquad (7.21)$$

and thus

$$g = \frac{\Delta Y}{Y} = \frac{\Delta X}{X}\left(\frac{\Delta Y}{Y} / \frac{\Delta M}{M}\right) = \frac{\Delta X}{X}\frac{1}{\Pi} = \frac{\hat{X}}{\Pi} \qquad (7.22)$$

Equation (7.22) says that, with the trade balance in equilibrium, the growth rate of GDP, g, is equal to the growth rate of exports divided by the income elasticity of demand for imports, which we call Π. This is the dynamic equivalent of Harrod's foreign trade multiplier, which Setterfield (2012, p. 84) claims to be for Kaldorians 'the basic "equation of motion" in growth theory'. The inverse of the income elasticity of demand for imports is thus the dynamic foreign trade multiplier. The reason the foreign trade multiplier and its dynamic version can be closely related to Kaldorians is that Kaldor (1970c), when discussing regional or national development, referred to Harrod's multiplier, linking it to Hicks's supermultiplier, which we mentioned briefly in Chapter 6, adding that output growth for a given region was tied to the growth rate of its exports.

> From the point of view of any particular region, the 'autonomous component of demand' is the demand emanating from *outside* the region; and Hicks's notion of the 'super-multiplier' can be applied so as to express the doctrine of the foreign trade multiplier in a dynamic setting. So expressed, the doctrine asserts that the rate of economic development of a region is fundamentally governed by the rate of growth of its exports. For the growth of exports, via the 'accelerator', will govern the rate of growth of industrial capacity, as well as the rate of growth of consumption; it will also serve to adjust (again under rather severe simplifying assumptions) both the level, and the rate of growth, of imports to that of exports. (Kaldor, 1970c, p. 342)

Palumbo (2009, pp. 350–51) and Setterfield (2012, p. 85) interpret the above statement with the help of the following set of equations, from which the public sector is absent:

$$M = \mu Y \qquad (7.18)$$

$$Y = C + I + X - M \qquad (7.23)$$

$$C = (1 - s_y)Y \qquad (7.24)$$

$$I = v_o \Delta Y = v_o g Y \qquad (7.25)$$

where s_y is, as is standard, the propensity to save out of income, v_o is the capital to output ratio, and g is the growth rate of the economy. Equation (7.24) is the consumption function, while equation (7.25) is an investment function, of the accelerator type.

Consumption and investment are both entirely induced expenditures. Putting together these four equations, we obtain

$$Y = \frac{X}{s_y - v_o g + \mu} \tag{7.26}$$

Since Kaldor claims that such an equation can be brought back to equation (7.20), $Y = X/\mu$, and something like its dynamic version given by equation (7.22), it has to be so because he assumes that $s_y = v_o g$; that is, he assumes that private saving equals private investment. This indeed became a key assumption of the New Cambridge approach, for which Kaldor was an inspiration.

7.6.2 Godley's Trade Performance Ratio and the Fiscal Stance

Godley's approach in a one-country model

We mentioned the New Cambridge approach in Chapter 4, where it was associated with the fundamental identity (equation 4.7) and the eventual creation of the post-Keynesian SFC approach. New Cambridge was also mentioned when discussing trade restrictions in the previous section of the current chapter. Members of the New Cambridge School were heavily involved in policy advice and forecasting in the 1970s, and one of their empirical claims at the time was that the discrepancy between private domestic saving and private domestic investment was of a small magnitude at any time (except in a period of crisis) and tended towards zero. In the terminology used by Godley, the net accumulation of financial assets of the domestic private sector (*NAFA*) tended towards zero; that is, domestic net private lending, $(S - I)$, tended towards zero. This meant that all the action had to do with the external and the public sectors.

We can provide a reinterpretation of the New Cambridge model, and of its variant found in Godley and Cripps (1983, ch. 14), by making use of the previous equations, more specifically equations (7.18), (7.24) and (7.25), by modifying equation (7.23) to take government expenditures G into account, and by adding a tax function with a tax rate τ:

$$Y = C + I + G + X - M \tag{7.23A}$$

$$T = \tau Y \tag{7.27}$$

Solving the model, we get

$$Y = \frac{G + X}{s_y + \tau - v_0 g + \mu} \tag{7.28}$$

If we assume once more that the domestic private sector, taken overall, that is, with households and private enterprises being consolidated, does not accumulate net financial assets ($s_y = v_o g$), equation (7.28) gets simplified down to equation (7.29), which determines what Godley and Cripps (1983, p. 295) call the quasi-steady-state level of income, or rather, a quasi-stationary state:

$$Y = \frac{G+X}{\tau+\mu} \qquad (7.29)$$

A slightly more complicated equation, which takes interest payments on public debt into consideration, is derived in Godley and Lavoie (2007a, p.178), but the above equation will be sufficient for our purposes. For Godley and Cripps (1983, p. 292), 'government expenditure and exports are the main *exogenous* variables (together with the government's income share, [τ], and the import share, μ)'. All income and expenditure flows will adjust to these. There are thus two crucial ratios to consider: the fiscal stance, which is defined as the ratio G/τ, and the trade performance ratio, which is X/μ.

For the moment, note that equation (7.29) corresponds to the case where equation (4.10) applies; that is, the economy encounters a particular case of the fundamental identity, so that the economy is either in a twin-deficit position (a budget and a current account deficit) or in a twin-surplus position. Only by a fluke, or through some additional adjustment process, will the public budget and the trade balance (or the current account balance) be in equilibrium simultaneously. For this to happen, the fiscal stance and the trade performance ratio have to be equal. In other words, we need equation (7.30) to be realized:

$$\frac{G}{\tau} = \frac{X}{\mu} \qquad (7.30)$$

As Godley and Cripps (1983, p. 296) point out, when the fiscal stance is lower than the trade performance ratio, the economy will be in a twin-surplus position. This can be seen by checking under which condition the inequality $T = \tau Y > G$ is verified. Substituting Y for its value in equation (7.29), it can be shown that the inequality requires $(G/\tau) < (X/\mu)$. In this case, the public debt to income ratio will be decreasing and the domestic economy will be accumulating foreign assets. As already indicated a number of times, such a situation can last a long time, since there is nothing to force a change. By contrast, when the fiscal stance is higher than the trade performance ratio, $(G/\tau) > (X/\mu)$, the economy will be in a twin-deficit position, with rising debt to GDP ratios and with a rising external debt. Unless the economy in question is the US economy, whose currency is the major international trade and reserve currency, such a situation is unlikely to be perpetuated, and one of the two ratios will have to change. Pérez Caldentey (2007, p. 210) shows that the condition given by equation (7.30) can be reinterpreted in a dynamic framework, when considering the growth rates of G and X, and by construing τ and μ as the income elasticities of taxes and imports.

The equality given by (7.30) can be restored either by a reduction in the fiscal stance or by a rise in the trade performance ratio. In the latter case, exports will need to increase, or the propensity to import will have to decrease. New Cambridge authors thought that this could be achieved through tariffs and quotas, or through subsidies for exports. If the adjustment is made through the fiscal stance, by reducing government expenditure or increasing the tax rate, the economy will obviously slow down. Indeed, Godley and Cripps (1983, p. 283) declare that 'in the long run fiscal policy can only be used to sustain growth of real income and output in an open economy provided that foreign trade performance so permits. This is the most important practical conclusion of our book.' As we shall see in the next subsection, several Kaldorians believe that the trade performance ratio, that is the balance of payments, is the ultimate constraint on economic activity for an individual country.

Godley's approach in a two-country model

We have so far assumed that exports were exogenous. The Godley and Cripps model can be slightly amended by considering two areas – North and South, denoted by N and S subscripts, which trade with each other. Once again, we omit interest flows for simplification, and we assume away exchange rate complications by assuming either that we deal with two regions of the same country or with two countries within a common currency area. In each area, the quasi-stationary level of GDP is determined by the following two equations, in analogy with equation (7.29):

$$Y_N = \frac{G_N + X_N}{\tau_N + \mu_N} \qquad (7.31)$$

$$Y_S = \frac{G_S + X_S}{\tau_S + \mu_S} \qquad (7.32)$$

Exports can now be made endogenous by presuming that exports from one area are the imports of the other area. In analogy with equation (7.18), we have the following two export equations:

$$X_N = M_S = \mu_S Y_S \qquad (7.33)$$

$$X_S = M_N = \mu_N Y_N \qquad (7.34)$$

Making use of equations (7.31), (7.32), (7.33) and (7.34), we can now solve for Y_N, noting that the only exogenous variables left are the government expenditures in the two areas. We thus have

$$Y_N = \frac{(\tau_S + \mu_S)G_N + \mu_S G_S}{(\tau_N + \mu_N)(\tau_S + \mu_S) - \mu_N \mu_S} \qquad (7.35)$$

We can easily compute three government expenditure multipliers. The first one still assumes that exports are exogenous, as in equation (7.31); the other two multipliers are derived from equation (7.35): the second multiplier deals with the domestic government expenditure; the third multiplier deals with the multiplier related to foreign government expenditure. We get

$$\frac{\Delta Y_N}{\Delta G_N} = \frac{1}{\tau_N + \mu_N} \qquad (7.36)$$

$$\frac{\Delta Y_N}{\Delta G_N} = \frac{1}{(\tau_N + \mu_N) - (\mu_N \mu_S)/(\tau_S + \mu_S)} \qquad (7.37)$$

Table 7.9 Multiplier values in the Godley and Cripps model with and without feedback

Propensities to import μ_N and μ_S	$\Delta Y_N/\Delta G_N$ Without feedback Equation (7.36)	$\Delta Y_N/\Delta G_N$ With feedback effects Equation (7.37)	$\Delta Y_N/\Delta G_S$ With feedback effects Equation (7.38)
0.1	2.00	2.08	0.42
0.2	1.66	1.87	0.62
0.3	1.43	1.75	0.75
0.4	1.25	1.67	0.83
0.5	1.11	1.61	0.89
0.6	0.83	1.56	0.94

$$\frac{\Delta Y_N}{\Delta G_S} = \frac{\mu_S}{(\tau_N + \mu_N)(\tau_S + \mu_S) - \mu_N \mu_S} \quad (7.38)$$

Obviously, comparing equations (7.36) and (7.37), the domestic government multiplier is larger when one takes into account the feedback effects from one area to the other. Equation (7.38) also shows the favourable effect that increased expenditures from a foreign government have on the domestic economy. Table 7.9 illustrates for heuristics purposes the values that these multipliers take for different values of the propensity to import, assuming in all cases that the tax rate is set at $\tau = 0.40$. One notices that the greater the propensities to import of the two trade areas, the more the multiplier without feedback underestimates the true value of the multiplier with the feedback effects.

What are the implications of the above for a currency union such as the eurozone, where propensities to import from other members of the eurozone can be large? If countries of the South are being forced to pursue austerity policies and thus reduce government expenditures, the negative effects of these reductions for economic activity are likely to be underestimated for the countries making the cuts. The negative effects of these cuts on countries of the North are also likely to be underestimated by the North politicians who are advocating such reductions in South government expenditure.

A further lesson can be drawn from this model. Starting from a situation where both regions of the eurozone (countries of the North and countries of the South) are running balanced budgets and enjoying balanced trade, it is clear that any country of the eurozone that experiences an increase in its propensity to import will end up with a government deficit. With virtually no growth, as has been nearly the case in the eurozone for some time, and excluding any third party, it is impossible for both regions of the eurozone to simultaneously enjoy government budget surpluses or balanced budgets.

This proposition is rarely understood, in contrast to another, more obvious, proposition, which says that all countries in the world cannot simultaneously have a trade surplus or a balance-of-payments surplus. But while everyone recognizes that, in a two-country monetary union, one of the partners will be running a trade deficit, it is not always understood that, in that same two-country monetary union, the laws of accounting are such that the country running a trade deficit must be running a government budget deficit as well, once the quasi-stationary position is reached. Despite this accounting law, all countries of the eurozone are strongly encouraged, with financial penalties imposed otherwise, to run balanced budgets or budgets with surpluses. Such rules make no sense at the macroeconomic level.

7.6.3 Thirlwall's Law or the Balance-of-payments Growth Constraint

Deriving Thirlwall's law

Harrod's foreign trade multiplier and Kaldor's (1970c) views on the constraints on growth have given rise to a large theoretical and empirical literature, which has its origins in equation (7.22), which may be called the dynamic variant of the foreign trade multiplier. Recall that this equation, obtained under very strict conditions, claims that the growth rate of an economy is equal to the growth rate of its exports divided by its income elasticity of the demand for imports.

Thirlwall (1979) unwittingly rediscovered this equation when attempting to explain differences in long-term international growth rates. The main purpose of his paper was to provide an alternative to the neoclassical explanations based on supply-side arguments that relied on the growth rate of factors of production, or what we called the natural rate of growth in Chapter 6. In a post-Keynesian fashion, Thirlwall (1979, p. 45) argued that, as a general statement, 'it is demand that "drives" the economic system, to which supply, within limits, adapts'. Thus, if there are differences in international growth rates, they must be explained by demand factors. Some countries can expand demand faster than others. They face lesser constraints on demand.

But why is this so? Thirlwall's answer was that, 'in an open economy, the dominant constraint is the balance of payments', and that this constraint was well approximated by 'the rate of growth of exports divided by the income elasticity of demand for imports', that is, equation (7.22). Thirlwall (1979, p. 46) argued that, 'if a country gets into balance of payments difficulties as it expands demand, before the short term capacity is reached, then demand must be curtailed'. As a consequence, 'some countries will have to constrain demand sooner than others for balance of payments equilibrium'. Thirlwall went so far as to claim that 'the rate of growth of exports divided by the income elasticity of demand for imports gives such a good approximation to the actual growth experience of major developed countries since 1950 that a new economic law might almost be formulated'. Indeed, no more than one year later, a paper referred to this relationship as 'Thirlwall's law' (Thirlwall, 2011, p. 310). The name was quickly endorsed by Davidson (1992, p. 93), and then an explosion of contributions was devoted to confirming or questioning the empirical results initially obtained by Thirlwall (McCombie and Thirlwall, 1994; Thirlwall, 2019).

Thirlwall's law and its more general versions also became known at the theory of the balance-of-payments growth constraint. It can be split into two parts. First, one can determine what is the growth rate that would sustain an equilibrium of the balance of payments, starting from an equilibrium position. This growth rate will be called g_B. Second, one needs to verify that, indeed, the actual growth rates of various countries roughly correspond to this computed balance-of-payments equilibrium growth rate. In the original and simpler versions – the only one that we shall consider here – the constraint is understood as the growth rate that keeps the trade balance in equilibrium. It would thus be more correct to refer to a balance-of-trade growth constraint. This means that, at all times, as in Harrod's formulation, we need exports in value terms to be equal to imports in value terms. Thus we need the following equation to be fulfilled:

$$p_d X = e p_f M \qquad (7.39)$$

where p_d is the price of domestic goods and hence the price of exports in domestic currency, while p_f is the price of foreign goods and hence the price of imports in foreign currency; thus the value of imports in foreign currency must be multiplied by the exchange rate e, which represents the value of the foreign currency expressed in units of the home currency (as was the case with s in equation (7.5), a depreciation of the home currency implies a rise in the value taken by e). X and M must now be interpreted in real terms.

In a growing economy, the same condition can be expressed in growth rates:

$$\hat{p}_d + \hat{X} = \hat{e} + \hat{p}_f + \hat{M} \qquad (7.40)$$

The import and export functions are now assumed to be more sophisticated than the ones we had before, and take the usual multiplicative form with constant elasticities, as in the Cobb–Douglas function. Using nearly the same notations as Thirlwall (2011) and Setterfield (2012), we have

$$M = \left(\frac{ep_f}{p_d}\right)^\psi Y^\Pi \qquad (7.41)$$

$$X = \left(\frac{p_d}{ep_f}\right)^\eta Z^\varepsilon \qquad (7.42)$$

Parameter ψ is the price elasticity of the demand for imports, and η is the price elasticity of the demand for exports. As expressed, these two parameters take the standard negative sign, since imports depend negatively on the price of imports in the home currency (ep_f), while exports depend negatively on the price of exports relative to the price of foreign products in the home currency. As before, Y is the income of the home country and Π is the income elasticity of its demand for imports. Z stands for world income (and not the autonomous capitalist consumption, as it did in Chapter 6 – we start to run out of letters!), while ε is the income elasticity of the world demand for the exports coming out of the home country.

Taking the logarithms of the above two equations and differentiating with respect to time, we obtain the import and export functions in growth terms:

$$\hat{M} = \psi(\hat{e} + \hat{p}_f - \hat{p}_d) + \Pi \hat{Y} \qquad (7.43)$$

$$\hat{X} = -\eta(\hat{e} + \hat{p}_f - \hat{p}_d) + \varepsilon \hat{Z} \qquad (7.44)$$

Combining equations (7.40), (7.43) and (7.44), we obtain the condition that is necessary for the trade balance to stay in equilibrium:

$$\hat{p}_d - \eta(\hat{e} + \hat{p}_f - \hat{p}_d) + \varepsilon \hat{Z} = \hat{e} + \hat{p}_f + \psi(\hat{e} + \hat{p}_f - \hat{p}_d) + \Pi \hat{Y} \qquad (7.45)$$

Solving for $\hat{Y}$, we obtain the balance-of-payments equilibrium growth rate g_B:

$$g_B = \frac{(1 + \eta + \psi)(\hat{p}_d - \hat{p}_f - \hat{e}) + \varepsilon \hat{Z}}{\Pi} \qquad (7.46)$$

If the standard Marshall–Lerner condition of trade theory holds, meaning that the sum of the absolute values of the price elasticities of exports and imports is greater than one ($|\eta| + |\psi| > 1$), the first term in parentheses in equation (7.46) is negative. Thus, with depreciation of the home currency, $\hat{e} > 0$, as long as the second term in parentheses remains negative, depreciation will have a positive effect on the trade balance, and hence g_B will be greater. As is often noted, however, for the balance-of-payments equilibrium growth rate to remain at its higher level, the currency depreciation cannot be only a one-time event, such as a one-time devaluation; the currency must keep on depreciating through time. Thus, for a time-limited depreciation to have a permanent effect on g_B, the depreciation must have some indirect effect on either the income elasticity of exports or of imports (on ε or Π). An alternative, which we shall not pursue, but which is spelled out by Boggio and Barbieri (2017) and endorsed by Blecker and Setterfield (2019, pp. 414–5), is that the growth rate of exports of a country depends on the *level* of its industry costs or prices relative to those of its competitors, rather than on *changes* in relative unit costs or prices. This is reminiscent of the claims of New developmentalism, according to which an under-valued exchange rate will help manufacturing exports and induce technical progress (along the lines of the Kaldor-Verdoorn effect), allowing middle-income countries to catch up with advanced economies.

Finally, if either equations (7.47A) or (7.47B) are verified

$$1 + \eta + \psi = 0 \qquad (7.47A)$$

$$\hat{p}_d - \hat{p}_f - \hat{e} = 0 \qquad (7.47B)$$

we get Thirlwall's law proper, where the numerator of equation (7.48) ends up being the growth rate of exports:

$$g_B = \frac{\varepsilon \hat{Z}}{\Pi} \qquad (7.48)$$

Figure 7.10 illustrates Thirlwall's law. The larger the ε to Π ratio, the higher the balance-of-payments constrained growth rate for a given growth rate of the world economy.

Interpreting Thirlwall's law
Equations (7.46) and (7.48) can be interpreted in two ways. First we can understand them for what they were derived from: g_B is the growth rate of the economy that will keep the trade balance in equilibrium (if we started from there). This first interpretation is not controversial. It is simply an equilibrium condition. But there is a second interpretation,

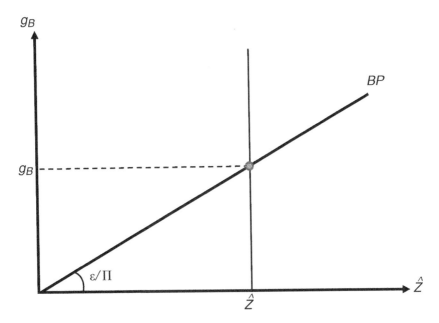

Figure 7.10   Thirlwall's law: the externally constrained growth rate as a function of the growth rate of the world economy

which is more open to criticism: g_B is the growth rate towards which an economy will tend. This seems quite reasonable when dealing with the case where the actual growth rate of the economy initially exceeds g_B, so that the economy is running a trade deficit. As noted when discussing Godley's fiscal stance and trade performance ratio, when the economy has a trade deficit, it has to borrow from abroad, whatever the exchange rate regime, and thus one would expect the authorities to take some deliberate measures to slow down the economy and wage increases, thus, it is hoped, reducing the current account deficit. But, as Palumbo (2011, p. 246), says,

> what seems problematic is the implicit hypothesis that the opposite situation – i.e. a weak stimulus to growth from domestic sources or in any case a persistent tendency of the economy towards trade surpluses – also proves unsustainable in the long run and therefore has to be corrected by means of expansionary policies.

Thus, if the initial actual growth rate is below the balance-of-payments growth rate g_B, corrective measures are unlikely to be taken by the country enjoying trade surpluses, and the actual growth rate will not tend towards g_B. Therefore it seems best to interpret g_B as the maximum growth rate that can be sustained over the long run, due to the external constraints imposed by the trade balance.

This said, what are some of the implications of Thirlwall's law as represented by equation (7.48), assuming that it has a close enough empirical validity (see McCombie and Thirlwall, 1994, ch. 5; and a list of empirical studies in Thirlwall, 2011, pp. 341–2)? First, as already pointed out, if Thirlwall's law is verified, then it means that either the equality given by (7.47A) or that given by (7.47B) (or both) is (are) verified. Equation (7.47A) implies that the sum of the absolute values of the price elasticities of imports and exports is equal to one. This may or may not happen. Equation (7.47B) implies that the real exchange rate ($e_R = ep_f/p_d$) is constant, and hence that relative purchasing power parity holds. This could occur because of pure competition or because of oligopolistic behaviour, but we know that relative purchasing power parity does not perform well empirically. Thus, although Thirlwall's law is seductive, because its relationship is so parsimonious and because it is plausible that 'simple laws make good economics' (Thirlwall, 2011, p. 310), I would venture that equation (7.48) provides only a rough guide to what happens to actual growth rates.

If, however, we accept the validity of Thirlwall's law, then the following consequences, outlined by Setterfield (2012, p. 88), must follow: price changes or international financial flows have an effect only in the short run; policies put forth to increase capacity will have no long-run effect on growth because the growth rate is determined by the demand side; however, policies to increase the growth rate of domestic demand will also fail in the long run, as the actual growth rate will have to revert to the rate constrained by the equilibrium of the trade balance. Most importantly, perhaps, the only way to increase the growth rate in the long run is to make the home products more attractive to the rest of the world (raise ε) or to make foreign products less attractive (lower Π), which Setterfield calls 'supply-side Keynesianism'. The alternative is 'global Keynesianism', meaning faster growth rates throughout the world (a higher $\hat{Z}$).

Some authors, starting with McCombie himself initially, have wondered whether (some of) the numerous empirical tests that have been performed to check the validity of Thirlwall's law reflect a near identity or a near tautology. It has been argued that comparing the balance-of-payments equilibrium growth rate with the actual growth rate of a country and assessing the correlation rates for a set of countries is a very weak test. This is because, while a country may face ever rising trade deficits, it may well be that over a long enough period the growth rates of exports and imports are the same, $\hat{X} = \hat{M}$. If in addition the econometrically estimated income elasticities turn out to be close to the values obtained through the algebraic calculation of the mean growth rates, then Thirlwall's equilibrium growth rate will always be very close to the actual growth rate.

This can be seen by defining the algebraically-calculated elasticities as $\bar{\varepsilon} = \hat{X}/\hat{Z}$ and $\bar{\Pi} = \hat{M}/\hat{Y}$, and assuming that $\hat{X} = \hat{M}$. Combining these three equations, we get: $\hat{Y} = \bar{\varepsilon}\hat{Z}/\bar{\Pi}$. Thus, so long as the income elasticities estimated through the export and import econometric equations are near the calculated elasticities $\bar{\varepsilon}$ and $\bar{\Pi}$, it will seem that Thirlwall's law is verified. McCombie (2019), however, shows through simulations that the estimated and calculated elasticities need not be close to each other in general. Blecker (2021) provides an extended analysis of this question, and a shortened analysis can be found in Blecker and Setterfield (2019, pp. 473–6). Since the essence of Thirlwall's law is that the convergence between the balance-of-payments equilibrium growth rate and the actual growth rate of an economy happens through quantities (national incomes) rather than by relative prices (the real exchange rate), a more convincing test may be to check how this convergence occurs.

Alternative export and import equations

Before closing this subsection, we underline a simplification of the standard account of export and import functions, as can be found in the derivation of Thirlwall's law and in the determination of the Marshall-Lerner condition. In equations (7.41) and (7.42), it is assumed that export prices and domestic prices are identical. But this may not be the case. When the home currency is depreciating, import prices denominated in the home currency may or may not rise, meaning that foreign producers who export their wares may decide to take a cut in their costing margins, so as to remain competitive and preserve their market shares; they may, however, let their prices rise if their competitors also raise theirs. A 10 per cent depreciation is thus likely to be accompanied by a less than 10 per cent increase in import prices. The 'pass-through' is likely to be well below 100 per cent. Similarly, producers at home may decide to take advantage of their improved competitiveness to increase their costing margins and hence their export prices (Godley, 1999b; Godley and Lavoie, 2007a, ch. 12). Thus one should take into account the existence of two additional prices, the export price p_x and the import price p_m, both expressed in domestic currency. In that sense, we can thus say that the prices of the goods which are being exported are subjected to a flexible mark-up, which depends on the evolution of the exchange rate. Furthermore, p_d and p_f should be understood as the prices of the domestic goods that compete with the foreign products which are being imported. As a consequence, equations (7.41) and (7.42) would have to be rewritten as

$$M = \left(\frac{p_m}{p_d}\right)^\psi Y^\Pi \tag{7.41A}$$

$$X = \left(\frac{p_x}{ep_f}\right)^\eta Z^\varepsilon \tag{7.42A}$$

Godley (1999b) further argues that logical consistency requires that the growth rates of import and export prices be written in the following way:

$$\hat{p}_m = \upsilon_m (\hat{e} + \hat{p}_f) + (1 - \upsilon_m)\hat{p}_d \tag{7.41B}$$

$$\hat{p}_x = \upsilon_x (\hat{e} + \hat{p}_f) + (1 - \upsilon_x)\hat{p}_d \tag{7.42B}$$

Godley's argument is that, if domestic and foreign prices grow at the same rate, export and import prices should also grow at that rate. In addition, if the domestic currency depreciation (a rise in e) is accompanied by an equal rate of increase in domestic prices, one would expect import and export prices to rise by the full amount of the depreciation rate. Otherwise, if we are to believe Coutts and Norman (2007), as discussed in Chapter 3, p_d and p_f themselves will hardly react to changes in the exchange rate unless imports are mainly intermediate goods and raw materials. What the above shows is that the formula for g_B that one would obtain with these modifications would not turn out to be as neat as that of equation (7.46), as shown by Blecker and Setterfield (2019, p. 458).

In the case of the determination of the Marshall-Lerner condition, the assumption of a complete exchange rate pass-through to import prices is implicit. It is assumed that the price of imports will increase one on one with the depreciation of the domestic currency, so that $v_m = 1$. As to the price of exports, expressed in the domestic currency, it will not be modified, so that $v_x = 0$, meaning that the price in the currency of the importer will drop one on one with the change in the exchange rate. With the terms of trade being defined as p_x/p_m (the ratio of the export to import prices, both defined in the same currency), the elasticity of the terms of trade with respect to the currency devaluation, is equal to $v_x - v_m$. With the full pass-through, this elasticity is negative and equal to unity. With a partial pass-through, the fall in the terms of trade will be less than proportional to the depreciation; the terms of trade might even improve.

These newly defined import and export prices have a further impact on international trade theory. The Marshall–Lerner condition is usually understood as saying that the the sum of the absolute values of the price elasticities of the demand for imports and exports must exceed unity if the trade balance is to improve following a devaluation of the domestic currency. With equations (7.41A) and (7.42A), what matters is the elasticity of the terms of trade with respect to the currency devaluation, the terms of trade being defined as p_x/p_m, the ratio of the export and import prices, both defined in the same currency. For instance, if a 10 per cent devaluation leads to a 5 per cent increase in import prices and a 2 per cent increase in export prices, the terms of trade have gone down by 3 per cent. The elasticity of the terms of trade with respect to the exchange rate would thus be −0.3. For the trade balance to improve, we need $\hat{p}_x\hat{X} - \hat{p}_m\hat{M} > 0$. By using this relationship and the above four equations, as demonstrated by Carnevali et al. (2020, p. 912) and Blecker and Setterfield (2019, p. 458), the trade balance is improved if the weighted sum of the absolute values of the price elasticities of the demand for imports and exports are greater than the negative of the elasticity of the terms of trade with respect to the nominal exchange rate (here 0.3 instead of 1), where the weights are the pass-through coefficients:

$$(1 - v_x)|\eta| + v_m|\psi| > v_m - v_x \qquad (7.49)$$

In the words of Carnevali et al. (2020, p. 895), the trade balance of a country 'improves *if and only if* the sum of its *weighted* price elasticities of export and import is greater than the difference between the pass-through coefficients of import and export prices'. Thus, to follow on our previous example and our own notation, if we assume in addition that $|\eta| = |\psi| = 0.3$, so that $|\eta| + |\psi| = 0.6 < 1$, meaning that the Marshall-Lerner condition clearly fails, the trade balance will still get improved with depreciation because the condition given by equation (7.49) will be fulfilled, since we get: $(0.8)(0.3) + (0.5)(0.3) = 0.37 > 0.3$. In the case of a full pass-through ($v_m = 1$, $v_x = 0$), for the trade balance to improve following devaluation, the absolute value of the price elasticity of imports would need to be very high: $|\psi| > 1$.

Carnevali et al. (2020) make use of a two-country stock-flow consistent model inspired by Godley and Lavoie (2007a, ch. 12) to confirm the relevance of condition (7.49) and to analyse through simulations what happens under different pass-through assumptions. In the case of a fixed exchange rate regime, they generally observe the standard J-curve effects associated with a currency devaluation, with the trade and current account balances recovering only after a short-period drop. All key variables improve better and much faster with a low pass-through. Similarly, with flexible exchange rates, following an exogenous drop in exports, the current account balance is more likely to stabilize with a low pass-through. The strategic behaviour of firms, in their attempt to keep their market shares by mitigating changes in their foreign currency-denominated prices, thus plays a fundamental role. The more sticky are these prices (the lower the pass-through), the faster and the more likely there will be an adjustment towards equilibrium. This is what we called the third paradox of flexibility in Chapter 1.

7.6.4 Thirlwall's Law in a Two-country Framework

Several extensions of the balance-of-payments equilibrium growth rate have been proposed by various authors. A weakness of the model presented above is that it does not take financial flows into account. This was noted very early on by Thirlwall and Hussain (1982), who applied a modified model to developing countries, with capital inflows financing the trade deficit. Other variants have subsequently been proposed, assuming that countries can run permanent trade deficits, provided that the trade deficit to GDP ratio remains roughly constant, and thus assuming that financial flows grow at the same rate as GDP (Moreno-Brid, 1998–99). But if a country benefits from foreign capital inflows, it also means that interest payments must be made on foreign debt, so that the foreign constraint on growth is now related to the current account balance rather than the trade balance (Moreno-Brid, 2003). Still, despite this, the newly found balance-of-payments equilibrium rate of growth is not very different from the one arising from Thirlwall's law. Equation (7.48) remains a fair approximation of the external constraint on growth.

On that basis, let us examine McCombie's (1993) proposal of a two-country extension of the model, where other autonomous growth components are taken into consideration, with their feedback effects from one area to another, not unlike the exercise pursued in a static framework with the model of Godley and Cripps (1983) in the previous subsection. McCombie's model will help us to understand once more that it is imperative to design an international financial architecture that will displace the burden of adjustment from countries with trade deficits towards countries with trade surpluses.

Let us assume that the world is divided into two regions, the North and the South, denoted by N and S. Assuming further that Thirlwall's law (taken from equation 7.22) is verified for both countries, we have

$$g_{BN} = \hat{X}_N / \Pi_N \tag{7.50}$$

$$g_{BS} = \hat{X}_S / \Pi_S \tag{7.51}$$

Since the exports of the South are the imports of the North, we must have

$$\hat{X}_S = \hat{M}_N \tag{7.52}$$

Since net exports are nil, the exports and the imports of the North are equal to each other, and thus, inversing equation (7.50), we have

$$\hat{M}_N = \Pi_N g_{BN} \tag{7.53}$$

Putting together these equations, we obtain

$$g_{BS} = \frac{\Pi_N}{\Pi_S} g_{BN} \qquad (7.54)$$

This equation is shown in Figure 7.11 as the *BP* curve. It represents all the growth rates of the two countries such that trade remains balanced. The country or region that has the lowest income elasticity of imports has the highest balance-of-payments constrained growth rate. Now what about the actual growth rate? The actual growth rate in each country depends on the growth rate of autonomous domestic expenditures and on the growth rate of exports; it also depends on the growth rate of imports and on the growth rate of induced domestic expenditures, which McCombie (1993) assumes to be the same as the overall growth rate of the economy. Without going into the algebra, we can assert that the actual growth rate of an economy depends on the growth rate of autonomous domestic expenditures and on the growth rate of its exports, and therefore on the actual growth rate of the other country. This gives rise to the other two upward-sloping curves, denoted by A_S and A_N, A_S representing the actual growth rate of the South economy as a function of the growth rate of the North economy. In the initial position of these curves, it is assumed that the A_S and A_N curves cross each other precisely on the *BP* curve, at point E_0, so that the two countries enjoy balanced trade.

Suppose now that the South sees a faster growth rate of its autonomous components, either because consumers and entrepreneurs now have higher animal spirits, or because the government has decided to pursue expansionary policies. The A_S curve will now shift upwards, as shown by the dotted line, and the world economy will be driven to point E_1,

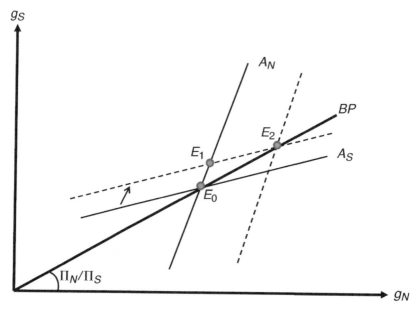

Figure 7.11 Thirlwall's law in a two-country economy

with both economies now enjoying faster growth rates. At E_1, however, the growth rate in the South is above the growth rate (g_{BS}) that warrants balanced trade at the existing growth rate of the North. As a consequence, the South is running a growing trade deficit; by symmetry, the North is running a growing trade surplus. There are two exits to this disequilibrium: a low one and a high one.

In the low exit, the South region will be forced to pursue austerity policies, and the world economy will go back to point E_0, with the lower growth rates. With the high exit, the North can take advantage of its trade surpluses to increase the growth rate of its autonomous domestic expenditures, thus shifting its A_N curve outwards, as shown by the dotted line, until the two dotted lines cross each other on the BP curve once again, but this time at point E_2. Both countries will then enjoy even higher growth rates, with balanced trade. The model shows that concerted expansionary Keynesian policies – global Keynesianism – do indeed manage to overcome balance-of-payments constraints.

More sophisticated extensions of such two-country models can be made. For instance, Vera (2006) provides a version with financial flows and where the terms of trade are determined endogenously. The North exports manufacturing goods, with mark-up pricing, benefiting from Kaldor–Verdoorn productivity effects, while the South exports primary commodities, the price inflation of which is assumed to be determined by the differential in the growth rate of the two regions.

7.6.5 Thirlwall's Law and the Natural Rate of Growth

In Chapter 6, we discussed the fact that the Kaleckian growth model did not generate a rate of growth equal to the natural rate of growth, as defined by equation (6.69). This meant that the rate of unemployment was either continuously rising or falling, an unlikely eventuality. We thus examined mechanisms that would either bring the demand-led Kaleckian growth rate towards the supply-led natural rate of growth or that would instead push the natural rate of growth towards the demand-determined growth rate of the Kaleckian model. The same problem arises with respect to the balance-of-payments constrained growth rate. If indeed the actual growth rate is determined or approximately determined by Thirlwall's law, unless by fluke, this rate and the natural rate of growth will differ and the rate of unemployment will be moving continuously upwards or downwards. This led Palley (2002, p.120) to argue that the balance-of-payments constrained growth model 'embodies an internal inconsistency owing to its failure to consistently incorporate the supply side of the economy'.

A way out of this conundrum has been suggested by Palley himself. We start with his main proposal. Palley (2002, p.123) simply suggests that, when the actual growth rate determined by external constraints is below the natural rate of growth, 'the increase in excess capacity pulls down the elasticity of demand for imports, [Π], thereby relaxing the external constraint on growth'. It is not quite clear why this should be so: why would an increase in excess capacity lead to a reduction in the long-run income elasticity of demand for imports? Assuming the presence of this mechanism for discussion purposes, we have a differential equation:

$$\hat{\Pi} = -\xi_1(g_n - g), \xi_1 > 0 \tag{7.55}$$

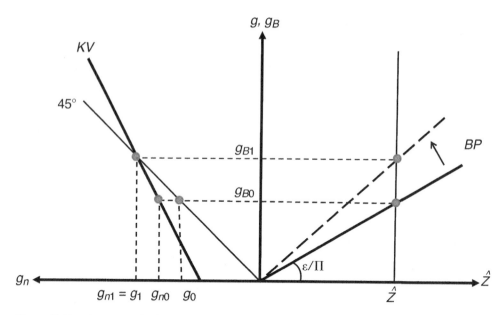

Figure 7.12 Reciprocal adjustments between the balance-of-payments constrained growth rate and the natural rate of growth

This first mechanism is illustrated on the right-hand side of Figure 7.12. The natural rate of growth g_n is shown by a horizontal dotted line. The balance-of-payments constrained growth rate, given by Thirlwall's law, is shown as the upward-rising curve denoted *BP*, which starts from the origin. That rate, as we know, depends on the ratio of the income elasticities of exports and imports, and on the growth rate of the rest of the world, which appears on the horizontal axis of the graph. Thus, for a given growth rate of the world economy, $\hat{Z}$, there is a unique growth rate for the domestic economy, set by the external constraints. With Palley's solution, the *BP* curve rotates upwards until the constrained growth rate equals the natural growth rate (here, until g_B rises to $g_{B1} = g_{n1}$). Obviously, this is an instance of aggregate demand adapting to aggregate supply.

The above was a simplified version of Palley's adjustment process. In fact, he incorporates a Kaldor–Verdoorn equation into his model, as would do and as have done many Kaldorians. Here we repeat for convenience this equation, which says that the growth rate of labour productivity is a positive function of output growth. We also recall the definition of the natural rate of growth, which is the sum of the rate of growth of the labour force and the rate of growth of labour productivity:

$$\lambda = \lambda_0 + \lambda_g g \tag{6.81}$$

$$g_n = \hat{N} + \lambda \tag{6.69}$$

Putting these two equations together, we get

$$g_n = \hat{N} + \lambda_0 + \lambda_g g \tag{7.56}$$

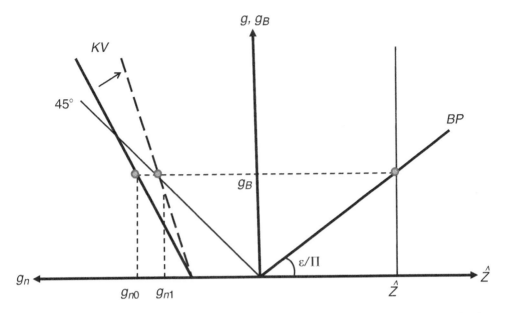

Figure 7.13 The natural rate of growth adjusts to the balance-of-payments constrained growth rate

Equation (7.56) is represented by the *KV* upward-sloping line in the quadrant situated on the left-hand side of Figure 7.12. This figure, proposed by Setterfield (2012, p. 103), illustrates the complete adjustment process proposed by Palley (2002). The figure assumes that initially the actual growth rate of the domestic economy, assumed to be the growth rate determined by Thirlwall's law, as shown on the right-hand side of the figure, is lower than the natural rate of growth determined by the Kaldor–Verdoorn equation ($g_0 < g_{n0}$). With excess capacity appearing, this triggers the mechanism described earlier by equation (7.55). The end result is a higher natural rate of growth and a higher balance-of-payments constrained growth rate, such that $g_1 = g_{n1}$.

Because both the balance-of-payments constrained growth rate and the natural rate of growth are endogenous, it would seem that the model is now demand-led. Setterfield (2012, p. 104) argues, however, that the model generates a '*semi* supply determined' rate of growth, because 'the demand-side is robbed of its status as the unambiguous "leading element" in the determination of long-run growth'.

As a consequence, Setterfield proposes an alternative solution, where the natural rate of growth adjusts to the growth rate constrained by the trade balance. Palley (2002, p. 124) briefly mentions that labour participation rates tend to fall when unemployment rises, thus affecting $\hat{N}$, but he thought that this could be only a short-term or medium-term solution to the problem. Setterfield (2012) looks at the other element of the natural rate of growth, and argues that the rate of growth of labour productivity λ is influenced by the growth rate of the economy, as suggested by the Kaldor–Verdoorn equation, but also by the evolution of the rate of unemployment. His adjustment process is a slight variant of a demand-led adjustment process determined by equations (6.71) and (6.76) already suggested in Chapter 6:

$$\dot{\lambda}_g = -\chi_8 \dot{U} = \chi_8(g - g_n), \chi_8 > 0 \tag{7.57}$$

This last adjustment process is illustrated with the help of Figure 7.13, also suggested by Setterfield (2012, p.105). Here, the actual growth rate is determined by the constraint imposed by balanced trade. The natural rate of growth is presumed to adjust to this demand-determined rate through a variation of the coefficients of the Kaldor–Verdoorn function. The plausibility of this adjustment process was discussed extensively in Chapter 6, so we shall say no more about it in the context of the Thirlwall model.

7.7 KALECKIAN MODELS OF AN OPEN ECONOMY

So far in this chapter we have not dealt with issues of income distribution. But income distribution and possible distributional conflicts are crucial elements of post-Keynesian economics, so something must be said about these within the context of an open economy. This is the topic of this section, and, to handle income distribution, it is natural to go back to the Kaleckian model developed in Chapters 3, 5 and 6. We start by dealing with simple identities, then a subsection will be devoted to an analysis of what happens to the wage share and the profit share when the value of the currency changes; finally, we deal with a simplified two-country Kaleckian model. Much of our inspiration comes from the work of Blecker (1989; 1999; 2011), who some time ago extended Kaleckian analysis to the open economy.

7.7.1 Simple Income-led Equations Once Again

As early as 1934, in a paper published in Polish, Kalecki (1971, p.15) pointed out that an increase in exports, or rather net exports, could generate an increase in the profits obtained by domestic entrepreneurs. As he said then, omitting saving out of wages and the public sector, 'aggregate profits are equal to capitalists' consumption *plus* investment *plus* the balance of foreign trade'. Kalecki (ibid., p.84) later wrote that 'it follows directly that an increase in the export surplus will raise profits *pro tanto* if other components are unchanged'. This is true, but the trade surplus is not generally considered to be the exogenous element, since imports are endogenous to economic activity. The equilibrium level of output will be found by equating injections to leaks, that is, by equating investment plus exports to saving and imports, all expressed in nominal terms:

$$I + X = S + M \tag{7.58}$$

In volumes, or in real terms, we need to take into account the fact that imports are associated with a different price index. Going back to the price assumptions used by McCombie and Thirlwall, we suppose that, while real consumption, investment and exports are associated with a price index p_d, nominal imports are equal to $ep_f M$, where

M is now imports in volumes. We retain the notation used in Chapter 5, that is, with q being real output, I real investment, π the share of profits and s_p the propensity to save out of profits. Furthermore, X is the exogenous amount of real exports, e is the nominal exchange rate and μ is the propensity to import foreign goods as a function of real output, so that real imports are $M = \mu q$. With this notation, equation (7.58) is now rewritten as

$$p_d I + p_d X = s_p \pi p_d q + e p_f M = s_p \pi p_d q + e p_f \mu q \qquad (7.58A)$$

Dividing nominal exports and imports throughout by p_d, and remembering that the real exchange rate e_R is defined as $e p_f / p_d$, we note that the trade balance TB reduces to

$$TB = (p_d X / p_d) - (e p_f M / p_d) = X - e_R M \qquad (7.59)$$

Solving equation (7.58A) for q, we can recover two equations that are quite analogous to those we had in Chapter 5 when assessing output and real profits:

$$q = \frac{I + X}{s_p \pi + e_R \mu} \qquad (7.60)$$

$$P = \frac{I + X}{s_p + \mu e_R / \pi} \qquad (7.61)$$

As in Chapter 5, we see that a decrease in the share of profits raises output and, once again, that an increase in exports leads to an increase in output. Furthermore, an increase in the real exchange rate e_R, that is, a decrease in the terms of trade, under the current assumption that imports in volume depends on output in volume, will lead to a reduction of real output and in real profits in the short run, all else equal.

Furthermore, equation (7.61) shows two things. First, it shows that a decrease in the profit share, or an increase in the wage share, leads to a decrease in real profits. Thus induced imports, just like induced taxes or saving out of wages, modify the results achieved within a closed economy without government and saving out of wages, where the level of real profits did not change when income distribution changed. The positive impact of a higher profit share on profits can once again be assessed with the help of Figure 5.12. The second interesting feature of equation (7.61) is that higher exports, for a given propensity to import, lead to higher profits. Thus policies whose objective is to achieve trade surpluses have a positive impact on business profits. Policies that reduce the growth rate of nominal wages relative to labour productivity, and thus increase the profit share, will also have a positive impact on profits, although they will have a negative impact on output and employment. There is thus a double incentive for corporations to give their support to policies of wage restraint. Such wage-restraint policies may succeed in making the domestic economy more competitive relative to foreign countries, thereby leading to an increase in exports, output and employment. At the same time, firms will benefit from a higher profit share and higher overall profits, but this will have a negative impact on output and employment. There is thus a clear possibility of conflict of interest between workers and their employers. The overall effect of such a policy of wage restraint on output or growth thus needs to be re-examined, this time within the context of an open economy.

Besides this internal conflict, Kaleckians also emphasize the international conflict that arises within the arena of trade relations. As Blecker (1999, p. 130) points out, 'any improvement in one country's competitive position takes profit income as well as market shares and employment opportunities from the other'. Blecker calls this an 'analysis of international conflict over profit realizations'. Bhaduri (1986, p. 139) similarly refers to 'conflicting national economic interests in trade relations', where such 'a clash of national interests becomes inevitable, because *all* countries cannot enjoy trade surplus at the same time'. For those who remain unconvinced, we can recover the equations that we used to define the two-country model of Godley and Cripps, but with investment and saving playing the role of government expenditure and taxes. We again assume that there are two regions, North and South, using N and S subscripts, and we set aside for now all the complications associated with the real exchange rate, assuming that it is fixed and equal to unity. Following a suggestion of Bhaduri (1986, p. 140), let us rewrite the export and import equations, as shown below, with $\bar{M}_i$ standing for an exogenous level of imports, and μ_i now standing for the marginal propensity to import:

$$X_N = M_S = \bar{M}_S + \mu_S q_S \tag{7.62}$$

$$X_S = M_N = \bar{M}_N + \mu_N q_N \tag{7.63}$$

$\bar{M}_i$ is a shift parameter in the import function that corresponds to an autonomous increase in imports going beyond the increase in imports induced by an increase in domestic income. The addition of $\bar{M}_i$ provides a simple way to assess the impact of a gain or a loss in competitiveness. In analogy with equation (7.35), we get the determination of the level of output for the North:

$$q_N = \frac{\left(s_{pS}\pi_S + \mu_S\right)I_N + \mu_S I_S + s_{pS}\pi_S\left(\bar{M}_S - \bar{M}_N\right)}{\left(s_{pN}\pi_N + \mu_N\right)\left(s_{pS}\pi_S + \mu_S\right) - \mu_N\mu_S} \tag{7.64}$$

The North will obviously benefit from its gain of competitiveness (that is, the loss of competitiveness of the South) when the South is subjected to an increase in its autonomous imports $\bar{M}_S$, as its output will rise, but at the expense of the South. This can be seen by examining equation (7.64) and checking that, reciprocally, the North would have lost out had its autonomous imports $\bar{M}_N$ increased. With profits a proportion π of income, one can conclude, as did Kalecki (1954, p. 51), that 'the capitalists of a country which manages to capture foreign markets from other countries are able to increase their profits at the expense of the capitalists of the other countries'. However, as we noted when dealing with the Godley and Cripps model, an increase in the investments I_S of the South will have a beneficial impact on the output of the North. Thus as Bhaduri (1986, p. 139) indicates, the conflict 'arises in a setting of *economic interdependence* among the trading nations'. There is conflict, but there is also complementarity.

Viewed in terms of the principle of effective demand, the trading nations would then appear to be locked in contradictory relations. They are *rivals* in trade with conflicting national interests in so far as each tries to obtain a trade surplus at the cost of others. They are also *partners* in trade in so far as the economic prosperity of each spills over to the others in the form of higher exports for all. (Bhaduri, 1986, p. 140)

We have yet to deal with the consequences of a change in the exchange rate, and this is what we do in the next subsection.

7.7.2 The Impact of the Trade Balance on the Rate of Capacity Utilization

The addition of international trade, net exports and the exchange rate when assessing the impact of changes in income distribution certainly adds a degree of complexity. First, the possibly favourable domestic impact of an increase in the wage share may be reversed once we consider the effects on net exports. Within the post-Kaleckian model of Chapter 6, as long as the negative impact of a higher wage share on profitability is not too large, we may be easily persuaded that economies are wage-led, and that real wages and employment can be increased at the same time as realized profits. 'This comforting conclusion must be drastically revised in the light of the model of an open economy . . . The possibility of a conflict between a redistribution towards wages and maintaining international competitiveness greatly reduces the prospects for a happy coincidence of worker's and capitalists' interests' (Blecker, 1989, pp. 406–7).

Our analysis of income distribution within an open economy is based on the work of Hein and Vogel (2008) and is also inspired by the post-Kaleckian growth model proposed by Blecker (2011). Our focus will be the rate of utilization rather than the growth rate. We start with the saving and investment equations used in Chapter 6:

$$g^s = s_p \pi u / v \tag{6.14}$$

$$g^i = \gamma + \gamma_u u + \gamma_\pi \pi \tag{6.25}$$

We now have to take into account the trade balance, *tb*, which is expressed as a ratio of the stock of capital. The trade balance, as shown in equation (7.65) below, is a linear function of the real exchange rate e_R, the domestic rate of utilization u and the foreign rate of utilization u_f, with parameters β_u and β_{uf} assumed to be positive. Since β_u is accompanied by a negative sign, this means, as we would expect, that a higher domestic rate of utilization induces a smaller trade surplus. The trade balance is thus considered to be endogenous, as it should be. On the other hand, a larger foreign rate of utilization means that the domestic trade surplus ought to be larger. The β_e parameter could be positive or negative. If it is positive, it implies that the Marshall–Lerner condition, or rather the new condition as defined by equation (7.49), is fulfilled: a depreciation of the home currency – an increase in the real exchange rate e_R – leads to an improvement of the trade balance. When $\beta_e = 0$, the effect on the trade balance is neutral.

$$tb = \frac{TB}{K} = \frac{X - e_R M}{K} = \beta_0 + \beta_e e_R - \beta_u u + \beta_{uf} u_f \tag{7.65}$$

With injections once again required to equate leaks, we have

$$g^s = g^i + tb \tag{7.66}$$

Thus, in analogy with equation (7.58A), we get

$$s_p\pi/v = \gamma + \gamma_u u + \gamma_\pi \pi + \beta_0 + \beta_e e_R - \beta_u u + \beta_{uf} u_f \tag{7.67}$$

Solving for the domestic rate of utilization, we have

$$u^* = \frac{(\gamma + \gamma_\pi \pi + \beta_0 + \beta_{uf} u_f + \beta_e e_R)v}{s_p\pi + (\beta_u - \gamma_u)v} \tag{7.68}$$

This equation closely resembles equation (6.29) since the present model is a post-Kaleckian model, but set in an open economy. As in the post-Kaleckian growth model, an increase in the profit share π has an ambiguous impact on the rate of utilization of the economy. Naturally, higher economic activity abroad, as reflected in a higher u_f, has a positive impact on the domestic rate of utilization, as we have already noted several times. What remains to be discussed is the impact of the real exchange rate e_R. We also need to clarify the relationship between the real exchange rate and income distribution. But obviously, from equation (7.68), a depreciation of the home currency (an exogenous increase in e_R, all else equal) has a positive impact on the rate of utilization if β_e is positive. Finally, it can be noted that the stability conditions in an open economy are less stringent than in a closed economy, as can be asserted from the additional presence of the positive β_u term in the denominator (which needs to be positive, for stability). As Blecker (2011, p. 219) says, 'the openness of a country to trade has a stabilising impact because higher domestic utilisation (output) increases imports and decreases the trade balance, thereby dampening further increases in demand'.

7.7.3 Income Distribution and the Real Exchange Rate

To achieve quick results, we rely on an assumption of Hein and Vogel (2008, p. 482), that is, we assume an open economy 'which depends on imported inputs for production purposes and the output of which competes in international markets', and we also assume that 'the prices of imported inputs and of the competing foreign final product to be exogenously given and to be moving in step', these prices being p_f. The nominal exchange rate e and economic activity abroad u_f are also taken to be exogenously given. In what follows, we wish to establish the relationship between the real exchange rate e_R and the profit share π.

We start by recalling the pricing equation of a firm, not fully vertically integrated, that has to purchase commodities or semi-finished products as inputs. As we saw in Chapter 3, for such a firm it is convenient to distinguish material inputs from labour inputs, the pricing equation being written as

$$p = (1 + \theta)(UDLC + UMC) \tag{3.16}$$

Denoting the ratio of material costs per unit to direct labour costs per unit by $j = UMC/UDLC$, as we did in Chapter 3, and with unit labour costs being $UDLC = w/y$ at the macroeconomic level (noting that here indirect labour costs are assumed away), equation (3.24) reduces to

$$p = (1 + \theta)(1+j)(w/y) \qquad (7.69)$$

The j ratio can be decomposed by noting that the unit material cost is equal to the number of material inputs per unit that are required (that is, the material input to output ratio), call this v_m, times the price of each input in domestic units, which is given by ep_f. Equation (7.69), where p is now the domestic price p_d, can thus be rewritten as

$$p_d = (1+\theta)\left(\frac{w}{y} + ep_f v_m\right) = (1+\theta)\left(1 + \frac{ep_f v_m}{w/y}\right)\frac{w}{y} \qquad (7.70)$$

This implies that the j ratio is equal to

$$j = \frac{ep_f v_m}{w/y} \qquad (7.71)$$

Let us recall the definition of the real exchange rate $e_R = ep_f/p_d$, where p_d stands for domestic prices while p_f denotes foreign and raw material prices. The real exchange rate is thus equal to

$$e_R = \frac{ep_f}{(1+\theta)\left(1 + \frac{ep_f v_m}{w/y}\right)\frac{w}{y}} \qquad (7.72)$$

Finally, let us further recall the relationship between the gross profit share in value added and the ratio of unit material cost to unit labour cost, from which we know that a higher j ratio implies a higher profit share π (since we assume away overhead labour, and that the gross and the net profit shares in value added are equal):

$$\pi = m_{va} = \frac{\theta(1+j)}{1+\theta(1+j)} \qquad (3.26)$$

In this open economy, the profit share can change for two main reasons: either the mark-up is changed or the j ratio is modified. Let us first deal with a change in income distribution caused by an increase in the mark-up θ. Obviously, in this case, the profit share π is now higher. What happens to the real exchange rate? Checking equation (7.72), the increase in the profit share due to the higher mark-up is accompanied by a fall in the real exchange rate, meaning a real appreciation of the domestic currency. There is a fall in international competitiveness. The profit share and the real exchange rate are inversely related.

Let us now deal with an increase in nominal wages (all else being constant). This means that the j ratio is smaller and hence that the profit share is smaller. Furthermore, domestic prices are now higher, and hence there is a fall in the real exchange rate, meaning a real appreciation of the domestic currency and a fall in international competitiveness. In this case there is thus a positive relationship between the profit share and the real exchange rate.

Finally, income distribution can change as a consequence of a change in the nominal exchange rate e. Equation (7.71) clearly shows that an increase in e leads to an increase in the j ratio, which means that the profit share is now larger, as long as the mark-up does not change as a consequence of the higher cost of raw materials or intermediate goods. But, as already discussed, empirical work shows that firms are likely to pass on such cost increases. What will be the impact on the real exchange rate? Taking the derivative of equation (7.72) with respect to e, it can be shown that it is positive. The increase in the nominal exchange rate leads to an increase in the real exchange rate. Thus, once again, there is a positive relationship between the profit share and the real exchange rate.

7.7.4 The Consequences of a Change in Income Distribution

We can use our standard graphs to illustrate what happens when there is a change in income distribution. This is done in Figure 7.14. The starting position is point A where the saving and investment curves of a closed economy intersect. We assume that the initial position is one where the trade balance is in equilibrium, so that the curve $g^i + tb$ that represents the sum of the investment and trade balance functions intersects the saving function at the same point A, and at the same rate of utilization u_0. This $g^i + tb$ curve is

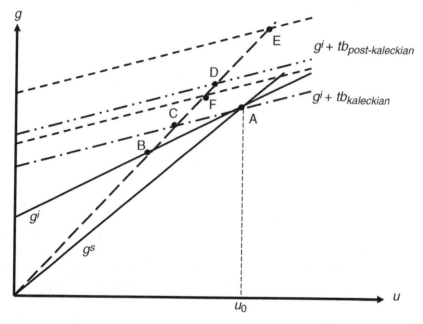

Figure 7.14 The impact of an increase in the profit share in an open-economy post-Kaleckian model

flatter than the closed-economy g^i curve because of the effect of the β_u term. Let us now impose a higher profit share π. As usual, the saving function rotates inwards. In a closed economy, with the canonical Kaleckian model, the new equilibrium would be given by point B. In an open economy, again with the canonical Kaleckian model, but omitting the impact of the induced change in the real exchange rate (or assuming that $\beta_e = 0$ in equation 7.65), the new equilibrium would be given by point C. In an open-economy post-Kaleckian model, which now incorporates the positive effect of a rise in the profit share on the investment function (the impact of the γ_π parameter), but still omitting the impact of the induced change in the real exchange rate (or assuming again that $\beta_e = 0$ in equation 7.65), the new equilibrium would be given by point D.

The full model also incorporates the impact of the change in international competitiveness due to the change in income distribution. Here we assume that $\beta_e > 0$; in other words, we assume that a real depreciation of the domestic currency (a higher e_R) improves the trade balance, which would lead to an additional upward shift of the $g^i + tb$ curve. This is what will happen when the higher profit share is caused by a nominal depreciation of the domestic currency (a higher e) or by a fall in the nominal wage rate. The final equilibrium would then be given by point E. By contrast, when the higher profit share is caused by an increase in the mark-up, we know that there is an inverse relationship between the profit share and the real exchange rate. The $g^i + tb$ curve will then shift back inwards, with a final equilibrium given by point F.

These results are rather disconcerting. For given parameters, a higher profit share or lower real wages in the open economy may end up being associated with lower or higher economic activity, depending on the source of the change in real wages (Hein and Vogel, 2008, p. 483). We end up in a nearly 'anything-goes' situation. The above theoretical results may help to explain, however, why empirical studies on whether a country is wage-led or profit-led sometimes arrive at different conclusions. The source of the change in income distribution is an important consideration, not taken into account in those empirical studies.

> For any given country, under a set of behavioural parameters, shocks to different exogenous variables that affect distribution (such as the bargaining power of labour, the market power of oligopolistic firms or the target real exchange rate of the monetary authorities) are likely to have different effects on distribution and utilisation. Thus the same country could exhibit wage-led behaviour in response to one type of shock . . . and profit-led behaviour in response to another sort of shock. (Blecker, 2011, p. 233)

Thus what we have here is a problem somewhat resembling the one we encountered when attempting to assess the demand regime in a closed economy when it was realized that overhead labour costs made such an assessment much more delicate than it seemed at first sight. Still, in the discussion of the next subsection, we shall rely on the results of an empirical study of these demand regimes.

In the model presented here, we did not take into account the possible feedback effects of a currency depreciation on wage demands and hence on domestic price inflation. This will be done in Chapter 8, which deals specifically with inflation.

7.7.5 Two-country Neo-Kaleckian Models

So far, we have examined the neo-Kaleckian or post-Kaleckian growth model within the framework of a single economy trading with some exogenous entity, thus avoiding the consideration of feedback effects. The Global Financial Crisis has encouraged even more countries to pursue, implicitly or explicitly, policies designed to achieve external surpluses in the hope of keeping employment at home. These policies are often based on wage restrictions, which are relatively easy to implement given the weakness of the labour market and given the increased globalization and international outsourcing of production, the hope being that reduced real wages or wage shares will lead to increases in the real exchange rate, which then will generate increases in economic activity and employment through the export sector.

Calls for wage austerity within a country may make sense if this economy is in a profit-led total demand regime, assuming, in contrast to what we just saw, that this can be ascertained with certainty. But does it make sense when feedback effects from the rest of the world economy are taken into account? The possibility of a macroeconomic paradox was pointed out a long time ago:

> A situation in which competitive wage cuts (or 'wage restraints') are pursued in all countries will potentially harm the interests of workers everywhere: real wages will be sacrificed, as long as mark-ups are flexible; but employment will not increase, as long as the competitive gains cancel each other out. In this case, the regressive effect of multilateral wage cuts on income distribution could well lead to a world-wide depression of demand and employment. On the one hand, if workers in all countries increase their money wages, and if the international competitive effects roughly cancel out, then the world economy as a whole can potentially enjoy wage-led growth – provided that firms still feel sufficient competitive pressures to compel them to cut their mark-ups in response to the wage increases. (Blecker, 1989, p. 407)

It turns out that while all G-20 countries are in a wage-led domestic demand regime, several of them are in a profit-led total demand regime (the increase in the profit share has a positive impact on the sum of domestic and foreign demand). Indeed, as Capaldo and Izurieta (2013) put it, it may be more appropriate to call the latter regime an 'export-led' demand regime, since most countries where total demand is profit-led achieve this nearly solely through the impact of income distribution on net exports, and thus through price effects related to international trade. It may thus be tempting for these countries to pursue pro-capital economic policies that restrain wage growth, as it may be for small countries that believe they are in a similar total demand regime. We can better understand the strategy of wage moderation pursued by 'export-led' countries by making use of Figure 7.15. The figure describes the implicit relation between real wages (at a given level of labour productivity) and the rate of capacity utilization of a single economy. The relationship between the two variables is assumed to be positive when only domestic demand is taken into consideration; in other words, domestic demand is wage-led. By contrast, the relationship between real wages and the rate of capacity utilization can be either positive or negative when the effects of the trade balance are taken into account, so that total demand can be either wage-led or profit-led.

The two possibilities are illustrated in Figure 7.15. The three curves are drawn under the assumption that the trade balance is in equilibrium when the real wage is at its initial position, at ω_0, with a rate of utilization u_0. A fall in the real wage rate, down to ω_1, would

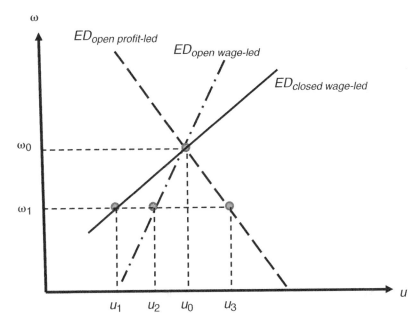

Figure 7.15 Effect of wage moderation policies on the rate of utilization in an export-led demand regime

have led to a decrease in the rate of utilization as far as u_1 if only domestic demand effects were considered. In a total demand wage-led regime, the rate of utilization only falls to u_2. However, in a profit-led (or export-led) open economy, the rate of capacity utilization rises instead to u_3, so that pro-capital policies that weaken trade unions and facilitate wage moderation policies do indeed achieve higher rates of economic activity.

To assess Blecker's above comment, it may be interesting to examine what happens when an increase in the profit share is imposed on one country at a time and then on all trading partners simultaneously. This is indeed what Onaran and Galanis (2012) have done. Table 7.10 compares the impact of a one percentage point increase in the profit share on domestic demand (consumption plus investment) and on total (adding net exports), including the income-multiplier effect, when this increase occurs in a single country and when this increase occurs in all members of the G-20 simultaneously. Because these G-20 countries represent around 80 or 85 per cent of world economic activity, this is nearly akin to a one percentage point increase in the profit share of the whole world economy.

Table 7.10 shows clearly that domestic demand is wage-led in all countries, or at least, that it is not profit-led. In other words, the positive impact of a higher profit share on investment never surpasses the strong negative impact that it has on consumption.

In addition, Table 7.10 demonstrates that a simultaneous increase in the profit share of all countries may have a negative effect on the aggregate demand of countries that were deemed to be in a profit-led total demand regime when the increase in the profit share was made in isolation. This is the case of Argentina, Canada, Mexico and India. Only Australia, China and South Africa remain profit-led (although Jetin and Reyes Ortiz

Table 7.10 Comparison of the effects of an isolated and of a simultaneous one percentage point increase in the share of profit

Country	Isolated effect On domestic demand	Isolated effect On total demand	Simultaneous effect on total demand
Eurozone-12	−0.223	−0.133	−0.245
Germany	−0.134	−0.031	
France	−0.301	−0.027	
Italy	−0.390	−0.173	
United Kingdom	−0.219	−0.030	−0.214
USA	−0.886	−0.808	−0.921
Japan	−0.166	−0.034	−0.179
Canada	−0.175	+0.148	−0.269
Australia	−0.116	+0.268	+0.172
Turkey	−1.084	−0.459	−0.717
Mexico	−0.315	+0.106	−0.111
South Korea	−0.770	−0.115	−0.161
Argentina	−0.014	+0.075	−0.103
China	−0.076	+1.932	+1.115
India	−0.157	+0.040	−0.027
South Africa	−0.005	+0.729	+0.390

Source: Adapted from Onaran and Galanis (2012, Tables 11–13).

(2020), with the same method but more recent data, come to the conclusion that the Chinese economy is now in a wage-led demand regime and that the Chinese authorities ought to pursue pro-labour policies as a strategy). Furthermore, Onaran and Galanis (2012, p. 40) calculate that a one percentage point increase in the profit share in all G-20 countries leads to a drop of 0.36 percentage points in their global GDP. Similar empirical results are obtained by Onaran and Obst (2016) when dealing with European Union countries, the EU15, and comparing the effects of isolated and simultaneous increases in the profit share. They also show that all EU15 countries would benefit from a coordinated increase in the wage share, provided the increase is smaller in small countries such as Belgium and Denmark.

This implies that, while some individual countries can successfully pursue beggar-thy-neighbour policies through wage moderation, such wage moderation policies do not constitute a viable strategy at the European or world level. If countries simultaneously pursue policies that lead to lower real wages and higher profit shares, only a fraction of the countries that are in a profit-led total demand regime will still benefit from their pro-capital distributional policies. At the global level, the only viable strategy is one of high wages, pre-empting a race to the bottom in wages. Austerity and wage moderation policies are suicidal when considering the global picture.

A number of post-Keynesian authors have formalized this insight within a two-country Kaleckian growth model, with a full description of both countries (Capaldo and Izurieta, 2013; von Arnim et al., 2014; Rezai, 2015; Bagnai and Rieber, 2019). While the models proposed by these authors are far from identical, the results that they draw from these models are very similar and are in line with the empirical results shown in Table 7.10. Here we do not go through the algebra of any of these models, but we try to reproduce the gist of their conclusions with the help of Figure 7.16.

All the authors just mentioned above examine what happens if both countries of a two-country world economy decide to pursue wage restriction policies and reduce their real wages simultaneously. This is illustrated with the help of Figure 7.16, which extends Figure 7.15 to two countries, N and S. We assume that both countries are in a wage-led domestic demand regime (in autarky), but in a profit-led total demand regime (with trade). Let us first deal with the case where the countries are identical. An isolated decrease in real wages, with real wages staying put in the other country, would have driven each economy from point A to point B, one at a time, and hence to an increase in the rate of utilization. This would thus seem to justify wage moderation policies. However, if both identical countries pursue simultaneously the same reduction in real wages (or the same increase in profit shares), both countries will remain on their original *ED* curve, and will thus end up at point C, with lower rates of capacity utilization. In the general case, with non-identical countries, it could be that, looking at total demand, one country remains profit-led (here country S, on the right-hand side of the figure) while the other country turns out to be wage-led (here country N, on the left-hand side of the figure), as shown in Figure 7.16 with the additional shifts of the *ED* curve and points D. This corresponds to some of the empirical results achieved by Onaran and Galanis (2012) and Onaran and Obst (2016).

Von Arnim et al. (2014, p. 455) provide a good summary of the difficulties inherent in wage-led strategies and international cooperation. They claim that 'globalization – increases in trade shares – strengthen the incentive to engage in relative wage suppression. This happens despite the fact that, on the one hand, coordinated redistribution towards

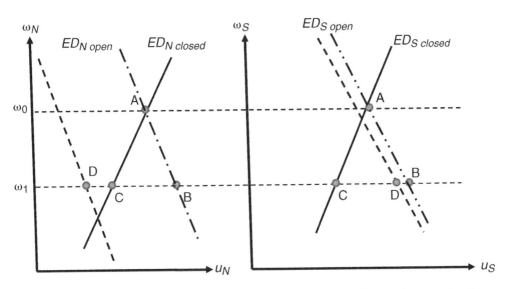

Figure 7.16 Impact on rates of utilization of a simultaneous real wage decrease in all countries

labor would achieve larger global aggregate demand gains and, on the other hand, coordinated redistribution may provide global demand gains even in profit-led economies'. This is another example of coordination failure, an instance of the prisoner's dilemma. Preferable outcomes could be achieved if individual countries were willing to cooperate by raising real wages, but wage suppression seems to be the dominant strategy for each individual country.

Some authors question the paradox of profit-led demand as it has been presented here, that is, the claim that 'even if there are some countries that are profit-led, the global economy as a whole is wage-led because the world is a closed economy' (Onaran, 2016, p. 464). In particular, Arslan Razmi (2015; 2016; 2018a), in a series of papers based on variants of the post-Kaleckian model, and even within a stock-flow consistent framework (Razmi, 2018b), has investigated the likelihood of wage-led demand regimes. Razmi (2015) first questioned the possibility of wage-led growth in low-income economies, arguing that they have a non-tradable sector and that the output of the tradable sector is supply-constrained by the amount of machines – a standard objection against Kaleckian models in the context of developing economies and a consideration that we already noted in section 5.1.3 of Chapter 5. By contrast, Dutt (2017, p. 191) doubts that the trading sectors of such an economy 'can sell any amount they want to at a given price', and he argues that the presence of non-traded goods is more likely to be conducive to a wage-led demand regime because 'the economy can expand without at least some of the increase in demand leaking abroad'.

More interestingly, Razmi (2018a) also questions Onaran's statement to the effect that, as a closed economy, Planet Earth as a whole is likely to be wage-led. While Razmi presents a full model with all the standard post-Kaleckian assumptions to demonstrate that aggregate demand at the world level may not be wage led, the gist of his argument can be told in words. His point is that two countries may have quite different structures. An extreme case is when consumption goods in one country are entirely imported, implying that this country only produces investment goods. 'Then a redistribution towards profits in the first country increases investment spending without affecting the (non-existent) consumer demand for the domestic good. Utilization rises as a result, and demand in that country is profit-led. Moreover, the boost in utilization increases consumer demand in the second country's goods, increasing utilization there as well. The world as a whole then appears to be profit-led' (Razmi, 2018a, p. 290).

In reality, if we are to believe the empirical results of Onaran and Galanis (2012) shown in Table 7.10, all G-20 countries are in a wage-led domestic demand regime. This is because it turns out that investment in most countries responds only weakly to a change in the profit share. The analysis designed by Razmi (2018a) is thus immaterial to the real world, since he assumes a profit-led domestic demand. And because the bigger G-20 members are still in a wage-led regime when taking international trade into account, there is room for cooperation that could bring about a wage-led growth strategy (Lavoie and Stockhammer, 2013b). Government officials, however, need to realize that wages are not only a cost to entrepreneurs, but also a crucial component of aggregate demand, as we have tried to underline throughout this book.

Increases in real wages and the wage share may end up having a smaller effect on aggregate demand than is ascertained by research, but any global negative impact is very unlikely. Therefore we should go forward with policies that generate higher real wages and a reduction in income inequality. Policies should be put in place to avoid the race to the bottom that has characterized the advent of financialization since the 1980s. Planet Earth is a closed economy, so what matters at the global level is the domestic demand regime. Since we know that all countries, or nearly all of them, are under a wage-led domestic demand regime, a wage-led growth strategy is the best strategy worldwide.

NOTE

* Full sentences have been taken from the following publications: 'The reflux mechanism in the open economy', in L.P. Rochon and M. Vernengo (eds), *Credit, Interest Rates and the Open Economy: Essays on Horizontalism*, Cheltenham, UK and Northampton, MA, USA: Edward Elgar Publishing, 2001, pp. 215–42; 'A Post Keynesian view of interest parity theorems', *Journal of Post Keynesian Economics*, **23** (1), Fall 2000, pp. 163–79; 'Interest parity, risk premia and Post Keynesian analysis', *Journal of Post Keynesian Economics*, **25** (2), Winter 2002–03, pp. 237–49.

8. Inflation theory

Not much has been said so far about price inflation. The main references to inflation were made in Chapter 6, when discussing Joan Robinson's inflation barrier, Duménil and Lévy's adjustment mechanism towards the normal rate of utilization and Dutt's adjustment mechanism bringing aggregate demand towards aggregate supply. Some hints about the impact of inflation on the prices of imported raw materials or intermediate commodities were also mentioned in Chapter 7. It is now time to say more about wage and price inflation.

8.1 THE QUANTITY THEORY VERSUS THE WAGE–COST MARK-UP RELATION

8.1.1 The Rejection of the Accelerationist Thesis

In mainstream economics, price inflation is essentially an excess demand phenomenon. In its simplest form, excess demand arises from an excess supply of money, or rather from an excessive growth rate of the money supply. This is the quantity theory of money in its various incarnations, including monetarism. In its Wicksellian version, associated with the New Consensus, excess demand arises from a market rate of interest that is too low compared to the natural rate of interest. More precisely, a negative discrepancy between the market and the natural rate of interest opens up an output gap that leads to an acceleration of the inflation rate, supported by growth in the money supply. This is akin to the accelerationist thesis and the vertical Phillips curve, based on the natural rate of unemployment or the non-accelerating inflation rate of unemployment (NAIRU). Whenever the actual rate of unemployment is below this rate, wage and price inflation speeds up. The change in the rate of inflation is thus determined by the level of the rate of unemployment relative to its presumed natural value. There are other incarnations of this accelerationist thesis, tied to the rate of capacity utilization, which carries several names: the non-accelerating inflation rate of capacity utilization (NAIRCU, Nahuis, 2003; NAICU, Hein, 2014, p. 461) and the steady-inflation rate of capacity utilization (SIRCU, McElhattan, 1985; Hein, 2008, ch. 17).

In post-Keynesian theory, the level of the money supply does not determine the level of prices; nor does the rate of growth of the money supply determine the rate of inflation. Excess money or monetized government deficits are not a proximate cause of inflation, not even in the case of the German hyperinflation of the 1920s, as already argued by Joan Robinson (1938) and more recently by Burdekin and Burkett (1992) and Wray (2012, pp. 246–57), nor in the case of the 'Great Inflation' in England in the 1500s, usually attributed to gold discoveries (Arestis and Howells, 2001–02). The major justification for this rejection of the quantity theory of money, as we have seen in Chapter 4, is that the supply of money is endogenous in the post-Keynesian framework.

Furthermore, as we also saw in Chapter 4, post-Keynesians reject the concept of the natural rate of interest, and they have very little faith in the natural rate of unemployment or the NAIRU, as we already saw towards the end of Chapter 1. There is ample empirical evidence showing that the accelerationist hypothesis required for the existence of a NAIRU – the restriction that expected or past inflation is into a one-to-one relation with actual inflation – just does not hold (Stanley, 2005b; Fair, 2004, ch. 4). At most, as explained by Stockhammer (2008, pp. 500–1), if inflationary expectations are fully incorporated in wage growth, one could 'probably accept that there is a NAIRU at any point in time, but it is neither exogenous nor is it a strong attractor for actual unemployment'. What is meant is that such a NAIRU is influenced and attracted by the actual rate of unemployment; there is hysteresis. Scepticism about the existence and the uniqueness of the NAIRU, as reflected recently in Lang et al. (2020), has long been a tenet of post-Keynesianism, as the following quote shows. Indeed, the second part of the quote shows that even the traditional Phillips curve has been questioned by post-Keynesians:

> Indeed *if* it is true that there is a unique NAIRU, that really is the end of discussion of macroeconomic policy. At present I happen *not* to believe it and there is no evidence of it. And I am prepared to express the value judgment that moderately higher inflation rates are an acceptable price to pay for lower unemployment. *But I do not accept that it is a foregone conclusion that inflation will be higher if unemployment is lower*. (Godley, 1983, p. 170)

There are thus 'doubts about the connection of inflation and unemployment' (Forder, 2014, p. 218). What then is the basis of the post-Keynesian theory of inflation? Post-Keynesians argue that the 'economy is primarily a money-wage system' (Weintraub, 1978, p. 66). The money wage rate is the exogenous factor explaining the price level that the orthodox authors have sought. As Robinson (1962, p. 70) said, 'in our model, as in reality, the level of the money-wage rate obtaining at any particular moment is an historical accident', although she also endorsed a traditional Phillips curve, prior to Phillips. when she wrote that 'movements of the level of employment are the chief influence determining movements in the level of money wages' (Robinson, 1947, p. 4). Departing on this issue from the quantity theory, Keynes wrote that 'the long run stability or instability of prices will depend on the strength of the upward trend of the wage-unit (or, more precisely, of the cost-unit) compared with the rate of increase in the efficiency of the productive system' (1936, p. 309).

That wages are the main determinant of prices does not necessarily imply that wage increases are the main cause of price inflation. Most post-Keynesians view inflation as a conflict over the distribution of income. Two of these conflicts appear to be crucial: that between different groups of workers on the one hand, and that between labour taken overall and the non-labour constituents of the firm on the other hand. To the first distributional conflict is associated the wage–wage spiral, and to the second conflict is associated the wage–price spiral. Here we shall focus on the second spiral. But before we tackle conflicting-claims inflation, let us consider some simple relations, starting with an identity, which is the counterpart to the identity of the quantity theory of money. This identity was put forward by Weintraub (1978, p. 45) as the wage–cost mark-up equation, which can be written as

$$p = \kappa w/y \tag{8.1}$$

where κ is the average mark-up of prices over unit labour costs.

Equation (8.1) is a macroeconomic identity in which w/y represents actual unit labour costs, rather than standard unit costs. It cannot explain inflation. Just like the quantity equation, it is a truism, that is, an identity which is an interesting way to put things but one that requires to be backed by a theory. Taking growth rates, we may, however, derive an *ex post* assessment of the proximate sources of inflation.

$$\hat{p} = \hat{w} - \hat{y} + \hat{\kappa} \tag{8.2}$$

While inflation could occur because of rising mark-ups ($\hat{\kappa} > 0$) – what Davidson (1972, p. 343) calls profit inflation – it is clear that, in the long run, as Keynes had it, the rate of inflation hinges on the differential between the first two terms of equation (8.2), since one would not expect the share of profit to increase forever. 'The proximate determinant of inflation is then the rate at which nominal money wages rise in excess of the growth of average labor productivity' (Moore, 1979, p. 133). This is what Keynes called 'semi-inflation', arising from an upward wage drift, not to be confused with what he called 'absolute inflation', which occurred as a consequence of excess demand. In semi-inflation, wages and prices rise without either full employment or full capacity having been reached. Semi-inflations, according to Keynes (1936, p. 302), have 'a good deal of historical importance', but they 'do not readily lend themselves to theoretical generalisations'. A number of post-Keynesians agree with Keynes and consider that the level of the money wage rate is an exogenous datum, given by historical and sociological circumstances that are almost outside the realm of economics. 'Post-Keynesian theory accepts Keynes's view that the nominal wage is for the most part exogenously determined' (Eichner and Kregel, 1975, p. 1305). Still, in the rest of the section, we shall try to provide an explanation of the evolution of wage inflation.

The key difference, then, between the mainstream and the post-Keynesian views of inflation is that, for the former, inflation is an excess-demand phenomenon, whereas for the latter it is basically a supply-side issue. In the post-Keynesian view, while price or wage inflation may accompany increased activity, excess demand is generally not the cause of continually rising prices. Inflation is not the result of an objective scarcity; it arises from conflicting views about the proper distribution of income. The influence of demand is only an indirect one. This is consistent with the Kaleckian model that has been presented in previous chapters. 'Excess demand provides at most only a minor component of a comprehensive explanation' (Cripps, 1977, p. 110).

The different interpretations of the well-known Phillips curve exemplify the divergences between the mainstream and post-Keynesian approaches to inflation. For mainstream authors, the Phillips curve is an example of the impact of scarcity and market forces. For post-Keynesian authors, higher levels of activity that give rise to lower rates of unemployment, or to falling unemployment rates, give labour more bargaining strength. The stronger bargaining strength can be implemented in the form of higher real wages because firms make more profits and are more likely to yield to the wage demands of labour when times are good (Kaldor, 1959, p. 293). This was also recognized by Keynes when he claimed that wage increases were discontinuously related to increased activity, the discontinuities being 'determined by the psychology of the workers and by the policies of employers and trade unions' (1936, p. 302). This is because relative bargaining power is strongly influenced by institutions, labour laws and history. The main feature of the post-Keynesian theory of inflation, then, is that it is based on a conflictual view of income distribution. As Eichner and Kregel (1975, p. 1308) said, 'At the heart of the inflationary process is the question of relative income distribution.'

8.1.2 The Wage–Cost Mark-up Equation Extended to the Open Economy

Things get slightly more complicated when considering an economy where firms import commodities or semi-finished products from abroad as inputs. As we saw in Chapter 7, in such a case, the pricing equation of a firm can be written as

$$p = (1 + \theta)(1 + j)(w/y) \tag{7.69}$$

where j is the ratio of material costs per unit to unit labour costs (omitting again the distinction between direct and indirect labour costs). Taking growth rates once more, we get

$$\hat{p} = \hat{w} - \hat{y} + \hat{\kappa} + \hat{J} \tag{8.3}$$

where $\kappa = (1 + \theta)$ and $J = (1 + j)$.

Seen from this angle, price inflation can occur for three reasons: the nominal wage rate grows faster than the productivity of labour; the mark-up rises; or the share of imported materials used as inputs relative to total labour costs rises. As Hein and Mundt (2012, p. 15) recall, the latter can happen for three reasons: the price of raw materials rises in the currency of the foreign producer; the domestic currency depreciates relative to the currency of the producer of raw materials; the amount of raw material which is required per unit of production rises. Thus, as is obvious from equations (8.2) and (8.3), everything else being equal, the actual real-wage rate w/p will be lower whenever j is higher, for any of the three reasons just given. In this economy where raw materials are imported from abroad, even though firms keep constant the mark-up θ, an increase in the world prices of commodities will cause real wages to fall. This will also cause an increase in the profit share of firms, unless they decide to reduce their mark-ups, as already pointed out in Chapter 3.

Thus what we wish to say here is that inflation in the prices of raw materials, which are essentially determined on world markets, are likely to jeopardize whatever distributional arrangement exists between profits and wages, or between the profit share and the real wage. This is important because post-Keynesians argue, following Kalecki, that, while the prices of manufactured goods and services are only weakly affected by the level or the growth rate of economic activity, this is not so with the prices of commodities. This means that, when economic growth is strong, the prices of commodities will rise, and hence an increase in the material cost per unit relative to the unit direct labour cost is likely to occur; that is, j is likely to rise. This will then produce a feedback effect on the prices of finished goods through higher costs and with a lag, through higher wages, as labour organizations try to catch up (Bloch and Sapsford, 1991–92, p. 259). This is well explained by Kalecki, who also underlines the speculative forces at work, which are particularly strong in our modern world.

> Generally speaking, changes in the prices of finished goods are 'cost-determined' while changes in the prices of raw materials inclusive of primary foodstuffs are 'demand-determined'. The prices of finished goods are affected, of course, by any 'demand-determined' changes in the prices of raw materials but it is through the channel of *costs* that this influence is transmitted ... The production of finished goods is elastic as a result of existing reserves of productive capacity. When demand increases it is met mainly by an increase in the volume of production while prices tend to remain stable ... The situation with respect to raw materials is different ... With supply inelastic in short periods, an increase in demand causes a diminution of stocks and a consequent increase in price. The initial price movement may be enhanced by the addition of a speculative element. The commodities in question are normally standardized and are subject to quotation at commodity exchanges. A primary rise in demand which causes an increase in prices is frequently accompanied by secondary speculative demand. (Kalecki, 1971, pp. 43–4)

The problem this poses for inflation theory and inflation policy is that 'primary commodity prices reflect conditions in world markets' (Bloch et al., 2004, p. 525). The evolution of commodity prices is strongly procyclical with respect to the growth of world aggregate demand. In other words, monetary authorities have no or little control over one of the main sources of price inflation in a country – the rising cost of raw materials, since the inflation rate of commodity prices depends on world demand for commodities and not on domestic demand, as argued already by Kaldor (1976). An increase in the growth rate of commodity prices has a direct effect on the domestic prices of finished goods, and it will have an additional indirect effect through its impact on the profit shares sought by firms and the response of workers to the changes in their real wage. Perry and Cline (2016) show that falling commodity prices have been a major cause of the 'great moderation' in inflation in the USA since the early 1990s, while monetary policy played virtually no role. Stable inflation was not the result of improvements in orthodox macroeconomic and monetary theories and policies!

8.2 INDUCTIVE REASONS FOR INFLATION

There are two major inductive reasons for inflation: equity requirements and the diffusion of information. We shall treat each of these two reasons in turn.

8.2.1 Fairness

One of the main distinguishing features between mainstream and heterodox theories of pay and of inflation is that the latter attach great importance to the notion of equity and justice, whereas the former do not (Wood, 1978, p. 7). Another way to put this distinction is to say that heterodox theories of pay emphasize customary rules whereas orthodox theories focus on market forces. In the neoclassical theory of inflation, the focus of the analysis rests on the anomic forces of competition. These are peripheral to the post-Keynesian explanation of inflation. At the core of heterodox theories of inflation are the normative pressures of fairness. In post-Keynesian theory, inflation is explained by normative values, that is, pay norms, customs, equity and justice. These norms have an impact on the perception of what is a fair relative wage, a fair real wage, and a fair profit share. They have an impact on both the wage–price spiral and the wage–wage spiral. The lucid consumer, developed in Chapter 2, concerned about her rank in the consumption hierarchy and about upholding her earnings to make ends meet, reappears under the guise of a lucid worker concerned about her status in the workforce, both in real terms and relatively to other workers (Baxter, 1988, pp. 211–50). My own experience with collective bargaining has revealed that most of the action around salaries evolves around a comparison with the salaries in other similar organizations.

Fair real wages are difficult to define. They depend to a large extent on historical experience. Fairness, both in absolute and in relative terms, is often established by history and custom (Hicks, 1974, p. 65). It is quite customary to associate fair increases in real wages with productivity hikes, but such an association is also sometimes refuted. It is then argued that fair real wages are unrelated to sectoral productivity, and are tied instead to the overall productivity of the economic system. Past experience plays an important role in determining the fairness of a wage offer. Rising real wages may have seemed unfair in the 1970s because their rate of growth was lower than in the 1960s. Since the early 1990s, stagnating real wages may have seemed quite just. Fairness depends on what is expected. The ultimate instance of a fair real wage is the real-wage resistance put up by workers in the case of an inflation barrier.

> The wage-earner's test for fair wages is not simply a comparison with other people's earnings; it is also a matter of comparison with his own experience, his own experience in the past. It is this which makes him resist a reduction in his money wage; but it also makes him resist a reduction in the purchasing power of his wage, and even a reduction in the growth of that purchasing power to which he has become accustomed. Thus there is a back lash of prices on wages – a Real Wage Resistance, it may be called. (Hicks, 1975, p. 5)

Nonetheless, however difficult it is to formalize or to test models based on fair wages, fairness is an essential feature of the labour market. As we saw in Chapter 5, the efficiency of a firm relies on the perception by the workers that they are treated fairly. Wage demands are based on what the workers perceive to be a just remuneration, both relative to what the firm can offer and relative to what other workers get or are expected to get. That workers are concerned with the fairness of their wage rate relative to that of other workers was recognized from very early on in the post-Keynesian literature. It is well known that Keynes himself underlined the importance of relative wages for the behaviour of workers and of their unions.

> Any individual or group of individuals, who consent to a reduction of money-wages relatively to others, will suffer a *relative* reduction in real wages, which is a sufficient justification for them to resist it . . . In other words, the struggle about money-wages primarily affects the *distribution* of the aggregate real wage between different labour-groups . . . The effect of combination on the part of a group of workers is to protect their *relative* real wage. (Keynes, 1936, p. 14)

While Robinson focused her attention mainly on the inflation barrier, she also recognized the importance of relative wages when she wrote that 'the causes of movements in money-wages are bound up with the competition of different groups of workers to maintain or improve their relative positions' (1962, p. 70). Although he seems to have changed his mind later, Kaldor (1964a, p. 143) initially attached only marginal importance to the wage–wage spiral, considering 'the outcome of the struggle of wage-earners in different industries and occupations to secure an improvement, or to prevent a deterioration of, their earnings relative to the wages paid in other occupations', as only a minor possible explanation of price inflation. The clearest and earliest exponent of wage–wage inflation was Richard Kahn. In his memorandum to the Radcliffe Committee in 1958, he argued that, apart from periods of marked shortage of labour, the main cause of inflation is 'the competitive struggle between trade unions and different sections of labour, exacerbated by the absence of an agreement about relative wages' (1972, p. 143). As Keynes before him, Kahn (ibid., p. 142) said that 'restraint displayed by any one section of labour taken in isolation operates at the expense of their real wages, which are reduced as a result of wage increases secured elsewhere'.

Some readers may wonder how a theory of inflation based on conflict between workers and entrepreneurs can be arrived at. Was it not demonstrated that real wages and profits could be simultaneously increased? The causes of the conflict are the following. First, high profits should encourage workers to ask for even higher real wages. If there were no limits to this process, full capacity would be reached and the inflation barrier underlined by the Marxian and neo-Keynesian models of growth and distribution would become pertinent. Second, and this is the mechanism that will be emphasized in the inflation model to be presented, the real wage that is targeted by the workers is in conflict with the margin of profit, which is the target of firms. One may wonder then why firms target a margin of profit rather than a rate of profit. The fact is that firms may set a target rate of profit, as in the target-return pricing formula, but this target profit rate is translated into a target margin of profit based on the normal rate of utilization of capacity. The real-wage targets of the workers and the percentage mark-up targets of the firms may thus clash, even though real wages and the actual rate of profit rise together. This will be better understood in a later section of the chapter, when target-return pricing will be explicitly introduced into a conflicting-claims model of inflation.

There is an additional reason why entrepreneurs and workers may be in conflict over the distribution of income. Rentiers also make claims over part of the profits realized by firms. Higher real rates of interest may induce entrepreneurs to raise the mark-up, and hence reduce the real-wage rate (Pivetti, 1985; Smithin, 1996; 2009; Hein, 2012). There is then the possibility of a conflict between entrepreneurs and rentiers over the distribution of profits, and this conflict may spill over into a conflict between rentiers and workers. Indeed, the conflict between workers and rentiers is often seen as a force that induces the state to take measures to slow down the economy and the rate of inflation, rentiers exhorting the state to protect their fixed incomes from the erosion of rising prices (Kalecki, 1971, ch. 12; Rowthorn, 1977).

8.2.2 Information

While the notion of fairness is the first of our two inductive reasons for inflation, the transmission of information is the second. Since fairness is, to a large extent, a relative notion, comparisons are required. These comparisons, in turn, require information about the profits of the firm, their margins of profit, the profits of the industry, the structure of wages, the deals negotiated elsewhere, the value of marginal benefits obtained elsewhere, the recent trend in earnings and so on. Some post-Keynesians have recognized the importance of the diffusion of information in the inflationary process. Davidson (1972, p. 344) writes that 'the increasingly readily information on the earnings of others . . . has created pressures which make wage–price inflation the most dangerous of current economic problems'. This is nowhere more evident than in the realm of top managers' remuneration, which has led to an explosion of the income share going to the top 1 per cent.

One may suspect, assuming available information is correct, that the larger the set of information, the larger is the potential for inflation. The positive relationship is explained by the fact that if wages within a group are compared to those of a larger set of labour unions, there is a higher probability for a group to find its wages unfair relative to another group (Wood, 1978, p. 23). The larger the reference group, the larger the absolute differentials in rates of productivity increases, and hence the larger the potential differential between wage increases and productivity increases in a given industry. On the other hand, when information is generally incorrect, better information may reduce rather than increase inflation pressures. For instance, the information to which the ordinary person or the ordinary union member has access is usually biased. The media have a tendency to publicize only the most spectacular and most outrageous wage deals, contributing somewhat to the inflationary forces by providing a biased informational content of wage spillovers. In any case, even if information could be accurate and comprehensive, only part of it can be processed by the union leaders and the members of the opposing negotiating team. Because there are limits to the information that can be processed in a world dominated by procedural rationality, only the base rates of a subset of occupations and of industries are taken into consideration when bargaining takes place. This explains why the wage increases struck in some key industries often have such an impact on all sectors of the economy.

The post-Keynesian view of how wage increases are transmitted from one part of the labour market to another is borrowed from the Institutional analysis of wage inflation (Burton and Addison, 1977; Piore, 1979). Whereas neoclassical authors consider market forces to be the determinants of pay structure, customs being frictions to the market mechanisms, Institutionalists believe that the wage structure is fundamentally determined by historical norms, the competitive pressures of demand and supply exercising frictions on the customary system. In contrast to the neoclassical framework, where wage transmission can occur only through market forces and price expectations, Institutionalist labour economists believe that there are wage spillover mechanisms whereby wage increases are transmitted to markets that experience very different economic conditions.

Broadly speaking, two variants of the spillover mechanism may be presented. In the first variant, the generalized spillover hypothesis, the wage bargain in an industry depends on past wage bargains of all industries, in particular the rate of wage increase struck at the bargaining table. There is then a substantial amount of interdependence between all sectors of the labour market. This interdependence is justified by the desire of each labour group to keep its place within the wage-earners' hierarchy. Any pressure at any point in the wage matrix is likely to be felt throughout. In a tuned-down version of the generalized spillover hypothesis, only the labour groups with the same contour enter the spillover matrix. These labour groups have similar characteristics, defined either by the type of product made or by the size of the firm to which they belong. Labour unions keep track of their relative position in the hierarchy by making comparisons with the other groups of the wage contour.

The other major variant of the spillover mechanism, perhaps a more realistic one, is that of the wage-leadership industry. This mechanism asserts that one industry, or just a few of them, enters the spillover matrix. All other wage bargains are struck in reference to a select group of key leading sectors. This is the counterpart, for the labour market, of the price-leadership hypothesis of the product market. Post-Keynesians are fond of this type of transmission mechanism. As in the case of price-leaders, wage-leaders may be chosen for various reasons. Sometimes the most economically important industries will be chosen, as a kind of demonstration effect: if the strongest firms in the country yield to the demands of the labour unions, why should less powerful corporations refuse to grant identical wage increases? Eichner (1976, p. 159) calls those the bellwether industries. Other times, in the hope of obtaining greater benefits, the designated wage leader is in an industry that is in a most favourable position: sales and profits are high, and productivity increases have been rapid (Kaldor, 1959, p. 294).

Whatever the exact form of the spillover mechanisms, a major feature of the various wage bargains is their imitative character. The spillover forces may have been reduced by weakened trade unions, but they still exist.

8.3 THE BASIC CONFLICTING-CLAIMS MODEL

The intention of the rest of the chapter is to present a conflicting-claims model of inflation based on the inconsistent income claims of firms and workers, that is, based on what has often been called 'real-wage resistance' by some and 'aspiration gap' by others. In standard terminology, the focus of the analysis is on the wage–price spiral. As a first approximation, the feedback effects from the real economy will be omitted. The wage–wage spiral will be examined in a later section. The chapter will end with an application of the conflicting-claims model to the international sector.

The basic post-Keynesian model of inflation based on conflicting claims has some affinity with Kalecki's (1971, ch. 14) last article, titled 'Class struggle and distribution of national income'. Whereas earlier he took the degree of monopoly to be an exogenous variable, Kalecki argues in this article that trade unions have the power to achieve reductions in the mark-up by demanding and achieving large increases in money wage rates. As was briefly discussed in Chapter 3, it is Kalecki's view that firms are able to shift to consumers a large part of the increase in wage costs, but that some redistribution in favour of workers occurs when trade unions have sufficient bargaining power, at least in a world with excess capacity. This view has been summarized by Rowthorn (1977, p. 224) in the following way: 'The working class can shift distribution in its favour by fighting more vigorously for higher wages, although the cost of such militancy is a faster rate of inflation, as capitalists try, with only partial success, to protect themselves by raising prices.'

As Dalziel (1990) recalls, several post-Keynesian, Marxian and even mainstream authors have constructed models of conflicting-claims inflation. In all these models, the rate of inflation is a function of the size of the inconsistency between the mark-up that firms wish to target and the real-wage rate that the leading key labour bargaining units consider to be fair. This was at the heart of the macroeconometric model of the Cambridge Economic Policy Group (Godley and Cripps, 1976). As is clear from the mark-up pricing equation, $p = (1 + \theta)w/y$, a target set in terms of real wages can always be made equivalent to a target set in terms of a mark-up. Provided there is no change in productivity, it is thus indifferent to assume that both firms and workers set real-wage targets, or that they both set mark-up targets. In our model, real-wage targets will be assumed and, to simplify notation, we shall call ω the real-wage rate w/p. The adopted representation follows Dutt (1987a). Several other authors in the Kaleckian tradition partially or fully adopt the same depiction, for instance Sawyer (1982), Taylor (1985; 1991), Sarantis (1990–91), Smithin (1994, ch. 9), Cassetti (2003), Setterfield (2007; 2009), Godley and Lavoie (2007a), Bastian and Setterfield (2016), Nah and Lavoie (2019b), Blecker and Setterfield (2019) and Brochier (2020).

The basic model of conflict inflation is based on two equations. It is assumed first that the growth rate of money wages that labour unions wish to negotiate is a function of two elements: the discrepancy between their real-wage target and the actual real-wage rate, and the price inflation rate of the previous period. This second element is different from the assumption that is standard in such models, whereby wage inflation is said to depend on price inflation expectations. Arestis and Sawyer (2005, p. 962) argue that the experience of inflation, rather than inflation expectations, is a much more satisfactory variable to enter into such a wage equation, considering that the future is uncertain and the world is non-ergodic. As Neville and Kriesler (2008, p. 314) point out, expected inflation is not an issue in labour bargaining:

> Where inflation is explicitly acknowledged, it is usually the previous period's inflation, so that the negotiation is an attempt to recover real wages to the pre-inflation level, rather than to have them anticipate inflation ... Wage demands usually represent an attempt to regain previous losses caused by inflation, they do not attempt to anticipate inflation.

This also corresponds to my own experience in collective bargaining with a university professors' association.

Let us call ω_w the real wage targeted by the labour unions and the workers. Suppose that the actual real-wage rate of the previous period was ω_{-1}. In general the new actual real-wage rate will not be equal to what has been targeted by workers. Wages may not be fully indexed and workers may not manage to obtain what they consider to be their fair real wage. We may thus formalize this by writing the following equation determining the rate of wage inflation:

$$\hat{w} = \Omega_1 (\omega_w - \omega_{-1}) + \Omega_2 \hat{p}_{-1} \tag{8.4}$$

The Ω_1 parameter indicates to what extent labour unions react to a discrepancy between the actual and the desired real-wage rate. Ω_1 may thus be considered as the bargaining power of the workers. This must be distinguished from the fair wage that the labour unions feel they should obtain. Workers may feel that the real wage is much too low compared to what they consider to be the just rate, but they may have few means to implement their beliefs. The Ω_2 parameter is the rate of wage 'indexation'. It is equal to unity in the case of full indexation, and is generally less than unity. Since the analysis is barely modified by the introduction of the indexation parameter, the equation determining the rate of wage inflation can be rewritten in its simplest form as

$$\hat{w} = \Omega_1 (\omega_w - \omega) \qquad (8.5)$$

We may proceed in a similar way for the equation determining the rate of price inflation. First, it may be assumed that firms wish to pass through increases in wage costs. In addition, they may wish to increase prices whenever the actual mark-up is below the mark-up they would ideally desire to set, and that the larger the differential between those two mark-ups, the higher the rate of price inflation. This may be formalized in terms of target real-wage rates, which for the firm we may denote as ω_f. When firms aim for lower real-wage rates, given the actual real-wage rate, they speed up the rate of price inflation, depending on their bargaining power on both the labour and the product markets. With Ψ_1 and Ψ_2 adjustment parameters playing a role symmetric to the Ω parameters, the rate of price inflation is given by

$$\hat{p} = \Psi_1 (\omega_{-1} - \omega_f) + \Psi_2 \hat{w} \qquad (8.6)$$

As was the case of the wage inflation equation, a simplified version of the price inflation equation can very well represent conflicting-claims price inflation without losing much substance. Omitting indexation, equation (8.6) becomes

$$\hat{p} = \Psi_1 (\omega - \omega_f) \qquad (8.7)$$

Some readers may be somewhat puzzled by equation (8.7). In a world dominated by large corporations, it would seem that firms can exact price increases of their liking. How is it possible for firms not to achieve their targeted mark-up or real-wage rate if they have ultimate control on prices? As Tarling and Wilkinson (1985, p. 179) put it, 'why should distributional shares change in a system where wages are determined unilaterally by capitalists and where in the time sequence prices follow wages?', as assumed here. One must conclude that, in historical time, prices do not always follow wages, or that firms face constraints on prices that have not yet been discussed. In the latter case, foreign competition would be a good example. There is also the fact that not all firms are homogeneous; workers in highly productive firms may target higher nominal and real wages, which less productive firms must match without being able to raise prices. In the former case, one may think of firms having to publish price lists in advance, before wage bargaining is over. There could be a lag period between the increase in costs and the increase in prices.

While most post-Keynesians seem to adopt the specification of the inflation process presented here, Hein and Stockhammer (2010; 2011) propose an alternative specification which is nevertheless also based on conflicting-claims inflation. Besides some minor features, the key difference is that they assume that the wage indexation parameter must be $\Omega_2 = 1$. This apparently small change implies that price inflation will rise ($\Delta \hat{p} > 0$) until the triple equality $\omega_w = \omega_f = \omega_{-1}$ is achieved, as can be verified by introducing equation (8.4) into equation (8.6) and setting $\Omega_2 = 1$. This means that a form of the accelerationist hypothesis is embedded in their model. Assuming that the wage target is a negative function of the rate of unemployment, stable inflation can only be achieved when the economy reaches a specific rate of unemployment – the dreaded NAIRU. There is a vertical long-term Phillips curve, although it is said not to be an attractor. In the Hein and Stockhammer model, as pointed out by Blecker and Setterfield (2019, pp. 259–60), unexpected inflation plays an important role, the level of the inflation rate is indeterminate as it is defined by the inertial effects of inflation expectations, and the inflation rate gets stabilized when distributional conflict is eliminated. All these features contrast with the specification being proposed here, as we shall see in the next section. It is true that there are small countries that entertain some form of automatic wage indexation schemes in contracts, but without full coverage and usually without full indexation. Furthermore, besides the lack of empirical evidence regarding a one-to-one relation between price inflation expectations and actual price inflation, already mentioned at the beginning of the chapter, empirical evidence regarding wage Phillips equations is quite clear. Whatever the econometric specification, the wage indexation coefficient is always much smaller than unity (Cunningham et al., 2019; Galí and Gambetti, 2020), so that assuming $\Omega_2 < 1$ appears to be justified.

8.4 SOLUTIONS TO THE CONFLICTING-CLAIMS MODEL

8.4.1 Equilibrium Inflation Regimes

Different situations will thus arise, depending on the bargaining positions of firms and of unions, and depending on the time lags or reverse time lags between wage bargaining and price setting. We may consider that there is a long-run equilibrium in a model without technical progress when the actual real-wage rate is a constant, that is, when the rate of wage inflation is equal to the rate of price inflation. In such an equilibrium, that is, with $\hat{w}$ and $\hat{p}$ equal to each other, the margin of profit is a constant; that is, the $\hat{\kappa}$ variable in equation (8.2) is equal to zero. In inflation accounting terms, it would seem that there is no profits inflation, but it is clear from equations (8.4) and (8.6) that firms and labour unions are equally responsible for the rise in prices. They both use their bargaining power or their possibilities of indexation to obtain what they consider to be their fair share of income. When $\hat{w} = \hat{p}$, the long-run equilibrium real-wage rate will be given by

$$\omega^* = (\Omega \omega_w + \Psi \omega_f) / (\Omega + \Psi) \tag{8.8}$$

where $\Omega = \Omega_1/(1 - \Omega_2)$ and where $\Psi = \Psi_1/(1 - \Psi_2)$.

Solving for wage and price inflation, using the value of ω^* found above, we discover that the steady-state price and wage inflation rates are positively related to the discrepancy between the two real-wage targets and to the size of the two indexation parameters Ω_2 and Ψ_2:

$$\hat{w} = \hat{p} = \frac{\Omega \Psi (\omega_w - \omega_f)}{\Omega + \Psi} = \frac{\Omega_1 \Psi_1 (\omega_w - \omega_f)}{\Omega_1 (1 - \Psi_2) + \Psi_1 (1 - \Omega_2)} \tag{8.9}$$

As Dalziel (1990) notes, at least three cases can be derived from the above equilibrium relation, two of which are in fact extreme cases. In the first case, firms have either an infinite bargaining power – Ψ_1 tends to infinity – or they are able to fully index any wage increase, when Ψ_2 is equal to unity. The latter case is the one chosen by Setterfield (2009) in a slightly different setup. In either situation, the actual real-wage rate, as defined by equation (8.8), will tend towards ω_f, the target real-wage rate of firms. Firms do not let the margin of profit fall below its target level and they can respond immediately to any increase in their wage costs. This situation corresponds to the one that has been implicitly assumed throughout this book. It is also how mark-up pricing is viewed by most economists. The case of the infinite power of firms over the real-wage rate is illustrated in Figure 8.1. A vertical line illustrates the fact that the actual real-wage rate can be no different from the target real-wage rate of firms, ω_f. The steady-state rate of inflation depends on the bargaining power of trade unions, as well as on the discrepancy between the real wage targeted by firms and the real wage targeted by unions.

We have:

$$\hat{w}^* = \hat{p}^* = \Omega(\omega_w - \omega_f) \tag{8.9A}$$

which can be obtained either from equation (8.4) by assuming that $\omega = \omega_f$ or from the first term of equation (8.9), by assuming that Ψ tends towards infinity.

The other extreme case arises when labour unions have absolute power over the real-wage rate. This can happen either because they have infinite bargaining power, or because they are able to fully index nominal wages to nominal prices. In either situation, the actual real-wage rate gets infinitely close to the real-wage rate targeted by the labour unions. To this case would seem to correspond the inflation barrier, where 'organised labour has the power to oppose any fall in the real-wage rate' (Robinson, 1962, p. 58). Firms are absolutely unable to raise the mark-up and hence reduce the real-wage rate. The situation

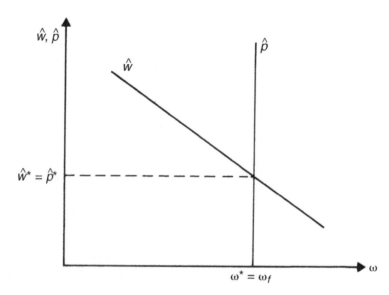

Figure 8.1 Conflicting-claims inflation when firms have absolute bargaining power over the real-wage rate

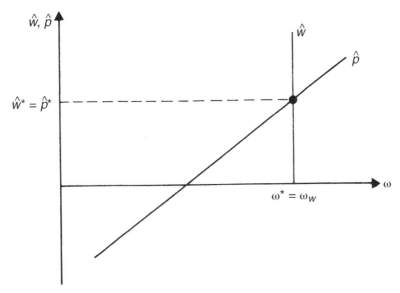

Figure 8.2 Conflicting-claims inflation when labour unions have absolute bargaining power over the real-wage rate

is shown graphically in Figure 8.2. The vertical line illustrates the ability of the trade unions to set the actual real-wage rate at the level they consider to be the fair one. In symmetry to the other extreme case, the rate of inflation is determined by the bargaining power of the firms and the discrepancy between the actual real-wage rate and the real-wage rate targeted by the firms.

We have:

$$\hat{w}^* = \hat{p}^* = \Psi(\omega_w - \omega_f) \tag{8.9B}$$

which can be obtained either from equation (8.6) by assuming that $\omega = \omega_w$ or from the first term of equation (8.9), by assuming that Ω tends towards infinity.

Finally, there is the general case, in which the actual real wage is somewhere in between the targets fixed by the firms and the trade unions. The general case arises when neither group has absolute bargaining power nor the ability to index fully wage or price increases. The inconsistent wage claims are made good by inflation and a compromise in the actual real-wage rate. This situation is particularly easy to illustrate when there is no indexation, that is, when equations (8.5) and (8.7) are the relevant ones. This is shown in Figure 8.3. The upward-sloping curve denoted by $\hat{p}$ represents the rate of price inflation at different actual real wages. If the actual real wage were equal to the target real wage of the firm, the rate of inflation would be zero. The downward-sloping curve marked $\hat{w}$ represents the rate of wage inflation at various actual real wages. The rate of wage inflation would be zero only if the actual and the target real wage of the trade unions were equal. This never occurs in the general case, unless the targets of the firms and of labour unions coincide.

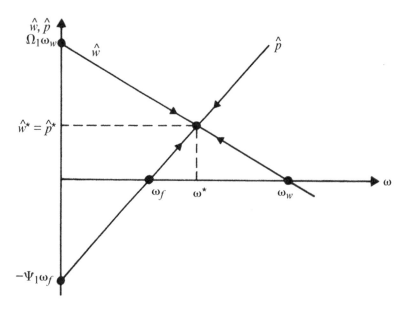

Figure 8.3   Conflicting-claims inflation when neither firms nor labour unions have absolute bargaining power over the real-wage rate

The rate of price inflation $\hat{p}$ is at its steady-state level when it is equal to the rate of wage inflation $\hat{w}$ that is, where the two curves intersect. At this intersection, one also finds the real-wage rate ω^*, which equates the two inflation rates. It is easily found that ω^* is a stable equilibrium. If the actual wage rate were to be in excess of ω^*, for instance, that is, to the right of ω^* in Figure 8.3, it can be seen that the rate of price inflation would be higher than the rate of wage inflation. It follows that the real-wage rate would eventually fall back to its steady-state value ω^*.

8.4.2   Hyper-inflation Regimes

It was argued earlier that instances of high inflation or of hyper-inflation could not be attributed to an excess supply of money, arising possibly from monetized government deficits. What then is the post-Keynesian story behind hyper-inflation? Going back to Figures 8.1 and 8.2, we can guess that a mixture of these two extreme cases will generate runaway inflation. Combining those two cases, with both the Ω_2 and the Ψ_2 parameters of indexation being very close to unity, implies that the $\hat{w}$ and $\hat{p}$ curves would be very steep. So high inflation would arise because of the conflict over the shares of income, a conflict that would be exacerbated by full or nearly full indexation, the detrimental consequences of which are well described in Taylor (1991, ch. 4).

Bastian and Setterfield (2016) argue that in general both firms and the trade unions do not exercise their full bargaining power and will compromise for some real wage (or profit share) acceptable to both parties. However, if the distance between the actual real wage and the target real wage becomes too large, this might trigger what they call a process of strato-inflation, where 'social groups increase the intensity with which they bargain in order to maintain their real incomes' (ibid., p. 643). When there is a rise in the inflation rate, the group which is most likely to observe a fall in their real income is that of the workers. As illustrated by Godley and Cripps (1983, p. 201) and Taylor (1991, pp. 90–91), with no indexation or partial indexation, the real value of wages received by workers as a result of a given wage settlement will be gradually eroded as time passes. The loss will be bigger when price inflation is higher and when the contract is of a longer duration. There may thus be a point at which the actual real wage will be so far away from the real wage target that workers and their trade unions will be induced to strike harder bargains, thus raising the value of the Ω_2 parameter. In formal terms, where ε is the admissible distance between the target and the actual real wage, if the term in square brackets is positive, we will have:

$$\dot{\Omega}_2 = f_\Omega [\omega_w - (\omega^* + \varepsilon)] \tag{8.4A}$$

Then, however, firms may decide to retaliate, and react more strongly to a change in wage inflation, in which case we would have:

$$\dot{\Psi}_2 = f_\Psi \dot{\Omega}_2 \tag{8.6A}$$

If such a process occurs, then both the $\hat{w}$ and $\hat{p}$ curves rotate around their respective axis given by ω_w and ω_f, both becoming ever steeper. While what will happen to the real wage with the stronger indexation parameters is not clear, one thing is certain, this process will generate rising wage and price inflation – the strato-inflation of Bastian and Setterfield (2016) – and eventually hyper-inflation.

What could bring about such a situation? Two factors come to mind. The first one is a dramatic supply-side shock, due to wars for instance or due to an agricultural crisis or a natural disaster. The second factor is a shock to the terms of trade or a foreign exchange crisis. As we have seen in previous chapters, a currency depreciation makes raw materials and intermediate goods more expensive and is likely to lead to a fall in real wages, which could trigger equation (8.4A).

Post-Keynesian authors who discuss hyper-inflation (Câmara and Vernengo, 2001; Charles and Marie, 2016; Bastian and Setterfield, 2020), all refer to Joan Robinson's understanding of the propagation mechanism of this phenomenon. In her 1938 book review on the topic of the German hyper-inflation, she 'introduces the notion of wage/foreign exchange spirals and distributive conflict' (Câmara and Vernengo, 2001, p. 149) and proceeds with the following analysis.

> Neither exchange depreciation nor a budget deficit can account for inflation by itself. But if the rise in money wages is brought into the story, the part which each plays can be clearly seen. With the collapse of the mark in 1921, import prices rose abruptly, dragging home prices after them. The sudden rise in cost of living led to urgent demands for higher wages.... Rising wages, increasing home costs and home money incomes, countered the effect of exchange depreciation in stimulating exports and restricting imports. Each rise in wages, therefore, precipitated a further fall in the exchange rate, and each fall in the exchange rate called forth a further rise in wages. The process became automatic when wages began to be paid on a cost-of-living basis. (Robinson, 1938, p. 510)

When the post-Keynesian approach to hyper-inflation is combined with the hierarchy of currencies view, along with the high pass-throughs associated with developing nations, the dangers of adopting a pure floating exchange regime, subject to brisk depreciations, become more obvious. To the problems arising from the trade balance must be added the 'flight out of domestic currency into a foreign currency' (Charles and Marie, 2016, p. 363), due to the dissolving trust *vis-à-vis* the depreciating currency – another recurrent theme among post-Keynesians from emerging economies. For Robinson (1938, p. 508), as perhaps for Latin-American structuralists when discussing the case of their own countries, 'whatever the cause of the collapse of the exchange, it seems clear that it was the collapse of the exchange which inaugurated the great inflation'. This justifies the calls for either fixed or managed floating exchange regimes for developing or emerging countries, with the accumulation of large foreign exchange reserves, so as to avoid detrimental wage/price/foreign exchange spirals.

8.5 IMPACT OF CHANGES IN BARGAINING POSITIONS

In the basic model of conflicting-claims inflation presented above, the rate of inflation depends only on the bargaining strength of firms and labour unions and on the discrepancy between their respective target real wages. The rest of the economy, the rate of growth, for instance, is assumed not to have any impact on the rate of inflation. Although this is an extreme assumption, which will be relaxed in the next section, it should be noted that Robinson adopts a similar stance in her growth analysis. Referring to Kalecki, she argues that money wages 'follow their own history more or less independently of what is happening to the equilibrium position in real terms', and that the rate of increase of money wages 'can react upon the real position by changing the distribution of real income' (1962, p. 17). We shall follow her intuitions on this issue and examine the impact of changes in bargaining positions on the distribution of income, and hence on the real rate of growth of the economy. To do so, we shall rely on equations (8.5) and (8.7), as we did in Figure 8.3, since these two equations are simpler to represent graphically and since indexation changes little to the analysis.

Let us first examine changes in the bargaining position of workers. The top part of Figure 8.4 illustrates an increase in the target real-wage rate of workers, from ω_{w1} to ω_{w2}. This is represented by a parallel upward shift of the $\hat{w}$ curve. It can be seen that an increase in the real wage targeted by labour unions would lead in the end to a higher rate of price and wage inflation, shown on the graph by $\hat{p}_2^*$. Furthermore, the new actual wage rate, given by ω_2^*, would be higher than before the change in the bargaining position of trade unions. None of these results is very surprising. They correspond to what one would expect from a more militant workforce. The analysis of an increase in the bargaining power of the workers would lead to similar results, except that the new upward-shifted $\hat{w}$ curve would not be parallel to the old one, as both curves would originate from the same point on the ω axis.

It is interesting to examine the effect that a more militant workforce would exert on the real economy. Accompanying the higher rate of inflation, there is a redistribution in favour of the workers, since the real-wage rate is now higher than it was before the change in the bargaining position of workers. In line with the canonical Kaleckian model

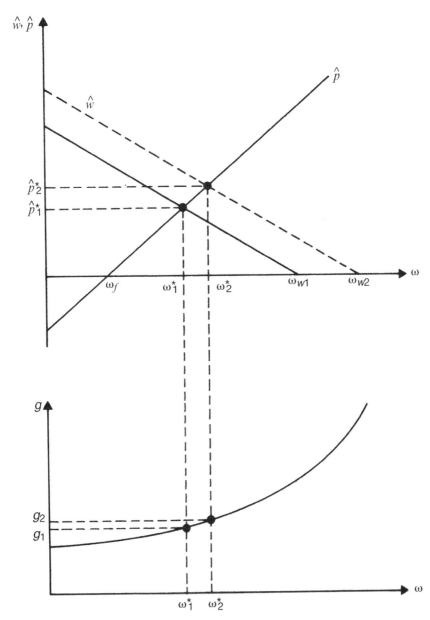

Figure 8.4 Higher rate of wage and price inflation and higher rate of accumulation resulting from an increase in the real wage sought by labour unions

of growth and distribution, the increase in the real-wage rate leads to a higher rate of utilization of capacity and to a higher rate of growth of the economy. This positive relationship is illustrated in the bottom part of Figure 8.4. The exact form of the positive relation between the real-wage rate and the real rate of growth depends on the derivatives of the equilibrium growth rate. In the case of the canonical Kaleckian model (which is wage-led), this equilibrium growth rate can be found by making use of the steady-state rate of capacity utilization (equation 6.16), and introducing it into the saving equation, thus obtaining

$$g^* = \frac{s_p \pi (\gamma - \gamma_u u_n)}{(s_p \pi - \gamma_u v)} \tag{8.10}$$

The above relation may be rewritten in terms of the real-wage rate ω. The share of wages is wL/pq; that is, $(w/p)(L/q) = \omega/y = 1 - \pi$. Thus the equilibrium growth rate is

$$g^* = \frac{s_p \left(1 - \frac{\omega}{y}\right)(\gamma - \gamma_u u_n)}{s_p \left(1 - \frac{\omega}{y}\right) - \gamma_u v} \tag{8.11}$$

The first and the second derivatives of equation (8.11) are positive, yielding the shape of the relationship between the real-wage rate and the rate of growth shown in Figure 8.4. There is thus a positive relationship between the strength of the bargaining position of the workers and the rate of growth of output and of employment up to full capacity. This is consistent with Kalecki's (1971, p. 163) belief that 'a wage rise showing an increase in the trade union power leads . . . to an increase in employment'. This seems also to be consistent with the results of the mainstream analysis of inflation, as well as with the results obtained by Marglin (1984b) in his analysis of inflation in economies constrained by a fixed ratio of capacity utilization. An increase in economic activity – higher rates of utilization or growth rates – is accompanied by an increase in price inflation. Inflation moves procyclically. The Great Moderation of the 1990s and 2000s – low levels of inflation and low variability in inflation – may thus be interpreted as a period during which the bargaining power of labour unions was considerably reduced as a consequence of the large recessions of the early 1980s and early 1990s endured by workers, as well as a consequence of globalization, Low inflation, despite the promises of its advocates, did not generate faster output and productivity growth.

There is, however, a second case that remains to be discussed – that of a change in the bargaining position of firms. Suppose that firms decide to accept a lower mark-up; that is, they set themselves a higher target real-wage rate, ω_{f2} instead of ω_{f1}. This could happen, for instance, when the unit cost of raw materials diminishes relative to unit wage costs, as explained when discussing equation (8.2), and as it did during the Great Moderation. This case is illustrated in the top half of Figure 8.5. The $\hat{p}$ curve shifts down. It leads to higher actual real-wage rates (ω_2^* instead of ω_1^*) and to lower rates of price and wage inflation ($\hat{p}_2^*$ instead of $\hat{p}_1^*$). Looking now at the bottom half of Figure 8.5, we see that lower rates of inflation accompany higher rates of growth. Inflation is countercyclical (Dutt, 1987a, p. 81). The mainstream view finds no support in this case.

Inflation theory

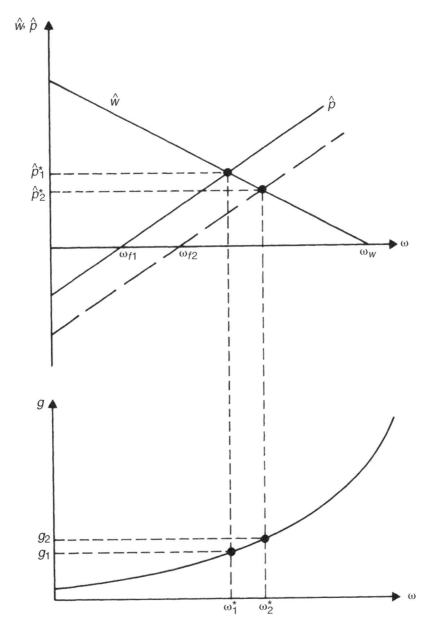

Figure 8.5 Lower rate of wage and price inflation and higher rate of accumulation resulting from a decrease in the costing margin sought by firms

This surprising result is due to the complementary effects of two key post-Keynesian propositions: a redistribution of income claims in favour of workers speeds up growth (when demand is wage-led); and less conflict over income slows down inflation. If firms accept a reduction in their target mark-up, both of these effects should occur until full

Table 8.1 Growth regimes and exogenous changes in bargaining positions

Growth regime	Stronger trade unions	Stronger firms
Wage-led	Faster accumulation Higher inflation	Slower accumulation Lower inflation
Profit-led	Slower accumulation Higher inflation	Faster accumulation Lower inflation

utilization of capacity is reached. Naturally, a rise in the target mark-up of firms, that is, a decrease in the real-wage rate targeted by firms, would have the opposite effects: the rate of growth would be lower and the rate of inflation would be higher. The transition to this new situation may be called stagflation.

Besides changes in the unit cost of raw materials, why would firms want to increase or reduce their costing margins and hence the target real wage? The various possibilities were outlined in Chapter 3, with Table 3.2. It can be noted in particular that an increase in interest rates could lead to higher targeted costing margins and hence to lower real-wage targets for firms, thus inducing slower growth and faster inflation. This was first noted within the present model by Dutt and Amadeo (1993), and the idea has been developed most fully by Hein (2008).

The analysis so far has been conducted on the basis of the canonical Kaleckian model. What if the post-Kaleckian model is the relevant one and the economy is in a profit-led growth regime? Then, obviously, our conclusions need to be reversed, as they are shown in Table 8.1. Every combination becomes possible.

8.6 ENDOGENOUS REAL-WAGE TARGETS OF WORKERS

It has been assumed up to now that the real-wage targets set by the trade unions and the firms are not influenced by the pressures or the absence of pressures from demand. In view of the standard Phillips curve, this appears to be a somewhat extreme assumption. It may be interesting to see to what extent the model is modified when demand considerations enter into it. In his own presentation of conflicting-claims inflation, Rowthorn (1977, p. 219) considers that the real wage targeted by workers is reduced when surplus labour arises; similarly, the mark-up targeted by firms is reduced when there is surplus capacity. The model could be made more complicated by also taking into account the reaction function of the central bank, since, as pointed out in Chapter 3, higher interest rates should induce firms to set higher percentage costing margins and hence a lower target real wage ω_f. But such a lower target would normally lead to faster inflation rates, not slower ones, and could thus jeopardize the operation of traditional monetary policy and the stability of the NAIRU, if it exists (Hein, 2008).

In what follows, however, we shall leave aside the target of firms, and examine the relation between wage inflation and the rate of unemployment. In the traditional Phillips curve, a change in the rate of wage inflation requires a change in the level of unemployment, and indeed this is how Arestis and Sawyer (2005, p. 962), for instance, describe wage inflation. Thus, while it could be said that post-Keynesians also have a NAIRU theory, as Stockhammer (2008) claims, there is a multiplicity of possible NAIRUs, rather than a unique one. But, as Stanley (2002) points out, this deprives the NAIRU of any predictive value. If we were to suppose that the real-wage target of workers depends on the level of unemployment, as is done by some post-Keynesian authors (Dutt, 1992c), complex interactions with limit cycles and the like would arise. This is because, as was shown earlier with the help of equation (6.71), the change in the rate of unemployment is roughly equal to the discrepancy between the natural rate of growth and the actual growth rate of output, so that the rate of unemployment keeps changing as long as these two rates are not equal to each other.

Some authors avoid this problem by assuming that they deal only with a short-run situation, where the capital stock and the available labour force are constant, so that the rate of utilization can be taken as a proxy for the rate of employment. Within this framework, as already pointed out earlier in section 6.5.4 in the case of empirical studies, many post-Keynesians consider that there is a range of rates of unemployment or of rates of utilization such that the Phillips curve is flat (Hein, 2002; 2008; Freedman et al., 2004; Fontana and Palacio-Vera, 2007; Kriesler and Lavoie, 2007; Herr, 2009; Hein and Stockhammer, 2011). As argued by Peach et al. (2011) in their empirical work, the Phillips curve has three segments, two exterior segments which have the standard negative (positive) relationship between inflation and unemployment (capacity utilization), and one interior segment where this relationship does not exist. Richard Lipsey (2016, p. 426), whose work in the early 1960s did so much to popularize the concept of the Phillips curve, also rejects the NAIRU and calls this flat segment the non-inflationary band of unemployment (although he uses the acronym NAIBU). Within the present model, in its short-run version, this means that the target real wage of workers reacts to the rate of utilization or to the rate of unemployment only when it is outside the flat segment, and hence that wage inflation changes only outside that range. This is illustrated in Figure 8.6, where the Phillips curve with respect to the rate of utilization has a distinctive shape.

Let us come back to the long-run version. We shall simply suppose that the real-wage rate targeted by workers is a function of the change in the unemployment rate, rather

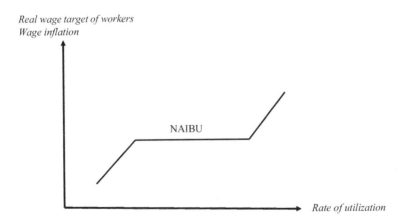

Figure 8.6 The post-Keynesian Phillips curve with its middle flat segment

than the level of unemployment. Recalling the approximation given by equation (6.71), we have

$$\omega_w = \omega_{w0} + \Omega_g(g - g_n) \tag{8.12}$$

Omitting for simplification the indexation term, wage inflation is thus determined in the following way:

$$\hat{w} = \Omega_1 [\omega_{w0} + \Omega_g(g - g_n) - \omega] \tag{8.13}$$

Equation (8.12) is illustrated with the help of Figure 8.7. The real-wage target of workers reacts positively to the growth rate of the economy, as shown on the graph, while the real-wage target of firms is assumed to be a constant. The actual real wage ω^* is a weighted average of these two targets, as determined by equation (8.8), and can thus be found in between the two target real wages. An identical proposal is made by Cassetti (2003), except that targets of workers and firms are expressed in terms of profit shares.

As to equation (8.13), we may call it a quasi-Phillips curve. From very early on in the history of the Phillips curve, it was empirically shown that the rate of wage inflation is significantly influenced by the rate of change of unemployment (Bowen and Berry, 1963), as also confirmed by Bloch et al. (2004). The main justification for equations (8.12) and (8.13) is that only a global recession or the threat to affluence may slow down inflationary forces. If the rate of unemployment is constant, those still having a job do not feel that their job or their income is threatened. Employed workers, who generally constitute the majority of workers, have little reason to fear the possibility of unemployment. There will be little pressure on trade union leaders to sacrifice wage

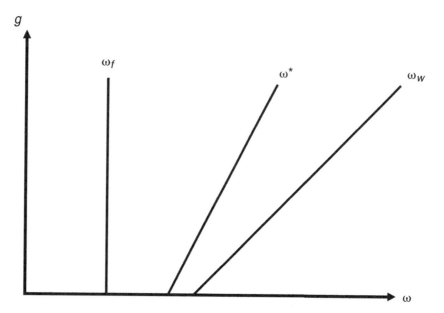

Figure 8.7 The endogenous real-wage target of workers and the actual real-wage rate

increases for the hope of a better employment outlook, even if the rate of unemployment is high. By contrast, workers may fear the possibility of losing their job if the rate of unemployment is rising. The faster it rises, the more threatened workers feel, and the more likely they are to waive real-wage objectives. 'The mechanism of the reserve army, in other words, requires not only the existence of unemployment but a *threat* to those still employed' (Boddy and Crotty, 1975, p. 10). It must be recognized, however, that the rate of unemployment cannot rise (or fall) forever. As pointed out in in section 6.6 of Chapter 6, some other mechanisms will make the natural rate of growth endogenous and converge towards the actual rate of growth.

We now examine how equations (8.11) and (8.12) interact with each other. This interaction is illustrated with the help of Figure 8.8. The real-wage rate that arises from the bargaining process between workers and firms is represented by the ω* curve and is the same as that described in Figure 8.7. The growth rate that arises from the effective-demand process, that is, the growth rate determined by the real wage and the other parameters of the canonical Kaleckian growth model, is represented by the g^* curve. As drawn, there are two possible long-run equilibria, given by points A and B, at the intersection of the two curves. Point A is the stable equilibrium, while point B is an unstable one. To see why, start with some historically given real wage rate, ω_0, as shown in the graph. At this real wage, effective-demand conditions will generate a growth rate equal to g_0. With this growth rate, however, workers will be forced to revise downward their estimate of the target real wage, thus leading to a new, lower, actual real-wage rate of ω_1. This in turn will generate a growth rate lower than g_0. This process will keep going on until point A is reached. Thus A is the stable equilibrium.

Readers can proceed to the usual comparative exercises. If there is a positive shock to effective demand, the g^* curve being shifted up, both real wages and output growth

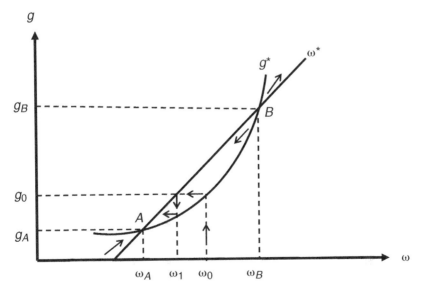

Figure 8.8 Combining the real-wage bargaining process with the impact of real wages on effective demand

will be higher at the new *A* equilibrium. Similarly, if the bargaining power of workers improves, thus tilting the ω* curve towards the right, real wages and output growth will also be higher. Thus, as Cassetti (2003, p. 462) has concluded, despite the addition of a conflict theory of inflation, 'the standard Kaleckian results are confirmed', as long as the rate of capacity utilization remains below unity.

8.7 WAGE–WAGE INFLATION AND PRODUCTIVITY GROWTH

Up to now, the rate of inflation has been explained solely in terms of a conflict between wage-earners on one side and firms on the other. No attention was paid to the conflicts within the labour class, arising because of the importance of retaining one's position in the socio-economic hierarchy. The intention of the present section is to accommodate the presence of wage–wage inflation in a conflicting-claims model of inflation. As we do so, technical progress will also be discussed.

The major characteristic of wage–wage inflation is that inflation would continue even if firms and trade unions in general agreed on a real-wage target. Past attempts at catching up create a backlog of recriminations, some groups of workers believing that they have been left behind in the previous round of negotiations. The attempt by each group of workers to re-establish what they consider to be their rightful place in the social hierarchy leads to a trend of rising wages. The wage inflation curve, previously written in its basic form under equation (8.5), thus needs an additional constant term, reflecting the wage–wage inflation trend, here called Ω_{ww}.

$$\hat{w} = \Omega_1 (\omega_w - \omega) + \Omega_{ww} \tag{8.14}$$

As is obvious in Figure 8.9, once wage–wage inflation is taken into account, it is impossible for the rate of inflation to reach zero unless the real wage targeted by firms is smaller than the real wage targeted by workers. It can be seen on the graph that, when workers and firms agree on the same real-wage target ω_w, the rate of wage and price inflation is $\hat{p}_1^*$ whereas there is no inflation when firms set a real-wage target of $\omega_f > \omega_w$. This inequality would seem to be a rather peculiar situation, which would arise very rarely indeed. Yet, before the Second World War, it was not uncommon to observe long periods of stable prices. Since it is very unlikely that firms would set target real-wage rates in excess of those fixed by trade unions for a long period of time, one must either conclude that the hypothesis of wage–wage inflation is incorrect or that some omitted factor must also be added to the basic conflicting-claims inflation model. Increases in productivity are perhaps the required additional element in favour of the wage–wage inflation hypothesis, as we shall now see.

There are many ways in which technical progress can be added to the basic model of inflation. Here we argue that the higher the rate of technical progress, the higher the wage inflation induced by wage–wage conflict, that is, the higher Ω_{ww} in equation (8.14). This would be caused by the large nominal wage increases that would be demanded in sectors with large productivity increases. Workers in sectors with low increases in productivity would ask for similar increases in wages, based on those obtained in sectors with high rates of technical progress. This is what some authors have called productivity-led

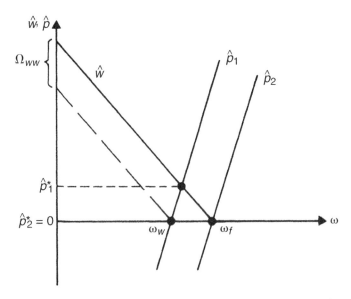

Figure 8.9 Adding wage–wage inflation to a conflict model of inflation: the rate of inflation is positive although firms and workers agree on their real-wage targets

inflation (Hicks, 1955). It is tightly linked to wage–wage inflation. Let λ denote, as before, the growth rate of labour productivity. Also, from now on in this section, so as to take into account changes in productivity, we redefine ω, which is now such that $\omega = (w/p)/y$. Thus ω is now the wage share, or what is sometimes called the level of efficient wages. With these assumptions, the $\hat{w}$ curve can be rewritten as

$$\hat{w} = \Omega_1(\omega_w - \omega) + \Omega_{ww0} + \Omega_\lambda \lambda \qquad (8.15)$$

On the side of the firms, one may suppose that productivity increases are partially or fully passed on to consumers. If a proportion Ψ_λ of the productivity gains are passed on in the form of lower prices, the $\hat{p}$ equation can be rewritten as

$$\hat{p} = \Psi_1(\omega - \omega_f) - \Psi_\lambda \lambda \qquad (8.16)$$

With technical progress, a constant ω requires that $\hat{w} = \hat{p} + \lambda$. Solving for ω, the above two equations yield

$$\omega^* = \frac{\Omega_1 \omega_w + \Psi_1 \omega_f + \Omega_{ww0} + [\Omega_\lambda - (1 - \Psi_\lambda)]\lambda}{\Omega_1 + \Psi_1} \qquad (8.17)$$

The elements in the square brackets of equation (8.17) show that an increase in productivity would have no impact on the actual wage share (the efficient wage rate) whenever the share of productivity gains $(1 - \Psi_\lambda)$ that firms decline to pass on to consumers is equal to the share Ω_λ of these gains that workers wish to translate into nominal wage increases. When $\Omega_\lambda > (1 - \Psi_\lambda)$, the economy is a Fordist regime, as it is called by the French Regulation school (Boyer, 1988): there is a positive relation between technical progress and the wage share. When $\Omega_\lambda < (1 - \Psi_\lambda)$, the economy is in an anti-Fordist regime: faster technical progress drives down the labour share. There is some evidence that inflation-targeting regimes tend to promote this anti-Fordist regime. 'Through the announcement effect of the inflation target, the central bank promotes a labour-market behaviour that anchors expectations and establishes a reference point for wage bargaining' (Lavoie and Seccareccia, 2021, p. 26). With productivity growth, wage growth targets that are anchored by the price inflation target set by the central bank will necessarily generate a falling wage share.

When there is technical progress and wage–wage inflation, a zero rate of price inflation does not require the equality of the profit margin targets set by labour unions and firms; that is, the wage shares targeted by unions and firms do not have to be equal. Figure 8.10 offers one of the many possibilities arising when there is no price inflation. The level of efficient wages ω^* that ensures a constant profit margin is given by the intersection of the $\hat{w}$ curve and of the curve marked $\hat{p} + \lambda$. This yields the steady-state rate of wage inflation $\hat{w}^*$. The vertical projection on the $\hat{p}$ curve yields the steady-state rate of price inflation $\hat{p}^*$, here zero. Because of the presence of technical progress and of wage–wage inflation, situations that would seem impossible in the basic inflation model may arise. Here, wage and price curves have been so constructed that there is no price inflation, despite the fact that the actual wage share is above the wage share targeted by firms ($\omega^* > \omega_f$). On the other hand, there is wage inflation despite the actual wage share being equal to the wage share targeted by labour unions ($\omega^* = \omega_w$). Blecker and Setterfield (2019, p. 217) propose

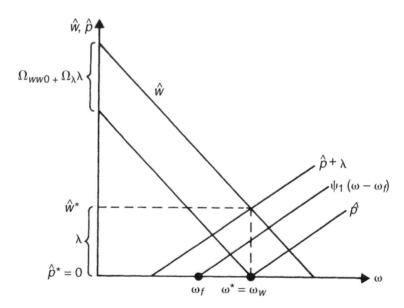

Figure 8.10 Wage–wage inflation and technical progress combined in a conflict model of inflation: a divergence between wage inflation and price inflation

a similar analysis of productivity growth and provide a figure illustrating the general case where price inflation is positive.

8.8 TARGET-RETURN PRICING AND BARGAINING

We return to endogenous real-wage targets and target-return pricing procedures. While endogenous real-wage targets may not modify the basis analysis of conflicting-claims inflation, it helps to solve a puzzle encountered earlier. The puzzle arose in the discussion of the implications of target-return pricing. The reader may recall from Chapter 6 that, if firms adjust the target rate of return to the actual rate of profit, along the lines given by equations (6.40) and (6.41), the rate of capacity utilization of the economy eventually comes to rest at precisely its normal rate, which is predetermined by convention. In this antinomic variant of the Kaleckian model of growth and distribution, the trade-off between real wages and the rate of growth reappears. The rate of utilization becomes exogenous, as in neoclassical, neo-Marxian and neo-Keynesian models. To save the Kaleckian features of the model, it had to be assumed that the adjustment of the target rate of return is non-existent or sluggish.

We are now in a position to explain why the target rate of return may fully adjust to the actual rate of profit, without the rate of utilization of capacity becoming exogenous. To do so, it must be recognized once again that firms are not in a position to set the exact mark-up of their choice. One must thus distinguish between two sorts of costing margins: the actual costing margin, which arises from the bargaining process; and the target costing margin, which corresponds to the target rate of return and the normal rate of utilization of capacity that firms would like to incorporate into their pricing strategy. In terms of wage rates, one would have to distinguish between two wage rates: the actual real-wage rate arising from bargaining, called ω^* as before; and the real-wage rate targeted by firms, called ω_f, corresponding to the target rate of return r_n assessed by firms.

Let us assume, then, that firms slowly adjust the target rate of return (or the normal profit rate) according to the actual rate of profit, as is shown in the expression below:

$$\dot{r}_n = \phi_2(r^* - r_n), \phi_2 > 0 \qquad (8.18)$$

A long-run steady-state position is reached when the target rate of return is the same in two successive periods, that is, when the target rate of return and the actual rate of return are equal. In a world where trade unions have some bargaining power, the target rate of return does not correspond to the actual real-wage rate but corresponds instead to the real-wage rate targeted by firms. The process described by equation (8.18) may thus come to an end without the steady-state target rate of return being actually incorporated in prices. This means that the rate of capacity utilization emerging from the adjustment process of the target rate of return is not necessarily the normal rate of utilization, and that, as a consequence, the rate of utilization is endogenous despite the existence of this adjustment process. Going back to the formula defining target-return pricing, that is, equation (5.67), we can make the following distinction.

The real wage targeted by firms is equal to

$$\omega_f = y_v \left(\frac{u_n - r_n v}{u_n + \sigma f} \right) \qquad (8.19)$$

while the real wage which arises from the bargaining process is equal to

$$\omega^* = y_v \left(\frac{u_n - r_n^* v}{u_n + \sigma f} \right) \qquad (8.20)$$

where r_n^* is the target rate of return which is actually incorporated to the pricing formula.

The adjustment process, when the actual rate of profit is initially larger than the target rate of return, is illustrated in Figure 8.11. Let us start from a situation in which the real-wage rates desired by firms and by workers coincide, as shown on the left-hand side of the graph. There the $\hat{p}_1$ and the $\hat{w}$ curves intersect the ω axis at the same point, the real-wage rate ω_w. We have the triple equality: $\omega_w = \omega_{f1} = \omega_1^*$. This implies, as is obvious from equations (8.19) and (8.20), that the target rate of return initially assessed by firms, called r_{n1}, and the target rate of return incorporated in the pricing formula, called r_{n1}^* are equal. We can draw the profits cost curve corresponding to this situation, shown on the right-hand side of the graph as $PC(\omega_w)$. For the given effective-demand conditions, illustrated by the ED curve, the actual rate of utilization of capacity is u_1, and the actual rate of profit is r_1. The actual rate of profit r_1 is thus much larger than the target rate of return r_{n1}. As a result, firms will slowly revise upwards the target rate of return r_n, along the lines of equation (8.18). The real-wage rate ω_f targeted by firms, as defined by equation (8.19), would thus start to fall.

Two phenomena will now arise. First, as firms revise their estimate of the target rate of return, a discrepancy arises between the real-wage rate targeted by firms and the real-wage rate targeted by workers. As a consequence, the actual real-wage rate becomes different from the real wage targeted by firms, and hence a similar discrepancy arises between the target rate of return assessed by firms and the target rate of return incorporated into prices. Second, as real wages diminish, the actual rate of profit falls. There is thus a convergence between the actual rate of profit, which falls, and the target rate of return, which rises.

The end result is shown in Figure 8.11. Firms are targeting a real-wage rate of ω_{f2}, and hence a target rate of return of r_{n2}. Because of the bargaining power of labour, inflation occurs at a rate of $\hat{p}_2^*$ while the actual real wage rate is ω_2^*. At that rate, the new profits cost curve $PC(\omega_2^*)$ is such that the actual rate of profit, r_2 and the target rate of return assessed by firms, r_{n2}, are equated. The adjustment process of the target rate of return has led to a new rate of utilization of capacity, u_2, which is different from the standard rate, u_n. The rate of utilization in the very long run is thus still endogenous, despite the presence of a price-adjustment mechanism.

Real-wage resistance in this example brings in inflation, but it also preserves the distinctive features of the Kaleckian model when this model is associated with an adaptative normal profit rate. The presence of bargaining power on the part of the workers allows us to respond to a criticism of the Kaleckian model of growth and distribution: there cannot be a true long-run steady state unless the normal profit rate and the actual profit

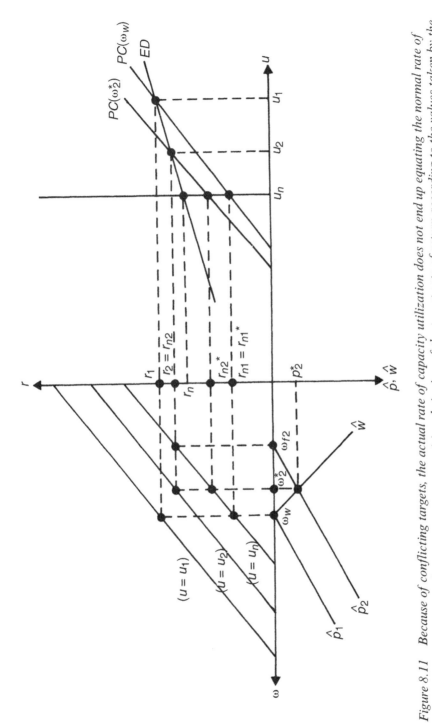

Figure 8.11 Because of conflicting targets, the actual rate of capacity utilization does not end up equating the normal rate of utilization, despite entrepreneurs revising their view of the target rate of return according to the values taken by the actual rate of profit

rate are equated. In the above model, the two rates are equated; that is, the actual profit rate and the target rate of return assessed by firms become equal. Despite this, the rate of utilization of capacity is still free to vary from its standard or normal value. The key characteristic of the Kaleckian model, the endogeneity of its rate of capacity utilization, is thus preserved.

8.9 INFLATION IN THE OPEN ECONOMY

8.9.1 The Impact of the Real Exchange Rate on Wage and Price Inflation

As a final topic for this chapter, we go back to the Kaleckian model in an open economy, discussed in Chapter 7. Readers may recall that the model presented there did not take into account the possible feedback effects of a currency depreciation on wage demands and hence on domestic price inflation. We revisit some of the results that we achieved in the previous chapter, taking as a start the two wage and price inflation equations, given by equations (8.5) and (8.7) of the basic conflict inflation model. We take our cues from Blecker (2011), who builds a model which has many similarities with the model of Hein and Vogel (2008) that was the basis of our open-economy Kaleckian model.

We slightly revise those two equations, by taking into account the impact that the real exchange rate may have on the behaviour of wages and domestic prices. Blecker assumes that a higher real exchange rate will induce firms to target a lower real wage, and hence a higher profit share. This is indeed consistent with the claim that we made in Chapter 7, where we showed that a depreciation of the domestic currency (a rise in the nominal exchange rate e) would lead to a lower real-wage rate, through the effect on the cost of imported raw materials and intermediate commodities. In Blecker's account, the real wage targeted by firms is

$$\omega_f = \omega_{f0} - \Psi_2 e_R \qquad (8.21)$$

Putting together equations (8.7) and (8.21), the domestic price inflation, which we denote by $\hat{p}_d$ to distinguish it from foreign price inflation, denoted by $\hat{p}_f$, is thus

$$\hat{p}_d = \Psi_1 (\omega - \omega_{f0} + \Psi_2 e_R) \qquad (8.22)$$

To assess wage inflation, we rely on the specification of Bastian and Setterfield (2020, p. 1280). The real wage targeted by workers becomes:

$$\omega_w = \omega_{w0} + \Omega_2 e_R \qquad (8.23)$$

where the parameter Ω_2 'will be relatively large in countries where imports of wage goods are important and labour unions are strong, and low otherwise' (Blecker, 2011, p. 224). Combining equations (8.5) and (8.23), wage inflation is given by:

$$\hat{w} = \Omega_1(\omega_{w0} + \Omega_2 e_R - \omega) \qquad (8.24)$$

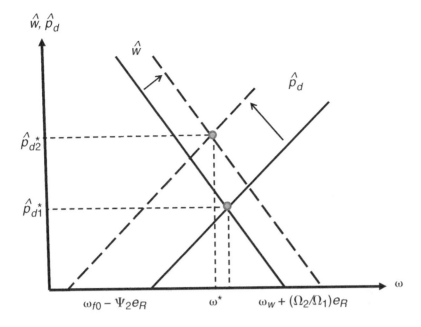

Figure 8.12 A higher real exchange rate (a real depreciation of the domestic currency) leads to faster wage and price inflation

Under these conditions, we can see right away that a higher real exchange rate e_R (a real depreciation of the domestic currency) will lead to faster wage and price inflation. This is shown with the help of Figure 8.12, which illustrates equations (8.22) and (8.24). With a higher real exchange rate e_R, the $\hat{w}$ and $\hat{p}_d$ curves shift as shown by the dotted lines. The new equilibrium rate of inflation is necessarily higher than what it was before the depreciation. This effect of depreciation on domestic inflation helps to explain why several economists from emerging economies doubt that the policies suggested by MMT advocates can easily be put in place in these countries (Vernengo and Pérez Caldentey, 2020, p. 337).

8.9.2 The Real-wage Rate in an Open-economy Conflict Inflation Model

What about the real-wage rate? As we did for the basic conflict inflation model, we can find the conditions under which the real-wage rate is a constant. This will happen when $\hat{\omega} = 0$ and hence, because the real wage in domestic terms is $\omega = w/p_d$ the real wage will be constant when $\hat{w} = \hat{p}_d$. Making use of this relation, as well as equations (8.22) and (8.24), we find what Blecker calls the distribution curve, or *DC* curve, which is the set of all values of the real wage and the real exchange rate such that the real wage remains constant. This relationship is given by equation (8.25):

$$\omega = \frac{\Omega_1 \omega_{w0} + \Psi_1 \omega_{f0} + (\Omega_1 \Omega_2 - \Psi_1 \Psi_2) e_R}{\Omega_1 + \Psi_1} \tag{8.25}$$

Similarly, we can look at all the doublets of real wages and real exchange rates for which the real exchange rate remains constant. Since the real exchange rate is $e_R = ep_f/p_d$, the evolution of the real exchange rate is given by

$$\hat{e}_R = \hat{e} + \hat{p}_f - \hat{p}_d \tag{8.26}$$

While we can assume price inflation abroad to be given exogenously, we know what domestic inflation is. Now what about the change in e, the nominal exchange rate? As a simplification device, Blecker examines only the case of a managed floating exchange rate, where the monetary authorities target a real exchange rate $\bar{e}_R$ trying to slowly bring back the actual real exchange rate towards its target. The adjustment that the monetary authorities will impose on the nominal exchange rate thus becomes

$$\hat{e} = \Gamma(\bar{e}_R - e_R) \tag{8.27}$$

Putting together equations (8.27) and (8.22), and setting equation (8.26) equal to zero, we find what Blecker calls the foreign exchange curve, or FE curve, which is the set of all values of the real wage and the real exchange rate such that the real exchange rate remains constant. We get

$$e_R = \frac{\hat{p}_f + \Psi_1 \omega_{f0} + \Gamma \bar{e}_R - \Psi_1 \omega}{\Psi_1 \Psi_2 + \Gamma} \tag{8.28}$$

The DC and FE curves are shown on the right-hand side of Figure 8.13. The FE curve (equation 8.28) is necessarily downward-sloping. The DC curve (equation 8.25) could

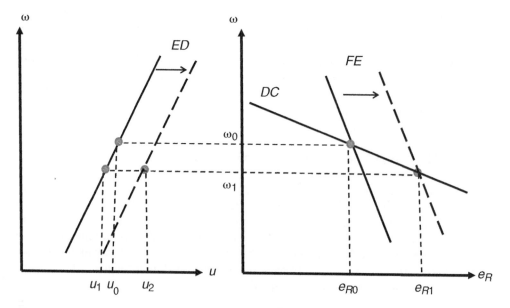

Figure 8.13 Effect of an increase in the targeted real exchange rate on the real exchange rate and the rate of utilization in a wage-led domestic demand regime

have a positive or a negative slope, or it could be flat if a depreciation of the home currency had no impact whatsoever on the real wage. Here we assume that labour unions are not strong enough to obtain higher real wages when there is a currency depreciation, and therefore we assume that the *DC* curve also has a negative slope (that is, $\Omega_1\Omega_2 < \Psi_1\Psi_2$). Blecker (2011, p. 225) assures us that the configuration shown on the right-hand side of Figure 8.13 exhibits dynamic stability, and so we shall take his word for it. The left-hand side of Figure 8.13, with the *ED* curve, illustrates equation (7.68) of Chapter 7, that is, the relationship between the rate of utilization and income distribution in an open economy, which we repeat here for convenience:

$$u^* = \frac{\left(\gamma_0 + \gamma_\pi \pi + \beta_0 + \beta_{uf} u_f + \beta_e e_R\right)v}{s_p \pi + \left(\beta_u - \gamma_u\right)v} \qquad (7.68)$$

But whereas the profit share stood for the variable representing income distribution in equation (7.68), here the chosen variable is the wage share, or more precisely the real-wage rate, under the assumption that there is no change in labour productivity, as was done in Chapter 7. The *ED* curve in Figure 8.13 is shown as being upward-sloping, thus assuming that the economy has a positive relationship between real wages and the rate of utilization, at a given real exchange rate. This economy is thus assumed to be in a wage-led domestic demand regime.

We conduct a single experiment with the model so constructed: what happens if the real exchange rate targeted by the central bank increases? In other words, what happens if the monetary authorities go for a depreciation of the real value of the home currency? Figure 8.13 shows what may happen with a higher target exchange rate $\bar{e}_R$. There is now a rightward shift of the *FE* curve, which will eventually achieve the higher target rate, but which will also bring about a lower real-wage rate as it moves from ω_0 to ω_1. In a domestic wage-led demand regime, this in itself moves the rate of utilization from u_0 to u_1. If the β_e coefficient of equation (7.68) is nearly zero, this means that the devaluation is unable to modify the balance of trade in nominal terms and thus, if we remain within the confines of the standard Marshall-Lerner condition, that the sum of the absolute values of the price elasticities of imports and exports is exactly equal to one. In this case, the *ED* curve stays put, and the rate of utilization after the depreciation is stuck at u_1. We could thus say that this economy has a wage-led domestic demand regime and a wage-led global demand regime, because a lower real-wage rate is associated with a lower rate of utilization, even when the open-economy effects are taken into consideration.

For the economy to move towards a profit-led global demand regime, a strong value for the β_e coefficient is necessary. In other words, the price elasticities of imports and exports need to have high absolute values. This would be the case illustrated with the strong rightward shift of the *ED* curve, now shown as a dotted line, inducing a new rate of utilization $u_2 > u_0$. In this case, the lower real-wage rate is associated with a higher rate of capacity utilization. Such an economy would be in a wage-led domestic demand regime but in a profit-led global demand regime. This possibility was underlined early on by Blecker (1989) and Bhaduri and Marglin (1990). Indeed, the empirical study of Onaran and Galanis (2012), as shown in Table 7.10, did show that a number of countries switched from a wage-led domestic demand regime to a profit-led regime when international trade was taken into consideration.

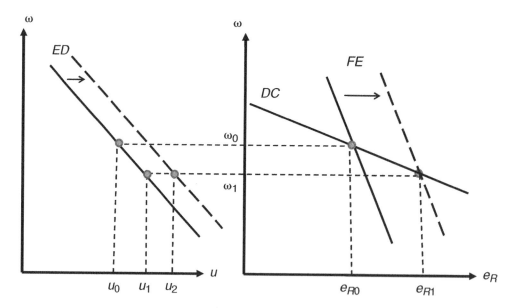

Figure 8.14 Effect of an increase in the targeted real exchange rate on the real exchange rate and the rate of utilization in a profit-led domestic demand regime

Figure 8.14 shows what would happen if the economy started out in a profit-led domestic demand regime. The *ED* curve would now be downward-sloping. The higher target real exchange rate once again drives down the real-wage rate from ω_0 to ω_1. This time, however, as can be seen on the left-hand side, the lower real-wage rate generates a higher rate of utilization, $u_1 > u_0$. As long as the β_e coefficient is non-negative, that is, as long as the *ED* curve does not shift leftwards, the new rate of utilization incorporating the real exchange effects will end up being $u_2 > u_0$, as shown in Figure 8.14. The global demand regime would thus normally remain profit-led.

We may thus conclude this section by saying that the introduction of induced wage and price inflation did not modify the essential results of the Kaleckian model in an open economy.

8.10 INFLATION: A RECAP

The inflation rate is usually explained through some kind of Phillips curve. The objective of the present section is to briefly recapitulate the various arguments regarding the inflation rate that have been offered so far. When discussing the Duménil and Lévy model in Chapter 6, we offered a demand-pull view of inflation, as reflected by equation (6.46), where the rate of inflation depends on the discrepancy between the actual and the normal rates of capacity utilization. The focus of the Kaleckian model of inflation developed in the present chapter has been a cost-push theory of inflation, based on the conflicting claims of workers and firms. This theory is also known as a real-wage resistance theory of inflation, or as a theory based on aspiration gaps. Its main elements are found in equations (8.4) and (8.6), where it is said that price inflation depends on current wage inflation, while current wage inflation depends on past price inflation, as well as the aspiration gaps of both groups of agents. A main feature of this Kaleckian model of inflation is that only partial indexing occurs. Finally, besides the bargaining power of workers and firms, we have also shown that the aspiration gap is likely to arise when the depreciation of the domestic currency leads to increases in (imported) commodity prices or to higher target costing margins, thus jeopardizing whatever distributional arrangement existed between profit recipients and workers.

How can we put all this in a form resembling that of the conventional Phillips curve? Serrano (2006) proposes a Phillips curve based on three components, which we can associate with the following equation:

$$\hat{p} = \alpha_1 \hat{p}_{-1} + \alpha_2 (u - u_n) + \alpha_3 (\omega_w - \omega_f) \tag{8.29}$$

It is understood that the third term on the right-hand side captures the aspiration gap as well as the other cost-push elements usually associated with supply-side shocks, such as imported inflation due to higher commodity prices such as oil or the higher prices of imported goods, increases in sales tax, a slowdown in productivity growth, or a rise in real interest rates.

Equation (8.29) is thus a kind of reduced form of the post-Keynesian view of inflation. The equation can be further simplified on two accounts. First, when the rate of utilization is close enough to its normal rate, the Phillips curve, as argued earlier, is likely to be flat so that the α_2 coefficient is likely to be zero. Second, Sraffians like Serrano would argue, as we saw in Chapter 6, that the actual rate of capacity utilization would trend towards the normal rate of utilization, through the mechanism developed with the help of equation (6.67), so that in the long-run we would have $u = u_n$. Thus, once again, the second term of equation (8.29) would disappear. Thus, whether the economy is in the middle flat zone of the Phillips curve, or whether it is indeed operating at the normal rate of capacity utilization, when present and past inflation rates are equated, the inflation rate is equal to

$$\hat{p} = \frac{\alpha_3 (\omega_w - \omega_f)}{1 - \alpha_1} \tag{8.30}$$

In the post-Keynesian view of inflation, price inflation is explained mainly by historical and cultural features, tied to the size and the strength of the aspiration gap, which itself may have been affected by the past evolution of aggregate demand. Finally, we may wish to consider the case where price inflation depends on price expectations. Lima and Setterfield (2008) and Summa and Braga (2020) suppose that there are anchored expectations, meaning that the expected rate of inflation $\hat{p}^e$ is a weighted average of past inflation and some conventional value of price inflation, which is a given constant (instead of the previous expected rate). With implicit or explicit inflation targeting, the anchor is likely to be the target rate of inflation $\hat{p}^T$ set by the central bank. With α_e being the weight attached to past inflation, we have:

$$\hat{p}^e = \alpha_e \hat{p}_{-1} + (1 - \alpha_e) \hat{p}^T \tag{8.31}$$

so that equation (8.29), assuming we are in the flat segment of the Phillips curve, can be rewritten as:

$$\hat{p} = \alpha_1 [\alpha_e \hat{p}_{-1} + (1 - \alpha_e) \hat{p}^T] + \alpha_3(\omega_w - \omega_f) \quad (8.32)$$

A steady state is reached when $\hat{p} = \hat{p}_{-1}$, that is, when the inflation rate does not change any more. The above equation then becomes:

$$\hat{p}^* = \frac{\alpha_1(1 - \alpha_e) \hat{p}^T + \alpha_3(\omega_w - \omega_f)}{(1 - \alpha_1 \alpha_e)} \quad (8.33)$$

The next question concerns what is required for the steady-state inflation rate to equate the target rate of inflation. To achieve $\hat{p}^* = \hat{p}^T$, the following equality is needed:

$$(\omega_w - \omega_f) = \frac{(1 - \alpha_1) \hat{p}^T}{\alpha_3} \quad (8.34)$$

In the case of equation (8.30), the causality could be understood as running from the distance between the two target real wages to the rate of inflation. The size of the distributive conflict gave rise to a certain inflation rate. By contrast, what equation (8.34) tells us is that if the inflation target is to be achieved, then the distributive conflict must be of a certain size. The lower the rate of inflation, the smaller must be the distributive conflict as represented by the distance $(\omega_w - \omega_f)$. What this implies is that if the monetary authorities wish to achieve a lower inflation target, the central bank and possibly the government will need to implement policies that will either increase ω_w or reduce ω_f. What is most likely to happen is that implemented policies will attempt to reduce the bargaining power of

Table 8.2 Factors that have weakened the bargaining power of workers

Factors whose increase have weakened the bargaining power of workers
Unemployment rates
Privatizations
Overall labour-market flexibility
Relative number of immigrant workers
International capital mobility
Free trade
Trade from low-wage developing countries
Direct investment into low-wage developing countries
Employment shift towards low-paid service industries
Factors whose decrease have weakened the bargaining power of workers
Share of full-time employment
Rates of unionization
Minimum wage relative to median wage
Overall progressivity of the tax system

Source: Slightly adapted from Pivetti (2013, Table 8.1) and Petri (2021, Table 8.1).

workers and thus reduce ω_w. Setterfield (2007) and Pivetti (2013) argue that this is exactly what has happened since the early 1980s, which would explain the Great Moderation and its low inflation rates in most industrialized countries. Table 8.2 provides a list of all the factors the changes of which have contributed to the decrease in the bargaining power of workers.

9. Concluding remarks*

I hope to have shown that post-Keynesian economics, with the addition of works made by members of other heterodox schools of thought, is a progressive research programme. Post-Keynesian economists are not forever dwelling on the past writings of Keynes or other founders of the post-Keynesian School; nor are they providing criticisms only of orthodox economics. Post-Keynesians have made substantial contributions of their own to economic theory; they are forging ahead, improving on past deficiencies, building bridges towards the other heterodox schools as well as providing policy and empirical analyses.

The book is my vision of what post-Keynesian economics is. Other self-identified post-Keynesians have no doubt a different view, perhaps not too far from what I have just presented. It should also be clear that several important works have been omitted, for lack of space, but also because some of these works were more complex and required a more in-depth understanding of economics or mathematics, not fitting for part of the readership of this book.

My intention in writing this book is not to produce clones, who would feverishly reproduce the ideas, the techniques and the models found here or in other post-Keynesian works. As Joan Robinson once said, we don't want students to replace one bag of tricks (the tricks of orthodox economics) by another. The purpose of the book is to help students find their way through the maze of publications. The goal is to convince readers that there is an alternative to orthodox economics out there and that quite a lot of relevant analysis can be gleaned through this alternative lens.

I close the book by commenting on three issues: the future of post-Keynesian economics; its relationship with ecological economics; and a summary of the main policy advice of post-Keynesianism.

9.1 THE FUTURE OF POST-KEYNESIAN ECONOMICS

9.1.1 A Dismal Future within a Dismal Science?

Thirty years ago, discussing the evolution of heterodox economics, which at the time I called the post-classical tradition, I wrote:

> There is now a great profusion of books written in that tradition. Several journals devoted to post-Keynesian economics or to the post-classical tradition at large have been created over the past 15 years, many of them very recently. Post-Keynesian journals have also diversified. Empirical work in post-Keynesian economics is now more prevalent than ever. Post-Keynesian economists seem to have gone beyond the criticizing stage. (Lavoie, 1992b, p. 423)

Exactly the same can be said today. Great strides have been made by all the researchers operating within the collective of post-Keynesian economics.

Still, as pointed out by King (2002) in his history of post-Keynesian economics, all heterodox schools of thought in economics, including post-Keynesian economists, face difficult times within academia. Twenty years later, Geoffrey Hodgson (2019) makes the same observation, writing a book with the revealing title: *Is there a future for heterodox economics?* Despite the large increase in journal outlets for work arising from alternative economic paradigms, and despite the substantial increase in the publication output of post-Keynesian and heterodox researchers, it seems to be ever more difficult to land jobs in economics departments of universities, especially those that run a PhD programme. This is the case, despite the advent of the Global Financial Crisis. What else is needed to convince deans and colleagues on hiring committees that their students would greatly benefit from being exposed to alternative views rather than being brainwashed in mathematics, technique and a consensual 'There Is No Alternative'? Two turns of events may improve the standing of heterodox economists within economics departments.

First, the financial crisis witnessed in 2007–08 may just be a warning of things to come. In an interview (Colander, 2001, p. 106), a rather pessimistic Paul Davidson argued nonetheless that the overall standing of post-Keynesian economics could improve if there were some cataclysmic crisis, suggesting that 'if there is a great depression, then clearly there's a possibility for an alternative'. The Global Financial Crisis certainly had a negative impact on orthodox theory, as journalists, government employers and financial firms realized that economic advice from mainstream sources had been futile. There was a 'return of the master', as Skidelsky (2009) would put it, about the renewed interest in Keynesian views and the ideas of Keynes. And the theories of several other heterodox authors, who had been more or less forgotten during their lifetime and after their death, such as those of Godley, Kalecki and Minsky, were again given some attention, in the media and on numerous blogs. Some contemporary heterodox authors, such as James Galbraith, Steve Keen, Stephanie Kelton, Mariana Mazzucato and Randy Wray, have also attracted a fair amount of attention and have become star economists in their own right, giving them an opportunity to disseminate their alternative views to a large non-academic public. It seems, however, that for things to really change within departments of economics, another global recession, or even possibly a global depression, would be needed. Luckily for ordinary citizens, even the COVID-19 pandemic has not produced such an economic depression, one reason being that governments have allowed the operation of the standard Keynesian automatic stabilizers while some countries even implemented counter-cyclical policies advocated by post-Keynesian economists, leaving aside previously-set fiscal deficit targets.

Besides such events, a second phenomenon could lead to the improvement of the lot of heterodox economics within economics departments. Ever since the early 1990s, economics departments throughout the world have been on the downslide, losing students to other departments, and sometimes being closed down or amalgamated with business schools. While the excesses of formalization are also entering other social sciences, Craufurd Goodwin (2000, p. 183) claims that economics departments are being supplanted by many new neighbouring fields, such as public administration, public affairs, social studies, industrial relations, international development, economic sociology, political economy and international political economy. The financial crisis has somewhat reversed the trend, as young adults, curious to know about the causes of and the remedies for the crisis, have flocked to undergraduate economics programmes. With a few exceptions, it is now obvious that these eager economics students have not been provided with any satisfactory answer, often getting no answer at all. Hence, in the medium run, there should be even fewer students than before in orthodox economics departments, as they will quickly become disenchanted with their choice. Economics departments will become like departments of theology or ancient studies, deprived of students and of funds. Some of them may thus decide to offer a greater variety of views and methods so as to attract and retain more students, thus hiring heterodox economists.

If economics departments act otherwise, with orthodox economists closing ranks as the number of available jobs shrinks, then heterodox dissenters might have to follow the advice that Hodgson used to give. They 'may have to abandon the economics label and find an alternative disciplinary description' (in Labrousse and Vercueil, 2008, p. 10)! In France, the creation of a new field, 'economics and society', under the leadership of the French Association of Political Economy, is still under consideration. There is a precedent, with the creation in some countries of the field of 'international political economy', a field at the border of political science and economics. Earl and Peng (2012, p. 466) have suggested a field of 'real-world economics'. It seems difficult to object to such a denomination, already put forth in Table 1.1.

Luckily for post-Keynesian economics, new information technologies available on the web and the existence of organizations such as Research Papers in Economics (RePEc) are helping considerably with the diffusion of heterodox works in economics. According to Novarese and Zimmerman (2008), heterodox papers have more downloads per paper than orthodox ones. Thus, even if heterodox authors are being constrained to publish in journals that are less known and that have fewer subscriptions in university libraries, heterodox ideas and post-Keynesian ones in particular can be disseminated through this medium. The same can be said about the contemporary use of the tools of social media and about online conferences. With the advent of the financial crisis, heterodox economists, their ideas and their students are also getting some additional financial support, in particular from the Institute for New Economic Thinking (INET). And as pointed out in the introduction to Chapter 1, a multitude of economics students are on the lookout for alternative theories and academic programs, participating in ever-rising numbers to summer schools in heterodox economics.

9.1.2 Strategies for the Future

The above has outlined the outside events that could help heterodox schools of thought and post-Keynesian economics to improve their position within academia. What could or should post-Keynesians themselves do? I have tackled this subject in a previous paper (Lavoie, 2012), along with several other authors (Lee and Lavoie, 2013). A limited assessment is offered in Table 9.1.

What the relationship of post-Keynesian economics with orthodox economics ought to look like is certainly the question that attracts the most diverse views. Here I would say that almost anything goes, since some post-Keynesian researchers may feel at ease in finding similarities or faults with some dissident orthodox views or theoretical

Table 9.1 Advice for heterodox or post-Keynesian economists

Suggestions	Authors
Stop trying to reform the mainstream	Stockhammer and Ramskogler (2009), Vernengo (2013), Hoang-Ngoc (2013)
Be eclectic and cooperate with other heterodox schools of thought	Dunn (2000), Lawson (2006), Stockhammer and Ramskogler (2009), Dobusch and Kapeller (2012)
Cooperate with other social sciences	Fine (2002), Hodgson (2019)
Expand the research agenda	Stockhammer and Ramskogler (2009)
Focus on real-world problems and be politically relevant	Stockhammer and Ramskogler (2009), Vernengo (2013)

developments, while others may prefer to abandon all efforts at reforming the mainstream. In any case, as indicated by a number of authors, it takes two to tango, and few orthodox authors pay any attention to heterodox economics, the only current exception perhaps being Modern Monetary Theory. On the other hand, doctoral students may prefer, for strategic reasons, to pursue some fashionable orthodox theme while subliminally introducing heterodox elements, omitted by mainstream authors, into their empirical analysis. This safe strategy, however, as pointed out by Duncan Foley (2013, p. 235), can turn out to be a risky one, because 'very few scholars shift their method or problem area successfully after they reach the Ph.D.'.

Whatever the case, 'dialogue with the best of the mainstream is not bad per se and *should* not be discouraged, but it is not essential to the development of the heterodox research agenda' (Vernengo, 2013, p. 162). Post-Keynesian economics is a lively tradition, in and of itself. As Lee (2013a, p. 106) contends, heterodox economics is not the negation of orthodox or neoclassical economics; it is 'a *positive* alternative to it. So if mainstream economics disappeared, heterodox economics would remain unaffected.'

There is substantially more agreement on the need to be more eclectic and to cooperate more with the other heterodox schools of thought. This implies pluralism within heterodox economics. Stockhammer and Ramskogler (2009, pp. 241–2) seek pluralism at both the strategic and theoretical levels. At the level of the former, they think that post-Keynesians 'should strengthen their ties with other heterodox economists to defend space for pluralism in the profession', while at the level of the latter, they claim that there are 'obvious potential gains from cooperation between post-Keynesians and other heterodox positions', notably institutional and evolutionary economics, ecological economics, and Marxism. Dunn (2000, p. 356) argues that there is a degree of incommensurability in the methodology of orthodox economics and post-Keynesian economics – a belief shared by Lee (2013a, p. 107) – and thus he believes that debates are more likely to be productive if conducted with the other heterodox traditions, which have a compatible methodology.

In the past, heterodox economists have had a tendency to either cite dead authors (Ricardo, Marx, Keynes) rather than living ones, or to cite well-known mainstream authors. Leonhard Dobusch and Jakob Kapeller (2012) show that post-Keynesian economists, when writing articles using formalization or econometrics, cite orthodox papers most often, then cite authors from the journal in which their paper is published, and last cite papers published in other heterodox journals. Allies are thus least cited! Dobusch and Kapeller argue that this is a road towards 'paradigmatic self-marginalization'. A concern with the rest of heterodox literature would no doubt improve the citation ranking of heterodox journals, and so would the situation of all heterodox economists. Of course there are time limitations in pursuing this strategy: deepening one's knowledge in all of post-Keynesian economics is already quite time-consuming! But a researcher who specializes in a single field may find the study of other schools of thought particularly rewarding, not so much to dismiss or criticize these other approaches, but rather to improve or complete some aspects of post-Keynesian theory.

An extended version of pluralism is to engage with other social sciences. Ben Fine (2002, p. 198) believes that heterodox economics 'has the potential to compete successfully with mainstream economics across the social sciences in view of its more acceptable methods and theory to them'. He contends that the methodology of heterodox economics is akin to that of the other social sciences, because heterodox economists are not obsessed with the individual agent, optimization, technical dexterity and resource allocation. Hodgson (2019, p. 163) calls this 'a very attractive proposal'. This may be so, but in the meantime, most social scientists seem to limit their assessment of what is economics to mainstream economics, and seem to be ill informed about alternative economic traditions. Fine argues nonetheless that heterodox dissenters have the potential to prosper across the social sciences, provided they make the effort to disseminate their views. As noted in previous chapters, a number of post-Keynesian authors, notably Hein and Stockhammer, have engaged with the literature on variants of capitalism which can be found in the field of international political economy, and some authors, such as Daniela Gabor or Anastasia Nesvetailova, are at the intersection of post-Keynesian economics and international political economy.

The last two elements of Table 9.1 point to an expansion of the themes treated by post-Keynesian economists and to a focus on real-world problems. This is what we tackle next.

9.2 ECOLOGICAL ECONOMICS AND THE POST-KEYNESIANS

Stockhammer and Ramskogler (2009, p. 241) propose to enlarge the range of problems tackled by post-Keynesians. They mention the effect of institutions on economic growth, the impact of information and communication technologies, globalization and outsourcing. Post-Keynesian economics also lacks a theory of the state, with the possible exception of Mazzucato (2013). The most pressing need is probably in relation to environmental issues, considering both the importance of the problem and the attraction that it generates among students and young scholars. So far, or at least until very recently, post-Keynesians have written little on the subject of the environment. There are perhaps two causes for this apparent lack of interest, as we shall see: first, ecological economists emphasize the (present or future) scarcity of natural resources, whereas scarcity is not a major theme of post-Keynesian economics; second, ecological economists aim for a slowdown in growth, zero growth or even de-growth, whereas post-Keynesians usually look for ways to speed up economic growth, so as to achieve full employment.

9.2.1 Past Engagements

In a sense, the lack of engagement of post-Keynesians with the environment is rather surprising because post-Keynesian economics has much in common with ecological economics, as already noted when discussing consumer choice in Chapter 2. Like ecological economists, post-Keynesians focus on production rather than on exchange, and on the complementarity of inputs in production as well as their non-substitutability. As pointed out by Perry (2013) in his survey of post-Keynesian ecological economics, there are many other common perceptions of the functioning of the economy, such as the presence of fundamental uncertainty along with the complexity of economic relations, which make prediction and in particular long-term predictions very difficult, and which ought to induce prudent decisions. Perry also mentions the irreversibility of several types of decisions and the importance of historical time, which can be associated with several phenomena such as hysteresis and path-dependence. In what was perhaps the first genuine post-Keynesian article dealing with environmental economics, Bird (1982) raises five issues: the choice of the proper social discount rate; the irreversibility of many environmental effects; the large informational requirements associated with environmental problems; the presence of multidimensional choices when pollution or the ecology is involved; and the necessity to satisfice rather than to optimize.

Keynes himself seems to have favoured and envisioned the appearance of a no-growth society. Galbraith was also concerned with the pollution effects of capitalism and consumerism. Minsky (1975, p. 166) did worry about consumption fads, leading to 'a fruitless inflationary threadmill, accompanied by what is taken to be deterioration in the biological and social environment'. Eichner (1987, ch. 13) devoted an entire chapter to what he called the exogenous supply constraints, with several sections devoted to the natural resource constraint, which Eichner held as a serious problem. Despite these, and despite the obvious links between post-Keynesian theory and authors such as Boulding and Georgescu-Roegen, who have been in the vanguard of ecological economics, post-Keynesians have paid little attention to environmental problems, the availability of raw materials and the biophysical sustainability of growth. There is no mention of natural resources or ecological problems in the new guide to post-Keynesian economics (Holt and Pressman, 2001), although the old guide (Eichner, 1979) contained a chapter on natural resources and Keynes's concept of user costs (Davidson, 1979). Keynes (1936) thought that user costs were highly relevant to production decisions of raw materials, meaning that expectations of rising (falling) future prices would slow down (speed up) current production decisions, thus helping to transform these expectations into self-fulfilling prophecies. There is controversy, however, about how useful the notion of user costs can be.

Ecological economists have expressed a number of times their interest in the Sraffian model of production, since it does not start with given endowments, but spells out instead the pricing and quantity interactions of the circular process of production, in which raw materials and energy resources can be embedded (Judson, 1989; Gowdy and Miller, 1990; Kemp-Benedict, 2014), although this is sometimes questioned (Patterson, 1998). Indeed, from very early on Sraffian authors have given some thought to the problems inherent in the use of exhaustible natural resources (Parrinello, 1983). Schefold (1985b) in particular was concerned with global climate and the greenhouse effect. Surprisingly for a school of thought that is not known for emphasizing the role of fundamental uncertainty, some Sraffians doubt the possibility of making valid predictions with regard to the evolution of the prices of natural resources. Schefold (2001, p. 316) points out that Hotelling's neoclassical theory of the price of exhaustible resources, which says that this price (net of extraction costs) rises over time at a rate equal to the interest rate, assumes perfect foresight, perfect competition and knowledge of future technology. All these assumptions are totally unrealistic. As an illustration of the difficulties of predicting the long-run evolution of exhaustible resources, Schefold recalls that oil and raw material prices have not risen as the Club of Rome had predicted back in 1972, and neither has their supply been exhausted 40 years later.

> The basic reason is simple: the surface of the globe is two dimensional, but the crust of the earth in which mineral deposits are stored is three dimensional. By digging a little deeper, more can be found, and the tendency to rising costs of extraction often is more than compensated by technical progress. Of course, the details of geology are vastly more complicated than such a consideration suggests, but the relevant factors are technology and costs of extraction, market power and demand. (Schefold, 2001, p. 317)

The recent evolution of natural gas and oil prices, and the generalization of new technologies of extraction reinforce Schefold's claim, which can also be found in Roncaglia (2003). Scepticism about the impending exhaustion of natural resources is reinforced by the confidence that the future holds inventions, innovations and the discovery of substitutes, especially in the domain of energy. I have taken this stance earlier: 'in the limit, even natural resources are reproducible: technical progress brings the discovery of new deposits or new substitutes, perhaps synthesized ones' (Lavoie, 1992a, p. 55). But, even if most exhaustible resources were not exhaustible after all, ecological economics is not only about access to raw materials or energy; it deals also with the preservation and the quality of the environment, as well as global warming and climate change. Why is it that post-Keynesians have not yet tackled these issues head on?

Spash and Ryan (2012) show that heterodox schools in general have not paid enough attention to the role of the environment in economic affairs. Mearman (2005) documents the causes of this lack of interest in the specific case of post-Keynesianism. From his survey of a number of well-known post-Keynesian economists, three explanations attract the most attention. First, post-Keynesians have been distracted by their fight against mainstream economics; second, they would have little to say on the environment; third, much of post-Keynesian economics deals with the growth of aggregate demand. In his useful survey of the links between post-Keynesian economics and ecological economics, Kronenberg (2010) points out that, while neoclassical economists define economics as the science of scarcity, which makes them naturally aware of the problem of depleting natural resources, this is not the case of post-Keynesians, who are rather concerned, as pointed out in Chapter 1, with the problem of how to use more of the existing production capacity.

Besides the Kronenberg and the Perry surveys, two books of essays have been published a decade ago about the interactions of ecological economics and post-Keynesian economics, illustrating the obvious emerging interest in tying environmental concerns to post-Keynesian theory (Lawn, 2009; Holt et al., 2009). The sticking point is that 'post-Keynesians generally recommend policies that are intended to promote growth', while 'ecological economists often argue that growth needs to be slowed down' (Kronenberg, 2010, p. 1492). This area of conflict was recognized very early on (Gowdy, 1991). The challenge is to reconcile the full-employment objective of post-Keynesians with the no-growth objective of environmentalists. This challenge must also incorporate a constraint: the fact that most members of our consumer society wish to improve their living standards or their relative living standards. Voluntary simplicity may not be so easy to generalize (Kallis et al., 2012). To square the circle, there are not many solutions: income inequalities need to be reduced, the world population has to decrease or at least to stop growing, and consumers have to be convinced that more leisure is preferable to the accumulation of material goods. This will also require the legislated reduction of working hours. The conflicting goals of society are no better illustrated than by the debate that occurs between those who hope for a total decoupling between production and gas emissions and hence promote a Green New Deal that will provide full employment and economic growth (Pollin, 2019), and those who are sceptical of decoupling and who believe that de-growth is the only solution to achieve temperature targets (Schor and Jorgenson, 2019).

9.2.2 Current Engagements

Post-Keynesians
Over the last few years there has been an acceleration in the study of ecological issues by post-Keynesian economists or closely-related allies, as exemplified by Priewe (2022); in addition, there has been a similar acceleration in the incorporation by ecological economists of post-Keynesian theories and tools, such as the theory of endogenous money, demand-led economic activity and the stock-flow consistent approach.

Less than a decade ago, Kronenberg was calling attention to the fact that most post-Keynesians focus on macroeconomic themes, whereas environmental problems are often studied within the context of microeconomics. Indeed, Kronenberg (2010, p. 1492) was lamenting that ecological economics 'has not yet had time to come up with a well-developed macroeconomic theory of its own'. However, environmental issues, notably all the questions around the zero-growth imperative and de-growth, clearly necessitate a macroeconomic analysis. Kronenberg suggested at the time that ecological economists should consider adopting the post-Keynesian theory of growth and macroeconomic dynamics, instead of trying to develop one from scratch.

The timid beginnings of such a joint program could be found in the paper of Rezai et al. (2013). They provided a useful survey of the works that connect macroeconomics to ecological works, pointing out that 'while it is important to infuse ecological thinking into macroeconomics, it is also important to infuse macroeconomic thinking into ecological theories' (2013, p. 75). Rezai et al. also contended that an ecological macro theory should incorporate post-Keynesian macroeconomics, because it includes relevant phenomena such as the paradox of thrift and involuntary unemployment. Their call has been heard, with Rezai and Stagl (2016) organizing a symposium on ecological macroeconomics, pointing out to the necessity of reaching out to the toolbox of post-Keynesian macroeconomics. Fontana and Sawyer (2013; 2016) were among the first post-Keynesians to attempt to merge ecological concerns with post-Keynesian growth theory. They conclude, not surprisingly, that 'the achievement of lower growth would require control over the volume and composition of investment' and argue that 'government policies and changing social norms are likely to be more successful than market forces in bringing the growth of output towards a sustainable path' (Fontana and Sawyer, 2016, p. 193). Naqvi and Stockhammer (2018, p. 168), by contrast, in a stock-flow consistent model with endogenous technical progress, suggest that 'a mix of market-based and centralized policies may be optimal'. Taylor et al. (2016) and Rezai et al. (2018) offer models linking climate change, the possibility of emission mitigation, endogenous productivity growth, employment and income distribution within a framework where the economy is in a profit-led demand regime with profit squeeze.

Thus, besides growth and income distribution, another topic of importance for ecological economics that was mentioned by Rezai and Stagl (2016) is the importance of financial markets for the non-financial sector. Post-Keynesians have dealt with at least five such problems. How will banks finance the transition towards a greener economy (Campiglio, 2016)? Will the issue of sovereign green bonds make any difference (Monasterolo and Raberto, 2018)? Will the transition towards decarbonization and climate change lead to financial instability (Dafermos et al., 2018) and will it generate a large set of stranded financial assets that will further intensify the financial crisis (Cahen-Fourot et al., 2021; Semieniuk et al., 2021)? Does the existence of positive real interest rates on debt preclude a transition towards a zero-growth economy, a question which has been given the name of the growth imperative by some well-known ecological economists (Douthwaite, 2012; Loehr, 2012; Farley et al., 2013). Post-Keynesians have delivered a negative answer to this question (Cahen-Fourot and Lavoie, 2016), as have some ecologists who have adopted the stock-flow consistent methodology (Jackson and Victor, 2015; Richters and Siemoneit, 2017), thus demonstrating an obvious need for a better comprehension of the credit and money creation process. Some of these papers have attracted a lot of attention.

Post-Keynesians have started to diversify their works in ecological economics. Besides the attempt to combine the stock-flow consistent approach with Georgescu-Roegen's distinction between stock-flow resources and fund-service resources (Dafermos et al., 2017), post-Keynesians have now ventured into an open-economy analysis of ecological issues. Althouse et al. (2020) consider a two-country model where countries are constrained by Thirlwall's law, as we saw in Chapter 7, and where there is a need to reduce global carbon emissions. Their most revealing scenario is the one where the centre industrialized country initiates a green-growth strategy that succeeds in reducing the absolute amount of domestic carbon emissions, thus decoupling its emissions from its domestic output, but without coordinating with the less carbon-efficient peripherical country. In this case, it is likely that as production in the peripherical country also rises, the global amount of emissions will rise unsustainably despite the fall in the emissions of the centre country. A sustainable scenario, but a less attractive one, is for the centre industrialized country to enter into de-growth, so as to allow the periphery country to keep on growing, with an overall reduction in emissions. The most attractive scenario is for the centre country to provide improved technology to the peripherical country, in the hope that both countries can enjoy growth. Obviously, such a scenario requires considerable international cooperation, as well as an optimistic view of future progress in decoupling technology, which many deny, as pointed out earlier when mentioning the debate between Pollin (2019) and Schor and Jorgenson (2019). Carnevali et al. (2021) also examine the consequences of greening policies in a two-country SFC model that takes into account financial cross-border transactions. They consider the cases of both flexible and fixed exchange rates. They find the feared rebound effect, already emphasized by Rezai et al. (2013), where the adoption of greener technology leads to more carbonization, as well as the possibility of other counter-intuitive effects, for instance when the search for green financial assets by portfolio holders in a flexible exchange rate regime worsens climate change. As Carnevali et al. (2021, p. 16) conclude, 'currency fluctuations bring about unintended implications from uncoordinated green actions, thus possibly making the final net effects on the economy, the financial sector, the society, and the broader ecosystem, unpredictable'.

Ecological economists
In a paper attempting to redirect the future of ecological economics away from what he considers to be incompatible mainstream economics, Clive Spash (2020, p. 4) has been complaining that the flagship journal of the International Society for Ecological Economics, *Ecological Economics*, 'has attracted and published increasing quantities of neoclassical economics', perhaps a symptom of its success and a reflection of the pragmatic and pluralistic approach of many of its leaders. In the specific field of ecological macroeconomics, there appears to be a realization, however, that 'the scientific validity of a theory is not based on who believes it, but lies in how it matches up to reality' (ibid., p. 12). The search for an alternative realistic approach has generated a rapprochement with post-Keynesian economics.

Pollitt and Mercure (2018) and Mercure et al. (2019) contend that, broadly speaking, there are two classes of models that assess the economy-wide impact of energy and climate policies and which can draw conclusions on the likely macroeconomic effects of a transition towards a low-carbon regime. These two classes of quantitative energy-environment-economy models, the 3E models, have been categorized as equilibrium and non-equilibrium models. Equilibrium models are essentially the computable general equilibrium (CGE) models, based on neoclassical assumptions such as utility maximization, optimal allocation and strong substitution and price effects. These mainstream models are still dominant among policymakers or international organizations to evaluate climate policy, but they are increasingly rejected by ecological economists who are looking for something else than marginal analysis or the marginal changes which are recommended by neoclassical economists. This something else is the so-called non-equilibrium models, which, as pointed out earlier, are more and more referred to as ecological or new ecological macroeconomics, even if the term is not always used in publications (Hardt and O'Neill, 2017, p. 201).

Hafner et al. (2020, p. 3) claim that there is a call for new approaches in economics in general and that the call is 'particularly relevant in the case of a low-carbon energy transition' since the long-term structural changes that will be needed are by necessity 'a complex out-of-equilibrium transition' – the study of the *traverse* as we named it earlier. They provide a list of features that this new approach should be embedded with: complexity, non-linearity, fundamental uncertainty, path-dependence, lock-in effects, irreversibility, heterogeneous agents or classes, heuristic or reasonable rationality with adaptative behaviour, a role for institutions, multiple equilibria with feedback loops, explicit monetary and financial flows with stock-flow consistency. This list extends the list provided earlier by Perry (2013), and it certainly resembles many of the features that post-Keynesians have been concerned with. As a consequence, it is no surprise to read from leading ecologists that the majority of models that can be associated with ecological macroeconomics rely on post-Keynesian theories (Hardt and O'Neill, 2017, p. 202) and that 'if a single modelling approach is applied, at present the post-Keynesian approach looks more appropriate' (Pollitt and Mercure, 2018, p. 194). Hafner et al. (2020, p. 13) add that while some ecological macroeconomic models still use the neoclassical CES production function – a choice, whatever its justification, which is criticized by ecological economists such as Pirgmaier (2017) and Morgan (2017) – the majority of these models rely on fixed technical coefficients. This, they say, is presumably because of the post-Keynesian critique of the neoclassical production function which was outlined in Chapter 1. Hafner et al. also confirm that virtually all of these ecological macroeconomic models are demand led.

One can also note that the main *macroeconometric* models dealing with energy use, materials consumption and greenhouse gas emissions are 'derived from a post-Keynesian background' (ibid., p. 186). Of particular interest is the E3MG (E3 Model at the Global level) run by Cambridge Econometrics, and developed by the Cambridge Centre for Climate Change Mitigation Research (4CMR), sited at the Department of Land Economy, where Philip Arestis and John McCombie are located. E3MG arose from the work of Terry Barker within the Department of Applied Economics, as part of the Cambridge Growth Project (CGP) launched by Richard Stone, a purpose of which was to create an alternative to computable general equilibrium based on SAM. The post-Keynesian pedigree of E3MG is no surprise since the other research group at the Department of Applied Economics was the Cambridge Economic Policy Group with Wynne Godley at its helm, as previously noted.

Speaking of Godley, Hardt and O'Neill (2017, p. 202) argue that 'stock-flow consistent modelling is a specific approach to macroeconomics ... that has proven popular in ecological macroeconomics, concluding from their survey of ecological macroeconomics that 'overall, the combination of input-output analysis with stock-flow consistent modelling was identified as a promising avenue for developing macroeconomic models for a post-growth economy' (ibid., p. 198). Similarly, Pollitt and Mercure (2018, p. 192) argue that 'SFC models have parallels with the way that system dynamics approaches are used in accounting of physical stocks and flows, and there are linkages between the two', a remark which is also endorsed by Hardt and O'Neill (2017, p. 202) when they write that 'the stock-flow consistent approach to macroeconomic modelling lends itself well to an implementation in a system dynamics framework', referring to the work of Jackson and Victor (2016), who use a system-dynamics software to run simulations on their SFC model to assess the possible effects of climate change and slow growth on income inequality. Other recent instances of combining the SFC approach and a software based on system dynamics are Jackson and Victor (2020) and D'Alessandro et al. (2020). Needless to say, ever since the report of the Club of Rome on the limits to growth (Meadows et al., 1972), system dynamics has been associated with ecological economics.

It was mentioned that a promising avenue for ecological macroeconomics was to combine input-output analysis, with its interdependence between industrial sectors, and SFC analysis. Perhaps one of the first papers to do so with an energy sector is the article by Berg et al. (2015), who recall that the econometrician Lawrence Klein advocated the combination of national income and product accounting with flow-of-funds accounts and input-output analysis. The authors suggest a path towards integrating these diverse approaches with the physical world, by building a SFC/IO model, distinguishing between an industrial sector and an energy sector, identifying their technical coefficients, and assessing the impact of an increase in the markup of energy costs. The impact is a fall in real wages, which generates a fall in consumer demand and an unintended rise in inventories, and then, through the intersectoral interlinkages, a substantial fall in overall economic activity due to the multiplier effects. Along similar lines, Jackson and Jackson (2021) have produced a sophisticated SFC/IO model that incorporates three sectors: an energy sector, an investment good sector which provides fixed capital goods to all sectors, and a third sector which produces consumption and intermediary goods. The authors assume that the energy sector can transit towards a more ecological regime, by purchasing a greater proportion of green capital goods that allow them to produce energy with zero emission, and hence by purchasing a smaller proportion of fossil fuel capital goods. Households have fixed preferences regarding their choice of consumer goods, including their choice between green and brown energy, but this is modulated by relative prices. The authors also assume that green energy requires a greater quantity of energy inputs to produce its energy output than does brown energy. This induces a fall in the wage share during the transition, and a concomitant increase in the unemployment and inflation rates.

In contrast to several other models, the negative impact on economic activity is not due to some form of crowding out, where investment in green energy can only be achieved by a reduction in investments in brown energy, nor is it due to the assumption that any increase in investment is only possible if there is a previous increase in saving. While this is consistent with post-Keynesian economics, a number of ecological economists attribute this feature to what they call the post-Schumpeterian school, where credit creation by banks is at the heart of the economic system, and where entrepreneurial innovations which are likely to increase productivity are being financed by bank loans. Pollitt and Mercure (2018, p.188), for instance, argue that 'the post-Schumpeterian school complements post-Keynesian thinking ... it is a micro economic counterpart of the same theory'. All in all, the combination of these two strands of heterodox economics 'apply a treatment of the financial system that is more consistent with reality' (ibid., p. 184), which for this reason appeals to ecological economists.

As one would expect due to its rising popularity, there are now stock-flow consistent agent-based models that are part of ecological macroeconomics, as can be found in Ponta et al. (2018) to give one example, which is an extension of the complex EURACE model.

9.3 POST-KEYNESIAN ECONOMIC POLICIES

The other advice provided by Stockhammer and Ramskogler (2009), and endorsed by Vernengo (2013), is to do more work relevant to decision-makers. It may thus be a good idea to end this book by summarizing the main policy lines advocated by post-Keynesian economists, in particular in the field of macroeconomic policies. Most of what follows is drawn from Hein (2012, ch. 7) and Arestis (2013), although some proposals have been discussed in earlier chapters. It could be said that, besides ecological sustainability, there are five policy objectives:

1. A fair distribution of income and wealth
2. Financial stability
3. Full employment of labour
4. A sustainable rate of inflation
5. External balance.

As such, these policy objectives are not really specific to post-Keynesian economics. For instance, a fair income distribution is likely to mean something entirely different for mainstream economists, who will probably associate proper income distribution with marginal productivity. Similarly, the means to achieve financial stability are likely to differ from one economist to another. So let us try to be slightly more specific.

It should now be clear to all that debt-led consumption booms are not sustainable and may lead to financial crises. Besides the increased facility in getting credit, post-Keynesians attribute the origins of rising consumer debt to the rise in inequality generated by the increased share of profits and the rising dispersion of wage income, in particular the rising share going to overhead managerial income. In addition, post-Keynesians believe in the benefits of wage-led growth. On the income distribution front, post-Keynesians thus advocate policies to correct the inequitable distribution of income and wealth. This can be done by modifying laws so as to reinforce the bargaining power of labour unions, by creating laws imposing or raising the minimum wage, by regulating the spreads between top salaries and the median salary of a company, and by forbidding performance-related bonuses for managers (stock-market options and other such incentives). In other words, the purpose of this legislation is to bring back income distribution to what it was before the advent of financialization and of the agency theories that legitimized the extraordinary rise in income inequality. Much higher income tax rates for the rich and wealth taxes are also likely to be needed to attain this objective (Piketty, 2014).

Post-Keynesians also favour the re-regulation of the financial sector, both because it should help in diminishing the power and importance of the financial sector, which should further reduce income inequality, and because it should contribute to a more stable financial system. Many of the financial innovations that bankers claim that they cannot do without, such as the possibility to 'originate and distribute', securitization of the second type, over-the-counter derivatives, ought to be outlawed. Shadow banks should all be brought back under the control of the regulated sector. Financial institutions that are too big to fail should be dismantled, just as quasi-monopolies were dismantled in the past. All off-balance-sheet operations ought to be brought back on balance sheets. It is clear that the financial system was much more stable when banks were pursuing only 'plain vanilla' operations. The subprime financial crisis has also demonstrated that the rules that used to be imposed on borrowers (to get a mortgage, for instance) had a stabilizing effect until they were removed, and hence that they ought to be reinstated, as they have been in some countries.

The main goal of governments should be full employment. While this seems to have been the main objective after the end of the Second World War, over the years this has given way to inflation targeting and balancing public budgets. Indeed, the leitmotiv of central bankers is that ensuring price stability is the best contribution that central banks can make to sustaining economic activity and technical progress – a claim repeatedly disconfirmed empirically. Mainstream economists have managed to persuade decision-makers to abandon demand-led full-employment policies, promoting instead supply-side structural reforms of the labour market, by invoking the inevitable constraint of the natural rate of unemployment. But this concept, and that of the NAIRU, has also been disconfirmed empirically. There is thus an urgent need to reorient macroeconomic policy. Taking for granted that full employment ought to be the primary goal of economic policy, which policy instrument should take charge of this objective?

As already argued at the end of Chapter 5, post-Keynesians generally contend that fiscal policy is the appropriate tool, in line with functional finance. As a long-term perspective, some post-Keynesians argue that the fiscal stance – the ratio of government expenditure to the average tax rate – is a crucial determinant of economic activity and employment (Godley and Cripps, 1983). Greater public investment spending is also suggested, such as public housing, public senior residences, hospitals, as well as more and better infrastructure. The COVID-19 crisis has clearly shown that large public investments in health and medical infrastructures are constantly needed to avoid catastrophes. Public investment so as to achieve a better environment also fits here. Public investment spending adds to the stability of the economic system as long as these public expenditures are not procyclical, in contrast to private investment expenditures, as Keynes (1936, p. 378) pointed out when he vaguely suggested the 'socialization' of investment. Within a short-term perspective, strong automatic stabilizers need to be put in place. For instance, unemployment insurance programmes need to be financially generous and accessible to all those who have lost their jobs, so that effective demand is sustained even when the economy is slowing down. Unemployment insurance premiums paid by workers or employers must not be raised when unemployment rates rise. A highly progressive tax system also generates an automatic stabilizer.

Over the last few years, there has been much discussion around two particular policies designed to improve income distribution and the functioning of the economy. These are: the proposal for a job guarantee programme, also called government as an employer of last resort (ELR), to which we already alluded to in Chapter 5; and the proposal for a guaranteed basic income, that could be means-tested, or in its more ambitious version, a universal basic income which would be unconditional. Post-Keynesians are usually more tempted to support a job guarantee programme rather than a guaranteed income programme. Still, while MMT authors have provided a strong case for a job guarantee programme (Tcherneva, 2020), a number of their post-Keynesian colleagues have questioned the feasibility of such a scheme. Critics fear that such a programme could only apply to jobs that are inessential, since their holders would move to the private sector whenever the economy is in the upswing; as a consequence, the programme could only be relevant to long-term unemployed workers, and not to temporarily unemployed workers or to highly-qualified workers. In the case of essential jobs, there is the fear that there would be a financial incentive for local governments to gradually replace well-paid unionized jobs by low-paid ELR jobs, with their holders becoming second-class civil servants (Seccareccia, 2004; Sawyer, 2019).

Universal basic income, despite its apparent appeal for economic freedom, has also some possible drawbacks. Besides its potentially enormous financial cost if poverty levels are to be superseded, guaranteed income might induce firms to reduce the wages of poor workers in times of high job scarcity and soften employee resistance to wage cuts. By contrast, in times of low unemployment, a sufficiently high guaranteed income is likely to induce more leisure, thus generating a negative labour supply response (as experienced in the few countries that have set up strong income replacement programmes during the COVID-19 crisis). This could persuade employers with vacant positions to raise real wages to attract employees. Seccareccia (2020) thus argues that it is imperative for any kind of guaranteed income programme to be accompanied by a full-employment commitment from the government based on public investment. But as we know from Kalecki's 1943 article on the political aspects of full employment, pressures from the business sector may make it complicated for a government to sustain a commitment to full employment (Kalecki, 1971, ch. 12).

What role is left for monetary policy? Most post-Keynesians would argue that its role is rather downgraded. As pointed out in Chapter 4, many post-Keynesians would argue that the target interest rate should be such that the nominal interest rate, meaning here the prime lending rate or AAA corporate bond rates, remains slightly above the inflation rate or in line with the inflation rate plus the growth rate of labour productivity. By acting in such a way, the central bank would not disrupt income distribution. Moving the interest rate on a one-to-one basis with inflation would still allow the monetary authorities to have some moderate countercyclical influence on the economy since empirical studies show that the nominal interest rate, more than the real interest rate, has some impact on private expenditures.

Post-Keynesians have long argued that monetary policy, meaning here changes in interest rates, have only a weak and indirect effect on wage and price inflation. Raising interest rates is effective only when large increases are imposed on the economy, but these changes are usually so drastic that they provoke economic recessions rather than just a slowdown of the inflation rate. The Global Financial Crisis has once more demonstrated that reducing the target interest rate, which is a short-term rate, does not do much for the real economy, in part because interest rate spreads tend to rise in a recession. If anything, central banks ought to set a long-term interest rate target, announce it, and act to enforce it, although even such a move is likely to be insufficient to get out of a deep recession.

Since standard monetary policy is unable to control inflation, according to the post-Keynesian view, some other tools must be provided to do so. Credit controls may be needed, or as suggested earlier, macro-prudential rules, such as stricter limitations on the capacity of borrowers to go into debt. A return to incomes and wage policies has been suggested. Wages would rise according to a benchmark, roughly equal to the sum of productivity growth and price inflation, while dividends would be allowed to grow at no higher a rate. With real interest rates being kept in line with productivity growth, income distribution would not be overly disturbed by these incomes and wage policies. This could be done through guidelines or through legal means, if needed. Hein (2012, p. 140), especially in the context of the eurozone, suggests that wage growth should exceed the benchmark in countries that run current account surpluses, while countries with current account deficits should target wage growth below the benchmark. As he points out, this may require large changes in existing institutions that link labour unions and employer associations, but it could kill several birds at once, including large global imbalances. On the subject of the eurozone policy strategies, Stockhammer et al. (2020) provide an interesting table where they compare the policies which have been advocated by various schools of thought, including post-Keynesians, to deal with external balance, the labour market, fiscal policy, monetary policy and financial markets. Lavoie and Seccareccia (2021), as other post-Keynesians such as James Galbraith, advocate a dual mandate, inflation and employment, for central banks, given that the Phillips curve has a flat segment.

International cooperation will need to be improved. As of now, countries that try to pursue a high-end exit, by adopting expansionary policies, are facing problems of external imbalances, partly caused by the austerity policies carried out by their trading partners. In the absence of proper mechanisms of international cooperation, trade restrictions and especially capital movement restrictions will have to be imposed, as discussed in Chapter 7. There is also the problem of commodity price inflation, which, as argued in Chapter 8, is a global phenomenon, and not one that can be tackled by individual countries or their central banks. We know that fast increases in world aggregate demand can generate great volatility in commodity prices such as food grains and metals. Kaldor (1996, p. 88) has suggested the creation of international buffer stocks to help mitigate these fluctuations and to combat destabilizing speculation in commodities.

Many of these policy proposals seem to be out of line with what is acceptable now to decision-makers. Such an agenda needs, however, to be put forward, detailed and debated, even if it appears to be unfashionable. The ideas defended by Hayek and Friedman were also out of fashion in the late 1940s and in the 1950s: still they continued pressing for them. It is the social duty of post-Keynesian economists to keep promoting alternative views on economic theory and economic policy, whatever the likelihood of their adoption, because these views are based on real-world economics, and not on some speculative idealization of markets.

9.4 EPILOGUE

What better way to conclude this book on post-Keynesian economics than to quote Luigi Pasinetti, currently one of the oldest post-Keynesian economists, along with Paul Davidson. In his latest article, Pasinetti argues that post-Keynesian economics is best equipped to unify economic theory and institutional analysis, and provides a powerful tool to assess contemporary problems.

> Neo-classical economics is not the only source of economic theory. There exist other alternative sources. In particular there is a brand of economic theory that is based on the idea of production, and more generally of economic activity as a process, which goes back to the glorious tradition of classical economics, and is continued by Keynesian and post-Keynesian economics. This alternative is at least as powerful as neo-classical economics. (Pasinetti, 2021, p. 438)

NOTE

* Full sentences have been taken from the following publication: 'Perspectives for post-Keynesian economics', *Review of Political Economy*, **24** (2), May 2012, pp. 321–36.

References

Ábel, I., K. Lehmann and A. Tapaszti (2016), 'The controversial treatment of money and banks in macroeconomics', *Financial and Economic Review*, **15** (2), 33–58.

Adrian, T. and H.S. Shin (2010), 'Liquidity and leverage', *Journal of Financial Intermediation*, **19** (3), July, 418–37.

Agliardi, E. (1988), 'Microeconomic foundations of macroeconomics in the post-Keynesian approach', *Metroeconomica*, **39** (3), October, 275–97.

Aglietta, M. (1996), 'Systemic risk, financial innovations, and the financial safety net', in G. Deleplace and E.J. Nell (eds), *Money in Motion: The Post Keynesian and Circulation Approaches*, London: Macmillan, pp. 552–81.

Aizenman, J. and R. Glick (2009), 'Sterilization, monetary policy, and global financial integration', *Review of International Economics*, **17** (4), September, 777–801.

Akerlof, G.A. (1982), 'Labor contracts as partial gift exchange', *Quarterly Journal of Economics*, **97** (4), November, 543–69.

Akerlof, G.A. and R.J. Shiller (2009), *Animal Spirits*, Princeton, NJ: Princeton University Press.

Akhtar, M.A. (1997), *Understanding Open Market Operations*, New York: Federal Reserve Bank of New York, Public Information Department.

Alary, P., J. Blanc, L. Desmedt and B. Théret (eds) (2020), *Institutionalist Theories of Money: An Anthology of the French School*, Cham, Switzerland: Palgrave Macmillan.

Alessie, R. and A. Kapteyn (1991), 'Habit formation, interdependent preferences and demographic effects in the almost ideal demand system', *Economic Journal*, **101** (406), May, 404–19.

Allain, O. (2009), 'La modération salariale: le point de vue (néo-)kaleckien', *Revue Économique*, **60** (1), January, 81–108.

Allain, O. (2015), 'Tackling the instability of growth: a Kaleckian-Harrodian model with an autonomous expenditure component', *Cambridge Journal of Economics*, **39** (5), September, 1351–1371.

Allain, O. (2019), 'Demographic growth, Harrodian (in)stability and the supermultiplier', *Cambridge Journal of Economics*, **43** (1), January, 85–106.

Allain, O. (2021a), 'Heterogeneous unit labor costs and profit margins in an economy with vintage capital: an amended neo-Kaleckian model', *Journal of Post Keynesian Economics*, **44** (4), 537–68.

Allain, O. (2021b), 'A supermultiplier model of the natural rate of growth', *Metroeconomica*, **72** (3), 612–34.

Allain, O., J. Hartwig and M.G. Hayes (2013), 'Effective demand: securing the foundations, introduction to the symposium', *Review of Political Economy*, **25** (4), December, 650–52.

Allen, P.R. and P.B. Kenen (1980), *Asset Markets and Exchange Rates: Modeling an Open Economy*, Cambridge: Cambridge University Press.

Althouse, J., G. Guarini and J.G. Porcile (2020), 'Ecological macroeconomics in the open economy: sustainability, unequal exchange and policy coordination in a center-periphery model', *Ecological Economics*, **172**, June, article 106628, 1–12.

Altman, M. (1998), 'A high-wage path to economic growth and development', *Challenge*, **41** (1), January–February, 91–104.

Altman, M. (2001), 'A behavioral model of labor supply: casting some light into the black box of income–leisure choice', *Journal of Socio-Economics*, **33** (3), May, 199–219.

Altman, M. (2006), 'Introduction', in M. Altman (ed.), *Handbook of Contemporary Behavioral Economics: Foundations and Development*, Armonk, NY: M.E. Sharpe, pp. xv–xxii.

Amable, B., R. Boyer and F. Lordon (1997), 'The *ad hoc* in economics: the pot calling the kettle black', in A. d'Autume and J. Cartelier (eds), *Is Economics Becoming a Hard Science?*, Cheltenham, UK and Lyme, USA: Edward Elgar, pp. 252–75.

Amadeo, E.J. (1986), 'Notes on capacity utilization, distribution and accumulation', *Contributions to Political Economy*, **5** (1), March, 83–94.

Amadeo, E.J. (1987), 'Expectations in a steady-state model of capacity utilization', *Political Economy: Studies in the Surplus Approach*, **3** (1), 75–89.

Amado, A.M. and M.L.R. Mollo (2015), 'The "developmentalism" debate in Brazil: some economic and political issues', *Review of Keynesian Economics*, **3** (1), Spring, 77–89.

Amstad, M. and A. Martin (2011), 'Monetary implementation: common goals but different practices', *FRBNY Current Issues in Economics and Finance*, **17** (7), 1–11.

Anand, P. (1991), 'The nature of rational choice and The Foundations of Statistics', *Oxford Economic Papers*, **43** (2), April, 199–216.

Anderson, S.J. and S.P. Dunn (2006), 'Galbraith and the management of specific demand: evidence from the tobacco industry', *Journal of Institutional Economics*, **2** (3), 273–96.

Andini, C. (2009), 'Teaching Keynes's principle of effective demand within the real wage vs employment space', *Forum for Social Economics*, **38** (2–3), July, 209–28.

Andreff, W. (1996), 'Hétérodoxies ou critique en économie', *Économies et Sociétés*, **30** (9), September, 239–52.

Andrews, P.W.S. (1949), *Manufacturing Business*, London: Macmillan.

Andrews, P.W.S. and E. Brunner (eds) (1975), *Studies in Pricing*, London: Macmillan.

Angrick, S. (2018), 'Global liquidity and monetary autonomy: an examination of open-economy policy constraints', *Cambridge Journal of Economics*, **42** (1), January, 117–35.

Anyadike-Danes, M. and W. Godley (1989), 'Real wages and employment: a sceptical view of some recent econometric work', *Manchester School*, **57** (2), June, 172–87.

Appelbaum, E. (1979), 'The labor market', in A.S. Eichner (ed.), *A Guide to Post-Keynesian Economics*, White Plains, NY: M.E. Sharpe, pp. 100–119.

Arena, R. (1987), 'L'école international d'été de Trieste (1981–1985): vers une synthèse classico-keynésienne?', *Économies et Sociétés*, **21** (3), March, 205–38.

Arena, R. and S. Blankenburg (2013), 'Sraffa, Keynes, and post-Keynesians: suggestions for a synthesis', in G.C. Harcourt and P. Kriesler (eds), *The Oxford Handbook of Post-Keynesian Economics: Volume 1: Theory and Origins*, Oxford: Oxford University Press, pp. 74–100.

Arestis, P. (1990), 'Post-Keynesianism: a new approach to economics', *Review of Social Economy*, **48** (3), Fall, 222–46.

Arestis, P. (1992), *The Post-Keynesian Approach to Economics*, Aldershot, UK and Brookfield, VT, USA: Edward Elgar.

Arestis, P. (1996), 'Post-Keynesian economics: towards coherence', *Cambridge Journal of Economics*, **20** (1), January, 111–35.

Arestis, P. (2013), 'Economic theory and policy: a coherent post-Keynesian approach', *European Journal of Economics and Economic Policy*, **10** (2), 243–55.

Arestis, P., S.P. Dunn and M. Sawyer (1999), 'Post Keynesian economics and its critics', *Journal of Post Keynesian Economics*, **21** (4), Fall, 527–49.

Arestis, P. and A.S. Eichner (1988), 'The Post-Keynesian and Institutionalist theory of money and credit', *Journal of Economic Issues*, **22** (4), 1003–22.

Arestis, P., A.R. González and Ó. Dejuán (2012), 'Modelling accumulation: a theoretical and empirical application of the accelerator principle under uncertainty', *European Journal of Economics and Economic Policies: Intervention*, **9** (2), November, 255–76.

Arestis, P. and P. Howells (2001–02), 'The 1520–1640 "Great Inflation": an early case of controversy on the nature of money', *Journal of Post Keynesian Economics*, **24** (2), Winter, 181–204.

Arestis, P. and M. Sawyer (1993), 'Political economy: an editorial manifesto', *International Papers in Political Economy*, **1** (1), 1–38.

Arestis, P. and M. Sawyer (2003), 'Reinventing fiscal policy', *Journal of Post Keynesian Economics*, **26** (1), Fall, 3–26.

Arestis, P. and M. Sawyer (2004), 'On fiscal policy and budget deficits', *European Journal of Economics and Economic Policies: Intervention*, **1** (2), November, 61–74.

Arestis, P. and M. Sawyer (2005), 'Aggregate demand, conflict and capacity in the inflationary process', *Cambridge Journal of Economics*, **29** (6), November, 959–74.
Arestis, P. and M. Sawyer (2006), 'Interest rates and the real economy', in C. Gnos and L.P. Rochon (eds), *Post-Keynesian Principles of Economic Policy*, Cheltenham, UK and Northampton, MA, USA: Edward Elgar, pp. 3–20.
Arestis, P. and M. Sawyer (2010), 'The return of fiscal policy', *Journal of Post Keynesian Economics*, **32** (3), Spring, 327–46.
Ariely, D., U. Gneezy, G. Loewenstein and N. Mazar (2009), 'Large stakes and big mistakes', *Review of Economic Studies*, **76** (2), April, 451–69.
Armstrong, P. (2020). *Can Heterodox Economics Make a Difference?*, Cheltenham, UK and Northampton, MA, USA: Edward Elgar.
Arnon, A. (1993), 'The policy implications of classical monetary theory: between the two hands', in G. Mongiovi and C. Rühl (eds), *Macroeconomic Theory: Diversity and Convergence*, Aldershot, UK and Brookfield, VT, USA: Edward Elgar, pp. 110–22.
Arnon, A. (2011), *Monetary Theory and Policy from Hume and Smith to Wicksell*, Cambridge: Cambridge University Press.
Arrous, J. (1978), 'Imperfection de l'information, incertitude et concurrence', doctoral dissertation, Université de Strasbourg et Université des Sciences Sociales de Grenoble.
Asimakopulos, A. (1970), 'A Robinsonian growth model in one sector notation – an amendment', *Australian Economic Papers*, **9** (15), December, 171–6.
Asimakopulos, A. (1975), 'A Kaleckian theory of income distribution', *Canadian Journal of Economics*, **8** (3), August, 313–33.
Asimakopulos, A. (1986), 'Finance, liquidity, saving, and investment', *Journal of Post Keynesian Economics*, **9** (1), Fall, 79–90.
Asimakopulos, A. (1988), 'Post-Keynesian theories of distribution', in A. Asimakopulos (ed.), *Theories of Income Distribution*, Boston, MA: Kluwer, pp. 133–58.
Astarita, C., C. Capuano and F. Purificato (2018), 'The macroeconomic impact of organised crime: A post-Keynesian analysis', *Economic Modelling*, **68**, January, 514–28.
Atesoglu, S. (2003–04), 'Monetary transmission – federal funds rate and prime rate', *Journal of Post Keynesian Economics*, **26** (2), Winter, 357–62.
Atesoglu, S. (2005), 'Monetary policy and long-term interest rates', *Journal of Post Keynesian Economics*, **27** (3), Spring, 533–40.
Auerbach, P. and P. Skott (1988), 'Concentration, competition and distribution', *International Review of Applied Economics*, **2** (1), January, 42–61.
Backhouse, R.E. (2004), 'A suggestion for clarifying the study of dissent in economics', *Journal of the History of Economic Thought*, **26** (2), June, 261–71.
Backhouse, R.E. (2014), 'MIT and the other Cambridge', *History of Political Economy*, **46** (annual supplement), 252–71.
Baddeley, M. (2017), 'Keynes's psychology and behavioural macroeconomics: theory and policy', *Economic and Labour Relations Review*, **28** (2), 177–96.
Baert, P. (1996), 'Realist philosophy of the social sciences and economics: a critique', *Cambridge Journal of Economics*, **20** (5), September, 513–22.
Bagehot, W. (1873), *Lombard Street – A Description of the Money Market*, Homewood, IL: Richard D. Irwin, 1962.
Bagnai, A. and A. Rieber (2019), 'Killing two birds with one currency: Income and fiscal policies in a growth model of a currency union', *Journal of Post Keynesian Economics*, **42** (2), 274–96.
Bakker, B.B. (1993), 'Net foreign assets of Dutch commercial banks, 1984–1990', *De Economist*, **141** (3), September, 431–42.
Banco Central de Chile (2016), *Basic Constitutional Act, Central Bank of Chile*.
Bank of Canada (2004), 'Intervention in the foreign exchange market', available at http://www.baileycapitalfund.com/Money%20Facts/InterventionExchangeMarket.php.
Baran, P.A. and P.M. Sweezy (1968), *Monopoly Capital*, London: Penguin, 1966.
Baranzini, A. and A. Mirante (2013), 'The Cambridge post-Keynesian school of income and wealth distribution', in G.C. Harcourt and P. Kriesler (eds), *Oxford Handbook of Post-Keynesian Economics*, volume 1, Oxford: Oxford University Press, pp. 288–361.

Baranzini, A. and R. Scazzieri (1986), 'Knowledge in economics: a framework', in M. Baranzini and R. Scazzieri (eds), *Foundations of Economics: Structures Inquiry and Economic Theory*, Oxford: Basil Blackwell, pp. 1–89.

Barba, A. and M. Pivetti (2009), 'Rising household debt: its causes and macroeconomic implications – a long period analysis', *Cambridge Journal of Economics*, **33** (1), January, 113–37.

Barbosa-Filho, N.H. and L. Taylor (2006), 'Distributive and demand cycles in the U.S. economy – a structuralist Goodwin model', *Metroeconomica*, **57** (3), July, 389–411.

Barnes, M. and G. Olivei (2003), 'Inside and outside bounds: threshold estimates of the Phillips curve', *Federal Reserve Bank of Boston New England Economic Review*, 3–18.

Barro, R.J. and H.I. Grossman (1971), 'A general disequilibrium model of income and employment', *American Economic Review*, **61** (1), March, 82–93.

Barzel, Y. and R.J. McDonald (1973), 'Assets, subsistence and the supply curve of labor', *American Economic Review*, **63** (4), September, 621–33.

Baskoy, T. (2011), 'Business competition and the 2007–08 financial crisis: a Post Keynesian approach', in J. Leclaire, T.H. Jo and J.E. Knodell (eds), *Heterodox Analysis of Financial Crisis and Reform: History, Politics and Economics*, Cheltenham, UK and Northampton, MA, USA: Edward Elgar, pp. 124–36.

Baskoy, T. (2012), 'Market governance', in J.E. King (ed.), *The Elgar Companion to Post Keynesian Economics*, 2nd edn, Cheltenham, UK and Northampton, MA, USA: Edward Elgar, pp. 387–91.

Bastian, E.F. and M. Setterfield (2016), 'A simple analytical model of the adverse real effects of inflation', *Journal of Post Keynesian Economics*, **38** (4), 637–65.

Bastian, E.F. and M. Setterfield (2020), 'Nominal exchange rate shocks and inflation in an open economy: towards a structuralist inflation targeting agenda', *Cambridge Journal of Economics*, **44** (6), 1271–99.

Baudrillard, J. (1972), *Pour une critique de l'économie politique du signe*, Paris: Gallimard.

Baumol, W.J. (1959), *Business Behavior, Value and Growth*. New York: Macmillan.

Baumol, W.J. (1982), 'Contestable markets: an uprising in the theory of industry structure', *American Economic Review*, **72** (1), March, 178–83.

Baumol, W.J. and A. Blinder (2006), *Macroeconomics: Principles and Policy*, 10th edn, Mason, OH: Thomson Higher Education.

Baxter, J.L. (1988), *Social and Psychological Foundations of Economic Analysis*, London: Harvester-Wheatsheaf.

Beed, C. and C. Beed (1996), 'Measuring the quality of academic journals: the case of economics', *Journal of Post Keynesian Economics*, **18** (3), Spring, 369–96.

Behringer, J. and T. van Treeck (2019), 'Income distribution and growth models: a sectoral balances approach', *Politics and Science*, **47** (3), 303–32.

Bell, S. (2000), 'Do taxes and bonds finance government spending?', *Journal of Economic Issues*, **34** (3), September, 603–20.

Bell-Kelton, S. and R. Ballinger (2006), 'The monetary policy outcome curve: can the size and structure of public debt undermine policy objectives?', in P. Arestis, M. Baddeley and J. McCombie (eds), *The New Monetary Policy: Implications and Relevance*, Cheltenham, UK and Northampton, MA, USA: Edward Elgar, pp. 129–48.

Bellofiore, R. (2013), 'Endogenous money, financial Keynesianism and beyond', *Review of Keynesian Economics*, **1** (2), Summer, 153–70.

Bénassy, J.P. (1975), 'Neo-Keynesian disequilibrium theory in a monetary economy', *Review of Economic Studies*, **42** (4), October, 503–23.

Bengston, D.N. (1994), 'Changing forest values and ecosystem management', *Society and Natural Resources*, **7** (6), 515–33.

Berg, M., B. Hartley and O. Richters (2015), 'A stock-flow consistent input-output model with applications to energy price shocks, interest rates, and heat emissions', *New Journal of Physics*, doi:10.1088/1367-2630/17/1/015011.

Berg, N. and G. Gigerenzer (2010), 'As-if behavioral economics: neoclassical economics in disguise?', *History of Economic Ideas*, **18** (1), January, 133–66.

Berger, P. (1972a), 'Rapports entre l'évolution de la balance des paiements et l'évolution de la liquidité interne', in A. de Lattre and P. Berger (eds), *Monnaie et balance des paiements*, Paris: Armand Colin, pp. 89–110.

Berger, P. (1972b), 'Interdépendance entre les mouvements de devises et les variations des crédits bancaires', in A. de Lattre and P. Berger (eds), *Monnaie et balance des paiements*, Paris: Armand Colin, pp. 171–6.

Berle, A.A. and G.C. Means (1933), *The Modern Corporation and Private Property*, New York: Harcourt, Brace and World.

Bertocco, G. (2011), 'Are banks special? Some notes on Tobin's theory of financial intermediation', *Journal of the Asia Pacific Economy*, **16** (3), 331–53.

Bezemer, D. (2010), 'Understanding financial crisis through accounting models', *Accounting, Organizations and Society*, **35** (7), October, 676–88.

Bhaduri, A. (1986), *Macroeconomics: The Dynamics of Commodity Production*, Armonk, NY: M.E. Sharpe.

Bhaduri, A. (2006), 'Endogenous economic growth: a new approach', *Cambridge Journal of Economics*, **30** (1), January, 69–83.

Bhaduri, A. (2008), 'On the dynamics of profit-led and wage-led growth', *Cambridge Journal of Economics*, **32** (1), January, 147–60.

Bhaduri, A. (2011a), 'Prices or quantities? The common link in the method of Sraffa, Keynes and Kalecki', in R. Ciccone, C. Gehrke and G. Mongiovi (eds), *Sraffa and Modern Economics, Volume II*, London: Routledge, pp. 89–96.

Bhaduri, A. (2011b), 'A contribution to the theory of financial fragility and crisis', *Cambridge Journal of Economics*, **35** (6), November, 995–1014.

Bhaduri, A., K. Laski and M. Riese (2006), 'A model of interaction between the virtual and the real economy', *Metroeconomica*, **57** (3), July, 412–27.

Bhaduri, A. and S. Marglin (1990), 'Unemployment and the real wage: the economic basis for contesting political ideologies', *Cambridge Journal of Economics*, **14** (4), December, 375–93.

Bhaduri, A. and J. Robinson (1980), 'Accumulation and exploitation: an analysis in the tradition of Marx, Sraffa and Kalecki', *Cambridge Journal of Economics*, **4** (2), June, 103–15.

Bianchi, M. (1990), 'The unsatisfactoriness of satisficing: from bounded rationality to innovative rationality', *Review of Political Economy*, **2** (2), July, 149–67.

Bianco, A. and C. Sardoni (2018),'Banking theories and macroeconomics', *Journal of Post Keynesian Economics*, **41** (2), 165–84.

Bibow, J. (2002), 'The markets versus the ECB, and the euro's plunge', *Eastern Economic Journal*, **28** (1), Winter, 45–57.

Bibow, J. (2009), *Keynes on Monetary Policy, Finance and Uncertainty: Liquidity Preference and the Global Financial Crisis*, London: Routledge.

Bindseil, U. (2004a), *Monetary Policy Implementation: Theory, Past, and Present*, Oxford: Oxford University Press.

Bindseil, U. (2004b), 'The operational target of monetary policy and the rise and fall of reserve position doctrine', Working Paper series No. 372, European Central Bank.

Bindseil, U. (2014), *Monetary Policy Operations and the Financial System*, Oxford: Oxford University Press.

Bird, P.J.W.N. (1982), 'Neoclassical and post Keynesian environmental economics', *Journal of Post Keynesian Economics*, **4** (4), Summer, 586–93.

BIS (2013a), 'Basel III liquidity coverage ratio', available at http://www.bis.org/publ/bcbs238.htm.

BIS (2013b), 'Basel III: A global regulatory framework for more resilient banks and banking systems', available at http://www.bis.org/publ/bcbs189.pdf.

Bjørnstad, R. and R. Nymoen (2008), 'The New Keynesian Phillips curve tested on OECD panel data', *Economics: The Open-Access, Open-Assessment E-Journal*, **2** (23), July.

Black, F. (1970), 'Banking and interest rates in a world without money', *Journal of Banking Research*, **1** (3), Autumn, 8–20.

Black, W.K. (2005), 'Control frauds as financial super-predators: how pathogens make financial markets inefficient', *Journal of Socio-Economics*, **34** (6), December, 734–55.

Blanchard, O. (2015), 'Looking forward, looking back', *IMF Survey Magazine*, 31 August, http://www.imf.org/external/pubs/ft/survey/so/2015/RES083115A.htm.
Blatt, J. (1982), *Dynamic Economic Systems*, Armonk, NY: M.E. Sharpe.
Bleaney, M. (1976), *Underconsumption Theories: A History and Critical Analysis*, New York: International Publishers.
Blecker, R.A. (1989), 'International competition, income distribution and economic growth', *Cambridge Journal of Economics*, **13** (3), September, 395–412.
Blecker, R.A. (1999), 'Kaleckian macro models for open economies', in J. Deprez and J.T. Harvey (eds), *Foundations of International Economics: Post Keynesian Perspectives*, London: Routledge, pp. 116–50.
Blecker, R.A. (2002), 'Distribution, demand and growth in neo-Kaleckian macro-models', in M. Setterfield (ed.), *The Economics of Demand-led Growth: Challenging the Supply-side Vision of the Long Run*, Cheltenham, UK and Northampton, MA, USA: Edward Elgar, pp. 129–52.
Blecker, R.A. (2005), 'International economics after Robinson', in B. Gibson (ed.), *Joan Robinson's Economics: A Centennial Celebration*, Cheltenham: Edward Elgar, pp. 309–49.
Blecker, R.A. (2011), 'Open economy models of distribution and growth', in E. Hein and E. Stockhammer (eds), *A Modern Guide to Keynesian Macroeconomics and Economic Policies*, Cheltenham, UK and Northampton, MA, USA: Edward Elgar, pp. 215–39.
Blecker, R.A. (2021), 'Thirlwall's law is not a tautology, but some empirical tests of it nearly are', *Review of Keynesian Economics*, **9** (2), Summer, 175–203.
Blecker, R.A. and M. Setterfield (2019), *Heterodox Macroeconomics; Models of Demand, Distribution and Growth*, Cheltenham, UK and Northampton, MA, USA: Edward Elgar.
Blinder, A.S. and R. Solow (1973), 'Does fiscal policy matter?', *Journal of Public Economics*, **2** (4), November, 319–37.
Blinder, A.S., E.R.D. Canetti, D.E. Lebow and J.B. Rudd (1999), *Asking About Prices: A New Approach to Understanding Price Stickiness*, New York: Russell Sage Foundation.
Bliss, C.J. (1975), *Capital Theory and the Distribution of Income*, Amsterdam: North-Holland.
Bloch, H., M. Dockery and D. Sapsford (2004), 'Commodity prices, wages, and U.S. inflation in the twentieth century', *Journal of Post Keynesian Economics*, **26** (3), Spring, 523–45.
Bloch, H. and M. Olive (1996), 'Can simple rules explain pricing behaviour in Australian manufacturing?', *Australian Economic Papers*, **35** (66), June, 1–19.
Bloch, H. and D. Sapsford (1991–92), 'Postwar movements in prices of primary products and manufactured goods', *Journal of Post Keynesian Economics*, **14** (2), Winter, 249–66.
Bloomfield, A.I. (1959), *Monetary Policy under the International Gold Standard: 1880–1914*, New York: Federal Reserve Bank of New York.
Boddy, R. and J. Crotty (1975), 'Class conflict and macro-policy: the political business cycle', *Review of Radical and Political Economics*, **7** (1), Spring, 1–19.
Boggio, L. (1980), 'Full cost and Sraffa prices: equilibrium and stability in a system with fixed capital', *Monte dei Paschi di Siena Economic Notes*, **9** (1), 3–33.
Boggio, L. (1986), 'Stability of production prices in a model of general dependence', in W. Semmler (ed.), *Competition, Instability, and Nonlinear Cycles*, New York: Springer Verlag, pp. 83–114.
Boggio, L. (1990), 'The dynamic stability of production prices: a synthetic discussion of models and results', *Political Economy: Studies in the Surplus Approach*, **6** (1–2), 47–58.
Boggio, L. (1992), 'Production prices and dynamic stability: results and open questions', *Manchester School of Economic and Social Studies*, **60** (3), September, 264–94.
Boggio, L. and L. Barbieri (2017), 'International competitiveness in post-Keynesian growth theory: controversies and empirical evidence', *Cambridge Journal of Economics*, **41** (1), January, 25–47.
Bonizzi, B. and A. Kaltenbrunner (2020), 'Critical macro-finance, Post Keynesian monetary theory and emerging economies', *Finance and Society*, **6** (1), 76–86.
Bonizzi, B. and A. Kaltenbrunner (2021), 'A Minskyan framework for the analysis of financial flows to emerging economies', in B. Bonizzi, A. Kaltenbrunner and R.A. Ramos (eds), *Emerging Economies and the Global Financial System: Post-Keynesian Analysis*, London: Routledge, pp. 43–55.
Bonizzi, B., A. Kaltenbrunner and J. Michell (2019), 'Monetary sovereignty is a spectrum: Modern monetary theory and developing countries', *Real-World Economics Review*, **89**, October, 46–61.

Bonizzi, B., A. Kaltenbrunner and R.A. Ramos (2021), 'Introduction', in B. Bonizzi, A. Kaltenbrunner and R.A. Ramos (eds), *Emerging Economies and the Global Financial System: Post-Keynesian Analysis*, London: Routledge, pp. 3–13.

Borio, C. (2019), 'On money, debt, trust and central banking', BIS Working Papers 863, Bank for International Settlement.

Borio, C. and P. Disyatat (2010), 'Unconventional monetary policies: an appraisal', *Manchester School*, **78**, Supplement, September, 53–89.

Bortis, H. (1997), *Institutions, Behaviour and Economic Theory: A Contribution to Classical-Keynesian Political Economy*, Cambridge: Cambridge University Press.

Botta, A. (2020), 'The short- and long-run inconsistency of the expansionary austerity theory: a post-Keynesian/evolutionist critique', *Journal of Evolutionary Economics*, **30** (1), January, 143–77.

Botta, A., E. Caverzasi and D. Tori (2015), 'Financial-real-side interactions in an extended circuit with shadow banking: loving or dangerous hugs?', *International Journal of Political Economy*, **44** (3), Winter, 196–227.

Botta, A., E. Caverzasi and D. Tori (2020), 'The macroeconomics of shadow banking', *Economic Dynamics*, **24** (1), 161–90.

Botte, F. and T. Dallery (2019), 'Analyse systématique du modèle de Bhaduri et Marglin à prix flexibles', *Revue de la Régulation*, **26**, Autumn, 1–36.

Bougrine, H. and M. Seccareccia (2004), 'Alternative exchange rate arrangements and effective demand: an important missing analysis in the debate over greater North American monetary integration', *Journal of Post Keynesian Economics*, **26** (4), Summer, 655–78.

Bouguelli, R. (2018), 'A note on "Rethinking liquidity creation: banks, shadow banks and the elasticity of finance"', *Journal of Post Keynesian Economics*, **41** (4), 648–53.

Bouguelli, R. (2020), 'Is shadow banking really akin to banking? A critical analysis in light of monetary theory', *Journal of Post Keynesian Economics*, **43** (1), 1–27.

Bowen, W.G. and R.A. Berry (1963), 'Unemployment and movements of the money wage level', *Review of Economics and Statistics*, **45** (2), May, 163–72.

Bowles, S. and R. Boyer (1988), 'Labor discipline and aggregate demand: a macroeconomic model', *American Economic Review*, **78** (2), May, 395–400.

Bowles, S. and R. Boyer (1990), 'A wage-led employment regime: income distribution, labour discipline, and aggregate demand in welfare capitalism', in S.A. Marglin and J.B. Schor (eds), *The Golden Age of Capitalism: Reinterpreting the Postwar Experience*, Oxford: Clarendon Press, pp. 187–217.

Bowles, S. and R. Boyer (1995), 'Wages, aggregate demand, and employment in an open economy: an empirical investigation', in G. Epstein and H. Gintis (eds), *Macroeconomic Policy After the Conservative Era*, Cambridge: Cambridge University Press, pp. 143–71.

Boyer, R. (1988), 'Formalizing growth regimes', in G. Dosi, C. Freeman, R. Nelson, G. Silverberg and L. Soete (eds), *Technical Change and Economic Theory*, New York and London: Pinter, pp. 608–30.

Boyer, R. (2005), 'From shareholder value to CEO power: the paradox of the 1990s', *Competition and Change*, **9** (1), March, 7–47.

Boyer, R. (2011), 'Post-Keynésiens et régulationnistes: une alternative à la crise de l'économie standard', *Revue de la régulation*, **10**, Autumn, available at http://regulation.revues.org/9377#text.

Boyer, R., M. Dehove and D. Plihon (2005), *Les crises financières*, Paris: La Documentation Française.

Boyer, R. and P. Petit (1988), 'The cumulative growth model revisited', *Political Economy: Studies in the Surplus Approach*, **4** (1), 23–43.

Brennan, D.J. (2014), 'Too bright for comfort: a Kaleckian view of profit realisation in the USA: 1964–2009', *Cambridge Journal of Economics*, **38** (2), March, 239–55.

Bresser-Pereira, L.C. (2020a), 'Neutralizing the Dutch disease', *Journal of Post Keynesian Economics*, **43** (2), 298–316.

Bresser-Pereira, L.C. (2020b), 'New Developmentalism: development macroeconomics for middle-income countries', *Cambridge Journal of Economics*, **44** (3), May, 629–46.

Brierley, J.A., C.J. Cowton and C. Drury (2006), 'Reasons for adopting different capacity levels in the denominator of overhead rates: a research note', *Journal of Applied Accounting Research*, **4** (2), 53–62.
Brinkman, H.J. (1999), *Explaining Prices in the Global Economy: A Post-Keynesian Model*, Cheltenham, UK and Northampton, MA, USA: Edward Elgar.
Brochier, L. (2020), 'Conflicting-claims and labour market concerns in a supermultiplier SFC model', *Metroeconomica*, **71** (3), July, 566–603.
Brochier, L. and A.C. Macedo e Silva (2019), 'A supermultiplier Stock-Flow Consistent model: the return of the paradoxes of thrift and costs in the long run?', *Cambridge Journal of Economics*, **43** (2), 413–42.
Brown, C. (1997), 'Consumer credit and the propensity to consume: evidence from 1930', *Journal of Post Keynesian Economics*, **19** (4), Summer, 617–38.
Brown, C. (2003–04), 'Toward a reconcilement of endogenous money and liquidity preference', *Journal of Post Keynesian Economics*, **26** (2), Winter, 325–40.
Brown, C. (2007), 'Financial engineering, consumer credit, and the stability of effective demand', *Journal of Post Keynesian Economics*, **29** (3), Spring, 427–55.
Brown, C. (2008), *Inequality, Consumer Credit and the Saving Puzzle*, Cheltenham, UK and Northampton, MA, USA: Edward Elgar.
Brown, E.K. (1981), 'The neoclassical and post-Keynesian research programs: the methodological issues', *Review of Social Economy*, **39** (2), October, 111–32.
Brown, J.R., S.M. Fazzari and B.C. Petersen (2009), 'Financing innovation and growth: cash flow, external equity and the 1990s R&D boom', *Journal of Finance*, **64** (1), February, 151–86.
Brunner, E. (1952), 'Competition and the theory of the firm', *Economia Internazionale*, **5** (3 and 4), 509–22 and 727–44.
Brunner, E. (1975), 'Competitive prices, normal costs and industrial stability', in P.W.S. Andrews and E. Brunner (eds), *Studies in Pricing*, London: Macmillan, pp. 18–34.
Bruno, O. (1999), 'Long-run positions and short-run dynamics in a classical growth model', *Metroeconomica*, **50** (1), February, 119–37.
Buiter, W. (2009) 'The unfortunate uselessness of most "state of the art" academic monetary economics', *Financial Times*, 3 March, available at http://blogs.ft.com/maverecon/2009/03/the-unfortunate-uselessness-of-most-state-of-the-art-academic-monetary-economics/#more-667.
Bundesbank (2017), 'The role of banks, non-banks and the central bank in the money creation process', *Monthly Report*, April, 13–33.
Burdekin, R.C.K. and P. Burkett (1992), 'Money, credit, and wages in hyperinflation: post-World War I Germany', *Economic Inquiry*, **30** (3), July, 479–95.
Burkett, P. (1994), 'Book review of *The Economic Surplus in Advanced Economics*, edited by John B. Davis', *Review of Social Economics*, **52** (2), Summer, 114–24.
Burton, J. and J. Addison (1977), 'The Institutionalist analysis of wage inflation: a critical appraisal', *Research in Labor Economics*, **1** (1), July, 333–76.
Buttet, S. and U. Roy (2014), 'A simple treatment of the liquidity trap for intermediate macroeconomics courses', *Journal of Economic Education*, **45** (1), 36–55.
Buttet, S. and U. Roy (2015), 'Macroeconomic stabilization when the natural real interest rate is falling', *Journal of Economic Education*, **46** (4), 376–93.
Cagatay, N. (1994), 'Themes in Marxian and post-Keynesian theories of international trade: a consideration with respect to new trade theory', in M. Glick (ed.), *Competition, Technology and Money: Classical and Post-Keynesian Perspectives*, Aldershot, UK and Brookfield, VT, USA: Edward Elgar, pp. 237–50.
Cahen-Fourot, L., E. Campiglio, E. Dawkins, A. Godin, E. Kemp-Benedict and S. Tresk (2019), 'Capital stranding cascades: the impact of decarbonisation on productive asset utilisation', *Energy Economics*, November, article 105581.
Cahen-Fourot, L. and M. Lavoie (2016), 'Ecological monetary economics: a post-Keynesian critique', *Ecological Economics*, **126**, June, 163–68.
Caldwell, B.J. (1989), 'Post-Keynesian methodology: an assessment', *Review of Political Economy*, **1** (1), March, 43–64.

Câmara, A. and M. Vernengo (2001), 'The German balance of payments school and the Latin American neo-structuralits', in L.P. Rochon and M. Vernengo (eds), *Credit, Interest Rates and the Open Economy: Essays on Horizontalism*, Cheltenham, UK and Northampton, MA, USA: Edward Elgar, pp. 143–59.

Caminati, M. and S. Sordi (2019), 'Demand-led growth with endogenous innovation', *Metroeconomica*, **70** (3), July, 405–22.

Campiglio, E. (2016), 'Beyond carbon pricing: The role of banking and monetary policy in financing the transition to a low-carbon economy', *Ecological Economics*, **121**, January, 120–30.

Capaldo, J. and A. Izurieta (2013), 'The imprudence of labour market flexibilization in a fiscally austere world', *International Labour Review*, **152** (1), March, 1–26.

Capoglu, G. (1991), *Prices, Profits and Financial Structure: A Post-Keynesian Approach to Competition*, Aldershot, UK and Brookfield, VT, USA: Edward Elgar.

Card, D. and A.B. Krueger (1995), *Myth and Measurement: The New Economics of the Minimum Wage*, Princeton, NJ: Princeton University Press.

Carnevali, E. (2021), 'A new, simple SFC open economy framework', *Review of Political Economy*, DOI: 10.1080/09538259.2021.1899518.

Carnevali, E., M. Deleidi, R. Pariboni and M. Veronese Passarella (2021), 'Cross-border financial flows and global warming in a two-area ecological SFC model', *Socio-Economic Planning Sciences*, **75**, June, article 100819.

Carnevali, E., G. Fontana and M. Veronese Passarella (2020), 'Assessing the Marshall-Lerner condition within a stock-flow consistent model', *Cambridge Journal of Economics*, **44** (4), July, 891–918.

Carney, M. (2008), 'From hindsight to foresight', 17 December 2008, Bank of Canada, available at http://www.bankofcanada.ca/wp-content/uploads/2010/03/sp08–16.pdf.

Carrión Álvarez, M. and D. Ehnts (2016), 'Samuelson and Davidson on ergodicity: a reformulation', *Journal of Post Keynesian Economics*, **39** (1), 1–16.

Carson, J. (1990), 'Kalecki's pricing theory revisited', *Journal of Post Keynesian Economics*, **13** (1), Fall, 146–52.

Carvalho, F. Cardim de (1992), *Mr Keynes and the Post Keynesians: Principles of Macroeconomics for a Monetary Production Economy*, Aldershot, UK and Brookfield, VT, USA: Edward Elgar.

Caserta, M. (1990), 'The steady-state model of capital utilisation: a comment', *Studi Economici*, **41** (2), 139–53.

Caserta, M. (2002), 'Transitional steady states: a contradiction in terms?', in P. Arestis, M. Desai and S. Dow (eds), *Money, Macroeconomics and Keynes: Essays in Honour of Victoria Chick, Volume One*, London: Routledge, pp. 173–81.

Caskey, J. and S. Fazzari (1987), 'Monetary contractions with nominal debt commitments: is wage flexibility stabilizing?', *Economic Inquiry*, **25** (4), 583–97.

Cassetti, M. (2003), 'Bargaining power, effective demand and technical progress: a Kaleckian model of growth', *Cambridge Journal of Economics*, **27** (3), May, 449–64.

Cassetti, M. (2006), 'A note on the long-run behaviour of Kaleckian models', *Review of Political Economy*, **18** (4), October, 497–508.

Cassetti, M. (2020), 'Fiscal policy as a long-run stabilization tool: simulations with a stock-flow consistent model', Working Paper 2003, Post-Keynesian Economics Society.

Castillo-Palermo, L.A. and T.P. Schmidt (2019), 'The process of endogenous liquidity in developing economies: the case of Mexico', *Review of Keynesian Economics*, **7** (3), Autumn, 369–87.

Cauvel, M. (2019), 'The neo-Goodwinian model, reconsidered'. FMM Working Paper, No 47, https://www.econstor.eu/bitstream/10419/213403/1/1670248771.pdf.

Cavana, R.Y., B.C. Dangerfield, O.V. Pavlov, M.J. Radzicki and I.D. Wheat (eds) (2021), *Feedback Economics: Economic Modeling with System Dynamics*, Cham, Switzerland: Springer Nature.

Caverzasi, E., A. Botta and C. Capelli (2019), 'Shadow banking and the financial side of financialisation', *Cambridge Journal of Economics*, **43** (4), July, 1029–51.

Cecchetti, S.G. (2006), *Money, Banking, and Financial Markets*, New York: McGraw-Hill Irwin.

Cesaratto, S. (2013), 'The implications of TARGET2 in the European balance of payments crisis and beyond', *European Journal of Economics and Economic Policy: Intervention*, **10** (3), 359–82.

Cesaratto, S. (2015a), 'Neo-Kaleckian and Sraffian controversies on accumulation theory', *Review of Political Economy*, **27** (2), April, 154–182.

Cesaratto, S. (2015b), 'Balance of payments or monetary sovereignty? In search of EMU's original sin: Comment on Marc Lavoie', *International Journal of Political Economy*, **44** (2), 142–56.

Cesaratto, S. (2017), 'Alternative interpretations of a stateless currency crisis', *Cambridge Journal of Economics*, **41** (4), 977–98.

Cesaratto, S. (2020), *Heterodox Challenges in Economics: Theoretical Issues and the Crisis of the Eurozone*, Cham, Switzerland: Springer.

Cesaratto, S. and S. Di Bucchianico (2020), 'Endogenous money and the theory of long-period effective demand', *Bulletin of Political Economy*, **14** (1), 1–38.

Chandler, A.D. (1977), *The Visible Hand: The Managerial Revolution in American Business*, Cambridge, MA: Harvard University Press.

Chang, H.J. (2003), *Kicking Away the Ladder: Development Strategy in Historical Perspective*, London: Anthem Press.

Chang, H.J. (2008), *Bad Samaritans: The Myth of Free Trade and the Secret History of Capitalism*, New York: Bloomsbury Press.

Charles, S. (2008), 'Corporate debt, variable retention rate and the appearance of financial fragility', *Cambridge Journal of Economics*, **32** (5), September, 781–95.

Charles, S. and J. Marie (2016), 'Hyperinflation in a small open economy with a fixed exchange rate: a post Keynesian view', *Journal of Post Keynesian Economics*, **39** (3), 361–86.

Charles, S., T. Dallery and J. Marie (2021), 'Teaching the economic impact of COVID-19 with a simple short-run macro-model: simultaneous supply and demand shocks', *Review of Political Economy*, **33** (3), July, 462–79.

Chattopadhyay, N., A. Majumder and D. Coondoo (2009), 'Demand threshold, zero expenditure and hierarchal model of consumer demand', *Metroeconomica*, **60** (1), February, 91–118.

Chaundy, D. (1999), 'What is the accommodating item in the balance of payments?', Working Paper No. 122, ESRC Centre for Business Research, University of Cambridge.

Chick, V. (1977), *The Theory of Monetary Policy*, Oxford: Parkgate Books.

Chick, V. (1983), *Macroeconomics After Keynes: A Reconsideration of the General Theory*, London: Philip Allan.

Chick, V. (1986), 'The evolution of the banking system and the theory of saving, investment and interest', *Économies et Sociétés*, **20** (8–9), August, 111–26.

Chick, V. (1995), 'Is there a case for Post Keynesian economics?', *Scottish Journal of Political Economy*, **42** (1), February, 20–36.

Chick, V. (1998), 'On knowing one's place: the role of formalism in economics', *Economic Journal*, **108** (451), November, 1859–1959.

Chick, V. and M. Caserta (1997), 'Provisional equilibrium and macroeconomic theory', in P. Arestis, G. Palma and M. Sawyer (eds), *Markets, Employment and Economic Policies: Essays in Honour of G.C. Harcourt, Volume Two*, London: Routledge, pp. 223–37.

Chirat, A. (2022), 'The correspondence between Baumol and Galbraith (1957–1958): an unsuspected source of managerial theories of the firm', *Research in the History and Methodology of Economics*.

Ciccone, R. (1986), 'Accumulation and capacity utilization: some critical considerations on Joan Robinson's theory of distribution', *Political Economy: Studies in the Surplus Approach*, **2** (1), 17–36.

Claassen, E.M. (1996), *Global Monetary Economics*, Oxford: Oxford University Press.

Clarke, Y. and G.N. Soutar (1981–82), 'Consumer acquisition patterns for durable goods: Australian evidence', *Journal of Consumer Research*, **8** (4), March, 456–60.

Clifton, J.A. (1977), 'Competition and the evolution of the capitalist mode of production', *Cambridge Journal of Economics*, **1** (2), June, 137–51.

Clifton, J.A. (1983), 'Administered prices in the context of capitalist development', *Contributions to Political Economy*, **2**, March, 23–38.

Clinton, K. (1991), 'Bank of Canada cash management: the main technique for implementing monetary policy', *Bank of Canada Review*, January, 3–32.

Coddington, A. (1982), 'Deficient foresight: a troublesome theme in Keynesian economics', *American Economic Review*, **72** (3), June, 480–87.

Cohen, A. and G.C. Harcourt (2003), 'Whatever happened to the Cambridge capital controversies?', *Journal of Economic Perspectives*, **17** (1), Winter, 199–214.
Colander, D. (2000), 'The death of neoclassical economics', *Journal of the History of Economic Thought*, **22** (2), June, 127–43.
Colander, D. (2001), 'An interview with Paul Davidson', *Eastern Economic Journal*, **27** (1), Winter, 85–114.
Colander, D., R.P.F. Holt and J.B. Rosser (2007–08), 'Live and dead issues in the methodology of economics', *Journal of Post Keynesian Economics*, **30** (2), Winter, 303–12.
Cömert, H. (2013), *Central Banks and Financial Markets: The Declining Power of US Monetary Policy*, Cheltenham, UK and Northampton, MA, USA: Edward Elgar.
Cömert, H. (2019), 'From trilemma to dilemma: monetary policy after the Bretton Woods world', in L.-P. Rochon and V. Monvoisin (eds), *Finance, Growth and Inequality: Post-Keynesian Perspectives*, Cheltenham, UK and Northampton, MA, USA: Edward Elgar, pp. 210–34.
Commendatore, M. (2006), 'Are Kaleckian models relevant for the long run?', in N. Salvadori and C. Panico (eds), *Classical, Neoclassical and Keynesian Views on Growth and Distribution*, Cheltenham, UK and Northampton, MA, USA: Edward Elgar, pp. 288–307.
Committeri, M. (1986), 'Some comments on recent contributions on capital accumulation, income distribution and capacity utilization', *Political Economy: Studies in the Surplus Approach*, **2** (2), 161–86.
Committeri, M. (1987), 'Capacity utilization, distribution and accumulation: a rejoinder to Amadeo', *Political Economy: Studies in the Surplus Approach*, **3** (1), 91–5.
Cook, S. (2008), 'Econometric analysis of interest rate pass-through', *Applied Financial Economic Letters*, **4** (4), 249–51.
Copeland, M.A. (1949), 'Social accounting for money flows', *The Accounting Review*, 24 (July), 254–64. Reproduced in J.C. Dawson (ed.) (1996), *Flow-of-Funds Analysis: A Handbook for Practitioners*, Armonk, NY: M.E. Sharpe, pp. 7–18.
Copeland, M.A. (1974), 'Concerning the origin of a money economy', *American Journal of Economics and Sociology*, **33** (1), January, 3–18.
Cordonnier, L. and F. Van de Velde (2015), 'The demands of finance and the glass ceiling of profit without investment', *Cambridge Journal of Economics*, **39** (3), May, 871–85.
Cornwall, J. (1972), *Growth and Stability in a Mature Economy*, London: Martin Robertson.
Cornwall, J. (1977), *Modern Capitalism: Its Growth and Transformation*, New York: St. Martin's Press.
Costa-Font, J., A. McGuire and T.D. Stanley (2013), 'Publication selection in health policy research: the winner's curse hypothesis', *Health Policy*, **109** (1), January, 78–87.
Cottrell, A. (1994), 'Post-Keynesian monetary theory', *Cambridge Journal of Economics*, **19** (6), December, 587–605.
Coulbois, P. (ed.) (1972), *Le change à terme: technique, théorie, politique*, Paris: Cujas.
Coulbois, P. (1979), *Finance internationale: le change*, Paris: Cujas.
Coulbois, P. (1982), 'Central banks and foreign-exchange crises today', in C.P. Kindleberger and J.P. Laffargue (eds), *Financial Crises: Theory, History and Policy*, New York: Cambridge University Press, and Paris: Éditions de la Maison des Sciences de l'Homme, pp. 195–216.
Coulbois, P. and P. Prissert (1974), 'Forward exchange, short term capital flows and monetary policy', *De Economist*, **122** (4), July, 283–308.
Coulbois, P. and P. Prissert (1976), 'Forward exchange, short term capital flows and monetary policy: a reply', *De Economist*, **124** (4), December, 490–92.
Couppey-Soubeyran, J. (2020), 'Helicopter money to combat economic depression in the wake of the Covid-19 crisis', Veblen Institute for Economic Reforms, May.
Courbis, B., E. Froment and J.M. Servet (1991), 'Enrichir l'économie politique de la monnaie par l'histoire', *Revue Économique*, **42** (2), March, 315–38.
Coutts, K., W. Godley and W. Nordhaus (1978), *Industrial Pricing in the United Kingdom*, Cambridge: Cambridge University Press.
Coutts, K. and N. Norman (2007), 'Global influences on UK manufacturing prices: 1970–2000', *European Economic Review*, **51** (5), July, 1205–21.

Coutts, K. and N. Norman (2013), 'Post-Keynesian approaches to industrial pricing: a survey and critique', in G.C. Harcourt and P. Kriesler (eds), *Oxford Handbook of Post-Keynesian Economics*, Volume 1, Oxford: Oxford University Press, pp. 443–66.
Cowling, K. (1982), *Monopoly Capitalism*, London: Macmillan.
Craig, B. and O. Humpage (2001), 'Sterilization intervention, nonsterilized intervention, and monetary policy', Working Paper No. 0110, Federal Reserve Bank of Cleveland.
Cramp, A.B. (1971), 'Monetary policy: strong or weak?', in N. Kaldor (ed.), *Conflicts in Policy Objectives*, Oxford: Basil Blackwell, pp. 62–74.
Cripps, F. (1977), 'The money supply, wages and inflation', *Cambridge Journal of Economics*, **1** (1), March, 101–12.
Cripps, F. and W. Godley (1978), 'Control of imports as a means to full employment and the expansion of world trade: the UK's case', *Cambridge Journal of Economics*, **2** (3), September, 327–34.
Crivelli, R. (1993), 'Hysteresis in the work of Nicholas Georgescu-Roegen', in J.C. Dragan, E.K. Sweifert and M.C. Demetrescu (eds), *Entropy and Bioeconomics*, Milan: Nagard, pp. 107–29.
Cross, R. (1995), 'Is the natural rate hypothesis consistent with hysteresis?', in R. Cross (ed.), *The Natural Rate of Unemployment: Reflections on 25 Years of the Hypothesis*, Cambridge: Cambridge University Press, pp. 181–200.
Crotty, J.R. (1990), 'Owner–manager conflict and financial theories of investment instability: a critical assessment of Keynes, Tobin and Minsky', *Journal of Post Keynesian Economics*, **12** (4), Summer, 519–42.
Cunningham, R., V. Rai and K. Hess (2019), 'Exploring wage Phillips curves in advanced economies', Bank of Canada Staff Discussion Paper 2019-8.
Cyert, R.M. and J.G. March (1963), *A Behavioral Theory of the Firm*, Englewood Cliffs, NJ: Prentice-Hall.
Cyert, R.M. and H.A. Simon (1983), 'The behavioral approach: with emphasis on economics', *Behavioral Science*, **28** (1), January, 95–108.
Cynamon, B.Z. and S.M. Fazzari (2008), 'Household debt in the consumer age: source of growth – risk of collapse', *Capitalism and Society*, **3** (2), July, 1–30.
Dafermos, Y, M. Nikolaidi and G. Galanis (2017), 'A stock-flow-fund ecological macroeconomic model', *Ecological Economics*, **131**, January, 191–207.
Dafermos, Y, M. Nikolaidi and G. Galanis (2018), 'Climate Change, Financial Stability and Monetary Policy', *Ecological Economics*, **152**, October, 219–34.
Dallery, T. (2009), 'Post-Keynesian theories of the firm under financialisation', *Review of Radical Political Economics*, **41** (4), December, 492–515.
Dallery, T. and T. van Treeck (2011) 'Conflicting claims and equilibrium adjustment processes in a stock–flow consistent macroeconomic model', *Review of Political Economy*, **23** (2), April, 189–212.
Dalziel, P.C. (1990), 'Market power, inflation, and incomes policy', *Journal of Post Keynesian Economics*, **12** (3), Spring, 424–38.
Dalziel, P. and M. Lavoie (2003), 'Teaching Keynes's principle of effective demand using the aggregate labor market diagram', *Journal of Economic Education*, **34** (4), Fall, 333–40.
Danby, C. (2004), 'Toward a gendered Post Keynesianism: subjectivity and time in a nonmodernist framework', *Feminist Economics*, **10** (3), November, 55–75.
Danby, C. (2009), 'Post-Keynesianism without modernity', *Cambridge Journal of Economics*, **33** (6), November, 1119–33.
D'Alessandro, S., A. Cieplinski, T. Distefano and K. Dittmer (2020), 'Feasible alternatives to green growth'. *Nature Sustainability*, **3** (4), April, 329–35.
D'Arista, J. (2000), 'Reforming the privatized international monetary and financial architecture', *Challenge*, **43** (3), May–June, 44–82.
D'Arista, J. (2004), 'Dollars, debt, and dependence: the case for international monetary reform', *Journal of Post Keynesian Economics*, **26** (4), Summer, 557–72.
Davidson, P. (1960), *Theories of Aggregate Income Distribution*, New Brunswick, NJ: Rutgers University Press.
Davidson, P. (1972), *Money and the Real World*, London: Macmillan.

Davidson, P. (1979), 'Natural resources', in A.S. Eichner (ed.), *A Guide to Post-Keynesian Economics*, White Plains, M.E. Sharpe, pp. 151–64.
Davidson, P. (1982–83), 'Rational expectations: a fallacious foundation for studying crucial decision-making processes', *Journal of Post Keynesian Economics*, **5** (2), Winter, 182–98.
Davidson, P. (1983), 'The marginal product curve is not the demand curve for labor and Lucas's labor supply function is not the supply curve for labor in the real world', *Journal of Post Keynesian Economics*, **6** (1), Fall, 105–17.
Davidson, P. (1984), 'Reviving Keynes's revolution', *Journal of Post Keynesian Economics*, **6** (4), Summer, 561–75.
Davidson, P. (1985), 'Liquidity and not increasing returns is the ultimate source of unemployment equilibrium', *Journal of Post Keynesian Economics*, **7** (3), Spring, 373–84.
Davidson, P. (1989), 'The economics of ignorance or the ignorance of economics?', *Critical Review*, **3** (3–4), Summer/Fall, 467–87.
Davidson, P. (1992), *International Money and the Real World*, 2nd edn, London: Macmillan.
Davidson, P. (1993a), 'The elephant and the butterfly: or hysteresis and Post Keynesian economics', *Journal of Post Keynesian Economics*, **15** (3), Spring, 309–23.
Davidson, P. (1993b), 'Austrians and Post Keynesians on economic reality: rejoinder to critics', *Critical Review*, **7** (2–3), Spring–Summer, 423–44.
Davidson, P. (1994), *Post Keynesian Macroeconomic Theory*, Aldershot, UK and Brookfield, VT, USA: Edward Elgar.
Davidson, P. (1996), 'Reality and economic theory', *Journal of Post Keynesian Economics*, **18** (4), Spring, 479–508.
Davidson, P. (1998), 'Post Keynesian employment analysis and the macroeconomics of OECD employment', *Economic Journal*, **108** (448), May, 817–31.
Davidson, P. (1999), 'Keynes's principle of effective demand versus the bedlam of the New Keynesians', *Journal of Post Keynesian Economics*, **21** (4), Summer, 571–88.
Davidson, P. (2000), 'There are major differences between Kalecki's theory of employment and Keynes's general theory of employment interest and money', *Journal of Post Keynesian Economics*, **23** (1), Fall, 3–26.
Davidson, P. (2003–04), 'Setting the record straight on *A History of Post Keynesian Economics*', *Journal of Post Keynesian Economics*, **26** (2), Winter, 245–72.
Davidson, P. (2008), 'Cruder oil prices: market fundamentals or speculation?', *Challenge*, **51** (4), July–August, 110–18.
Davidson, P. (2009), *The Keynes Solution*, Basingstoke: Palgrave Macmillan.
Davidson, P. (2010–11), 'Behavioral economists should make a turn and learn from Keynes and the Post Keynesians', *Journal of Post Keynesian Economics*, **33** (2), Winter, 251–4.
Davidson, P. (2010), 'Black swans and Knight's epistemological uncertainty: are these concepts also underlying behavioral and post-Walrasian theory?', *Journal of Post Keynesian Economics*, **32** (4), Summer, 567–70.
Davidson, P. and S. Weintraub (1978), 'A statement of purposes', *Journal of Post Keynesian Economics*, **1** (1), Fall, 3–7.
Davies, J.E. and F.S. Lee (1988), 'A post-Keynesian appraisal of the contestability criterion', *Journal of Post Keynesian Economics*, **11** (1), Fall, 3–24.
Davis, J.B. (2006), 'The nature of heterodox economics', *Post-Autistic Economic Review*, **40**, December, 23–30.
Davis, J.B. (2008), 'The turn in recent economics and return of orthodoxy', *Cambridge Journal of Economics*, **32** (2), April, 349–66.
Deaton, A. and J. Muellbauer (1980), *Economics and Consumer Behavior*, Cambridge: Cambridge University Press.
de Boyer, J. (1998), 'Endogenous money and shareholders' funds in the classical theory of banking', *European Journal of the History of Economic Thought*, **5** (1), Spring, 60–84.
De Grauwe, P. and M. Grimaldi (2006), *The Exchange Rate in a Behavioral Finance Framework*, Woodstock, UK: Princeton University Press.
Dejuán, Ó. (2005), 'Paths of accumulation and growth: towards a Keynesian long-period theory of output', *Review of Political Economy*, **17** (2), April, 231–52.

de Largentaye, J. (1979), 'A note on the *General Theory of Employment, Interest and Money*', *Journal of Post Keynesian Economics*, **1** (3), Spring, 6–15.
Deleidi, M. (2018), 'Post Keynesian endogenous money theory: a theoretical and empirical investigation of the credit demand schedule', *Journal of Post Keynesian Economics*, **41** (2), 185–209.
Deleidi, M. (2020), 'Post-Keynesian endogenous money theory: horizontalists, structuralists and the paradox of illiquidity', *Metroeconomica*, **71** (1), February, 156–75.
Del Monte, A. (1975), 'Grado di monopolio e sviluppo economico', *Rivista Internazionale di Scienze Sociali*, **83** (3), May–June, 231–63.
De Lucchi, J.M. (2013), 'Endogenous money and public foreign debt during the Argentinean convertibility', *Review of Keynesian Economics*, **1** (3), Autumn, 322–46.
Deprez, J. (1996), 'Davidson on the labor market in a monetary production economy', in P. Arestis (ed.), *Keynes, Money and the Open Economy: Essays in Honour of Paul Davidson: Volume One*, Cheltenham, UK and Brookfield, VT, USA: Edward Elgar, pp. 123–43.
Dequech, D. (1999), 'Expectations and confidence under uncertainty', *Journal of Post Keynesian Economics*, **21** (3), Spring, 415–30.
Descamps, C. and J. Soichot (2003), 'Monnaie endogène et réglementation prudentielle', in P. Piegay and L.P. Rochon (eds), *Théories monétaires post Keynésiennes*, Paris: Économica, pp. 99–120.
de Soto, H. (2000), *The Mystery of Capital*, London: Bantam Press.
De Vroey, M. (1975), 'The transition from classical to neoclassical economics: a scientific revolution', *Journal of Economic Issues*, **9** (3), September, 415–39.
Dhar, R. (1999), 'Choice deferral', in P.E. Earl and S. Kemp (eds.), *The Elgar Companion to Consumer Research and Economic Psychology*, Cheltenham, UK and Northampton, MA, USA: Edward Elgar, pp. 75–81.
Di Guilmi, C. (2017), 'The agent-based approach to Post Keynesian macro-modeling', *Journal of Economic Surveys*, **31** (5), December, 1183–1203.
Dixon, R. (1986), 'Uncertainty, unobstructedness, and power', *Journal of Post Keynesian Economics*, **8** (4), Summer, 585–90.
Dobrev, D. (1999), 'The currency board in Bulgaria: design, peculiarities and management of foreign exchange cover', Discussion Paper DP/9/1999, Bulgarian National Bank.
Dobusch, L. and J. Kapeller (2012), 'A guide to paradigmatic self-marginalization: lessons from post-Keynesian economists', *Review of Political Economy*, **24** (1), July, 469–87.
Domar, E.D. (1944), 'The burden of the debt and national income', *American Economic Review*, **34** (4), December, 798–827.
Domowitz, I., R.G. Hubbard and B.C. Petersen (1986), 'Business cycles and the relationship between concentration and the price–cost margin', *Rand Journal of Economics*, **17** (1), Spring, 1–17.
Dore, R. (2000), 'Will global capitalism be Anglo-Saxon capitalism?', *New Left Review*, November–December, 101–19.
Dore, R. (2002), 'Stock market capitalism and its diffusion', *New Political Economy*, **7** (1), March, 115–21.
Dorfman, R., P.A. Samuelson and R.M. Solow (1958), *Linear Programming and Economic Analysis*, New York: McGraw-Hill.
Dosi, G. and M. Egidi (1991), 'Substantive and procedural uncertainty: an exploration of economic behaviours in changing environments', *Journal of Evolutionary Economics*, **1** (2), April, 145–68.
Dosi, G., C. Freeman, R. Nelson, F. Silverberg and L. Soete (eds) (1988), *Technical Change and Economic Theory*, London and New York: Pinter.
Dosi, G., M. Napoletano, A. Roventini, J.E. Stiglitz and T. Treibich (2020), 'Rational heuristics? Expectations in evolving economies with heterogeneous interacting agents', *Economic Inquiry*, **58** (3), July, 1487–516.
Dosi, G., M.C. Pereira, A. Roventini and M.E. Virgillitoa (2017), 'When more flexibility yields more fragility: the microfoundations of Keynesian aggregate unemployment', *Journal of Economic Dynamics and Control*, **81**, August, 162–86.
Dos Santos, C.H. (2006), 'Keynesian theorising during hard times: stock–flow consistent models as an unexplored "frontier" of Keynesian macroeconomics', *Cambridge Journal of Economics*, **30** (4), July, 541–65.

Dostaler, G. (1988), 'La théorie post-Keynésienne, la Théorie Générale et Kalecki', *Cahiers d'Economie Politique*, **14–15**, 123–42.
Doucouliagos, H. and T.D. Stanley (2009), 'Publication selection bias in minimum-wage research? A meta-regression analysis', *British Journal of Industrial Relations*, **47** (2), June, 406–28.
Doucouliagos, H. and T.D. Stanley (2013), 'Are all economic facts greatly exaggerated? Theory competition and selectivity', *Journal of Economic Surveys*, **27** (2), April, 316–39.
Douthwaite, R. (2012), 'Degrowth and the supply of money in an energy-scarce world', *Ecological Economics*, **84**, December, 187–93.
Dow, A.C. and S.C. Dow (1989), 'Endogenous money creation and idle balances', in J. Pheby (ed.), *New Directions in Post-Keynesian Economics*, Aldershot, UK and Brookfield, VT, USA: Edward Elgar, pp. 147–64.
Dow, S.C. (1987) 'Money and regional development', *Studies in Political Economy*, **23**, Summer, 73–94.
Dow, S.C. (1991), 'The Post-Keynesian school', in D. Mair and A.G. Miller (eds), *A Modern Guide to Economic Thought*, Aldershot, UK and Brookfield, VT, USA: Edward Elgar, pp. 176–206.
Dow, S.C. (1996), 'Horizontalism: a critique', *Cambridge Journal of Economics*, **20** (4), July, 497–508.
Dow, S.C. (1999), 'International liquidity preference and endogenous credit creation', in J. Deprez and J.T. Harvey (eds), *Foundations of International Economics: Post Keynesian Perspectives*, London: Routledge, pp. 153–70.
Dow, S.C. (2000), 'Prospects for the progress of heterodox economics', *Journal of the History of Economic Thought*, **22** (2), June, 157–70.
Dow, S.C. (2005), 'Axioms and Babylonian thought: a reply', *Journal of Post Keynesian Economics*, **27** (3), Spring, 385–92.
Downward, P. (1999), *Pricing Theory in Post Keynesian Economics: A Realist Approach*, Cheltenham, UK and Northampton, MA, USA: Edward Elgar.
Downward, P. (2000), 'A realist appraisal of post-Keynesian pricing theory', *Cambridge Journal of Economics*, **24** (2), March, 211–24.
Downward, P. and F.S. Lee (2001), 'Post Keynesian pricing "reconfirmed"? A critical review of Asking About Prices', *Journal of Post Keynesian Economics*, **23** (3), Spring, 465–84.
Drakopoulos, S.A. (1990), 'The implicit psychology of the theory of the rational consumer', *Australian Economic Papers*, **29** (55), December, 182–98.
Drakopoulos, S.A. (1992a), 'Psychological thresholds, demand and price rigidity', *Manchester School of Economics and Social Studies*, **60** (2), June, 152–68.
Drakopoulos, S.A. (1992b), 'Keynes' economic thought and the theory of consumer behaviour', *Scottish Journal of Political Economy*, **39** (3), August, 318–36.
Drakopoulos, S.A. (1994), 'Hierarchical choice in economics', *Journal of Economic Surveys*, **8** (2), June, 133–53.
Drakopoulos, S.A. (1999), 'Post-Keynesian choice theory', in P.A. O'Hara (ed.), *Encyclopedia of Political Economy*, Volume 2, London: Routledge, pp. 887–9.
Drakopoulos, S.A. (2008), 'The paradox of happiness: toward an alternative explanation', *Journal of Happiness Studies*, **9** (2), June, 303–15.
Drakopoulos, S.A. and A.D. Karayiannis (2004), 'The historical development of hierarchical behavior in economic thought', *Journal of the History of Economic Thought*, **26** (3), September, 363–78.
Dray, M. and A.P. Thirlwall (2011), 'The endogeneity of the natural rate of growth for a selection of Asian countries', *Journal of Post Keynesian Economics*, **33** (3), Spring, 451–68.
Duesenberry, J. (1949), *Income, Saving and the Theory of Consumer Behavior*, Cambridge, MA: Harvard University Press.
Dullien, S. (2010), '*Macroeconomic Theory and Macroeconomic Pedagogy* – a review of the book edited by Giuseppe Fontana and Mark Setterfield', *European Journal of Economics and Economic Policies: Intervention*, **7** (2), November, 266–71.
Dullien, S. (2011), 'The New Consensus from a traditional Keynesian and post-Keynesian perspective: a worthwhile foundation for research or just a waste of time?', *Économie Appliquée*, **64** (1), March, 173–200.

Dullien, S. (2017), 'How to promote alternative macroeconomic ideas: are there limits to running with the (mainstream) pack?', *European Journal of Economics and Economic Policies: Intervention*, **14** (2), 238–49.

Duménil, G. and D. Lévy (1990), 'Convergence to long-period positions: an addendum', *Political Economy: Studies in the Surplus Approach*, **6** (1–2), 265–78.

Duménil, G. and D. Lévy (1993), *The Economics of the Profit Rate: Competition, Crises and Historical Tendencies in Capitalism*, Aldershot, UK and Brookfield, VT, USA: Edward Elgar.

Duménil, G. and D. Lévy (1999), 'Being Keynesian in the short term and classical in the long term: the traverse to classical long-term equilibrium', *The Manchester School*, **67** (6), December, 684–716.

Duménil, G. and D. Lévy (2004), *Économie marxiste du capitalisme*, Paris: La Découverte.

Dumouchel, P. and J.-P. Dupuy (1979), *L'enfer des choses: René Girard et la logique de l'économie*, Paris: Editions du Seuil.

Dunn, S.P. (2000), 'Wither Post Keynesianism?', *Journal of Post Keynesian Economics*, **22** (3), Spring, 343–64.

Dunn, S.P. (2001), 'Bounded rationality is not fundamental uncertainty: a Post Keynesian perspective', *Journal of Post Keynesian Economics*, **23** (4), Summer, 567–88.

Dunn, S.P. (2008), *The 'Uncertain' Foundations of Post Keynesian Economics*, London: Routledge.

Dunn, S.P. (2011), *The Economics of John Kenneth Galbraith: Introduction, Persuasion and Rehabilitation*, Cambridge: Cambridge University Press.

du Tertre, R. and Y. Guy (2019), 'Gouvernance d'entreprise et finance', in M. Aglietta (ed.), *Capitalisme: Le temps des ruptures*, Paris: Odile Jacob, pp. 267–343.

Dutt, A.K. (1984), 'Stagnation, income distribution and monopoly power', *Cambridge Journal of Economics*, **8** (1), March, 25–40.

Dutt, A.K. (1986–87), 'Wage-rigidity and unemployment: the simple diagrammatics of two views', *Journal of Post Keynesian Economics*, **9** (2), Winter, 279–90.

Dutt, A.K. (1987a), 'Alternative closures again: a comment on growth, distribution and inflation', *Cambridge Journal of Economics*, **11** (1), March, 75–82.

Dutt, A.K. (1987b), 'Competition, monopoly power and the uniform rate of profit', *Review of Radical Political Economics*, **19** (4), Winter, 55–72.

Dutt, A.K. (1987c), 'Keynes with a perfectly competitive goods market', *Australian Economic Papers*, **26** (49), December, 275–93.

Dutt, A.K. (1990a), *Growth, Distribution and Uneven Development*, Cambridge: Cambridge University Press.

Dutt, A.K. (1990b), 'Growth, distribution and capital ownership: Kalecki and Pasinetti revisited', in B. Datta, S. Gangopadhyay, D. Mookherjee and D. Ray (eds), *Economic Theory and Policy*, Bombay: Oxford University Press, pp. 130–45.

Dutt, A.K. (1991–92), 'Expectations and equilibrium: implications for Keynes, the neo-Ricardian Keynesians, and the Post Keynesians', *Journal of Post Keynesian Economics*, **14** (2), Winter, 205–24.

Dutt, A.K. (1992a), 'Stagnation, growth and unproductive activity', in J.B. Davis (ed.), *The Economic Surplus in Advanced Economics*, Aldershot, UK and Brookfield, VT, USA: Edward Elgar, pp. 91–113.

Dutt, A.K. (1992b), 'Rentiers in post Keynesian models', in P. Arestis and V. Chick (eds), *Recent Developments in Post-Keynesian Economics*, Aldershot, UK and Brookfield, VT, USA: Edward Elgar, pp. 95–122.

Dutt, A.K. (1992c), 'Conflict inflation, distribution, cyclical accumulation and crises', *European Journal of Political Economy*, **8** (4), December, 579–97.

Dutt, A.K. (1995), 'Internal finance and monopoly power in capitalist economies: a reformulation of Steindl's growth model', *Metroeconomica*, **46** (10), February, 16–34.

Dutt, A.K. (1997), 'Equilibrium, path dependence and hysteresis in post-Keynesian models', in P. Arestis, G. Palma and M. Sawyer (eds), *Markets, Unemployment and Economic Policy: Essays in Honour of Geoff Harcourt, Volume Two*, London: Routledge, pp. 238–53.

Dutt, A.K. (2003), 'On post Walrasian economics, macroeconomic policy and heterodox economics', *International Journal of Political Economy*, **33** (2), Summer, 47–64.

Dutt, A.K. (2006a), 'Aggregate demand, aggregate supply and economic growth', *International Review of Applied Economics*, **20** (3), July, 319–36.
Dutt, A.K. (2006b), 'Maturity, stagnation and consumer debt: a Steindlian approach', *Metroeconomica*, **57** (3), July, 339–64.
Dutt, A.K. (2010), 'Equilibrium, path dependence and hysteresis in post-Keynesian models of economic growth', in A. Birolo, D. Foley, H.D. Kurz and I. Steedman (eds), *Production, Distribution and Trade: Alternative Perspectives. Essays in Honour of Sergio Parrinello*, London: Routledge, pp. 233–53.
Dutt, A.K. (2011), 'Growth and income distribution: a post-Keynesian perspective', in E. Hein and E. Stockhammer (eds), *A Modern Guide to Keynesian Macroeconomics and Economic Policies*, Cheltenham, UK and Northampton, MA, USA: Edward Elgar, pp. 61–87.
Dutt, A.K. (2012), 'Growth, distribution and crises', in H. Herr, T. Niechoj, C. Thomasberger, A. Truger and T. van Treeck (eds), *From Crisis to Growth? The Challenge of Debt and Imbalances*, Marburg: Metropolis, pp. 33–59.
Dutt, A.K. (2017), 'Income inequality, the wage share, and economic growth', *Review of Keynesian Economics*, **5** (2), Summer, 170–95.
Dutt, A.K. (2019), 'Some observations on models of growth and distribution with autonomous demand growth', *Metroeconomica*, **70** (2), May, 288–301.
Dutt, A.K. and E.J. Amadeo (1990), *Keynes's Third Alternative: The Neo-Ricardian Keynesians and the Post Keynesians*, Aldershot, UK and Brookfield, VT, USA: Edward Elgar.
Dutt, A.K. and E.J. Amadeo (1993), 'A post-Keynesian theory of growth, interest and money', in M. Baranzini and G.C. Harcourt (eds), *The Dynamics of the Wealth of Nations: Growth, Distribution and Structural Change, Essays in Honour of Luigi Pasinetti*, London: Macmillan, pp. 181–205.
Dyson, B., G. Hodgson and F. van Lerven (2016), 'A response to critiques of full reserve banking', *Cambridge Journal of Economics*, **40** (5), September, 1351–61.
Earl, P.E. (1983), *The Economic Imagination: Towards a Behavioural Analysis of Choice*, Armonk, NY: M.E. Sharpe.
Earl, P. (1986), *Lifestyle Economics: Consumer Behaviour in a Turbulent World*, Brighton, UK: Wheatsheaf.
Earl, P.E. (ed.) (1988), *Behavioural Economics, Volume 1*, Aldershot, UK and Brookfield, VT, USA: Edward Elgar.
Earl, P.E. (1995), *Microeconomics for Business and Marketing*, Aldershot, UK and Brookfield, VT, USA: Edward Elgar.
Earl, P.E. and T.-C. Peng (2012), 'Brands of economics and the Trojan horse of pluralism', *Review of Political Economy*, **24** (3), July, 451–68.
Ederer, S. and M. Rehm (2020), 'Making sense of Piketty's "fundamental laws" in a Post-Keynesian framework: the transitional dynamics of wealth', *Review of Keynesian Economics*, **8** (2), Summer, 195–219.
Editors (2011), 'Editorial note', *Cambridge Journal of Economics*, **35** (3), May, 635.
Edwards, S.F. (1986), 'Ethical preferences and the assessment of existence values: does the neoclassical model fit?', *Northeastern Journal of Agricultural and Resource Economics*, **15** (2), October, 145–50.
Eggertsson, G.B. and P. Krugman (2012), 'Debt, deleveraging, and the liquidity trap: a Fisher–Minsky–Koo approach', *Quarterly Journal of Economics*, **127** (3), August, 1469–513.
Eichengreen, B. (1984), 'Keynes and protection', *Journal of Economic History*, **44** (2), June, 363–73.
Eichengreen, B., R. Hausmann and U. Panizza (2002), 'Original sin: the pain, the mystery and the road to redemption', available at http://www.financialpolicy.org/financedev/hausmann2002.pdf.
Eichner, A.S. (1976), *The Megacorp and Oligopoly: Micro Foundations of Macro Dynamics*, Cambridge: Cambridge University Press.
Eichner, A.S. (1978), 'Review of *Studies in Pricing* by Andrews and Brunner', *Journal of Economic Literature*, **16** (4), December, 1436–8.
Eichner, A.S. (ed.) (1979), *A Guide to Post-Keynesian Economics*, White Plains, NY: M.E. Sharpe.
Eichner, A.S. (1986a), *Toward a New Economics: Essays in Post-Keynesian and Institutionalist Theory*, London: Macmillan.

Eichner, A.S. (1986b), 'A comment on a Post Keynesian view of average direct costs', *Journal of Post Keynesian Economics*, **8** (3), Spring, 425–6.

Eichner, A.S. (1987), *The Macrodynamics of Advanced Market Economies*, Armonk, NY: M.E. Sharpe.

Eichner, A.S. and J.A. Kregel (1975), 'An essay on post-Keynesian theory: a new paradigm in economics', *Journal of Economic Literature*, **13** (4), December, 1293–311.

Eisner, R. (1996), 'The retreat from full employment', in P. Arestis (ed.), *Employment, Economic Growth and the Tyranny of the Market: Essays in Honour of Paul Davidson*, Volume 2, Cheltenham, UK and Brookfield, VT, USA: Edward Elgar, pp. 106–30.

Encarnación, J. (1964), 'A note on lexicographic preferences', *Econometrica*, **32** (1–2), January–April, 215–17.

Ennis, H.M. and T. Keister (2008), 'Understanding monetary policy implementation', *Federal Reserve Bank of Richmond Economic Quarterly*, **94**, Summer, 235–63.

Epstein, G. (1994), 'A political economy model of comparative central banking', in G. Dymski and R. Pollin (eds), *New Perspectives in Monetary Macroeconomics: Explorations in the Tradition of Hyman P. Minsky*, Ann Arbor, MI: University of Michigan Press, pp. 231–77.

Epstein, G. (2010), 'Financial flows must be regulated', in H. Bougrine and M. Seccareccia (eds), *Introducing Macroeconomic Analysis: Issues, Questions, and Competing Views*, Toronto: Emond Montgomery, pp. 283–306.

Epstein, G.A. (2019), *What's Wrong with Modern Money Theory? A Political Critique*, Cham, Switzerland: Palgrave Macmillan.

Ethier, W.J. (1988), *Modern International Economics*, 2nd edn, New York: Norton.

Etzioni, A. (1988), *The Moral Dimension: Toward a New Economics*, New York: The Free Press.

Evans, D. (1981), 'Unequal exchange and economic policies: some implications of the neo-Ricardian critique of the theory of comparative advantage', in J. Livingstone (ed.), *Development Economics and Policy: Readings*, London: Allen and Unwin, pp. 117–28.

Fabo, B., M. Jančoková, E. Kempf and L. Pástor (2020), 'Fifty shades of QE: Conflicts of interest in economic research', NBER Working Paper No. 27849.

Fair, R.C. (2004), *Estimating How the Macroeconomy Works*, Cambridge, MA: Harvard University Press.

Fanti, L. and L. Zamparelli (2021), 'The paradox of thrift in a two-sector Kaleckian growth model', *Metroeconomica*, **72** (3), July, 526–38.

Farley, J., M. Burke, G. Glomenhoft, B. Kelly, D.F. Murray, S. Posner, M. Putnam, A. Scanlan and A. Witham (2013), 'Monetary and fiscal policies for a finite planet', *Sustainability*, **5**, 2008–26.

Fazzari, F.M. (1994–95), 'Why doubt the effectiveness of Keynesian fiscal policy?', *Journal of Post Keynesian Economics*, **17** (2), Winter, 231–48.

Fazzari, S.M., P. Ferri and E. Greenberg (1998), 'Aggregate demand and firm behavior: a new perspective on Keynesian microfoundations', *Journal of Post Keynesian Economics*, **20** (4), Summer, 527–59.

Fazzari, S.M., P. Ferri and E. Greenberg (2008), 'Cash flow, investment, and Keynes–Minsky cycles', *Journal of Economic Behavior and Organization*, **65**, March, 555–72.

Fazzari, S.M., P. Ferri, E. Greenberg and A.M. Variato (2013), 'Aggregate demand, instability, and growth', *Review of Keynesian Economics*, **1** (1), Spring, 1–21.

Fazzari, S., P. Ferri and A.M. Variato (2020), 'Demand-led growth with accommodating supply', *Cambridge Journal of Economics*, **44** (3), May, 583–605.

Fazzari, S.M. and T.L. Mott (1986–87), 'The investment theories of Kalecki and Keynes: an empirical study of firm data, 1970–1982', *Journal of Post Keynesian Economics*, **9** (2), Winter, 171–87.

Febrero, E., J. Uxó and F. Bermejo (2018), 'The financial crisis in the eurozone: a balance-of-payments crisis with a single currency?', *Review of Keynesian Economics*, **6** (2), 221–39.

Feiwel, G.R. (1972), 'Introduction: notes on the life and work of Michal Kalecki', in M. Kalecki, *The Last Phase in the Transformation of Capitalism*, New York: Monthly Review Press.

Felipe, J. and J.S.L. McCombie (2001), 'The CES production function, the accounting identity, and Occam's razor', *Applied Economics*, **33** (10), August, 1221–32.

Felipe, J. and J.S.L. McCombie (2005), 'How sound are the foundations of the aggregate production function?', *Eastern Economic Journal*, **31** (3), Summer, 467–88.
Felipe, J. and J.S.L. McCombie (2006), 'The tyranny of the identity: growth accounting revisited', *International Review of Applied Economics*, **20** (3), July, 283–99.
Felipe, J. and J.S.L. McCombie (2009), 'Are estimates of labour demand functions mere statistical artefacts?', *International Review of Applied Economics*, **23** (2), March, 147–68.
Felipe, J. and J.S.L. McCombie (2011–12), 'On Herbert Simon's criticisms of the Cobb–Douglas and the CES production functions', *Journal of Post Keynesian Economics*, **34** (2), Winter, 275–93.
Felipe, J. and J.S.L. McCombie (2013), *Aggregate Production Function and the Measurement of Technical Change: Not Even Wrong*, Cheltenham, UK and Northampton, MA, USA: Edward Elgar.
Ferguson, C.E. (1969), *The Neoclassical Theory of Production and Distribution*, Cambridge: Cambridge University Press.
Fernández-Huerga, E. (2008), 'The economic behavior of human beings: the Institutional/Post Keynesian model', *Journal of Economic Issues*, **42** (3), September, 709–26.
Fernández-Huerga, E. (2019), 'The post-Keyneisan view on labour demand in micro and macroeconomic fields', *Economics and Sociology*, **12** (2), 109–28.
Fernández-Huerga, E., J. Garcia-Arias and A. Slavador (2017), 'Labor supply: toward the construction of an alternative conception from post Keynesian and institutional economics', *Journal of Post Keynesian Economics*, **40** (4), 576–99.
Fiebiger, B. (2016a), 'Fiscal policy, monetary policy and the mechanics of modern clearing and settlement systems', *Review of Political Economy*, **28** (4), October, 590–608.
Fiebiger, B. (2016b), 'Rethinking the financialisation of non-financial corporations: a reappraisal of US empirical data', *Review of Political Economy*, **28** (3), July, 354–79.
Fiebiger, B. (2018), 'Semi-autonomous household expenditures as the causa causans of postwar US business cycles: the stability and instability of Luxemburg-type external markets', *Cambridge Journal of Economics*, **42** (1), January, 155–75.
Fiebiger, B. (2020), 'Some observations on endogeneity in the normal rate of capacity utilisation', *Review of Keynesian Economics*, **8** (3), Autumn, 385–406.
Fiebiger, B. and M. Lavoie (2017), 'The IMF and the new fiscalism: was there a U-turn?', *European Journal of Economics and Economic Policies: Intervention*, **14** (3), 314–32.
Fiebiger, B. and M. Lavoie (2019), 'Trend and business cycles with external markets: non-capacity generating semi-autonomous expenditures and effective demand', *Metroeconomica*, **70** (2), May, 247–62.
Fiebiger, B. and M. Lavoie (2020), 'Helicopter Ben, monetarism, the New Keynesian credit view and loanable funds', *Journal of Economic Issues*, **54** (1), March, 77–96.
Fiebiger, B. and M. Lavoie (2021), 'Central bankers and the rationale for unconventional monetary policies: reasserting, renouncing or recasting monetarism?', *Cambridge Journal of Economics*, **45** (1), January, 37–52.
Filardo, A.J. (1998) 'New evidence on the output cost of fighting inflation', *Federal Reserve Bank of Kansas City Quarterly Review*, **83** (3), 33–61.
Fine, B. (2002), 'Economic imperialism: a view from the periphery', *Review of Radical Political Economics*, **34** (2), Spring, 187–201.
Fishburn, P.C. (1974), 'Lexicographic orders, utilities and decision rules: a survey', *Management Science Theory*, **20** (11), July, 1442–71.
Fisher, F.M. (1971), 'Aggregate production functions and the explanation of wages', *Review of Economics and Statistics*, **53** (4), November, 305–25.
Fisher, I. (1933), 'The debt-deflation theory of great depressions', *Econometrica*, **1** (4), October, 337–57.
Flaschel, P. (2009), *The Macrodynamics of Capitalism: Elements for a Synthesis of Marx, Keynes and Schumpeter*, 2nd edn, Berlin: Springer-Verlag.
Fleming, J.M. (1962), 'Domestic financial policies under fixed and flexible exchange rates', *IMF Staff Papers*, **9** (3), November, 369–80.
Fog, B. (1956), 'A study of cost curves in industry', *Weltwirtshaftliches Archiv*, **77**, 44–53.

Foley, D. (2013), 'Notes on ideology and methodology, with addendum', in F.S. Lee and M. Lavoie (eds), *In Defense of Post-Keynesian Economics and Heterodox Economics: Responses to their Critics*, London: Routledge, pp. 230–40.
Fontana, G. (2003), 'Post Keynesian approaches to endogenous money: a time framework explanation', *Review of Political Economy*, **15** (3), 291–314.
Fontana, G. (2009), *Money, Uncertainty and Time*, London: Routledge.
Fontana, G. and B. Gerrard (2004), 'A Post Keynesian theory of decision making under uncertainty', *Journal of Economic Psychology*, **25** (5), October, 619–37.
Fontana, G. and B. Gerrard (2006), 'The future of Post Keynesian economics', *Banca Nationale del Lavoro Quarterly Review*, **59** (236), 49–80.
Fontana, G. and A. Palacio-Vera (2007), 'Are long-run price stability and short-run output stabilization all that monetary policy can aim for?', *Metroeconomica*, **58** (2), May, 269–98.
Fontana, G. and M. Sawyer (2013), 'Post-Keynesian and Kaleckian thoughts on ecological macroeconomics', *European Journal of Economics and Economic Policies: Intervention*, **10** (2), September, 256–67.
Fontana, G. and M. Sawyer (2016), 'Towards post-Keynesian ecological economics', *Ecological Economics*, **121**, January, 186–95.
Fontana, G. and M. Sawyer (2017), 'A rejoinder to a "A response to critiques of full reserve banking"', *Cambridge Journal of Economics*, **41** (6), November, 1741–8.
Fontana, G. and M. Setterfield (eds) (2009a), *Macroeconomic Theory and Macroeconomic Pedagogy*, Basingstoke: Palgrave Macmillan.
Fontana, G. and M. Setterfield (2009b), 'Macroeconomics, endogenous money and the contemporary financial crisis: a teaching model', *International Journal of Pluralism and Economics Education*, **1** (1–2), 130–47.
Forder, J. (2014), *Macroeconomics and the Phillips Curve*, Oxford: Oxford University Press.
Forstater, M. (1998), 'Flexible full employment: structural implications of discretionary public sector employment', *Journal of Economic Issues*, **32** (2), June, 557–63.
Forstater, M. and W. Mosler (2005), 'The natural rate of interest is zero', *Journal of Economic Issues*, **39** (2), June, 535–42.
Fox, J. (2009), *The Myth of the Rational Market: A History of Risk, Reward, and Delusion on Wall Street*, New York: HarperCollins.
Francis, A. (1980), 'Company objectives, managerial motivations and the behaviour of large firms: an empirical test of the theory of "managerial" capitalism', *Cambridge Journal of Economics*, **4** (4), December, 349–61.
Franke, R. (2015), 'An examination of Professor Shaikh's proposal to tame Harrodian instability', *European Journal of Economics and Economic Policies: Intervention*, **12** (1), 7–19.
Franke, R. (2017a), 'A simple approach to overcome the problems arising from the Keynesian stability condition', *European Journal of Economics and Economic Policies: Intervention*, **14** (1), 48–69.
Franke, R. (2017b), 'What output-capital ratio to adopt for macroeconomic calibrations?', *International Review of Applied Economics*, **31** (2), 208–224.
Franke, R. (2018), 'Can monetary policy tame Harrodian instability?', *Metroeconomica*, **69** (3), July, 593–618.
Franke, R. (2020), 'An attempt at a reconciliation of the Sraffian and Kaleckian views on desired utilization', *European Journal of Economics and Economic Policies: Intervention*, **17** (1), 61–77.
Franke, R. (2021), 'Pure Harrodian dynamics: heterogeneous expectations and the loss of three established propositions', Working Paper, DOI: 10.13140/RG.2.2.17746.07365.
Franke, R. and W. Semmler (1991), 'A dynamical macroeconomic growth model with external financing of firms: a numerical stability analysis', in E.J. Nell and W. Semmler (eds), *Nicholas Kaldor and Mainstream Economics: Confrontation or Convergence?*, London: Macmillan, pp. 335–59.
Fratini, S.M. (2019), 'On the second stage of the Cambridge capital controversy', *Journal of Economic Surveys*, **33** (4), September, 1073–93.
Freedman, C., G.C. Harcourt and P. Kriesler (2004), 'Has the long-run Phillips curve turned horizontal?', in G. Argyrous, M. Forstater, and G. Mongiovi (eds), *Growth, Distribution and Effective Demand: Alternatives to Economic Orthodoxy*, Armonk, NY: M.E. Sharpe, pp. 144–62.

Freitas, F. and F. Serrano (2015), 'Growth rate and level effects: the stability of the adjustment of capacity to demand and the Sraffian supermultiplier', *Review of Political Economy*, **27** (3), July, 258–81.
Frenkel, R. (2006), 'An alternative to inflation targeting in Latin America: macroeconomic policies focused on employment', *Journal of Post Keynesian Economics*, **28** (4), Summer, 573–92.
Frenkel, R. (2007), 'The sustainability of monetary sterilization policies', *CEPAL Review*, **93**, December, 29–36.
Friedman, M. (1953), 'The methodology of positive economics', in *Essays in Positive Economics*, Chicago, IL: Chicago University Press, pp. 3–43.
Fritz, B., L.F. de Paula and D. Prates (2018), 'Global currency hierarchy and national policy space: a framework for peripheral economies', *European Journal of Economics and Economic Policies: Intervention*, **15** (2), 208–18.
Frydman, R. and M.D. Goldberg (2014), *Imperfect Knowledge Economics: Exchange Rates and Risk*, Princeton: Princeton University Press.
Fujimoto, T. and D. Leslie (1983), 'A two-class model of Keynesian unemployment', *Metroeconomica*, **35** (1–2), February, 54–71.
Fujita, S. (2019), 'Mark-up pricing, sectoral dynamics, and the traverse process in a two-sector Kaleckian economy', *Cambridge Journal of Economics*, **43** (2), March, 465–79.
Fullbrook, E. (2003), *The Crisis in Economics: The Post-Autistic Economics Movement: The First 600 Days*, London; Routledge.
Fullbrook, E. (2009), 'Introduction: Lawson's reorientation', in E. Fullbrook (ed.), *Ontology and Economics; Tony Lawson and His Critics*, London: Routledge, pp. 1–12.
Fullbrook, E. (2013), 'New paradigm economics', *Real-World Economics Review*, **65**, September, 129–31.
Fuller, D. and D. Geide-Stevenson (2003), 'Consensus among economists: revisited', *Journal of Economic Education*, **34** (4), Fall, 369–87.
Fullwiler, S.T. (2003), 'Timeliness and the Fed's daily tactics', *Journal of Economic Issues*, **37** (4), December, 851–80.
Fullwiler, S.T. (2005), 'Paying interest on reserve balances: it's more significant than you think', *Journal of Economic Issues*, **39** (2), June, 543–50.
Fullwiler, S.T. (2006), 'Setting interest rates in the modern money era', *Journal of Post Keynesian Economics*, **28** (3), Spring, 496–525.
Fullwiler, S.T. (2013), 'An endogenous money perspective on the post-crisis monetary policy debate', *Review of Keynesian Economics*, **1** (2), Summer, 171–94.
Fullwiler, S.T. (2017), 'Modern central-bank operations: the general principles', in L.P. Rochon and S. Rossi (eds), *Advances in Endogenous Money Analysis*, Cheltenham, UK and Northampton, MA, USA: Edward Elgar, pp. 50–87.
Fung, M.V. (2006), 'Developments in behavioral finance and experimental economics and post Keynesian finance theory', *Journal of Post Keynesian Economics*, **29** (1), Fall, 19–39.
Gabor, D. (2016), 'The (impossible) repo trinity: the political economy of repo markets', *Review of International Political Economy*, **23** (6), 967–1000.
Gabor, D. (2020), 'Critical macro-finance: a theoretical lens', *Finance and Society*, **6** (1), 45–55.
Gabor, D. and C. Ban (2016), 'Banking on bonds: the new links between states and markets', *Journal of Common Market Studies*, **54** (3), 617–35.
Galbraith, James K. (1994–95), 'John Maynard Nosferatu', *Journal of Post Keynesian Economics*, **17** (2), Winter, 249–60.
Galbraith, James K. (2008), *The Predator State*, New York: Free Press.
Galbraith, John K. (1952), *A Theory of Price Control*, Cambridge, MA: Cambridge University Press.
Galbraith, John K. (1958), *The Affluent Society*, Boston, MA: Houghton Mifflin.
Galbraith, John K. (1972), *The New Industrial State*, New York: New American Library, 2nd edn (first published 1967).
Galbraith, John K. (1975), *Economics and the Public Purpose*, Harmondsworth: Penguin Books (first published 1973).

Galbraith, John K. (1978), 'On post Keynesian economics', *Journal of Post Keynesian Economics*, **1** (1), Fall, 8–11.
Galbraith, John K. (1990), *A Short History of Financial Euphoria*, Harmondsworth: Penguin Books.
Galbraith, John K. (2004), *The Economics of Innocent Fraud: Truth for Our Time*, Boston, MA: Houghton Mifflin.
Galí, J. and L. Gambetti (2020), 'Has the U.S. wage Phillips curve flattened? A semi-structural exploration', in G. Castex, L. Galí and D. Saravia (eds), *Changing Inflation Dynamics, Evolving Monetary Policy*, Santiago, Chile: Banco Central de Chile, pp. 149–72.
Gallagher, K.P. (2015), 'Contesting the governance of capital flows at the IMF', *Governance*, **28** (2), April, 185–98.
Garber, P. (2010), 'The mechanics of intra euro capital flight', Deutsche Bank, 10 December, available at http://fincake.ru/stock/reviews/56090/download/54478.
Garegnani, P. (1970), 'Heterogeneous capital, the production function and the theory of distribution', *Review of Economic Studies*, **37** (3), July, 407–36.
Garegnani, P. (1979), 'Notes on consumption, investment and effective demand II', *Cambridge Journal of Economics*, **3** (1), January, 63–82.
Garegnani, P. (1983), 'Two routes to effective demand', in J.A. Kregel (ed.), *Distribution, Effective Demand and International Economic Relations*, London: Macmillan, pp. 69–80.
Garegnani P. (1990a), 'Quantity of capital', in J. Eatwell, M. Milgate and P. Newman (eds), *Capital Theory: The New Palgrave*, London: Macmillan, pp. 1–78.
Garegnani, P. (1990b), 'Sraffa: Classical versus marginalist analysis', in K. Bharadwaj and B. Schefold (eds), *Essays on Piero Sraffa: Critical Perspectives on the Revival of Classical Theory*, London: Unwin Hyman, pp. 112–41.
Garegnani, P. (1992), Some notes for an analysis of accumulation', in J. Halevi, D. Laibman and E.J. Nell (eds), *Beyond the Steady State: A Revival of Growth Theory*, New York: St. Martin's Press, pp. 47–71.
Georgescu-Roegen, N. (1950), 'The theory of choice and the constancy of economic laws', *Quarterly Journal of Economics*, **64** (1), February, 125–38.
Georgescu-Roegen, N. (1954), 'Choice, expectations and measurability', *Quarterly Journal of Economics*, **68** (4), November, 503–34.
Georgescu-Roegen, N. (1966), 'The nature of expectations and uncertainty', in *Analytical Economics*, Cambridge, MA: Harvard University Press, pp. 241–75.
Georgescu-Roegen, N. (1971), *The Entropy Law and the Economic Process*, Cambridge, MA: Harvard University Press.
Gerrard, B. (1995), 'Probability, uncertainty and behaviour: a Keynesian perspective', in S. Dow and J. Hillard (eds), *Keynes, Knowledge and Uncertainty*, Aldershot, UK and Brookfield, VT, USA: Edward Elgar, pp. 177–95.
Gigerenzer, G. (2008), *Rationality for Mortals: How People Cope with Uncertainty*, Oxford: Oxford University Press.
Gigerenzer, G. and R. Selten (2001), 'Rethinking rationality', in G. Gigerenzer and R. Selten (eds), *Bounded Rationality: The Adaptive Toolbox*, London: MIT Press, pp. 1–12.
Giotis, G. and M. Chletsos (2015), 'Is there publication selection bias in minimum wage research during the five-year period from 2010 to 2014?', *Economics: The Open Access, Open Assessment E-Journal*. No 2015-58, August.
Giovannoni, O. (2008), 'What did the Fed do when inflation died?', *International Journal of Political Economy*, **37** (2), Summer, 49–70.
Girardi, D. and R. Pariboni (2019), 'Normal utilization as the adjusting variable in Neo-Kaleckian growth models: a critique', *Metroeconomica*, **70** (2), May, 341–58.
Girardi, D. and R. Pariboni (2020), 'Autonomous demand and the investment share', *Review of Keynesian Economics*, **8** (3), Autumn, 428–53.
Godley, W. (1983), 'Keynes and the management of real national income and expenditure', in D. Worswick and J. Trevithick (eds), *Keynes and the Modern World*, Cambridge: Cambridge University Press, pp. 135–77.

Godley, W. (1992), 'Maastricht and all that', *London Review of Books*, **14** (19), 8 October, 3–4. Reprinted in M. Lavoie and G. Zezza (eds), *The Stock–Flow Consistent Approach: Selected Writings of Wynne Godley*, Basingstoke: Palgrave Macmillan, pp. 189–93.

Godley, W. (1993), 'Time, increasing returns and institutions in macroeconomics', in S. Biasco, A. Roncaglia and M. Salvati (eds), *Market and Institutions in Economic Development: Essays in Honour of Paolo Sylos Labini*, New York: St. Martin's Press, pp. 59–82.

Godley, W. (1996), 'Money, finance and national income determination: an integrated approach', Working Paper No. 167, The Levy Economics Institute of Bard College.

Godley, W. (1999a), 'Money and credit in a Keynesian model of income determination', *Cambridge Journal of Economics*, **23** (4), April, 393–411.

Godley, W. (1999b), 'Open economy macroeconomics using models of closed systems', Working Paper No. 281, Jerome Levy Economics Institute of Bard College.

Godley, W. (1999c), 'Seven unsustainable processes', Special Report, Jerome Levy Economics Institute of Bard College. Reproduced in Lavoie and Zezza (eds), *The Stock–Flow Consistent Approach: Selected Writings of Wynne Godley*, Basingstoke: Palgrave Macmillan, pp. 216–54.

Godley, W. (2004), 'Weaving cloth from Graziani's thread: endogenous money in a simple (but complete) model', in R. Arena and N. Salvadori (eds), *Money, Credit and the Role of the State: Essays in Honour of Augusto Graziani*, Aldershot, UK and Brookfield, US: Ashgate, pp. 127–35.

Godley, W. (2012), 'Macroeconomics without equilibrium or disequilibrium', in M. Lavoie and G. Zezza (eds), *The Stock–Flow Consistent Approach: Selected Writings of Wynne Godley*, Basingstoke: Palgrave Macmillan, pp. 90–122.

Godley, W. and F. Cripps (1976), 'A formal analysis of the Cambridge Economic Policy Group Model', *Economica*, **43** (172), September, 335–48.

Godley, W. and F. Cripps (1983), *Macroeconomics*, London: Fontana.

Godley, W. and M. Lavoie (2005–06), 'Comprehensive accounting in simple open economy macroeconomics with endogenous sterilization or flexible exchange rates', *Journal of Post Keynesian Economics*, **28** (2), Winter, 241–76.

Godley, W. and M. Lavoie (2007a), *Monetary Economics: An Integrated Approach to Credit, Money, Income, Production and Wealth*, Basingstoke: Palgrave Macmillan.

Godley, W. and M. Lavoie (2007b), 'Fiscal policy in a stock–flow consistent (SFC) model', *Journal of Post Keynesian Economics*, **30** (1), Fall, 79–100.

Godley, W. and M. Lavoie (2007c), 'A simple model of three economies with two currencies: the Eurozone and the USA', *Cambridge Journal of Economics*, **31** (1), January, 1–23.

Godley, W., D.B. Papadimitriou and G. Zezza (2008), 'Prospects for the United States and the world: a crisis that conventional remedies cannot resolve', Strategic Analysis, Levy Economics Institute of Bard College, December.

Goldstein, J.P. (1999), 'The simple analytics and empirics of the cyclical profit squeeze and cyclical underconsumption theories: clearing the air', *Review of Radical Political Economics*, **31** (2), Spring, 74–88.

Goldstein, J.P. and M.G. Hillard (2009), 'Introduction: a second-generation synthesis of heterodox macroeconomic principles', in J.P. Goldstein and M.G. Hillard (eds), *Heterodox Macroeconomics: Keynes, Marx and Globalization*, London: Routledge, pp. 3–23.

Goodhart, C.A.E. (1984), *Monetary Theory and Policy: The U.K. Experience*, London: Macmillan.

Goodwin, C. (2000), 'Comment: it's the homogeneity, stupid!', *Journal of the History of Economic Thought*, **22** (2), June, 179–83.

Goodwin, N., J.A. Nelson, F. Ackerman and T. Weisskopf (2009), *Microeconomics in Context*, 2nd edn, Armonk, NY: M.E. Sharpe.

Goodwin, R. (1967), 'A growth cycle', in C.H. Feinstein (ed.), *Socialism, Capitalism and Economic Growth*, Cambridge: Cambridge University Press, pp. 54–8.

Gordon, D.M. (1994), 'Putting heterodox macro to the test: comparing post-Keynesian, Marxian, and Social Structuralist macroeconometric models of the post-war US economy', in M.A. Glick (ed.), *Competition, Technology and Money: Classical and Post-Keynesian Perspectives*, Aldershot, UK and Brookfield, VT, USA: Edward Elgar, pp. 143–85.

Gordon, M.J. (1987), 'Insecurity, growth, and the rise of capitalism', *Journal of Post Keynesian Economics*, **9** (4), Summer, 529–51.
Gowdy, J.M. (1991), 'Bioeconomics and post Keynesian economics: a search for common ground', *Ecological Economics*, **3** (1), March, 77–87.
Gowdy, J.M. (1993), 'Georgescu-Roegen's utility theory applied to environmental economics', in J.C. Dragan, E.K. Seifert and M.C. Demetrescu (eds), *Entropy and Bioeconomics*, Milan: Nagard, pp. 230–40.
Gowdy, J.M. and K. Mayumi (2001), 'Reformulating the foundation of consumer choice theory and environmental valuation', *Ecological Economics*, **39** (2), November, 223–37.
Gowdy, J.M. and J.L. Miller (1990), 'Harrod–Robinson–Read measures of primary input productivity theory and evidence from U.S. data', *Journal of Post Keynesian Economics*, **12** (4), Summer, 591–604.
Grabel, I. (1996), 'Financial markets, the state and economic development: controversies within theory and policy', *International Papers in Political Economy*, **3** (1), 1–42.
Grabel, I. (2006), 'A post-Keynesian analysis of financial crisis in the developing world and directions for reform', in P. Arestis and M. Sawyer (eds), *A Handbook of Alternative Monetary Economics*, Cheltenham, UK and Northampton, MA, USA: Edward Elgar, pp. 403–19.
Grabel, I. (2015), 'The rebranding of capital controls in an era of productive incoherence', *Review of International Political Economy*, **22** (1), 7–43.
Granger, C.W.J. and P. Newbold (1974), 'Spurious regressions in econometrics', *Journal of Econometrics*, **2** (2), July, 111–20.
Gray, J. and R. Chapman (2004), 'The significance of segmentation for Institutionalist theory and public policy', in D.P. Champlin and J.T. Knoedler (eds), *The Institutionalist Tradition in Labor Economics*, Armonk, NY: M.E. Sharpe, pp. 117–30.
Graziani, A. (1984), 'The debate on Keynes's finance motive', *Economic Notes by Monte dei Paschi di Siena*, **1** (1), 5–33.
Graziani, A. (2003), *The Monetary Theory of Production*, Cambridge: Cambridge University Press.
Gregg, P., S. Jewell and I. Tonk (2012), 'Executive pay and performance: did bankers' bonuses cause the crisis?', *International Review of Finance*, **12** (1), March, 89–122.
Grossman-Wirth, V. (2019), 'What monetary policy operational frameworks in the new financial environment? A comparison of the US Fed and the Eurosystem perspective', *International Journal of Political Economy*, **48** (4), Winter, 336–52.
Gu, G.C. and F.S. Lee (2012), 'Prices and pricing', in J.E. King (ed.), *The Elgar Companion to Post Keynesian Economics, Second Edition*, Cheltenham, UK and Northampton, MA, USA: Edward Elgar, pp. 456–63.
Gualerzi, D. (2001), *Consumption and Growth: Recovery and Structural Change in the US Economy*, Cheltenham, UK and Northampton, MA, USA: Edward Elgar.
Guerrien, B. (1989), *Concurrence, flexibilité et stabilité*, Paris: Economica.
Guerrien, B. (2009), 'Irrelevance and ideology', in E. Fullbrook (ed.), *Ontology and Economics: Tony Lawson and His Critics*, London: Routledge, pp. 158–61.
Gyöngyössy, I. (1984), *International Money Flows and Currency Crises*, The Hague: Martinus Nijhoff.
Hafner, S., A. Anger-Kraavi, I. Monasterolo and A. Jones (2020), 'Emergence of new economics energy transition models: a review', *Ecological Economics*, **177**, November, article 1006779, 1–25.
Hagemann, H. (1991), 'A Kaldorian saving function in a two-sectoral linear growth model', in E.J. Nell and W. Semmler (eds), *Nicholas Kaldor and Mainstream Economics*, London: Macmillan, pp. 449–68.
Hahn, F.H. (1972), *The Share of Wages in National Income*, London: Weidenfeld & Nicolson.
Haight, A.D. (2007–08), 'A Keynesian angle for the Taylor rule: mortgage rates, monthly payment illusion, and the scarecrow effect of inflation', *Journal of Post Keynesian Economics*, **30** (2), Winter, 259–78.
Haines, W.M. (1982), 'The psychoeconomics of human needs: Maslow's hierarchy and Marshall's organic growth', *Journal of Behavioral Economics*, **11** (2), Winter, 97–121.

Haldane, A.G. and V. Madouros (2012), 'The dog and the frisbee', in Federal Reserve Bank of Kansas City, *The Changing Policy Landscape*, Jackson Hole Economic Policy Symposium, pp.109–59, https://www.kansascityfed.org/documents/6926/DogFrisbee_Haldane_JH2012.pdf.
Halevi, J. (1985), 'The contemporary significance of Baran and Sweezy's notion of monopolistic capitalism', in M. Jarsulic (ed.), *Money and Macro Policy*, Boston. MA: Kluwer–Nijhoff, pp. 109–34.
Halevi, J. and P. Kriesler (1991), 'Kalecki, classical economics and the surplus approach', *Review of Political Economy*, **3** (1), January, 79–92.
Hall, R.L. and C.J. Hitch (1939), 'Price theory and business behaviour', *Oxford Economic Papers*, **1** (2), May, 12–45.
Hamermesh, D.S. (1986), 'The demand for labor in the long run', in O. Ashenfelter and R. Layard (eds), *Handbook of Labor Economics*, Amsterdam: North-Holland, Vol. 1, pp. 429–71.
Hamouda, O.F. and G.C. Harcourt (1988), 'Post Keynesianism: from criticism to coherence?', *Bulletin of Economic Research*, **40** (1), January, 1–33.
Hanmer, L.C. and A.H. Akram-Lodhi (1998), 'In "the house of the spirits": toward a Post Keynesian theory of the household?', *Journal of Post Keynesian Economics*, **20** (3), Spring, 415–434.
Hanson, J.D. and D.A. Kysar (1999a), 'Taking behavioralism seriously: the problem of market manipulation', *New York University Law Review*, **74**, 630–749.
Hanson, J.D. and D.A. Kysar (1999b), 'Taking behavioralism seriously: some evidence of market manipulation', *Harvard Law Review*, **112** (7), May, 1420–572.
Harcourt, G.C. (1972), *Some Cambridge Controversies in the Theory of Capital*, Cambridge: Cambridge University Press.
Harcourt, G.C. (1987), 'Foreword', in P. Kriesler, *Kalecki's Microanalysis: The Development of Kalecki's Analysis of Pricing*, Cambridge: Cambridge University Press, pp. xi–xii.
Harcourt, G.C. (2001a), 'Post-Keynesian thought', in *50 Years a Keynesian and Other Essays*, Basingstoke, UK: Palgrave, pp. 263–85.
Harcourt, G.C. (2001b), 'On Keynes and Chick on prices in modern capitalism', in P. Arestis, M. Desai and S. Dow (eds), *Money, Macroeconomics and Keynes: Essays in Honour of Victoria Chick, Volume One*, London: Routledge, pp. 115–23.
Harcourt, G.C. (2006), *The Structure of Post-Keynesian Economics: The Core Contributions of the Pioneers*, Cambridge: Cambridge University Press.
Harcourt, G.C. (2012), *The Making of a Post-Keynesian Economist: Cambridge Harvest*, Basingstoke: Palgrave Macmillan.
Harris, D.J. (1974), 'The price policy of firms, the level of employment and distribution of income in the short run', *Australian Economic Papers*, **13** (22), June, 144–51.
Harcourt, G.C. and P. Kenyon (1976), 'Pricing and the investment decision', *Kyklos*, **29** (3), September, 449–77.
Hardt, L. and S.W. O'Neill (2017), 'Ecological macroeconomic models: assessing current developments', *Ecological Economics*, **134**, April, 198–211.
Harris D.J. (1978), *Capital Accumulation and Income Distribution*, Stanford, CA: Stanford University Press.
Harrod, R.F. (1933), *International Economics*, Cambridge: Cambridge University Press.
Harrod, R.F. (1939), 'An essay in dynamic theory', *Economic Journal*, **49** (193), March, 14–33.
Harrod, R.F. (1952), *Economic Essays*, London: Macmillan.
Harrod, R.F. (1972a), 'Imperfect competition, aggregate demand and inflation', *Economic Journal*, **82** (325), March, 392–401.
Harrod, R.F. (1972b), 'Uncertainty and dynamic axioms', in C.F. Carter and J.L. Ford (eds), *Uncertainty and Expectations: Essays in Honour of G.L.S. Shackle*, Oxford: Basil Blackwell, pp. 122–35.
Harrod, R.F. (1973), *Economic Dynamics*, London: Macmillan.
Hart, N. and P. Kriesler (2016), 'Keynes, Kalecki, Sraffa: coherence within pluralism?, in J. Courvisanos, J. Doughney and A. Millmow (eds), *Reclaiming Pluralism in Economics*, London: Routledge, pp. 186–202.

Harvey, J.T. (1991), 'A Post Keynesian view of exchange rate determination', *Journal of Post Keynesian Economics*, **14** (1), Fall, 61–71.
Harvey, J.T. (1993), 'Daily exchange rate variance', *Journal of Post Keynesian Economics*, **15** (4), Summer, 515–40.
Harvey, J.T. (1998–99), 'The nature of expectations in the foreign exchange market: a test of competing theories', *Journal of Post Keynesian Economics*, **21** (2), Winter, 181–200.
Harvey, J.T. (1998), 'Heuristic judgment theory', *Journal of Economic Issues*, **32** (1), March, 47–64.
Harvey, J.T. (2012), 'Exchange rates', in J.E. King (ed.), *The Elgar Companion to Post Keynesian Economics*, 2nd edn, Cheltenham, UK and Northampton, MA, USA: Edward Elgar, pp. 185–9.
Hayek, F.A. (1941), *The Pure Theory of Capital*, Chicago, IL: University of Chicago Press.
Haynes, W.W. (1964), 'Pricing practices in small firms', *Southern Economic Journal*, **30** (4), April, 315–24.
Hein, E. (2002), 'Monetary policy and wage bargaining in the EMU: restrictive ECB policies, high unemployment, nominal wage restraint and inflation above the target', *Banca Nazionale del Lavoro Quarterly Review*, **55** (222), 229–337.
Hein, E. (2008), *Money, Distribution Conflict and Capital Accumulation*, Basingstoke: Palgrave Macmillan.
Hein, E. (2012), *The Macroeconomics of Finance-dominated Capitalism and its Crisis*, Cheltenham, UK and Northampton, MA, USA: Edward Elgar.
Hein, E. (2014), *Distribution and Growth After Keynes: A Post-Keynesian Guide*, Cheltenham, UK and Northampton, MA, USA: Edward Elgar.
Hein, E. (2017), 'Post-Keynesian macroeconomics since the mid 1990s: main developments', *European Journal of Economics and Economic Policies: Intervention*, **14** (2), 131–73.
Hein, E. (2018), 'Autonomous government expenditure growth, deficits, debt and distribution in a neo-Kaleckian growth model', *Journal of Post Keynesian Economics*, **41** (2), 316–38.
Hein, E. (2020), 'Gender issues in Kaleckian distribution and growth models: on the macroeconomics of the gender gap', *Review of Political Economy*, **32** (4), October, 640–64.
Hein, E., M. Lavoie and T. van Treeck (2011), 'Some instability puzzles in Kaleckian models of growth and distribution: a critical survey', *Cambridge Journal of Economics*, **35** (1), May, 587–612.
Hein, E., M. Lavoie and T. van Treeck (2012), 'Harrodian instability and the normal rate of capacity utilization in Kaleckian models of distribution and growth – a survey', *Metroeconomica*, **63** (1), February, 39–69.
Hein, E. and J. Martschin (2021), 'Demand and growth regimes in finance-dominated capitalism and the role of the macroeconomic policy regime: a post-Keynesian comparative study on France, Germany, Italy and Spain before and after the Great Financial Crisis and the Great Recession', *Review of Evolutionary Political Economy*, **2** (3), December, 493–527.
Hein, E. and M. Mundt (2012), 'Financialisation and the requirements and potentials for wage-led recovery – a review focusing on the G20', Working Paper No. 37, Conditions of Work and Employment series, International Labour Office.
Hein, E., W. Paternesi Meloni and P. Tridico (2021), 'Welfare models and demand-led growth regimes before and after the financial and economic crisis', *Review of International Political Economy*, **28** (5), 1196–1223.
Hein, E. and E. Stockhammer (2010), 'Macroeconomic policy mix, employment and inflation in a post-Keynesian alternative to the New Consensus model', *Review of Political Economy*, **22** (3), July, 317–54.
Hein, E. and E. Stockhammer (2011), 'A post-Keynesian macroeconomic model of inflation, distribution and employment', in E. Hein and E. Stockhammer (eds), *A Modern Guide to Keynesian Macroeconomics and Economic Policies*, Cheltenham, UK and Northampton, MA, USA: Edward Elgar, pp. 112–36.
Hein, E. and A. Tarassow (2010), 'Distribution, aggregate demand and productivity growth: theory and empirical results for six OECD countries based on a post-Kaleckian model', *Cambridge Journal of Economics*, **34** (4), July, 727–54.

Hein, E. and L. Vogel (2008), 'Distribution and growth reconsidered: Empirical results for six OECD countries', *Cambridge Journal of Economics*, **32** (3), May, 479–511.
Hein, E. and R. Woodgate (2021), 'Stability issues in Kaleckian models driven by autonomous demand growth—Harrodian instability and debt dynamics', *Metroeconomica*, **72** (2), May, 388–404.
Heiner, R.A. (1983), 'The origin of predictable behavior', *American Economic Review*, **73** (4), September, 560–95.
Heinsohn, G. and O. Steiger (1983), 'Private property, debts and interest or: the origin of money and the rise and fall of monetary economics', *Studi Economici*, **21**, 5–55.
Heinsohn, G. and O. Steiger (2000), 'The property theory of interest and money', in J. Smithin (ed.), *What is Money?*, London; Routledge, pp. 67–100.
Hendry, D.F. (1980), 'Econometrics – alchemy or science?', *Economica*, **47**, November, 387–406.
Henry, J. (1987), 'Equilibrium as a process', *Économie appliquée*, **40** (3), 463–82.
Henry, J. (1991), *La théorie du commerce extérieur dans le temps historique: une analyse post-Keynésienne*, Paris: Presses Universitaires de France.
Henry, J. (1993), 'Post-Keynesian methods and the post-classical approach', *International Papers in Political Economy*, **1** (2), 1–26.
Henry, J. and M. Seccareccia (1982), 'Introduction: la théorie post-keynésienne: contributions et essais de synthèse', *Actualité Économique*, **58** (1–2), January–June, 5–16.
Herndon, T., M. Ash and R. Pollin (2014), 'Does high public debt consistently stifle economic growth? A critique of Reinhart and Rogoff', *Cambridge Journal of Economics*, **38** (2), March, 254–79.
Herr, H. (2009), 'The labour market in a Keynesian economic regime: theoretical debate and empirical findings', *Cambridge Journal of Economics*, **33** (5), September, 949–65.
Hewitson, G. (1997), 'The post-Keynesian "demand for credit" model', *Australian Economic Papers*, **36** (68), June, 127–43.
Hey, J.D. (1982), 'Search for rules for search', *Journal of Economic Behavior and Organization*, **3** (1), March, 65–81.
Hicks, J.R. (1950), *A Contribution to the Theory of the Trade Cycle*, Oxford: Clarendon Press.
Hicks, J.R. (1955), 'The economic foundations of wage policy', *Economic Journal*, **65** (259), September, 389–404.
Hicks, J. (1974), *The Crisis in Keynesian Economics*, Oxford: Basil Blackwell.
Hicks, J.R. (1975), 'What is wrong with Monetarism?', *Lloyds Bank Review*, October, 1–13.
Hicks, J. (1982), *Money, Interest and Wages*, Cambridge, MA: Harvard University Press.
Hicks, J. (1985), 'Sraffa and Ricardo: a critical view', in G.A. Caravale (ed.), *The Legacy of Ricardo*, New York: Basil Blackwell, pp. 305–19.
Hicks, J. (1990), 'Ricardo and Sraffa', in K. Bharadwaj and B. Schefold (eds), *Essays on Piero Sraffa: Critical Perspectives on the Revival of Classical Theory*, London: Unwin Hyman, pp. 99–102.
Hoang-Ngoc, L. (2013), 'Whither heterodoxy? Or where is heterodox economics going?, in F.S. Lee and M. Lavoie (eds), *In Defense of Post-Keynesian Economics and Heterodox Economics: Responses to their Critics*, London: Routledge, pp. 241–52.
Hodgson, G. (1982), 'Theoretical and policy implications of variable productivity', *Cambridge Journal of Economics*, **6** (3), September, 213–26.
Hodgson, G.M. (1988), *Economics and Institution: A Manifesto for a Modern Institutional Economics*, Cambridge: Polity Press.
Hodgson, G. (1989), 'Post-Keynesianism and Institutionalism: the missing link', in J. Pheby (ed.), *New Directions in Post-Keynesian Economics*, Aldershot, UK and Brookfield, VT, USA: Edward Elgar, pp. 94–123.
Hodgson, G.M. (2004), 'Reclaiming habits for Institutional economics', *Journal of Economic Psychology*, **25** (5), October, 651–60.
Hodgson, G.M. (2011), 'The eclipse of the uncertainty concept in mainstream economics', *Journal of Economic Issues*, **45** (1), March, 159–75.
Hodgson, G.M. (2019), *Is There a Future for Heterodox Economics? Institutions, Ideology and a Scientific Community*, Cheltenham, UK and Northampton, MA, USA: Edward Elgar.

Holmes, A. (1969), 'Operational constraints on the stabilisation of money supply growth', in *Controlling Monetary Aggregates*, Boston, MA: Federal Reserve Bank of Boston, pp. 65–77.

Holt, R.P.F. (2007), 'What is Post Keynesian economics?', in M. Forstater, G. Mongiovi and S. Pressman (eds), *Post-Keynesian Macroeconomics: Essays in Honour of Ingrid Rima*, London: Routledge, pp. 89–107.

Holt, R.P.F. and S. Pressman (eds) (2001), *A New Guide to Post Keynesian Economics*, London: Routledge.

Holt, R.P.F., S. Pressman and C.L. Spash (eds) (2009), *Post Keynesian and Ecological Economics: Confronting Environmental Issues*, Cheltenham, UK and Northampton, MA, USA: Edward Elgar.

Houthakker, H.S. and L.D. Taylor (1970), *Consumer Demand in the United States: Analyses and Projections*, 2nd edn, Cambridge, MA: Harvard University Press.

Howells, P. (2009), 'Money and banking in a realistic macro model', in G. Fontana and M. Setterfield (eds), *Macroeconomic Theory and Macroeconomic Pedagogy*, Basingstoke: Palgrave Macmillan, pp. 160–87.

Howells, P. (2010), 'The money supply in macroeconomics', in M. Galindo-Martin and C. Spiller (eds), *Issues in Economic Thought*, New York: Nova Science, pp. 161–84.

Hudson, M. (2010), *America's Protectionist Takeoff, 1815–1914: The Neglected American School of Political Economy*, ISLET.

Hunt, E.K. (1992), 'Analytical Marxism', in B. Roberts and S. Feiner (eds), *Radical Economics*. Boston: Kluwer Academic, pp. 91–107.

Ihrig, J. and S. Wolla (2020), 'Let's close the gap: revisiting teaching materials to reflect how the Federal Reserve implements monetary policy', Finance and Economics Discussion Series 2020–092, Federal Reserve Board.

Innes, A.M. (1913), 'What is money?', *Banking Law Journal*, May, 377–408. Reproduced in L.R. Wray (ed.), *Credit and State Theories of Money: The Contributions of A. Mitchell Innes*, Cheltenham, UK and Northampton, MA, USA: Edward Elgar, 2004, pp. 14–49.

Ioannidis, J.P.A., T.D. Stanley and H. Doucouliagos (2017), 'The power of bias in economics research', *Economic Journal*, **127**, October, F236-F265.

Ironmonger, D.S. (1972), *New Commodities and Consumer Behaviour*, Cambridge: Cambridge University Press.

Isaac, A.G. and Y.K. Kim (2013), 'Consumer and corporate debt: a neo-Kaleckian synthesis', *Metroeconomica*, **64** (2), May, 244–71.

Isard, P. (1995), *Exchange Rate Economics*. Cambridge: Cambridge University Press.

Jackson, A. and T. Jackson (2021), 'Modelling energy transition risk: the impact of declining energy returns on investment (EROI)', *Ecological Economics*, **185**, July, article 107023, 1–27.

Jackson, T. and P.A. Victor (2015), 'Does credit create a "growth imperative"? A quasi-stationary economy with interest-bearing debt', *Ecological Economics*, **120**, December, 32–48.

Jackson, T. and P.A. Victor (2016), 'Does slow growth lead to rising inequality? Some theoretical reflections and numerical simulations', *Ecological Economics*, **121**, January, 206–19.

Jackson, T. and P.A. Victor (2020), 'The transition to a sustainable prosperity – a stock-flow consistent ecological macroeconomic model for Canada', *Ecological Economics*, **177**, November, article 106787, 1–14.

Jakab, Z. and M. Kumhoff (2015), 'Banks are not intermediaries of loanable funds – and why this matters', Staff Working Paper 529, Bank of England.

Jakab, Z. and M. Kumhoff (2019), 'Banks are not intermediaries of loanable funds – facts, theory and evidence', Staff Working Paper 761, Bank of England.

Jean, Y. and M. Vernengo (2008), 'Puzzles, paradoxes, and regularities: cyclical and structural productivity in the United States (1950–2005)', *Review of Radical Political Economics*, **40** (3), Summer, 237–43.

Jefferson, T. and J.E. King (2010–11), 'Can Post Keynesians make better use of behavioral economics?', *Journal of Post Keynesian Economics*, **33** (2), Winter, 211–34.

Jespersen, J. (2009), *Macroeconomic Methodology: A Post-Keynesian Perspective*, Cheltenham, UK and Northampton, MA, USA: Edward Elgar.

Jetin, B. and L. Reyes Ortiz (2020), 'Wage-led demand as a rebalancing strategy for economic growth in China', *Journal of Post Keynesian Economics*, **43** (3), 341–66.

Johnson, M.D. (1988), 'Comparability and hierarchical processing in multialternative choice', *Journal of Consumer Research*, **15** (3), December, 303–14.

Johnson, R.D. (2010), 'Extracting a revised labor supply theory from Becker's model of the household', *Journal of Socio-Economics*, **39** (2), April, 241–50.

Johnston, J. (1960), *Statistical Cost Analysis*, London: McGraw-Hill.

Jorion, P. (2008), *L'Implosion: la finance contre l'économie, ce que révèle et annonce la crise des subprimes*, Paris: Fayard.

Jossa, B. (1989), 'Class struggle and income distribution in Kaleckian theory', in M. Sebastiani (ed.), *Kalecki's Relevance Today*, New York; St. Martin's Press, pp. 142–59.

J.P. Morgan (2016), 'It's time to reassess your hurdle rate', November, http://ejvanalytics.com/wp-content/uploads/2018/08/2016-JPMorgan-Reassess.pdf.

Judson, D.H. (1989), 'The convergence of neo-Ricardian and embodied energy theories of value and price', *Ecological Economics*, **1** (3), October, 261–81.

Kahn, R.F. (1972), *Selected Essays on Employment and Growth*, Cambridge: Cambridge University Press.

Kahn, R.F. (1977), 'Malinvaud on Keynes', *Cambridge Journal of Economics*, **1** (4), December, 375–88.

Kahneman, D. (2011), *Thinking Fast and Slow*, Toronto: Doubleday.

Kahneman, D. and J.L. Knetsch (1992), 'Valuing public goods; the purchase of moral satisfaction', *Journal of Environmental Economics and Management*, **22** (1), January, 57–70.

Kahneman, D. and A. Tversky (1979), 'Prospect theory: an analysis of decision under risk', *Econometrica*, **47** (2), March, 263–91.

Kaldor, N. (1934a), 'A classificatory note on the determinateness of equilibrium', *Review of Economic Studies*, **1** (2), February, 122–36.

Kaldor, N. (1934b), 'The equilibrium of the firm', *Economic Journal*, **44** (173), March, 60–76.

Kaldor, N. (1938), 'Stability and full employment', *Economic Journal*, **48** (192), December, 642–57.

Kaldor, N. (1956), 'Alternative theories of distribution', *Review of Economic Studies*, **23** (2), 83–100.

Kaldor, N. (1957), 'A model of economic growth', *Economic Journal*, **67** (268), December, 591–624.

Kaldor, N. (1959), 'Economic growth and the problem of inflation: Part 2', *Economica*, **26** (4), November, 287–98.

Kaldor, N. (1960), 'Characteristics of economic development', in *Essays on Economic Stability and Growth*, London: Duckworth, pp. 233–42.

Kaldor, N. (1961), 'Capital accumulation and economic growth', in F.A. Lutz and D.C. Hague (eds), *The Theory of Capital*, New York: St. Martin's Press, pp. 177–228.

Kaldor, N. (1964a), 'Monetary policy, economic stability and growth', in *Essays on Economic Policy*, Vol. 1, London: Duckworth, pp. 128–53.

Kaldor, N. (1964b), 'Introduction', in *Essays on Economic Policy*, Vol. 1, London: Duckworth, pp. vii–xxi.

Kaldor, N. (1966), 'Marginal productivity and the macro-economic theories of distribution', *Review of Economic Studies*, **33** (4), October, 309–19.

Kaldor, N. (1970a), 'Some fallacies in the interpretation of Kaldor', *Review of Economic Studies*, **37** (1), January, 1–7.

Kaldor, N. (1970b), 'The new monetarism', *Lloyds Bank Review*, July, 1–17.

Kaldor, N. (1970c), 'The case for regional policies', *Scottish Journal of Political Economy*, **17** (3), November, 337–48.

Kaldor, N. (1972), '"The irrelevance of equilibrium economics"', *Economic Journal*, **82** (328), December, 1237–52.

Kaldor, N. (1976), 'Inflation and recession in the world economy', *Economic Journal*, **86** (344), December, 703–14.

Kaldor, N. (1978a), 'Introduction', in *Further Essays on Economic Theory*, London: Duckworth, pp. 7–24.

Kaldor, N. (1978b), 'Causes of the slow rate of economic growth in the United Kingdom', in *Further Essays on Economic Theory*, London: Duckworth, pp. 100–138.

Kaldor, N. (1978c), 'Introduction', *Further Essays on Applied Economics*, London: Duckworth, pp. vii–xxix.
Kaldor, N. (1980), 'Monetarism and UK monetary policy', *Cambridge Journal of Economics*, **4** (4), December, 293–318.
Kaldor, N. (1981), *Origins of the New Monetarism*, Cardiff: University College Cardiff Press.
Kaldor, N. (1982), *The Scourge of Monetarism*, Oxford: Oxford University Press.
Kaldor, N. (1983a), 'Keynesian economics after fifty years', in D. Worswick and J. Trevithick (eds), *Keynes and the Modern World*, Cambridge: Cambridge University Press, pp. 1–28.
Kaldor, N. (1983b), *Limitations of the 'General Theory'*, London: The British Academy.
Kaldor, N. (1985), *Economics Without Equilibrium*, Armonk, NY: M.E. Sharpe.
Kaldor, N. (1986), 'Limits on growth', *Oxford Economic Papers*, **38** (2), July, 187–98.
Kaldor, N. (1996), *Causes of Growth and Stagnation in the World*, Cambridge: Cambridge University Press.
Kaldor, N. and J. Trevithick (1981), 'A Keynesian perspective on money', *Lloyds Bank Review*, July, 1–19.
Kalecki, M. (1937), 'The principle of increasing risk', *Economica*, **4** (76), November, 441–7.
Kalecki, M. (1944), 'Professor Pigou on the classical stationary state: a comment', *Economic Journal*, **54** (213), April, 131–2.
Kalecki, M. (1954), *Theory of Economic Dynamics: An Essay on Cyclical and Long-Run Changes in Capitalist Economies*, New York: Monthly Review Press Classics, 2009.
Kalecki, M. (1969), *Studies in the Theory of Business Cycles 1933–1939*, Oxford: Basil Blackwell.
Kalecki, M. (1971), *Selected Essays in the Dynamics of the Capitalist Economy*, Cambridge: Cambridge University Press.
Kallis, G., C. Kershner and J. Martinez-Alier (2012), 'The economics of degrowth', *Ecological Economics*, **84**, December, 172–80.
Kania, J.J. and J.R. McKean (1976), 'Ownership, control, and the contemporary corporation: a general behavior analysis', *Kyklos*, **29** (2), June, 272–91.
Kant, S. (2003), 'Extending the boundaries of forest economics', *Forest Policy and Economics*, **5** (1), January, 39–56.
Kapeller, J. and B. Schütz (2015), 'Conspicuous consumption, inequality and debt: the nature of consumption-driven profit-led regimes', *Metroeconomica*, **66** (1), February, 51–70.
Kapeller, J., B. Schütz and S. Steinerberger (2013), 'The impossibility of consumer choice: a problem and its solution', *Journal of Evolutionary Economics*, **23** (1), January, 39–60.
Kapeller, J. and F. Springholz (eds) (2016), *Heterodox Economics Directory*, 6th edition, http://heterodoxnews.com/directory/#entry-14.
Kaplan, A.D.H., J.B. Dirlam and R.F. Lanzillotti (1958), *Pricing in Big Business: A Case Approach*, Washington, DC: Brookings Institution.
Kappes, S.A. and M. Milan (2020), 'Dealing with adaptative expectations in stock-flow consistent models', *Journal of Post Keynesian Economics*, **43** (1), 76–89.
Karacaoglu, G. (1984), 'Absence of gross substitution in portfolios and demand for finance: some macroeconomic implications', *Journal of Post Keynesian Economics*, **6** (4), Summer, 567–89.
Kaufman, B.E. (2004), 'The Institutional and Neoclassical schools in labor economics', in D.P. Champlin and J.T. Knoedler (eds), *The Institutionalist Tradition in Labor Economics*, Armonk, NY: M.E. Sharpe, pp. 13–38.
Kaufman, B.E. (2010a), 'The theoretical foundations of industrial relations and its implications', *Industrial and Labor Relations Review*, **64** (1), October, 74–108.
Kaufman, B.E. (2010b), 'Institutional economics and the minimum wage: broadening the theoretical and policy debate', *Industrial and Labor Relations Review*, **63** (3), April, 427–53.
Kaufman, B.E. (2020), 'Richard Lester's institutional-industrial relations model of labor markets and the near-zero minimum wage employment effect: the model Card and Krueger ignored but shouldn't have', *Journal of Economic Issues*, **54** (4), December, 1002–32.
Keen, S. (2017), *Can We Avoid Another Financial Crisis?*, Cambridge: Polity Press.
Keister, T., A. Martin and J. McAndrews (2008), 'Divorcing money from monetary policy', *FRBNY Economic Policy Review*, **14** (2), September, 41–53.

Kelton, S. (2020), *The Deficit Myth: Modern Monetary Theory and the Birth of the People's Economy*, New York: Public Affairs.
Kelton, S. and L.R. Wray (2009), *Can Euroland Survive?*, Public Policy Brief 106, Levy Economics Institute of Bard College.
Kemp-Benedict, E. (2013), 'Material needs and aggregate demand', *Journal of Socio-Economics*, **44**, June, 16–26.
Kemp-Benedict, E. (2014), 'The inverted pyramid: a neo-Ricardian view of the economy-environment relationship', *Ecological Economics*, **107**, November, 230–41.
Kenyon, P. (1979), 'Pricing', in A.S. Eichner (ed.), *A Guide to Post-Keynesian Economics*, White Plains, NY: M.E. Sharpe, pp. 34–45.
Kesting, S. (2011), 'What is "green" in the green new deal? Criteria from ecofeminist and post-Keynesian economics', *International Journal of Green Economics*, **5** (1), 49–64.
Keynes, J.M. (1930a), *A Treatise on Money, Volume I, The Pure Theory of Money*, New York: Harcourt, Brace and Company.
Keynes, J.M. (1930b), *A Treatise on Money, Volume II, The Applied Theory of Money*, New York: Harcourt, Brace and Company.
Keynes, J.M. (1936), *The General Theory of Employment, Interest, and Money*, London: Macmillan.
Keynes, J.M. (1973), *The Collected Writings of John Maynard Keynes*, London: Macmillan, St. Martin's Press and Cambridge University Press.
iv: *A Tract on Monetary Reform* (1923)
viii: *Treatise on Probability* (1921)
ix: *Essays in Persuasion* (1931)
xii: *Economic Articles and Correspondence: Investment and Editorial*
xiii: *The General Theory and After: Part I, Preparation*
xiv: *The General Theory and After: Part II, Defence and Development*
xxv: *Activities 1940–1944: Shaping the Post-War World: The Clearing Union*
xxix: *The General Theory and After: A Supplement*
Khan, N. (2022), 'Does inflation targeting really promote economic growth?', *Review of Political Economy*, 2022, **34** (4).
Kiefer, D. and C. Rada (2015), 'Profit maximising goes global: the race to the bottom', *Cambridge Journal of Economics*, **39** (5), September, 1333–50.
Kim, H. (2019), 'Interest-rate causality between the federal funds rate and long-run market interest rates', *Review of Keynesian Economics*, **7** (3), Autumn, 388–401.
Kim, J.H. and M. Lavoie (2016), 'A two-sector model with target-return pricing in a stock-flow consistent framework', *Economic Systems Research*, **28** (3), 403–27.
Kim, J.H. and M. Lavoie (2017), 'Demand-led growth and long-run convergence in a two-sector model', Demand-led growth and long-run convergence in a neo-Kaleckian two-sector model, *Korean Economic Review*, **33** (1), Summer, 179–206.
Kim, Y. (2012), 'Emulation and consumer debt: implications of keeping up with the Joneses', Working Paper 12–08, Trinity College Department of Economics.
King, J.E. (1995), *Conversations with Post Keynesians*, Basingstoke: Macmillan.
King, J.E. (2001), 'Labor and unemployment', in R.C. Holt and S. Pressman (eds), *A New Guide to Post Keynesian Economics*, London: Routledge, pp. 65–78.
King, J.E. (2002), *A History of Post Keynesian Economics Since 1936*, Cheltenham, UK and Northampton, MA, USA: Edward Elgar.
King, J.E. (2012a), *The Microfoundations Delusion: Metaphor and Dogma in the History of Macroeconomics*, Cheltenham, UK and Northampton, MA, USA: Edward Elgar.
King, J.E. (2012b), 'Post Keynesians and others', *Review of Political Economy*, **24** (2), April, 305–19.
King, J.E. (2013), 'Should post-Keynesians make a behavioural turn?', *European Journal of Economics and Economic Policies: Intervention*, **10** (2), September, 231–42.
King, J.E. (2015), *Advanced Introduction to Post-Keynesian Economics*, Cheltenham, UK and Northampton, MA, USA: Edward Elgar.
King, J.E. (2017), 'Post Keynesian economics in Cambridge', in R.A. Cord (ed.), *The Palgrave Companion to Cambridge Economics, Volume One*, London: Palgrave Macmillan, pp. 135–55.

King, J.E. (2019), 'Some obstacles to wage-led growth', *Review of Keynesian Economics*, **7** (3), Autumn, 308–20.

Kirman, A. (1989), 'The intrinsic limits of modern economic theory: the emperor has no clothes', *Economic Journal*, **99**, Supplement, 126–39.

Klamer, A. and D. Colander (1990), *The Making of an Economist*, Boulder, CO: Westview Press.

Kleinknecht, A. (2020), 'The (negative) impact of supply-side labour market reforms on productivity: an overview of the evidence', *Cambridge Journal of Economics*, **44** (2), March, 445–64.

Knapp, G.F. (1924), *The State Theory of Money*, New York: Augustus M. Kelley, 1973.

Knetsch, J.L. (1990), 'Environmental policy implications of disparities between willingness to pay and compensation demanded measures of values', *Journal of Environmental Economics and Management*, **18** (3), May, 227–37.

Knight, F. (1940), *Risk, Uncertainty and Profit*, London: The London School of Economics and Political Science; first published 1921.

Kohler, K. (2020), 'Gross capital flows and the balance-of-payments: a balance sheet perspective', Working Paper 2019, Post-Keynesian Economics Society.

Koo, R.C. (2009), *The Holy Grail of Macroeconomics: Lessons from Japan's Great Recession*, Singapore: Wiley.

Kornai, J. (1980), *Economics of Shortage*, Amsterdam: North Holland.

Koutsoyiannis, A. (1975), *Modern Microeconomics*, London: Macmillan.

Koutsoyiannis, A. (1984), 'Goals of oligopolistic firms: an empirical test of competing hypotheses', *Southern Economic Journal*, **51** (2), October, 540–67.

Krassoi-Peach, E. and T.D. Stanley (2009), 'Efficiency wages, productivity and simultaneity: a meta-regression analysis', *Journal of Labor Research*, **30** (3), September, 262–8.

Kregel, J.A. (1973), *The Reconstruction of Political Economy: An Introduction to Post-Keynesian Economics*, London: Macmillan.

Kregel, J.A. (1984–85), 'Constraints on the expansion of output and employment: real or monetary?', *Journal of Post Keynesian Economics*, **7** (2), Winter, 139–52.

Kregel, J.A. (1986), 'Shylock and Hamlet or are there bulls and bears in the circuit?', *Économies et Sociétés*, **20** (8–9), August–September, 11–22.

Kregel, J.A. (2017), '"Isms" and "Zations": on fictitious liquidity and endogenous financialization', *Economia e Sociedade, Campinas*, **26**, December, 879–93.

Kregel, J.A. (2019), 'MMT: the wrong answer to the wrong question', *Real-World Economics Review*, 89, October, 85–96.

Kregel, J.A. (2020), 'External debt matters: what are the limits to monetary sovereignty?', *Japanese Political Economy*, **46** (4), 287–99.

Kriesler, P. (1987), *Kalecki's Microanalysis: The Development of Kalecki's Analysis of Pricing*, Cambridge: Cambridge University Press.

Kriesler, P. and M. Lavoie (2007), 'The new view on monetary policy: the New Consensus and its post-Keynesian critique', *Review of Political Economics*, **19** (3), July, 387–404.

Kronenberg, T. (2010), 'Finding common ground between ecological economics and post-Keynesian economics', *Ecological Economics*, **69** (7), May, 1488–94.

Krugman, P. (1998), 'It's baaack! Japan's slump and the return to the liquidity trap', *Brookings Papers in Economic Activity*, No. 2, 137–205.

Krugman, P. (2009), 'Deficits saved the world', *The New York Times Opinion Pages*, 15 July, available at http://krugman.blogs.nytimes.com/2009/07/15/deficits-saved-the-world/.

Krugman, P. (2012), *End This Depression Now!*, New York: W.W. Norton.

Krugman, P. (2013), 'The 1 percent solution', *The New York Times Opinion Pages*, 25 April, available at http://www.nytimes.com/2013/04/26/opinion/krugman-the-one-percents-solution.html?hp&_r=0.

Kumar, R., C. Schoder and S. Radpour (2018), 'Demand driven growth and capital distribution in a two class model with applications to the United States', *Structural Change and Economic Dynamics*, **47**, December, 1–8.

Kurz, H.D. (1986), 'Normal positions and capital utilization', *Political Economy: Studies in the Surplus Approach*, **2** (1), 37–54.

Kurz, H.D. (1990), 'Technical change, growth and distribution: a steady state approach to unsteady growth', in H.D. Kurz (ed.), *Capital, Distribution and Effective Demand: Studies in the Classical Approach to Economic Theory*, Cambridge: Polity Press, pp. 210–39.

Kurz, H.D. (1993), 'Modèle classique et projet Keynésien: réponse à C. Tutin', *Cahiers d'économie politique*, **22**, May, 93–103.

Kurz, H.D. (1994), 'Growth and distribution', *Review of Political Economy*, **6** (4), October, 393–420.

Labrousse, A. and J. Vercueil (2008), 'Fostering variety in economics: entretien avec Geoffrey Hodgson', *Revue de la régulation*, **2**, January, available at http://regulation.revues.org/document2853.html.

Labrousse, A. and T. Lamarche (2009), 'Vers une association d'économie politique hétérodoxe? Entretien avec Nicolas Postel et Richard Sobel', *Revue de la Régulation*, **5**, 1st Semester, 1–9.

Lachmann, L.M. (1977), *Capital, Expectations and the Market Process*, Kansas City, MO: Sheed, Andrews and McMeel.

Lah, M. and A. Sušjan (1999), 'Rationality of transitional consumers: a Post Keynesian view', *Journal of Post Keynesian Economics*, **21** (4), Summer, 589–602.

Laina, P. (2019), 'Money creation under full-reserve banking: a stock-flow consistent model', *Cambridge Journal of Economics*, **43** (5), September, 1219–49.

Lainé, M. (2017), 'The heterogeneity of animal spirits: a taxonomy of entrepreneurs with regard to investment decisions', *Cambridge Journal of Economics*, **41** (2), March, 595–636.

Lakomski-Laguerre, O. (2016), 'Joseph Schumpeter's credit view of money: a contribution to a monetary analysis of capitalism', *History of Political Economy*, **48** (3), September, 489–514.

Lancaster, K. (1971), *Consumer Demand: A New Approach*, New York: Columbia University Press.

Lancaster, K. (1991), 'Hierarchies in goods-characteristics analysis', in *Modern Consumer Theory*, Aldershot, UK and Brookfield, VT, USA: Edward Elgar, pp. 69–80.

Lang, D. (2009), 'Involuntary unemployment in a path-dependent system: the case of strong hysteresis', in P. Arestis and M. Sawyer (eds), *Path Dependency and Macroeconomics*, Basingstoke: Palgrave Macmillan, pp. 80–118.

Lang, D., M. Setterfield and I. Shikaki (2020), 'Is there scientific progress in macroeconomics? The case of the NAIRU', *European Journal of Economics and Economic Policies: Intervention*, **17** (1), 19–38.

Lanzillotti, R.F. (1958), 'Pricing objectives in large companies', *American Economic Review*, **48** (5), December, 921–40.

Lavoie, M. (1984), 'The endogenous credit flow and the Post Keynesian theory of money', *Journal of Economic Issues*, **18** (3), September, 771–97.

Lavoie, M. (1985a), 'La distinction entre l'incertitude Keynésienne et le risque néoclassique', *Économie Appliquée*, **38** (2), 493–518.

Lavoie, M. (1985b), 'Credit and money: the dynamic circuit, overdraft economics, and post-Keynesian economics', in M. Jarsulic (ed.), *Money and Macro Policy*, Boston, MA: Kluwer-Nijhoff, pp. 63–84.

Lavoie, M. (1985c), 'The Post Keynesian theory of endogenous money: a reply', *Journal of Economic Issues*, **19** (3), September, 843–8.

Lavoie, M. (1986a), 'Minsky's law or the theorem of systemic financial fragility', *Studi Economici*, **29**, 3–28.

Lavoie, M. (1986b), 'Chômage classique et chômage Keynésien: un prétexte aux politiques d'austérité', *Économie Appliquée*, **39** (2), 203–38.

Lavoie, M. (1987), *Macroéconomie: Théorie et controverses postkeynésiennes*, Paris: Dunod.

Lavoie, M. (1992a), 'Towards a new research programme for post-Keynesianism and neo-Ricardianism', *Review of Political Economy*, **4** (1), January, 37–79.

Lavoie, M. (1992b), *Foundations of Post-Keynesian Economic Analysis*, Aldershot, UK and Brookfield, VT, USA: Edward Elgar.

Lavoie, M. (1994), 'A Post Keynesian theory of consumer choice', *Journal of Post Keynesian Economics*, **16** (4), Summer, 539–62.

Lavoie, M. (1995a), 'The Kaleckian model of growth and distribution and its neo-Ricardian and neo-Marxian critiques', *Cambridge Journal of Economics*, **19** (6), December, 789–818.

Lavoie, M. (1995b), 'Interest rates in post-Keynesian models of growth and distribution', *Metroeconomica*, **46** (2), June, 146–77.
Lavoie, M. (1996–97), 'Real wages, employment structure and the aggregate demand curve in a Kaleckian short-run model', *Journal of Post Keynesian Economics*, **19** (2), Winter, 275–88.
Lavoie, M. (1996a), 'Mark-up pricing versus normal cost pricing in post-Keynesian models', *Review of Political Economy*, **8** (1), January, 57–66.
Lavoie, M. (1996b), 'Unproductive outlays and capital accumulation with target-return pricing', *Review of Social Economy*, **54** (3), Fall, 303–21.
Lavoie, M. (1996c), 'Traverse, hysteresis, and normal rates of capacity utilization in Kaleckian models of growth and distribution', *Review of Radical Political Economics*, **28** (4), December, 113–47.
Lavoie, M. (1996d), 'Horizontalism, structuralism, liquidity preference and the principle of increasing risk', *Scottish Journal of Political Economy*, **43** (3), August, 275–301.
Lavoie, M. (1996e), 'Monetary policy in an economy with endogenous credit money', in G. Deleplace and E.J. Nell (eds), *Money in Motion: The Post Keynesian and Circulation Approaches*, Basingstoke: Macmillan, pp. 532–45.
Lavoie, M. (1997), 'Loanable funds, endogenous money and Minsky's financial fragility hypothesis', in A.J. Cohen, H. Hagemann and J. Smithin (eds), *Money, Financial Institutions and Macroeconomics*, Boston, MA: Kluwer Academic, pp. 67–82.
Lavoie, M. (1998), 'Simple comparative statics of class conflict in Kaleckian and Marxist short-run models', *Review of Radical Political Economics*, **30** (3), Summer, 101–13.
Lavoie, M. (2000a), 'Le chômage d'équilibre: réalité ou artefact statistique?', *Revue Économique*, **51** (6), November, 1477–84.
Lavoie, M. (2000b), 'A Post Keynesian view of interest parity theorems', *Journal of Post Keynesian Economics*, **23** (1), Fall, 163–79.
Lavoie, M. (2001), 'The reflux mechanism in the open economy', in L.P. Rochon and M. Vernengo (eds), *Credit, Growth and the Open Economy: Essays in the Horizontalist Tradition*, Cheltenham, UK and Northampton, MA, USA: Edward Elgar, pp. 215–42.
Lavoie, M. (2002–03), 'Interest parity, risk premia and Post Keynesian analysis', *Journal of Post Keynesian Economics*, **25** (2), Winter, 237–49.
Lavoie, M. (2003a), 'The tight links between post-Keynesian and feminist economics', in E. Fullbrook (ed.), *The Crisis in Economics: The Post-Autistic Economics Movement: The First 600 Days*, London: Routledge, pp. 189–92.
Lavoie, M. (2003b), 'Real wages and unemployment with effective and notional demand for labour', *Review of Radical Political Economics*, **35** (2), June, 166–82.
Lavoie, M. (2003c), 'Kaleckian effective demand and Sraffian normal prices: towards a reconciliation', *Review of Political Economy*, **15** (1), January, 53–74.
Lavoie, M. (2003d), 'A primer on endogenous credit-money', in L.P. Rochon and S. Rossi (eds), *Modern Theories of Money: The Nature and Role of Money in Capitalist Economies*, Cheltenham, UK and Northampton, MA, USA: Edward Elgar, pp. 506–43.
Lavoie, M. (2006a), 'Do heterodox theories have anything in common? A post-Keynesian point of view', *European Journal of Economics and Economic Policies: Intervention*, **3** (1), May, 87–112.
Lavoie, M. (2006b), *Introduction to Post-Keynesian Economics*, Basingstoke: Palgrave Macmillan.
Lavoie, M. (2006c), 'A post-Keynesian amendment to the New Consensus on monetary policy', *Metroeconomica*, **57** (2), May, 165–192.
Lavoie, M. (2006d), 'Endogenous money: accommodationist', in P. Arestis and M. Sawyer (eds), *Handbook on Alternative Monetary Economics*, Cheltenham, UK and Northampton, MA, USA: Edward Elgar, pp. 17–34.
Lavoie, M. (2006e), 'A fully coherent post-Keynesian model of currency boards', in C. Gnos and L.P. Rochon (eds), *Post Keynesian Principles of Economic Policy*, Cheltenham, UK and Northampton, MA, USA: Edward Elgar, pp. 185–207.
Lavoie, M. (2008), 'Neoclassical empirical evidence on employment and production laws as artefact', *Rivista Economía Informa*, **351**, March–April, 9–36.

Lavoie, M. (2009a), 'Post Keynesian consumer choice theory and ecological economics', in R.P.F. Holt, S. Pressman and C.L. Spash (eds), *Post Keynesian and Ecological Economics: Confronting Environmental Issues*, Cheltenham, UK and Northampton, MA, USA: Edward Elgar, pp. 141–57.

Lavoie, M. (2009b), 'Cadrisme within a Kaleckian model of growth and distribution', *Review of Political Economy*, **21** (3), July, 371–93.

Lavoie, M. (2009c), 'Taming the New Consensus: hysteresis and some other post-Keynesian amendments', in G. Fontana and M. Setterfield (eds), *Macroeconomic Theory and Macroeconomic Pedagogy*, Basingstoke: Palgrave Macmillan, pp. 191–212.

Lavoie, M. (2009d), 'Towards a post-Keynesian consensus in macroeconomics: reconciling the Cambridge and Wall Street views, in E. Hein, T. Niechoj and E. Stockhammer (eds), *Macroeconomic Policies on Shaky Foundations – Whither Mainstream Economics?*, Marburg: Metropolis Verlag, pp. 75–99.

Lavoie, M. (2010a), 'The possible perverse effects of declining wages', *International Journal of Pluralism and Economics Education*, **1** (3), 260–75.

Lavoie, M. (2010b), 'Surveying short-run and long-run stability issues with the Kaleckian model of growth', in M. Setterfield (ed.), *Handbook of Alternative Theories of Economic Growth*, Cheltenham, UK and Northampton, MA, USA: Edward Elgar, pp. 132–56.

Lavoie, M. (2011a), 'History and methods of post-Keynesian economics', in E. Hein and E. Stockhammer (eds), *A Modern Guide to Keynesian Macroeconomics and Economic Policies*, Cheltenham, UK and Northampton, MA, USA: Edward Elgar, pp. 1–33.

Lavoie, M. (2011b), 'Should Sraffians be dropped out of the post-Keynesian school?', *Économies et Sociétés*, **44** (7), July, 1027–59.

Lavoie, M. (2012), 'Perspectives for post-Keynesians', *Review of Political Economy*, **24** (2), April, 321–36.

Lavoie, M. (2013a), 'The monetary and fiscal nexus of neo-chartalism: a friendly critique', *Journal of Economic Issues*, **47** (1), March, 1–32.

Lavoie, M. (2013b), 'Sraffians, other post-Keynesians, and the controversy over centres of gravitation', in E.S. Levrero, A. Palumbo and A. Stirati (eds), *Sraffa and the Reconstruction of Economic Theory: Volume Three*, Basingstoke: Palgrave Macmillan, pp. 34–54.

Lavoie, M. (2015a), 'The eurozone: similarities to and differences from Keynes's plan', *International Journal of Political Economy*, **44** (1), 3–17.

Lavoie, M. (2015b), 'The eurozone crisis: A balance-of-payments problem or a crisis due to a flawed monetary design? A reply to Sergio Cesaratto', *International Journal of Political Economy*, **44** (2), 157–60.

Lavoie, M. (2016a), 'Frederic Lee and post-Keynesian pricing theory', *Review of Political Economy*, **28** (2), April, 169–86.

Lavoie, M. (2016b), 'Convergence towards the normal rate of capacity utilization in neo-Kaleckian models: the role of non-capacity creating autonomous expenditures', *Metroeconomica*, **67** (1), February, 172–201.

Lavoie, M. (2017a), 'The origins and evolution of the debate on wage-led and profit-led regimes', *European Journal of Economics and Economic Policies: Intervention*, **14** (2), 200–21.

Lavoie, M. (2017b), 'Prototypes, reality and the growth rate of autonomous consumption expenditures: a rejoinder', *Metroeconomica*, **68** (1), February, 194–99.

Lavoie, M. (2018), 'Rethinking macroeconomic theory before the next crisis', *Review of Economic Policies*, **6** (1), Spring, 1–21.

Lavoie, M. (2019a), 'Modern monetary theory and post-Keynesian economics', *Real-World Economics Review*, **89**, October, 97–108.

Lavoie, M. (2019b), 'Advances in the post-Keynesian analysis of money and finance', in P. Arestis and M. Sawyer (eds), *Frontiers of Heterodox Macroeconomics*, Cham (CH): Palgrave Macmillan, pp. 89–129.

Lavoie, M. (2020), 'Was Hyman Minsky a post-Keynesian economist?', *Review of Evolutionary Political Economy*, **1** (1), 85–102.

Lavoie, M. (2022), 'Stock-flow consistent macroeconomic modeling and Post-Keynesian Institutionalism', in C.J. Whalen (ed.), *A Modern Guide to Post-Keynesian Institutional Economics*, Cheltenham, UK and Northampton, MA, USA: Edward Elgar, pp. 253–72.

Lavoie, M. and G. Daigle (2011), 'A behavioural finance model of exchange rate expectations within a stock–flow consistent framework', *Metroeconomica*, **62** (3), July, 434–58.

Lavoie, M. and B. Fiebiger (2018), 'Unconventional monetary policies, with a focus on quantitative easing', *European Journal of Economics and Economic Policies: Intervention*, **15** (2), 139–46.

Lavoie, M. and W. Godley (2001–02), 'Kaleckian models of growth in a coherent stock–flow monetary framework: a Kaldorian view', *Journal of Post Keynesian Economics*, **24** (2), Winter, 277–312.

Lavoie, M. and P. Kriesler (2007), 'Capacity utilization, inflation and monetary policy: the Duménil and Lévy macro model and the New Consensus', *Review of Radical Political Economics*, **39** (4), Fall, 586–98.

Lavoie, M. and W.J. Nah (2020), 'Overhead labour costs in a neo-Kaleckian model with autonomous non-capacity creating expenditures', *Review of Political Economy*, **32** (4), October, 511–37.

Lavoie, M. and P. Ramírez-Gastón (1997), 'Traverse in a two-sector Kaleckian model of growth with target return pricing', *Manchester School of Economic and Social Studies*, **55** (1), March, 145–69.

Lavoie, M. and S. Reissl (2019), 'Further insights on endogenous money and the liquidity preference theory of interest', *Journal of Post Keynesian Economics*, **42** (4), 503–26.

Lavoie, M. and M. Seccareccia (1999), 'Interest rate: fair', in P. O'Hara (ed.), *Encyclopedia of Political Economy*, Vol. 1, London: Routledge, pp. 543–5.

Lavoie, M. and M. Seccareccia (2001), 'Minsky's financial fragility hypothesis: a missing macroeconomic link?', in R. Bellofiore and P. Ferri (eds), *Financial Fragility and Investment in the Capitalist Economy: The Economic Legacy of Hyman Minsky, Volume II*, Cheltenham, UK and Northampton, MA, USA: Edward Elgar, pp. 76–96.

Lavoie, M. and M. Seccareccia (2019), 'Macroeconomics and natural rates: some reflections on Pasinetti's fair rate of interest', *Bulletin of Political Economy*, **13** (2), 139–62.

Lavoie, M. and M. Seccareccia (2021), 'Going beyond the inflation-targeting mantra: *a dual mandate*', https://www.mcgill.ca/maxbellschool/files/maxbellschool/7_lavoie_0.pdf.

Lavoie, M. and E. Stockhammer (2013a), 'Wage-led growth: concepts, theories and policies', in M. Lavoie and E. Stockhammer, *Wage-led Growth: An Equitable Strategy for Economic Recovery*, Basingstoke: Palgrave Macmillan, pp. 13–39.

Lavoie, M. and E. Stockhammer (2013b), *Wage-led Growth: An Equitable Strategy for Economic Recovery*, Basingstoke: Palgrave Macmillan.

Lavoie, M. and P. Wang (2012), 'The "compensation" thesis, as exemplified by the case of the Chinese central bank', *International Review of Applied Economics*, **26** (3), May, 287–302.

Lawn, P. (ed.) (2009), *Environment and Employment: A Reconciliation*, London: Routledge.

Lawson, T. (1985), 'Uncertainty and economic analysis', *Economic Journal*, **95** (380), December, 909–27.

Lawson, T. (1994), 'The nature of Post Keynesianism and its links to other traditions: a realist perspective', *Journal of Post Keynesian Economics*, **16** (4), Summer, 503–38.

Lawson, T. (1997), *Economics and Reality*, London: Routledge.

Lawson, T. (2006), 'The nature of heterodox economics', *Cambridge Journal of Economics*, **30** (4), July, 483–505.

Lawson, T. (2009a), 'The current economic crisis: its nature and the course of academic economics', *Cambridge Journal of Economics*, **33** (4), July, 759–77.

Lawson, T. (2009b), 'Heterodox economics and pluralism: reply to Davis', in E. Fullbrook (ed.), *Ontology and Economics: Tony Lawson and His Critics*, London: Routledge, pp. 93–129.

Lawson, T. (2009c), 'The mainstream orientation and ideology: reply to Guerrien', in E. Fullbrook (ed.), *Ontology and Economics: Tony Lawson and His Critics*, London: Routledge, pp. 162–74.

Lawson, T. (2009d), 'Provisionally grounded critical ontology: reply to Vroemen', in E. Fullbrook (ed.), *Ontology and Economics: Tony Lawson and His Critics*, London: Routledge, pp. 335–53.

Lawson, T. (2009e), 'On the nature and role of formalism in economics: reply to Hodgson', in E. Fullbrook (ed.), *Ontology and Economics: Tony Lawson and His Critics*, London: Routledge, pp. 189–231.

Layard, R., S. Nickell and R. Jackman (1991), *Unemployment: Economic Performance and the Labour Market*, Oxford: Oxford University Press.

Lazonick, W. (2022), 'Is the most unproductive firm the foundation of the most efficient economy? Penrosian learning confronts the neoclassical fallacy', *International Review of Applied Economics*, DOI: 10.1080/02692171.2021.2022296.

Lazonick, W. and M. O'Sullivan (2000), 'Maximizing shareholder value: a new ideology for corporate governance', *Economy and Society*, **29** (1), February, 13–35.

Lazzarini, A. (2011), *Revisiting the Cambridge Capital Controversies: A Historical and Analytical Study*, Pavia: Pavia University Press.

Lea, S.E.G., R.M. Tarpy and P. Webley (1987), *The Individual in the Economy: A Survey of Economic Psychology*, Cambridge: Cambridge University Press.

Leamer, E.E. (2015), 'Housing really is the business cycle: what survives the lessons of 2008–09?', *Journal of Money, Credit and Banking*, **47** (1), Supplement, 43–50.

Le Bourva, J. (1992), 'Money creation and credit multipliers', *Review of Political Economy*, **4** (4), October, 447–66.

Lee, F. (1986), 'Post Keynesian view of average direct costs: a critical evaluation of the theory and the empirical evidence', *Journal of Post Keynesian Economics*, **8** (3), Spring, 400–424.

Lee, F.S. (1984), 'The marginalist controversy and the demise of full cost pricing', *Journal of Economic Issues*, **18** (4), December, 1107–32.

Lee, F.S. (1985), 'Full cost prices, classical price theory, and long period method analysis: a critical evaluation', *Metroeconomica*, **37** (2), June, 199–219.

Lee, F.S. (1988), 'Costs, increasing costs, and technical progress: response to the critics', *Journal of Post Keynesian Economics*, **8** (3), Spring, 489–91.

Lee, F.S. (1994), 'From post-Keynesian to historical price theory, part I: facts, theory and empirically grounded pricing model', *Review of Political Economy*, **6** (3), July, 303–36.

Lee, F.S. (1998), *Post Keynesian Price Theory*, Cambridge: Cambridge University Press.

Lee, F.S. (2009), *A History of Heterodox Economics: Challenging the Mainstream in the Twentieth Century*, London: Routledge.

Lee, F.S. (2011), 'Old controversy revisited: pricing, market structure, and competition', MPRA Working Paper, available at http://mpra.ub.uni-muenchen.de/30490/.

Lee, F.S. (2013a), 'Heterodox economics and its critics', in F. Lee and M. Lavoie (eds), *In Defense of Post-Keynesian and Heterodox Economics: Response to their Critics*, London: Routledge, pp. 104–32.

Lee, F.S. (2013b), 'Competition, going enterprise, and economic activity', in J.K. Moudud, C. Bina and P.L. Mason (eds), *Alternative Theories of Competition: Challenges to the Orthodoxy*, London: Routledge, pp. 160–73.

Lee, F.S. and J. Irving-Lessman (1992), 'The fate of an errant hypothesis: the doctrine of normal-cost prices', *History of Political Economy*, **24** (20), Summer, 273–309.

Lee, F.S., J. Irving-Lessman, P. Earl and J.E. Davies (1986), 'P.W.S. Andrews' theory of competitive oligopoly: a new interpretation', *British Review of Economic Issues*, **8** (19), Autumn, 13–39.

Lee, F.S. and M. Lavoie (eds) (2013), *In Defense of Post-Keynesian and Heterodox Economics: Responses to their Critics*, London: Routledge.

Le Héron, E. (1986), 'Généralisation de la préférence pour la liquidité et financement des banques', *Économies et Sociétés*, **20** (8–9), August–September, 67–93.

Le Héron, E. and T. Mouakil (2008), 'A post-Keynesian stock–flow consistent model for dynamic analysis of monetary policy shock on banking behaviour', *Metroeconomica*, **59** (3), July, 405–40.

Leibenstein, H. (1950), 'Bandwagon, snob and Veblen effects in the theory of consumer's demand', *Quarterly Journal of Economics*, **64** (1), February, 183–207.

Leibenstein, H. (1978), *General X-Efficiency Theory and Economic Development*, London: Oxford University Press.

Leijonhufvud, A. (1973), 'Life among the econ', *Western Economic Journal*, **11** (3), September, 327–37.

Leijonhufvud, A. (1976), 'Schools, revolutions and research programmes in economic theory', in S. Latsis (ed.), *Method and Appraisal in Economics*, Cambridge: Cambridge University Press, pp. 65–108.
León-Ledesma, M.A. and A.P. Thirlwall (2002), 'The endogeneity of the natural rate of growth', *Cambridge Journal of Economics*, **26** (4), July, 441–59.
Lerner, A. (1943), 'Functional finance and the federal debt', *Social Research*, **10** (1), February, 38–51.
Lerner, A. (1947), 'Money as a creature of the state', *American Economic Review*, **37** (2), May, 312–17.
Levine, A.L. (1988), 'Sraffa, Okun, and the theory of the imperfectly competitive firm', *Journal of Economic Behavior and Organization*, **9** (1), January, 101–5.
Levrero, S.E. (2021), 'Estimates of the natural rate of interest and the stance of monetary policies: a critical assessment', *International Journal of Political Economy*, **50** (1), 5–27.
Levrero, E.S. and M. Deleidi (2021), 'Monetary policy and long-term interest rates: evidence from the U.S. economy', *Metroeconomica*, **72** (1), February, 121–47.
Li, H., Y. Xu and Y. Zhuang (2021), 'China's trilemma: monetary policy autonomy in an economy with a managed floating exchange rate', *Asian-Pacific Economic Literature*, **35** (1), May, 99–107.
Libânio, G.A. (2009), 'Aggregate demand and the endogeneity of the natural rate of growth: evidence from Latin American economies', *Cambridge Journal of Economics*, **33** (5), September, 967–84.
Lima, G.T. and M. Setterfield (2008), 'Inflation targeting and macroeconomic stability as a Post Keynesian economy', *Journal of Post Keynesian Economics*, **30** (3), Spring, 435–61.
Lima, G.T. and M. Setterfield (2016), 'Expectations and stability in the Kaleckian growth model', *Brazilian Keynesian Review*, **2** (1), 11–25.
Lipsey, R.G. (2016), 'The Phillips curve and an assumed unique macroeconomic equilibrium in historical context', *Journal of the History of Economic Thought*, **38** (4), December, 415–29.
Littleboy, B. (2013), 'Rhetoric in the spirit of Keynes: metaphors to persuade economists, students and the public about fiscal policy', in J. Jespersen and M.O. Madsen (eds), *Teaching Post Keynesian Economics*, Cheltenham, UK and Northampton, MA, USA: Edward Elgar, pp. 117–33.
LK (2014), 'Post Keynesian Economics: a diagram', http://socialdemocracy21stcentury.blogspot.com/2014/04/post-keynesian-economics-diagram.html.
Loasby, B.J. (1976), *Choice, Complexity and Ignorance*, Cambridge: Cambridge University Press.
Lockwood, M. (1996), 'Non-compensatory preference structures in non-market valuation of natural area policy', *Australian Journal of Agricultural Economics*, **40** (2), August, 85–101.
Loehr, D. (2012), 'The euthanasia of the rentier – a way towards a steady-state economy', *Ecological Economics*, **84**, December, 232–9.
Lombra, R.E. and R.G. Torto (1973), 'Federal Reserve defensive behavior and the reverse causation argument', *Southern Economic Journal*, **40** (1), July, 47–55.
Lucas, R. (1981), *Studies in Business Cycle Theory*, Cambridge, MA: MIT Press.
Lutz, M.A. and K. Lux (1979), *The Challenge of Humanistic Economics*, Menlo Park, CA: Benjamin/Cummings.
Lux, K. and M.A. Lutz (1999), 'Dual self', in P. Earl and S. Kemp (eds), *The Elgar Companion to Consumer Research and Economic Psychology*, Cheltenham, UK and Northampton, MA, USA: Edward Elgar, pp. 164–70.
Macedo e Silva, A.C. and C.H. Dos Santos (2011), 'Peering over the edge of the short period? The Keynesian roots of stock–flow consistent macroeconomic models', *Cambridge Journal of Economics*, **35** (1), January, 105–24.
Mäki, U. (1989), 'On the problem of realism in economics', *Ricerche Economiche*, **43** (1–2), 176–98.
Malinvaud, E. (1977), *The Theory of Unemployment Reconsidered*, Oxford: Basil Blackwell.
Mandarino, G.V., C.H. Dos Santos and A.C. Macedo e Silva (2020), 'Workers' debt-financed consumption: a supermultiplier stock-flow consistent model', *Review of Keynesian Economics*, **8** (3), Autumn, 339–65.
Marangos, J. (2004), 'A post-Keynesian approach to the transition process', *Eastern Economic Journal*, **30** (3), Summer, 441–65.

March, J.G. (1978), 'Bounded rationality, ambiguity, and the engineering of choice', *Bell Journal of Economics*, **4** (2), Autumn, 587–610.
Marchal, J. (1951), 'The construction of a new theory of profit', *American Economic Review*, **41** (4), September, 549–65.
Marchal, J. and F. Poulon (1987) *Monnaie et crédit dans l'économie française*, Paris: Cujas.
Marcuzzo, M.C. and E. Sanfilippo (2009), 'Profit maximization in the Cambridge tradition of economics', in M. Forstater and G. Mongiovi (eds), *Post-Keynesian Macroeconomics: Essays in Honour of Ingrid Rima*, London: Routledge, pp. 70–86.
Marglin, S.A. (1984a), *Growth, Distribution and Prices*, Cambridge, MA: Harvard University Press.
Marglin, S.A. (1984b), 'Growth, distribution and inflation: a centennial synthesis', *Cambridge Journal of Economics*, **8** (2), June, 115–44.
Marglin, S.A. and A. Bhaduri (1990), 'Profit squeeze and Keynesian theory', in S. Marglin and J. Schor (eds), *The Golden Age of Capitalism: Reinterpreting the Postwar Experience*, Oxford: Clarendon Press, pp. 153–86.
Marquetti, A. (2004), 'Do rising real wages increase the rate of labour-saving technical change? Some econometric evidence', *Metroeconomica*, **55** (4), November, 432–41.
Marris, R. (1964a), *The Economic Theory of Managerial Capitalism*, New York: Free Press of Glencoe.
Marris, R. (1964b), *The Economics of Capital Utilization*, Cambridge: Cambridge University Press.
Marselli, R. (1993), 'Treasury financing and bank lending-reserves causality: the case of Italy, 1975–1990', *Journal of Post Keynesian Economics*, **15** (4), Summer, 571–88.
Martin, B. (2008), 'Fiscal policy in a stock–flow consistent model: a comment', *Journal of Post Keynesian Economics*, **30** (4), Summer, 649–68.
Maslow, A.H. (1954), *Motivation and Personality*, New York: Harper and Row.
Mason, P.L. (1993), 'Variable labor effort, involuntary unemployment, and effective demand: irreconcilable concepts?', *Journal of Post Keynesian Economics*, **15** (3), Spring, 427–42.
Mason, R. (1998), *The Economics of Conspicuous Consumption*, Cheltenham, UK and Northampton, MA, USA: Edward Elgar.
Mata, T. (2004), 'Constructing identity: the Post Keynesians and the capital controversies', *Journal of the History of Economic Thought*, **26** (2), June, 241–59.
Mazier, J. (2020), *Global Imbalances and Financial Capitalism: Stock-Flow-Consistent Modelling*, Milton Park: Routledge.
Mazzucato, M. (2013), *The Entrepreneurial State: Debunking Public vs. Private Myths*, London: Anthem Press.
McCallum, B.T. (1996), *International Monetary Economics*, Oxford: Oxford University Press.
McCloskey, D.N. (1983), 'The rhetoric of economics', *Journal of Economic Literature*, **21** (2), June, 481–517.
McCombie, J.S.L. (1987), 'Does the aggregate production function imply anything about the laws of production? A note on the Simon and Shaikh critiques', *Applied Economics*, **19** (8), August, 1121–36.
McCombie, J.S.L. (1993), 'Economic growth, trade interlinkages, and the balance-of-payments constraint', *Journal of Post Keynesian Economics*, **15** (4), Summer, 471–506.
McCombie, J.S.L. (1998), 'Are there laws of production? An assessment of the early criticisms of the Cobb–Douglas production function', *Review of Political Economy*, **10** (2), April, 141–73.
McCombie, J.S.L. (2000–2001), 'The Solow residual, technical change, and aggregate production functions', *Journal of Post Keynesian Economics*, **23** (2), Winter, 267–97.
McCombie, J.S.L. (2001), 'What does the aggregate function show? Further thoughts on Solow's second thoughts on growth theory', *Journal of Post Keynesian Economics*, **23** (4), Summer, 589–616.
McCombie, J. (2002), 'Increasing returns and the Verdoorn law from a Kaldorian perspective', in J. McCombie, M. Pugno and B. Soro (eds), *Productivity Growth and Economic Performance: Essays on Verdoorn's Law*, Basingstoke: Palgrave Macmillan, pp. 64–114.
McCombie, J.S.L. (2019), 'Why Thirlwall's law is not a tautology: more on the debate over the law', *Review of Keynesian Economics*, **7** (4), Winter, 429–43.

McCombie, J.S.L. and R. Dixon (1991), 'Estimating technical change in aggregate production functions: a critique', *International Review of Applied Economics*, **5** (1), January, 24–46.
McCombie, J.S.L. and M.R.M. Spreafico (2016), 'Kaldor's technical progress function and Verdoorn's law revisited', *Cambridge Journal of Economics*, **40** (4), 1117–36.
McCombie, J.S.L. and A.P. Thirlwall (1994), *Economic Growth and the Balance-of-Payments Constraint*, London: Macmillan.
McCulley, Paul A. (2009), 'The shadow banking system and Hyman Minsky's economic journey', in *Insights into the Global Financial Crisis*, CFA Institute Research Foundation, pp. 257–68.
McElhattan, R. (1985), 'Inflation, supply shocks and the stable inflation rate of capacity utilization', *Economic Review, Federal Reserve Bank of San Francisco*, Winter, 45–63.
McKenzie, R.A. (2011), 'Casino capitalism with derivatives: fragility and instability in contemporary finance', *Review of Radical Political Economics*, **43** (2), June, 198–215.
McLeay, M., A. Radia and R. Thomas (2014), 'Money creation in the modern economy', *Bank of England Quarterly Bulletin*, First Quarter, 14–27.
Meadows, D.H., D.L. Meadows, J. Randers and W. Behrens (1972), *Limits to Growth*, New York: Potomas Associates.
Means, G.C. (1936), 'Notes on inflexible prices', *American Economic Review*, **26** (1), March, Supplement, 23–35.
Means, G.C. (1992), 'Corporate power in the marketplace', in F.S. Lee and W.J. Samuels (eds), *The Heterodox Economics of Gardiner Means: A Collection*, Armonk, NY: M.E. Sharpe, pp. 318–34.
Mearman, A. (2005), 'Why have post-Keynesians had (relatively) little to say on the economics of the environment?', *International Journal of Environment, Workplace and Employment*, **1** (2), 131–54.
Mearman, A. (2006), 'Critical realism in economics and open-systems ontology: a critique', *Review of Social Economics*, **64** (1), March, 48–75.
Mearman, A. (2009), 'Who do heterodox economists think they are?', available at http://carecon.org.uk/DPs/0915.pdf.
Mearman, A. (2012a), 'Heterodox economics and the problems of classification', *Journal of Economic Methodology*, **19** (4), December, 407–24.
Mearman, A, (2012b), 'Econometrics', in J.E. King (ed.), *Post Keynesian Economics*, 2nd edn, Cheltenham, UK and Northampton, MA, USA: Edward Elgar, pp. 132–8.
Mearman, A., S. Berger and D. Guizzo (2019), *What is Heterodox Economics? Conversations with Leading Economists*, London: Routledge.
Mehlum, H. and R. Torvik (2021), 'The macroeconomics of COVID-19: a two-sector interpretation', *Review of Keynesian Economics*, **9** (2), Summer, 165–74.
Mehrling, P. (2017), 'Financialization and its discontents', *Finance and Society*, **3** (1), 1–10.
Melmiès, J. (2010), 'New Keynesians versus Post Keynesians on the theory of prices', *Journal of Post Keynesian Economics*, **32** (3), Spring, 445–66.
Mercure, J.F., F. Knobloch, H. Pollitt, L. Paroussos, S.S. Scrieciu and R. Lewney (2019), 'Modelling innovation and the macroeconomics of low-carbon transitions: theory, perspectives and practical use', *Climate Policy*, **19** (8), 1019–37.
Metcalfe, J.S. (2013), 'Schumpeterian competition', in J.K. Moudud, C. Bina and P.L. Mason (eds), *Alternative Theories of Competition: Challenges to the Orthodoxy*, London: Routledge, pp. 111–26.
Michell, J. (2017), 'Do shadow banks create money? Financialisation and the monetary circuit', *Metroeconomica*, **68** (2), May, 354–77.
Michl, T.R. (1985), 'International comparisons of productivity growth: Verdoorn's law revisited', *Journal of Post Keynesian Economics*, **7** (4), Summer, 474–92.
Milberg, W. (1994), 'Is absolute advantage passé? Towards a post-Keynesian/Marxian theory of international trade', in M. Glick (ed.), *Competition, Technology and Money: Classical and Post-Keynesian Perspectives*, Aldershot, UK and Brookfield, VT, USA: Edward Elgar, pp. 219–36.
Minsky, H.P. (1957), 'Central banking and money market changes', *Quarterly Journal of Economics*, **71** (2), May, 171–87.

Minsky, H.P. (1964), 'Financial crisis, financial systems, and the performance of the economy', in Commission on Money and Credit, *Private Capital Markets*, Englewood Cliffs, NJ: Prentice-Hall, pp. 173–289.
Minsky, H.P. (1975), *John Maynard Keynes*, New York: Columbia University Press.
Minsky, H.P. (1977), 'The financial instability hypothesis: an interpretation of Keynes and an alternative to standard theory', *Challenge*, **20** (1), March–April, 20–27.
Minsky, H.P. (1982a), *Can 'It' Happen Again? Essays on Instability and Finance*, Armonk, NY: M.E. Sharpe.
Minsky, H.P. (1982b), 'The financial-instability hypothesis: capitalist processes and the behavior of the economy', in C.P. Kindleberger and J.-P. Laffargue (eds), *Financial Crises: Theory, History and Policy*, New York: Cambridge University Press, pp. 13–47.
Minsky, H.P. (1986a), *Stabilizing an Unstable Economy*, New Haven, CT: Yale University Press.
Minsky, H.P. (1986b), 'Global consequences of financial deregulation', *Wallenberg Papers in International Finance*, **2** (1), 1–19.
Minsky, H.P. (1991), 'The endogeneity of money', in E.J. Nell and W. Semmler (eds), *Nicholas Kaldor and Mainstream Economics: Confrontation or Divergence?*, London, Macmillan, pp. 207–20.
Minsky, H.P. (1995), 'Financial factors in the economics of capitalism', *Journal of Financial Services Research*, **9** (3–4), December, 197–208.
Minsky, H.P. (1996), 'The essential characteristics of Post Keynesian economics', in E.J. Nell and G. Deleplace (eds), *Money in Motion*, London: Macmillan, pp. 552–81.
Mirowski, P. (2011), 'The spontaneous methodology of orthodoxy, and other economists' affliction in the Great Recession', in J.B. Davis and D.W. Hands (eds), *The Elgar Companion to Recent Economic Methodology*, Cheltenham, UK and Northampton, MA, USA: Edward Elgar, pp. 473–513.
Mises, L. von (1976), *Epistemological Problems in Economics*, New York: New York University Press.
Mitchell, W. (2007), 'Econometrics, realism and policy in Post Keynesian economics', Working Paper, Centre of Full Employment and Equity (CofFEE), available at http://e1.newcastle.edu.au/coffee/pubs/wp/2007/07–02.pdf.
Mitchell, W. and J. Muysken (2008), *Full Employment Abandoned: Shifting Sands and Policy Failures*, Cheltenham, UK and Northampton, MA, USA: Edward Elgar.
Mitchell, W., L.R. Wray and M. Watts (2019), *Macroeconomics*, London: Red Globe Press.
Mohun, S. (2014), 'Unproductive labor in the U.S. economy: 1964–2010', *Review of Radical Political Economics*, **46** (3), 355–79.
Monasterolo, I. and M. Raberto (2018), 'The EIRIN flow-of-funds behavioural model of green fiscal policies and green sovereign bonds', *Ecological Economics*, **144**, February, 228–43.
Mongiovi, G. (1991), 'Keynes, Sraffa and the labour market', *Review of Political Economy*, **3** (1), January, 25–42.
Mongiovi, G. (2012), 'Sraffian economics', in J.E. King (ed.), *Post Keynesian Economics*, 2nd edn, Cheltenham, UK and Northampton, MA, USA: Edward Elgar, pp. 499–504.
Moore, B.J. (1973), 'Some macroeconomic consequences of corporate equities', *Canadian Journal of Economics*, **6** (4), November, 529–44.
Moore, B.J. (1979), 'Monetary Factors', in A.S. Eichner (ed.), *A Guide to Post-Keynesian Economics*, White Plains, NY: M.E. Sharpe, pp. 120–38.
Moore, B.J. (1988), *Horizontalists and Verticalists: The Macroeconomics of Credit Money*, Cambridge: Cambridge University Press.
Moore, B.J. (1989), 'On the endogeneity of money once more', *Journal of Post Keynesian Economics*, **11** (3), Spring, 479–87.
Moore, B.J. (1991), 'Money supply endogeneity: reserve price setting or reserve quantity setting?', *Journal of Post Keynesian Economics*, **13** (3), Spring, 404–13.
Moore, B.J. (1994), 'The demise of the Keynesian multiplier: a reply to Cottrell', *Journal of Post-Keynesian Economics*, **17** (1), Fall, 121–34.
Moore, B.J. (2001), 'Some reflections on endogenous money', in L.P. Rochon and M. Vernengo (eds), *Credit, Interest Rates and the Open Economy: Essays on Horizontalism*, Cheltenham, UK and Northampton, MA, USA: Edward Elgar, pp. 11–30.

Moore, B.J. (2004), 'A global currency for a global economy', *Journal of Post Keynesian Economics*, **26** (4), Summer, 631–54.

Moore, B.J. (2006), *Shaking the Invisible Hand: Complexity, Endogenous Money and Exogenous Interest Rates*, Basingstoke: Palgrave Macmillan.

Moosa, I.A. (2002), 'A test of the Post Keynesian hypothesis on expectation formation in the foreign exchange market', *Journal of Post Keynesian Economics*, **24** (3), Spring, 443–58.

Moosa, I.A., (2004), 'An empirical examination of the Post Keynesian view of forward exchange rates', *Journal of Post Keynesian Economics*, **26** (3), Spring, 395–418.

Moosa, I.A. (2017a), *Econometrics as a Con Art; Exposing the Limitations and Abuses of Econometrics*, Cheltenham, UK and Northampton, MA, USA: Edward Elgar.

Moosa, I.A. (2017b), 'Covered interest parity: the untestable hypothesis', *Journal of Post Keynesian Economnics*, **40** (4), 470–86.

Moreno-Brid, J. (1998–99), 'On capital flows and the balance of payments constrained growth model', *Journal of Post Keynesian Economics*, **21** (2), Winter, 283–98.

Moreno-Brid, J. (2003), 'Capital flows, interest payments and the balance of payments constrained growth model: a theoretical and empirical analysis', *Metroeconomica*, **54** (2–3), May, 346–65.

Morgan, J. (2017), 'Piketty and the growth dilemma revisited in the context of ecological economics', *Ecological Economics*, **136**, June, 169–77.

Mosler, W. (1995), *Soft Currency Economics*, West Palm Beach, available at http://mosler economics.com/mandatory-readings/soft-currency-economics/.

Mosler, W. (1997–98), 'Full employment and price stability', *Journal of Post Keynesian Economics*, **20** (2), Winter, 167–82.

Mosler, W. (2002), 'A critique of John B. Taylor's "Expectations, open market operations, and changes in the federal funds rate"', *Journal of Post Keynesian Economics*, **24** (3), Spring, 419–22.

Mosler, W. (2010), *The 7 Deadly Innocent frauds of Economic Policy*, USA: Valance Co.

Mosler, W. and M. Forstater (1999), 'General framework for the analysis of currencies and commodities', in P. Davidson and J. Kregel (eds), *Full Employment and Price Stability*, Cheltenham, UK and Northampton, MA, USA: Edward Elgar, pp. 166–77.

Moss, S.J. (1978), 'The post-Keynesian theory of income distribution in the corporate economy', *Australian Economic Papers*, **17** (31), December, 303–22.

Moss, S.J. (1980), 'The end of orthodox capital theory', in E.J. Nell (ed.), *Growth, Profits, and Property: Essays in the Revival of Political Economy*, Cambridge: Cambridge University Press, pp. 64–79.

Mott, T. (1985–86), 'Towards a post-Keynesian formulation of liquidity preference', *Journal of Post Keynesian Economics*, **8** (2), Winter, 222–32.

Mott, T. and E. Slattery (1994), 'The influence of changes in income distribution on aggregate demand in a Kaleckian model: stagnation vs exhilaration reconsidered', in P. Davidson and J.A. Kregel (eds), *Employment, Growth and Finance*, Aldershot, UK and Brookfield, VT, USA: Edward Elgar, pp. 69–82.

Mundell, R. (1961a), 'The international disequilibrium system', *Kyklos*, **14** (2), May, 153–72.

Mundell, R. (1961b), 'Flexible exchange rates and employment policy', *Canadian Journal of Economics and Political Science*, **27** (4), November, 509–17.

Mundell, R. (1963), 'Capital mobility and stabilization policy under fixed and flexible exchange rates', *Canadian Journal of Economics and Political Science*, **29** (4), November, 475–85.

Munier, F. and Z. Wang (2005), 'Consumer sovereign and consumption routine: a reexamination of the Galbraithian concept of the dependence effect', *Journal of Post Keynesian Economics*, **28** (1), Fall, 65–82.

Murau, S. and T. Pforr (2020), 'What is money in a critical macro-finance framework?', *Finance and Society*, **6** (1), 56–66.

Myatt, A. (1986), 'On the non-existence of a natural rate of unemployment and Kaleckian underpinnings of the Phillips curve', *Journal of Post Keynesian Economics*, **8** (3), Summer, 447–62.

Naastepad, C.W.M. and S. Storm (2010), 'Feasible egalitarianism: demand-led growth, labour and technology', in M. Setterfield (ed.), *Handbook of Alternative Theories of Economic Growth*, Cheltenham, UK and Northampton, MA, USA: Edward Elgar, pp. 311–30.

Nah, W.J. and M. Lavoie (2017), 'Long-run convergence in a neo-Kaleckian open-economy model with autonomous export growth', *Journal of Post Keynesian Economics*, **40** (2), 223–38.

Nah, W.J. and M. Lavoie (2018), 'Overhead labour costs in a neo-Kaleckian growth model with autonomous expenditures', Working Paper, No. 111/2018, Hochschule für Wirtschaft und Recht Berlin, Institute for International Political Economy (IPE), Berlin.

Nah, W.J. and M. Lavoie (2019a), 'Convergence in a neo-Kaleckian model with endogenous technical progress and autonomous demand growth', *Review of Keynesian Economics*, **7** (3), Autumn, 275–91.

Nah, W.J. and M. Lavoie (2019b), 'The role of autonomous demand growth in a neo-Kaleckian conflicting-claims framework', *Structural Change and Economic Dynamics*, **51**, December, 427–44.

Nahuis, N.J. (2003), 'An alternative demand indicator: the "nonaccelerating inflation rate of capacity utilization"', *Applied Economics*, **35** (11), 1339–44.

Naples, M.I. (1987), 'Cyclical and secular productivity slowdown', in *The Imperiled Economy*, Book 1, New York: Union for Radical Political Economics, pp. 159–70.

Naqvi, A. and E. Stockhammer (2018), 'Directed technological change in a post-Keynesian ecological macromodel', *Ecological Economics*, **154**, December, 168–88.

Ndikumana, L. (1999), 'Debt service, financing constraints, and fixed investment: evidence from panel data', *Journal of Post Keynesian Economics*, **21** (3), Spring, 455–78.

Neilson, D.H. (2019), *Minsky*, Cambridge: Polity Press.

Nell, E.J. (1978), 'The simple theory of effective demand', *Intermountain Economic Review*, **9** (2), Fall, 1–33.

Nell, E.J. (1985), 'Jean Baptiste Marglin: a comment on growth, distribution and inflation', *Cambridge Journal of Economics*, **9** (2), June, 173–8.

Nell, E.J. (1988), *Prosperity and Public Spending: Transformational Growth and the Role of Government*, Boston, MA: Unwin Hyman.

Nell, E.J. (1992), 'Demand, pricing and investment', in *Transformational Growth and Effective Demand: Economics After the Capital Critique*, London: Macmillan, pp. 381–451.

Nell, E.J. (1998), *The General Theory of Transformational Growth: Keynes After Sraffa*, Cambridge: Cambridge University Press.

Nell, E.J. (2003), 'Anchors aweigh: from real to nominal money and from market to government stabilization', in E.J. Nell and M. Forstater (eds), *Reinventing Functional Finance: Transformational Growth and Full Employment*, Cheltenham, UK and Northampton, MA, USA: Edward Elgar, pp. 171–210.

Nell, E.J. and M. Forstater (eds) (2003), *Reinventing Functional Finance: Transformational Growth and Full Employment*, Cheltenham, UK and Northampton, MA, USA: Edward Elgar.

Nenovsky, N. and K. Hristov (1998), 'Financial repression and credit rationing under currency board arrangements for Bulgaria', Discussion Paper DP/2/1998, Bulgarian National Bank.

Nersisyan, Y. and F. Dantas (2017), 'Rethinking liquidity creation: banks, shadow banks and the elasticity of finance', *Journal of Post Keynesian Economics*, **40** (3), 279–99.

Nersisyan, Y. and L.R. Wray (2017), 'Cranks and heretics: the importance of an analytical framework', *Cambridge Journal of Economics*, **41** (6), November, 1749–60.

Nesvetailova, A. (2007), *Fragile Finance: Debt, Speculation and Crisis in the Age of Global Credit*, London: Palgrave Macmillan.

Neville, J.W. and P. Kriesler (2008), 'Expectations and unemployment', in L.R. Wray and M. Forstater (eds), *Keynes and Macroeconomics After 70 Years: Critical Assessments of The General Theory*, Cheltenham, UK and Northampton, MA, USA: Edward Elgar, pp. 309–20.

Nichols, L.M. and N. Norton (1991), 'Overhead workers and political economy macro models', *Review of Radical Political Economics*, **23** (1–2), Spring–Summer, 47–54.

Nikiforos, M. (2013), 'The (normal) rate of capacity utilization at the firm level', *Metroeconomica*, **64** (3), July, 513–38.

Nikiforos, M. (2016), 'On the "utilization controversy": a theoretical and empirical discussion of the Kaleckian model of growth and distribution, *Cambridge Journal of Economics*, **40** (2), March, 437–67.

Nikiforos, M. (2017), 'Uncertainty and contradiction: an essay on the business cycle', *Review of Radical Political Economics*, **49** (2), 247–64.

Nikiforos, M. (2018), 'Some comments on the Sraffian supermultiplier approach to growth and distribution', *Journal of Post Keynesian Economics*, **41** (4), 659–75.

Nikiforos, M. and D.K. Foley (2012), 'Distribution and capacity utilization: conceptual issues and empirical evidence', *Metroeconomica*, **63** (1), February, 200–229.

Nikiforos, M. and G. Zezza (2017), 'Stock-Flow consistent macroeconomics models: a survey', *Journal of Economic Surveys*, **31** (5), December, 1204–39.

Nikolaidi, M. (2015), 'Securitisation, wage stagnation and financial fragility: a stock-flow consistent perspective', GPERC27, Greenwich Papers in Political Economy. https://gala.gre.ac.uk/id/eprint/14078/1/GPERC27_Paper-Securitisation.pdf.

Nikolaidi, M. and E. Stockhammer (2017), 'Minsky models: a structured survey', *Journal of Economic Surveys*, **31** (5), December, 1301–31.

Nisticò, S. (2002), 'Classical-type temporary positions: a cost-plus model', *Journal of Post Keynesian Economics*, **25** (1), Fall, 83–102.

Nordhaus, W. and W. Godley (1972), 'Pricing in the trade cycle', *Economic Journal*, **82** (327), September, 853–82.

Norman, N. (1996), 'A general Post Keynesian theory of protection', *Journal of Post Keynesian Economics*, **18** (4), Summer, 509–32.

Norman, N. (2008), 'How to recognize a good Post Keynesian', Working Paper, available at http://www.postkeynesian.net/ucamonly/Norman180111paper4.pdf.

Novarese, M. and C. Zimmerman (2008), 'Heterodox economics and the dissemination of research through the Internet: the experience of RePEc and NEP', *On the Horizon*, **16** (4), 198–204.

Nurkse, R. (1944), *International Currency Experience: Lessons of the Inter-War Period*, Geneva: League of Nations.

Obstfeld, M. and K. Rogoff (1995), 'The mirage of fixed exchange rates', *Journal of Economic Perspectives*, **9** (4), Autumn, 73–96.

Obstfeld, M., J.C. Shambaugh and A.M. Taylor (2005), 'The trilemma in history: tradeoffs among exchange rates, monetary policies, and capital mobility', *Review of Economics and Statistics*, **87** (3), August, 423–38.

O'Donnell, R.M. (1989), *Keynes: Philosophy, Economics and Politics*, London: Macmillan.

O'Donnell, R.M. (1991), 'Keynes on probability, expectations and uncertainty', in R.M. O'Donnell (ed.), *Keynes as Philosopher-Economist*, New York: St. Martin's Press, pp. 3–102.

O'Donnell, R.M. (2013), 'Two post-Keynesian approaches to uncertainty and irreducible uncertainty', in G.C. Harcourt and P. Kriesler (eds), *Oxford Handbook of Post-Keynesian Economics*, Volume 2, Oxford: Oxford University Press, pp. 124–42.

O'Hara, P.A. (2007a), 'Heterodox political economy specialization and interconnection – concepts of contradiction, heterogeneous agents, uneven development', *European Journal of Economics and Economic Policies: Intervention*, **4** (1), May, 99–120.

O'Hara, P.A. (2007b), 'Principles of institutional-evolutionary political economy – converging themes from the schools of heterodoxy', *Journal of Economic Issues*, **41** (1), March, 1–41.

Okun, A.M. (1981), *Prices and Quantities*, Washington, DC: The Brookings Institution.

Onaran, Ö. (2011), 'Globalisation, macroeconomic performance and distribution', in E. Hein and E. Stockhammer (eds), *A Modern Guide to Keynesian Macroeconomics and Economic Policies*, Cheltenham, UK and Northampton, MA, USA: Edward Elgar, pp. 240–66.

Onaran, Ö. (2016), 'Wage- versus profit-led growth in the context of globalization and public spending: the political aspects of wage-led recovery', *Review of Keynesian Economics*, **4** (4), Winter, 458–74.

Onaran, Ö. and G. Galanis (2012), 'Is aggregate demand wage-led or profit-led? National and global effects', Working Paper No. 40, Conditions of Work and Employment Series, International Labour Office.

Onaran, Ö. and T. Obst (2016), 'Wage-led growth in the EU15 member-states: the effects of income distribution on growth, investment, trade balance and inflation', *Cambridge Journal of Economics*, **40** (6), November, 1517–51.

Oreiro, J.L. and J.F. Costa Santos (2020), 'The term structure of interest rate in SFC model with inflation targeting and zero money financing of government deficit', *Revista Praticas de Administração Pública*, **4** (3), 3–42.

Oreiro, J.L., G.J. Silva and J.F. Costa Santos (2020), 'The debate about Sraffian Supermultiplier Model and the future of heterodox growth models', *Brazilian Journal of Political Economy*, **40** (3), July-September, 510–31.

Orléan, A. (1999), *Le pouvoir de la finance*, Paris: Odile Jacob.

Orléan, A. (2014), *The Empire of Value: A New Foundation for Economics*, Cambridge, MA: MIT Press.

Osberg, L. (1995), 'Concepts of unemployment and the structure of employment', *Économie Appliquée*, **48** (1), 133–56.

Ostry, J.D., P. Lougani and D. Furceri (2016), 'Neoliberalism oversold?', *Finance and Development*, June, 38–41.

Oyvat, C., O. Öztunalı, and C. Elgin (2020), 'Wage-led versus profit-led demand: a comprehensive empirical analysis', *Metroeconomica*, **71** (3), July, 458–86.

Palley, T.I. (1991), 'The endogenous money supply: consensus and disagreement', *Journal of Post Keynesian Economics*, **13** (3), Spring, 397–403.

Palley, T.I. (1994), 'Competing views of the money supply process: theory and evidence', *Metroeconomica*, **45** (1), February, 67–88.

Palley, T.I. (1996b), 'Accommodationism versus structuralism: time for accommodation', *Journal of Post Keynesian Economics*, **18** (4), Summer, 585–94.

Palley, T.I. (2002), 'Pifalls in the theory of growth: an application to the balance-of-payments-constrained growth model', in M. Setterfield (ed.), *The Economics of Demand-led Growth: Challenging the Supply-side Vision of the Long Run*, Cheltenham, UK and Northampton, MA, USA: Edward Elgar, pp. 115–25.

Palley, T. (2005), 'Class conflict and the Cambridge theory of distribution', in B. Gibson (ed.), *Joan Robinson's Economics: A Centennial Celebration*, Cheltenham, UK and Northampton, MA, USA: Edward Elgar, pp. 203–24.

Palley, T.I. (2006), 'A post-Keynesian framework for monetary policy: why interest rate operating procedures are not enough', in C. Gnos and L.P. Rochon (eds), *Post-Keynesian Principles of Economic Policy*, Cheltenham, UK and Northampton, MA, USA: Edward Elgar, pp. 78–98.

Palley, T.I. (2008), 'Institutionalism and new trade theory: rethinking comparative advantage and trade policy', *Journal of Economic Issues*, **42** (1), March, 195–208.

Palley, T.I. (2010), 'Inside debt and economic growth: a neo-Kaleckian analysis', in M. Setterfield (ed.), *Handbook of Alternative Theories of Economic Growth*, Cheltenham, UK and Northampton, MA, USA: Edward Elgar, pp. 293–308.

Palley, T.I. (2011), 'A theory of Minsky super-cycles and financial crises', *Contributions to Political Economy*, **30**, June, 31–46.

Palley, T.I. (2012), 'Wealth and wealth distribution in the neo-Kaleckian growth model', *Journal of Post Keynesian Economics*, **34** (3), Spring, 453–74.

Palley, T.I. (2016a), *Post Keynesian Economics: Debt, Distribution and the Macro Economy*, London: Macmillan.

Palley, T.I. (2017), 'Wage- vs profit-led growth: the role of the distribution of wages in determining regime character'. *Cambridge Journal of Economics*, **41** (1): 49–61.

Palley, T. (2019), 'The economics of the super-multiplier: a comprehensive treatment of labor markets', *Metroeconomica*, **70** (2), May, 325–40.

Palley, T.I. (2021), 'The economics of New Developmentalism: a critical assessment', *Investigación Económica*, **80** (317), July-September, 3–33.

Palley, T.I., L.P. Rochon and M. Vernengo (2012), 'Statement of the co-editors, economics and the economic crisis: the case for change', *Review of Keynesian Economics*, **1** (1), October, 1–4.

Palumbo, A. (2009), 'Adjusting theory to reality: the role of aggregate demand in Kaldor's late contributions to economic growth' *Review of Political Economy*, **21** (3), July, 341–68.

Palumbo, A. (2011), 'On the theory of the balance-of-payments-constrained growth', in R. Ciccone, C. Gehrke and G. Mongiovi (eds), *Sraffa and Modern Economics, Volume II*, London: Routledge, pp. 240–59.
Palumbo, A. and A. Trezzini (2003), 'Growth without normal capacity utilization', *European Journal of the History of Economic Thought*, **10** (1), Spring, 109–36.
Panagopoulos, Y. and A. Spiliotis (2017), 'New insights on the money-supply-endogeneity debate and the new "equity" multiplier: some evidence from the euro area', in L.-P. Rochon and S. Rossi (eds), *Advances in Endogenous Money Analysis*. Cheltenham, UK and Northampton, MA, USA: Edward Elgar, pp. 129–44.
Panico, C. (1985), 'Market forces and the relation between the rates of interest and profits', *Contributions to Political Economy*, **4**, March, 37–60.
Panico, C. (1988), *Interest and Profit in the Theories of Value and Distribution*, London: Macmillan.
Parenteau, R. (2010), 'Of Godley geometry and the fatal deceit of the eurozone', powerpoint presentation, 28 June.
Parguez, A. (1980), 'Profit, épargne, investissement: éléments pour une théorie monétaire du profit', *Économie Appliquée*, **33** (2), 425–55.
Parguez, A. (1999), 'The expected failure of the European Economic and Monetary Union: a false money against the real economy', *Eastern Economic Journal*, **25** (91), Winter, 63–76.
Parguez, A. (2012–13), 'The fundamental and eternal conflict: Hayek and Keynes on austerity', *International Journal of Political Economy*, **41** (4), Winter, 54–68.
Parguez, A. and M. Seccareccia (2000), 'The credit theory of money: the monetary circuit approach', in J. Smithin (ed.), *What is Money?*, London: Routledge, pp. 101–23.
Pariboni, R. (2016a), 'Autonomous demand and the Marglin-Bhaduri model: a critical note', *Review of Keynesian Economics*, **4** (4), Winter, 409–28.
Pariboni, R. (2016b), 'Household consumer debt, endogenous money and growth: a supermultiplier-based analysis', *PSL Quarterly Review*, **69** (278), September, 211–33.
Park, M.S. (1995), 'A note on the Kalecki–Steindl steady-state approach to growth and distribution', *Manchester School*, **63** (3), September, 297–310.
Park, M.S. (1997), 'Accumulation, capacity utilisation and distribution', *Contributions to Political Economy*, **16**, 87–101.
Paroush, J. (1965), 'The order of acquisition of durable goods', *Econometrica*, **33** (1), January, 225–35.
Parrinello, S. (1983), 'Exhaustible natural resources and the classical method of long-period equilibrium', in J.A. Kregel (ed.), *Distribution, Effective Demand and International Economic Relations*, London: Macmillan, pp. 186–99.
Pasinetti, L.L. (1974), *Growth and Income Distribution: Essays in Economic Theory*, Cambridge: Cambridge University Press.
Pasinetti, L.L. (1977), *Lectures in the Theory of Production*, Cambridge: Cambridge University Press.
Pasinetti, L.L. (1981), *Structural Change and Economic Growth*, Cambridge: Cambridge University Press.
Pasinetti, L.L. (1993), *Structural Economic Dynamics: A Theory of the Economic Consequences of Human Learning*, Cambridge: Cambridge University Press.
Pasinetti, L.L. (2007), *Keynes and the Cambridge Keynesians: A Revolution in Economics to be Accomplished*, Cambridge: Cambridge University Press.
Pasinetti, L.L. (2002), 'An analytical approach to the "just" rate of interest: the priority of labour over capital', *Rivista Internazionale di Scienze Sociali*, **110** (3), 323-329.
Pasinetti, L.L. (2021), 'Economic theory and institutions', *Structural Change and Economic Dynamics*, **56**, March, 438–42.
Patinkin, D. (1965), *Money, Interest and Prices*, 2nd edn, New York: Harper and Row.
Patterson, M. (1998), 'Commensuration and theories of value in ecological economics', *Ecological Economics*, **25** (1), April, 105–25.
Payne, J.E. (2006–07), 'More on the transmission mechanism: mortgage rates and the federal funds rate', *Journal of Post Keynesian Economics*, **29** (2), Winter, 247–59.

Peach, R., R. Rich and A. Cororaton (2011), 'How does slack influence inflation?', *Federal Reserve Bank of New York Current Issues in Economics and Finance*, **17** (3), 1–7.
Pedrosa, I. and D. Lang (2021), 'To what extent does aggregate leverage determine financial fragility? New insights from an agent-based stock-flow consistent model', *Journal of Evolutionary Economics*, **31** (4), September, 1221–75.
Pencavel, J. (1986), 'Labor supply of men: a survey', in O. Ashenfelter and R. Layard (eds), *Handbook of Labor Economics*, Vol. 1, Amsterdam: North-Holland, pp. 3–102.
Penrose, E.T. (1959), *The Theory of the Growth of the Firm*, Oxford: Basil Blackwell.
Peps-Economie (2013), 'L'enseignement de l'économie dans le supérieur: bilan et perspectives', *L'Économie politique*, **58**, April, 6–23.
Pérez Caldentey, E. (2007), 'Balance of payments constrained growth within a stock–flow framework', in United Nations ECLAC, *Caribbean Development Report*, Volume 1, pp. 196–221, available at http://www.eclac.cl/publicaciones/xml/3/32653/l.155rev1a.pdf.
Perrotini, I. and H.Y.D. Tlatelpa (2003), 'Crecimiento endógeno y demanda en las economías de américa del norte', *Momento Económico*, **128**, July–August, 10–15.
Perry, N. (2013), 'Environmental economics and policy', in G.C. Harcourt and P. Kriesler (eds), *The Oxford Handbook of Post-Keynesian Economics*, Volume 2, Oxford: Oxford University Press, pp. 390–411.
Perry, N. and N. Cline (2016), 'What caused the great inflation moderation in the US? A post-Keynesian view', *Review of Keynesian Economics*, **4** (4), Winter, 475–502.
Petit, P. (2005), 'Managerial capitalism by any other name', *Challenge*, **48** (5), September–October, 62–78.
Petri, F. (2021), *Microeconomics for the Critical Mind*, Cham, Switzerland: Springer Nature.
Phelps-Brown, E.H. (1957), 'The meaning of the fitted Cobb–Douglas function', *Quarterly Journal of Economics*, **71** (4), November, 546–60.
Piketty, T. (2014), *Capital in the Twenty-First Century*, Cambridge, MA: Harvard University Press.
Piore, M. (ed.) (1979), *Unemployment and Inflation: Institutionalist and Structuralist Views*, White Plains, NY: M.E. Sharpe.
Pirgmaier, E. (2017), 'The neoclassical Trojan horse of steady-state economics', *Ecological Economics*, **133**, March, 52–61.
Pivetti, M. (1985), 'On the monetary explanation of distribution', *Political Economy: Studies in the Surplus Approach*, **1** (2), 73–103.
Pivetti, M. (2013), 'On advanced capitalism and the determinants of the change in income distribution: a classical interpretation', in E.S. Levrero, A. Palumbo and A. Stirati (eds), *Sraffa and the Reconstruction of Economic Theory: Volume One. Theories of Value and Distribution*, Basingstoke: Palgrave Macmillan, pp. 176–91.
Pizano, D. (2009), 'A conversation with Professor Joan Robinson', in D. Pizano, *Conversations with Great Economists*, New York: Jorge Pinto Books, pp. 81–108.
Plihon, D. (2002), *Rentabilité et risque dans le nouveau régime de croissance*, Paris: La Documentation Française.
Pollin, R. (1991), 'Two theories of money supply endogeneity: some empirical evidence', *Journal of Post Keynesian Economics*, **13** (3), Spring, 366–96.
Pollin, R. (1996), 'Money supply endogeneity: what are the questions and why do they matter?', in G. Deleplace and E.J. Nell (eds), *Money in Motion: The Post Keynesian and Circulation Approaches*, London: Macmillan, pp. 490–515.
Pollin, R. (2005), 'Evaluating living wage laws in the United States: good intentions and economic reality in conflict?', *Economic Development Quarterly*, **19** (3), August, 3–24.
Pollin, R. (2008), 'Considerations on interest rate exogeneity', Working Paper No. 177, Political Economy Research Institute, University of Massachusetts in Amherst.
Pollin, R. (2019), 'Advancing a viable global climate stabilization project: degrowth versus the Green New Deal', *Review of Radical Political Economics*, **51** (2), 311–319.
Pollitt, H. and J.F. Mercure (2018), 'The role of money and the financial sector in energy-economy models used for assessing climate and energy policy', *Climate Policy*, **18** (2), 184–97.

Ponta, L., M. Raberto, A. Teglio and S. Cincotti (2018), 'An agent-based stock-flow consistent model of the sustainable transition in the energy sector', *Ecological Economics*, **145**, March, 274–300.

Poole, W. (1970), 'Optimal choice of monetary policy instruments in a simple stochastic macro model', *Quarterly Journal of Economics*, **84** (2), May, 197–216.

Posner, R.A. (2009a), *A Failure of Capitalism*, Cambridge, MA: Harvard University Press.

Posner, R.A. (2009b), 'How I became a Keynesian: second thoughts in the middle of a crisis', *The New Republican*, 23 September, available at http://www.tnr.com/print/article/how-i-became-keynesian.

Prasch, R. (1996), 'Reassessing the theory of comparative advantage', *Review of Political Economy*, **8** (1), January, 37–56.

Prasch, R. (2000), 'Reassessing the labor supply curve', *Journal of Economic Issues*, **34** (3), September, 679–92.

Prasch, R. (2004), 'How is labor distinct from broccoli? Some unique characteristics of labor and their importance for economic analysis and policy', in D.P. Champlin and J.T. Knoedler (eds), *The Institutionalist Tradition in Labor Economics*, Armonk, NY: M.E. Sharpe, pp. 146–58.

Prates, D. (2020), 'Beyond Modern Money Theory: A Post-Keynesian approach to the currency hierarchy, monetary sovereignty, and policy space', *Review of Keynesian Economics*, **8** (4), Winter, 494–511.

Pratten, S. (1996), 'The closure assumption as a first step: Neo-Ricardian economics and Post-Keynesianism', *Review of Social Economy*, **54** (4), Winter, 423–43.

Prescott, E.C. (1998), 'Needed: a theory of total factor productivity', *International Economic Review*, **39** (3), August, 525–52.

Priewe, J. (2022), 'Growth in ecological transition: green, zero or de-growth', *European Journal of Economics and Economic Policies: Intervention*, **19** (1), 19–40.

Prissert, P. (1972), 'Politiques monétaires, mouvements de capitaux à court terme et euro-dollars en régime de taux de change fixes', *Économie Appliquée*, **25** (2–3), 299–323.

Rabinovich, J. (2019), 'The Financialization of the nonfinancial corporation: a critique to the financial turn of accumulation hypothesis', *Metroeconomica*, **70** (4), November, 738–75.

Rabinovich, J. (2021), 'Financialisation and the "supply-side" face of the investment-profit puzzle', *Journal of Post Keynesian Economics*, **44** (3), 434–62.

Rada, C. (2017), 'Pension funding in a Keynesian model of growth', *Review of Keynesian Economics*, **5** (1), Spring, 94–106.

Rada, C. and L. Taylor (2006), 'Empty sources of growth accounting and empirical replacements à la Kaldor and Goodwin with some beef', *Structural Change and Economic Dynamics*, **17** (3), September, 486–500.

Radonjić, O. and S. Kokotović (2014), *Keynes, Minsky and Financial Crises in Emerging Markets*, Belgrade: University of Belgrade.

Radzicki, M.J. (2008), 'Institutional economics, post-Keynesian economics, and system dynamics: three strands of a heterodox braid', in J.T. Harvey and R.F. Garnett (eds), *Future Directions for Heterodox Economics*, Ann Arbor, MI: The University of Michigan Press, pp. 156–84.

Rahimi, A., M. Lavoie and B. Chu (2016), 'Linear and nonlinear Granger-causality between short-term and long-term interest rates during business cycles', *International Review of Applied Economics*, **30** (6), 714–28.

Rahimi, A., B.M. Chu and M. Lavoie (2017), 'Linear and non-linear Granger causality between short-term and long-term interest rates: a rolling window strategy', *Metroeconomica*, **68** (4), November, 882–902.

Rahmatian, A. (2020), *Credit and Creed: A Critical Legal Theory of Money*, London: Routledge.

Rassuli, A. and K. Rassuli (1988), 'The realism of Post Keynesian economics: a marketing perspective', *Journal of Post Keynesian Economics*, **10** (2), Spring, 455–73.

Razmi, A. (2015), 'The limits to wage-led growth in a low-income economy', *Metroeconomica*, **66** (4), November, 740–70.

Razmi, A. (2016), 'Growth and distribution in low-income economies: modifying post-Keynesian analysis in light of theory and history', *Review of Keynesian Economics*, **4** (4), Winter, 429–49.

Razmi, A. (2018a), 'Is planet Earth as a whole likely to be wage-led?', *Review of Keynesian Economics*, **6** (3), Autumn, 289–307.
Razmi, A. (2018b), 'Does the demand regime matter over the medium run? Revisiting distributional issues in a portfolio framework under different exchange rate regimes', *Metroeconomica*, **69** (4), November, 708–36.
Reardon, J. (2009), 'Private equity firms and the irrelevance of traditional monopoly', *Economía Informa*, **351**, March-April, 102–12.
Reich, M. (1984), 'Segmented labour: time-series hypothesis and evidence', *Cambridge Journal of Economics*, **8** (1), March, 63–81.
Reinhart, C.M. and K.S. Rogoff (2010), 'Growth in a time of debt', *American Economic Review*, **100** (2), May, 573–8.
Renversez, F. (1996), 'Monetary circulation and overdraft economy', in G. Deleplace and E.J. Nell (eds), *Money in Motion: The Post Keynesian and Circulation Approaches*, London: Macmillan, pp. 465–88.
Reynolds, P.J. (1987), *Political Economy: A Synthesis of Kaleckian and Post Keynesian Economics*, Brighton, UK: Wheatsheaf Books.
Rezai, A. (2015), 'Demand and distribution in integrated economies', *Cambridge Journal of Economics*, **39** (5), September, 1399–414.
Rezai, A. and S. Stagl (2016), 'Ecological macroeconomics: introduction and review', *Ecological Economics*, **121**, January, 181–5.
Rezai, A., L. Taylor and D. Foley (2018), 'Economic growth, income distribution, and climate change', *Ecological Economics*, **146**, April, 164–72.
Rezai, A., L. Taylor and R. Mechler (2013), 'Ecological macroeconomics: an application to climate change', *Ecological Economics*, **85** (January), 69–76.
Riach, P. (1995), 'Wage-employment determination in a Post Keynesian world', in P. Arestis and M. Marshall (eds), *The Political Economy of Full Employment*, Aldershot, UK and Brookfield, VT, USA: Edward Elgar, pp. 163–75.
Ribeiro, R.S.M., J.S.L. McCombie and G.T. Lima (2020), 'Does real exchange rate undervaluation really promote economic growth?', *Structural Change and Economic Dynamics*, **52**, 408–17.
Ricardo, D. (1951), *Principles of Political Economy and Taxation*, 3rd edn, Vol. 1 of the *Works and Correspondence of David Ricardo*, edited by P. Sraffa, Cambridge: Cambridge University Press.
Richters, O. and A. Siemoneit (2017), 'Consistency and stability analysis of a monetary growth imperative', *Ecological Economics*, **136**, June, 114–25.
Rider, C. (1982), 'Trade theory irrelevance', *Journal of Post Keynesian Economics*, **4** (4), Summer, 594–601.
Rima, I. (1984a), 'Whatever happened to the concept of involuntary unemployment?', *International Journal of Social Economics*, **11** (3–4), 62–71.
Rima, I. (1984b), 'Involuntary unemployment and the respecified labor supply curve', *Journal of Post Keynesian Economics*, **6** (4), Summer, 540–50.
Rizvi, S.A.T. (2006), 'The Sonnenschein–Mantel–Debreu results after thirty years', *History of Political Economy*, **38** (Supplement), 228–45.
Robbins, L. (1932), *An Essay on the Nature and Significance of Economic Science*, London: Macmillan (3rd edn, 1984).
Robinson, J. (1937), *Introduction to the Theory of Employment*, London: Macmillan.
Robinson, J. (1938), 'The Economics of Inflation, by C. Bresciani-Turroni', *Economic Journal*, **48** (191), September, 507–13.
Robinson, J. (1947), *Essays in the Theory of Employment*, Oxford: Basil Blackwell.
Robinson, J. (1952), *The Rate of Interest and Other Essays*, London: Macmillan.
Robinson, J. (1956), *The Accumulation of Capital*, London: Macmillan.
Robinson, J. (1962), *Essays in the Theory of Economic Growth*, London: Macmillan.
Robinson, J. (1964), 'Pre-Keynesian theory after Keynes', *Australian Economic Papers*, **3** (1–2), June, 25–35.
Robinson, J. (1966), *An Essay on Marxian Economics*, 2nd edn, London: Macmillan (1st edn 1942).
Robinson, J. (1969), 'A further note', *Review of Economic Studies*, **36** (2), April, 260–62.

Robinson, J. (1970), 'Quantity theories old and new, a comment', *Journal of Money, Credit and Banking*, **2** (4), November, 504–12.
Robinson, J. (1971), *Economic Heresies: Some Old-fashioned Questions in Economic Theory*, London: Macmillan.
Robinson, J. (1973), *Collected Economic Papers, Volume IV*, Oxford: Basil Blackwell.
Robinson, J. (1975a), 'Introduction 1974: comments and explanations', in *Collected Economic Papers, volume III*, Oxford: Basil Blackwell.
Robinson, J. (1975b), 'The unimportance of reswitching', *Quarterly Journal of Economics*, **89** (1), February, 32–9.
Robinson, J. (1977), 'Michal Kalecki on the economics of capitalism', *Oxford Bulletin of Economics and Statistics*, **39** (1), February, 7–17.
Robinson, J. (1978), 'Keynes and Ricardo', *Journal of Post Keynesian Economics*, **1** (1), Fall, 12–18.
Robinson, J. (1980), 'Time in economic theory', *Kyklos*, **33** (2), May, 219–29.
Robinson, J. and J. Eatwell (1973), *An Introduction to Modern Economics*, London: McGraw-Hill.
Rochon, L.P. (1999), *Credit, Money and Production: An Alternative Post-Keynesian Approach*, Cheltenham, UK and Northampton, MA, USA: Edward Elgar.
Rochon, L.P. (2001), 'Horizontalism: setting the record straight', in L.P. Rochon and M. Vernengo (eds), *Credit, Interest Rates and the Open Economy: Essays on Horizontalism*, Cheltenham, UK and Northampton, MA, USA: Edward Elgar, pp. 31–68.
Rochon, L.P. and S. Rossi (2004), 'Central banking in the monetary circuit', in M. Lavoie and M. Seccareccia (eds), *Central Banking in the Modern World: Alternative Perspectives*, Cheltenham, UK and Northampton, MA, USA: Edward Elgar, pp. 144–63.
Rochon, L.P. and S. Rossi (2011), 'Monetary policy without reserve requirements: central bank money as means of final payment on the interbank market', in C. Gnos and L.P. Rochon (eds), *Credit, Money and Macroeconomic Policy: A Post-Keynesian Approach*, Cheltenham, UK and Northampton, MA, USA: Edward Elgar, pp. 98–115.
Rochon, L.P. and S. Rossi (2013), 'Endogenous money: the evolutionary versus the revolutionary views', *Review of Keynesian Economics*, **1** (2), Summer, 210–29.
Rochon, L.-P. and S. Rossi (eds) (2017), *Advances in Endogenous Money Analysis*, Cheltenham, UK and Northampton, MA, USA: Edward Elgar.
Rochon, L.P. and M. Setterfield (2008), 'The political economy of interest-rate setting, inflation, and income distribution', *International Journal of Political Economy*, **37** (2), Summer, 5–25.
Rochon, L.P. and M. Setterfield (2012), 'A Kaleckian model of growth and distribution with conflict-inflation and Post Keynesian nominal interest rate rules', *Journal of Post Keynesian Economics*, **34** (3), Spring, 497–520.
Rogé, C. (2020), 'Harrodian instability in a post-Keynesian growth and distribution model', *Metroeconomica*, **71** (1), February, 88–128.
Rogers, C. (1983), 'Neo-Walrasian macroeconomics, microfoundations and pseudo-production models', *Australian Economic Papers*, **22** (40), June, 201–20.
Rogers, C. (1989), *Money, Interest and Capital: A Study in the Foundations of Monetary Theory*, Cambridge: Cambridge University Press.
Rogers, C. (2018), 'The conceptual flaw in the microeconomic foundation of dynamic stochastic general equilibrium models', *Review of Political Economy*, **30** (1), January, 72–83.
Rolim, L.N. (2019), 'Overhead labour and feedback effects between capacity utilization and income distributions: estimations for the USA economy', *International Review of Applied Economics*, **33** (6), 756–73.
Romer, P. (2016), 'The trouble with macroeconomics', Working Paper, available at https://paul romer.net/wp-content/uploads/2016/09/WP-Trouble.pdf.
Roncaglia, A. (1978), *Sraffa and the Theory of Prices*, New York: John Wiley.
Roncaglia, A. (1995), 'On the compatibility between Keynes's and Sraffa's viewpoints on output levels', in G.C. Harcourt, A. Roncaglia and R. Rowley (eds), *Income and Employment in Theory and Practice*, New York: St. Martin's Press, pp. 111–25.
Roncaglia, A. (2003), 'Energy and market power: an alternative approach to the economics of oil', *Journal of Post Keynesian Economics*, **25** (4), Summer, 641–60.

Rosser, J.B. Jr (1999), 'Complex dynamics in New Keynesian and Post Keynesian models', in R.J. Rotheim (ed.), *New Keynesian Economics/Post Keynesian Alternatives*, London: Routledge, pp. 288–302.
Rossi, S. (2006), 'Cross-border transactions and exchange rate stability', in L.P. Rochon and S. Rossi (eds), *Monetary and Exchange Rate Systems: A Global View of Financial Crises*, Cheltenham, UK and Northampton, MA, USA: Edward Elgar, pp. 191–209.
Rousseas, S. (1986), *Post Keynesian Monetary Economics*, Armonk, NY: M.E. Sharpe.
Rowthorn, R.E. (1977), 'Conflict, inflation and money', *Cambridge Journal of Economics*, **1** (3), September, 215–39.
Rowthorn, B. (1981), 'Demand, real wages and economic growth', *Thames Papers in Political Economy*, Autumn, 1–39.
Roy, R. (1943), 'La hiérarchie des besoins et la notion de groupes dans l'économie de choix', *Econometrica*, **11** (1), January, 13–24.
Roy, R. (2005), 'The hierarchy of needs and the concept of groups in consumer choice theory', *History of Economics Review*, **42**, 50–56. Partial translation of Roy (1943).
Rumsfeld, D. (2003), available at http://www.youtube.com/watch?v=GiPe1OiKQuk.
Runde, J. (1990), 'Keynesian uncertainty and the weight of arguments', *Economics and Philosophy*, **6** (2), October, 275–92.
Runde, J. (1994), 'Keynesian uncertainty and liquidity preference', *Cambridge Journal of Economics*, **18** (2), June, 129–44.
Russo, E. (2020), 'Harrodian instability in decentralized economies: an agent-based approach', *Economia Politica*, **38** (2), July, 539–67.
Rymes, T.K. (1971), *On Concepts of Capital and Technical Change*, Cambridge: Cambridge University Press.
Ryoo, S. and P. Skott (2013), 'Public debt and full employment in a stock–flow consistent model of a corporate economy', *Journal of Post Keynesian Economics*, **35** (4), Summer, 511–28.
Saith, A. (2022), *Cambridge Economics in the Post-Keynesian Era: The Eclipse of Heterodox Traditions*, Cham, Switzerland: Springer Nature.
Salmon, F. (2009), 'A recipe for disaster: the formula that killed Wall Street', *Wired*, 17 March, available at http://www.wired.com/techbiz/it/magazine/17-03/wp_quant?currentPage=all.
Samuelson, P.A. (1962), 'Parable and realism in capital theory: the surrogate production function', *Review of Economic Studies*, **29** (3), June, 193–206.
Samuelson, P.A. (1969b), 'The role of money in national economic policy', in *Controlling Monetary Aggregates*, Boston, MA: Federal Reserve Bank of Boston, pp. 7–15.
Samuelson, P.A. (1979), 'Paul Douglas's measurement of production functions and marginal productivities', *Journal of Political Economy*, **87** (5), October, 923–39.
Samuelson, P.A. (2007), 'Reflections on how biographies of individual scholars can relate to a science's biography', in P.A. Samuelson and W.A. Barnett (eds), *Inside the Economist's Mind: Conversations with Eminent Economists*, Oxford: Blackwell, pp. viii–x.
Sarantis, N. (1990–91), 'Distribution and terms of trade dynamics, inflation, and growth', *Journal of Post Keynesian Economics*, **13** (2), Winter, 175–98.
Sardoni, C. (2002), 'On the microeconomic foundations of macroeconomics: a Keynesian perspective', in A. Arestis, M. Desai and S. Dow (eds), *Methodology, Microeconomics and Keynes: Essays in Honour of Victoria Chick, Volume Two*, London: Routledge, pp. 4–14.
Sargent, T.J. (1993), *Bounded Rationality in Macroeconomics*, Oxford: Oxford University Press.
Sarkar, P. (1993), 'Distribution and growth: a critical note on stagnationism', *Review of Radical Political Economics*, **25** (1), March, 62–70.
Sasaki, H. (2011), 'Conflict, growth, distribution, and employment: a long-run Kaleckian model', *International Review of Applied Economics*, **25** (5), September, 539–57.
Sasaki, H., J. Matsuyama and K. Sato (2013), 'The macroeconomic effect of the wage gap between regular and non-regular employment and minimum wages', *Structural Change and Economic Dynamics*, **26**, 61–72.
Sawyer, M.C. (1982), *Macro-Economics in Question*, Armonk, NY: M.E. Sharpe.
Sawyer, M.C. (1989), *The Challenge of Radical Political Economy*, London: Harvester Wheatsheaf.

Sawyer, M.C. (1995), 'Comment on Earl and Shapiro', in S. Dow and J. Hillard (eds), *Keynes, Knowledge and Uncertainty*, Aldershot, UK and Brookfield, VT, USA: Edward Elgar, pp. 303–11.

Sawyer, M.C. (2001a), 'Kalecki on money and finance', *European Journal of the History of Economic Thought*, **8** (4), Winter, 487–508.

Sawyer, M. (2001b), 'Minsky's analysis, the European single currency and the global financial system', in R. Bellofiore and P. Ferri (eds), *Financial Keynesianism and Market Instability: The Economic Legacy of Hyman Minsky, Volume I*, Cheltenham, UK and Northampton, MA, USA: Edward Elgar, pp. 179–93.

Sawyer, M. (2010), 'Crises and paradigms in macroeconomics', *European Journal of Economics and Economic Policies: Intervention*, **7** (2), November, 283–302.

Sawyer, M. (2011), 'Re-thinking macroeconomic policies', in C. Gnos and L.P. Rochon (eds), *Credit, Money and Macroeconomic Policy: A Post-Keynesian Approach*, Cheltenham, UK and Northampton, MA, USA: Edward Elgar, pp. 268–88.

Sawyer, M. (2019), 'Modern monetary theory: is there any added value?', *Real-World Economics Review*, **89**, October, 167–79.

Sawyer, M.C., S. Aaronovitch and P. Samson (1982), 'The influence of cost and demand changes on the rate of change of prices', *Applied Economics*, **14** (2), April, 195–209.

Sawyer, M. and M. Veronese Passarella (2017), 'The monetary circuit in the age of financialisation: a stock-flow consistent model with a twofold banking sector', *Metroeconomica*, **68** (2), May, 321–53.

Schefold, B. (1983), 'Kahn on Malinvaud', in J. Eatwell and M. Milgate (eds), *Keynes's Economics and the Theory of Value and Distribution*, Oxford: Oxford University Press, pp. 229–46.

Schefold, B. (1984), 'Sraffa and applied economics: are there classical supply curves?', Centro Di Studi Economice Avanzati, Conference on Streams of Economic Thought, Trieste–Udine.

Schefold, B. (1985a), 'On changes in the composition of output', *Political Economy: Studies in the Surplus Approach*, **1** (2), 105–42.

Schefold, B. (1985b), 'Ecological problems as a challenge to classical and Keynesian economics', *Metroeconomica*, **37** (1), February, 21–61.

Schefold, B. (1997), *Normal Prices, Technical Change and Accumulation*, London: Macmillan.

Schefold, B. (2001), 'Critique of the corn–guano model', *Metroeconomica*, **52** (3), August, 316–28.

Schefold, B. (2013), 'Only a few techniques matter! On the number of curves on the wage frontier', in E.S. Levrero, A. Palumbo and A. Stirati (eds), *Sraffa and the Reconstruction of Economic Theory, Volume 1, Theories of Value and Distribution*, Basingstoke: Palgrave Macmillan, pp. 46–69.

Schelling, T.C. (1946), 'Raise profits by raising wages', *Econometrica*, **14** (3), July, 227–34.

Scherer, F.M. (1970), *Industrial Market Structure and Economic Performance*, Chicago, IL: Rand McNally.

Schoder, C. (2017), 'A critical review of the rationale approach to the microfoundations of post-Keynesian theory', *Review of Political Economy*, **29** (2), April, 171–89.

Schor, J.B. (1987), 'Class struggle and the macroeconomy: the cost of job loss', in *The Imperiled Economy*, Book 1, New York: Union for Radical Political Economics, pp. 171–82.

Schor, J.B. (2008), *The Overworked American: The Unexpected Decline of Leisure*, New York: Basic Books.

Schor, J.B. and A.K. Jorgenson (2019), 'Is it too late for growth?', *Review of Radical Political Economics*, **51** (2), 320–329.

Schumpeter, J.A. (1934), *The Theory of Economic Development*, Cambridge, MA: Harvard University Press.

Schumpeter, J.A. (1943), *Capitalism, Socialism and Democracy*, New York: Harper.

Schumpeter, J.A. (1954), *History of Economic Analysis*, New York: Oxford University Press.

Schütz, B. (2021), 'Creating a pluralist paradigm: an application to the minimum wage debate', *Journal of Economic Issues*, **55** (1), March, 103–24.

Scitovsky, T. (1976), *The Joyless Economy*, Oxford: Oxford University Press.

Seccareccia, M. (1984), 'The fundamental macroeconomic link between investment activity, the structure of employment and price changes: a theoretical and empirical analysis', *Économies et Sociétés*, **18** (4), April, 165–219.

Seccareccia, M. (1991a), 'An alternative to labour-market orthodoxy: the post-Keynesian/institutionalist policy view', *Review of Political Economy*, **3** (1), January, 43–61.
Seccareccia, M. (1991b), 'Salaire minimum, emploi et productivité dans une perspective post-Keynésienne', *L'Actualité économique*, **67** (2), June, 166–91.
Seccareccia, M. (1994), 'Credit money and cyclical crises: the views of Hayek and Fisher compared', in M. Colonna and H. Hagemann (eds), *Money and Business Cycles: The Economics of F.A. Hayek, Volume I*, Aldershot, UK and Brookfield, VT, USA: Edward Elgar, pp. 53–73.
Seccareccia, M. (2004), 'What type of full employment? A critical evaluation of government as the employer of last resort', *Investigación Económica*, **63** (247), January–March, 15–44.
Seccareccia, M. (2012), 'Understanding fiscal policy and the new fiscalism', *International Journal of Political Economy*, **41** (2), Summer, 61–81.
Seccareccia, M. (2020), 'Dualism and economic stagnation: can a policy of guaranteed basic income return mature market economies to *les Trente glorieuses*?', in B.K. Maclean, H. Bougrine and L.P. Rochon (eds), *Aggregate Demand and Employment: International Perspectives*, Cheltenham, UK and Northampton, MA, USA: Edward Elgar, pp. 33–60.
Semieniuk, G., E. Campiglio, J.F. Mercure, U. Voltz and N.R. Edwards (2021), 'Low-carbon transition risks for finance', *WIREs Climate Change*, **12** (1), January–February, article e678, 1–24.
Semmler, W. (1984), *Competition, Monopoly and Differential Profit Rates*, New York: Columbia University Press.
Sen, A. (ed.) (1970), *Growth Economics*, London: Penguin.
Sen, A.K. (1977), 'Rational fools: a critique of the behavioral foundations of economic theory', *Philosophy and Public Affairs*, **6** (4), Summer, 317–44.
Sent, E.-M. (2004), 'Behavioral economics: how psychology made its (limited) way back into economics', *History of Political Economy*, **36** (4), Winter, 735–60.
Seppecher, P. (2012), 'Flexibility of wages and macroeconomic instability in an agent-based computational model with endogenous money', *Macroeconomic Dynamics*, **16** (2), Supplement S2, September, 284–97.
Serrano, F. (1995a), 'Long period effective demand and the Sraffian supermultiplier', *Contributions to Political Economy*, **14**, 67–90.
Serrano, F. (1995b), 'The Sraffian multiplier', PhD dissertation, Faculty of Economics and Politics, University of Cambridge.
Serrano, F. (2006), 'Mind the gap: hysteresis, inflation dynamics and the Sraffian supermultiplier', available at http://www.ie.ufrj.br/datacenterie/pdfs/download/texto_10_10.pdf.
Serrano, F. and F. Freitas (2017), 'The Sraffian supermultiplier as an alternative closure for heterodox growth theory', *European Journal of Economics and Economic Policies: Intervention*, **14** (1), 70–91.
Serrano, F. and R. Summa (2015), 'Mundell–Fleming without the LM curve: the exogenous interest rate in an open economy', *Review of Keynesian Economics*, **3** (2), Summer, 248–268.
Serrano, F., F. Freitas and G. Bhering (2019), 'The trouble with Harrod: the fundamental instability of the warranted rate in the light of the Sraffian multiplier', *Metroeconomica*, **70** (2), May, 263–87.
Setterfield, M. (1993), 'Towards a long-run theory of effective demand: modeling macroeconomic systems with hysteresis', *Journal of Post Keynesian Economics*, **15** (3), Spring, 347–64.
Setterfield, M. (1999), 'Expectations, path dependence and effective demand: a macroeconomic model along Keynesian lines', *Journal of Post Keynesian Economics*, **21** (3), Spring, 479–502.
Setterfield, M. (2002), 'Introduction: a dissenter's view of the development of growth theory and the importance of demand-led growth', in M. Setterfield (ed.), *The Economics of Demand-led Growth: Challenging the Supply-side Vision of the Long Run*, Cheltenham, UK and Northampton, MA, USA: Edward Elgar, pp. 1–18.
Setterfield, M. (2003), 'What is analytical political economy?', *International Journal of Political Economy*, **33** (2), Summer, 4–16.
Setterfield, M. (2006), 'Is inflation targeting compatible with Post Keynesian economics?', *Journal of Post Keynesian Economics*, **28** (4), Summer, 653–72.

Setterfield, M. (2007), 'The rise, decline and rise of income policies in the US during the post-war era: an institutional-analytical explanation of inflation and the functional distribution of income', *Journal of Institutional Economics*, **3** (2), August, 127–46.
Setterfield, M. (2009), 'Macroeconomics without the LM curve: an alternative view', *Cambridge Journal of Economics*, **33** (2), March, 273–93.
Setterfield, M. (2012), 'The remarkable durability of Thirlwall's Law', in E. Soukiakis and P.A. Cerqueira (eds), *Models of Balance of Payments Constrained Growth: History, Theory and Empirical Evidence*, Basingstoke: Palgrave Macmillan, pp. 83–110.
Setterfield, M. (2019), 'Long-run variation in capacity utilization in the presence of a fixed normal rate', *Cambridge Journal of Economics*, **43** (2), March, 443–63.
Setterfield, M. and J.D. Avritzer (2020), 'Hysteresis in the normal rate of capacity utilization: a behavioral explanation', *Metroeconomica*, **71** (4), November, 898–919.
Setterfield, M. and Y.K. Kim (2017), 'Household borrowing and the possibility of consumption-driven, profit-led growth', *Review of Keynesian Economics*, **5** (1), Spring, 43–60.
Shackle, G.L.S. (1971), *Expectations, Enterprise and Profit*, London: Allen and Unwin.
Shackle, G.L.S. (1972), *Epistemics and Economics*, Cambridge: Cambridge University Press.
Shackle, G.L.S. (1984), 'Comment on the papers by Randall Bausor and Malcolm Rutherford', *Journal of Post Keynesian Economics*, **6** (3), Spring, 388–93.
Shaikh, A. (1974), 'Laws of production and laws of algebra. The humbug production function', *Review of Economics and Statistics*, **56** (1), February, 115–20.
Shaikh, A. (1980a), 'Laws of production and laws of algebra: humbug II', in J. Nell (ed.), *Growth, Profits, & Property: Essays in the Revival of Political Economy*, Cambridge: Cambridge University Press, pp. 80–95.
Shaikh, A. (1980b), 'The laws of international exchange', in E.J. Nell (ed.), *Growth, Profits and Property: Essays in the Revival of Political Economy*, Cambridge: Cambridge University Press, pp. 204–35.
Shaikh, A. (1990), 'Humbug production function', in J. Eatwell, M. Milgate and P. Newman (eds), *Capital Theory*, London: Macmillan, pp. 191–4.
Shaikh, A. (2005), 'Non-linear dynamics and pseudo production functions', *Eastern Economic Journal*, **31** (3), Summer, 347–66.
Shaikh, A. (2007a), 'A proposed synthesis of classical and Keynesian growth', SCEPA Working Paper 2007-1, available at http://www.newschool.edu/scepa/publications/workingpapers/SCEPA%20Working%20Paper%202007-1.pdf.
Shaikh, A. (2007b), 'Globalization and the myths of free trade', in A. Shaikh (ed.), *Globalization and the Myths of Free Trade: History, Theory, and Empirical Evidence*, London: Routledge, pp. 50–68.
Shaikh, A. (2009), 'Economic policy in a growth context: a classical synthesis of Keynes and Harrod', *Metroeconomica*, **60** (3), July, 455–94.
Shaikh, A. (2010), 'Reflexivity, path dependence and disequilibrium dynamics', *Journal of Post Keynesian Economics*, **33** (1), Fall, 3–16.
Shaikh, A. (2016), *Capitalism: Competition, Conflict, Crises*, Oxford: Oxford University Press.
Shapiro, C. and J.E. Stiglitz (1984), 'Equilibrium unemployment as a worker discipline device', *American Economic Review*, **74** (3), June, 433–44.
Shapiro, N. (1977), 'The revolutionary character of post-Keynesian economics', *Journal of Economic Issues*, **11** (3), September, 541–60.
Shapiro, N. (1981), 'Pricing and the growth of the firm', *Journal of Post Keynesian Economics*, **4** (1), Fall, 85–100.
Shapiro, N. and T. Mott (1995), 'Firm-determined prices: the post-Keynesian conception', in P. Wells (ed.), *Post-Keynesian Economic Theory*, Amsterdam: Kluwer Academic, pp. 35–48.
Shapiro, N. and M. Sawyer (2003), 'Post Keynesian price theory', *Journal of Post Keynesian Economics*, **25** (3), Spring, 355–67.
Sharif, M. (2003), 'A behavioural analysis of the subsistence standard of living', *Cambridge Journal of Economics*, **27** (2), March, 191–207.

Sheard, P. (2013), 'Repeat after me: banks cannot and do not lend out reserves', Research Note, Standard and Poor's Rating Services, available at http://www.standardandpoors.com/spf/upload/Ratings_US/Repeat_After_Me_8_14_13.pdf.

Shefrin, H. (2016), 'Assessing the contribution of Hyman Minsky's perspective to our understanding of economic instability', in A.G. Malliaris, L. Shaw and H. Shefrin (eds), *The Global Financial Crisis and Its Aftermath: Hidden Factors in the Meltdown*, Oxford: Oxford Scholarship, pp. 104–42.

Sherman, H.J. (1979), 'A Marxist theory of the business cycle, *Review of Radical Political Economics*, **11** (1), 1–23.

Sherman, H.J. (2010), *The Roller Coaster Economy: Financial Crisis, Great Recession and the Public Option*, Armonk, NY: M.E. Sharpe.

Shiozawa, Y. (2016), 'The revival of the classical theory of values', in N. Yokokawa, K. Yagi, H. Uemura and R. Westra (eds), *The Rejuvenation of Political Economy*, New York: Routledge, pp. 151–72.

Shiozawa, Y., M. Morioka and K. Taniguchi (2019), *Microfoundations of Evolutionary Economics*, Tokyo: Springer.

Shipley, D.D. (1981), 'Pricing objectives in British manufacturing industry', *Journal of Industrial Economics*, **29** (4), June, 429–43.

Simon, H.A. (1955), 'A behavioral model of rational choice', *Quarterly Journal of Economics*, **69** (1), February, 99–118.

Simon, H.A. (1962), 'The architecture of complexity', *Proceedings of the American Philosophical Society*, **106** (6), December, 467–82.

Simon, H.A. (1976), 'From substantive to procedural rationality', in S.J. Latsis (ed.), *Method and Appraisal in Economics*, Cambridge: Cambridge University Press, pp. 129–48.

Simon, H.A. (1979a), 'On parsimonious explanations of production relations', *Scandinavian Journal of Economics*, **81** (4), 459–74.

Simon, H.A. (1979b), 'Rational decision making in business organizations', *American Economic Review*, **69** (4), September, 493–513.

Simon, H.A. (1991), 'Organizations and markets', *Journal of Economic Perspectives*, **5** (2), Spring, 25–44.

Simon, H.A. (1997), *An Empirically Based Microeconomics*, Cambridge: Cambridge University Press.

Sippel, R. (1997), 'An experiment on the pure theory of consumer's behaviour', *Economic Journal*, **107** (444), September, 1431–44.

Sissoko, C. (2017), 'The plight of modern markets: how universal banking undermines capital markets', *Economic Notes by Banca Monte dei Paschi di Siena*, **46** (1), 53–104.

Sissoko, C. (2019), 'Repurchase agreements and the (de)construction of financial markets', *Economy and Society*, **48** (2), 315–41.

Skidelsky, R. (1986), *John Maynard Keynes, Volume Two: The Economist as Saviour, 1920–1937*, London: Macmillan.

Skidelsky, R. (2009), *Keynes: The Return of the Master*, London: Allen Lane.

Skott, P. (1981), 'On the Kaldorian saving function', *Kyklos*, **34** (4), November, 563–81.

Skott, P. (1989a), *Conflict and Effective Demand in Economic Growth*, Cambridge: Cambridge University Press.

Skott, P. (1989b), *Kaldor's Growth and Distribution Theory*, Frankfurt am Main: Peter Lang.

Skott, P. (2010), 'Growth, instability and cycles: Harrodian and Kaleckian models of accumulation and income distribution' in M. Setterfield (ed.), *Handbook of Alternative Theories of Economic Growth*, Cheltenham, UK and Northampton, MA, USA: Edward Elgar, pp. 108–31.

Skott, P. (2012), 'Theoretical and empirical shortcomings of the Kaleckian investment function', *Metroeconomica*, **63** (1), February, 109–38.

Skott, P. (2017), 'Autonomous demand and the Harrodian criticism of the Kaleckian model', *Metroeconomica*, **68** (1), February, 185–93.

Skott, P. (2019), 'Autonomous demand, Harrodian instability and the supply side', *Metroeconomica*, **70** (2), May, 233–46.

Skott, P. and S. Ryoo (2008), 'Macroeconomic implications of financialisation', *Cambridge Journal of Economics*, **32** (6), November, 827–62.
Slade-Caffarel, Y. (2019), 'The nature of heterodox economics revisited', *Cambridge Journal of Economics*, **43** (3), May, 527–40.
Smithin, J. (1988), 'On flexible wage policies', *Économies et Sociétés*, **22** (3), March, 135–53.
Smithin, J. (1994), *Controversies in Monetary Economics: Ideas, Issues and Policy*, Aldershot, UK and Brookfield, VT, USA: Edward Elgar.
Smithin, J. (1996), *Macroeconomic Policy and the Future of Capitalism: The Revenge of the Rentiers and the Threat to Prosperity*, Cheltenham, UK and Brookfield, VT, USA: Edward Elgar.
Smithin, J. (1997), 'An alternative monetary model of inflation and growth', *Review of Political Economy*, **9** (4), October, 395–410.
Smithin, J. (2001), 'International monetary arrangements', in R.P.F. Holt and S. Pressman (eds), *A New Guide to Post Keynesian Economics*, London: Routledge, pp. 114–25.
Smithin, J. (2002–03), 'Interest parity, purchasing power parity, "risk premia", and Post Keynesian analysis', *Journal of Post Keynesian Analysis*, **25** (2), Winter, 219–36.
Smithin, J. (2004), 'Macroeconomic theory, (critical) realism, and capitalism', in P.A. Lewis (ed.), *Transforming Economics: Perspectives on the Critical Realist Project*, London: Routledge, pp. 55–75.
Smithin, J. (2009), *Money, Enterprise and Income Distribution: Towards a Macroeconomic Theory of Capitalism*, London: Routledge.
Smithin, J. (2020), 'Interest rates, income distribution and the monetary policy transmissions mechanism under endogenous money: what have we learned 30 years on from *Horizontalists and Verticalists*?', *European Journal of Economics and Economic Policies: Intervention*, **17** (3), 381–98.
Solow, R.M. (1957), 'Technical change and the aggregate production function', *Review of Economics and Statistics*, **39** (2), August, 312–20.
Solow, R.M. (2003), 'Dumb and dumber in macroeconomics', Working Paper for a Festschrift in honour of Joseph Stiglitz, https://www0.gsb.columbia.edu/faculty/jstiglitz/festschrift/Papers/Stig-Solow.pdf.
Solow, R.M. (2008), 'The state of macroeconomics', *Journal of Economic Literature*, **22** (1), 243–9.
Sonenshine, R., N. Larson and M. Cauvel (2016), 'Determinants of CEO compensation before and after the financial crisis', *Modern Economy*, **7** (12), November, 1455–77.
Soros, G. (2010), *The Soros Lectures at the Central European University*, New York: PublicAffairs.
Spash, C.L. (1998), 'Investigating individual motives for environmental action: lexicographic preferences, beliefs, attitudes', in J. Lemons, L. Westra and R. Goodland (eds), *Ecological Sustainability and Integrity: Concepts and Approaches*, Dordrecht, Boston, MA and London: Kluwer Academic Publishers, pp. 46–62.
Spash, C.L. (2020), 'A tale of three paradigms: realizing the revolutionary potential of ecological economics', *Ecological Economics*, **169**, March, article 106518, 1–14.
Spash, C.L. and N. Hanley (1995), 'Preferences, information and biodiversity preservation', *Ecological Economics*, **12** (3), March, 191–208.
Spash, C.L. and A. Ryan (2012), 'Economic schools of thought on the environment: investigating unity and division', *Cambridge Journal of Economics*, **36** (5), September, 1091–121.
Spaventa, L. (1970), 'Rate of profit, rate of growth and capital intensity in a simple production model', *Oxford Economic Papers*, **22** (2), July, 129–47.
Spencer, D.A. (2006), 'Work for all those who want it? Why the neoclassical labour supply curve is an inappropriate foundation for the theory of employment and unemployment', *Cambridge Journal of Economics*, **30** (3), May, 459–72.
Sraffa, P. (1960), *Production of Commodities by Means of Commodities: Prelude to a Critique of Economic Theory*, Cambridge: Cambridge University Press.
Stanford, J. (2017), 'The resurgence of gig work: historical and theoretical perspectives', *Economic and Labour Relations Review*, **28** (3), September, 382–401.
Stanley, T.D. (1998), 'New wine in old bottles: a meta-analysis of Ricardian equivalence', *Southern Economic Journal*, **64** (3), January, 713–17.

Stanley, T.D. (2002), 'When all are NAIRU: hysteresis and behavioural inertia', *Applied Economic Letters*, **9** (11), September, 753–7.
Stanley, T.D. (2004), 'Does unemployment hysteresis falsify the natural rate hypothesis? A meta-regression analysis', *Journal of Economic Surveys*, **18** (4), September, 589–612.
Stanley, T.D. (2005a), 'Beyond publication bias', *Journal of Economic Surveys*, **19** (3), July, 309–45.
Stanley, T.D. (2005b), 'Integrating the empirical tests of the natural rate hypothesis: a meta-regression analysis', *Kyklos*, **58** (4), November, 611–34.
Stanley, T.D. and S.B. Jarrell (1989), 'Meta-regression analysis: a quantitative method of literature surveys', *Journal of Economic Surveys*, **3** (2), 161–70.
Stanley, T.D., S.B. Jarrell and H. Doucouliagos (2010), 'Could it be better to discard 90% of the data? A statistical paradox', *American Statistician*, **64** (1), February, 70–77.
Steedman, I. (1979a), *Trade Amongst Growing Economies*, Cambridge: Cambridge University Press.
Steedman, I. (ed.) (1979b), *Fundamental Issues in Trade Theory*, London: Macmillan.
Steedman, I. (1980), 'Heterogeneous labour and classical theory', *Metroeconomica*, **32** (1), February, 39–50.
Steedman, I. (1992), 'Questions for Kaleckians', *Review of Political Economy*, **4** (2), April, 125–51.
Steindl, J. (1952), *Maturity and Stagnation in American Capitalism*, New York: Monthly Review Press, 1976.
Steindl, J. (1979), 'Stagnation theory and stagnation policy', *Cambridge Journal of Economics*, **3** (1), March, 1–14.
Steindl, J. (1982), 'The role of household saving in the modern household', *Banca Nazionale del Lavoro Quarterly Review*, March, 69–88.
Stenfors, A. (2019), 'The covered interest parity puzzle and the evolution of the Japan premium', *Journal of Economic Issues*, **53** (2), June, 417–24.
Stevens, T.H., J. Echeverria, R.J. Glass, T. Hager and T.A. More (1991), 'Measuring the existence value of wildlife: what do CVM estimates really show?', *Land Economics*, **67** (4), November, 390–400.
Stiglitz, J.E. (2015), 'Reconstructing macroeconomic theory to manage economic policy', in E. Laurent and J. Le Cacheux (eds), *Fruitful Economics: Papers in Honor of and by Jean-Paul Fitoussi*, Basingstoke, UK: Palgrave Macmillan, pp. 20–49.
Stiglitz, J.E. and B. Greenwald (2003), *Towards a New Paradigm in Monetary Economics*, Cambridge: Cambridge University Press.
Stilwell, F. (2019). 'From economics to political economy: contradictions, challenges and changes', *American Journal of Economics and Sociology*, **78** (1), January, 35–62.
Stockhammer, E. (2004), *The Rise of Unemployment in Europe: A Keynesian Approach*, Cheltenham, UK and Northampton, MA, USA: Edward Elgar.
Stockhammer, E. (2005–06), 'Shareholder value orientation and the investment–profit puzzle', *Journal of Post Keynesian Economics*, **28** (2), Winter, 193–216.
Stockhammer, E. (2008), 'Is the NAIRU theory a monetarist, New Keynesian, Post Keynesian or Marxist theory?', *Metroeconomica*, **59** (3), July, 479–510.
Stockhammer, E. (2011), 'The macroeconomics of unemployment', in E. Hein and E. Stockhammer (eds), *A Modern Guide to Keynesian Macroeconomics and Economic Policies*, Cheltenham, UK and Northampton, MA, USA: Edward Elgar, pp. 137–64.
Stockhammer, E. (2022), 'Post-Keynesian macroeconomic foundations for comparative political economy', *Politics and Society*, **56** (1), 156–187.
Stockhammer, E., C. Constantine and S. Reissl (2020), 'Explaining the Euro crisis: current account imbalances, credit booms and economic policy in different economic paradigms', *Journal of Post Keynesian Economics*, **43** (2), 231–66.
Stockhammer, E. and K. Kohler (2022), 'Learning from distant cousins? Post-Keynesian Economics, Comparative Political Economy and the growth models approach', Working Paper 2210, Post-Keynesian Economics Society.
Stockhammer, E. and J. Michell (2017), 'Pseudo-Goodwin cycles in a Minsky model', *Cambridge Journal of Economics*, **41** (1), January, 105–25.

Stockhammer, E. and P. Ramskogler (2009), 'Post-Keynesian economics – how to move forward', *European Journal of Economics and Economic Policies: Intervention*, **6** (2), November, 227–46.

Storm, S. (2021a), 'Cordon of conformity: why DSGE models are not the future of macroeconomics', *International Journal of Political Economy*, **50** (2), Summer, 77–98.

Storm, S. (2021b), 'A rejoinder', *International Journal of Political Economy*, **50** (2), Summer, 109–15.

Storm, S. and C.W.M. Naastepad (2012), *Macroeconomics Beyond the NAIRU*, Cambridge, MA: Harvard University Press.

Storm, S. and C.W.M. Naastepad (2013), 'Wage-led or profit-led supply: wages, productivity and investment', in M. Lavoie and E. Stockhammer (eds), *Wage-Led Growth: An Equitable Strategy for Economic Recovery*, Basingstoke: Palgrave Macmillan, pp. 100–124.

Storm, S. and C.W.M. Naastepad (2017), 'Bhaduri-Marglin meet Kaldor-Marx: wages, productivity and investment', *Review of Keynesian Economics*, **5** (1), Spring, 4–24.

Strotz, R.H. (1957), 'The empirical implications of a utility tree', *Econometrica*, **25** (2), April, 269–80.

Summa, R. and J. Braga (2020), 'Two routes back to the old Phillips curve: the amended mainstream model and the conflict augmented alternative', *Bulletin of Political Economy*, **14** (1), 81–115.

Summers, L. (1985), 'On economics and finance', *Journal of Finance*, **40** (3), July, 633–5.

Sylos Labini, P. (1949), 'The Keynesians', *Banca Nazionale del Lavoro Quarterly Review*, November, 238–42.

Sylos Labini, P. (1971), 'La théorie des prix en régime d'oligopole et la théorie du développement', *Revue d'économie politique*, **81** (2), mars–avril, 244–72.

Taleb, N.N. (2007), *The Black Swan: The Impact of the Highly Improbable*, New York: Random House.

Tarling, R. and F. Wilkinson (1985), 'Mark-up pricing, inflation and distributional shares: a note', *Cambridge Journal of Economics*, **9** (2), June, 179–85.

Tarshis, L. (1980), 'Post-Keynesian economics: a promise that bounced?', *American Economic Review*, **70** (2), May, 10–14.

Tatliyer, M. (2017), 'Inflation targeting and the need for a new central banking framework', *Journal of Post Keynesian Economics*, **40** (4), 512–39.

Tavani, D. and R. Vasudevan (2014), 'Capitalists, workers, and managers: wage inequality and effective demand', *Structural Change and Economic Dynamics*, **30**, 120–31.

Taylor, J.B. (1993), 'Discretion versus policy rules in practice', *Carnegie-Rochester Conference Series on Public Policy*, **39**, December, 195–214.

Taylor, L. (1983), *Structuralist Macroeconomics: Applicable Models for the Third World*, New York: Basic Books.

Taylor, L. (1985), 'A stagnationist model of economic growth', *Cambridge Journal of Economics*, **9** (4), December, 381–403.

Taylor, L. (1990), 'Real and money wages, output and inflation in the semi-industrialized world', *Economica*, **57**, August, 329–53.

Taylor, L. (1991), *Income Distribution, Inflation and Growth: Lectures on Structuralist Macroeconomic Theory*, Cambridge, MA: MIT Press.

Taylor, L. (2004), *Reconstructing Macroeconomics: Structuralist Proposals and Critiques of the Mainstream*, Cambridge, MA: Harvard University Press.

Taylor, L. (2008), 'A foxy hedgehog: Wynne Godley and macroeconomic modelling', *Cambridge Journal of Economics*, **32** (4), July, 639–63.

Taylor, L. (2012), 'Growth, cycles, asset prices and finance', *Metroeconomica*, **63** (1), February, 40–63.

Taylor, L. and S.A. O'Connell (1985), 'A Minsky crisis', *Quarterly Journal of Economics*, **100**, Supplement, 871–85.

Taylor, L. and C. Rada (2008), 'Debt–equity cycles in the 20th century: empirical evidence and a dynamic Keynesian model', in P. Flaschel and M. Landesmann (eds), *Mathematical Economics and Capitalist Dynamics: Goodwin's Legacy Continued*, London: Routledge, pp. 219–46.

Taylor, L., A. Rezai and D. Foley (2016), 'An integrated approach to climate change, income distribution, employment, and economic growth', *Ecological Economics*, **121**, January, 196–205.
Tcherneva, P.R. (2006), 'Chartalism and the tax-driven approach', in P. Arestis and M. Sawyer (eds), *A Handbook of Alternative Monetary Economics*, Cheltenham, UK and Northampton, MA, USA: Edward Elgar, pp. 69–86.
Tcherneva, P.R. (2020), *The Case for a Job Guarantee*, Cambridge: Polity Press.
Terzi, A. (2010), 'Keynes's uncertainty is not about white or black swans', *Journal of Post Keynesian Economics*, **32** (4), Summer, 559–66.
Thirlwall, A.P. (1979), 'The balance of payments constraint as an explanation of international growth rate differences', *Banca Nazionale del Lavoro Quarterly Review*, **32** (128), March, 45–53.
Thirlwall, A.P. (2011), 'Balance of payments constrained growth models: history and overview', *PSL Quarterly Review*, **64** (259), December, 307–51.
Thirlwall, A.P. (2019), 'Thoughts on balance-of-payments constrained growth models: history and overview', *Review of Keynesian Economics*, **7** (4), 554–67.
Thirlwall, A.P. and M.N. Hussain (1982), 'The balance of payments constraint, capital flows and growth rate differences between developing countries', *Oxford Economic Papers*, **34** (3), November, 498–509.
Thompson, S. (2020), 'Growth, external markets and stock-flow norms: a Luxemburg-Godley model of accumulation', *Cambridge Journal of Economics*, **44** (2), March, 417–43.
Tobin, J. (1963), 'Commercial banks as creators of money', in D. Carson (ed.), *Banking and Monetary Studies*, Homeward, IL: Richard D. Irwin, pp. 408–19.
Tobin, J. (1969), 'A general equilibrium approach to monetary analysis', *Journal of Money, Credit, and Banking*, **1** (1), February, 15–29.
Tobin, J. (1980), *Asset Accumulation and Economic Activity*, Chicago, IL: University of Chicago Press.
Tobin, J. (1982), 'Money and finance in the macroeconomic process', *Journal of Money, Credit, and Banking*, **14** (2), May, 171–204.
Todd, P.M. and G. Gigerenzer (2003), 'Bounding rationality to the world', *Journal of Economic Psychology*, **24** (2), April, 143–65.
Tomer, J.F. (2007), 'What is behavioral economics?', *Journal of Socio-Economics*, **36** (3), June, 463–79.
Toporowski, J. (2000), *The End of Finance*, London: Routledge.
Toporowski, J. (2005), *Theories of Financial Disturbances*, Cheltenham, UK and Northampton, MA, USA: Edward Elgar.
Toporowski, J. (2008), 'Minsky's induced investment and business cycles', *Cambridge Journal of Economics*, **32** (5), September, 725–37.
Trezzini, A. (2011a), 'The irreversibility of consumption as a source of endogenous-demand-driven economic growth', *Review of Political Economy*, **23** (4), October, 537–56.
Trezzini, A. (2011b), 'Steady state and the analysis of long-run tendencies: the case of neo-Kaleckian models', in R. Ciccone, C. Gehrke and G. Mongiovi (eds), *Sraffa and Modern Economics, Volume II*, London: Routledge, pp. 129–51.
Trezzini, A. and A. Palumbo (2016), 'The theory of output in the modern classical approach: main principles and controversial issues', *Review of Keynesian Economics*, **4** (4), Winter, 503–22.
Trigg, A.B. (1994), 'On the relationship between Kalecki and the Kaleckians', *Journal of Post Keynesian Economics*, **17** (1), Fall, 91–110.
Trigg, A.B. (2004), 'Deriving the Engel curve: Pierre Bourdieu and the social critique of Maslow's hierarchy of needs', *Review of Social Economy*, **62** (3), September, 393–406.
Trigg, A.B. (2008), 'Quantity and price systems: toward a framework for coherence between post-Keynesian and Sraffian economics', in J.T. Harey and R.F. Ganett Jr (eds), *Future Directions for Heterodox Economics*, Ann Arbor, MI: University of Michigan Press, pp. 127–41.
Tucker, P. (2004), 'Managing the central bank's balance sheet: where monetary policy meets financial stability', *Bank of England Quarterly Bulletin*, **44** (3), Autumn, 359–82.
Tuñez-Area, N. (2006), 'Does public deficit mean inflation? A reflection on the Kaleckian and Minskian tradition', *European Journal of Economics and Economic Policies: Intervention*, **3** (1), May, 151–67.

Tversky, A. (1972), 'Elimination by aspects: a theory of choice', *Psychological Review*, **79** (4), July, 281–99.
Tymoigne, E. (2009), *Central Banking, Asset Prices and Financial Fragility*, London: Routledge.
Unger, R. (2016), 'Traditional banks, shadow banks and the US credit boom – credit origination versus financing', Discussion Paper 11/2016, Deutsche Bundesbank.
United Nations (2009), *System of National Accounts 2008*, New York: United Nations.
van den Bergh, J.C.J.M., A. Ferrer-i-Carbonell and G. Munda (2000), 'Alternative models of individual behaviour and implications for environmental policy', *Ecological Economics*, **32** (1), January, 43–61.
van Treeck, T. (2009), 'A synthetic, stock–flow consistent macroeconomic model of financialisation', *Cambridge Journal of Economics*, **33** (3), May, 467–93.
van Treeck, T. and S. Sturn (2012), 'Income inequality as a cause of the Great Recession? A survey of current debates', Working Paper No. 39, Conditions of Work and Employment Series, International Labour Office.
Vatn, A. (2009), 'Combining Post Keynesian, ecological and institutional economic perspectives', in R.P.F. Holt, S. Pressman and C.L. Spash (eds), *Post Keynesian and Ecological Economics: Confronting Environmental Issues*, Cheltenham, UK and Northampton, MA, USA: Edward Elgar, pp. 114–38.
Veblen, T. (1899), *The Theory of the Leisure Class*, London: Macmillan.
Vera, L.V. (2006), 'The balance-of-payments-constrained growth model: a north–south approach', *Journal of Post Keynesian Economics*, **29** (1), Fall, 67–92.
Vergeer, R. and A. Kleinknecht (2010–11), 'The impact of labor market deregulation on productivity: a panel data analysis of 19 OECD countries (1960–2004)', *Journal of Post Keynesian Economics*, **33** (2), Winter, 371–407.
Vergnhanini, R. and B. De Conti (2018), 'Modern Monetary Theory: A criticism from the periphery', *Brazilian Keynesian Review*, **3** (2), 16–31.
Vernengo, M. (2013), 'Conversation or monologue? On advising heterodox economists, with addendum', in F.S. Lee and M. Lavoie (eds), *In Defense of Post-Keynesian Economics and Heterodox Economics: Responses to their Critics*, London: Routledge, pp. 158–71.
Vernengo, M. and E. Pérez Caldentey (2020), 'Modern Money Theory (MMT) in the Tropics: Functional finance in developing countries', *Challenge*, **63** (6), 332–48.
Vianello, F. (1985), 'The pace of accumulation', *Political Economy: Studies in the Surplus Approach*, **1** (1), 69–87.
Vianello, F. (1989), 'Effective demand and the rate of profit: some thoughts on Marx, Kalecki and Sraffa', in M. Sebastiani (ed.), *Kalecki's Relevance Today*, New York: St. Martin's Press, pp. 164–90.
Vickrey, W. (1997), 'A trans-Keynesian manifesto (thoughts about an asset-based macroeconomics)', *Journal of Post Keynesian Economics*, **19** (4), Summer, 495–510.
von Arnim, R., D. Tavani and L. Carvalho (2014), 'Redistribution in a neo-Kaleckian two-country model', *Metroeconomica*, **65** (3), July, 430–59.
Walsh, V. (2011), 'Rationality in reproduction models', in R. Ciccone, C. Gehrke and G. Mongiovi (eds), *Sraffa and Modern Economics, Volume I*, London: Routledge, pp. 453–67.
Watts, M.J. and N.G. Gaston (1982–83), 'The "reswitching" of consumption bundles: a parallel to the capital controversies?', *Journal of Post Keynesian Economics*, **5** (2), Winter, 281–8.
Webb, S. (1912), 'The economic theory of a legal minimum wage', *Journal of Political Economy*, **20**, December, 973–98.
Weeks, J. (2012), 'What is economics? Parable for our time', *Insight*, available at http://www.insightweb.it/web/content/what-economics-parable-our-time.
Weintraub, E.R. (1975), *General Equilibrium Analysis: Studies in Appraisal*, Cambridge: Cambridge University Press.
Weintraub, S. (1958), *An Approach to the Theory of Income Distribution*, Philadelphia, PA: Clifton.
Weintraub, S. (1978), *Capitalism's Inflation and Unemployment Crisis*, Reading, MA: Addison-Wesley.
Weintraub, S. and P. Davidson (1973), 'Money as cause and effect', *Economic Journal*, **83** (332), December, 1117–32.

Weiss, L.W. (1980), 'Quantitative studies of industrial organisations', in M. Intriligator (ed.), *Frontiers of Quantitative Economics*, Volume 1, Amsterdam: North-Holland, pp. 362–403.
Weisskopf, T.E. (1979), 'Marxian crisis and the rate of profit in the postwar US economy', *Cambridge Journal of Economics*, **3** (4), December, 341–78.
Weisskopf, T.E., S. Bowles and D.M. Gordon (1985), 'Two views of capitalist stagnation: underconsumption and challenges to capitalist control', *Science & Society*, **49** (3), 259–86.
Wells, P. (1983), 'A Post Keynesian view of liquidity preference and the demand for money', *Journal of Post Keynesian Economics*, **5** (4), Summer, 523–36.
Werner, R. (2005), *New Paradigm in Macroeconomics*, Basingstoke: Palgrave Macmillan.
Werner, R. (2012), 'Towards a new research program on banking and the new economy – implications of the Quantity Theory of Credit for the prevention and resolution of banking and debt crises', *International Review of Financial Analysis*, **25**, December, 1–17.
Werner, R. (2016), 'A lost century in economics: three theories of banking and the conclusive evidence', *International Review of Financial Analysis*, **46**, 361–79.
Whalen, C. (2013), 'Post-Keynesian Institutionalism after the Great Recession', *European Journal of Economics and Economic Policy: Intervention*, **10** (1), April, 12–27.
Whalen, C.J. (2020), 'Post-Keynesian institutionalism: past, present, and future', *Evolutionary and Institutional Economics Review*, **17** (1), 71–92.
Whelan, K. (2014), 'TARGET2 and central bank balance sheets', *Economic Policy*, **29** (77), January, 81–116.
Whitesell, W. (2006), 'Interest rate corridors and reserves', *Journal of Monetary Economics*, **53** (6), September, 1177–95.
Wiles, P. (1973), 'Cost inflation and the state of economic theory', *Economic Journal*, **83** (330), June, 377–98.
Wilson, M.C. (2010), 'Creativity, probability and uncertainty', *Journal of Economic Methodology*, **16** (1), March, 45–56.
Winslow, E.G. (1989), 'Organic interdependence, uncertainty and economic analysis', *Economic Journal*, **83** (396), June, 377–98.
Wojnilower, A.M. (1980), 'The central role of credit crunches in recent financial history', *Brookings Papers on Economic Activity*, **11** (2), 277–326.
Wojnilower, A.M. (1983), 'Transmuting profits into interest or how to free financial markets and bankrupt business', in L.H. Meyer (ed.), *Improving Money Stock Control: Problems, Solutions, and Consequences*, Boston, MA: Kluwer–Nijhoff, pp. 179–192.
Wojnilower, A.M. (1985), 'Private credit demand, supply, and crunches – how different are the 1980's?', *American Economic Review*, **95** (3), May, 351–6.
Wolfson, M.H. (1996), 'A Post Keynesian theory of credit rationing', *Journal of Post Keynesian Economics*, **18** (3), Spring, 443–70.
Wolfson, M.H. (2012), 'Credit rationing', in J. King (ed.), *The Elgar Companion to Post Keynesian Economics*, 2nd edn, Cheltenham, UK and Northampton, MA, USA: Edward Elgar, pp. 115–21.
Wood, A. (1975), *A Theory of Profits*, Cambridge: Cambridge University Press.
Wood, A. (1978), *A Theory of Pay*, Cambridge: Cambridge University Press.
Wray, L.R. (1989), 'Two reviews of Basil Moore', *Journal of Economic Issues*, **23** (4), December, 1185–9.
Wray, L.R. (1990), *Money and Credit in Capitalist Economies: The Endogenous Money Approach*, Aldershot, UK and Brookfield, VT, USA: Edward Elgar.
Wray, L.R. (1992a), 'Alternative theories of the rate of interest', *Cambridge Journal of Economics*, **16** (1), March, 69–91.
Wray, L.R. (1992b), 'Alternative approaches to money and interest', *Journal of Economic Issues*, **26** (4), 1145–78.
Wray, L.R. (1995) 'Keynesian monetary theory: liquidity preference or black box horizontalism?', *Journal of Economic Issues*, **29** (1), March, 273–80.
Wray, L.R. (1997), 'Deficits, inflation, and monetary policy', *Journal of Post Keynesian Economics*, **19** (4), Summer, 543–72.
Wray, L.R. (1998), *Understanding Modern Money*, Cheltenham, UK and Northampton, MA, USA: Edward Elgar.

Wray, L.R. (1999), 'The development and reform of the modern international monetary system', in J. Deprez and J.T. Harvey (eds), *Foundations of International Economics: Post Keynesian Perspectives*, London: Routledge, pp. 171–99.

Wray, L.R. (2000), 'Modern money', in J. Smithin (ed.), *What is Money?*, London: Routledge, pp. 42–66.

Wray, L.R. (2006a), 'When are interest rates exogenous?', in M. Setterfield (ed.), *Complexity, Endogenous Money and Macroeconomic Theory: Essays in Honour of Basil J. Moore*, Cheltenham, UK and Northampton, MA, USA: Edward Elgar, pp. 271–89.

Wray, L.R. (2006b), 'To fix or to float: theoretical and pragmatic considerations', in L.P. Rochon and S. Rossi (eds), *Monetary and Exchange Rate Systems: A Global View of Financial Crises*, Cheltenham, UK and Northampton, MA, USA: Edward Elgar, pp. 210–31.

Wray, L.R. (2008), 'Money manager capitalism and the commodities market bubble', *Challenge*, **51** (6), November–December, 52–80.

Wray, L.R. (2009), 'The rise and fall of money manager capitalism: a Minskian approach', *Cambridge Journal of Economics*, **33** (4), July, 807–28.

Wray, L.R. (2012), *Modern Money Theory: A Primer on Macroeconomics for Sovereign Monetary Systems*, Basingstoke: Palgrave Macmillan.

Wray, L.R. and Y. Nersisyan (2020), 'Does the national debt matter?', *Japanese Political Economy*, **46** (4), 261–86.

Wrenn, M.V. (2007), 'What is heterodox economics? Conversations with historians of economic thought', *Forum of Social Economics*, **36** (2), October, 97–108.

Wynarczyk, P. (1999), 'On Austrian–Post Keynesian overlap: Just as far is New York from Knoxville, Tennessee?', *Economic Issues*, **4** (2), September, 31–48.

Yellen, J. (1980), 'On Keynesian economics and the economics of post-Keynesians', *American Economic Review*, **70** (2), May, 15–19.

Yordon, W.J. (1987), 'Evidence against diminishing returns in manufacturing and comments on short-run models of output–input behavior', *Journal of Post Keynesian Economics*, **9** (4), Summer, 593–603.

You, J.I. (1994), 'Macroeconomic structures, endogenous technical change and growth', *Cambridge Journal of Economics*, **18** (2), April, 213–33.

Zambelli, S. (2004), 'The 40% neoclassical aggregate theory of production', *Cambridge Journal of Economics*, **28** (1), January, 99–120.

Zambelli, S. (2018a), 'The aggregate production function is NOT neoclassical', *Cambridge Journal of Economics*, **42** (2), March, 383–426.

Zambelli, S. (2018b), 'Production of commodities by means of commodities and non-uniform rates of profits', *Metroeconomica*, **69** (4), November, 791–819.

Zezza, G. (2008), 'U.S. growth, the housing market, and the distribution of income', *Journal of Post Keynesian Economics*, **30** (3), Spring, 375–402.

Name index

Ábel, I. 196, 200
Addison, J. 599
Adrian, T. 273
Agliardi, E. 384, 398
Aglietta, M. 23, 278
Aizenman, J. 506, 513
Akerlof, G. 10, 86, 89, 327
Akhtar, M.A. 224, 228
Akram-Lodhi, A.H. 103
Alary, P. 199
Alessie, R. 107
Allain, O. 163, 300, 305, 318, 384, 433, 436–9, 443, 462
Allen, P.R. 506
Altman, M. 13, 91, 297, 328, 341
Amable, B. 100
Amadeo, E.J. 42, 46, 372, 380, 382, 384, 386, 392, 398, 429, 612
Amado, A.M. 559
Amstad, M. 255
Anand, P. 81
Anderson, S.J. 107
Andini, C. 317
Andreff, W. 10
Andrews, P.W.S. 44, 45, 128–9, 155, 159, 165–6, 168
Angrick, S. 511, 514
Anyadike-Danes, M. 63–5
Appelbaum, E. 296, 338
Arena, R. 42, 189
Arestis, P. 4, 12, 25, 34, 36, 41, 43, 44, 47, 100–101, 102, 251, 263, 364, 477, 515, 518, 592, 601, 612, 640–41
Ariely, D. 137, 152
Armstrong, P. 6, 224
Arnon, A. 195, 207
Arrous, J. 101, 106, 119, 121
Asimakopulos, A. 41, 45, 163, 172, 337, 345, 349, 356, 358, 379, 381
Astarita, C. 383
Atesoglu, S. 247
Auerbach, P. 410, 424
Avritzer, J.D. 429–30

Backhouse, R.E. 9–10, 50
Baddeley, M. 85, 90, 96

Baert, P. 12
Bagehot, W. 229
Bakker, B.B. 503
Ballinger, R. 368
Ban, C. 550
Baran, P.A. 128, 182, 382
Baranzini, A. 12, 44, 370, 492
Barba, A. 17, 433
Barbieri, L. 559, 568
Barbosa-Filho, N.H. 405, 459
Barnes, M. 422
Barro, R.J. 2, 301–2, 364
Barzel, Y. 342
Baskoy, T. 132, 133
Bastian, E.F. 601, 606, 607, 622
Baudrillard, J. 107
Baumol, W. 130, 138, 159
Baxter, J.L. 339, 597
Beed, C. 30
Behringer, J. 383
Bell, S. 221, 543
Bell-Kelton, S. 368
Bellofiore, R. 195
Bénassy, J.P. 10, 308
Bengston, D.N. 114
Berg, N. 13, 16, 89, 93, 640
Berger, P. 511
Berle, A.A. 135
Berry, R.A. 614
Bertocco, G. 199
Bezemer, D. 295
Bhaduri, A. 4, 19, 41, 43, 45, 49, 168, 170, 186, 299, 391, 393–6, 398–9, 405–6, 417, 439, 444, 453, 485, 553, 580–81, 625
Bianchi, M. 97
Bianco, A. 199
Bibow, J. 45, 258–9, 529, 551
Bindseil, U. 48, 196–7, 226, 229–31, 233–4, 236
Bird, P.J.W.N. 114, 635
Bjørnstad, R. 98
Black, F. 195
Black, W.K. 152
Blanchard, O. 4
Blankenburg, S. 42
Blatt, J. 84
Bleaney, M. 301

708

Blecker, R.A. 18, 41, 45, 370, 384, 392, 396, 399, 433, 553, 568, 570–72, 578, 580–82, 585–7, 601, 603, 618, 622–5
Blinder, A. 159, 161–2, 164, 174, 179, 368
Bliss, C.J. 14
Bloch, H. 173, 596, 614
Bloomfield, A.I. 511
Boddy, R. 459, 461, 615
Boggio, L. 185, 188–9, 559, 568
Bonizzi, B. 275, 497, 541, 552
Borio, C. 200, 210, 234
Bortis, H. 5, 37, 431
Botta, A. 274, 292, 332
Botte, F. 404
Bougrine, H. 504
Bouguelli, R. 199, 273, 275
Bowen, W.G. 614
Bowles, S. 336, 344, 405, 469
Boyer, R. 8, 14, 44, 45, 136, 210, 336, 344, 375, 405, 464, 467, 469–70
Brennan, D.J. 454
Bresser-Pereira, L.C. 558
Brierley, J.A. 168
Brinkman, H.J. 131, 556
Brochier, L. 439, 462, 601
Brown, C. 17, 109, 246, 259, 271, 488, 490
Brown, E.K. 36, 39
Brown, J.R. 146
Brunner, E. 44, 128, 159, 162, 166, 168–9, 345
Bruno, O. 405
Buiter, W. 3
Burdekin, R.C.K. 592
Burkett, P. 447, 592
Burton, J. 599
Buttet, S. 325

Cagatay, N. 553
Cahen-Fourot, L. 638
Caldwell, B.J. 13
Câmara, A. 607
Caminati, M. 462
Campiglio, E. 638
Capaldo, J. 586, 588
Capoglu, G. 180
Card, D. 70
Carnevali, E. 18, 20, 535, 572, 638–9
Carney, M. 19, 21
Carrión Álvarez, M. 78
Carson, J. 178
Carvalho, F. Cardim de 34, 36, 45
Caserta, M. 411–14
Cassetti, M. 366, 429, 464–5, 470, 601, 614, 616
Castillo-Palermo, L.A. 502
Cauvel, M. 349, 461
Cavana, R.Y. 8

Cecchetti, S.G. 238
Cesaratto, S. 42, 291, 431, 435, 547, 550
Chandler, A.D. 131–2, 137
Chang, H.J. 553, 557
Chapman, R. 297
Charles, S. 316, 418, 607, 608
Chattopadhyay, N. 106
Chaundy, D. 503
Chick, V. 4, 31, 36, 41, 45, 197, 218, 231, 301, 305, 412
Chirat, A. 138
Chletsos, M. 70
Ciccone, R. 376, 393, 429
Claassen, E.M. 510
Clarke, Y. 110
Clifton, J.A. 130, 139
Cline, N. 596
Clinton, K. 230
Coddington, A. 85
Cohen, A. 51
Colander, D. 5, 9, 30, 631
Cömert, H. 249, 514
Commendatore, M. 414, 429
Committeri, M. 382, 387, 410–11
Cook, S. 247
Copeland, M.A. 199, 292
Cordonnier, L. 333
Cornwall, J. 44, 45, 444
Costa Santos, J.F. 226
Costa-Font, J. 73
Cottrell, A. 261
Coulbois, P. 514, 522–6, 529, 531–2
Couppey-Soubeyran, J. 243
Courbis, B. 199
Coutts, K. 45, 128, 131–2, 165, 169, 173, 175, 177, 556, 571
Cowling, K. 178
Craig, B. 509
Cramp, A.B. 194, 195
Cripps, F. 194, 211–12, 261, 286, 294, 555, 562–5, 573, 580, 594, 601, 607, 643
Crivelli, R. 109
Cross, R. 442
Crotty, J. 8, 136, 459, 461, 615
Cunningham, R. 603
Cyert, R.M. 91, 95, 129, 139, 171
Cynamon, B.Z. 109, 488

Daigle, G. 536
D'Alessandro, S. 640
Dallery, T. 145, 150–51, 153, 404, 414, 419, 429
Dalziel, P. 304, 600, 603
Danby, C. 36, 103
Dantas, F. 275, 276
D'Arista, J. 544, 545

Davidson, P. 4, 15, 22, 24, 32, 34, 36, 38, 41, 45–9, 75, 77–80, 86, 143, 159, 163, 194, 199, 245, 258, 260, 274, 278, 280, 290, 291, 300, 301, 305–6, 311–12, 325, 376, 416, 472, 518, 537–8, 544–7, 549, 566, 594, 599, 631, 635, 645
Davies, J.E. 130, 134
Davis, J.B. 5, 9–10
de Boyer, J. 210
De Conti, B. 541
De Grauwe, P. 534
de Largentaye, J. 48
De Lucchi, J.M. 517
De Soto, H. 199
De Vroey, M. 28
Deaton, A. 124
Dejuán, Ó. 431
Del Monte, A. 382, 390
Deleidi, M. 247, 250, 267
Deprez, J. 48, 305
Dequech, D. 45, 76, 83
Descamps, C. 210
Dhar, R. 103
Di Bucchianico, S. 291
Di Guilmi, C. 8
Disyatat, P. 210, 234
Dixon, R. 56, 63, 134
Dobrev, D. 517
Dobusch, L. 74
Domar, E.D. 366, 367
Domowitz, I. 175
Dore, R. 136
Dorfman, R. 50
Dornbusch, L. 633–4
Dos Santos, C.H. 286
Dosi, G. 18, 78, 94, 431, 461
Dostaler, G. 36, 37, 49
Doucouliagos, H. 70–72
Douthwaite, R. 638
Dow, A.C. 246
Dow, S.C. 19, 22, 30, 31, 36, 39, 45, 197, 210, 246, 261, 268, 537
Downward, P. 31, 161, 165, 174
Drakopoulos, S.A. 100–101, 103, 105, 109
Dray, M. 445
Du Tertre, R. 153–4
Duesenberry, J. 108, 110, 486
Dullien, S. 15, 40, 74, 194
Duménil, G. 8, 98, 187, 315, 346, 386, 420–23, 426, 442, 474, 592, 626
Dumouchel, P. 108
Dunn, S.P. 12, 35, 36, 39, 42, 45, 77, 107, 134–7, 633
Dupuy, J.-P. 108

Dutt, A.K. 31, 41–2, 45, 46, 182, 184, 300–301, 305, 323, 345, 381–2, 384, 396, 398, 402, 404, 412–13, 429, 435, 438, 441–2, 444, 446–7, 473–4, 485–6, 493–5, 590, 592, 601, 610, 612–13
Dyson, B. 198

Earl, P. 10, 43, 45, 85, 86, 90, 91, 99, 101, 105, 110, 113, 121, 185, 632
Ederer, S. 493
Edwards, S.F. 114, 116–18
Eggertsson, G.B. 325
Egidi, M. 78
Ehnts, D. 78
Eichengreen, B. 539, 551
Eichner, A.S. 4, 34–6, 38–9, 44–7, 100–102, 104–7, 122, 128–9, 135, 138, 141, 156–9, 163–4, 175, 179–80, 184–5, 194, 230, 251, 262–3, 268, 274, 280, 284–5, 296, 340, 376–7, 413, 416, 515, 518, 594–5, 600, 635
Eisner, R. 422
Encarnación, J. 106, 112
Ennis, H.M. 235
Epstein, G. 8, 251, 394, 552–3
Ethier, W.J. 505
Etzioni, A. 107, 114
Evans, D. 497

Fabo, B. 29
Fair, R.C. 593
Fanti, L. 172, 185
Farley, J. 638
Fazzari, S.M. 18, 41, 45, 109, 146, 250, 308, 323, 364, 425, 438, 444, 488
Febrero, E. 237, 550
Feiwel, G.R. 299
Felipe, J. 57, 63–6, 351
Ferguson, C.E. 52
Fernández-Huerga, E. 97, 101, 301, 338
Fiebiger, B. 151, 224, 241, 243, 282, 333, 363, 429–30, 440, 459–61
Filardo, A.J. 422
Fine, B. 633–4
Fishburn, P.C. 106
Fisher, F.M. 59, 61
Fisher, I. 19, 21, 22, 323, 325
Flaschel, P. 370, 455
Fleming, J.M. 506
Fog, B. 159, 162
Foley, D. 453, 455, 633
Fontana, G. 12, 31, 34–5, 36, 41, 43, 45, 77, 78, 85, 194, 197, 199, 211, 238, 266, 267, 613, 637–8
Forder, J. 593
Forstater, M. 44, 221, 224, 251, 364–5, 543

Fox, J. 11, 244
Francis, A. 141
Franke, R. 404, 413, 423, 424, 430, 474
Fratini, S.M. 53
Freedman, C. 613
Freitas, F. 382, 432, 438
Frenkel, R. 513
Friedman, M. 3, 10, 13, 16, 87, 89, 194–6, 198, 241–2, 245
Fritz, B. 541
Frydman, R. 78, 271, 535
Fujimoto, T. 301, 303
Fujita, S. 187
Fullbrook, E. 6, 12, 30
Fuller, D. 73
Fullwiler, S. 45, 208, 230, 231, 234–6, 243, 248
Fung, M.V. 85, 271

Gabor, D. 275, 280, 550, 634
Galanis, G. 301, 399, 587–90, 625
Galbraith, James K. 43, 45, 364, 631
Galbraith, John K. 4, 22, 24, 36, 43, 45, 107–8, 128, 133–8, 141–2, 150–51, 171
Gali, J. 603
Gallagher, K.P. 552
Gambetti, L. 603
Garber, P. 547
Garegnani, P. 4, 42, 45, 51–3, 182, 187, 382, 394, 416
Gaston, N.G. 120
Geide-Stevenson, D. 73
Georgescu-Roegen, N. 14, 45, 81, 83–4, 105–6, 109, 112–13, 119, 635, 638
Gerrard, B. 34, 36, 43, 77, 78, 81, 85
Gigerenzer, G. 13, 16, 86–93
Giotis, G. 70
Giovannoni, O. 250
Girardi, D. 429, 440
Glick, R. 506, 513
Godley, W. 4, 44–5, 63–5, 128, 154, 169, 193–4, 196–7, 211–12, 246, 255–8, 261, 268, 280–81, 285–8, 290–92, 294, 315, 366, 368–9, 433, 439, 475, 479, 485, 497, 499, 504, 508, 511, 515, 518, 520, 526, 535–6, 543–4, 555–7, 562–5, 569, 571–3, 580, 593, 601, 607, 631, 640, 643
Goldberg, M.D. 78, 535
Goldstein, J.P. 454, 455
Goodhart, C.A.E. 196
Goodwin, C. 631
Goodwin, N. 108
Goodwin, R. 44, 45, 405, 455
Gordon, D.M. 405
Gordon, M.J. 271
Gowdy, J.M. 107, 114, 115, 635, 637

Grabel, I. 44, 269, 552
Granger, C.W.J. 65, 247, 461, 465
Gray, J. 297
Graziani, A. 4, 41, 183, 274, 290–91, 315
Greenwald, B. 196
Gregg, P. 137
Grimaldi, M. 534
Grossman, H.I. 301, 302
Grossman-Wirth, V. 241
Gu, G.C. 164, 167
Gualerzi, D. 101, 106
Guerrien, B. 28, 53
Guy, Y. 153, 154
Gyöngyössy, I. 512

Hafner, S. 639–40
Hagemann, H. 391
Hahn, F.H. 14, 56
Haight, A.D. 250
Haines, W.M. 103
Halevi, J. 38, 382, 414
Hall, R.L. 128, 129, 130, 168, 174
Hamermesh, D.S. 56
Hamouda, O.F. 40–42, 44, 47
Hanley, N. 107, 114, 116, 118
Hanmer, L.C. 103
Hanson, J.D. 108
Harcourt, G.C. 4, 30, 40–42, 44, 46–7, 49, 51, 141, 180, 301, 305, 315, 416, 645
Hardt, L. 639, 640
Harris, D.J. 41, 45, 159, 301, 345, 373
Harrod, R.F. 25, 44, 45, 60, 128, 156, 159, 169, 183, 373, 401–2, 412, 462, 537, 560
Hart, N. 42
Harvey, J.T. 10, 43, 45, 85, 91, 108, 534
Hayek, F.A. 19, 24, 195, 645
Haynes, W.W. 170
Hein, E. 35–8, 41, 45, 167, 183, 252, 267, 370, 383–4, 423–4, 426–7, 438–9, 464–5, 470, 474, 477, 485, 490, 581, 582, 585, 592, 595, 598, 602–3, 612, 613, 622, 634, 641, 644
Heiner, R.A. 78, 88, 99
Heinsohn, G. 199, 261
Hendry, D.F. 65
Henry, J. 36, 37, 435, 497
Herndon, T. 67
Hewitson, G. 264
Hey, J.D. 87
Hicks, J. 46, 48, 130, 132, 189–90, 194, 217, 246, 412, 431, 561, 597, 617
Hillard, M.G. 454
Hitch, C.J. 128, 129, 130, 168, 174
Hoang-Ngoc, L. 633
Hodgson, G. 16, 17, 30, 39, 43, 85, 87, 91, 95, 327, 631–2, 633, 634

Holmes, A. 196, 230
Holt, R.P.F. 36, 40, 100, 635, 636
Houthakker, H.S. 124
Howells, P. 197, 206, 226, 267–8, 592
Hristov, K. 517
Hudson, M. 325, 557
Humpage, O. 509
Hunt, E.K. 32
Hussain, M.N. 573

Ihrig, J. 204, 240–41
Innes, A.M. 199
Ioannidis, J.P.A. 70, 72
Ironmonger, D.S. 106, 119
Irving-Lessman, J. 21, 129, 323
Isaac, A.G. 485
Isard, P. 530
Izurieta, A. 586, 588

Jackson, A. 641
Jackson, T. 638, 640, 641
Jakab, Z. 200, 273
Jarrell, S.B. 68
Jean, Y. 349
Jefferson, T. 86
Jespersen, J. 36, 39, 48
Jetin, B. 587
Johnson, M.D. 105
Johnson, R.D. 340
Johnston, J. 147, 158–9
Jorion, P. 245
Jossa, B. 182
Joyce, M. 674
Judson, D.H. 635
Juselius, K. 674

Kahn, R.F. 4, 33, 129, 131, 194–7, 272, 309, 381, 560, 598
Kahneman, D. 86, 88, 92, 109, 115, 116
Kaldor, N. 4, 15, 25, 32, 33, 44–6, 48–50, 60, 128, 129, 138, 140, 145–6, 154, 155, 159–61, 163, 173–4, 178, 180–81, 183, 194–7, 206–7, 242, 246, 261–2, 266, 272, 303, 317, 332–3, 349, 358–9, 370–71, 376, 380, 382, 393, 405, 415–16, 425–6, 429, 433, 444–5, 462–9, 471, 473, 491, 511, 532, 537, 539, 555, 557, 561–2, 568, 595–6, 598, 600, 654
Kalecki, M. 4, 18–21, 32, 33, 40–41, 45, 47, 48–9, 128–32, 142–3, 146, 159, 162, 172, 175, 178, 182, 265, 282, 299–301, 303, 308, 313, 323, 332, 334–5, 345, 363, 382–4, 405, 416, 440, 470, 493, 495, 578, 580, 595–6, 598, 600, 608, 631, 644
Kallis, G. 637
Kaltenbrunner, A. 275, 552

Kania, J.J. 136
Kant, S. 114
Kapeller, J. 6, 74, 109, 114, 490–91, 633–4
Kaplan, A.D.H. 44, 170
Kappes, S.A. 294
Kapteyn, A. 107
Karacaoglu, G. 256
Karayiannis, A.D. 103
Kaufman, B.E. 8, 298, 318, 343
Keen, S. 44, 268, 370, 631
Keister, T. 235, 236
Kelton, S. 45, 224, 364, 365, 551, 631
Kemp-Benedict, E. 127, 635
Kenen, P.B. 506
Kenyon, P. 140, 141, 180
Kesting, S. 119
Keynes, J.M. 3, 4, 10, 17–19, 22–4, 27, 29, 31–4, 39, 41, 45–9, 77, 80–84, 86, 90, 92, 95–100, 199, 201, 203–6, 236, 241, 245–6, 249, 251, 253, 261, 271, 274, 291, 297, 300–302, 305–8, 311, 320, 322–3, 325, 332–3, 349, 363–4, 371, 383, 497, 513, 518, 522, 539, 544–5, 551, 560, 593–5, 597–8, 630–31, 633, 635, 643
Khan, N. 250
Kiefer, D. 459
Kim, H. 247–8
Kim, J.H. 172
Kim, Y.K. 109, 485–6, 490–91
King, J.E. 5, 33, 36, 41–4, 46–7, 86, 187, 311, 400, 631
Kirman, A. 53, 55
Klamer, A. 30
Kleinknecht, A. 469, 472
Knapp, G.F. 199
Knetsch, J.L. 114, 115, 116
Knight, F. 23, 31, 77, 81, 83–4
Kohler, K. 383, 498
Kokotović, S. 514
Koo, R.C. 236, 243, 308
Kornai, J. 191, 316
Koutsoyiannis, A. 133, 139–40, 155, 158, 178–9, 427
Krassoi-Peach, E. 72, 327, 331
Kregel, J.A. 4, 34–6, 38–9, 45–7, 159, 199, 203, 246, 472, 476, 540, 543, 594–5
Kriesler, P. 38, 42, 45, 178, 414, 420, 422, 601, 613
Kronenberg, T. 119, 636–7
Krueger, A.B. 70
Krugman, P. 9, 10, 18, 29, 246, 284, 325, 332
Kumar, R. 493
Kumhof, M. 200, 273
Kurz, H.D. 42, 45, 345, 393–4, 398, 413, 416
Kysar, D.A. 108

Labrousse, A. 6, 632
Lachmann, L.M. 76
Lah, M. 101
Lainé, M. 300
Lakomski-Laguerre, O. 195
Lamarche, T. 6
Lancaster, K. 104, 106, 119, 121
Lang, D. 44, 442, 479, 593
Lanzillotti, R.F. 44, 128, 170, 174, 180, 189
Lavoie, M. 2, 12, 21, 34–6, 39, 41–2, 44, 46, 57, 68, 76, 101, 106, 129, 154, 165, 169, 172, 185, 194, 197, 199, 201, 221, 224, 232, 241, 243, 246, 251–3, 256–7, 262–3, 272, 285, 287–8, 292, 294, 300, 301, 304, 308, 315, 325, 334, 345, 362–3, 366, 368–9, 383, 384, 398–400, 402, 404, 414, 420, 422, 427, 429, 433, 438–40, 442, 444, 451, 454, 459–60, 462, 464, 470, 474–5, 477, 479, 484–5, 499, 504, 508, 511, 515, 517–18, 520, 523, 535–6, 544, 547, 550, 557, 563, 571–2, 590, 601, 613, 618, 630, 632, 636, 638
Lawn, P. 636
Lawson, T. 10–13, 15, 17, 28–31, 34, 39, 96, 633
Layard, R. 57, 63
Lazonick, W. 133, 136
Lazzarini, A. 51
Le Bourva, J. 194, 197, 207, 272, 274, 515
Le Héron, E. 45, 197, 246, 260, 275, 276
Lea, S.E.G. 104, 119
Leamer, E.E. 440
Lee, F.S. 6, 10, 13, 34–5, 44–6, 92, 128–32, 134, 158, 161–9, 171–2, 174, 178, 180, 185, 632–3
Leibenstein, H. 10, 91, 108, 148, 328
Leijonhufvud, A. 11, 30
León-Ledesma, M.A. 445
Lerner, A. 45, 364–6, 368, 539, 542, 568, 571–2, 581, 625
Leslie, D. 301, 303
Levine, A.L. 185
Levrero, E.S. 202, 247
Lévy, D. 8, 98, 187, 280, 315, 346, 386, 420–23, 426, 442, 474, 592, 626
Li, H. 511
Libânio, G.A. 445
Lima, G.T. 337, 404, 627
Lipsey, R.G. 613
Littleboy, B. 365
Loasby, B.J. 76
Lockwood, M. 114, 116–17, 119
Loehr, D. 638
Lombra, R.E. 196, 230
Lucas, R. 3, 13, 59, 84, 86, 100
Lutz, M.A. 86, 103–5, 107, 119
Lux, K. 103–5, 107, 119

Macedo e Silva, A.C. 286, 439
Mäki, U. 13
Malinvaud, E. 10, 308
Mandarino, G.V. 27
Marangos, J. 27
March, J.G. 91, 129, 139, 171
Marchal, J. 135, 211
Marcuzzo, M.C. 129
Marglin, S. 28, 97, 376, 380–81, 391, 393–6, 398–9, 406, 417, 439, 453, 459, 610, 625
Marie, J. 607, 608
Marquetti, A. 327, 465
Marris, R. 138, 144, 146, 148, 161
Marselli, R. 511
Martschin, J. 383
Martin, A. 255
Martin, B. 366, 368
Maslow, A.H. 103–4, 119, 121–2, 135
Mason, P.L. 336
Mason, R. 108
Mata, T. 33
Mayumi, K. 107, 114
Mazier, J. 8, 536
Mazzucato, M. 45, 631, 634
McCallum, B.T. 506, 522
McCloskey, D.N. 40
McCombie, J.S.L. 44, 45, 56–7, 60–66, 168, 351, 462–4, 555, 560, 566, 569–70, 573–4, 578, 640
McCulley, P.A. 19, 23–4, 271
McDonald, R.J. 342
McElhattan, R. 592
McKean, J.R. 136
McKenzie, R.A. 23
McLeay, M. 196, 200, 273
Meadows, D.H. 640
Means, G.C. 31, 44, 45, 128, 130–32, 135, 168
Mearman, A. 6, 11, 30–31, 40, 47, 119, 636
Mehlum, H. 316
Mehrling, P. 260, 273, 275
Melmiès, J. 131, 132, 164, 173–4
Mercure, J.F. 639–41
Metcalfe, J.S. 132
Michell, J. 274, 459
Michl, T.R. 463
Milan, M. 294
Milberg, W. 553
Miller, J.L. 134, 635
Minsky, H.P. 4, 8, 19, 21–3, 27, 36, 41, 43, 45, 46–7, 49, 75, 77, 82, 94, 196–7, 202, 214, 237, 261, 266, 268–73, 275, 278, 280, 290, 292, 308, 315, 323, 377, 459, 472–4, 477–84, 552, 631, 635
Mirante, A. 44, 370, 492

Mirowski, P. 16, 29, 74
Mitchell, W. 40, 44, 365, 442
Mohun, S. 346, 461
Mollo, M.L.R. 559
Monasterolo, I. 638
Mongiovi, G. 42, 45, 53, 338, 431
Moore, B.J. 41, 45, 78–9, 148, 178, 194, 197, 206, 210, 246–8, 250, 261–2, 311, 532, 538–9, 542–3, 594
Moosa, I.A. 29, 40, 65, 521, 523–5, 534
Moreno-Brid, J. 573
Morgan, J. 640
Mosler, W. 221–2, 224, 230–31, 234, 248, 251
Moss, S.J. 51, 145
Mott, T.L. 134, 146, 164, 246, 392, 398
Mouakil, T. 260
Muellbauer, J. 124
Mundell, R. 505–7, 512, 522
Mundt, M. 595
Munier, F. 110
Murau, S. 275
Muysken, J. 365, 442
Myatt, A. 345

Naastepad, C.W.M. 44, 45, 301, 328, 331, 462, 464–5, 469–70, 472
Nah, W.J. 345, 439, 444, 454, 459, 462, 601
Nahuis, N.J. 592
Naples, M.I. 327
Ndikumana, L. 477
Neilson, D.H. 209
Nell, E.J. 4, 34, 42, 44, 100, 102, 106, 107, 109, 184, 210, 301, 309–13, 317, 319, 328, 364, 365, 381, 398
Nenovsky, N. 517
Nersisyan, Y. 199, 225, 275, 542
Nesvetailova, A. 19, 22, 634
Neville, J.W. 45, 601
Newbold, P. 65
Nichols, L.M. 345, 454
Nikiforos, M. 286, 345, 429, 440, 453, 455
Nikolaidi, M. 43, 292, 483, 485
Nisticò, S. 188
Nordhaus, W. 169
Norman, N. 36, 39–40, 45, 128, 131, 132, 165, 173, 177, 556, 571
Norton, N. 345, 454
Novarese, M. 632
Nurkse, R. 511–12
Nymoen, R. 98

Obst, T. 588, 589
Obstfeld, M. 506
O'Connell, S.A. 474, 482
O'Donnell, R.M. 77, 79, 81, 90, 98

O'Hara, P.A. 43
Okun, A.M. 130–32, 165, 172, 174, 313, 347, 349
Olive, M. 173
Olivei, G. 422
Onaran, Ö. 45, 301, 399, 469, 553, 587–90, 625
O'Neill, S.W. 639–40
Oreiro, J.L. 226, 440
Orléan, A. 8, 17, 19, 45, 96
Osberg, L. 351
Ostry, J.D. 1–2
O'Sullivan, M. 136
Oyvat, C. 399, 490

Palacio-Vera, A. 613
Palley, T. 34, 36, 37, 43–5, 197, 219, 248, 266–7, 275–6, 278, 305, 323, 345, 438, 444, 454, 482, 484–5, 493, 543, 557, 559, 576–7
Palumbo, A. 382, 412, 424, 431, 561, 569
Panagopoulos, Y. 211
Panico, C. 45, 195, 254
Parenteau, R. 499
Parguez, A. 24, 41, 197, 282, 543–4
Pariboni, R. 429, 439–40, 485, 490–91
Park, M.S. 426, 429, 431, 435
Paroush, J. 110
Parrinello, S. 635
Pasinetti, L.L. 4, 25, 28, 36, 37, 42–3, 45, 47, 97, 100, 102, 106, 119, 145, 160, 181, 183–5, 189, 252–3, 370–71, 375, 391, 473, 475, 491–4, 645
Patinkin, D. 301, 323
Patterson, M. 635
Payne, J.E. 247
Peach, R. 422, 613
Pedrosa, I. 479
Pencavel, J. 338
Peng, T.-C. 10, 632
Penrose, E.T. 32, 137, 142, 148
Pérez Caldentey, E. 44, 541, 563, 623
Perrotini, I. 445
Perry, N. 596, 635–6, 639
Petit, P. 44, 45, 136, 464, 470
Petri, F. 45, 51, 628
Pforr, T. 275
Phelps-Brown, E.H. 56
Piketty, T. 491, 493, 642
Piore, M. 298, 599
Pirgmaier, E. 640
Pivetti, M. 17, 45, 182, 433, 543, 598, 628–9
Plihon, D. 8, 17
Pollin, R. 197, 201, 247–9, 266, 271, 343, 637–8
Pollitt, H. 639–41
Ponta, L. 641
Poole, W. 630

Posner, R.A. 3
Poulon, F. 211
Prasch, R. 296, 340, 553
Pratten, S. 31
Prescott, E.C. 56
Pressman, S. 44, 100, 635
Prissert, P. 514, 518, 522–5, 531–5

Raberto, M. 638
Rabinovich, J. 151, 333
Rada, C. 383, 459, 470, 475
Radonjić, O. 514
Radzicki, M.J. 8
Rahimi, A. 247
Rahmatian, A. 200, 210–11
Ramírez-Gastón, P. 172, 185
Ramskogler, P. 633–4, 641
Rassuli, A. 101
Rassuli, K. 101
Razmi, A. 590
Reardon, J. 137
Rehm, M. 493
Reich, M. 298
Reinhart, C.M. 67
Reissl, S. 262
Renversez, F. 217
Reyes Ortiz, L. 587
Reynolds, P.J. 34, 165, 184, 298
Rezai, A. 588, 637–9
Riach, P. 351
Ribeiro, R.S.M. 559
Ricardo, D. 5, 19, 25, 42, 126, 184, 189, 195, 320, 364, 633
Richters, O. 638
Rider, C. 553
Rima, I. 338, 339
Rizvi, S.A.T. 53, 55
Robbins, L. 6
Robinson, J. 4, 18, 19, 25, 32, 33–4, 36, 38, 41, 45–7, 49–51, 100, 102, 106–7, 123, 128–9, 133, 138–9, 142, 159–60, 163, 168, 170, 180–81, 183, 186, 189, 194, 196–7, 205, 207, 248–9, 258, 264, 266, 299–301, 313, 315, 317, 341, 358, 370–73, 375–6, 378–82, 384, 391, 405, 415, 417, 419–20, 425, 427, 445, 472, 493, 553, 555, 557, 592–3, 597, 604, 607–8, 630
Rochon, L.P. 44, 196–7, 216, 218, 230, 232, 249–52, 261, 474
Rogé, C. 418
Rogers, C. 25, 37, 53, 201
Rogoff, K. 67, 506
Rolim, L.N. 461
Romer, D. 59
Romer, P. 3
Roncaglia, A. 25, 42, 45, 126, 184, 189, 636

Rosser, J.B. Jr 44, 80, 370
Rossi, S. 197, 216, 218, 232, 545
Rousseas, S. 197, 272
Rowthorn, R.E. 4, 18–19, 157, 168, 345, 350, 355, 376, 382, 384, 387–8, 393, 451, 453, 464, 470, 598, 600, 612
Roy, R. 101, 103, 112, 124
Roy, U. 325
Rumsfeld, D. 77
Runde, J. 81–2, 254
Russo, E. 430–31
Ryan, A. 636
Rymes, T.K. 25, 463
Ryoo, S. 366, 402, 474

Saith, A. 4
Salmon, F. 14
Samuelson, P. 29, 46, 50, 56, 66, 196
Sanfilippo, E. 129
Sapsford, D. 596
Sarantis, N. 601
Sardoni, C. 48, 199
Sargent, T.J. 86, 87
Sarkar, P. 392, 393
Sasaki, H. 345, 444
Sawyer, M. 5, 12, 36, 37, 39, 41, 43, 45, 49, 131–2, 164, 172, 175, 199, 251–2, 292, 364, 543–4, 601, 612, 637–8, 643
Scazzieri, R. 12
Schefold, B. 42, 45, 66, 102, 124, 188–9, 301, 303, 635–6
Schelling, T.C. 337
Scherer, F.M. 170
Schmidt, T.P. 502
Schoder, C. 338
Schor, J. 327, 340, 637, 638
Schumpeter, J.A. 26, 32, 133, 195, 199, 202
Schütz, B. 109, 318, 490, 491
Scitovsky, T. 109
Seccareccia, M. 36, 37, 195, 197, 201, 202, 252–3, 296–7, 315, 330, 342, 363, 377, 479, 504, 618, 643, 644
Selten, R. 88
Semieniuk, G. 638
Semmler, W. 185, 474
Sen, A. 10, 107, 402
Sent, E.-M. 85–6, 89
Seppecher, P. 18
Serrano, F. 45, 382, 431–6, 438, 514, 518, 542, 627
Setterfield, M. 12, 31, 36, 44, 45, 109, 194, 249–52, 267, 300, 370, 399, 404, 412–13, 429–30, 433, 439, 444, 474, 490–91, 561, 567–8, 570–72, 577–8, 601, 603–4, 606–7, 618, 622, 627, 629

Shackle, G.L.S. 45, 76, 78, 85, 97, 412
Shaikh, A. 15–16, 32, 56–7, 59–61, 65, 96, 125, 414, 417–20, 423–4, 429, 454, 474, 476, 553–4, 556
Shapiro, C. 327, 343
Shapiro, N. 37, 131, 134, 149, 164, 172, 180
Sharif, M. 338, 340
Sheard, P. 194
Shefrin, H. 88, 270
Sherman, H.J. 455–6, 461
Shiller, R.J. 10, 86, 89
Shin, H.S. 273
Shiozawa, Y. 25, 189, 190, 191
Shipley, D.D. 133, 170, 174
Siemoneit, A. 638
Simon, H.A. 10, 11, 32, 48, 56, 78, 86–91, 93, 95, 98, 104, 137, 139, 148, 190, 346, 412, 427, 543
Sippel, R. 105
Sissoko, C. 278, 280
Skidelsky, R. 3, 30, 80, 203, 631
Skott, P. 44, 45, 161, 306, 366, 370, 376, 402–3, 410, 413, 424–6, 429, 438, 440, 442, 455–6, 460, 473–5, 477
Slade-Caffarel, Y. 30
Slattery, E. 392, 398
Smithin, J. 13, 31, 183, 201–2, 252–3, 323, 519–20, 523, 525–7, 529, 531, 537–9, 542, 598, 601
Soichot, J. 210
Solow, R. 3, 46, 50, 59, 368
Sonenshine, R. 137
Sordi, S. 462
Soros, G. 28, 96, 530
Soutar, G.N. 110
Spash, C.L. 107, 114, 116, 118, 636, 639
Spaventa, L. 391
Spencer, D.A. 338
Spiliotis, A. 211
Spreafico, M.R.M. 463–4
Springholz, F. 6
Sraffa, P. 4, 42–3, 45, 47, 50–51, 66, 126, 182, 184, 189–91, 285
Stagl, S. 637, 638
Stanford, J. 345
Stanley, T.D. 68, 70–72, 92, 214, 327, 331, 442, 593, 613
Steedman, I. 42, 45, 126, 187, 497
Steiger, O. 199, 261
Steindl, J. 4, 19, 21, 41, 45, 128, 149, 156, 160, 162, 173, 179, 181, 182, 282, 318, 345, 359, 382, 384, 411, 413–14, 416, 425, 470, 473, 474, 478–81, 483–4
Stenfors, A. 524
Stevens, T.H. 114, 116–17

Stiglitz, J.E. 3, 4, 9, 10, 28, 74, 196, 327, 343
Stilwell, F. 5
Stockhammer, E. 41, 45, 150–52, 299, 383, 398, 400, 442–3, 459, 483, 485, 590, 593, 602–3, 613, 633, 634, 638, 641, 644
Storm, S. 3, 4, 44, 45, 100, 301, 328, 331, 462, 464–5, 469–70, 472
Strotz, R.H. 104
Sturn, S. 488
Summa, R. 514, 518, 542, 627
Summers, L. 244
Sušjan, A. 101
Sweezy, P.M. 128, 182, 382
Sylos Labini, P. 45, 74, 128, 130, 141, 143, 160, 161, 169, 183, 184, 193

Taleb, N.N. 13, 15, 80, 88–9, 91
Tarassow, A. 464–5, 470
Tarling, R. 602
Tarshis, L. 178
Tatliyer, M. 250
Tavani, D. 351
Taylor, J.B. 231, 249
Taylor, L. 41, 45, 124, 183, 285, 286, 292, 299, 370, 382, 384, 392, 394, 405, 455–6, 459, 470, 474–5, 478–9, 482, 499, 515, 522, 601, 606–7, 638
Tcherneva, P. 45, 364, 365, 643
Terzi, A. 80
Thirlwall, A.P. 44, 45, 445, 462, 464, 497, 535, 555, 560, 566–71, 573, 575–8, 638
Thompson, S. 439
Tlatelpa, H.Y.D. 445
Tobin, J. 18, 46, 154, 199, 245, 255–6, 274, 285–6, 308, 323, 325, 526, 553
Todd, P.M. 88–9, 93
Tomer, J.F. 86, 91
Toporowski, J. 21, 41, 45, 260, 269, 271, 479
Torto, R.G. 196, 230
Torvik, R. 316
Trevithick, J. 194, 206
Trezzini, A. 110, 382, 412, 424, 431, 433, 435
Trigg, A.B. 42, 108, 334
Tucker, P. 196, 247
Tuñez-Aria, N. 315
Tversky, A. 88, 92–3
Tymoigne, É. 251

Unger, R. 274, 277–8

Van de Velde, F. 333
van den Bergh, J.C.J.M. 114
van Treeck, T. 383, 414, 419, 429, 475, 485, 488
Vasudevan, R. 351
Vatn, A. 119

Veblen, T. 32, 43, 45, 97, 108, 135, 139, 486
Vera, L.V. 575
Vercueil, J. 632
Vergeer, R. 469, 472
Vergnhanini, R. 541
Vernengo, M. 44, 349, 541, 607, 623, 633, 641
Vianello, F. 379, 393–5, 410, 543
Vickrey, W. 10–11, 364
Victor, P.A. 638, 640
Vogel, L. 581, 582, 585, 622
von Arnim, R. 588, 589
von Mises, L. 32, 195

Walsh, V. 55
Wang, P. 511
Wang, Z. 110
Watts, M.J. 44, 120
Webb, S. 328
Weeks, J. 6, 26
Weintraub, E.R. 76
Weintraub, S. 4, 41, 45, 46, 47, 76, 167, 172, 194, 197, 593–4
Weiss, L.W. 182
Weisskopf, T.E. 378, 454, 459–61
Wells, P. 246
Werner, R. 12, 26, 210, 242, 268, 272, 274

Whalen, C. 43, 45
Whelan, K. 547
Whitesell, W. 235
Wiles, P. 183
Wilkinson, F. 298, 602
Wilson, M.C. 79
Winslow, E.G. 96
Wojnilower, A.M. 17, 19, 23, 268, 272
Wolfson, M.H. 262, 263, 264, 266
Wolla, S. 204, 240, 241
Wood, A. 138, 142, 144–6, 148–9, 169, 180, 297, 416, 596, 599
Woodgate, R. 86, 439
Wray, L.R. 24, 44, 45, 136, 194–7, 199, 211, 221, 224–5, 230, 246, 251, 255–6, 266, 364–5, 475, 538–40, 542–3, 550–51, 592, 631
Wrenn, M.V. 32
Wynarczyk, P. 79

Yellen, J. 337, 358
Yordon, W.J. 162, 163
You, J.I. 394

Zambelli, S. 51, 66, 184
Zamparelli, L. 172, 185
Zezza, G. 17, 44, 286, 485
Zimmerman, C. 632

Subject index

accumulation
    and adjustment via monetary policy 420–23
    and animal spirits 372, 380–81, 384, 395, 418–19, 429, 488
    and business debt 472–5
    desired rate of 374–5
    model of Kaleckian 382–91
    model of neo-Keynesian 370–75
    model of post-Kaleckian 393–5
    model with Hicksian stock–flow investment 423
    model with stabilizing Marxian labour market 422–4
    see also Harrodian instability; Keynesian stability
agent-based models 7–8, 17–18, 20, 33, 430–31, 479, 641
aggregate demand–aggregate supply 322–5
anchored expectations 627
animal spirits 372, 380–81, 384, 395, 418–19, 429, 488
asset-based economies
    neo-chartalist vs post-chartalist views 221–4
    vs overdraft economies 217–18
auto-economies *see* asset-based economies
autonomous
    demand 308–9, 359, 433, 440
    non-capacity creating expenditure 435–9, 443, 453, 462

Banking School 183, 195, 206, 242, 503
banks
    and capital adequacy ratios 209–11
    and certificates of deposits and securitization 211–12
    and international transactions 500–503
    liquidity preference of 260–68
    profits of 207–9
    repos 216
beauty contest 17, 271, 534
behavioural economics
    new 5, 8, 10, 15, 16, 85–6, 88–9, 93, 109, 271
    old 7, 13, 16, 43, 76, 85–6, 89–92, 129, 139, 327, 427

cambist view 523–6
    in a fixed exchange rate regime 529–32
    in a flexible exchange rate regime 526–9
    practical consequences of 532–3
Cambridge
    capital controversies 25, 50–52, 53, 55, 497
    equation 145, 317, 371, 379
    price mechanism 415–17, 419
capacity
    constant rates of utilization in model of accumulation 375–9
    convergence towards normal rate 410–14
    endogenous normal rate 426–30
    engineer rated 156, 184
    planned excess 159–62
    profit maximizing rate of 413
    theoretical 156, 161
capital controls, in an asset-based economy 221–4
central banks 551–3
    ceiling system 237–8
    corridor system 232–4
    and credit easing 239–40
    defensive role 229–31
    floor system 236–8
    and government deposits 228–9
    interest rate targeting 231–2
    in an open economy 506–8
    in an overdraft economy 217–18
    and quantitative easing 239–44
    reaction function 249–53
    repos 228
common currency area 543–4
    and government expenditure 564–6
comparative advantage 553–5, 557
compensation thesis 503–4, 509, 515–18, 532
    critique of mainstream view 504–8
    extreme historical instances of 509–11
    limitations to 513–15
    in retrospect 511–13
competition
    flex price vs fix price markets 130–31
    non-price 132–3
    and the post-Keynesian firm 129–30
conflict inflation 601, 622, 623–6

consumers
  bandwagon effect 108
  choice, post-Keynesian principles of 103–10
  debt 483–95
  emulation 108–9
  formalization of theory 119–21
  snob and Veblen effects 108
conventions
  and banking 213
  and capacity utilization 412
  and consumer choice 102, 107
  and decision making 96–100
  and the firm 142, 143, 168, 171, 190
  and the labour market 342–3
cost curves, short run 157–9, 162–3
cost-plus pricing
  and competition 130
  critiques of 172–4, 178–9
  definition 164–5
  determinants of costing margin 178–83
  and prices of production 183–91
  and tariffs 556
  and tests of aggregate production function 62–5
COVID-19 2, 19, 73, 232, 234, 236, 240, 248, 316, 363, 400, 460, 631, 643–4
credit easing *see* central banks
credit rationing 15, 142, 200, 261–6
currency board 515–18
current account balance 20, 44, 281–3, 498–501, 533–4, 536–7, 539, 543, 545, 557, 560, 563, 572–3

data mining 67
  see also econometrics
debt-deflation effect 21–2, 269, 323
debt-led vs debt-burdened demand regimes 276–8
demand regimes *see* wage-led vs profit-led
direct costs 155, 157–9, 162–3, 165–8, 170–72, 174–6, 182, 187, 314, 353, 355–6, 358–9, 362, 383–4

ecological economics 6, 12, 100, 106, 320, 630, 633–41
  lexicographic ordering and 114–19
ecological macroeconomics 8, 637, 639–41
ecological rationality
  definition 90–91
  and modelling 100
  rules of 95–8
econometrics
  and aggregate production function 56–67
  and post-Keynesian economics 39–40
  and publication bias 67–73

effective demand
  and distribution 358–9
  and international trade 560–66, 578–82
  and labour demand 298–301
  point of 305–8
  and profits 334
efficiency wage hypothesis 297, 331, 343
  see also Webb effect
efficient market hypothesis 22, 38, 244, 543
employer of last resort 364, 643
endogenous money 33–4, 193–5, 204–31, 238, 264, 268, 275, 501–4, 514, 516, 547, 550, 555, 637
environment-consistent rationality and presuppositions 16
  see also ecological rationality; uncertainty
eurozone *see* common currency area; overdraft economics; TARGET2
expansion frontier 146–50

fair interest rates 252
fairness
  and inflation 596–8
  and labour markets 297
  and pricing 174, 596–8
feminist economics 6, 12, 103
finance, initial vs final 290–94
finance frontier 142, 145–7, 149–53, 179–81, 263, 475–6, 478
finance motive 203, 291, 297
financial fragility hypothesis 34–5, 268–71, 474, 478, 479–84, 552
financialization 145, 150–52, 249, 282, 538, 642
  management, ownership and 135–7
fiscal policy
  effectiveness in an open economy 504–5
  and exchange rate regimes 539
  importance of 363
  vs monetary policy 368–9
  see also government deficits
Fisher effect 325
foreign exchange rates
  and expectations 534–5
  and the forward rate 524–30
  and import, export prices 571–3
  and inflation 555, 622–3
  and pass-though 173, 542, 556, 571–3, 624
  and post-Keynesian support for fixed 537–8
  and post-Keynesian support for floating 538–40
  and profit share 584
  and trade deficits 556
  and trade flows 535–6
formalism 29–31
frown costs 235

full-cost pricing 130, 168, 181
functional finance 364–6, 539, 643
　sustainability of 366–8
fundamental identity 44, 281–5, 498–9

Global Financial Crisis
　and consumers and income distribution 17, 38, 362
　and economics 29, 49, 50, 67, 72–4, 362, 631
　history of 1–2
　and the monetary system 232, 234, 250, 251, 260, 271, 644
　and open economics 534, 552, 586
　and paradoxes 17–24
　reactions to 2–4
　see also subprime financial crisis
government deficits
　and money creation 221–4
　and profits 331–7, 363
　stability 366–8
gravitation 187–90
Great Moderation 596, 610
gross substitution, axiom of 105, 106, 114
growth imperative 637–8

Harrodian instability 401–3, 412, 417, 421–5, 427–8, 437–8
heredity principle 109–10
heterodox economics
　definition of 6–8
　vs orthodox dissenters 5–6
　presuppositions 11–32
heuristics 88–93
historical time 38, 98, 109, 163, 602, 635
hyper-inflation 606–8

ideology 2–3, 28–9, 73, 129
income effects
　and consumer theory 101, 102, 106–7, 123–4, 127
　and labour supply 338
infant-economy argument 557–8
inflation
　and bargaining positions 603–12
　barrier 379–82, 391, 420, 597–8, 604
　conflicting-claims model 600–603
　and consumer hierarchy 616–19
　and expectations vs experience 600–601
　and fairness 596–8
　and indexation 601–2, 606–7
　and information 598–600
　in an open economy 622–6
　post-Keynesian conception of 592–4
　and unemployment 612–16

Institutionalist economics
　and choice theory 91, 97, 100
　and the firm 128, 134–5, 141
　and heterodoxy 7, 9–10, 11, 13
　and labour markets 297–8, 301, 599
　old vs new 8
　and post-Keynesians 35, 38, 40, 43–4, 633
instrumentalism 13–16, 66, 163, 463
interest rates
　and distribution 251–3
　fair 252–3
　and liquidity preference 245–9, 253–60
　long-tern–short-term causality 247–9
　natural 51, 200–202, 250–52, 519, 533, 592–3
　parity 519–33
　and portfolio choice 254–7
　and risk premia 254–5, 265–8, 523, 526–8
　and target profit rate 180, 182–3
international buffer stocks 645
investment as a function of
　animal spirits 372
　expected rate of capacity utilization 384
　expected rate of profit 372–3
　growth rate of output 423
　normal rate of profit 394
　share of profits 394

job guarantee 364, 643

Kaldor's supermultiplier 560–62
Kaldor–Verdoon Law 444, 462–9, 471, 532, 557, 568, 575–8
Kaleckian economists 41, 46, 313, 345, 413
Keynes effect 308, 322
Keynesian stability 385, 387, 401–6, 408–9, 414, 419, 421, 428, 434, 438, 443, 477, 489, 493
Keynesian unemployment 308–9, 341
Keynes's Plan 544–7, 549

labour
　demand and efficiency 325–31
　demand and technology 318–20
　demand and the real wage 316–18
　demand notional vs effective 302–5
　market 296–8
　overhead 345–51
　shirking 343–5
　supply, heterodox views 340–43
　supply and consumer hierarchy 338–40
　supply curve, backward bending 341–2
　and work sharing 320–22

lexicographic ordering
  and ecological economics 114–19
  and needs 102, 105, 110–14
  and rationality 93, 99
liquidity preference 41, 49, 160, 200–201, 241–9
  and business debt 472–6
  and financial instability 268–71
  and foreign currencies 534
  and portfolio choice 253–60
  see also banks; interest rates
liquidity trap *see* monetary policy
luxury goods 125–6

managerial slack 152
mark-up pricing
  and competition 130
  and conflicting claims 604–5
  definition 165–8
  and inflation 595–6
  and New Keynesians 178
  and profit shares 356–9
  relative to other pricing formulas 171–2
  and rules of thumb 95, 99
Marshall–Lerner conditions 568, 571–2, 581, 625
Marx effect *see* Webb effect
Marxian economists 7–8, 11, 26, 35, 128, 134, 372, 398, 420
  and profit squeeze 398–9, 405, 408, 469–61, 638
  see also Radical economists
minimum wage 66, 70–72, 318, 328, 343, 380, 400, 628, 642
Modern Monetary Theory 35, 193, 196, 199, 221, 365, 539
  see also neo-chartalists
monetary circuit 290–92
monetary policy
  as adjustment mechanism in models of accumulation 420
  effectiveness in an open economy 504–8
  and the finance frontier 145
  vs fiscal policy 368–9
  and liquidity trap 246, 325
  recent developments 231–44
money
  and credit 197–200
  endogeneity 34, 193–5, 501–2
  history of post-Keynesian theory of 195–7
  principles of post-Keynesian theory of 197–203
Mundell–Fleming model 499, 504–8, 557

NAIRU 2, 25, 65, 72, 592–3, 602, 612–13, 643
natural growth rate 441–7, 462, 575–8, 613–14
needs
  and consumer theory 103–9
  overlap of 121–3
  vs wants 103–4
neo-Austrians 7, 8, 31–2, 76, 79, 198
neo-chartalists 44, 193, 221–5, 251, 365
  see also Modern Monetary Theory
neo-Pasinetti theorem 145, 473, 475
net costing margin 166, 168–71, 174–7, 179
net profit margin 176–7, 359
New Cambridge 44, 281, 286, 555, 562–3
New Classical 3, 13, 19, 299, 305
New Consensus 10, 16, 177, 194–5, 198, 201–2, 250–51, 322, 325, 363–4, 420, 474, 592
new fiscalism 362–3
New Keynesians 3, 9, 15, 28, 98, 172, 178, 194, 196, 242, 299, 323, 325, 327, 442, 474
  see also New Consensus; orthodox dissenters
New Paradigm Keynesians 196
normal-cost pricing 165, 168–72, 191, 354
  see also cost-plus pricing; target-return pricing
non-ergodicity 38, 78–80, 601
notional labour demand 303, 305–6, 308–9, 314

Okun's Law 313, 347–51
organicism 12, 17, 36, 96
orthodox dissenters
  definition 9–11
  and money 201
  reaction to heterodoxy 28, 31, 32, 74
orthodox economics
  and aggregate production function 50–60
  and consumer preferences 105–7, 114–15
  vs heterodox economics 5–6, 9–11
  and money 197–203
  presuppositions of 11–18, 24–31
  and publication bias 67–73
  rationality, bounded optimization 87–8
  rationality, cognitive illusions 88–90
  rationality, unbounded 16–17, 86–7
  and supply of labour 337–8
overdraft economics 219–21
  vs asset-based economics 217
  and liability management 218–19
  and sovereign debt crisis 259
overhead costs 155, 165–6, 168–9, 171–2, 174, 178–9, 182, 314, 345–62, 447–54, 456

paradox
  of costs 18–20, 387–91, 393, 396–7, 415, 419–20, 423, 429, 439, 447–50
  of debt 19, 21, 473, 479, 489
  of liquidity 19, 22–3, 272
  of profit-led demand 20, 590
  of public deficits 18, 19
  of risk 19, 23
  of thrift 18–19, 203, 285, 318, 375, 378–9, 381, 387–8, 390, 393, 415, 419–20, 423, 439, 637
  of tranquillity 19, 21, 22, 24, 268
path dependence 33, 38, 44, 109, 429, 635, 639
  see also unemployment hysteresis
Penrose effect 148
Phillips curve 2, 98, 420, 422, 592–4, 603, 612–14, 626–8
Pigou effect 20, 308, 322–3, 325
portfolio choice *see* interest rates
post-Keynesian economics
  definition 3–4, 46–9
  Fundamentalist 39–40, 46, 49, 75, 77–8, 193, 290, 301, 472
  future 630–34
  history of 33–5
  policies 641–5
  and presuppositions 35–40
  strategies for 632–4
power
  and financialization 135–7
  and growth 137–9
  and objectives of the firm 133–6
presuppositions 11–13, 17, 26–9, 31–7, 39, 55, 85, 96, 198, 203, 551
profit
  and the costing margin 337
  and goals of the firm 133, 139–42
  and government deficits 332–7
  in an open economy 582–5
  rate 51, 144–53, 190–91, 377–8, 387–93, 460
  share and business cycles 455–8
  share and overhead costs 447–50
  share in national income 331–4
  and wages in neo-Keynesian growth model 378
profit-led demand 20, 398–9, 408, 439, 459–61, 465, 467–8, 490, 495, 559, 590, 638
publication bias 67–73, 92

quantitative easing *see* central banks
quantity theory of money 2, 48, 193–6, 239, 243, 554, 592–3

Radical economists 7–9, 35
  and Radical price adjustment 407–9, 416, 426, 442
  see also Marxian economists
rationality *see* ecological rationality; environment-consistent rationality; orthodox economics
realism/realisticness 12–16, 28–9, 31, 34–5, 42, 87, 96, 426
real-world problems 633–4
recantations 2–3
reflux principle 195, 206–7, 229, 238, 242, 257, 503, 514, 518, 532–3, 545, 547, 555
Regulation School 7–8, 618
repos 23, 215–16, 225–8, 235, 237, 241, 254, 271, 273, 275, 278, 279–80, 292–4, 509, 526, 550
retained earnings
  and finance 139–42
  and the fundamental identity 282–3
retention ratio
  endogenous 417–19
  and finance frontier 147, 150
ROE 16, 142, 153–4
rules of thumb 91, 94–5, 99, 110, 140, 143, 171, 174; *see also* conventions; heuristics; satisficing

satisficing 12, 93, 95, 133, 139–41, 412
scarcity 6, 12, 24–6, 31, 51, 87, 101, 140, 164, 183, 191, 296, 398, 422, 594, 634, 636, 643
securitization *see* banks
shadow banking 23, 228, 264, 272–5, 278–80, 292–3
shadow banks 273, 280, 642
shareholder value 136, 151–2, 419
shirking 343–5
snob effect 108
Sraffian economics
  and choice theory 126
  criticism of neoclassical economics 50, 53
  and ecological economics 635
  and heterodox economics 25, 31
  and investment and capacity 382, 393–5, 398, 414, 417, 431–3, 435, 454, 627
  and post-Keynesian economics 35, 40–41, 42–3, 47
  and price theory 128, 165, 180, 182–5, 187–9, 380
  and wage/profit frontier 380
Sraffian supermultiplier 431–3, 438–40, 490
sterilization *see* compensation thesis
stock–flow consistent approach 8, 196–7, 286–90, 294

subprime financial crisis 38, 236, 245, 248, 264, 271–2, 284, 299, 308, 320, 473, 484, 488, 642
substitution effects
  and consumer theory 100–102, 104–7, 121, 123–6
  evidence for 72
  and the firm 155, 188
  and labour supply 155, 188
  and macroeconomics 51–2

TARGET2 209, 547, 549–50
target-return pricing
  and bargaining 618–22
  definition 170–71
  and heterodox economics 31
  in Kaleckian growth model 447–51
  and prices of production 184–7
  and profit maximization 179
  and profit shares 355, 359–62
  and rationality 99
technological progress
  and accumulation 461–2
  and employment growth 466–8
  function 462–4
  and inflation 616–17
technological unemployment *see* labour
Thirlwall's Law 566–71, 573–7, 638
total demand wage-led regimes 587
TSR 153–4

twin deficit 238, 500
  see also fundamental identity

uncertainty
  and chaos 79
  definition 75–7
  objections to 83–5
  ontological vs epistemic 77–9
  and ecological economics 635–6
  and exchange rates 534, 537–8
  and the firm 133–4, 141, 160, 412–13, 427
  and liquidity preference 254, 266, 269
  and presuppositions 17, 21–2, 31
  and the weight of an argument 81–3
unemployment hysteresis 72, 441–2
utilization function 346–7

valuation ratio 154, 475–6
Veblen effect 108

wage-led vs profit-led
  definition 20, 397
  empirical studies 399–400
  in models of accumulation 407–10, 417, 435, 442, 452–3, 457, 465–8
  in models of inflation 610, 612, 625, 626, 642
  in open economy models 581, 586–7, 588–9
Webb effect 327–31, 351, 465, 468–9, 471
weight of evidence 82, 83, 529
work sharing *see* labour

Printed and bound by CPI Group (UK) Ltd, Croydon, CR0 4YY
27/06/2022
03132188-0001